INTERNATIONAL POLITICS
AND FOREIGN POLICY

REVISED EDITION

INTERNATIONAL
POLITICS
AND FOREIGN POLICY

a reader in research and theory

edited by JAMES N. ROSENAU

THE FREE PRESS, NEW YORK [Fp] Collier-Macmillan Limited, London

Copyright © 1969 by THE FREE PRESS

A DIVISION OF THE MACMILLAN COMPANY

Printed in the United States of America

Collier-Macmillan Canada, Ltd., Toronto, Ontario

Library of Congress Catalog Card Number: 69–12120

printing number
3 4 5 6 7 8 9 10

To the students in Political Science 221
at Douglass College, whose readiness year after year
to roam around the frontiers of theory and research
in international relations stimulated the original
and present editions of this volume

Contents — an Overview

Contents

Contributors

Chadwick F. Alger
Northwestern University

Hayward R. Alker, Jr.
Massachusetts Institute of Technology

Lincoln P. Bloomfield
Massachusetts Institute of Technology

Kenneth E. Boulding
University of Colorado

Steven J. Brams
Syracuse University

David Braybrooke
Dalhousie University

Michael Brecher
McGill University

Richard A. Brody
Stanford University

H. W. Bruck
Department of Commerce

Philip M. Burgess
Ohio State University

William D. Coplin
Wayne State University

Karl W. Deutsch
Harvard University

Amitai Etzioni
Columbia University

Johan Galtung
*International Peace Research Institute,
Oslo*

Michael Haas
University of Hawaii

John C. Harsanyi
University of California, Berkeley

Charles F. and Margaret G. Hermann
Princeton University

John H. Herz
City College of New York

Roger Hilsman
Columbia University

Stanley Hoffmann
Harvard University

Gary D. Hoggard
University of Southern California

Ole R. Holsti
University of British Columbia

Robert Jervis
Harvard University

Morton A. Kaplan
University of Chicago

Herbert C. Kelman
Harvard University

Allen Kessler

Henry A. Kissinger
Harvard University

Werner Levi
University of Hawaii

Charles E. Lindblom
Yale University

Charles A. McClelland
University of Southern California

Roger D. Masters
Dartmouth College

T. B. Millar
Australian National University

Robert C. North
Stanford University

Glenn D. Paige
University of Hawaii

E. Raymond Platig
Department of State

Ithiel de Sola Pool
   Massachusetts Institute of Technology
Dean G. Pruitt
   State University of New York at Buffalo
John R. Raser
   Western Behavioral Sciences Institute
Fred W. Riggs
   University of Hawaii
James A. Robinson
   Ohio State University
Thomas W. Robinson
   RAND Corporation
Richard N. Rosecrance
   University of California, Berkeley
Rudolf J. Rummel
   University of Hawaii
Bruce M. Russett
   Yale University
Burton Sapin
   University of Minnesota

J. David Singer
   University of Michigan
Melvin Small
   Wayne State University
Paul Smoker
   Peace Research Center, Lancaster, England
Richard C. Snyder,
   University of California
Harold and Margaret Sprout
   Princeton University
Sidney Verba
   University of Chicago
Kenneth N. Waltz
   Brandeis University
Barton Whaley
Arnold Wolfers
Quincy Wright
   University of Virginia
Oran R. Young
   Princeton University

The purpose, scope, and contents of this book bear such little resemblance to its predecessor, published in 1961, that it might well be designated "Volume II" rather than "Revised Edition." The central aim of the original edition was "to narrow a large and persistent gap between scholarship and teaching in the field of international politics and foreign policy," while the primary goal of this collection is to heighten the interdependence of theory and research in the field. Whereas the 1961 edition consisted of fifty-five selections, here the scope has been expanded to fifty-seven selections. As for the contents, some of the selections of the previous edition have been reproduced, but the degree of overlap is very small indeed: only five of the original selections will be found here and thus fifty-two of these fifty-seven selections are new.

At first glance these thoroughgoing changes might appear to be cause for embarrassment to the editor. In the Introduction to the first edition it is asserted that the temptation to include articles dealing with current trends in world affairs was resisted, that articles were included "only if they seemed likely to be useful in twenty years," and that therefore "no selection in [the] book [could] be outdated by the course of events." How, then, to account for a new edition that, appearing only eight years after its predecessor, includes only 9 per cent of the original selections? The answer lies, quite plainly, in the editor's lack of foresight.

Further reflection about the reasons for this wide margin of error, however, reveals cause for satisfaction rather than embarrassment. It is now clear that I underestimated the rapid growth of the field during the 1960s. The gap between scholarly research and classroom teaching has narrowed so greatly that it has become quite commonplace for researchers to share their work with their students. Today even undergraduates are exposed to the complexities of systems theory, the premises of decision-making analysis, the applications of game theory, the techniques of quantitative inquiry, and the assumptions of internation simulations. No longer is it necessary to devote the early weeks of graduate seminars to breaking down and replacing ambiguous and unusable concepts acquired in the course of undergraduate training. The present-day student may be receptive or resistant to the idea of applying scientific methods to international phenomena, but in either event he is likely to be familiar with their uses as well as sensitive to their virtues and limitations.

This swift transformation in the teaching of international politics and foreign policy has been paralleled—and perhaps even fostered—by similar progress on the frontiers of theory and research. The 1960s have witnessed a remarkable growth in the scope and pace of the theoretical enterprise. Old models have been perfected and new ones have been developed; this has led to an increasingly sophisticated penetration of the mysteries of international life. Most significantly, theorists have begun to converge in their work, refining and clarifying their own models in terms of propositions framed by others. Nor have the advances at the empirical level been any less remarkable. The techniques of data-making have been perfected so rapidly that a growing wealth of systematic and relevant materials is becoming available. Whereas researchers were faced with an acute shortage of reliable data when the earlier edition of this book was compiled, now they are confronted with the problems of data storage and data retrieval. Furthermore, and perhaps even more significant, today a wide number of researchers are inclined to use each others' findings, both as tests for their own hypotheses and as the bases for new inquiries. As a consequence of these advances in theory and research, knowledge in the field is increasingly cumulative and decreasingly fragmented, a characteristic that is readily evident from a comparison of this volume and its predecessor.

In short, while innovation was the distinguishing feature of the 1961 edition, consolidation marks this new edition. The selections of the former have been largely replaced, not because they were made obsolete by the course of events, but because they were superseded by progress in the study of world politics. Many of the original selections continue to be useful and their utility may yet span the predicted twenty years, but even more useful materials have since become available. Thus the editor's embarrassment over the wholesale replacement of fifty selections gives way to satisfaction over the reasons for such a drastic revision.

Despite the extensive changes in the contents of the book, its basic organization has not been altered. The five parts used in the 1961 edition have been preserved and the breakdowns within the parts are also essentially the same. Most notably, the book continues to be organized in such a way as to concentrate on both the *actions* and the *interactions* of the actors who comprise the international system. Regardless of whether it is theory- or policy-oriented, most of the work in the field falls under either of these two foci. One group of theorists and researchers are interested in discerning regularities in the behavior of actors, in the common goals that are sought, in the means and processes through which the goal-seeking behavior is sustained, and in the societal sources of the goals and means selected. In other words, the members of this group are concerned with the study of *foreign policy*, and they tend to regard the condition of the international system at any moment in time as stemming from the foreign policy actions of nation-states. A second group of theorists and researchers are mainly concerned with the patterns that recur in the interaction of states, in the balances and imbalances that develop under varying circumstances, in the formation of coalitions and other factors that precipitate changes in the international system, and in the development of supranational institutions that might regulate one or another aspect of the international system. Stated differently, adherents of this approach are concerned with the study of *international politics*, and they tend to view the condition of the international

system at any moment in time as stemming from properties of the system that require conforming behavior on the part of its national components. While this distinction between the two foci is frequently either overlooked or dismissed, obviously it makes a difference whether one concentrates on the components of the system or on the system as a whole.* To overlook the distinction and use the terms *international politics* and *foreign policy* interchangeably is to lose touch with the phenomena one wishes to explain. To dismiss the distinction on the grounds that only one of the foci is capable of resolving the theoretical, research, and policy problems of the field is to risk the loss of valuable insights and findings that might have been yielded by the rejected focus. In short, there would seem to be ample room for both levels of analysis and thus the organization, as well as the title, of this revised edition continue to reflect this conception of the field. Part Three is composed of theories and approaches pertaining to the study of foreign policy, and Part Four contains materials addressed to the analysis of international politics.

Only two changes in the organization of the book are worthy of note. One is an expansion of Part Two on the international system. Conceptions of the system's properties and dynamics have become so much more sophisticated since 1961 that the addition of subsections C and D on its structural characteristics and regional subsystems seemed to be clearly necessary. The second change is to be found in the expansion of Part Five on research techniques and orientations. In the earlier edition this section contained only six selections; here it consists of seventeen and the number of research techniques identified has been expanded accordingly. This expansion reflects both the growth and the consolidation that marked the field during the 1960s. It reflects growth in the sense that students of international phenomena are more inclined than they were to subject their theoretical formulations to the test of systematic empirical data and they have thus adapted an ever-widening variety of research techniques to their needs. It reflects consolidation in the sense that these empirical orientations have led students to return to the older forms of research as well as to perfect the new ones, and thus the range of techniques presented in Part Five includes such traditional methods as the case study and the comparative assessment along with statistical analyses and mathematical formulations.

This expanded section on research methods also contributes to the primary purpose that this revised edition is designed to serve. As the field consolidated

---

* For an elaboration of this point, see Selection 3.

its gains during the 1960s, it became increasingly clear that only through a close and continuous interaction between theory and research could progress toward the comprehension of international phenomena be achieved. Some students may be more gifted as theorists and others may be more at home with empirical inquiries, but each needs the other to move forward. Theory divorced from data can never be more than idle speculation and research unguided by theory can never yield more than intriguing findings. Only through a full recognition of the interdependence of theory and research can an enduring and profound grasp of the complexities of world politics be developed, and it was the need to stress this interdependence that served as the prime motive to revise the 1961 volume. All the theoretical selections in Parts Three and Four evidence a pervasive sensitivity to empirical reality and all the methodological selections in Part Five rest on explicit theoretical foundations. Nowhere in this volume will the reader find a selection that attempts to construct a theory simply in order to interrelate ideas or one that seeks to perfect a method simply in order to manipulate data. The two types of selections are presented in separate clusters so as to facilitate comparison among different theories and among different methodological procedures, but every one of the seventeen selections in Part Five could just as easily have been interspersed throughout Parts Three and Four. Indeed, so interdependent are the theory and research components of all the selections that if the reader is not especially interested in comparing and assessing the various methodologies, he probably would be well advised to read Selections 41, 44, 46, 47, 50, 53, and 55 in connection with the relevant subsections of Part Three and Selections 42, 43, 45, 48, 49, 51, 52, 54, 56, and 57 in connection with the appropriate subsections of Part Four.

The main criteria for sifting the ensuing selections out of the vast welter of available materials follow from the foregoing considerations. In order to encourage further consolidation and to stress the interdependence of theory and research, again the temptation to include articles that examine transitory aspects of the current world scene was resisted in favor of others with more enduring theoretical or methodological foci. The utility of these selections may be diminished by continued progress in the field—and given the existing evidence of the editor's lack of foresight in this regard, it even seems hazardous to predict a life span of ten years for them—but none of them will be rendered obsolete by the course of events. Virtually all of the fifty-seven selections present theories, approaches, or methods that are relevant to one or another aspect of international politics and foreign policy and that, whatever their validity and usefulness, are applicable to a wider class of situations than prevail at any moment in time. Furthermore, in selections that originally turned from the development of theory or the application of method to the assessment of current events, the latter has been omitted in order to permit the inclusion of more materials consistent with the focus of the book.

Another criterion of selection stemmed from the wish to avoid, wherever possible, overlap with other collections of readings in the field. It seemed preferable to make more obscure materials available rather than to reproduce articles, however important, that had already been published in other anthologies. Consequently, a number of selections originally scheduled for inclusion were omitted when they subsequently appeared in other collections. At the same time, in the process of making this book a self-contained entity covering the entire field, a certain amount of overlap could not be avoided; a few of these selections will therefore be found elsewhere, although significant variations may obtain with regard to their abridgment.

One other criterion of selection needs to be mentioned: aside from the introductory articles presented in Part One, each selection had to be ultimately susceptible to empirical verification. No materials have been included that analyze the desirability of a particular course of action or that espouse the superiority of one set of policy goals over another. This is a book that seeks to explore the way international politics and foreign policy are or may be. It does not attempt to probe the way they ought to be. There is a place, to be sure, for normative theory in the study of world politics. One is a citizen as well as a student, so that questions of policy and morality can never be avoided. Yet, in the belief that the student will perform best as a citizen if the distinction between the two roles is clear, this volume is intended for the former and not the latter. It is assumed that a greater comprehension of why international politics and foreign policy unfold as they do will facilitate actions designed to influence how they ought to unfold. We live in troubled times, but this fact obligates us to apply our intelligence as well as our good will. The individual who feels that the world's problems are too urgent to allow for the pursuit of greater comprehension is likely to be neither a good student nor an effective citizen.

The task of developing the foregoing criteria and achieving such a thoroughgoing revision was aided greatly by a number of colleagues who responded at length to a questionnaire asking which selections in the original edition should be preserved and which ones should be replaced. In addition, several selections in this edition are the result of recommendations included in the responses to this questionnaire. Hence it is a pleasure to record my indebtedness to Professors William D. Coplin, Ernst B. Haas, Wolfram F. Hanrieder, Charles F. Hermann, Ole R. Holsti, Howard H. Lentner, Werner Levi, Lloyd Jensen, Morton A. Kaplan, Michael K. O'Leary, Norman J. Padelford, Willard Range, R. J. Rummel, Bruce M. Russett, J. David Singer, and Harold Sprout. An indebtedness to the Center of International Studies of Princeton University and the Research Council of Rutgers University for their support is also happily recorded. Maureen Berman, a political science major at Douglass College, and Ellen Grundfest, a Ph.D. candidate in Political Science at Rutgers University,

ably assisted in preparing the manuscript for publication, and the assistance of Mrs. Esther Rosenblum at all stages of the project is also gratefully acknowledged. A special word of thanks goes to Mr. Harry M. McConnell for his encouragement in undertaking such an extensive revision. Finally, my wife Norah has provided the kind of emotional and substantive support without which this revision could have been neither initiated nor completed. None of the foregoing, however, is responsible for any errors of judgment. The ultimate responsibility for the selection and organization of the readings is mine.

J.N.R.

January 15, 1969
NEW BRUNSWICK, NEW JERSEY

INTERNATIONAL
POLITICS
AND FOREIGN POLICY

Part One

International Politics and Foreign Policy as a Subject of Study

Every field of inquiry goes through an important and necessary stage during which scholars turn their attention to the kind of enterprise in which they are engaged. After a prolonged period of concern with substantive matters, self-consciousness of purpose develops and questions arise about the road which has been traveled to date and the direction which inquiry should follow in the future. At this point, histories of the field are written, explorations of its boundaries are undertaken, methods of research and analysis are scrutinized, the requirements of further theoretical concepts are reexamined and, if need be, rejected. While it is not always clear whether this process of maturation constitutes "healthy ferment" or "hopeless confusion," the nature and limits of the field eventually emerge with greater clarity, thus enabling its practitioners to move on to the central task of accumulating knowledge through the investigation and interpretation of substantive materials.

In the years since World War II the study of international politics and foreign policy experienced these inevitable growing pains and is beginning to show the signs of sophistication that mark the end of adolescence. Where the boundaries of the field were once a matter of considerable dispute, their ambiguity is no longer perplexing and instead it is recognized that the effort to draw them with great precision is at best arbitrary and at worst futile. Where the question of whether the field was a single autonomous discipline or a series of subfields scattered throughout the established disciplines once seemed extremely troublesome and important, it now seems superficial and trivial in contrast to the problem of comprehending substantive phenomena, whatever the discipline in which they may be formally located. Where the differences between the scientific and traditional approaches to the subject once appeared to pose a fateful choice among mutually exclusive premises and procedures, they are now seen to be complementary as well as conflictful and, accordingly, the existence of several viable routes to knowledge has come to be accepted.

On occasion, to be sure, "great debates" over such matters still find their way into print,* and some students thus still feel the need to adopt an inflexible stance toward those who employ different assumptions and methods. For the most part, however, the contentiousness of the 1960s has been replaced by an acceptance of

---

* Cf. Klaus Knorr and James N. Rosenau (eds.), *Contending Approaches to International Politics* (Princeton: Princeton University Press, 1969).

diversity and a readiness to get on with the job of conducting research and perfecting theory. Both the diversity and the acceptance of it are apparent in the seven selections that follow, particularly in the first two. Selection 1 differentiates between the traditional and scientific approaches to the field, but at the same time it accepts—even asserts—the notion that neither is inferior to the other and that, indeed, there is plenty of room for both approaches. Implicit in the reasoning, moreover, is the possibility that the two approaches may even serve each other—by the scientific investigators integrating the insights of the traditionalists into their hypotheses and by the traditionalists using the findings of the scientists to enrich and extend their analyses. Similarly, the second selection acknowledges the prevalence of diverse approaches in the process of attempting to summarize recent developments in the field through a tracing of its boundaries and contents.

The realization that international phenomena can be investigated at several levels of analysis (Selection 3), that theory and theorizing can take several forms (Selection 4), that several conceptions of the relationship between national actors and their environments can underlie inquiry (Selection 5), and that the generation of empirical data can be accomplished in a variety of imaginative ways (Selections 6 and 7) provides further evidence of the field's progress toward maturity. While modern students of international relations do not always agree on the best route to reliable knowledge, they do share an alertness to the differences between necessary and sufficient causes; between observation and influence; between historical accounts and quantified data; between pure research designed to extend comprehension and applied research intended to resolve immediate policy problems.

Furthermore, throughout the ensuing analyses it can readily be discerned that in addition to a growing acceptance of diversity, the maturing of the field has fostered a sense of confidence that the conceptual and methodological equipment with which to comprehend international politics and foreign policy is now available. A number of problems persist, but these are neither ignored nor depreciated by any of the authors. On the contrary, they are confronted directly and, given the tolerance, dedication, and sophistication that pervades all of the fifty-seven selections in this volume, it seems clear that workable solutions will eventually be found for even the most enduring problems.

A. Identifying the Boundaries and Contents of the Field

1. International Relations: Wisdom or Science?

Charles A. McClelland is Professor of International Relations at the University of Southern California. A longtime leader in the field, his many writings include *Theory and the International System* (1966). Recently Professor McClelland's research has consisted of an effort to chart basic patterns of interaction in the international system (see Selections 42 and 57). In this essay he outlines two basic approaches to the study of international politics and foreign policy that the student can follow. While the differences between the two approaches have been the source of considerable controversy, here their complementarity is also noted. [*Published for the first time in this volume*]

International relations as an academic field was established about forty years ago. During this period, a view has prevailed in European universities and, to an extent, among American scholars that this particular subject puts so many intellectual demands on its students that it should be approached seriously only by well-trained and mature graduate students. Even then, the idea of a general survey or a comprehensive introduction to the field continues to appear inappropriate to these people. The reasons for such an attitude have been advanced many times: one needs, first of all, an intensive grounding in the histories of many countries and this involves not only much careful study but also the mastery of several languages. It is often said that only through a knowledge of language can a person come to understand the ideas and feelings of a people. Secondly, in order to develop insights properly, one must have direct experience in living and working abroad. Travel is considered essential. Finally, it is thought that a secure knowledge can be obtained only in a few circumscribed areas—by a thorough and rigorous investigation of a few topics such as colonial administration in Indonesia under the Dutch or the diplomacy of the Nazi-Soviet agreement of 1939. Implicit is the notion that *no one man* can understand the sweep of international relations but that many specialists, each working in his own sphere, *together* have such knowledge. This, in unadulterated form, is what we shall call here the "wisdom outlook." Although we may not share these beliefs, they should not be discounted without investigation.

It is a fact that most of the concrete knowledge we have of international relations has been arrived at in the manner advocated in the wisdom outlook. For the most part, international relations knowledge has been a by-product of direct experience. The literature from ancient times—the Bible, the Homeric poems, the histories of Herodotus and Thucydides, and many others—show an accumulation of experience in dealing with foreigners. The ancient writings give much evidence of thought concerned with the management of relations between peoples. By 200 B.C., the Chinese literati were exploring many of the issues which agitate discussions of international affairs today—pacifism and militarism, isolation and intervention, political realism and political idealism, and imperialism—but these subjects appeared as part of the discourses on history and philosophy. The same is true of the knowledge which was given formal expression in the *Arthasastra*, a compilation of teachings and advice dealing with the relations between the kingdoms of ancient India.

In modern Europe, a long succession of commentators on international relations—Dante, Machiavelli, Guicciardini, Bacon, Grotius, Fenelon, Burke, Rousseau, Gentz, Bismarck, Lenin, Churchill, and a host of others—have set forth what they have understood the principles of international conduct to be as observed from the inside or close at hand. The usual literary form has been that of historical description of particular events and persons and joined to these, commentaries, generalizations, and statements of principles.

Present-day students who take the wisdom outlook are, in effect, reasserting the correctness of the old practice. What they are saying, in substance, is that reflections growing out of direct experience and historical study are two legitimate ways by which one gains access to a knowledge of international relations. Obviously, the wisdom approach puts great demands on the time and the intelligence of the student. The product of his study is an "understanding" that is not quite intuitive; it is more a synthesis constructed privately from both particular facts and general meanings. Each student must build up such understanding by his own individual intellectual effort sustained over a long period of time.

Perhaps the easiest way to explain the place of the wisdom outlook in the study of international relations is to argue that there is very little about the subject that earlier generations have not known and understood. The only important problem, therefore, is to recover this knowledge in each new generation and to apply it to current facts and situations. But there are no real shortcuts—no royal roads to knowledge—and always, we must learn by practical experience and the study of the past. Only a few men will be able to succeed; the experienced practical man who is also a competent scholar is a rarity. Ambitious young students are best advised, at the beginning, to concentrate their studies in diplomatic history, on the great books of commentary and

political philosophy, and on the biographies of famous practitioners of the diplomatic arts. Ill-advised are the attempts to learn by general principles and by searches for uniformities, recurrences, or likenesses in international affairs.

The scientific approach is very different in outlook and purpose. This has also been called the "behavioral" approach. Those specialists and scholars who have faith in the development of a science of international relations do not believe that it is necessary for everyone to go through the process the wisdom approach requires. The two approaches should not be thought of, however, as diametrically opposed. They are not mutually exclusive or even necessarily in conflict. The scientific assumptions and procedures are simply different.

The scientific point of view arises from the conviction that there are many new things to learn about international behavior and that discoveries about the flow of interaction we have defined previously as the reality of international relations are possible. The search is for the patterns of conduct, the recurring responses, and the regularities of action in international situations. The frank objective of the scientific approach is to learn about patterns and trends in order to be able to predict what is *likely* to happen in international relations. The goal is not to foretell exactly what events will take place in 1987 in China or in what year and under what specific circumstances the Cold War will end. The aim is to develop skill in showing "which way the wind is blowing" and, therefore, what might well happen under stated circumstances.

There is some parallel here with the science of meteorology. The weathermen have set up a system of observation so that the results give them an indication of whether it is likely to rain or shine in a particular area. With a little study, the layman can understand the general basis of meteorological work. Everyone knows the forecasts often turn out wrong, but we also understand that the meteorologist is dealing with a great many shifting variables and combinations. He, in brief, is a purveyor of *likelihoods*, not certainties. His science grows by unending struggles with the errors made in earlier predictions. The scientific approach to international relations proceeds from a similar preoccupation with the questions of how things work, of how the variables combine, and of possible and probable outcomes.

It was said earlier that the wisdom techniques include observations from the vantage point of practical experience and the study of the past. What, then, are the procedures of the scientific approach? There are, fundamentally, just three interdependent procedures. The first is the step of constructing testable hypotheses. A hypothesis is simply a statement about what is thought to exist, about how certain things appear to be related, or about how something operates. It is a guess in the sense that it is an explicit assertion that awaits proof or disproof. The second step involves the task of showing whether a hypothesis fits observable facts. A good hypothesis will include some indications of how the testing is to be carried out and it will be stated in a form so that there is a chance to show whether it is correct or not. The third step is merely the harvesting of results. This is the gathering, comparing, and integrating of the findings from numerous tests and hypotheses. When it seems warranted by the evidence, a prediction in terms of what is probable is announced. This is a circular cooperative game that goes on and on; anyone who is willing to abide by the rules may attempt to play. No extended apprenticeship in histories and languages is required as a prerequisite.

Now it must be pointed out, and without reservation, that the scientific (or behavioral) approach has failed to produce enough material to support a general survey of international relations. The accomplishment to date amounts to little "islands" of research and these little islands float in a "sea" of wisdom. Perhaps in another quarter of a century we shall see many links between the islands. These bridges, in other words, will be general explanations of how the international system works and of the directions in which it is moving.

Meanwhile, it is necessary to utilize both techniques and both approaches. It would be unwise to neglect the meaningful products of experience and history. Even if we should have grave doubts about the ability of the scientific approach to arrive ultimately at general statements concerning the regularities in international transactions, we need to respect the efforts of those who are already making contributions in this direction.

Every gain will make it simpler for increasing numbers of nonexperts to grasp the principles of international relations. Further, it is from the scientific outlook that encouragement is given to attempts to synthesize the imperfect knowledge already available into general patterns. A survey of the field or a simplified account of international relations becomes, in the scientific perspective, an interim public report. Although the idea may be argued in various ways, it is the scientific outlook which supports best the faith that large numbers of educated men who are not specialists may come to understand international relations, and from this knowledge, exert a wise influence in the struggles with international problems.

2. International Relations as a Field of Inquiry

E. Raymond Platig is presently Director of External Research in the U.S. Department of State. The ensuing delineation of the boundaries and contents of the international relations field is part of a larger evaluation that Dr. Platig prepared for the Carnegie Endowment for International Peace, where he held the position of Research Director for a number of years prior to taking up his present duties. In addition to outlining recent trends in the field, this essay sets forth the author's own position on how it should be defined and organized. The reader may not be inclined to accept Dr. Platig's formulation in its entirety, but its explicitness should encourage him to clarify his own conception of the phenomenon encompassed by the field. [*Reprinted from E. Raymond Platig, International Relations Research: Problems of Evaluation and Advancement (Santa Barbara: Clio Press, 1967), pp. 4–44, by permission of the author, the Carnegie Endowment for International Peace, and the publisher.*]

The field of international relations is currently experiencing a period of great research activity which some see as growth and others as dismemberment, which some see as intellectually invigorating and others as intellectual pretension, some as socially relevant and others as an escape into social irresponsibility.

It has not always been thus. To be sure, the brief history of international relations as a field of inquiry has been characterized by much internal dissension. But each phase of that history has appeared—at least to most observers—to have a dominant theme or central approach. Thus, insofar as American scholarship in the field is concerned, it is commonly said that the emphasis has shifted successively from diplomatic history in the early decades of this century, to current events combined with international law and organization in the interwar period, to international politics in the 1940s and 1950s.[1]

[1] For comments on changing emphases in the field, see the following sources: Kenneth W. Thompson, "The Study of International Politics: A Survey of Trends and

These past changes of emphasis took place within a fairly small scholarly community characterized more by the vigor of its internal debate than by the magnitude of its research activity. However, in the years since 1945, the research effort has grown apace. The forces effecting this change are familiar enough. From an American perspective they include the four intertwined revolutions of our time: (1) the revolution in the weaponry war; (2) the multifaceted scientific-technological revolution that is inexorably increasing the interdependence of peoples; (3) the growth of Communist power; (4) the anticolonial revolt and the associated revolution of rising expectations. These revolutions have, continuously since 1945, brought American society face to face

Developments," *Review of Politics*, 14 (1952), 433–467; Grayson Kirk, *The Study of International Relations in American Colleges and Universities* (New York, Council on Foreign Relations, 1947), pp. 2–8; William T. R. Fox, "Frederick Sherwood Dunn and the American Study of International Relations," *World Politics*, XV (1962), 1–19.

with innumerable problems and opportunities, some of them unprecedented in kind or in scale.

The mobilization of American scientific and scholarly talent in World War II aroused expectations that similar talent could be called upon to assist with the problems arising from increasing American involvement in a rapidly changing world arena. Private foundations and various agencies of the United States Government have shared these expectations with academic institutions and professional and learned societies, with the result that money for research and study has become available on an unprecedented scale.[2] These stimuli have resulted in the founding and growth of numerous research centers, institutes, and programs, primarily on university campuses but also in other places in American society, including the industrial world and the fascinatingly varied world of nonprofit institutions.[3] At the same time, the internal research

capabilities of government agencies have been enlarged and new relationships (involving a range of satisfactions and tensions) established between "practitioners" and scholars. To this rapidly expanding research enterprise there have come persons from various disciplines which previously demonstrated little concern for the practical and intellectual problems of the field.

Under the impact of these forces, a number of important developments have taken place in the past decade or two.[4] One striking change has been the emergence of numerous research programs, centers, and institutes concentrating on specific geographic areas. Such programs now exist for all of the major areas of the world and their output of studies and data has been truly impressive.[5] Since much of the stimulus for the growth of area studies has come

[2] This is not universally considered an unmixed blessing. For development of the thesis that "foundations are given to a 'policy of fashion' while government agencies to a 'policy of caution' in research sponsorship" see Gilbert Shapiro, "Social Science Research and the American University," *The American Behavioral Scientist* (October 1964), 29–35.

Figures on the funding of international relations and related research are not readily available. Recent efforts by the External Research Staff of the Department of State to compile information on social science research relating to foreign areas done on government contract demonstrate that even in this limited sector of the research enterprise it is necessary to place heavy reliance on estimates. These estimates do, however, suggest both the orders of magnitude involved and the accelerating pace of government-sponsored research. Thus, for example, 386 projects on Africa initiated in the years 1949–64 (59 per cent of them initiated in the years 1961–63) cost the government an estimated $76 million; 529 projects on Latin America initiated in the years 1957–64 (60 per cent of them initiated in the years 1961–63) cost an estimated $30 million; 381 projects on Communist China initiated in the years 1949–63 (18 per cent of them initiated in the years 1961–63) cost an estimated $12 million–$15 million; no estimate of cost is available for the approximately 1900 projects on the U.S.S.R. initiated in the years 1949–63 (35 per cent of them initiated in the years 1961–63). It is estimated that research of this type is currently being supported at the rate of $50 million per year. See "INR Leads in Research Coordination," *Department of State News Letter*, No. 45 (January 1965), 18–19. It should be stressed that these figures apply only to government contract research; they tell us nothing of the magnitude of government internal research or of privately funded research efforts.

[3] A recent survey has identified 140 organized, nongovernmental research programs dealing with the developing areas. U.S. Department of State, Bureau of Intelligence and Research, External Research Staff, *Research Centers*

on the Developing Areas (Washington, External Research Staff, November 1964).

[4] Neither international relations nor any of the other social sciences has yet had adequate treatment by historians and sociologists. It could be argued that the "sociology of the social sciences" is a seriously underdeveloped area of scholarship in view of the increasing social importance of these disciplines. Some aspects of the subject are explored in Daniel Lerner, ed., *The Human Meaning of the Social Sciences* (New York, Meridian Books, Inc., 1959), see especially Harry Alpert, "The Growth of Social Research in the United States," pp. 73–86; Pendleton Herring, Philip E. Mosely, and Charles J. Hitch, *Research for Public Policy* (Washington, The Brookings Institution, 1961); Leonard D. White, ed., *The State of the Social Sciences* (Chicago, The University of Chicago Press, 1956); Daniel Lerner and Harold D. Lasswell, eds., *The Policy Sciences: Recent Development in Scope and Method* (Stanford, Stanford University Press, 1951); Paul F. Lazarsfeld, "Observations on Organized Social Research in the United States," *Information* (December 1961), 3–37; Peter R. Senn, "What is 'Behavioral Science?'—Notes Toward a History," *Journal of the Behavioral Sciences*, 2 (1966), 107–22. For recent treatment of some aspects of particular disciplines see Elbridge Sibley, *The Education of Sociologists in the United States* (New York, The Russell Sage Foundation, 1963); Albert Somit and Joseph Tanenhaus, *American Political Science: A Profile of a Discipline* (New York, Atherton Press, 1961); Harold D. Lasswell, *The Future of Political Science* (New York, Atherton Press, 1963), esp. pp. 1–42; William D. Garvey and Belver C. Griffith, "Scientific Information Exchange in Psychology," *Science*, CXLVI (1964), 1655–59.

[5] A recent survey indicates that between 1954 and 1964 graduate language and area study programs have increased in number from 62 to 153. U.S. Department of State, Bureau of Intelligence and Research, External Research Staff, *Language and Area Study Programs in American Universities* (Washington, External Research Staff, 1964). See also, George M. Beckmann, "The Role of Foundations," The Non-Western World in Higher Education, *The Annals*, CCCXLVI (1964), 13–22.

from the needs of the times, there has been some unevenness in development. For example, partly owing to the interest of government agencies, the Human Relations Area Files, an increasingly valuable collection of data for crosscultural analysis, contain as many source pages on Vietnam as on the whole of South America.[6] Economic, educational, and sociological studies have been prominent in programs dealing with developing nations and areas. Along with country, area, and developmental studies, there has been a growing, though far from sufficient, number of comparative studies dealing with some of the basic processes of national and social life. Finally, there has been an impressive increase in strategic, tactical, and national security studies. Partly in response to these latter studies—and particularly in response to studies of strategy in the nuclear age—there has developed a somewhat amorphous "peace research movement."[7] One result has been a vociferous, if sterile, debate which now shows some signs of abating as those on all sides back away from questioning the dedication of others to the quest for peace—a quest which, it seems fair to assume, has been a major motivating factor in bringing individuals into the field of international relations from the very beginning.[8]

These developments have provided much raw material for the field of international relations which, more directly, is experiencing a mushrooming growth of new approaches to the study of the relations between and among nations.

The concept of political integration has provided a focus for attention to the processes and prospects for building larger communities of humankind.[9] Conflict resolution has attracted sufficient attention to support the institutionalization of a center for its study and the publication of a journal.[10] General systems theory has brought new perspectives to the study of the multistate system which have now deeply penetrated and multiplied within the field.[11] The political thought and practice of nonwestern multistate systems are being explored for suggestive and comparative purposes.[12] Decision making, long advocated as an important focus of study by Frederick S. Dunn, received new impetus in the mid-1950s.[13] Since then, that aspect of decision making involving the perceptions of actors has received increasing attention.[14] Game theory has undergone a rapid development and its applications to theory in the

---

[6] Donald Morrison, "Indexing the Human Relations Area Files," *The American Behavioral Scientist* (June 1964), 49–50.

[7] On strategic and national security studies see Gene M. Lyons and Louis Morton, *Schools for Strategy: Education and Research in National Security Affairs* (New York, Frederick A. Praeger, Publishers, 1965). For an account of the "peace research" response see L. Larry Leonard, "Development and Significance of Peace Research" (mimeo., November 25, 1964) and Arthur I. Waskow, "New Roads to a World Without War," *The Yale Review*, LIV (1964), 85–111.

[8] The unique contribution that has been or may be made by a "peace research" orientation is still a matter of much dispute. The thesis has recently been set forth that in the United States it can make no unique contribution to the study of international relations, but that in a European context it may serve as a vehicle to bring behavioral and natural scientists into the field. See John Burton, "'Peace research' and 'international relations,'" *The Journal of Conflict Resolution*, 8 (1964), 281–86. For a different but not contradictory view see Johan Galtung, "An Editorial," *Journal of Peace Research*, I (1964), 1–4.

[9] Karl W. Deutsch, *Political Community at the International Level*, Doubleday Short Studies in Political Science (Garden City, Doubleday & Company, Inc., 1954); Ernst B. Haas, *The Uniting of Europe* (Stanford, Stanford University Press, 1958); Ernst B. Haas, *Beyond the Nation-State: Functionalism and International Organization* (Stanford, Stanford University Press, 1964).

[10] The Center for the Study of Conflict Resolution at the University of Michigan and *The Journal of Conflict Resolution*, which began publication in 1957.

[11] Morton A. Kaplan, *System and Process in International Politics* (New York, John Wiley & Sons, Inc., 1957); Klaus Knorr and Sidney Verba, eds., *The International System: Theoretical Essays* (Princeton, Princeton University Press, 1961); Richard N. Rosecrance, *Action and Reaction in World Politics: International Systems in Perspective* (Boston, Little, Brown and Company, 1963); Kenneth S. Carlston, *Law and Organization in World Society* (Urbana, University of Illinois Press, 1962); Charles A. McClelland, "Systems Theory and Human Conflict," Elton B. McNeil, ed., *The Nature of Human Conflict* (Englewood Cliffs, Prentice-Hall Inc., 1965), pp. 250–73.

[12] Joel Larus, ed., *Comparative World Politics: Readings in Western and Pre-Modern Non-Western International Relations* (Belmont, Calif., Wadsworth Publishing Co., Inc., 1964); Adda B. Bozeman, *Politics and Culture in International History* (Princeton, Princeton University Press, 1960).

[13] Frederick S. Dunn, *Peace-Making and the Settlement with Japan* (Princeton, Princeton University Press, 1963); Richard C. Snyder, H. W. Bruck, and Burton Sapin, eds., *Foreign Policy Decision Making: An Approach to the Study of International Politics* (New York, The Free Press, 1962).

[14] Ole R. Holsti, Richard A. Brody, and Robert C. North, "Violence and Hostility: The Path to World War," Stanford University Studies in International Conflict and Integration (mimeo., February 1964).

field continue to be tested and assessed.[15] Simulation, in its various computerized and role-playing forms, has been used to explore the decision-making processes and to test and develop models of international political systems.[16] Arms control has provided the focus not only for much private academic study but also for the extensive research supported by the United States Arms Control and Disarmament Agency.[17] International organization, an established sector of the field of international relations, has in recent years been experiencing a revitalization and reorientation.[18] Elite studies, a product of the early postwar years, have been developed and refined through the use of survey techniques and sophisticated interviewing.[19]

This partial list of new approaches to the field should not be permitted to obscure the continuing vitality of scholarship making use of the more established analytical and narrative approaches. One impressionistic measure of this can be found in the nature of the volumes represented in the 1964 World

Affairs Book Fair. Of 935 volumes, approximately one-third are judged to fall wholly or in large part within the core of international relations as defined later in this chapter. Of these 300–350 volumes, probably less than 10 per cent makes significant use of one or more of the newer approaches.[20]

Most of the recent departures in theory and research rely upon concepts and techniques hitherto foreign to the field of international relations—concepts and techniques drawn from anthropology, communications, economics, operations research, psychology, and sociology.[21] Along with the new concepts have come new practitioners equipped with mathematical techniques of data handling and analysis: some applying probability models, some

[15] John von Neumann and Oskar Morgenstern, *Theory of Games and Economic Behavior*, 2nd edition 1947 (Princeton, Princeton University Press, 1944); Kaplan, *System and Process*; Anatol Rapoport, *Fights, Games, and Debates* (Ann Arbor, The University of Michigan Press, 1960), pp. 105–242; Knorr and Verba, *The International System*; Anatol Rapoport, *Strategy and Conscience* (New York, Harper and Row, Publishers, 1964).

[16] Harold Guetzkow *et al.*, *Simulation in International Relations: Developments for Research and Teaching* (Englewood Cliffs, Prentice-Hall Inc., 1963); Sidney Verba, "Simulation, Reality, and Theory in International Relations," *World Politics*, 16 (1964), 490–519; William D. Coplin, "The Northwestern Inter-Nation Simulation as a Theory-Building Exercise: An Evaluation Based on Contemporary Theories of International Relations" (mimeo. paper prepared for delivery at the 1965 Annual Meeting of the American Political Science Association).

[17] Donald G. Brennan, ed., *Arms Control, Disarmament, and National Security* (New York, George Braziller, 1961). A new international quarterly entitled *Disarmament and Arms Control* began publication in mid-1963. See also, U.S. Department of State, Bureau of Intelligence and Research, External Research Staff, *Studies in Progress or Recently Completed: Arms Control and Disarmament* (Washington, External Research Staff, 1964 ff.).

[18] "Research on International Organization: Program of a New Committee," *Items*, 7 (1963), 31–2. Large programs of research have recently been started at the Brookings Institution and the Maxwell Graduate School of Citizenship and Public Affairs at Syracuse University.

[19] Hans Speier, *German Rearmament and Atomic War: The Views of German Military and Political Leaders* (Evanston, Row, Peterson and Company, 1957); Raymond A. Bauer, Ithiel de Sola Pool, and Lewis Anthony Dexter, *American Business and Public Policy: The Politics of Foreign Trade* (New York, Atherton Press, 1963).

[20] *Catalogue of the Combined Book Exhibit* (New York, World Affairs Book Center of the Foreign Policy Association, 1964). Among recent works representative of theory and analysis firmly rooted in the more established approaches are William T. R. Fox, ed., *Theoretical Aspects of International Relations* (Notre Dame, University of Notre Dame Press, 1959); Horace V. Harrison, ed., *The Role of Theory in International Relations* (Princeton, D. Van Nostrand Company Inc., 1964); John H. Herz, *International Politics in the Atomic Age* (New York, Columbia University Press, 1959); Fred Charles Ikle, *How Nations Negotiate* (New York, Harper & Row, Publishers, 1964); Hans J. Morgenthau, *Politics in the 20th Century* (3 vols., Chicago, The University of Chicago Press, 1962), esp. 2, *The Impasse of American Foreign Policy*; Kenneth W. Thompson, *Political Realism and the Crisis of World Politics: An American Approach to Foreign Policy* (Princeton, Princeton University Press, 1960); Arnold Wolfers, *Discord and Collaboration: Essays on International Politics* (Baltimore, The Johns Hopkins Press, 1962). In the preface to his book Professor Herz makes a statement of more than passing interest:

> This is an old-fashioned kind of book. It is the result neither of teamwork nor of any similar type of group study or collective research. It is not the product of a seminar, nor that of a study conference for which the author acted as reporter. It has not issued from a lecture series, and it is not based on a field trip or any wide traveling whatsoever. The author has not used a single IBM facility in the book's preparation, nor has he conducted any interviews for it, whether in depth or otherwise. There has not been any polling, nor have questionnaires been distributed. As a matter of fact the book does not contain a single chart, graph, map, diagram, table, or statistical figure. It is simply the product of the application to problems and subject matter at hand of whatever intelligence was available.

[21] These developments are amply illustrated in two recent compendia: James N. Rosenau, ed., *International Politics and Foreign Policy: A Reader in Research and Theory* (New York, The Free Press of Glencoe, Inc., 1961) and Roger Fisher, ed., *International Conflict and Behavioral Science: The Craigville Papers* (New York, Basic Book, Inc., 1964).

searching for quantifiable indices of basic processes and factors, and some searching the storehouse of mathematical models for those that might fit arms races, negotiating behavior, etc. The electronic computer has been programmed for these purposes and for others, such as intensive analysis of the contents of diplomatic communications, the simulation of crises, and the analysis of voting records in international bodies. Though in some respects these "importations" (some might prefer to call them "interventions") have left the field of international relations in a state of conceptual and methodological disarray,[22] they have also served to make some of those workers in the vineyard whose original orientation was derived from the "hard core" disciplines of political science, history, law, and geography aware that other fields have some interesting and useful things to say about such central concepts as power, community, negotiation, administration, social change, acculturation, diplomacy, loyalty, opinion, violence, law, etc.[23] These "newer contributions" have not always been appreciated by the "traditionalists," not least of all because the new "frontiersmen" (the phrase is James Rosenau's) have sometimes appeared disinclined to assess with

care the adequacy of the maps prepared by their predecessors before discarding them and striking out on their own explorations.[24]

It would be an oversimplification to suggest that the current diversity and occasional acrimony in the field of international relations arise entirely from the challenge of and response to the forces of "behavioralism" and "quantification." Yet the vitality and inroads made by these forces form an important part of the picture; how much and how constructive a part of the picture is not readily agreed. Some see one or more of the newer approaches as useless, if not positively harmful, digressions; some see them as rediscovering old truths, some as refining old truths, and others as setting forth— or at least setting the stage for—new and more profound truths. In this respect international relations could well be characterized by the same terms that Harold Lasswell recently applied to political science. In many departments of political science, Lasswell writes:

. . . intellectual differences of scope and method are transmuted into fighting ideologies and slogans. In this way "philosophy," "morality," and "religion" manage to oppose "science," "pseudoscience," and "administrative triviality"; in reply, the "pursuit of verifiable truth" stands over against the "arrogance"

---

[22] J. D. B. Miller, in a recent mimeographed essay entitled "International Relations: Theory or comment?" has likened the present state of international relations to that in psychology in the 1920s when H. L. Mencken offered the following description:

Barring sociology (which is yet, of course, scarcely a science at all, but rather a monkeyshine which happens to pay, like playacting or theology), psychology is the youngest of the sciences, and hence chiefly guesswork, empiricism, hocus-pocus, poppycock. On the one hand, there are still enormous gaps in its data, so that the determination of its simplest principles remains difficult, not to say impossible; and, on the other hand, the very hollowness and nebulosity of it, particularly around its edges, encourages a horde of quacks to invade it, sophisticate it and make nonsense of it. Worse, this state of affairs tends to such confusion of effort and direction that the quack and the honest enquirer are often found in the same man. "The Genealogy of Etiquette," James T. Farrell, ed., *Prejudices: A Selection* (New York, Vintage Books, 1919, 1920, 1922, 1924, 1926, 1927, 1958 Alfred A. Knopf, Inc.), p. 17.

[23] A helpful overview of the forces that have been reshaping the study of international relations in the postwar years is provided in William T. R. Fox and Annette Baker Fox, "The Teaching of International Relations in the United States," *World Politics*, XIII (1961), 339–59. See also John Gange, *University Research on International Affairs* (Washington, American Council on Education, 1958).

[24] Kenneth N. Waltz, *Man, the State and War: A Theoretical Analysis* (New York, Columbia University Press, 1954, 1959), pp. 42–79, provides a critical review of much behavioral science literature in the field and concludes that even the "less extreme" behavioral scientists "often betray an unwillingness to study the political problems and theories of international relations before offering to contribute their insights" (p. 79). Professor Kenneth E. Boulding, economist at the University of Michigan, has long been in the vanguard of the "frontiersmen." In a recent review essay he both shows a willingness to reassess the contributions of the traditionalists and offers evidence of an earlier disinclination to assess their contributions with care. These tendencies are most clearly seen in his commendation of Hans J. Morgenthau for displaying in the 1960 edition of *Politics Among Nations* that he has "learned from his critics" some of those things that were in fact quite characteristic of Morgenthau's 1948 edition. Kenneth E. Boulding, "The content of international studies in college: a review," *The Journal of Conflict Resolution*. VIII (1964), 66–7. For additional comment on this problem of old and new approaches to the field see E. Raymond Platig, "Review of *International Politics and Foreign Policy: A Reader in Research and Theory*, edited by James N. Rosenau," in *The American Political Science Review*, 56 (1962), 431–32, and Gabriel A. Almond, "Anthropology, Political Behavior, and International Relations," *World Politics*, II (1950), 277–84.

of purported "truth by definition" and "private revelation." Even "mathematics" and "statistics" are fighting words, and "behavioral," "metaphysical," and "legalistic" are expressions of opprobrium or encomium. . . .

It is evident that the inner tensions of the recent decades of accelerated growth are to be explained in part by the tradition that political science is a microcosm of the macrocosm of law, the humanities, and the social and psychological sciences. Small wonder that scholars of diverse traditions have found it difficult to live with one another. If we examine the history of older departments of political science, we find that the original inhabitants usually migrated from elsewhere in the academic universe, often from history, philosophy, or law. Modern developments have broadened the intellectual antecedents or brought closer contact with sociology, psychiatry, psychology, social anthropology, and related disciplines.[25]

A necessary concomitant of this enlarged, diverse, and often divergent research effort has been the explosive growth of literature in and related to the field. The "publications explosion" has not been of the same order of magnitude as that in the natural sciences, but it is serious and has spewed forth a number of problems which place an additional burden on intellectual activity. Old bibliographic services have been unable to cope with either the increased volume of literature or the increased range of the literature that may be considered relevant. Nor have these services been able to incorporate adequately the new forms in which publication or distribution often take place, such as occasional papers, preprints, symposia, conference proceedings, and government reports. New bibliographic services have not yet taken up the slack, nor does the expanding literature on information retrieval reveal any firm consensus on how these problems ought to be handled in the social sciences or any part of them.[26] In addition, in the midst of this expanded research activity, it becomes both increasingly important and increasingly difficult to know what is currently being studied in order to have confidence that one's own research effort is sufficiently cognizant of and well articulated with others as to make its maximum contribution. The magnitude of this problem—even

within the limited sphere of government-supported research related to international relations—is suggested by the fact that an interagency committee established in the spring of 1964 and called the "Foreign Area Research Coordination Group" includes representatives of some twenty agencies.[27]

In brief, as a field of inquiry, international relations today resembles a poorly marked-out arena in which a multiplicity of research programs and strategies compete, coexist, overlap, or retain splendid isolation. In addition to being pretentious, it would also be quite undesirable for anyone at this point to propose a single research strategy for the field. Indeed, it is highly unlikely that any vital field of inquiry can or ever should have a single research strategy. Still the assumption which has inspired this volume—and which has not been disproved in the course of the inquiries and discussions on which it is based—is that the field of international relations would derive much intellectual profit from serious attempts to review and assess its various research strategies and scholarly activities and bring them into a more useful, if still flexible, relationship.[28] It is

---

[25] Lasswell, *The Future of Political Science*, pp. 36–7. For similar comments concerning sociology see Sibley, *The Education of Sociologists*, pp. 16–17.

[26] A good overview of the "state of the art" relevant to information problems in the social sciences can be found in *The American Behavioral Scientist* (June 1964), pp. 3–70.

[27] This group "will seek to insure cooperative effort in research activities, prevent duplication between agencies, encourage maximum use of research results, and promote efficient use of private research. Activities will focus on research in the social and behavioral sciences related to U.S. Foreign policy—political, military, economic and cultural." "State and Defense Carry Ball in Joint Foreign Area Research Program," *Armed Forces Management* (September 1964) p. 13. Not central but clearly related to the field of international relations is a recent inquiry into the "studies" activities of one of the armed services which concludes that eight separate "study efforts" produce approximately five hundred studies per year, full knowledge of which can be had—even by those with full access—only by consulting seventeen separate bibliographical sources which are not linked by any logical plan. Lt.-Col. Charles J. Davis, Annex C to the Army Study System, 2, *Study Documentation and Information Retrieval* (mimeo., March 1963), 6–10. One can take heart from these indications that government agencies not only are aware of the problems but are exerting themselves to analyze and cope with them.

[28] There have been and continue to be numerous reviews and assessments by individual scholars of those portions of the field that they find of greatest interest. These, however, like much of the work in the field, are widely scattered throughout the literature. Though often of great value, they generally suffer from the limitations imposed by the author's own immediate purpose. Thus even if one makes the considerable effort required to search them out, he finds it difficult to correlate their insights and arrive at anything resembling an integrated and reliable understanding of the current state of the field. More is said in Chapter III of this study about the way in which the field currently performs this function of review and evaluation.

even conceivable that a field which purports to understand the requirements of statesmanship might find the internal resources to hasten within its own confines the process, foreseen in the field of political science by Robert A. Dahl,[29] whereby the "behavioral mood" or "scientific outlook" ceases to be "a separate, somewhat sectarian, slightly factional outlook," and whereby the "new consensus" outlined by David B. Truman may emerge.[30]

The objective to be sought is not an overarching research plan, but rather a means of improving the research infrastructure of the field so that the knowledge being developed emerges efficiently, cumulatively, and in ways most relevant to those problems which cry out for intellectual analysis as well as those to which it can be applied. Attention needs to be focused on questions such as: What are the major trends in the field? By what standards are its thought and inquiry [in the field] to be evaluated? By whom and by whose writ? How, on a continuing basis, assess the field's accomplishments; reveal its weaknesses; mark out areas in need of rebuilding or ready for consolidation; identify directions that promise advance?

If the above description of the current state of the field[31] can be accepted as passably accurate,

then it might appear an exercise of foolish arrogance to attempt a definition of the field. Yet it is not a task that can be avoided if the writer expects his readers to follow his analysis, consider his prescriptions, and offer meaningful criticism. It is, therefore, to the task of constructing a working definition that we must turn.

International Relations Defined

Starting with the assumption that the natural, social, and cognitive life of man is a seamless fabric, and making the further assumption that this fabric is increasingly, if still loosely, global in scope, how does one identify those threads and isolate those sections which define a field of social inquiry? Clearly it is impossible to comprehend the entirety of human existence except at the very broadest level of generalization. Neither history, nor the social sciences nor the natural sciences, nor most of the humanities address themselves to the task of full comprehension. This remains the task of philosophy (and theology) which, when not preoccupied with logic chopping (or doctrinal disputation), remains the "queen of the sciences." But neither philosophy nor theology has concerned itself exclusively—nor should they—with offering propositions that can be used as hypotheses for empirical research. In their most profound tasks, they employ, but are not limited to, the approach of modern science; they assign some, and often crucial, validity to a world beyond reason and the senses. Science, it has been said, "is reason tempered by observation, and observation impregnated by thought; it is an orderly construction fitted to the world of the senses, an experiential search for a world of order."[32] Science in this broad attitudinal and methodological sense has demonstrated its utility in the social and psychological as well as in the natural realms. Whether the social sciences, as a body of theory and findings, provide an adequate base for social action and policy is a question to be addressed in the next chapter. But clearly there is much that can be learned about human social

[29] "The Behavioral Approach in Political Science: Epitaph for a Monument to a Successful Protest," *The American Political Science Review*, LV (1961), 770.

[30] "Disillusion and Regeneration: The Quest for a Discipline," *The American Political Science Review*, LIX (1965), 865–73.

[31] The reader interested in supplementing this sketch with some recent perspectives on the current state of the field—or parts of it—is referred to the following works, in addition to some of those already cited: Richard C. Snyder, "Some Recent Trends in International Relations Theory and Research," Austin Ranney, ed., *Essays on the Behavioral Study of Politics* (Urbana, University of Illinois Press, 1962), pp. 103–71; Stanley Hoffmann, ed., *Contemporary Theory in International Relations* (Englewood Cliffs, Prentice-Hall Inc., 1960); Charles A. McClelland, "The function of theory in international relations," *The Journal of Conflict Resolution*, IV (1960), 303–36; Harold D. Lasswell, "The Scientific Study of International Relations," *The Year Book of World Affairs 1958* (London, Stevens & Sons Limited, 1958), pp. 1–28; Robert C. North, "International Relations: Putting the Pieces Together," *Background*, VII (1963), 119–30; James N. Rosenau, "Convergence and cleavage in the study of international politics and foreign policy: a review," *The Journal of Conflict Resolution*, VI (1962), 359–67; Herbert McClosky, "Concerning Strategies for a Science of International Politics," *World Politics*, VIII (1956), 281–95; Kathleen Archibald, "Social Science Approaches to Peace: Problems and Issues," *Social Problems*, XI (1963), 91–104; Hans J.

Morgenthau, "International Relations, 1960–64," *The Annals*, CCCLX (1965), 163–71.

[32] Bixenstine, *Science*, 145, 466. For a definition on the same mode see Caryl P. Haskins, *The Scientific Revolution and World Politics* (New York, Harper & Row, Publishers, for the Council on Foreign Relations, 1964), p. 32.

behavior through application of the attitudes and methods of science. However, two things need to be noted: First, each of the natural and social sciences has been able to push back the frontiers of knowledge by limiting its search for order to only part of the totality of perceived reality. Second, this familiar partition of knowledge has been brought about less by the imposition or acceptance of arbitrary limiting factors than by considerations of relevance rooted in reason and experience. Thus two or more sciences beginning with quite different facets of reality have often found themselves dealing with many of the same phenomena.[33]

In other words, one can find little in the nature of things in reason or in experience on which to base the expectation that all the fields of inquiry can be sorted out into a neat pattern of disciplines, themes, areas, and problems. If we recognize that each field of inquiry is a developing human invention, and if we recognize that the fields of social inquiry in particular have mixed, varied, and often obscure origins, it is perhaps not surprising that there should be overlapping and competing claims among them. This absence of well-marked boundaries does not mean, however, that we must eschew all attempts at definition and settle for chaos. What it does mean is that no single definition of a particular field will encompass all of the work presented as a contribution to that field or exclude all of the work presented as a contribution to some other field. Any definition, therefore, is bound to alienate both those who feel unjustly excluded and those who see the integrity of their own fields threatened by the expansive claims of another. Perhaps these factors help explain a recent tendency to, in effect, settle for chaos under the guise of an operational definition which says that physics is what physicists do and international relations is what international relationists do.

We prefer to run the risks of alienation and controversy (risks which in any event we expect to encounter for reasons both more profound and more trivial than those related to questions of definition) and to approach the problem of definition by inquiring into the distinguishing core and the relevant scope of the field. Without a core there is no definable field; without attention to the scope there is danger of serious and unnecessary confusion with other fields of inquiry.

If what follows seems to some too basic and commonsensical, perhaps a moment's reflection will suggest that these characteristics are not inappropriate to the task at hand. A deliberate attempt has been made to minimize the use of specialized terminology in the hope that the few basic and broadly shared concepts actually employed here are sufficient to indicate the major realities for the analysis of which more refined and esoteric concepts may well be needed. The reader will note that the propositions to follow owe a great deal to the work of others in the field. However, since we aspire to a statement that is basic, synoptic, and coherent, no attempt has been made to provide a review of the large body of literature that has been perused, nor has an effort been made to identify seminal contributions. The author would be pleased if all who care to claim as their own any part of what follows would do so. He would be even more pleased if a large number were willing to accept what follows for what it purports to be: a workable though primitive definition of the field.

Some Preliminaries

1. As a field of inquiry international relations studies the distribution of power on a global scale and the interplay between and among power centers.

    1.0. *Power:* Power is used here in a very broad sense to encompass the entire range of man's influence and control over his fellow man. It includes both his ability to exert and his actual exertion of influence and control over the minds and actions of other men.[34] It might

---

[33] This is, of course, also characteristic of nonscientific disciplines. For some insight into the agonies it can create in the humanities see "Toward the Definition of 'Interdisciplinary,'" *ACLS Newsletter* (April 1963), pp. 9–11d.

[34] The fact needs to be faced that the social sciences suffer from a lack of precision in the agreed meaning of key concepts. Whether this stems primarily from the nature of the subject matter with which the social sciences deal, from the nature of the minds that have applied themselves to the subject matter, or from the "youth" of the disciplines is a question on which it is easy to stimulate debate. How this lack of precision relates to the scientific claims, aspirations, and potentialities of the social sciences is also a matter of some dispute. The concept of power is a case in point. Some would prefer that the term encompass influence or control, but not both; some would prefer that it denote only an *ability* to influence (and/or control); while others that it denote only *actual* influence (and/or control). Many have

be preferable to designate this "social power," but the simpler term will be retained with the understanding that power in this sense is distinguishable—if not always separable—from the physical, chemical, and biological power of the natural world.

1.0–1. To the extent men can command the power of the natural world, they may be able to use it as an element of their social power. To the extent men do not command the power of the natural world, it may serve to alter their social power and relations.

1.0–2. The physical ability to influence and control the minds and actions of men is one fundamental aspect of social power. This is epitomized by the instruments of physical violence.

1.0–3. The other fundamental aspect of social power is perhaps best called the psychocultural aspect. This is epitomized by the instruments of rational and emotional persuasion.

1.0–4. All other forms of power are compounded from these two fundamental aspects. It would serve no useful purpose here to present a new or repeat an old typology of forms of power. The point to be made is simply that in all of its forms social power is compounded of these two fundamental aspects—physical and psychocultural.

1.1. *Distribution of power:* Each person in contact with others is possessed of some degree of ability—however trivial—to influence others. Power is thus broadly diffused on a global scale. However, the thorough study of interpersonal relations on this scale has not been undertaken, presumably because it is considered unmanageable or likely to be unrewarding or both.

offered operational definitions of the term. [For a brief but provocative commentary on the concept of power see Karl W. Deutsch, *The Nerves of Government: Models of Political Communication and Control* (New York, The Free Press, 1963), pp. 110–27. For a different and more extensive analysis see George Modelski, *A Theory of Foreign Policy* (New York, Frederick A. Praeger, 1962), pp. 21–64.] Neither these nor a host of other issues concerning the meaning of power have been settled in the vast literature on the subject and they cannot be settled here, though it is recognized that both empirical research and the substantive discussion of theoretical or policy issues in international relations often require a more refined definition of power than is offered here.

1.1–1. In groups, men not only can combine—in an additive sense—some forms of the power each possesses but also can introduce a multiplier effect through organization and joint activity, thus creating new forms and orders of magnitude of social power. On a global scale, human groups are numerous, highly diverse in type, and often overlapping in membership and function. The thorough study of intergroup relations on this scale has not been undertaken, presumably because it, too, is considered essentially unmanageable.

1.1–2. In order to make manageable the unmanageable, it is necessary to select as a focus for study "those groups of greatest importance." If this phrase is not to mean everything and anything, it must refer, when we are speaking of international relations, to those groups which possess, in the global picture, major power.

1.1–3. Because man's command over the power of the natural world is one of the two fundamental aspects of social power, and because the power of the natural world is so closely associated with the physical characteristics of territory, it is not surprising that the extent and quality of territory under its control has traditionally been one of the significant indices of a group's power. Clearly the struggle for the exclusive or predominant control of territory has been one of the basic patterns of intergroup relations. Thus the territorially based group (whether tribe, city-state, empire, nation-state, or principality) has been, and continues to be, one of the centers of major power.

1.1–4. Because a group's ability to organize and direct its activities in a given territory is in part a function of psychocultural factors (which form the second of the two fundamental aspects of social power), it is not surprising that the most stable territorially based groups are often those having a large measure of ideological or cultural unity.

1.1–5. It is, of course, true that the world has never been divided among territorially based groups all founded exclusively on the principle of one territory, one culture, one ideology, one organization. But the exceptions, no matter how numerous and how important, do not invalidate the proposition that organized, territorially based groups belong to a class all members of which are, compared with all other classes of groups and most other discrete groups, major centers of power. Such groups, therefore, have constituted and continue to constitute a class of power units or centers which are important foci for the study of the distribution of power on a global scale.

1.2. *Government:* A territorially based group in which an identifiable organization provides over-all management of the power of the group and monitors the power relations of subgroups is said to have a government and is properly called a state.

1.2–1. Historically there have been stateless territories, ones in which there were no governments. There have also been territories in which two or more governments operated simultaneously through either a hierarchical arrangement (e.g., federations, colonies, protectorates), or a horizontal arrangement (e.g., condominia), or a situation of conflict (e.g., civil war); in such cases the statehood of the territory has often been in doubt.

1.2–2. However, the most persistent and common arrangement throughout recorded history is that of the territorial state, an arrangement wherein it has been relatively easy to identify a dominant (sovereign) center of power (government) within the territory. This was true in the ancient Far East, ancient India, and the ancient Mediterranean world, as well as at times and places in medieval Europe and predominantly in the modern era of nation-states.

1.2–3. In brief, it is governments which, for the most part, exercise the powers in so-called sovereign states and among which, therefore, one might expect to find many of the main power centers that interact on a global scale.[35]

1.3 *Sovereignty:* The concept of sovereignty defies brief analysis and its full meaning defies brief and noncontroversial statement. Thus its utility as an analytical concept is limited. However, it is a useful word for designating that class of states in which can be found most of the major centers of power on the contemporary global scene. A few additional words about it are, therefore, required.

1.3–1. In a legal sense, sovereignty means that the government of a state does not recognize the legitimacy of any external human restraints upon its behavior unless it has consented to those restraints.

1.3–2. In a political sense, sovereignty might be equated with autonomy, the full exercise of which requires that the government of a state command sufficient power to be able to reject external restraints or reverse its acceptance of them.

1.3–3. It is obvious that not all states that enjoy sovereignty in the legal sense command sufficient power to enjoy autonomy.[36] It is equally obvious that not even the government of the most powerful of states is able to avoid having some of its actions, both external and internal, influenced by external forces, especially

---

[35] All of the main power centers are not, of course, governments. See paragraph 2.2.

[36] Both the utility and the difficulty of distinguishing in practice the legal from the political meaning of sovereignty can be seen in the current phase of the Cyprus question. In a letter to *The New York Times* published on June 26, 1964, Ambassador Zenon Rossides pointed up the plight of a state that claims legal sovereignty but clearly does not enjoy autonomy. "Suffice it to say," wrote the Ambassador, "that a country that is deprived of the fundamental right to decide upon its own Constitution, or amend it even on matters of purely internal administration without the consent of three foreign powers, is obviously not an independent or sovereign country.

"It is an accepted principle of international law that a state cannot contract out of the substance of its internal independence and continue to be independent. Consequently either the treaties (the Zurich and London agreements of 1959–60) are valid and Cyprus is not independent but a territory under tutelage, or Cyprus is an independent country and the treaties, insofar as they negate or restrict that independence, are by that very fact rendered invalid . . .

"Once having been admitted to the U.N., Cyprus enjoys equal rights of full independence and sovereignty of a member of the UN, as prescribed by the Charter— including, of course, the right of self-determination.

"Aside from the legal aspect, the realities of life have shown that the conflict between the treaties and the provisions of the Charter has resulted in fighting and bloodshed in Cyprus.

"For a country cannot be independent and at the same time be subject to outside intervention, and be placed under an overhanging threat of invasion from another country on the preposterous claim that military intervention—in violation of the Charter—can be sanctioned as a lawful procedure under any treaty. Such logic would make nonsense of the Charter and of the main purpose for which the UN was established: the maintenance of peace in freedom."

those that can be brought to bear by the governments of other sovereign states.

1.3–4. It is because the governments of legally sovereign states are centers of great power (even though the amount of power located in each center varies over a wide range) without, at the same time, being immune to the influence that can be brought to bear by their "sovereign equals," that the interplay between and among the governments of sovereign states is properly thought of as lying at the core of international relations.

The Core of International Relations

2. Thus it can be said that the substantive core of international relations is the interaction of governments of sovereign states.

2.0 *Forms:* The interactions of governments of sovereign states take many forms, all of which are of concern to international relations. Among the many forms of governmental interactions the most important are diplomatic, military, and economic.

2.0–1. Except in rare cases, the interactions of governments of sovereign states take place within a framework of constant concern for the relative power of the interacting states vis-à-vis one another and other states. Therefore all interactions—whatever their outward form— are either frankly and intensely political or subject to becoming so on short notice.

2.1 *Political Systems:* For these reasons, the interactions of the governments of two or more sovereign states can be said to take place within a multistate system which, for most purposes, is a multinational political system.

2.1–1. International relations is concerned with past, present, emerging, and hypothetical multinational political systems.

2.1–2. International relations is concerned with all sizes of multinational political systems, ranging from two-state systems to all-inclusive (in the contemporary world, "global") international systems. In the contemporary world, local systems may usefully—but not exclusively—be thought of as subsystems of regional systems and the latter as subsystems of the international system.

2.1–3. International relations is concerned with all conditions of multinational political systems ranged along the continuum from violent conflict to peaceful integration.

2.1–4. International relations is concerned with all instrumentalities and forms of interaction among sovereign governments within multinational political systems: diplomatic, military, economic, psychological, legal, ethical, technical, and cultural.

2.2. *Actors:* The fact that governments of sovereign states are viewed as the most important actors in multinational political systems is not to be construed as meaning that they are the only important actors.

2.2–1. Governments have a virtual monopoly of the diplomatic and military forms of interaction.

2.2–1.0. International organizations play an increasingly important role in diplomatic relations not only by providing new settings for governmental interactions, but also as actors in their own right.

2.2–1.1. Multinational forces play an important role in military relations, as do rebel, guerrilla, volunteer, and mercenary forces.

2.2–2. In the economic, psychological, legal, ethical, technical, and cultural forms of interaction within a multinational political system, governments share participation with many other actors of various kinds.

2.2–2.0. No government of a sovereign state has total control over the people of the nation[37] it governs. To the extent a government's power is less than total, individuals and groups within the nation can and do enter into independent transnational relations and thus may become direct actors in multinational political systems.

2.2–2.1. In addition to nongovernmental actors based within the territory of a single sovereign state, there are also truly international groups that may play a direct role in a multinational political system. These may be organized religions (e.g., the Catholic Church),

---

[37] In keeping with common and convenient usage, we here and elsewhere use the term "nation" interchangeably with the term "state," even though the principle "one nation (in the cultural sense), one state" is little reflected in the realities of the contemporary world.

or organized political ideologies (e.g., communism) or international, intergovernmental organizations (e.g., the UN, the OAS, etc.) or international, nongovernmental organizations (e.g., international scientific unions, cartels, etc.).

2.2–3. From the point of view of a multinational political system, the importance of nongovernmental actors is a function of their power base, their independence from governmental power, and the ways in which their acts and goals are related to those of governments. To put it differently, the relevance of particular national subgroups and international groups to the core of international relations varies according to the extent to which their actions impinge upon the environment in which intergovernmental relations take place and upon the power and policies of governments of sovereign states.

2.2–4. In the contemporary world, governmental practices vary greatly as to when and to what degree they attempt to encourage, monitor, restrict, manage, or control these international transactions resulting from initiatives other than their own.

2.2–5. Thus the extent to which nongovernmental groups are direct and autonomous actors is a far-ranging but seldom an independent variable in contemporary multinational political systems.

The Scope of International Relations

3. In its attention to the actions and interactions of governments within a multinational political system, international relations cannot ignore the factors that influence those actions. These factors serve to define the scope of international relations and are of two kinds: (a) the characteristics of the governments that act—especially their relationships to the social entities they govern; (b) the context within which the multinational political system exists.

3.0. *Intranational factors:* Not only does the power available to a government depend upon its ability to organize and direct the populace of its state, but individuals and groups within a nation can and do exert influence upon

the government so that it will manage national power both internally and externally in ways that are supportive of the goals pursued by these individuals and groups. Hence such individuals and groups may play important roles as indirect actors in multinational political systems.

3.0 1. International relations penetrates as deeply into the internal life of a nation as is necessary to understand the actions of the government and other nationally based actors in a multinational political system.

3.0–2. The depth of penetration cannot be established *a priori;* it varies from nation to nation, from interaction to interaction.

3.0–3. International relations does not encompass all national studies, but it overlaps them, draws upon them, and at times generates its own essentially national studies in order to elucidate the actions, potentialities, vulnerabilities, and policies of governments and other actors in multinational political systems.

3.1. *The international social system:* International relations recognizes that each multinational political system—even the all-inclusive, global international political system—exists within an environment that influences the system and the actors and interactions within it. For the international political system this environment is most usefully thought of as a general international social system.[38]

3.1–1. The international social system, like other social systems, may be thought of as a series of interdependent, functional subsystems; the international political system is the most important of these subsystems for the field of international relations. Among the other constituent functional subsystems of the international social system are an economic system, a legal system, an ethnic system, and a scientific system; at a different but overlapping level there can be found an exchange system, a postal system, a public health system, a natural resources system, etc.

3.1–2. These functional subsystems have

---

[38] Each multinational political system may be thought of as having a corresponding multinational social system. However, for the sake of brevity and clarity, the discussion to follow deals only with the general international social system.

varying degrees of autonomy and coherence; each differs in the extent and nature of its dependence upon the others, especially in its dependence upon the international political system. Not all subsystems are relevant to every interaction in the international political system.

3.1–3. International relations encompasses all general and specific analyses of the international social system and its various subsystems. However, it assigns higher priorities to those analyses that bear most directly upon the behavior of actors in the international political system.

3.2. *Core and scope:* In its full scope, therefore, international relations has occasion to draw upon or supplement the social sciences, history, the humanities, and the natural sciences at numerous levels of analysis. Though its reach is great, it limits its empirical and intellectual load by grasping only those items that most illuminate the core—the interactions of the main actors in multinational political systems.

Some Implications: A Disciplined Multidisciplinary Approach[39]

4. Regardless of their origins, analytical methods and data processing techniques are characterized by a rapid rate of diffusion among the fields of social inquiry. Analytical methods are likely to remain more closely identified with specific fields of inquiry than are data processing techniques because the former employ the core concepts of a field; even so, diffusion of concepts and methods is more the rule than the exception. It is, therefore, as unrewarding to try to identify each and every field of social inquiry by its unique methodology or research

techniques as it is to search for an exclusive and clearly delinated subject matter for each field.

4.0. Since the core concepts of international relations are political concepts, the central method of analysis is political. The scholar or analyst whose primary method of analysis is other than political is most likely to contribute to the field of international relations when he either relates his results (both his data and his style of thinking) to the core political concepts or so presents them that others can easily establish the relationship.

4.0–1. International relations makes use of all data processing techniques appropriate to its historical, current, trend, and predictive interests.

4.0–2. International relations draws heavily upon those aspects of area studies that throw light upon local and regional multinational political systems; when necessary, it generates its own area studies.

4.0–3. International relations draws upon and stimulates those aspects of national studies that assist in the analysis of international political behavior; foreign policy, national security, and national economic studies are clearly the most relevant of these and are often undertaken directly as part of international relations inquiry.

4.0–4. International relations enriches its analysis of the conditions within multinational political systems by drawing upon the behavioral sciences for insights into the processes of conflict, cooperation, integration, transformation, pacification, negotiation, acculturation, communication, etc.

4.0–5. International relations draws upon and stimulates military, economic, and technological studies in order better to understand the material aspects of international political behavior; it draws upon psychological and cultural studies for the persuasive aspects; and ethical and legal studies for the normative aspects.

4.0–6. To enhance its understanding of the modes of interaction within multinational political systems, international relations draws upon and stimulates international organizational, administrative, small-group, and decision-making analyses.

4.0–7. International relations draws upon

[39] We disregard here the oft-debated question whether international relations is a discipline. An answer to the question is less a matter of intellectual necessity than a matter of academic structure and politics. Readers interested in the question may consult the basic treatment of it to be found in Wright, *The Study of International Relations*, pp. 16–61; C. A. W. Manning, *The University Teaching of Social Sciences: International Relations* (Paris, UNESCO, 1954); and Trygve Mathisen, *Methodology in the Study of International Relations* (New York, The Macmillan Company, 1959). For two recent perspectives see J. W. Burton, *The Year Book of World Affairs 1964*, pp. 213–29, and Ch. Boasson, *Approaches to the Study of International Relations* (Assen, the Netherlands, Van Gorcum & Comp. N. V., 1963).

and stimulates nonpolitical analyses of multinational systems where these are relevant to a more complete understanding of the operation of multinational political systems.

4.1. Ultimately, international relations scholars aspire to the same type of coherent analysis of the purposes, structures, and processes of the international social system as some social scientists[40] have recently been aspiring to for other social systems.[41]

[40] For a recent attempt to combine political science, sociology, and economics in a "tightly integrated approach" to society, see Alfred Kuhn, *The Study of Society* (Homeward, Ill., Richard D. Irwin, Inc., and the Dorsey Press, Inc., 1963). See also, Peter M. Blau, *Exchange and Power in Social Life* (New York, John Wiley & Sons, Inc., 1964).

[41] Some may be concerned that analysts of the international social system, in their desire for a coherent analysis, may find in the system itself greater coherence than actually exists, but there is no inescapable reason why they should. Indeed, this type of analysis is capable of generating valuable comparisons of systems by means of which the peculiar characteristics of the international social system can be elucidated.

3. The Level-of-Analysis Problem in International Relations

J. David Singer is Professor of Political Science at the University of Michigan. A pioneer in the effort to render the study of international politics more scientific, his many important works include authorship of *Deterrence, Arms Control, and Disarmament* (1962) and editorship of *Human Behavior and International Politics* (1965) and *Quantitative International Politics* (1968). As can be seen in Selections 7, 29, 35, and 45 as well as here, Professor Singer's contribution has been multifaceted and includes works that focus on theoretical problems, that present unique empirical data, that analyze crucial policy dilemmas, and that examine the methodological challenges confronting researchers. In addition, and perhaps no less important, Professor Singer's research has not curbed his involvement in political affairs. His commitment to the peace movement is as thoroughgoing as is his detachment in his scholarly and scientific inquiries, thus demonstrating that forfeiture of effective citizenship need not be the price of scientific research into international politics. In this essay Professor Singer argues persuasively that while the field consists of both international politics and foreign policy, the two are not the same and the differences between them are in certain respects unbridgeable. Indeed, the distinction that is drawn here between the two aspects of the field seems so basic that it has been introduced into both the title and the organization of this volume. [*Reprinted from Klaus Knorr and Sidney Verba (eds.),* The International System: Theoretical Essays (*Princeton: Princeton University Press, 1961*), *pp. 77–92, by permission of the author and Princeton University Press.*]

In any area of scholarly inquiry, there are always several ways in which the phenomena under study may be sorted and arranged for purposes of systemic analysis. Whether in the physical or social sciences, the observer may choose to focus upon the parts or upon the whole, upon the components or upon the system. He may, for example, choose between the flowers or the garden, the rocks or the quarry, the trees or the forest, the houses or the neighborhood, the cars or the traffic jam, the delinquents or the gang, the legislators or the legislature, and so on.[1] Whether he selects the micro- or macro-level of analysis is ostensibly a mere matter of methodological or conceptual convenience. Yet the choice often turns out to be quite difficult, and may well become a central issue within the discipline concerned. The complexity and significance of these level-of-analysis decisions are readily suggested by

[1] As Kurt Lewin observed in his classic contribution to the social sciences: "The first prerequisite of a successful observation in any science is a definite understanding about what size of unit one is going to observe at a given time." *Field Theory in Social Science*, New York, 1951, p. 157.

the long-standing controversies between social psychology and sociology, personality-oriented and culture-oriented anthropology, or micro- and macro-economics, to mention but a few. In the vernacular of general systems theory, the observer is always confronted with a system, its sub-systems, and their respective environments, and while he may choose as his system any cluster of phenomena from the most minute organism to the universe itself, such choice cannot be merely a function of whim or caprice, habit or familiarity.[2] The responsible scholar must be prepared to evaluate the relative utility—conceptual and methodological—of the various alternatives open to him, and to appraise the manifold implications of the level of analysis finally selected. So it is with international relations.

But whereas the pros and cons of the various possible levels of analysis have been debated exhaustively in many of the social sciences, the issue has scarcely been raised among students of our emerging discipline.[3] Such tranquillity may be seen by some as a reassuring indication that the issue is not germane to our field, and by others as evidence that it has already been resolved, but this writer perceives the quietude with a measure of concern. He is quite persuaded of its relevance and certain that it has yet to be resolved. Rather, it is contended that the issue has been ignored by scholars still steeped in the intuitive and artistic tradition of the humanities or enmeshed in the web of "practical" policy. We have, in our texts and elsewhere, roamed up and down the ladder of organizational complexity with remarkable abandon, focusing upon the total system, international organizations, regions, coalitions, extra-national associations, nations, domestic pressure groups, social classes, elites, and individuals as the needs of the moment required. And though

most of us have tended to settle upon the nation as our most comfortable resting place, we have retained our propensity for vertical drift, failing to appreciate the value of a stable point of focus.[4] Whether this lack of concern is a function of the relative infancy of the discipline or the nature of the intellectual traditions from whence it springs, it nevertheless remains a significant variable in the general sluggishness which characterizes the development of theory in the study of relations among nations. It is the purpose of this paper to raise the issue, articulate the alternatives, and examine the theoretical implications and consequences of two of the more widely employed levels of analysis: the international system and the national sub-systems.

I. The Requirements of an Analytical Model

Prior to an examination of the theoretical implications of the level of analysis or orientation employed in our model, it might be worthwhile to discuss the uses to which any such model might be put, and the requirements which such uses might expect of it.

Obviously, we would demand that it offer a highly accurate *description* of the phenomena under consideration. Therefore the scheme must present as complete and undistorted a picture of these phenomena as is possible; it must correlate with objective reality and coincide with our empirical referents to the highest possible degree. Yet we know that such accurate representation of a complex and wide-ranging body of phenomena is extremely difficult. Perhaps a useful illustration may be borrowed from cartography; the oblate spheroid which the planet earth most closely represents is not transferable to the two-dimensional surface of a map without *some* distortion. Thus, the Mercator projection exaggerates distance and distorts direction at an increasing rate as we move north or south *from* the equator, while the polar gnomonic projection suffers from these same debilities as we move *toward* the equator. Neither offers therefore a wholly accurate presentation, yet each is true enough to reality to be quite useful for certain specific purposes. The same

[2] For a useful introductory statement on the definitional and taxonomic problems in a general systems approach, see the papers by Ludwig von Bertalanffy, "General System Theory," and Kenneth Boulding, "General System Theory: The Skeleton of Science," in Society for the Advancement of General Systems Theory, *General Systems*, Ann Arbor, Mich., 1956, I, part I.

[3] An important pioneering attempt to deal with some of the implications of one's level of analysis, however, is Kenneth N. Waltz, *Man, the State, and War*, New York, 1959. But Waltz restricts himself to a consideration of these implications as they impinge on the question of the causes of war. See also this writer's review of Waltz, "International Conflict: Three Levels of Analysis," *World Politics*, XII (April 1960), pp. 453–61.

[4] Even during the debate between "realism" and "idealism" the analytical implications of the various levels of analysis received only the scantiest attention; rather the emphasis seems to have been at the two extremes of pragmatic policy and speculative metaphysics.

sort of tolerance is necessary in evaluating any analytical model for the study of international relations; if we must sacrifice total representational accuracy, the problem is to decide where distortion is least dysfunctional and where such accuracy is absolutely essential.

These decisions are, in turn, a function of the second requirement of any such model—a capacity to *explain* the relationships among the phenomena under investigation. Here our concern is not so much with accuracy of description as with validity of explanation. Our model must have such analytical capabilities as to treat the causal relationships in a fashion which is not only valid and thorough, but parsimonious; this latter requirement is often overlooked, yet its implications for research strategy are not inconsequential.[5] It should be asserted here that the primary purpose of theory is to explain, and when descriptive and explanatory requirements are in conflict, the latter ought to be given priority, even at the cost of some representational inaccuracy.

Finally, we may legitimately demand that any analytical model offer the promise of reliable *prediction*. In mentioning this requirement last, there is no implication that it is the most demanding or difficult of the three. Despite the popular belief to the contrary, prediction demands less of one's model than does explanation or even description. For example, any informed layman can predict that pressure on the accelerator of a slowly moving car will increase its speed; that more or less of the moon will be visible tonight than last night; or that the normal human will flinch when confronted with an impending blow. These *predictions* do not require a

particularly elegant or sophisticated model of the universe, but their *explanation* demands far more than most of us carry around in our minds. Likewise, we can predict with impressive reliability that any nation will respond to military attack in kind, but a description and understanding of the processes and factors leading to such a response are considerably more elusive, despite the gross simplicity of the acts themselves.

Having articulated rather briefly the requirements of an adequate analytical model, we might turn now to a consideration of the ways in which one's choice of analytical focus impinges upon such a model and affects its descriptive, explanatory, and predictive adequacy.

II. The International System as Level of Analysis

Beginning with the systemic level of analysis, we find in the total international system a partially familiar and highly promising point of focus. First of all, it is the most comprehensive of the levels available, encompassing the totality of interactions which take place within the system and its environment. By focusing on the system, we are enabled to study the patterns of interaction which the system reveals, and to generalize about such phenomena as the creation and dissolution of coalitions, the frequency and duration of specific power configurations, modifications in its stability, its responsiveness to changes in formal political institutions, and the norms and folklore which it manifests as a societal system. In other words, the systemic level of analysis, and only this level, permits us to examine international relations in the whole, with a comprehensiveness that is of necessity lost when our focus is shifted to a lower, and more partial, level. For descriptive purposes, then, it offers both advantages and disadvantages; the former flow from its comprehensiveness, and the latter from the necessary dearth of detail.

As to explanatory capability, the system-oriented model poses some genuine difficulties. In the first place, it tends to lead the observer into a position which exaggerates the impact of the system upon the national actors and, conversely, discounts the impact of the actors on the system. This is, of course, by no means inevitable; one could conceivably look upon

[5] For example, one critic of the decision-making model formulated by Richard C. Snyder, H. W. Bruck, and Burton Sapin, in *Decision-Making as an Approach to the Study of International Politics* (Princeton, N.J., 1954), points out that no single researcher could deal with all the variables in that model and expect to complete more than a very few comparative studies in his lifetime. See Herbert McClosky, "Concerning Strategies for a Science of International Politics," *World Politics*, VIII (January 1956), pp. 281–95. In defense, however, one might call attention to the relative ease with which many of Snyder's categories could be collapsed into more inclusive ones, as was apparently done in the subsequent case study (see note 11 below). Perhaps a more telling criticism of the monograph is McClosky's comment that "Until a greater measure of theory is introduced into the proposal and the relations among variables are specified more concretely, it is likely to remain little more than a setting-out of categories and, like any taxonomy, fairly limited in its utility" (p. 291).

the system as a rather passive environment in which dynamic states act out their relationships rather than as a socio-political entity with a dynamic of its own. But there is a natural tendency to endow that upon which we focus our attention with somewhat greater potential than it might normally be expected to have. Thus, we tend to move, in a system-oriented model, away from notions implying much national autonomy and independence of choice and toward a more deterministic orientation.

Secondly, this particular level of analysis almost inevitably requires that we postulate a high degree of uniformity in the foreign policy operational codes of our national actors. By definition, we allow little room for divergence in the behavior of our parts when we focus upon the whole. It is no coincidence that our most prominent theoretician—and one of the very few text writers focusing upon the international system—should "assume that [all] statesmen think and act in terms of interest defined as power."[6] If this single minded behavior be interpreted literally and narrowly, we have a simplistic image comparable to economic man or sexual man, and if it be defined broadly, we are no better off than the psychologist whose human model pursues "self-realization" or "maximization of gain"; all such gross models suffer from the same fatal weakness as the utilitarian's "pleasure-pain" principle. Just as individuals differ widely in what they deem to be pleasure and pain, or gain and loss, nations may differ widely in what they consider to be the national interest, and we end up having to break down and refine the larger category. Moreover, Professor Morgenthau finds himself compelled to go still further and disavow the relevance of both motives and ideological preferences in national behavior, and these represent two of the more useful dimensions in differentiating among the several nations in our international system. By eschewing any empirical concern with the domestic and internal variations within the separate nations, the system-oriented approach tends to produce a sort of "black box" or "billiard ball" concept of the national actors.[7] By discounting—or denying—the

differences among nations, or by positing the near-impossibility of observing many of these differences at work within them,[8] one concludes with a highly homogenized image of our nations in the international system. And though this may be an inadequate foundation upon which to base any *causal* statements, it offers a reasonably adequate basis for *correlative* statements. More specifically, it permits us to observe and measure correlations between certain forces or stimuli which seem to impinge upon the nation and the behavior patterns which are the apparent consequence of these stimuli. But one must stress the limitations implied in the word "apparent"; what is thought to be the consequence of a given stimulus may only be a coincidence or artifact, and until one investigates the major elements in the causal link—no matter how persuasive the deductive logic—one may speak only of correlation, not of consequence.

Moreover, by avoiding the multitudinous pitfalls of intra-nation observation, one emerges with a singularly manageable model, requiring as it does little of the methodological sophistication or onerous empiricism called for when one probes beneath the behavioral externalities of the actor. Finally, as has already been suggested in the introduction, the systemic orientation should prove to be reasonably satisfactory as a basis for prediction, even if such prediction is to extend beyond the characteristics of the system and attempt anticipatory statements regarding the actors themselves; this assumes, of course, that the actors are characterized and their behavior predicted in relatively gross and general terms.

concentrates upon the correlation between stimulus and response; these are viewed as empirically verifiable, whereas cognition, perception, and other mental processes have to be imputed to the individual with a heavy reliance on these assumed "intervening variables." The "billiard ball" figure seems to carry the same sort of connotation, and is best employed by Arnold Wolfers in "The Actors in International Politics" in William T. R. Fox, ed., *Theoretical Aspects of International Relations*, Notre Dame, Ind., 1959, pp. 83–106. See also, in this context, Richard C. Snyder, "International Relations Theory—Continued," *World Politics*, XIII (January 1961), pp. 300–12; and J. David Singer, "Theorizing About Theory in International Politics," *Journal of Conflict Resolutions*, IV (December 1960), pp. 431–42. Both are review articles dealing with the Fox anthology.

[8] Morgenthau observes, for example, that it is "futile" to search for motives because they are "the most illusive of psychological data, distorted as they are, frequently beyond recognition, by the interests and emotions of actor and observer alike" (*op.cit.*, p. 6).

[6] Hans J. Morgenthau, *Politics Among Nations*, 3rd ed., New York, 1960, pp. 5–7. Obviously, his model does not preclude the use of power as a dimension for the differentiation of nations.

[7] The "black box" figure comes from some of the simpler versions of S-R psychology, in which the observer more or less ignores what goes on within the individual and

These, then, are some of the more significant implications of a model which focuses upon the international system as a whole. Let us turn now to the more familiar of our two orientations, the national state itself.

III. The National State as Level of Analysis

The other level of analysis to be considered in this paper is the national state—our primary actor in international relations. This is clearly the traditional focus among Western students, and is the one which dominates almost all of the texts employed in English-speaking colleges and universities.

Its most obvious advantage is that it permits significant differentiation among our actors in the international system. Because it does not require the attribution of great similarity to the national actors, it encourages the observer to examine them in greater detail. The favorable results of such intensive analysis cannot be overlooked, as it is only when the actors are studied in some depth that we are able to make really valid generalizations of a comparative nature. And though the systemic model does not necessarily preclude comparison and contrast among the national sub-systems, it usually eventuates in rather gross comparisons based on relatively crude dimensions and characteristics. On the other hand, there is no assurance that the nation-oriented approach will produce a sophisticated model for the comparative study of foreign policy; with perhaps the exception of the Haas and Whiting study,[9] none of our major texts makes a serious and successful effort to describe and explain national behavior in terms of most of the significant variables by which such behavior might be comparatively analyzed. But this would seem to be a function, not of the level of analysis employed, but of our general unfamiliarity with the other social sciences (in which comparison is a major preoccupation) and of the retarded state of comparative government and politics, a field in which most international relations specialists are likely to have had some experience.

But just as the nation-as-actor focus permits us to avoid the inaccurate homogenization which often flows from the systemic focus, it also may lead us into

[9] Ernst B. Haas and Allen S. Whiting, *Dynamics of International Relations*, New York, 1956.

the opposite type of distortion—a marked exaggeration of the differences among our sub-systemic actors. While it is evident that neither of these extremes is conducive to the development of a sophisticated comparison of foreign policies, and such comparison requires a balanced preoccupation with both similarity and difference, the danger seems to be greatest when we succumb to the tendency to overdifferentiate; comparison and contrast can proceed only from observed uniformities.[10]

One of the additional liabilities which flow in turn from the pressure to overdifferentiate is that of Ptolemaic parochialism. Thus, in over-emphasizing the differences among the many national states, the observer is prone to attribute many of what he conceives to be virtues to his own nation and the vices to others, especially the adversaries of the moment. That this ethnocentrism is by no means an idle fear is borne out by perusal of the major international relations texts published in the United States since 1945. Not only is the world often perceived through the prism of the American national interest, but an inordinate degree of attention (if not spleen) is directed toward the Soviet Union; it would hardly be amiss to observe that most of these might qualify equally well as studies in American foreign policy. The scientific inadequacies of this sort of "we-they" orientation hardly require elaboration, yet they remain a potent danger in any utilization of the national actor model.

Another significant implication of the sub-systemic orientation is that it is only within its particular framework that we can expect any useful application of the decision-making approach.[11] Not all of us, of course, will find its inapplicability a major

[10] A frequent by-product of this tendency to over-differentiate is what Waltz calls the "second-image fallacy," in which one explains the peaceful or bellicose nature of a nation's foreign policy exclusively in terms of its domestic economic, political, or social characteristics (*op.cit.*, Chaps. 4 and 5).

[11] Its most well-known and successful statement is found in Snyder *et al.*, *op. cit.* Much of this model is utilized in the text which Snyder wrote with Edgar S. Furniss, Jr., *American Foreign Policy: Formulation, Principles, and Programs*, New York, 1954. A more specific application is found in Snyder and Glenn D. Paige, "The United States Decision to Resist Aggression in Korea: The Application of an Analytical Scheme," *Administrative Science Quarterly*, III (December 1958), pp. 341–78. For those interested in this approach, very useful is Paul Wasserman and Fred S. Silander, *Decision-Making: An Annotated Bibliography*, Ithaca, N.Y., 1958.

loss; considering the criticism which has been leveled at the decision-making approach, and the failure of most of us to attempt its application, one might conclude that it is no loss at all. But the important thing to note here is that a system-oriented model would not offer a hospitable framework for such a detailed and comparative approach to the study of international relations, no matter what our appraisal of the decision-making approach might be.

Another and perhaps more subtle implication of selecting the nation as our focus or level of analysis is that it raises the entire question of goals, motivation, and purpose in national policy.[12] Though it may well be a peculiarity of the Western philosophical tradition, we seem to exhibit, when confronted with the need to explain individual or collective behavior, a strong proclivity for a goal-seeking approach. The question of whether national behavior is purposive or not seems to require discussion in two distinct (but not always exclusive) dimensions.

Firstly, there is the more obvious issue of whether those who act on behalf of the nation in formulating and executing foreign policy consciously pursue rather concrete goals. And it would be difficult to deny, for example, that these role-fulfilling individuals envisage certain specific outcomes which they hope to realize by pursuing a particular strategy. In this sense, then, nations may be said to be goal-seeking organisms which exhibit purposive behavior.

However, purposiveness may be viewed in a somewhat different light, by asking whether it is not merely an intellectual construct that man imputes to himself by reason of his vain addiction to the free-will doctrine as he searches for characteristics which distinguish him from physical matter and the lower animals. And having attributed this conscious goal-pursuing behavior to himself as an individual, it may be argued that man then proceeds to project this attribute to the social organizations of which he is a member. The question would seem to distill down to whether man and his societies pursue goals of their own choosing or are moved toward those im-

posed upon them by forces which are primarily beyond their control.[13] Another way of stating the dilemma would be to ask whether we are concerned with the ends which men and nations strive for or the ends toward which they are impelled by the past and present characteristics of their social and physical milieu. Obviously, we are using the terms "ends," "goals," and "purpose" in two rather distinct ways; one refers to those which are consciously envisaged and more or less rationally pursued, and the other to those of which the actor has little knowledge but toward which he is nevertheless propelled.

Taking a middle ground in what is essentially a specific case of the free will vs. determinism debate, one can agree that nations move toward outcomes of which they have little knowledge and over which they have less control, but that they nevertheless do prefer, and therefore select, particular outcomes and *attempt* to realize them by conscious formulation of strategies.

Also involved in the goal-seeking problem when we employ the nation-oriented model is the question of how and why certain nations pursue specific sorts of goals. While the question may be ignored in the system-oriented model or resolved by attributing identical goals to all national actors, the nation-as-actor approach demands that we investigate the processes by which national goals are selected, the internal and external factors that impinge on those processes, and the institutional framework from which they emerge. It is worthy of note that despite the strong predilection for the nation-oriented model in most of our texts, empirical or even deductive analyses of these processes are conspicuously few.[14] Again, one might attribute these lacunae to the methodological and conceptual inadequacies of the graduate training which international relations

---

[12] And if the decision-making version of this model is employed, the issue is unavoidable. See the discussion of motivation in Snyder, Bruck, and Sapin, *op. cit.*, pp. 92–117; note that 25 of the 49 pages on "The Major Determinants of Action" are devoted to motives.

[13] A highly suggestive, but more abstract treatment of this teleological question is in Talcott Parsons, *The Structure of Social Action*, 2nd ed., Glencoe, Ill., 1949, especially in his analysis of Durkheim and Weber. It is interesting to note that for Parsons an act implies, *inter alia*, "a future state of affairs toward which the process of action is oriented," and he therefore comments that "in this sense and this sense only, the schema of action is inherently teleological" (p. 44).

[14] Among the exceptions are Haas and Whiting, *op. cit.*, Chaps. 2 and 3; and some of the chapters in Roy C. Macridis, ed., *Foreign Policy in World Politics*, Englewood Cliffs, N.J., 1958, especially that on West Germany by Karl Deutsch and Lewis Edinger.

specialists traditionally receive.[15] But in any event, goals and motivations are both dependent and independent variables, and if we intend to explain a nation's foreign policy, we cannot settle for the mere postulation of these goals; we are compelled to go back a step and inquire into their genesis and the process by which they become the crucial variables that they seem to be in the behavior of nations.

There is still another dilemma involved in our selection of the nation-as-actor model, and that concerns the phenomenological issue: do we examine our actor's behavior in terms of the objective factors which allegedly influence that behavior, or do we do so in terms of the actor's *perception* of these "objective factors"? Though these two approaches are not completely exclusive of one another, they proceed from greatly different and often incompatible assumptions, and produce markedly divergent models of national behavior.[16]

The first of these assumptions concerns the broad question of social causation. One view holds that individuals and groups respond in a quasi-deterministic fashion to the realities of physical environment, the acts or power of other individuals or groups, and similar "objective" and "real" forces or stimuli. An opposite view holds that individuals and groups are not influenced in their behavior by such objective forces, but by the fashion in which these forces are perceived and evaluated, however distorted or incomplete such perceptions may be. For adherents of this position, the only reality is the phenomenal—that which is discerned by the human senses; forces that are not discerned do not exist for that actor, and those that do exist do so only in the fashion in which they are perceived. Though it is difficult to accept the position that an individual, a group, or a nation is affected by such forces as climate, distance, or a neighbor's physical power only insofar as they are recognized and appraised, one must concede that perceptions will certainly affect the manner in which such forces are responded to. As has often been pointed out, an individual will fall to the ground when he steps out of a tenth-story window regardless of his perception of gravitational forces, but on the other hand such perception is a major factor in whether or not he steps out of the window in the first place.[17] The point here is that if we embrace a phenomenological view of causation, we will tend to utilize a phenomenological model for explanatory purposes.

The second assumption which bears on one's predilection for the phenomenological approach is more restricted, and is primarily a methodological one. Thus, it may be argued that any description of national behavior in a given international situation would be highly incomplete were it to ignore the link between the external forces at work upon the nation and its general foreign policy behavior. Furthermore, if our concern extends beyond the mere description of "what happens" to the realm of explanation, it could be contended that such omission of the cognitive and the perceptual linkage would be ontologically disastrous. How, it might be asked, can one speak of "causes" of a nation's policies when one has ignored the media by which external conditions and factors are translated into a policy decision? We may observe correlations between all sorts of forces in the international system and the behavior of nations, but their causal relationship must remain strictly deductive and hypothetical in the absence of empirical investigation into the causal chain which allegedly links the two. Therefore, even if we are satisfied with the less-than-complete descriptive capabilities of a non-phenomenological model, we are still drawn to it if we are to make any progress in explanation.

[15] As early as 1934, Edith E. Ware noted that ". . . the study of international relations is no longer entirely a subject for political science or law, but that economics, history, sociology, geography—all the social sciences—are called upon to contribute towards the understanding . . . of the international system." See *The Study of International Relations in the United States*, New York, 1934, p. 172. For some contemporary suggestions, see Karl Deutsch, "The Place of Behavioral Sciences in Graduate Training in International Relations," *Behavioral Science*, III (July 1958), pp. 278–84; and J. David Singer, "The Relevance of the Behavioral Sciences to the Study of International Relations," *ibid.*, VI (October 1961), pp. 324–35.

[16] The father of phenomenological philosophy is generally acknowledged to be Edmund Husserl (1859–1938), author of *Ideas: General Introduction to Pure Phenomenology*, New York, 1931, trans. by W. R. Boyce Gibson; the original was published in 1913 under the title *Ideen zu einer reinen Phänomenologie und Phänomenologischen Philosophie*. Application of this approach to social psychology has come primarily through the work of Koffka and Lewin.

[17] This issue has been raised from time to time in all of the social sciences, but for an excellent discussion of it in terms of the present problem, see Harold and Margaret Sprout, *Man-Milieu Relationship Hypotheses in the Context of International Politics*, Princeton University, Center of International Studies, 1956, pp. 63–71.

The contrary view would hold that the above argument proceeds from an erroneous comprehension of the nature of explanation in social science. One is by no means required to trace every perception, transmission, and receipt between stimulus and response or input and output in order to explain the behavior of the nation or any other human group. Furthermore, who is to say that empirical observation—subject as it is to a host of errors—is any better a basis of explanation than informed deduction, inference, or analogy? Isn't an explanation which flows logically from a coherent theoretical model just as reliable as one based upon a misleading and elusive body of data, most of which is susceptible to analysis only by techniques and concepts foreign to political science and history?

This leads, in turn, to the third of the premises relevant to one's stand on the phenomenological issue: are the dimensions and characteristics of the policy-makers' phenomenal field empirically discernible? Or, more accurately, even if we are convinced that their perceptions and beliefs constitute a crucial variable in the explanation of a nation's foreign policy, can they be observed in an accurate and systematic fashion?[18] Furthermore, are we not required by the phenomenological model to go beyond a classification and description of such variables, and be drawn into the tangled web of relationships out of which they emerge? If we believe that these phenomenal variables are systematically observable, are explainable, and can be fitted into our explanation of a nation's behavior in the international system, then there is a further tendency to embrace the phenomenological approach. If not, or if we are convinced that the gathering of such data is inefficient or uneconomical, we will tend to shy clear of it.

The fourth issue in the phenomenological dispute concerns the very nature of the nation as an actor in international relations. Who or what is it that we study? Is it a distinct social entity with well-defined boundaries—a unity unto itself? Or is it an agglomeration of individuals, institutions, customs, and procedures? It should be quite evident that those who view the nation or the state as an integral social unit could not attach much utility to the phenomenological approach, particularly if they are prone to concretize or reify the abstraction. Such abstractions are incapable of perception, cognition, or anticipation (unless, of course, the reification goes so far as to anthropomorphize and assign to the abstraction such attributes as will, mind, or personality). On the other hand, if the nation or state is seen as a group of individuals operating within an institutional framework, then it makes perfect sense to focus on the phenomenal field of those individuals who participate in the policy-making process. In other words, *people* are capable of experiences, images, and expectations, while institutional abstractions are not, except in the metaphorical sense. Thus, if our actor cannot even have a phenomenal field, there is little point in employing a phenomenological approach.[19]

These, then, are some of the questions around which the phenomenological issue would seem to revolve. Those of us who think of social forces as operative regardless of the actor's awareness, who believe that explanation need not include all of the steps in a causal chain, who are dubious of the practicality of gathering phenomenal data, or who visualize the nation as a distinct entity apart from its individual members, will tend to reject the phenomenological approach.[20] Logically, only those who disagree with each of the above four assumptions would be *compelled* to adopt the approach. Disagreement with any one would be *sufficient* grounds for so doing.

The above represent some of the more significant implications and fascinating problems raised by the adoption of our second model. They seem to indicate that this sub-systemic orientation is likely to produce richer description and more satisfactory (from the empiricist's point of view) explanation of international relations, though its predictive power would appear no greater than the systemic orientation. But the descriptive and explanatory advantages are

[18] This is another of the criticisms leveled at the decision-making approach which, almost by definition, seems compelled to adopt some form of the phenomenological model. For a comprehensive treatment of the elements involved in human perception, see Karl Zener *et al.*, eds., "Inter-relationships Between Perception and Personality: A Symposium," *Journal of Personality*, XVIII (1949), pp. 1–266.

[19] Many of these issues are raised in the ongoing debate over "methodological individualism," and are discussed cogently in Ernest Nagel, *The Structure of Science*, New York, 1961, pp. 535–46.

[20] Parenthetically, holders of these specific views should also be less inclined to adopt the national or sub-systemic model in the first place.

achieved only at the price of considerable methodological complexity.

IV. Conclusion

Having discussed some of the descriptive, explanatory, and predictive capabilities of these two possible levels of analysis, it might now be useful to assess the relative utility of the two and attempt some general statement as to their prospective contributions to greater theoretical growth in the study of international relations.

In terms of description, we find that the systemic level produces a more comprehensive and total picture of international relations than does the national or sub-systemic level. On the other hand the atomized and less coherent image produced by the lower level of analysis is somewhat balanced by its richer detail, greater depth, and more intensive portrayal.[21] As to explanation, there seems little doubt that the sub-systemic or actor orientation is considerably more fruitful, permitting as it does a more thorough investigation of the processes by which foreign policies are made. Here we are enabled to go beyond the limitations imposed by the systemic level and to replace mere correlation with the more significant causation. And in terms of prediction, both orientations seem to offer a similar degree of promise. Here the issue is a function of what we seek to predict. Thus the policy-maker will tend to prefer predictions about the way in which nation x or y will react to a contemplated move on his own nation's part, while the scholar will probably prefer either generalized predictions regarding the behavior of a given class of nations or those regarding the system itself.

Does this summary add up to an overriding case for one or another of the two models? It would seem not. For a staggering variety of reasons the scholar may be more interested in one level than another at any given time and will undoubtedly shift his orient-ation according to his research needs. So the problem is really not one of deciding which level is most valuable to the discipline as a whole and then demanding that it be adhered to from now unto eternity.[22] Rather, it is one of realizing that there *is* this preliminary conceptual issue and that it must be temporarily resolved prior to any given research undertaking. And it must also be stressed that we have dealt here only with two of the more common orientations, and that many others are available and perhaps even more fruitful potentially than either of those selected here. Moreover, the international system gives many indications of prospective change, and it may well be that existing institutional forms will take on new characteristics or that new ones will appear to take their place. As a matter of fact, if incapacity to perform its functions leads to the transformation or decay of an institution, we may expect a steady deterioration and even ultimate disappearance of the national state as a significant actor in the world political system.

However, even if the case for one or another of the possible levels of analysis cannot be made with any certainty, one must nevertheless maintain a continuing awareness as to their use. We may utilize one level here and another there, but we cannot afford to shift our orientation in the midst of a study. And when we do in fact make an original selection or replace one with another at appropriate times, we must do so with a full awareness of the descriptive, explanatory, and predictive implications of such choice.

A final point remains to be discussed. Despite this lengthy exegesis, one might still be prone to inquire whether this is not merely a sterile exercise in verbal gymnastics. What, it might be asked, is the difference between the two levels of analysis if the empirical referents remain essentially the same? Or, to put it another way, is there any difference between international relations and comparative foreign policy? Perhaps a few illustrations will illuminate the subtle but important differences which emerge when one's level of analysis shifts. One might, for

[21] In a review article dealing with two of the more recent and provocative efforts toward theory (Morton A. Kaplan, *System and Process in International Politics*, New York, 1957, and George Liska, *International Equilibrium*, Cambridge, Mass., 1957), Charles P. Kindleberger adds a further—if not altogether persuasive—argument in favor of the lower, sub-systemic level of analysis: "The total system is infinitely complex with everything interacting. One can discuss it intelligently, therefore, only bit by bit." "Scientific International Politics," *World Politics*, XI (October 1958), p. 86.

[22] It should also be kept in mind that one could conceivably develop a theoretical model which successfully embraces both of these levels of analysis without sacrificing conceptual clarity and internal consistency. In this writer's view, such has not been done to date, though Kaplan's *System and Process in International Politics* seems to come fairly close.

example, postulate that when the international system is characterized by political conflict between two of its most powerful actors, there is a strong tendency for the system to bipolarize. This is a systemic-oriented proposition. A sub-systemic proposition, dealing with the same general empirical referents, would state that when a powerful actor finds itself in political conflict with another of approximate parity, it will tend to exert pressure on its weaker neighbors to join its coalition. Each proposition, assuming it is true, is theoretically useful by itself, but each is verified by a different intellectual operation. Moreover—and this is the crucial thing for theoretical development—one could not add these two kinds of statements together to achieve a cumulative growth of empirical generalizations.

To illustrate further, one could, at the systemic level, postulate that when the distribution of power in the international system is highly diffused, it is more stable than when the discernible clustering of well-defined coalitions occurs. And at the sub-systemic or national level, the same empirical phenomena would produce this sort of proposition: when a nation's decision-makers find it difficult to categorize other nations readily as friend or foe, they tend to behave toward all in a more uniform and moderate fashion. Now, taking these two sets of propositions, how much cumulative usefulness would arise from attempting to merge and codify the systemic proposition from the first illustration with the sub-systemic proposition from the second, or vice versa? Representing different levels of analysis and couched in different frames of reference, they would defy theoretical integration; one may well be a corollary of the other, but they are not immediately combinable. A prior translation from one level to another must take place.

This, it is submitted, is quite crucial for the theoretical development of our discipline. With all of the current emphasis on the need for more empirical and data-gathering research as a prerequisite to theory-building, one finds little concern with the relationship among these separate and discrete data-gathering activities. Even if we were to declare a moratorium on deductive and speculative research for the next decade, and all of us were to labor diligently in the vineyards of historical and contemporary data, the state of international relations theory would probably be no more advanced at that time than it is now, unless such empirical activity becomes far more systematic. And "systematic" is used here to indicate the cumulative growth of inductive and deductive generalizations into an impressive array of statements conceptually related to one another and flowing from some common frame of reference. What that frame of reference should be, or will be, cannot be said with much certainty, but it does seem clear that it must exist. As long as we evade some of these crucial *a priori* decisions, our empiricism will amount to little more than an ever-growing potpourri of discrete, disparate, non-comparable, and isolated bits of information or extremely low-level generalizations. And, as such, they will make little contribution to the growth of a theory of international relations.

4. Theory and International Relations

Stanley Hoffmann is Professor of Government at Harvard University. A specialist in the politics of France and of international organizations as well as general theory, his many writings include *Contemporary Theory in International Politics* (1960), *The State of War* (1965), and *Gulliver's Troubles, or the Setting of American Foreign Policy* (1968). In this essay he notes that various kinds of theories can be constructed to explain international politics and that each kind presents the student of the subject with both opportunities and limitations. Professor Hoffmann's analysis clearly demonstrates that theory does not come into existence on its own, that the student must make basic choices in order to probe at the theoretical level, and that in making these choices he imposes limits on the kind of knowledge he can uncover. [*Reprinted from Stanley Hoffmann*, The State of War (*New York: Frederick A. Praeger, Inc., 1965; London: Pall Mall Press, 1966), pp. 3–21, by permission of the author and the publishers.*]

I

The theory of international relations is both very old and very young. It is old in the sense that, with the end of the medieval dream of a Christian Community, political philosophers very soon began to reflect on the "state of nature" in which states found themselves. These philosophers presented on the one hand interpretations of past and present relations among states; the question from which their interpretations flowed was whether these relations were such as to assure a minimum of order and peace (or under which conditions and thanks to which practices this minimum would obtain) or whether, on the contrary, the division of the world into discrete units condemned mankind to virtually permanent war. They looked for the causes of conflicts, as a recent book reminds us,[1] in human nature, in the nature of

[1] Kenneth Waltz, *Man, the State and War* (New York, 1959).

political or economic regimes, or in the very structure of the international milieu. On the other hand, these philosophers reflected on the future of relations among states either as philosophers of history certain of the direction history would take, or as reformers convinced that there were institutions, methods, and ideas which could ensure that harmony prevailed among nations and whose triumph it was necessary to insure.

But the theory of international relations is new, if one takes it in the sense of a systematic study of observable phenomena that tries to discover the principal variables, to explain the behavior, and to reveal the characteristic types of relations among national units. Such efforts of empirical theory, as opposed to philosophical theory, really began only after World War II. Why did they come so late? Why are they so important?

They came so late for a number of reasons,

among them the fact that the study of international relations only recently began to free itself from the disciplines of history and law. For a long time, the systematic analysis of world politics had been smothered by the history of international relations and by the study of the legal norms which attempt to order these relations but which, both insofar as they succeed and insofar as they fail, ought themselves to be included in a properly political study of international relations. Secondly, empirical theory developed in reaction to the ideologies that flourished before World War II, when the liberal vision of democratic and reconciled nationalities, the socialist vision of peoples finally united after the proletarian revolution, and the myth of international order—not to speak of ideologies forged by fascism and national socialism— all coexisted with and competed against each other. These ideologies were based on some of the philosophies I have already mentioned; they were well stocked with predictions and recommendations; they bolstered prejudices, they inspired statesmen, they were instruments for action as well as objects of belief. The reaction against them, when it came, naturally was to debunk them; understandably, it began in countries where ideologies had wreaked most damage in men's minds but where the social sciences were free to carry out their task to disclose and disenchant, and at a time when the differences between favorite utopias and international reality could no longer be reconciled: i.e., in the England of E. H. Carr and the United States of Spykman and Morgenthau. It was also normal that an empirical theory of international relations should have developed most rapidly in the country where the grip of history and law on the social sciences was weakest —that is, where political science had long enjoyed academic autonomy—i.e., in the United States.

As to the scope and significance of the effort, it is easily explained. First, in every discipline, empirical research and theoretical elaboration go hand in hand. Any good empirical study is no mere conglomeration of facts but is the verification of an implicit or explicit hypothesis, or at least it is the answer to a preliminary question and contributes to the construction of a hypothesis. In traditional political science, the relation of research to theory has always been close: thus, Aristotle's study of the political life of his time is mixed with a typology of regimes that is both a theory of forms of government and a theory of the relations between the social structure and the political system; in Tocqueville, we find both a detailed study of the United States and a theory of democracy.

Secondly, in the study of international relations itself, a certain haste in theoretical formulation can be accounted for both by the subject matter and by the country in which these formulations have been attempted. So many disciplines—law and sociology, geography and cybernetics, history and demography —impinge upon the study of international relations that priorities are indispensable; even if one considers political science as a science of synthesis rather than as an autonomous discipline, one must acknowledge that there is a basic difference between synthesis and juxtaposition, science and chaos. Each discipline tries to answer a different series of questions, and these questions and answers are not of the same kind: they differ in subject matter (man as a biological unit, or relations among men or goods, or geographical factors) and in aim (description, or explanation, or philosophy). To achieve synthesis, there must be a common denominator, a currency unit into which one can change the currencies of all the other disciplines. In the study of international relations, this standard is the *theory* of international relations, a body of statements aimed at elucidating phenomena that are studied in political science or in other relevant disciplines. In the United States, the theory of international relations has developed apace partly because the contemporary orientation of *all* political science is theoretical, due to its reaction to earlier "hyperfactualism," and also because of the influence of the physical sciences, sociology, and the new communications sciences.

At present, one can classify the main theoretical attempts as follows:

1. *According to degree of elaboration.* Some "theories" consist only of methodological *questions* for the study of international relations. On a more complex level, we find *hypotheses* meant to guide research. The last stage is that of *laws* that purport to explain phenomena and that are thus answers to questions or definitive hypotheses.

2. *According to scope.* In each of the preceding three categories, we can distinguish efforts to develop *partial theories* and attempts at a *general theory*. The respective advantages and disadvantages here are the same as in sociology or domestic political science.

Some theories of foreign policy, such as those on "decision-making," are partial, elementary theories; theories of strategy are partial, middle-range theories.

3. *According to object.* Here we find on the one hand *empirical theory*, oriented to the study of concrete phenomena, and on the other hand *philosophical theory*, which is oriented to the realization of an ideal, or which judges reality according to certain values, or which provides a description of reality based on *a priori* concepts of the nature of man or of various institutions. A third category is created by the "policy sciences," that is, action-oriented theory, the study of reality not for the pure pleasure of understanding but in order to act on it through power.

Among these empirical theories—whether partial or total; questions, hypotheses, or laws—we can make further distinctions: (a) *according to method:* the contrast here is between the deductive method, which tries to build abstract models from a small number of postulates so as to discover the rules of rational conduct in different situations; and the inductive method, which tries rather to start from concrete reality and to identify its significant features so as to make it intelligible; (b) *according to focus:*[2] certain theories are above all conceptualizations; their aim is to analyze and refine the main concepts used in the effort to understand relations among states. These conceptualizations provide the material for the two other types of theories: schematizations, which try to define the characteristic rules of conduct and the different types of relations from which these rules follow; and those concerned with determining factors, with a systematic analysis of the forces that account for events occurring as they do, for certain types of international relations emerging when they do, or for the actors behaving as they do.

These distinctions apply, of course, to all theory in the social sciences; the problems they pose (Can and should one concentrate first on such-and-such a category? Can and should one combine different types? What is the best method? *Et cetera*) are in particular common to theory in political science. Nevertheless, the theory of international relations is

in certain ways deeply original; the general problems of the social sciences are raised in it in special ways and with special sharpness.

II

This is not the place for a history or detailed critique of the principal attempts to formulate a theory of international relations.[3] Briefly stated *general* theories—or theories that attempt to be general—have appeared in two forms. On the one hand, there is the work of Hans Morgenthau, which is presented as at the same time empirical *and* philosophical, as a conceptualization, a schematization, a study of determining factors, *and* a series of laws. On the other hand, there are the apparently more modest theories, growing out of conceptual frameworks designed to identify the main variables and provide the organizational scheme for research —the theme of "decision-making," the theory of equilibrium, the notions of international systems or of "calculated control." As for *partial* theories, some of the most interesting of them focus on international integration (which owes a great debt to communications theory) and on strategy (based on game theory). These attempts raise, it seems to me, a number of logical problems.

1. Conceptualization is often not rigorous enough. A basic concept is sometimes troublesome because the analysis has not been fully carried out. Thus, the basic concept of power, dear to Morgenthau, suffers from multiple confusions: not only does the author fail to distinguish among different forms of power, but he confuses the quest for power which is the consequence of a human instinct common to all men in all societies, and the quest for power which is directly attributable to the structure of the international milieu. He also confuses power as the object or goal of politics and power as the means used to achieve a whole range of goals (of which power may or may not be one). Similarly, the concept of the international system—a useful concept, now very much in vogue—has not yet been sufficiently worked out, perhaps because the author who has carried it

[2] Here I am borrowing a very important distinction from Raymond Aron. See *Paix et guerre entre les nations* (Paris, 1962), "Introduction." (Published in 1966 in New York under the title *Peace and War*.)

[3] I take the liberty to refer the reader to the second part of Hoffmann, *Contemporary Theory in International Relations* (New York, 1960), as well as to my article "Vers l'étude systématique des mouvements d'intégration internationale" in *Revue française de science politique* (June, 1958), and to my review of books by John Herz and Morton Kaplan (*Op. cit.*, December, 1959).

furthest, Morton Kaplan, has proceeded deductively without paying too much attention to concrete phenomena. Three issues in particular need to be investigated here: the temporal limits to international systems (the criteria of historical definitions and determinations), spatial limits, and, finally, the exact nature of the relations between the international system and the actors in it; one of the dangers of the concept as it is now formulated is that it makes one believe that the system tyrannically determines the policy of national units within it, thus underestimating the autonomy of nations and the diversity of their actions at any given moment.

At other times, a basic concept is not useful because it is based on an unjustified generalization of an idea that is valid for a limited historical period only: such is the case with the concept of national interest, developed by Hans Morgenthau and Kenneth Thompson. This concept, if it is to be useful at all, presupposes a period of stability in international relations, limited objectives, national regimes that are similar enough to have roughly similar goals, and foreign policies that can be and are free from domestic passions and pressures.

Lastly, a basic concept may be faulty because it was taken from another discipline where it has a precise meaning and put into the framework of international relations where it is hardly more than an evocative metaphor: this is the problem with the concept of equilibrium, whose meaning is uncertain when the phenomena to which it is applied are not measurable and are as disparate as, for instance, military potential, relations between social classes, structures of international organizations, and a state's international commitments. Detailed empirical analysis of the "balance of power" reveals a multiplicity of practices that can hardly be subsumed under this single heading. In the same way, the notion of message, used so much in theories of "decision-making" and integration, suffers from a formalism that makes it difficult to apply to the complexities of international life.

2. A second problem, that of the level of abstraction of the schematizations, is raised by the widespread resort to deductive models. True, any schematization tends toward abstract models; examples from economic theory are often given in order to show how useful they can be. But, as Jean Meynaud has said, there is an essential difference between models that differ from reality only by a few degrees of abstraction and those whose divergence from reality amounts to a difference in kind.[4] The difference is one only of degree when the model deals with a measurable reality whose elements—goods or services—can be expressed in monetary terms, and with a relatively simple form of behavior expressed in monetary terms—such as maximization of the national product when one focuses on the over-all community, or the maximization of profit if one speaks of individual enterprises.[5] There is a difference in kind when the model attributes questionable objectives to the actors—the maximization of power or maintenance of the system—and above all when it eliminates variables that are extremely important but difficult to measure—the role of institutions, the decisions of political leaders, the ideologies that so often determine the choice of objectives (that is, the hierarchy of values which the gross national product, the nation's power, and its actions within the international system are meant to serve)—in other words, everything that distinguishes political phenomena from other processes of communication, political systems from other systems. The usefulness of a method that requires a re-introduction of essential variables when one wants to pass from the model to reality is very dubious.

This is why the use of deductive models has been important until now in only one area: in the study of strategy, where the analogy between the behavior of nations in conflict and firms in competition may be fruitful. Many writers see game theory as another systematization of strategies that is valuable both for theoretical understanding and for action. But there are two limitations. In the first place, game theory has still not progressed much beyond situations in which the antagonists are completely opposed, in contrast to conflicts where the partners are interdependent in certain ways, which is much

[4] *Introduction à la science politique* (Paris, 1959), p. 285, à propos the model of Anthony Downs. It may also happen that an apparently deductive model merely describes in abstract terms the main features of a concrete situation or system but does not really reach the situation's or system's essence; thus, it is not a real schematization. Mr. Kaplan's first two models are of this kind.

[5] On this point, see the excellent remarks of Charles P. Kindleberger in William T. R. Fox (ed.), *Theoretical Aspects of International Relations* (South Bend, Ind., 1959), chap. 5, pp. 78 ff.

closer to reality.[6] Secondly, all of international life cannot be studied as a single strategy of conflict: it is made up of a series of competitions, and the stakes are too varied to be reduced to a common measure; cooperation and conflict, coordination and bargaining are mixed in many and diverse ways; the prevailing uncertainty requires that the actors make a complex choice of means to attain whatever range of goals they have selected.

3. A third problem concerns the search for determining factors. Some of the theories that attempt to be at the same time schematizations and analyses of determining factors in international affairs stress one special factor. An interesting and little-known theory advanced by Panayis Papaligouras[7] posits an extremely strong tie between the behavior of states toward one another and the degree to which their political structures are similar or different. The international system is homogeneous when they are similar and stable (that is, when all the states comprising it have strong institutions, an effective legal order, and a generally accepted moral code); otherwise, the system is heterogeneous. More recently, George Modelski has emphasized the economic and social order by constructing two models of international systems, agrarian and industrial, which differ in size, composition, from the viewpoint of the division of labor, their stratification, and the methods used in each to assure order.[8] Both these theories tend to attribute to one determining factor consequences that could equally well be due to other factors and effects that can occur only when additional other conditions are present.

Inversely, theories such as those of Kaplan, which try to formulate the logic of national conduct without indicating which correlations are the most significant and which variables the main ones, remain in some way incomplete. This flaw is related to the tendency mentioned above of turning the international system into a kind of closed and rigorously deterministic society that dictates its laws to the states that make it up.

4. Some theoreticians (particularly those concerned with strategy, but also some writing on international law or integration) raise the cardinal issue of the relation between empirical theory and the so-called policy sciences. Research oriented to action requires both an analysis of reality and a definite choice of values. Unfortunately, these values are not always made as explicit as they should be. The theory may be based on the postulate that men should act according to the author's own ideals, or that the foreign policy of the nation for which he writes should adopt as its goal the achievement of these ideals—whether the maximization of power according to the criterion of greatest efficiency, or the growing integration of the Atlantic Community.[9] If, on the other hand, the values are made explicit, the orientation of the study raises another problem: were the Author to adopt the Prince's values and goals, he would become a professional apologist and an official propagandist; were he to start by defining his own values but subsequently shift to the study of how they could be achieved by his country's leaders and institutions, he might stumble into an even more dangerous nationalist perversion, trying to prove that the measures taken by the Prince actually do serve those values or that the triumph of those values would serve the national interest.

5. There is also the acute problem of the relation of empirical to philosophical theory. Some writers have denounced in "modern" (i.e., empirical) political theory a perversion of "classical" political theory that replaces comprehension of the essential nature of things with perception of process and of causal laws that allegedly determine man's behavior; the result, according to these critics, is to depreciate the value of prudence and to emphasize a utilitarian approach to research; it encourages a mushrooming of hypotheses that assume man's infinite malleability, a simplified view of power, and the abstraction of man from the polity.[10] Some of these critics would be more convincing if they were less indiscriminate, if they did not virtually condemn the very idea of empirical theory. And their views would be most respectable if they told us how philosophical theory

---

[6] See Thomas C. Schelling's important work *The Strategy of Conflict* (Cambridge, Mass., 1960), in particular, Chaps. 1, 3, 4, 9, and 10.

[7] *Théorie de la société internationale* (Geneva, 1941).

[8] See his essay in Klaus Knorr and Sidney Verba, eds., *The International System* (Princeton, N.J., 1961), pp. 118–43.

[9] See, for instance, Henry Kissinger, *Nuclear Weapons and Foreign Policy* (New York, 1957), and Karl Deutsch et al., *Political Community and the North Atlantic Area* (Princeton, N.J., 1957).

[10] See Richard Cox, "The Role of Political Philosophy in the Theory of International Relations," *Social Research* (Autumn, 1962), pp. 261–92.

all by itself penetrates to the "essence" of things, and what the order established in and by nature is. Unfortunately, we are only told that we have been "corrupted" so completely by modern theory and modern philosophy that we no longer have any way of finding out!

A second approach, not much more helpful, is provided by Morgenthau. His work does not exclude one theory to the benefit of the other but suffers from a confusion of the two. An *a priori* concept of human nature leads him to find, always and everywhere, forms of behavior whose permanence he states rather than proves. As a result, he confuses the present form of competition among rival units (the contest among nation-states) with a permanence of such competition in history; he considers as the chief techniques for accommodation and international order practices whose efficiency is neither complete nor everlasting. Any theory based on a belief in eternal truths of human nature brings us back to Bossuet's providential reading of history; it tends to find in concrete investigation only the evidence for those truths which had been smuggled in at the start. Neither philosophy nor science makes headway thereby: science ought not to be the mere demonstration of philosophical presuppositions; philosophy should not be satisfied with the assertions that all human actions are ambiguous and vitiated by original sin and that "moral absolutism" in inter-state relations therefore should be avoided. For, when incompatible values are locked in battle, an invitation to universal tolerance, to pure relativism, or to abstention is of little philosophical or practical help.[11]

However, the kind of empirical theory that tries to cut itself off from political philosophy completely and aims at total objectivity and neutrality is that which falls most readily into the previously mentioned errors—imitating the physical sciences, postulating a closed society, and tending to consider what is as what must be, since the international system it advances is ruled by laws that dictate their values and objectives to the units. Conversely, an insufficient analysis of reality has led a whole series of normative theorists—international jurists who follow

Hans Kelsen or Georges Scelle—into the opposite mistake, that of believing that what ought to be already exists.

Thus, the radical divorce between the two kinds of research results in confusions between "is" and "ought" which are as serious as their deliberate mixture.

6. Most theories of international relations rest on an insufficiently developed study of the notion of rational behavior in international affairs. They all try to describe the rules of rational behavior—Hans Morgenthau even states that this is in fact the ultimate aim. But the difficulty is to know what kind of rationality one is talking about. Some theorists (including strategic theorists) simply describe what would be rational conduct if the objectives they postulated were actually those of the nations under discussion— the quest for power, the achievement of the national interest, or the maintenance of the present international system. But do those nations really resemble these models? If they have different goals, or especially if the priorities of those goals have not been coherently and clearly set out, or if the goals are incompatible, the model of rational behavior loses much of its usefulness. This is why Morgenthau's and Kaplan's theories are most appropriate for stable systems with virtually fixed national objectives, when rational conduct consists almost entirely in the choice of the best means. In other periods, the first problem is the choice of goals: in such cases, one is no longer necessarily within the realm of rationality; values matter then, and they are often irrational —or unreasonable. Only if the system determines the goals which states must pursue even in such periods will we have a more or less satisfactory yardstick for judging rational behavior. Decision-making theory, on the other hand, presents a model of a rational decision-maker but without any reference to national goals and without asking whether the model conforms to the real world, in which many leaders often lack the information they need to make a wise choice of rational means after the goals have been set, and where decisions determining both ends and means are made collectively and are not always coherent.

There is another difficulty. The theorist tries to explain the behavior of the actors. But the system he analyzes, the logic of which seems unimpeachable to him, is to a certain extent his own artificial (if heuristic) construct: the actors themselves live in the

[11] This is Kenneth Thompson's tendency, under the influence of Hans Morgenthau and Reinhold Niebuhr. See *Political Realism and the Crisis of World Politics* (Princeton, N.J., 1960).

daily uncertainty of competition; they perceive the rules but dimly; and they have the power to affect, indeed change, the conflicts. The theorist tends to set forth what would be the most rational behavior for the actor given the laws of the system; the actor tries to set his course according to his own goals, which are only partially determined by the system and which also derive from all sorts of domestic forces. What is rational to the theorist may not be rational to the actor, for their frames of reference are not identical. Theorists, thus, at times consider as rational (hence, commendable) moves which presuppose that the nations recognize their common interests in the framework of the system—whereas the nations, involved as they are in international conflict, try to make gains at each other's expense and define their interests in terms of these contests.

These are the main difficulties. What kinds of research, accomplished in what way, could overcome them?

III

The starting point of any valid theory of international relations is the recognition of the radical difference between the domestic and the international milieu. There are circumstances where this difference tends to vanish—in nations whose cohesiveness is so weak that relations among its social or political groups resemble international relations. Also, at certain points in history, the two milieus are interlocked: at the present time, international politics borrows various institutions from domestic politics (parliamentarism, pressure groups, parties, unions); domestic politics is often subordinated to and, in some cases, even determined by international competition. However, a discipline must be based on a kind of ideal-type, a representation of the essence of the phenomena that are studied and of the essential difference between these and other phenomena. This does not exclude a subsequent analysis of instances in which the difference is blurred, but we find such an ideal-type at the starting point of any theory. "Domestic" political science and sociology are based on the model of the integrated society—a Community (a basic, if imprecise, consensus among the members, a fairly elaborate division of labor, and belief in a common good that is more or less broadly and clearly defined) endowed

with Power (a monopoly of the legitimate use of force which the state exerts directly on the citizens). The model from which a theory of international relations must start is that of a decentralized milieu divided into separate units. It is not a Community, but at best it is a society with limited and conditional cooperation among its members, whose primary allegiance is to the constituent parts and not to the body formed by their sum total; at worst, it is a battlefield. It has no central Power—hence, resort to violence by each unit is legitimate, and the institutions established among the units have no direct authority over individuals within the units.

Only if one starts from this point can one understand not merely (and obviously) the characteristic processes or institutions of international relations—war and diplomacy—but also the *internationales* of political parties and labor unions, or the legal and institutional efforts to rule out the use of force by nations. For the differences between *internationales* and domestic parties or unions, and the many failures of international juristic efforts, can be explained only if the difference between the two kinds of milieus is kept at the center of one's study.

From this starting point, it follows that:

1. The theory of international relations, since it asks questions common to all political science but in a unique framework, cannot simply transpose into this framework the hypotheses or laws of "domestic" political science. For there is an essential difference between the science of Power (or of "authority structures") and the science of the absence of Power (or of the multiplicity of powers, which amounts to the same thing). The decline of so-called idealist theories is due to their neglect of this distinction.

2. The theory of international relations—understood as a body of organizing principles allowing one to select from the contributions of the many disciplines dealing with relations among separate units and to use those contributions wisely—is a political rather than economic or sociological theory. Economic or sociological theory could provide the study of international relations with organizing principles only if a well-developed international community existed; at present, economic phenomena among nations and trans-national relations among individuals and social groups of different countries clearly reveal the latter's separation and rivalries. In some sociological theories of industrial society

(especially Parsons'), there is little room for the political sector; certainly, political life is not at the center of the theory. While this may be valid for some national societies (certainly not for all), one cannot conceive a theory of international relations that did not place in a central position the political phenomena deriving from the fragmentation of the world into separate units.[12]

Where does one go from there? Three possibilities occur almost at once. The first concerns the very purpose of theoretical research: it is essential that its first objective be understanding rather than action; pure theory must precede applied theory. Of course, the theorist should not lock himself in an ivory tower. The questions he asks in order to elucidate international relations are often provided by current events—indeed, each generation tends to study the events occurring about it in order to find answers to the pressing questions of the day—and the conclusions he reaches will probably, if they are correct, be useful for action. But if action becomes his goal, his research may be entirely distorted. To advise the Prince presupposes adequate empirical knowledge and a discussion of values. "Policy scientists" tend to skip over the latter and to be premature about the former. Moreover, there is a wide gap between the intellectual solution of a problem—i.e., a conclusion that allows us to understand the nature, origins, development, and effects of a problem—and its political solution. Theory tries to rise above events; action must take the events into account. From a given theory, multiple actions can be deduced; its main usefulness is negative—it shows what cannot be done. To move from empirical theory to action requires the re-introduction of events and values.

A second choice, related to the first, concerns the scope of theory. Should one begin with limited theories or with general theory? The former can be misleading, if they somewhat arbitrarily isolate one sector amidst all the phenomena of world politics and reach erroneous conclusions due to the neglect or distortion of the bonds that link this sector to the rest; policy scientists have not always been careful enough in this respect. Moreover, general theory is never built up from a mere sum total of more limited theories—scientific discovery usually proceeds the other way around—and the accumulation of partial theories raises the same problem of "convertibility" as the accumulation of disciplines. But we do not have any general theory, in the sense of a set of hypotheses covering all the data or in the sense of validated laws—far from it. We ought, then, to begin with a more modest general theory—a framework of concepts and questions dealing with all the phenomena and capable of orienting research by placing partial sectors in the context of the whole. From this point, efforts to produce well worked-out partial theories and efforts to refine the general theory by filling the framework with increasingly precise hypotheses could be made side by side.

A third choice concerns method. There are two schools of thought here, as we know. On one side, we find deductive theorists eager to provide us with a few highly general abstract propositions, from which predictions could be derived. They consider theory meaningful only if it makes prediction possible, and they regard theory's main function to discover regularities. On the other side, there are theorists who are concerned at least as much with differences as with similarities, and who do not believe that in the social sciences the bond between understanding and prediction or prescription is very close.[13] What they try to construct is a theory that distinguishes different categories or types of foreign policies and international relations and shows both the regularities—the rules—within each such category or type and the specific features that distinguish one from another. This kind of theory can, of course, at a high level of abstraction, use deductive models, but only in those areas where the difference between the model and reality is one of degree; in other words, at the level of general theory, these theorists prefer to take history as their point of departure. Of course, the concepts they apply may be both abstract and very general, but the schematizations they aim for and the hypotheses they try to verify will be much nearer reality than models of the first type. I, for one, prefer the second approach; its fruitfulness has been well demonstrated by Raymond Aron.

[12] Hence the flaws of theories that try to find in the economic structure of society the clue to international relations—for instance, the theory of imperialism and the theories of peace through trade or industrialization.

[13] The difference can be formulated as follows: for the first school, the more we understand, the better we should be able to predict; for the second, the more we understand, the clearer we should be about the limits and uncertainties of prediction.

What can, indeed, be accomplished by this kind of general theory, aimed at understanding rather than action? Three tasks ought to be performed by empirical theory:

To sharpen concepts. It is necessary, not to revise our vocabulary or invent a new one, but to analyze, indeed to dissect, the phenomena covered by terms such as power, interest, system, war, peace, alliance, equilibrium, international law. These efforts should lead to typologies as precise as it is possible to make them. None is needed more than the typology of national aims pursued in international relations: as we have seen, it is the absence of any classification of such aims that falsifies the concepts of power, of interest, and of rational conduct. There could be distinguished, I believe, the goals pursued by units in competition, and the tasks (or functions) accomplished through the process of international relations —the latter either a consequence of national drives to attain certain objectives or independent of such policies (trade and commerce, the diffusion of ideas and political systems, economic development).

To prune and sort out. An enormous number of models and hypotheses have accumulated over the years. Political philosophers and philosophers of history have provided us with models of international relations. Other social scientists have worked out theories that are filled with assumptions about world politics, usually with respect to the influence that a given variable (geography, population, or economic systems) exerts on world politics. The great ideologies that claim to make clear the present and future of inter-state relations and that continue to affect the actions of political leaders are another rich source of materials. A serious theory of international relations must filter out these explanations and predictions, determine the amount of truth in them, explain their flaws, and draw from all this hypotheses about the relations among different variables which can be tested by methodical research.

To study international systems. The idea of systems is probably the most fruitful of all the conceptual frameworks. It makes it possible to separate the theory of international relations from foreign-policy analysis, and yet it allows both to advance. Relations among states are not merely the peaceful or bellicose convergence of separate foreign policies. Important elements of the system—the structure of the world (the nature of the basic units, the distribution of power), supranational or transnational forces—may be neglected if one focuses exclusively on the competing units. Furthermore, the units' policies are themselves conditioned by the system—to what extent is a question to be reassessed with each new case. The comparative study of international systems should also allow one to define the main kinds of typical national behavior and the relative importance of the determining factors, as well as how the influence of each factor on national policy and consequently on the international system combines with the influence of other factors. Finally, the study of systems raises the problem of change from one system to another. Each element of an international system is in constant motion; one must, therefore, distinguish changes within the system from changes of systems. To do so requires a rigorous selection of criteria— that is, of the essential features selected to define each system,[14] a problem analogous to the characterization of types of political regimes in Aristotle or Montesquieu.

The theory of the contemporary international system also remains to be worked out. Here, we find some very original features—a revolutionary transformation in military technology; heterogeneous political regimes and economic systems; a change in the role of the state, which has practically ceased to be a unit of military defense; a dual evolution toward the formation of blocs and toward an increasing fragmentation into independent units; the coexistence of different ages of world politics; the presence of an international organization in which disparities are supposed to fade and the unity of the world is intended to emerge.

IV

These are the most urgent tasks of a general empirical theory of international relations, but there remains the important problem of the relations between empirical and philosophical theory. As we have seen, confusion between the two is as bad as their total separation. I would like to emphasize how grave the latter error is for empirical theory. It makes neither neutrality possible nor objectivity certain. As many writers have shown, the choice of concepts,

[14] Richard Rosecrance's *Action and Reaction in World Politics* (Boston, 1963) suffers from the author's neglect of the problems of delimitation between systems.

the selection of data, the interpretation of reality are always partly subjective. Reality is susceptible to multiple "readings"; each reading reflects the reader's personality and his more or less explicit philosophy. If total neutrality is beyond reach, the theorist must be saved from the antinomies which tore Max Weber between the universe of science—with its neutrality, its rationality, and its devotion to truth—and the world outside, a battlefield given over to conflicts of the gods, laid waste by prophets and demagogues, a terrain where one must choose between undemonstrable values. Such dichotomies tend to impel the scholar, outside his work, to nihilism and even to let chaos creep into his research in the social sciences; for understanding, which gives pride of place to some of the correlations research has produced, implies a choice among the possible interpretations of reality, since reality does not entirely dictate this choice, irrationality can insinuate itself.[15] The more generalized the research becomes, the more the choice risks being arbitrary.

The formula I would suggest as a way out of this vicious circle is the permanent and reciprocal warning by each kind of theory against the other. General empirical theory provides a first resort against the risk of arbitrariness, against the tendency to prophecy and political bias within empirical research itself: "The road to objectivity passes through theory,"[16] through the rigorous and systematic examination of the whole, through the construction of a framework in which even very general hypotheses can be submitted to a critical test. Empirical theory has its own laws, which require that biases be restrained and that taboos erected by society be ignored or destroyed. The point is to keep our prejudices from becoming obstacles to the search for truth, but this does not mean the values we believe in should not serve as our guide. The usefulness of philosophical theory for the empirical theorist is precisely that it helps him to make explicit the preferences subsumed in the categories he uses and the relationships he stresses, to reveal to him the postulates about the nature of man, of society, of the state, or of relations among states that are deeply rooted in him and that cannot but affect his work.

A genuine understanding of philosophical theory will therefore operate as a methodological warning system. Moreover, since political philosophers have been concerned primarily with issues at the heart of international relations—order, peace, the effects of the absence of power—the empirical theorists will find models for study and comparison in their works.

Conversely, the philosophical theorist ought to know and accept the results which empirical theorists reach, for, if there is a chasm between "is" and "ought," the theoretician of "is" nevertheless can suggest to the philosopher what is and is not possible, what follows from our desires, and what actual contradictions are hidden in them. Philosophy that ignores this advice ends up floating in a vacuum or becoming an escape from the political world (cf. various philosophies of international law), or its concluding tenets are unacceptable—excessively idealistic, or overly resigned to violence or to the ambiguity of all action precisely because it over simplified reality.

Does this mean that the empirical theorist should become a philosopher? If he is capable of it, why not? "The conclusions reached by scientific understanding lead spontaneously to wisdom."[17] Furthermore, the political philosophy of international relations is in such a lamentable state that help is sorely needed. In the past, the great theorists of international law were also philosophers of interstate relations; today, at the very time that the theory of international relations takes as its basic assumption the difference between domestic affairs and relations among states, prevailing theorists tend to ignore this contrast, either because they belong to the natural-law tradition or because they proclaim the unity of all law and reduce the state to a mere reference point of legal norms. The gap that has thus been opened can be filled only by integrating political philosophy to the issues of world order instead of to the problems of national foreign policies on which it focused under the influence of so-called realism.

Faced with the problem of order in a fragmented world, political philosophy must not ignore the difficulties which the very uniqueness of the international milieu poses and which frustrate the three conditions any political order tries to fulfill: security,

[15] See Raymond Aron's introduction to Max Weber, *Le Savant et le politique* (Paris, 1959).
[16] Aron, "Science et conscience de la société," *European Journal of Sociology*, I, 1 (1960).

[17] *Ibid.*

satisfaction, and flexibility. The history of international relations is a graveyard of theoretical and practical attempts to establish order despite the psychological, moral, and legal problems that render inoperable so many of the solutions worked out within nations. But the very values that any serious empirical theorist accepts and tries to promote in his work—respect for truth, freedom to investigate and to criticize, belief that mankind's history is not mere sound and fury (a belief without which there can be no social science)—guide him toward a certain kind of philosophy: if the multiplicity of gods and beliefs cannot be denied, yet how can the theorist refuse to embrace those values that make it possible to produce his work and that give it meaning? To opt for theory is to choose in favor of the universal, of reason, and of freedom against "carnivorous idols". Since universal imperatives are always threatened by excessive formalism, it is essential for political philosophy to discover how, within what limits, and at what cost these imperatives can be introduced into the world as it is: such philosophy must therefore both judge and condemn any solution that would restrict human freedom or increase violence in the world, and it must also recognize that whatever ignores the limitations the world imposes on rational action to promote these values works against the very ideal whose victory is sought. Political philosophy must be, therefore, both the quest for an ideal that corresponds to the values which inspire it, and constant awareness of the limitations.

To refer to the limits of action is to evoke Albert Camus—a man concerned with justice, with the dialogue between nations as well as within them, and concerned about limits, precisely because he saw nihilism threatening any artist or any philosopher who neglected either such imperatives or such modesty. Indeed, is the situation of the empirical or philosophical theorist so different from that of the artist which Camus so eloquently described in his essays and in his Nobel Prize speech at Stockholm? The theorist and the artist are both witnesses to man's longing for liberty and for order; both are torn between the need to isolate themselves from other men in order to create and the conviction that their work will contribute to that liberation of others which any effort guided by the "most humble and the most universal truth" will foster; both cannot fail to be aware of their own weaknesses; neither can become the servant of those who make history; nor can they abandon the right to proclaim that the men who make history do not always serve the values to which artistic or scientific research thus understood are dedicated.

5. Environmental Factors in the Study of International Politics*

Harold and Margaret Sprout have long been among the leaders on the frontiers of theory and research. Harold Sprout is Henry G. Bryant Professor of Geography and International Relations at Princeton University; Margaret Sprout has collaborated with her husband on a number of books and articles. Interested mainly in the geographical aspects of the field, they have co-authored such works as *The Rise of American Naval Power* (1939), *Toward a New Order of Sea Power* (1940), *Foundations of National Power* (1945), *Foundations of International Politics* (1962), and *The Ecological Perspective on Human Affairs* (1965). Among their central concerns in recent years have been the epistemological and theoretical problems that arise in the analysis of international politics and foreign policy. A number of these problems are identified in this selection. Especially useful is their delineation of five theories employed by researchers in the field that pertain to the role of environmental factors. Since several of these theories are mutually exclusive, the student entering the field is provided here with an opportunity to contrast them directly and to assess which one or ones he finds most congenial. [*Reprinted from* The Journal of Conflict Resolution, *I (1957), 309–28, by permission of the authors and the publisher. Copyright 1957 by the University of Michigan.*]

Those who practice statecraft, as well as those who study and write about it, seem generally to take for granted that the phenomenon called "international politics" is meaningfully related to the setting or environment or milieu in which political decisions are taken and executed.

Let us start with some illustrative examples.

* This paper is a sequel to *Man-Milieu Relationship Hypotheses in the Context of International Politics*, published in 1956 by the Center of International Studies at Princeton University. Both studies are products of a research program supported jointly by the Rockefeller Foundation and Princeton University. An earlier draft of the present paper served as basis for a panel discussion at the annual meeting of the American Political Science Association, in September 1957.

First, the words of a German diplomat, Richard von Kühlmann, that "geographical position and historical development are so largely *determining* factors of foreign policy that, regardless of the kaleidoscopic change of contemporary events, and no matter what form of government has been instituted or what political party may be in power, the foreign policy of a country has a *natural tendency* to return again and again to the same general and fundamental alignment" (our italics) (3).

Next, the French diplomat, Jules Cambon: "The geographical position of a nation . . . is the principal factor *conditioning* its foreign policy—the principal reason why it must have a foreign policy at all" (our italics) (1).

Third, from a recent text on sea power: "England *driven* to the sea by her sparse resources to seek a livelihood and to find homes for her burgeoning population, and sitting athwart the main sea routes of Western Europe, seemed *destined by geography* to command the seas" (our italics) (4, p. 44).

Fourth, from a highly regarded work on Japan: "The mountains of Japan have *pushed* the Japanese out upon the seas, *making* them the greatest seafaring people of Asia. . . . Sea routes have *beckoned* the Japanese abroad. . . . The factor of geographic isolation during . . . two thousand years has *helped fashion* national traits which eventually, and *almost inevitably*, *led* Japan to political isolation and to crushing defeat in war" (our italics) (5, pp. 5, 8).

Fifth, from a standard treatise on resources, the assertion that invention of the basic steel furnace (which made it possible to produce good steel from the acidic ores of Alsace-Lorraine) "*led inevitably* to Germany's industrial hegemony on the continent [of Europe]" (our italics) (11, p. 648).

In all such statements (and one could extend the list indefinitely), a causal relationship is asserted between some environmental factor or set of factors, on the one hand, and some attitude, action, or state of affairs, on the other. Some of the statements are phrased in deterministic language—"determined," "drove," "led inevitably," etc. Others, probably more numerous, are phrased in terms compatible with some degree of choice—"influence," "pressure," etc.

Such forms of speech and the causal relationships which they state or imply delineate the main issues with which this study is concerned: How are environmental factors related to political phenomena? And what forms of speech are most fruitful in expressing such relationships?

In approaching these questions, it will be helpful to draw a distinction between political attitudes and policy decisions, on the one hand, and, on the other hand, the layouts in space or other states of affairs which we shall call the "operational results of decisions." We regard this distinction as important, indeed as prerequisite to fruitful investigation of ecological viewpoints, concepts, and theories in connection with politics in general and international politics in particular.

Within these terms of reference, we shall attempt to establish the following propositions or theses:

1. Environmental factors become related to the attitudes and decisions which, in the aggregate, comprise a state's foreign policy *only* by being apperceived and taken into account by those who participate in the policy-forming process.

2. Conclusions as to the manner in which apperceived environmental factors are dealt with in foreign-policy-making depend on the theory or theories of decision-making which the analyst brings to bear on the case under consideration.

3. Hypotheses as to the manner in which apperceived environmental factors enter into the decision-making process can provide fruitful linkages between ecological and behavioral approaches to the study of international politics.

4. Environmental factors can be significantly related to the operational results of policy decisions, even though such factors are not apperceived and taken into account in the policy-forming process.

5. What is called analysis of state power or international power relations or (preferably, in our view) analysis of state capabilities consists essentially of calculating opportunities and limitations latent, or implicit, in the milieu of the state under consideration.

6. Capability calculations or estimates are always carried out within some framework of assumptions regarding the policy objectives, operation strategy, and political relations of the state under consideration.

7. Conclusions as to the opportunities and limitations which are implicit in a state's milieu and which may affect the operational results of its policy decisions depend on the ecological theory and the topical explanatory premises which the analyst brings to bear in the specific case under consideration.

The Problem in General

In the preceding paragraphs we have used numerous ecological terms—"environment," "milieu," "environmental factors," "man-milieu relationship hypotheses," etc. This terminology suffers from ambiguous and conflicting usage in the special vocabularies of ecological and behavioral sciences and in the vocabulary of human geography, which has ecological aspects but is not regarded by its principal spokesmen as primarily an ecological science.

We have attempted to straighten out this semantic tangle in a previous study (8). Because "environment" has come to mean different things to different specialists, we have substituted the French word *milieu* to designate the general concept. Since there is no corresponding French adjective, we have retained the English adjective "environmental." But we have restricted the noun "environment" (modified by qualifying adjectives) to limited aspects of the milieu, as, for example, "physical environment," "social environment," "non-human environment," "psychological environment," "operational environment," etc.

We define the general concept of "milieu" to include all phenomena (excepting only the environed unit's own hereditary factors) to which the environed unit's activities may be related. So defined, milieu includes both tangible objects, non-human and human, at rest and in motion, and the whole complex of social patterns, some embodied in formal enactments, others manifest in more or less stereotyped expectations regarding the behavior of human beings and the movements and mutations of non-human phenomena. This definition of milieu includes the environed unit's own ideas or images of the milieu, a concept designated herein as "psychological environment."

This aggregate of physical objects and social patterns is conceived as comprising the potential maximum set of environmental factors that might be deemed relevant to any given human state of affairs. What specific components of this aggregate are judged to be significantly relevant in a particular context depends on how the analyst defines the problem in hand and on the relationship of the theory, or theories, which he brings to bear.

Environment, or milieu, connotes some idea of relationship, both in popular usage and in technical vocabularies of special fields. Something is conceived to be encompassed—that is to say, environed—by something else in some meaningful relationship. In the discussion of human affairs, the "something environed" may be defined as a single human being or as some human group. In the context of diplomacy and other aspects of international politics, the

environed unit may be conceived as a single policy-making agent of the state, as some *ad hoc* policy-making group, as a formal agency of government, as some non-official group within the body politic, as the population of the state as a whole, as the state itself viewed as a corporate entity, or as some supra-state grouping such as, for example, the "Atlantic Community."[1]

What phenomena are included in the milieu depends in part on how one defines the environed unit. If, for example, the unit is a formal agency of government or some *ad hoc* policy-making group in the government, a great many factors physically internal to the state as well as factors external thereto may be significantly relevant elements of the milieu of such policy-making units. On the other hand, if the environed unit is conceived as the corporate entity of the state, only factors external to that entity are components of the milieu. For certain purposes —for example, the analysis of policy decisions—it may be more fruitful to proceed in terms of the concepts of decisional unit and internal and external setting.[2] For other purposes—for example, analysis of certain aspects of state capability—it may be more fruitful to conceive the state as an entity in relation to its external setting alone.

All too often in discussions of foreign policy and state capability, the precise referent is obscure. But some concept of environed unit there must be. Otherwise, by definition, there is no concept of milieu, no ascertainable set of relevant factors, no concept of environmental relationship.

Relationships between man and milieu have been hypothesized in various ways. In our earlier study, cited above, we identified and discussed five more or less distinct relationship theories: environmental determinism, free-will environmentalism, environmental possibilism, cognitive behaviorism, and environmental probabilism.

[1] The concept of a group or a corporate entity as the environed unit presents numerous difficulties. A group is not a biological entity endowed with hereditary characters in any sense analogous to the human beings who comprise the group. Nevertheless, the concept of a group as an environed unit conforms to almost universal usage; and, if properly qualified, it is a fruitful concept in the analysis of foreign policy and state capabilities in international relations.

[2] For an example of the use of this distinction between internal and external setting in foreign-policy analysis see Snyder *et al.* (6, pp. 34 ff.).

Environmental determinism hypothesizes an invariable correlation between some set of environmental "causes" and environing "effects." Man, by this hypothesis, has no choice; indeed, he is, by definition, incapable of choice. The properties of the milieu determine his activities. Hence his past activities are explicable and his future activities predictable by reference to the variation of some set of environmental causes.

Construed literally, two of the statements quoted at the beginning of this essay would appear to be exhibits of environmental determinism: the quotations regarding British sea power (Potter *et al.*), and regarding Germany's "industrial hegemony" (Zimmermann). The authors of these statements, we are confident, would deny that they are environmental determinists.

Looking at the matter more broadly, one notes that the determinist label has been pinned on numerous interpretations of history. Such names as Demolins, Tatzel, Semple, and Huntington immediately come to mind. Huntington, for example, has been called a determinist because he claimed to discover regular correlations between climatic variables and "civilization."

Neither Huntington nor any other alleged determinist known to us has denied man's capacity to choose among alternative courses of action. We have never discovered any interpretation of history that even closely approaches rigorous environmental determinism. We would contend that both general interpretations of history and specific statements phrased in deterministic rhetoric are simply rhetoric and nothing more. A little later on, we shall attempt to show that most man-milieu relationships expressed in deterministic rhetoric are also and more fruitfully explicable in non-deterministic terms.

Free-will environmentalism, or simply environmentalism, represented in its origin a retreat from strict determinism. The environmentalist substituted in place of "determine," "control," and other deterministic verbs, such verbs as "influence," "push," "beckon," etc., which admit the concept of choice among alternatives.

Most environmentalists have concerned themselves mainly with man's relations to the physical environment. Environmentalist discourse often displays a certain teleological coloration. "Nature" is conceived as a wise and purposeful entity guiding human destiny. Man is the target of Nature's signals. If he is wise, he heeds them. But the environmentalist conceives man is capable of choosing the "wrong road"—albeit to his future sorrow and frustration.

One encounters environmentalist rhetoric in many fields. We have quoted several examples. We are confident that the authors of those passages would reject the teleology implicit in a literal interpretation of their words. Again, we suspect, these authors have indulged in a poetic license which, in our view, has no justification in serious explanations of human activities. At any rate, environmentalist rhetoric explains nothing that is not more satisfactorily explicable in terms of other relationship theories yet to be considered.

Environmental possibilism is the relationship theory that took form in reaction against determinism and environmentalism. In the possibilist theory, the issue of choice is bypassed. The milieu as a whole or some set of environmental factors is conceived as a sort of matrix which limits the operational results of whatever is attempted.

These environmental limits are conceived to vary from place to place and from time to time. The limits implicit in one set of factors (for example, Atlantic winds and currents) may vary with changes in other factors (for example, changes in ship design and mode of propulsion). But, at any given place and time, possibilism postulates some set of limits that affect the outcome of any attempted course of action.

A particular set of limits may circumscribe broadly or narrowly; that is to say, they may leave room for considerable, or very little, range of effective choice. Under conditions of primitive technology, the range tends to be narrow. As men attain more efficient tools and skills, accumulate capital, and perfect their social organization, the limits may be pushed back, and the range of effective choice widens.

In the possibilist hypothesis, environmental limitations on accomplishment are assumed to be discoverable. But methodological discussion of possibilism is rarely explicit as to how one goes about discovering them. One may assume that a hypothetical omniscient observer could identify and delineate *all* the interrelations between milieu and environed unit. But, of course, no observer is in fact omniscient. The most that one can do is to frame hypotheses as to what environmental factors are significantly relevant to the action under consideration and how these set limits to the operational results thereof.

Thus the example just above rests upon some such set of hypotheses or premises, as follows: north of about 40° north latitude, Atlantic winds and currents move generally toward the east. These westerly winds and currents presented formidable obstacles to westbound sailing ships unable to sail close to the wind. In that state of marine technology, the normal westbound course across the Atlantic included a long detour southward to the latitudes of the northeasterly trade winds. Development of sailing ships capable of sailing closer to the wind reduced somewhat the limiting effects of headwinds and adverse currents. The development of externally powered ships eventually reduced the wind-current limitation to a level where it no longer substantially affected the westbound movement of ships across the Atlantic.

In possibilist theory, *environmental limitations* may exist and be operative irrespective of human knowledge and decisions. In the example just cited, Atlantic winds and currents indubitably limited certain movements of a fifteenth-century ship, irrespective of the desires and decisions of the ship's master. But *hypotheses to account for this state of affairs* do not exist apart from human observation and thought. Such hypotheses are formulated by someone. They have been called acts of creative imagination. Generally, though not necessarily, they are generalizations derived from observed events. But there is no certainty that any two observers will formulate identical explanatory hypotheses. However, in any given society and period, there is likely to be considerable agreement as to how things work and why.

Environmental possibilism carries no built-in assumption that a given environed unit will discover the limits of fruitful choice prior to reaching a decision. Nor is there any assumption that prior discovery would necessarily affect the decision taken. In the possibilist frame of reference, motives and decisions are *always taken as given*, not as phenomena to be explained or predicted.

Broadly speaking, environmental possibilism is the frame of reference within which the capabilities of states are calculated. But possibilism provides no basis for analyzing environmental factors in the

context of policy formation. We shall return to this point later.

Cognitive behaviorism is the label that we have selected to designate the simple and familiar principle that a person reacts to his milieu as he apperceives it—that is, as he perceives and interprets it in the light of past experience.[3] This concept of milieu is variously designated in the special vocabularies of psychological science: "life-space," "psychological field," "behavioral environment," "psychological environment," etc.

Cognitive behaviorism per se postulates no particular theory of human motivation and no particular mode of utilizing environmental knowledge. It simply draws a sharp distinction between the *psychological environment* (with reference to which an individual defines choices and takes decisions) and the *operational environment* (which sets limits to what can happen when the decision is executed).

This distinction was at issue in a recent rejoinder to a familiar passage in R. C. Collingwood's work on *The Idea of History*. Collingwood argued that "the fact that certain people live . . . on an island has in itself no effect on their history; what has an effect is the way they conceive of that position" (2, p. 200). To this the geographer, O. H. K. Spate, replied that "people cannot conceive of their insular position in any way unless they live on an island" (7).

Spate's rejoinder plainly runs contrary to a great deal of well-authenticated human experience. From time immemorial, men have formed opinions and taken decisions on some inaccurate image of the milieu. One thoroughly investigated demonstration of this phenomenon and its operational consequences was the now all-but-forgotten panic that was triggered off in New Jersey in 1938 by Orson Welles's rather too realistic radio description of the landing, near Princeton, of imaginary invaders from Mars. To contend that "people cannot conceive of their insular position in any way unless they live on an island" is equivalent to insisting that they cannot perceive nonexistent "flying saucers."

Cognitive behaviorism simply affirms the elementary first principle that what matters in decision-making is not how the milieu is but how the decision-maker imagines it to be. The next step in linking environmental factors to decisions involves

[3] The term "cognitive behaviorism" is open to certain objections considered in our earlier study (8, p. 58).

application of some hypothesis as to the decision-maker's environmental knowledge and his mode of using it.

Environmental probabilism is a general label for various behavioral models by which choices and decisions are explained or predicted on the basis of probable conformity to a hypothetical norm. Such a model may be simple or complex. It may be set forth explicitly or (what is more likely) left implicit. The analyst may even deny that he has any behavioral model in mind at all. But such denials are largely quibbles over terminology; for every explanation of past action and every prediction that is more than a throw of the dice are based on some set of assumptions regarding what is normally expectable behavior in the situation under consideration.

Some historians, geographers, and political scientists contend that every human being is unique and hence that human decisions are unpredictable. But such persons generally do not hesitate, for example, to cross a busy street when the traffic light turns green. In stepping from the curb, they are making a prediction that adverse traffic will obey the signal. In effect, such a prediction is simply an inference (generally subconscious) from a generalized model (rarely articulated) of how a "typical" motorcar driver behaves in the milieu under consideration. The pedestrian generally knows nothing about the lives of the specific drivers of oncoming cars. Nor does he usually know anything about their specific individual driving behavior. But he does have some notion of how drivers generally behave in that city and country; and he predicts driving behavior on the expectation of probable conformity to that hypothetical norm. That is all any behavioral model provides.

Before considering some of the assumptions incorporated into models of decision-making, we should like to stress a little further the probabilistic nature of such a model. The model is not a description of any specific person's behavior, and it carries no built-in assumption that the generalized description of "typical" behavior fits any particular person. In the present state of knowledge, no behavioral model can possibly anticipate idiosyncratic deviations from the hypothetical norm.

Norms are derived by generalization of past experience. Such a generalization is initially a trial hypothesis to be tested. When (in the example cited above) further observation confirms that car drivers almost invariably obey traffic signals, the hypothesis is said to be confirmed to a high degree of probability. In due course the hypothesis evolves into an assumption accepted without further proof and eventually hardens into a firm expectation. At any stage in the evolution from trial hypothesis to firm expectation, the proposition may constitute the general premise (also called "explanatory hypothesis," "principle," "law") from which future decisions are predicted by logical deduction.

No model can eliminate uncertainty from the prediction of decisions. This holds with special force for decisions formulated in complex organizations. One's closest approach to certainty can be expressed by some such sentence as "A will almost certainly choose x." Generally, if deliberation is involved in the decision-making process, the most one is justified in predicting is that A will probably choose x. Often one can find no justification for more than "The odds are about even that A will choose x." In every gradation of certainty to uncertainty, prediction consists essentially of making rough estimations of the betting odds for or against a certain choice being made.

Probabilistic behavioral models generally include at least three categories of assumptions: (1) assumptions regarding motivation; (2) assumptions regarding environmental knowledge; and (3) assumptions regarding the mode of utilizing such knowledge in defining alternatives and taking decisions.

Ideological or other characteristics of the model depend, it is clear, on the content of these assumptions. The assumption regarding motivation, for example, can have an acquisitive, power-seeking self-denying, Marxist, racist, or other content. The assumption regarding the extent of the decision-maker's environmental knowledge can range anywhere between total ignorance and omniscience of relevant factors. The assumption regarding the mode of utilizing environmental knowledge in making decisions can be that the hypothetical "typical" person is predominantly rational or that his behavior is explicable by the "theory of games" or by "Freudian theory" or by some other theory of human behavior.

A very familiar American version of the decision-making model is one that might be called "common-sense probabilism." In this model, men are assumed to be predominantly acquisitive, adequately know-ledgeable, and generally rational. In the context of daily living, the assumption of acquisitiveness usually shows a strong pecuniary coloration. People are assumed to want money and the things money buys. Common-sense probabilism further assumes that men generally have environmental knowledge that is adequate for their purposes. That is to say, the actor's psychological environment is assumed to correspond in essential respects to the operational environment in which his decisions are executed. Third, common-sense probabilism assumes that the individual applies his environmental knowledge rationally to the choice of ends achievable with the means at his command and to the choice of appro-priate means to achieve possible ends. That is to say, he calculates rationally the opportunities and limitations implicit in his operational environment. Finally, built into common-sense probabilism is the implicit assumption that the actor upon the stage and the analyst who observes and interprets from the sidelines both perceive and evaluate the milieu of the actor in substantially the same way.

Some such behavioral model, we submit, is implicit in Griffith Taylor's so-called "scientific determinism" and in the rhetoric of all those who employ deterministic or environmentalistic modes of speaking. Let us consider Taylor's familiar example of Antarctica as a milieu which largely determines man's choices and actions with reference to it. The purport of what he says appears to be about as follows: *If* the choice of fruitful means to a desired end in a given milieu is narrowly circumscribed (as in establishing a permanent settlement in Antarctica), and *if* (as Taylor clearly assumes) persons involved in the enterprise are adequately cognizant of what is possible (that is, cognizant of limitations set by that milieu), and *if* (as he also appears to assume) such persons take their environmental knowledge ration-ally into account in making choices, *then* it follows that there will be close correlation between environ-mental limits and human action.

If, as the common-sense probabilist also ap-pears to assume, his (the analyst's) own knowledge of the milieu in question and his mode of thinking about it correspond in essential respects to his sub-ject's, the analyst can explain the subject's past choices and predict his probable future choices simply by informing himself as to the milieu and by imagining how a "rational man" like himself would react to it. Thus, starting with a given action and the set of environmental factors which he deems relevant, the common-sense probabilist reasons backward to an explanation of the action, as indicated above. Starting with a set of environmental factors, he reasons forward to the probable correlated behavior. This, we submit, is substantially what underlies most statements in which environmental factors are asserted to "determine" or to "influence" choices and other actions.

Now, in the light of this discussion, let us re-examine some of the statements quoted in the opening paragraphs. Von Kühlmann, it is recalled, cited "geographical position" as one of the factors "determining" a state's foreign policy. Reischauer contended that the "mountains of Japan pushed the Japanese out on the seas" and that "sea routes beckoned the Japanese abroad." The sea-power text spoke of England "driven to the sea by her sparse resources, . . ."

How should one construe such rhetoric? One possibility is to brand it as pure teleology. Read in context, however, such seemingly teleological state-ments as those just quoted rarely appear to justify the conclusion that the author intended to ascribe human-like purposes and behavior to non-human phenomena. Sometimes, it would appear, teleo-logical rhetoric represents simply a sort of poetic license, designed perhaps to infuse an atmosphere of struggle and drama into the subject in hand.

However, there is still a third way of interpret-ing such rhetoric. Quite often, it would appear, authors employ action-verbs with an environ-mental factor or set of factors as the grammatical subject, but in a sense neither teleological nor poetic. Take the verb "influence," for example. This is probably the most commonly used verb in seemingly teleological environmentalistic rhetoric. The essence of dictionary definitions of influence is "*Some activity* on the part of a person or thing, that produces without apparent force an *effect* on another person or thing." The father speaks and thereby influences the child. The traffic officer blows his whistle and thereby influences the motorist. Then, by a sort of analogical extension, an author speaks of geographical location or climate or a new machine or some other non-human factor influencing people to do so-and-so.

Construed in context, such seemingly teleological statements appear frequently to be a sort of verbal shorthand to connote that the "influenced" person or group perceived the environmental factor or aggregate in question; that he, or they, evaluated it with reference to their purposes; and that he, or they, acted in the light of the conclusions reached. One could similarly construe the whole battery of action-verbs when employed with environmental subjects. In such usage, the force of the verb—ranging from determine, or control, to influence—may be construed merely as expressing the speaker's estimate of the odds that the environed unit would recognize and heed the limitations implicit in the environmental factors in question.[4]

When one reads in the Reischauer book that "sea routes have beckoned the Japanese abroad," perhaps all that the passage was intended to communicate is that, at a certain stage in Japanese history, substantial numbers of Japanese envisaged more attractive opportunities in sea-faring than in farming or other pursuits ashore.

Our conclusion is that these and other examples of environmentalistic rhetoric, when not construed as teleology or poetic license, are equivalent to saying that the environed persons *envisaged* certain ends; that they *perceived and comprehended* adequately the opportunities and limitations latent in their milieu; and that they applied such knowledge *rationally* in choosing ends that were possible and in formulating means appropriate to the ends selected.

All the probabilistic models with which we are here concerned carry an assumption that the environed unit is capable of choosing among alternatives. But that is *not* equivalent to assuming that *all* choices which, by definition, are *possible* choices are equally *probable* choices. The essence of such a model is that some choices are more probable than others. The function of the model is to enable the analyst to arrange a set of possible choices on a sort of continuum of estimated degrees of probability. By reference to the assumptions of normally expectable behavior, incorporated into the model, the analyst eliminates

as very improbable or less improbable those choices which would represent greater or lesser deviations from the hypothetical norm.

Probabilistic models, it may be argued, are manifestly better suited to predicting the odds of occurrence in a large aggregate of units than to "pinpointing" the actions of a specific unit. A market analyst, for example, may be able to predict within a more or less calculable range of error how many persons in a given society will buy new automobiles next year. But if the analyst should attempt to identify the specific prospective purchasers, the incidence of error would increase greatly, and the statistical methods employed in handling large aggregates of data might prove quite fruitless for predicting the behavior of particular individuals.

From this position it is an easy step to skepticism concerning all models for predicting the behavior of specific individuals and small groups.[5] But, as previously emphasized, a recurrent and inescapable feature of our day-by-day living in society is precisely that kind of prediction. Hardly anyone would contend that the scores of predictive judgments which each of us makes every day are merely blind guesses, like pulling numbers out of a hat. We argued from the street-crossing example that such predictions consist essentially of deductions from assumptions of typical, or normally expectable, behavior respecting particular aspects of the total behavior of our fellow men. The question posed for the next section is whether and to what extent such models are fruitful for explaining and predicting the decisions of foreign policy taken in the more complex milieu of international politics.

Environmental Factors in Foreign-Policy Analysis

Our thesis, as stated at the outset, is that environmental factors become related to the attitudes and decisions which comprise a state's foreign policy only by being perceived and taken into account in the policy-forming process. The statesman's *psychological* environment (that is, his image, or estimate, of the situation, setting, or milieu) may or may not correspond to the *operational* environment (in which

---

[4] It should be carefully noted that there is a certain class of environmental factors to which standard dictionary definitions of influence and other action-verbs can be applied with no teleological coloration. We refer, of course, to the other human beings in the milieu of the unit under consideration—such as the father and the police officer in the examples used in the text.

[5] This issue was recently discussed in a paper by Dr. William Warntz (10) on "The Unity of Knowledge, Social Science, and the Role of Geography."

his decisions are executed). But in policy-making, as we have stressed before, what matters is how the policy-maker imagines the milieu to be, not how it actually is.

The American debacle at Pearl Harbor is a historic example of this principle: The American commanders there remained totally ignorant of the approaching Japanese task force. Their psychological environment contained no hostile force readying its planes for a dawn attack on the great American base. Hence that force, though indubitably part of the operational environment, was *not related* in any way whatsoever to the *decisions* of the American commanders to the moment the attack began.

Many other examples come to mind. The United States-Canadian boundary was originally drawn in ignorance of the geographic layout and had subsequently to be corrected. The Battle of New Orleans was fought in January, 1815, in the erroneous belief that a state of war still continued. The Battle of the Bulge caught the Allied Command unprepared in December, 1944, because of faulty evaluation of intelligence reports. The Monroe Doctrine was promulgated in 1823, with reference to a threat of aggression that had largely subsided. American missile and satellite research after World War II proceeded on a widely held, but erroneous, assumption of a comfortable margin of superiority over Russian technology. Attitudes are formed and decisions of foreign policy are constantly being taken on fragmentary and often quite defective estimates of the situation.

The British Cabinet's decision to re-occupy the Suez Canal, in October, 1956, illustrates the same principle, but with a complicating dimension. Let us assume, for purposes of this discussion, that the decision to intervene was predicated on some such set of assumptions as these: that the operation could be executed swiftly; that the Egyptians would be unable either to offer effective resistance or to block the canal; that other Arab peoples would not disrupt the production and flow of oil to Europe contrary to their manifest economic interest; that the Soviet government would keep its hands off; that the United States and Commonwealth governments and peoples would accept a *fait accompli*; that the United Nations could offer no serious opposition; and that public opposition, which was dividing Britain internally, would speedily collapse as soon

as British forces were re-established in the Canal Zone.

In the Suez case the significant environmental factors included potential human responses to the decision under consideration. These responses, when they did occur, became part of the operational environment in which the British decision was executed. That they did not exist prior to the decision added a complicating element of uncertainty to the decision-makers' problem. But that in no way invalidates the thesis that environmental factors are related to policy decisions only to the extent that they are taken into account in the decision-making process. The Suez example rather emphasizes that the decision-maker's estimate of the situation may frequently (perhaps generally) have to include not merely phenomena existent prior to the decision but also his predictions as to how the situation will develop as the decision is carried into execution.

Discrepancies between the policy-maker's estimate of the situation (that is, his psychological environment) and the operational environment become highly significant when the problem is to explain or to predict the results of a given decision. We shall consider that issue further in the next section. For the present it is sufficient to emphasize once again that what matters in policy-making is how the milieu appears to the policy-maker, not how it appears to some sideline analyst or how it might appear to a hypothetical omniscient observer. Hence, excluding the special problem of self-analysis by the policy-maker himself, the first step in linking environmental factors to policy decisions is to find out how the given policy-maker, or policy-making group, conceives the milieu to be and how that unit interprets the opportunities and limitations implicit therein with respect to the ends to be accomplished.

This task presents formidable difficulties. The task is to construct at second hand, from what the decision-maker says and does, a description of his image, or estimate, of the situation and his orientation to it. The analyst functions at some distance, often at a great distance, from his subject. He may have to contend with linguistic, ideological, or other social barriers to communication and understanding. As a rule, he has to work with insufficient, incomplete, and often contradictory evidence. At best, the analyst's inferences regarding his subject's image of the milieu and his orientation to it rest invariably and inescapably on more or less arbitrary decisions as to the relevance and weight to be given to various kinds of evidence perceived and filtered through the analyst's own (and usually several intermediaries') culture-biased spectacles.

Even when one comes to grips in some fashion with the methodological difficulties inherent in imagining the "universe of the decision-makers"— or, in less technical idiom, the "pictures in their heads"—he is still only on the threshold of explaining or predicting how environmental factors enter into the policy-forming process. In order to take another step, he must apply some theory of decision-making; and, in order to be relevant for this purpose, the theory must include assumptions as to (a) the purposes or ends toward which the policy-maker's efforts are oriented; (b) the environmental data which the policy-maker deems relevant to his purposes and from which he derives his estimate of the situation; and (c) his mode of utilizing such data in deciding what ends are feasible and in formulating strategy calculated to attain the ends envisaged.

Discussion of the relation of environmental factors to policy decisions has tended in the past to follow more or less in the pattern which we have called "common-sense probabilism." Rarely have the guiding assumptions been clearly articulated. Often they have been obscured by environmentalistic rhetoric, as in the examples quoted early in this essay. But scratch the surface of almost any discussion of foreign policy, and one is apt to discover the familiar assumptions that men are predominantly acquisitive, adequately knowledgeable, and generally rational.

In the specific context of foreign policy, the assumption of acquisitiveness typically appears as power orientation. Politics is defined as a struggle for power. Desire to enhance the power of one's own state over other states is said to be the paramount objective of the foreign policies of all states. At a lower level of generality, this struggle for power is described in terms of expansion and protection— expansion at the expense of other states, protection of things previously acquired against encroachment by other states.

Whether this assumption is adequately descriptive of the typical orientation of policy-makers in all countries and whether the assumption is a fruitful one at still more specific levels of policy definition are both debatable. But these issues are marginal to the present discussion. The point here is that *some* concept of ends to be accomplished underlies all foreign-policy analysis and that the analyst's assumptions as to the general orientation and specific objectives envisaged by the policy-makers in a given situation will affect his conclusions as to what environmental factors probably were (or probably will be) taken into account in the deliberations under consideration.

Turning, now, to the issue of the policy-maker's environmental knowledge, the common-sense model assumes that policy-making units normally command data that are sufficiently complete and accurate for their purposes. This assumption is implicit in the venerable cliché that "politics is the art of the possible." That cliché is sometimes quoted as a description of typical policy-making behavior, sometimes as a precept for policy-makers. In either context it implies that those who make decisions for the state can be assumed, in general, to know what is possible. That is to say, their estimates of a situation can be assumed to represent close enough approximations of opportunities and limitations implicit in their operational environment.

This is a dubious assumption. It is one thing, for example, to assume that farmers generally know the elements of good farming in a given milieu. It is something else again to assume that a specific individual farmer commands such knowledge. It is still more dubious, in our judgment, to assume that a head of state or a foreign minister or a legislative committee commands *effectively* the vastly greater range of environmental data required to conduct adequately the foreign relations of a modern state.

The higher one moves in the hierarchy of a great power's government, the more one is impressed by the remoteness of executives from the operational environment in which their decisions are executed. What passes for knowledge of the situation at the higher levels consists mainly of generalized descriptions and abstracts, several degrees removed from on-the-spot observations. On most issues the individual or group responsible for decisions will have little time and only the most general knowledge for checking what is prepared at lower working levels of the organization.

Let us assume (and we think it is a reasonable assumption) that the British Cabinet's decision to send military forces to reoccupy Suez was predicated on a firm expectation that the job could be finished quickly. How did Eden and his colleagues come to such a conclusion? One can only speculate, of course. They probably received estimates of the situation prepared by civil servants and military staffs. Such estimates probably included statements regarding the strength and deployment of land, sea, and air forces, their state of readiness, landing craft and other transportation and handling equipment on hand, liaison arrangements with the French Command, the condition of Egyptian defenses, the morale of Egyptian troops and civil population, etc. In addition, we may perhaps assume that Eden and his immediate associates had some general notions of their own about British military power, conditions in the Arab countries, and what it would take to re-occupy the canal. But is it likely that they had much fresh knowledge of these matters or the time necessary to check up on their experts?

These questions immediately pose others. To what extent is a top-level executive a virtual prisoner of the civil and military officials who provide data for him? On the other hand, how may his known preferences affect the substance and coloration of what his staffs decide to tell him? To what extent may their own attitudes and preferences bias their observations and calculations? In other words, to what extent is the "wish father to the thought" in statecraft as in other walks of life? And to what extent do such considerations affect the whole chain of communications in a complex foreign-policy-making situation?

Such questions raise doubts as to the common-sense assumption of adequate environmental knowledge. The proposition that a head of state, foreign minister, legislative committee, or other decision-making unit in a complex modern government commands such knowledge effectively is no more than a hypothesis to be confirmed—rarely, if ever, an assumption to be taken for granted.

With reference to past actions, it is sometimes possible for the historian to discover what environmental data were actually available, recognized as relevant, and taken into account. But with reference to past actions about which evidence is scanty and untrustworthy and with reference to all future

contingencies, the analyst has no alternative but to supplement empirical research with some hypothesis or model as to the manner in which information is "normally" or "typically" gathered, interpreted, and communicated upward through the organization under consideration.

We come finally to the closely related issue of how environmental data are utilized in foreign-policy-making. Here one encounters a wide range of opinions. At one pole stand those who are generally skeptical of all explicit models for explaining or predicting how individuals or groups are likely to *react* to a perceived state of affairs. This skepticism is especially marked with respect to interpreting the behavior of persons functioning in a milieu radically different from the analyst's own. This view is reflected in the argument that it is useless to try to understand or to forecast the reactions of Chinese or Russians or other "inscrutable" foreigners. The classic expression of this pessimism is Churchill's description of Soviet foreign policy as a "riddle wrapped in an enigma."

At the opposite pole one hears it optimistically contended that "human nature" is everywhere the same and that one can (within limits, to be sure) intuit how other people (even the "inscrutable foreigners") are likely to react. The analyst has simply to imagine how he himself would react to the state of affairs in question. This intuitive hypothesis rests upon assumptions previously discussed in connection with the difficulty of reconstructing another's image of the milieu. It involves assuming that persons of different social class, different educational background, different functional role, different nationality, etc., will nevertheless perceive *and react* in substantially similar ways. When doubts are voiced, these are resolved by assuming that analyst and subject analyzed, alike, function rationally in accord with universal principles of "human nature."

Some such view seems to be implicit in much of the environmentalistic rhetoric which encumbers the literature of foreign policy. We opened this discussion by quoting numerous examples of such rhetoric. Later on, we contended that environmentalistic statements in the context of foreign affairs can be construed as teleology or as poetic license but that such statements are just as likely to be no more than a sort of short-hand for longer and more cumbersome descriptions of human *reactions* to *perceived* environmental conditions. We concluded, it will be recalled, that when an author speaks of some environmental factor or set of factors influencing foreign policy or the makers of foreign policy, what he seems generally to be saying is that the policy-makers desired to achieve certain ends; that they imagined the milieu to be so-and-so; that their image of the milieu corresponded substantially with the operational environment; and that they employed their environmental knowledge rationally in framing a strategy to accomplish the desired end.

In general, this concept of man-milieu relationship takes for granted that policy-making is a deliberative process and that it is carried on within an intellectual framework of rationality and logic. There is much evidence to confirm these assumptions. But they do present difficulties, for there is also evidence that policy decisions may reflect not only defective environmental knowledge but also illogical reasoning as well. For example, how often do executives discount overtones of caution, warning, or pessimism in staff advice which casts a shadow on the choice to which they are predisposed? What are the odds that the top-level decision-maker will disregard, for quite illogical reasons, the estimates and recommendations prepared for his guidance?

Such questions go to the heart of systematic foreign-policy analysis. They raise the issue whether attempting to forecast the choices of a single individual or decision-making group by means of assumptions regarding "typical," or normally expectable, behavior is any more fruitful than throwing the dice. Analogies drawn from various kinds of macro-prediction are not especially helpful. The economic geographer predicting crop distributions, the demographer projecting population trends, the market analyst, or the election forecaster rarely, if ever, attempt to predict reactions of specific individuals but only the odds that certain choices will recur in large aggregates of behavior. The foreign-policy analyst, on the contrary, deals (by definition) with the choices of specific individuals or relatively small organized groups.

Nor is it very helpful to compare street-crossing behavior (see preceding section) and foreign-policy analysis. In the street-crossing example, it is true, the analyst drew a predictive inference from assumptions as to what he regarded as normally expectable behavior. But the significant variables involved in predicting when a man will cross a busy street are probably much fewer and simpler than those involved in predicting what a foreign minister will do about disarmament, nuclear-bomb tests, technical assistance to underdeveloped countries, etc.

Even though it may be generally unfruitful (in the present state of knowledge about human behavior) to attempt to "pin-point" the *specific* choices of *specific* decision-making *units* operating in *complex* situations, it does not necessarily follow that throwing the dice is the only alternative. Under these conditions, negative prediction can become a useful product of analysis. By applying suitable premises regarding what is "typical," or normally expectable, behavior in the kind of situation under consideration, the analyst attempts to narrow the range within which specific choices will probably fall. By this method (described in the preceding section), the foreign-policy analyst eliminates as *very* improbable or as *quite* improbable those choices which would represent greater or lesser deviation from the hypothetical norm. If he cannot forecast precisely what the British Cabinet will do about the European "common market" during the next five years, the foreign-policy analyst can perhaps reach fruitful conclusions as to what they are more or less likely *not* to do.

Negative prediction to narrow the range of probable choice, no less than positive prediction of specific choice, involves the application of general hypotheses, or premises, of typical or normally expectable behavior. The value of such premises will depend, in part, on the analyst's knowledge of the setting and functions under consideration, in part on the imagination he displays in drawing generalizations from such knowledge that are relevant and significant for the problem in hand. If the problem is to compare the collection, communication, and utilization of environmental data in all governmental systems, the model would obviously have to be pitched at the highest level of generality. But the problem may be to compare the effective command and use of such data in all totalitarian governments or in all democratic governments or in all democratic governments of the parliamentary type. Or the problem may be to compare democratic and totalitarian types, Western and non-Western types or more specifically, for example, the British and Chinese systems of foreign-policy-making. Or the problem may be to form conclusions regarding the command

and use of environmental data within a single form of government or even within a single specific system.

In every case the issue is what set of premises (hypotheses or assumptions) will yield the most fruitful insights as to the ways in which environmental data are related to policy decisions. Such premises, we emphasized previously, are not found in "nature"; they are formulated. In the main, they are generalized descriptions of typical, or normally expectable, behavior either at the level of a single system or at the level of two or more systems. In the context of foreign-policy analysis, premises regarding man-milieu relationships focus mainly on the policy-maker's knowledge of the milieu and the uses he makes of that knowledge. At these two points of focus, the ecological approach gives way to behavioral concepts and theories for the further development of knowledge and understanding of the relation of environmental factors to the foreign policies of states.

Environmental Factors in Capability Analysis

We drew a distinction at the outset between capability analysis and foreign-policy analysis. The latter consists essentially of explaining or predicting policy decisions. Capability analysis, on the other hand, is directed to the calculation of the opportunities and limitations implicit in the milieu, which will affect the operational results of whatever is attempted, irrespective of whether such factors are known and heeded by the decision-makers in question.[6]

The Japanese task force approaching Pearl Harbor, for example, was unknown to, and hence formed no part of the psychological environment of, the American commanders there. But that hostile

[6] We prefer the term "state capability" to the more common term "state power." The latter term is used loosely, and usage varies. Power may be defined simply as superior military force. Or it may be conceived more broadly to include non-military instrumentalities and techniques of statecraft, such as negotiation, subversive activities, economic inducements and pressures, etc. In its broadest connotation, power can be defined as the sum total of a state's capacities to affect the behavior of other states. In this sense, influence as well as coercion are subcategories of the concept "power." So defined, power approximates capability as we use this term herein.

fleet was indubitably part of their operational environment and (though not related in any way to their decisions) affected the results of those decisions.

Put in general terms, the distinction is this. If the problem is to explain or to predict a policy decision, the analyst has to answer such questions as: What environmental factors (or aspects of the situation) did the decision-maker recognize and consider to be significant? What *use* did he make of his environmental *knowledge* in defining what was to be attempted and the means to be employed? If, on the other hand, the problem is to explain or to predict the operational results of a *given* policy decision or set of decisions (actual or hypothetical), the question he must answer is: How may the properties present or latent in the milieu affect the operational results of that decision, even though these factors are not known or taken into account in the decision-making process?

Capability analysis, so defined, involves application of the frame of reference and ecological theory commonly known in geographic science as "environmental possibilism," whereas foreign-policy analysis involves application of the theory which we have called "environmental probabilism."

Statements about state capabilities, like statements about foreign policy, are frequently couched in deterministic or environmentalistic rhetoric. Zimmermann (quoted earlier) asserted that invention of the basic steel furnace "*led inevitably* to Germany's industrial hegemony" on the Continent. The sea-power text spoke of England being "*destined by geography* to command the seas" (our italics).

In reviewing the sea-power book, we contended that "geography did not destine England to command the seas." We construed the passage to mean simply that "available resources ashore, configuration of lands and seas, and other conditions in the milieu *enabled* Englishmen to achieve the kind of history which they did in fact make for themselves" (9).

One could similarly recast the Zimmermann statement in non-deterministic terms. The invention of the basic steel furnace *made it possible* to produce good steel out of acidic ores. A lot of such ore *was present* inside Germany (that is, latent in the German milieu). German industrialists *took advantage* of the new process to expand steel production. Thus a change in one environmental factor (steel-making process) enabled German industrialists to make use of another environmental factor (acidic iron ore) and thereby to outstrip the steel production of other European countries and achieve the "industrial hegemony" which they did, in fact, achieve.

One can analyze state capabilities either historically or predictively. In the former context, the task is to formulate an explanation of how it was possible for certain functions to be performed, which were in fact performed, as exemplified above. In a predictive context (and most capability analysis is predictive), the task is to calculate the odds for or against ability to perform certain functions in the future.

At this point some analytical distinctions should be made. Capability calculations normally enter into the policy-making process. A foreign-policy analyst (who studies the process from the sidelines) will normally attempt to find out how the policy-makers and their staffs themselves envisage the opportunities and limitations implicit in their milieu. Such an inquiry is *not* capability analysis but rather an aspect of foreign-policy analysis, considered in the preceding section. But the operation becomes capability analysis when the sideline observer makes an *independent* judgment as to what those opportunities and limitations are and how they will affect the course of events, irrespective of whether or how these factors are conceived or taken into account by the decision-makers in question.

Perhaps an analogy from medicine will help to make this distinction clearer. The physician may ask the patient to describe his symptoms. From the latter's responses, the physician learns how the patient conceives his illness. The physician may also deduce from the patient's description of symptoms some conclusions as to what the illness really is. But he may also make various laboratory tests—blood pressure, metabolism, etc.—from which to confirm or modify the inferences drawn from the patient's verbalization. Similarly, the capability analyst may make his own independent assessment of the opportunities and limitations implicit in the milieu of the state under consideration.

It should be clear by now that we conceive capabilities to be calculable only with reference to some set of policies and some operational situation. It is utterly meaningless to speak of capabilities in the abstract. Capability is always capability to do

something, to bring about or perpetuate some state of affairs. Policy assumptions may be left implicit. But, unless some set of ends and means is envisaged, no calculation is possible, no inventory of environmental factors has any significance.

Failure to keep the discussion of state capabilities within some policy frame of reference is one of the reasons why a good deal that has been said about the so-called "elements" or "foundations" of national power is footless and unconvincing. The data of physical geography have no intrinsic political significance whatever. Nor have demographic, technological, economic, or other environmental data. Such factors acquire political significance only when related to some frame of assumptions as to what is to be attempted, by what means, when and where, and vis-à-vis what adversaries, associates, and bystanders.

The policy framework may be short-term and rather specific. What factors, for example, will set limits to the results of the declared American intention to regain ground lost to the Russians in science and military technology? What factors will affect the outcome of the French policy of holding the line in Algeria? What factors will limit British military expenditures during the next five years? By what criteria may one judge the proposition asserted in the British Defense Statement of 1957, that "there is at present no means of providing adequate protection for the people of Britain against the consequences of an attack with nuclear weapons"?

Such relatively short-term capability questions shade off into longer-term and more general questions. By what criteria, for example, may one evaluate the thesis, propounded by a prominent geographer, that "permanent environmental restrictions of cold, drought, and continentality will never permit [the Soviet Union] to achieve strictly first-class rank"? Or Sir Halford Mackinder's historic thesis that "the grouping of lands and seas, and of fertility and natural pathways, is such as to lend itself to the growth of empires, and in the end of a single world empire"?

Putting the problem within a suitable policy framework constitutes only the first step in capability analysis. Given the most explicit policy assumptions —as to what is to be attempted, by what means, when and where, etc.—one still has very little basis for judging the significance of a state's geographical position, material resources, population, economic plant, social structure, and similar data regarding other states. Such data acquire significance for capability analysis only when subjected to the criteria of appropriate explanatory propositions or hypotheses.

What do we mean by explanatory capability hypotheses? We mean such propositions as, for example: The growth of air power has progressively diminished the military value of insular bases. Or: In the present state of military technology there is no effective tactical defense against nuclear missiles. Or: Democratic systems of government are less able than dictatorships to execute quick changes of policy. Or: Size of population is not per se an index of military or economic capacity. Such hypotheses, which are the essence of capability calculations, comprise the logical premises from which the analyst deduces what environmental factors are significantly relevant and what they signify with respect to the policy objectives and strategy under consideration.

Like models of normally expectable *policy-making* behavior, discussed in the preceding section, capability hypotheses or premises are not found full-blown in nature. They are creative acts of imagination, generally, though not necessarily, derived by generalization from observed events. Many of the premises employed in capability analysis have been so repeatedly confirmed as to be accepted as truisms. But in our era of rapid technological and other social changes, most capability premises have become more or less debatable. Take, for example, the thesis that scientists in a totalitarian communist state operate under ideological and other handicaps that prevent them from keeping pace with their counterparts in a "free society." Only yesterday that proposition seemed as sound as the Rock of Gibraltar. Today it is at most no more than a working hypothesis to be confirmed.

The propositions which an analyst adjudges confirmed and fruitful depend, as a rule, on his previous experience with the problem's antecedents or on generalizations derived from other problems which, in his judgment, exhibit fruitful analogies. There is no guaranty whatever that any two analysts will reason from exactly the same premises or reach the same conclusions. The most that one can expect is that explanatory premises will be made explicit, that environmental factors considered significantly relevant will be so designated, and that logical procedures will be observed. Only thus is it possible for one analyst to check the work of another, to identify the sources of conflicting conclusions regarding the capabilities of states.

Consider, for example, the prediction quoted above, that "permanent environmental restrictions of cold, drought, and continentality will never permit [the Soviet Union] to achieve strictly first-class rank." Read in context, that prediction seems to be derived from a number of hypotheses—regarding future trends in science and technology, regarding the Russian people's tolerance of austerity, regarding the pace of development of other nations, etc. But these strategic hypotheses are not explicitly articulated. Greater explicitness would have rendered the exposition more fruitful, by removing doubt and uncertainty as to the premises from which the final conclusion was derived.

This is not a plea for elaboration of the obvious. It is rather a plea for more sophisticated discrimination between what is obvious and noncontroversial and what is significant and controversial. It might be instructive to re-examine from this point of view some of the many disconfirmed capability predictions of our time. One might reflect, for example, on the generally implicit assumptions from which observers predicted that Nazi Germany could not stand the financial and moral strains of a long war; that the Red Army would collapse in a few weeks under the hammer-blows of the Wehrmacht; that it would take Russian scientists and engineers twenty years or more to produce an atomic bomb; etc.

It is easy to be wise after the event. Some degree of uncertainty is probably inherent in all complex capability calculations, at least in the present state of knowledge. But the burden of our argument in this section is that clearer understanding of the steps involved in capability analysis, more sophistication in formulation of capability premises, more explicitness in articulating strategic premises, and more rigor in their application to environmental data should help to avoid such gross miscalculations as have characterized capability predictions in the past.

Conclusions

The first conclusion that emerges from this discussion is our conviction that the ecological viewpoint and frame of reference—the concept of man-milieu relationship and certain relationship theories—provide a fruitful approach to the analysis of foreign policy and the estimation of state capabilities.

Our second conclusion is that it is fruitful to distinguish analytically between the relation of environmental factors to policy decisions, on the one hand, and to the operational results of decisions, on the other. With respect to policy-making and the content of policy decisions, our position is that what matters is how the policy-maker imagines the milieu to be, not how it actually is. With respect to the operational results of decisions, what matters is how things are, not how the policy-maker imagines them to be. In our judgment, a good deal of the confusion which has clouded the discussion of environmental factors in international politics derives from failure to keep this distinction explicit and to observe it rigorously.

Third, we conceive of the ecological approach as a system of concepts and theory that is useful to the student of international politics, not as a substitute for, but as a complement to, the behavioral and other approaches to the study of foreign policy and the international capabilities of states.

Finally, we see in the ecological approach a useful bridge for bringing to the study of international politics relevant theories and data from geography, psychology, sociology, and other systems of learning.

References

1. Cambon, J. "The Permanent Bases of French Foreign Policy," *Foreign Affairs*, VIII (1930), 174.

2. Collingwood, R. C. *The Idea of History*. New York: Oxford University Press, 1946.

3. Kühlmann, R. von. "The Permanent Bases of German Foreign Policy," *Foreign Affairs*, IX (1931), 179.

4. Potter, E. B., *et al. The United States and World Sea Power*. New York: Prentice-Hall, 1955.

5. Reischauer, E. O. *Japan: Past and Present*. New York: Knopf, 1946.

6. Snyder, R. C., Bruck, H. W., and Sapin, B. *Decision-making as an Approach to the Study of International Politics*. Princeton: Princeton University Press, 1954.

7. Spate, O. H. K. "Toynbee and Huntington: A Study in Determinism," *Geographical Journal*, CXVIII (1952), 406, 423.

8. Sprout, H. and M. *Man-Milieu Relationship Hypotheses in the Context of International Politics*. Princeton: Center of International Studies, 1956.

9. Sprout, H. Review of Potter *et al., op. cit.* in *United States Naval Institute Proceedings*, February, 1956, p. 213.

10. Warntz, W. "The Unity of Knowledge, Social Science, and the Role of Geography," paper presented at the Geography Session of the National Council for the Social Studies, November 29, 1957.

11. Zimmermann, E. W. *World Resources and Industries*. Rev. ed. New York: Harper, 1951.

6. On Writing About Foreign Policy

T. B. Millar is Senior Fellow in the Department of International Relations of the Australian National University. In this article he candidly assesses the difficulties that must be overcome in probing foreign policy activities at both the theoretical and empirical levels. Here it can be seen that the problems of analyzing the behavior of a single actor in the international system are hardly less complex than those inherent in analyzing the interaction of its many actors. [*Reprinted from* Australian Outlook, *XXI (1967), 71–84, by permission of the author and the publisher.*]

I once had a professor who strongly objected to defining terms. We all know what we mean, he would say, by "peaceful change," or "domestic jurisdiction," or whatever the topic was. Do we, in fact, all know what we mean by "foreign policy"? When we talk about the foreign policy of Britain or Botswanaland, do we know with some exactness which of the many policies and actions of the respective governments we are referring to? Or, if we do not, does it matter that we leave the boundaries indistinct?

Foreign policy is presumably something less than the sum of all policies which have an effect upon a national government's relations with other national governments. The United Nations General Assembly has long ago asserted the principle that if the sensitivities of enough members are affected by the action of one country towards its own nationals, that action ceases to be domestic; yet we still would not say that *apartheid* is a part of the foreign policy of South Africa. Many kinds of domestic actions have external effects but are not foreign policy. On the other hand, the Commonwealth Immigrants Act is part of the foreign policy of the United Kingdom (leaving aside the question of whether Commonwealth countries are foreign), as it directly impinges on the nationals of other countries and affects the way their governments behave towards Britain. Similarly the Australian restricted immigration policy has undoubted foreign policy implications, *is*, in effect, foreign policy. Foreign trade policy is part of the corpus of foreign policy, but is usually only included in a discussion of foreign policy when it has some evident bearing on the security of the country or its capacity to get along in the world. Thus people who become disturbed by Australia's trade with Communist China do so in terms of its effects on our foreign policy decisions, on our defence, or our relations with other countries such as India or the United States. Here our trade policy has foreign policy effects, *is* foreign policy, in the way that our trade policy with Rhodesia is but our trade policy with Brazil is not. At least in Australia, the processes whereby trade policy is decided are usually totally separate from the processes whereby foreign (political or diplomatic) policy is decided, except at the very top, and this can have some unfortunate results. Large political oaks from small trade acorns can grow, but until the political branches appear we are justified in calling the matter "trade" and not "foreign."

Many other kinds of actions can have a direct effect on foreign relations. Foreign aid policy is clearly a part of foreign policy, and is customarily so recognized. Foreign investment is equally relevant but not always equally recognized. Defence policy becomes foreign policy when it begins to operate across the border or appears to carry a threat of doing so, or when by its inadequacy it suggests a vacuum waiting to be filled from outside. Today, nations also compete with each other with the weapons of culture and travel. The British Council has long been a barely concealed arm of the Foreign Office (or, strictly, of foreign policy). Of longer heritage, Alliance Francaise associations have for decades helped convey a congenial "school-friend" image of la belle France. Goethe societies are designed for similar ends. In Australia we periodically send an orchestra or other entertainment group off on tour and invite foreign journalists or academics to "junket" around our continent at our taxpayers' expense. No strings are attached; we merely hope that greater understanding and goodwill will result, and our place in the world become so much more secure. This hope could, of course, be misplaced. The way in which one of our coloured visitors is treated in a hotel could spoil the effect of the money and effort expended.

The most important aspects of foreign policy are still those contained in the daily diplomatic contacts, the sense or goodwill or apathy or illwill expressed towards other governments publicly or privately, the comparative attitudes taken towards political or security issues. Yet to write on foreign policy involves looking at the other aspects mentioned—at whatever affects the attitude of governments towards each other, whether it be an aircraft carrier steaming ostentatiously off the coast, a critical postcard dropped in the bazaar by a homesick Peace Corps girl, or a spy satellite circling the globe every few minutes and sending back its tell-tale pictures.

Facts and Factors

All writing on foreign policy which is not theoretical and abstract is a collection of approximations to the truth incompletely assessed on the basis of inadequate evidence. This applies whether the article is in *Foreign Affairs* or the *Daily Blow*, whether it comes from Chatham House or Printing House Square or the research section of the foreign office.

The Foreign Minister's public analysis (usually ghost-written by a senior civil servant) peddles his country's viewpoint and promotes his own image. The journalist accentuates what he believes (or what he believes his editor and employer believe) is newsworthy. The political scientist may write according to his educated approach or may equally declaim from a rationalized prejudice or passion. The commentator rarely has time to give more than a bubble explanation in the teeth of his paper's deadline. This does not mean that such writing is unimportant; merely that it is incomplete and must be subjected to scrutiny and scepticism. Unfortunately the writers who are most widely read are those who have least time to prepare what they write—journalists and commentators. It is doubtful whether an academic writing in journals of reasonably serious comment is read by many people who are not also academics or undergraduates. This may help his prospects for advancement, but is unlikely to affect the policies of the governments he is writing about. Few people actually engaged in foreign policy—diplomats, foreign service officers, Ministers—read such articles; they have no time. Probably the only general exception to this rule is *Foreign Affairs*, because of the appointments or the quality of its contributors. Particular exceptions also occur with particular officers, and with the article which is sufficiently controversial to get reproduced or summarized in the press.

Sad and unjust though this state of affairs may be, it does not reduce the obligation on every writer on foreign policy to provide as many relevant facts as he can, assessed as validly and objectively as he can, and to write as lucidly as he can. The more that is so written, the more will filter out to the public or the policy makers. It is surprising how many scholars see little need for proper research, academic integrity and objectivity when writing on contemporary political events.

The difficulties of getting at the facts in foreign policy before the files are opened are obvious enough. Australia is one of the hardest of the democracies in this respect. In Britain there are more outside experts with the ear of relevant Ministers or officials, a larger corps of discerning academics and pressmen. Periodically a former Cabinet Minister will write his reminiscences in the Sunday papers or publish a book of memoirs to supplement regular source material. Such memorials are helpful, even if they must be treated with reserve. (It is not only that "old men forget," as Duff Cooper emphasized. Younger men also forget, and any man sees the world through one set of eyes. A retired important personage can hardly fail to be tempted, consciously or unconsciously, to put the best light on his own actions. It is not unknown for an autobiographer to leave out a significant point in the state paper which as yet only he has permission to mention, and one recently gave long extracts from Hansard without any ellipses to mark passages omitted.) Confidential documents are also often made available far in advance of the fifty-year period. In the United States, especially since the Kennedy era began, it is open season almost all the time. So many amateurs are brought into the political process—either full time or on a periodical consulting basis—and then proceed to publish all the intimate details of their office, that foreign policy is carried on in a kind of glass bowl. The problem here is not a poverty of source material but an embarrassment of riches, and the distorting refraction of the glass. Again, the reliability of the witnesses can never be assumed, even where they agree with each other which is not invariable. In Australia, we have inherited and reinforced the British concept of a permanent professional civil service immune from public criticism and debarred from public comment. We have almost unchanging governments reluctant to admit the public into their confidence and perhaps often not sufficiently articulate to do so. (An exception—a prominent Minister who leaks Cabinet secrets for years with impunity—does not invalidate the principle.) We have no Official Secrets Act but we have a catch-all Crimes Act whose provisions frighten senior or retired civil servants into silence. Yet, true though this all is, the persistent enquirer can get at very nearly all the points about an aspect of foreign policy, as J. G. Starke showed in his book on ANZUS.[1] By reading the debates in Parliament, official records of ministerial press conferences, other official documents, press accounts, and material obtainable from similar sources overseas; by interviewing relevant people on a non-attribution basis (and the personage who will not reveal a corner of his mind in public is often delighted to get things off his chest in private)—one can get the general picture of what the policy is and how it developed. It only takes patience, time and judgment.

Judgment—because of the inevitable problem of selection and assessment of facts, of determining how true the "facts" are, and which "facts" are "factors" in a foreign policy. A "fact," true or partly true, becomes a factor only when it is taken into account. A respected Oxford scholar, Mr G. F. Hudson, has written that the "primary factor in all foreign policy is geographical location."[2] If he means that geographical location *ought to be* the primary factor in all foreign policy, one could perhaps agree. Yet examples abound of nations whose foreign policies have been worked out in bland disregard of geographical considerations. Certainly one cannot escape one's geography, but one can misunderstand it or forget it. One may even overcome it somewhat. And the importance of geography changes as technology changes. The nuclear-powered missile-carrying submarine has robbed the globe of its safe pockets.

There are no immutable or absolute factors in foreign policy. This is what makes writing theoretically about foreign policy so difficult. Perhaps nations ought to determine their policies in accordance with set principles—geographic, demographic, military, economic, ideological, and so on. Prime Ministers ought to be rational, however that may be judged, but they are not always so. To find the basis for the foreign policy of a country, therefore, it is necessary to ascertain why relevant decisions were actually made. This means looking at the thinking of the people who make the decisions, their image of the world and of their own polity, of finding which facts were factors to them, and how they took them into account. One can no more explain foreign policy from a basis of "objective" facts than one can explain Shakespeare from the basis of a grammar book. A New York professor who keeps a record of UN voting told me that he is occasionally telephoned by some of the smaller delegations to ask how they voted on a particular issue last time, and the reasons they then gave.

Yet it is still usually helpful in understanding a country's foreign policy to be aware of the basic considerations such as geography, population,

---

[1] J. G. Starke, *The ANZUS Treaty Alliance* (Melbourne: M.U.P., 1965).

[2] G. F. Hudson, *British and American Policies in the Far East since 1900*, University of Leeds, Thirteenth Montagu Burton Lecture on International Relations, 1955.

economic resources,[3] culture, history, etc. Actions in defiance of these are the exception rather than the rule.

Perhaps I should here make the distinction between the facts of a foreign policy—what the policy is—and the facts on which it is based. For the latter, the facts which are factors, the writer on foreign policy must remember that there can also be factors which may not be particularly factual. The Prime Minister's image of the world may be substantially erroneous, but he will act on it. We do not know whether the Menzies Liberal-Country Party government in its early years believed that a Communist-inspired world war could engulf Australia at short notice. In retrospect, such a belief would seem to be inadequately supported by the facts. Yet the government spoke as though it believed this to be true. Perhaps it was only the Country Party, or the Country Party's leaders, who believed it, and the Liberals could not afford to deny them the policy which such a belief involved. Alternatively, perhaps no-one believed it, but the government jointly felt the belief to be a good one to propagate in order to retain power. Anyone other than Sir Robert Menzies who asserts one of these three alternatives categorically to be true is, in fact, guessing. Similarly one could cite many foreign policies which have appeared to be based on an erroneous picture of the situation— Nehru's decision to "throw the Chinese out of India," Chou En-lai's encouragement of revolution in Africa, Eden's action at Suez, Kennedy's at the Bay of Pigs, Khrushchev's over the rockets to Cuba, Johnson's over the Dominican Republic. It is what people believe to be true, not what *is* true, that is most relevant to their actions. It is easier to appreciate this over situations that are past than over those which are current or impending. It is vitally important that the decision makers of foreign policy, and the public which elects or replaces them, should have an image of the world which corresponds as closely to the facts as possible. Hence not only the absurdity but the criminality of the foreign service officers who report what they believe their minister wants

to hear rather than the unpleasant truth he ought to hear. . . .

The academic trying to get quickly at the facts suffers from the disadvantage that he cannot get access (in Australia at least) to the confidential reports of his own and other country's experts. Yet confidential reports are not *ipso facto* more correct than public ones, and there are built-in obstacles to objectivity within a foreign office. Living in a foreign country tends steadily to sap, in one direction or the other, the impartiality of the ambassador and thus of his telegrams and reports. No Pakistani has ever put his country's case on Kashmir as well as a Commonwealth high commissioner did to me in Karachi. And at home there develops a conventional wisdom (or perhaps two on some issues), a series of myths which can be powerful instruments for the containment of overdue policy changes.

Academics may not be as affected by such considerations, but national factors can enter their assessment. At one famous university I visited, each of the two lecturers on the history and government of India and of Pakistan took with some heat the viewpoint over Kashmir taken by the nation whose politics he taught. International gatherings of political scientists are likely to see some strong nationalisms manifested. It would be surprising if this were not so since, apart from emotional factors such as patriotism, the world looks different and the importance of situations varies according to the vantage point. We can hardly expect a West German, political scientist or not, to get any more worked up over Viet Nam than an Australian does over the Oder-Neisse line. To a Frenchman, the important point about China is to learn to live with it; to an Australian, the important question is *where*. The closeness or remoteness of a situation tends to affect one's assumptions about it. Europeans on the whole are much readier than Americans or Australians to give China the benefit of the doubt about whether it is aggressive or not, or whether it is merely reacting to American actions. Yet a considerable number of academics on both sides of that argument appear to claim a divine veracity for their assumptions. Thus the problem again may be less one of viewpoint or interpretation than of proper academic scepticism about the facts—difficult enough as these are to obtain—and due restraint in their interpretation.

[3] Lord Attlee said of his Foreign Secretary, Ernest Bevin: "Our economic weakness was a great handicap to him in his work. I have often heard him say that a few million tons of coal at his disposal would have made all the difference to the outcome of some of his negotiations." *As it Happened* (London: Odhams, undated), p. 197.

Making Foreign Policy Decisions

I have suggested that it is as relevant to find out why decisions were actually made as what were the facts which ought to have influenced the decision makers. It is usually not particularly difficult to find out what a foreign policy is (except in the case of secret treaties) and broadly how it was arrived at. Yet to get a sophisticated analysis of the decision-making process involves not only the patient research mentioned but a lengthy study of the policy-making environment.

The majority of foreign policy decisions are like Topsy—they just grow. They grow out of past policies, are moulded somewhat in the bureaucratic (or other) machine, are heavily circumscribed by the logic of events. The enthusiast for change or for using scientific methods to determine the most rewarding foreign policy irrespective of past events is often unaware just how much of a country's foreign policy is inherited. It is not of course totally circumscribed and inevitable. Personalities, pressures and chance all have their effect.

The logic of events and the legacy of the past will explain most foreign policy actions, and where they do not explain, they may be called in to justify, as Hitler used Versailles and Japan used geography. Chance is an element without a valency, unassessable. The others—the action of the machine, the effects of personalities and pressures on government—are more concealed and thus more difficult and more important to study.

The role of a foreign office is never easy to determine, and books or articles on it are usually factual without being very informative.[4] They tell us how it functions; they do not tell us how it *works*, lives, palpitates; what alternatives to existing policy it puts up; which members are listened to and which are not; how reliable are its methods for collecting and assessing information; what are its continuing myths; what effect the office has on its minister and through him on the government. Important as these

aspects are, the study of the "family tree" of the department can only hint at them. The problem usually is that only the serving officer really knows what is happening and he is forbidden from reporting it. In the United States, the practice of having non-career men in several top positions in the State Department does make them readier to talk about foreign policy but it rarely seems to make them readier to talk about the State Department.[5] The real amateurs who come in to advise the President, such as Arthur Schlesinger Jr., and who are delighted to burst into print about it all, are unlikely to be knowledgeable about the foreign policy machine, in which they are not especially welcome.

It takes a good deal of historical research and perspective to bring out the role of the foreign office at any time, or the role of alternative channels which a head of government may use (as Hitler and Roosevelt did). You have to wait for the memoirs and the opening of collections of personal papers. Here the scholar in the United States is probably best served of any country. In Australia, perhaps because of the very short period in which we have had a Department of External Affairs, it is virgin territory.[6]

The role of a foreign office will vary with its expertise, with the personality of its head and of the head of government, and according to the way the government is organized. It provides continuity of policy and diplomacy as ministers change; it helps to educate ministers. Where the minister and his permanent head are in conflict on major policy issues, the permanent head must defer or resign or may be removed. Thus Lord Vansittart was removed from office in the Chamberlain government in January

---

[4] For example, Lord Strang, *The Foreign Office* (London: Allen & Unwin, 1955), and *The Diplomatic Career* (London: Andre Deutsch, 1962). Strang is more informative about the workings of the Foreign Office in his autobiographical work, *Home and Abroad* (London: Andre Deutsch, 1956). A useful (official) article on the organization and functions of the Australian Department of External Affairs appeared in *Current Notes on International Affairs*, vol. XXXVI, 5 (May 1965).

[5] The American system of congressional inquiries does produce some informative testimony. See for example the contributions of Dean Rusk, Averell Harriman and others in *The Secretary of State and the Ambassador*, Jackson Subcommittee Papers on the Conduct of American Foreign Policy (New York: Frederick A. Praeger, 1964). See also H. Field Haviland Jr., *The Formulation and Administration of United States Foreign Policy* (Washington: Brookings Institution, 1960).

[6] Fortunately, this is not for long. Sir Alan Watt, a former Secretary of the Department of External Affairs and currently Director of the Australian Institute of International Affairs has written a chapter on "The Australian Diplomatic Service" which will appear in the 1961–65 volume of *Australia in World Affairs*, edited by Gordon Greenwood and Norman Harper. Sir Alan also has references to Australian foreign policy-making in his book now being published by Cambridge University Press, *The Evolution of Australian Foreign Policy 1938–1965*.

1938, over his views on Germany; in Australia, Dr. John Burton ceased to be Secretary of the Department of External Affairs shortly after the Menzies government came to power in 1949. But a minister cannot easily change a whole foreign office, and the more established it is the more pressure will it exert on him, despite its constitutionally inferior position. Where he is inexpert or inexperienced, he will usually have no alternative to accepting the position and the brief prepared for him by his office.[7] Whether he does or not, it is both legitimate and desirable that the writer on foreign policy should be aware of the minister's relationship with the foreign office, and their respective contributions to the content of the country's foreign policy.

The policy-making machinery is obviously influenced by the personalities who are within it or who act upon it, and their individual attitudes and contributions are fair game for the researcher. Yet he must remind himself constantly of the pitfalls of emphasizing the personality rather than the policy. The portion of a policy which is directly dependent upon an individual is usually slight, even though it is impossible to assert the alternative—that the policies would have been adopted irrespective of the personalities involved.[8]

A sociologically more interesting task is to assess the role of an elite in foreign policy. But it is also much more difficult and involves a good deal of assumption. There are not many Cabinet members who would be prepared to assert publicly or perhaps even to believe that "what is good for General Motors is good for the United States of America." As Wright Mills shows,[9] it is much easier to deduce the effect of an elite on domestic politics than on foreign politics. The fact that a high proportion of a Cabinet or of the "oligocratic society"[10] of which it is the centre, have been (say) to Eton and Oxbridge is more likely to affect the tone than the content of foreign policy, but it is very difficult to be precise about either.[11] One can more readily draw up an acceptable list of the Establishment than show what policies it has collectively helped to establish, and why.

Finally, there are the pressure groups—the churches, the trade unions, the ex-soldiers' organizations, and so on, perhaps even the political parties. It is right that the attitudes of such organizations towards foreign affairs should be examined. To determine how they affect Government policy is however a far more difficult matter than to see where they agree with Government policy; and even if policy is changed there may be many more reasons than the fact that a particular interest group has been pressing for it. The Returned Servicemen's League in Australia is an example of a pressure group granted special facilities by the government for presenting its views. On matters of preferential treatment for ex-servicemen, it is very effective. On defence issues, with which the League also concerns itself and on which it makes regular submissions to the federal Cabinet, its advice is more often ignored than accepted. The fact that in 1964 the Government exempted from taxation the pay of part-time Citizen Forces could be related to RSL pressure on the point, but the pressure was exerted for fifteen years before the policy was adopted, and there were undoubtedly other factors in its adoption at that time.[12]

Similarly with churches or religious groups, especially powerful minority ones, it is easier to discern cases in which a government activity is in accord with their interests and policies than to be sure where the activity is due to sectarian pressure. Kennedy's action at the Bay of Pigs is sometimes seen to be due to his religious sympathies, but this becomes less convincing when one remembers that Nixon, a Protestant, who very nearly became President, would have been at least as enthusiastic as Kennedy for the operation. Certainly, pressure

---

[7] Although not to the extent, one hopes, that a British Minister did, who, when suddenly asked for his opinion at a Cabinet meeting, looked at his brief and allegedly began: "The Minister is advised to say . . ." Anthony Sampson, *Anatomy of Britain* (London: Hodder and Stoughton, 1962), p. 235.

[8] Some interesting examples of the effect of individuals on the conduct of foreign relations are contained in D. C. Watt, *Personalities and Policies* (London: Longmans, 1965).

[9] C. Wright Mills, *The Power Elite* (New York: O.U.P., 1956). The same deduction could be drawn from Sampson, *op. cit.*

[10] The phrase is D. C. Watt's, *op. cit.*, p. 1, where he refers to Britain as such a society, an elite group being

responsible for the exercise rather than the possession of power.

[11] D. C. Watt, in a chapter "The Nature of the Elite," *op. cit.*, is equally vague except when referring to specific people such as the King or Geoffrey Dawson of *The Times*.

[12] The role of the RSL as a pressure group is discussed in G. L. Kristianson, *The Politics of Patriotism* (Canberra: A.N.U. Press, 1966).

is often exerted by minorities on majorities, but the writer on foreign policy, who is fully entitled to report correlation of policies or events, has to be careful not to deduce causation from correlation without adequate evidence. One must be sure of the *effect* before declaring the *cause*. As Bernard Cohen has written:

At the present time, the study of particular interest groups *as a way of determining policy influence* is premature, and would inevitably result in so many distorted and negative findings as to be a prohibitively costly method of research. The same is true for the study of influential individuals: to trace the career pattern of a person who is influential in foreign policy matters one has to start at the end where the influence is demonstrated, and work backwards to community, organizational and personal antecedents.[13]

Science, Theory and Philosophy

"It is for the collector of data to know the fact," Aristotle said, "and for the mathematicians to establish the reason."[14] This is a claim which some students of international politics today would support, as scientific method is applied to information about international systems and sub-systems.[15] My concern is not with international society, but with the foreign policy of any given nation, and the extent to which scientific method, theoretical analysis or philosophical discussion can be used to understand what a particular foreign policy is and what it is based on, to forecast a policy, or to assess the "best" policy in any situation.

To deny any validity to scientific approaches to the study of foreign policy is like saying (as a provocative Australian astronomer did) that "space travel is bunk." They may be difficult, they may not attain

what their proponents claim or wish, but they are here to stay. Some writing of this kind admittedly appears to be pretentious nonsense; some, a way of employing pseudo-scientific jargon or even properly scientific terminology and method to say what could be said more simply and more understandably with a lot less effort. Some of it is primarily an intellectual exercise. But modern mathematical techniques, and machinery for the storage and treatment of information, are tools for the using. The questions are how to use them, and how to avoid misusing them.

It is unlikely that there are many foreign offices around the world which are using computers for information storage and retrieval.[16] The time-honoured system of the dog-eared file, with a maximum of security classification and a minimum of ease in discovering quickly what the file contains, will be with us for a long time. Yet one would imagine that a computer could be immensely useful in recording the actions and policies of particular nations during any situation, and the various factors which appeared to bear on them. You do not have to believe in history repeating itself to be aware of the value of such information when a similar, comparable or related situation occurs at a later date. In the same way, the ability to forecast, which can never be perfect, can be improved by greater access to information. A specialist on a given country can gradually build up his techniques, indulging in forecasts on the basis of information fed into the machine and comparing the results with the reality as it occurs. Such information could include indices of the composition and coherence and ideology of the elite, aspects of the political system, figures of economic and military potential, demographic movements, known reactions to external influences, degrees of traditionalist influence, other national characteristics, etc. Game theory is another tool. It is a way of putting into mathematical form the conflict or competition of interests and strategies between a small number of "players" (i.e. nations) in order to deduce which strategy will yield the result most satisfactory to each one's interest. It is thus an attempt at making predictions about the behaviour (the foreign policy) of a country by showing which

[13] Bernard C. Cohen, *The Influence of Non-Governmental Groups on Foreign Policy-Making* (Boston: World Peace Foundation, 1960), p. 23.

[14] *The Organum*, quoted by Hayward R. Alker, Jr., *Mathematics and Politics* (New York: Macmillan, 1965), who analyzes some of Aristotle's pretensions.

[15] I am not here going into the claims of the scientific and traditional schools, which are broadly compared and confronted in two issues of *World Politics*: Hedley Bull, "International Theory: The Case for a Classical Approach," XVII, no. 3, April 1966, and Morton A. Kaplan, "The New Great Debate. Traditionalism vs. Science in International Relations," XIX, no. 1, October 1966. The difficulties associated with the quantification of international relationships are discussed in Hayward R. Alker, Jr., "The Long Road to International Relations Theory. Problems of Statistical Nonadditivity," *World Politics*, XVIII, 4 (July 1966).

[16] An interesting assessment of the problems and possibilities is given by Fisher Howe, *The Computer and Foreign Affairs. Some First Thoughts* (Washington: Center for International Systems Research, 1966).

policy would be most rational; it gives a guide to the scientific and theoretical study of international relations and can expose the limitations of particular approaches. Deductions carefully drawn from quantified international transactions may also throw some light on international relationships and thus on the foreign policies of the countries concerned.

All but the most dogmatic of the proponents of these and other mathematical techniques admit that no such method is wholly convincing or adequate. It can only be a guide. There are always imponderable and variable factors, each of which adds to the difficulties of precision. One can make adjustments for irrationality or chance, but can never be sure in which direction to make them. In game theory, the number of players is almost always far smaller than in real life, where the effects of changes in one country's foreign policy are usually quickly related to the policies of many others. Models can be so simplified as to be useless. Theorizing, mathematically or otherwise, in order to determine policy, may add a measure to the basis of judgment, but can never allow for the personalized intuition or hunch on which a leader may act, rightly or wrongly. Scientific method is thus rather like a torch in a zoo at night. It may give you a good picture of one animal or one cage, but you cannot be sure what is going on in the rest of the zoo at the same time. And, of course, machines can go wrong.

Kaplan complains[17] that the theorist is unfairly criticized for mistaking his model for the reality; yet it is very easy to do just that, and it is easy for the man who analyzes his problems by factors at each stage, placing values on various actions and their alternatives, to forget how subjective or unreal his analysis may be. The problem here is not the tool, but in its use, and the lesson is that someone who knows a lot about mathematics but only a little about the world is as unlikely to prescribe correctly for the body politic as is someone who knows a lot about chemicals but only a little about man to prescribe correctly for the body physical.

Non-mathematical theorizing or philosophizing about foreign policy can be another useful corrective to preoccupation with the day's telegrams or press reports. It is important to keep analyzing the objectives of policy and the principles underlying it, to get at the basis of action and reaction, of interest and power and organization. So long as one's feet are on the ground, thought can add cubits to one's analytical stature. Only when ideas are muffled or distorted by words, and theory is devoid of reference to the real world, does it cease to be relevant to foreign policy.

There are many aspects to writing on foreign policy which are not touched on here. My plea is that all honest approaches be acknowledged and investigated. We need our Toynbees, Kaplans, Churchills, and the host of conventional historians and political analysts. We need to recognize the fact of "subjectivity" for writer and reader alike, for there is no totally objective writer on the actions of man; if there were, he would be immensely dull to read and would teach us nothing. The problems of writing about national policies and national secrets are formidable but not impregnable. We still have the responsibility to ask, as Foch did, "De quoi s'agit-il?" We still have the duty to exercise a disciplined caution in our conclusions.

---

[17] *Loc. cit.* The theories for which he is criticized and which he justifies are those contained in *System and Process in International Politics* (New York: John Wiley and Sons, Inc., 1957).

7. The Behavioral Science Approach to International Relations: Payoff and Prospects

J. David Singer elaborates here on his previously indicated (in Selection 3) interest in the relevance of scientific method for the study of international phenomena. The case he makes for the use of this method is brief; yet it cannot be readily ignored, especially since Professor Singer succinctly demonstrates that such an approach can be used to alleviate as well as to comprehend the conflict and suffering that prevail in the international arena. [*Reprinted from* SAIS Review, *X (Summer 1966), 12–20, by permission of the author and the* SAIS Review. *Copyright 1966 by the School of Advanced International Studies of the Johns Hopkins University.*]

A careful observer of the scholarly scene in International Relations today might discern the existence of two distinct intellectual styles or cultures. One of these cultures is, of course, the traditional one: scholars trained in history, law, and political science, bringing the laboriously acquired wisdom and insights of these disciplines to bear on contemporary questions of theory or policy. The other and more recently developed culture is that of the behavioral sciences; here we see a much smaller, but now expanding, number of scholars trying to apply a new array of methods, concepts, and data to these same intellectual and policy concerns.

The purpose of this essay is to compare these two intellectual styles, appraise their relevance for our discipline, and evaluate the desirability and probability of their convergence. More specifically, the comparisons will be made in terms of: methods for data-making and data-analysis; concepts for theory-building, and foreign policy problem-solving.

Basically, the purpose of any scholarly activity is the acquisition and codification of knowledge, whether that knowledge is intended, in turn, to aid in solving certain human problems or to satisfy the intellectual or aesthetic objectives of the researcher. Regardless of ultimate application (and this is often unknown and unforeseen) knowledge cannot be said to exist—and certainly cannot be codified or accumulated—without data.

Data making is one of the first critical distinctions between the traditional and the behavioral cultures. The typical researcher in International Relations has, of course, a solid respect for facts and reveals in his writings a remarkable combination of resourcefulness and meticulous diligence in seeking out those diplomatic, military and economic facts which seem most germane to his interests. But mere facts (a given event did or did not occur, it occurred at a given point in time and space, etc.) do not constitute data, nor can they in and of themselves be said to constitute knowledge in any but the most modest and fragmentary sense of the word.

Some will insist that this is the best we can do; that no two events, situations, or conditions are quite alike, and that each is discrete, unique and essentially incomparable. Happily this viewpoint has few supporters and their numbers appear to be fading fast. Most of us *are* interested in comparisons and generalizations and *do* seek to discern whatever regularities and uniformities exist; quite clearly, we cannot theorize without making comparisons and generalizations. At the same time, we recognize that all comparability is indeed only relative and approximate, and that no two events or conditions are *exactly* alike. That need not deflect us though, since similarity need not extend to *every* attribute of the subject cases, but only those which concern us at the moment; simple statistical techniques and standard sampling procedures permit us to "control" for the dissimilar attributes.

The question, then, is how we can ascertain whether or not there is a sufficient degree of similarity among many cases, events or conditions to permit us to generalize across such cases. That, in turn, cannot be done in any reliable fashion by the fact-finding techniques of the traditional International Relations scholar. Because they are impressionistic, unique, and fail to classify events and conditions according to explicit and rigorous coding rules, we cannot be sure that our descriptions are comparable. This liability extends not only from case to case when the *same* researcher is involved, but, more seriously, absolutely precludes any legitimate comparability and generalization—and therefore any cumulativeness of results—when *several* scholars are at work on the same theoretical problem. In other words, unless our basic observation and classification procedures (by which cases are described) are explicit and replicable, we cannot convert interesting—but theoretically useless—facts into data, and without data, we cannot generalize.

To carry the data-making point just a step further, we can say that when the political scientist or historian does employ explicit, visible and reproducible coding rules to convert a welter of facts into data, his procedures are "operational." And, by definition, once we begin to use operational procedures, we have begun to quantify our variables. That is, we select some finite number of cases which we would like to use as a basis for generalization, justify that selection on grounds of completeness or representativeness, and then proceed to ascertain the presence, strength, or direction of a given single variable at a time in each of the cases; when that variable has been

measured for each of the cases, the procedure is repeated for each additional variable, until all the independent, intervening, and dependent variables necessary to the analysis have been observed, measured and recorded. Until such steps as these have been completed, any comparative or general statement just cannot be treated as anything more serious than an interesting hypothesis or hunch. Furthermore, until the sampling criteria for case selection and the operational indicators of our variables meet certain stringent methodological requirements, we still remain short of a scientifically useful state of affairs.

While careful (yet imaginative) selection of cases, and rigorous measurement of variables, are quite necessary to good research, they remain far from sufficient. Until our data have been analyzed, we cannot claim to have presented sufficient evidence to support a descriptive or correlational (no less a causal) statement. And needless to say, the more variables we have to cope with, the more difficult the analysis. It is at this point that the importance of the "N/V ratio" becomes critical; the traditional researcher tends to look at a very few cases (and often only one) at a time, producing a very small N (number of cases) while trying to cope with and analyze a fairly large V (number of variables). This may make for interesting narrative but not for compelling theory. The modern social scientist, on the other hand, tries to limit himself to a few variables (V) at a time, but seeks to measure their role in the largest feasible number of cases (N), seeking an N/V ratio with maximum organizing efficiency.

Once the basic research design has been set up, the key variables operationalized, and the data generated via those operational procedures, analysis can proceed. Very often, a simple plotting of the data on a scatter diagram or in one or more tables (showing, for example, how many cases which are high on one variable are also high on another) will reveal the general nature of the co-variation between and among the variables. But to get a finer measurement of these co-variations or correlations, a wide range of statistical analyses is available, and with the introduction of electronic computers these correlations can be ascertained quickly and reliably.

Computing such correlations, however, is by no means the end of the inquiry. For example, to know (whereas we originally only suspected or hypothesized) that the amount of war in the twentieth-century international system increases as the amount of alliance involvement increases is an interesting finding, but no matter how strong (or predictable, or plausible) the correlation coefficient, we are still a long distance from demonstrating causality. The next problem is to ascertain how likely it was that the observed correlation occurred by sheer chance. This is now easily (and more or less automatically) discerned by computation of the correlation score's level of statistical significance; thus, if the computer print-out sheet shows the number .001 alongside of a given correlation coefficient, we know that the laws of probability say that such a coefficient had only one chance in a thousand of occurring by sheer chance or accident, and may therefore be taken quite seriously.

In addition to controlling for sheer statistical accident, we must also control for the effects of other factors which could not only have helped to produce the high co-variation, but may well have been more potent in producing that outcome than the independent variable(s) used in the particular correlation. This is a relatively complicated matter, requiring not only methodological sophistication, but a solid grasp of the theoretical problem and the ingenuity to think of alternative explanations for the observed correlations.

Without going any further into the procedural details of a more or less typical piece of scientific research (circa 1966), the key point should now be clear: Science is not a substitute for insight, and methodological rigor is not a substitute for wisdom. Research which is *merely* rigorous may well be routine, mechanical, trivial, and of little theoretical or policy value. However—and here we must note the second major difference between the traditionalists and the social scientists—in the absence of such rigorous and controlled analysis, even the most operational data are of limited value. The historian and political scientist will typically look at a large number of facts, constantly reappraise and rearrange them in his mind, and then, on the basis of what *may* have been a highly disciplined sequence of mental calculations, come up with an interpretation of them. But no one else will ever *know*; we may find his interpretation plausible or even compelling, and we may be persuaded or put off by his reputation, but

no one could consciously reproduce his intellectual processes. In sum, both imagination and rigor are necessary, but neither is sufficient.

To this point, my emphasis has been upon what I consider to be the most important contribution of the behavioral sciences. But the methodological payoffs are essentially of short-term concern. Within a decade, almost every graduate school in the country will have some faculty who have been trained in scientific method, and assertions to the effect that "you can't quantify diplomatic variables," or "international politics are too complicated to be treated scientifically" will sound as absurd as they now do when said of biology, psychology, or economics. Moreover, we will by then be well on the road to methodological and statistical adaptations of our own, to meet the problems which, despite their *general* similarity to those of other disciplines, are distinct enough to require considerable innovations and departure from the other social sciences.

The more long-run payoffs for us will probably come from the *concepts* and the *findings* of the behavioral sciences, and it is to these that I should now like to turn, however briefly. Taking the latter class of contributions first, it is worth noting the obvious point that the behavior of nations is, at bottom, a result of the behavior of individuals, small groups, and social organizations, including not only such familiar actors as defense ministers, chiefs of state, political parties, foreign ministries, legislatures, and international organizations, but families, schools, labor unions, professional societies and the like. How much does the average political scientist know about such human groups and about their associated phenomena: socialization, attitude change, group dynamics, social stratification, or role differentiation? The chances are that he has had almost no formal training and that his *in*formal training probably includes as much of the erroneous or dubious folklore of the political curbstone as it does of rigorously tested and well validated scientific findings. To illustrate my point, where in our literature is even the most partial theory of foreign policy decision making, with the central roles, relationships and structure carefully described and the causal links among these factors articulated? And where did one find any social analysis of citizen attitudes toward foreign affairs before the social psychologists began to move into our field? How often we hear scholars and practitioners try to explain or predict with a passing and casual reference to "human nature:" we attribute to this catch-all variable a bewildering, incoherent, incompatible, and often downright erroneous set of inclinations and capabilities.

The point should need no further elaboration. For decades now, sociologists, psychologists, and anthropologists have been studying with varying degrees of rigor and creativity the behavior of individuals and groups in a wide variety of settings. Would we not do well to have a general idea of what these scholars have found, so that we can use knowledge—rather than folklore—as inputs into our theorizing and policy making?

Equally critical in the long run are the *concepts* which have emerged out of the behavioral scientist's work. Without concepts, no two pieces of information can be meaningfully related, and without powerful ones we can achieve only the most modest understanding, no matter how abundant our facts. But as our concepts, organizing schema, and models become more sophisticated, and anchored in behavioral science research, we can maximize our comprehension and codify our knowledge. Quite clearly, men of action (such as policymakers) and men of ignorance or indifference (such as many citizens) are unlikely to do much abstract theorizing about international relations; as long as their concepts and constructs *seem* to work for problem solving purposes, they are unlikely to either scrap the old ones or invent new ones. Yet many of us limp along, trying to understand and explain the complex phenomena of global politics with the pitifully small and inadequate conceptual repertory of the practitioner or of the layman.

This is doubly unfortunate inasmuch as a treasure chest of ideas, constructs, and schema lies ready at hand in the behavioral science (and engineering and mathematical) literature. Some (such as pattern maintenance, stratification, status congruence, dissonance, or anomie) may very well be put to work directly, while others (such as homeostasis, zero-sum, transference, diffusion, internalization, or permeability) may require modification and adaptation before they can be applied to our particular problems. In sum, concepts are tools for organizing information, and the traditional researcher goes to work year after year with a kit which is meagre and obsolete. Little

wonder that we continue to be baffled by the complexity of it all?

My main preoccupation here is with the extent to which a behavioral science approach might lead to fuller knowledge and more powerful theory. But the payoffs need not end with the intellectual and the scholarly. There are important policy payoffs, with critical implications for human welfare.

Suppose, for example, that we think of war as a combination of epidemic and auto accident, rather than as a moral struggle between good and evil, or as the inevitable and regular consequence of man's depravity and greed. Such a formulation immediately suggests that war's occurrence or not at a given time is a function of voluntaristic, deterministic, and probabilistic phenomena. If we knew, for example, which of the elements were at the deterministic end of the continuum and which were more susceptible to individual and group intervention in the short or middle run, we might well be able to prevent these human catastrophes even while protecting certain national interests. If we knew what sorts of diplomatic immunization and sanitary engineering methods could prevent (or make less likely) the typical pre-war situation, and if we knew (to shift metaphors) which steering, braking, and signaling techniques tend to minimize the likelihood of collision, the odds on our survival might improve dramatically. Of course, we do *not* know these things; we all have hunches and hypotheses, but where is the evidence which would permit the rejection of certain competing explanations and the tentative or firm acceptance of others? Despite the confident (and generally inconsistent) assertions of publicists, ideologues, and policymakers, the causes of war's beginning or ending remain as much a mystery as do the causes of cancer or the causes of sunspots.

Were the implications not so ominous, it would be humorous that in recent months, both Peking and Washington have been sounding the call to avert another "Munich"; each asserts with apparent sincerity that if "the aggressor" is not stopped now, he will have to be stopped later and at much greater cost. Both usages of the parallel are probably ridiculous, yet where is the codified knowledge which could be used to measure the extent to which the analogue does hold? Or, how do we ascertain that the case at hand is not more closely analogous to

Fashoda, or Sarajevo, or the Spanish Civil War, or the recent Algerian struggle?

If, for example, we now had available the results of one or more rigorous operational analyses of all (or even many) prior cases of limited and partly internationalized civil wars, with the knowledge that some escalated into more severe wars and others found a negotiated solution, we could make our policy judgments with considerably greater confidence. What are the key variables: the polarity of the larger international system, the ethnic differences between the combatants, the populace's attitude toward the regime, the economic intervention of third parties, the tactical ploys of the insurgents, or what? In the absence of the hard evidence that scientific research *could* have established, national policymakers and their supporters get away with what will probably turn out to be the most arrant nonsense. What we see in diplomacy and strategy today is the equivalent of what the medical profession was able to expose as quackery, once its practitioners began to "go scientific."

We must, however, be careful not to claim too much. First of all, there is so little scientifically generated knowledge about International Relations, and so few researchers trained or inclined to add to it, that we are decades away from the kind of diagnostic and prescriptive base that would be necessary. Secondly, the world (social and physical) is indeed a probabilistic one, and the best we can do is explain in terms of tendencies, and predict in terms of odds. And it might well be that the last great crisis before oblivion will be so distinctive in character that no prior cases or combination of cases will be sufficiently similar to offer much guidance. These are indeed possibilities, but with so much at stake, any chance of improving our odds would seem to be worth pursuing.

A fuller understanding of the causes of war (or specific classes of war) is not, of course, the only potential payoff of a behavioral science approach to our subject. Considerable knowledge could (and will) be generated such as to ease the problem of the aggrandizer, or hinder the growth of a global community, or permit greater exploitation at home and abroad, and so on. But this sort of research could (and will) also help the weak to resist the strong, the peace lovers to defend their own interests, and the nations to build a more just and stable order. Which

of these classes of problems will be solved first is, of course, a function of research support, data availability, scientific ingenuity, theoretical serendipity, scholars' values, and many other factors. Just as high energy physics and biochemistry have generated both kinds of knowledge, a social science of International Relations will also produce both kinds of knowledge. But with some prior attention to human values on the part of governments and researchers, we may come out with a somewhat more wholesome ratio than did the creators of the atomic bomb and biological warfare.

It should be apparent by now that we speak more of promise than of performance, more of future prospects than of past payoffs. Space precludes any full summary of the theoretical knowledge that has already been generated, however limited its quantity may be.[1] . . . But in a handful of universities and research centers in America (and in Western Europe and Japan) scientific research in International Relations goes on, and slowly the ratio between the traditional and the scientific cultures begins to change, with the pace quickening as the scholarly possibilities become more evident and the policy needs become more pressing.

As important as such developments may be, it is equally important that they not proceed at the expense of, and unrelated to, the excellent work that the traditional scholars have done for decades (or centuries, depending upon one's point of view) and will continue to do. As I suggested at the outset, no product of ingenuity, craftmanship, and diligence can be safely dismissed or ignored. Even though some of the more enthusiastic devotees of the newer culture in our field may convey the contrary impression, it is unlikely that we will follow that tendency. We cannot afford to. Rather, we can be expected to move steadily in an integrative direction, with the "traditionalist" and the "behavioralist" both reaching out in the other's direction, borrowing, adapting, and recombining in such a way as to gain the great benefits of the newer approach while retaining all that is valuable in the older. Sound scholarship would seem to demand no less, and humanity can ask for no more.

[1] A representative sampling of such research, plus a fairly complete bibliography, will be found in this author's *Quantitative International Politics: Insights and Evidence* (New York: The Free Press, 1968).

Part Two

The International System

Of all the advances that have occurred in the study of international phenomena, perhaps none is more important than the ever-growing tendency to regard the world as *the international system*. For many years, scholars referred to the "family of nations," the "international society," or the "world community." Such designations were used loosely, interchangeably, and analogically; ordinarily, they did not represent serious efforts to conceptualize the organization of international relations along familial, societal, or communal lines. The designation of the world as a "system," however, does reflect an explicit attempt to adapt a precise concept which has proved valuable to other social sciences and to the physical sciences as well. Furthermore, it is a neutral concept. Whereas the terms "family," "society," and "community" all suggest the existence of a basic unity and coherence, the notion of a system does not quite as readily imply characteristics which may mislead the observer. More important, a "systems perspective" facilitates a clearer formulation of the main variables with which students of international politics and foreign policy must contend. For a system is considered to exist in an environment and to be composed of parts which, through interaction, are in relation to each other. Consequently, a system has a structure and encompasses processes through which it is either sustained or changed. By conceiving of international phenomena in this way, the main variables of the field can be meaningfully and fruitfully clustered under three major foci. Stated briefly, a systemic conception allows us to focus upon the actions of nations as the components of the system; upon the structure and functioning of the system which results from the interaction of nations; or upon the environmental factors which condition both the actions of nations and the operation of the system.

It may be useful to note that we are more familiar than we realize with the notion of a system. It is quite commonplace, for example, to think in terms of an economic system, a political system, a personality system, or even of inanimate systems, such as a subway or an electrical system. Most of us are accustomed to discussing the ways in which the components of a system contribute to, or detract from, its stability, flexibility, and durability. Contrariwise, we frequently refer to ways in which a system "requires" its components to perform certain functions or otherwise fulfill their role in the system. Indeed, even the concept of an international system is not unfamiliar. Most of us, in our casual conversations, implicitly conceive of world affairs in such a framework. When, for instance, we remark that "the cold war is getting hotter" or that "world tension is lessening," we are referring to states of a system, just as the economist is when he talks of booms and busts, or the psychologist when he refers to depressions and euphorias. In other words, it should not be difficult for the student to accept and adopt a systemic (as well as a systematic) approach to the phenomena of international politics and foreign policy. In so doing, he may find that new dimensions of his subject have become manifest.

Notwithstanding its essential simplicity, the concept of an international system gives rise to some methodological problems which need to be mentioned. In the first place, the question arises as to whether the nations of the world should be regarded as a single international system, or whether it is preferable to view them as forming several international systems. It would be quite logical, for example, to posit the existence of a Southeast Asian system, a West European system, a small-nation system, a Communist-nation system, an agrarian-nation system, and so on. Indeed, any continued interaction between two nations can properly be viewed in a systemic framework, so that theoretically the one hundred-plus nations of the world can form more than five thousand dyadic international systems. In addition, if individuals, officials, or groups are considered international actors along with nations, then the potential number of international systems becomes virtually incalculable.

These various possibilities indicate that the classification of systems is somewhat arbitrary and depends upon the purposes of the observer. Faced with countless systems, most observers find it convenient to assume that all the units which engage in international action constitute *the* international or global system, and to regard less comprehensive patterns of interaction as its subsystems. Thus it is possible to analyze the special situations involving, say, the nations of Southeast Asia in systemic terms and, at the same time, place them within the larger framework of international politics. In addition to its convenience, this classification scheme is logically sound. All the subsystems are, after all, affected by their membership in the global system, whereas the latter does not conform to the functional requirements of any larger system. Perhaps in an earlier day, when communication and transportation facilities were poor, several autonomous international systems, such as the Chinese and the Aztecs, existed simultaneously. And, conceivably, some day new systems will be discovered through space exploration. For the present, however, there is only one international system which does not also have the characteristics of a subsystem. Consequently, for reasons of both substance and manageability, we shall henceforth distinguish between *the* international system and the many international subsystems. Most of the ensuing selections also make this distinction, either explicitly or implicitly.

Identification of the units or actors of the international system presents a second methodological problem. A variety of kinds of units can be considered as initiators of action which sustains the international system. Obviously individuals, whether they function as government officials or private citizens, acquire the attributes of international actors whenever they engage in behavior that transcends national boundaries. Viewed in a broader framework, many types of collectivities, ranging from groups, to governments, to nation-states, to supranational organizations, can also be regarded as actors. There are, of course, advantages and drawbacks inherent in both the individual and collectivity perspectives. On the one hand, collectivities are abstractions and do not engage in the observable actions that identifiable individuals may undertake in fulfilling certain social roles. To speak of Germany wanting this, or France avoiding that, is to run the risk of oversimplifying, of ascribing human characteristics to nonhuman, abstract entities. On the other hand, many individuals act on behalf of governments, which, in turn, represent units called nation-states that for centuries have been the focal point of man's highest loyalties and thus are the political agencies that supersede all others in their capacity to make binding decisions for their members. If it is done carefully, then, to speak of what Germany wants or what France avoids is to account in an abbreviated and useful way for the collective preferences or behavior of large social systems with a legal and political base. Unfortunately, as Harold and Margaret Sprout have shown, many students of international politics and foreign policy do not exercise care in this regard and indiscriminately attribute individual qualities to collective actors.*

Assuming that the observer exercises care and manages to avoid the dangers of reification and anthropomorphism, it follows that his goals will determine whether he treats individuals or collectivities as international actors. If he is interested in high-level theories of stability and change in the international system, he will probably concentrate on states as actors. But if he is concerned with the behavior of a single nation-state, or with a particular pattern of interaction among several nation-states, then his attention will doubtless be drawn to those persons who are duly constituted to make decisions for the state. So as to move back and forth among these levels, most observers combine them by, in effect, positing a state-as-decision-makers model of the actors who comprise the international system. That is, action in the international system is ordinarily attributed to states, but these states are recognized to be a complex of governmental officials who act on behalf of and in response to their national societies. Virtually all of the remaining selections in the book employ this combined conception of the international actor and, despite the qualifications set forth in the next paragraph, this conception also underlies the use of the word "state" in the titles and introductions to Parts Three, Four, and Five.

Although it is comprehensive and helpful, the states-as-decision-makers model does not entirely resolve the problem of identifying international actors. Developments since World War II have fostered the emergence of units which cannot, by any stretch of the imagination, be regarded as nation-states, but which nevertheless initiate actions central to the international system. Nation-states continue to be the predominant source of international action, and certainly many decades will elapse before they are overshadowed by some other form of political organization. Yet, the development of nuclear weapons and long-range missiles, the rapid technological advances in other areas, and the achievement of independence by formerly colonial peoples in Asia and Africa have precipitated two tendencies which classifiers of international actors cannot ignore. One is an integrative tendency, whereby the military and non-military technology of the space age has led groups of nation-states to an increased awareness of their interdependence and, consequently, to a greater readiness to coordinate their efforts. The other is a disintegrative tendency among those newly independent states of Asia and Africa which, rightly or wrongly, were created prior to the emergence of national loyalties and a political agency which could make decisions binding upon its sectional or tribal components. The former tendency has resulted in the establishment of supra-national organizations which act in ways that cannot be treated as merely the sum of behaviors undertaken by national actors. For example, action can be traced back increasingly to the United Nations, to the Organization of African Unity, to the European Coal and Steel Community, or to the many other formal organizations comprised of national members. To be sure, actions resulting from the votes cast by, say, more than one hundred and twenty members of the General Assembly of the United Nations are most fruitfully

---

* Harold and Margaret Sprout, *The Ecological Perspective on Human Affairs: With Special Reference to International Politics* (Princeton: Princeton University Press, 1965), pp. 33–8.

viewed as the net product of some one hundred and twenty separate actions. This would not be true, however, of much of the activity of the Secretary General of the United Nations or of the ranking officials of other international organizations whose loyalties and responsibilities would be characterized as supranational. Contrariwise, the disintegrative tendency has produced international situations in which the key actors are tribal chiefs or leaders of breakaway provinces. It is awkward to classify rebel leaders as national leaders, albeit they often initiate or sustain interaction sequences that are international in character. In short, nation-states may be the most predominant international actors, but they are no longer the only actors. Both larger and smaller units have come into existence and allowance must be made, both conceptually and empirically, for their presence in any international situation.

Still another set of methodological problems that must be faced concerns the international environment and its relation to the international system. Ordinarily the environment of a system is viewed as consisting of everything that exists outside of that system. When it is applied to a system that comprises all the nations of the world, however, this conception may not seem very useful. It would appear to equate outer space with the environment of the international system (and to an ever-increasing extent even outer space is becoming a part of the system). However, it must be remembered that the student of international politics and foreign policy is primarily interested in political phenomena and that all other types of phenomena are investigated only in order to shed light on the political dimensions of behavior. In effect, when students of the subject refer to an international system, they are using a shorthand description; what they actually have in mind is an international *political* system. From this perspective, therefore, the environment of the international system consists of all those events and conditions, both human and nonhuman, which are nonpolitical in nature and which affect the behavior of nation-states and the operation of the international system. Hence, for example, population trends, the development of new weapons, the emergence of new cultural norms, changes in climate, and geographical realities are all considered environmental factors. An even more succinct illustration is that of the world economy: its ups and downs constitute one aspect of the environment of the global system, a vitally important aspect to which the global system must adjust and over which it attempts to maintain a minimum of control.

The question arises as to how the boundaries—and thus the environment—of an international system are to be defined, by the student or by the actors he observes. Practice differs in this regard. Some observers conceive of the international environment as consisting of all the nonpolitical events and conditions that they perceive to be operative in the world, irrespective of whether or not the existence of the events and conditions is recognized by the decision-makers who act on behalf of nation-states or other political actors in the system. Other observers limit their conception to the events external to a nation-state that its decision-makers perceive. The latter, for example, would argue that while the world's population explosion has long been smoldering, it did not become part of the global environment until its potential danger came to be appreciated by those in high political offices. Depending on their purposes, still other observers find that it is quite possible to employ both objective and subjective conceptions of the environment. While there is some validity in all of these approaches, the distinctions between them are important and stem from profound philosophical differences regarding the nature of causation. Thus, whichever approach one adopts, its implications and limitations must be identified and accepted if the role of environmental factors in international politics and foreign policy is to be properly analyzed.

A systemic perspective gives rise to one other problem that needs to be mentioned. There would appear to be a bias in favor of stability inherent in the systems concept. That is, in asking what functions must be performed for a system to persist, the analyst runs the danger of organizing his data in such a way that he takes note only of those factors within a system or its environment that foster its continuance. Strictly speaking, however, such a bias is not built into the systems concept. The systems analyst does not assume that the requisite functions will be performed. He allows—even looks—for the possibility that they will not be performed. Hence he is ever ready to take note of instability that leads either to the collapse of a system into its environment or to its transformation. In other words, it is both possible and desirable to view any international system as located at any moment in time somewhere on a continuum that ranges from perfect stability (i.e., constancy) to perfect instability (i.e., nonexistence) and to treat the shifts in its location that occur through time as systemic transformations. Indeed, the most interesting aspects of international systems are those involving the dynamics whereby they shift back and forth between different degrees and forms of stability and instability.

The eight articles that follow elaborate on the foregoing aspects of the global system. The first two are concerned with the problem of identifying the actors in the system; taken together, they clearly reveal that this problem requires careful consideration and is not simply a matter of formulating a brief definition of a nation-state. The third examines some of the more salient features of the global environment in the present era. The next four investigate structural characteristics of the international political system itself, including those that underlie systemic transformation. The last selection of Part Two probes at the subsystemic level and reveals the close interrelatedness of the global system to its regional components. Further insights into the international system can be developed from some of the selections in Part Four—especially in its first section—that focus on the stability and instability of international interaction patterns.

A. Actors Comprising the System

8. The Territorial State Revisited: Reflections on the Future of the Nation-State

John H. Herz is Professor of Government at the City College of New York. His work in the international field stemmed from an interest in political philosophy and such basic problems as the "security dilemma" and the "idealism-realism conflict." After examining these concepts at a general level in *Political Realism and Political Idealism* (1951), Professor Herz sought to apply them to the postwar international scene and to evaluate the consequences of rapid technological advance for the structure and functioning of the international system. One result of this effort was *International Politics in the Atomic Age* (1959), from which an excerpt was reproduced in the first edition of this reader. In that excerpt Professor Herz forecast that modern technology would lead to the demise of the nation-state as an international actor. Impelled by international developments in the 1960s, Professor Herz reconsidered this thesis a decade later and, as can be seen in the ensuing selection, backed away from it. What follows, then, presents not only a cogent estimate of the viability of the nation-state as an actor, but it also offers—especially if contrasted with Selection 9 of the first edition of this book—an impressive illustration of how theory is developed and revised when a flexible and open-minded scholar is at work. [*Reprinted from* Polity, The Journal of the Northeastern Political Science Associations, *I, 1 (1968), pp. 12–34, by permission of the author and the publisher. Copyright 1968 by the University of Massachusetts Press.*]

Despite the conspicuous rise of international organization and supranational agencies in the postwar world and despite the continuing impact on international affairs of subnational agents such as business organizations (in the West) and "international" parties (in the East), the states remain the primary actors in international relations. Indeed, as the rush into "independent" statehood shows, being a sovereign nation seems to be the chief international status symbol as well as to furnish the actual entrance ticket into world society.

In 1957 I published an article entitled—perhaps rashly—"Rise and Demise of the Territorial State."[1] Its chief thesis was to the effect that for centuries the characteristics of the basic political unit, the nation-state, had been its "territoriality," that is, its being identified with an area which, surrounded by a "wall of defensibility," was relatively impermeable to outside penetration and thus capable of

[1] *World Politics*, IX (1957), 473 ff.; elaborated upon in my *International Politics in the Atomic Age* (New York, 1959).

satisfying one fundamental urge of humans—protection. However, so my argument proceeded, territoriality was bound to vanish, chiefly under the impact of developments in the means of destruction which render defense nugatory by making even the most powerful "permeable." What was going to take the place of the now obsolete nation-state? I said that, rationally speaking, only global "universalism," affording protection to a mankind conceiving of itself as one unit, was the solution.

This thesis was subsequently referred to by many who seemed to agree with its main thrust—that of the demise of the nation-state. The nuclear age seemed to presage the end of territoriality and of the unit whose security had been based upon it.[2] Naturally there was less agreement concerning what (if anything) would take its place. "Futurology" (to use the term—now accepted into the language of social science in Europe—coined by Ossip K. Flechtheim for a science or art of prognostic) provides uncertain standards of predicting developments. But it is clear that, at least in a negative way, the "demise" thesis seemed to preclude a revival of something close to the traditional political unit. Rather, it seemed to anticipate trends toward international interdependence, if not global integration.

Developments have rendered me doubtful of the correctness of my previous anticipations. The theory of "classical" territoriality and of the factors threatening its survival stands. But I am no longer sure that something very different is about to take its place. There are indicators pointing in another direction: not to "universalism" but to retrenchment; not to interdependence but to a new self-sufficiency; toward area not losing its impact but regaining it; in short, trends toward a "new territoriality." The following constitutes an attempt to analyze the trends that point in the direction of a possible territorial world of the future and to present something like a model of such a world with the aid of hypotheses, which, on the basis of demonstrable facts, do not seem entirely implausible. There will

be a variety of hypotheses, each probably open to some doubt, but the sum-total seems at least minimally plausible.

I. Considerations

Consider the following: (a) In the spring of 1967 there was on the shore of the eastern Mediterranean a unit that appeared under any customary standard unviable. Endowed with an "impossible" strategic configuration it faced encircling units not merely hostile but solemnly sworn to destroy the "alien" unit in their midst at first opportunity. The opportunity seemed to have come when two obstacles suddenly vanished that so far had enabled Israel to live: the protective force of UNEF and the proverbial disunity of the Arabs. The world anticipated the second stage of Hitler's "final solution" of the "Jewish question." What happened? Determined to face death and extinction, a population deeply attached to its "homeland" not only resisted but beat all comers. The latter, *not* faced with the choice of victory or national extinction, fled.

(b) There was, in 1967, one of the poorest countries extant, chiefly agrarian, little developed, long under colonial rule, never, in modern times, politically organized as an independent unit. Split in half, it was also split in its approach to the problem of its unification and independence. Then the most powerful nation on earth undertook to impose one solution upon the Vietnamese. Whereupon one half, so far only half-heartedly resigned to Communist rule, became united as one in resistance to the "aggressor" (even to the point of permitting the controlling group to risk arming the people), while in the other half guerrilla war and the "fish-in-water" situation frustrated the "invader's" efforts to such an extent that even the marshalling of overwhelming force failed to enable him to achieve his goal of subjection.

What are we to conclude from the above? That in an age of nationalism nations are invincible? That the nuclear arsenal is "unavailable" as an effective means of forcing decisions? That a new type of warfare restores the protective function to entities that, at least in the eyes of large portions of the people, legitimately represent the nation, or to the group that strives for national autonomy? Before trying to establish hypotheses, let us look further into the two

[2] See, for instance, the similar conclusion reached by Klaus Knorr in *On the Uses of Military Power in the Nuclear Age* (Princeton, 1966), p. 174. See also Raymond Aron, *Peace and War: A Theory of International Relations* (New York, 1966), pp. 395–96, and even Hans J. Morgenthau in, for example, "The Four Paradoxes of Nuclear Strategy," *American Political Science Review*, LVIII (1964), 23 ff.

situations used as examples. In neither case has nuclear power been used. But the other type of weapon and warfare which causes the decline of classical territoriality by enabling belligerents to circumvent the "hard shell" of defense and to destroy the enemy "vertically"—airpower—has been clearly in evidence. What has been its effect? In the case of Israel control of the air, established at the very beginning of hostilities, was decisive in her victory. What did it achieve? Survival of one national unit, certainly. But also defeat of the enemy in the traditional sense of compelling him to abide by the will of the victor? The present plight of Israel, not knowing what to do with its "victory" in the face of apparent Arab determination not to negotiate a settlement, is significant. In an age of nationalism and guerrilla war one seems to be able to counter aggression but not to subdue. Supposing Israel had occupied Cairo and Damascus, might she have forced her enemies' hands? For example, by establishing, in the classical fashion, complaint regimes with which to negotiate? In all likelihood, little would have been gained. In such cases, the "Algerian" type of situation is liable to ensue, with the victor facing the "territorial" urge of a nationalistic population, its readiness to bear any hardship rather than submit.

The same applies to Vietnam. There, too, the Algerian analogy is correct, and not the far-fetched one of Hitlerian expansionism and a possible Munich. Nuclear power so far has proved "unavailable" because it would be "overproductive." While United States control of the air has been the primary cause of its and its client's forces not being defeated on the ground, it has proved incapable of defeating the enemy. The resulting stalemate, in the long run, is likely to be more frustrating to the side that fights away from home halfway around the globe for a cause that, at best, is confused in its mind, than for those who are convinced that they fight for their homes, ground, country, nation.

Israel, the Arabs, Algeria, Vietnam—we may add, from recent years, Poland, Hungary, Rumania, China, France, Panama, Cuba: nation-state and nationalism, territorial urge and the urge to maintain (or establish, or regain) one's "sovereignty" and "independence"—all of these do not seem to have diminished in importance in these decades of the nuclear age. Let us try to develop some hypotheses concerning their role in the future.

II. The End of Empire

By "empire" we mean control of areas and populations outside those one considers as constituting one's own nation; the term also indicates the (non-national or multinational) entities thus formed. It is our first hypothesis that remnants of empire, where it still survives, are bound to disappear, in this way rendering the entire surface of the globe (inasmuch as it is under governmental control of specific, separate political units) a mosaic of nation-states. (On the problem of their identity, coherence, and legitimacy see below.)

Let us distinguish empires of the old style from those formed under the impact of nuclear and bipolar factors. The old empires were chiefly founded by and based upon territorial conquest and domination. They were successful because of the then prevailing strategic-technological and/or cultural-civilizational superiorities of the expansionist countries and the simultaneous absence of nationalism in the modern sense from the areas into which the imperial countries expanded (with tribalism in Africa, for instance, or feudal systems with weak national coherence in India). At a certain stage of industrial and capitalistic development there were strong economic motivations for such expansion and control. The importance of foreign resources and manpower, and of capital export and investment, to technologically and industrially developing nations led theorists of "imperialism" such as Lenin and other Marxists, but also non-Marxist ones, to believe that imperialist expansion and colonial control were features innate in and congruous with the advance of industrial systems. We know now that this conjunction was characteristic of only one phase in this development, a phase which under new technological developments (such as substitution of synthetic for natural raw materials) is drawing to a close.[3]

[3] See, for example, Knorr, op. cit., p. 21 ff. In Knorr's convincing presentation this is only one of several factors making for the diminished value of territorial expansion. Others are: the decline of offensive foreign-political goals, with welfare societies, no longer led by military elites, turning to domestic affairs; the growth of an antiwar spirit, due to the more direct impact on people at large of the costs and suffering of war; restraints through world opinion; and decreased submissiveness of ruled populations (pp. 29 ff., 57 ff.). I shall deal with some of these factors, in particular the last one (which, of course, is closely related to the rise and spread of nationalism), below. A similar line of argument is to be found in E. O.

Thus, beginning with a pre-Western empire, the Ottoman, and then extending to the great "classical" empires of the British, French, Dutch, etc., the process of liquidation has been going on relentlessly, spurred by the triumphant march of nationalism over the globe. Indeed, so little "interest" remains in the imperial stance that nowadays we sometimes find the imperial country in the somewhat absurd situation of trying hard to "get out of there," and as soon as possible, but having a difficult time doing so without leaving behind chaos or strife (for example, Britain and its few remaining possessions "East of Suez"). And even the conclusion of arrangements on retention of bases which may be more vital to the defense and/or the economy of the newly independent unit than to its former ruler, often proves difficult because of the extreme nationalism found in the area. Such areas thus tend to become useless to the former owner, untenable, or both. (On their role in regard to "new-style" empires see below.)

We may thus anticipate the extension of this trend to still existing areas of old-style empire, such as that of the Portuguese in Africa. Only where original empire led to white settlement on a large scale which subsequently developed its own separate territoriality will there be serious problems concerning the liquidation of these settlers' control over (numerically minority or majority) indigenous populations (as in South Africa). There it is, however, no longer a problem of imperialism or colonialism but rather one of racial adjustment and ethnic integration in a territorial unit.

The demise of old-style empire is now largely achieved, and few doubt the completion of the process in the future. But many will say that this has not meant the disappearance of empire as such; that it merely indicates a change in appearance and aspects. Territorial conquest and expansion may no longer be the fashion of the day. But has not indirect penetration, with indirect controls, taken their place when totalitarian regimes try to conquer the world

through propaganda and subversion and when the nuclear superpowers extend the "hard shell of defensibility" from the traditional territorial unit, the nation-state, to blocs that, under bipolarity, tend to comprise halves of the globe? One effect of this "new-style" imperialism was that, within each of the two blocs that gave the postwar international system its bipolar character, the relation between a leading power and nations that formerly would have been allies on an equal plane became one of dominating unit to client, or satellite unit. I have previously tried to trace the novel features of intrabloc relationships which prevail under bipolar and nuclear conditions (for example, the novel features of NATO, as compared with alliances of the old style[4]), while the "imperialistic," expansionist tendencies of world-revolutionary systems have been vividly described by authors such as Hans J. Morgenthau.[5]

I still believe that my description of postwar bipolarity and its effects was correct in reference to a situation in which two, and only two, powers held a nuclear monopoly, and the development of weapons and delivery systems required the establishment of empires complete with forward areas of troops stationed at or near their rim and bases lining their frontiers. Even at that time, however, there were forces at work that counteracted the empire-consolidating factors. They have since turned out to be extremely important. One category is primarily military-strategic. With the development of intercontinental ballistic missiles and the corresponding delivery systems the importance of missile bases outside the territory of the superpowers themselves has diminished. With the emergence of second-strike capacity on both sides and the ensuing stabilization of mutual deterrence, the usefulness of nuclear weapons as umbrellas protecting areas outside the superpowers has become doubtful. I shall

[4] *International Politics in the Atomic Age*, pp. 112–43.

[5] This author uses the somewhat misleading term "nationalist universalism"; see, for example, *Politics Among Nations*, 4th ed. (New York, 1967), p. 323 ff. World-revolutionary expansionism does constitute a new type of expansionist nationalism, but the term "universalism" might better be reserved to an antinationalist or nonnationalist, *internationalist* attitude. The ensuing confusion can be seen in a book like J. W. Burton's *International Relations: A General Theory* (Cambridge, 1965), where Morgenthau and I are referred to throughout as joint advocates of "nationalist universalism" in a sense in which neither of us has used the term; see, for example, pp. 110, 132, 149.

Czempiel, *Das amerikanische Sicherheitssystem 1945–1949* (Berlin, 1966), for example, on p. 12: "In its initial phase capitalism depended on raw materials, so that there was temptation to compel their possessors to exploit them.... In the era of mass consumption raw material production as well as capital exports recede in importance behind promotion of sales. For the sale of private cars, that symbol of mass society, territorial expansion is not necessary ..." (translation mine).

have more to say about the impact of such "unavailability of force" on nation-states and the nation-state system. Suffice it here to draw attention to the ensuing lesser importance of allies (or clients) and their inclusion in organized blocs or defense systems, and to the equally diminishing value of bases on foreign soil and of integrated forces. Even where the latter are still strategically meaningful, their maintenance becomes more difficult under the impact of the second type of factors: the resurgence of nationalism within the blocs. Resistance of nations to being reduced to client or satellite status by now has meant their emergence from such a status to genuine autonomy (especially in the East) or to the traditional nationalism and the national independence of prenuclear times (as in the West). To this must be added the trend toward nuclear multipolarity through nuclear proliferation—a joint effect of the spread of technological know-how and of nationalism. What this presages will be discussed in more detail below. What had to be pointed out here is the trend away from the coherence and consolidation of the new-style empires that had been founded on nuclear monopolies or nuclear superiorities, toward the assertion, or reassertion, of nationhood and independence.

III. The Unavailability of Force

"The dangerousness of war has reduced the danger of war."[6] The overkill machinery of nuclear armament, with all its potential pervasiveness in regard to the territory and boundaries of traditional international units, has had the unexpected, paradoxical, and encouraging effect of stabilizing a world most had believed destabilized in the extreme through the advent of the new weapon. At the dawn of the atomic age, when the new machinery for destruction had first become available to powers utterly at odds in regard to ways of life, types of regimes, and objectives of foreign policy, there had been general expectation that the holocaust was inevitable unless the enormity of the threat would make the superpowers agree on radical measures of disarmament and control. They did not, and yet, in twenty years of nuclear confrontation, the world has escaped nuclear war and even conventional war among major nations.

[6] Inis L. Claude, *The Changing United Nations* (New York, 1967), p. 9.

Chief cause of this development, of course, has been nuclear stalemate through nuclear deterrence. The boundaries of the blocs turned out to be the limits of spheres of tacitly agreed upon nonintervention. The United States and the Soviet Union emerged as the two great "conservatives," both intent on consolidating the status quo as it had been established after World War II, including its often abstruse and seemingly unmanageable arrangements, settlements, and boundaries (for example, the two Germanies, Berlin, and access routes to West Berlin; or the 38th parallel in Korea). A nuclear war, or any war that might escalate into one, was not to be risked over issues located in the sphere conceded to the other side (such as the crises concerning Hungary, Berlin, or Cuba). In this way, at least in intention, the bloc frontiers have taken the place of the "trip-wire" lines of protection which national boundaries used to constitute in the age of territorial impermeability.

But this also meant protection of the respective actors and regimes and, by way of indirection, of the units controlled by these regimes. If Castro is protected in Cuba, or Chiang on Taiwan, or Ulbricht in East Germany, or whoever is in power at Seoul, this entails also the preservation of Cuba, the Republic of China, the German Democratic Republic, and the Republic of Korea *qua* territorial units. Force in the relationship between the United States and the Soviet Union, or their respective blocs, has been "unavailable" in the sense that the effects of nuclear action are considered unacceptable to either side. Although the weapon must remain available as a retaliatory threat, one not merely hopes that it will never be used but is more or less agreed that it will not function—except as retaliation—in one's policy calculations.

One can go a step further. Realization that any kind of hostilities involving the major powers or their bloc affiliates can easily get out of control and escalate into nuclear war has made them discount, to some extent, the use even of conventional force. It is kept up for balance and held in readiness for defense but its actual use has become unlikely. We can further observe that even outside the blocs (or whatever remains of them) the use of force has declined in the relations between the big and the small. There certainly has been growing hesitation to resort to it, ironically above all on the part of the big toward those who would appear to be at their mercy. Compared with prenuclear imperialistic practices, the forbearance of the United States toward Panama or that of the Soviets toward Albania or Rumania has been quite astonishing. Some of the reasons are nuclear, to be sure. Less forbearance might lead to nuclear "confrontation" or worse things. But there are additional reasons. Thus, in former times the powerful could afford to disregard hostile reaction on the part of what is loosely referred to as "world opinion." They can no longer discount it today exactly because, with force less available, they must look for substitute means of safeguarding interests and conducting policy. These may be found in areas such as "parliamentary diplomacy," where—as in the debates and votes of the United Nations—the goodwill of the small may turn out to be important. In this way, a hostile reaction to warlike policies of the mighty can be brought to bear on the international plane. A growing conviction that force used for national purposes is "outlawed"—whatever the legal nature of this principle—reinforces the impact of opinion, as does, in a particular region, the belief that old-style interventionism is outlawed in inter-American relations. Exceptions prove the rule: American intervention in Vietnam and the Dominican Republic has led to tragic isolation of the United States in world opinion.

But the effect of the "unavailability of force" on the territorial stability of countries is not exclusively positive. It is somewhat ambiguous. For instance, we can see that, by way of curious reaction, force unavailability to the large may encourage the small to defy them and use force with impunity. What hampers the powerful—anxiety concerning nuclear confrontations, anticolonialist opinion, etc.—favors the small. They leave the nuclear worrying to the nuclear powers and bank on being backed up by world opinion and the world organization. To this may be added a frequent lack of responsibility or the parochialism of new nations and their leaders, who may be tempted to pursue grievances to the point of violence in disregard of the dangers this involves for world peace. They may even set out to create threats to the peace so as to draw attention to their particular problems.

Another ambiguity lies in the combined effect of nuclear "unavailability" and second-strike capacity. The latter protects the super-powers but seems to deprive the others, in and outside the blocs, of reliance on nuclear protection. This has been one of the reasons for the assertion of independence of bloc members and, in some instances, for the development of their own nuclear forces. While this has added strength to them *qua* nation-states, it also endangers them vis-à-vis the other superpower. Their getting out from under the wings of the protecting power leaves them out in the cold, more independent but also more endangered.

What about nuclear proliferation as such, and its effect on the nation-state system? Undoubtedly, acquisition of a nuclear arsenal adds to the relative strength of the acquiring nation, in particular in its relation to the remaining nonnuclear ones. Even countries like France, which, because of lack of sufficient economic base or for similar reasons, are destined to remain inferior to the nuclear super-powers, gain in status and thus, to some extent, in freedom of foreign-political action. And those which, like China, are on the way to "superpowerdom" comparable to that of the United States and the Soviets, may perceive an opportunity to try out the path of "new-style empire." This, in turn, threatens others, such as India, and thus reinforces the tendency toward proliferation.

Even should a nonproliferation treaty come about, its effect on the stability of the present international system must be doubted. If France and China cannot be brought under the agreement, it is hard to see what protection can be effectively given to countries like India, which would assume a status of permanent nuclear inferiority. If the nuclear umbrella furnished their own allies by the United States and the Soviet Union has become dubious, can there be one for nonaligned countries? Verbal assurances of this sort tend to become "incredible," and even though they may be given in good faith, a counterpower not believing in them may be lured into risking confrontations that may end in nuclear war. In this way, far from creating protection and stability, a system of such guarantees may actually increase the danger of war. More likely than not, and whether there are nonproliferation agreements or not, if a nuclear power threatens a nonnuclear one, the latter will quickly be transformed into a nuclear power by a nuclear "friend" (who, in a case like that of the United States and West Germany, has merely to make bombs or missiles in the area accessible to the nonnuclear power already in possession of delivery systems and trained personnel); in such an event, a treaty is unlikely to make much difference.[7]

Thus we are warranted in anticipating a world of nuclear proliferation, with increasing numbers of both greater and lesser nuclear powers. This will certainly involve great instability and growing risks of actual nuclear war.[8] On the other hand, it is at least imaginable that what happened in the postwar decades may repeat itself; that is, that at least for a period of time, *systems* of mutual deterrence may stabilize the situation. There may be regional systems, with regional nuclear balances, there may be agreed upon and inspected denuclearized areas, and so forth. Details depend on factors that are difficult to predict, such as the identity and distribution of the nuclear powers, the stage and level of their nuclear equipment, and the internal cohesion of the units in question. In any event, we may, by way of hypothesis, assume the emergence of a multipolar world of nuclear proliferation in which the territorial nature of the component units is preserved and is not entirely in jeopardy. The global victory of the nationalism of the self-determining and self-limiting variety (in contrast to expansionist nationalism), in addition, would clearly circumscribe the units and thus provide this world with the underpinning of enhanced stability of the constituent entities. This presupposes uncontested boundaries and the settlement of outstanding territorial issues. International organization and international law might here come to the rescue. But the emergence of a world of nationally defined and delimited units requires a number of additional hypotheses.

---

[7] See also L. Beaton, "Nuclear Fuel for All," *Foreign Affairs*, XLV (1967), 4, 662 ff.; Beaton points out that even a legal commitment to nonproduction of nuclear weapons will mean little, especially after some lapse of time and possible change of the commitment-making regime, if the country can use plutonium derived from nuclear power stations in its territory. The only safe guarantee against proliferation would be nuclear disarmament of the "halves," but this is not in the cards.

[8] Among the most dangerous risks a multiplication of variables under nuclear proliferation would bring about are those of a personal nature (insanity or incapacity or emotional overreaction of leaders, unintentional or unauthorized action of subordinates, etc.). For a summing up of these factors see Jerome D. Frank, *Sanity and Survival: Psychological Aspects of War and Peace* (New York, 1967).

IV. Legitimacy of Nations

So far we have dealt with trends and phenomena that provide the exterior environment in which a new territoriality may arise. Decline of empires, reduction in the role of penetrating force—developments such as these create preconditions for continuation of a national role as a basic constituent of international relations. They are necessary but not sufficient factors. In a positive way, nations, in order to be effective actors in international relations, must prove to be "legitimate" units, that is, entities which, generically and individually, can be and are being considered as basic and "natural" for the fulfillment of essential purposes, such as the protection and welfare of people. We must therefore, search for factors that enable them to play this role, and also deal with the obstacles they encounter.

Why do we speak of "*new* territoriality"? If territory and statehood are to continue or resume their accustomed role, in what respect are they new? I suggest the term because now they will exist in an environment of nuclear penetrability, and they will have to assert themselves in an environment of vastly and rapidly increasing technological, economic, and general interrelationships of a shrinking world.

To one watching the seemingly unending appearance of (by now over 130) "nation-states" upon the international scene—a veritable population explosion of nations—raising doubts about the ongoing power of the nation-state idea may sound strange. But all of us are aware of the turmoil and travail, the difficulties and doubts that accompany the process. Can one put into one and the same category The Gambia and France, Barbados and China, the Congo and Argentina? It is a commonplace to point out the synthetic nature of units formed on the accidental basis of boundaries drawn at the European conference table in the age of colonialism; the artificiality of "nations" built on the tearing apart or throwing together of several coherent entities, such as tribes; the doubtful identity of nations themselves proclaiming to be parts of an overarching nation (such as Arab states in relation to an overall "Arab nation"); the linguistic and similar centrifugal forces that threaten even apparently solid nations such as India; the nonviability of tiny or excessively weak nations, devoid of sufficient population and/or resources; the lack of territorial integration of widely separate island groups.

But these problems do not appear entirely insoluble. There is the problem of the "microstates" (especially those still unborn, in the Pacific and elsewhere). There is a parallel here to the mini-units that emerged as "sovereign" entities in the area of the Holy Roman Empire after the Peace of West-phalia; most of these were eventually consolidated or absorbed. It should not prove beyond human (even political) ingenuity to find solutions here through federation, semiautonomy under other units, etc. More complex seem the problems of larger and yet highly synthetic units, many of them in Africa. We shall discuss some of the more basic questions relating to their nationhood below. It is sufficient to point here to the analogous condition of at first equally synthetic units in another continent, South (and Central) America; they originated in similarly artificial colonial districts, an origin which did not prevent their exhibiting, in due course, the sentiments and characteristics of nationhood. They might have grown into one or two overall "nations" on the pattern of the North American colonies (which originally had, perhaps, even more distinctive characteristics of their own than those in Latin America); instead they grew into the genuinely distinct nations most of them constitute today.[9] Raymond Aron is probably right in pointing out that some of the smaller among the new African states are more viable than they would have been had they been established as bigger and therefore (economically, etc.) seemingly more viable entities. In this way it is easier for them to overcome tribalism. The contrast between the relative success of, let us say, Ghana, on the one hand, and Nigeria or the Congo, on the other hand, illustrates what he means.

What, then, renders a nation-state legitimate? Legitimacy originates from the feelings and attitudes of the people within as well as neighbors and others abroad in regard to the unit, its identity and co-herence, its political and general "way of life." Where there is positive valuation, that is, an impression or even a conviction that the unit in question "should be" the one on the basis of which a particular group organizes its separate and distinct existence as a "nation," there is legitimacy. The legitimacy of the territorial state that emerged from the Middle Ages in Europe was chiefly founded on defensibility against foreign attack (its protective function) and on the two successive principles of "legitimate" dynastic rule and, later, common nationality. One might distinguish between the legitimacy of the unit as such and that of its internal system (regime, socio-political structure). In regard to the former, in an age of nationalism units may range all the way from illegitimacy to complete legitimacy. Mere possession of the outward paraphernalia of statehood (independent government in *de facto* control of an area) does not suffice. For instance, with the growth of national unification movements in the areas later constituting the German Empire and the Italian Kingdom, existing sovereign states in these areas became increasingly illegitimate. Today, the partition of Germany leaves the legitimacy of both German units in doubt.[10] Independence movements rendered empires increasingly illegitimate as indigenous nationalism rose against colonialism. But in many of the new states that emerged from decolonization, absence of minimally strong feelings of identity and solidity still prevents their being considered as fully legitimate. There is, of course, a good deal of variation. Where, as in Algeria, or now in Vietnam, a population previously little integrated even in its own image has to fight long and doggedly for independence, it is likely to emerge more strongly consolidated as a national entity than where a "nation," carved out with accidental boundary lines, had independence thrown upon it without much popular exertion. Being compelled to fight for or defend one's territory generates true nationhood.

Internal legitimacy (without which the legiti-macy of the unit as such can provide little real solidity) in our day is closely related to democracy in the broad sense of people having the conviction that they control their destinies and that government operates for their welfare. Old-fashioned autocracy, once legitimate in the eyes of the people in many parts of the world, today hardly survives anywhere as legitimate. Even Ethiopia, Saudi Arabia, and Iran

---

[9] It is true, however, that in those Latin American countries where Indians—not yet mobilized politically and otherwise—constitute a high proportion of the population we have the problem of nationhood still to be established out of ethnically diverse constituent groups.

[10] Even more spurious, of course, would be West Berlin as an independent "third German state" (a sugges-tion of the Soviets and their friends).

have to "modernize" themselves in this respect. And modern dictatorship, as appears clearly from trends and developments everywhere and in respect of the most diverse types of that form of government (from Spain through Eastern Europe to the Soviet Union), feels compelled to shed its more authoritarian and totalitarian traits in order to establish a popular image of legitimate rule. In the democracies themselves, legitimacy is the stronger the older and more safely rooted democratic habits and processes actually are. In many new countries legitimacy is in doubt not only because of the problematic nature of the unit but also because of the nature of the regime, which may be oppressive (military control as the only way to keep the unit together) and/or unrepresentative (in the sense of rule by one among several ethnic groups). Thus one can arrange the countries of the world along a continuum ranging all the way from externally and internally stable and legitimate to "soft," "spongy" units and regimes.[11] Only as the latter ones "harden," that is, with the spread of national self-determination and democracy, will the "new territoriality" arise in regard to them. For, as Rupert Emerson has put it, "the nation has in fact become the body that legitimizes the state."[12]

But these developments are not autonomous or self-contained. The outside world can, and does, influence them, for instance, through the extension or denial of "recognition" or through the grant of membership in international agencies, particularly the United Nations.[13] There is reason for the German Democratic Republic to try so desperately to gain recognition (and therewith the status of a legitimate international unit) from other than Communist countries, and, by the same token, for the Federal Republic to try to prevent this and thus remain the only German unit recognized by the majority of nations. The older nations of the world, in this way, have a chance, through policies of

recognition and acceptance to membership based upon whether or not the applicants are viable as nationally coherent entities, to promote the emergence of some legitimate units and hamper that of others. The U.N. in particular, might devise objective admission standards for such purposes. But such policies can also be used for the power-political objectives of particular nations, as is shown by the history of United States "recognition policies." The same applies to policies of foreign aid. Such help would seem to lend itself to stabilizing and thus legitimatizing new and/or underdeveloped countries. But aid *policy* can be used also to make these units "penetrable" through the creation of economic, technological, or military dependencies. Thus the future of the legitimacy of nations is intimately tied to problems of intervention and indirect penetration.

V. Intervention and Nonalignment

At this juncture, foreign intervention, especially by "indirect penetration,"[14] constitutes, perhaps, the most serious threat to the future of nations and their "new territoriality."

In addition to nuclear permeability, certain new technological penetrabilities (for example, through observation and collection of information from space satellites and through telephotography) and the manifold opportunities created through economic, technical and military assistance, indirect penetration adds the power-political opportunities that emerge from an "international civil war" situation among competing systems and ideologies. This quasi-war situation renders possible political-military penetration of a country through promoting or lending assistance to indigenous insurrectionist forces, an assistance which, in turn, may range from diplomatic aid (for example, recognition) rendered to a rebel regime to making portions ("volunteer" or otherwise) of one's own armed forces available. It may further mean penetration of the top level of a country's regime through bribery or similar "purchase" of top personnel, or the doctrinal penetration of such levels on the part of revolutionary regimes. In the pursuance of such policies one may exploit all

---

[11] Referring to the domino theory of aggression in Southeast Asia, Kenneth Waltz remarks: "States in the area of the fighting lack the solidity, shape, and cohesion that the image suggests. Externally ill-defined, internally fragile and chaotic, they more appropriately call to mind sponges..." ("The Politics of Peace," *International Studies Quarterly*, XI [1967], 3, 205).

[12] Rupert Emerson, *From Empire to Nation* (Boston, 1960), p. 96.

[13] On the effect of what he calls "collective legitimization" through acceptance into the U.N. see Inis Claude, op. cit., p. 83 ff.

[14] In his truly penetrating and enlightening study, *The Revolution in Statecraft* (New York, 1965), Andrew M. Scott calls this phenomenon "informal access" or "informal penetration."

the weaknesses and dissensions which exist in the penetrated unit, whether they originate in ethnic, religious, or other groups discriminated against, in depressed socio-economic classes, or among ideologically opposed or alienated groups or individuals. As Scott puts it, "in a period of increasing informal access, a situation sometimes develops in which the critical boundary may not be the geographic one but one defined by the circumstances of the market, the location of the adherents of an opposing ideology, the location of a given racial or religious group, or the zone of effectiveness of counter-penetration efforts. ...In an era of informal penetration, the attack on the legitimacy of the government in the target country frequently denies the very principle of legitimacy on which that government is based."[15]

Such penetration assisting the "revolutionary" side, or its threat, may in turn provoke similar penetration by powers interested in shoring up the existing unit and its regime. Defense agreements, military aid, training of troops, establishment of bases, economic-financial ties through investments, aid, exclusive or predominant trade relations, currency arrangements, all of these are common means to establish or maintain influence which, especially in the case of the newly independent, small, and weak units, frequently amounts to dependency coming close to what the "revolutionary" side (although engaging in similar policies in regard to "its" clients) denounces as "neo-colonialism." Not only American penetration of countries allegedly or actually threatened with "subversion," but also continued French influence in formerly French African units are cases in point. On the "Eastern" side, in addition to (and even in competition with) Soviet (and their clients') efforts, Chinese and Castroite forces may be at work.

Civil war assisted from abroad in this way may result in the dissolution of statehood (through secession) or of the prevailing regimes (through revolution). Could there be a more glaring example of the "demise" of the territorial state?

While not playing down the importance of these phenomena, one can point out countertendencies and advance the hypothesis that they may prevail in the long run.

One of these is the lessening of revolutionary

penetration and interference that has resulted from the "deradicalization" of Communist regimes. Of late, there has been much discussion of a worldwide trend toward "deideologization," the "end" or, at least, the "erosion" or "decline" of ideologies and of the corresponding movements, whether leftist or rightist, West or East. There is little doubt of the presence of this phenomenon as far as the once world-revolutionary doctrines and policies of the core-Communist power are concerned.[16] It has been apparent not only in doctrines of peaceful coexistence, peaceful liberation from colonialism, and peaceful transition from capitalism to socialism but, more importantly, in Soviet moderation of her actual attitudes in the face of tempting situations abroad, most strikingly, perhaps, in Vietnam. Inasmuch as there has been aid to revolutionary forces, this has been due chiefly to the Chinese factor, the felt necessity not to lose face in the eyes of leftist movements and parties throughout the world. Even with the Chinese themselves, for whom Soviet deradicalization has been a golden opportunity to claim world-revolutionary leadership, action has not matched proclamation. In a situation as close as the Vietnamese, assistance has consisted mainly of verbal advice rather than more forceful and substantial intervention. Only when danger struck really close to home, as in Korea after the U.N. forces crossed the 38th parallel, did they intervene more massively.

There seems to be growing realization among *all* Communist regimes that interference is promising only where conditions in the respective country or area are "ripe" for a revolution (or "war of liberation"), and that ripeness presupposes the readiness and ability of the indigenous forces to carry the

[15] Op. cit., pp. 168–69.

[16] As Robert C. Tucker has pointed out, the process should be referred to as "deradicalization" rather than "deideologization," because less radicalism in action may be accompanied by doctrinal emphasis on symbols of "nonchange." "Intensified *verbal* allegiance to ultimate ideological goals belongs to the pattern of deradicalization" ("The Deradicalization of Marxist Movements," *American Political Science Review*, LXI [1967], 2, pp. 343 ff., 358). But even in this connection there is a decreasing line in regard to amount of and emphasis on doctrine running from Stalin through Khrushchev to the present Soviet rulers, and a corresponding decrease in expected reference and obeisance to ideology on the part of writers and scholars. Cf. Jean-Yves Calvez, "La place de l'idéologie," *Revue française de science politique*, XVII (1967), 1050 ff.

brunt of the struggle. This has been stated repeatedly by both Soviet and Chinese spokesmen,[17] and it does not seem to be mere subterfuge. A long history of disappointment with Moscow-initiated and foreign-guided coups, uprisings, and riots from the Twenties (Hungary, Bavaria, Hamburg, China) to more recent times seems to have taught the Communist regimes a lesson. The situation that promises success cannot be created artifically; it must be based upon the "territorial imperative" motivating an indigenous population together with its leadership's revolutionary objectives.

But where indigenous forces are primarily responsible for a revolutionary victory, they are not likely to accept control or influence on the part of an assisting power—*vide* Yugoslavia and China herself. This, in turn, may lessen the temptation to intervene. And, by the same token, lessening of Communist interventionism may in due course diminish the West's concern with "world Communism" and its alleged "conspiracy" to control the world, and thus affect its policies of counter-interventionism. For twenty years there has not been a single Communist attempt to revolutionize a developed nation or society, or a corresponding attempt on the part of the West to "liberate" a Communist unit. Even in regard to the Third World there seems to be a decrease in such ventures. The United States has not seriously tried to "regain" a Communized country as close as Cuba. Much, however, in respect to the underdeveloped, overpopulated "South" of the world depends on its chances of development and modernization. On this vital problem see below.

We seem to be in a stage of transition from doctrinal-political splits, confrontations, and interventions toward a world of lessened antagonisms. In such a world, nation-states would be left in peace to develop their own systems and remain neutral themselves in regard to the great powers. Nonalignment is in line with nationalism as a legitimizing force; it also lessens the concern of the big that, by leaving small states alone, they might simply hand the opponent a chance to extend his influence. Under bipolar conditions, nonalignment could appear risky to the small because of absence of protection and guarantees. But even then alignment was not without dangers of its own—of becoming, for example, a target for the other side because of bases on one's soil. With the disintegration of the blocs noninvolvement will appear preferable to more and more of the weaker states. Finland and Cambodia, each very close to an ideologically antagonistic superpower, illustrate the degree of security that can be gained through nonalignment where the objective of the superpower is not expansion but security. Alignment, in such a case, cannot help but create concern in one superpower about the other's aggressive intentions, and may this way lead to "preventive" intervention; nonalignment reassures.[18] If this tendency should spread, increased stability of nations and of the nation-state system would ensue.

VI. Outlook and Conclusions

A good deal of attention has recently been paid to discoveries in the relatively young science of animal behavior (ethology); they relate to the so-called territorial nature of certain animal species. Biologists such as Konrad Lorenz and, following their lead, popularizers such as Robert Ardrey, have given us vivid descriptions of how animals in every major category (fish, birds, mammals) stake out an area as "their own," fix boundaries, defend their territory (singly, with a mate, or in small groups) against intruders, are motivated by their "territorial instinct" more powerfully when close to the center of their territory than when at a distance from it, and so forth. To perceive analogies to these striking phenomena in human affairs, and particularly in relations of nations to each other, is tempting, and the authors mentioned have not hesitated to jump to such conclusions. "The territorial nature of man is genetic and ineradicable."[19] The "territorial imperative" not only motivates individuals, such as peasants threatened with collectivization of their holdings, but accounts for the behavior patterns of nations and other human collectivities. For those

---

[17] Interestingly, Trotsky, than whom no one was more "world-revolutionary," had declared in the Twenties that "only that revolution is viable which wins out of its own strength"—quoted in Ossip K. Flechtheim, *Bolschewismus 1917–1967: Von der Weltrevolution zum Sowjetimperium* (Vienna, 1967), p. 47.

[18] J. W. Burton, op. cit., has developed a theory according to which the international system of the future will be distinguished by a lessening of alliances and the substitution for "power politics" of nonalignment based chiefly on nationalism.

[19] Robert Ardrey, *The Territorial Imperative: A Personal Inquiry into the Animal Origins of Property and Nations* (New York, 1966), p. 116.

of us in the social sciences who have previously emphasized the role of "territoriality," especially in international relations, it is tempting to find in these phenomena a biological and thus vastly more fundamental confirmation of their theories. If the "territorial imperative" that motivates the basic units of international relations is rooted in the nature of humans as animal species we do not have to worry about the future of the nation-state. Contrariwise, approaches that look forward to eventual replacement of territorial units with something nonterritorial, such as world government, would truly be proved utopian.

I suggest that we suspend judgment, however—at least for the time being. It seems that the ethological findings themselves are contested exactly in the area of our ancestors, or closest relatives, the primates.[20] And an unwarranted jumping to conclusions becomes patent when no evidence is offered that a genetically inherited instinct prevails in humans as it does in certain, but *only* certain animal species, or that what motivates individual animals (or possibly humans) or very small groups (like families or clans) the same way, that is, instinctively, motivates large societies, such as nations. Ardrey, for instance, is inconsistent when he claims that the territorial imperative that motivated Russian peasants tenaciously clinging to their plot of land was destroyed by collectivization (thus "proving" the eternal, because instinct-based, nature of private property) while at the same time asserting that the much larger collectivity, the nation, as such reacts instinctively to intrusion on "its" territory. Why, then, do not *kholchozes* develop their territorial instinct? True, in cases of threats to their very existence (such as we have discussed in connection with Israel, Algeria, etc.) nations' defensive behavior seems to be motivated by very elementary and powerful "imperatives." But even here there is no proof of *instinctive* behavior. And outside such marginal and truly "existential" situations the analogy is even less convincing. The more "normal" condition of nations competing for power (including territory) and thus getting involved in expansionism, armament races, and wars seems to go back rather to what I have called the "security dilemma," that is, the fear

that competing units may deprive them of their land, resources, independence, and political existence. Animals do not "know"—as does man—that conspecific groups may become competitors for "hunting grounds" or other means of living; they do not "realize" that, if "their" territory proves insufficient to support a given number of them, they can solve this problem by invading others' territory, or, by the same token, that conspecific groups may attack them for these purposes.

It is thus a realization specific and unique to man that explains (in part, at least) competition for territory and scarce resources and accounts for intergroup conflicts, territorial defense and aggrandizement, and so forth. The social constellation deriving from this realization is different from one that would derive from genetically inherent instincts. For, if it is conscious competition for scarce resources rather than a territorial and/or aggressive instinct[21] that in the past has been the prime motive of humans and human societies, the outlook for the future of international relations must differ vastly from one based on the assumption of biological drives. Under the latter, territorial units must forever go on fighting for land and resources. But the security dilemma can at least be attenuated through scientific-technological progress that "modernizes" mankind and thus frees it from scarcity. Modernization thus raises the hope that nationhood could become stabilized, not on the basis of a territorial instinct, but on that of providing plenty for those it comprises. Our final hypothesis, therefore, refers to the modernization of the premodern world.

As we have pointed out before, industrial technology renders modernized nations ever more independent from natural resources outside their boundaries; they need no longer expand and conquer. For the presently underdeveloped nation modernization means liberation from economic dependencies (such as those of the present one-crop and one-resource countries). Modernization and economic development would also serve to confer on many units that legitimacy which, as pointed out before, they lack because of the absence or weakness of a "national" elite that would integrate them, despite

[20] See, for example, S. Carrighar, "War is not in Our Genes," *The New York Times Magazine*, September 10, 1967.

[21] Aggressiveness is likewise claimed by Lorenz and others to be a genetically inherited human instinct; in this article, which deals primarily with territoriality, I cannot deal with this theory in detail.

ethnic and similar disparities, into a modern nation. Once national self-determination and national integration has been achieved all over the globe, expansionist nationalism will be discredited and, if practiced, will encounter the overriding strength of other, defensive, nationalism. The latter is likely to remain the effective ideology of an age of technological modernity in which the hold of other traditional ideologies, creeds, and value systems tends to vanish.

But whether such consolidation of the nation-state and corresponding stability of the state system will be attained depends on whether at least a large proportion of the underdeveloped will be able to modernize themselves. Modernized countries have proved relatively stable; also, generally, they do not desire territory from others: not the Soviet Union from the United States, or vice versa, nor even, by now, Germany from France. But the underdeveloped are beset by every type of turmoil, radicalism, and foreign interventionism. It is therefore a problem of development and development policies; a question of whether the affluent nations will be able and willing to make the sacrifices that are required of them even though they themselves have their own problems of development and equity; above all, it is the problem of preventing overpopulation. The rapidly growing pressure of population outrunning resources not only prevents the underdeveloped from modernizing but may actually lead to conditions deteriorating so badly that territory may assume overwhelming importance again. Unless there is rapid and drastic population planning, excess populations will press against boundaries separating them from—for the most part equally overpopulated—neighbors, and wars may ensue with the violence of the primitive, elementary struggle for "hunting grounds" and "water holes," only now on a global plane. Territory would become an object of expansionism and conquest again, and nationalism assume, or reassume, the nature of antagonism and despair. The big and wealthy would withdraw into their poverty-surrounded nuclear fortresses, or else engage in renewed "international civil war." For the time being, so it appears, it is not internationalism, "universalism," or any other supranational model that constitutes the alternative to the territorial, or nation-state, system, but genuine, raw chaos.

Such chaos would lead to a system or, rather, a nonsystem of international relations in which the terms territoriality and statehood would hold scant meaning. If we consider how little has been done in these decisive decades to forestall such a development—hardly anything, for instance, in the vital areas of population control and of the widening gap between the underdeveloped and the affluent nations —the pessimistic conclusion that it is almost too late for the development of a system of "new territoriality" seems, realistically, to impose itself. Assuming, however, that the "almost" still leaves room for more hopeful potentialities, let us recall the hypotheses made above by summing up the most basic requirements for a development under which the new-old nation-state, the polity of the last decades of this century, might emerge.

First among these, I would list the spread of political, economic, and attitudinal modernity to the areas where legitimate nation-states have still to be established through such processes of modernization. What this presupposes demographically, technologically, economically has already been mentioned.

Second, to make sure that new states, as well as some of the old, do not fall prey to continual quarrels over territorial issues, such issues among them must be settled in such a way that boundaries encompass populations which consider themselves and are recognized by others as nationally satisfied and self-sufficient entities. This is a large order, and all devices of diplomacy, all procedures of international organization, all rules of law and institutions of adjudication must be utilized, developed, and possibly improved for their solution.

Third, we must count upon the continuing deradicalization of systems originally based on world-revolutionary doctrines, and a corresponding inclination of the other states to leave the choice of internal structure to the respective nations without trying to influence, interfere, or control. Among other things, this would imply that programs of foreign assistance be separated from political policies and/or transferred increasingly to international agencies, and that even in case of civil war outside powers abstain from assisting either side, including the one they consider the "legitimate government" of the unit in question; new international law might be developed to spell out the corresponding legal rules and commitments.

Last, but not least, under such hypotheses

recourse to international violence would be reduced to two major categories: action in self-defense when, and only when, one's own territory is directly attacked or invaded; in the event the invader succeeds in occupying the area, continued resistance of its population through a combination of guerrilla warfare and nonviolent resistance to render the aggressor the "fly on the flypaper." The unavailability of the "big" instrumentalities of international violence—in the sense of our discussion above—might induce their possessors to forego intervention in such situations, just as they might forego intervening in civil wars according to our third hypothesis. If genuine, legitimate nations in this way become units of their own protection, urged on by a "territorial imperative" of the pattern set by countries like Switzerland and Israel, they may have a better chance to survive as independent states than under the system of alliances and similar pacts, in which "collective self-defense" all too often serves as a subterfuge for big-power intervention.

The function, then, of the future polity would still or again be that of providing group identity, protection, and welfare; in short, the legitimate function of the nation. And this neo-territorial world of nations, in addition, might salvage one feature of humanity which seems ever more threatened by the ongoing rush of mankind into the technological conformity of a synthetic planetary environment: diversity of life and culture, of traditions and civilizations. If the nation can preserve these values, it would at long last have emerged as that which the philosophers of early nationalism had expected it to be: the custodian of cultural diversity among groups mutually granting each other their peculiar worth. In the past that other, opposite type of nationalism, the exclusivist, xenophobic, expansionist, oppressive one, has rendered their expectation nugatory, causing instability and infinite suffering of nations and people. This small world of ours can no longer live with it. Chaotic instability is too high a price to pay for its fleeting triumphs in an inflammable world. Neo-territoriality will function only if and when the danger of nuclear destruction and the interdependence of humans and their societies on the globe will have made nations and their leaders aware that the destiny awaiting us is now common to all.

9. The Nation-State and Other Actors

Fred W. Riggs is Professor of Political Science at the University of Hawaii and a leading student of comparative politics. Besides his many articles on this subject, his books include *Ecology of Public Administration* (1961) and *Administration in Developing Countries* (1964). In this selection Professor Riggs turns his talents upon the problem of identifying international actors in a world where the coherence of nation-states can no longer be taken for granted. Here it becomes clear that the boundaries which divide international actors from each other present the observer with a methodological challenge hardly less complex than the political challenge they present to the actors themselves. [*Reprinted from Klaus Knorr and Sidney Verba (eds.),* The International System: Theoretical Essays (*Princeton; Princeton University Press, 1961*), *pp. 144–48, by permission of the author and the Princeton University Press.*]

I. Introduction: The Inter-State System

Conventional theories of international relations assume, implicitly, the model of an "inter-state system."... A classic formulation is contained in a speech given by former Secretary of State John Foster Dulles at a meeting of the American Society for International Law.[1] In it Mr. Dulles identified six characteristics of the nation-state: (1) laws which "reflect the moral judgment of the community"; (2) political machinery to revise these laws as needed; (3) an executive body able to administer the laws; (4) judicial machinery to settle disputes in accord with the laws; (5) superior force to deter violence by enforcing the law upon those who defy it; and (6) sufficient well-being so that people are not driven by desperation to ways of violence. The international system, Mr. Dulles pointed out, in large part lacks these characteristics. He went on to assess the limited success of attempts, ranging from the League of Nations and Kellogg-Briand Pact through the United Nations, to create such a "state system" or

[1] *Department of State Bulletin*, xxxiv (May 7, 1956), p. 740.

"order" at the international level. Mr. Dulles sadly reported that, despite notable progress in the development of international law and judicial machinery, the desired international order does not, as yet, exist.

This statement rather strikingly uncovers the implicit model of an inter-state system. In effect, Mr. Dulles depicted two contrasting "ideal" or "constructed" types. At one extreme is the political *order* characteristic of the nation-state; at the other an *anarchic* system of inter-state relations.

Let us examine this model from two perspectives: first from above, the *systemic* point of view; and then from below, in terms of the component *units*, the states.

The Systemic Perspective

The "inter-state system" is seen, in Mr. Dulles' model, as lacking the basic characteristics of a "state system," although it may have an embryonic legal system, as expressed by international law, and a fragmentary judicial machinery.

Let us imagine that the organizations of the

United Nations and the specialized agencies are able gradually to extend their effective power. The U.N. becomes a primary actor in the politics of Palestine, Libya, Korea, the Congo. Its technical agencies begin to carry out agricultural and health programs in underdeveloped countries. We become aware of limited spheres of action in which it is almost possible to speak of world "public opinion," of policies which are universally applicable—for the control of epidemics or the distribution of mail—and of machinery for the enforcement of order. There may even be sufficient enjoyment of these benefits so that no state will be disposed to destroy them by violence.

Suppose that the sphere of these specialized activities gradually widens further, and the extent of world consensus together with appropriate decision-making and enforcement machinery increases, but that no unitary world government is yet formed. We should then still have an "inter-state system," but it would begin to share, however imperfectly, some of the qualitative characteristics of a state. It would not be a pure "anarchy." In other words, however anarchic contemporary world politics, is it inherent in the model of an inter-state system that it should always be anarchic? If not, then might not an inter-state system approximate the characteristics of a state system?

An alternative view of world politics takes this possibility into account. Instead of regarding international relations as an anarchy of states, it postulates an integrated "world order." Under this postulate the organs of "world government" acquire a direct relationship to individuals as actors, just as the United States government deals with individual citizens, without, of course, ceasing to deal also with the governments of its fifty component "states." In this view, world government and world law are the "ideal forms" of world politics, and our failure to achieve this condition reflects a pathological condition which must be changed as quickly as possible. Indeed, such a "world state" is what Mr. Dulles portrayed as our policy goal, to be achieved by destroying the contemporary inter-state anarchy.

This model—however good as a normative view—is as unrealistic as the model which perceives world politics in terms only of an inter-state system. Nor can the difficulty be overcome by a compromise which recognizes both states and individuals as actors in world politics. Such a formulation fails to identify many crucial characteristics of the system. We need a model that will provide a more specific picture of how states and individuals are related to each other in an international system. Moreover, there may be other entities—neither states nor individuals—which ought also to be included in our image of the system.

The Unit Perspective

The second perspective, viewing the system from below, in terms of its component units, the "states," draws upon our image of the Western nation-states. The model is certainly not far from reality if we use it to organize data about the United States, England, France, or a number of other Western democracies. It is when we start applying it to the non-Western world, and especially to the new states of Asia and Africa, that we run into difficulties.

We have all been struck and alarmed, I am sure, by events since the summer of 1960 in the new Republic of Congo. Here, by acknowledgment of the United Nations, a new "state" was born. If it is in truth a "state," then by Mr. Dulles' definition we must expect it to defend itself against attack from abroad and revolution from within, to adopt and enforce laws reflecting the moral judgment of the Congolese people, to organize a government, participate in the U.N., and conduct a foreign policy capable of safeguarding the "national interest" of the Congo.

But do not recent events contradict this image? What is the moral judgment of the Congolese community? Is there even such a community, or do we see rather a congeries of tribal communities brought into temporary administrative connection by Belgian imperial policy, and now suddenly released from control and expected to act like a "nation-state" in our anarchic world? The "government," recognized by foreign powers, turns out to be a group of individuals drawn from the minuscule Congolese intelligentsia, vested with formal "authority" but lacking the requisites for effective control over the population, to say nothing of a capacity to formulate laws based on public opinion and knowledge of problems and alternatives, to enforce these laws, and provide for their testing by judicial process. Nor can it be said that the population has a sufficient sense of well-being to cause it to reject violence.

If these criteria, so clearly itemized by Mr. Dulles, are not present in the Congo and are also not present in the sphere of world politics, then Congolese politics share some basic characteristics of world politics. This is a rather shattering conclusion because it suggests that if the study of inter-state and of state politics are to be differentiated, then the study of Congolese politics belongs with the study of international relations rather than of domestic politics. This seems to be a contradiction in terms. We resist the idea that the Congo is an "inter-state system." How shall we struggle out of this trap into which we have apparently slipped?

We might, first of all, fall back on the popular maxim that "the exception proves the rule." Apart from the fallacy in a foolish interpretation of this proverb which takes the word "prove" to mean "establish" rather than "test," the fact is that the Congolese case is not really exceptional except for its dramatic quality. Many new states and even some old ones qualify only imperfectly as "states" under the Dulles criteria.

The Republic of Congo, Congo Republic (Brazzaville), Chad, Niger, Nigeria, Mali, Togo, Dahomey, Ivory Coast, Upper Volta, Central African Republic, Malagasy, and Somalia have recently attained their "independence" in Africa. With many of these names we are scarcely familiar. Together with Laos and other new Asian countries—some of which come but little closer to the model of a nation-state—they have major voting power in the U.N. General Assembly. It may shortly appear that the model "state" can be used to describe only a minority of the countries in our "inter-state" system. But if they do not satisfy the basic conditions of a state, how can we call them states? Can we have

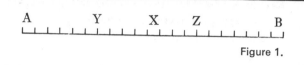

Figure 1.

an inter-state system many of whose members are not states?

The X Perspective

How shall we escape from this awkward position? On the one hand, we discover that the inter-state system may exhibit many characteristics of a state, whereas many "states" lack these characteristics to a considerable degree. The sharp distinction between the study of domestic politics and of international relations breaks down.

The position may be clarified if we use a scale instead of a simple dichotomy. In Figure 1, let position A represent a polar type of political structure having all the characteristics enumerated by Mr. Dulles—i.e., a "nation-state." Let the opposite polar type, B, represent a structure having none of these characteristics—i.e., an "anarchy." Then a wide range of intermediate positions having these characteristics in various degrees may be imagined, as at X, Y, and Z. Perhaps the political characteristics of a state like the Congo, or an international system like the modern world, could best be classified at an intermediate point—X, for example.

This possibility suggests a different line of investigation. If there is any similarity between the basic political structure of government in a new state and in our international system, then perhaps models developed for one might shed light on the other. An analysis of the contemporary inter-state system might help us understand the underdeveloped country, and models for politics in these countries may illuminate aspects of international relations....

B. Environmental Limitations and Opportunities

10. The Ecology of Future International Politics*

Bruce M. Russett is Professor of Political Science at Yale University. One of those in the forefront of the effort to subject international phenomena to scientific analysis, he has written a number of important works in the field. In addition to his other contributions to this volume (Selections 12 and 33) his writings include authorship of *Trends in World Politics* (1965) and *International Regions and the International System* (1967), as well as coauthorship of *World Handbook of Political and Social Indicators* (1964). In this article Professor Russett examines some of the features of the international environment that have undergone rapid change and offers some creative assessments of the consequences of these changes for the international political system. [*Reprinted from Bruce M. Russett, "The Ecology of Future International Politics," International Studies Quarterly, XI (March 1967), 12–31, by permission of the author and the Wayne State University Press. Copyright 1967 by Wayne State University Press, Detroit, Michigan.*]

The Range and Probability of Future Outcomes

The prediction of future world events is frequently an exercise in political sociology. Or perhaps more accurately, it is a problem in political ecology, one concerned with the relationship between the political system and its social and physical environment.

A statement that nothing will change over the next few decades would hardly be credible, and anyway it would be boring. On the other hand, to quote one of my favorite books on prediction, "If a man predicts large but not very large changes, the public will regard him as a man of imagination; but if he predicts extremely large changes, his audience will replace imagination by phantasy."[1] I would like, in this paper, to avoid both extremes. In any case, my recent menus have offered neither sheep livers nor chicken entrails, so I am unable to engage in prophecy. I will not attempt to foretell a specific event on a specific occasion, nor to paint a detailed picture of a particular political future. But I am a restrained believer in the outlook aptly labelled by Charles Burton Marshall as "the limits of foreign policy."[2]

* An earlier version of this paper was given as an address to the Annual Meeting of the American Sociological Association at Miami Beach, August 29, 1966. Marc Pilisuk, J. David Singer, Harold Sprout, and Guy E. Swanson offered valuable comments. I wrote the paper while Visiting Research Political Scientist at the Mental Health Research Institute, University of Michigan, and am grateful for its stimulating environment.

[1] H. Thiel, *Economic Forecasts and Policy* (Amsterdam: North Holland, 2nd edition, 1961), p. 156.
[2] Charles Burton Marshall, *The Limits of Foreign Policy* (New York: Henry Holt, 1954).

Without getting into the determinist-free will debate—which in the still youthful state of our sciences is largely irrelevant anyway—we can, I think, agree generally with the idea that political prediction is best concerned with the future state of *milieu* within which decisions have to be made. In this context we are interested in *negative* prediction— we aspire to narrow the range of possibilities, to eliminate some events as unlikely, and to produce a range of outcomes within which future developments will lie.[3]

In effect, we want to do what we do as scientists when generalizing from our samples to larger populations; we want to make a prediction that states both a *range* of possibilities—the confidence interval —and the probability, or *significance level*, that we attach to the likelihood that the true value will fall within that range. If we give as a "best guess" some point within that interval, we recognize that it is really only shorthand for a much more complicated statement. I think this is true whether we are making explicitly quantitative statements, such as the number of people who would be killed in a nuclear war, or whether we are talking about apparently discrete events, such as whether or not "war" will occur. We may simplify our analytical models to talk about war *vs.* peace, but we know that there are many shades and varieties of each, and that in *many* respects the "war" we refer to is less a step-level jump from previous states than the mode of a distributional curve. We have learned this well from our recent experiences with civil unrest and insurgency. All of us know too about the problem of subjective probabilities and the inappropriateness of assigning a probability to a unique event; when we make a

prediction that is not based on a sample from a known universe we are beyond the limits within which the assignment of precise probability levels is permissible. Yet without some such effort, however crude and subjective, the analysis is incomplete and misleading.

Suppose that we have a prediction that a particular kind of war promises to bring death to between 5 and 25 million Americans. The President of the United States must decide in a crisis whether that is a price the country should pay in order to defend Western Europe. However he chooses to phrase his question, he must ask further, "What are the *probabilities* that the casualty level will actually fall within this range?" Presumably his decision would be quite different if his advisor could say he was *very* confident (say, a 99 per cent probability) that casualties would not exceed the upper limit of this range, than if he thought there was as much as one chance in three that the upper limit might be exceeded. Without both elements, the apparent precision of a quantitative confidence interval smacks of scientism, and the consumer would be better off with a vague but honest, "I am rather confident" or "only moderately confident" that the actual casualty level will be within the range, than he would be with a statement that gives no inkling whatever of the probability the forecaster may have had in mind.[4]

But this is not meant to be a treatise on the statistics of deadly quarrels, nor on scientific method either. I now want to consider another kind of prediction—how one can examine smooth changes in order to identify more or less discrete ones, in effect to anticipate system change. I will, however, stay within the framework outlined at the beginning—we will not be trying to predict particular events, but changes in the social and technological environment that will produce political and further social changes of one sort or another, changes that will lead to quite different social and political systems and present to future decision-makers the opportunity, and usually the necessity, for choice.

[3] See Harold and Margaret Sprout, *The Ecological Perspective on Human Affairs* (Princeton, N.J.: Princeton University Press, 1965), pp. 180, 199. See also Thiel, *op. cit.*, Chap. 1; and Nicholas Rescher, "Discrete State Systems, Markov Chains, and Problems in the Theory of Scientific Explanation and Prediction," *Philosophy of Science*, 30 (1963), pp. 325–45; and, for a similar if less rigorous and overly cautious statement, Saul Friedlander, "Forecasting in International Relations," in Bertrand de Jouvenel, ed., *Futuribles: Studies in Conjecture*, II (Geneva: Droz, 1965), p. 99. On the difficulties of predicting particular events, relevant comments include those by Wilbert E. Moore, *Social Change* (Englewood Cliffs, N.J.: Prentice-Hall, 1963), pp. 3–4; and Kenneth E. Boulding, "Expecting the Unexpected: The Uncertain Future of Knowledge," in Edgar Morphet and Charles Ryan, eds., *Conference on Designing Education for the Future*, Denver, Colo., July 1966.

[4] I am thinking, of course, of Herman Kahn, *On Thermonuclear War* (Princeton, N.J.: Princeton University Press, 1960), though he is by no means the only offender, and his use of ranges was a notable improvement over all previous efforts in this area.

Rigor, Information, and Imagination

Imagination is often useful, and sometimes essential, for accurate prediction. Yet there have *always* been some men who had imagination, and only in recent decades has prediction been dramatically improved in many areas. We now predict economic conditions, elections, demographic trends, with imperfect but notably better success than we used to. This success is dependent less upon flights of imagination than upon a mixture of information and rigor.

Formal rigor means eliminating contradictions, preventing obscurity, and avoiding leaps in logic. Perhaps even more important, the rigorous formulation of a problem very often identifies a trend that wouldn't be apparent from mere intuition or imaginative speculation. Deductive reasoning has been the great strength of traditional sociology, and, sometimes without the sociologists' rigor, of traditional political science too. Now, rigor is frequently supplied by mathematics or symbolic logic. Despite the occasional abuse of mathematics and symbols, these tools have a remarkable ability to show up relationships that would otherwise escape notice. A primary reason for the greater success of economists and demographers in predicting future developments has undoubtedly been their increased use of rigorous —that is, mathematical—theories.[5]

One of the most striking and popular applications has long been the projection of exponential growth rates from the past into the future. An exponential growth rate is of course simply like compound interest, where a quantity regularly increases by some *proportion* of itself, rather than by a standard absolute *amount*. Hence, when graphed, the pattern is of a rising and ever-steeper curve, rather than an upwardly sloping straight line. It is in fact one of the simplest of all models, known in the trade as a first-order system.[6] Yet for limited periods of time, and under stable conditions, it is an extraordinarily useful model. Probably the

most familiar example is that for the population explosion, where the world's current annual rate of population increase, about two per cent or a doubling every 35 years, is projected forward and the density of the land areas of the globe is projected to a level exceeding present-day Hong Kong's by the year 2200. Similar growth rates have been publicized by Derek Price for the expansion of science. The household phrase about "almost 90 per cent of all scientists who ever lived are alive today" comes directly from his work.[7] As we go on I shall identify some other social phenomena that have grown at exponential, and often remarkably steady, rates for years or decades.

The fact that so many processes have exhibited exponential growth rates is no accident, nor is the rate itself merely a coincidence or a statistical construct forced on the unwilling data. Science feeds upon itself, with some scientific progress making possible the cumulation of further progress. The growth of *science* has made possible many *technological* changes, as of course the demand for these improvements has provided the material basis for science to grow. While all the rates have not been precisely the same, and as we shall see the recent doubling periods vary between about every 35 years (for population) and every four years (scientific expenditures, and the destructive radius of weapons), a neat identity would be too much to expect. The rapid growth in each of them is nevertheless closely interrelated and interdependent. As such they comprise a system in dynamic but stable equilibrium; change is interrelated in a highly dependable manner, and if we can for a moment forget the *rapidity* of change about us, looking backward over recent decades the highly "predictable" nature of that change is impressive. It has been like a rocket taking off from its launching pad—slowly gathering momentum until very great speeds are attained, but the acceleration has been quite steady and not at all fortuitous.

Yet *rigor* is only a part of the modern success story in prediction. The other major element is simply *information*, scads of it, precisely, in fact, one of the exponentially-growing phenomena being

---

[5] Obviously there are plenty of examples where economists and demographers have fallen on their faces in prediction, though not so grossly in recent years as in the earlier stages of their sciences' development. In general, it is fairer to compare present social science's predictive power with that of its predecessors than to disparage it by comparing it with its natural science contemporaries. See Bernard Barber, *Science and the Social Order* (New York: The Free Press, 1952) p. 243.

[6] Boulding, *op. cit.*

[7] Derek J. de Sola Price, *Science Since Babylon* (New Haven, Connecticut: Yale University Press, 1961), chap. 5. See also his *Little Science, Big Science* (New York: Columbia University Press, 1963).

measured. Price's statements about scientists are primarily inferences from the volume of scientific information; the most familiar set of data in his presentation refer to the number of scientific and technical journals, which has now reached over 100,000. Without this information explosion we would not know in a precise and detailed way, even to the degree necessary for fitting very rough exponential growth curves, about all the other changes. It has made possible the *inductive* generalization that marks so much current work in both sociology and political science. (Though many historians and political scientists have always held to a notion that "the facts speak for themselves.")[8] But large bodies of quantitative information are expensive and time-consuming to produce, and could never have been gathered by scholars working under nineteenth century conditions.

And curve-fitting is a tricky business. Formally speaking, many possible curves can be fitted to a single set of points.[9] The "best" curve is highly ambiguous, and if one has only a few observations, gathered perhaps for only a short period of time and subject to substantial error in measurement, the hazards are multiplied. With little data a straight line, an exponential growth rate, or even a cyclical pattern of hills and valleys superimposed on a rising trend may all be equally "correct" mathematically, and we may have little basis for preferring one or another. Even the fact of a rising trend may be misleading, especially as it may be related to a longer-term cycle. So the information-gathering side of things is crucial, and we need all the public and private data-gathering services in existence—at the same time that we need to devise means to prevent being snowed under in a blizzard of trivia.

Even rigor and information, the twin pillars of modern social wisdom, suffice only for limited tasks. The uncritical projection of exponential growth rates provides some of the worst examples of simple-minded curve-fitting. Quite obviously the world's rate of population increase will *not* continue

unabated until the earth's density exceeds Hong Kong's; some kind of control, deliberate or natural, felicitous or disastrous, will prevent it.[10] Still, the ease and attractions of simple projection have subverted many a would-be prophet. G. K. Chesterton, in his slightly pompous Victorian way, amply satirized the outlook:

> When we see a pig in a litter larger than the other pigs, we know that by an unalterable law of the Inscrutable it will some day be larger than an elephant,—just as we know, when we see weeds and dandelions growing more and more thickly in a garden, that they must, in spite of all our efforts, grow taller than the chimney-pots and swallow the house from sight, so we know and reverently acknowledge, that when any power in human politics has shown for any period of time any considerable activity, it will go on until it reaches the sky.[11]

Some political and social predictions based on the extrapolation of apparent growth rates are only a little less absurd, yet even a sensible-appearing use may go very far wrong.[12] Upward trends do *not* go on forever, but at some point, for some reason, level off, oscillate, or go into a downturn. A child doubles in height between the ages of 2 and 18—but he won't (I trust) double his height again before he is 35. But political history is full of examples of failures to

---

[8] This strain is exemplified by Henry Adams' writings on American history, especially his *History of the United States of America* (London: Putnam, 1891–92, 9 vols.).

[9] Arthur C. Clarke, *Profiles of the Future* (New York: Harper and Row, 1962), chap. 1 is a popular but sophisticated statement of this problem. He notes (p. 7) "Mathematics is only a tool, though an immensely powerful one. No equations, however impressive and complex, can arrive at the truth if the initial assumptions are incorrect."

[10] Such a density would imply a total world population above 400 billion. Actually the upper limit to a population living "moderately well" is probably around 50 billion. One of the more buoyant pro-natalists (Colin Clark, "Agricultural Productivity in Relation to Population," in Gordon Wolstenholme, ed., *Man and His Future* [Boston: Little, Brown, 1963], pp. 23–35), and one of the most creative minds working on the problem of how that population might be sustained (Richard L. Meier, *Science and Economic Development: New Patterns of Living* [Cambridge: M.I.T. Press, 1966, 2nd ed.], p. 147), seem to have arrived at this figure independently. Both describe the prospective living conditions in some detail; they might be characterized as appreciably better than those now prevailing in Latin America but probably inferior to—and certainly different from—those now typical of Europe.

[11] G. K. Chesterton, *The Napoleon of Notting Hill* (London: John Lane, 1904), p. 19.

[12] One of the most forceful statements about the utility of prediction *via* extrapolating exponential growth curves is Hornell Hart, "Predicting Future Trends," (New York: Appleton-Century Crofts, 1957), pp. 455–73, and a good argument for caution, trying instead to anticipate jumps and quantum leaps, is Gardner Murphy, "Where is the Human Race Going?" in Richard E. Farson, ed., *Science and Human Affairs* (Palo Alto, Calif.: Science and Behavior Books, 1965), pp. 7–17. A more general treatment of how exponential growth rates change is Daniel Bell, "Twelve Modes of Prediction: A Preliminary Sorting of Approaches in the Social Sciences," *Daedalus*, XCIII, 3 (1964), 845–80.

anticipate the system break, the turning point, when what used to be appropriate is no longer so. Generals' alleged preparedness to fight the last war is just such an instance. A national population policy which stressed producing large numbers was appropriate for an era when the number of soldiers a state could field was a major basis of its power; some countries, like Italy, carried that policy over into an age when per capita wealth was equally important as a power base. Political goals, as well as political methods, must be adapted to changes in the social and technological environment. Perhaps we have reached a period when the simple goal of maximizing the "national interest"—whatever that is—has become inappropriate in a world where heavy symbiosis and cooperation are unavoidable. We also must have sufficient discrimination to know which growth rates are important to us. By 1870 there was, within the British government, a clear awareness that Germany's growing steel production would intersect with Britain's before the end of the nineteenth century. For another decade, however, they thought that the country they had to worry about, for political reasons, was France, not Germany. Here then, are still a variety of crucial roles for imagination.

This is the kind of thing to which I want to devote the rest of this article: to examining some of the features of the environment of the international political system that have undergone very rapid change in recent years, suggesting what the prospects are for their continued growth, and what their political consequences may be. There are at least four possible ways in which a smooth, continuous rate of growth in something may eventually have a discontinuous effect on other aspects of the system, producing what may be called step-level change or system transformation.[13]

Crossing a Threshold

One is an increase which crosses a threshold, a rate of growth that continues until, on reacting with some other aspect of the social or political system, it produces a discrete change. A given equilibrium may be unstable. In forest ecology, forms of life, adapted to their environment, grow and develop in an area, but in so doing they modify their environment until it has changed so that they are no longer adapted to it. Hardwood trees, for instance, first become established in sunny, relatively open areas. But as they grow up and mature over many decades, they shade the ground beneath them, and in the shade young conifer trees thrive better than new hardwoods. In time, as the large hardwoods die out they are replaced by conifers, which in turn create even deeper shade that prevents the growth of any more hardwoods. The resulting "climax" forest is then in a static equilibrium, and will maintain itself indefinitely except for exogenous change introduced by the activities of man, fire, or other natural disaster. An obvious political example is the slow growth of a voting bloc that, on passing the 50 per cent mark, is able then to effect a sharp change in policy.[14] Even here the change may not be all that discontinuous—some political change is likely to occur in response to the pressure of any large bloc, and some further change will arise in anticipation of its majority status as it approaches the half-way mark. But the principle, even though not entirely unambiguous in most empirical examples, is clear enough.

If in the future we have a world government, with effective authority over its member states or over individuals, this example might be of more importance for international politics than it now seems to be. Already the poor states (those with a per capita income of less than $300 a year) form more than a majority in the United Nations, and actually they have the two-thirds majority which is required for issues defined as "important." If they were able to enforce their collective will they doubtless would expand United Nations assessments many times over, spreading the new revenues around for economic development. But though for years they have had the votes necessary to pass this assessment—and have been able to band together to defeat the rich powers on other occasions—they have not done so with the tax rate. It is one thing to assess taxes, quite another, in the current state of international organization, to collect them. So for the present they avoid a show of parliamentary strength that would merely expose their executive weakness.

---

[13] An early use of this approach in political science is, of course, Morton Kaplan's *System and Process in International Politics* (New York: Wiley, 1957).

[14] Bertrand de Jouvenel, "Political Science and Prevision," *American Political Science Review*, LIX, 1 (1965), 34.

Another example of this phenomenon which might have more immediate effect is provided by relative power relationships in the Middle East. Despite Israel's numerical inferiority to her neighbors (on the order of one to twenty) her wealth, organization, and external assistance, plus the divisions among the Arabs, allow her to remain militarily equal to her antagonists. But a sustained growth in income and organizational efficiency in Egypt could over the long run tip that balance in the Arabs' favor. The notion of a sharp system change or step-level jump is an over-simplification, but at least subjectively, if not objectively, Egypt could reach a point where its leader could decide that from then on he had the power to crush Israel. Whether he really was able to do it, whether he miscalculated and was beaten again, or whether Israel changed the whole threat system by going nuclear, the effect would nevertheless be of a slow and smooth change in one parameter that had, at some pretty clearly identifiable point, produced a discrete change in the system.

More generally, something of this sort has happened in the international system as a whole. Kenneth Boulding has adapted from economics what he calls the "loss of strength gradient," or the rate at which a nation's power declines with distance from its borders.[15] For the major industrial powers this gradient has been steadily pushed outward since the Napoleonic Wars, as fewer and fewer states have remained "unconditionally viable." (He calls a nation unconditionally viable if it can prevent foreign imposition of a drastic change of political or social organization inside it own borders.) The ability of one nation to coerce another even at a great distance was strengthened first by social changes (such as the *levée en masse*, the aggregation of large nation-states, and revolutionary ideology), and then technological innovation (the steamship, tanks, aircraft, and finally the atomic bomb). For many years this meant that only six or so great powers were viable against any opponent, and that these great powers could conquer even far away small states.

The cumulative effect of these trends, however, produced a dramatic system-change at the end of World War II, when only the two superpowers could dependably resist the domination of any other state. The erosion of all other nations' unconditional viability is in effect what we mean by the transformation of the international system in the early postwar years.

And the bipolar system as we knew it only a decade ago has itself become transformed by the maintenance of the very same trends that first produced it. Continuing technological change, moving from atom bombs and manned bombers to thermonuclear weapons and intercontinental missiles, has removed the sanctuaries that the superpowers used to enjoy in their homelands. Thus there has been a limited revival in the independence of the middle powers, as the great powers can no longer provide such a credible deterrent umbrella. Yet though smaller states are not now so dependent on the big powers for protection—not dependent simply because they are not so confident in it—they still could never hope to *defeat* a superpower. Thus we are somewhere between a bipolar situation and a balance of power world with many foci of more or less equal strength.

Changes in transportation and destructive capacities produced fairly discontinuous changes in the political system, first by cutting the number of great powers to two, and then by restoring to those at the middle level *some* of the independence they had possessed before bipolarity. The elimination of *all* states from the "unconditionally viable" category makes the need for new political forms for the international system more pressing than ever. We hear less about this now than a few years ago when the balance of terror was thought to be unstable, but I think the passing of extreme bipolarity *increases* the long-run requirement for political change.

Possibly these trends will have further sharp effects on the international system. The most likely way would be if technology were for a while to favor strongly the defender, especially in the development of an anti-ballistic missile system for continental defense. Apparently such development has progressed a good bit farther than most of us would have expected a couple of years ago, and an effective anti-ICBM defense no longer seems utterly out of the question for the two big and rich powers.[16] If

[15] Kenneth E. Boulding, *Conflict and Defense* (New York: Harper and Row, 1960).

[16] See Jeremy J. Stone, *Containing the Arms Race* (Cambridge: M.I.T. Press, 1966), pp. 224–32, and Bruce M. Russett, "The Complexities of Ballistic Missile Defense," *Yale Review*, Spring 1967.

successful, and if not merely outflanked by chemical or bacteriological weapons, it would return its possessor to the unconditional viability of the good old days. But at the moment that still seems to be a long shot, and I suspect we must look in other directions for new ecological influences on the political system.

Demand and Supply as Limits to Growth

The previous example was of a smooth trend that, on reacting with some other characteristics, produced a marked change in the system. There are in addition several possibilities for trends to stop moving along at their previously established rates—the growth stops, or at least is drastically modified. Our *second* class, then, is of a development that reaches a so-called "logical" ending point, where it stops because of a change in the needs, perception, and behavior of men, because the *demand* which initiated it has essentially been fulfilled. One such is probably in the destructiveness of modern weapons that I alluded to a moment ago. During the century preceding World War II the destructive radius of the biggest weapons then available grew at a doubling rate faster than every 10 years, with the perfection of explosive chemicals and the development first of large cannons and finally of blockbuster bombs. The explosion of the first atomic bomb marked a certain discontinuous jump here, and in the two decades following it the doubling period shortened, to about every four years, culminating in the 100 megaton weapon that can collapse an ordinary frame house within 30 miles of its explosion point. But there is an obvious limit to the destructiveness of modern weapons—the size of anything worth destroying. At the doubling rate of four years, another twenty would be quite sufficient for a weapon capable of obliterating an entire continent; less than a decade more would produce a doomsday machine with a destructive radius exceeding that of the globe. More than that would appear to be a waste of scarce resources. Weapons development and improvement might well continue, but along other dimensions like reliability, discrimination (as between men and structures in the neutron bomb), and "cleanliness."[17]

Many of the characteristics of what has been termed the "mobiletic" revolution are likely also to fall into this category, and also rather soon. Mobiletics is a slightly inelegant but useful term coined to cover the whole range of movement—of things, of energy, and of information.[18] One of its components is the transportation of men and other high value-per-unit-volume goods. In the nineteenth century the speed at which men could travel over transcontinental or intercontinental distances doubled more or less every twenty-five years. It began at the speed of the sailing ship or horse and carriage (depending on the medium), which was hardly more than five miles an hour over sustained distances in the early 1800s. This progressed through the perfection of clippers, the steamship and the railroad. After the Wright brothers this rate speeded up, with a doubling about every ten years, reaching around 600 miles an hour in the late 1940s and the 2000-mile-an-hour bomber in the early 1960s. The built-in limits to the trend are fuzzy but fairly obvious, at least on this small earth. Something like a man-carrying intercontinental rocket is the top; 5000 mile missiles make the entire trip from point to point in under 30 minutes or roughly 10,000 miles per hour. Extrapolation of the 10-year doubling rate since the turn of the century would bring us to this limit sometime in the 1980s. Since the 2000-mile-per-hour airliner is not expected to be operational until after 1970 this projection for the rocket seems rather over-optimistic, and the social demand for human travel at 10,000 miles per hour instead of 200 miles per hour is not likely to be so great as to require that the "schedule" imposed by extrapolating past changes be kept. In the longer run faster speeds for manned travel to the planets and beyond are to be expected, but even here the extrapolation to 30,000 miles per hour in the year 2000 is, give or take a few years and tens of thousands of miles, about as long as current rates of growth can go unabated. According to most scientific authorities, by then there would appear to be more payoffs in suspended animation, or interstellar travel by colonies that would reproduce themselves en route. The real upper limit to man's travel capabilities may be only at the speed of light, but it

---

[17] The data in this and the following paragraph are from Bruce M. Russett, *Trends in World Politics* (New York: The Macmillan Company, 1965), Chap. 1.

[18] Bertram E. Gross, *Space-Time and Post-Industrial Society* (Syracuse, N.Y.: Syracuse University, Maxwell School of Citizenship and Public Affairs, 1966, mimeo.), p. 4.

is unlikely to be approached at the current high rates of increase. This, then, is another rate of change that will, within the lifetimes of some of us, slow down drastically.

With the advent of the telegraph, communication became virtually instantaneous, at the speed of light plus processing time, over short distances. The changes are not so orderly that any simple exponential growth curve can be fitted to this one, but modern improvements have concentrated on eliminating the need for fixed channels of communication such as wires, on lengthening the distance that could be covered, and on providing facilities for transmitting a wider variety of messages, from electrical impulses that had to be translated from Morse code into letters, to impulses that could be made into faithful reproductions of sound and sight. When these developments culminate, as they will shortly, in the installation of a world-wide system of satellite relays to carry television impulses around the earth within two seconds, the most important dimension of the communication revolution will be completed.[19] Further work will be left to clean up the quality and variety of transmission possibilities and to proliferate transmitters and receivers. These mobiletic changes, therefore, are now approaching their natural completion. Probably they will pick up again on some now hardly imaginable dimensions,[20] but it is unlikely that in the next fifty years or so they will again produce such a sudden change in the environment of international politics as they have just put us through.

These are growth rates that will slow down essentially as the *demand* is satisfied. Making an effective decision to speed up or slow down their growth is not always within the capabilities of our social and political systems, but at least the growth is not so autonomous that we need anticipate any particular difficulties when the "natural" slowdown points approach. This is by no means universally the case with rapidly growing social phenomena, so we are led to a *third* category—growth rates that come to a halt because the *supply* of some basic commodity is exhausted.

Behind all the changes just listed has been the explosion of science and technology. Since the eighteenth century the number of scientists in the world at large has doubled approximately every 15 years; in the United States alone the doubling rate has been faster, roughly every 10 years. This clearly can't go on. The number of scientists and engineers has now reached almost one per cent of the total population,[21] and if one eliminates the temperamentally and intellectually unfit (eliminates them only for analytical purposes), they amount to possibly one-fifth of those who have the capacities to become productive scientists. Even if we forget about leaving high-IQ individuals for commerce, administration, and the arts, it is clear that this exponential growth curve has a built-in ceiling. We will see the end of it well before the century is out; it will affect our professional lives and especially those of our graduate students. Some mitigation may be in sight; for instance, utilizing the brain-drain of high-IQ people from underdeveloped countries, a reservoir that may not dry up for another fifty years or so; or extremely sophisticated computer usage; or hiring more secretaries; or improving information retrieval; or various ways of relieving scientists of the substantial drudgery that still remains in their work. Yet this kind of relief only postpones the day when surgery will be necessary. Federal obligations for research and development in the United States doubled roughly every four years between 1950 and 1964.[22] But for the past three years they have levelled off at about three per cent of national income. This is nearly a third of what we now spend on defense, and even allowing for growth in real national income (perhaps a doubling every 20 years at an annual rate of about four per cent) it is hard to see how science spending can grow very much more. Depending upon how it is handled, the levelling-off of this trend could lead to a period of regrouping and digestion in science, as better means are perfected for making us aware of other people's research and avoiding some of the duplication that is

[19] See John R. Platt, "The Step to Man," *Science*, CXLIX (August 6, 1965), 608.

[20] Sometimes this mutation and revival is called "escalation." See Gerald Holton, "Scientific Research and Scholarship: Notes Towards the Design of Proper Scales," *Daedalus*, XCI, 2 (1962), 369–99.

[21] This is from a projection and adaptation of figures for 1962–64 in U.S. Bureau of the Census, *Statistical Abstract of the United States, 1966* (Washington, D.C.: U.S. Government Printing Office, 1966), p. 547–48. I am assuming that the potential talent pool includes all those of working age with an IQ of at least 120.

[22] *Ibid.*, p. 544, and *Statistical Abstract of the United States, 1959*, p. 539. The figures are not fully comparable, but the general pattern is unmistakable.

currently so prevalent. In the world at large, it is conceivable that a levelling-off of the growth in science could slow down some of the more wasteful and dangerous aspects of international technological competition. In any case, the levelling has already begun.

The Social Control of Growth

This leads us to a distinction which ushers in our *fourth* class of growth patterns—between growth rates that are brought to a halt *only* by resource limitations, and rates that are controlled, short of the physical limits, by deliberate social policy.[23] John Platt's fascinating essay on "The Step to Man" also mentions some of the growth curves I have detailed, and forecasts their orderly levelling-off.[24] But orderly transition may be the exception. A growth rate may reach its ceiling and in the absence of social control or an escalation that picks up again on some other dimension, bump along the ceiling. In effect this is oscillation around the equilibrium level, and I will illustrate it with the outcome foreseen for the population explosion according to one model.

Imagine an island with no foreign trade and where there is neither emigration nor immigration—a closed system. The area of agricultural land is fixed, and for some time it has supported a population, growing at a constant rate, that has not yet required all of the available land. As land utilization reaches 100 per cent and the level of technology remains constant, the population will approach the maximum that the island can support. But if technology is evolving, as it has been in the Western world over the past several centuries, the ceiling may continually

be pushed upward and the population may continue to grow at its exponential rate. Let us assume, however, that at some point the local farmers' ingenuity gives out and they exhaust all methods for substantially increasing the yield of their land. When this point is reached the population of the island will have attained its ceiling. Growth may not stop absolutely short in its tracks, for there may be some belt-tightening possible. But it must stop soon, and not necessarily as a simple levelling-off to a smooth plateau. On the contrary, after the first steps of belt-tightening the next consequence is likely to be a disease epidemic in a population made vulnerable by malnutrition, or there may occur a natural disaster which drastically cuts food production in a situation where there is no margin to spare. Instead of simply levelling-off, the population will drop sharply in response to the sudden rise in death rates. But after this immediate disaster is past, there will again, at the advanced technological level achieved, be a surplus of land relative to population. So, for a short period, unless reproductive habits have been changed, the population will again shoot upward, at the previous rate, until the gap is filled once more. And again, the population will become vulnerable to disease or nature, will fall once again, and so on. Here is the classic Malthusian trap in which population is forced into equilibrium with limited productive resources. The pattern, however, is one of violent oscillations to and from a ceiling imposed by "nature."[25]

Such a perpetual unhappy fate is nevertheless not the only possible denouement to the exponential growth curve. If, instead of allowing resource limitations to determine the situation, it is subjected to human volition and social control, a better solution is feasible. If the birth rate is brought down fairly quickly and made equal to the death rate before the ceiling is reached, the curve can be made to taper

[23] I distinguish between this *planned diminution* and the simple relatively autonomous slackening of demand discussed as the second category. Note too that the first and third categories apply to environmental limitations that act regardless of human cognition, whereas the second and fourth operate only as a consequence of perceptions. This useful distinction between different environmental effects is made by Sprout and Sprout, *op. cit.*

[24] Platt, *op. cit.* An initially exponential curve that bends over smoothly in an S-shape is the logistic curve. An early example in demographic prediction is Lowell J. Reed, "Population Growth and Forecasts," *Annals of the American Academy of Political and Social Science*, CLXXXVIII (November, 1936), 159–66. The logistic curve may have looked applicable to U.S. population in the 1930s, but it does not fit later developments. The article is nevertheless useful as an explicit answer to the projection of exponential rates to infinity.

[25] A good example of thinking that hitting the ceiling is the only probable outcome to such demographic pressures is Sir Charles Darwin, "Forecasting the Future," in Edward Hitchings, Jr., *Frontiers in Science* (New York: Basic Books, 1958), pp. 100–16. Richard L. Meier, *Modern Science and the Human Fertility Problem* (New York: Wiley, 1959), pp. 53–63, forecasts something much like this happening in certain areas of the world, notably the island of Mauritius. For a similar result with a different mechanism (the stress syndrome) see Hudson Hoagland, "Mechanisms of Population Control," *Daedalus*, XCIII, 3 (1964), 812–29.

off smoothly and culminate in an even plateau without wild oscillation. Presumably there will be some fluctuation for a while, as the social controls are perfected and the right mix is found to depress the birth rate just to, and not beyond, the equilibrium level. But in principle the proper procedures could be worked out.

Going from the abstract model of the isolated island to the current world demographic situation brings, I would guess, substantial cause for optimism. Many sociologists and economists are more expert on demographic matters than I, and I will not try to encroach on their territory. It appears to me, however, that this represents a growth rate that is on the verge of being brought under control, at least sometime before the end of the century. I doubt very much that the world will look like our mythical island, or even like Hong Kong. For what is, by comparison with the funds expended for military research and development, a very modest investment, we have come up with a variety of extremely promising methods for population control, and have still more in the works. Even a cosmic pessimist would have to admit that the technical side of this problem is being licked before our eyes. The social side—how to bring about widespread acceptance and use—is not so easy, but with the new attitudes in developed and underdeveloped countries alike, it does not seem so formidable as it did only a few years ago. I should perhaps say these things in a still small voice, since I am assuming a high degree of public awareness and determination to defeat the threat, a degree that has not yet been reached and must be maintained for decades if my prediction is to come true. It could, if it makes us complacent, become a self-defeating prophecy. And I am aware that the details of solving this problem could yet be very difficult, and that the quality of life on earth may well depend less on *whether* the demographic revolution is brought to its thermidor, than on how quickly. A delay of a generation will mean almost twice as many people to accommodate, and give us some very serious economic and political crises throughout Asia—crises that may be partly avoided by more rapid action. Thus I am very much in sympathy with those who are in a hurry. But this is nevertheless a promising area. With some luck, determination, and dedication, it may become an example of how a social pattern, an exponential growth rate of enormous import, was brought under control before it reached its built-in ceiling and burdened mankind with its oscillations.

Here then is a prediction, imbued with I think only a small component of over-optimism, for the turn of the coming century. The population explosion will be, at least for macro-purposes, ended. We may not have reached the state of equal birth and death rates and hence a stable population, but the rate of growth should be much reduced. The world food crisis will have been met and surmounted. (Notice, however, that I did *not* say avoided. I do not think we will get off that easily. Before population control takes full effect we will have had to deal with mass famine in Asia.) The problem of economic development will still be with us, and perhaps in even more pressing form. But it will be in *different* form, for rapid population growth will no longer be a major break on the developmental process, demanding heavy inputs of capital investment just to stay in place. The major problems instead will be in the areas of organization, determination, and the difficulties of controlling the social and political unrest that is associated with the middle stages of economic development. How to cope with rising expectations, with wants that increase even faster than growing satisfactions, will not be an easy question. The last stages of the mobiletic revolution, in bringing to even the poorest members of world society images of how foreign and domestic rich live, will enormously exacerbate problems we can already see.

The End of Stable Change

For the past century men in the Western world, and more recently over the rest of the globe, have lived in a period when change was the usual state of affairs. Though the change has been exciting, disruptive, and demanding for the individuals undergoing it, all of us have become accustomed to it; our parents with some head shaking, our children in a way that takes space travel and other wonders in stride as normal and utterly expectable events. Prediction of the ecology of international politics has been difficult primarily because for most of the time we have been so ignorant about the precise magnitudes of change and its predictable regularities. Had we before us accurate information about past experience, and courage enough to extrapolate, much of the present situation could have been predicted merely by expecting more of the same that had prevailed—not the same levels, but the same change rates. Relatively speaking, *political* prediction would have been easy (given today's data sources and theoretical achievements). Persistence forecasting, or the extrapolation of mildly sloping trends, would have been accurate. But until recently much of the necessary quantitative information simply had not been assembled, and since one can hardly extrapolate a trend without knowing what the trend is, we have a clear example of a case where neither imagination nor rigor were, by themselves, sufficient for adequate forecasting. Where precise data are still lacking, the normal difficulties of forecasting have been compounded recently by the rapid changes implied in the high levels now reached on many of the exponential growth curves, where a doubling in eight years instead of twelve can make a very great difference in the absolute changes with which society must cope.

Some of these problems will remain in future years, but as more and better data become available, and as social science develops greater rigor and a better understanding of our environment, they are being eased. For a brief period prediction may have great success in a world of rapid but dependable change. It will soon be shaken, however, by the system breaks that can be discerned in the not so distant future. Then new qualities of imagination will be required, both to *predict* and to *determine* what the world will be like. Much of the future will depend upon which growth rates change first, and whether by orderly deliberate control that brings them to a plateau with a minimum of oscillation, or whether they bump up and down against a ceiling imposed by the environment. Doubtless we all would prefer a world where population growth was brought to a regulated halt, rather than one where Malthus reigned supreme and the population rose and fell with epidemics and bad harvests. And because many of these growth rates *are* interrelated, an uncontrolled change in one is likely to have far-ranging effects.

For several generations we have been living in an era of transition between great system changes. That era is now coming to a close, and a period of instability is ahead. We have a limited amount of time to break loose from habit, inertia, and administrative routine, to decide which trends we most need to control, and to devise ways of doing it. Without adopting a naive eighteenth-century faith in the omnipotence of science, it is nonetheless true that when a social need is strongly felt *some* solution is often found, even though no one could have predicted in advance precisely what that solution would be.[26] On the whole, I am hopeful that the necessary social and technological innovations can be found under pressure, although the time is short and the margin for error not at all wide. The population control experience is a good omen here. Only ten years ago one could not have said which, if any, of the possibilities then being explored might pay off; now we find unanticipated degrees of freedom. Maybe something of the sort will arise for international politics and world order. Right now no one can produce a scheme for the year 2000 that really looks workable, but as the pressure comes on, ingenious men may be able to develop something.

While trying to improve our predictive powers we must, at the same time, avoid *depending* on a high level of predictive success. We must maintain a pluralist approach so as to be able to adapt to the unexpected; we must have several possible alternatives and "keep our options open." It is worth recalling a statement by Alfred North Whitehead that is even more appropriate now than when he wrote it forty years ago:

We must expect that the future will be dangerous. It is the business of the future to be dangerous, and it is among the merits of science that it equips the future for its duties. ... The middle class pessimism over the future of the world comes from a confusion between civilization and security. In the immediate future there will be less security than in the immediate past, less stability. ... There is a degree of instability which is inconsistent with civilization. But, on the whole, the great ages have been unstable ages.[27]

26 See Bell, *op. cit.*, and John R. Platt, *The Excitement of Science* (Boston: Houghton Mifflin, 1962), Chap. 4, for good discussion of how this may be true, and also L. B. Slobodkin, "On the Present Incompleteness of Mathematical Ecology," *American Scientist*, LIII, 3 (1965), 347–59. It is important, however, to distinguish between what an *observer* might diagnose as social needs, and effective social *demands*.

27 Alfred North Whitehead, *Science and the Modern World* (New York: The Macmillan Company, 1925), p. 291.

C.   Structural Characteristics

11.   World Politics as a Primitive Political System[*]

Roger D. Masters is Associate Professor of Government at Dartmouth College. A student of political philosophy as well as international affairs, his recent works include *The Nation Is Burdened* (1967) and *The Political Philosophy of Rousseau* (1968). In this essay Professor Masters uses an intriguing set of comparisons to explore the structure and functioning of the international system. Whether or not the reader agrees with the conclusion that primitive societies and world politics are sustained by similar processes, he will find that Professor Master's analysis offers revealing insights into the dynamics of modern international systems. [*Reprinted from* World Politics, *XVI (July 1964), 595–619, by permission of the author and the publisher.*]

I. Reasons for Comparing Primitive and International Politics

Many primitive peoples have political systems which are very much like the international political system. If the characterization of world politics as mere "anarchy" is an exaggeration, surely anarchy moderated or inhibited by a balance of power is a fairly accurate description of the rivalry between sovereign nation-states. The Nuer, a primitive African people, have been described as living in an "ordered anarchy" which depends on a "balanced opposition of political segments."[1] It is commonplace to describe the international system as lacking a government, so that "might makes right." "In Nuerland legislative, judicial and executive functions are not invested in any persons or councils";

hence, throughout the society, "the club and the spear are the sanctions of rights."[2]

To be sure, politics among the Nuer—or any other primitive people—is not identical to world politics, but however important the differences may be, a number of writers have suggested the possibility of comparing the two kinds of political systems.[3] Curiously enough, however, there has been virtually

The author's research has been undertaken with the assistance of a grant from the Stimson Fund, Yale University.

[1] E. E. Evans-Pritchard, *The Nuer* (Oxford 1940), 181, idem, "The Nuer of the Southern Sudan," in M. Fortes and E. E. Evans-Pritchard, eds., *African Political Systems* (London 1940), 293.

[2] Evans-Pritchard, *The Nuer*, 162, 169. Cf. R. F. Barton, "Ifugao Law," *University of California Publications in American Archaeology and Ethnology*, XV (February 1915), 15.

[3] E.g., Hans Morgenthau, *Politics Among Nations* (1st edn., New York 1953), 221; George Modelski, "Agraria and Industria: Two Models of the International System," in Klaus Knorr and Sidney Verba, eds., *The International System* (Princeton 1961), 125–26; and David Easton, "Political Anthropology," in Bernard J. Siegel, ed., *Biennial Review of Anthropology 1959* (Stanford 1959), 235–36. At least one anthropologist was aware of the analogy: see R. F. Barton, *The Half-Way Sun* (New York 1930), 109–10; idem, *The Kalingas* (Chicago 1949), 101; and idem, "Ifugao Law," 100, 103. In his introduction to *The Kalingas*, E. A. Hoebel wrote: "International law is primitive law on a world scale" (p. 5). Cf. Hoebel's *The Law of Primitive Man* (Cambridge, Mass., 1954), 125–26, 318, 321, 330–33.

no effort to elaborate these similarities comprehensively from a theoretical point of view.[4]

It should be noted in passing that there are three more general reasons for comparing primitive and international political systems. An attempt to bridge the gap between political science and anthropology has merits because such cross-disciplinary endeavors may free one from unnecessarily narrow assumptions which often dominate research in a given field. This is particularly true with respect to political anthropology, since the political aspects of primitive society have often been only imperfectly analyzed.[5]

Secondly, it may not be amiss to point out that long before anthropology was established as a discipline, political philosophers analyzed the social and political antecedents of existing states and governments.[6] The idea of a "state of nature," in which men lived before the establishment of governments, plays an important role in the history of political philosophy. Although recent students of primitive society have argued that "the theories of political philosophers" are "of little scientific value,"[7] the existence of a tradition which considered the "state of nature" as relevant to any political theory may indicate that political scientists should consider primitive politics more fully than they now do.

This general point is of specific importance for the theory of international politics because it can be said that the modern theory of international relations took the notion of a "state of nature" as its model.[8] Since anthropologists have asserted that such a "state of nature" never existed, consideration of the empirical and theoretical relevance of the concept may well be in order; not the least of the advantages of a comparison between primitive and international politics would be a fuller understanding of the relevance of modern political philosophy to a theory of world politics.[9]

Finally, as Ragnar Numelin has shown, "international relations" (or its analog) exists among uncivilized peoples; the "discovery" of diplomacy cannot be attributed, as it customarily is, to the "historical" cultures of the Mediterranean or Orient.[10] Thus any exhaustive theory of world politics would have to comprehend the rivalry, warfare, and diplomacy of primitive peoples as genuine examples of "international politics."

II. Similarities Between Primitive and International Politics

At the outset, four elements common to politics within a number of primitive societies and international relations deserve mention: first, the absence of a formal government with power to judge and punish violations of law; second, the use of violence and "self-help" by the members of the system to achieve their objectives and enforce obligations; third, the derivation of law and moral obligations either from custom or from explicit, particular bargaining relationships (i.e., the absence of a formal legislative body operating on the basis of—and making—general rules); and fourth, a predominant organizational principle which establishes political units serving many functions in the overall social system.

The first three of these similarities between

[4] Since this study was undertaken, an article has been published that marks a first step in this direction. See Chadwick F. Alger, "Comparison of Intranational and International Politics," *American Political Science Review*, LVII (June 1963), 414–19.

[5] In 1940, A. R. Radcliffe-Brown said: "The comparative study of political institutions, with special reference to the simpler societies, is an important branch of social anthropology which has not yet received the attention it deserves" (Preface, in Fortes and Evans-Pritchard, eds., *African Political Systems*, XI). More recently, David Easton has written: "Such a subfield [as political anthropology] does not yet exist" ("Political Anthropology," 210).

[6] E.g., Montaigne, *Essays*, I, XXIII ("Of Custom, and that We Should Not Easily Change a Law Received"), and I, xxxi ("Of Cannibals"); Rousseau, *Second Discourse*, esp. First Part and notes c–q; and Locke, *Second Treatise of Civil Government*, esp. Chaps. 2 and 3.

[7] Fortes and Evans-Pritchard, *African Political Systems*, 4. See also Henry Sumner Maine's sharp criticism of Rousseau's conception of the "state of nature" in *Ancient Law* (New York 1874), 84–8, 299.

[8] On the relations between the concept of a "state of nature" and the prevailing theory of politics among sovereign states, see Kenneth N. Waltz, *Man, the State, and War* (New York 1959), esp. Chaps. 6–8; and Richard H. Cox, *Locke on War and Peace* (Oxford 1960), esp. Chap. 4.

[9] Cf. Kenneth N. Waltz, "Political Philosophy and the Study of International Relations," in William T. R. Fox, ed., *Theoretical Aspects of International Relations* (Notre Dame, Ind., 1959), 51–68; and Arnold Wolfers, "Political Theory and International Relations," in Arnold Wolfers and Laurence W. Martin, eds., *The Anglo-American Tradition in Foreign Affairs* (New Haven 1956), esp. xi–xiii.

[10] Ragnar Numelin, *The Beginnings of Diplomacy* (New York 1950), 125 *et passim*.

primitive and international politics are relatively self-evident when one considers those primitive societies which lack fully developed governments. The fourth, however, may not be as clear. In certain primitive societies, territorial political units are largely defined, especially in the eyes of their members, in terms of kinship groups which are reckoned either "unilaterally" (i.e., groups such as the "lineage," in which descent is in either the male or female line from a common ancestor), or "bilaterally" (i.e., the family group includes relatives of both mother and father, as in modern, "Western" society).[11] Different combinations or divisions of these groups, on a territorial basis, often provide the basic structure of the entire political system.

Although it is not normally noted, the international system of sovereign states is also organized largely on the basis of a single principle. In this case, the principle is that of "territorial sovereignty"—i.e., the conception that sovereignty "is always associated with the proprietorship of a limited portion of the earth's surface, and that 'sovereigns' *inter se* are to be deemed not *paramount*, but *absolute* owners of the state's territory."[12] This ultimate authority can, of course, be divided, as it is in federal states; but so, too, with the lineage principle in some primitive systems which are divided into different levels of units.[13]

In primitive societies like the Nuer, lineage or kinship groups perform a wide variety of functions, so that it is not possible to point to a specific action and define it as "political,"[14] rather, there is a political element in many actions which simultaneously serve other purposes. This characteristic has been described in recent sociological literature as the "functional diffuseness" of traditional social structures.[15] The conception of "diffuseness" is thus opposed to "functional specificity" (i.e., the organization of a special group or institution to perform a given activity or function), which is supposed to prevail in all modern societies.

An extreme example of this usage is found in Riggs's polar conceptions of a "fused" system, in which "a single structure performs all the necessary functions," and a "refracted society," in which "for every function, a corresponding structure exists."[16] Riggs argues that traditional, agrarian societies are "fused," whereas modern, industrialized societies are "refracted." While such a distinction may indicate an important tendency, it is a radical exaggeration to imply that in modern political systems, "for every function, a corresponding structure exists." The political unit of the modern state system has a "fused" character which parallels the "diffuse" role of kinship groups in primitive societies like the Nuer.[17] Moreover, just as an industrial civilization does not presuppose a perfectly

[11] See Fortes and Evans-Pritchard, *African Political Systems*, 11; and Barton, "Ifugao Law," 92–4, 110. Carl Landé, in a stimulating unpublished paper entitled "Kinship and Politics in Pre-Modern and Non-Western Societies," has emphasized the different effects of these two types of kinship groups.

[12] Maine, *Ancient Law*, 99 (original italics).

[13] The foregoing comparison may appear to come strikingly close to the formulations of Maine (*ibid.*, 124–25) and Lewis H. Morgan (*Ancient Society* [New York 1877], 6–7)—formulations which have been criticized in recent years by anthropologists. See I. Schapera, *Government and Politics in Tribal Societies* (London 1956), 2–5. Despite the inadequacies of the conceptions of Maine and Morgan, especially with reference to their presumption of progress in human development, some distinction between primitive or traditional society, in which kinship and personal "status" play a predominant role, and modern territorial states, based on citizenship and contract, is today accepted by many social scientists. Indeed, it is paradoxical that while anthropologists have been attacking the Maine-Morgan dichotomy (by showing that all societies have a territorial element), sociologists and political scientists have been adopting the distinction from the works of Tönnies, Weber, Parsons, or Levy. E.g., see Fred W. Riggs, "Agraria and Industria—Toward a Typology of Comparative Administration," in William J. Siffin, ed.,

Toward the Comparative Study of Public Administration (Bloomington 1959), 28–30, 111.

[14] E.g., according to Evans-Pritchard, "We do not therefore say that a man is acting politically or otherwise, but that between local groups there are relations of a structural order that can be called political" (*The Nuer*, 264–65).

[15] See Talcott Parsons, *The Social System* (Glencoe, Ill., 1951), 65–7.

[16] Fred W. Riggs, "International Relations as a Prismatic System," in Knorr and Verba, eds., *The International System*, 149. Cf. Modelski, "Agraria and Industria," in *ibid.*, for a stimulating adaptation of Riggs's concepts.

[17] To be sure, it is easier to specify what actions are "political" in the twentieth-century world than it was for Evans-Pritchard among the Nuer. Nonetheless, as Karl Deutsch has remarked, the nation-state is itself "functionally diffuse," performing an extraordinary range of economic, social, and political functions. See "Towards Western European Integration: An Interim Assessment," *Journal of International Affairs*, XVI (1962), 95–6. Cf. Gabriel A. Almond, "Introduction," in Gabriel A. Almond and James S. Coleman, eds., *The Politics of the Developing Areas* (Princeton 1960), 11, 63.

"refracted" society, traditional societies are rarely totally "fused."[18]

Up to this point we have tried to show two things: first, that there is a striking similarity between some primitive political systems and the modern international system; and second, that one element of this similarity is the "functional diffuseness" of political units in both types of system. If this is so, one cannot employ the polar opposites of "primitive" and "modern" or "functionally diffuse" and "functionally specific" as the basis of a comparative analysis of primitive political systems. Because primitive political systems vary enormously, one must explicitly distinguish the particular *kind* of primitive society which is supposed to present the greatest similarity to world politics.

In order to compare primitive and international politics, therefore, one needs a classification which distinguishes primitive societies in terms of their political structure. Although the typologies of primitive political systems hitherto developed by anthropologists have been imperfect, it will be useful to accept provisionally the distinction between primitive peoples which have developed some form of governmental institutions and those which have generally been called "stateless societies."[19]

The following comparison will focus on primitive societies that lack formal governments. Such systems may be described as having "diffuse leadership," since individuals or groups have influence without formally institutionalized coercive authority. There may be a "titular chief" in these societies, but such an individual, even together with other influential men, does not act as a ruler. Since the modern world, as a political system, shares this structural characteristic of "statelessness," a résumé

of political life in primitive stateless societies will show the utility of comparing them to the international political system.

III. "Self-Help" and Violence in Primitive Stateless Societies

In stateless systems, disputes cannot be referred to an impartial government backed by a police force. The characteristic pattern of responding to criminal or civil wrongs is "self-help": the individual or group which feels injured considers himself or itself legitimately responsible for punishing a crime or penalizing a tort. Self-help in these circumstances involves two stages which appear to be directly comparable to the functions of adjudication and enforcement in modern legal systems. In either system, first it is necessary to determine that a wrong has occurred and that a particular individual or group will be punished in a particular way; second, the punishment or penalty for that wrong must be enforced or implemented.

In the simplest primitive societies, both stages are accomplished by the individual or family that has been wronged. For example, when a kinship group discovers that one of its members has been murdered, the guilty individual and his kinship group will be identified and a retaliatory killing (or other punishment) will be inflicted by the wronged group. As Barton indicated in his study of Philippine headhunters, such self-enforcement of legal penalties[20] raises a crucial problem among stateless primitive peoples. The kinship group which enforces the *lex talionis* by killing a murderer or one of his kin sees this act as not only necessary, but also legitimate. Although unrelated bystanders may accept this interpretation, since retaliatory killing is customary, the kinship group which is penalized may not consider the retaliation to be a legitimate punishment.[21] When this occurs, there is often a

---

[18] It is simply incorrect to assert that nonliterate peoples, however traditionally minded, were incapable of developing "functionally specific roles," "achievement norms of recruitment," or the "state" as a formal organization; each of these attributes, so readily described as "modern," can be found in societies which must be described as "primitive." For an example, see S. F. Nadel, *A Black Byzantium: The Kingdom of the Nupe in Nigeria* (London 1942). Cf. Riggs, "Agraria and Industria," 28. . . .

[19] See Fortes and Evans-Pritchard, *African Political Systems*, 5–23; John Middleton and David Tait, eds., *Tribes Without Rulers* (London 1958), 1–3; Lucy Mair, *Primitive Government* (Baltimore 1962), Part I, Schapera, *Government and Politics*, 63–4, 208–14; and Robert Lowie, *Social Organization* (New York 1948), Chap. 14. For a critique of the categories used by anthropologists, see Easton, "Political Anthropology," 210–26.

[20] It must be emphasized that the retaliation is *legal*, being sanctioned by customary law (or, in Weber's terms, "traditional legitimacy"). Cf. Mair, *Primitive Government*, 16–19; and A. R. Radcliffe-Brown, *Structure and Function in Primitive Society* (Glencoe, Ill., 1952), Chap. 12.

[21] See Barton, *The Kalingas*, 231. Note the parallel tendency in world politics: "One state's aggression is always another state's 'legitimate use of force to defend vital national interests'" (Inis L. Claude, Jr., "United Nations Use of Military Force," *Journal of Conflict Resolution*, VII [June 1963], 119).

tendency for crime and punishment to "escalate" into a more or less permanent relation of "feud" between the kinship groups involved.[22]

In feuds, violence usually takes the form of sporadic surprise attacks by individuals or small groups. Hence a condition of feud should not be equated too completely with what we call "war,"[23] rather, it is a condition of rivalry in which intermittent violence and aggression (e.g., seizure of property or person as well as retaliatory killing) appear legitimate to those who attack, and illegitimate to the victims. The similarity of this "state of feud" and a Hobbesian "state of nature" is obvious, with the important difference that kinship groups are often involved, instead of isolated individuals.

Although the notion of modern warfare cannot be accurately applied to all primitive intergroup fighting, primitive violence sometimes approximates a civilized war. The gradations of conflict arising out of self-help have been clarified by Tait and Middleton, who suggest that primitive feuds and wars be distinguished because only in the latter is there no obligation to attempt to settle the dispute.[24] They argue that within a restricted range (which varies from one primitive society to another) the

more or less permanent condition of feud rivalry is rendered unlikely, if not impossible, by the existence of close kinship ties and relationships of "administrative organization."

At this level there may be a duel or the requirement that ritual acts of atonement be performed, but prolonged group rivalry is unlikely since the individuals concerned are all members of a single "nuclear group" (which is, normally, a local community, a kinship group, or both). Within such a local or family unit, disputes culminating in violence are not self-perpetuating; as in modern states, a punishment or penalty "atones" for a crime and thereby completes the legal case.[25]

Outside of this range, punishment does not terminate the rivalry arising out of a dispute; although retaliatory violence tends to be self-perpetuating, Tait and Middleton suggest that there is a zone in which violence can be described as a feud because the opposed groups recognize an obligation to settle their dispute. In this range of social interaction there are normally procedures for arriving at a settlement. Hence, among the Nuer, the "leopard-skin chief" holds an office which serves the function of settling feuds on the basis of compensation.[26] The "go-between" among the Ifugao serves a similar function.[27]

This does not mean that such means of settling the feud are always successful, nor that the settlement is in fact permanent. On the contrary, Evans-Pritchard concludes: "Though the chief admonishes the relatives of the dead man at the ceremonies of settlement that the feud is ended and must not be renewed, Nuer know that 'a feud never ends'.... There is no frequent fighting or continuous unabated hostility, but the sore rankles and the feud, though formally concluded, may at any time break out again."[28] Hence the settlement of a feud amounts to a truce—one might say a treaty, given the impermanence of similar settlements in international politics—between rival groups. Such a settlement

[22] Cf. Barton, *The Half-Way Sun*, Chaps. 5 and 6. In some situations, however, a group may refrain from counterretaliation, either because the kinsman who was punished was offensive to his own kin or because the group lacks the power to react....

[23] Numelin argues that organized, continuous warfare of the type known to civilized man is practically unknown among primitive peoples (*The Beginnings of Diplomacy*, Chap. 2). Cf. Schapera, *Government and Politics*, 215, 219; and Melville J. Herskovits, *Cultural Anthropology* (New York 1955), 207–8.

[24] "Introduction," *Tribes Without Rulers*, 20–2. Cf. Radcliffe-Brown, *African Political Systems*, XX. A similar though not identical distinction is made by Barton, "Ifugao Law," 77–8. Kinds of violence in primitive society could also be distinguished in terms of the extent to which groups act as corporate units and the degree to which violence is continuous. In this sense, a true "war" would consist of more or less continuous hostilities between corporate groups, whereas "feuds," in the purest case, would be intermittent conflicts between individuals (albeit with the support of kinship groups). Although such an approach would take into consideration the fundamental issue raised by Rousseau's criticism of Hobbes's concept of a "state of war" (see *L'État de guerre*, in C. E. Vaughan, ed., *The Political Writings of Rousseau* [2 vols., Cambridge, Eng., 1915], I, 293–307), it raises theoretical questions which require a more exhaustive analysis than is here possible. For the present, therefore, it is useful to accept provisionally the distinction between feud and war as elaborated by anthropologists.

[25] Tait and Middleton, *Tribes Without Rulers*, 19–20. See Barton, "Ifugao Law," 14–15, and the example, 120–21.

[26] Evans-Pritchard, *The Nuer*, 152–54.

[27] Barton, *The Half-Way Sun*, 109–10, and the example described on 70 ff.

[28] *The Nuer*, 155. Cf. Barton, "Ifugao Law," 75: "Once started, a blood feud was well-nigh eternal (unless ended by a fusion of the families by means of marriage)."

may occur because feuding segments need to co-operate on other matters, but it cannot unite them into a harmonious unit without further steps, such as a marriage between the feuding families.[29]

Tait and Middleton use the term "jural community" to describe the unit within which disputes take the form of feuds to be settled by an established procedure.[30] Violence on this level tends to be limited in a way which presents very revealing similarities to procedures in international affairs: as with "limited war," there is a restriction on the means of violence used and the ends sought, and like some interstate treaties, each rival group is willing to end violence (if only temporarily) because of the need to cooperate with its rivals. Hence the settlement of a feud does not ordinarily preclude the recurrence of violence; as in international treaties, the parties are their own judges of the maintenance of the conditions of the peaceful settlement.[31]

The feuding condition is thus a relationship between rival groups in which violence is a latent but ever-present threat should disputes arise. War, as defined by Tait and Middleton, is a more extreme form of competition, since there is no obligation to settle conflict, however temporarily. Among many peoples with leaders instead of rulers and govern-ments, a distinction is made between those groups with whom violence is limited to feuding and those with whom there is a continuous condition of war. A given group is not bound by common procedures of dispute settlement with foreigners or with individuals from different parts (or "jural com-munities") of the same nation. For example, whereas conflicting groups from the same Nuer tribe could only be in a state of feud, individuals or groups from different Nuer tribes are always in a potential state of war with each other. When spatially or culturally distant groups are involved, violence is likely to emerge at any time, even in the absence of a formal dispute.[32]

Among stateless primitive peoples, therefore, social distance (which is highly correlated with geographical distance) decreases the likelihood that violence, should it occur, will be limited.[33] This spatial distinction between those who are "far" and those who are "near" tends to produce a series of concentric zones around each group in many primi-tive worlds.[34] Where such zones have been found, the specific boundaries of each region are often unclear. Thus there is considerable evidence that, for a member of many primitive societies without a government, the group or "political community" to which allegiance is owed varies, depending on the dispute in question.[35]

This characteristic is related to one of the fundamental differences between many primitive political systems and world politics—namely, the fusion of various levels of social intercourse which we are accustomed to distinguish. In modern life, one can speak of a distinction between the level of a society (normally organized as a nation-state), that of a local community, and that of a family. For the primitive, the family or kinship group may include all residents of a locality; even if it does not, the kinship group or locality will tend to have many of the functions of a modern society without having either the political structure or the unique claim to allegiance of the modern state. As a consequence, parallels drawn between primitive political systems and international politics, however useful they may be in other respects, must take into consideration differences in the scope and powers of units in the two kinds of systems.[36]

[29] See the example in Barton, *The Half-Way Sun*, 115.
[30] "The jural community . . . is the widest grouping within which there are a moral obligation and a means ultimately to settle disputes peaceably" (*Tribes Without Rulers*, 9).
[31] Cf. the rarity of the emergence of what has been called a "security community" in international politics. Karl Deutsch, *et al.*, *Political Community and the North Atlantic Area* (Princeton 1957), Chap. 1.
[32] Evans-Pritchard, *The Nuer*, 121–22. Cf. Lewis H. Morgan, *League of the Iroquois* (Rochester 1851), 73.

[33] The conquest of physical space by modern techno-logy has altered the character of "social distance" without destroying it. Today differences in the kind of political regime tend to have effects similar to those of geographical distance between primitive tribes; because of their political principles, Communist regimes are those farthest from the United States even when they are close to us in miles. Cf. the concepts of "structural distance" (Evans-Pritchard, *The Nuer*, 113 ff.) and "social distance" (Emory S. Bogar-dus, *Sociology* [4th edn., New York 1954]. 535–36).
[34] See the similar diagrams in Barton, *The Half-Way Sun*, 114, and Evans-Pritchard, *The Nuer*, 114. Note that Barton distinguishes a "neutral zone" between the "home region" and the zone of feuding.
[35] See Mair, *Primitive Government*, 46–8, 104–6.
[36] The problem of units and levels of analysis has had surprisingly little attention in recent theorizing on international politics. For exceptions, see Karl Deutsch, *Political Community at the International Level* (Garden City, N.Y., 1954); Waltz, *Man, the State, and War;* and

Despite these differences, however, there are some striking similarities between primitive stateless societies and international political systems with respect to the role of violence in intergroup conflict. In both, there is a range of social relationships which is relatively exempt from self-perpetuating violence; within the "nuclear groups" composing both systems, the procedures for settling disputes or atoning for crimes are terminal, at least in principle. In both types of systems, intermittent, violent conflict between nuclear groups can be temporarily settled without removing the potentiality of further attacks. Violence is justified in the eyes of the aggressive group because the legal system permits self-help as a means of enforcing one's rights. Since the punished group denies this justification, there is a tendency for a conflict to erupt into an exchange of hostilities, a tendency which is restrained between those groups which consider themselves to be similar or "near" each other. These similarities indicate that the analogy between primitive political systems without governments and international politics is not merely fanciful; both appear to belong to a general class of political systems in which self-help or violence is an accepted and legitimate mode of procedure.

IV. Order in Primitive Stateless Societies

In discussing the characteristics of violence in primitive societies which lack rulers, there has been an emphasis on the competitive relationship of opposed groups. When seen in this light, primitive society may seem to be a barely controlled anarchy in which security of life and limb is scarcely to be expected. Since this impression is inaccurate, it is of the greatest importance to emphasize the variety of political functions performed in primitive stateless societies.

Even if one disputes Barton's estimate that the life of the Philippine headhunter was more secure than that of a citizen in modern societies, it is undoubtedly true that, as he says, "a people having no vestige of constituted authority and therefore living in literal anarchy, [can] dwell in comparative peace and security of life and property."[37] Whatever the logical merits of Hobbes's conception of a "state of nature," it does not seem to follow, at least among primitive peoples, that the anarchy of social life without a government produces a violent war of all against all. Quite the contrary, it would appear that violence in such primitive societies often serves the function of maintaining law and order according to customary procedures.

The pacific functions of self-help can be clearly seen if one considers the circumstances in which violence does *not* arise out of conflict in a stateless primitive system. In the simplest of such societies, the necessities of cooperation tend to preclude violence within the family and locality, while the limitations of technology tend to restrict social intercourse to these relatively narrow groups; hence, among the technologically least developed primitives, feuding relations are rare and wars virtually unknown. In this kind of system, self-help and retaliation function effectively as the only forcible means for punishing crimes because social opprobrium is, in itself, a strong punishment.[38]

Among primitive peoples with a more complex stateless system, such as the Ifugao studied by Barton, there are many occasions for feuding or warfare, but actual violence does not arise out of every dispute. The limitation of violence between potentially feuding groups is related to the institutions which serve the function of settling feuds. The Ifugao "go-between" not only acts as a mediator in feuds which have caused deaths on either side, but also acts prior to the eruption of violence in an effort to prevent such killings. In negotiating disputes which have not yet led to killing, he emphasizes at every stage the dangers implicit in open feuding; by describing these dangers in detail, the "go-between" (with the backing of his own family and the local community at large) attempts to deter an attack by either of the opposed families.

Institutionalized pressures to prevent the outbreak of violence also occur within the rival groups

J. David Singer, "The Level-of-Analysis Problem in International Relations," in Knorr and Verba, eds., *The International System*, 77–92. Of particular importance is the relationship between a cultural community or "people" and organized "political communities." Cf. Gabriel A. Almond, "Comparative Political Systems," *Journal of Politics*, XVIII (August 1956), 393–408.

[37] Barton, "Ifugao Law," 6. Barton calculated the annual death rate from head-hunting at 2 per 1000 during a period of "abnormally high" activity (*The Half-Way Sun*, 200). In the United States, accidental deaths from all causes during 1963 were at the rate of 5.3 per 1000.

[38] E.g., A. R. [Radcliffe-] Brown, *The Andaman Islanders* (Cambridge, Eng., 1922), 48–52, 84–7.

themselves. Thus, while the closest relatives of an offended individual may insist on the need for killing as a punishment for such wrongs as adultery, sorcery, or refusal to pay debts, more wealthy relations (who, according to Ifugao custom, may be more vulnerable to counterretaliation than the killer should a feud occur) frequently counsel moderation.[39] Since retaliation is an action decided upon by the family as a unit, and since feuds are difficult to settle, "the accuser is usually not overanxious to kill the accused."[40]

Whether originating with a "go-between" or a member of a wronged group, advice that open feuding be avoided, or at least limited, is characteristic of a phenomenon which has recently received extensive attention in foreign affairs—namely, deterrence. Although it has sometimes been assumed that deterrence requires a rational calculation of the consequences of an attack, deterrence and self-help among primitive peoples do not presuppose a conscious strategic calculation of the type formalized by game theorists.[41] Thus the possibility of violent counterretaliation may, in itself and without further calculation, stabilize rivalries and limit conflicts when there is no governmental arbiter to enforce law and order.

In order to avoid an overemphasis on either the stability produced by deterrence or the violence resulting from self-help, it will be useful to view both as necessarily related consequences of a political system which lacks authoritative governmental institutions. In political regimes of this kind, self-help and deterrence have the function of regulating bargaining between opposed groups, but they also serve as a means of organizing social intercourse in a predictable fashion. This latter function is especially important, though it tends to be overlooked in analyses of deterrence from the standpoint of a theory of strategy.

[39] On the characteristics of self-help and retaliation among the Ifugao, see Barton, *The Half-Way Sun*, Chaps. 3, 5, and 6; and "Ifugao Law," 75–87, 92–5, 99–109.

[40] *Ibid.*, 95. Compare the Cuban crisis of October 1962.

[41] Sophisticated students of strategy have never assumed, of course, that rivals can deter each other only if their calculations are formulated in terms of game theory. Cf. Thomas Schelling's analogy of deterring a child, *The Strategy of Conflict* (Cambridge, Mass., 1960), 11. Nonetheless, popular analyses often assert that deterrence implies—and requires—rational calculation on both sides. E.g., Seymour Melman, *The Peace Race* (New York 1961), 22.

Retaliation by an offended group, both as a means of deterring wrongs and as a method of punishment, can therefore be studied in terms of its social consequences. As Barton points out with reference to headhunting, these consequences are multiple, and are sometimes not consciously perceived by those concerned.[42] Consciously, retaliation is a means of maintaining the well-being of an offended group and of responding to a specific wrong. Unintentionally or unconsciously, self-help serves to preserve and unite a group which has been threatened by another, to fix responsibility for wrongs, and thus to maintain a legal order. For a specific individual who executes retaliation, the dangerous exploits required for self-help may consciously be a means of gaining glory and influence as well as a means of preserving his legal rights.[43] Since all of these functions have analogies in the self-help conducted by sovereign nation-states, it would be unwise to see in retaliation and deterrence merely a means of maximizing the advantage gained by one of two or more rivals.

The essential character of both self-help and deterrence in primitive society is thus political in the broadest sense: when there is no government, retaliation and the threat of violence serve to unite social groups and maintain legal or moral criteria of right and wrong. This use of might to make right seems repugnant to civilized men, for it has been largely (though not completely) superseded within modern society; nonetheless, such a procedure is consonant with a particular kind of social order and cannot be dismissed as having been surpassed with the formation of the first political society. Primitive legal procedures may largely be confined to the international political system today, but on this level the uncivilized notions of self-help and retaliation continue to play a decisive role.[44]

Indeed, the example of primitive societies which have successfully developed governmental institutions shows how difficult it is to substitute hierarchical legal procedures for self-help. Even

[42] For the distinction between latent and manifest functions which is here implied, see Marion J. Levy, Jr., *The Structure of Society* (Princeton 1952), 83–5. Cf. Barton, *The Half-Way Sun*, 196–7.

[43] *Ibid.* Barton also notes that headhunting served the latent function of providing "relief from the monotony of daily life."

[44] Cf. Aristotle, *Nicomachean Ethics*, V.1130^{b}30–1134^{a}15.

among peoples like the Alur, who are ruled by chiefs, a significant category of wrongs are punished, at least in the first instance, by retaliation on the part of the offended group.[45] Only if the consequences of retaliation and counterretaliation threaten the security of innocent bystanders do the chiefs intervene, making the conflict a matter of "public law" punishable by an authority acting in the name of the tribe as a whole. In this eventuality, punishment may be meted out impartially to both parties to a feud; the creation of specifically governmental institutions represents a departure from the principle of self-help, and requires a minimal awareness that there is an organized community at a higher level than that of the contending groups.[46]

V. International Politics as a Primitive, Stateless System

The foregoing analysis has attempted to show how self-help, retaliation, and deterrence can be viewed as a characteristically primitive approach to law and order. Through this focus on stateless primitive peoples, the reliance upon self-help and deterrence in international relations appears to be evidence that the world forms a political system that is in many respects similar to primitive systems. Although it is often argued that international law and politics are *sui generis*,[47] the utility of a comparison between international affairs and stateless primitive societies is shown by two characteristic similarities: first, the relation of law to violence as a means of organizing a coherent social system; and second, the relationship of custom to rivalry and bargaining as means of making and applying known rules.[48]

Although it is fashionable to describe inter-national relations as a lawless anarchy,[49] and to admit that international law exists only on condition that it be called "weak" law,[50] these habitual opinions must be questioned. It is true that the international system permits and even sanctions a considerable amount of violence and bloodshed; but, as has been seen, there is a class of stateless political systems which have this characteristic because they depend upon self-help for the enforcement of law. In such systems law and violence are related in a way that is quite different from the internal political order under which civilized man is accustomed to live; if we speak of international "anarchy," it would be well to bear in mind that it is an "ordered anarchy."

To prove that international law is not necessarily "weak," one need only consider the functions of law in a political system. Hoffmann has suggested that any legal order has three functions: it should produce "security," "satisfaction," and "flexibility."[51] According to these criteria, a legal system dependent upon the self-enforcement of rights by autonomous groups (be they families or nation-states) is "strong" in all three respects.

Most obviously, "flexibility" is assured in a system which recognizes any change in power; to the extent that might makes right, changes in might produce changes in right. It may be somewhat less evident that international law produces a "satisfactory" solution for disputes, yet this is on the whole true because of the admitted impossibility of reversing the verdict of brute force.[52] And, finally, the stateless international system even produces a modicum of security, most especially through deterrence based upon a mutual recognition that rival nations will both be harmed (if not destroyed) by the use of their legitimate right to self-help. In

[45] Aidan W. Southall, *Alur Society*, (Cambridge Eng., n.d.), 144. See also 122–36, 160–65.

[46] *Ibid.*, 144–46, 23–4, 237–39.

[47] E.g., Stanley Hoffmann, "International Systems and International Law," in Knorr and Verba, eds., *The International System*, 205.

[48] The second of these characteristics is concerned, speaking crudely, with the relationship between what Almond has called the "political functions" of rule-making, rule application, and interest articulation, while the first corresponds roughly to his functions of interest aggregation and rule adjudication. The last of these functions, in a stateless system, should really be spoken of as rule enforcement, for obvious reasons. Cf. "Introduction," in Almond and Coleman, eds., *The Politics of the Developing Areas*, 17; and see note 82 below.

[49] Cf. Waltz, *Man, the State, and War*, Chaps. 6 and 7. While the present essay is in complete agreement with Waltz's major theme (i.e., that war is a necessary consequence of the state system, since "in anarchy there is no automatic harmony"), his emphasis on the problem of war tends to understate the elements of legality and order in world politics.

[50] E.g., Hoffmann, "International Systems and International Law," 206–7.

[51] *Ibid.*, 212.

[52] Although the "satisfaction" with defeat in war may be of short duration, this is not a necessary consequence of military defeat (as the pro-Western attitude of West Germany and Japan after World War II indicates). The limited durability of "satisfactory" settlements will be discussed below.

this respect it is worth emphasizing that the nuclear age, with its awesome potentialities for destruction, has also seen a corresponding increase in the un-willingness of powerful nation-states to resort to overt war.[53]

To reveal more clearly the orderly (if violent) aspects of a stateless international system, several elements of the relationship between force and law need to be spelled out in greater detail. As in primitive stateless societies, not only does violence erupt intermittently from a continuing condition of poten-tial feud or war between autonomous groups; cooperation also occurs sporadically. While such cooperation is sometimes limited to actions which prepare for or prosecute warfare (as in most alliances), the members of the interstate system have also been capable of making mutually binding cooperative decisions in *ad hoc* multilateral conferences.[54] The Concert of Europe provides a more institutionalized example of such intermittent structures, which act as a kind of temporary "government" while pre-serving the sovereignty of the major states in the international system.[55]

This type of cooperative decision-making, subject to veto by a participating state, must be seen as a feasible—if obviously limited—method of procedure; it is present not only in *ad hoc* bilateral or multilateral meetings, but also in the continuously functioning international organizations (the League of Nations and the UN) which have been developed in this century.[56] It should also be noted that the

emergence of so-called "functional" organizations represents a trend toward continuously functioning institutions capable of limited but very real coopera-tion in the international political system.[57]

The limitations as well as the importance of both violence and cooperation in world politics must therefore be equally emphasized in any total assessment of the international system. In so doing, the comparison with stateless primitive peoples serves the useful purpose of identifying the characteristic properties of a political system in which law is sanctioned by self-help. As among the primitives, retaliation is an acceptable means of righting a wrong, though it is true that civilized nations regard strict retaliation—"an eye for an eye"—as a more extreme recourse than do savage peoples.[58] As among state-less primitives, neutrality is possible, and non-involved groups often attempt to mediate conflict and induce rivals to cease fighting. As among stateless primitives, finally, the very possibility that conflict may escalate serves to deter violence on some occa-sions.[59] Hence the relation of law to force in the multistate system, like the "ordered anarchy" of primitive societies without governments, is derived from the lack of authoritative political institutions.

When we turn more directly to the decision-making process—the second characteristic mentioned above—it may be recalled that in many primitive political systems, especially those lacking govern-mental institutions, custom and bargaining are related in a crucial way, since they are the only

[53] Since World War II there have been numerous international incidents which, under prenuclear conditions, would probably have resulted in open warfare. Cf. Herman Kahn, "The Arms Race and Some of Its Hazards," in Donald G. Brennan, ed., *Arms Control, Disarmament, and National Security* (New York 1961), 93 ff. On the security offered by the "impermeable" nation-state before the development of nuclear weapons, see John H. Herz, *International Politics in the Atomic Age* (New York 1959), Part 1.

[54] Most notably, of course, in peace conferences terminating major wars.

[55] On the Concert of Europe, see Richard N. Rose-crance, *Action and Reaction in World Politics* (Boston 1963), Chap. 4, and the references there cited. Compare the specialized, intermittent political agencies in many stateless primitive societies: Robert H. Lowie, "Some Aspects of Political Organization Among American Aborigines," *Journal of the Royal Anthropological Institute*, LXXVII (1948), 17–18; and Radcliffe-Brown, *African Political Systems*, xix.

[56] Note the similarity between the Iroquois Con-federacy, which could act as a unit only if a decision was

unanimous, and the UN Security Council. See Morgan, *League of the Iroquois*, 111–14; and Inis L. Claude, Jr., *Swords into Plowshares* (2nd edn., New York 1959), Chap. 8.

[57] Cf. the limited but continuous role of the *pangats* and "pact-holders" among the Kalinga, which Barton contrasts with the intermittent action of the Ifugao "go-betweens" and "trading partners" (*The Kalingas*, 144–46). On the question of the "continuity" or "contingency" of political structures, see Easton, "Political Anthropology," 235–38, 245–46.

[58] Henry S. Maine, *International Law* (New York 1888), 174–75. Primitive peoples do not always exact strict retaliation, however; the institution of a "weregild" or payment in lieu of retaliation is paralleled in international politics by reparations and other penalties exacted in the negotiation of peace treaties. Also, compare Morton A. Kaplan, "The Strategy of Limited Retaliation," Policy Memorandum No. 19 (Princeton, Center of International Studies, 1959), and, more generally, recent strategic discussions of "graduated deterrence"—e.g., Henry A. Kissinger, *The Necessity for Choice* (New York 1961), 65–70.

[59] Cf. Schelling, *The Strategy of Conflict*, Chap. 8.

methods for establishing enforceable rules. The same can be said of the international political system, for it too lacks an authoritative legislature or an all-powerful executive. International law can be said to be created in two major ways: a practice or rule either becomes a custom, having been followed for a considerable time, or it is adopted by mutual consent, as binding specific groups under particular circumstances. While the second of these legislative methods is relatively unambiguous to the extent that it produces formal treaties and agreements, the first produces customary law slowly and imperceptibly, so that in periods of rapid change one may wonder if any such law really exists. Over time, nonetheless, specific legal rules have been adopted and accepted as valid by the nation-states composing the modern international system.[60]

At any moment of time, international law seems to be chaotic and uncertain; "double standards" often appear to bind weak or law-abiding states, while permitting the ruthless or strong to satisfy their demands with impunity.[61] But when a longer-range view is taken and the world is considered as a stateless political system in which self-help is a legitimate means of legal procedure, disputes over the content of international law (like disputes over the legitimacy of each killing in a primitive feud) become a predictable consequence of the system's structure. As the world is now organized, international law almost requires conflict concerning the substantive provisions relating to a given dispute, and warfare is a legal means of bargaining prior to the conclusion of more of less temporary settlements.[62]

One peculiar characteristic of laws in a stateless political system is thus the legitimization of dispute concerning the application of legal rights to particular circumstances. While it is usual in this context to emphasize the relationship of force to law (by pointing out that "might makes right" in anarchy), the frequency and necessity of disputes over the substance of rights have another consequence: the primacy of political rivalry. Within a society with a government, men whose interests conflict must channel their demands through a specific institutional structure, ultimately recognizing (in principle) the legitimacy of political attitudes which have been sanctioned by governmental decision.[63]

In international politics, this relatively terminal character of intra-state political decisions is often lacking; the policies of one's rivals need not be legitimized even by victory in warfare. In a sense, therefore, might does *not* make right in international politics (as, indeed, the French insisted after 1871 and the Germans after 1918). Like primitive feuds, international disputes are only temporarily settled; a settlement which precludes the possibility of further conflict is rare.[64] This means that political differences, and the interests upon which these differences are based, are often more visible in world politics than in intra-state politics. Conflicting

[60] On the character of international law and its sources, see James L. Brierly, *The Law of Nations* (4th edn., London 1949), 1–91, 229–36; Percy E. Corbett, *Law and Society in the Relations of States* (New York 1951), 3–52; and Morton A. Kaplan and Nicholas de B. Katzenbach, *The Political Foundations of International Law* (New York 1961), Chap. 9. Some observers of international relations, following John Austin's legal theory, have doubted that a system without a single sovereign authority could have "true" law. For a criticism of this application of Austin's view, see Maine, *International Law*, 47–51.

[61] William Foltz has pointed out to me that there is also a parallel "reverse double standard" in both primitive and international systems; weak and unimportant groups are often permitted actions which major groups would not commit (or which would be strongly criticized if committed). . . .

[62] From the point of view of a systematic analysis, law

need not be a "good." Indeed, law need not produce peaceful "order," though as civilized men we infer from our political experience that this *should* be so. Hence authorities on international law often feel compelled to go beyond mere restatements of accepted legal principles; the international law texts, long an important method of codifying customary international law, are frequently animated by a desire for reform. Cf. Maine, *International Law*, Lectures I, XII, *et passim*. Unlike the sphere of domestic politics, in which relativism sometimes seems tenable to scholars, international law and politics are difficult to treat in a wholly positivist fashion without thereby accepting as justifiable a condition of legal self-help and war which civilized men tend to reject as barbarous, if not unjust. Hence world politics is perhaps *the* area in which it is most evident that satisfactory political theory cannot divorce objectivity (and especially freedom from partisanship) from the quest for standards of justice.

[63] But note that, even in domestic politics, the legitimacy of governmental decisions may be challenged by those who are willing to be "bellicose." Cf. Bertrand de Jouvenel, *The Pure Theory of Politics* (New Haven 1963), 180 ff.

[64] For the prerequisites for these rare cases, see the study cited in note 31. Note the function of "marriage" (between representatives of rival kinship groups in primitive societies and between ruling families in the earlier period of modern state system) as a means of formalizing such a settlement.

demands for the satisfaction of the desires of one's own group—politics and rivalry—are therefore the prime factors in international relations.[65]

This primacy of political conflict in world affairs is especially important because of a further similarity between primitive and international politics. Just as some stateless primitive societies are differentiated into spatial "zones" of increasing opposition, so the world can be divided into areas which are politically "far" from each other.[66] Here again, a characteristic of world politics which often appears to be *sui generis* can be understood more broadly in the context of a comparison between primitive and international politics.

VI. Some Differences Between Primitive and International Political Systems

In arguing that stateless primitive political systems resemble the international political system in many ways, the search for analogies should not obscure the massive differences which must have been only too easily noticed by the reader. By specifying some of these differences, however, it will be possible to distinguish those aspects in which world politics is unique from those that are due to the absence of a formally constituted world government. In particular, there are two general differences between primitive and international politics which will make it easier to see the limits of the structural similarity between the two. It will be necessary to consider, first, the role of political culture, and second, the impact of change.

Although it is usually assumed that the beliefs, manners, and customs of nonliterate peoples are homogeneous, many primitive societies are composed of heterogeneous ethnic stocks; indeed, such heterogeneity is particularly important, for it appears to be related to the emergence of governmental institutions, at least among many African peoples.[67] Nonetheless, there is a marked tendency toward cultural homogeneity in primitive stateless societies,

since most individuals accept without question the established way of life.[68] Although the application of traditional rules to specific cases may be and frequently is disputed, the relative stability of culture limits the kinds of change occurring in most primitive systems.[69]

In contrast, the international political system currently includes radically different political cultures. As Almond has shown, national political systems which face the task of integrating different political cultures are subject to strains that are absent in more homogeneous societies; *a fortiori*, this problem is even greater in a system which permits many antagonistic political cultures to organize themselves into autonomous nation-states.[70] In general, therefore, it could be argued that self-help and structural decentralization tend to produce a greater degree of instability in world politics than in most primitive stateless societies.[71]

An additional feature compounds this problem. The historical development of Western civilization, as it has increased man's control over nature and spread the effects of modern science throughout the world, has produced particularly sharp differences between political cultures, at the same time that it has brought these cultures into closer contact than was possible before the advent of modern technology. And, simultaneously with this intensification of the contact between different cultures, it has become apparent that technologically advanced societies are capable of what seems to be virtually infinite material progress, so that the most powerful nations can continuously increase their technological superiority over "backward" or "underdeveloped" states.

The main consequence of the interaction of modern, scientific technology upon cultural differences has been extraordinarily rapid change in world politics, of which the great increase in the number of

---

[65] Cf. the "principle of political primacy" emphasized by Robert E. Osgood, *Limited War* (Chicago 1957), 13–15.

[66] "Blocs" and regional systems are, of course, ready examples. On the relationship between the global system and regional systems in international politics, see George Liska, *Nations in Alliance* (Baltimore 1962), 19–20, 22–4, 259–62.

[67] See Schapera, *Government and Politics*, 124–25; and Mair, *Primitive Government*, Chap. 5.

[68] Cf. Fortes and Evans-Pritchard, *African Political Systems*, 9–10.

[69] Hence there may be disputes concerning the power and influence of opposed groups, but these conflicts are rarely ideological in character.

[70] See Almond, "Comparative Political Systems," 400–2. Cf. the importance of the nationality problem in the U.S.S.R.

[71] Note, however, that many primitive societies are not as stable and unchanging as is often believed. E.g., see Southall, *Alur Society*, 224–27, 236, *et passim*; and J. A. Barnes, *Politics in a Changing Society* (London 1954), Chap. 2.

nation-states is out the most superficial index.[72] The stateless structure of a primitive political system may be tolerably stable, despite the reliance upon self-help enforcement; a similar structure, in the changing context of international politics, may well lead to chaos. Even in a primitive world, the contact of a more "advanced" people with a society without governmental institutions has often produced a rapid domination of the latter by the former.[73] It is all the more to be expected, therefore, that the present structure of the international system is essentially transitional, and that quite considerable changes must be expected in the next century.

VII. Conclusion: Directions for Research

The reader may well wonder, at this point, whether the foregoing analysis has any theoretical significance: can the contrast between primitive stateless societies and the interstate system provide any substantive insights otherwise missed by students of world politics? The relative novelty of the comparison here proposed is not, in itself, sufficient justification of the endeavor. Almost eighty years ago, Henry Sumner Maine saw this parallel when he remarked: "Ancient jurisprudence, if perhaps a deceptive comparison may be employed, may be likened to international Law, filling nothing, as it were, except the interstices between the great groups which are the atoms of society."[74] While the parallels noted above may be nothing but a "deceptive comparison," Maine's formulation itself suggests the important element of similarity which promises to clarify our understanding of world politics.

Although both primitive and international politics can take place in "the interstices between the great groups which are the atoms of society," the "groups" which are "atoms" are not always the same. While this has obviously been true in international affairs at different times and places, it is no less so in primitive societies. As a result, there are an immense variety of types of primitive political systems, just as there have been widely different international political systems.

The question, then, is whether there are different patterns of groups—or different political structures—which can be identified as typical alternatives among primitive peoples; if this is the case, then perhaps the types of primitive political systems have similarities to the possible types of international political systems.

To date, there have been two major approaches to the construction of typologies of international systems: on the one hand, models of the international system have been defined in terms of behavioral rules,[75] and on the other, types of international systems have been distinguished on the basis of historical evidence.[76] Without entering into methodological discussion, it can be wondered whether both of these approaches have shortcomings: the former tends to be *ad hoc*, and the latter to be restricted to the periods one studies.[77] Given the orientation of recent theoretical efforts in political science, the construction of a structural typology of political systems would seem to be a useful supplement to other approaches.[78]

Because such a typology appears to derive from "structural-functional" theory, developed especially by some British anthropologists,[79] it would be well to specify more precisely what is meant by "structure," and why it is emphasized rather than "function." As Marion J. Levy, Jr., has suggested, the term "structure," in its most general sense, "means a pattern, i.e., an observable uniformity, of action or operation."[80] Levy adds: "Functions refer to what is done, and structure refers to how (including in the meaning of 'how' the concept 'by what')

---

[72] On the distinction between "stable" and "revolutionary" international systems, see Hoffmann, "International Systems and International Law," 208–11. . . .

[73] Southall, *Alur Society*, 229–34.

[74] *Ancient Law*, 161.

[75] The most well-known example of this approach is, of course, Morton A. Kaplan's *System and Process in International Politics* (New York 1957), Chap. 2.

[76] See Hoffmann, "International Systems and International Law," 215–33; and Rosecrance, *Action and Reaction in World Politics*, esp. Part II.

[77] Cf. *ibid.*, Chap. I, and Stanley Hoffman, ed., *Contemporary Theory in International Relations* (Englewood Cliffs, N.J., 1960), 40–50, 174–84.

[78] It seems, for example, that the distinction between stateless systems and fully developed states is insufficient because it ignores an intermediary type which Southall called "pyramidal" or "segmentary states." In such systems, of which feudalism is but one example, there are a multiplicity of levels of authority, the most comprehensive of which is "paramount" without being "sovereign." See Southall, *Alur Society*, 241–60; and Barnes, *Politics in a Changing Society*, 47–53.

[79] E.g., see Radcliffe-Brown, *Structure and Function in Primitive Society*, esp. Introduction and Chap. 10.

[80] Levy, *The Structure of Society*, 57.

what is done is done. One refers to the results of actions (or empirical phenomena in general), and the other to the forms or patterns of action (or empirical phenomena in general).... The same empirical phenomenon may be an example of either a function or a structure, depending upon the point from which it is viewed.... An interest in the results of operation of a unit focuses attention on the concept of function. An interest in the patterns of operation focuses attention on structure. An interest in the results of operation of a unit and the implications of those results focuses attention on both function and structure since the implications that can be studied scientifically lie in their effects on observable uniformities."[81] As is evident, from the point of view of sociological theory it is impossible to develop a general theory which emphasizes solely either "structure" or "function." Nonetheless there are good reasons for suggesting that a structural typology precede refined "functional" analysis.

This advantage can best be shown by referring to Alger's analysis of the similarities between intra-national and international politics. Although Alger suggests that Almond's list of political functions is useful for such a comparison,[82] when he turns to the parallel between primitive and international politics, he emphasizes three factors, derived from Easton's work, which are ultimately structural in character: namely, the differentiation of political roles and the contingency or continuity of their operation, the specialization of roles which control physical force, and the character of overlapping memberships.

The reason why Almond's political functions are not immediately useful in comparing primitive and international politics is not hard to see. As Alger remarked, "A headman of a primitive society may perform intermittently as interest articulator, aggregator, and rule-maker."[83] If Almond's functions are not performed by specialized individuals in many primitive societies, concentration on these functions may only emphasize the "diffuseness" of roles, without indicating the different patterns which emerge in different systems. It is necessary to see in what kinds of situations different individuals act in different ways; functional categories derived from "modern" complex political systems may be simply inappropriate for the study of primitive societies.[84]

As Almond himself was at pains to point out, "The functional categories which one employs have to be adapted to the particular aspect of the political system with which one is concerned."[85] Since a comparison of primitive and international political systems must identify the "particular aspects" of each type of system which are analogous, the use of functional categories would seem to be unpromising at the outset. In contrast, the use of a structural typology of political systems, if it proves possible to define kinds of political structures which exist in *both* primitive and international politics, has a double advantage: this approach should permit one to see not only the similarities between systems, but also the sources of the differences between modern international politics and primitive political systems.[86]

Finally, it should be pointed out that research in this direction, while it appears to utilize recent

---

[81] *Ibid.*, 60–62.

[82] Alger emphasizes the similarities between international politics and the internal politics of both developing nations and primitive societies ("Comparison of Intranational and International Politics," 410–19). He suggests that the "input functions" ("political socialization and recruitment, interest articulation, interest aggregation, and political communication") are more relevant than the "output functions" ("rule-making, rule application, and rule adjudication"). Cf. Almond and Coleman, eds., *The Politics of the Developing Areas*, 16–17; and note 48 above.

[83] Alger, "Comparison of Intranational and International Politics," 412. Cf. Almond and Coleman, eds., 19.

[84] An additional critique which might be made is that the Almond functions imply a political teleology: since traditional, "diffuse" systems tend to be replaced by modern, "functionally specific" ones, analysis may be oriented toward finding those activities which favor the trend toward "modernity." Cf. Almond and Coleman, eds., 16–7....

[85] *Ibid.*, 16.

[86] In addition, an emphasis on structure should permit one to handle more explicitly the troublesome problem of defining the "actors" in the international system. Cf. Arnold Wolfers, "The Actors in International Politics," *Discord and Collaboration* (Baltimore 1962), 3–24. Alger seems to adopt the so-called "individuals-as-actors" approach, which raises some severe methodological problems; for example, he suggests (in applying Easton's work) that "international systems would tend to be distributed toward the contingent end of the continuum" which ranges from "contingent" to "continuous." This is a questionable conclusion if one considers that not only international organizations, but specific roles within national governments (e.g., "foreign minister"), function continuously in the modern state system. Cf. Alger, "Comparison of Intranational and International Politics," esp. 416, with the discussion above, p. 610....

theoretical approaches derived from anthropology, sociology, and behavioral political science, is not divorced from the problems posed by traditional political philosophy. By emphasizing the existence of a class of social systems in which no formally instituted governments are established, the relevance of the notion of a "state of nature" to international politics can be shown to be more than a mere by-product of "normative" theories developed by political philosophers.

At the same time, however, since the apparent "anarchy" of a "state of nature" is found in primitive societies, analysis of the various kinds of primitive political structures suggests that some of the implications of the "state of nature" doctrine in political philosophy are questionable. In particular, the phenomenon of stateless societies implies that even if one can speak of a "state of nature," such a condition cannot be used to prove that man is by nature an asocial being; as a result, the "state of nature" (whether in primitive or international politics) need not be considered the *natural* human condition, as opposed to the purely *conventional* political community or state. Hence the comparison of international and intranational politics—and, more specifically, the analysis of similarities between primitive and world politics—among other things leads us to a reassessment of the sufficiency of the theory of politics established by Hobbes and elaborated by Locke, Rousseau, and Kant.[87]

[87] For a sophisticated attempt to show the continuing relevance of the philosophy of Rousseau as the basis of a theory of international politics, see Stanley Hoffmann, "Rousseau on War and Peace," *American Political Science Review*, LVII (June 1963), 317–33. Cf. Kenneth N. Waltz, "Kant, Liberalism, and War," *ibid.*, LVI (June 1962), 331–40.

12. Toward a Model of Competitive International Politics*

Bruce M. Russett does not use the same method to generate insights into the international system here as he did in Selection 10. Rather he follows the example of the previous selection and compares international structures and processes with other types of political systems. Here, however, modern national systems with a developed form of party competition serve as the focus of comparison. While the reader may question the wisdom of restricting the comparison to two-party systems rather than extending it to include multiparty systems, he is bound to be again impressed by the thought that world politics is not totally different from other, less encompassing types of politics. In addition, in evaluating the suitability of the two-party comparison, the reader will extend and deepen his comprehension of the international system. [*Reprinted from* Journal of Politics, *XXV* (*May 1963*), *226–47, by permission of the author and the publisher.*]

I. A Two-Party System?

A number of attempts have been made in recent years to construct rigorous models of the international system, among which some of the more precise are various models of international equilibrium and other examples of systems analysis.[1] Most of these efforts have been directed to the application of models more or less directly derived from economics or the natural sciences.

It may be, however, that we have overlooked a number of possibilities from closely related aspects of political science. For example, there is a substantial body of theory about competitive national political systems which might profitably be applied to international politics. The relevance may not be immediately apparent. National systems are characterized by institutions empowered to make, execute, and interpret decisions binding on their citizens. Though these institutions are not entirely absent from the international system, they are undeniably weak. But in any society cooperative behavior results not only from the actual or potential threat of sanctions applied by authority. Nor would such institutions guarantee cooperation. In their comparative study of political integration Karl W. Deutsch *et al.* found the establishment of common governmental institutions and a "monopoly of violence" often more of a hindrance than a help.[2] Of the wars between 1820 and 1949 involving more than 31,000 casualties, at least half were internal rather than international.[3]

Rules of order are often followed, in both local and international society, because of social pressures.

* This article is in the nature of a working paper, part of an intensive study of politics in the United Nations. I am indebted to James D. Barber, Talcott Parsons, and Richard Van Wagenen for comments, and to the Social Science Research Council for financial support.

[1] See especially George Liska, *International Equilibrium* (Cambridge, Mass., 1957) and Morton Kaplan, *System and Process in International Politics* (New York, 1957).

[2] *Political Community and the North Atlantic Area* (Princeton, 1957), p. 105.

[3] See Lewis F. Richardson, *Statistics of Deadly Quarrels* (Chicago and Pittsburgh, 1960), pp. 32–50.

A reputation for morality and law-abidingness can be useful, and the contrary reputation damaging. In this respect the United States has an important asset not lightly to be squandered, for with most of its international audience America's word carries a certain presumption of sincerity. Similarly, rules may be followed to avoid reciprocal non-compliance by others with respect to common interests. Despite their hostility, the United States and the Soviet Union regularly avoid certain forms of threatening behavior (sinking "spying" trawlers, "spoofing" each others radar). On another level, interference with the regular channels of international commerce and postal exchange is generally avoided even though short-term gains might accrue from interference. If particular interference were countered from many sources, all parties might well lose.

Nor is even the threat of reciprocal sanctions all that restrains an actor. Cooperative behavior results from common values, and there are values, such as economic development, political autonomy, and equality, which seem to be held by virtually all governments (see below). Furthermore, what Talcott Parsons calls "an underlying structure of cross-cutting solidarities" produces restraint.[4] Even some firmly anti-Communist governments in Latin America refuse to apply sanctions to Castro—in part because of their established cultural and political ties with Cuba which cut across the Communist—non-Communist dimension. We shall discuss these and other sources of restraint in the following pages. It simply is erroneous to think of international politics as anarchic, chaotic, and utterly unlike national politics. Let us examine some of the similarities, as well as some differences, between national competitive systems and the international system.[5]

As a working hypothesis, consider the world as a political system in which the two power blocs, Communist and Western, are analogous to two parties which compete for the favor of the uncommitted "voters." Each party, including a leader and loyal party members or "partisans," tries to convince voters that it is best able to fulfill their needs and respect their normative prescriptions. At this stage of the analysis we shall consider a voter, whether neutral or partisan, as equivalent to the government of a particular nation. The United Nations is, obviously, a major arena of the competition—it is the principal instance where the parties do vie for votes, and where the one-nation-one-vote principle holds. In fact, by providing an arena where the parties must participate in a continuing electoral competition for the allegiance of the neutrals the United Nations performs a major function in preserving the system's stability. But the United Nations is not the only arena for this kind of competition. By stretching the analogy somewhat we may extend the case to the competition for foreign military bases and allies. Those readers who are disturbed by the one-nation-one-vote simplification as applied to conditions outside the United Nations may imagine some kind of weighted "voting" system.

Note that we speak of a two-party rather than a multi-party system. While there may be some objection, it would seem that on the whole the present distribution of power is bi-polar, albeit in a "loose" rather than a "tight" bi-polar system.[6] Half of the world's independent political entities are at present militarily allied with one or the other of the two great blocs. More important, members of these alliances together account for over 70 per cent of the world's population and nearly 90 per cent of its income. Furthermore, as Thomas Hovet, Jr. has pointed out, even the "neutrals" do not form any really coherent grouping.[7] According to their voting records in the United Nations, they must be subdivided into "pro-Western," "pro-Eastern" and "neutral" neutrals. And if one goes on to distinguish different voting patterns on various issues, even the last subdivision loses much of its meaning.[8] On this

[4] "Order and Community in the International Social System," in James N. Rosenau, ed., *International Politics and Foreign Policy* (New York, 1961), p. 126. Also see his article, "Voting and the Equilibrium of the American Political System," in Eugene Burdick and Arthur J. Brodbeck, eds., *American Voting Behavior* (Glencoe, 1959).

[5] Several recent pieces have examined the similarities of other political systems to international politics. For comparison with primitive societies and developing nations see Chadwick F. Alger, *Comparison of Intranational and International Politics*, paper delivered at the Annual Meeting of the APSA, September 1962, and Fred Riggs, "International Politics as a Prismatic System," *World Politics*, XIV (1961), pp. 141–81.

[6] Kaplan, *op. cit.*

[7] *Bloc Politics in the United Nations* (Cambridge, Mass., 1960). See also Arnold Wolfers, ed., *Neutralism* (Washington, 1961).

[8] Sydney D. Bailey (*The General Assembly of the United Nations*, New York, 1960, p. 28) refers in passing to an "embryonic" party system in the Assembly, but then

basis it is difficult to make a very convincing argument for the existence of a third party of a power and coherence comparable to that of either of the great power blocs. There are, of course, "independents" and "minor parties," and their existence is crucial to the functioning of the two-party system hypothesized, but that is quite a different matter.[9]

Naturally there are differences between national systems and the international model here suggested. First, the international electorate, with each nation considered as a single voter, is in this sense much smaller than any national electorate; each voter considers himself to have, and does in fact have, more influence on the parties' behavior than do single voters in the national systems. Thus in parts of the following analysis the similarity is more often between domestic blocs or interests and international "voters" than between single "voters" on both levels.

Second, and more important, there are no periodic elections at which the voters decide between the parties, and thus no long periods of relative quiescence during which the parties prepare for the next election. Instead, voting is practically continuous. Many major votes occur during every session of the General Assembly, and equally important opportunities for alignment arise outside the United Nations. Yet these are merely electoral skirmishes comparable to votes in a national legislature; complete victory for either side would imply the end of the electoral process, at least between those particular parties.

Because there is no powerful, permanent supranational government to gain control of, "victory" is likely to have meaning only as the destruction of the other party's power base. Similarly, the inability of a United Nations majority actually to enforce many of its decisions—the absence of much legislative power—encourages use of the Assembly as a propaganda forum rather than as an arena for close political bargaining. Many varied interests are represented, but often there is insufficient legislative power to force compromise for the achievement of a common parliamentary program.[10]

At least one institutional difference should be noted. Seymour Lipset suggests that a major contributor to the emergence of radical politics is the existence of effective channels of communication, informing voters of a potential community of interest and possibilities of joint action.[11] The United Nations, as a forum for promoting debate and the international exchange of ideas, certainly serves as an important means of facilitating communication among the underdeveloped nations. Yet the attitudes of individual voters are the subject of public communication in a way that they are not in democratic societies—on most issues the vote is open, not secret. The secret ballot protects a subordinate from reprisal by his superiors, and it equally protects him from social ostracism by his fellows.[12] A laborer in the "reddest" mining area can vote conservative without his choice becoming known to his co-workers unless he chooses to make it known. Bloc members in the United Nations have no such protection.

II. Legitimacy and Consensus

In referring to some of the differences between national competitive systems and the international one we have, in the process, also alluded to some of the similarities. Let us now examine the similarities somewhat more systematically. We shall draw heavily on analyses of the American system, both because it has been intensively studied and because observers agree that it is characterized by much underlying diversity of opinion.

Most voters, including all the neutrals and even many of the partisans, regard continuing competition and the avoidance of a final resolution as the most desirable outcome. They probably have a preference as to the party they would wish to see win in a showdown, but it is far better for their self-perceived

dismisses the idea on the grounds that because voting alignments differ so greatly on different classes of issues one cannot really call it a party system. Perhaps his conclusion is due to his greater familiarity with the relatively homogeneous British parties than with heterogeneous American parties where shifting alignments from one issue to the next are commonplace.

[9] We cannot at this stage dismiss entirely the possibility that in some respects a multi-party model would have a higher explanatory power in international politics than a two-party model. Its applicability is, however, a matter to be settled by empirical research, and one of the chief purposes of this paper is to indicate some of the questions which might be asked.

[10] See Arthur N. Holcombe, "The Role of Politics in the Organization of Peace," Commission to Study the Organization of Peace, 11th Annual Report, *Organizing Peace in the Nuclear Age* (New York, 1959), p. 79.

[11] *Political Man* (Garden City, 1960), p. 238.

[12] See Stein Rokkan, "Mass Suffrage, Secret Voting, and Political Participation," *European Journal of Sociology*, II (1961), pp. 132–52.

interests that neither party eliminate the other.[13] This is not only because of a fear that final victory would be achieved only by the military destruction of at least one leader, with the concomitant destruction of many neutrals and partisans. More important, in a competitive world there are many potentialities to be exploited by the voters. Under many conditions competition between the parties is likely to produce concessions to the neutrals and the offer of substantial favors in the form of foreign aid, support for anti-colonial movements, and help in the achievement of other goals such as security from a local enemy. As we shall see below, conditions of competition may also serve to moderate the ideologies or platforms of the major parties; insofar as the original ideology of neither party appeals to the needs of a neutral, this moderating influence is likely to result in a nearer approximation of his wishes.

Not only does competition provide the neutral with parties who become eager suitors for his favor, it provides him with numerous opportunities actively to seek the fulfillment of his wishes. By the promise of his vote, or the implicit or explicit threat to give it to the other party, he may significantly influence the platform or performance of one or both of the parties in his favor. His influence may be dependent upon his ability to maintain his lobby in some kind of uncommitted position. This is analogous to a major question about interest group politics in national systems—under what conditions will a lobby be more influential as a partisan than with a foot in both camps? The partisan may, or may not, have substantial control over the politics of his leader; the uncommitted may, by playing his hand shrewdly, influence both leaders.

This is not very different from what goes on in democratic national politics, where neither the neutrals nor, in most cases, even the partisans will aid in the elimination of either party. No matter how deeply committed a party is to achieving final victory

over its opponents, when it discovers that victory is not a real possibility for the foreseeable future it must become active in a different kind of politics. In Ernst Haas' terms, the result may be "a delicate negotiating process, with the world organization the forum, not of a community conscience or a concert of power, but of counterbalancing forces unwilling to seek a showdown, fearful of alienating friends or neutrals, and therefore willing to make concessions."[14]

Yet the system's stability may be quite fragile. Though neutral voters may much prefer a world where neither party wins final victory, even more vital may be the desperate necessity, in case one side *does* win, of being on the winning side. Thus if either side appeared to be winning one might witness an extremely powerful "bandwagon" effect far in excess of that in stable democracies where no one expects the victors to take drastic reprisals on their former opponents.

In domestic politics, of course, stability is maintained not only by a realization that the long term interests of most voters depend on the maintenance of an effective opposition, but by a normative element as well. Concepts of legitimacy as well as of interest restrain the partisans. Even Communist parties, in nations where they form a major part of the parliamentary Opposition, must at least pay deference to generally accepted norms.

If the idea of competition and the existence of competing forces is ever to be legitimized, it must be through the recognition that all voters share at least some interests in common. A principal mutual interest in the current international arena, though not the only one, is the avoidance of general war. Probably every government can conceive of some conditions to which war is preferable, but also of many other outcomes which are definitely more desirable than war. Unavoidably there is considerable overlap of the views of the two sides, so that there are many circumstances both would prefer to general war. The balance of terror, if it remains stable over a long period, may eventually convince each side of its inability to destroy the other at an acceptable cost. From there, and recognizing their mutual interest in avoiding war, each may eventually develop a sense of the legitimacy of the opposition. One may

---

[13] For evidence that this applies to partisans as well as neutrals see Lloyd Free, *Six Allies and a Neutral* (New York, 1959), pp. 33–56. Free cites numerous interviews with members of the Japanese Diet who affirm their attachment to the Western Alliance but nevertheless believe that the continuance of two-bloc competition serves Japanese interests best by making the Americans sensitive to Japanese needs. A similar situation surely applies to Poland, including many Polish Communists, who are well aware that even their limited independence is due to the existence of a rival to the Russians.

[14] "Regionalism, Functionalism, and Universal International Organization," *World Politics*, VIII, 2 (January 1956), p. 240.

not approve of the opposition's policies, but may grudgingly admit its right to exist and, within limits, to proselytize. Such a development would be aided by the above-mentioned conscious recognition by the neutrals and many of the partisans that their own interests are best served in a system where two or more opposing parties exist. Some such recognition seems to have occurred in England and America. The existence of the United Nations, and the "right" of the other side to take its case to the world body, may eventually contribute to some such development.

Even short-run stability, without the legitimization of conflict, depends on some degree of consensus on basic values as well as immediate interests. At present there is such a *limited* common "frame of reference" between East and West. Without such a consensus, in fact, the idea of competition for the favor of voters would make little sense. As Talcott Parsons has pointed out, both the Communist and Western ideologies place high value on each of the following: economic productivity, political autonomy, and equality.[15] What is more, the elites of the emerging nations, even when they are not confirmed believers in either Marxism or Western liberalism, usually accept these same values. This might not have been the case. Neither productivity nor equality is highly regarded in the traditional cultures of much of Asia and the Middle East, but in most countries those who are at least nominally committed to "modernization" are in power and not the traditionalists.

Obviously there are sharp limits to this basic consensus. Principally the conflict arises over two values: socialism vs. free enterprise, and the political freedoms of liberal democracy. Even here, however, the differences can be exaggerated. Western states have, in recent decades, abandoned or restricted free enterprise in many areas of their economies; free enterprise is often valued largely as an instrumental goal, a means of securing political freedom, rather than an aim in itself. Communist societies, on the other hand, give a kind of defence to liberal democracy. However restricted political liberties may be at present, full freedom is promised for the day when the state withers away. Communist leaders are often

15 "Polarization and the Problem of International Order," in Quincy Wright, William Evan, and Morton Deutsch, *Preventing World War III* (New York, 1962).

highly cynical in discussing that day, but the acknowledgment that such a state is desirable does at least show that freedoms are *valued*. Every apparently liberal statement that they make tends, by encouraging popular hopes, to strengthen this very tenuous consensus.

A related factor which may promote system stability by narrowing the extremes of polarity is what Parsons calls "cross-cutting solidarities." Insofar as voters who adhere to one party belong to or are emotionally attached to organizations including many voters of the other party, this may reduce their demands for fear of losing those with cross-cutting solidarities or by causing disbelief in the ranks about the extremists' charges against the other party. There are rather few of these solidarities between the blocs at present, with the chief exception of Poland's cultural and emotional predilections for the West and Cuba's ties to the Soviet bloc while remaining linked with many Latin American states. On the unofficial level such bonds as those of the Holy See with Roman Catholics in Eastern Europe also should not be ignored. Many more attachments exist, however, between neutrals and members of the two major blocs. They include formal organizations like the Nordic Council and the British Commonwealth, as well as non-governmental bonds such as Yugoslavia's Communist party ties, and links between neutralist and pro-Western Moslem nations. The role of these cross-cutting solidarities may well expand.

Yet another possible stabilizing factor might be the degree to which decision-makers develop broader institutional loyalties, as to the United Nations. One is reminded of the way Senators will rally to the defense of "the club." Does a similarity of background and profession common to many diplomats contribute to mitigating their conflicts? One would not expect this factor to have a very strong influence, but it ought not to be dismissed prematurely.

But any development of a consensus or sense of legitimacy in the international system is likely to be a fragile thing. The Soviets' defiance of "public opinion" to resume nuclear testing illustrates an important difference between democratic politics and the international system as presently constituted —there are, in international politics, sometimes major gains to be achieved by threatening to defy the consensus or destroy the stability of the system. By threatening to attempt a violent seizure of power one may promote a desire on the part of the independents to placate the violent party. Even this, however, sometimes applies in times of domestic crisis and impending revolution or civil war (e.g. the United States before 1861). The possibility of violence, from riot to coup d'etat to social revolution, is never entirely absent from domestic politics.

III. Issues and Ideology

If the parties are to woo voters successfully they must be concerned both with making promises and seeing that their performances, their records, are such that their promises seem plausible. Each party may put a different emphasis on the two elements, and each may stress different aspects (the Soviet Union, for instance, was willing to accept a bad blot on its record of international action in its movement against Hungary), but both are nevertheless important. And if there is a substantial number of voters who do not share their ideological goals, the partisans' arguments are likely to turn increasingly away from ideological discussion in favor of particular pragmatic platforms and promises. Parties may become increasingly reluctant to commit themselves openly to the goals of a particular set of voters if there is another large set of voters whose goals are competitive (e.g., American reluctance to make an unequivocal commitment either to colonial powers or to anti-colonialists).

As ideologies are de-emphasized they are likely also to become more ambiguous. This may produce a split between an esoteric ideology for the inner party members which remains relatively pure and internally consistent and an exoteric, or public, ideology designed to appeal to or at least not to offend a wide variety of sentiments.[16] In recruiting new Party members American Communists, for instance, place little emphasis on the class-conflict elements of traditional Marxist thought but rather play to the desires of special groups wanting civil rights, civil liberties, or the avoidance of "imperialist" war. Yet this difference between the esoteric and exoteric ideologies may cause a nearly intolerable

strain producing either a weakening of even the leadership's attachment to the ideology or a situation where it is impossible for the party to hold most of its special-interest converts.[17] In the former case conflict between "revisionist" leaders and those who wish to hold fast to the basic ideology is certain. All these possibilities can be discerned both in the history of the American Communist Party and on the present-day international scene. Of course, in current international politics neither party seems really to anticipate the continued existence of both parties throughout the foreseeable future of the polity. The hope of final victory, eliminating the need for any subsequent elections, may circumscribe the true, as compared with the apparent, modification of ideology. Once "absolute power" was achieved the forces of ideology would reassert themselves. Yet a contrary hypothesis is also plausible—the real fear of annihilation may induce a party to jettison its ideology in the pursuit of survival.

The fear of alienating neutral voters may contribute to the formation of party platforms in other ways. In an effort to appeal to competing groups parties may make inconsistent promises, analogous to platforms which call both for more welfare spending and for lower taxes. Or a party may select only certain elements of its ideology for campaign emphasis. It is likely to ignore those issues which seem so divisive that almost any position the party might take would alienate more voters than it would attract. The United States government, which stands to antagonize someone whatever its position on colonialism, would surely be not unhappy to see the whole matter dropped. The Soviets, however, who depend upon quite a different set of partisans for their basic support, stand to make a net gain by being anti-colonial, so they play up the issue as much as possible.

Any proliferation in the number of workable issues brought before the United Nations should also, in the long run, contribute to stabilizing the system. While the United Nations was used primarily as a forum for promoting Western security interests the independents and neutral-leaning partisans found themselves in a relatively weak bargaining position. But now, with the intrusion of economic development and colonialism as major issues in their

[16] Gabriel Almond, *The Appeals of Communism* (Princeton, 1954), pp. 68–74, distinguishes between esoteric and exoteric communications.

[17] See George Liska, *The New Statecraft* (Chicago, 1961), pp. 48, 206–07.

own right, many nations have substantial freedom of maneuver. They may bargain and engage in log-rolling, exchanging support on security issues for votes against colonialism. As the authors of *The American Voter* declare,

If an electorate responds to public affairs in terms of one or a few well-defined and stable ideological dimensions on which there is little movement of opinion, political controversy will be relatively tightly bounded and the possibilities of party maneuver . . . relatively circumscribed. But if an electorate responds to public affairs in a less structured fashion, politics will be more fluid, party strategy will include or may consist primarily of exploiting new dimensions of opinion, and the likelihood of party alternation in power will be greater.[18]

The emergence of new issues might eventually contribute to a sharp shift in alignments. Leaders and partisans of both major blocs may some day decide that they share a common interest in preserving their wealth from confiscation by an aroused underdeveloped bloc. This could conceivably produce the emergence of a new "have-not" party followed by the merger of the former opponents into a single party. Or it might mean simply that the voting alignment on some types of issues would be radically different from that on other matters.

The proliferation of issues contributes in other ways. A cumulative pattern of compromises and concessions can set up expectations of peace, stability, and co-existence which may constrain the leaders. Even if the leaders make concessions purely as temporary expedients and not out of any desire to promote such expectations, they are likely to give rise to hopes which it will be costly to disappoint.[19]

The intrusion of issues other than the military security one may make it possible for some partisans even of the tightly organized Communist bloc occasionally to deviate from the party norm. One can hardly conceive of the Soviets tolerating deviation on a major security measure in the near future, but on some other matters a vote against the bloc, or an abstention, might possibly be overlooked. By providing opportunities for deviation on issues which are not central to the Soviet Union's security we may

contribute to a wholesome precedent. Once deviation is tolerated at all it may be difficult to stop it short of a certain fluidity even on rather vital matters.

The United States could conceivably gain in another way from the proliferation of issues, properly controlled. The West is in many ways a conservative group, seeking to restrain the pace and scope of economic and social change. Conservative groups traditionally have maintained themselves in part by yielding significantly to the program of their opponents, but also by promoting issues not directly bound up with class or status issues. Essentially conservative parties tend to emphasize "style" issues as efficiency in government or morality, or to stress personality in their campaigns.[20] To protect their own positions and to avoid disruption of the society they must prevent the lines of political division from becoming identical with those of economic cleavage. Both the Republicans and the British Conservatives expect to get about one-third of the working-class vote; their ability to do so both indicates and helps to maintain their societies' underlying consensus.

For these reasons it becomes vital to make a close analysis of current voting patterns in the United Nations. One would like to know at least the following: 1. How great a diminution has there been in the proportion of votes and debating time devoted to issues of East-West military security? 2. How high is the correlation between *per capita* income and voting with the Western Bloc? What other variables correlate with voting patterns?[21] 3. How greatly does the voting pattern on such issues as colonialism diverge from that on East-West relations?

Party competition not only may affect the issues chosen for stress and the positions taken, it may produce a tendency to avoid the explicit discussion of policy. Attention and effort may be concentrated on nominating politics and on electing men to office. Heterogeneous groups who could not be brought together on any explicit set of policy statements may nevertheless be able to combine for the purpose of winning elections and distributing offices. This too might be investigated by examining debates and votes in the United Nations. Is there

[18] A. Campbell, P. Converse, W. Miller, and D. Stokes, *The American Voter* (New York, 1960), p. 550.

[19] Note, however, that to serve this function the issues must be ones about which there is *disagreement*. Matters about which there is consensus contribute in other ways. See Haas, *op. cit.*, p. 250.

[20] Lipset, *op. cit.*, pp. 281–82.

[21] In the absence of high income, is some measure of "status" (white race, European culture) correlated with pro-Westernism?

more intra-bloc cohesion on such matters as admitting new nations ("convention credentials") than on most substantive issues?[22] Is the proportion of debate time on such matters increasing over the years, indicating a tendency to avoid discussion of some divisive substantive matters?

We shall refer below to the effect of various distributions of attitudes among the population, but it is important also to recognize the effect of various *intensities* of preference. If those who hold the most extreme attitudes also hold them most intensely, a serious threat to the system's stability may exist, especially if the extremists are numerous.[23] Quite possibly the influx of new voters, the emergent nations, into the international arena has meant not only that most voters now prefer a "middle" solution to East-West problems, but that most voters are relatively apathetic in a particular sense. That is, the particular issues presented by the two parties' ideologies really have little appeal to them, so that they would not care greatly which was the victor. Their strong preferences are reserved for what are to them private matters—the development and modernization of their own countries, by whatever methods. They are thus not apathetic toward politics in general, but merely to the issues presented by the parties.[24] As noted above, in their eyes the achievement of their goals may depend upon the absence of a clearcut victory for either side. This necessity for two-party competition might, in the long run, be turned into a virtue, as the existence of the competitors took on important aspects of legitimacy in the neutrals' eyes.

One is here reminded of the argument by the authors of *Voting* about the role of the "independent" or, more accurately, the apathetic voter.[25] If the majority of voters held strong preferences the system might quickly become unworkable; only so long as most voters are relatively uninvolved in the ideological arguments of the partisans is the peaceful resolution of conflict possible.

[22] Party cohesion in legislative voting is higher on such issues than on more substantive matters. See Julius Turner, *Party and Constituency* (Baltimore, 1951), p. 53.

[23] See Robert A. Dahl, *A Preface to Democratic Theory* (Chicago, 1956), Chap. 4.

[24] They may also share the attitude, rather widespread in some democracies, that politics is disreputable, and really played only by "professionals."

[25] Bernard Berelson, Paul Lazarsfeld, and William McPhee, *Voting* (New York, 1954), pp. 314–15.

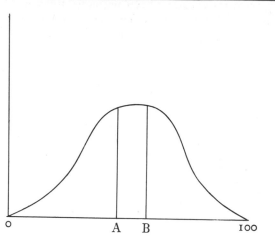

Figure 1. Two-party convergence when preferences are distributed unimodally.

IV. The Distribution of Preferences

Whether the two parties will become more or less extreme in their stands is a crucial question. Currently there is substantial evidence that the international party leaders have moderated their policies, at least those parts which are explicitly stated. Most of this can be seen as an attempt to win the support of neutrals and to hold that of the less extreme partisans. But whether these developments merely represent temporary tendencies, likely to be reversed in the near future, depends in large part upon the underlying distribution of voters' preferences. This leads to discussion of a variable which could promote system stability, but could also lead to the breakdown of the system and either to conflict or to the emergence of a polycentric system.

As Anthony Downs has shown,[26] if most voters favor moderate or middle-of-the-road policies

[26] *An Economic Theory of Democracy* (New York, 1957), p. 118. I owe to Downs, Chap. 8, the method of presentation and many of the insights in the following paragraphs.

Donald E. Stokes has made a penetrating criticism of the Downs model (*Spatial Models of Party Competition*, paper presented to the Annual Meeting of the APSA, September 1962). Among his points are: 1. More than one dimension (issue) may be politically relevant, with different preference distributions for each dimension. 2. The salience of various dimensions may change over time. 3. Leaders, partisans, and neutrals all may have different perceptions of salience and preference distributions. These possibilities were, however, dealt with in the previous section of this article.

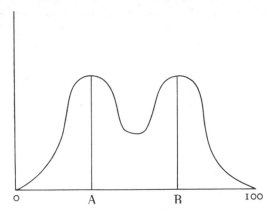

Figure 2. Two-party divergence when preferences are distributed bimodally.[27]

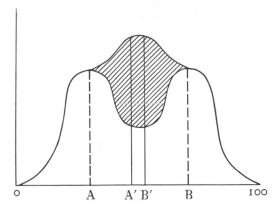

Figure 3. Two-party convergence with the creation of a single center mode by the enfranchisement of new voters.

the two parties' policies will converge toward the center. The possible loss of extremists will not deter their movement toward the center and toward each other because there will be so few voters to be lost at the margin compared with the number to be gained in the middle. This situation is illustrated in the following figure. The vertical axis measures numbers of voters and the horizontal axis measures degree of preference for some policy, the extent to which economic control ought to be centralized, for instance, with zero representing no centralization and 100 complete central control. If voters' preferences are such that most voters are found at a single mode around 50, then both party A and party B will tend, over time, to move toward that mode.

But if preferences are distributed bimodally, as

in Figure 2, the outcome is likely to be quite different. Attempted shifts to the center may meet with the refusal of extremists to support either party if both become alike, or at least similar. Since the potential loss at the margin is so great, the parties may retain quite different programs.

The recent moderation of some of the two international parties' policies might be traced to a world preference pattern like that indicated in Figure 1, which the parties have just now begun to recognize. But if we introduce a dynamic element, the moderation may be traceable to a shift in the world preference pattern caused by the "enfranchisement" of new voters. As the African and Asian countries have achieved independence and admission to the United Nations they have become new voters for whom the parties must compete. Whereas at the end of World War II preferences were distributed bimodally as in Figure 2, by the end of the 1950's the addition of new voters to the ranks had created another peak toward the center.

Figure 3 above illustrates one possible outcome of the enfranchisement of new voters. With the emergence of a new single mode at the center, the parties shift their policies from A to B and A' and B'. But the result need not be that above, for the size of the center mode is crucial. If it were much smaller, not significantly higher than the modes at A and B and separated from each of the original peaks by a valley, the most likely outcome would be not the convergence of A and B but the creation of a third party, a "neutral bloc" C.

[27] In a digression, note the relevance of this distribution to suggestions that if Southern Negroes can get the right to vote, normal party competition will force Southern politicians to modify their anti-Negro positions. Assume for a moment that the mode at A represents the advocates of integration, and the mode at B represents the segregationists. Assume further that most of the people near mode A are at present disenfranchised, so that both parties' policies naturally gravitate toward mode B. If the A people gain the right to vote, one party may well shift to them, but given the basic distribution of preferences *only* one party will make the move, and there will be a wide gulf between party policies as well as basic preferences. If one assumes further that there really are fewer people at A than at B—the mode is lower—(not a bad assumption for the South, where Negroes are substantially less than 50 per cent of the population) the integrationists are condemned to be a minority as long as preferences remain unchanged.

V. The Electoral System

Institutions also are relevant. It has often been said that single-member constituencies promote the emergence of two parties since small minorities in any district cannot hope, by themselves, to gain power. Do the "single-member districts" of the international system (one country, one government) make a similar contribution?

Federalism, it is sometimes alleged, contributes to the stability of a system which is threatened by many potential cleavages.[28] Nowhere in the American federal government is there a single locus of power, not even the Presidency, from which commands will receive obedience from officials everywhere. National leaders can control the nomination of local candidates only by enlisting the support of local leaders, and they are often unsuccessful. Federalism, reinforced by the electoral college, forces parties to have a decentralized structure appropriate for campaigning on a state-by-state basis. This encourages them to make contradictory promises, or at least to emphasize different aims in different areas. These factors reinforce the tendency noted above for the parties in a two-party system to concentrate on winning elections rather than on making explicit policy formulations. And the fact that national, state, and local elections are staggered is likely to prevent a party from getting complete control throughout the nation—there is always a new election taking place somewhere. To switch to the international arena, would it make any difference if all Free World elections were held simultaneously?

By forcing partisans to avoid great emphasis on issues which might divide the polity these institutional factors can contribute heavily to the long-run stability of the system, even if they sometimes exasperate the partisans. And the federal system, superimposed on a political system characterized by regional cleavages, contributes to the maintenance of long-run competition in another way. Just because there are various state elections as well as national ones, each party can depend on a safe "home base" from which it can hope to expand. Under competitive conditions the existence of safe regional bases may contribute to the moderation of party policies. Because the leaders know their regional bases are

secure they may tend to neglect their home interests in order to woo the uncommitted, and under many circumstances people in the regional bases may find there is little they can do to remedy the neglect. If regional demands should become too forceful, however, or should the leaders of either party despair of attracting the neutrals, these regional home bases could of course become disruptive forces leading to possible "civil" war.

VI. The Individual Voter

To this point we have for the most part been concerned with propositions about the international system as a whole, and broad trends in the behavior of voters in the mass. Yet it is also important to suggest hypotheses about the behavior of particular voters. One aspect of this problem is the relation between a single government's constituency and the policies it pursues in the international system. In trying to affect the behavior of another state one government may appeal either directly to another government or to the constituency beneath it. Thus the American government bargains directly with other delegations in the United Nations, and also uses the General Assembly as a propaganda forum to influence world opinion. To examine this we may draw upon some of the hypotheses advanced by students of legislative behavior.

Turner's study of Congressional voting noted that representatives from districts which are socioeconomically most typical of their parties tend to show the highest degree of party loyalty on roll calls and those who come from districts atypical of their parties tend to cross party lines often.[29] Voting patterns in the United Nations should provide an excellent opportunity for testing this. "Typicality" might be measured in a number of ways. Several possible indices, as applied to members of the Western bloc, would be *per capita* income, "democratic" form of government, or perhaps some measurement of the degree to which each member shares the European cultural heritage. Different ways of making these indices operational should be experimented with, and several indices tried to see

[28] Several of the hypotheses in this section I owe to Austin Ranney and Willmoore Kendall, *Democracy and the American Party System* (New York, 1956). pp. 490–99.

[29] Turner, *op. cit.*, See however, Samuel P. Huntington's conclusion ("A Revised Theory of American Party Politics," *American Political Science Review*, XXXXIV, 3 (September 1950), pp. 669–77) that party differences in liberalism and conservatism are greatest where elections are closest.

the patterns produced by each. One would expect party loyalty to be greatest where the member was typical on all dimensions, and diminish as he was atypical on one or more.[30]

Even if this hypothesis should hold generally true, one would nevertheless be required to explain a significant number of exceptions. One interesting line of thought is suggested by Duncan MacRae's finding that members of the Massachusetts state legislature whose previous election margins were close tended to reflect constituency socio-economic characteristics in their votes more closely than did those with wider margins.[31] He indicates that this may be due either to a heightened sensitivity to constituents' wishes resulting from anxiety about re-election or from a general rise in the level of interest in constituencies where there is a continuing political contest.

Quite the opposite conclusion is suggested by Leon Epstein's examination of the characteristics of British M.P.s who defied their parties' stand on the Suez issue.[32] He found that constituency parties in safe districts were much more likely to retaliate against M.P.s who defied the party Whips than were the constituency organizations in marginal districts. It is generally felt in British politics that no candidate can add by his personal characteristics more than 500 votes to what any other candidate from the same party could poll. Thus the party organization in a safe constituency can win with any other candidate—its M.P.s need it more than it needs him. On the other hand, the constituency party of a marginal district may be loath to purge an M.P. and provoke an intra-party battle.

These contrary hypotheses might well be tested on United Nations voting. The equivalent of "closeness of election margin" might be measured either by some index of degree of "democracy" in a particular country or by the electoral margin of the

government and/or the amount of party alternation in government. Did Britain vote more regularly with the Western Alliance than the Philippines (close margin, atypical)? Did the Dominican Republic (wide margin, atypical) vote more regularly with other members of the Alliance than Brazil (close margin, a typical)? These questions would have to be applied to all members of the bloc.

Part of the difference between the findings of MacRae on American politics and Epstein on British politics is surely explicable in terms of differences between the national systems. Local party organizations tend to be far more autonomous in the United States than Britain; a representative is better able to build up a local machine specifically for *his* support. The local party is more closely controlled by the central party organization, and thus more likely to reflect its views, in Britain than in the United States. Because he is more closely tied to the national party, a representative in the British system would be less likely to reflect the socio-economic characteristics of an atypical constituency than of a typical constituency regardless of the "closeness" of his election.

On the international scene, governments most directly faced with a foreign-sponsored alternative to their rule—such as the divided states of China, Germany, Korea, and Vietnam—might be most dependent upon their alliances for support. Thus they might tend to be most extreme in the advocacy of their parties' policies. This does not mean that there would necessarily be great harmony between leader and partisan—both Chinas exemplify just the opposite—but that the dependence of the partisan on the strength of his party for protection would tend to make him at least as doctrinaire, and possibly more so, than his leader.

A somewhat different hypothesis is suggested by David Truman's finding that Congressmen who come from close districts and have low seniority tend to agree with the Democratic majority leaders.[33] That is, Congressmen who lacked power bases of their own followed the party leadership. The converse is shown by the fact that Republican Congressmen who were first elected in a Presidential year 1932–48 (i.e. against a strong Democratic national trend) were less likely to agree with the Republican

[30] This would be consistent with Turner's findings, and also with the effect of demographic "cross-pressures" uncovered by the voting studies.

[31] Duncan R. MacRae, "The Relation Between Roll Call Votes and Constituencies in the Massachusetts House of Representatives," *American Political Science Review* XXXXVI, 4 (December 1952), pp. 1046–55. See also MacRae, *Dimensions of Congressional Voting* (Berkeley and Los Angeles, 1958), p. 286.

[32] "British M.P.s and Their Local Parties: The Suez Cases," *American Political Science Review*, LIV, 2 (June 1960), pp. 374–90.

[33] *The Congressional Party* (New York, 1959), pp. 214–24.

House Leader than were Congressmen first elected in non-presidential years. Those with independent power bases tended to be either noticeably more conservative or significantly more liberal than G.O.P. Leader Martin.

VII. Toward a Model

The hypotheses suggested on these pages are all tentative, and need to be refined and tested. Not all are readily testable, but it would appear that data on voting patterns in the UN General Assembly would prove a uniquely valuable aid in the testing.

In any case I certainly do not wish to suggest that propositions may be transferred eclectically and uncritically from one kind of political system to another. But I do hope that this exercise has indicated some of the fruits which might be obtained for international relations from awareness of the findings of studies of other systems. I have made rather extensive reference to such studies in order to suggest the wealth of material that is there. Perhaps as these hypotheses are tested more rigorously on national political systems—for their validity has not even been firmly established there—they may be tried out on the international system as well.

13. A Functional Approach to International Organization*

Michael Haas is Associate Professor of Political Science at the University of Hawaii and the author of a number of provocative articles on international political behavior. Here he undertakes a searching examination of international organizations from the theoretical perspective of structural-functional analysis. The result is not only suggestive of the wide uses to which this form of analysis can be put; but, more importantly, it also develops a number of interesting insights into the organizational aspects of international systems. Again it is clear that such systems have much in common with other types of political systems. [*Reprinted from* Journal of Politics, *XXVII* (*August 1965*), *498–517, by permission of the author and the publisher.*]

Developments in theory building in international relations in recent years seem to have neglected the subject of international organization. Since the first step in theory construction is to specify basic concepts and hypotheses, a step not yet taken systematically in the field of international organization,[1] it should perhaps be no surprise that international organization theory has lagged. In the following discussion an attempt is made to delineate fundamental terms and propositions which may serve as a springboard for a theory of international organization as a subset of a broader structural-functional approach to international relations.[2]

* The author wishes to acknowledge the helpful criticisms of Werner Levi and the support of the Office of Research Administration, University of Hawaii.

[1] The standard "functional" treatment of international organization was presented by Sir Alfred Zimmern; it has been extended by Herbert Nicholas and Inis Claude. See Sir Alfred Zimmern, *The League of Nations and the Rule of Law, 1919–1935* (2nd ed., London, 1945); H. G. Nicholas, *The United Nations as a Political Institution* (2nd ed., London, 1963); Inis L. Claude, Jr., *Swords into Plowshares* (3rd ed., New York, 1964), Chaps. 11–17.

[2] For some current systemic approaches to international relations, see Morton A. Kaplan, *System and Process in International Politics* (New York, 1957); Klaus

"International Organization" Defined

The very term "international organization" is ambiguous. In the conventional sense, an international organization is an institution or structure similar to Congress or to a city council; it has a definite set of rules, members, agenda, places and times of meeting.

A second meaning of the concept is implied as well. If "organization" is an arrangement of parts into a unified whole, then there is a noninstitutional aspect to the phrase "international organization." The purpose of organization is conscious coordination of activity;[3] the method of organization is to routinize coordination by such techniques as division of labor and task specialization. Coordination can be performed either formally or informally. When coordination is formal, it takes place within official structures and institutional machinery; this is the conventional significance of the term "organization"

Knorr and Sidney Verba, eds., *The International System* (Princeton, 1961); Richard N. Rosecrance, *Action and Reaction in World Politics* (Boston, 1963).

[3] Chester I. Barnard, *The Functions of the Executive* (Cambridge, 1962), 73.

in international relations. Informal coordination involves an unwritten system of practices in which units of the system assume such roles as those of leader or nonleader. "International organization" in the second sense refers to informal role differentiation in the world polity. Often this second meaning has been called "world organization."[4]

When a system has an operative formula that determines "who gets what, when and how,"[5] it is definitely organized politically. In international relations, units that are most powerful take leadership roles; weak units are nonleaders. Thus, it may be hypothesized safely that international organization in the first sense is a dependent variable of world organization, the second interpretation of the term. Informal organization is more basic than formal organization; characteristics of international structures are a function of the nature of the international arena. In the subsequent portion of this discussion the term "international organization" will be used to refer only to the meaning of the term in the conventional sense.

Not all organizations are international, so a complete definition of "international organization" should specify the meaning of the term "international." Historically the types of units in the world political system have changed in form and in number. Traditionally, an international organization has been said to exist when many nation states are linked together structurally. If this criterion were adopted, the study of international organization would date only from the year 1648, when the nation state system was officially christened in the Peace of Westphalia.[6] Previously there were other basic units—the empire, the city state, the free city, the dynastic state and the *sui generis Holy See*.[7] A loose definition of international organization, then, would say that it consists of intergovernmental institutions, members of which perceive each other to be basic units of the world polity.[8] Any world system, hence, may contain international organizations.

A final problem is to determine the minimum number of units that must belong to an organization before it can be called "international." Bilateral, trilateral, plurilateral, regional or universal relationships could be included. There is little controversy in placing the latter terms under the rubric "international." If the former terms are accepted, transient coalitions of states or caucusing but uncohesive blocs in United Nations voting would qualify as well as tightly organized alliances and monolithic blocs. So long as permanent structures are involved, it would be consistent with the above formulation to refer to even a dyadic institution as an international organization in the conventional sense. If there is a stable role structure in a dyad, world organization in the second, or systemic, sense may be said to exist. International organizations differ empirically in number of members, but they all share a common characteristic: there is conscious coordination of common activities. International structures and complementary role differentiation fall into disuse when their purposes are unfulfilled.

International Organization as a Variable

After designing tools for ascertaining when an international organization is present, a second step in conceptualization is to suggest basic propositions. International organization may be investigated as a dependent or as an independent variable. As a dependent variable, it is a reflection of world organization; as an independent variable, it is a factor which may alter world organization (see Fig. 1). Until states are willing or coerced to surrender their sovereignty to international organizations, however, effects of international institutions will not transform the world polity. Powerful states keep the effectiveness of international structures within bounds.

In studying international organizations as a dependent variable, one should classify their inputs and outputs. Two types of independent variables,

---

[4] Pitman B. Potter, "Origin of the Term 'International Organization,'" *American Journal of International Law*, XXXIX (October, 1945), 803–04; Werner Levi, *Fundamentals of World Organization* (Minneapolis, 1953).

[5] Harold D. Lasswell, *Politics: Who Gets What, When, How* (New York, 1958).

[6] John H. Herz, "The Rise and Demise of the Territorial State," *World Politics*, IX (April, 1957), 473–93.

[7] Adda B. Bozeman, *Politics and Culture in International History* (Princeton, 1960).

[8] This definition would exclude nongovernmental, private international associations, such as the Inter-Parliamentary Union and the International Red Cross. Since their role in international system function performance is minimal, their analysis is not included herein. Similarly, intergovernmental international organizations perform many nonpolitical functions.

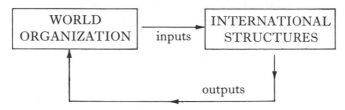

Figure 1. International organization within the world polity

types of international systems and various features of international institutions, also must be enumerated.

To identify differences between international systems, it is useful to begin with their common properties. International systems resemble other social systems in that their existence requires the performance of certain functions. Since international systems are highly politicized,[9] these functions are the same as those in other political systems. With some modifications of Almond's formulation,[10] it can be said that functions of international systems are eight in number—articulation, aggregation, socialization, recruitment, transaction, rule making, rule application and rule supervision.

A description of the state of an international system at any one time, therefore, will include statements about the way in which each of the eight functions is performed. First of all, one would specify which structures perform each function. Since the structures which might perform the functions vary from particularistic units to universalistic organizations, a second characteristic of an international system is the degree to which there is institutionalization of function performance. What percentage of articulation, for example, occurs within international organizations and what part is external and noninstitutionalized? In examining the informal organization of world polities, the relevant question to ask is the extent and locus of specialization and division of labor in function performance.

Several problems for empirical research follow from this formulation. What structures are most likely to perform which functions, and under what conditions? What can account for increases and decreases in the institutionalization of function

performance over time? Which kinds of informal world organization accompany which patterns in function performance? In which kinds of power stratification systems do international organizations transform world organization, and vice versa? Clearly answers to these questions would tell us how near to world government an international system is at any one time. In the absence of specific research in these matters there are few opportunities to make more than "educated guesses."[11] In the discussion to follow an attempt is made to set the stage for such an exploration. Each function is defined and illustrated; the degree to which its performance can be institutionalized is specified next. Finally, there will be speculation on the impact of types of informal world power stratification on function performance and institutionalization.

Input Functions

The functions fall into two groups. Input functions, those that are performed to obtain rewards from governmental institutions in domestic political systems, include articulation, aggregation, socialization, recruitment and transaction. Output functions include rule making, rule application and rule supervision. In international systems it is common for nearly all functions to be performed outside formal universalistic structures, which accounts for the impermeability of world organization to operations of international organizations.

Articulation

"Articulation" is the stating of a demand on a political system. Internationally relevant demands may be voiced by private individuals, by national

[9] Werner Levi, "On the Causes of Peace," *Journal of Conflict Resolution*, VIII (March, 1964), 27–30.

[10] Gabriel A. Almond and James S. Coleman, eds., *The Politics of the Developing Areas* (Princeton, 1960).

[11] Cf. George Modelski, "Agraria and Industria: Two Models of the International System," in Knorr and Verba, eds., *The International System*.

decision makers and by spokesmen for nongovernmental, regional or universal international organizations. Articulation may occur in such arenas as undergraduate "bull sessions," negotiating conferences and meetings of the General Assembly of the United Nations.

In the present nation state system the basic actors are those that have the elusive properties of "sovereignty." International systems and international organizations differ according to the rules of membership in the system, the number of units that are members, and the demographic homogeneity of the units. Any unit may articulate as legitimately as any other unit, but there is some role specialization or division of labor, depending on the demographic stratification of the actors: industrial, agrarian, riparian, major, middle and minor powers concentrate their articulation on matters of most vital interests.

Due to low expectation and aspiration levels nongovernmental articulation is much less frequent than articulation of decision makers on behalf of their units within the world polity. Subnational groups, such as the United States Chamber of Commerce, and cross-national associations, such as international cartels and professional societies, in practice work through their own governments rather than articulating independently in international relations. The types of institutions that articulate vary from governments of empires, city states, dynastic states, nation states, and of other actors that are recognized as legitimate participants in an international conference or other formal inter-unit gathering. When one unit absorbs all parts of the world into one system, local representatives, satraps or members of a centralized colonial administration engage in articulation of international interests within the system.

The locus, specificity and institutionalization of the arena of effective articulation, hence, is a function of world power stratification. Directive hierarchical systems, with one unit autocratically supreme, fuse articulation of core area interests with articulation of interests of the dependent, peripheral areas, the former being more frequently selected at the expense of the latter. Since it is the nature of an autocracy to suppress independent centers of power, there is reluctance to establish structures specialized in articulation; the colonial administration fills the vacuum in such cases as did the

Roman Empire. Under tight bipolarity, bloc leaders articulate with greater frequency than bloc followers, establishing intrabloc structures for formal statement of some of these demands in order to give the impression that they are articulated on behalf of the entire bloc interest. In non-directive democratic blocs this institutional appearance reflects reality, while in directive (authoritarian) blocs it masks dictation. Loose bipolar articulation is performed by bloc leaders, by international actors and by actors aligned with neither bloc; peacetime articulation takes place within universalistic international organizations than under tight bipolarity, since the major effective forum for the nonaligned articulator is the international institution. The greater the number of autonomous centers of power in the world system, thus, the more functional diffusion in frequency and locus of performance of articulation. In multipolar or multibloc systems powerful actors monopolize articulation; other units may state their demands, but they are largely dependent upon the major powers or blocs for their attainment, so their aspiration level is low as independent articulators. As affairs of a world system become more complex, a "concert" or a council of representatives of regional blocs may arise as an institutional arena for articulation in multipolar systems. In a polypolar system, where each unit is roughly equal in strength, articulation is least stratified. If there are many units interacting with high frequency in the world polity, the unwieldiness of articulation outside institutional frameworks makes the establishment of an organizational arena for articulation seem rational. It has been said, in fact, that the idea of the "grand debate" of the United Nations is based upon the assumption of a polypolar international system.[12]

To sum up, governments of basic units of world polities are the structures that articulate. The more concentrated the stratification of power, the more some units will articulate more effectively than others. Institutional arenas for articulation are most common as systems approach nondirective and polypolar forms.

Aggregation

When demands of several units are combined, harmonized to reduce inter-unit inconsistencies, and collectively advocated as a single "package,"

[12] See Claude, *Swords into Plowshares*, Chap. 15.

aggregation may be said to have occurred. Aggregation involves cooperation in the articulation of demands by two or more units of a political system. It may be performed initially at the ambassadorial level, by "gentlemen's agreements," and it may be formalized later in a treaty, alliance or caucusing group of an international organization. Voting blocs and regional international organizations are examples of the structural effects of aggregation.[13]

Aggregation at the international level is informally pursued, but it can result in the formation of institutional frameworks within which it can be performed systematically. Within groups that aggregate, role specialization is frequent: some units may be more committed to particularistic ideological or economic goals, while others act as brokers or mediators. The latter would be expected to assume leadership roles;[14] the former set the boundaries within which aggregation may proceed.

The aggregation function is performed by decision makers of governments on behalf of their units in the international political system; autonomous leaders of intergovernmental organizations may also encourage aggregation among countries by behind-the-scenes negotiation, as has the United Nations Secretary General. When the need for close collaborative aggregation between allies reaches some threshold, international machinery is established to provide a regularized framework for aggregation. The growth in regionalism, in part, reflects aspirations for regularized aggregation of goals within international subsystems.

International power stratification can account for patterns of aggregation. In directive hierarchical systems decision makers at the seat of the empire aggregate core and periphery interests to achieve a satisfactory balance between the two. Lacking accountability, there is no reason to display performance of aggregation by setting up institutions open to public view; aggregation can be performed in secret. Tight bipolar aggregation is performed by the bloc leaders to insure bloc solidarity and strength;

foreign ministries play dominant roles in the strategy of aggregation. Both directive and nondirective blocs have institutional frameworks for aggregation. The former use meetings of bloc countries to ratify aggregated packages of demands previously agreed upon; the latter use such structures for negotiating aggregation. In loose bipolarity the role of international actors can be successful in aggregating cross-bloc interests, while nonaligned countries try to achieve an aggregated "third force" position mediatory between the opposing blocs. Use of universalistic international organizations as arenas for aggregation increases as bipolarity loosens. So long as there is no intensive "struggle for power" between members of multipolar and multibloc systems, aggregation of military goals proceeds at a low rate. Close aggregation between two or more major members triggers a counter-coalition to check threats to the system's ambiguous structure. Institutionalized aggregation by all the major powers as executive directors of the international political system is practiced so long as a common front is believed useful in maintaining the system against actions of minor powers. Institutionalized aggregation fades when major powers can no longer patch over disagreements between them. In polypolarity each unit is equally likely to engage in aggregation. As the number of units and the world volume of inter-unit transactions increases, an institutional framework for aggregation is more probable.

Hence, aggregation is performed by governmental units, especially those that play mediatory or leadership roles within the international polity. Functional specificity of institutions in aggregation declines as power is more evenly distributed in the world.

Socialization

What conditioning of units in the world polity can account for the way they behave? The process of learning what roles one is to play, what behavior patterns one is to follow, is referred to as "socialization." Where religions captivate the minds of peoples, units in the international system will attempt to conform to certain moral standards, as was the case in ancient imperial systems and in the medieval international system.[15] If rulers are genetically

[13] Regional alliances have multifunctional aspects. NATO conference deliberations consist initially in articulation, later aggregation, and at final stages plurilateral rules concerning NATO countries may emerge or an aggregated demand may be placed on non-NATO countries.

[14] Cf. David B. Truman, *The Congressional Party* (New York, 1959).

[15] Bozeman, *Politics and Culture in International History*.

related, kinship loyalties and beliefs may determine behavior, as in seventeenth and eighteenth century Europe.[16] The rise of the capitalistic ethic has meant an emphasis on individual aggrandizement, resulting in national acquisitiveness. Whereas the family and group life of a domestic political system are the main arenas for national socialization, there are two sources of international socialization. Particularistic national foreign policy traditions and principles of domestic socialization transferred to the international level constitute an inner-oriented source; the second type of socialization occurs as decision makers attempt to steer their countries in various roles within the world polity, learning the constraints and possibilities of action. There is evidence today that participation in international organization may also be an outer-oriented socialization experience that modifies particularistic behavior of actors within the system.[17]

In directive unipolar systems, outer-oriented socialization to international politics is obtained by specialists at the core and periphery of the empire. Core leaders learn techniques for maintaining dominance, and periphery socialization consists in learning how to balance local pressures against core needs. Training of a specialized corps of colonial and military administrators within institutionalized settings insures more efficient dominance of the central unit of a unipolar system. In tight bipolarity inner-oriented socialization tends to consist of learning the ideological superiority of one's bloc and its interests. Bloc institutions are arenas for socialization of followers in directive blocs and for leaders in non-directive blocs. Both inner- and outer-oriented socialization in multipolar systems is mainly particularistic, but some outer-oriented socialization may accrue from experiments of directorates of major powers in reshaping the international system through joint consultation and action. The history of multipolar (balance of power) systems is one of lack of such experiences. In polypolar international systems the heavy utilization of universalistic organizations entails a considerable degree of outer-oriented international socialization within institutional frameworks.

Most international socialization is particularistic. Outer-oriented socialization experiences within universalistic structures are least common in multipolar systems, and are very frequent in unipolar or polypolar systems. Bipolar systems have regional or bloc organizations within which there is a socialization that is neither completely particularistic nor universalistic.

Recruitment

The process of leadership selection may explain why some actors are mediators in aggregation or leaders in socialization. Characteristically, the leaders of international systems are the most "powerful." The components of effective power, however, have shifted over time and have been difficult to define with precision.[18] Military power has been the ultimate test of leadership positions from the ancient imperial systems to the present age of nuclear weapons. When units are not fighting, other factors assume immediate importance. In the medieval international system, ideological rectitude was responsible for the influence of the papacy. In the present "balance of terror" era, economic superiority has elevated such nation states as Canada, Japan and West Germany to leadership roles despite their military inferiority.

Leadership selection, in short, is seldom performed within a specialized structure in international systems. The battlefield is a more important arena than the ballot box. The categories of national resources that are most salient in the recruitment process deal with material deprivations and rewards.

In unipolar systems military power establishes dominance of the core areas whence other influence resources agglutinate in the central region, such as economic wealth and administrative skill. Leaders in various peripheral subsystems of directive empires are appointed by institutions of the central government. Tight bipolar leaders are the most economically stable and prosperous members of ideologically distinct blocs. In directive blocs a threat to a leader is handled militarily; in nondirective blocs economic sanctions would be more frequent in controlling bloc

[16] Rosecrance, *Action and Reaction in World Politics*, Chap. 2.

[17] Chadwick F. Alger, "United Nations Participation as a Learning Experience," *Public Opinion Quarterly*, XXVII (Fall, 1963), 411–26.

[18] A complete set of components of "influence" has been specified to include power, respect, rectitude, affection, well-being, wealth, skill, and enlightenment. Harold D. Lasswell and Abraham Kaplan, *Power and Society* (New Haven, 1950), 87 (table 2).

deviants. In either case the most powerful units, with the most diverse sets of interests to promote, have more resources to mobilize to meet challenges to their position, so they are likely to assume central roles in reconciling intrabloc conflict. The United States is the mediator-leader of the Western bloc; the Soviet Union, within the Communist camp. The same principle applies to nonaligned countries in loose bipolarity. To some extent India and Egypt are leaders and mediators within the African-Asian group of countries.[19] Although the election of a Secretary General of a universalistic international actor gives the formal appearance of institutionalized recruitment, if the official is to be effective he must gain the approval of both blocs and of neutral countries in a loose bipolar system. Since international actors are constrained under multipolarity, differentiated leadership roles emerge only among the five or more major powers. The scope of the leadership tends to be specialized geographically into spheres of influence in order to avoid conflict between major powers. The "concert" of Europe was an institutional recognition of leadership roles played by the five major powers in post-Napoleonic Europe. Further role differentiation into factional leaders and followers around issues of common interest resulted in decreased regularity in use of the concert. In polypolar systems institutionalized recruitment of leaders, with genuine nomination and election procedures, would arise and persist. Since distinctions between states in power and wealth are minimal in polypolarity, the most "popular" countries would be leaders, and a true election process would undoubtedly emerge.

The fewer the centers of power in an international system, the more likely will leaders be chosen outside international structures. Ordinarily, however, countries with superior military power and economic resources are leaders; others are nonleaders.

Transaction

"Transaction" means the exchange of symbols, goods or persons between units. In Almond's original formulation, political communication is postulated as one of the functions of a political system. In international relations, trade and interchanges of nationals are as significant as communication, the transmission and receipt of messages. In domestic systems, commercial relations and travel are representative forms of behavior within the economic and cultural subsets of the social system, thus separable analytically from events in the political subset of the social system. International relations are so highly politicized, however, that it would be difficult to ignore international trade, labor mobility and cultural exchange in analyzing functions of international political systems.

World politics may be differentiated by the degree of interaction between units. In ancient civilizations there was little contact between empires, so there was not much need for interimperial international organization. In modern times the interaction between actors is so frequent that universal membership in international organization is expected.

The communication subfunction is performed usually in dyads between official representatives of two basic units. Newspapers of one country are seldom read by nationals of another,[20] and the stamp on goods "made in the United States" has less meaning for ordinary citizens than does a large volume of trade to government elites. Increasingly, transaction of symbols, persons and even goods occurs in meetings of international organizations, in corridors and conference rooms of the headquarters of such bodies and through technical and other assistance agencies of these organizations. Frequent meetings between plenipotentiaries of such dissimilar nation states as Bolivia and Belgium date from the first meeting of the League of Nations Assembly. Secretariats of international organizations contribute a substantial amount of international transactions through publications, political activities and technical services. International transactions are stratified in fidelity: universal international organizations are ideologically neutral sources of information and activities, while individual members and their bloc organizations are ideologically biased.

[19] Jan F. Triska and Howard E. Koch, Jr., "Asian-African Coalition and International Organization: Third Force or Collective Impotence?" *Review of Politics*, XXI (July, 1959), 417–55.

[20] Ithiel de Sola Pool, Suzanne Keller and Raymond A. Bauer, "The Influence of Foreign Travel on Political Attitudes of American Businessmen," *Public Opinion Quarterly*, XX (Spring, 1956), 163 (Table 5); Bernard C Cohen, *The Press and Foreign Policy* (Princeton, 1963).

Powerful actors are more prolific in international transactions than weak actors.[21]

Transaction volume reflects power stratification. In unipolar systems there is only one core area; in bipolar systems, two; in multipolar systems, five to eight; in polypolar systems, no definable core areas. Institutionalized performance of transaction is most likely in directive unipolar systems, where independent sources can be controlled and suppressed. Tight bipolar systems have two bloc-wide international organizations as frameworks for transaction. In a directive bloc, the flow of transactions is organizationally centralized; in nondirective blocs, it is more administratively decentralized, though there may be some concentration within the dominant power of the bloc. In loose bipolarity the two blocs are joined by an ambiguously arranged nonaligned set of countries, and a universal actor that provides institutionalized machinery for international transactions. In multipolarity, universalistic institutionalization of transaction is constrained by the oligarchy of major powers at the command of about five dense transactional nodes in the world polity. The more the volume of transactions in polypolar systems, the more need to establish organizations with functional differentiation and division of labor in transaction between units of the international system in order to prevent overloaded channels.

The number of centers of power in international arenas corresponds to the frequency of concentrated nodes in the world transactional network. Institutionalization of transaction is common when the system is either so simple as to be easily controlled or too complex to be self-managing.

Other Functions

Output functions deal with rules within political systems. An orderly social existence depends upon predictable behavior in the exchange of goods, symbols and services. Societies inevitably contain a kind of operational code,[22] which sorts out behavior that conforms to, or deviates from, the attainment of man's needs in a particular society. The operational code constitutes a set of conventional rules of conduct that enable individuals to achieve certain substantive aims.

A deficiency of international systems has been that rules of international operational codes are perceived as unjust by those on whom they are imposed. Latin American suspicion of "Yankee imperialism" is a well known example. Nonacceptance of rules has meant international anarchy. Unlike domestic political systems, most of the functions dealing with international rules are not performed within formal institutions. These functions are rule making, rule application and rule supervision.

Rule Making

In political systems there are two types of rules. *Procedural* rules specify the constitutional structures and practices through which inputs flow. *Substantive* rules are the concrete outputs of political decisions which allocate rewards in the resolution of interest conflicts. An example of a procedural rule is the provision in the United Nations Charter that says that the General Assembly may not make any recommendation with regard to a dispute or situation while the Security Council is considering it. Examples of substantive rules are decisions of a world court, resolutions calling for a plebiscite in Kashmir, or proclamations that no atomic weapons shall be shipped to Cuba.

Procedural rules in modern diplomacy were developed by Richelieu, and most of them have been codified or expanded within such structures as conferences of international bodies. The procedures of pacific settlement which emerged from the Hague conferences are examples of outputs of procedural rule making institutions.[23] Their utilization has been successful at times, but great powers have been reluctant to accept their substantive results. Most substantive rules are declared originally as foreign policy goals of powerful nations, though resolutions of international bodies play an increasing role. What distinguishes a goal that is merely articulated from a rule of the international system is its authoritatively prescribed observance. The most powerful states assume the roles of rule makers or rule breakers; less powerful states must be content

[21] Rudolph J. Rummel, "Dimensions of International Relations in the Mid-1950's," *American Political Science Review*, forthcoming.

[22] Nathan Leites, *The Operational Code of the Politburo* (New York, 1951).

[23] Zimmern, *The League of Nations and the Rule of Law, 1919–1935*, 110–17.

to be rule observers or rule amenders. There is further role specialization within international organizations. Plenary sessions do more rule making, and other bodies perform different functions connected with rules of the international system. International organizations constitute an arena for some substantive rule making, especially where small countries and nonvital interests are involved, but institutionalization of rule making in international structures is in a primitive stage. Few such rules, even the resolution providing for a plebiscite in Kashmir, are observed.[24]

The more substantive rules are made between any group of nations, the more procedural rules will be needed to make the rule making more routine and efficient. The number of procedural rules is doubtless an exponential function of the number of substantive rules. Since a procedural rule is an indicator of the degree of institutionalization of rule making, the more complex an international organization's procedures the greater its ability to resolve a large variety of international conflicts.

Procedural and substantive rules are made by the central unit of unipolar international systems. The rules confer particularistic benefits to the center at the expense of the periphery in directive empires. Tight bipolar systems have two competing sets of rules, made either by fiat in the dominant unit of a directive bloc on behalf of a bloc organization, or by a process of negotiation in an organization of a nondirective bloc. The few cross-bloc rules are concerned with procedures for interbloc transaction. In loose bipolarity the two blocs try to entice the uncommitted countries to adopt one of the competing sets of substantive rules. An institutional arena for resolution of conflicts is less successful in dealing with interbloc conflicts than with conflicts between nonaligned states. In multipolar systems the major powers jointly make rules in a concert framework when they come to an agreement; if there are disagreements among major powers, the concert is abandoned, and rule making occurs within spheres of great powers' influence.

Although "unit veto" polypolarity could be accompanied either by chaotic, disconnected attempts by countries to impose particularistic rules on each other, such systems would not last very long. In other polypolar systems democratic institutionalized procedures for rule making would arise, and the substantive decisions would tend to be more universalistic in character.

Rules are made by the most powerful units in a world polity. Institutionalization of rule making occurs when there is stability in a unit's dominance or when no single unit is able to dominate the international system.

Rule Application

When rules are implemented, or put into practice, they may be said to be applied. Implementation of a procedural rule may involve, for example, the convening of a special session of the General Assembly, when legal requirements for such a move have been fulfilled. An execution of a substantive rule occurs when an arbitral award is made, a plebiscite held, or a naval blockade established.

Once rules are made and carried out, violations of the rule are possible. When individuals detect these infractions or misinterpretations of the rule, a decision may be made to deal with the violators. Accordingly, a new rule will be issued about the particular case; the rule will then be implemented. Rule application, hence, has two manifestations. The initial execution of a rule is *execution*, the translation of a general rule into specific forms of behavior, whereas the application of a rule administered to a violator may be referred to as *enforcement*. The order to prevent flow of nuclear weapons to Cuba is executed by sending a fleet of ships to the Caribbean, but if a ship attempts to break through the blockade, implementation of the order may mean firing on the challenger of the rule (enforcement).

Procedural rules are applied by ministerial officials of units in the international system or by officers of international organizations—by foreign ministers, plenipotentiaries, secretaries general or by committee chairmen. Substantive rules are implemented by subordinate officials in bureaucracies, such as plebiscite election clerks and naval personnel.

Pacific settlement, thus, may be distinguished more precisely from collective security. In peaceful

[24] The same proposition is applicable to world courts. Shabtai Rosenne, "The International Court and the United Nations: Reflections on the Period 1946–1954," *International Organization*, IX (May, 1955), 244–56.

settlement a dispute is resolved by a rule which is implemented voluntarily by all parties. In collective security a rule that no country shall go to war is violated, whereupon enforcement of the rule is initiated by many countries to defeat the aggressor and stop the war.

In directive unipolar systems rule implementation is imposed upon the periphery of the system. Enforcement of rules is necessary when rules are regarded as unduly favorable to the center; all available means are mobilized to coerce the disobedient. In tight bipolar systems there is little implementation of interbloc rules because means for effective enforcement are lacking. Directive bloc leaders monopolize enforcement capabilities to insure compliance with their particularistic bloc rules. In nondirective blocs there is such dispersion of means of enforcement that implementation of rules is voluntary; a lone deviant can be easily coerced by the rest of the bloc if its expulsion from the bloc is seen as the greater evil. In loose bipolarity there is more specialization in rule implementation and enforcement. Representatives of neutral nations, usually in official roles of universalistic institutions, assume mediatory roles to reduce conflict between the two blocs. The "leave it to Dag" approach was a recognition that Hammarskjold, as United Nations Secretary General, was effective in securing consent to General Assembly rules precisely because his official role was nonpolitical. Collective security, however, has operated through traditional diplomatic channels in the absence of an international police force. Under multipolarity, rule implementation can be assured when the major powers are unanimously behind a rule, willing to enforce it. But when major powers cannot all agree, a recalcitrant state can avoid implementation so long as it is supported by one or two major powers. If the fundamental rule of stable multipolarity—that no unit or coalition may approach a predominance in strength—is violated, the other major powers must mobilize collective security measures to enforce the rule. Voluntary compliance and international enforcement institutions are most likely in polypolar, democratic international systems.

Implementation of rules is a function of the degree of concentration of influence within the system, because enforcement capability insures compliance with international rules. So long as rules shift in content over time due to changes in the world polity, rules will not assume a traditional character which enables an actor to internalize them, making implementation more automatic and enforcement less necessary.

Rule Supervision

The final function is rule supervision, not rule adjudication as in Almond's framework. The reason for this alteration can be explained by examining the functions performed by courts and by law enforcement officers.

Judges hear facts of a case, thus overseeing how particular behavior measures up to prescribed legal standards; secondly, they make rulings concerning how behavior should be altered, if necessary. Police officers supervise public conduct and also apply general rules to specific cases. Because judicial and administrative processes are bifunctional, the Almond framework may be modified by eliminating "rule adjudication" from the list of functions of political systems. One part is recategorized as rule making; the other is designated as rule supervision.

Procedural rule supervision is performed by a parliamentarian in rule making bodies. Supervisors of procedural rule appliers are officials whose responsibility it is to see that orders are neither countermanded nor deficient or excessive of specified limits of competence. If the Economic and Social Council spends too much or too little for an authorized field project, supervision of its error may be performed by auditors in the secretariat budget staff or by a General Assembly committee.

The central unit of a unipolar system delegates the task of rule supervision to colonial and military administrators in each province. Spies, fifth column elements, members of the diplomatic corps and members of non-governmental private associations supervise rule observance for leaders of directive blocs in tight bipolar systems; the diplomatic network is the major structure performing the rule overseeing function for nondirective bloc leaders. In loose bipolarity the power possessed by an international organization enables it to establish supervisorial organs even when it cannot enforce rules. Indeed, the closest thing to a functional innovation within the League of Nations and the United Nations has been the increase in supervisorial powers of constituent and special organs. The use of "preventive diplomacy" with such bodies as UNEF in Suez and ONUC in the Congo has depended upon nonaligned nations for support.[25] In nineteenth century multipolarity the concert was a supervisorial institution to insure that the balance of power was not upset. When major powers disband the institution of the concert, information about rule compliance is no longer pooled in a regular fashion; it is particularistically analyzed. The efficiency of a polypolar system of interdependent, mutually interacting states points toward functional specificity in performance of the supervisorial function by an international organization.

The locus of rule supervision is deconcentrated territorially, but its management lies in the hands of any unit of the international system that has representatives abroad. Institutionalization occurs when centers of power are linked organizationally, or when they agree to establish a functionally specific organ.

Summary

The major actors in international systems are the basic units, whether, empires, city states or nation states. Most functions are performed outside international structures; they are performed instead within each particularistic unit. Institutionalization in particularistic structures is very likely if the number of power centers is one or two; universalistic structures are most likely to contain functionally specific universalistic institutions when power is diffused throughout an international system.

Conclusion

A unified approach to the study of international organization has been long overdue. The usual criticism of a theoretical scheme which contains tentative observations about the findings it anticipates is that it blocks, rather than opens, new avenues for research. The intention of the framework presented above is the contrary.

Structural-functional case studies of international organizations in many time periods are needed in order to provide a descriptive literature. Propositions can be tested definitively only later. The power approach of Hans Morgenthau[26] is interjected above to suggest the most plausible hypotheses, given the current state of knowledge in the field of international relations.

Interrelations between functions remain to be specified. The conditions under which institutionalization of functions in international systems will increase or decrease are not well known. Finally, the degree to which international organizations transform, rather than reinforce, the power stratification of the world polity is an unanswered question.

The functional approach is only one route for attacking such problems. Its only claim is that it offers certain conveniences in categorization, hypothesis-suggesting and in placing international organization in its proper perspective within international systems.

[25] Claude, *Swords into Plowshares*, 285-303.

[26] Hans J. Morgenthau, *Politics Among Nations* (3rd ed., New York, 1962).

14. International Law and Assumptions About the State System*

William D. Coplin is Associate Professor of Political Science at Wayne State University. A specialist in the application of simulation techniques to the study of international politics, his work also includes authorship of *The Functions of International Law* (1966). In this article Professor Coplin analyzes key juridical aspects of the international system, concluding that, like the system for which it provides legal structure, international law is in itself undergoing change. His thought that this evolving body of law facilitates as well as reflects the changing political scene points to yet another facet of the complexity of international systems. [*Reprinted from* World Politics, *XVII (July 1965), 615–34, by permission of the author and the publisher.*]

Most writers on international relations and international law still examine the relationship between international law and politics in terms of the assumption that law either should or does function only as a coercive restraint on political action. Textbook writers on general international politics like Morgenthau,[1] and Lerche and Said,[2] as well as those scholars who have specialized in international law like J. L. Brierly[3]

and Charles De Visscher,[4] make the common assumption that international law should be examined as a system of coercive norms controlling the actions of states. Even two of the newer works, *The Political Foundations of International Law* by Morton A. Kaplan and Nicholas deB. Katzenbach[5] and *Law and Minimum World Public Order* by Myres S.

* I want to thank Dr. Robert W. Tucker of the Johns Hopkins University and Richard Miller of Wayne State University Law School for their constructive criticism of the first draft of this article.

[1] Hans J. Morgenthau, *Politics Among Nations* (New York 1961), 275–311. The entire evaluation of the "main problems" of international law is focused on the question of what rules are violated and what rules are not.

[2] Charles O. Lerche, Jr., and Abdul A. Said, *Concepts of International Politics* (Englewood Cliffs, N.J., 1963), 167–87. That the authors have employed the assumption that international law functions as a system of restraint is evident from the title of their chapter which examines international law, "Limitations on State Actions."

[3] J. L. Brierly, *The Law of Nations* (New York 1963), I. Brierly defines international law as "the body of rules and principles of action which are binding upon civilized states in their relations. . . ."

[4] Charles De Visscher, *Theory and Reality in Public International Law* (Princeton 1957), 99–100.

[5] Morton A. Kaplan and Nicholas deB. Katzenbach, *The Political Foundations of International Law* (New York 1961), 5. In a discussion of how the student should observe international law and politics, the authors write: "To understand the substance and limits of such constraining rules (international law), it is necessary to examine the interests which support them in the international system, the means by which they are made effective, and the functions they perform. Only in this way is it possible to predict the areas in which rules operate, the limits of rules as effective constraints, and the factors which underlie normative change." Although the authors are asking an important question—"Why has international law been binding in some cases?"—they still assume that international law functions primarily as a direct restraint on state action. For an excellent review of this book, see Robert W. Tucker, "Resolution," *Journal of Conflict Resolution*, VII (March 1963), 69–75.

McDougal and Florentino P. Feliciano,[6] in spite of an occasional reference to the non-coercive aspects of international law, are developed primarily from the model of international law as a system of restraint. Deriving their conception of the relationship between international law and political action from their ideas on the way law functions in domestic communities, most modern writers look at international law as an instrument of direct control. The assumption that international law is or should be a coercive restraint on state action structures almost every analysis, no matter what the school of thought or the degree of optimism or pessimism about the effectiveness of the international legal system.[7] With

an intellectual framework that measures international law primarily in terms of constraint on political action, there is little wonder that skepticism about international law continues to increase while creative work on the level of theory seems to be diminishing.[8]

Therefore, it is desirable to approach the relationship between international law and politics at a different functional level, not because international law does not function at the level of coercive restraint, but because it also functions at another level. In order to illustrate a second functional level in the relationship between international law and politics, it is necessary to examine the operation of domestic law. In a domestic society, the legal system as a series of interrelated normative statements does more than direct or control the actions of its members through explicit rules backed by a promise of coercion. Systems of law also act on a more generic and pervasive level by serving as authoritative (i.e., accepted as such by the community) modes of communicating or reflecting the ideals and purposes, the acceptable roles and actions, as well as the very processes of the societies. The legal system functions on the level of the individual's perceptions and attitudes by presenting to him an image of the social system—an image which has both factual and normative aspects and which contributes to social order by building a consensus on procedural as well as on substantive matters. In this sense, law in the domestic situation is a primary tool in the "socialization"[9] of the individual.

International law functions in a similar manner: namely, as an institutional device for communicating to the policy-makers of various states a consensus on the nature of the international system. The purpose of this article is to approach the relationship between international law and politics not as a system of direct restraints on state action, but rather as a system of quasi-authoritative communications to the policy-makers concerning the reasons for state

[6] Myres S. McDougal and Florentino P. Feliciano, *Law and Minimum World Public Order* (New Haven 1961), 10. The authors suggest that if any progress in conceptualizing the role of international law is to be made, it is necessary to distinguish between the "factual process of international coercion and the process of authoritative decision by which the public order of the world community endeavors to regulate such process of coercion." This suggestion is based on the assumption that international law promotes order primarily through the establishment of restraints on state actions.

[7] There are a few writers who have tried to approach international law from a different vantage point. For a survey of some of the other approaches to international law and politics, see Michael Barkun, "International Norms: An Interdisciplinary Approach," *Background*, VIII (August 1964), 121–29. The survey shows that few "new" approaches to international law have developed beyond the preliminary stages, save perhaps for the writings of F. S. C. Northrop. Northrop's works (e.g., *Philosophical Anthropology and Practical Politics* [New York 1960], 326–30) are particularly significant in their attempt to relate psychological, philosophical, and cultural approaches to the study of law in general, although he has not usually been concerned with the overall relationship of international political action. Not mentioned in Barkun's survey but important in the discussion of international law and politics is Stanley Hoffmann, "International Systems and International Law," in Klaus Knorr and Sidney Verba, eds., *The International System* (Princeton 1961), 205–38. However, Hoffmann's essay is closer in approach to the work by Kaplan and Katzenbach than to the approach developed in this article. Finally, it is also necessary to point to an article by Edward McWhinney, "Soviet and Western International Law and the Cold War in a Nuclear Era of Bipolarity: Inter-Bloc Law in a Nuclear Age," *Canadian Yearbook of International Law*, I (1963), 40–81. Professor McWhinney discusses the relationship between American and Russian structures of action, on the one hand, and their interpretations of international law, on the other. While McWhinney's approach is basically similar to the one proposed in this article in its attempt to relate international law to politics on a conceptual level, his article is focused on a different set of problems, the role of national attitudes in the contemporary era on ideas of international

law. Nevertheless, it is a significant contribution to the task of analyzing more clearly the relationship between international law and politics.

[8] See Richard A. Falk, "The Adequacy of Contemporary International Law: Gaps in Legal Thinking," *Virginia Law Review*, L (March 1964), 231–65, for a valuable but highly critical analysis of contemporary international legal theory.

[9] See Gabriel A. Almond and James S. Coleman, eds., *The Politics of the Developing Areas* (Princeton 1960), 26–31, for an explanation of the concept of socialization.

actions and the requisites for international order. It is a "quasi-authoritative" device because the norms of international law represent only an imperfect consensus of the community of states, a consensus which rarely commands complete acceptance but which usually expresses generally held ideas. Given the decentralized nature of law-creation and law-application in the international community, there is no official voice of the states as a collectivity. However, international law taken as a body of generally related norms is the closest thing to such a voice. Therefore, in spite of the degree of uncertainty about the authority of international law, it may still be meaningful to examine international law as a means for expressing the commonly held assumptions about the state system.

The approach advocated in this article has its intellectual antecedents in the sociological school, since it seeks to study international law in relation to international politics. Furthermore, it is similar to that of the sociological school in its assumption that there is or should be a significant degree of symmetry between international law and politics on the level of intellectual constructs—that is, in the way in which international law has expressed and even shaped ideas about relations between states. It is hoped that this approach will contribute to a greater awareness of the interdependence of international law and conceptions of international politics.

Before analyzing the way in which international law has in the past and continues today to reflect common attitudes about the nature of the state system, let us discuss briefly the three basic assumptions which have generally structured those attitudes.[10] First, it has been assumed that the state

is an absolute institutional value and that its security is the one immutable imperative for state action. If there has been one thing of which policy-makers could always be certain, it is that their actions must be designed to preserve their state. Second, it has been assumed that international politics is a struggle for power, and that all states seek to increase their power. Although the forms of power have altered during the evolution of the state system, it has been generally thought that states are motivated by a drive for power, no matter what the stakes. The third basic assumption permeating ideas about the international system has to do with maintaining a minimal system of order among the states. This assumption, symbolized generally by the maxim "Preserve the balance of power," affirms the necessity of forming coalitions to counter any threat to hegemony and of moderating actions in order to avoid an excess of violence that could disrupt the system.

It is necessary at this point to note that an unavoidable tension has existed between the aim of maintaining the state and maximizing power, on the one hand, and of preserving the international system, on the other. The logical extension of either aim would threaten the other, since complete freedom of action by the state would not allow for the limitation imposed by requirements to maintain the system, and a strict regularization of state action inherent in the idea of the system would curtail the state's drive for power. However, the tension has remained constant, with neither norm precluding the other except when a given state was in immediate danger of destruction. At those times, the interests of the system have been subordinated to the drive for state survival, but with no apparent long-range effect on the acceptance by policy-makers of either set of interests, despite their possible incompatibility. The prescriptions that states should be moderate, flexible, and vigilant[11] have been a manifestation of the operation of the system. Together, the three basic assumptions about the state system have constituted the conceptual basis from which the policy-makers have planned the actions of their state.

[10] The following discussion of the assumptions of the state system is brief, since students of international politics generally agree that the three assumptions listed have structured most of the actions of states. This agreement is most complete concerning the nature of the "classical" state system. The author is also of the opinion that these assumptions continue to operate today in a somewhat mutated form. (See his unpublished manuscript "The Image of Power Politics: A Cognitive Approach to the Study of International Politics," Chaps. 2, 4, 8.) Note also the agreement on the nature of classical ideas about international politics in the following: Ernst B. Haas, "The Balance of Power as a Guide to Policy-Making," *Journal of Politics*, XV (August 1953), 370–97; Morton A. Kaplan, *System and Process in International Politics* (New York 1957), 22–36; and Edward Vose Gulick, *Europe's Classical Balance of Power* (Ithaca, N.Y., 1955).

[11] See Gulick, 34; and for a discussion of the principles of moderation, flexibility, and vigilance, *ibid.*, 11–16.

I. Classical International Law and the Image of the State System

Almost every legal aspect of international relations from 1648 to 1914 reinforced and expressed the assumptions of the state system. State practices in regard to treaties, boundaries, neutrality, the occupation of new lands, freedom of the seas, and diplomacy, as well as classical legal doctrines, provide ample illustration of the extent to which the basic assumptions of the state were mirrored in international law.

The essential role of treaties in international law reflected the three assumptions of the state system. First, treaty practices helped to define the nature of statehood. Emanating from the free and unfettered will of states, treaties were the expression of their sovereign prerogatives. Statehood itself was defined in part as the ability to make treaties, and that ability presupposed the equality and independence usually associated with the idea of the state. Moreover, certain definitive treaties, like those written at the Peace of Augsburg (1515) and the Peace of Westphalia (1648), actually made explicit the attributes of statehood. The former treaty affirmed the idea that the Prince had complete control over the internal affairs of the state, while the latter emphasized that states were legally free and equal in their international relationships.[12] Even the actual wording of treaties expressed the classical assumption about the sanctity of the state. Whether in the formal references to the "high contracting parties" or in the more vital statements about the agreement of sovereigns not to interfere with the actions of other sovereigns, treaties were clear expressions of the classical idea of the state.[13]

Treaty law also contributed to the evolution of the classical assumption regarding the maintenance of the international system. Both explicitly and implicitly, treaties affirmed the necessity of an international system. Whether or not they contained such phrases as "balance of power," "just equilibrium," "universal and perpetual peace,"[14] "common and public safety and tranquillity,"[15] "public tranquillity on a lasting foundation,"[16] or "safety and interest of Europe,"[17] the most important treaties during the classical period affirmed the desirability of maintaining the international system.[18] Also, many treaties reaffirmed earlier treaty agreements, contributing to the idea that the international system was a continuing, operative unity.[19] Therefore, treaties usually reminded the policy-maker that the maintenance of the international system was a legitimate and necessary objective of state policy.

Finally, treaties affirmed the necessity and, in part, the legality of the drive for power. The constant juggling of territory, alliances, and other aspects of capability was a frequent and rightful subject of treaty law. Treaties implicitly confirmed that power was the dynamic force in relations between states by defining the legal criteria of power and, more important, by providing an institutional means, subscribed to by most of the members of the system, which legalized certain political transactions, such as territorial acquisition and dynastic exchange.

A second state practice which contributed to the classical assumptions about the state system was the legal concept of boundaries. Inherent in the very idea of the boundary were all three assumptions of the classical system. First, the boundary marked off that most discernible of all criteria of a state's existence—territory.[20] A state was sovereign within its territory, and the boundary was essential to the demarcation and protection of that sovereignty. Freedom and equality necessitated the delineation of a certain area of complete control; the boundary as conceptualized in international law was the

---

[12] For the effects of the two treaties, see Charles Petrie, *Diplomatic History, 1713–1939* (London 1949), 111; David Jayne Hill, *A History of Diplomacy in the International Development of Europe* (New York 1924), 603–6; and Arthur Nussbaum, *A Concise History of the Law of Nations* (New York 1961), 116.

[13] E.g., *The Treaty of Ryswick, 1697* in Andrew Browning, ed., *English History Documents*, VIII (New York 1963), 881–83.

[14] *Treaty of Ryswick*, Article 1, in *ibid.*

[15] *Barrier Treaty of 1715*, Article 1, in *ibid.*, Vol. X.

[16] *Treaty of Vienna, 1713*, in *ibid.*, Vol. VIII.

[17] *Treaty of Quadruple Alliance, 1815*, in *ibid.*, Vol. XI.

[18] Leo Gross ,"The Peace of Westphalia, 1648–1948," *American Journal of International Law*, XLII (January 1948), 20–40.

[19] For a treaty which expressed the necessity of keeping prior obligations, see *Treaty of Aix-la-Chapelle, 1748*, in Browning, ed., Vol. X.

[20] See John H. Herz, *International Politics in the Atomic Age* (New York 1962), 53, for a discussion of the role of territory in the classical state system and the international legal system.

institutional means through which that necessity was fulfilled. Second, the boundary was essential for the preservation of the international system.[21] After every war the winning powers set up a new or revised set of boundaries which aided them in maintaining order by redistributing territory. More important, the boundary also provided a criterion by which to assess the intentions of other states. Change of certain essential boundaries signified a mortal threat to the whole system, and signaled the need for a collective response.[22] Finally, the legal concept of boundaries provided a means through which the expansion and contraction of power in the form of territory could be measured. Since the boundary was a legal means of measuring territorial changes, international law in effect reinforced the idea that the struggle for power was an essential and accepted part of international politics. All three assumptions of the state system, therefore, were mirrored in the classical legal concept of boundaries. . . .

The assumptions of the state system were reinforced not only by the legal practices of states but also by the major international legal theories of the classical period. Three general schools of thought developed: the naturalists, the eclectics or Grotians, and the positivists.[23] In each school, there was a major emphasis on both the state and the state system as essential institutional values. Whether it was Pufendorf's insistence on the "natural equality of state,"[24] the Grotians' concept of the sovereign power of state,[25] or Bynkershoek and the nineteenth-century positivists' point that treaties were the prime, if not the only, source of international law,[26] the state was considered by most classical theorists to be the essential institution protected by the legal system. At the same time, almost every classical writer on international law either assumed or argued for the existence of an international system

of some kind.[27] Along with Grotians, the naturalists maintained that a system of states existed, since man was a social animal. Vattel, probably the most famous international lawyer in the classical period, asserted that a balance of power and a state system existed.[28] Even the positivists of the nineteenth century assumed that there was an international system of some kind. This is apparent from their emphasis on the balance of power,[29] as well as from their assumption that relations between nations could be defined in terms of legal rights and duties.[30]

Therefore, there was a consensus among the classical theorists of international law that international politics had two structural elements: the state, with its rights of freedom and self-preservation; and the system, with its partial effectiveness in maintaining a minimal international order. That the theorists never solved the conflict between the idea of the unfettered sovereign state, on the one hand, and a regulating system of law, on the other, is indicative of a conflict within the assumptions of the state system,[31] but a conflict which neither prevented international lawyers from writing about an international legal order nor kept policy-makers from pursuing each state's objectives without destroying the state system.

[21] See Hoffmann, 212, 215, for a discussion of the way in which territorial settlements in treaties aided stability within the system. He calls this function part of the law of political framework.

[22] E.g., the English and French attitude toward Belgium.

[23] For a discussion of the precise meaning of these classifications, see Nussbaum.

[24] Ibid., 149.

[25] Hugo Grotius, The Rights of War and Peace, ed. with notes by A. C. Campbell (Washington 1901), 62.

[26] Cornelius Van Bynkershoek, De dominio maris dissertatio, trans. by Ralph Van Deman Mogoffin (New York 1923), 35.

[27] De Visscher, 88. For similar interpretations of classical and pre-twentieth-century theorists, see Walter Schiffer, The Legal Community of Mankind (New York 1951), Chap. I; or Percy E. Corbett, Law and Society in the Relations of States (New York 1951).

[28] Emeric de Vattel, The Laws of Nations (Philadelphia 1867), 412–14.

[29] G. F. Von Martens, The Law of Nations: Being the Science of National Law, Covenants, Power & Founded upon the Treaties and Custom of Modern Nations in Europe, trans. by William Cobbett (4th ed., London 1829), 123–24.

[30] Almost all of the nineteenth-century positivists assumed that relations between nations were systematized enough to allow for a system of rights and duties. E.g., William Edward Hall, A Treatise on International Law (Oxford 1904), 43–59; Henry Wheaton, Elements of International Law (Oxford 1936), 75. Wheaton does not discuss duties as such, but when he talks about legal rights he distinguishes between "absolute" and "conditional" rights. According to Wheaton, the "conditional" rights are those resulting from membership in the international legal system. This formulation implies the existence of corresponding duties.

[31] See Von Martens, 123–34, for the intellectual and legal problems growing out of the assumption that states may legally maximize power but that they also have a responsibility "to oppose by alliances and even by force of arms" a series of aggrandizements which threaten the community.

Although the norms of classical international law sometimes went unheeded, the body of theory and of state practice which constituted "international law as an institution" nonetheless expressed in a quasi-authoritative manner the three assumptions about international politics. It legalized the existence of states and helped to define the actions necessary for the preservation of each state and of the system as a whole. It reinforced the ideas that vigilance, moderation, and flexibility are necessary for the protection of a system of competing states. And finally, international law established a legalized system of political payoffs by providing a means to register gains and losses without creating a static system. In fact, this last aspect was essential to the classical state system. With international law defining certain relationships (territorial expansion, empire-building, etc.) as legitimate areas for political competition, other areas seemed, at least generally in the classical period, to be removed from the center of the political struggle. By legitimizing the struggle as a form of political competition rather than as universal conflict, international law sanctioned a form of international system that was more than just an anarchic drive for survival.

II. Contemporary International Law and the Assumptions of the State System

As a quasi-authoritative system of communicating the assumptions of the state system to policy-makers, contemporary international law no longer presents a clear idea of the nature of international politics. This is in part a result of the tension, within the structure of contemporary international law itself, between the traditional legal concepts and the current practices of states. International law today is in a state of arrested ambiguity—in a condition of unstable equilibrium between the old and the new. As a result, it no longer contributes as it once did to a consensus on the nature of the state system. In fact, it adds to the growing uncertainty and disagreement as to how the international political system itself is evolving. The following discussion will attempt to assess the current developments in international law in terms of the challenges those developments make to the three assumptions of the state system. It is realized that the three assumptions themselves have already undergone change, but our purpose is to show where contemporary international legal practice and theory stand in relation to that change.

The Challenge to the State and the System

The current legal concept of the state is a perfect example of the arrested ambiguity of contemporary international law and of the threat that this condition represents to the assumptions of the state system. On the one hand, most of the traditional forms used to express the idea of statehood are still employed. Treaty-makers and statesmen still write about "respect for territorial integrity," the "right of domestic jurisdiction," and the "sovereign will of the high contracting parties." Moreover, most of the current substantive rights and duties, such as self-defense, legal equality, and territorial jurisdiction, that are based on the assumption that states as units of territory are the irreducible institutional values of the system continue to be central to international legal practice.[32] On the other hand, certain contemporary developments contrast sharply with the traditional territory-oriented conceptions of international law.[33] With the growth of international entities possessing supranational powers (e.g., ECSC), the legal idea of self-contained units based on territorial control lacks the clear basis in fact that it once enjoyed. Many of the traditional prerogatives of the sovereign state, such as control over fiscal policy,[34] have been transferred in some respects to transnational units. While the development of supranational powers is most pronounced in Europe, there is reason to believe, especially concerning international cooperation on technical matters, that organizations patterned on the European experience might occur elsewhere.

Another significant manifestation of ambiguity in the territorial basis of international law is found in

[32] E.g., Charles G. Fenwick, *International Law* (New York 1952), Chap. II.

[33] For a survey of current challenges to traditional international law, see Wolfgang Friedmann, "The Changing Dimensions of International Law," *Columbia Law Review*, LXII (November 1962), 1147–65. Also see Richard A. Falk, *The Role of the Domestic Courts in the International Legal Order* (Syracuse 1964), 14–19, for a discussion of the fact that while there is a growing "functional obsolescence" of the state system, the assumptions of the state system continue to operate for psychological and political reasons.

[34] E.g., Articles 3 and 4 of the *Treaty Establishing the European Coal and Steel Community* (April 18, 1951).

post-World War II practice of questioning the validity of the laws of other states. The "act of state doctrine" no longer serves as the guideline it once did in directing the national courts of one state to respect the acts promulgated in another.[35] Once based on the assumption of the "inviolability of the sovereign," the "act of state doctrine" today is the source of widespread controversy. The conflicting views of the doctrine are symptomatic of the now ambiguous role of territoriality in questions of jurisdictional and legal power. Although these developments in current legal practice are only now emerging, they nonetheless can be interpreted as a movement away from the strictly and clearly defined legal concept of the state that appeared in classical international law.

Other developments in contemporary international law represent, theoretically at least, a challenge to the assumption that the state and its freedom of action are an absolute necessity for the state system. Most noticeable has been the attempt to develop an international organization which would preserve a minimal degree of order. Prior to the League of Nations, there had been attempts to institutionalize certain aspects of international relations, but such attempts either did not apply to the political behavior of states (e.g., the Universal Postal Union) or did not challenge the basic assumptions of the state system (as the very loosely defined Concert of Europe failed to do). As it was formulated in the Covenant and defined by the intellectuals, the League represented a threat to the assumptions of the state system because it sought to settle once and for all the tension between the policy-maker's commitment to preserve his state and his desire to maintain the state system by subordinating his state to it through a formal institution.

Proponents of the League saw it as a means to formalize a system of maintaining international order by committing states in advance to a coalition against any state that resorted to war without fulfilling the requirements of the Covenant. If it had been operative, such a commitment would have represented a total revolution in the legal concept of the state as an independent entity, since it would have abolished the most essential of all sovereign prerogatives, the freedom to employ coercion. However, the ideal purpose of the League, on the one hand, and the aims of politicians and the actual constitutional and operational aspects of the League, on the other, proved to be quite different. Owing to certain legal formulations within the Covenant (Articles 10, 15, 21) and the subsequent application of the principles (e.g., in Manchuria and Ethiopia), the hoped-for subordination of the state to the system was not realized.[36]

Like the League, the United Nations was to replace the state as the paramount institutional value by establishing a constitutional concert of powers. However, it has succeeded only in underscoring the existing tension between the drive to maintain the state and the goal of maintaining the system. In the Charter itself, the tension between the state and the system remains unresolved.[37] Nor does the actual operation of the United Nations

[35] For an excellent discussion of the legal and political problems related to the question of the "act of state doctrine" in particular, and of territorial supremacy as a concept in general, see Kenneth S. Carlston, *Law and Organization in World Society* (Urbana, Ill., 1962), 191–93, 266–69. Also, for a discussion of the problem in a larger framework, see Falk, *Role of the Domestic Courts*. Since World War II, states, especially on the European continent, have found increasingly broader bases to invalidate the effect of foreign laws. Traditionally, states have refused to give validity to the laws of other lands for a small number of narrowly constructed reasons (e.g., refusal to enforce penal or revenue laws). Today many states have declared foreign laws invalid for a variety of reasons, the most important being the formulation that the national court cannot give validity to a foreign law that is illegal in terms of international law (see *"The Rose Mary Case," International Law Report* [1953], 316 ff.), and the most frequent being a broad interpretation of "sense of public-order" (see Martin Domke, "Indonesian Nationalization Measures Before Foreign Courts," *American Journal of International Law*, LIV [April 1960], 305–23). The most recent case in American practice, the *Sabbatino* decision (Supplement, *International Legal Materials*, III, No. 2 [March 1964], 391), appears to reaffirm the traditional emphasis on the territorial supremacy of the national legal order in these matters, but is actually ambiguous. On the one hand, the Opinion of the Court applied the "act of state doctrine" in declaring the Cuban law valid, but on the other hand, the Court stated that "international law does not require application of the doctrine."

[36] For a useful discussion of the relationship between the idea of collective security and the assumption of the balance of power system, see Inis L. Claude, *Swords into Plowshares* (New York 1962), 255–60; and Herz, Chap. 5. It is necessary to make a distinction between the theory of collective security, which certainly would challenge the basic assumptions of the state system, and its operation, which would not.

[37] Compare Articles 25–51, or paragraphs 2–7 in Article 2, for the contrast between system-oriented and state-oriented norms.

provide a very optimistic basis for the hope that tension will be lessened in the future.

In terms of international law, regional organizations constitute a mixed challenge to the traditional relationship between the state and the system. Although certain organizations represent an attempt to transcend the traditional bounds of their constituent members on functional grounds, this does not necessarily mean that those members have rejected the state as a political form. In reality, if regional organizations represent any transformation at all in the structural relationship between the state and the system, they constitute an attempt to create a bigger and better state, an attempt which is not contrary to the traditional assumptions of the state system. In spite of the fact that some organizations are given supranational power and present a challenge in that sense, most of the organizations are as protective of the sovereign rights of the state as is the United Nations Charter (e.g., the OAS Charter) or are not regional organizations at all, but military alliances.[38]

A more serious challenge, but one somewhat related to the challenge by regional organizations, is the changing relation of the individual to the international legal order. In the classical system, international law clearly relegated the individual to the position of an object of the law. Not the individual, but the state had the rights and duties of the international legal order.[39] This legal formulation was in keeping with the classical emphasis on the sanctity of the state. Today, however, the development of the concepts of human rights, international and regional organizations, and the personal responsibility of policy-makers to a higher law not only limit the scope of legally permissible international action but, more important, limit the traditional autonomy of the leaders of the state over internal matters.[40] The

idea that the individual rather than the state is the unit of responsibility in the formulation of policy has a long intellectual tradition;[41] however, it is only recently that the norms associated with that idea have become a part of international law.

Although the role of the individual in international law is small and the chances for its rapid development in the near future slight, it represents a more vital challenge to traditional international law and to the assumptions of the state system than either international or regional organizations. Since the principle of collective responsibility (of the state) rather than individual responsibility has traditionally served as the infrastructure for the rights and duties of states,[42] the development of a place for the individual in the international legal system that would make him personally responsible would completely revolutionize international law. At the same time, by making the individual a higher point of policy reference than the state, the development of the role of the individual represents a challenge to the assumption once reflected in classical international law that the preservation and maximization of state power is an absolute guideline for policy-makers. The evolving place of the individual in the contemporary international legal system, then, is contrary to the traditional tendency of international law to reaffirm the absolute value of the state.

The Challenge to the Concept of Power

One of the most significant developments in international law today relates to the assumption that states do and should compete for power. In the classical period, international law, through the legal concepts of neutrality, rules of warfare, occupation of new lands, rules of the high seas, and laws of diplomacy, reinforced the idea that a struggle for power among states was normal and necessary. Today, many of these specific legal norms still

[38] This is not to say that regional organizations do not represent a challenge to the concept of the state on psychological or social grounds. Obviously, the type of allegiance to a United Europe would be different in kind and degree from the traditional allegiance to a European state. However, in terms of the challenge to the legal concept of the state, regional organizations still adhere to the idea that the constituent members are sovereign in their relationship with states outside the organization.

[39] See Corbett, 53–6, for a discussion of the place of the individual in classical international law.

[40] Most modern writers have noted that the individual no longer stands in relation to international law solely as the object (e.g., Corbett, 133–35, or Friedmann, 1160–62),

though they are agreed that, to use Friedmann's words, "the rights of the individual in international law are as yet fragmentary and uncertain."

[41] According to Guido de Ruggiero, *The History of European Liberalism* (Boston 1959), 363–70, the liberal conception of the state has always assumed that the individual was the absolute value, though this idea has not always been operative.

[42] For an excellent discussion of the role of collective responsibility in international law, see Hans Kelsen, *Principles of International Law* (New York 1959), 9–13, 114–48.

apply, but the overall permissible range of the struggle for military power[43] has been limited by the concept of the just war.

The idea of the just war is not new to international law. Most of the classical writers discussed it, but they refused to define the concept in strict legal terms and usually relegated it to the moral or ethical realm.[44] The nineteenth-century positivists completely abandoned the doctrine with the formulation that "wars between nations must be considered as just on both sides with respect to treatment of enemies, military arrangements, and peace."[45] However, with the increased capability of states to destroy each other, a movement has grown to regulate force by legal means.

This movement developed through the Hague Conventions and the League of Nations and, in some respects, culminated in the Kellogg-Briand Pact of 1928. Today, the just war is a more or less accepted concept in international law. Most authors write, and most policy-makers state, that aggression is illegal and must be met with the sanction of the international community. The portent of this formulation of the assumption regarding power is great since, theoretically at least, it deprives the states of the range of action which they once freely enjoyed in maximizing their power and in protecting themselves. If the only legal justification for war is self-defense, or authorization of action in accordance with the Charter of the United Nations,[46]

then a war to preserve the balance of power or to expand in a limited fashion is outlawed. While the traditional formulation of international law provided a broad field upon which the game of power politics could be played, the new formulations concerning the legal use of force significantly limit and, one could argue, make illegal the military aspects of the game of power politics.[47] The freedom to use military power, once an essential characteristic of sovereignty and an integral part of international law, is no longer an accepted international legal norm.

The concept of the just war directly challenges the assumptions of the state system, because it implies that the military struggle for power is no longer a normal process of international politics. No longer does international law legitimize the gains of war, and no longer do policy-makers look upon war as a rightful tool of national power.[48] This is not to say that states do not use force in their current struggles or that the doctrine of the just war would deter them in a particular case. However, the doctrine does operate on the conceptual level by expressing to the policy-makers the idea that the use of force is no longer an everyday tool of international power politics. In terms of the traditional assumption about the state's natural inclination to maximize power, the contemporary legal commitment to the just-war doctrine represents a profound and historic shift.

III. International Law and the Reality of Contemporary International Politics

Contemporary international legal practice, then, is developing along lines which represent a threat not only to traditional concepts of international

---

[43] Although the military struggle today is considered to be only one aspect of the struggle for power, it is the one most closely related to the problem of order in both the classical and the contemporary system, and therefore the most crucial in the relationship between law and politics.

[44] See D. W. Bowett, *Self-Defense in International Law* (Manchester 1958), 156–57; and Nussbaum, 137, 153–55, 171.

[45] See Nussbaum, 182–83. Also see Ian Brownlie, *International Law and the Use of Force by States* (Oxford 1963), 15–18.

[46] Actually, the range of action provided by the contemporary formulation, especially regarding the authorization in accordance with the United Nations Charter, could be broad and could conceivably take in "balancing" action if the deadlock in the Security Council were broken. The reason for this is the very ambiguous mandate for Security Council action spelled out in the Charter. It is possible under this mandate to call the limited "balancing" action, typical of the eighteenth century, an action taken to counter a "threat to the peace." Nonetheless, given the current stalemate within the Security Council, and the nature of the General Assembly actions

to date, it is safe to conclude that contemporary international law has greatly limited the wide-ranging legal capacity that states once had in deciding on the use of force.

[47] See Brownlie, 251–80, for a discussion of the contemporary legal restrictions on the use of force. Also see Kaplan and Katzenbach, 205, for a discussion of the just-war doctrine and its compatibility with the balance of power system.

[48] Certainly, technological developments have been primarily responsible for the rejection of war as a typical tool of international power. In this case, as in most, international legal doctrine mirrors the existing attitudes and helps to reinforce them.

law but also to the assumptions of the state system. The sporadic developments in international and regional organizations, the evolving place of the individual in the international legal system, and the doctrine of the just war are manifestations of the transformation occurring today both in the structure of international law and in attitudes about the state system. Actually, of course, the traditional conceptions of international law and the classical assumptions about international politics are not extinct.[49] Rather, there is in both international law and politics a perplexing mixture of past ideas and current developments. The only thing one can be sure of is that behind the traditional legal and political symbols which exist today in a somewhat mutated form, a subtle transformation of some kind is taking place.

It is not possible to evaluate the line of future development of the assumptions about the state system or the international legal expression of those assumptions from the work of contemporary theorists of international law. The most apparent new expressions are those that propose increased formalizations of world legal and political processes.[50] On the other hand, much international legal theory today seems to be dedicated to an affirmation of the traditional assumptions of international politics. Political analysts like Hans Morgenthau,[51] E. H.

Carr,[52] and George F. Kennan,[53] and legal theorists like Julius Stone,[54] P. E. Corbett,[55] and Charles De Visscher,[56] are predisposed to "bring international law back to reality."

This trend toward being "realistic" occupies the mainstream of current international legal theory,[57] and to identify its exact nature is therefore crucial. Many writers who express this viewpoint seem to fear being labeled as overly "idealistic." They utter frequent warnings that international law cannot restore international politics to order, but, on the contrary, can exist and flourish only after there is a political agreement among states to maintain order. In short, it is assumed that international law cannot shape international political reality, but can merely adjust to it. Although there are complaints of too much pessimism in current legal theory,[58] most writers, given the initial

---

[49] As in the past, international lawyers are still concerned with definitions and applications of concepts of territorial integrity, self-defense, and domestic jurisdiction, and policy-makers are still motivated by the traditional ideas of state security and power. However, the traditional political and legal symbols have been "stretched" to apply to current conditions. For a development of this position see Coplin, Chaps. 4 and 8.

[50] E.g., Arthur Larson, *When Nations Disagree* (Baton Rouge, La., 1961); or Grenville Clark and Louis B. Sohn, *World Peace Through World Law* (Cambridge, Mass., 1960). These theorists and others who fall under this classification are "radical" in the sense that what they suggest is antithetical to the assumptions of the state system as traditionally developed. These writers are not necessarily utopian in their radicalism. This is especially true since adherence today to the traditional assumptions might itself be considered a form of (reactionary) radicalism. However, the radical scholars, in the sense used here, are very scarce, especially among American students of international law. Today there is a very thin line separating the few radical scholars from the more numerous radical polemicists of world government.

[51] Morgenthau writes (277): "To recognize that international law exists is, however, not tantamount to assessing that . . . it is effective in regulating and restraining the struggle for power on the international scene."

[52] E. H. Carr, in *The Twenty Years' Crisis, 1919–1939* (London 1958), 170, writes: "We are exhorted to establish 'the rule of law' . . . and the assumption is made that, by so doing, we shall transfer our differences from the turbulent political atmosphere of self-interest to the purer, serener air of impartial justice." His subsequent analysis is designed to disprove this assumption.

[53] George F. Kennan, *Realities of American Foreign Policy* (Princeton 1954), 16.

[54] Julius Stone, *Legal Control of International Conflict* (New York 1954), introduction.

[55] Corbett, 68–79, 291–92.

[56] De Visscher writes (xiv): "International law cannot gather strength by isolating itself from the political realities with which international relations are everywhere impregnated. It can only do so by taking full account of the place that these realities occupy and measuring the obstacle which they present."

[57] The programs of the last two annual meetings of the American Society of International Law exemplify the way in which the concern for reality (as power) has come to dominate international legal theory. In the 1963 program, the relationship between international law and the use of force was not discussed by international legal theorists but by two well-known writers on the role of conflict in international politics. The 1964 program manifested the same tendency. It centered on the question of compliance with transnational law, a topic treated in a socio-political framework by most panelists. This point is not to be taken as a criticism of the two programs, both of which were excellent and very relevant, but as proof of the assertion that the mainstream of contemporary theory of international law is significantly oriented to the role of power.

[58] Many writers, even realists like Morgenthau (*op. cit.*, 275) and others like McDougal and Feliciano (*op. cit.* 2–4), decry the modern tendency toward "cynical disenchantment with law," but it is obvious from their subsequent remarks that they are reacting more against the "utopianism" of the past than the cynicism of the

predisposition to avoid "idealism," do not heed them.

The desire of contemporary theorists to be "realistic" has been crucial to the relationship between contemporary international law and the assumptions of the state system. In their effort to achieve realism, current theorists have not examined their traditional assumptions about international politics. When they talk about adjusting international law to the realities of power, they usually have in mind the traditional reality of international politics. Today, a large share of the theoretical writing on international law that is designed to adapt law to political reality is in effect applying it to an image of international politics which itself is rapidly becoming outmoded. Much contemporary international legal theory, then, has not contributed to the development of a new consensus on the nature

present. There have been a few who have attacked the "realist" position on international law (e.g., A. H. Feller, "In Defense of International Law and Morality," *Annals of the Academy of Political and Social Science*, Vol. 282 [July 1951], 77–84). However, these attacks have been infrequent and generally ineffective in starting a concerted action to develop more constructive theory. For another evaluation of the "realist" trend, see Covey T. Oliver, "Thoughts on Two Recent Events Affecting the Function of Law in the International Community," in George A. Lipsky, ed., *Law and Politics in the World Community* (Berkeley 1953).

of international politics but instead has reinforced many of the traditional ideas.

In order to understand more fully the relation of international law to world politics, it is necessary to do more than examine law merely as a direct constraint on political action. The changes in the conceptual basis of international law that are manifested in current practice and, to a lesser extent, in current legal theory are symptomatic of a series of social and institutional revolutions that are transforming all of international politics. To conclude that international law must adjust to political reality, therefore, is to miss the point, since international law is part of political reality and serves as an institutional means of developing and reflecting a general consensus on the nature of international reality. In the contemporary period, where the international legal system is relatively decentralized, and international politics is subject to rapid and profound development, it is necessary to avoid a conceptual framework of international law which breeds undue pessimism because it demands too much. If international law does not contribute directly and effectively to world order by forcing states to be peaceful, it does prepare the conceptual ground on which that order could be built by shaping attitudes about the nature and promise of international political reality.

D. Regional Subsystems

15. The Subordinate State System of Southern Asia[*]

Michael Brecher is Professor of Political Science at McGill University.
The author of *Nehru: A Political Biography* (1959) and *The New States of Asia*
(1963), he is among the few students of international politics who combines a
theoretical interest in the field in general with a high degree of competence in
analyzing the politics of a particular region. This combination is plainly evident
in the ensuing selection, which applies the logic and concepts of systems analysis
to the interrelationships of one specific set of geographically proximate nation-
states. Here it can be seen that the concept of an international system can be
fruitfully applied on a less than global scale. Indeed, Professor Brecher's analysis
indicates that comprehension of the global system cannot be achieved unless
inquiry also proceeds at the subsystemic level. [*Reprinted from* World Politics,
XV (January 1963), 213–35, by permission of the author and the publisher.]

I. Introduction

Asian studies have long since ventured beyond the
traditional limits of Orientalia to embrace history
and the social sciences; they have not as yet, however, applied the insights of international relations
to an area framework. Similarly, international
relations specialists have all but ignored the relevance
of their discipline to Asia.[1] The purpose of this
article is to help bridge the serious gap between
these two fields.

Until a few years ago the sole level of analysis
in international relations was the nation-state. Almost
all texts adopted this approach,[2] and many included
surveys of the foreign policy of selected states.[3]
One reason was the relative abundance of data on
the state actors. Another was the lack of effective

[*] I am grateful to Dr. Howard Wriggins for inviting
me to prepare this paper, which was presented, in a slightly
different form, to the Fourteenth Annual Meeting of the
Association for Asian Studies in Boston on April, 3 1962.
An earlier draft also benefited from the comments of
Professor Michael Oliver, Dr. Blema Steinberg, and Mr.
Paul Noble of McGill University.

[1] Whether or not international relations is an autonomous discipline, an emerging discipline, or simply a
branch of political science is still subject to sharp controversy. See C. A. W. Manning, *The University Teaching
of Social Sciences: International Relations* (Paris 1954);
P. D. Marchant, "Theory and Practice in the Study of
International Relations," *International Relations*, 1 (April
1955), 95–102; Charles A. McClelland, "Systems and

History in International Relations: Some Perspectives for
Empirical Research and Theory," *General Systems:
Yearbook of the Society for General Systems Research*, III
(1958), 221–47 [these two articles are reprinted in whole or
in part in James N. Rosenau, ed., *International Politics and
Foreign Policy* (New York 1961), 18–23 and 24–35, re-
spectively]; and Morton A. Kaplan, "Is International
Relations a Discipline?" *Journal of Politics*, XXIII
(August 1961), 462–76.

[2] A notable partial exception is Hans J. Morgenthau,
Politics Among Nations: The Struggle for Power and Peace
(3rd edn., New York 1960).

[3] See, for example, Frederick L. Schuman, *International Politics: The Western State System and the World
Community* (6th edn., New York 1958).

supra-state authority to ensure orderly relations among them, thereby accentuating their individual roles.

The unit or actor focus is not without great merit. It can provide studies in depth of state behavior that are essential to a comparative analysis of foreign policy.[4] It encourages the gathering of data useful for the study of decision-making, motives, and elite images of the external world. And it permits an inquiry into the content of "national interest."[5] This focus, micro-analysis, will probably continue to be the most widely used because "as things stand today—and are likely to remain for an indefinite period—there can be no serious doubt about the paramount position of the nation-state or about the superiority of its influence and power."[6] Yet new macro-perspectives have emerged.

Some of the ablest minds in international relations have set out on "the long road to theory," as part of the general search for a science of politics.[7] Their most suggestive innovation, creating a new level of analysis, is the concept of an "international system." As so often in the past, the more rigorous models of economic theory have provided both a challenge and an assumed analogy. Since an inter-national economic system exists apart from the national economic systems within it, there must also be an international political system related to, but distinct from, the political systems of nation-states; such is a rationale of the new approach.[8]

The body of literature is already impressive and the range of method striking. At one extreme is the pure theory of Morton Kaplan, who postulates six types of system: "balance of power," loose bipolar, tight bipolar, universal, hierarchical, and unit veto; only the first two have historical counterparts and "essential rules," but all are logically plausible.[9] At the other extreme is the inductive method of Stanley Hoffmann, based on "systematic historical research" or a comparative historical sociology.[10] Others concentrate on the contemporary international system, the most stimulating model being that of John Herz in *International Politics in the Atomic Age.*[11]

The basic features of this contemporary system, as viewed by Herz and others, may be noted briefly. *First* is its universality, its geographic expansion to global terms with the coming of independence to Asia and Africa; the state membership has more than doubled in fifteen years. *Second* is the continued absence of law and order within the system and a fragmentation of power; this is in sharp contrast with the authority pattern in the state units of the system, where a monopoly of the means of violence usually obtains. *Third* is a unique pyramid of power, which takes the form of bipolarity, with two superpowers acting as centers of decision, military organization, economic coordination, and diplomatic cooperation involving a large segment of the system—though not all its members. *Fourth* is the presence of new types of actors; states still predominate in number and influence, but there are also bloc actors, a universal actor (the United

[4] A preliminary effort in this direction, not entirely satisfactory, is Roy C. Macridis, ed., *Foreign Policy in World Politics* (2nd edn., Englewood Cliffs, N.J., 1962).

[5] This has long been concealed by the exponents of metaphysical realism. See Hans J. Morgenthau, *In Defense of the National Interest* (New York 1951).

[6] Arnold Wolfers, "The Actors in International Politics," in William T. R. Fox, ed., *Theoretical Aspects of International Relations* (Notre Dame 1959), 101. For dissenting views on this point, see Edward Hallett Carr, *Nationalism and After* (London 1945), esp. 53 ff.; and John H. Herz, *International Politics in the Atomic Age* (New York 1959), Part 1, esp. 96 ff.

[7] The rapidly growing interest in theory and method is well reflected in five recent collections of papers and one volume: Fox, ed.; Stanley Hoffmann, ed., *Contemporary Theory in International Relations* (Englewood Cliffs, N.J., 1960); *The Place of Theory in the Conduct and Study of International Relations*, special issue of *Journal of Conflict Resolution*, IV (September 1960); Rosenau, ed.; Klaus Knorr and Sidney Verba, eds., *The International System: Theoretical Essays*, special issue of *World Politics*, XIV (October 1961); and Quincy Wright, *The Study of International Relations* (New York 1955).

Among the notable illustrations of model-building in international relations are Morton A. Kaplan, *System and Process in International Politics* (New York 1957); and George Liska, *International Equilibrium* (Cambridge, Mass., 1957). For a critique of "scientism" in American political science, see Bernard Crick, *The American Science of Politics: Its Origins and Conditions* (London 1959).

[8] See Fred A. Sondermann, "The Linkage Between Foreign Policy and International Politics," in Rosenau, ed., 10. A notable earlier example of the use of economics concepts for the analysis of international politics is the "developmental" and "equilibrium" concepts in Harold D. Lasswell, *World Politics and Personal Insecurity* (New York 1935), Chap. 1.

[9] Kaplan, *System and Process*, Chap. 2. See also his "Problems of Theory Building and Theory Confirmation in International Politics," in Knorr and Verba, eds., 6–24.

[10] Stanley Hoffmann, "International Relations: The Long Road to Theory," *World Politics*, XI (April 1959), esp. 366 ff.

[11] New York 1959.

Nations), and various regional actor organizations. *Fifth* is the decline of Europe, a shift in the power center from the continental core of the Western state system to the periphery (Soviet Union) and beyond the seas (United States); this was due partly to the end of empire, partly to the division of Europe by power and ideology into two blocs, and partly to a technological revolution, the *sixth* and most vital feature of the contemporary system.

Massive technological change, especially the development of nuclear weapons and missiles, has tended to undermine (Herz says, has ended) the physical defensibility or impermeability of states, the material basis of the preceding system. Even if exaggerated as far as the superpowers are concerned, the "decline of the territorial state" and the technology responsible for it have had a tremendous impact on the system. They have created both the possibility and the necessity for the creation of blocs, in order to provide greater security for related units; they have produced the new type of actor, the superpower, which raises the level of fear for all other units and thereby induces bloc formation; and they have destroyed the classical balance of power. The very presence of superpowers eliminates the role of balancer—in global terms—and the traditional balancing process. What exists today is a balance of terror, which performs only the negative function of the classical balance—namely, to deny preponderance of power to states seeking to change the *status quo* by violence—not the positive function of facilitating preponderance on the side of the *status quo*.[12]

A *seventh* characteristic of the contemporary system is the rise of ideology to prominence, another component of the multiple revolution still in progress. In the Europe-centered nineteenth-century system, interstate conflict was for limited power, prestige, and profits, with exceptions—notably, Napoleonic France. The coming of Fascism, Nazism and Communism, however, sundered the value consensus of the international system. The last, especially, helped to accentuate intra-bloc rigidity and inter-bloc rivalry—in short, underpinned the fragmentation of the system into blocs. Ideology and power became intertwined, each strengthening the intensity of the

other; the result was to aggravate the tendency of actors to seek unlimited power, now possible because of the technological revolution.

This, in turn, points up *another* critical feature —the total character of the political process in the contemporary system, in every sense. The goals have become total, whether defined in terms of Morgenthau's "nationalistic universalism" or "liberation" or world communism; the instruments have become total, with weapons of unparalleled destructive capacity; and the consequences have become total, for people everywhere on the planet.[13] The globalization of politics, referred to earlier, has also marked the disappearance of the colonial frontier, at least in the traditional meaning of that term.[14] *Finally*, there is an ever-widening gap between the rate of progress in means of destruction and the rate of progress towards international order, incomparably greater than at any other time in history.

Much of the literature on international relations in the past decade or more reveals an almost pathological concern with Soviet-American relations, most of it policy-oriented and transitory. Even among the few, like Herz, who have constructed a sophisticated model, there is evident a preoccupation with the dominant system of inter-state politics, i.e., the bipolar bloc system. This is natural and appropriate, for as William Fox observed many years ago, ". . . we will never reach [a well-ordered world] by ignoring the differences between the elephants and the squirrels of international politics."[15] Apart from assisting a rational process of framing policy, the primary stress on the Dominant (bipolar bloc) System provides data to test and refine models of international systems—notably, Kaplan's loose and tight bipolar types.

By the same token, it is dangerous to assume that the elephants are the only members of the system or to ignore the squirrels by virtue of a specious claim that the elephants determine all or most of their actions. Yet this is often done. The focus on the superpowers rests on the premise, rarely stated,

---

[12] Ernst B. Haas, "The Balance of Power: Prescription, Concept or Propaganda?" *World Politics*, V (July 1953), 442–77.

[13] Morgenthau, *Politics Among Nations*, Chap. 22.

[14] For a stimulating general analysis of the Western colonial epoch in Asia and Africa, see Rupert Emerson, *From Empire to Nation: The Rise to Self-assertion of Asian and African Peoples* (Cambridge, Mass., 1960), esp. Part 1.

[15] W. T. R. Fox, *The Super Powers—The United States, Britain and the Soviet Union: Their Responsibility for Peace* (New York 1944), 3.

that the Dominant System is synonymous with the International System. This assumption is then elevated to the status of truth and is invoked to justify the exclusion or neglect of all other inter-state patterns. For certain features of contemporary international politics the assumption is valid. But there is an array of interstate problems, conflicts, and relationships among actors outside the blocs that have nothing or little to do with the bloc system, in the Americas, Africa, Asia, and even in Europe; and these are ignored, or distorted, by a model that identifies the bipolar bloc system with the totality of inter-state politics. More important, this assumption obscures another vital pattern of relations—the *Subordinate State System.*

The existence of this pattern would seem to be obvious. A few writers pay lip service to it.[16] Kaplan's type-models and Hoffmann's historical systems can theoretically be applied with this focus. Yet thus far there have been few efforts to explore a specific subordinate system of inter-state politics.[17] This gap in both international relations and Asian studies suggests a need to apply the combined skills of a discipline and area knowledge.[18]

The foregoing discussion gives rise to the following propositions: (a) There are two broad levels of analysis, the unit (nation-state) level and the systems level; the latter, however, reveals three distinct foci of attention—in ascending order, Subordinate Systems, the Dominant System, and the World or Global Political System; in theory, the Dominant System may be geographically and organizationally coterminous with the Global System, but this threefold classification is valid for the contemporary world.[19] (b) There are at least five definable subordinate systems at present—Middle Eastern, American, Southern Asian, West European, and West African. (c) The World System is not merely the sum of relations within the Dominant (bipolar bloc) System and in all subordinate systems; rather, there is a need to link a model of the Dominant System with those of the subordinate systems in order to devise a comprehensive model of the World System. This task has not even been started.

The focus of this article is the Subordinate State System of Southern Asia. Some of its features will be sketched and, where appropriate, comparisons with other systems will be drawn. The strokes will be sweeping, as befits a preliminary inquiry. The operative terms are "structure" and "texture." "Structure" will be used here to denote the basic features of the pattern of relations among and between the units of the system.[20] "Texture" connotes the broad characteristics of the environment—material, political, ideological—in which those relationships function.

What is the rationale for exploring the Southern Asian System or any Subordinate System? In the broadest sense, it will enrich both area study and international relations. The concept of system gives the one-country Asian specialist a region-wide perspective that can deepen his insight into the foreign relations of his particular state. Moreover, this approach can contribute a common analytical framework and hence comparable data to all students of Asia with an international relations interest, and thereby enrich the study of inter-state relations in the region as a whole; the area has too long been characterized by isolated, one-country, compartmentalized study. Stated in different terms, this focus will permit a study of the *interaction* among states in Southern Asia rather than *action* alone, i.e., the foreign policy of one state. To the international relations specialist, the application of systems concepts to a region will increase greatly the data for case studies of state systems. There have been relatively few Dominant Systems in history; the Subordinate System focus will permit tentative hypotheses about unit behavior in comparable milieux. It will, therefore, be a step towards an empirically oriented theory of comparative systems.

Various specific reasons strengthen the case for this approach. *First*, a system sets limits to the foreign policy choices of all actors within it—i.e., it creates external givens that impinge on both the

[16] See, for example, Rosenau, ed., 77–8.

[17] Leonard Binder, "The Middle East as a Subordinate International System," *World Politics*, X (April 1958), 408–29; George Modelski, "International Relations and Area Studies: The Case of South-East Asia," *International Relations*, II (April 1961), 143–55; and Thomas Hodgkin, "The New West Africa State System," *University of Toronto Quarterly*, XXXI (October 1961), 74–82.

[18] A thoughtful policy-oriented paper is Guy J. Pauker, "Southeast Asia as a Problem Area in the Next Decade," *World Politics*, XI (April 1959), 325–45.

[19] For a discussion of levels of analysis, see J. David Singer, "The Level-of-Analysis Problem in International Relations," in Knorr and Verba, eds., 77–92.

[20] Used in this way, "structure" is very similar to Herz's "system." (Herz, 7.)

content (goals) and the conduct (techniques) of all actors' foreign policy. Some writers attach great importance to the notion of "system determinism"— i.e., that policy is determined by the character and distribution of power within the system of which it is a member.[21] Although this may be exaggerated, it points up the vital fact that a state's foreign policy is the product of external, as well as internal, conditions. A *second* factor is that states operate at different levels and usually have various associations. Aside from being part of the Global System, they may be members of the Dominant System and one or more subordinate systems. Different actions and decisions derive from different associations; it is useful to separate and correlate policy acts with specific membership roles. Thus, for example, Pakistan belongs to two subordinate systems (Southern Asian and, marginally at least, Middle Eastern), the Dominant (bipolar bloc) System, and the Global System. Its policy on Kashmir, Israel, Germany, and nuclear tests may be viewed in terms of these four associations respectively.

A *third* justification, noted earlier, is that an exclusive Dominant System focus distorts all inter-state relations except those within the bipolar bloc system—and most exist outside that framework. The constant intrusion of that focus leads to errors of judgment and, frequently, of policy as well. *Finally*, the study of subordinate systems would help to resolve a sterile debate on the merits of deductive and inductive approaches to a more rigorous discipline of international relations.[22] Both methods have a legitimate place in this quest. An application of existing models will test their validity and lead to refined theory. The accumulation of data about subordinate inter-state politics will facilitate inductive hypotheses to be tested frequently in the light of steadily increasing data. In the cross-fertilization of international relations and Asian studies, both will benefit.

II. Definition of the Southern Asian System

Any concept must be defined precisely if it is to serve a useful analytical purpose. Yet, as James Rosenau

observed, since all bilateral interaction may be viewed in a systems framework, the one hundred contemporary states can theoretically form almost five thousand dyadic systems.[23] The concept of Subordinate State System is more rigorous and requires six conditions: (1) its scope is delimited, with primary stress on a geographic region; (2) there are at least three actors; (3) taken together, they are objectively recognized by other actors as constituting a distinctive community, region, or segment of the Global System; (4) the members identify themselves as such; (5) the units of power are relatively inferior to units in the Dominant System, using a sliding scale of power in both; and (6) changes in the Dominant System have greater effect on the Subordinate System than the reverse. In the present Global System, as we have said, there are five subordinate systems—Middle Eastern, American, Southern Asian, West European, and West African; others may emerge.

Using conventional geographic terminology, Southern Asia extends from Pakistan to Indonesia; the state members are Pakistan, India, Nepal, Ceylon, Burma, Thailand, Cambodia, Laos, North Viet Nam, South Viet Nam, Malaya, the Philippines, and Indonesia. China is not formally within the region and is usually excluded from the designation "South and Southeast Asia" or the more recent category, "Southern Asia." However, the Subordinate System is a political as well as a geographic concept; the region is a necessary but not a sufficient basis for definition.

China is a vital peripheral state, analogous to Russia in the eighteenth-century European system, Macedon in the Greek city-state system, and Ch'in in the Chou system of China before the seventh century B.C. Moreover, the subsequent roles of Macedon and Ch'in are not wholly irrelevant to China and the present Southern Asian System.[24]

There are other persuasive reasons for China's inclusion in this system. The presence of 12 million Chinese in the states of Southeast Asia gives China great influence within that region, comparable to that of the scattered German communities in Eastern Europe in the past half-century; more pointed is the analogy of the Chinese in Singapore-Malaya

---

[21] See, for example, Herz, 115; and Sondermann, in Rosenau, ed., 13.

[22] For extreme formulations, see Singer, 92, and Hoffmann, "International Relations," 356–58, respectively.

[23] Rosenau, ed., 77.

[24] A brief description of inter-state politics in antiquity is to be found in Schuman, Chap. 1.

and the Germans in Sudetenland. Closely related is the unstabilizing effect of China's minorities on the internal politics of various states; this accentuates her influence in the system. Another reason derives from Chinese territorial contiguity with many states of the region; this permits continuous Chinese interaction with these weaker units, a vital test of membership in any international political system. This pattern assumes special significance in the light of China's historic hegemony in Southeast Asia and its goal of renewed domination of that area.[25] Thus, this article treats China as a member of the Southern Asian System.[26] She is, of course, a member of other systems, too.

China's inclusion suggests a system comprising three overlapping fields—South Asia, Southeast Asia, and China.[27] Only two actors, India and China, have a high intensity relationship to and influence on most actors in all three fields, both through bilateral links.

The selection of a date for the *origin* of the system is somewhat arbitrary. The year 1959 would seem to be valid, for it marks the rounding out of the system—with the coming of independence to Indonesia and the emergence of a united mainland China, following on the transfer of power to the Philippines, Ceylon, Pakistan, India, and Burma. The remaining two phases, the creation of four weak units in Indo-China in 1954 and the end of British rule in Malaya in 1957, were marginal to the system. Prior to the end of World War II, the entire area, except Thailand and a weakened China, was totally dependent on European actors; Southern Asia was a geographic, economic, and political appendage of the Dominant (European) System. The countries of the region were objects, not subjects, of politics;

they lacked autonomy of power and freedom of decision-making in external affairs.

Having delineated the State System of Southern Asia in space and time, we may now turn to its salient structural and textural characteristics.

III. Structural Features

A key structural feature of any system is the *Configuration (Distribution and Level) of Power*. The general level in Southern Asia is low, in both absolute and relative terms. No member of the system appears to be capable of producing nuclear weapons or missiles; the armed forces of all states, except China, are small in number and severely limited as to skills and weapons. All units are characterized by an arrested economy, a low standard of living, a stagnant agriculture, a shortage of capital and skills, little heavy industry, and (most states) a disturbing rate of population growth.[28] Only India and China are potential "Great Powers"; Pakistan, Indonesia, and the Philippines are "Middle Powers"; all the rest are squirrels.

In systems of advanced technology—for example, where two actors possess thousands of H-bombs and adequate delivery systems—the power margin is inconsequential. In Southern Asia the differences *tend* to be accentuated by the low general level. Yet this tendency is offset by other factors. Vast geographic distances, along with an underdeveloped economy, confine the effectiveness of India's and China's power to their respective fields; India's superior military strength may be effective vis-à-vis Nepal, Pakistan, and Ceylon, but it diminishes rapidly and steadily farther east. For China's influence, the barriers of distance and technology are especially noticeable in the offshore island areas of Southeast Asia; there, the lack of naval and air power is crucial. For all other actors in the system, their low level of power and technology restricts the exercise of influence, at best, to neighboring states.

This general weakness also invites intervention by superpowers and blocs to fill the power vacuum,

[25] See Victor Purcell, *The Chinese in Southeast Asia* (London 1951).

[26] For a different view, excluding Great Powers from subordinate systems—in this case, India and China—see Modelski, 148–50.

[27] Neither Japan nor either of the Koreas is included in the Southern Asian Subordinate System. Unlike China, they do not meet conditions (3) or (4) as noted earlier—i.e., they are not (usually) treated as part of that system by outside actors and do not so identify themselves. They do of course, have relations with some states in Southern Asia and, in theory, could become full members of the system. Apart from periods of disunity, by contrast, China has regarded itself as part of the Southern Asia System and has, throughout history, played a major role therein.

[28] Strictly speaking, the level of technology and economy is an environmental or textural feature. However, the level of power is a direct function of technological and economic characteristics in the area covered by this system. In short, this is an overlapping feature, falling into both Structure and Texture categories.

a penetration that is resented and feared by many states in the Subordinate System.[29] Indeed, it is the low level of power in Southern Asia that gives China, an extra-area actor, virtual *carte blanche* access to the system, as well as *de facto* membership in it. Moreover, the presence of a relatively powerful peripheral state, China, further diminishes the application of India's power, not only in Southeast Asia but also with respect to immediate neighbors, such as Nepal and Pakistan. There is, then, diffusion of power in Southern Asia, with neither of two potential Great Powers able to dominate the system because of technological underdevelopment.

How does this power configuration compare with other systems? The pattern in Southern Asia is much more pyramidal than in *nineteenth-century Europe*, where there were five relatively equal Great Powers—England, France, Prussia (Germany), Austria, and Russia. Another striking difference was the absence of a major peripheral state upsetting all power calculations within the system proper; Russia had by then become a formal member, and the United States, the only possible analogy to China vis-à-vis Southern Asia today, remained a passive onlooker until the last years of the European system's century of peace. Like China in Southern Asia, when the United States became an active participant in 1917, it, too, acquired *de facto* membership in the system.

The distribution of power also differed in the state system of *ancient China*. Among the multiplicity of states were seven major units—notably, leagues of states under the leadership of Ch'u, Chin, Ch'in, and Wu. Gradually, over the course of centuries, a bipolar pattern emerged, with Chin and Ch'u as the superpowers—until the peripheral state, Ch'in, established its hegemony.[30] A similar pattern is observable in *ancient Greece*, with most city-states ultimately being linked to Athens or Sparta—and Macedon destroying the system. Southern Asia today does not reveal a bipolar pattern. Moreover, neither China nor Greece was a subordinate system; both were autonomous during most of their existence.

[29] An extreme illustration of resentment was Krishna Menon's comment on SEATO: "... this is not a regional organization.... It is a modern version of a protectorate. ..." (*Daily Indiagram* [Ottawa], August 30, 1954).

[30] On this and other aspects of inter-state politics in that autonomous system, see Richard L. Walker, *The Multi-State System of Ancient China* (Hamden, Conn., 1953).

The hierarchy of power in Southern Asia is superficially akin to the *contemporary Dominant System*, with its two superpowers, its four "Middle Powers"—England, France, Germany, and China—and the host of squirrels. There are, however, striking differences. The general level of power in the Dominant System is infinitely higher. And the power margin of the superpowers in the Dominant System is greater both quantitatively and qualitatively. This, in turn, has two vital consequences: it makes each a hegemonial state within each bloc, to a much greater degree than India in South Asia; and it enables both to exert a life-and-death influence on all actors in the Dominant System, which neither India's nor China's power margin permits in the Subordinate System. The substantive differences, then, are very great indeed.

The level of power in Southern Asia is comparable to that of the *Middle East System*, but the distribution is markedly different. There is no Great Power in the Middle East, real or potential. Most units in the Arab core are of the same order of power; Egypt and Iraq are the strongest, but neither has the power status of India or China in Southern Asia. In fact, two of the peripheral states, Turkey and Israel, are at present stronger than any single Arab actor—though the margin is not decisive. The distribution of power in the *American System* reveals still another pattern, that of a superpower whose superior technology and military and economic strength give it hegemonial status. Not even the Soviet Union can claim such unqualified domination within its bloc in the Dominant System.

Another structural feature concerns *organizational integration* (as distinct from social integration). Southern Asia is acutely underdeveloped in this respect. There is no system-wide political institution, judicial body, or security machinery. And neither of the two economic organizations embracing almost all units plays a vital role. Indeed, the process of integration has barely begun.

The *political* sphere is characterized by infrequent conferences among the actors of the system. Noteworthy events were the Asian Relations Conference in 1947, the Delhi Conference on Indonesia in 1949, and the Bandung Conference of 1955. No permanent machinery for regional cooperation emerged, despite serious efforts at the first and third of these conclaves. One reason was the rivalry of India and China, neither willing to concede Asian leadership to the other. A second was fear among the smaller states that one or both giants would dominate the system. As for the Colombo Powers, formed in 1954, or the Asian Group within the Afro-Asian bloc at the United Nations, they lack organic unity or even a common attitude to the Dominant System and its conflicts. Yet Bandung was a turning point in the evolution of the Southern Asian System, for it symbolized rejection of the Western view that everything was secondary to the Cold War. By asserting the primacy of anti-colonialism, the Conference proclaimed the regional autonomy of this Subordinate System and its non-involvement, where possible, in the bipolar struggle for power.[31]

The lack of integration in the *security* field is even more striking. The only formal organization, SEATO, includes but three units of the system—Pakistan, Thailand, and the Philippines—and is dominated by extra-area Powers; it is also opposed by various states within Southern Asia. Nor are the members' obligations impressive—"to meet the common danger in accordance with [their] constitutional processes" in case of aggression, and to consult immediately on appropriate measures in case of subversion (Article 4); and even this is aimed at only one kind of danger, the threat from Communist China. Finally, the organizational links are minimal and the military power of the Southern Asian members grossly inadequate; it is extra-area power, that of the United States, which gives SEATO meaning.[32]

The efforts to forge *economic* unity are more impressive and more successful. The UN Economic Commission for Asia and the Far East (ECAFE)

have functioned since 1947, and the Colombo Plan since 1950. Both include most states in Southern Asia, as well as extra-area units. Both were designed to assist the process of economic development, but both are advisory in character. ECAFE possesses a permanent secretariat that conducts valuable research and recommends policies to members, who meet annually in formal conference and more frequently in sundry committees; the Commission proposes, but the states dispose. As for the Colombo Plan, really a collection of individual state plans, the organizational links are even less developed. A Consultative Committee meets annually to hear reports and to facilitate an exchange of views. The Bureau in Colombo acts as a clearing house for information, technical assistance, and the like. Both institutions have achieved much in promoting international cooperation and in creating a climate of opinion conducive to the granting of aid by wealthier actors outside the area.[33]

The level of organizational integration in Southern Asia is much lower than in other systems. Although not highly institutionalized, the Concert of Europe performed security and political functions from 1815 to 1848, and in a modified form throughout the nineteenth century. The Permanent Court of Arbitration provided quasi-judicial services towards the close of the *European System*, and a series of technical inter-state organizations emerged to serve member needs.[34] Each bloc in the *current Dominant System* has a high degree of integration. Thus, in the U.S.-led bloc there is a sophisticated security institution (NATO), a judicial body (European Court), a host of economic organizations (OECD, Schuman Plan, Common Market, etc.), and a legislative-executive organ (Council of Europe).[35] The Soviet bloc also possesses a security

[31] For accounts of Bandung, see George McTurnan Kahin, *The Asian-African Conference* (Ithaca 1956); and A. Appadorai, *The Bandung Conference* (New Delhi 1955). On the steps taken in the direction of political integration see Russell H. Fifield, *The Diplomacy of Southeast Asia, 1945–1958* (New York 1958), Chap. 10; Guy Wint, "South Asia: Unity and Disunity," *International Conciliation,* No. 500 (November 1954), 162–73; and William Henderson, "The Development of Regionalism in Southeast Asia," *International Organization,* IX (November 1955), 463–76.

[32] See Ralph Braibanti, "The Southeast Asia Collective Defense Treaty," *Pacific Affairs,* XXX (December 1957), 321–41; and Royal Institute of International Affairs, *Collective Defence in South East Asia: The Manila Treaty and Its Implications* (London 1956).

[33] For the work of ECAFE and the Colombo Plan, see, respectively, United Nations: *Economic Survey of Asia and the Far East for . . .* (annual since 1947, New York); and Colombo Plan: Consultative Committee, *Annual Report,* Colombo Plan for Co-operative Economic Development in South and Southeast Asia (London, Wellington, Singapore, *et al.*). See also P. S. Lokanathan, "ECAFE—The Economic Parliament of Asia," in *Indian Year Book of International Affairs, 1953,* 11 (Madras 1953), 3–26.

[34] See Gerard J. Mangone, *A Short History of International Organization* (New York 1954), Chaps. 2 and 3.

[35] See Ernst B. Haas, *The Uniting of Europe: Political, Social, and Economic Forces, 1950–1957* (London 1958) and *Consensus Formation in the Council of Europe* (London 1960).

machine (Warsaw Pact), an economic organization (Council for Economic Mutual Assistance), specialized organs (Danube Commission and the Institute for Nuclear Research), and a multitude of bilateral agreements covering a wide range of inter-state cooperation. Underpinning these institutional aspects is the Communist Party; frequent meetings of Politburo (Presidium) members and gatherings at Congresses enhance the integration process.[36]

An extreme contrast to Southern Asia in this respect is the *American System*. Indeed, the Organization of American States (OAS) provides the most comprehensive, formal machinery in the history of state systems. There is a legislative organ (Inter-American Conference), a permanent executive body (the Council), a secretariat (Pan American Union), a multifaceted security machinery (Foreign Ministers' meetings, Inter-American Peace Committee, Defense Board and Advisory Defense Committee), specialized organs (Economic and Social Council, Cultural Council and Council of Jurists), and specialized agencies (Commission of Women, Statistical Institute, Sanitary Bureau, etc.), and, finally, an abundance of conferences and congresses on functional matters. The structure is impressive on paper, but its effectiveness as an instrument of cooperation among the twenty-one republics is often wanting.[37] Similar duality obtains in the *Middle East System*. The counterpart of the OAS is the Arab League, which has an organ of consultation (Majlis or Council), seven permanent committees to deal with political, economic, social, cultural, and health matters, a secretariat, a security machine (Joint Defense Council, Military Organization, Chiefs of Staff Committee, etc.), and a growing number of specialized agencies. The League is even less effective than the OAS in security and other spheres,

but it has the organizational foundations that are still lacking in Southern Asia.[38]

The degree of integration is closely related to a third structural feature—*Character and Frequency of Interaction* among the members. Of all the states in the system, only India has active relations with almost all other units. Apart from formal diplomatic ties, other actors have limited inter-state relations— for example, Pakistan with India and, through SEATO, with Thailand and the Philippines; Ceylon with India; Burma with India and China; the Philippines with her SEATO partners; Malaya with Indonesia; Thailand with Burma and Cambodia, etc. Interaction among the members is, then, incomplete or spatially discontinuous within the system. Moreover, it is almost entirely bilateral in form, the only examples of multilateralism being ECAFE and the Colombo Plan, SEATO, and the United Nations, which do not bind the actors. Most inter-state relations are of low intensity, though there are variations, the extremes being near-continuous tension between India and Pakistan and rarely disturbed tranquillity between India and Indonesia. Mainland China has resumed active relations with many states in Southern Asia since Bandung, but these remain less stable than those of India.[39]

In this sphere, too, Southern Asia is less developed than other systems. In the *Middle East*, for example, relations among the core Arab members are spatially continuous and complete, intense and acutely multilateral. The half-dozen actors are in constant contact, at every level, and use every form of interaction—diplomatic, political, social, economic, cultural, personal; the process of interaction even includes close links between domestic politics in any one state and the internal and external affairs of all others. At the same time, there are no relations with one peripheral unit, Israel, and limited ties with two others, Turkey and Iran.[40]

[36] See Zbigniew Brzezinski, "The Organization of the Communist Camp," *World Politics*, XIII (January 1961), 175–209; and George Modelski, *The Communist International System* (Center of International Studies, Princeton University, 1960).

[37] See Manuel S. Canyes, ed., *The Organization of American States and the United Nations* (4th edn., Washington 1958); C. G. Fenwick, "The Inter-American Regional System: 50 Years of Progress," *American Journal of International Law*, L (January 1956), 18–31; Martin B. Travis, Jr., "The Organization of American States: A Guide to the Future," *Western Political Quarterly*, X (September 1957), 491–511; and Arthur P. Whitaker, *The Western Hemisphere Idea: Its Rise and Decline* (Ithaca 1954).

[38] See T. R. Little, "The Arab League: A Reassessment," *Middle East Journal*, X (Spring 1956), 138–50; and Paul Seabury, "The League of Arab States: Debacle of a Regional Arrangement," *International Organization*, III (November 1949), 633–42.

[39] On China's role in international politics, see H. Arthur Steiner, "Communist China in the World Community," *International Conciliation*, No. 533 (May 1961); and Howard L. Boorman, "Peking in World Politics," *Pacific Affairs*, XXXIV (Fall 1961), 227–41.

[40] Binder, 423–26.

The pattern differs somewhat in *America*. All actors have continuous bilateral ties with the hegemonial power. Multilateral lines in the system as a whole are channeled through the OAS. And contact among the twenty Latin units varies in intensity. It is at a high level in Central America, which resembles the Arab core in this respect, fairly high in the deep south of the hemisphere, and declines sharply among the others.

Apart from these three basic structural features, which apply to all systems of inter-state politics, there is the question of the *linkage between the Subordinate and Dominant Systems* of the time. An inquiry into the nature and extent of penetration (or interpenetration) of the two systems will shed light on the degree of autonomy of the Subordinate System and its units. It will also represent a first step towards achieving the goal noted earlier—an all-inclusive model of the World Political System.

All states in Southern Asia are members of the Global System, and almost all belong to the universal international organization, the United Nations. Some also participate in the Dominant System—Pakistan, Thailand, the Philippines (and South Viet Nam) via SEATO; China and North Viet Nam via the Soviet bloc. Others are relatively free actors—India, Indonesia, Burma, Ceylon, and Malaya.[41] All, of course, are also units of a subordinate system.

Perhaps the most important feature of the Southern Asian Subordinate System is the constant penetration by the Dominant System. The Western bloc penetrates through a security instrument (SEATO), an economic organization (Colombo Plan), a multipurpose association (Commonwealth), bilateral aid, and propaganda. The Soviet bloc penetrates through a security instrument (Communist military bloc), bilateral aid from Moscow and Peking, subversion (Chinese minority), a political organization (Communist Party), and propaganda. Both blocs court the uncommitted states in Southern Asia—notably, India and Indonesia. Both blocs also intrude in the problems of the area—directly in Laos and Viet Nam, indirectly in Kashmir and West New Guinea (West Irian).[42] This intervention

is facilitated by three conditions: the dire need of Southern Asian states for economic aid, which can be provided only by extra-area Powers; ideological disunity and the lack of integration; and the political instability of most units within the system.

Among all members of the Subordinate System, only India reciprocates actively. Indeed, it penetrates the Dominant System effectively and continuously, through a conscious mediatory role at the United Nations and elsewhere, in regard to the Middle East, the Congo, Laos, disarmament, and Berlin. For all states but India and China, the Subordinate System is the primary, if not exclusive, framework for foreign policy. Even those units that are militarily linked to a bloc are motivated essentially by regional considerations—Pakistan fears India and desires aid in the struggle for Kashmir; Thailand and the Philippines fear Chinese expansion.

India's policy towards some issues reflects a local ("national interest") or subordinate system outlook—for example, Goa, Kashmir, and the treatment of Indians in Ceylon, Burma, or Malaya. On other vital questions, however, there is a primary stress on implications for the Global System or the Dominant System—Tibet in 1950, Laos since 1954, South Viet Nam today.

China's motivations are more difficult to unravel. In some cases, her role in the Dominant (bipolar bloc) System is primary, as with her aid to Castro and the F.L.N. in Algeria, and her attitude in the Congo and in Hungary in 1956. In others, her membership in the Subordinate System is decisive —for example, the border disputes and settlements with Burma and Nepal, her performance at Bandung, and the placatory offer to Asian states on the double nationality problem. But in another category the lines are blurred, with both systems appearing to fuse; the outstanding examples are Formosa and the border conflict with India. China's aim of hegemony in Southern Asia is clearly involved, but so is the larger struggle in the Dominant System—between the blocs in the Formosa case, within the Communist bloc in the Indian border case. For the two giants of Southern Asia, then, interpenetration is frequent and vital.

The *Middle East Subordinate System* is similar

---

[41] Nepal, Cambodia, and Laos are too exposed to be termed "free actors." At the same time, they do not participate formally in bloc military alliances.

[42] As reflected in various Anglo-American-sponsored resolutions on Kashmir in the Security Council and the

Soviet vetoes, and the U.S. (Bunker) mediation between the Netherlands and Indonesia.

to Southern Asia in this respect, but not altogether. The blocs penetrate through security or military ties (CENTO and Soviet arms aid to Egypt), economic assistance, and propaganda. They also intervene in regional problems—the Arab-Israel conflict continuously, Jordan and Lebanon in 1958, Kuwait in 1961, etc. The basic difference is the absence of a reverse penetration, except by Egypt on a rare occasion, as a prominent Afro-Asian neutralist. The *American System* was strikingly different until 1959. Apart from limited diplomatic contacts and the presence of some weak Communist parties, effective Soviet bloc penetration was prevented by United States hegemony; this is simply another way of saying that Southern Asia was a power vacuum, open to extra-area pressure, and that America was not. This has changed somewhat with the rise of Castro, facilitating Soviet bloc entry into the American Subordinate System on an unparalleled scale. Like the Middle East, and unlike Southern Asia, reverse penetration is nonexistent, except at the United Nations, for no Latin American state is powerful enough or sufficiently uncommitted to play India's role.

IV. Textural Features

Various textural features of Southern Asia merit attention, however brief. One is the *low intensity of communications and transport* within the system. Another is the complex of *common and conflicting ideologies and values*. A third is the *diversity of political systems*. And a fourth is *internal instability within the member-units*. Contrasts and similarities with other systems are striking.

Distances are vast in Southern Asia, topographic barriers are great, means of transport are limited, and extreme poverty restricts travel to a few. Inter-state radio contact is minimal, except for India-Pakistan, India-Ceylon, India-Burma, and bilateral links in parts of Southeast Asia. Press communications are also minimal, though some leading Indian, Pakistani, and Ceylonese newspapers may be available in the other countries. Television is practically nonexistent. And the language barrier is formidable, not only within the system, but often within individual states as well—for example, fourteen languages in India, two or more in Pakistan and Ceylon, and no less diversity in other lands. Indeed,

inter-state communication is confined to the elite—at the United Nations, diplomatic conclaves, regional conferences, and the like. The communications network of each unit is virtually closed to the others, hardly an inducement to integration and cooperation.

The *Middle East System* lies at the other extreme of communications interaction. Distances are much less, states are territorially contiguous, and topography, though a barrier, is not insurmountable. The great contrast, however, is the common language of the Arab core, which eases communication via press, radio, visiting leaders, and the spoken and written word generally. Face-to-face contact is much greater. Arabic is also widely understood in the peripheral states—Israel, Turkey, and Iran. There is, in short, an open communications system, which strengthens the interaction process. The *American System* is similarly endowed with an integrated communications network. A common language is an asset, though the hegemonial power and Brazil stand apart. A developed air transport service assists the process. And radio, press, and TV knit the actors together in an information sense.

All states in Southern Asia share the goals of economic development, social progress, and a viable political order; this permits widespread cooperation in such associations as ECAFE and/or the Colombo Plan. Most have a common experience of foreign, white rule, inducing a common reaction to many international issues involving the ills of colonialism and racism. They are also deeply attached to nationalism and fear renewed domination. In all these important intangibles they are psychologically knit together in a community, fulfilling the fourth condition of a Subordinate System; this is also a temporary substitute for organizational integration.

Beyond these, however, is a wide gulf in regard to values. There is a clash between the secular and religious orientation to public policy, as illustrated in Indian and Pakistani constitution-making.[43] A variant is the conflict between modernist and traditionalist approaches to the achievement of common goals. Some follow the liberal path in politics and economics, others the Communist way, and still others various types of a "middle way."

[43] See, for example, Leonard Binder, *Religion and Politics in Pakistan* (Berkeley and Los Angeles, 1961).

There are sharp cleavages within the system on the proper attitude to the bloc struggle within the Dominant System. Unlike Western Europe or America, there are several distinct civilizations —Buddhist, Muslim, and Hindu. Their economies are competitive. Enormous distance is a barrier to close contact. Racial, linguistic, and cultural differences are numerous and deep. Historic antagonisms persist, especially fear and resentment by the weaker peoples and states in Southern Asia. And, as in Africa, there are zones of English, French, and Dutch influence, with different traditions of education, law, and administration. No wonder, then, that the initiative for inter-state organizations in Southern Asia has usually come from outside the system, as with SEATO, ECAFE, and the Colombo Plan.[44] Yet their existence testifies to the presence of the third condition of a Subordinate System—objective treatment by outside actors as a distinct system or community.

In *nineteenth-century Europe*, too, there were differing values and ideologies—liberalism versus conservatism, revolution versus legitimacy, democracy versus absolutism. It is true that Christian civilization provided a unifying thread and common standards of behavior—until 1917. And yet the great gulf in values between the blocs today does not detract from their membership in a system— indeed, the *Dominant System*. Nor does ideological diversity, *per se*, deny the existence of a Southern Asian System. The *Middle East* Arab core is far more united in values and ideology; it has a common religion, for the most part, a common way of life, thought, and action, and the common experience, problems, and aspirations of Southern Asian states. Yet there is a basic clash in values with other members of the system. Apart from the United States, the *American System* is immeasurably more homogeneous in terms of cultural and ideological foundations —a common history, religion, way of life, and basic values.

There are three general types of political system in Southern Asia. Democracy, based on the Anglo-American models, may be found with deviations in India, the Philippines, Malaya, and Ceylon. The Soviet or Communist model is evident in

[44] Exceptions are the quiescent Asian Relations Organization and the Association of Southeast Asian States.

China and North Viet Nam. All other states reveal some form of authoritarianism. It may be mild, as in Pakistan since 1958, or severe, as in South Viet Nam since 1955. It may be military rule, as in Thailand and Burma, or civilian dictatorship, as in South Viet Nam, or an uneasy blend of civil-military control, as in Indonesia, or absolute monarchy, as in Nepal. In all of these cases the essential components of democracy are absent, in whole or in part. In some, the disregard for civil liberties is as great as in Communist lands, and the instruments of control are no less oppressive. In most, the army has become a major political force, either exercising power directly or standing in the wings ready to seize control from a faltering civil authority and acting as guardian of the political order. But in none of these states is authoritarianism total; this is one vital distinction between Communist governments and those of the middle zone. Another is the commitment in principle to democracy, though this has lessened in recent years. For the present, however, they remain almost as far removed from democracy as is communism; and many are less welfare-oriented than either of the polar models. All three types of political system in Southern Asia are "Western" in the sense that they are legacies of the Western epoch in Asian history. Democracy is the direct intrusion of colonial rulers. Communism is the product of Western ideas and the example of a non-Asian state. And even the non-Communist authoritarians use Western-derived techniques and political forms to maintain power.

Diversity in political forms and substance is not unique to Southern Asia. Nor is it a necessary source of conflict within the system. *Nineteenth-century Europe* had constitutional democracy (England) coexisting with autocracy, constitutional and other (Prussia, Austria, Russia, etc.). In the *Middle East* today there is democracy (Israel and, with qualifications, Lebanon) and non-Communist authoritarianism of different forms—military (Egypt, Iraq, Turkey, and Yemen), absolute monarchy (Saudi Arabia), and constitutional autocracy (Iran and Jordan). As for *America*, all three types are represented—democratic (U.S., Uruguay, and occasionally, others), Communist (Cuba), and authoritarian (the majority, most of the time).

The dominant feature of internal politics in Southern Asia is instability. The record is emphatic

on this theme.[45] Pakistan and Indonesia are the most persuasive illustrations. In the first eleven years of statehood, Pakistan had four heads of state and eight cabinets; there were seven Chief Ministers of Sind from 1947 to 1955. Constitutional government broke down in the provinces three times—in the Punjab (1948–1951), in Sind (1951–1953), and in East Bengal (1954–1955). No national election was ever held. A grave constitutional crisis occurred in 1954. Politics was controlled by a club of 150 opportunistic men engaged in a dismal game of political chairs. The rot was swept aside in 1958 by Mohammed Ayub Khan. The military remained in power until 1962, and Field Marshal Ayub continues to rule as President under the new constitution.[46]

The crisis of instability was as severe in Indonesia. Violence has been endemic since the Japanese departed in 1945. Banditry has never been stamped out. Nor has guerrilla war. The main area of disorder has been the outer islands, scene of four major insurrections in the 1950's. In the political arena, too, fragmentation has been the keynote. None of the three major parties—the Nationalists, Masjumi, and the Communists—was strong enough to establish a firm majority, leading to coalition government, often the bane of political order. Only Sukarno, President since independence, created the image of continuity. With the coming of "Guided Democracy" in 1958, the search for a viable polity took a new path.[47]

The pattern of instability in the *Middle East System* is similar—if anything, more acute. There, it has led to sharp change in foreign policy, as with Nasser in Egypt and Kassem in Iraq since 1958. In the *American System*, only when the entire political order is transformed, as in Cuba, does instability lead to a new path in external affairs. Thus far, the ubiquitous flux of Southern Asian politics has not seriously undermined the continuity of foreign policy—in Burma, Pakistan, or Indonesia, for example. However, this is a potential effect on the actors. Moreover, political change within the states makes a prediction of probable actor behavior more difficult. It also accentuates the image of power weakness in the system as a whole.

V. Conclusion

The foregoing analysis suggests certain observations. The state system of Southern Asia consists of fourteen units, most of which are weak and under grave internal stress. Each jealously guards its newly won status and asserts the primacy of national interests over group interests that could induce organizational integration. The process is rudimentary and is likely to remain so in the foreseeable future. Indeed, Southern Asia is clearly the most underdeveloped of all contemporary Subordinate State Systems.

The vast majority of states lack sufficient power to ensure their independence. Apart from India and China, it is certain that no actor will have the surplus power to play a major role outside the system in the coming decades. The region of Southern Asia is a power vacuum buffeted by both blocs in the Dominant System. The presence of American and Soviet-Chinese power, real and potential, creates a precarious equilibrium and a dangerously rigid link between Dominant and Subordinate Systems.

Viewed in these terms, Southern Asia bears a striking resemblance to the Balkans before 1914. It lies between two centers of power and ideology. Its units are very weak compared with extra-area powers, three of which have actively intervened—like Germany and Russia in the Balkans; indeed, one of them is a member of the system. And conflicts within Southern Asia—for example, in Laos and Viet Nam—attract intervention by the superpowers.

The real danger in such an unstable system of power is that one or more of the units will disintegrate or even come under the control of outside states. If this were to occur in a unit like India or Indonesia, the consequences would be far-reaching. The whole system would be unsettled, and pressure

[45] The record and the causes are examined in Michael Brecher, "Political Instability in the New States of Asia," in David E. Apter and Harry Eckstein, eds., *Comparative Politics: A Reader* (New York 1963).

[46] For acute analyses of Pakistan's politics, see Keith Callard, *Pakistan: A Political Study* (London 1957) and *Political Forces in Pakistan, 1957–1959* (New York 1959); Mushtaq Ahmad, *Government and Politics in Pakistan* (Karachi 1959); and Khalid bin Sayeed, "Collapse of Parliamentary Democracy in Pakistan," *Middle East Journal*, XIII (Autumn 1959), 389–406.

[47] See George McTurnan Kahin, ed., *Major Governments of Asia* (Ithaca 1958), Chaps. 21–3; Guy J. Pauker, "U.S. Foreign Policy in South-East Asia," in *United States Foreign Policy: Asia* (Conlon Report, Washington 1959), esp. 56–62; and John D. Legge, *Problems of Regional Autonomy in Contemporary Indonesia* (Ithaca 1957).

from without would increase for all Southern Asian states. The line dividing Dominant from Subordinate System would disappear, and bloc rigidity would be further accentuated. In case of Indian disintegration, probably nothing could prevent the rapid assertion of Sino-Soviet domination over the whole system. In brief, the domestic stability of most units in Southern Asia is necessary for the maintenance of a system at all. And the maintenance of an autonomous system in Southern Asia is conducive to stability in the World Political System.

One final observation is in order. Space limitations have not permitted discussion of the next two logical stages of the analysis. The first is a demonstration of how the Subordinate System of Southern Asia *qua* system helps to shape the broad outlines and specific acts of the foreign policy of member-states. The other is a projection of the likely evolution of the system as a whole. This article has attempted only to provide an analytical framework within which these tasks can be performed fruitfully. It is now up to those with special knowledge of individual states in Southern Asia to link the system and the foreign policy of a particular unit. Only then can the broader task of charting the future of the system be undertaken.

Part Three

The Actions of States: Theories and Approaches

Most studies of foreign policy concern themselves with either the purposes of state action, the form it takes, the processes which initiate it, or the societal sources from which it derives. Taken together or singly, these areas present a number of substantive and methodological problems, not the least of which is the nature of the linkages between them. Obviously, the goals of foreign policy are a function of the processes by which they are formulated, just as these, in turn, are influenced by the objectives which were sought in the past and the society's aspirations for the future. Similarly, the form of state action is determined partly by the goals toward which it is directed, partly by the resources available to sustain it, and partly by the organizational and intellectual processes through which it was selected. Indeed, the inter-relationship of the various aspects of foreign policy is so intricate that the societal factors which underlie state action are affected, through feedback, by the action itself, and thus operate differently as sources of future action. In short, like all behavior, foreign policy action is sequential. It does not have a beginning, an existence, and an end. Rather, it is constantly unfolding, and at any given moment is partly a function of what it was previously and what it may become in the future. While the observer is obliged to segment this sequence for analytic purposes, he can profit by remembering that in so doing he runs the risk of exaggerating the causal and independent character of the variables that he has separated out for examination.

Few aspects of the field are more resistant to clarifying analysis than the objectives that states pursue in their international relationships. Foreign policy goals have been the subject of extensive investigation and have been classified and conceptualized in countless ways. Peace, security, power, and prosperity have been identified as long-range goals and differentiated from short-range objectives. Similar distinctions have been drawn between goals that are general and specific, absolute and relative, humanitarian and national, stated and actual, unified and divergent, and so on through a seemingly endless list of possible combinations. These subcategories have in turn been placed within the framework of the national interest, which is often posited as the key to any explanation of goal-seeking behavior. However, despite their usefulness as refinements of an otherwise unmanageable subject, none of these formulations is entirely satisfactory. All of them are either too simple or too elaborate. Simplification results when such all-inclusive goals as, say, peace and security are cited as the goals sought by states. Because these concepts are so general, they fail to differentiate one type of goal-seeking action from another. Not infrequently, in fact, states enter into military action and accept the resulting anxieties in an effort to establish conditions which are free of war and tension. If any kind of behavior can be undertaken in the name of peace and security, then what do these terms distinguish? Contrariwise, excessive elaboration results when attention is focused on, say, short-range rather than long-range goals. For then it is difficult to raise analysis above the level of the particular situation. The short-range goals of a state tend to correspond to its notions of how outstanding issues should be resolved; hence, it has as many goals as there are issues. And, since other states have different conceptions of how the same issues ought to be resolved, it is virtually impossible to develop a model of short-range goals that is applicable to most states.

However, even if a workable model of foreign policy goals could be developed, there would still remain the difficult problem of distinguishing between ends and means. For every goal can also be viewed as a means to some other goal. Short-range objectives are instruments to the realization of long-range objectives; specific ends are designed to serve more general ends; divergent goals are considered necessary to the achievement of unified goals; and so on. In other words, the same phenomena can be classified as both ends and means; and, of course, the way they are classified will significantly affect the interpretation of them. It makes a difference, for example, whether one posits power as the goal of a society's foreign policy, or whether it is regarded as instrumental to the achievement of other ends.

No list of the problems involved in analyzing foreign policy goals would be complete without mention of those which inevitably attend use of the concept of national interest. Stated briefly, the problem here is to determine whether the best interests of a nation are other than those delineated by its officials and, if they are, how these interests are to be discerned and investigated. Are we to conceive of an objective national interest which exists apart from subjective interpretations? Obviously, there is no "correct" answer to this question. It is essentially a philosophical problem, and one which each researcher must resolve for himself. If he is a logical positivist, he will deny the existence of an objective reality called *the* national interest which may or may not be discernible. Rather, he will insist that the question of what is best for a society is a value question which might be resolved differently by each individual and which, insofar as the society's operation is concerned, is resolved by those individuals who are able to commit it to a course of action, i.e., government officials. The logical positivist would say that private citizens who describe the national interest are merely attaching a fancy label to their own personal views of what is best for the nation. On the other hand, if he does not subscribe to the tenets of logical positivism, the researcher would regard it as valid and necessary to posit an objective national interest and to undertake a search for its components. He would contend that certain conditions abroad are better for the country than others, that some interests are more important than others, and that therefore some conditions and interests have the highest priority and can be properly labeled "in the national interest." In short, whatever school of thought one may prefer, the problem of classifying the national interest encompasses choices which are crucial to the organization and analysis of empirical data. Hence it is a problem which no student in the field can afford to ignore.

Nor will the difficulty of analyzing foreign policy goals come to an end once the various conceptual and philosophical problems are settled. For then it is necessary to determine what kinds and amounts of data will constitute evidence of the existence of foreign policy goals, however the latter may be defined. This is not an easy task.

Decisions must be made as to the reliability of official pronouncements of goals, with regard to the handling of discrepancies between past behavior and announcements of revised plans for the future, concerning the relative weight to be attached to historical, political, economic, social, geographic, and a host of other factors. Foreign policy goals do not leap out at the observer from the mass of data he has accumulated. They must be inferred, and sound inferences require the use of careful and explicit research procedures. Indeed, if hasty and implicit methods are used, there is always the danger that one will "prove" what one was predisposed to believe. The data which are potentially evidential of goals are so extensive that they can be structured to yield virtually any interpretation the observer, knowingly or otherwise, may be intent on finding. If he has already committed himself to the view that the nation under examination aspires to conquest, then through careful selection of appropriate "facts" he can demonstrate that this is the underlying purpose of its current action. More importantly, if the observer is already inclined toward a contrary position, there are always sufficient data to enable him to conclude that a particular nation is desirous of accommodation rather than conquest.

Unlike the goals of state action, its forms have proved easy to clarify and analyze. The nature, implications, and consequences of diplomatic action, for example, are the subject of a vast literature not marked by controversy or confusion. The purposes, types, and limits of diplomacy are readily classified, and one is hard put to think of any major methodological problems which might inhibit the investigation of diplomatic practices and processes. Much the same can be said of the other tools and techniques of "statecraft." Propaganda, subversion, economic action, military action (or the threat of it), and other techniques have all been thoroughly explored, and none has presented insoluble substantive or procedural problems.

Still another major area that has held the attention of researchers is the process by which states formulate their foreign policies. Students in the field have become increasingly sensitive to the close relationship between the "what" and the "how" of foreign policy. For many years, the policy-making process was simply assumed as a necessary prerequisite to the initiation of state action. Today, however, it is common-place to presume that *what* a state does is in no small way a function of *how* it decides what to do. At any point in time, for example, not only is American foreign policy a response to perceived aspects of the international environment, but it is also very much a result of the prevailing state of executive-legislative relations. In other words, foreign policy action is a product of decisions, and the ways decisions are made may substantially affect their contents.

The analysis of foreign policy decision-making has proceeded on several levels. Some observers have focused on the interaction of officials and agencies, or what might be regarded as the *organizational* process whereby decisions are reached. Others have held these variables constant and dwelt upon the interaction of ideas, or what might be called the *intellectual* process by which policies acquire structure and content. Still other observers have combined these two foci and, through case studies, outlined the close linkage between them. It must be emphasized, however, that the various levels of decision-making analysis rest on a common assumption, namely, that the making of foreign policy is not simply a matter of individuals assessing a situation and calculating the best way to cope with it. In the first place, the individuals are officials, which means they occupy particular roles or offices that—either formally or informally—limit and guide their behavior. Secondly, at least in industrialized societies, their roles are enacted in large, complex agencies that are part of an even larger and more complex structure called government. Among other things, this means that the responsibility for decision is widely dispersed and that communication and coordination must occur before policies can be adopted. Thirdly, the communication networks of large-scale organizations are so complex that the facilities for circulating ideas within the decision-making system can be an important determinant of the policies which are ultimately adopted. For example, the soundness of the policy alternatives which are fashioned out of intelligence reports will depend to some extent on whether the right officials receive the right information at the right time. Fourthly, officials and agencies develop a stake in their particular responsibilities and the resulting conflicts greatly complicate the tasks of coordination. In fact, not infrequently policies cannot be framed without the prior construction of a delicate, albeit perhaps momentary, consensus within and among the various agencies that exercise the dispersed authority.

Notwithstanding the myriad implications which flow from the assumption that foreign policy-making takes place in large-scale organizations, many critics of decision-making analysis insist that essentially it involves the study of how a few top-ranking persons in government respond to situations abroad. In its worst form, this criticism posits students of decision-making as amateur psychoanalysts who probe the psyches of policy-making officials. Nothing could be further from the truth. While the analysis of decision-making processes does have limitations, as noted below, a preoccupation with personality and past experience is not among them. On the contrary, an initial premise is that much, if not all, of the behavior of decision-makers can be explained without reference to idiosyncratic factors. What happened to a foreign minister in college, or his latest blow-up with his wife, or his aspiration to become prime minister may be relevant in explaining his actions in a diplomatic crisis, but to the student of decision-making such data belong at the very bottom of his list of items for investigation. Moreover, he assumes that he will satisfactorily account for the foreign minister's behavior before he reaches the bottom of the list. The requirements of the office of foreign minister, the historical foreign policies of his society, the values held by the foreign minister's political party, the relationship of events abroad to existing commitments and future plans—factors such as these have considerable explanatory power, and their careful analysis will usually render superfluous any inquiry into the unique personality and background which distinguish the foreign minister from everyone else.

This is not to say that the researcher has no interest in the motives of decision-makers. On the contrary, he regards motives as central to his investigations and motivational analysis of foreign ministers as a mandatory routine practice. But it is not so much the private, idiosyncratic motives that are investigated as those that are built into the decision-maker's role, that derive from the organizational process, that stem from treaty obligations and traditional values, that are inherent in the goals toward which policy is oriented, and so on. For example, built into the offices of a foreign and a treasury minister are, respectively, the motives to strengthen alliances and balance budgets. If these two officials should clash repeatedly over proposed foreign aid expenditures, presumably it would be because their role-derived motives are in conflict, not because their personalities are antagonistic. The student of decision-making, in other words, is concerned primarily with political motivation and only secondarily with personal motivation.

One other misconception of decision-making analysis should be clarified. It is often alleged that, in focusing on the organizational and communication processes of the decision-making system, researchers lose sight of developments abroad and that they therefore cannot hope to account for the dynamics of state action. It is the requirements imposed by external events, so the argument goes, that primarily determine decision-makers' responses; concern with how the decision-making system operates only serves to divert attention from these far more important variables. Whatever validity this criticism may have with respect to specific empirical studies, it cannot be generally applied to the analysis of decision-making. For the latter does regard events in the external setting as crucial determinants of state action. Its main focus is the world as decision-makers see it, and this includes events and trends abroad as well as those at home or within the agencies of government. If officials are sensitive to the external setting and guide their actions accordingly, then the researcher also examines these phenomena. But he does so by observing closely what happens to the external stimuli, from the time they feed into the decision-making system until they culminate in the response of officials. To be sure, at this point he might become excessively preoccupied with communication and organizational processes. If this occurs, however, the fault is the researcher's and is not inherent in the analysis of decision-making.

This is not to imply that the student of decision-making encounters no difficulties. The extent and utility of his empirical investigations may be limited in several important ways. Some observers, for example, question whether the foreign policy behavior of non-Western, unindustrialized societies can be explained through the use of a model which is geared mainly to the large-scale decision-making systems of the industrialized West. Others wonder about the usefulness of a model that relies heavily upon governmental sources that are classified as secret and are thus unavailable to the researcher. Still others have reservations about the utility of a model that depends upon sociological and psychological concepts that are unfamiliar to many students in the international field and thereby create a problem in communication. Concern has also been voiced as to whether the study of decision-making involves so many categories and subcategories that empirical investigation cannot proceed in an orderly and economical manner. Another criticism focuses on the question of whether the retrospective examination of decision-making processes can ever yield meaningful predictions of future events and developments.

In short, there are a number of problems that the student of decision-making must face. None of them seems insurmountable, however. While certain concepts may not be applicable to non-Western decision-makers, the processes by which they assess information, frame alternatives, and adopt policies can nevertheless be observed and analyzed. The problem of classified materials is indeed a serious one, but some data are available and, as will be seen in Part Five, there are techniques that enable the researcher to draw reliable inferences about the missing links. The problems of communication and excessive categorization can be minimized through self-conscious efforts to cope with them. The quantification of cases involving decision-making should facilitate the testing of hypotheses and the derivation of accurate and useful predictions. Stated differently, these problems emphasize that decision-making analysis has limitations and must be applied with care, but certainly these limitations do not warrant the conclusion that studies of the processes which initiate state action are bound to be unproductive.

The researcher and the decision-maker share one analytic problem in common. Both have a need to estimate and compare the human and nonhuman resources of states. The decision-maker must analyze the capabilities of foreign nations in order to assess what they are likely to do and whether they will be able to implement their goals. In addition, of course, the decision-maker must constantly evaluate the capabilities of his own society and attempt to keep them in balance with the policies which are being framed or serviced. Similarly, the researcher must analyze the state's capabilities in order to anticipate the choices of decision-makers and to calculate the potentialities of particular policies. However, capability analysis is not as easy as it sometimes seems. A number of factors, ranging from military equipment to group solidarity, from population size to capacity for sacrifice, can be relevant to the capabilities of a society. Thus there is the ever-present problem of which resources to analyze and how they can best be categorized. Furthermore, some resources are extremely difficult to measure. National morale or intelligence-gathering facilities, to cite but two of many possible examples, do not lend themselves readily to quantification and comparison. Equally difficult is the problem of how much weight should be attached to the various factors which are said to determine a state's capabilities. For example, are mineral resources more or less important than national morale as determinants of capability? And how much more or less important? Such problems confront the decision-maker and the researcher in virtually the same form, and both, each for his own reasons, are constantly engaged in the process of revising estimates to account for technological and other changes, as well as for new ways of analyzing and comparing resources.

As decision-making processes and capabilities have come under more extensive and sophisticated scrutiny, more attention has been paid to the societal sources of state action. For many years, the composition, structure, and operation of a society were not considered particularly relevant to the formulation or conduct of its foreign policies. These tasks were performed by policy-makers and diplomats in response to events abroad, and developments at home seemed to have little bearing upon policy content or diplomatic style. With the development of capability and decision-making analysis, however, it came to be recognized that what transpires within a society has a great deal of bearing on the contents of its policies and its capacity to implement these policies. That is, in the case of capabilities, the systematization of variables led to the recognition that the ability of a state to achieve its goals and service its policies is dependent upon intangible aspects of societal organization as well as upon such tangible factors as military equipment or population size. Today, for example, it is commonplace to investigate such factors as the extent of national unity, the viability of labor-management relations, and the adequacy of high school science training if one wishes to assess, respectively, a society's capacity for sacrifice in a cold war, its economic productivity, and its ability to develop a nuclear weapons system.

Similarly, in the case of decision-making analysis, broad-gauged inquiries into the social, political, and economic structure of societies have been fostered by the need to isolate those factors within the internal setting that condition and limit the behavior of foreign policy officials. In part, of course, this involves a study of public opinion and the way in which a society and its officials are directly responsible to each other's wants and fears. It must be emphasized, however, that students of decision-making are interested in much more profound processes than the standard methods by which policy-makers are made aware of public sentiment. Rather, they assume that a society's economic institutions, social structure, educational system, major value orientations, even its family life—to cite but a few of the possible factors— underlie the actions of its decision-makers, not to mention the individual and group behavior of those who, as private citizens, act and react in an international context.

Hence a major task of researchers who focus on the societal sources of foreign policy has been to identify and conceptualize the linkages which bind decision-makers to the internal setting. They have not been satisfied simply to assume that somehow the nature of a society is reflected in its foreign policies. Nor have they been content to posit foreign policy as a response to abstractions such as nationalism. Instead, researchers have proceeded on the assumption that attempts to link decision-makers to the internal setting must be as precise as efforts to trace the influence of factors in the external setting. Stated differently, it is no more meaningful to assert that officials acted as they did because of nationalism than to contend that their actions were a result of a crisis abroad. The dynamics of both nationalism and the crisis must be uncovered if distinctions are to be drawn between one foreign policy action and another.

These linkages to the internal setting are not easily discerned. Virtually all of them confront the researcher with complex problems of social scientific analysis. If, for example, nationalism is a meaningful concept, then presumably it subsumes such phenomena as historical tradition, ideological fervor, societal unity, and group processes precipitated by political leaders and mass media of communication. Each of these components, in turn, encompasses elaborate social and psychological processes which are difficult to trace and integrate into a coherent framework. Moreover, after the contents and sources of nationalism have been identified and conceptualized, there remains the no less difficult task of isolating the points at which the phenomena of nationalism enter and shape the decision-making process. The related problem of identifying the common value orientations and characteristic behavior patterns that distinguish a society and condition the actions of its foreign policy officials complicates analysis even further. How widely shared are the common values? How characteristic are the behavior patterns? How are the former transmitted to policy-makers, and how do the latter influence the decision-making process? Are there, so to speak, "cultural compulsions" which might be expected to affect individual decision-makers? Does the national character concept advance or confound comprehension of the internal setting? If its usefulness is judged to be limited, how then shall we account for, say, the reactions of societies to crisis or their behavior in situations short of the acute? Clearly, questions such as these lead the student of foreign policy into uncharted areas of inquiry. Moreover, because they are complex and challenging, he runs the risk of becoming so engrossed in social processes and societal structures that he loses sight of his purpose in investigating them.

The task of tracing linkages between decision-makers and their internal settings is further complicated by the fact that the political and social processes of industrialized Western nations differ greatly from those which are operative in the modernizing societies of the non-West. Students of United States or Soviet foreign policy may therefore need to develop an entirely new set of categories and concepts when they seek to uncover the sources of non-Western foreign policies. If, for example, they are concerned with the role that elite groups play in mobilizing public opinion and otherwise sustaining the policy-making process, their mode of analyzing American and Russian elites will probably not suffice when their attention turns to the performance of leadership functions in Asian and African societies. Indeed, even the identity of the elites may be different, as is evident in the tendency of student leaders and military officers to play a much more important role in non-Western politics than they do in the politics of industrialized societies.

The following eleven selections, with one exception, are designed to cover the major areas and problems with which studies of foreign policy have been concerned. The first three selections present different formulations of the ends and means that states pursue or employ in their external relationships. The next six focus upon various aspects of decision-making and the problems of capability analysis. The last two deal with some of the societal sources which may shape the content and conduct of foreign policy. Only the forms of state action do not fall within the scope of these selections. As noted, diplomacy, foreign economic policy, and the other tools and techniques of statecraft are the subject of a vast literature and do not pose major theoretical or methodological problems. Thus it seemed appropriate to allocate this space to the less clear-cut aspects of foreign policy and to suggest that the reader consult the standard texts for thorough discussions of the forms of state action.

16. The Pole of Power and the Pole of Indifference

Arnold Wolfers, recently deceased, was long a leader of theory and research in the international field. Formerly Sterling Professor of International Relations at Yale University and Director of the Washington Center of Foreign Policy Research, his works include *Britain and France Between Two Wars* (1940) and *Discord and Collaboration* (1962). He was also the author of a number of important articles which attempted to reformulate and clarify the major concepts and problems of the field. In this selection Professor Wolfers tackled the task of analyzing and classifying the various ends toward which state action may be directed.   [*Reprinted from* World Politics, *IV (1951), 39–63, by permission of the author and the publisher.*]

In international relations, two opposing schools of thought have fought each other throughout the modern age. Ever since Machiavelli published the *Prince*, his "realistic" views have shocked "idealist" thinkers. As a battle of the mind, fought by and large outside the political arena, the dispute between the two schools was of great concern to philosophers and moralists; but not until Woodrow Wilson set out to bring Utopia down to earth did it become a political issue of the first magnitude. For the first time, the responsible head of one of the leading powers acted as though the world were on the verge of crossing the threshold from sordid "power politics" to a "new era" in which the admonitions of the idealist philosophers would suddenly become the political order of the day.

No amount of disillusionment has been able to wipe out the deep marks left by the outburst of idealist enthusiasm which Woodrow Wilson's leadership evoked. Today more than ever American statesmen and the American public find themselves torn between the conflicting pulls of idealist and realist thought. Often the same event—as the war in Korea has vividly demonstrated—is interpreted simultaneously in terms of both schools, as an incident in the age-old struggle for power on the one hand, as a great venture in community action against an aggressor on the other. . . .

The two schools are obviously far apart, if not diametrically opposed on many issues. Yet, despite striking differences, their views are closely related to each other, at least in one significant respect. Both approach international politics on the same level—which might briefly be called the power level—though they approach it from opposite ends.[1]

[1] The term "power" is used here and throughout this article in the restricted sense in which it occurs in the popular use of such word combinations as "power politics" or "struggle for power," meaning to cover the ability to coerce or, more precisely, to inflict deprivations on others. This leaves out other ways of exerting influence, e.g., by bestowing benefits which are not ordinarily connected with or condemned as "power politics." (See Harold and Margaret Sprout, in the new 2d rev. edition of *Foundations of National Power*, New York, 1951, p. 39, where they explain their reasons for choosing a

By way of simplification, it can be said that while the realist is primarily interested in the quest for power—and its culmination in the resort to violence —as the essence of all politics among nations, the idealist is concerned above all with its elimination. On this level there can be no meeting of the minds. But the question arises whether to start off with the quest and struggle for power does not mean tying up the horse at its tail.

Normally, power is a means to other ends and not an end in itself. Where it becomes an end, as it does in the case of the "mad Caesars," one is faced with what Toynbee would call an "enormity." Therefore, to treat the quest for power, positively or negatively, outside the context of ends and purposes which it is expected to serve, robs it of any intelligible meaning and, by the way, also makes it impossible to judge its appropriateness or excessiveness. It is as if an economist, in developing economic theory, were to concentrate on the accumulation and expenditure of money. He could not avoid painting a picture of a world of misers or spendthrifts, as the political scientist on the power level can see little but a world of insatiably power-hungry or unconditionally power-hostile political actors.[2]

One gets a very different picture, as the further discussion should show, if one considers first the values and purposes for the sake of which policy-makers seek to accumulate or use national power, as they may also seek alternative or supplementary means.

This suggests beginning with a "theory of ends" and proceeding from there to the analysis of the quest for power as it develops in conjunction with and under the impact of the ends it is meant to promote. It must be kept in mind, however, that one is not dealing with a simple cause-and-effect relationship. The degree to which power is available or attainable frequently affects the choice of ends. Prudent policy-makers will keep their ends and aspirations safely within the power which their

country possesses or is ready and willing to muster.[3] Statesmen with a respect for moral principles, or under pressure from people who have such respect, may hesitate to pursue goals which demand the sacrifice of these principles or of other values in the process of power accumulation or use.[4]

There is little reason to expect that all actors on the international stage will orientate themselves uniformly toward one and the same goal, whether it be peace, security, or "power as an end in itself." However, the possibility will have to be considered that they may be operating under some form of "compulsion" which may force them in the long run to fall in line with each other.

States are not single-purpose organizations like hospitals, golf clubs, or banking establishments.[5] At one and the same time people expect from them not only external security, but such widely differing things as colonial conquest, better control over foreign markets, freedom for the individual, and international lawfulness. Between goals such as these, relatively scarce means must be parceled out in order of preference and by a constant process of weighing, comparing, and computing of values. Because policy-makers, like all men, seek to maximize value in accordance with ever-fluctuating value patterns, one would anticipate great variation in their choice unless something compelled them to conform.[6]

[3] Walter Lippmann has consistently advocated such prudence. "The thesis of this book," he says in reference to his *U.S. Foreign Policy: Shield of the Republic* (Boston, 1943), "is that a foreign policy consists in bringing into balance, with a comfortable surplus of power in reserve, the nation's commitments and the nation's power. The constant preoccupation of the true statesman is to achieve and maintain this balance."

[4] For some of the ethical problems involved, see my article on "Statesmanship and Moral Choice," *World Politics*, I, No. 2 (January, 1949), pp. 175–95.

[5] In speaking of the actors on the international stage, I shall use the term "states" as a means of abbreviation. The real actors are aggregates of decision-makers acting in the name of states or nations, including in a varied order of influence such persons as statesmen, legislators, lobbyists, and common citizens. There are also, today, as there were in medieval times, actors other than states, like the Cominform, the Vatican, the United Nations, or the Anglo-Iranian Oil Company, which one could not afford to ignore in any complete theory of international politics. One might call them subnational, transnational, and supernational centers of influence and often of power.

[6] As Harold D. Lasswell and Abraham Kaplan put it in *Power and Society* (New Haven, 1950): "No generalizations can be made a priori concerning the scale of

much broader definition.) The term "resort to power" will be used to mean reliance on the ability to inflict deprivations, "resort to violence" as actual coercion by the use of physical force.

[2] Some political scientists would exclude by definition from what they call "political" anything but the problems of power. But the consequence is that a "foreign policy" must then be called political in one respect and non-political in all others, the latter including all policy ends other than power itself.

The number of conceivable ends is much larger than is indicated by broad categories such as "security," "aggrandizement," or "international order." Policy-makers must decide whether a specific increment of security is worth the specific additional deprivations which its attainment through power requires. However, for purposes of analysis it is permissible to limit the discussion to a few representative types of goals. It need only be kept in mind that these typical bundles of related ends are not sharply divided from one another and that no actor is likely to be found pursuing a single type of objectives all the time. He may be out for security today, for conquest tomorrow.

The goals of foreign policy can be classified under the three headings of "goals of national self-extension," "goals of national self-preservation," and "goals of national self-abnegation." For actors other than states, corresponding categories would have to be chosen.[7]

The term "self-extension" is not used here in a derogatory sense, although some goals which belong in this category may deserve moral condemnation. It is meant to cover all policy objectives expressing a demand for values not already enjoyed, and thus a demand for a change of the status quo. The objectives may vary widely. The aim may be more "power as an end in itself" or domination over other peoples or territorial expansion; but it may also represent a quest for the return of lost territory, or the redress of legitimate grievances, such as termination of unjust discriminations, the emancipation from foreign control or imposition on others of an ideology or way of life.[8]

Self-preservation is meant to stand for all demands pointing toward the maintenance, protection, or defense of the existing distribution of values, usually called the status quo. The term "self-preservation" is not without ambiguity. The national "self" which states seek to preserve can undergo a wide variety of interpretations. It may be considered to include only national independence and the territorial integrity of the homeland; or it may be held to embrace a whole catalogue of "vital interests," from safety belts and influence zones to investments and nationals abroad. Another variable makes the notion of self-preservation even more elusive and therefore often convenient as a cloak for other purposes. To preserve possessions does not merely mean to defend them when they are actually under attack. Status quo powers regularly demand that the threat of such attack be reduced at least to the point of giving them a reasonable sense of security.

Thus, the quest for security—the preservation goal *par excellence*—points beyond mere maintenance

---

values of all groups and individuals. What the values are in a given situation must in principle be separately determined for each case." Though they state earlier that a certain element of invariance must be assumed to "make a political science possible," they cannot be pleading for the assumption that all actors uniformly prefer one single value, such as power. For they also say (p. 57) that: "It is impossible to assign a universally dominant role to some value or other."

[7] There will be little room in the following to discuss the factors that account for the choice of goals by the decision-makers. There is need for much more study of these factors. Growing awareness that policy cannot arise except through choices and decisions of individuals has led recently to a tendency to stress the psychological factor. But it is probable that the understanding of national foreign policies, as well as any long-run predictions concerning such policies, will be found to depend on knowledge of antecedents to action that are more general and more constant than the psychological traits and predispositions of frequently changing individuals, or even of groups, elites, and nations. To give an illustration, the pressures which the Soviet Government has placed in recent years on Turkey could have been predicted, even at the time when Moscow disclaimed any future concern with Constantinople and the Straits, on the basis of a geopolitical and historical analysis of the environment in which the Kremlin acts today and acted in Czarist days. Spykman's prediction of 1942 that "a modern, vitalized and militarized China . . . is going to be a threat not only to Japan, but also to the position of the Western Powers in the Asiatic Mediterranean," which sounded almost blasphemous to some of his critics when it was made, could not have been made if it had depended on the knowledge of the future political fortunes, the psychology, and the doctrine of one who was then a little-known Communist agitator with the name of Mao Tse-tung

(Nicholas John Spykman, *America's Strategy in World Politics*, New York, 1942, p. 469).

[8] The literature on the causes of imperialism is extensive. Studies have also been made bearing on such problems as the relationship between dictatorship and expansionist foreign policies; but one would wish studies like that of Edmond N. Cahn (*The Sense of Injustice*, New York, 1949) to be extended to the international field. For where is the "sense of injustice" more "alive with movement and warmth" (p. 13) and where is the "human animal" more "disposed to fight injustice" (p. 25) than in international relations? Status quo countries will continue to live in a fool's paradise if they fail to understand the deep and manifold causes which account for demands for change and self-extension even through violence.

and defense.[9] It can become so ambitious as to transform itself into a goal of unlimited self-extension. A country pursuing the mirage of absolute security could not stop at less than world domination today.[10] A change to self-extension in the name of security often occurs at the close of a war. Victims of attack who were entirely satisfied before hostilities started are rarely content, if victorious, to return to the *status quo ante*.

Self-abnegation, finally, is meant to include all goals transcending—if not sacrificing—the "national interest," in any meaningful sense of the term. It is the goal of those who place a higher value on such ends as international solidarity, lawfulness, rectitude, or peace than even on national security and self-preservation. It is also the goal of individuals, groups, or regimes who at the expense of the nation as a whole use their influence within the decision-making process to promote what might be called "subnational" interests.

This may appear to be a category which only a Utopian could expect to find in international politics, at least as far as idealistic self-abnegation is concerned. How could any nation dare indulge in altruistic pursuits—or allow its interests to be sacrificed to interest of a group—and yet hope to survive? While the discussion of compulsion and penalties must be further postponed, it is worth pointing out, nevertheless, that the United States was powerful enough in 1918 to permit Woodrow Wilson to in-

dulge in self-abnegation goals without much harm to American interests and that little Denmark, too, weak to seek self-preservation through power, limited its foreign policy largely to humanitarian causes and yet in the end survived Hitler's conquest. There is also the case of governments like that of Communist Czechoslovakia which for the sake of party doctrine and power are ready to promote the transnational cause of world communism, though it means sacrificing all but the outward appearances of national sovereignty and independence. Highest devotion to national interests and aspirations, even if spread more widely over the globe today than ever, is not the only possible attitude of actors in international affairs. Exponents of world government are not necessarily Utopians for hoping that peoples and governments some day will commit an act of radical national self-abnegation and abdicate as sovereign entities in favor of a world state.

Cases in which self-abnegation goals have precedence over national self-preservation may be rare in an era in which nationalism and the ethics of patriotism continue unabated.[11] This does not preclude the possibility, however, that where influential groups of participants in the decision-making process place high value on a universal cause such as peace, pressures exerted by these groups may affect the course of foreign policy. It may lead to a more modest interpretation of the national interest, to more concern for the interests of other nations, to more concessions for the sake of peace, or to more restraint in the use of power and violence. Whether the nation will profit or suffer in the end from the success of such "internationalist," "humanitarian," or "pacifist" pressures depends on the circumstances of the case; whichever it does, the abnegation goals will have proved themselves a reality.

[9] I am employing the term "security" as it is used in the everyday language of statesmen to signify not "high value expectancy" generally—as Lasswell and Kaplan define the term (*op. cit.*, p. 61)—but high expectancy of value *preservation*. The two authors may have had the same thing in mind, because they specify that security means a realistic expectancy of *maintaining* influence. One would not say that Nazi Germany either came to be or came to feel more secure as her expectancy of successful self-*extension* through conquest of territory increased.

[10] The degree of security-mindedness of different countries and of groups within countries depends on many circumstances which would be worth studying. Looking at the United States and France in recent times, it would seem as if countries become more ambitious in their desire for security either for having enjoyed a high degree of it over a long period or for having had much and recent experience with the sad consequences of insecurity. James Burnham in *The Struggle for the World* (New York, 1947), argues that in the atomic age, there can be no security short of world empire, with only two candidates for such empire available today. "In the course of the decision," he says, "both of the present antagonists may . . . be destroyed. But one of them must be" (pp. 134 f.).

[11] As Hermann Goering is reported to have said, cynically (see G. M. Gilbert, *The Psychology of Dictatorship*, New York 1950, p. 117): "Voice or no voice, the people can always be brought to do the bidding of the leaders. That is easy. All you have to do is to tell them they are being attacked and denounce the pacifists for lack of patriotism. . . ."

According to Charles A. Beard (*The Idea of National Interest*, New York, 1943), the interest of the nation as a whole, if it can be defined at all, is constantly being sacrificed to the interests of groups which are powerful enough to have their special interests pass for the "national interest." If he were right, most countries would be engaged most of the time, involuntarily, in a process of national self-abnegation—and still survive.

Now let us suppose that a government has picked its objective or objectives and has also decided to rely on the accumulation and use of power as the chief means of reaching its goal. We can then ask ourselves what will determine the scope of its quest for power. Would it not stand to reason—provided the government in question was acting rationally—that it would seek to preserve or acquire as much power as appeared adequate to assure the success of its policy? It would not aim at a higher level of power, because every increment adds to the burdens the country has to bear, cuts down on the chances of attaining other objectives, and tends to provoke counteraction. To seek less than adequate power would mean giving up the chance of attaining one's goal.

Because adequacy is a matter of subjective estimates, the factors which influence these estimates are of major interest. Two countries with the same goals and acting under similar circumstances may differ widely in their views on adequacy of power. But this need not invalidate some general theses concerning the relationship between the main categories of policy goals and the quest for power.

Goals of national self-abnegation—provided they are not set by subnational groups parading their interests as the "national interest"—call for the approval and support of more than a single nation. Accumulation, show, or use of national power are likely to defeat rather than to promote such ends. Nations pursuing ends that fall into this category—including the end of eliminating "power politics"!—will tend to play down their own national power or to reduce it. "Disarmament by example" pursued by Britain prior to 1932 was a way of trying to promote world peace by a policy of self-abnegation.

Obviously, cases will be rare in which for the sake of goals of self-abnegation a nation refuses to resort to power even when the inner core of the national self comes under serious threat of attack. This means that under stress self-preservation usually gains the upper hand. However, even then idealistic pressures at home in favor of self-denying policies may persist and either delay or reduce the effort to enhance defensive national power.

Statesmen and peoples who hold—or profess to hold—strong beliefs in universal causes, religious or ideological, are not always found to minimize reliance on national power. On the contrary, striking cases have become only too familiar in this age of revolutionary and ideological strife in which goals appearing to be of a self-transcending kind have revealed themselves as the most ambitious goals of self-extension. Whenever a nation goes out on a "crusade" for some universal cause, claiming to have a mission of imposing its ideas and institutions on others, there is practically no limit to the enhancement of national power it deems necessary. National power is looked upon or advertised here as the chosen instrument with which to bring salvation to mankind!

Goals of self-extension generally place an extremely high premium on the resort to power as a means. The chances of bringing about any major change of the international status quo by means other than power or even violence are slim indeed. Because it is also true that self-extension is often sought passionately if not fanatically and by actors of various sort and motivation, the tendency is toward frequent and intensive quests for enhanced power by nations belonging to this category. No phenomenon in international politics calls for more study and attention.

Adequate power, in this instance, means power deemed adequate to overcome the power of resistance put up by those who desire to preserve things which they possess and cherish. Where such resistance is expected to be feeble, as it is when the demand is directed against weak or complacent and isolated countries, the nation seeking self-extension may be expected to be satisfied with far less than the maximum power for which it has potentialities. However, in view of the fact that other and stronger countries, as a rule, are awake to their interest in preserving well beyond their own borders the established distribution of values, resistance to change is usually not easy to break. It may be so forbidding as to deter countries from making the attempt. Thus, fervently "revisionist" Hungary after 1919 was sufficiently impressed by the power and resolution of the Little Entente not to attempt to regain her lost territories by means of power. The whole idea of the balance of power as a guarantor of peace rests on the assumption that the costs of adequate power for self-extension may at a certain point become excessive or prohibitive.

Many a "satisfied" country would better be called a country "resigned to non-extension," as can be seen whenever easy opportunities for gain present themselves. Not many belligerents, even if they were victims of attack when the war started, fail to come forth with "historic claims" and strategic demands once they are victorious. It would be exaggerated, however, to say that self-extension will always take place where no resistance is expected, or where no serious costs are involved. While Switzerland may stand alone in having refused to consider an increase of territory, even as a gift, it is well known how consistently influential groups in the United States Senate, and in the American public at large, have opposed territorial annexations.

Because of the fact that self-extension almost invariably calls for additional power, countries of the type discussed here tend to be the initiators of power competition and the resort to violence. Herein lies the significant kernel of truth in the idealist theory of aggression.[12] Cases are conceivable, of course, in which the initiative rests with a country concerned with self-preservation which starts enhancing its defensive power for fear of an imagined threat; the resort to violence, too, may be the preventive act of a nation that believes itself to be menaced by an attack on its own values or those of its friends.[13] If two countries are both eager to gain advantages at each other's expense, or are both haunted by fears and suspicions, it may be difficult to decide where the initiative lay and where the first move was made that led to a race for higher levels of power and ultimately to war.

Turning, finally, to the goals of self-preservation, they will be found to be most elusive when it comes to setting up general hypotheses concerning their effect on the quest for power. Depending on the circumstances, countries in this category may run the whole gamut from a frantic concern with the enhancement of power at one extreme to complete indifference to power at the other. Britain offers an excellent example of a swing of the pendulum from complacency under Baldwin and Chamberlain to spectacular and heroic total mobilization of power under Churchill.

[12] See also Robert Strausz-Hupé and Stefan T. Possony, *International Relations*, New York 1950, p. 9.

[13] ". . . a government with no appetite whatsoever," writes W. T. R. Fox ("Atomic Energy and International Relations," in *Technology and International Relations*, ed. by W. F. Ogburn, Chicago 1949, p. 118), "may start a conflict if its leaders feel sure that the opponent has for a long time been unscrupulously trading on their general unwillingness to start a war."

The reason why self-preservation calls forth such a variety of attitudes toward power lies in the fact that countries which are satisfied to let things stand as they are have no immediate incentive for valuing power or for wishing to enhance it. Whether they become interested in power at all—and the extent to which they do—depends on the actions which they expect from others. It is a responsive interest which takes its cue from the threats, real or imagined, directed at things possessed and valued. If policy is rationally decided, the quest for power here increases and decreases in proportion to these external threats.

One can bring out the peculiarities of this responsive attitude most clearly if one starts out by postulating a situation in which all of the major actors are assumed to be concerned with nothing but self-preservation. In the mid-twenties, when the "revisionist" nations were still impotent, this situation was closely approximated. Under such conditions, policy-makers are inclined toward keeping the costs of power at a minimum and toward avoiding any move which might provoke a race for power from which, after all, they have nothing to gain. If there was no reason to fear that one or more within the group might switch to goals of self-extension, and particularly if there was no danger of dissatisfied and potentially strong countries outside the group regaining actual power, the estimates of what constitutes adequacy would drop very low. The unguarded border between Canada and this country serves as a striking reminder of the indifference to power in the relations between two nonextension-seeking and nondistrustful neighbors.[14]

The conditions postulated here describe a configuration in which peace strategies such as the idealist school advocated in the twenties would have an excellent chance of success, provided no country feared the early ascendancy of a presently impotent and dissatisfied nation. All would be interested in disarmament to the lowest level compatible with internal security, in the promotion of mutual confidence and understanding, and in the collective organization of "watchfulness." Only hysteria could produce a race for power within a group of countries

[14] W. T. R. Fox points out that "One state's security is not necessarily every other state's insecurity. . . . Greater security . . . is an objective toward which it is at least conceivable that all states can move simultaneously" (*The Super-Powers*, New York, 1944, p. 11).

intent upon self-preservation. The chances are that the high degree of security which they would believe to be enjoying would lull them into a state of such indifference toward power that they might be overtaken by a self-extension seeking outsider. So slow is the "security dilemma" in catching up with those who are content with mere security!

History does not indicate that conditions of all-round satisfaction are either frequent or persistent. They certainly are not in our age, which among other ways of creating dissatisfaction has produced a surprising contempt for the art of satisfying defeated enemies. As a consequence, threats to the established order are almost constantly forcing those who seek preservation of cherished values to muster power of resistance if they wish to assure the success of their defensive objective. In this sense, one can say that their quest for power is the result of external "compulsion."

However, this "compulsion" is not some kind of mechanical force which would rob the actors of their freedom of choice. No decision-maker is forced by anything except his own value preferences or his conscience to defend by means of power either national independence or any other threatened values. There are plenty of Europeans today—and there may be European governments tomorrow— who prefer to risk their country's freedom and institutions rather than embark on a policy of armed resistance which they consider hopeless or too costly. What the penalties are for not ceding to the "compulsion" is another question.

Those who interpret international politics as being essentially a struggle for survival, similar to the "survival of the fittest" in business competition or in the Darwinian world of competing animal species, are thereby suggesting that the penalty consists in the loss of independent existence. This has been true in some instances; but there is plenty of historical evidence to show that a threat to "existence," of great powers at least, has occurred only in the exceptional though cataclysmic eruption of

revolutionary or imperialist ardor characteristic of a Napoleon or a Hitler.[15] In our era such eruptions have become not only frequent, but capable of spreading out over the entire globe and of drawing all nations into a single struggle for survival. There have been other times—and they cover much of the maligned history of European "power politics"— when the demands for self-extension, though ubiquitous as far as the major powers of the time were concerned, have remained limited in scope. Even if successful, the penalties on the loser rarely ranged beyond such deprivations as the loss of a strip of territory or the shift of a neighboring country to a less friendly dynasty. Whether such limitation was imposed solely by the lack of means for more ambitious self-extension, or whether it also expressed a prudent and conservative spirit on the part of the decision-makers, cannot be discussed here. In any case, the contrast with the "struggles for survival" of an age of revolutionary and total wars is striking.

Even when the penalty is not annihilation—and defeat today, as in remote ages, may actually mean physical extermination—countries usually feel compelled by their judgment and conscience not to allow possessions they value to go by default. They may enhance and use their power in defense of everything from prestige and colonies to free institutions and moral principles. The loss of values for which a people is ready to fight and die becomes a "compelling" penalty. "Collective security," as practiced recently, can be understood as an effort not only to equal in scope and speed the power drive of the "initiators," but to bring the "free peoples" to a point where they will identify their "selves" with the entire non-Communist world and its institutions and feel compelled to fight for the preservation of their larger "selves." . . .

[15] See Hans J. Morgenthau, *Scientific Man vs. Power Politics*, Chicago, 1946, p. 107, on the difference between "the great international conflicts" and the "secondary conflicts."

17. National Interests*

Thomas W. Robinson is affiliated with the RAND Corporation.
In this article he focuses on a concept frequently used to interpret and explain the
goals of foreign policy, the national interest. His assessment of the concept is
especially useful because it is based on a careful analysis of the ideas that a leading
student of the subject, Professor Hans J. Morgenthau, has set forth in various
writings. [*Reprinted from Thomas W. Robinson, "A National Interest Analysis
of Sino-Soviet Relations,"* International Studies Quarterly, *XI (June 1967),
135–75, by permission of the author and the Wayne State University Press. Copyright by Wayne State University Press, Detroit, Michigan.*]

I. Introduction

In the last decade and a half, elaboration of a number
of theoretical approaches to international relations
has perhaps been the major development in that
field. Quite a number of separate and, for the most
part, fruitful theoretical orientations have been
devised, and the obvious gap which had existed for
so many years has now begun to be filled. At present it
appears that a period of consolidation and expansion
from within has set in, in which the various theories
must be interrelated and tested through practical
application.

At least four problems remain to be overcome in
the period ahead. The most serious, perhaps, is the
split between "traditional" political analysis and the
"behavioral" or "scientific" approach. These are
obviously complementary, but so far there has been
a dearth of attempts to integrate the two and to use
the insights of one as inputs into the other. It is true
that there are theorists who for most of their careers

approached international relations either from the
point of view of traditional political analysis or of
"moralism-legalism" but who now have begun to
write in the newer idiom. (Quincy Wright is the
example that comes immediately to mind.) But for
the most part the gulf of misunderstanding and, on
the part of some, deliberate ignorance, remains. To
the extent that this is a generational problem, based
on the fear of being outmoded and on the reluctance,
late in one's career, to retool, the problem will solve
itself with the mere passage of time. But not only
would it be a pity from the point of view of creative
cross-fertilization were the "traditionalists" and the
"behavioralists" not to make an early attempt at
unification, but also the problem appears to be of
broader scope than mere passage of time. For the
older approach has both much to offer which must not
be lost sight of and presents at every point a healthy
challenge to the newer series of approaches to show
their concrete relevance to issues of the moment.
The time is therefore ripe for new attempts to bring
together the poles, which have too long remained
apart.

A similar problem, it seems to me, exists inside
the confines of the "behavioral" camp itself. Here we
find a multitude of theoretical approaches to international relations, only a few of which attempt to

* This paper was prepared for presentation at the
Western Political Science Association conference held in
Reno, Nevada, March 25, 1966. Any views expressed in
this paper are those of the author. They should not be
interpreted as reflecting the views of The RAND Corporation or the official opinion or policy of any of its governmental or private research sponsors.

build on the work that has come before. This goes for both theoretical models and for some of the newer methodologies. There seems to be a dual compartmentalization—of theory from theory and method from method, on the one hand, and theory from method, on the other. This, too, is probably a product of the speed and richness of progress in the recent period, but it must be rectified before approaches become schools and schools find traditions to defend. New combinations of theory and method must be tried out: let us, for instance, marry systems analysis to simulation and "power politics" to game theory. We may obtain some bastard offsprings but perhaps a genius or two will also emerge.

A third problem—laden with danger but presenting opportunities—is the application of the new theories and methodologies to the real world, especially to topics in contemporary world politics. In a period when the theoretical and methodological base of international relations is in flux, it is very tempting, but quite dangerous, to draw immediate policy implications from theoretical work. Most current models and methods are as yet too rough and therefore unequal to standing up in competition with sophisticated traditional political analysis. Testing by reference to reality should not be made in all cases for the additional reasons that it not only encourages an "I-told-you-so" attitude on the part of opponents to the new experimentation but also carries with it the danger of leading policy-makers astray, thereby harming national interests and policy. But, on the other hand, there should be no unwillingness to consult international political reality whenever it appears that a test promises to advance the field. The trick is to build a model with enough sophistication, to combine it with a workable method and then to find an historical case which will provide a good test. . . .

In this paper, we shall attempt to contribute to the solution of . . . [the first of these problems by examining] Hans Morgenthau's national interest formulation as representative of the best which the "traditional" approach has to offer. . . .

II. Hans Morgenthau's Conception of the National Interest

In discussing Morgenthau's view of the national interest, let us divide the subject as follows: (1)

Definition and analysis of the national interest; (2) basic statement of the relation between interest and power; (3) national interest and morality; (4) propositions about the national interest; (5) national interest and nuclear weapons; (6) national interest and international organization.

Definition and Analysis of the National Interest

At first it seems that Morgenthau uses the term "national interest" in many different ways to cover a bewildering variety of meanings. This seems to be evidenced by the following array of terms: common interest and conflicting interest, primary and secondary interest, inchoate interest, community of interests, identical and complementary interests, vital interests, legitimate interests, specific or limited interests, material interests, hard-core interests, necessary and variable interests.[1] Upon further investigation, however, these terms can be collapsed into two general categories—the national interests of a single nation and the degree of commonality of

[1] (Note: All footnote references are to Hans J. Morgenthau; the author's name will therefore not be repeated.)
(a) Common and conflicting interests: *The Restoration of American Politics* (Chicago: The University of Chicago Press, 1964), p. 203; "Alliances in Theory and Practice," in Arnold Wolfers, ed., *Alliance Policy in The Cold War* (Baltimore: The Johns Hopkins Press, 1959), p. 188.
(b) Primary and secondary interests: *The Impasse of American Foreign Policy* (Chicago: The University of Chicago Press, 1962), p. 191; "The Crisis in the Western Alliance," *Commentary*, Vol. 35 (1963), pp. 185–98.
(c) Inchoate (rudimentary, incipient) interests: *The Restoration of American Politics, op. cit.*, p. 198.
(d) Community of interests: *Ibid.*, p. 204; "Alliances in Theory and Practice," *op. cit.*, p. 189.
(e) Identical and complementary interests: *The Impasse of American Foreign Policy, op. cit.*, p. 173; "The Impotence of American Power," *Commentary*, Vol. 36 (1963), p. 385; "Alliances in Theory and Practice," *op. cit.*, p. 189; *In Defense of the National Interest* (Chicago: The University of Chicago Press, 1950), p. 146.
(f) Vital interests: *Dilemmas of Politics* (Chicago: The University of Chicago Press, 1958), p. 274.
(g) Legitimate interests: *The Impasse of American Foreign Policy, op. cit.*, p. 214.
(h) Specific (limited) interests: "Alliances in Theory and Practice," *op. cit.*, p. 201.
(i) Material interests: *Ibid.*, p. 188.
(j) Hard core interests: *Dilemmas of Politics, op. cit.*, p. 66.
(k) Necessary (permanent) and variable interests: "Another 'Great Debate': The National Interest of the United States," *The American Political Science Review*, Vol. XLVI (1952), p. 973.

interests among two or more nations. Under the heading of the national interest of a single state we can group together several interests, according to: (1) the degree of primacy of the interest; (2) the degree of permanence of the interest; (3) the degree of generality of the interest. These may be represented according to the following diagram:

	Primary[1]	Secondary[3]
Permanent	Specific[2] General	
Variable	Specific[2] General	

(a) Includes as synonyms: vital, legitimate, hard-core, and necessary national interests.
(b) Includes as synonyms: material and limited interests.
(c) Includes as a synonym: non-vital interests.

Thus, for example, primary interests can be either permanent or variable in time as well as specific or general. This gives us eight different types of interests which a given nation may hold. Note, however, that only three adjectives are needed to describe a national interest. For instance, an interest can be designated as primary, permanent, and specific, or secondary, variable, and general (but not, note, as primary, permanent, and variable or secondary, specific, and general). All of the interests of a given nation expressed at any given moment are called the total interests of that nation.[2]

The degree or lack of commonality of interests between two or more states, may be represented geometrically as in the following diagram:

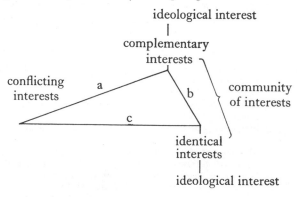

Thus, there exist three continua of interests between two or more nations, represented by the sides a, b, and c of the triangle. Inchoate interests cannot be represented since, by definition, they have yet to be expressed. Once they are defined they will appear as an interest representable as a point on one of the lines of the diagram. Ideological interests are always built on the foundation of some commonly-felt interests. This is shown in the diagram.

It remains to define more closely each of the interests mentioned. We have the following six "national" interests.

(a) *Primary interests* include protection of the nation's physical, political, and cultural identity and survival against encroachment from the outside.[3] Primary interests can never be compromised or traded. All nations hold these same interests and must defend them at any price.[4]

(b) *Secondary interests* are those falling outside of *a* but contributing to it. For example, protecting citizens abroad and maintaining proper immunities for a nation's diplomats are secondary interests.

(c) *Permanent interests* are those which are relatively constant over long periods of time; they vary with time, but only slowly.[5] For instance, Great Britain for many centuries has had an interest in the freedom to navigate the seas and in a narrow definition of coastal waters.

(d) *Variable interests* are those which are a function of "all the cross currents of personalities, public opinion, sectional interests, partisan politics, and political and moral folkways" of a given nation.[6] In other words, they are what a given nation at any particular time chooses to regard as its national interests. In this respect the variable interest may diverge from both primary and permanent interests. For example, Great Britain in 1938 chose to regard certain events bearing on the security of Czechoslovakia as not within its interest.

(e) *General interests* are those which the nation can apply in a positive manner to a large geographic area, to a large number of nations, or in several specific fields (such as economics, trade, diplomatic

[3] *Dilemmas of Politics*, op. cit., pp. 50, 51, 66, 178; "Another Great Debate," op. cit., p. 973.
[4] *The Impasse of American Foreign Policy*, op. cit., p. 291.
[5] *Dilemmas of Politics*, op. cit., p. 66.
[6] *Ibid.*, p. 66; "Another Great Debate," op. cit., p. 973.

[2] "Alliances in Theory and Practice," op. cit., p. 188.

intercourse, international law, etc.). An example would be the British interest in the maintenance of a balance of power on the European continent.

(f) *Specific interests* are those positive interests not included in *e*. Specific interests are usually closely defined in time and/or space and often are the logical outgrowth of general interests.[7] For instance, Britain historically has regarded the continued independence of the Low Countries as an absolute prerequisite for the maintenance of the balance of power in Europe.

We also have the following three "international" interests:

(g) *Identical interests* between nations obviously are those national interests (that is, one or more of *a* through *f* above) which those nations hold in common.[8] For example, Great Britain and the U.S. have had an interest in assuring that the European continent is not dominated by a single power.

(h) *Complementary interests* between nations are those which, although not identical, at least are capable of forming the basis of agreement on specific issues.[9] England has an interest in maintaining the independence of Portugal from Spain as a means of controlling the regions of the Atlantic Ocean off the Iberian peninsula, while Portugal has an interest in British maritime hegemony as a means of defense against Spain.

(i) *Conflicting interests* are those not included in *g* and *h*. It should be noted, however, that today's conflicting interests can be transformed tomorrow, through diplomacy, occurrence of events, or the passage of time into common or complementary interests.[10] The same thing might be said about the possibility of transforming identical or complementary interests into conflicting interests.

The Relation Between Interest and Power

In Morgenthau's political theory, the starting place for a discussion of most subjects is a consideration of human nature. This is the case also with his derivation of the basic proposition of his theory that politicians and statesmen, if they wish to be successful must in the first instance equate their own and their states' interests with the pursuit and use of power. The derivation of this proposition is as follows. Since human nature is imperfect, society also is imperfect, as it is human nature writ large. Hence, abstract moral principles can never be realized fully but can only be approximated through the balancing of interests and by temporary settlements. Two good methods exist to this end. On the one hand, one can attempt to set up a system of checks and balances among the various contending parties. On the other hand, one may strive for the lesser attainable evil in preference to the absolute good which is always beyond reach.[11] In international relations, too, this method must be followed. Foreign policy goals must not range beyond the power available, for although national desires for good and for evil are infinite, the resources for obtaining them are strictly limited. It is therefore necessary to distinguish desirable goals from essential goals. The list of essential national goals is called the total national interest. Once this is done, it remains only to establish a hierarchical order among them according to the purposes of the nation and then to allocate the power resources of the nation accordingly.[12]

Bringing the desires of a nation into line with the power available for their pursuit, and the designation of those interests which are to be pursued at all costs, is the focus of Morgenthau's theory of international politics and of his statement of political realism.[13] This is all that is meant by "the concept of interest defined in terms of power."[14] It is, therefore, not a vague concept with no real meaning, as alleged by some. It is merely prudence operating in international relations, resulting in "a rational, discriminating understanding of the hierarchy of national interests and the power available for their support."[15] It is true that these interests tend to be

---

[7] "Alliances in Theory and Practice," *op. cit.*, p. 191.

[8] *Ibid.*, pp. 188, 189, 191; *In Defense of the National Interest*, *op. cit.*, p. 146; "The Impotence of American Power," *op. cit.*, p. 385; *The Impasse of American Foreign Policy*, *op. cit.*, p. 173.

[9] *In Defense of the National Interest*, *op. cit.*, p. 146; *The Impasse of American Foreign Policy*, *op. cit.*, p. 173.

[10] *The Restoration of American Politics*, *op. cit.*, pp. 198, 203.

[11] *Dilemmas of Politics*, *op. cit.*, p. 261; "Goldwater—The Romantic Regression," *Commentary*, Vol. 38 (1964), pp. 65–8.

[12] *In Defense of the National Interest*, *op. cit.*, pp. 117–18.

[13] *Dilemmas of Politics*, *op. cit.*, pp. 47, 50, 51, 54; *Politics Among Nations* (New York: Alfred A. Knopf, 1963, 3rd edition), p. 5.

[14] *Ibid.*, p. 14.

[15] "War With China?" *The New Republic*, Vol. 152, April 3, 1965, p. 14.

relatively constant over long periods of time. This is due to: (1) the nature of the interests themselves, especially the primary interests defined above; (2) the relative constancy of the political environment within which policies made in pursuit of those interests operate; (3) the limited number of policy alternatives available to pursue them.[16] Since these are by no means constant, even the most "permanent" interests change in time. The fact is that national interests are constant only as long as the latter two factors themselves do not vary. In other words, although the national interest is a prime variable, it is dependent on the state of the political environment and on the variation in the number of policy alternatives available. It is the relative constancy in these just as much as the root desire to protect one's national security and identity that allows Morgenthau to conclude that by thinking in terms of interest defined as power "we think as [the statesman] does, and as disinterested observers we understand his thoughts and actions perhaps better than he does. . . ."[17] It is not necessary, for instance, to know all the secrets of the Chinese foreign office, in order to know China's national interests in regard to Korea or Formosa.[18] But Morgenthau also concludes, as we shall see below, that many components of the national interest may change very quickly, when, as at present, the political environment and the available policy alternatives themselves fluctuate rapidly. The implication is clear that in periods of rapid change, we shall have much more difficulty in putting ourselves in the shoes of statesmen and figuring out, on the basis of a national interest analysis what their policy was, is, or will be. Finally, the national interest is by no means the only factor to be considered when making or ascertaining policy. The relative power of the parties concerned is the other primary element and we must also consider such factors as personalities of the members of the decision-making groups, national traditions, and situationally-based "opportunities" that may suddenly appear.[19]

National Interest and Morality

Even though it may sometimes be difficult to determine the national interest for the reasons

cited, Morgenthau warns us to distinguish clearly between this type of thinking, which is necessary and correct, and moralistically-based thinking, which is politically dangerous and morally wrong.[20] The choice, of course, is not between moral principle and the national interest, but between two types of political morality, the one divorced from political reality and taking as its standard the abstract formulation of universal moral principles, and the other intimately concerned with political reality and taking as its standard not only those same moral principles but also the political consequences that may flow from their application.[21] Thinking in terms of the national interest is morally necessary, for the state in contradistinction to the individual has no moral right to risk sacrifice of the nation for the sake of certain moral principles. Instead, its highest moral principle must be survival, for the state is entrusted with the very lives of its citizens, and therefore must in every instance insure their well-being.[22] Thinking in terms of the national interest also guards against the pitfall of equating the interests of the nation with the sort of moral-ideological crusade which assumes that the national interest of the nation is the same as the universal interest of all.[23]

Propositions About the National Interests

Morgenthau makes use of national interest analysis in many different contexts, and we can only illustrate the mode of analysis here by selected examples. These will be divided into three parts:

    A. War and the use of force;
    B. Alliances;
    C. Diplomatic negotiations.

A. *Use of force.*   War and peace form a continuum of means by which nations pursue their interests.[24] Whether a nation protects those interests by peaceful or violent means, however, is not only its own choice but is also a function of certain objective conditions over which it has no control.[25] Every great power—even in the nuclear age—must at times defend its

---

[16] *Dilemmas of Politics, op. cit.,* p. 66.
[17] *Ibid.,* p. 67; *Politics Among Nations, op. cit.,* p. 5.
[18] *Dilemmas of Politics, op. cit.,* p. 308.
[19] "Another Great Debate," *op. cit.,* p. 969.

[20] *Politics Among Nations, op. cit.,* p. 146.
[21] "Another Great Debate," *op. cit.,* p. 986; *In Defense of the National Interest, op. cit.,* p. 133.
[22] "Another Great Debate," *op. cit.,* p. 985.
[23] *In Defense of the National Interest, op. cit.,* p. 35.
[24] *Dilemmas of Politics, op. cit.,* p. 256.
[25] *The Impasse of American Foreign Policy, op. cit.,* p. 186.

national interests with the threat or use of force.[26] Still, although it often occurs that the interests of nations are irreconcilable (and diplomacy has had a chance to show that they are), war can sometimes be avoided merely by the passage of time.[27]

B. *Alliances*. The purpose of an alliance is to explicate and make precise an existing community of interests among two or more nations,[28] and to transform that community of interests into legal obligations. It follows immediately that if there is no such community of interests—either common or complementary—either the alliance will fail or naked power must be substituted; and the latter does not provide a firm foundation for any alliance.[29] An alliance, of course, is a function of the large variety of interests—primary, permanent, variable and so on—that every nation possesses the generality and duration of a given alliance will therefore depend on the relative strengths of those interests which favor the alliance and those that oppose it. Such an estimation must be made by every statesman when he considers whether or not to engage in alliance ties.[30] The advantage of pursuing the national interests through alliances, of course, lies in the translation of inchoate, common, or complementary interests into common policy[31] and in bringing the nation's power directly to bear on questions of national interest.

Alliances can be classified, in regard to their relationship to the interests of the nation involved, according to the following table.[32]

Presumably the types of alliances noted here are polar types so that, for instance, one could also speak of alliance which is *more* complementary than ideological, *rather* one-sided, *somewhat* limited, of *medium* duration, and *partially* operative. Presumably, also, one can write the history of a given alliance in terms of the variability of these factors. Morgenthau adduces the following propositions concerning the relation of alliances to national interests.

National Interest	Alliances
1. Type of shared interest: Identical (common), complementary, ideological	Identical or complementary and/or ideological
2. Increment of power and benefit added:	
Mutual increase	Mutual alliance
One-sided increase	One-sided alliance
3. Degree of totality of national interests covered:	
Primary or general	General alliance
Secondary or specific	Limited alliance
4. Coverage of national interests in terms of time:	
Variable national interests	Temporary alliance
Permanent national interests	Permanent alliance
5. Degree of effectiveness in operation in terms of common policies and actions.	Operative or Inoperative alliance

1. The degree of generality of common interests expressed in alliance form is inversely related to the duration of the alliance: general alliances (founded on general interests) will be of short duration while limited alliances will be long-lasting.[33]

2. The relative degree of primacy of national interests expressed in an alliance is inversely proportional to the power of the nation: a weak nation and a strong one will enter into an alliance to defend primary and secondary interests, respectively.[34]

3. In this case, however, the weaker is dependent on the stronger; this will be tolerable only if there is complete identity of interests between the two, a condition which is rare.[35]

4. Even though an alliance may be based on equality (that is, not one-sided in the distribution of power and benefits), it will not succeed unless (a) there is an identity of interests, reflected in the goals of the alliance and (b) an awareness of this identity exemplified through "common measures" and "spontaneous cooperation."[36]

5. A one-sided alliance, where one party receives most of the benefits and the other party carries most of the burden, often results from complementary national interests. Treaties of guarantee are often of this variety.[37]

26 *Ibid.*, p. 44.
27 *The Restoration of American Politics, op. cit.*, p. 202.
28 *Politics Among Nations, op. cit.*, p. 182; "Alliances in Theory and Practice," *op. cit.*, p. 186.
29 *Ibid.*, p. 206.
30 *Ibid.*, p. 191.
31 *The Impasse of American Foreign Policy, op. cit.*, p. 123.
32 "Alliances in Theory and Practice," *op. cit.*, p. 189; *Politics Among Nations, op. cit.*, p. 182.

33 "Alliances in Theory and Practice," *op. cit.*, p. 191.
34 *Ibid.*, p. 190.
35 "The Crisis in the Western Alliance," *op. cit.*, p. 186.
36 "The Impotence of American Power," *op. cit.*, p. 385.
37 "Alliances in Theory and Practice," *op. cit.*, p. 189.

6. The degree of cohesion of alliances is a function only of the relative community of interests felt by the participants and not of the degree of integration achieved or of the quality of legal ties expressed in the alliance.[38]

7. Not every community of interests need be codified into an alliance.[39] Conversely, the existence of certain legal ties binding one nation to another can never overbalance the national interests of the nation; at some time these may lead the nation to pursue policies fundamentally opposed by those by which the nation is legally bound.[40]

8. Ideology is related to interest in alliance in the following manner. An ideological commitment is often added to an alliance already firmly grounded on specific common or complementary interests. In this case it will probably strengthen the alliance. It may, however, weaken it by "obscuring the nature and limits of common interests that the alliance was supposed to make precise and by raising expectations bound to be disappointed for the extent of concerted policies and actions." If, however, a community of interests is absent, an alliance based on ideology alone will be stillborn.[41]

9. The interests that unite two nations against a third and therefore the alliance built on their base are usually precise concerning the designation of the enemy but relatively vague concerning the concrete objectives and policies to be pursued against that enemy.[42]

C. *Diplomatic negotiations and peaceful settlement.* Conflict of interest, to Morgenthau, is the basic factor of international society. Morgenthau defines diplomacy as the technique for accommodating such conflicts of interests.[43] Diplomacy attempts to make the best of a bad situation by attempting to reconcile one's own national interests with those of the other side; that is, it first attempts to define the differences of those interests and then tries to delimit, codify, and emphasize common and complementary interests.

At the same time it separates commonly held interests from conflicting interests and manipulates conditions so as to minimize the danger stemming from those conflicts.[44] Negotiations are an attempt to reconcile divergent interests through a process of give-and-take in which either or both sides concede minor points while leaving the substance of their interests, or else one side receives through compensations from the other at least the equivalent of what it concedes.[45] National interest is directly related to diplomacy not only through definition but in the probabilities as to whether the outcome will be peaceful or not. For only those agreements will last which express the common or complementary interests of the parties concerned and they will last only so long as "their terms coincide with those interests."[46] Although relative power is also a central factor in the outcome of negotiations[47] (from which the conclusion is immediately apparent that settlements must be negotiated only by those whose interests and power are involved, and by no others), it is less important to a successful (i.e. peaceful) outcome than the ability to reconcile apparently irreconcilable interests. The supreme task of diplomacy, therefore, is to "assess correctly the chances for peaceful settlement by asertaining the vital interests of the opposing nations and their relations to each other."[48]

There exist three possible outcomes of diplomatic negotiations between two nations according to the type and degree of compatibility of interests involved. These are either: primary and incompatible (i.e. conflicting) interests, in which case negotiations are impossible; primary and compatible (i.e. either common or complementary) interests, in which case negotiations redefine seemingly incompatible interests; secondary (compatible or incompatible) interests, in which case a compromise is arrived at through trading of interest for interest.[49]

---

[38] *The Impasse of American Foreign Policy, op cit.,* p. 219.

[39] "Alliances in Theory and Practice," *op. cit.,* p. 186; *Politics Among Nations, op. cit.,* p. 182.

[40] *In Defense of the National Interest, op. cit.,* p. 144.

[41] "Alliances in Theory and Practice," *op. cit.,* pp. 188–89.

[42] *Ibid.,* p. 187.

[43] *Dilemmas of Politics, op. cit.,* p. 274; *The Restoration of American Politics, op. cit.,* p. 202.

[44] *Ibid.,* pp. 203–4; *The Impasse of American Foreign Policy, op. cit.,* p. 214.

[45] *Ibid.,* p. 190.

[46] *Ibid.,* p. 173; *In Defense of the National Interest, op. cit.,* p. 146.

[47] *The Impasse of American Foreign Policy, op. cit.,* p. 171.

[48] *In Defense of the National Interest, op. cit.,* pp. 136, 149.

[49] *The Impasse of American Foreign Policy, op. cit.,* p. 191; *Dilemmas of Politics, op. cit.,* pp. 274–75; *The Restoration of American Politics, op. cit.,* pp. 202–3.

Such a compromise may or may not be fruitful. A misleading settlement occurs when one of the parties, pursuing a policy end through appeasement, misjudges its interests or those of its opponent as well as misjudging the power situation. The result is that the nation may surrender a vital interest without obtaining anything worthwhile from the other side.[50]

National Interest and Nuclear Weapons

It was stated above that the primary interest of all nations consists in the security of national territory and in the safeguarding of the lives and values of the citizens. This is true in the nuclear age as it was true previously. But in contrast to the era which ended in 1945 it is no longer physically possible to guarantee this result.[51] This is due, of course, to the technological revolution in transportation, communication, and war, and in particular to the advent of nuclear weapons.[52] In consequence, all nations—large, small, communist, non-communist—for the first time have an overriding common interest in the avoidance of war.[53] Nuclear weapons have not modified the range of traditional interests pursued by powers, nor have they changed the problems associated therewith. They have, however, modified the means for pursuing those interests: for the most part these must now be peaceful (and therefore) diplomatic in character.[54] All nations whether they like it or not now must redefine their national interests in terms of the interests of all the others; for contemporary war not only means possible defeat in the traditional sense but also certain destruction of domestic society and of the political regimes and civilizations built on them.[55] This means, in particular, that nations will no longer go to war (and thus will not risk their existence) in pursuit of secondary interests. Now these must all be subjected to the process of diplomatic settlement.[56]

This process of redefinition and accommodation is imperative not only because of the nuclear-technological revolution but also because of the post-World War II political revolution. The latter has wrought five basic destabilizing transformations in the international political system, which together and separately serve to make precarious the connection between violence and foreign policy. These are: (1) expansion of the formerly Europe-centered balance of power system to include the entire world; (2) transfer of the center of gravity of that system to the extra-European peripheries; (3) collapse of the previous multipolar system into a bipolar one; (4) disappearance of the crucial role of the balancer, formerly held by Great Britain, without prospects for a successor; (5) the rise of Asia and Asian nationalism as a major factor in world politics.[57] These radical changes indeed have made the present era revolutionary and force every nation to modify its conduct accordingly. Instead of ignoring these factors of revolution or working in opposition to them (policies which were possible before 1945), it now becomes the interest of each nation to work with these powerful forces and, if possible, direct them toward the attainment of national goals.[58]

The nature of alliances also changes in the nuclear age. Previously, nations became allied with one another because they shared some common or complementary interests. Today, on the other hand, alliances—especially those made between one of the bipolar core powers and a peripheral member of its system—carry unacceptable risks to the smaller, less powerful nation. Therefore, in contrast to the past, nations with similar interests today may *not* ally.[59] For instance, European nations today have an interest in *separating* themselves from the United States, or at least not allying themselves too closely.[60] There is thus a tug of war between, on the one hand, the common interest felt among the alliance partners against Soviet pressures and, on the other, the interest in not coming under bombardment in a nuclear war between the giants. So far the interests felt in common have overbalanced the divergent ones

[50] *In Defense of the National Interest, op. cit.*, p. 137.

[51] *Dilemmas of Politics, op. cit.*, p. 178.

[52] *In Defense of the National Interest, op. cit.*, pp. 152–60.

[53] *The Restoration of American Politics, op. cit.*, p. 283; *Dilemmas of Politics, op. cit.*, p. 277.

[54] *The Restoration of American Politics, op. cit.*, p. 138; *Dilemmas of Politics, op. cit.*, p. 277.

[55] *The Restoration of American Politics, op. cit.*, p. 275; *In Defense of the National Interest, op. cit.*, p. 162.

[56] "Cuba—The Wake of Isolation," *Commentary*, Vol. 33 (1962), pp. 427–30.

[57] *In Defense of the National Interest, op. cit.*, pp. 40–52.

[58] "We are Deluding Ourselves in Vietnam," *New York Times Magazine*, April 18, 1965, p. 85.

[59] "The Four Paradoxes of Nuclear Strategy," *The American Political Science Review*, Vol. LVII (1964), p. 33.

[60] "The Crisis in the Western Alliance," *op. cit.*, p. 185.

but the trend is in the other direction.[61] (Presumably, many of these same pressures are also being felt in the Eastern bloc.) Thus, in the nuclear age, alliances tend to lose their efficacy as instruments for the pursuit of the national interest and as a result nations tend to become more and more isolated from each other.

National Interest and International Organization

However, there is an instrument for pursuing the national interest that may take up the slack. This is the United Nations, to which Morgenthau turns next.[62] As we have noted, national interests in the nuclear age do not change, except for the addition of the overriding interest to avoid thermonuclear war. The two core powers in a bipolar world must pursue their national interests by retaining their allies (or at least not allow them to join the opposite camp) and preparing for conflict with the enemy. On the other hand, they must justify their interests and policies to their allies—who now have interests different from the core power—by means of appealing to the general interests of all. These general interests may or may not in reality agree with those of the core power but they must be appealed to nevertheless. This usually means that the core power must ideologically justify and rationalize its interests in terms of supranational interests.[63] The United Nations, a supra-national institution, is a good place to pursue this task. The United Nations thus becomes an arena both for the traditional pursuit of national interests, and the rationalization thereof. Nations, to be sure, must be careful to submit for United Nations debate and consideration only those problems for which they *a priori* are sure of obtaining Security Council approval. This means, of course, that issues of dispute between the two camps will not be submitted for solution to the United Nations.[64] But because all matters are debatable by the organs of the United Nations, the national interests of the core powers and the policies made in accordance with them must be defined in terms transcending these interests. That is, these two powers must appeal to those whose support the core power seeks on the basis of national interests of the latter and not on the basis of interests in common with the core power,[65] for the United Nations is an instrument for the pursuit of those national interests which nations have in common.[66] Treating the United Nations instrumentally, however, has the somewhat unintended effect of "blunting," "reformulating," and "adaptation" of policies made in consonance with the national interest. While this does not of course preclude continued pursuit of the national interest outside of the United Nations, that organization does have a real, if subtle, effect on the interests of nations.[67] This is a liability to the core powers since it limits their freedom to define those interests. . . .[68]

[61] "Alliances in Theory and Practice," *op. cit.*, p. 193.
[62] *The Impasse of American Foreign Policy, op. cit.*, p. 122.
[63] *In Defense of the National Interest, op. cit.*, p. 104.
[64] *The Impasse of American Foreign Policy, op. cit.*, p. 121.
[65] *Ibid.*, pp. 124, 126.
[66] *Ibid.*, p. 125.
[67] *In Defense of the National Interest, op. cit.*, p. 104.
[68] *The Impasse of American Foreign Policy, op. cit.*, p. 127.

18. The Relative Irrelevance of Moral Norms in International Politics

Werner Levi is Professor of Political Science at the University of Hawaii and a longtime student of international relations. The author of a number of inquiries into the subject, his books include *Fundamentals of World Organization* (1950) and *Free India in Asia* (1952). In this article he tackles the difficult task of assessing the extent to which moral values, as distinguished from national interests, serve as goals of foreign policy. Whether or not the reader agrees with Professor Levi's interpretation of the relative importance of norms and interests, he will find his thinking about the problem enlivened by the ensuing discussion. [*Reprinted from* Social Forces, *XLIV (1965), 226–33, by permission of the author and the University of North Carolina Press.*]

The Unverified Assumptions

There exists a widespread belief that the absence of common moral norms among the peoples of the world is largely responsible for the hostilities and the violence characteristic of international relations. The hopeful assertion is made that cooperative behavior and a more peaceful solution of international conflicts would be assured if only the nations could agree on common moral norms. The reasoning is, more or less, that moral norms prescribe the propriety of action. When the use of violence in human affairs is morally condemned and the maintenance of peace is elevated to a high moral value, people who adhere to these norms can always come to an agreement on whether they should or should not behave in a certain manner. In any case, acceptance of these norms would make it very difficult for either side in a conflict to engage in evil action toward the other. Ideally, these moral norms would become so embedded in international institutions and become so much part of the decision-makers' social environment, that interests and goals incompatible with these norms would never be allowed to reach the

acute stage in which their realization would be attempted. They would be discarded as soon as they were conceived. Swords may be beaten into plowshares.[1]

This belief may be considered an oversimplified and specialized aspect of the theory that the foundation of any integrated society is the normative structure of a common value-orientation among its members.[2] So broadly stated, that is when all values are included, this theory can be justified at least on the grounds that if all the members of a society had differing and conflicting values, there could hardly be cohesion of any kind. The real problem in discovering the role played by values in maintaining a relatively peaceful society is to determine which

[1] For some examples see F. Ernest Johnson, ed., *World Order: Its Intellectual and Cultural Foundation* (New York: Harper & Bros., 1945), p. 22; Thomas Merton *et al. Breakthrough to Peace* (Norfolk, Va.: New Directions, 1962), p. 29; Arthur I. Waskow, *The Worried Man's Guide to World Peace* (New York: Doubleday & Co., 1963), p. 49.

[2] E.g., Talcott Parsons and Edward A. Shils, eds., *Toward a General Theory of Action* (New York: Harper & Rowe, 1962), pp. 159–89; Talcott Parsons, *The Social System* (Glencoe, Ill.: The Free Press, 1951), pp. 41–2.

values are relevant and in what manner they are relevant. Of special interest here is the somewhat narrower question whether moral norms are relevant and why and how?

A slightly different, though related theory is that the possession of common values is a community building factor.[3] This is presumably true because almost anything people have in common has such a propensity. Common values would then contribute to the integration—and therewith possibly peacefulness—of a community not because they are values or because of their substance, but because they are something shared by the members. Their effectiveness would rest on the same basis that the flag as a common symbol to the enjoyment of a national sport could contribute to integration. Whether also the content, the substance of moral norms would have the effect of producing more peaceful behavior leads exactly to the crux of the hopeful assertion that common moral norms would produce a peaceful society.

The assumption that they do implies an extraordinary confidence in the ability of moral norms to work as determinants of behavior. They would not merely be the rules and precepts according to which all behavior ought to be shaped, they would be expected, in fact, to shape behavior. They are envisaged as the checkpoint through which all decisions to act have to pass successfully. The moral norms would represent a superstructure over all social behavior, controlling it in its totality. An even furtive look at international behavior throughout the ages would raise serious doubts about the effectiveness of such a control or else raise serious doubts about the nature of moral norms applying to the international society. On this last point, the answer can quickly be provided that, at least as far as public confessions everywhere are concerned, the basic moral norms alleged to apply to international behavior are the same as are presumably to apply to any behavior. This reduces the scope of this investigation to the effectiveness of moral norms as controls in

international behavior. In its pursuit a distinction can usefully be made between moral norms and interests.[4] Both are classes of values and motivators of behavior. But they are psychologically and functionally different. Moral norms are evaluative. They are the rules according to which behavior ought to be shaped and, as long as they remain untranslated into law, their enforcement is a matter of conscience. Their function is to maintain the individual in coexistence with his fellow individuals in a society. Interests are the wants and desires of an essentially non-ethical-normative nature. They relate to—usually—material needs, directly or indirectly, and they function to produce behavior intended to satisfy these needs. The relationship between moral values and interests is hierarchical, with interests, or at least their realization, subordinated to morality.[5] One of the most striking features of international behavior is the obvious disturbance in this hierarchy. Wherein may lie its causes—whether in the nature of international politics or in the nature of moral norms or in a combination of both—is the object of this investigation. For, if it should turn out that the influence of moral norms on international behavior is nonexistent or very limited, the acceptance of common norms by the nations as the remedy of international ills would not be very helpful; respectively, the prevailing ills must be due to other causes than the absence of common norms.

The Empirical Evidence

History provides at best an inconclusive answer to the question. There is evidence that in the course of time men have attempted to humanize their relations. There is the counter-evidence also that they have treated each other with increasing dishonesty and cruelty. The same civilization which raised the status of the common man has also perfected his destruction. Still, until that destruction takes place, from time to time statesmen appear to find it increasingly necessary to justify their international acts in moral terms. The records of international agencies abound

[3] Rudolf Smend, *Verfassung und Verfassungsrecht* (München: Duncker & Humblot, 1928), pp. 34–45; Karl W. Deutsch *et al.*, *The Political Community and the North Atlantic Area* (Princeton, New Jersey: Princeton University Press, 1957), p. 123; Philip E. Jacob and James V. Toledano, *The Integration of Political Communities* (Philadelphia: J. B. Lippincott Co., 1964), pp. 209–46; Werner Levi, *Fundamentals of World Organization* (Minneapolis: University of Minnesota Press, 1950), p. 21.

[4] For examples of the discussion of this vexing problem see Vernon Van Dyke, "Values and Interests," *American Political Science Review*, 56 (September 1962), pp. 567–76; Jacob and Toledano, *op. cit.*, pp. 224–25.

[5] The important point here is not to state a final definition of morality and interests as different types of values. It is, rather, to emphasize that they differ as motivational forces of behavior.

in moral appeals and in moral justifications of international actions. The content of international law reflects more and more the improvement of international methods of coexistence from a moral viewpoint. Charitable impulses can be discovered behind grants of mutual aid. Those who look desperately for a greater moralization of the international society may find some hope in this development. But they should not be under any illusion that the order of things is becoming very favorable for the ascendancy of moral norms. There have been statesmen who have shaped their foreign policy according to moral prescriptions, which has all too often earned them the derogatorily meant sobriquet of "idealist" or "dreamer." The evidence is overwhelming that in making their decisions most statesmen have asked, first, what needed to be done to preserve the interests of the country, and only second, if ever, what the moral thing might be to do. When there was incompatibility in the answers, the interests almost always carried the day. Mostly for reasons of expediency or to satisfy public demands for moral behavior, the interests may have been reformulated or adjusted, but most rarely changed and never abandoned—unless different interests, judged higher, but interests nevertheless, made it advisable to adhere to moral norms in the given instant. Such indirect tribute to moral norms may be a compliment to the public and better than none. It may eventually lead to institutions which have the "sober and tried goodness of the ages, the deposit, little by little, of what has been found practicable in the wayward and transient outreachings of human idealism."[6] But this is not the ruling influence of morality that those have in mind who hope for a better world from the predominance of common norms. There may be this minimal moral influence, but the hierarchy is reversed, with the interests commanding the moral values. Perhaps it may be said, to use a metaphor of Max Weber's, that the moral norms have acted as switchmen to affect no more than the tracks along which the interests were running.[7]

"The deposit" which the normative system prevalent in a society may leave "little by little" in the social institutions becomes an integral part of the social environment in which those participating in the making of foreign policy decisions—from statesman to the man in the street—live. They are in part the product of this environment and "the deposit" will affect the frame of reference within which they judge their situations and make their decisions.[8] Moral norms through some process of absorption, and socialization thus gain some influence upon decisions, regardless of whether in any given case or in general a person deliberately and consciously evaluates his actions by moral standards. This is a very imponderable influence. It hardly justifies the optimistic belief that knowledge of the norms "opens the way to identifying with considerable precision one major distinguishable and vital element in the determination of human behavior."[9] Such knowledge may be helpful when normative standards have been deliberately applied to a decision. But there are many cases where this is not true of individuals; and there are overwhelming numbers of cases—as will be seen—where this is not true in collective decisions on foreign policy.

Even granting, as one obviously must, that moral norms are instrumental, together with many other forces in shaping social institutions, there still remains the question in what manner they are effective. This refers not only to the intensity of the influence but to its substance. Uncertainty exists on both counts. On the first, because moral norms have to compete with many other forces in shaping behavior. On the second, because in the translation of the norms into behavior a vast choice of actions becomes possible. As these points are examined, it will become evident that there are reasons why the influence of moral norms in general, as it has just been discussed, and in the sense of directing behavior toward the assumed high standards of the norms, are likely to be quite insignificant in international politics. Unfortunately for those who are hoping for great improvements in the international society from commonly accepted moral norms, the reasons for this insignificance are more abundant as well as more cogent than those permitting the assumption of some vague, moral influence upon internationally important decisions.

[6] Charles H. Cooley, *Social Organization* (New York: Schocken Books, 1962), p. 322.

[7] H. H. Gerth and C. Wright Mills, *From Max Weber, Essays in Sociology* (New York: Oxford University Press, 1946), p. 63.

[8] Muzafer Sherif, *The Psychology of Social Norms* (New York: Harper & Bros, 1936), pp. 25, 66, 85, 142.

[9] Jacob and Toledano, *op. cit.*, p. 220.

The evidence, not conclusive but revealing, to be culled from the memoirs and occasional statements of statesmen indicates that they felt the foremost consideration in shaping foreign policy must be and was the interests of the nation. The deliberate application of moral standards to foreign policy decisions has usually been on second thought, if it took place at all. In security measures to guarantee a nation's survival, there is little room for moral considerations, as alliances between the strangest ideological bedfellows or the manufacture of the H Bomb clearly show. In a balance of power policy, the most widely accepted and practiced of all policies, moral considerations must be deliberately avoided, as its manipulators fully realize. To quote Sir Winston Churchill: the balance of power "has nothing to do with rulers or nations." It is "a law of public policy which we are following, and not a mere expedient dictated by accidental circumstances, or likes and dislikes, or any other sentiment."[10] The principle underlying the idea that "Great Britain has no permanent friends, Great Britain has no permanent enemies, Great Britain has only permanent interests" becomes, sooner or later, the guideline in the formulation of any nation's foreign policy. Mr. John Foster Dulles expressed this in his defense of the State Department, whose task, he said, was not to make friends for the United States, but to take care of her interests. Even the newest nations, while still seized by their nationalistic fervor, in a righteous mood, and quite idealistic about their future and mission in the world, very quickly recognize the need to be coldblooded and coolheaded about the preservation of their interests on the international scene. With all his moralizing about foreign policy, Mr. Nehru, for instance, reminded his Parliament on every occasion that interests are the dominant determinants of a nation's foreign policy. Hopefully, and presumably as a result of that vague influence of moral norms on social institutions, a nation's interests may be formulated to avoid a clash with prevailing moral norms, or may be reconciled with them through some process of rationalization. And quite possibly, the conception of the interests or, where these are fairly rigidly given through the international system, the conception of the means and methods to realize these interests, are in some not easily definable manner affected by the residue of the moral norms embedded in the social structure. All this, however, is a far cry from the image of moral norms as the superstructure forcing all behavior into its allegedly clearly visible framework.

The Function of Moral Norms

The rank order given by statesmen to interests and moral norms in the making of foreign policy is not a matter of cynicism or immorality, nor is it alone a result of the international system which forces each nation to guarantee its own survival. It is, to some extent, the hardly avoidable consequence of the way in which most moral norms must function. With a few exceptions (e.g., the precept to engage in charitable action) which rarely apply to international politics anyway, moral norms are qualifiers, not initiators or ends of behavior.[11] Honesty, reliability, trustworthiness, neighborly love cannot be established or demonstrated in the abstract. They need an apropos. They can only find expression as qualities of behavior aiming at some other goal. Moral norms are not ends in themselves. Nations do not act to translate moral norms into reality. A treaty is not signed to demonstrate trustworthiness, nor a transaction undertaken to prove honesty. Instead, these actions are engaged in to pursue some interest, and moral norms can then be applied to the pursuit or the interest. Ralph Barton Perry pointed out that the "solid meaning" of morality lies in "doing good."[12] Morality is related to behavior, and (rational) behavior is end oriented, an end most of the time not moral per se, though subject to judgment by moral standards. This kind of end and behavior represent the bulk in international relations. The usual sequence: defining the interest first, choosing the behavior to realize it second, examining both in the light of morality third (assuming that all three processes are deliberate) creates itself a tendency to give interests primacy over morality. This becomes truer the stronger the interest. And there are no more compelling social interests than those called national

[10] Winston S. Churchill, *The Second World War*, Vol. I, *The Gathering Storm* (Boston: Houghton Mifflin Co., 1948), pp. 207–8.

[11] This is to be distinguished from moral norms motivating certain types of behavior, a behavior which has been stimulated or initiated by other forces.

[12] Ralph Barton Perry, *One World in the Making* (New York: A. A. Wyn, 1945), p. 45.

interests. Moral norms would have to be extraordinarily powerful to match their strength and overcome them. There are no such to be seen. The rule not to kill is probably more strongly held and less equivocally held than any other. Even it gave way to "just wars" in defense of national interests.

This degradation of moral norms to serve rather than master interests is enhanced by their social function. This function is to be effective as a social control and thereby contribute to the preservation of the society. By accepting and internalizing the set of moral norms, the members of the society are expected to act in solidarity and unison, giving the society cohesion, solidity, integration, and permanence. It can happen that social change produces needs for the perpetuation of the society which cannot be filled or are actually contravened by the prevailing behavior. The norms supporting such behavior then become dysfunctional and, as the behavior adjusts to new needs, devoid of social significance. Such norms, if they last, become "survivals" whose nature cannot be explained by present utility, but only by their historical function in the past.[13] International relations provide abundant examples of changes in behavior which are not easily reconcilable with traditional norms. One only has to think of the numerous activities taking place in international agencies in contravention of the nationalistically influenced norms implied in the concept of sovereignty and its demands for the untouchability of "domestic" or "internal" affairs, or of the fate of women and children in warfare with modern weapons. As in this case so in all others. When norms and necessary social practice move so far apart that tension is created in the society, either the norms or the practice has to give. Almost invariably, because of the pressure of interests and for other reasons (soon to be demonstrated) the norm passes into oblivion or, if it is strongly embedded in institutions and consciences, is being reinterpreted to suit new interests, as it has to be if it is to remain socially useful.

The assertion that the function of moral norms is to produce and support behavior useful for the perpetuation of the society in which they exist may appear contradicted by the apparent general and universal validity of these norms. For the needs of a given society are usually specific while the norms are formulated in broad terms. But this is a surface appearance. There are several reasons for this kind of formulation, though none interferes in practice with the specific purpose of the norm for specific societies. The general formulation improves the functionality of the norm for the same reason that a broadly worded national constitution is more serviceable and enduring than a specific one. Secondly, certain fundamental norms (e.g., you shall not kill) are essential to the maintenance of any society. Thirdly, the formulation of norms in universal terms aims at strengthening their appeal. Finally, the unpredictability of situations in which the norms must exercise their controlling influence upon behavior on the one hand, and the advisability of having the norm internalized in advance of the situations on the other, make it mandatory to state the norm in general terms. It must also not be forgotten that for purposes of international propaganda broadly stated norms lend themselves nicely to nationalistic missionary activity.

It is, however, clearly evident from the practice of nations that in specific application and interpretation, the social norms are geared to the preservation of the national society. So much so that they permit the subordination and, if need be, disturbance and destruction of the international society. Since most of the citizens cherish the preservation of their nation as their highest interest, their social moral norms are made to function, or more correctly are intended to function in support of the nation. They cannot at the same time function also in support of the wider international society, since the peoples of the world are interested in its maintenance only insofar as this may serve the higher interest of maintaining their own nations.[14]

Leaving aside for a moment the question of the efficiency of moral norms, an interesting conclusion emerges from the general formulation and the specific application of moral norms for those who hope for a better world from commonly held norms. The most fundamental norms designed to support a society are mostly held in common across the globe already —of necessity so because of the basically similar characteristics and requirements of human societies. Almost everywhere, they are formulated in general terms, unrestrained by national considerations. The

[13] Sherif, *op. cit.*, pp. 199–200 and W. H. R. Rivers quoted there.

[14] Werner Levi, "On the Causes of Peace," *Journal of Conflict Resolution*, 8 (March 1964), pp. 30–31.

rule is that you shall not kill, regardless of the victim's nationality. On the international scene, the evidence is in article 38 of the Statute of the International Court of Justice empowering the Court to decide cases in accordance with the "general principles of law recognized by civilized nations," which represent a part of a moral, normative system. Thus, the responsibility for the much criticized state of international relations and politics can hardly be placed upon the absence of commonly held norms. Instead, it appears more justifiable to put the blame upon the manner in which the norms are interpreted and applied. Not common norms must be postulated, but their interpretation and application must be in such a manner as to produce potentially the desired result. And since these are related to the function the norms are intended to perform, that is to say: since the interpretation and application are dependent upon the interests the norms are designed to safeguard, the call should really go out for a growing community of interests and for an emphasis upon common interests already established as the key factor in the integration toward a peaceful international society.[15] Once there is awareness of common interests, the norms already accepted by most nations in their abstract form will be specified to assist these interests and may perform their socially beneficial functions—inasmuch as they may do so at all—for the international society. Whether they do so is now to be considered further.

The Nature of Moral Norms

There are a number of reasons, inherent in the nature of moral norms (and in addition to those already discussed), tending to make norms servants more often than guides of interests and of the behavior to realize these.[16]

The first reason is that moral norms are of necessity stated in broad, general terms. They become thereby subject to widely differing interpretation in a given case, as the slogan "we are all against sin" indicates very well. As a consequence, a wide range of behavior is possible, all in the name of the

[15] Werner Levi, "On the Causes of Peace," *Journal of Conflict Resolution*, 8 (March 1964), pp. 31–32.

[16] On the following see Gunnar Myrdal, *An American Dilemma* (New York: Harper & Bros., 1944), Appendix 1 and 2; Levi, *op. cit.*, pp. 167–72; see also Marian D. Irish, ed., *World Pressures on American Foreign Policy* (Englewood Cliffs, New Jersey; Prentice-Hall, 1964), pp. 24, 26.

same moral norm, except perhaps in the rare cases when the norm is stated in narrow, specific, and unequivocal terms. But then the urge to broaden its scope is always great, as is demonstrated by the new translation of the commandment "You shall not kill" into "You shall not murder." From the standpoint of the norm's social function, the flexibility in behavior the variety of interpretation permits may be unfavorable, since the desired or expected behavior may not be produced. It may, however, have its compensating virtue for the social system. It allows for easier social change. And where there are two norms in conflict when stated in the abstract, the range of behavior permissible under each may nevertheless lead to nonconflicting behavior. The peaceful coexistence between the United States and the Soviet Union, with each side claiming to base its behavior upon mutually exclusive normative value systems, contains innumerable examples of this situation. It would be difficult to project the likely behavior simply from knowledge of the moral norms confessed to by the actors. Just as compatible behaviors may prevail in spite of normative value systems incompatible in the abstract, so is subscription to common norms no guarantee that compatible or peaceful behaviors will result.

The second reason for the subservient role of moral norms is the composition of the normative system of many individual values. They change. As social needs develop and require new norms, these are added, others are forgotten, and yet others are adjusted. These individual norms are not necessarily all compatible with one another any more than some of the behaviors they support. This may be true of that part of the system applying to all members of the society, or of the parts applying to special actors and their roles. The business ethics of modern capitalism, for instance, is in many respects not easily reconcilable with the ethics of many religions. Chaplains have found it difficult to bless the guns of their nation in wartime. Communists can adjust the internationalist tenets of their creed to their traditional nationalism only with the ample help of sophistry. The pledge of professional secrecy by a psychiatrist may readily clash with his patriotic duty to inform the police on his client's traitorous activities.[17] Different values refer to different roles, and

[17] See Waldo V. Burchard, "Role Conflicts in Military Chaplains," *American Sociological Review*, 19 (October

though the roles may harmonize, the ethics practiced in each may not. Such compartmentalization permits the use of different moral norms in different situations. Depending upon how two nations see the situation in which they find themselves, they may select and apply different norms, supporting different behavior, although the total value system of the parties in the abstract may be fairly similar. The definition of the situation which determines the applicable norms introduces many kinds of non-normative factors, such as a nation's culture, environment, and historical experience. How nations view each other or their situations is the result of many factors in which moral norms may be quite irrelevant. There can be very great and legitimate differences, leading to entirely different judgments regarding what moral norms, even from among the set held in common, should apply. Again: moral norms in such situations would not be the primary determinants of behavior.

The third reason why moral norms are weak directors of behavior is the different intensity with which individual norms are held. The command not to kill is more strictly obeyed than the command not to cheat an insurance company. It appears that the hierarchy of intensities is in part determined by the importance of the norm for the preservation of the society and, to a very large part, by the culture and the interests of the group. In a bureaucratized and militarized society such as old Prussia, obedience to the orders of superior officers was considered more important than following the dictates of humanitarianism. In Communist societies, theft of public property has been considered a worse crime than taking human life. As a consequence, one group may more readily compromise its norms or substitute others than another group on the same issue. Each group would justify, within the framework of its normative system, a totally different behavior. In other words, the intensity with which each moral norm in a system is held is a relevant factor (in addition to the content of the norm) in estimating the result the influence of a norm may have on behavior. Norms held in common may still not be held with the same intensity and would, for that reason too, not necessarily produce the same behavior.

1954), pp. 528–535; Ralph B. Little and Edward A. Strecker, "Moot Questions in Psychiatric Ethics," *American Journal of Psychiatry*, 113 (November 1956), pp. 455–60.

Interests as Determinants of Moral Norms

The total picture emerging from this analysis in regard to the influence of moral norms on international behavior can not be very encouraging to those whose hope for a more peaceful world is largely based upon the power of morality. Statesmen are inclined to give moral norms secondary consideration in making policy decisions or to use morality expediently. Interests have chronological precedence over norms in the shaping of national behavior. National interests overpower morality. Norms support rather than produce institutions. Finally, the nature of norms and of norm systems permits widely differing interpretations, the selection of expediently useful norms from the total system, and the suppression of inconvenient and not too intensely held norms. Each of these factors permits a great variety of behaviors, which is further increased by the combination of these factors. It is likely therefore that the influence of moral norms is mostly to permit behavior along a vast range, but short of extremes which cannot be rationalized in the terms of the norms. The extermination of millions of people in Germany in the 1930's and 1940's, for instance, seemed to have gone beyond the points to which ordinary German norms could be stretched so that the whole theoretical structure of a "super race" with new moral norms had to be built before the act of killing could be justified.

The wide choice of behavior available under moral norms raises the question of what determines the choice. The answer may be easier for international than for individual behavior because of the overwhelming strength of national interests and the endeavor of official decision-makers to act—in accordance with their estimation of these interests—for the realization of the national interests. The behavior of nations indicates that most of the time interests, judged generally apart from and sometimes in deliberate disregard of moral norms, have been decisive in shaping behavior. It could hardly be otherwise, if the foregoing analysis is reasonably close to the truth. Mostly for reasons of public acceptance of foreign policies, international propaganda, and others related to psychological warfare, have the choices based on interests been cloaked in the language of morality. But this, in some cases demonstrably, has been an afterthought and moral norms served, to use Jeremy Bentham's expression, as "fig leaves of the mind." When, historically, international behavior conformed to moral norms, there may have been no conflict, or else it is more likely that interests and ulterior motives demanded such conformity than that the force of morality produced it.

This analysis could also help to explain why it is so difficult to discover the influence moral norms, as compared to interests, may have on national behavior on the international scene. The interpretability, flexibility, and selectivity of moral norms and moral systems makes it possible to find a moral justification for almost any national behavior. Hence the familiar phenomenon that statesmen can claim, and often rightly so, to act in accordance with moral norms, and accuse their opposites for failing to do the same. Under the circumstances, commitment by nations to common norms, as postulated and, indeed, as already existing to some extent, does not hold out the hoped-for great promise of more peaceful international relations. These are more likely to come with the growth and awareness of common interests. Thucydides recognized over two thousand years ago that "identity of interests is the surest bond, whether between states or individuals."

B. Decision-Making and Decision-Makers

19. The Decision-Making Approach to the Study of International Politics

Richard C. Snyder, H. W. Bruck and Burton Sapin
were affiliated with the Foreign Policy Analysis Project of Princeton University
when they collaborated on the monograph from which this selection is drawn.
Since then they have become associated, respectively, with the University of
California, the U.S. Department of Commerce, and the University of Minnesota.
From the moment of its publication this monograph was recognized as a major
addition to the literature of the field. It was the first extended and systematic
attempt to conceptualize the role of decision-making in the formulation of
foreign policy and in the processes of international politics. As such, and like
any pioneering document, it has had the effect of compelling students in the field
to reexamine the concepts and procedures whereby they assess the deliberations
and actions of policy-makers. Many have since found reasons to go beyond the
decision-making approach as a basis for their own research, but few would deny
that this document continues to be a major work and that the variables it encompasses must somehow be taken into account. The excerpt presented here sets forth
the major premises of the decision-making approach and places it within the larger
context of international politics and foreign policy. An application of this approach
to empirical phenomena can be found in Selection 41. [*Reprinted from Richard
C. Snyder, H. W. Bruck, and Burton Sapin (eds.), Foreign Policy Decision-Making:
An Approach to the Study of International Politics (New York: The Free Press,
1962), pp. 60–74, by permission of the authors and the publisher. Copyright 1962
by The Free Press, A Division of The Macmillan Company.*]

We believe that those who study international
politics are mainly concerned with the actions,
reactions, and interactions among political entities
called national states. Emphasis on action suggests
process analysis, i.e., the passage of time plus continuous changes in relationships—including the
conditions underlying change and its consequences.
Since there is a multiplicity of actions, reactions
and interactions, analysis must be concerned with a
number of processes.

Action arises from the necessity to establish,
to maintain, and to regulate satisfying, optional
contacts between states and to exert some control
over unwanted yet inescapable contacts. Action is
planful[1] in the sense that it represents: an attempt to
achieve certain aims, and to prevent or minimize the
achievement of the incompatible or menacing aims of
other states.

[1] Frank Knight, *Freedom and Reform* (1947), pp.
335–69.

The action-reaction-interaction formulation suggests that sequences of action and interaction are always closed or symmetrical. This may be diagrammed State A ⟷ State B which implies a reciprocal relationship. Such is clearly not always the case. Many sequences are asymmetrical, i.e., State A ⟶ State B ⟶ in which case State A acts, State B reacts but there is no immediate further action by A in response to B's action. With more than two states involved, of course, there are other possibilities—as suggested by

$$A \longleftrightarrow B$$
$$\diagdown \quad \diagup$$
$$C$$

Given the fact that relationships may be symmetrical or asymmetrical and given the fact that action sequences though initiated at different times are nonetheless carried on simultaneously, there will be both the appearance and the possibility of *discontinuity* (i.e., discontinuous processes) within the total set of processes which link any one state with all others. The process of state interaction is not, to repeat, always a sequence of action and *counter-action*, of attempt and frustration, of will opposing will. Nor should it be assumed that the process *necessarily* has an automatic, chess-game quality or that reactions to action are necessarily immediate or self-evident. Not all national purposes are mutually incompatible, that is, it is not necessary that one nation's purposes be accomplished at the expense of another set of national purposes. One state may respond to the action of another without opposing that action *per se*; it may or may not be able to block that action effectively, it may or may not want to do so. The response may be in the form of inaction (calculated inaction we shall regard analytically as a form of action), or it may be in the form of action quite unrelated to the purposes of the state which acted first. Much diplomacy consists in probing the limits of tolerance for a proposed course of action and in discovering common purposes. As action unfolds, purposes may change due to resistances or altered circumstances and hence, often, head-on conflicts are avoided or reduced in impact. For these reasons the processes of state interaction are much less orderly than—hopefully—the analysis of these processes.

State action and therefore interaction obviously takes many forms—a declaration, a formal agreement, regulation of relationships, discussion, a gift or loan, armed conflict, and so on. Reactions take the same forms only they are viewed as responses. Since we are dealing with planful actions (rather than random behavior),[2] interaction is characterized by *patterns*, i.e., recognizable *repetitions* of action and reaction. Aims *persist*. Kinds of action become *typical*. Reactions become *uniform*. Relationships become *regularized*. Further comment on the identification and characterization of patterns will be made below.

Thus far, there would probably be little disagreement except relatively minor ones on specific terminology. Now the question is: how is the political process (remembering always that this connotes multiple processes and *kinds* of processes) at the international level to be analyzed? Clearly there are *what*, *how* and *why* questions with respect to state interaction. In order to be true to our previously stated philosophy, we should recognize that there is more than one possible approach depending on the purposes of the observer and on the kinds of questions which interest him most.

"The State as Actor in a Situation"

Figure 1 will serve as a partial indication of the fundamental approach adopted in this essay. . . .

Commentary 1. The first aspect of this diagrammatic presentation of an analytical scheme is the *assumption* that the most effective way to gain perspective on international politics and to find ways of grasping the complex determinants of state behavior is to pitch the analysis on the level of *any state*. An understanding of *all* states is to be founded on an understanding of *any one* state through the use of a scheme which will permit the analytical construction of properties of action which will be shared in common by all specific states. That is, the model is a fictional state whose characteristics are such as to enable us to say certain things about all real states regardless of how different they may appear to be in some ways. Therefore if the scheme is moderately successful, we should be able to lay the foundation for analyzing the impact of cultural values on British foreign and on Soviet foreign policy even though the

[2] The distinction between social action and behavior is an important one analytically, though we shall continue to use state action and state behavior synonymously.

values are different in each case and produce quite different consequences. "State X," then, stands for all states or for any one state. We have rejected the assumption that two different analytical schemes are required simply because two states behave differently.

It should be added immediately that theoretical progress in the study of international politics will require eventually a *typology* of states based on: basic political organization, range of decision-making systems, strengths and weaknesses of decision-making systems, and types of foreign policy strategies employed. This will facilitate comparison, of course, but it will also make it possible to take into account certain significant differences among states while at the same time analyzing the behavior of all states in essentially the same way.

2. We are also assuming that the nation-state is going to be the significant unit of political action for many years to come. Strategies of action and commitment of resources will continue to be decided at the national level. This assumption is made on grounds of analytical convenience and is not an expression of preference by the authors. Nor does it blind us to the development or existence of supra-national forces and organizations. The basic question is solely how the latter are to be treated. We prefer to

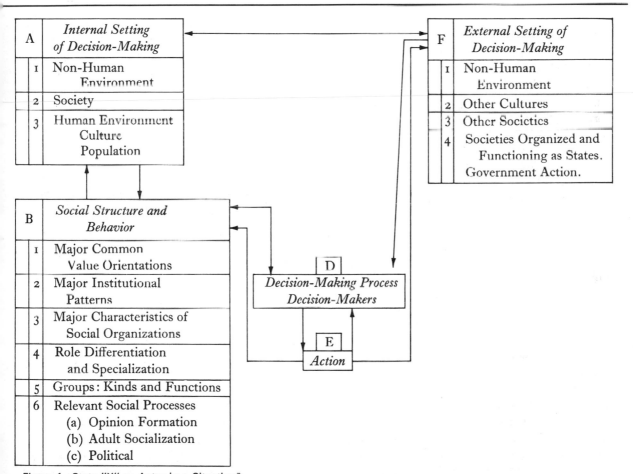

Figure 1. State "X" as Actor in a Situation*
(Situation is comprised of a combination of selectively relevant factors in the external and internal setting as interpreted by the decision-makers.)

* This diagram is designed only to be crudely suggestive. Detailed explanation must be deferred. The term non-human environment is construed to mean all physical factors (including those which result from human behavior) but not relationships between human beings or relationships between human beings and these physical factors. The latter relationships belong under society and culture.

view the United Nations as a special mode of inter-action in which the identity and policy-making capacity of individual national states are preserved but subject to different conditioning factors. The collective action of the United Nations can hardly be explained without reference to actions in various capitals.

3. The phrase "state as actor in a situation" is designed primarily as a short hand device to alert us to certain perspectives while still adhering to the notion of the state as a collectivity.[3] Explicit mention must be made of our employment of action analysis and (both here and in the detailed treatment of decision-making) *of some of the vocabulary* of the now well-known Parsons-Shils scheme.[4] We emphasize vocabulary for two reasons. First, as new schemes of social analysis are developed (mostly outside of political science) there is a great temptation to apply such schemes quickly, one result being the use of new words without comprehension of the theoretical system of which they are a part. Second, we have rejected a general application of the Parsons-Shils approach as an organizing concept—for reasons which will emerge later. At this point we may simply note that our intellectual borrowings regarding fundamental questions of method owe much more to the works of Alfred Schuetz.[5]

Basically, action exists (analytically) when the following components can be ascertained: actor (or actors), goals, means, and situation. The situation is defined by the actor (or actors) in terms of the way the actor (or actors) relates himself to other actors, to possible goals, to possible means, and in terms of the way means and ends are formed into strategies of action subject to relevant factors in the situation. These ways of relating himself to the situation (and thus of defining it) will depend on the nature of the actor—or his orientations. Thus "state X" mentioned above may be regarded as a participant in an action system comprising other actors; state X is the focus of the observer's attention. State X orients to action according to the manner in which the particular situation is viewed by certain officials and according to what they want. The actions of other actors, the actor's goals and means, and the other components of the situation are related meaningfully by the actor. His action flows from his definition of the situation.

4. We need to carry the actor-situation scheme one step further in an effort to rid ourselves of the troublesome abstraction "state." It is one of our basic methodological choices to define the state as its official decision-makers—those whose authoritative acts are, to all intents and purposes, the acts of state. *State action is the action taken by those acting in the name of the state.* Hence, the state is its decision-makers. State X as *actor* is translated into its decision-makers as actors. It is also one of our basic choices to take as our prime analytical objective the re-creation of the "world" of the decision-makers as *they* view it. The way *they* define situations becomes another way of saying this is the way the state oriented to action and why. This is a quite different approach from trying to re-create the situation and interpretation of it *objectively*, i.e., by the observer's judgment rather than that of the actors themselves.

To focus on the individual actors who are the state's decision-makers and to reconstruct the situation as defined by the decision-makers requires of course that a central place be given to the analysis of the behavior of these officials. One major significance of the diagram is that it calls attention to the sources of state action and to the essentially subjective (i.e., from the standpoint of the decision-makers) nature of our perspective.

5. Now let us try to clarify a little further. We have said that the key to the explanation of why the state behaves the way it does lies in the way its decision-makers as actors define their situation. *The definition of the situation*[6] is built around the projected action as well as the reasons for the action. Therefore, it is necessary to analyze the actors (the official decision-makers) in the following terms:

(a) their *discrimination* and *relating* of objects, conditions and other actors—various things are perceived or expected in a relational context;

---

[3] Some social scientists argue that a collectivity cannot properly be regarded as an actor, as the term is used in the analysis of social action. However, see Talcott Parsons and Edward Shils, *Toward a General Theory of Action*, pp. 192–95.

[4] The vocabulary of action analysis has become fairly common, yet there are several kinds of action theories (for example, note the differences between Marion J. Levy, *The Structure of Society*, and Parsons and Shils, *op. cit.*).

[5] In particular, "Choosing Among Projects of Action," *Philosophy and Phenomenological Research*, 12:161–84 (December 1951) and "Common-Sense and Scientific Interpretation of Human Action," *Philosophy and Phenomenological Research* 14: 1–37 (September 1953).

[6] Compare this concept with Arthur Macmahon, *Administration in Foreign Affairs* (1953) Chap. I entitled "The Concert of Judgment."

(b) the existence, establishment or definition of *goals*—various things are wanted from the situation;

(c) attachment of *significance* to various courses of action suggested by the situation according to some criteria of estimation;

(d) application of *"standards of acceptability"* which (1) narrow the range of perceptions; (2) narrow the range of objects wanted; and (3) narrow the number of alternatives.

Three features of all orientations emerge: *perception*, *choice*, and *expectation*.

Perhaps a translation of the vocabulary of action theory will be useful. We are saying that the actors' orientations to action are reconstructed when the following kinds of questions are answered: what did the decision-makers think was relevant in a particular situation? how did they determine this? how were the relevant factors related to each other—what connections did the decision-makers see between diverse elements in the situation? how did they establish the connections? what wants and needs were deemed involved in or affected by the situation? what were the sources of these wants and needs? how were they related to the situation? what specific or general goals were considered and selected? what courses of action were deemed fitting and effective? how were fitness and effectiveness decided?

6. We have defined international politics as processes of state interaction at the governmental level. However, there are non-governmental factors and relationships which must be taken into account by any system of analysis, and there are obviously non-governmental effects of state action. Domestic politics, the non-human environment, cross-cultural and social relationships are important in this connection. We have chosen to group such factors under the concept of setting. This is an analytic term which reminds us that the decision-makers act upon and respond to conditions and factors which exist outside themselves and the governmental organization of which they are a part. Setting has two aspects: *external* and *internal*. We have deliberately chosen setting instead of environment because the latter term is either too inclusive or has a technical meaning in other sciences. Setting is really a set of categories of *potentially relevant factors and conditions* which may affect the action of any state.

External setting refers, in general, to such factors and conditions beyond the territorial boundaries of the state—the actions and reactions of other states (their decision-makers) and the societies for which they act and the physical world. Relevance of particular factors and conditions *in general* and *in particular situations* will depend on the attitudes, perceptions, judgments and purposes of State X's decision-makers, i.e., on how they react to various stimuli. It should be noted that our conception of setting does *not* exclude certain so-called environmental limitations such as the state of technology, morbidity ratio and so on, which *may* limit the achievement of objectives or which *may* otherwise become part of the conditions of action *irrespective* of *whether* and *how* the decision-makers perceive them.[7] However—and this is important—this does not in our scheme imply the substitution of an omniscient observer's judgment for that of the decision-maker. Setting is an analytical device to suggest certain enduring kinds of relevances and to limit the number of non-governmental factors with which the student of international politics must be concerned. The external setting is constantly changing and will be composed of *what the decision-makers decide is important*. This "deciding" can mean simply that certain lacks—such as minerals or guns— are imposed on them, i.e., must be *accepted*. A serious native revolt in South Africa in 1900 was not a feature of the external setting of U.S. decision-makers; it would be in 1954. Compare, too, the relatively minor impact of Soviet foreign activities on the U.S. decision-makers in the period 1927 to 1933 with the present impact.

Usually the factors and conditions referred to by the term *internal setting* are loosely labeled "domestic politics," "public opinion" or "geographical position." A somewhat more adequate formulation might be: some clues to the way any state behaves toward the world must be sought in the way its society is organized and functions, in the character and behavior of its people and in its physical habitat. The list of categories under B (Social Organization) may be somewhat unfamiliar. There are two reasons for insisting that the analysis of the society for which State X acts be pushed to this fundamental level. First, the list invites attention to a much wider range of potentially relevant factors than the more familiar terms like morale, attitudes, national power, party

[7] We are indebted to Professor Harold Sprout for calling our attention to this point.

politics, and so on. For example, the problem of vulnerability to subversive attack is rarely discussed by political scientists in terms of the basic social structure of a particular nation, i.e., in terms of B3. Nor is recruitment of man-power often connected up with the way the roles of the sexes are differentiated in a society. Second, if one is interested in the fundamental "why" of state behavior, the search for reliable answers must go beyond the *derived* conditions and factors (morale, pressure groups, production, attitudes, and so on) which are normally the focus of attention.

7. The diagram suggests another important point. Line BD is a two-way arrow connoting rightly an interaction between social organization and behavior on the one hand and decision-making on the other. Among other things this arrow represents the impact of domestic social forces on the formulation and execution of foreign policy. BD implies that the influence of conditions and factors in the society is felt through the decision-making process. But line EB is also important because it indicates that a nation experiences its own external actions. State action is designed primarily to alter factors and behavior or to otherwise affect conditions in the external setting, yet it may have equally serious consequences for the society itself. We need only suggest the range of possibilities here. Extensive foreign relations may enhance the power of the central government relative to other regulatory institutions. Particular programs may contribute to the redistribution of resources, income, and social power. For example, the outpouring of billions in foreign aid by the United States since 1945 has contributed to the increased power and influence of scientists, military leaders, engineers and the managerial group. The people of a state experience foreign policy in other ways—they may feel satisfaction, alarm, guilt, exhilaration or doubt about it. There will be non-governmental *interpretations*—perhaps several major ones—shared by various members or groups of the society. Such interpretations may or may not be identical with the prevailing official interpretation. There will also be non-governmental *expectations* concerning state action which, again, may not correspond to official expectations. Discrepancies between non-governmental and governmental interpretations and expectations may have important ramifications. For one thing, public support and confidence may be

undermined if state action produces consequences which fundamentally violate public expectations.

The point to be made here is that the diagrammatic expression of our scheme shows that the impact of domestic social factors (line BDE) must be viewed also as a part of a larger feedback process as indicated by line BDEBD.

8. Another significant set of relationships emerges from the diagram in line AB-F. The external and internal setting are related to each other. Among others, two implications may be stressed here. First, because we have defined international politics as interaction process at the governmental level, it may appear that we are making the focus unduly narrow, thus ignoring a whole host of private, non-governmental interactions. Nothing could be further from the truth. Societies interact with each other in a wide range of ways through an intricate network of communications—trade, family ties, professional associations, shared values, cultural exchanges, travel, mass media and migration. While all of these patterns may be subject to governmental regulation (in some form), they *may* have very little to do with the origins and forms of state action. At any rate, the question of the political significance of inter-societal, intercultural non-governmental interactions requires an analytical scheme which will make possible some understanding of how such interactions condition official action. This in turn requires a much more systematic description of interactions than we now have, plus a way of accounting for their connection with state action.

One can however study the interactions connoted by line AB-F for their own sake with only a slight interest in their political aspects. In this case, it seems proper to say that the focus is international relations rather than international politics.

Non-governmental international relations do not enter the analysis of state behavior *unless* it can be shown that the behavior of the decision-makers is in some manner determined by or directed toward such relations. For example, assume a bitter, hostile campaign against a foreign government by powerful U.S. newspapers and assume the campaign is well publicized in the other nation. By itself this would constitute an asymmetrical interaction between two societies. It would not become a matter of state interaction unless or until the following happened: (a) an official protest to the U.S. State Department by the foreign government; (b) retaliation against U.S. citizens in the foreign country; (c) disturbance of negotiations between the two governments on quite another issue; (d) arousal of public opinion in the foreign country to the point where the effectiveness of U.S. policies toward that country was seriously affected; (e) the pressure generated by the campaign in the U.S. caused the decision-makers to modify their actions and reactions vis-à-vis the other state; (f) the U.S. government officially repudiated the criticism and apologized to the other government. This same *kind* of argument would hold for all types of non-governmental relations except that there would be varying degrees of directness (i.e., change in intersocietal relations——→change in state action) and indirectness (i.e., change in intersocietal relations——→change in social organization and behavior——→derived condition or factor——→change in state action) and therefore different time-sequences.

Second, while the most obvious consequences of state action are to be looked for in the reactions of other states along the lines DEF_4D in the diagram, changes in the external setting can influence state action along the lines of DEF_3A_3BD, that is, indirectly through changes in non-governmental relations which ultimately are recognized and taken into account by the decision-makers.

9. To get back to the center of the diagram, it should be noted that DE is a two-way arrow. The rest of this essay is concerned with the nature of decision-making, but it can be said here that in addition to the feedback relationships DEBD and DEF_3A_3, ED connotes a direct feedback from an awareness by the decision-makers of their own action and from assessments of the progress of action. This is to say that state action has an impact on decision-making apart from subsequent reactions of other states and apart from effects mediated through the state's social organization and behavior.

10. So far as this diagram is concerned, most attention in the field of international politics is paid to interactions DEF_4DE. DE represents action(s); EF (particularly EF_4) represents consequences for, or impact upon, the external setting; FD represents new conditions or stimuli—reactions or new actions (F_4D). Therefore, DEFDE represents the action-reaction-interaction sequence.

Obviously these lines stand for a wide range of relationships and kinds of action. What should be

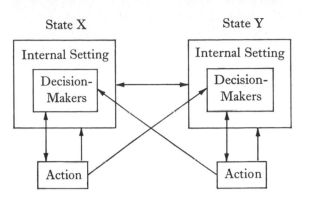

Figure 2

emphasized here is that interactions can be really understood fully only in terms of the decision-making responses of states to situations, problems, and the actions of other states. The combination of interaction and decision-making can be diagrammed as shown in Figure 2.

Naturally if one thinks of all the separate actions and reactions, all the combinations involved in the governmental relationships between one state and all others, it seems unrealistic and somewhat absurd to let a few lines on a diagram represent so much. Indeed, all would be lost unless one could speak of *patterns* and *systems*. Patterns refer to *uniformities* and *persistence* of actions and sets of relationships. "Nationalism," "imperialism," "internationalism," "aggression," "isolationism," "peace," "war," "conflict," and "cooperation" are familiar ways of characterizing kinds of actions and reactions as well as patterned relationships among states. These terms are, of course, both descriptive and judgmental— they are shorthand expressions covering complicated phenomena and also may imply approval or disapproval, goodness or badness.

System in this context refers to the modes, rules and nature of reciprocal influence which structure the interaction between states. Five kinds of system— there are others—may be mentioned: *coalitions* (temporary and permanent); *supranational organization; bilateral; multilateral* (unorganized); and *ordination-subordination* (imperial relationships and satellites). Once again, the way these interactions and relationships arise and the particular form or substance they take would seem to be explainable in terms of the way the decision-makers in the participating political organisms "define their situation." As we have said elsewhere,[8] there seem to be only two ways of scientifically studying international politics: (1) the description and measurement of interaction; and (2) decision-making—the formulation and execution of policy. Interaction patterns can be studied by themselves without reference to decision-making except that the "why" of the patterns cannot be answered.

Summary. To conclude this brief commentary, it may be said that the diagram presented above entitled "the state as actor in a situation" is designed in the first instance to portray graphically the basic perspectives of our frame of reference: *any* state as a way of saying something about *all* states; the central position of the decision-making focus; and the integration of a wide range of factors which may explain state action, reaction and interaction.

The lines of the diagram carry *two* suggestive functions. First, they alert the observer to possible (known and hypothetical) relationships among empirical factors. Thus the diagram simultaneously invites attention to three interrelated, intersecting

[8] Introduction to Karl Deutsch, *Political Community at the International Level*, Foreign Policy Analysis Series No. 2, 1953.

empirical processes—state interaction (DEFD) at the governmental level, inter-societal interaction (ABF) at the non-governmental level, and intra-societal interaction (BDEB) at both the governmental and non-governmental level. These processes arise, to put the matter another way, from decision-makers interacting with factors which constitute the dual setting, from state interaction as normally conceived, and from the factors which constitute internal and external settings acting upon each other.

Second, the diagram is intended to suggest possible analytic and theoretical relationships as well. The boxes indicate ways of specifying the relevant factors in state behavior through the employment of certain concepts—decision-making, action, setting, situation, society, culture, and so on—which provide, if they are successfully developed, criteria of relevance and ways of handling the empirical phenomena and their inter-relationships. There are in existence a large number of tested and untested hypotheses, general and "middle range" theories, applicable within each of the categories comprising the diagram. The central concept of decision-making may provide a basis for linking a group of theories which hitherto have been applicable only to a segment of international politics or have not been susceptible of application at all. . . .

20. Types of Decision-Making

David Braybrooke and Charles E. Lindblom were, respectively, Assistant Professor of Philosophy and Professor of Economics at Yale University at the time they collaborated on the work from which this selection is drawn. The former has since become Associate Professor of Philosophy and Politics at Dalhousie University in Nova Scotia. In this excerpt from an elaborate inquiry into the dynamics of policy-making, the authors proceed on the assumption that decisions in the political realm do not always follow a careful consideration and comparison of the desirability of alternative courses of action—what they call the "synoptic ideal." Rather they convincingly outline four different types of decision-making and suggest that perhaps the most widely practiced type involves marginal adjustments to changing circumstances—what they call "disjointed incrementalism." Their analysis here does not focus specifically on foreign policy decision-making, but such phenomena are not excluded from the scope of their argument, and the reader will doubtless find it instructive to ponder the circumstances under which each of the four types of decision-making are likely to be characteristic of foreign policy. [*Reprinted from David Braybrooke and Charles E. Lindblom*, A Strategy of Decision: Policy Evaluation as a Social Process (*New York: The Free Press, 1963*), *pp. 61–79, by permission of the authors and the publisher. Copyright 1963 by the Free Press, A Division of The Macmillan Company.*]

In view of the obstacles frustrating an approximation to the synoptic ideal, it is not surprising to find problem solvers exploiting in quite systematic ways, adaptive strategies for decision-making. They do not simply give up. A commonplace strategy is one to which we give the name "disjointed incrementalism." It is not the only set of adaptations to the difficulties of policy analysis—others range from coin tossing to the employment of game theory—but it is undoubtedly a most important one, no less important for not having been explicitly codified. Our aim is not to present it in the spirit of invention but to show that it is indeed an observable system—despite the fact that social scientists tend to employ it apologetically, as though their deviations from the synoptic ideal were regrettable.

Our first move in presenting the strategy, however, is indirect. Disjointed incrementalism is best understood in terms of the kinds of political decisions and situations to which it is adapted. The patterns of decision-making that circumstances allow vary from situation to situation, and the principal characteristics of the pattern that we identify as the strategy of disjointed incrementalism display themselves more emphatically in some kinds of situations and decisions rather than others. At this point, therefore, we shall look into a variety of situations and decisions.

I. Decisions Effecting Small Changes

In some situations, political decisions effect large changes and in other situations effect only small ones.

For our purposes, this distinction is so crucial that we must take the time necessary to make it more precise.

When is a change small? When is a difference in social states small? Is a change in the Federal Reserve's rediscount rate a small change? A change in eligibility for unemployment compensation? Dropping a bomb on Hiroshima? Limiting the President of the United States to two terms in office? Building a national highway network? Integrating public schools? If "small" seems easy to define, consider the difficulty that arises if we declare that restricting the President to two terms in office is only a small reform—and you declare that the restriction, through its effects on the balance of power between President and Congress during his second term, will seriously weaken the Presidency, drastically impair the nation's capacity to act vigorously in foreign policy, and finally threaten our survival in the cold war. Or consider the possibility that we regard a change in habits of church attendance as small because we find it unimportant, while you consider it large because you deem it important.

These examples suggest that, whether a change is called "large" or "small" depends on the value attached to it, and this value can vary from person to person. But the notion of "small" is not so subjective and personal as this conclusion implies, for in any society there develops a strong tendency toward convergence in estimates of what changes are important or unimportant. The convergence is of a particular kind that gives the judgment of "importance" an objective quality. Convergence develops for two reasons: because, while people favor (or disfavor) contrary things, they make issues of the same topics and because they tend to agree on which factors are important for theoretical explanations of change.

"Theoretical" may be too elegant a word; "ideological," on the other hand, is too abusive. What we mean to say is that individuals in a society have ways of describing and explaining important social change, ways that give prominence to some factors rather than others, including factors that affect people's values. These ways of describing and explaining tend to be roughly the same for most members of the society. Thus, in the United States, almost everyone would assume such factors as private property, the two-party system, separation of church and state, civil liberties, and American attitudes toward personal success to be relevant to a description and explanation of important social change. Almost everyone would also agree that such factors as rate of progression in income taxation, school lunch programs, a particular election, or parental attitudes toward comic books belong to a discussion of somewhat less important social change. And almost everyone would dismiss such factors as today's weather, a particular municipal election, or the current popular evaluation of a recent movie as appropriate only to the discussion of the most trivial social change. At this extreme, one might even refuse to think of such a discussion as descriptive of social change at all.

We come very close here to suggesting that our distinction between "small" and "large" change is the difference, as it is sometimes put, between structural changes and changes within a given structure. We prefer our formulation because we are not confident that the difference between structural changes and intrastructural changes can be established objectively. Depending on one's view of society, a change, for example, in language habits could be structural (for what social pattern is more fundamental than language?) or not structural (for ways of speech can and do change without evident consequences either for other elements of social structure or for the community's values). The view of society we take for purposes of defining "large" and "small" change, then, is the converging view that rests on widespread agreement concerning what is or is not important change.

We have advanced in our task of definition only to the point where we now propose to say that a "small" change is a change in a relatively unimportant variable or relatively unimportant change in an important variable. To introduce another term we shall want to use heavily, we add that a small change in an important variable will also be denoted as an "increment of change." We consider the introduction through public policy of what is considered to be a new and important element (in the combination of elements to which people refer in explaining important social change) to be a large or nonincremental change. On the other hand, a somewhat greater or reduced use of an existing social technique or a somewhat higher or lower level of attainment of some existing values is a small or incremental change.

It could be argued that any change is nonincremental if one counts its indefinitely cumulating consequences from here to eternity. We therefore wish to specify that a small or incremental change is one that, within some short time period, such as five years, is small or incremental, regardless of the indefinite future.

We draw no sharp line between the incremental and nonincremental; the difference is one of degree. Hence we imagine a continuum between, at one extreme, quite trivial changes (either because no important variables are altered or because the change of important variables is of trivial magnitude) and, at the other extreme, large changes in important variables. In such a continuum, we would place the kind of change we wish to identify as small toward the left. At the extreme left, however, are changes of such little importance that they do not even raise policy problems. Strictly speaking, they are incremental; but we take no interest in them, for they include such public problems as — to mention a popular example of triviality — what kind of paper clips the Department of Agriculture should purchase.

Within the range of incremental changes, two types are worth distinguishing. The first is social change that largely repeats (with respect to the elements altered and with respect to the character and scope of the changes) frequent previous change. Changes in interest rates, tax rates, severity of court sentences, school curricula, budget allocations to various public services, or traffic regulations achieve changes of this kind. On a continuum, the more repetitive the change, other things being equal, the more it is incremental. It is, of course, not logically necessary for a repetitive change that stays within a given range to be considered small or incremental. Sometimes repetitive changes of this kind can, because of changed circumstances, be regarded as nonincremental. The typical situation is, however, that repetitive changes become part of a game played by rule; they are not viewed as important in "theories" of social change, even if they are important from other points of view. In example, manipulation of the interest rate, while of no small consequence in maintaining full employment, represents only small social change.

The second kind of incremental change is the nonrepetitive change that is viewed either as a permanent small alteration in policy or as one small step in an indefinite nonrepetitive sequence. In the United States, present desegregation policies are achieving changes that might be termed incremental, although some people would argue that they go beyond the incremental; the changes contemplated in recent revisions of the antitrust laws and laws on federal funds for research, agricultural prices, and foreign aid are also within the incremental spectrum.

One can distinguish very roughly between changes in patterns of behavior or policies that are limited by their containment within another "larger" pattern of behavior or policies—and changes in the "larger" pattern that are held in turn to be variations within another still "larger" fixed pattern, and so forth. Viewed in this way, incremental changes include any changes permitted within the smallest set of patterns, as well as some of the smaller changes within the larger patterns, including very small changes in the very largest. Thus any change in the rediscount rate authorized by the Federal Reserve System, most changes in rules governing congressional procedure, some changes in the major governing principles of the U.S. Constitution, and very minor changes of degree in fundamental political attitudes would be considered marginal or incremental.

II. Political Decision-Making

Imagine now another continuum, on which political decisions can be arrayed according to the degree to which the decision-makers can be supposed to understand all the features of the problem with which they are faced. Near one extreme, information is generally lacking; values (goals, objectives, constraints, side conditions) are neither well understood nor well reconciled, and intellectual capacity generally falls far short of grasping and thinking through the problem. Near the other extreme, all aspects of the problem are quite well grasped in the decision-maker's mind.

We can combine this continuum with the first by altering the latter to refer explicitly to *decisions* that achieve a range from small to large change. We now have four recognizable types of decisions: (a) decisions that effect large change and are guided by adequate information and understanding; (b) decisions that effect large change but are not similarly guided—hence, at an extreme, blind or unpredictable

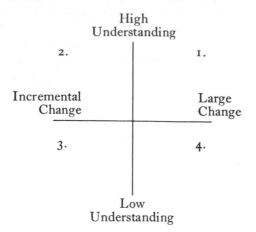

High
Understanding

2.   1.

Incremental   Large
Change   Change

3.   4.

Low
Understanding

Figure 1

decisions; (c) decisions that effect only small change and are guided by adequate information and understanding; and (d) decisions that effect small change but are not similarly guided, being therefore subject to constant reconsideration and redirection. In Figure 1 these types appear in quadrants 1, 4, 2, and 3, respectively.

To what kinds of political situation can we match each of these kinds of decision?

With respect to the first quadrant, the likelihood that decisions can accomplish large social changes and, at the same time, be guided by a high level of intellectual comprehension of the problem is slim. Such decisions require prodigious feats of synoptic analysis, beyond human capacities. To be sure, we are competent enough to produce catastrophes; with nuclear energy in our hands, we may be able, if we choose, to extinguish human life on earth—a very large change indeed. The kinds of large changes that lie within the range of what a government might wish to accomplish, however, are immensely more difficult, for reasons outlined in the preceding chapter. For although one needs to be able to predict only one disastrous consequence of a policy decision in order to be sure of a disaster, to attain some positive large-scale change, one needs to predict (unless one counts on luck) that none of a number of possible disasters will ensue.

Decisions designed to achieve desired large changes are, of course, made: for example, the decision of the southern states to secede from the Union

and the decision of the Lincoln administration to use force to stop them; the Soviet decision to move rapidly to the collectivization of agriculture; or the decision of some high-ranking French officers in Algeria in 1961 to challenge the authority of the civil government. That decisions to achieve large change are not guided by a high level of understanding, however, is illustrated by these very decisions, all of which brought quite unanticipated consequences.

Although we can think of many decisions to accomplish large changes that produced consequences subsequently applauded by the decision-makers—including some of the examples already given—is there a single example of a decision for which it can be claimed both that it accomplished a large change and that its implications were comprehensive and clearly understood beforehand?

In short, the only political context in which a decision of this kind could be made is the imaginary society of the philosopher king or some other utopian society in which, as in B. F. Skinner's *Walden Two*,[1] one group in the society—in Skinner's book, the psychologists—has achieved extraordinary comprehension of social change. One might, of course, argue that when circumstances are intolerable enough, available understanding is sufficient for large—specifically revolutionary—social change. An analyst might believe, without denying his incompetence to trace through the consequences of revolution, that any new situation likely to develop is preferable to the *status quo*. Aside from this possibility, however, the first quadrant is the realm of superhuman decision-makers.

Decisions in the fourth quadrant, decisions marked by large change and quite imperfect understanding, are not rare, even if they are not the typical instrument of policy-making. Nor are such decisions made only in error or by foolish decision-makers. On the contrary, such decisions are sometimes inescapable, forced on decision-makers by circumstances. In addition, such decisions are sometimes deliberately taken by decision-makers because the potential rewards seem attractive enough to outweigh the perils posed by imperfect understanding. If, in an important sense, Pearl Harbor forced the United States into war with Japan, nothing similar forced the United States to bomb Hiroshima and Nagasaki.

[1] B. F. Skinner, *Walden Two* (New York: Macmillan, 1948).

The political situations or circumstances that stimulate decisions affecting large but poorly understood change include crises, some revolutions, and war, as well as what decision-makers might call "grand opportunities." (Lest we fail to appreciate the blindness of such decisions, let us note that crises, wars and revolutions are often the results rather than the antecedent circumstances of such decisions.) The political locus for decisions of this kind lies in the deliberations of policy-makers and their advisers at the highest level. There is some circularity in such a statement, for anyone who carries off a revolution becomes a top-level policy-maker, even if he was not recognized as such before. All we mean to say is that, typically, the decision effecting large change is not made at the lower levels of government, nor, specifically, is it made in the middle or lower ranks of the administrative service.

The fourth quadrant, therefore, is clearly not the area or context of politics as usual, not even in the dictatorships, where the large decision seems more feasible than it normally does in the democracies. In the Soviet system, for example, decisions do not typically fall into the fourth quadrant: Foreign policy, for example, is typically carried forward by endless small moves; economic planning too is a process of unending calculation and step-by-step adjustment.

What is the political context for decisions in the second quadrant, decisions that effect small or incremental changes on the basis of a high level of intellectual comprehension of problem and decision? In the first place, it appears that decisions effecting only small or incremental changes are the daily business of governmental machinery: decisions to build a new veterans' hospital, increase foreign aid to Latin America, amend our farm-price legislation, schedule a summit conference, continue with a small increase or decrease of the annual appropriation to the navy, liberalize benefits under Old Age and Survivors' Insurance, provide health insurance for the aged, lower the banking system's reserve requirements, call a conference on the problems of small business, order office equipment or furniture for government offices, assign tasks to administrative subordinates, provide paid sick-leave for government employees, deny or grant workmen's compensation to an applicant, undertake an anti-trust action against a corporation, condemn a building, reroute traffic, make a loan, or arrest a speeding motorist. Even if we drop from this list all those decisions that are not to be dignified in the name of policy, the remaining items and countless other examples that could be cited leave no doubt that policy is usually made through decisions that in any given instance achieve only small or incremental changes.

But for how many of these decisions can we say that the decision-maker attains a high level of understanding of his problem, including the implications of all the various alternative possible decisions? Not for all, certainly. When policy makers, fearful of inflation, opt for higher taxes, they know that before the new legislation can be implemented, business conditions may call for antidotes to recession rather than for curbs on inflation. They can only hope to have an opportunity to act again if they are in error; they can hardly hope to read the future with confidence. When policy-makers try to woo Latin America with more generous foreign aid, they act largely on the supposition that more funds will not do any damage to our relations with the American republics and might help. How often can they be said to have diagnosed correctly the particular ills they wished to remedy and to have predicted what the direct and indirect consequences of the new flow of funds would be? Even when policy-makers attempt something so simple as grants-in-aid for state highway construction, they cannot foresee the whole range of important consequences for urban congestion and the amenities of life. We need only call to mind the arguments of the preceding chapters to establish that, even for decisions effecting only small changes, information and understanding will be limited.

Where a decision effecting an incremental change does indeed seem to fall within a recognized competence—rather than to depend largely on imponderables or preferences—the decision is often delegated to a specialized group: engineers, economists, physicians, accountants—or one or another subgroup of that very large and internally differentiated group of experts on small policy decisions, the public administrators. We can say, therefore, that for decisions of the second quadrant, the decision-maker is typically not at the highest levels of the government bureaucracy and may be a professional specialist of some sort.

Bearing in mind the difficulties of comprehending a problem as envisaged in the synoptic ideal, however, we should recognize that many decisions of the administrative service of government, even at middle and low levels, many decisions of professional experts are not decisions of the second quadrant. If a decision is a second quadrant decision, it is probably an administrative or professional decision, but many administrative and professional decisions are too complex to fall into the second quadrant.

III. Incremental Politics

We are thus brought to the third quadrant: decisions effecting small or incremental change and not guided by a high level of understanding. These decisions, we now see, are the decisions typical of ordinary political life—even if they rarely solve problems but merely stave them off or nibble at them, often making headway but sometimes retrogressing. Decisions like these are made day by day in ordinary political circumstances by congressmen, executives, administrators, and party leaders.

Let us describe this kind of political decision-making in more detail. It is decision-making through small or incremental moves on particular problems rather than through a comprehensive reform program. It is also endless; it takes the form of an indefinite sequence of policy moves. Moreover, it is exploratory in that the goals of policy-making continue to change as new experience with policy throws new light on what is possible and desirable. In this sense, it is also better described as moving *away* from known social ills rather than as moving *toward* a known and relatively stable goal. In any case, it is policy-making that chooses those goals that draw policies forward in the light of what recent policy steps have shown to be probably realizable; the utopian goal, chosen for its attractiveness without thought of its feasibility, is not a heavy influence on this kind of policy-making. In the frequency with which past moves are found wanting and new moves debated, it reveals both man's limited capacities to understand and solve complex problems and an unsettled, shifting compromise of conflicting values. Woodrow Wilson describes the process at its best:

We shall deal with our economic system as it is and as it might be modified, not as it might be if we had a clean sheet of paper to write upon; and step by step we shall make it what it should be, in the spirit of those who question their own wisdom and seek council and

knowledge, not shallow self-satisfaction or the excitement of excursions whither they cannot tell.[2]

Incremental policy-making is illustrated less flatteringly in legislation for old-age security in the United States. Our "program" for the aged is not a program at all; it is not a comprehensively considered and co-ordinated policy. Rather, it consists of Old Age and Survivors' Insurance, special provisions for the aged under the income tax law, old-age assistance provided through the cooperation of state and federal government, and county and municipal provision of medical care and other particular services for the needy aged. It is therefore a product of a number of small, specific moves. It has been developed—and goes on developing—as a sequence of decisions, illustrated in the endless stream of congressional decisions that liberalizes benefits and extends incrementally the coverage of Old Age and Survivors' Insurance.

To pursue the illustration, policy-makers have never been confident—and certainly have never agreed—on what goals for old-age income and security they wish to pursue. Nor have they understood exactly what consequences would flow from their decisions. During the great depression of the 1930's, they were stirred into important steps to appease a politically restless group of aged voters, and they were stirred again to remedy the real reduction in old-age benefits that attended post-World War II inflation—and to head off an increasingly strong movement for industry-financed pensions that trade unions were pushing at the bargaining table. During all these years, decision-makers have presumably also been motivated by their perceptions of the ways in which programs existing at any one time still left the aged inadequately cared for. The proportion of those uncared for has no doubt diminished, but the programs are incomplete while some remain; furthermore, new matters of concern appear once all the aged have been assured the minimum decencies. Never sure how far they wished to go in liberalization, policy-makers nevertheless have known what they wanted to move away from. Increases in coverage of OASI have clearly been influenced by growing skill in administering the

[2] Woodrow Wilson, *First Inaugural Address*, 1913, cited by John R. Moore in testimony before the Kefauver subcommittee on antitrust and monopoly, July 16. 1957.

program—a clear example of goals following the emergence of means.

We shall call this typical pattern incremental politics for two reasons. In the first place, we have referred to its preoccupation with small or incremental changes as one of its defining characteristics. Secondly, some of the other characteristics of this pattern of politics are rooted in its preoccupation with small or incremental change. In short, the incremental character of this political pattern is central and fundamental, even if it does not wholly characterize it.

For a democracy like the United States, the commitment to incremental change is not surprising. Nonincremental alternatives usually do not lie within the range of choice possible in the society or body politic. Societies, it goes without saying, are complex structures that can avoid dissolution or intolerable dislocation only by meeting certain preconditions, among them that certain kinds of change are admissible only if they occur slowly. Political democracy is often greatly endangered by nonincremental change, which it can accommodate only in certain limited circumstances.

In incremental politics, political parties and leaders compete for votes by agreeing on fundamentals and offering only incrementally different policies in each policy area in which they wish to compete. Since this phenomenon has been frequently demonstrated to be a prerequisite for the survival of democracy itself, it can hardly be questioned as a characteristic of political life in the Western democracies. Moreover, each of the competing political parties shifts its own policies only incrementally at any one time. Such incremental alteration of party policies is in fact the normal, though not invariable, rule in all two-party democracies and in some multiparty democracies.[3] In addition, policy-making proceeds through a sequence of approximations. A policy is directed at a problem, it is tried, altered, tried in its altered form, altered again, and so forth. In short, incremental policies follow one upon the other in the solution to a given problem.

These are easily recognizable fundamental

processes in American democracy and indeed in most, if not all, of the stable, deeply rooted democracies of the world. To be sure, ideological rhetoric pervades political debate and runs through general statements of purpose in legislative enactments; but the preponderance of incremental politics is evident from the manner in which the legislators themselves, as well as administrators and judges, implement those purposes.

It becomes clearer now why political policy, in its focus on increments of change, also shows the other characteristics—it is remedial, serial, and exploratory, for example—that we identified as part of incremental politics. To pursue incremental changes is to direct policy toward specific ills—the nature of which is continually being re-examined— rather than toward comprehensive reforms; it is also to pursue long-term changes through sequences of moves. Avoiding social cleavage along ideological lines, which is exacerbated when issues of ultimate principle are raised, incremental politics explores a continuing series of remedial moves on which some agreement can be developed even among members of opposing ideological camps.

Even though we speak of small or incremental changes as the kind of change that is made in incremental politics, we should like to caution against identifying incremental change only with change that is immediately acceptable to political decision-makers. Discussing national water resources policy, James Fesler goes through a list of possible administrative reorganizations and reaches the conclusion that

The indications that Congress cannot be appeased by any administrative arrangement so far devised simplifies our immediate task of drawing conclusions about national water resources administration. Until further political analyses disclose a way in which Congress might accommodate the patent need for more reasonable arrangements for consideration of water resource programs, we can revert to relatively apolitical modes of analysis.[4]

He proceeds to discuss, in despair of finding any program on which Congress might look favorably, the possibility of organizing water-resource administration into a single major national department with

---

[3] A more exact statement of the conditions and the explanation of their necessity to democracy will be found in R. A. Dahl and C. E. Lindblom, *Politics, Economics and Welfare* (New York: Harper and Bros., 1953), pp. 294 ff.

[4] James W. Fesler, "National Water Resources Administration," *Law and Contemporary Social Problems*, XXII (Summer, 1957), 468 ff.

program formulation at the secretarial level of the contemplated department. These suggestions remain, despite their immediate political unacceptability, within the bounds of incremental politics as we define the term.

Just how far the practice of incremental politics permeates the activity of our government can be illustrated even by decisions that, on superficial inspection, appear to be nonincremental. The decision to convert from a peacetime to a wartime economy would, at first glance, appear to be one of the largest and most consequential decisions a nation might make, hardly an incremental decision. Yet, in the United States, the actual process of transformation was incremental.[5] A sequence of decisions began in fact before the country was actually at war, when this country took up the task of supplying its future allies from "the arsenal of democracy." The Neutrality Act was revised in November, 1939, to permit "cash and carry" purchases of arms by the Allies, and the federal government set up an interdepartmental committee to co-ordinate foreign and domestic purchases. The government began applying informal pressure to expand the machine-tool industry, even before Congress authorized new appropriations for "defense"; after these appropriations were made, "educational contracts" were issued "through which industry was led into war production step by step, somewhat against its desires, if not against its will."[6]

The President reacted to the Nazi triumphs in the spring of 1940 by declaring a state of "unlimited national emergency." What this meant, immediately, was a number of incremental moves—a demand for "night and day production" of machine tools; creation of new administrative agencies to deal with petroleum and food; and the founding of an Office of Civilian Defense. Other developments came soon after. In addition to passing increased appropriations, Congress made various laws to facilitate the financing of war contracts. The Selective Service Administration commenced operations. (At roughly the same time, the United States exchanged fifty destroyers for island bases within the British Empire.) As the summer of 1940 ended, voluntary priorities on military orders began to give way to regulation; the Council of National Defense established a Priorities Board.

In January, 1941, the President put forward the "lend-lease" program, which was approved by Congress in March. An Office of Production Management was set up. As agitation began for the conversion of the automobile industry to aircraft production, the government began acting to expand steel and aluminum capacity. To speed up the conversion of existing plants to war production, a Supply Priorities and Allocations Board was superimposed in August, 1941, on the Office of Production Management, which in its several months of operation had proved unable to deal effectively with "the military opposition to lend-lease and . . . industrial opposition

---

[5] In other countries, incremental characteristics may have been less prominent. Speaking partly from his own experience, one of the critics who helped us most with useful and penetrating comments on a draft of this book cited the change in Great Britain from a peace economy to a war economy as a striking example of comprehensive plans smoothly and successfully applied. That his impressions had some foundation we do not wish to deny. Yet the testimony of other participants seems to reflect an incremental process. Professor E. A. G. Robinson, for example, writing on "The Overall Allocation of Resources," in *Lessons of the British War Economy*, ed. D. N. Chester (Cambridge: Cambridge University Press, 1951), maintains that "The development in the years 1939 to 1945 was wholly empirical. There was no . . . conscious thought in the early stages of a definite goal in the form of the perfect war economy towards which we were moving. At each stage we relied on the working of the normal incentives so far as they were practicable, and replaced them only to the extent that they appeared at a particular moment to be working badly in a particular field" (p. 35). Although Robinson considers that "the manpower survey and the manpower allocations" that were "the backbone of the central planning in the later phases of the war" (p. 52) were on the whole quite effective, he writes that manpower planning was "always done for comparatively short periods only. There was no official and agreed long-term appreciation of the manpower position two years or more ahead. The departments had to use their own judgment about the planning of extensions of capacity, in almost complete darkness as to the likelihood that a sufficient proportion of the progressively diminishing manpower resources would come their way" (pp. 54–55). Robinson goes on immediately to make the interesting comment, "While this is a valid criticism, it would not be true to say that it was a criticism often advanced during the actual course of the war. It may be that departments, irked by central control, did not wish to add yet another link to their fetters. It remains that I have no recollection of actual demands for longer-term manpower forecasts or of refusals to undertake them" (p. 55). Our argument in this book will invest this comment with a great deal of added significance.

[6] Luther Gulick, *Administrative Reflections from World War II* (University, Ala.: University of Alabama Press, 1948), p. 3. The data about industrial mobilization in the United States in this and succeeding paragraphs are taken from Gulick.

to war conversion."[7] An Office of Price Administration began functioning, although it did not obtain specific statutory powers until some months later. The first Liberty ship was launched, nonessential building was brought to an end, and steel plate was put under "complete allocation."

All these steps were taken before the war officially began; it was in the midst of an unfinished series of such developments that the Japanese struck at Pearl Harbor. The War and Navy Departments had prepared an industrial mobilization plan against the eventuality of being officially at war, and the plan was revised as late as September, 1939. This gesture at over-all planning was not, however, effective in the sense of producing a plan that was actually applied—even though, in making the gesture, the planners had foreseen most of the functions that the government would have to take on in a wartime economy. The planners had not envisioned—even during the revisions of mid-1939—what Gulick calls "our crab-like progress into 'defense' and war." Equally important, they had not realized how complex and extensive—and how variable—the institutions necessary to organize mobilization would turn out to be. They underestimated the importance, for example, of political leadership by the President, omitted to consider the need for a food administration, and treated price controls as an optional possibility. Apparently they did not contemplate any "economic dealings with allies"—thus ignoring what became, as we have seen, the leading stimulus to industrial mobilization before the war officially began.

The incremental pattern of mobilization continued as an accelerated process after the United States became fully involved. Indeed, one could hardly hope for more spectacular evidence of incremental adjustments than the continual reorganizations of the war production agencies themselves. The Office of Production Management, as we have seen, was superseded, at least in part, even before the war began by the Supply Priorities and Allocations Board. The co-ordinating functions of those two agencies were taken over, once the war began, by still another *ad hoc* agency—the War Production Board; then by the Office of Economic Stabilization; and finally by the Office of War Mobilization. The last became, as new needs emerged, the Office of War Mobilization and Reconversion. Waves of reorganization also characterize the history of other wartime agencies. Gulick claims to detect in these waves a "sequence of evolution" or "rhythm of growth and adaptation,"

starting with (a) planning and advisory agencies, (b) passing to action agencies with extensive power of issuing coordinating directives to other action agencies, (c) improvising bottleneck-breaking agencies for individual programs and then (d) correcting the conflicts thus engendered by setting up co-ordinating agencies of limited jurisdiction, and finally (e) creating a super co-ordinating agency in the White House, with complete authority over the domestic economy.[8]

We may append to this account Gulick's comment, "Our administrative structure for war . . . was not established like a new building and completed before occupancy, but was built while occupied and remodeled from time to time as we waged the war."[9] Whether or not large-scale operations like mobilization are launched according to a general plan, there seem to be indefeasible incremental features about them.

The incremental character of political policy-making is often disguised, more often in the Soviet Union than in the United States, by much talk of plans and planning. Often a plan is no more than a loosely stated set of goals and possible steps. It is relevant to the kind of actual decision-making we have been describing, but its goals and steps ordinarily have to be reformulated with each policy move. Even in the Soviet Union, economic planning is highly sequential and incremental like the kind of policy-making we have been describing for the United States.

IV. Types of Decision-Making

We can now ask, What methods for analysis are suitable to each of the kinds of decisions and situations represented in the four quadrants? We are going to present the strategy of disjointed incrementalism as an analytical strategy adapted, as the name we give it suggests, to the third quadrant—adapted, that is to say, to incremental politics.

---

[7] *Ibid.*, p. 6.

[8] *Ibid.*, pp. 27 ff.
[9] *Ibid.*, pp. 37 ff.

Synoptic methods, we suggest, are limited to the second quadrant, that is, to those happy if limited circumstances in which decisions effect sufficiently small change to make synoptic understanding possible. Synoptic methods are called for in the first quadrant, to be sure; for all the reasons given in this and the preceding chapter, however, the information and comprehension requirements of synoptic problem-solving simply cannot be met for large-scale social change. It is of course the careless assumption that man's competence is unlimited that makes utopian reconstruction so attractive.

As for the fourth quadrant, crises, wars, revolutions, and grand opportunities call for kinds of analytical strategy quite different from the synoptic, but we cannot claim that the strategy of disjointed incrementalism is suited to these situations. At the present juncture in the study of decision-making, one would be hard put to formalize the methods appropriate to that quadrant. We represent these conclusions roughly in Figure 2. . . .

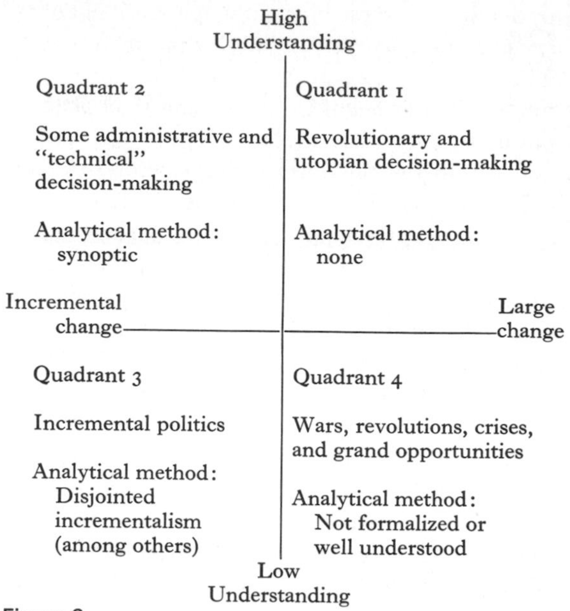

High
Understanding

Quadrant 2	Quadrant 1
Some administrative and "technical" decision-making	Revolutionary and utopian decision-making
Analytical method: synoptic	Analytical method: none

Incremental change ———————————————— Large change

Quadrant 3	Quadrant 4
Incremental politics	Wars, revolutions, crises, and grand opportunities
Analytical method: Disjointed incrementalism (among others)	Analytical method: Not formalized or well understood

Low
Understanding

Figure 2

21. Assumptions of Rationality and Non-Rationality in Models of the International System

Sidney Verba is Professor of Political Science at the University of Chicago and a distinguished scholar in the field of comparative politics. He has written *Small Groups and Political Behavior* (1961), coauthored *The Civic Culture* (1963), and co-edited *The International System* (1961) and *Political Culture and Political Developments* (1965). In this article Professor Verba assesses the degree to which foreign policy decision-making is grounded in rational processes, but, unlike the previous selection, here the problem is approached from the perspective of the individual policy-maker, his attitudes, his personality, his skills, and his responsiveness to the requirements of his official role. [*Reprinted from Klaus Knorr and Sidney Verba (eds.),* The International System: Theoretical Essays (*Princeton: Princeton University Press, 1961), pp. 93–117, by permission of the author and the Princeton University Press.*]

I

It is a truism that all action within the international system can be reduced to the action of individuals. It is also true, however, that international relations cannot be adequately understood in terms of individual attitudes and behaviors. Models of the international system usually deal with larger units, nation-states, as prime actors. To what extent can such models give us adequate explanations of international relations without some built-in variables to deal with individual decision-making?

It may be that some processes in international relations can be adequately explained on the level of social structure without explicit consideration of the personality, predispositions, attitudes, and behavior of the individual decision-maker. In that case, the introduction of variables dealing with individual behavior would complicate the model without commensurate payoff in terms of increased understanding and prediction. This would be true if the impact of individual decision-making on the behavior of nations in their relations with other nations were slight, or if the impact varied randomly (because, for instance, of idiosyncratic factors) among the population of international events that one was trying to explain. If, on the other hand, models of the international system that either ignore or make grossly simplifying assumptions about individual decision-making can explain international relations only very imperfectly, it may well be worth the additional effort to build variables about individual decision-making into them.[1]

This paper will deal with the place of assumptions and theories about individual decision-making

[1] We ask that a model give adequate explanation and prediction of international events, not perfect explanation and prediction. There are, however, no hard and fast rules as to what is adequate explanation. In a sense, the test is a psychological one: an explanation is adequate when the "mind comes to rest." And this will depend upon the nature of the problem, its importance, complexity, and the interests of the people working on it.

in models of the international system. The individuals in whose behavior we are interested are all those whose activities either alone or with others have some perceptible impact upon the international system. This then includes masses and elites, governmental and non-governmental figures. Behaviors that will be considered as affecting the international system range from the minimal one of holding an opinion about an international situation as a member of the public to the authoritative decision made by some major government official. If one conceives of the international system as consisting of activities involving interaction among two or more nation-states, and the act of any single state is considered an input into that system, it is clear that the main impact of the activities of individuals upon the international system takes place on the level of the internal decision-making process that determines what input a nation will make into the international system. This is the case because with rare exceptions the roles of individuals within their own nations and the norms associated with these roles outweigh in importance their roles within the international system. We shall therefore concentrate on the individual as a role-holder in the foreign policy-formulating structure of his own nation.

Theories that attempt to explain and understand the course of international relations make varying assumptions about the actions and motivations of individual actors. Two approaches can be called the rational and the non-rational. Each makes a simplifying assumption about the way in which individuals act in international situations. Non-rational models assume that when an individual is faced with a choice situation in relation to an international event (a governmental decision-maker faced with a threat from an adversary nation, an ordinary citizen hearing about an insult to his head of state), he responds in terms of what we shall call non-logical pressures or influences. These are pressures or influences unconnected with the event in question. A gross case occurs when an individual responds aggressively to an international event because of internal psychological pressures toward aggression having their root in childhood experiences. A non-logical influence is any influence acting upon the decision-maker of which he is unaware and which he would not consider a legitimate influence upon his decision if he were aware of it. The latter criterion is difficult to make operational, but inferences can be

drawn from the individual's value system. In any case, the former criterion will serve as an adequate indicator of the existence of such non-logical influences.[2]

Rational models of individual decision-making are those in which the individual responding to an international event bases his response upon a cool and clearheaded means-ends calculation. He uses the best information available and chooses from the universe of possible responses that alternative most likely to maximize his goals. The rational decision-maker may, for instance, respond aggressively to an international event, but the aggressive response will have its source in calculations based upon the nature of the international situation. It will be directed against the real enemy—the nation threatening or inflicting damage to one's interests—and the decision-maker will have some reasonable expectation of achieving his ends through the aggressive response. Furthermore, the decision will either have no psychological side-effects on the decision-maker (he will not experience tension release or guilt because of it), or, if there are psychological side-effects, they will be irrelevant as far as the nature of the decision is concerned.[3]

In most cases, neither of these models of individual behavior represents a complete description of

[2] An attitude or behavior rooted in such non-logical influences may be considered to be a "symptom," in the Freudian sense of the word; that is, ". . . an overt tension-reducing response whose relationship to an unconscious motive is not perceived by the individual." See Irving Sarnoff, "Psychoanalytic Theory and Social Attitudes," *Public Opinion Quarterly*, XXIV (Summer 1960), pp. 251–79. It may be useful to distinguish between motives that are non-logical and motives that are inappropriate. If, for instance, an individual responds to an international decision-making situation in terms of his desire for organizational promotion rather than the welfare of his nation, his motives may be considered inappropriate even in terms of his own value structure (he may feel guilty), but they are not non-logical as long as they are conscious motives.

[3] An individual may respond to an international event in terms of the event itself and still not behave "rationally," as the term is ordinarily used. (We shall consider the concept of rationality more fully below.) He may respond foolishly because of inadequate information. Or he may respond in anger and haste—not in the cool manner of the rational decision-maker—but the anger may be due to the acts of the adversary nation rather than to the previous existence of latent aggression in the individual. This type of behavior, while not rational, fits easily into the model of rational behavior, for its deviation from rationality is along the dimensions considered significant in the model of rationality.

actual behavior. They are presented rather as simplifying assumptions about individual behavior. But the choice of assumption has serious consequences for the adequacy and usefulness of the theory of which it is a part. For even if we are interested in the behavior of nation-states, the implicit or explicit assumptions we make about individual behavior will affect our understanding of state behavior. Let us consider the non-rational models first.

II

The attitudes and behaviors of an individual often perform functions for him that are not apparent in the attitude or act itself. They may work to resolve problems that are not the overt topic of the attitude or the manifest object of the behavior. Non-rational models of individual attitudes and behaviors in relation to international affairs are built upon this insight.

These models postulate certain needs whose roots lie in innate drives or early experiences. These needs are then projected into public affairs, where their fulfillment is sought through attitudes and behaviors relevant to international events. Individuals, for instance, are described as having a need for an aggressive outlet. This need is met through the expression of aggressive feelings toward some foreign nation, going even as far as a desire for war. In this way, attitudes toward international affairs are explained in terms of certain personality-oriented pressures, not in terms of reactions to international events. The international system becomes the arena into which unresolved personal problems are projected.[4] Evidence from clinical studies of individuals as well as from correlational studies of larger groups suggests that there is indeed a relationship between personality variables and early childhood experiences, on the one hand, and attitudes on a wide range of topics, including international relations, on the other. A tendency to adopt hostile attitudes toward other groups, including other nations, has been correlated with such variables as patterns of child-rearing, level of latent aggression, scores on the F-scale, personal

insecurity, and so forth. In most cases, however, the correlations—though in the expected direction—have been insufficient to explain the attitude. This fact, plus the fact that many of these studies have been of special populations, such as college students, and deal with verbal responses to hypothetical situations, suggests that one must be cautious in extrapolating to explanations of the way in which nations will behave in their relations with other nations.[5]

What we can say on the basis of these studies is that, at minimum, personality variables affect attitudes and behaviors in the international sphere. Each individual brings with him into the situations relevant to international relations in which he may be involved a set of predispositions, previous experiences, and the like, all of which are irrelevant in terms of his own model of the situation. But it is more difficult to say how strong the effects are likely to be, in what direction they will operate, and under what conditions the non-logical influences are likely to be significant. And, above all, it is hard to connect theories of non-logical influence on political decisions with the way in which nations act in the international system. At best the evidence on these influences deals with the behavior of individuals and, even at this level, it is difficult to explain why one decision and not another was taken by a particular individual in a particular situation. The connection between these influences and the actions of nation-states is much more difficult to detect. The simplest model connects the hypothesized predispositions of individuals directly with the position that a nation takes vis-à-vis other nations. Thus, a high (but unspecified) proportion of individuals in Nation A have aggressive tendencies; these tendencies are displaced on an external object; for a variety of reasons, a foreign nation is a convenient object; ergo: Nation A goes to war with Nation B. This sort of model has little predictive or explanatory power, and little need be said about it. The question is not whether personality and predispositional variables determine the action of nation-states, but how these variables can

---

[4] For a fuller discussion of these theories and, in particular, of the origins of these personality-oriented needs and the ways in which these needs are translated into attitudes toward international affairs, see Maurice Farber, "Psychoanalytic Hypotheses in the Study of War," *Journal of Social Issues*, I (1955), pp. 29–35; and Bjørn Christiansen, *Attitudes Towards Foreign Affairs as a Function of Personality*, Oslo, Oslo University Press, 1959.

[5] For examples of these studies, see Christiansen, *op. cit.*; Charles D. Farris, "Selected Attitudes on Foreign Affairs as Correlates of Authoritarianism and Political Anomie," *Journal of Politics*, XXII (February, 1960), p. 50; Arthur I. Gladstone, "The Possibility of Predicting Reactions to International Events," *Journal of Social Issues*, I (1955), pp. 21–28; and Daniel Levinson, "Authoritarian Personality and Foreign Policy," *Journal of Conflict Resolution*, I (March, 1957), pp. 37–47.

usefully be fitted into models of the international system.[6]

There is, however, a previous question that can be asked—a question that begs the one just raised and that may be easier to answer. Although non-logical variables have an effect on the course of international relations, is it desirable to bring these variables into models of the international system? That they have some effect on that system is certainly insufficient reason for incorporating them into theories of the system, for to include all variables that have some effect on international relations would be to create a model so complex as to be useless. The question we raise is one of the economics of research design. Does the increase in explanatory power that would accompany the introduction of such variables into a model of the international system justify the increased complexity of the model? How significant is the impact of these non-logical influences on the sorts of events we are trying to explain in our models of the international system?

Let us assume that individuals have a variety of psychological needs and that these needs can be filled through public activities, including activities related to international affairs. For example, to take the most frequently mentioned need, assume that every individual has some need to manifest aggression. The level of the need varies from individual to individual, ranging from such a low level that there are no discernible behavioral consequences to such a high level that it dominates most behavior. Each individual is so situated that his behavior affects the international system, but he is also involved in a host of other relationships. His aggressive needs can find outlet in his behavior in relation to the international system; they can also find outlet in his behavior in relation to the other systems with which he interacts. Thus we have a simple table:

| | | *Level of Aggressive Needs* | |
		High	Low
The International	High	x	x
System as Outlet	Low	x	x

[6] One can distinguish between the effects on the course of international relations of the nature of man and of *the hypotheses held by men about the nature of man.* It may be that the latter have as great an effect as the former, though, of course, the two are not completely unrelated. A belief that basic predispositions are learned as a child and cannot be changed or that aggression has its roots in human nature might well affect decisions in international affairs.

People can therefore vary in terms of their level of aggressive needs and in terms of the extent to which aggressive needs find their expression within the sphere of international relations. What this table suggests is that such variables are relevant only among those individuals whose level of aggressive needs is high and whose outlet for the need is their behavior in regard to the international system. If the combination High/High is rare, one will lose little by ignoring the effects of non-logical influences.

In order to assess the probability of a significant number of individuals falling in the High/High category, one would have to develop a series of hypotheses as to the probability that an individual will be high in terms of the impact of a particular non-logical force and high in terms of its projection into the international sphere. On the first problem, it is of course possible through clinical studies to spell out the types of non-logical forces to which individuals are subject. Such studies, however, are of limited use unless they can supply us with rules, albeit rough ones, as to the likely level of a particular influence in individuals whom we cannot submit to detailed clinical analysis. Such rules would have to enable us to predict what particular non-logical force is likely to be more widespread among what groups. There is some evidence that certain non-logical forces are more prevalent among some national groups than among others, and some evidence that political elites tend to manifest a different set of non-logical forces than non-elites. But, in most cases, the research backing up these propositions is quite scanty. In any case, the extent to which any group or individual manifests a particular non-logical need takes us into questions of general psychology and far from our consideration of political psychology. Of greater relevance to our study is the second variation—the extent to which attitudes and behaviors relevant to international affairs rather than attitudes and behaviors in other areas serve as the outlet for non-logical needs.

To what extent is the sphere of international relations likely to serve as the outlet for the externalization of non-logical needs? This will depend upon the extent to which such non-logical needs can be satisfied by attitudes and behaviors toward international affairs and the extent to which the projection of such needs into the international arena does not conflict with other more instrumental functions of attitudes and behaviors in that field.[7] The following hypotheses deal with the conditions that affect the probability that attitudes and behaviors in relation to international affairs will represent the externalization of an individual's personality-oriented needs. The first set of hypotheses deals with the relationship of the individual to the international situation:

(1) The greater the involvement of an individual in a situation, the greater will be the effect of non-logical and predispositional influences. At the one extreme, if the individual is completely apathetic to the course of international events, they can afford little or no outlet for the release of his personality-oriented tensions. But if he is deeply involved, his relations to the course of international events will be affect-laden and there will be more opportunity for the projection of non-logical influences into the international sphere. It is, of course, possible for involvement in international affairs to follow from some personality-oriented need. If the need were strong enough, one might expect search behavior in order to find an object of orientation for that need, and such an object might, for instance, be a foreign nation. But in general one would expect such needs to be oriented toward some object in which the individual is already involved.

The hypothesis that involvement will be directly related to the degree to which attitudes and behaviors in relation to international affairs perform personality-oriented functions requires qualification. Involvement refers to the degree to which an indi-

vidual feels concerned and interested in an event. Involvement increases the impact of personality factors if everything else is equal. But it rarely is. Involvement tends to go along with other relationship characteristics that inhibit the degree to which personality variables affect behavior.

(2) The more information an individual has about international affairs, the less likely is it that his behavior will be based upon non-logical influences. In the absence of information about an event, decisions have to be made on the basis of other criteria. A rich informational content, on the other hand, focuses attention on the international event itself. The personality-oriented functions of the attitude would, under such circumstances, be more likely to conflict with the more cognitive and instrumental functions that attitudes also perform—functions having to do with our understanding of the world of international affairs and our manipulation of that world in the direction of our conscious interests. Such conflict might, of course, be resolved by an adjustment of one's perceptions of the international scene; one might, for instance, seek and find only that information that supported one's personality-oriented attitude. But the richer and more differentiated the informational content, the more difficult this would be.

(3) The higher the level of skill in handling international problems, the less likely it will be that attitudes on international affairs will be free to perform personality-oriented functions. Skill is, of course, closely related to information, but it is not the same. It refers to specific techniques relevant to international affairs as well as to the more general intellectual ability to deal with complex and abstract problems. Insofar as a problem is handled within an intellectual structure—a particular event related to other events and to a class of events, historical perspective brought to bear, consequences calculated, and so forth—the impact of personality on the decision will be inhibited.

(4) The more an individual values rationality as a decision-making process, the less personality factors will play a role in his decision. That an individual values rationality as a means of making decisions does not mean that he is necessarily rational in his behavior, nor does it mean that he has some complete model of scientific rationality in his mind which he mechanically follows. Rather it refers to a

[7] The underlying theory of attitude formation that we are using here is a functional one. This makes it difficult for us to ask the question that really interests us: under what conditions are attitudes toward international affairs likely to be caused by non-logical needs? We would fall into a teleological trap if we were to assume that because an attitude performs certain psychological functions for an individual, we have explained the cause or genesis of that attitude. Nevertheless, although one cannot assume causality, attitudes that do serve as the outlets for some psychological need are more likely to be determined at least in part by that need than attitudes that do not perform such functions. Theories of learning, for instance, suggest that individuals will adopt those attitudes and behaviors that perform functions for them. See M. Brewster Smith, Jerome S. Bruner, and Robert W. White, *Opinions and Personality*, New York, 1956; M. Brewster Smith, "Opinions, Personality and Political Behavior," *American Political Science Review*, LII (March 1958), pp. 1–17; and Daniel Katz, "The Functional Approach to the Study of Attitudes," *Public Opinion Quarterly*, XXIV (Summer, 1960), pp. 163–204.

general tendency to value as the basis of a decision such modes of decision-making as seeking information, controlling one's emotions (insofar as one is consciously able), trying to calculate at least some of the effects of a decision, and so forth. These modes of decision will be imperfectly observed, but insofar as they are valued, they will conflict with the formally irrelevant criteria upon which non-logical attitudes are formed.

(5) The more influence a person believes himself to have over events, the less he will orient himself toward those events in terms of personality variables. A low level of influence, especially when coupled with high involvement, is anxiety-producing. This will bring personality variables to the fore.

(6) Closely related to the degree of influence that an individual has over events is the degree of responsibility he feels for the decisions he makes. Those who are expected to be responsible for the consequences of their decisions will be more inhibited in admitting criteria that are not supposed to be relevant. Insofar as responsibility is felt, there will be greater calculation of the effects of decisions, and they will be more likely to be made in terms of the events themselves than in terms of extrinsic non-logical factors.

The second set of hypotheses as to when international relations decision-making and attitudes will perform personality-oriented functions has to do with the nature of the decision.

(1) The more detailed a decision an individual is expected or required to make, the less likely is it that personality variables will have an effect. Personality-oriented needs are non-political in origin. They have their roots in early socialization or are perhaps, instinctive. The actions or attitudes that those personality factors can directly generate are, therefore, in political terms quite diffuse. They have no political content. At best they can direct a general policy one way or another; they offer little guide to specific policies.

Probably for this reason, most studies of the psychological roots of international relations have stressed rather gross distinctions—whether or not an individual's reaction was likely to be aggressive or not. More precisely, the studies have usually tried to explain the origins of war; to see under what circumstances individuals tend to choose warlike responses. But the decision to go to war is a rare one,

and it is usually the result of a large number of previous decisions in which the alternative of an aggressive response vs. a non-aggressive response was not so clear. In the specific choice situations in which individuals find themselves, there may be no one alternative that better allows expression of a psychological need. To link underlying motives with an attitude on a specific public issue—atomic testing, foreign aid, and so forth—is difficult, if not impossible. The alternatives available to an individual may be so closely delimited that personality can have little or no effect.

Though general orientation toward international affairs might be linked to non-logical influences, in the process of the translation of that general orientation into specific policy choices, such cognitive factors as information and communications structure will play a part.[8]

(2) The more ambiguous the cognitive and evaluative aspects of the decision-making situation, the more scope there is for personality variables. Insofar as the "logic of the situation" is compelling, the decision-maker will have less leeway for the play of psychological forces. Thus if the values which the decision-maker consciously considers relevant to a decision are vital ones, personality will play less of a role in determining the response to an action than if the values involved are of less importance. One need not have a high level of latent aggression to respond violently to a direct attack. The level of latent aggression may, however, play a larger role in determining the reaction to some more limited provocation.

[8] Take the example of national stereotypes. As Boulding has pointed out, these are important components of decisions in international relations. Stereotypes of other nations tend to be long-lasting and to color interpretations of a nation's acts. But while stereotypical thinking as a mode of thought (tendency to maintain rigid categories, lack of receptivity to contradictory information, fixed evaluations) can be linked to personality variables, the particular object and content of the stereotype are harder to derive from such psychological roots. For instance, the American image of Russia changed considerably between 1942 and 1948. Such change can best be traced to the activities of the Russians during that period and the changing relations of the United States and Russia. It would be hard to trace such a specific change from a largely favorable image to an unfavorable one to the psychological roots of stereotypical thinking. See Kenneth E. Boulding, "National Images and International Stereotypes," *Journal of Conflict Resolution*, III (June, 1959), pp. 120–31; and Milton Rokeach, *The Open and the Closed Mind*, New York, 1960.

This is in turn dependent upon the degree to which the ends believed relevant in the particular situation are clear and unambiguous—i.e., are known to the participant, are few in number, and/or are clearly ordered in the participant's mind. (As will be discussed below, such lack of ambiguity is not usual.) Insofar as one has such a goal or set of goals in mind, the situation itself will be more compelling. Attention will be focused on the choice situation and the effect of unrecognized influences upon the individual will be reduced—if for no other reason than that it will be harder for these influences to remain unrecognized, since their effect on lowering the maximization of the relevant values will be more obvious. This is not to imply that where the goal is unambiguous and the way to maximize it is clear, non-logical forces might not operate and be unrecognized (by distorting perceptions and the like). But their influence would tend to be less under those circumstances.

Lastly, one can point to several effects that the social structure of the decision-making situation will have upon the probability that attitudes and behaviors in relation to international affairs will serve as an outlet for non-logical pressures. Insofar as a decision is made within a group context in which the individual's decision or attitude is visible to others, the opportunity for a decision or attitude to perform personality-oriented functions will be limited. In situations of this sort, attitudes that served such functions might be unable to perform the social adjustment functions that attitudes also perform—that is, an attitude that represented an externalization of an individual's personal problems might conflict with group expectations. The literature on group pressures for conformity is too well known to be repeated here. Suffice it to say that in group situations where attitudes are not private, and even in cases where they are, there will be both internal and external pressure upon the individual to adjust his attitudes somewhat in the direction of the group.

A group context for decision-making and attitude formation will, however, act to inhibit the effects of non-logical forces only under the assumption that these non-logical forces are idiosyncratic. If, on the other hand, a large number of the members of a group are subject to similar pressures and share attitudes that perform a personality-oriented func-tion, the attitude in question will be reinforced by the group situation. Furthermore, personality-oriented attitudes may spread to those group members who do not share the personality need upon which the attitude was originally based. The perception, for instance, that a particular out-group is hostile may have as its origin a projection of internal aggressive tendencies, but it may also originate in the communi-cations about that out-group to which the individual has been exposed. If the individual is a member of a group in which the general opinion of some other group is negative, he will tend to view the other group negatively. Furthermore, if all the information he has received about the other group from the members of his own group is negative, his negative view of the out-group will be quite reasonable. If this is the case, it is possible for attitudes toward international affairs having their roots in the personality character-istics of some individuals to be generalized through-out a group all of whose members do not share those characteristics. An individual in a group containing a significant number of members with personality predispositions that lead them to take hostile views toward other groups will be more likely to take such hostile views himself (even if he does not personally share the predisposition) than will a similar individual in a group with a low rate of such personality types. In this way such social-structure variables as com-munication networks and group norms interact with personality type to affect the set of predispositions with which a group approaches international poli-tics.

What do these hypotheses as to the situations in which attitudes and behaviors are likely to be rooted in non-logical needs suggest about the extent to which understanding of such needs is relevant for the understanding of international relations? On the one hand, they do help to explain the popularity of non-logical models of decision-making in inter-national relations. Attitude formation and decision-making in relation to international affairs do meet some of the conditions that, according to the above hypotheses, would tend to maximize the impact of non-logical forces. Some international issues are ones in which there is high involvement. Attachment to national symbols has a high affective content. Furthermore, the existence in international issues of an "out-group"—the other nation—presents the individual with an object toward which aggressive feelings can be directed with the minimum of such unpleasant side-effects as the guilt that might accompany aggression toward some closer object. And, lastly, international issues are often ones of high ambiguity about which information is hard to come by.

Despite these characteristics of international relations that tend to heighten the impact of non-logical influences, the non-logical models of international decision-making offer far from adequate explanations of attitudes and behaviors toward international affairs. As we have noted, the more detailed the policy situation with which we are dealing, the less useful non-logical models of decision-making become. At best they deal with rather gross distinctions and with the type of policy decision that is rarely made—the choice between a warlike or a non-warlike response. But, most important of all, the above hypotheses suggest that attitudes and behaviors in the international sphere perform many other functions for the individual than the one of serving as an external outlet for some non-logical pressure and that these other functions may be more significant.

Furthermore, the personality-oriented functions of attitudes on international affairs are probably of small significance in terms of prediction or explanation. This is largely the case because of the forces inhibiting the extent to which international attitudes and behaviors can perform personality-oriented functions for the individual. As was suggested above, the less involved an individual is in international affairs, the more information and skills he has, the greater the extent to which he accepts rationality as a valued model of decision-making, the greater his felt responsibility and influence, and the greater the extent to which his decision is made within a structured social situation, the less likely will it be that non-logical influences will play a major role in his attitude or behavior. This in turn suggests that such non-logical pressures are more inhibited among foreign policy elites than among the mass of average citizens.[9] With the exception of the

degree of involvement, foreign policy elites are subject to more of the conditions that tend to inhibit the impact of personality-oriented pressures. They have greater knowledge, skills, responsibility, and influence; and, what may be most important, operate generally within bureaucratic social situations that tend to limit the scope of the decisions they can make and the criteria they can apply to these decisions. If one concentrates on explaining the behaviors and attitudes of foreign policy elites—and if one wants to explain the behaviors of nation-states as actors within the international system, this is the most strategic approach[10]—it is clear that non-logical explanations, while not completely irrelevant are of little use. As *the* model of international relations, the non-logical model represents a great oversimplification with little explanatory power. As *part* of a broader model of the international system, the non-logical explanation of international behavior probably does not add enough to the explanatory power of the larger model to compensate for the added complexity of incorporating such variables.

III

An alternative simplifying assumption about the processes by which individuals make decisions relevant to international affairs is an assumption of rationality. Essentially, this assumption is that the decision-maker will follow a specified set of rules in making his decisions. The particular set differs in

[9] We mean by a foreign policy elite roughly all individuals whose activities and attitudes have a perceptible effect on the course of international relations. In most cases, this refers to a small group of high government officials, and some high communications and interest group leaders. It is important to keep in mind that on the mass level any theory of the effects of personality factors on behavior must

be able to explain the modal personality in a group. Idiosyncratic variation will have no discernible effect on policy. On the elite level, as we have defined it, idiosyncratic variation might have a great effect upon policy and a study of it might prove fruitful.

[10] This is not to deny the possible impact of non-elite opinion on foreign policy. Several commentators, for instance, have described the foreign-policy formulation process in the United States as one in which mass or public opinion, dominated by mood, affective reactions, and non-logical predispositions, impedes rational decision-making by the foreign policy elite. But, insofar as non-logical factors have their greatest effect on the non-elite level, such factors can be more easily incorporated into models that assume that policy choices are based upon more rational criteria. The non-logical aspects of non-elite behavior may be considered as informational input into the elite level and a factor to be taken into account in the elite's calculations. Since one of the elite's goals will be maintenance of their position, their perception of "public opinion" may induce them to initiate policies that they might not otherwise undertake. However, in terms of the model used to explain the formation of foreign policy, it can be a rational decision-making model.

various models of rationality, but the crucial point is that the rules can be specified. These rules indicate what information the decision-maker will use and how much further information he will seek. They specify the way in which calculations will be made, and, given the set of values that the decision-maker holds, they also specify the decision that will be arrived at, or at least the parameters within which it will fall. In this way, the varied decisional situations within the international system can be reduced to more manageable proportions. No model and no theorist, no matter how committed to holistic principles, can encompass the totality of a situation. The rationality model simplifies by specifying which variables are to be considered by decision-makers. Furthermore, by specifying the rules to be used by a decision-maker, it defines his behavior by these rules. All other behaviors—other information he seeks or receives, other modes of calculation, his personality, his preconceptions, his roles external to the international system—are irrelevant to the model. This eliminates an entire set of variables that are particularly hard to deal with in a systematic manner. Furthermore it allows one to consider all decision-makers to be alike. If they follow the rules, we need know nothing more about them. In essence, if the decision-maker behaves rationally, the observer, knowing the rules of rationality, can rehearse the decisional process in his own mind and, if he knows the decision-maker's goals, can both predict the decision and understand why that particular decision was made. Knowing, then, the process by which decision-makers respond to various turns in international affairs, the observer can concentrate on the events in the international system and greatly simplify his task of observation.

But to assess the usefulness and limitations of the rationality model in the understanding of international relations it is necessary to deal with three questions: What are the rules of rationality that are used to define the decision-making process? To what extent do individuals live up to the rationality model? And insofar as they do not live up to it—that is, insofar as the actual behavior of states in concrete situations cannot be predicted and/or explained by the model—to what extent is it still a useful tool of analysis? The answer to the last question will depend upon such factors as the extent to which deviations from the model are significant

in terms of their effects on the behaviors of individuals and states and, if some of the deviations are significant, the extent to which corrections for them can be built into the model, perhaps at some later stage of analysis.

There are numerous definitions of rational behavior. These range from complete sets of rules to be followed in making decisions to more limited definitions centering around the state of psychic tension of the decision-maker (a rational decision is a cool and clearheaded decision) or specifying one aspect of the decision-making process (a rational decision-maker calculates the effects of his decisions). We will examine some of the characteristics attributed to rational decision-making and then consider the way in which such rationality models fit into models of the international system.

The most usual concept of rationality is that it is a process of means-ends analysis. The simplest case of means-ends analysis involves a single goal sought by the decision-maker. In this case, insofar as the goal is empirical (i.e., insofar as it is possible to tell if it has been attained), rational choice is the selection, among alternatives, of the action that maximizes the goal. If more than one value is relevant in the situation, it is necessary to add several steps to the model. The various values have to be listed in order of importance, and alternatives have to be compared not in terms of which maximizes one value, but in terms of which provides the best value-mix.

The means-end model, especially insofar as it specifies that one chooses the alternative that best attains one's ends, implies several other decision-making characteristics. Ideally all possible alternatives must be considered—or, if that is impossible, certainly a great number or at least all the obvious ones. Furthermore, the alternatives must be considered on their merits—that is, in terms of their contribution to the values of the decision-maker. This latter point presents some serious difficulties: if the decision-maker has a variety of goals, the alternative that would maximize the goal most relevant to the decision at hand—e.g., in a market decision, the alternative that would maximize the monetary gain—may at the same time involve great costs in terms of some other value (say, prestige or leisure) that would make it rational to reject the alternative. Since all values that may be affected by a decision are relevant to that decision, we must specify more carefully what is meant by considering an alternative on its merits. Doing so implies: (1) considering only those values that will in fact be affected by the alternative—i.e., having accurate information and making correct assessments of the outcomes—and (2) making such calculations consciously. If the individual chooses an alternative that does not maximize the goals he consciously considers to be pertinent in the situation, the decision cannot be called rational even though it maximizes others of his values which he did not consider. On the other hand—in a market situation, for instance—if an individual does not choose the alternative that maximizes monetary gain, the decision will still be rational so long as the other values relevant to the situation are consciously considered. If he refuses to drop some unprofitable activity of the family business because he believes such action would be disloyal to the memory of his father, and if the goal of loyalty is consciously invoked in the situation, the decision is rational, given his set of values. But if the relationship with family tradition is not consciously invoked and if it has effects in a situation in which it would be considered irrelevant by the decision-maker if he were aware of it, the decision will have been made on other than rational grounds. The criterion of consciousness has been added to avoid the problem of having to accept all acts as rational for which the observer or participant could, with hindsight, think of a goal that it maximized.

Thus the notion of means-ends calculations introduces the need for accurate information, correct evaluation, and consciousness of calculation. Another usual characteristic attached to this set of rational characteristics is that decisions be made coolly, with a clear head. Essentially this derives from the requirement of accurate calculations. It does not specify that the individual must avoid emotional involvement in the outcome or experience no emotion during the process of deliberation. Whether or not he does so is irrelevant as long as his calculations are not affected by his emotion. (This problem is more complex than can be gone into here, for an emotional state may change an individual's value hierarchy and thus affect his calculations. Though one can argue that emotion ought not to affect the means selected, it is more difficult to dismiss as irrational the effect of emotion on one's goals.)

The means-ends rationality model is a simplification. Individuals do not in fact make decisions in this way. However, this in itself does not make the model useless as a tool, since all theories and models involve simplification. What is necessary is to look at the nature and extent of the simplification. A growing body of theoretical and empirical work on decision-making suggests that though individuals do calculate advantages when making decisions, the method of calculation is quite different from that postulated in the means-ends rationality model.[11]

One set of reasons why the rationality model is not an adequate description of decision-making lies in human frailty. The type of calculation required by the model for anything but the simplest choices is beyond the powers of any individual, group, or presently designed individual-computer system. There may be too many significant variables, inadequate information, variables that are not easily quantifiable, or decisional methods that are not advanced enough. This raises serious problems for the use of rationality models, for to make the concept of means-ends rationality operational, some rules must be specified for judging whether or not such a decision-making technique has been used. Since the rules of means-ends rationality specify that one selects from the universe of alternatives the alternative that maximizes one's values, the objective observer, trying to decide if this approach to decision-making has been followed, would have to be able to make the same calculations that the method demands from the actual decision-maker. He would have to know the "right" decision, even if the actual decision-maker did not. If there are grossly different alternatives, one of which clearly maximizes the values believed by the decision-maker to be relevant to the situation

[11] The following discussion draws upon a variety of works dealing with rationality, including the work of Herbert Simon and James G. March and their associates on organizational decision-making (see, in particular, March and Simon, *Organizations*, New York, 1958, and Cyert and March, "A Behavioral Theory of Organizational Objectives," in Mason Haire, ed., *Modern Organization Theory*, New York, 1959); Thomas C. Schelling, "Toward a Strategy of International Conflict," The RAND Corporation, P-1648, 1959; Harold Garfinkel, "The Rational Properties of Scientific and Commonsense Activities," *Behavioral Science*, V (January, 1960), p. 72; Charles E. Lindblom, "Policy Analysis," *American Economic Review*, XLVIII (June, 1958), pp. 298–313; and Lindblom, "The Science of Muddling Through," *Public Administration Review*, XIX (Winter, 1959), pp. 79–88.

while the others do not, the invocation of the "objective scientific observer" test of rationality is meaningful. But such situations are rare. They occur most frequently when one is dealing with a group that is, from the point of view of modern Western scientific thought, "foolish"—that is, a group that makes no serious attempt to approximate the rationality model in its decision-making because of lack of commitment to such an approach. Even in these situations it is often difficult to tell if the rules of rationality are being followed, for the calculations that the objective observer must make will founder on the question of the values that are operative in the situation. Usually the assumption will have to be made that there is a single overriding goal, such as increased economic production, whereas in reality a variety of other goals may be involved. But when faced with a decision made by an individual or group as highly trained and sophisticated as he is, the outside observer is probably no more able to judge whether the resulting decision meets the criteria of rationality than are the actual decision-makers. Their frailty is his frailty too. And, as was pointed out in the previous section, the foreign policy elites will usually have high levels of information, be committed to rationality values, and so forth. Therefore, either one needs an objective observer whose wisdom and omniscience are much greater than those of the policy-maker or one has to assume that what the policy-maker selects is the best (most rational) alternative—a definition of rationality that is circular and gets us nowhere.[12]

But human frailty is perhaps the least important reason why the rationality model is inadequate to explain decision-making. Individuals fail to make decisions according to the criteria of the model not merely because they are foolish, or not well enough trained, or because they just do not try hard enough. Deviations from the model of rationality may take several other significant forms.

The first such deviation involves the value structure required for the rationality model. In order for a decision-maker to maximize a particular value or a set of values, he must be aware of his own values and be able to order them in terms of their significance to him. Such clear self-awareness is rare. This is true not merely because values conflict—because peace may conflict with prosperity or defense may conflict with deterrence—but because individuals do not have a clear set of value preferences that exist independently of the situation and can be matched against a variety of alternatives to see which gives the best value outcome. Instead, one's values depend in part upon the situation one is facing and what is attainable in that situation. One's preferences may change during a decision process. In actual policy decisions, as Lindblom points out, means and ends are not isolated from each other and handled independently. A policy choice is usually a choice of a set of means as well as a set of ends.[13]

Means-ends calculations are made more difficult by the fact that policy decisions—especially in international relations—represent collective decisions. As numerous authors have shown, if arriving at a value ordering for an individual is difficult, arriving at a joint preference ordering for a group is even more difficult, if not logically impossible. Different members will prefer different goals, and policy will often be formulated by bargaining among the members of a foreign-policy coalition. Furthermore, for any member of the foreign policy-making coalition, a particular policy decision affects both his goals in regard to the external system (i.e., what sort of foreign policy he prefers) as well as his goals in regard to the

---

[12] In terms of training, skills, values, and information, there is no reason to expect higher levels of rationality among detached observers than among decision-makers. There are, however, certain important structural characteristics of the situations in which decision-makers and detached observers operate that make it likely that the detached observer will more closely approximate the rationality model. This will be discussed below.

[13] Lindblom, "Policy Analysis" and "The Science of Muddling Through," *loc. cit.* This suggests why the rational model of economic man, though also inadequate, is not as inadequate as the rational model of political man. Though it oversimplifies economic choice situations to say that there is a single goal which is easily quantifiable and under which various alternatives can be rated one against another, nevertheless this is more closely approached in economic calculation, where the sphere of activity is essentially defined by its concentration around a set of values having to do with maximizing economic gain, than it is in political affairs, where the sphere is not defined by a set of values relevant to it but by the employment of certain means for the maximization of any or all values held by the individual or the group. This may also explain why rationality models have been used in international relations largely in connection with military problems—more specifically, in connection with the problems of nuclear deterrence. The reason may be that the relevant goals within this limited sphere are less ambiguous (deterring an attack, avoiding nuclear destruction) and easier to place in a hierarchy.

internal policy-making system (i.e., what position he wants to attain or maintain within the organization). Any policy alternative will therefore be considered in relation to a variety of goal systems that may not be consistent. It is not only that deterrence may conflict with defense, but that some members of the coalition may prefer deterrence to defense, others may prefer defense to deterrence, and others may prefer both though they conflict. And in each case the preference will be based upon both the type of foreign policy that the individual would like to see his nation follow and the effects of choosing one alternative over the other on the position he would like to attain within the foreign policy-making organization. This situation is most obvious when one considers the process of foreign policy-making in the United States, where bargaining among the various branches of the government, between government and non-governmental groups, and within the various branches of the Executive has become the normal means of reaching policy decisions.[14] But it is probable that in all decision-making systems within a bureaucratic structure (and this then applies to all modern states, democratic or non-democratic) such coalition formation is a standard part of decision-making.

One of the requirements of means-ends rationality is that a set of goals be mutually consistent. This requirement is violated both when members of the coalition have goals inconsistent with those of other members (and insofar as various members each have some influence over organization policy, the organization will have conflicting goals), and when individuals themselves have goals that are inconsistent. Under the means-ends rationality model, the only way to handle such a goal conflict is to adjust the goal structure so that it is consistent. One goal must be dropped or downgraded. In such situations, however, rearranging goals to form a consistent set is not the only mechanism of adjustment; the relationship between the conflicting goals can, for instance, be denied. This can be done by separating the goals in

one's mind either in terms of time (maximize X today and Y tomorrow) or in terms of spheres of activity (maximize X in relation to foreign policy, and Y in relation to domestic policy).[15] When decisions are made within a group bargaining situation, it becomes easier for a variety of conflicting values to coexist and form the basis of policy. Different goals can be pursued by different subgroups of the organization and in this way the conflict among them obscured. Since the rationality model cannot deal with inconsistent goal structures and since such structures are not uncommon, the model is limited in explaining much organizational decision-making.

Another weakness in the rationality model is that it makes unrealistic assumptions about the way in which information, and in particular information about alternatives, is acquired. Policy alternatives are not simply presented to the decision-maker for his selection. He must seek them, a process that is difficult and time-consuming. Studies of decision-making suggest that individuals do not consider all possible alternatives and, what is more important, make no attempt to do so. Rather they scan alternatives with persistence and simplicity biases. They seek alternatives that are as similar as possible to past choices so that experience can be used as a guide. Few alternatives are considered. In fact, the process is not one of narrowing down the range of choice by eliminating possible alternatives as time goes on. Fewer alternatives are considered at the beginning of a decision than toward the end. It is only when a particular alternative is close to being accepted as policy and its implications become clear that other alternatives will be brought up by coalition members who fear injury from the proposed decision.[16]

Lastly, the model of means-ends rationality treats each decision as if it were a separate entity. But a decision-maker cannot do so. He operates

[14] On bargaining as a process of making foreign policy, see Samuel P. Huntington, "Strategy and the Political Process," *Foreign Affairs*, XXXVIII (January, 1960), pp. 285–99; and Roger Hilsman, "The Foreign-Policy Consensus: An Interim Research Report," *Journal of Conflict Resolution*, III (December 1959), pp. 361–82. On the general subject of bargaining as a characteristic of the American political process, see Robert A. Dahl, *A Preface to Democratic Theory*, Chicago, 1956, Chap. 5.

[15] See, in this connection, Robert Abelson and M. Rosenberg, "Symbolic Psychologic: A Model of Attitudinal Cognition," *Behavioral Science*, III (January, 1958), pp. 1–13.

[16] See R. M. Cyert, W. R. Dill, and J. G. March, "The Role of Expectations in Business Decision-Making," *Administrative Science Quarterly*, III (December, 1958), pp. 307–40; Richard C. Snyder and Glenn D. Paige, "The United States Decision to Resist Aggression in Korea," *ibid.*, pp. 341–78; and John W. Gyr, "The Formal Nature of a Problem-Solving Process," *Behavioral Science*, V (January, 1960), p. 39.

within a structure in which there has been previous commitment to policy and organizational vested interests in policy. A new policy will therefore tend to be not the best of all possible policies, but a relatively small variation on a present policy; it will be, to use Lindblom's word, an "incremental" policy. The choice will often be between two alternatives—the *status quo* or some limited modification of the *status quo*. And the criterion of choice will not be: "Is it the best possible action?" but "Is it better or, at least, no worse than the present policy?"[17]

It is clear that when the decision-maker begins to search for an adequate choice rather than for the best choice—when decision-makers stop maximizing and begin "satisficing," to use Simon's term—it becomes very difficult to use the rationality model. When the operating rule was to find the best alternative, the observer, as we saw, could both predict and explain the decision that was made. There is only one best alternative. There may, however, be many adequate alternatives, and the rules of rationality do not specify how one chooses among them.

As the above description suggests, rationality models can give us only imperfect explanations and predictions of international events. Does this mean that they ought to be abandoned? Our discussion of rational decision-making should make us hesitate to do so. Like the decision-maker who accepts an adequate decision (a decision that is better, or at least no worse, than no decision), the theorist may have to accept an adequate theory (one that is better, or at least no worse, than no theory). The assumption of rationality within theories of international relations may still be a useful assumption despite the limitations mentioned above (and it will, of course, be more useful if its limitations are made explicit than if they are ignored).

Rationality models of decision-making, we have seen, would be extremely useful if only individuals behaved rationally. This suggests that the closer behavior comes to the model, and the more one is able to specify the ways in which behavior deviates from the model, the more useful the rationality model will be.

One reason for the frequent use of the rationality model in international relations theory may be that

decision-making in international relations, though it deviates from rationality, approaches it more closely than does decision-making in other areas. The earlier section of this article that dealt with non-logical models of decision-making suggested that there are numerous inhibitions on the sway of non-logical factors in international decision-making. Insofar as such non-logical factors are inhibited from affecting decision-making, the probability of decision-making that approaches the rationality model is increased. Of course, as our intervening discussion will have made clear, the absence of non-logical factors affecting a decision may make rational decision possible, but it does not imply that the decision will be made according to the rules of means-ends rationality. There are, however, several characteristics of international relations decision making which suggests that the rationality model is more appropriate for this area than for, say, domestic political decision-making.

The more generally accepted the values involved in a political decision made within a group bargaining context and the simpler their structure, the more likely the decision is to approach the rationality model. Though there are many values operative in international decision-making, the fact that the decision involves an external power, in relation to which the members of the foreign policy-making coalition all occupy the same status as citizens of the nation, increases the salience of norms associated with the individual's role within the nation rather than within the sub-system of which he is also a member. In connection with foreign policy, these norms require that an individual act to further the interest of the entire nation, not his own organization. It is true that what is best for the over-all system is often equated with what is best for the unit of which the individual is a member (whether it be General Motors or the Navy or Air Force). And the over-all goals of the system, such as "maintaining the national interest," are often little better than slogans to which it is difficult to give operational meaning or, more likely, to which it is only too easy to give many different meanings. Nevertheless the existence of these emotion-laden slogans does give the system some cohesion, in that it provides a common language in which demands can be expressed and facilitates bargaining over the specific shape of the demands. Furthermore it legitimizes appeals to serve the general

[17] Lindblom, "The Science of Muddling Through."

and not the sub-unit interest, and makes illegitimate overt invocation of sub-unit interest over the interests of the entire system. While this does not eliminate the identification of sub-unit and over-all interests, it does inhibit the extent to which the latter can be ignored in the name of the former.[18]

The salience of system norms over sub-system norms in foreign policy formation is further heightened by the existence of concrete groups and organizations in the government whose explicit function is to co-ordinate and control the bargaining process among the various members of the foreign policy coalition. These co-ordinating groups and organizations— and there probably are more of them in connection with foreign than domestic policy—may be oriented to either of two types of norm: they may be oriented to the improvement of the quality of foreign policy decisions and the furtherance of system over sub-system values, or they may be oriented to the maintenance of the bargaining process among the participants in the foreign policy formation system. If they are oriented to the former, it is clear that decision-making will tend more closely to approximate the rationality model. If oriented to the latter, their effect on the degree of rationality of the decision-making process is more ambiguous, though by facilitating communications they may also increase rationality. The extent to which the mechanisms limiting parochialism will work depends in part on the nature of the policy situation. It may be suggested that the more pressing the decision, the more these mechanisms will come into play (though, of course, decisions in an emergency are affected by decisions made before the emergency). The greater the sense of stress, the greater will be the legitimacy of the over-all norms of the system and the greater the illegitimacy of parochial norms. Furthermore, the greater the emergency, the more likely is decision-making to be

concentrated among high officials whose commitments are to the over-all system.[19] Thus it may be, paradoxically, that the model of means-ends rationality will be more closely approximated in an emergency when the time for careful deliberation is limited. Though fewer alternatives will be considered the values invoked during the decision period will tend to be fewer and more consistent, and the decision will less likely be the result of bargaining within a coalition.

The ways in which actual decision-making deviates from the means-ends rationality model suggests the importance of decision-making or, at least, decision-recommending outside of a bureaucratic context. Means-ends rationality as a process of decision-making is more closely approximated in research and in decisions that are "unattached" rather then bureaucratic.[20] The search for policy alternatives by unattached intellectuals is less inhibited by organizational coalitions. A wider range of alternatives is likely to be considered, and the values invoked are likely to be more explicit and consistent. And, because of the over-all norms of loyalty to the system, the more explicit the values operative in a particular decision situation, the more they will tend to be non-parochial. Unattached intellectual research, therefore, can introduce a higher level of means-ends rationality into foreign-policy decision-making. And in foreign policy problems, much more than in connection with most domestic problems, there is a large amount of such work being done. But one caution: it may be just because this research approaches the rationality model that it is often not translatable into actual policy. By approximating the model of means-ends rationality—by making the values to be served explicit and by calculating explicitly the possible consequences of alternative policies—this type of policy formulation is more likely to arouse opposition among members of the foreign policy coalition whose value preferences are different.

These characteristics of international relations decision-making ought not to be taken to imply that such decision-making follows the means-ends

---

[18] Writing about the role of interest groups in foreign policy, Cohen has noted that "Since most foreign policy is by nature designed to deal with large national interests rather than special group interests, then it may turn out that the motivations of interest groups, the intensity of their involvement, and the extent to which they can advance legitimate claims to share official power tend to be more circumscribed in these foreign policy situations than they would be under typical conditions of domestic policy-making." (Bernard C. Cohen, *The Political Process and Foreign Policy*, Princeton, N.J., 1957, p. 283.) Though this was written about non-governmental interest groups, it probably applies as well to organizations within the government.

[19] See Hilsman, *op. cit.*, and Snyder and Paige, *op. cit.*
[20] The term "unattached" is taken from Robert Merton, "The Role of the Intellectual in Bureaucracy," in *Social Structure and Social Theory*, Glencoe, Ill., 1957, pp. 207–24.

rationality model. Such we found earlier would be very unlikely, if not impossible. It does suggest, however, that such a model may be a not inappropriate first approximation. But it will be useful only if one does not forget that it *is* an approximation. It may be useful to consider how nations would behave if decisions were made rationally, but too heavy concentration on such decisions may lead to sterile theorizing. It is important also to begin to build into the rationality model propositions as to the ways in which decision-making will deviate from the model—the circumstances under which deviation will be maximized, the types of individuals most likely to deviate, the ways in which deviation will take place. These dimensions of deviation are of course just those aspects of decision-making that were eliminated from the rationality model in order to develop a simpler and more manageable model. But their reintroduction as extensions of the rationality model does not imply a return to the chaos of looking at "raw" decisions in terms of all their aspects. One of the major values of

the rationality model may be that it facilitates the systematic consideration of deviations from rationality. Some such deviations have been specified above in connection with our discussion of the factors that impede or enhance the impact of non-logical influences on decisions and in connection with our discussion of the differences between actual decision-making and decision-making according to the rationality model.

The rationality model is useful, but it is useful only if its limitations are appreciated. It may be convenient under certain circumstances to assume that nations make decisions as if they were following the rules of means-ends rationality. But if the simplification of the rationality model leads one to believe that an adequate model of the international system can be developed without consideration of the complex ways in which policy is formulated within the nations that are members of that system, the model will ill serve the cause of theory in international relations.

22. Policy-Making Is Politics

Roger Hilsman is among the few professional students of foreign policy who has also shouldered important policy-making responsibilities in government. The scholarly side of this rare combination included an affiliation with Princeton University, the Library of Congress, and Columbia University, where he is now Professor of Public Law and Government. The policy-making side occurred in the early 1960s when he served as Director of the Bureau of Intelligence and Research in the State Department and Assistant Secretary of State for Far Eastern Affairs. Both sides of this combination can also be seen in this excerpt from his account of his government experiences. Here Professor Hilsman makes explicit what is only implicit in the previous selections, namely, that foreign policy decision-making is rooted deeply in the political and organizational processes of a society. His focus is the United States, but his central point seems applicable to any society. [*Reprinted from Roger Hilsman*, To Move a Nation (*Garden City and New York: Doubleday and Company, Inc., 1964*), *pp. 4–13. Copyright 1964, 1967 by Roger Hilsman. Reprinted by permission of the author and Doubleday and Company, Inc.*]

Decisions

The business of Washington is making decisions that move a nation, decisions about the direction American society should go and decisions about how and where and for what purposes the awesome power—economic, political, and military—of this, the world's most powerful nation, shall be used. The decisions are about social security and medicare and labor laws and the rules for conducting business and manufacture. Or they are about moving a nation toward war or peace—a test ban treaty, intervening in Vietnam, the UN in the Congo, or Soviet nuclear missiles in Cuba. Where the power to move a nation is, there also are the great decisions.

What is decided is policy. It is policy about problems and issues that may make or break powerful interests in our society—organized labor or the medical profession or the massive interests represented by the "military-industrial complex" that President Eisenhower warned about in his farewell address. Or it is policy that will cost American lives in some foreign jungle and result either in our continued survival and success as a nation or, conceivably, in our downfall in a nuclear holocaust that takes much of the rest of the world with us. In the business of Washington, the stakes are high.

The Process of Policy-Making

The nature and importance of the business done in Washington are obvious. The process by which that business is done and the nation is moved is more obscure.

As Americans, with our flair for the mechanical and love of efficiency combined with a moralistic Puritan heritage, we would like to think not only that policy-making is a conscious and deliberate act, one of analyzing problems and systematically examining grand alternatives in all their implications, but also that the alternative chosen is aimed at achieving overarching ends that serve a high moral purpose. Evidence that there is confusion about goals or evidence that the goals themselves may be competing or mutually incompatible is disquieting, and we hear repeated calls for a renewed national purpose, for a unifying ideology with an appeal abroad that will rival Communism, or for a national strategy that will fill both functions and set the guidelines for all of policy. As Americans, we think it only reasonable that the procedures for making national decisions should be orderly, with clear lines of responsibility and authority. We assume that what we call the "decisions" of government are in fact decisions—discrete acts, with recognizable beginnings, and sharp, decisive endings. We like to think of policy as rationalized, in the economist's sense of the word, with each step leading logically and economically to the next. We want to be able to find out who makes decisions, to feel that they are the proper, official, and authorized persons, and to know that the really big decisions will be made at the top, by the President and his principal advisers in the formal assemblage of the Cabinet or the National Security Council and with the Congress exercising its full and formal powers. And we feel that the entire decision-making process ought to be a dignified, even majestic progression, with each of the participants having roles and powers so well and precisely defined that they can be held accountable for their actions by their superiors and eventually by the electorate.

The reality, of course, is quite different. Put dramatically, it could be argued that few, if any, of the decisions of government are either decisive or final. Very often policy is the sum of a congeries of separate or only vaguely related actions. On other occasions, it is an uneasy, even internally inconsistent compromise among competing goals or an incompatible mixture of alternative means for achieving a single goal. There is no systematic and comprehensive study of all the implications of the grand alternatives—nor can there be. A government does not decide to inaugurate the nuclear age, but only to try to build an atomic bomb before its enemy does. It does not make a formal decision to become a welfare state, but only to take each of a series of steps—to experiment with an income tax at some safely innocuous level like 3 per cent, to alleviate the hardship of men who have lost their jobs in a depression

with a few weeks of unemployment compensation, or to lighten the old age of industrial workers with a tentative program of social security benefits. Rather than through grand decisions on grand alternatives, policy changes seem to come through a series of slight modifications of existing policy, with the new policy emerging slowly and haltingly by small and usually tentative steps, a process of trial and error in which policy zigs and zags, reverses itself, and then moves forward in a series of incremental steps.[1] Sometimes policies are formulated and duly ratified only to be skewed to an entirely different direction and purpose by those carrying them out—or they are never carried out at all. And sometimes issues are endlessly debated with nothing at all being resolved until both the problem and the debaters disappear under the relentless pyramiding of events.

The Power of the President

One result of all this is that in spite of the great power they wield, presidents can very rarely command, even within what is supposedly their most nearly absolute domain, the Executive Branch itself. President Truman, as he contemplated turning the presidency over to Eisenhower, used to say, "He'll sit here and he'll say, 'Do this! Do that!' And nothing will happen. Poor Ike—it won't be a bit like the Army."[2]

Presidents, being human, sometimes find the system frustrating. Once at a press conference, President Kennedy surprised us all by answering a question about allied trade with Cuba with a promise to take certain measures that were still under discussion. "Well!" he said afterward with some exasperation. "Today I actually made a little policy." But mainly, presidents maneuver, persuade, and pressure—using all the levers, powers, and influences they can muster. And most presidents recognize that this is what they must do. . . .

On some occasions presidents do not succeed in getting the others to come around, and they must then

[1] See Charles E. Lindblom, "The Science of 'Muddling Through,'" *Public Administration Review*, XIX, 1959, and his book *The Intelligence of Democracy*, 1965.

[2] Richard E. Neustadt, *Presidential Power*, 1960, p. 9.

either pay the political costs of public disunity or make some concession to achieve the unity of compromise. In the Kennedy administration, for example, the State Department was convinced that high-level visits to Vietnam were politically bad. They felt, in particular, that visits by so high-ranking an official as Secretary of Defense McNamara would get United States prestige hooked too tightly to the roller coaster of events in Vietnam in spite of the fact that we had only limited influence on those events. Visits by so high-ranking an official would also tend to make a bad situation look even worse by showing our concern too openly. And, finally, such visits would tend to make a Vietnamese struggle conducted with only our aid and advice look in the world's eyes like a purely American war.

The President was only too well aware of these probable consequences, but in the circumstances, he indicated that he was prepared to pay the price. For the only way of keeping the higher-ranking military officers in the Pentagon from an increasingly public display of discontent with the President's decision not to enlarge the war was to keep the Secretary of Defense fully content with the policy. And the only way to do that, apparently, was to let him see for himself.

On some occasions, the President clearly makes the decision, even if he cannot make it exactly as he might wish. On other occasions, the decision is just as clearly made by Congress. But in action after action, responsibility for decision is as fluid and restless as quicksilver, and there seems to be neither a person nor an organization on whom it can be fixed. At times the point of decision seems to have escaped into the labyrinth of governmental machinery, beyond layers and layers of bureaucracy. Other times it seems never to have reached the government, but remained in either the wider domain of a public opinion created by the press or in the narrower domain dominated by the maneuverings of special interests.

Turmoil

Just as our desire to know who makes a decision is frustrated, so is our hope that the process of policy-making will be dignified. A decision, in fact, may be little more than a signal that starts a public brawl by people who want to reverse it. President Eisenhower's

"New Look" decision to concentrate on air power at the expense of ground forces, for example, had no visible result for the first year except semipublic fights with the Joint Chiefs of Staff, an eruption of the so-called "Colonels' revolt," and frequent leaks of top secret information. The whole strategy was completely reversed when the Kennedy administration came into responsibility in 1961, and the reversal was fought by the same technique of leaks, but this time it was Air Force rather than Army partisans doing the leaking. At the very beginning of the Kennedy administration, for example, Rusk wrote McNamara a memorandum seeking an interdepartmental discussion of the basic problem, and a distorted version of the memo was promptly given to Air Force sympathizers in the press in an obvious attempt at sabotage.

Leaks, of course, are the first and most blatant signs of battle, and they are endemic in the policy process. When it became clear, for example, that the report of the Gaither Committee, set up by Eisenhower in 1957 to study civil defense in terms of the whole of nuclear strategy, would be critical of the "New Look" and the entire Eisenhower defense policy, the crucial battle between the different factions within the administration took place, not on the substance of the report, but on the issue of whether there would be two hundred top secret copies of the report or only two. For everyone knew without saying so that if the President did not accept the Gaither Committee's recommendations, it might be possible to keep the report from leaking to the press if there were only two copies, but never if there were two hundred. The committee won the battle, and two hundred top secret copies were distributed within the Executive Branch. The President did not accept the recommendations; and, sure enough, within a few days Chalmers Roberts of the Washington *Post* was able to write a story, covering almost two newspaper pages, that contained an accurate and comprehensive version of both the top secret report and its recommendations.

Not surprisingly, it was these continual leaks that especially puzzled and angered Eisenhower. In 1955, he said, "For some two years and three months I have been plagued by inexplicable undiscovered leaks in this Government." But so are all presidents, before and after Eisenhower. Not only are there leaks of secret information, but leaks that distort secret information so as to present a special view that is often totally false. There flows out of Washington a continuous stream of rumor, tales of bickering, speculation, stories of selfish interest, charges and countercharges. Abusive rivalries arise between the government agencies engaged in making policy, and even within a single agency different factions battle, each seeking allies in other agencies, among the members of Congress, from interest associations, and among the press. Officialdom, whether civil or military, is hardly neutral. It speaks, and inevitably it speaks as an advocate. The Army battles for ground forces, the Air Force for bombers; the "Europe faction" in the State Department for policy benefiting NATO, and the "Africa faction" for anticolonialist policies unsettling to our relations with Europe. All of these many interests, organizations, and institutions—inside and outside the government—are joined in a struggle over the goals of governmental policy and over the means by which these goals shall be achieved. Instead of unity, there is conflict. Instead of a majestic progression, there are erratic zigs and zags. Instead of clarity and decisiveness, there are tangle and turmoil, instead of order, confusion.

Sources of the Turmoil

But even though we deplore the disorder and confusion, the seeming disloyalty of leaks, the noise and untidiness, and all the rest, it would be well to look more deeply into the nature of the process before condemning it.

Partly, of course, the turbulence derives from the nature of our constitution itself. As Richard E. Neustadt has pointed out, the constitutional convention of 1787 did not really create a government of "separated powers" as we have been taught, but a government of separated institutions sharing powers.[3] The Executive, for example, is clearly part of the legislative process—almost all major bills today are drafted and put forward by the Executive department concerned, and the President still has the veto. The courts, too, legislate—much to the annoyance of many congressmen, especially die-hard segregationists. And the Congress is equally involved in administration, in both its investigative function

[3] Richard E. Neustadt, *op. cit.*, p. 33.

and its appropriation of money and oversight of spending. To the head of a department or agency, the Congress, with its power to reward and punish, is as much his boss as is the President. And some agency heads can build enough power on the Hill to put themselves beyond the reach of a President even to fire them—as J. Edgar Hoover succeeded in doing with his job as director of the FBI. Different institutions sharing powers, getting involved in each others' business, provide the checks and balances sought by the founding fathers and many other benefits besides. But they also contribute to the phenomenon of turbulence.

The Multiplicity of Actors

Still another dimension is the now familiar fact that many more people are involved in the process of government than merely those who hold the duly constituted official positions. It is no accident that the press, for example, is so often called the "fourth branch of government." The press plays a role in the process of governance. It performs functions which are a necessary part of the process and which it sometimes performs well and sometimes badly.

There are also lobbies, the spokesmen of special interests of every kind and description from oil producers and farmers to the Navy League and Women Strike for Peace. Their efforts on Capitol Hill are more familiar, but the lobbies work just as hard to influence the Executive, although in different ways. In any case, they play a role in the process of governance and perform necessary functions, often for good but sometimes for evil.

And there are others who play a role. The academic world, the world of research in the universities, has an influence and participates in the process, both formally and informally. In the presidential campaigns of 1960 and 1964, for example, no candidate could be without his own team of university advisers —Kennedy and Nixon each had such a team, and so did both Johnson and Goldwater. Most of the more effective senators on Capitol Hill have academic friends, experts in the universities, whom they regularly consult. And there is a whole new set of institutions doing research of all kinds on contract with the government, organizations staffed with people who have governmental clearances for secret work but who are neither in the armed services nor the civil service—quasi-governmental organizations such as the RAND Corporation, in Santa Monica, California, the Institute of Defense Analyses, in Washington, and the Hudson Institute, just outside New York. All of these people and organizations influence policy. Although not accountable to the electorate, they have power and they are as much a part of the governmental process as the traditional legislative, judicial, and executive branches of government. There are many more people involved in making policy than those who hold official positions, in sum, and they have more subtle ways for shaping policy.

Policy Convictions

But all this is only the beginning. Among the principal findings of a British government committee appointed to study the powers of ministers was that most men find it easier to go against their own pecuniary interests than they do to go against a deep conviction on policy. As we have said, in the business of Washington, the stakes are high and the issues fundamental, both to our society and to the question of war and peace for the entire world. In such circumstances it is not surprising that passions run strong and full. It is not even surprising that men occasionally feel so deeply that they take matters into their own hands, leaking secret materials to the Congress or the press in an attempt to force the President to adopt what they are convinced is the only right path, the salvation of the nation. When in the late 1950s, for example, intelligence officials leaked secret information foreshadowing an upcoming "missile gap" to Democratic senators and sympathetic members of the press, it was not because they were disloyal, but because they were deeply convinced that the nation was in peril. They had tried and failed to convince the top levels of the Eisenhower administration of the validity of their projections, and they felt completely justified in taking matters into their own hands by going over the President's head to Congress, the press, and the public. Colonel Billy Mitchell was doing the same in the 1920s when he provoked a court-martial so he could present the case for air power to the nation at large. But none of this is new. Throughout history, the motive for such deeds —for mankind's greatest achievements, but also, unhappily, for mankind's greatest crimes—has rarely been to benefit the individual, but for the glory of something the individual thinks of as bigger than himself, for his God, his nation, or his ideology.

There is nothing in this to nullify the point that selfish interests are also involved in these decisions, and that the decisions affect such powerful interests as labor, the farmers, the medical profession, and the "military-industrial complex." But society is made up of its different parts, and it is not merely a rationalization when farmers, for example, argue that a healthy nation depends on a healthy agriculture. There is nothing wrong in the people of a democracy expressing their interests, their values hopes, and fears through "interest" organizations. How else, save through some such hierarchy of representative organizations, can the needs and desires of so many millions of people be aggregated?

Nor is there anything wrong in the fact that the bureaucracy itself is divided, that it represents special interests, and that its parts speak as advocates, fighting hard for their constituencies. The Department of Labor is inevitably and rightly more oriented toward workingmen than management; the Bureau of Mines more toward extractive industry than the industrial users of minerals; the Children's Bureau more toward restrictions on employers than permissiveness. Indeed some segments of society that are poorly organized for exercising leverage on either public opinion or the Congress would have a much smaller voice if the bureaucracy of the federal government did not represent their interests, and many of the long-range, more general interests of society as a whole have no other spokesman at all. But all this also contributes to the turbulence of the Washington scene.

Inadequacy of Knowledge

Still another dimension of the confusion and turbulence of the policy-making process is the complexity of the problems and the inadequacy of our knowledge of how and why things work in the social affairs of men, our limited capacity to foresee developments that bring problems or to predict the consequences of whatever action we do take. Partly this is because in the field of foreign affairs, especially, there are so many other people and nations involved, friends and enemies, with goals of their own and tactics of their own. But it is more than this. More and better understanding will not always or necessarily lead to sure solutions to knotty problems, but it sometimes does. If our understanding of the workings of a modern industrial economy had been better in the 1920s, the Great Depression could very probably have been avoided; and if our knowledge had been only slightly greater in the 1930s than it was, the measures to meet the Depression would probably have been more effective and quicker-acting. Winston Churchill called World War II the "unnecessary war," by which he meant that if we had better understood what Hitler and Nazism were really about and particularly their compelling dynamism leading toward war, it would have been politically possible to take the necessary preventive measures—which however hard and costly, would have been better than the horror of what actually occurred.

When knowledge is inadequate, when problems are complex, and especially when they are also new — presenting a challenge with which there has been no experience—there is in such circumstances room to spare for disagreement, conflict, and turmoil. It is not the only cause of disagreement, much less the central cause, but it is one of them. McGeorge Bundy once said that policy in Vietnam was "the most divisive issue in the Kennedy administration." He meant *inside* the administration, and he was right. And the cause of the dissension was precisely inadequate understanding and a failure of analysis. Modern guerrilla warfare, as the Communists practice it, is *internal* war, an ambiguous aggression that avoids direct and open attack violating international frontiers but combines terror, subversion, and political action with hit-and-run guerrilla raids and ambush. It is new to the Western world, and not yet fully understood. In the Kennedy administration there were those who saw it as a modified form of traditional war, but war nevertheless to be fought primarily with traditional military measures. Others saw guerrilla warfare as essentially political in nature, aimed at winning the people while terrorizing the government, and they believed that in fighting against a guerrilla insurgency military measures should be subordinated to political action. But there was simply not enough knowledge and experience with such matters to prove who was right, and the struggle within the administration became increasingly bitter.

Policy-Making Is Politics

These are some of the facets of policy-making and the decisions that move nations—separate institutions sharing powers, the press, experts, and others who influence policy without holding formal power, selfish and unselfish interest groups that exert a different kind of power, the difficulties and complexities of analysis, prediction, and judgment. These many facets help to explain the turmoil, and they flag a warning to those who would be cynical about Washington and the hurly-burly that is disquieting or even repugnant to so many. But they do not completely explain even the surface phenomena of Washington, nor is what explanation they do give completely satisfying. As Americans, we aspire to a rationalized system of government and policy-making. This implies that a nation can pursue a single set of clearly perceived and generally agreed-to goals, as a business organization is supposed to pursue profits. Yet is this realistic? Is the problem of making policy in a highly diversified mass society really one of relating the different steps in making a decision to a single set of goals or is it precisely one of choosing goals—of choosing goals not in the abstract but in the convoluted context of ongoing events, with inadequate information, incomplete knowledge and understanding, and insufficient power—and doing so, in all probability, while we are pitted against opposition both at home and abroad? If so, the making of national decisions is not a problem for the efficiency expert, or of assembling different pieces of policy logically as if the product were an automobile. Policy faces inward as much as outward, seeking to reconcile conflicting goals, to adjust aspirations to available means, and to accommodate the different advocates of these competing goals and aspirations to one another. It is here that the essence of policy-making seems to lie, in a process that is in its deepest sense political.

Recognizing the political nature of policy-making might help us to a better understanding of the diversity and seeming inconsistency of the goals that national policy must serve. It might also help us to understand the powerful but sometimes hidden forces through which these competing goals are reconciled, why the pushes and pulls of these cross-currents are sometimes dampened or obscured, and why they are sometimes so fiercely public. Even the roles of such "unrational" procedures as bargaining and power might also become more clear.

President Kennedy once said, "There will always be the dark and tangled stretches in the decision-making process—mysterious even to those who may be most intimately involved . . ."[4] Yet it is equally true that we can understand better than we now do how a nation is moved and that better understanding can lead to more effective policy and perhaps even to improvements in the policy-making process itself. . . .

[4] In his foreword to Theodor C. Sorensen's *Decision-Making in the White House*, Columbia University Press, 1963.

23. Hypotheses on Misperception*

Robert Jervis is Assistant Professor of Government at Harvard University. His analysis in this article stresses that decision-making in foreign policy involves intellectual as well as political and organizational processes. These mental calculations, however, do not necessarily conform to the dictates of logic and Professor Jervis persuasively demonstrates that a number of factors can distort the intellectual operations that undergird decision-making. If the reader has been disappointed by the implied conclusion of the previous selections that psychological studies of personality are of little value to the student of international politics, he will be pleased to find here that sociopsychological inquiries into the processes of perception have a great deal to offer. [*Reprinted from* World Politics, *XX (1968), 454–79, by permission of the author and the publisher*]

In determining how he will behave, an actor must try to predict how others will act and how their actions will affect his values. The actor must therefore develop an image of others and of their intentions. This image may, however, turn out to be an inaccurate one; the actor may, for a number of reasons, misperceive both others' actions and their intentions. In this research note I wish to discuss the types of misperceptions of other states' intentions which states tend to make. The concept of intention is complex, but here we can consider it to comprise the ways in which the state feels it will act in a wide range of future contingencies. These ways of acting usually are not specific and well-developed plans. For many reasons a national or individual actor may not know how he will act under given conditions, but this problem cannot be dealt with here.

* I am grateful to the Harvard Center for International Affairs for research support. An earlier version of this research note was presented at the International Studies Association panel of the New England Political Science Association in April 1967. I have benefited from comments by Robert Art, Alexander George, Paul Kecskemeti, Paul Leary, Thomas Schelling, James Schlesinger, Morton Schwartz, and Aaron Wildavsky.

I. Previous Treatments of Perception in International Relations

Although diplomatic historians have discussed misperception in their treatments of specific events, students of international relations have generally ignored this topic. However, two sets of scholars have applied content analysis to the documents that flowed within and between governments in the six weeks preceding World War I. But the data have been put into quantitative form in a way that does not produce accurate measures of perceptions and intentions and that makes it impossible to gather useful evidence on misperception.[1]

The second group of theorists who have explicitly dealt with general questions of misperception in international relations consists of those, like

[1] See, for example, Ole Holsti, Robert North, and Richard Brody, "Perception and Action in the 1914 Crisis," in J. David Singer, ed., *Quantitative International Politics* (New York, 1968). For a fuller discussion of the Stanford content analysis studies and the general problems of quantification, see my "The Costs of the Quantitative Study of International Relations," in Klaus Knorr and James N. Rosenau, eds., *Contending Approaches to International Politics* (Princeton, 1969).

Charles Osgood, Amitai Etzioni, and, to a lesser extent, Kenneth Boulding and J. David Singer, who have analyzed the cold war in terms of a spiral of misperception.[2] This approach grows partly out of the mathematical theories of L. F. Richardson[3] and partly out of findings of social and cognitive psychology, many of which will be discussed in this research note.

These authors state that their case in general, if not universal, terms, but do not provide many historical cases that are satisfactorily explained by their theories. Furthermore, they do not deal with any of the numerous instances that contradict their notion of the self-defeating aspects of the use of power. They ignore the fact that states are not individuals and that the findings of psychology can be applied to organizations only with great care. Most important, their theoretical analysis is for the most part of reduced value because it seems largely to be a product of their assumption that the Soviet Union is a basically status-quo power whose apparently aggressive behavior is a product of fear of the West. Yet they supply little or no evidence to support this view. Indeed, the explanation for the differences of opinion between the spiral theorists and the proponents of deterrence lies not in differing general views of international relations, differing values and morality,[4] or differing methods of analysis,[5] but in differing perceptions of Soviet intentions.

II. Theories—Necessary and Dangerous

Despite the limitations of their approach, these writers have touched on a vital problem that has not been given systematic treatment by theorists of international relations. The evidence from both psychology and history overwhelmingly supports the view (which may be labeled Hypothesis 1) that decision-makers tend to fit incoming information into their existing theories and images. Indeed, their theories and images play a large part in determining what they notice. In other words, actors tend to perceive what they expect. Furthermore (Hypothesis 1a), a theory will have greater impact on an actor's interpretation of data (a) the greater the ambiguity of the data and (b) the higher the degree of confidence with which the actor holds the theory.[6]

For many purposes we can use the concept of differing levels of perceptual thresholds to deal with the fact that it takes more, and more unambiguous, information for an actor to recognize an unexpected phenomenon than an expected one. An experiment by Bruner and Postman determined "that the recognition threshold for . . . incongruous playing cards (those with suits and color reversed) is significantly higher than the threshold for normal cards."[7] Not only are people able to identify normal (and therefore expected) cards more quickly and easily than incongruous (and therefore unexpected) ones, but also they may at first take incongruous cards for normal ones.

However, we should not assume, as the spiral theorists often do, that it is necessarily irrational for actors to adjust incoming information to fit more closely their existing beliefs and images. ("Irrational" here describes acting under pressures that the actor would not admit as legitimate if he were conscious of them.) Abelson and Rosenberg label as "psycho-logic" the pressure to create a "balanced" cognitive structure—i.e., one in which "all relations among 'good elements' [in one's attitude structure] are positive (or null), all relations among 'bad elements' are positive (or null), and all relations between good and bad elements are negative (or null)." They correctly show that the "reasoning [this

[2] See, for example, Osgood, *An Alternative to War or Surrender* (Urbana, 1962); Etzioni, *The Hard Way to Peace* (New York, 1962); Boulding, "National Images and International Systems," *Journal of Conflict Resolution*, III (June, 1959), 120–31; and Singer, *Deterrence, Arms Control, and Disarmament* (Columbus, 1962).

[3] *Statistics of Deadly Quarrels* (Pittsburgh, 1960) and *Arms and Insecurity* (Chicago, 1960). For nonmathematicians a fine summary of Richardson's work is Anatol Rapoport's "L. F. Richardson's Mathematical Theory of War," *Journal of Conflict Resolution*, I (September 1957), 249–99.

[4] See Philip Green, *Deadly Logic* (Columbus, 1966); Green, "Method and Substance in the Arms Debate," *World Politics*, XVI (July 1964), 642–67; and Robert A. Levine, "Fact and Morals in the Arms Debate," *World Politics*, XIV (January 1962), 239–58.

[5] See Anatol Rapoport, *Strategy and Conscience* (New York, 1964).

[6] Floyd Allport, *Theories of Perception and the Concept of Structure* (New York, 1955), 382; Ole Holsti, "Cognitive Dynamics and Images of the Enemy," in David Finlay, Ole Holsti, and Richard Fagen, *Enemies in Politics* (Chicago, 1967), 70.

[7] Jerome Bruner and Leo Postman, "On the Perceptions of Incongruity: A Paradigm," in Jerome Bruner and David Krech, eds., *Perception and Personality* (Durham, N.C., 1949), 210.

involves] would mortify a logician."[8] But those who have tried to apply this and similar cognitive theories to international relations have usually overlooked the fact that in many cases there are important logical links between the elements and the processes they describe which cannot be called "psycho-logic." (I am here using the term "logical" not in the narrow sense of drawing only those conclusions that follow necessarily from the premises, but rather in the sense of conforming to generally agreed-upon rules for the treating of evidence.) For example, Osgood claims that psycho-logic is displayed when the Soviets praise a man or a proposal and people in the West react by distrusting the object of this praise.[9] But if a person believes that the Russians are aggressive, it is logical for him to be suspicious of their moves. When we say that a decision-maker "dislikes" another state this usually means that he believes that that other state has policies conflicting with those of his nation. Reasoning and experience indicate to the decision-maker that the "disliked" state is apt to harm his state's interests. Thus in these cases there is no need to invoke "psycho-logic," and it cannot be claimed that the cases demonstrate the substitution of "emotional consistency for rational consistency."[10]

The question of the relations among particular beliefs and cognitions can often be seen as part of the general topic of the relation of incoming bits of information to the receivers' already established images. The need to fit data into a wider framework of beliefs, even if doing so does not seem to do justice to individual facts, is not, or at least is not only, a psychological drive that decreases the accuracy of our perceptions of the world, but is "essential to the logic of inquiry."[11] Facts can be interpreted, and indeed identified, only with the aid of hypotheses and theories. Pure empiricism is impossible, and it would be unwise to revise theories in the light of every bit of information that does not easily conform to them.[12]

No hypothesis can be expected to account for all the evidence, and if a prevailing view is supported by many theories and by a large pool of findings it should not be quickly altered. Too little rigidity can be as bad as too much.[13]

This is as true in the building of social and physical science as it is in policy-making.[14] While it is terribly difficult to know when a finding throws serious doubt on accepted theories and should be followed up and when instead it was caused by experimental mistakes or minor errors in the theory, it is clear that scientists would make no progress if they followed Thomas Huxley's injunction to "sit down before fact as a mere child, be prepared to give up every preconceived notion, follow humbly wherever nature leads, or you will learn nothing."[15]

As Michael Polanyi explains, "It is true enough that the scientist must be prepared to submit at any moment to the adverse verdict of observational evidence. But not blindly. . . . There is always the possibility that, as in [the cases of the periodic system

---

[8] Robert Abelson and Milton Rosenberg, "Symbolic Psycho-logic," *Behavioral Science*, III (January, 1958), 4–5.

[9] P. 27.

[10] *Ibid.*, 26.

[11] I have borrowed this phrase from Abraham Kaplan who uses it in a different but related context in *The Conduct of Inquiry* (San Francisco, 1964), 86.

[12] The spiral theorists are not the only ones to ignore the limits of empiricism. Roger Hilsman found that most consumers and producers of intelligence felt that intelligence should not deal with hypotheses, but should only provide the policy-makers with "all the facts" (*Strategic*

Intelligence and National Decisions [Glencoe, 1956], 46). The close interdependence between hypotheses and facts is overlooked partly because of the tendency to identify "hypotheses" with "policy preferences."

[13] Karl Deutsch interestingly discusses a related question when he argues, "Autonomy . . . requires both intake from the present and recall from memory, and selfhood can be seen in just this continuous balancing of a limited present and a limited past. . . . No further self-determination is possible if either openness or memory is lost. . . . To the extent that [systems cease to be able to take in new information], they approach the behavior of a bullet or torpedo: their future action becomes almost completely determined by their past. On the other hand, a person without memory, an organization without values or policy . . . —all these no longer steer, but drift: their behavior depends little on their past and almost wholly on their present. Driftwood and the bullet are thus each the epitome of another kind of loss of self-control . . ." (*Nationalism and Social Communication* [Cambridge, Mass., 1954], 167–68). Also see Deutsch's *The Nerves of Government* (New York, 1963), 98–109, 200–56. A physicist makes a similar argument: "It is clear that if one is too attached to one's preconceived model, one will miss all radical discoveries. It is amazing to what degree one may fail to register mentally an observation which does not fit the initial image. . . . On the other hand, if one is too open-minded and pursues every hitherto unknown phenomenon, one is almost certain to lose oneself in trivia" (Martin Deutsch, "Evidence and Inference in Nuclear Research," in Daniel Lerner, ed., *Evidence and Inference* [Glencoe, 1958], 102).

[14] Raymond Bauer, "Problems of Perception and the Relations Between the U.S. and the Soviet Union," *Journal of Conflict Resolution*, V (September 1961), 223–29.

[15] Quoted in W. I. B. Beveridge, *The Art of Scientific Investigation*, 3rd ed. (London, 1957), 50.

of elements and the quantum theory of light], a deviation may not affect the essential correctness of a proposition. . . . The process of explaining away deviations is in fact quite indispensable to the daily routine of research," even though this may lead to the missing of a great discovery.[16] For example, in 1795, the astronomer Lalande did not follow up observations that contradicted the prevailing hypotheses and could have led him to discover the planet Neptune.[17]

Yet we should not be too quick to condemn such behavior. As Thomas Kuhn has noted, "There is no such thing as research without counter-instances."[18] If a set of basic theories—what Kuhn calls a paradigm—has been able to account for a mass of data, it should not be lightly trifled with. As Kuhn puts it: "Lifelong resistance, particularly from those whose productive careers have committed them to an older tradition of normal science [i.e., science within the accepted paradigm], is not a violation of scientific standards but an index to the nature of scientific research itself. The source of resistance is the assurance that the older paradigm will ultimately solve all its problems, that nature can be shoved into the box the paradigm provides. Inevitably, at times of revolution, that assurance seems stubborn and pig-headed as indeed it sometimes becomes. But it is also something more. That same assurance is what makes normal science or puzzle-solving science possible."[19]

Thus it is important to see that the dilemma of how "open" to be to new information is one that inevitably plagues any attempt at understanding in any field. Instances in which evidence seems to be ignored or twisted to fit the existing theory can often be explained by this dilemma instead of by illogical or nonlogical psychological pressures toward consistency. This is especially true of decision-makers' attempts to estimate the intentions of other states, since they must constantly take account of the danger that the other state is trying to deceive them.

The theoretical framework discussed thus far, together with an examination of many cases, suggests Hypothesis 2: scholars and decision-makers are apt to err by being too wedded to the established view and too closed to new information, as opposed to being too willing to alter their theories.[20] Another way of making this point is to argue that actors tend to establish their theories and expectations prematurely. In politics, of course, this is often necessary because of the need for action. But experimental evidence indicates that the same tendency also occurs on the unconscious level. Bruner and Postman found that "perhaps the greatest single barrier to the recognition of incongruous stimuli is the tendency for perceptual hypotheses to fixate after receiving a minimum of confirmation. . . . Once there had occurred in these cases a partial confirmation of the hypothesis . . . it seemed that nothing could change the subject's report."[21]

---

[16] *Science, Faith, and Society* (Chicago, 1964), 31. For a further discussion of this problem, see *ibid.*, 16, 26–41, 90–94; Polanyi, *Personal Knowledge* (London, 1958), 8–15, 30, 143–68, 269–98, 310–11; Thomas Kuhn, *The Structure of Scientific Revolution* (Chicago, 1964); Kuhn, "The Function of Dogma in Scientific Research," in A. C. Crombie, ed., *Scientific Change* (New York, 1963), 344–69; the comments on Kuhn's paper by Hall, Polanyi, and Toulmin, and Kuhn's reply, *ibid.*, 370–95. For a related discussion of these points from a different perspective, see Norman Storer, *The Social System of Science* (New York, 1960), 116–22.

[17] "He found that the position of one star relative to others . . . had shifted. Lalande was a good astronomer and knew that such a shift was unreasonable. He crossed out his first observation, put a question mark next to the second observation, and let the matter go" (Jerome Bruner, Jacqueline Goodnow, and George Austin, *A Study of Thinking* [New York, 1962], 105).

[18] *The Structure of Scientific Revolution*, 79.

[19] *Ibid.*, 150–51.

[20] Requirements of effective political leadership may lead decision-makers to voice fewer doubts than they have about existing policies and images, but this constraint can only partially explain this phenomenon. Similar calculations of political strategy may contribute to several of the hypotheses discussed below.

[21] P. 221. Similarly, in experiments dealing with his subjects' perception of other people, Charles Dailey found that "premature judgment appears to make new data harder to assimilate than when the observer withholds judgment until all data are seen. It seems probable . . . that the observer mistakes his own inferences for facts" ("The Effects of Premature Conclusion Upon the Acquisition of Understanding of a Person," *Journal of Psychology*, XXX [January 1952], 149–50). For other theory and evidence on this point, see Bruner, "On Perceptual Readiness," *Psychological Review*, LXIV (March 1957), 123–52; Gerald Davidson, "The Negative Effects of Early Exposure to Suboptimal Visual Stimuli," *Journal of Personality*, XXXII (June 1964), 278–95; Albert Myers, "An Experimental Analysis of a Tactical Blunder," *Journal of Abnormal and Social Psychology*, LXIX (November 1964), 493–98; and Dale Wyatt and Donald Campbell, "On the Liability of Stereotype or Hypothesis," *Journal of Abnormal and Social Psychology*, XLIV (October 1950), 496–500. It should be noted that this tendency makes "incremental" decision-making more likely (David Braybrooke and

However, when we apply these and other findings to politics and discuss kinds of misperception, we should not quickly apply the label of cognitive distortion. We should proceed cautiously for two related reasons. The first is that the evidence available to decision-makers almost always permits several interpretations. It should be noted that there are cases of visual perception in which different stimuli can produce exactly the same pattern on an observer's retina. Thus, for an observer using one eye the same pattern would be produced by a sphere the size of a golf ball which was quite close to the observer, by a baseball-sized sphere that was further away, or by a basketball-sized sphere still further away. Without other clues, the observer cannot possibly determine which of these stimuli he is presented with, and we would not want to call his incorrect perceptions examples of distortion. Such cases, relatively rare in visual perception, are frequent in international relations. The evidence available to decision-makers is almost always very ambiguous since accurate clues to others' intentions are surrounded by noise[22] and deception. In most cases, no matter how long, deeply, and "objectively" the evidence is analyzed, people can differ in their interpretations, and there are no general rules to indicate who is correct.

The second reason to avoid the label of cognitive distortion is that the distinction between perception and judgment, obscure enough in individual psychology, is almost absent in the making of inferences in international politics. Decision-makers who reject information that contradicts their views—or who develop complex interpretations of it—often do so consciously and explicitly. Since the evidence available contains contradictory information, to make any inferences requires that much information be ignored or given interpretations that will seem tortuous to those who hold a different position.

Indeed, if we consider only the evidence available to a decision-maker at the time of decision, the view later proved incorrect may be supported by as much evidence as the correct one—or even by more. Scholars have often been too unsympathetic with the people who were proved wrong. On closer examination, it is frequently difficult to point to

differences between those who were right and those who were wrong with respect to their openness to new information and willingness to modify their views. Winston Churchill, for example, did not open-mindedly view each Nazi action to see if the explanations provided by the appeasers accounted for the data better than his own beliefs. Instead, like Chamberlain, he fitted each bit of ambiguous information into his own hypotheses. That he was correct should not lead us to overlook the fact that his methods of analysis and use of theory to produce cognitive consistency did not basically differ from those of the appeasers.[23]

A consideration of the importance of expectations in influencing perception also indicates that the widespread belief in the prevalence of "wishful thinking" may be incorrect, or at least may be based on inadequate data. The psychological literature on the interaction between affect and perception is immense and cannot be treated here, but it should be noted that phenomena that at first were considered strong evidence for the impact of affect on perception often can be better treated as demonstrating the influence of expectations.[24] Thus, in international relations, cases like the United States' misestimation of the political climate in Cuba in April 1961, which may seem at first glance to have been instances of

Charles Lindblom, *A Strategy of Decision* [New York, 1963]), but the results of this process may lead the actor further from his goals.

[22] For a use of this concept in political communication, see Roberta Wohlstetter, *Pearl Harbor* (Stanford, 1962).

[23] Similarly, Robert Coulondre, the French ambassador to Berlin in 1939, was one of the few diplomats to appreciate the Nazi threat. Partly because of his earlier service in the USSR, "he was painfully sensitive to the threat of a Berlin-Moscow agreement. He noted with foreboding that Hitler had not attacked Russia in his *Reichstag* address of April 28. . . . So it went all spring and summer, the ambassador relaying each new evidence of the impending diplomatic revolution and adding to his admonitions his pleas for decisive counteraction" (Franklin Ford and Carl Schorske, "The Voice in the Wilderness: Robert Coulondre," in Gordon Craig and Felix Gilbert, eds., *The Diplomats*, Vol. III [New York, 1963], 573–74). His hypotheses were correct, but it is difficult to detect differences between the way he and those ambassadors who were incorrect, like Neville Henderson, selectively noted and interpreted information. However, to the extent that the fear of war influenced the appeasers' perceptions of Hitler's intentions, the appeasers' views did have an element of psycho-logic that was not present in their opponents' position.

[24] See, for example, Donald Campbell, "Systematic Error on the Part of Human Links in Communications Systems," *Information and Control*, I (1958), 346–50; and Leo Postman, "The Experimental Analysis of Motivational Factors in Perception," in Judson S. Brown, ed., *Current Theory and Research in Motivation* (Lincoln, Neb., 1953), 59–108.

wishful thinking, may instead be more adequately explained by the theories held by the decision-makers (e.g., Communist governments are unpopular). Of course, desires may have an impact on perception by influencing expectations, but since so many other factors affect expectations, the net influence of desires may not be great.

There is evidence from both psychology[25] and international relations that when expectations and desires clash, expectations seem to be more important. The United States would like to believe that . . . the U.S.S.R. is ready to give up what the United States believes is its goal of world domination, but ambiguous evidence is seen to confirm the opposite conclusion, which conforms to the United States' expectations. Actors are apt to be especially sensitive to evidence of grave danger if they think they can take action to protect themselves against the menace once it has been detected.

III. Safeguards

Can anything then be said to scholars and decision-makers other than "Avoid being either too open or too closed, but be especially aware of the latter danger"? Although decision-makers will always be faced with ambiguous and confusing evidence and will be forced to make inferences about others which will often be inaccurate, a number of safeguards may be suggested which could enable them to minimize their errors. First, and most obvious, decision-makers should be aware that they do not make "unbiased" interpretations of each new bit of incoming information, but rather are inevitably heavily influenced by the theories they expect to be verified. They should know that what may appear to them as a self-evident and unambiguous inference often seems so only because of their preexisting beliefs. To someone with a different theory the same data may appear to be unimportant or to support another explanation. Thus many events provide less independent support for the decision-makers' images than they may at first realize. Knowledge of this should lead decision-makers to examine more closely evidence that others believe contradicts their views.

Second, decision-makers should see if their attitudes contain consistent or supporting beliefs that are not logically linked. These may be examples of true psycho-logic. While it is not logically surprising nor is it evidence of psychological pressures to find that people who believe that Russia is aggressive are very suspicious of any Soviet move, other kinds of consistency are more suspect. For example . . . in Finland in the winter of 1939, those who felt that grave consequences would follow Finnish agreement to give Russia a military base also believed that the Soviets would withdraw their demand if Finland stood firm. And those who felt that concessions would not lead to loss of major values also believed that Russia would fight if need be.[26] In this country, those who favored a nuclear test ban tended to argue that fallout was very harmful, that only limited improvements in technology would flow from further testing, and that a test ban would increase the chances for peace and security. Those who opposed the test ban were apt to disagree on all three points. This does not mean, of course, that the people holding such sets of supporting views were necessarily wrong in any one element. The Finns who wanted to make concessions to the USSR were probably correct in both parts of their argument. But decision-makers should be suspicious if they hold a position in which elements that are not logically connected support the same conclusion. This condition is psychologically comfortable and makes decisions easier to reach (since competing values do not have to be balanced off against each other). The chances are thus considerable that at least part of the reason why a person holds some of these views is related to psychology and not to the substance of the evidence.

Decision-makers should also be aware that actors who suddenly find themselves having an important shared interest with other actors have a tendency to overestimate the degree of common interest involved. This tendency is especially strong for those actors (e.g., the United States, at least before 1950) whose beliefs about international relations and morality imply that they can cooperate only with "good" states and that with those states there will be no major conflicts. On the other hand, states that have either a tradition of limited cooperation with others (e.g., Britain) or a strongly held

[25] Dale Wyatt and Donald Campbell, "A Study of Interviewer Bias as Related to Interviewer's Expectations and Own Opinions," *International Journal of Opinion and Attitude Research*, IV (Spring 1950), 77–83.

[26] Max Jacobson, *The Diplomacy of the Winter War* (Cambridge, Mass., 1961), 136–39.

theory that differentiates occasional from permanent allies[27] (e.g., the Soviet Union) find it easier to resist this tendency and need not devote special efforts to combating its danger.

A third safeguard for decision-makers would be to make their assumptions, beliefs, and the predictions that follow from them as explicit as possible. An actor should try to determine, before events occur, what evidence would count for and against his theories. By knowing what to expect he would know what to be surprised by, and surprise could indicate to that actor that his beliefs needed reevaluation.[28]

A fourth safeguard is more complex. The decision-maker should try to prevent individuals and organizations from letting their main task, political future, and identity become tied to specific theories and images of other actors.[29] If this occurs, subgoals originally sought for their contribution to higher ends will take on value of their own, and information indicating possible alternative routes to the original goals will not be carefully considered. For example, the U.S. Forest Service was unable to carry out its original purpose as effectively when it began to see its distinctive competence not in promoting the best use of lands and forests but rather in preventing all types of forest fires.[30]

Organizations that claim to be unbiased may not realize the extent to which their definition of their role has become involved with certain beliefs about the world. Allen Dulles is a victim of this lack of understanding when he says, "I grant that we are all creatures of prejudice, including CIA officials, but by entrusting intelligence coordination to our central intelligence service, which is excluded from policy-making and is married to no particular military hardware, we can avoid, to the greatest possible extent, the bending of facts obtained through intelligence to suit a particular occupational viewpoint."[31] This statement overlooks the fact that the CIA has developed a certain view of international relations and of the cold war which maximizes the importance of its information-gathering, espionage, and subversive activities. Since the CIA would lose its unique place in the government if it were decided that the "back alleys" of world politics were no longer vital to U.S. security, it is not surprising that the organization interprets information in a way that stresses the continued need for its techniques.

Fifth, decision-makers should realize the validity and implications of Roberta Wohlstetter's argument that "a willingness to play with material from different angles and in the context of unpopular as well as popular hypotheses is an essential ingredient of a good detective, whether the end is the solution of a crime or an intelligence estimate."[32] However, it is often difficult, psychologically and politically, for any one person to do this. Since a decision-maker usually cannot get "unbiased" treatments of data, he should instead seek to structure conflicting biases into the decision-making process. The decision-maker, in other words, should have devil's advocates around. Just as, as Neustadt points out,[33] the decision-maker will want to create conflicts among his subordinates in order to make appropriate choices, so he will also want to ensure that incoming information is examined from many different perspectives with many different hypotheses in mind. To some extent this kind of examination will be done automatically through the divergence of goals, training, experience, and information that exists in any large organization. But in many cases this divergence will not be sufficient. The views of those analyzing the data will still be too homogeneous and the decision-maker will have to go out of his way not only to cultivate but to create differing viewpoints.

While all that would be needed would be to have some people examining the data trying to validate unpopular hypotheses, it would probably be

[27] Raymond Aron, *Peace and War* (Garden City, 1966), 29.

[28] Cf. Kuhn, *The Structure of Scientific Revolution*, 65. A fairly high degree of knowledge is needed before one can state precise expectations. One indication of the lack of international relations theory is that most of us are not sure what "naturally" flows from our theories and what constitutes either "puzzles" to be further explored with the paradigm or "anomalies" that cast doubt on the basic theories.

[29] See Philip Selznick, *Leadership in Administration* (Evanston, 1957).

[30] Ashley Schiff, *Fire and Water: Scientific Heresy in the Forest Service* (Cambridge, Mass., 1962). Despite its title, this book is a fascinating and valuable study.

[31] *The Craft of Intelligence* (New York, 1963), 53.

[32] P. 302. See Beveridge, 93, for a discussion of the idea that the scientist should keep in mind as many hypotheses as possible when conducting and analyzing experiments.

[33] *Presidential Power* (New York, 1960).

more effective if they actually believed and had a stake in the views they were trying to support. If in 1941 someone had had the task of proving the view that Japan would attack Pearl Harbor, the government might have been less surprised by the attack. And only a person who was out to show that Russia would take objectively great risks would have been apt to note that several ships with especially large hatches going to Cuba were riding high in the water, indicating the presence of a bulky but light cargo that was not likely to be anything other than strategic missiles. . . .

Of course all these safeguards involve costs. They would divert resources from other tasks and would increase internal dissension. Determining whether these costs would be worth the gains would depend on a detailed analysis of how the suggested safeguards might be implemented. Even if they were adopted by a government, of course, they would not eliminate the chance of misperception. However, the safeguards would make it more likely that national decision-makers would make conscious choices about the way data were interpreted rather than merely assuming that they can be seen in only one way and can mean only one thing. Statesmen would thus be reminded of alternative images of others just as they are constantly reminded of alternative policies.

These safeguards are partly based on Hypothesis 3: actors can more easily assimilate into their established image of another actor information contradicting that image if the information is transmitted and considered bit by bit than if it comes all at once. In the former case, each piece of discrepant data can be coped with as it arrives and each of the conflicts with the prevailing view will be small enough to go unnoticed, to be dismissed as unimportant, or to necessitate at most a slight modification of the image (e.g., addition of exceptions to the rule). When the information arrives in a block, the contradiction between it and the prevailing view is apt to be much clearer and the probability of major cognitive reorganization will be higher.

IV. Sources of Concepts

An actor's perceptual thresholds—and thus the images that ambiguous information is apt to produce—are influenced by what he has experienced and learned about.[34] If one actor is to perceive that another fits in a given category he must first have, or develop, a concept for that category. We can usefully distinguish three levels at which a concept can be present or absent. First, the concept can be completely missing. The actor's cognitive structure may not include anything corresponding to the phenomenon he is encountering. This situation can occur not only in science fiction, but also in a world of rapid change or in the meeting of two dissimilar systems. Thus China's image of the Western world was extremely inaccurate in the mid-nineteenth century, her learning was very slow, and her responses were woefully inadequate. The West was spared a similar struggle only because it had the power to reshape the system it encountered. Once the actor clearly sees one instance of the new phenomenon, he is apt to recognize it much more quickly in the future.[35] Second, the actor can know about a concept but not believe that it reflects an actual phenomenon. Thus Communist and Western decision-makers are each aware of the other's explanation of how his system functions, but do not think that the concept corresponds to reality. Communist elites, furthermore, deny that anything *could* correspond to the democracies' description of themselves. Third, the actor may hold a concept, but not believe that another actor fills it at the present moment. Thus the British and French statesmen of the 1930's held a concept of states with unlimited ambitions. They

[34] Most psychologists argue that this influence also holds for perception of shapes. For data showing that people in different societies differ in respect to their predisposition to experience certain optical illusions and for a convincing argument that this difference can be explained by the societies' different physical environments, which have led their people to develop different patterns of drawing inferences from ambiguous visual cues, see Marshall Segall, Donald Campbell, and Melville Herskovits, *The Influence of Culture on Visual Perceptions* (Indianapolis, 1966).

[35] Thus when Bruner and Postman's subjects first were presented with incongruous playing cards (i.e., cards in which symbols and colors of the suits were not matching, producing red spades or black diamonds), long exposure times were necessary for correct identification. But once a subject correctly perceived the card and added this type of card to his repertoire of categories, he was able to identify other incongruous cards much more quickly. For an analogous example—in this case, changes in the analysis of aerial reconnaissance photographs of an enemy's secret weapons-testing facilities produced by the belief that a previously unknown object may be present—see David Irving, *The Mare's Nest* (Boston, 1964), 66–67, 274–75.

realized that Napoleons were possible, but they did not think Hitler belonged in that category. Hypothesis 4 distinguishes these three cases: misperception is most difficult to correct in the case of a missing concept and least difficult to correct in the case of a recognized but presumably unfilled concept. All other things being equal (e.g., the degree to which the concept is central to the actor's cognitive structure), the first case requires more cognitive reorganization than does the second, and the second requires more reorganization than the third.

However, this hypothesis does not mean that learning will necessarily be slowest in the first case, for if the phenomena are totally new the actor may make such grossly inappropriate responses that he will quickly acquire information clearly indicating that he is faced with something he does not understand. And the sooner the actor realizes that things are not—or may not be—what they seem, the sooner he is apt to correct his image.[36]

Three main sources contribute to decision-makers' concepts of international relations and of other states and influence the level of their perceptual thresholds for various phenomena. First, an actor's beliefs about his own domestic political system are apt to be important. In some cases, like that of the U.S.S.R., the decision-makers' concepts are tied to an ideology that explicitly provides a frame of reference for viewing foreign affairs. Even where this is not the case, experience with his own system will partly determine what the actor is familiar with and what he is apt to perceive in others. Louis Hartz claims, "It is the absence of the experience of social revolution which is at the heart of the whole American dilemma. . . . In a whole series of specific ways it enters into our difficulty of communication with the rest of the world. We find it difficult to understand Europe's 'social question'. . . . We are not familiar with the deeper social struggles of Asia and hence tend to interpret even reactionary regimes as 'democractic.'"[37] Similarly, George Kennan argues that in World War I the Allied powers, and especially America, could not understand the bitterness and violence of others' internal conflicts: ". . . The inability of the Allied statesmen to picture to themselves the passions of the Russian civil war [was

partly caused by the fact that] we represent . . . a society in which the manifestations of evil have been carefully buried and sublimated in the social behavior of people, as in their very consciousness. For this reason, probably, despite our widely traveled and outwardly cosmopolitan lives, the mainsprings of political behavior in such a country as Russia tend to remain concealed from our vision."[38]

Second, concepts will be supplied by the actor's previous experiences. An experiment from another field illustrates this. Dearborn and Simon presented business executives from various divisions (e.g., sales, accounting, production) with the same hypothetical data and asked them for an analysis and recommendations from the standpoint of what would be best for the company as a whole. The executives' views heavily reflected their departmental perspectives.[39] William W. Kaufmann shows how the perceptions of Ambassador Joseph Kennedy were affected by his past: "As befitted a former chairman of the Securities Exchange and Maritime Commissions, his primary interest lay in economic matters. . . . The revolutionary character of the Nazi regime was not a phenomenon that he could easily grasp. . . . It was far simpler, and more in accord with his own premises, to explain German aggressiveness in economic terms. The Third Reich was dissatisfied, authoritarian, and expansive largely because her economy was unsound."[40] Similarly it has been argued that Chamberlain was slow to recognize Hitler's intentions partly because of the limiting nature of his personal background and business experiences.[41]

[36] Bruner and Postman, 220.

[37] *The Liberal Tradition in America* (New York, 1955), 306.

[38] *Russia and the West Under Lenin and Stalin* (New York, 1962), 142–43.

[39] DeWitt Dearborn and Herbert Simon, "Selective Perception: A Note on the Departmental Identification of Executives," *Sociometry*, XXI (June, 1958), 140–44.

[40] "Two American Ambassadors: Bullitt and Kennedy," in Craig and Gilbert, 358–59.

[41] Hugh Trevor-Roper puts this point well: "Brought up as a business man, successful in municipal politics, [Chamberlain's] outlook was entirely parochial. Educated Conservative aristocrats like Churchill, Eden, and Cranborne, whose families had long been used to political responsibility, had seen revolution and revolutionary leaders before, in their own history, and understood them correctly; but the Chamberlains, who had run from radical imperialism to timid conservatism in a generation of life in Birmingham, had no such understanding of history or the world: to them the scope of human politics was limited by their own parochial horizons, and Neville Chamberlain could not believe that Hitler was fundamentally different from himself. If Chamberlain wanted peace, so must Hitler"

The impact of training and experience seems to be demonstrated when the background of the appeasers is compared to that of their opponents. One difference stands out: "A substantially higher percentage of the anti-appeasers (irrespective of class origins) had the kind of knowledge which comes from close acquaintance, mainly professional, with foreign affairs."[42] Since members of the diplomatic corps are responsible for meeting threats to the nation's security before these grow to major proportions and since they have learned about cases in which aggressive states were not recognized as such until very late, they may be prone to interpret ambiguous data as showing that others are aggressive. It should be stressed that we cannot say that the professionals of the 1930's were more apt to make accurate judgments of other states. Rather, they may have been more sensitive to the chance that others were aggressive. They would then rarely take an aggressor for a status-quo power, but would more often make the opposite error.[43] Thus in the years before World War I the permanent

officials in the British Foreign Office overestimated German aggressiveness.[44]

A parallel demonstration in psychology of the impact of training on perception is presented by an experiment in which ambiguous pictures were shown to both advanced and beginning police-administration students. The advanced group perceived more violence in the pictures than did the beginners. The probable explanation is that "the law enforcer may come to accept crime as a familiar personal experience, one which he himself is not surprised to encounter. The acceptance of crime as a familiar experience in turn increases the ability or readiness to perceive violence where clues to it are potentially available."[45] This experiment lends weight to the view that the British diplomats' sensitivity to aggressive states was not totally a product of personnel selection procedures.

A third source of concepts, which frequently will be the most directly relevant to a decision-maker's perception of international relations, is international history. As Henry Kissinger points out, one reason why statesmen were so slow to recognize the threat posed by Napoleon was that previous events had accustomed them only to actors who wanted to modify the existing system, not overthrow it.[46] The other side of the coin is even more striking: historical traumas can heavily influence future perceptions. They can either establish a state's image of the other state involved or can be used as analogies. An example of the former case is provided by the fact that for at least ten years after the Franco-Prussian War most

("Munich—Its Lessons Ten Years Later," in Francis Loewenheim, ed., *Peace or Appeasement?* [Boston, 1965], 152–53). For a similar view see A. L. Rowse, *Appeasement* (New York, 1963), 117.

But Donald Lammers points out that the views of many prominent British public figures in the 1930's do not fit this generalization (*Explaining Munich* [Stanford, 1966], 13–140). Furthermore, arguments that stress the importance of the experiences and views of the actors' ancestors do not explain the links by which these influence the actors themselves. Presumably Churchill and Chamberlain read the same history books in school and had the same basic information about Britain's past role in the world. Thus what has to be demonstrated is that in their homes aristocrats like Churchill learned different things about politics and human nature than did middle-class people like Chamberlain and that these experiences had a significant impact. Alternatively, it could be argued that the patterns of child-rearing prevalent among the aristocracy influenced the children's personalities in a way that made them more likely to see others as aggressive.

[42] *Ibid.*, 15.

[43] During a debate on appeasement in the House of Commons, Harold Nicolson declared, "I know that those of us who believe in the traditions of our policy, . . . who believe that one great function of this country is to maintain moral standards in Europe, to maintain a settled pattern of international relations, not to make friends with people who are demonstrably evil . . . —I know that those who hold such beliefs are accused of possessing the Foreign Office mind. I thank God that I possess the Foreign Office mind" (quoted in Martin Gilbert, *The Roots of Appeasement* [New York, 1966], 187). But the qualities Nicolson mentions and applauds may be related to a more basic attribute of "the Foreign Office mind"—suspiciousness.

[44] George Monger, *The End of Isolation* (London, 1963). I am also indebted to Frederick Collignon for his unpublished manuscript and several conversations on this point.

[45] Hans Toch and Richard Schulte, "Readiness to Perceive Violence as a Result of Police Training," *British Journal of Psychology*, LII (November, 1961), 392 (original italics omitted). It should be stressed that one cannot say whether or not the advanced police students perceived the pictures "accurately." The point is that their training predisposed them to see violence in ambiguous situations. Whether on balance they would make fewer perceptual errors and better decisions is very hard to determine. For an experiment showing that training can lead people to "recognize" an expected stimulus even when that stimulus is in fact not shown, see Israel Goldiamond and William F. Hawkins, "Vexierversuch: The Log Relationship Between Word-Frequency and Recognition Obtained in the Absence of Stimulus Words," *Journal of Experimental Psychology*, LVI (December, 1958), 457–63.

[46] *A World Restored* (New York, 1964), 2–3.

of Europe's statesmen felt that Bismarck had aggressive plans when in fact his main goal was to protect the status quo. Of course the evidence was ambiguous. The post-1871 Bismarckian maneuvers, which were designed to keep peace, looked not unlike the pre-1871 maneuvers designed to set the stage for war. But that the post-1871 maneuvers were seen as indicating aggressive plans is largely attributable to the impact of Bismarck's earlier actions on the statesmen's image of him.

A state's previous unfortunate experience with a type of danger can sensitize it to other examples of that danger. While this sensitivity may lead the state to avoid the mistake it committed in the past, it may also lead it mistakenly to believe that the present situation is like the past one. Santayana's maxim could be turned around: "Those who remember the past are condemned to make the opposite mistakes." As Paul Kecskemeti shows, both defenders and critics of the unconditional surrender plan of World War II thought in terms of the conditions of World War I.[47] Annette Baker Fox found that the Scandinavian countries' neutrality policies in World War II were strongly influenced by their experiences in the previous war, even though vital aspects of the two situations were different. Thus "Norway's success [during World War I] in remaining non-belligerent though pro-Allied gave the Norwegians confidence that their country could again stay out of war."[48] And the lesson drawn from the unfortunate results of this policy was an important factor in Norway's decision to join NATO.

The application of the Munich analogy to various contemporary events has been much commented on, and I do not wish to argue the substantive points at stake. But it seems clear that the probabilities that any state is facing an aggressor who has to be met by force are not altered by the career of Hitler and the history of the 1930's. Similarly the probability of an aggressor's announcing his plans is not increased (if anything, it is decreased) by the fact that Hitler wrote *Mein Kampf*. Yet decision-makers are more sensitive to these possibilities, and thus more apt to perceive ambiguous evidence as indicating they apply to a given case, than they would have been had there been no Nazi Germany.

Historical analogies often precede, rather than

follow, a careful analysis of a situation (e.g., Truman's initial reaction to the news of the invasion of South Korea was to think of the Japanese invasion of Manchuria). Noting this precedence, however, does not show us which of many analogies will come to a decision-maker's mind. Truman could have thought of nineteenth-century European wars that were of no interest to the United States. Several factors having nothing to do with the event under consideration influence what analogies a decision-maker is apt to make. One factor is the number of cases similar to the analogy with which the decision-maker is familiar. Another is the importance of the past event to the political system of which the decision-maker is a part. The more times such an event occurred and the greater its consequences were, the more a decision-maker will be sensitive to the particular danger involved and the more he will be apt to see ambiguous stimuli as indicating another instance of this kind of event. A third factor is the degree of the decision-maker's personal involvement in the past case—in time, energy, ego, and position. The last-mentioned variable will affect not only the event's impact on the decision-maker's cognitive structure, but also the way he perceives the event and the lesson he draws. Someone who was involved in getting troops into South Korea after the attack will remember the Korean War differently from someone who was involved in considering the possible use of nuclear weapons or in deciding what messages should be sent to the Chinese. Greater personal involvement will usually give the event greater impact, especially if the decision-maker's own views were validated by the event. One need not accept a total application of learning theory to nations to believe that "nothing fails like success."[49] It also seems likely that if many critics argued at the time that the decision-maker was wrong, he will be even more apt to see other situations in terms of the original event. For example, because Anthony Eden left the government on account of his views and was later shown to have been correct, he probably was more apt to see as Hitlers other leaders with whom he had conflicts (e.g., Nasser). A fourth factor is the degree to which the analogy is compatible with the rest of his belief system. A fifth is the absence of alternative concepts and analogies. Individuals and states vary in the

[47] *Strategic Surrender* (New York, 1964), 215–41.
[48] *The Power of Small States* (Chicago, 1959), 81.

[49] William Inge, *Outspoken Essays*, First Series (London, 1923), 88.

amount of direct or indirect political experience they have had which can provide different ways of interpreting data. Decision-makers who are aware of multiple possibilities of states' intentions may be less likely to seize on an analogy prematurely. The perception of citizens of nations like the United States which have relatively little history of international politics may be more apt to be heavily influenced by the few major international events that have been important to their country.

The first three factors indicate that an event is more apt to shape present perceptions if it occurred in the recent rather than the remote past. If it occurred recently, the statesman will then know about it at first hand even if he was not involved in the making of policy at the time. Thus if generals are prepared to fight the last war, diplomats may be prepared to avoid the last war. Part of the Anglo-French reaction to Hitler can be explained by the prevailing beliefs that the First World War was to a large extent caused by misunderstandings and could have been avoided by farsighted and nonbelligerent diplomacy. And part of the Western perception of Russia and China can be explained by the view that appeasement was an inappropriate response to Hitler.[50]

V. The Evoked Set

The way people perceive data is influenced not only by their cognitive structure and theories about other actors but also by what they are concerned with at the time they receive the information. Information is evaluated in light of the small part of the person's memory that is presently active—the "evoked set." My perceptions of the dark streets I pass walking home from the movies will be different if the film I saw had dealt with spies than if it had been a comedy. If I am working on aiding a country's education system and I hear someone talk about the need for economic development in that state, I am apt to think

he is concerned with education, whereas if I had been working on, say, trying to achieve political stability in that country, I would have placed his remarks in that framework.[51]

Thus Hypothesis 5 states that when messages are sent from a different background of concerns and information than is possessed by the receiver, misunderstanding is likely. Person A and person B will read the same message quite differently if A has seen several related messages that B does not know about. This difference will be compounded if, as is frequently the case, A and B each assume that the other has the same background he does. This means that misperception can occur even when deception is neither intended nor expected. Thus Roberta Wohlstetter found not only that different parts of the United States government had different perceptions of data about Japan's intentions and messages partly because they saw the incoming information in very different contexts, but also that officers in the field misunderstood warnings from Washington: "Washington advised General Short [in Pearl Harbor] on November 27 to expect 'hostile action' at any moment, by which it meant 'attack on American possessions from without,' but General Short understood this phrase to mean 'sabotage.'"[52] Washington did not realize the extent to which Pearl Harbor considered the danger of sabotage to be primary, and furthermore it incorrectly believed that General Short had received the intercepts of the secret Japanese diplomatic messages available in Washington which indicated that surprise attack was a distinct possibility. Another implication of this hypothesis is that if important information is known to only part of the government of state A and part of the government of state B, international messages may be misunderstood by those parts of the receiver's government that do not match, in the information

---

[50] Of course, analogies themselves are not "unmoved movers." The interpretation of past events is not automatic and is informed by general views of international relations and complex judgments. And just as beliefs about the past influence the present, views about the present influence interpretations of history. It is difficult to determine the degree to which the United States' interpretation of the reasons it went to war in 1917 influenced American foreign policy in the 1920's and 1930's and how much the isolationism of that period influenced the histories of the war.

[51] For some psychological experiments on this subject, see Jerome Bruner and A. Leigh Minturn, "Perceptual Identification and Perceptual Organization," *Journal of General Psychology*, LIII (July 1955), 22–28; Seymour Feshbach and Robert Singer, "The Effects of Fear Arousal and Suppression of Fear Upon Social Perception," *Journal of Abnormal and Social Psychology*, LV (November 1957), 283–88; and Elsa Sippoal, "A Group Study of Some Effects of Preparatory Sets," *Psychology Monographs*, XLVI, No. 210 (1935), 27–28. For a general discussion of the importance of the perceiver's evoked set, see Postman, 87.

[52] Pp. 73–74.

they have, the part of the sender's government that dispatched the message.[53]

Two additional hypotheses can be drawn from the problems of those sending messages. Hypothesis 6 states that when people spend a great deal of time drawing up a plan or making a decision, they tend to think that the message about it they wish to convey will be clear to the receiver.[54] Since they are aware of what is to them the important pattern in their actions, they often feel that the pattern will be equally obvious to others, and they overlook the degree to which the message is apparent to them only because they know what to look for. Those who have not participated in the endless meetings may not understand what information the sender is trying to convey. George Quester has shown how the German and, to a lesser extent, the British desire to maintain target limits on bombing in the first eighteen months of World War II was undermined partly by the fact that each side knew the limits it was seeking and its own reasons for any apparent "exceptions" (e.g., the German attack on Rotterdam) and incorrectly felt that these limits and reasons were equally clear to the other side.[55]

Hypothesis 7 holds that actors often do not realize that actions intended to project a given image may not have the desired effect because the actions themselves do not turn out as planned. Thus even without appreciable impact of different cognitive structures and backgrounds, an action may convey an unwanted message. For example, a country's representatives may not follow instructions and so may give others impressions contrary to those the home government wished to convey. The efforts of Washington and Berlin to settle their dispute over Samoa in the late 1880's were complicated by the provocative behavior of their agents on the spot. These agents not only increased the intensity of the local conflict, but led the decision-makers to become more suspicious of the other state because they tended to assume that their agents were obeying instructions and that the actions of the other side represented official policy. In such cases both sides will believe that the other is reading hostility into a policy of theirs which is friendly. Similarly, Quester's study shows that the attempt to limit bombing referred to above failed partly because neither side was able to bomb as accurately as it thought it could and thus did not realize the physical effects of its actions.[56]

VI. Further Hypotheses From the Perspective of the Perceiver

From the perspective of the perceiver several other hypotheses seem to hold. Hypothesis 8 is that there is an overall tendency for decision-makers to see other states as more hostile than they are.[57] There seem to be more cases of statesmen incorrectly believing others are planning major acts against their interest than of statesmen being lulled by a potential aggressor. There are many reasons for this which are too complex to be treated here (e.g., some parts of the bureaucracy feel it is their responsibility to be suspicious of all other states; decision-makers often feel they are "playing it safe" to believe and act as though the other state were hostile in questionable cases; and often, when people do not feel they are a threat to others, they find it difficult to believe that others may see them as a threat). It should be noted, however, that decision-makers whose perceptions are described by this hypothesis would not necessarily further their own values by trying to correct for this tendency. The values of possible outcomes as well as their probabilities must be considered, and it may be that the probability of an unnecessary arms-tension cycle arising out of misperceptions, multiplied by the costs of such a cycle, may seem less to decision-makers than the probability of incorrectly believing another state is friendly, multiplied by the costs of this eventuality.

Hypothesis 9 states that actors tend to see the behavior of others as more centralized, disciplined, and coordinated than it is. This hypothesis holds true in related ways. Frequently, too many complex

---

[53] For example, Roger Hilsman points out, "Those who knew of the peripheral reconnaissance flights that probed Soviet air defenses during the Eisenhower administration and the U-2 flights over the Soviet Union itself . . . were better able to understand some of the things the Soviets were saying and doing than people who did not know of these activities" (*To Move a Nation* [Garden City, 1967], 66). But it is also possible that those who knew about the U-2 flights at times misinterpreted Soviet messages by incorrectly believing that the sender was influenced by, or at least knew of, these flights.

[54] I am grateful to Thomas Schelling for discussion on this point.

[55] *Deterrence Before Hiroshima* (New York, 1966), 105–22.

[56] *Ibid.*

[57] For a slightly different formulation of this view, see Holsti, 27.

events are squeezed into a perceived pattern. Actors are hesitant to admit or even see that particular incidents cannot be explained by their theories.[58] Those events not caused by factors that are important parts of the perceiver's image are often seen as though they were. Further, actors see others as more internally united than they in fact are and generally overestimate the degree to which others are following a coherent policy. The degree to which the other side's policies are the product of internal bargaining,[59] internal misunderstandings, or subordinates' not following instructions is underestimated. This is the case partly because actors tend to be unfamiliar with the details of another state's policy-making processes. Seeing only the finished product, they find it simpler to try to construct a rational explanation for the policies, even though they know that such an analysis could not explain their own policies.[60]

Familiarity also accounts for Hypothesis 10: because a state gets most of its information about the other state's policies from the other's foreign office, it tends to take the foreign office's position for the stand of the other government as a whole. In many cases this perception will be an accurate one, but when the other government is divided or when the other foreign office is acting without specific authorization, misperception may result. For example, part of the reason why in 1918 Allied governments incorrectly thought "that the Japanese were preparing to take action [in Siberia], if need be, with agreement with the British and French alone, disregarding the absence of American consent,"[61] was that Allied

ambassadors had talked mostly with Foreign Minister Motono, who was among the minority of the Japanese favoring this policy. Similarly, America's NATO allies may have gained an inaccurate picture of the degree to which the American government was committed to the MLF because they had greatest contact with parts of the government that strongly favored the MLF. And states that tried to get information about Nazi foreign policy from German diplomats were often misled because these officials were generally ignorant of or out of sympathy with Hitler's plans. The Germans and the Japanese sometimes purposely misinformed their own ambassadors in order to deceive their enemies more effectively.

Hypothesis 11 states that actors tend to overestimate the degree to which others are acting in response to what they themselves do when the others behave in accordance with the actor's desires; but when the behavior of the other is undesired, it is usually seen as derived from internal forces. If the *effect* of another's action is to injure or threaten the first side, the first side is apt to believe that such was the other's *purpose*. An example of the first part of the hypothesis is provided by Kennan's account of the activities of official and unofficial American representatives who protested to the new Bolshevik government against several of its actions. When the Soviets changed their position, these representatives felt it was largely because of their influence.[62] This sort of interpretation can be explained not only by the fact that it is gratifying to the individual making it, but also, taking the other side of the coin mentioned in Hypothesis 9, by the fact that the actor is most familiar with his own input into the other's decision and has less knowledge of other influences. The second part of Hypothesis 11 is illustrated by the tendency of actors to believe that the hostile behavior of others is to be explained by the other side's motives and not by its reaction to the first side. Thus Chamberlain did not see that Hitler's behavior was related in part to his belief that the British were weak. More common is the failure to see that the other side is reacting out of fear of the first side, which can lead to self-fulfilling prophecies and spirals of misperception and hostility.

This difficulty is often compounded by an implication of Hypothesis 12: when actors have intentions

---

[58] The Soviets consciously hold an extreme version of this view and seem to believe that nothing is accidental. See the discussion in Nathan Leites, *A Study of Bolshevism* (Glencoe, 1953), 67–73.

[59] A. W. Marshall criticizes Western explanations of Soviet military posture for failing to take this into account. See his "Problems of Estimating Military Power," a paper presented at the 1966 Annual Meeting of the American Political Science Association, 16.

[60] It has also been noted that in labor-management disputes both sides may be apt to believe incorrectly that the other is controlled from above, either from the international union office or from the company's central headquarters (Robert Blake, Herbert Shepard, and Jane Mouton, *Managing Intergroup Conflict in Industry* [Houston, 1964], 182). It has been further noted that both Democratic and Republican members of the House tend to see the other party as the one that is more disciplined and united (Charles Clapp, *The Congressman* [Washington, 1963], 17–19).

[61] George Kennan, *Russia Leaves the War* (New York, 1967), 484.

[62] *Ibid.*, 404, 408, 500.

that they do not try to conceal from others, they tend to assume that others accurately perceive these intentions. Only rarely do they believe that others may be reacting to a much less favorable image of themselves than they think they are projecting.[63]

For state A to understand how state B perceives A's policy is often difficult because such understanding may involve a conflict with A's image of itself. Raymond Sontag argues that Anglo-German relations before World War I deteriorated partly because "the British did not like to think of themselves as selfish, or unwilling to tolerate 'legitimate' German expansion. The Germans did not like to think of themselves as aggressive, or unwilling to recognize 'legitimate' British vested interest."[64]

Hypothesis 13 suggests that if it is hard for an actor to believe that the other can see him as a menace, it is often even harder for him to see that issues important to him are not important to others. While he may know that another actor is on an opposing team, it may be more difficult for him to realize that the other is playing an entirely different game. This is especially true when the game he is playing seems vital to him.[65]

The final hypothesis, Hypothesis 14, is as follows: actors tend to overlook the fact that evidence consistent with their theories may also be consistent with other views. When choosing between two theories we have to pay attention only to data that cannot be accounted for by one of the theories. But it is common to find people claiming as proof of their theories data that could also support alternative views. This phenomenon is related to the point made earlier that any single bit of information can be interpreted only within a framework of hypotheses and theories. And while it is true that "we may without a vicious circularity accept some datum as a fact because it conforms to the very law for which it counts as another confirming instance, and reject an allegation of fact because it is already excluded by law,"[66] we should be careful lest we forget that a piece of information seems in many cases to confirm a certain hypothesis only because we already believe that hypothesis to be correct and that the information can with as much validity support a different hypothesis. For example, one of the reasons why the German attack on Norway took both that country and England by surprise, even though they had detected German ships moving toward Norway, was that they expected not an attack but an attempt by the Germans to break through the British blockade and reach the Atlantic. The initial course of the ships was consistent with either plan, but the British and Norwegians took this course to mean that their predictions were being borne out.[67] This is not to imply that the interpretation made was foolish, but only that the decision-makers should have been

[63] Herbert Butterfield notes that these assumptions can contribute to the spiral of "Hobbesian fear. . . . You yourself may vividly feel the terrible fear that you have of the other party, but you cannot enter into the other man's counter-fear, or even understand why he should be particularly nervous. For you know that you yourself mean him no harm, and that you want nothing from him save guarantees for your own safety; and it is never possible for you to realize or remember properly that since he cannot see the inside of your mind, he can never have the same assurance of your intentions that you have" (*History and Human Conflict* [London, 1951], 20).

[64] *European Diplomatic History 1871–1932* (New York, 1933), 124. It takes great mental effort to realize that actions which seem only the natural consequence of defending your vital interests can look to others as though you are refusing them any chance of increasing their influence. In rebutting the famous Crowe "balance of power" memorandum of 1907, which justified a policy of "containing" Germany on the grounds that she was a threat to British national security, Sanderson, a former permanent undersecretary in the Foreign Office, wrote, "It has sometimes seemed to me that to a foreigner reading our press the British Empire must appear in the light of some huge giant sprawling all over the globe, with gouty fingers and toes stretching in every direction, which cannot be approached without eliciting a scream" (quoted in Monger, 315). But few other Englishmen could be convinced that others might see them this way.

[65] George Kennan makes clear that in 1918 this kind of difficulty was partly responsible for the inability of either the Allies or the new Bolshevik government to understand

the motivations of the other side: "There is . . . nothing in nature more egocentric than the embattled democracy. . . . It . . . tends to attach to its own cause an absolute value which distorts its own vision of everything else. . . . It will readily be seen that people who have got themselves into this frame of mind have little understanding for the issues of any contest other than the one in which they are involved. The idea of people wasting time and substance on any *other* issue seems to them preposterous" (*Russia and the West*, 11–12).

[66] Kaplan, 89.

[67] Johan Jorgen Holst, "Surprise, Signals and Reaction: The Attack on Norway," *Cooperation and Conflict*, No. 1 (1966), 34. The Germans made a similar mistake in November 1942 when they interpreted the presence of an Allied convoy in the Mediterranean as confirming their belief that Malta would be resupplied. They thus were taken by surprise when landings took place in North Africa (William Langer, *Our Vichy Gamble* [New York, 1966], 365).

aware that the evidence was also consistent with an invasion and should have had a bit less confidence in their views.

The longer the ships would have to travel the same route whether they were going to one or another of two destinations, the more information would be needed to determine their plans. Taken as a metaphor this incident applies generally to the treatment of evidence. Thus as long as Hitler made demands for control only of ethnically German areas, his actions could be explained either by the hypothesis that he had unlimited ambitions or by the hypothesis that he wanted to unite all the Germans. But actions against non-Germans (e.g., the takeover of Czechoslovakia in March 1938) could not be accounted for by the latter hypothesis. And it was this action that convinced the appeasers that Hitler had to be stopped. It is interesting to speculate on what the British reaction would have been had Hitler left Czechoslovakia alone for a while and instead made demands on Poland similar to those he eventually made in the summer of 1939. The two paths would then still not have diverged, and further misperception could have occurred.

C. Capability Analysis

24. On the Concepts
of Politics and Power*

Karl W. Deutsch is Professor of Government at Harvard University and one of the most original and stimulating scholars in the international field. His many writings include *Nationalism and Social Communication* (1954), *The Nerves of Government* (1963), and *The Analysis of International Relations* (1968). Here Professor Deutsch examines two central concepts in the field of international politics and, as is the case in subsequent selections (29 and 44), his searching analysis reveals that the concepts are considerably more complex than they appear at first glance. This article clearly shows that the ends and means of foreign policy and the decision-making that leads to their selection are intimately related to the capabilities available to a society. Equally plain is the point that these capabilities only become meaningful in relation to those possessed by the actors over whom influence is sought. If the reader is persuaded by Professor Deutsch's formulation of the concepts of politics and power, he will henceforth find it difficult to proceed as if the analysis of capabilities can be accomplished merely by taking inventory of the human and nonhuman resources of a society. [*Reprinted from the* Journal of International Affairs, *XXI (1967), 332–41, by permission of the author and the publisher.*]

Some Concepts About Politics

Among the vast number of human relations, which ones are *political?* What does politics do that other human activities and institutions do not do?

Politics consists of the more or less incomplete control of human behavior through voluntary habits of *compliance* in combination with threats of probable *enforcement*. In its essence, politics is based on the interplay of these two things: habits and threats.

* This attempt at a somewhat more unified restatement of certain concepts from recent theories of politics and international relations is a draft for part of a forthcoming book on *The Analysis of International Relations* (Englewood Cliffs, N.J.: Prentice-Hall, 1968). Research drawn upon in its preparation was supported in part by the Carnegie Corporation and by the National Science Foundation through the Yale Political Data Program.

The *habits* of behaving, cooperating, obeying the law, or respecting some decision as binding tend to be voluntary for most people. For habits are part of our nature and of the way we more or less automatically act. Without these habits, there could be no law and no government as we know them. Only because most drivers stick to the right-hand side of the road and stop at red lights can the traffic code be enforced at a tolerable cost. Only because most people do not steal cars can the police protect our streets against the few who do. If a law is not obeyed voluntarily and habitually by, say, at least 90 per cent of the people, either it becomes a dead letter, or it becomes very expensive to enforce, or it becomes a noble but unreliable experiment like Prohibition. The voluntary or habitual compliance of the mass of the population is the invisible but very real basis of power for every government.

Although this compliance is largely voluntary, it is not entirely so. If it were, we would be dealing not with politics but with folkways, custom, and morality. In politics, the compliance habits of the many are preserved and reinforced by the *probability* of *enforcement* against the few who may transgress the law or disobey the government.

Enforcement consists of the threat or the use of rewards or punishments. In practice, punishments are used more often than rewards. Punishments are usually cheaper; some people enjoy applying them under an ideological pretext, such as Communism or anti-Communism; and many people think they are more reliable. Clearly, where most people are in the habit of obeying the law anyhow, it would seem costly and needless to offer them rewards for it; it seems cheaper and more efficient to threaten penalties for the few who disobey. Punishments may deter some transgressors from repeating their offense, but it is more important that they deter others from following their example.

Enforcement usually is not certain; it is only probable. But ordinarily the likelihood of enforcement, together with the compliance habits of most of the population, is enough to keep the proportion of serious transgressions down to a tolerable level. The punishment of nine out of ten murderers might be enough to deter a good share of those who might otherwise commit premeditated murder. And convictions in only one-fourth of the automobile-theft cases might suffice, together with the law-abiding habits of most people, to prevent most automobile thefts.

Even the most certain or most cruel punishments, of course, do not deter those murderers who are too thoughtless, too confident, or too passionately excited to care or think realistically about the chance of getting caught. This fact points up one of the weaknesses of deterrence, whether against murder or war.

The conditions that determine the effectiveness of enforcement are much the same as those that determine the frequency of obedient or law-abiding behavior. Most significant among these are the strength of the compliance habits of the bulk of the people, and their willingness to give active support to the government in upholding its commands and laws. Next in importance are all the other conditions that influence the relative probabilities of law-abiding vs. law-breaking behavior to which the threat of enforcement is being applied. (E.g., if there is hunger among the poor, more people are likely to steal bread.) The size and efficiency of the enforcement apparatus ranks only third in importance. Least important are the processes of changing rules, passing new laws, or threatening more severe punishments.

However, mass habits of compliance and general social conditions, the most powerful long-run influences on the behavior of the population, are the most difficult to manipulate. Even the size, training, equipment, and morale of the enforcement personnel—the armed forces, police, judiciary, and to some extent the civil service—can be changed only slowly and at great cost. The weakest lever of control thus becomes attractive because it is the easiest to use. Passing another law, threatening a more severe penalty, or relaxing the standards of legal justice are much cheaper and quicker, and hence often more attractive than the longer and harder task of effecting more fundamental changes in the situation.

Politics, then, is the interplay of enforcement threats, which can be changed fairly quickly, with the existing loyalties and compliance habits of the population, which are more powerful but harder to change. Through this interplay of habitual compliance and probable enforcement, societies protect and modify their institutions, the allocation and reallocation of their resources, the distribution of values, incentives, and rewards among their population, and the patterns of teamwork in which people cooperate in the production of goods, services, and offspring.

Rule or Dominion. With this concept of politics clearly in mind, we can readily understand the two related concepts of *rule* or *dominion*. By the rule or dominion of a leader, the German sociologist Max Weber meant the chance or probability of his being obeyed. Of two leaders or governments, according to Weber's reasoning, the one more likely to be obeyed by a given population has more dominion over them.

If we carry this reasoning a little further, we recognize what T. W. Adorno once called "the implicit mathematics in Max Weber's thought."[1] A

[1] T. W. Adorno, "Oral Communication," 15th German Congress of Sociology (Max Weber Centenary), Heidelberg, May 1964.

probability, strictly speaking, is a number denoting the frequency, usually expressed as a percentage, with which events of a certain type (in this case acts of obedience to the commands of the ruler) occur within a larger ensemble of events (in this case the general behavior of the population). Weber's concept of rule can therefore be expressed as a number. At least in principle, it can be measured in quantitative terms.

At the same time, we can see the close relationship between Weber's idea of the chance or frequency of acts of obedience and our own concept of the rate of compliance. The latter concept is somewhat broader, in that it includes passively compliant behavior as well as the more positive acts of obedience emphasized by Weber, whenever such behavior significantly influences the outcome of the political process.

Our concept of *habitual* compliance, however, is somewhat narrower than Weber's "chance of being obeyed," excluding as it does acts of submission to the immediate threat of naked force. People obey a gunman in a holdup or a foreign army of occupation so long as they have guns pointed at them. Weber's concept of "rule" or "dominion" covers such cases of obedience under duress. But it should be noted that the obedience is exacted through processes of force, not of politics. They become political only insofar as the obedient behavior continues after the gunman's or the invader's back is turned. Only then, in the interplay of remembered fear and continuing compliance, are we dealing with politics.

When we say that politics is that realm of human affairs where domination and habitual compliance overlap, we are implying that politics, owing to its double nature, is apt to be an area of recurrent tension between centralization and decentralization. For domination or rule usually can be exercised more easily by centralized organizations; threats of enforcement, too, can be manipulated more effectively from a single center. But the dependable habits of large numbers of people can be created rarely, if ever, through a single center of command; nor can they be created quickly. Habits more often develop from a multitude of different experiences repeated over time in many ways. The centralized use of threats or force rarely creates, therefore, a durable community of politically relevant habits; it is much

more often such a community of habits that provides the possibilities for the exercise of centralized power.

The Concept of Power

Recognizing the dual nature of politics also helps us to see the limits of the concept of political power. Some brilliant writers have tried to build a theory of politics, and particularly of international relations, largely or entirely upon the notion of power. This is the approach of classical theorists like Machiavelli and Hobbes, as well as of contemporary theorists like Morgenthau and Schuman. The notion of power as the basis of international politics is also widespread in the popular press and even in the foreign services and defense establishments of many countries. What is the element of truth contained in this notion, and what are its limits?

Power, put simply and crudely, is the ability to prevail in conflict and to overcome obstacles. It was in this sense that Lenin, before the Russian Revolution, posed to his followers a key problem of politics with the question, "Who Whom?" Who was to be the master of actions and events, and who was to be their object and victim? In the 1932 depression, a German protest song called up a related image: "We shall be hammers, not anvils," it announced. Who is stronger and who is weaker? Who will get his way and who will have to give in?

Such questions as these, when asked about actual or possible encounters among a limited number of competitors, lead to rank lists, such as the rankings of baseball clubs in the pennant races, of chickens in the pecking order, and of great powers in world politics. The fewer actual encounters that have occurred, of course, the more such rank lists must be built up from hypotheses based upon the past performance and the existing or potential resources of the contestants.

Potential Power, as Inferred from Resources

An example of the relative power potential of two coalitions of nations appears in Table 1.[2] Here the power of the Allied and Axis countries in World War II is measured, or at least suggested, by the

[2] Klaus E. Knorr, *The War Potential of Nations* Princeton: Princeton University Press, 1956), p. 34.

TABLE 1

Combat-Munitions[1] Output of the Main Belligerents, 1938–1943 (percentage of total)

Country	1938	1939	1940	1941	1942	1943
United States	6	4	7	14	30	40
Canada	0	0	0	1	2	2
Britain	6	10	18	19	15	13
U.S.S.R.	27	31	23	24	17	15
TOTAL, United Nations	39	45	48	58	64	70
Germany[2]	46	43	40	31	27	22
Italy	6	4	5	4	3	1
Japan	9	8	7	7	6	7
TOTAL, Axis Countries	61	55	52	42	36	30
GRAND TOTAL	100	100	100	100	100	100

[1] Includes aircraft, army ordnance and signal equipment, naval vessels, and related equipment.
[2] Includes occupied territories.

millions of tons of munitions that each side produced each year.

The table reveals that the Axis powers produced far more munitions than the Allies in 1938, 1939, 1940, and 1941, but that their lead diminished in 1942 and was decisively lost in 1943, the year Winston Churchill aptly dubbed "the hinge of

TABLE 2

Some Hypothetical Rank Orderings of the Power Potential of Major Countries, 1960–63 and 1980

(Based on Energy Production, Steel Output, and Population)

Index Values: U.S. 1960 = 100
Computed from:

Actual Figures for 1960–63		Projections for 1980	
Rank			
1. U.S.	100	1. China	250
2. U.S.S.R.	67	2. U.S.	160
3. China	41	3. U.S.S.R.	120
4. German Federal Republic	15	4. Japan	39
5. Japan	14	5. German Federal Republic	25
6. Britain	12	6. Britain	19
7. France	7	7. France	11
TOTAL	256	TOTAL	624

fate." After this turning point, the Axis powers fell ever further behind until their collapse in 1945.

Table 2 provides a hypothetical ranking of the power potential of the major nations for the period 1960 to 1963 and projects another one for 1980.[3]

The 1980 estimates are based on projected increases in per-capita steel and energy production and total population in each country. (E.g., for China an annual per-capita steel output of about 400 lbs., or roughly one-half the 1963 level of the U.S.S.R. and of Japan, and a population of about 1,100 million are projected.) No one, of course, can yet be sure whether these projections are realistic. In any case, it seems noteworthy that the power of the strongest single country in both periods is rated at well below one-half of the total power of the first seven countries.

The Weight of Power, as Inferred from Results

Power potential is a rough estimate of the material and human resources available for power. Indirectly, it can be used to infer how successful a country should be in a contest of power, if it uses its resources to advantage. Conversely, the *weight* of an actor's power can be inferred from his success at influencing outcomes in the international system.

The weight of an actor's power or influence over some process is the extent to which he can change the probability of its outcome. This can be measured most easily when we are dealing with a repetitive class of similar outcomes, such as votes in the UN General Assembly. Suppose, for instance, that in the Assembly motions supported by the United States pass on the average of three times out of four, or with a probability of 75 per cent, while those motions not supported by the United States pass only 25 per cent of the time. We then might say that U.S. support can shift a motion's chances of success on the average of from 25 to 75 per cent, that is, by 50 percentage points. These 50 percentage points then would be a rough measure of the average weight of U.S. power in the General Assembly. (The measure is a rough one, and it may understate the real influence of the United States, since anticipated U.S.

[3] From data in Wilhelm Fucks, *Formeln zur Macht: Prognosen über Vökler, Wirtschaft, Potentiale* (Stuttgart: Deutsche Verlagsanstalt, 1965), Figs. 37–38, pp. 129–31.

opposition may be enough to discourage many motions from even being proposed.)

Estimating the weight of power is more difficult when we are dealing with a single event. How much power did the dropping of an atom bomb on Hiroshima, for example, exert in terms of its influence on the Japanese decision to surrender? An outstanding expert on Japan, former Ambassador Edwin O. Reischauer, concludes that the bomb shortened the war by only a few days.[4] To make such a judgment, it is necessary to imagine that the unique event—the attack on Hiroshima at a time when Japan was exhausted and seeking a way to surrender—had occurred many times. One would then try to imagine the average outcome for two sets of hypothetical cases: those in which a bomb was dropped, and those in which it was not.

This might seem farfetched, but it is not. Indeed, it is not very different from the reasoning of an engineer trying to determine why a bridge collapsed, or of a physician trying to determine why a patient died. In order to estimate the effect of what was done, and perhaps to estimate what should have been done, we convert the unique event into a member of a repetitive class of similar hypothetical events. We then try to estimate the extent and probability of alternative outcomes in the presence and in the absence, respectively, of the action or condition whose power we wish to gauge. Finally, we infer the power of the actor in the situation from the power of the act or the condition he controls. Power considered in this way is much the same thing as causality; and the weight of an actor's power is the same as the weight of those causes of an outcome that are under his control.

Modern governments have greatly increased the weight of their power over their own populations. Taxes are collected, soldiers drafted, laws enforced, and lawbreakers arrested with a much higher probability than in the past. By the same token, the weight of government power in industrially advanced countries usually is much greater than that in the developing nations, although there are wide variations among the latter.

In world politics, on the contrary, the weight of the power of most governments, and particularly of the great powers, has been declining ever since 1945. No government today has as much control over the probable outcome of world affairs as had Great Britain, say, between 1870 and 1935. At present Britain cannot control India, Pakistan, Nigeria, or Rhodesia; the United States cannot control Cuba, and certainly not France; the Soviet Union cannot control Albania, Yugoslavia, or China; and China cannot control Indonesia or Burma.

At a closer look, the weight of power may actually include two different concepts. The first deals with the ability to *reduce* the probability of an outcome *not* desired by an actor. In domestic politics we sometimes speak of "veto groups" that can prevent or make unlikely the passage of some piece of legislation they dislike. In international politics, we find a very considerable veto power of the five permanent members of the UN Security Council formally embodied in the UN Charter. Less formally, we may speak of the power of a government to deny some territory or sphere of influence to some other government or ideological movement. Thus the United States in the 1950's successfully denied South Korea to its North Korean attackers, and it is currently denying much of South Vietnam to the Viet Cong.

It should be easy to see why this is so. The specific outcome that we may wish to prevent may not be very probable in the first place. Suppose that Communist guerrillas in an Asian or African country had roughly one chance in three (33 per cent) of establishing a stable Communist regime. In that case, an anti-Communist intervention carried out with limited power—say with a weight of about 28 per cent—could reduce the guerrillas' chances of success from 33 per cent to only 5 per cent. In other words, the probability of their failure would be 19:1. Outcomes that are already moderately improbable thus can be made highly improbable by the application of a relatively limited amount of power. In such situations, the change in the probabilities of a particular outcome will seem quite drastic. The limited use of power will seem to have changed great uncertainty into near certainty and thus to have produced spectacular results.

The same weight of power produces far less impressive results, however, when it is used to promote an outcome that is fairly improbable in the first place. Suppose we wish to produce a stable

[4] Edwin O. Reischauer, *The United States and Japan*, rev. ed. (Cambridge: Harvard University Press, 1957), p. 240.

constitutional, democratic regime in that strife-torn Asian or African country of our example. With the knowledge that only about one out of every twenty of the developing countries has a stable democratic government, we can estimate that such a venture will have about a 5 per cent chance of success. Thus, applying power with a weight of 28 per cent would still only produce a 33 per cent probability that a democratic regime could be established. We would still be left with a 2:1 chance for its failure.

Even this calculation is far too optimistic. For it has unjustifiably assumed that power to promote one outcome can be transformed without loss into the same amount of power to produce another. We all know very well that this is not true. The power to knock a man down does not give us the power to teach him to play the piano. The power to bomb and burn a village cannot be completely or easily transformed into the power to win the sympathies of its inhabitants, to govern it with their consent, or even less to produce among them the many skills, values, and freely given loyalties that are essential to democratic government.

The more specific a desired positive outcome is, the more alternatives are excluded by it. Hence, it usually is less probable; and, moreover, the application of limited power cannot ordinarily make it highly probable. Limited power is most effective when used negatively to veto or deny some specific outcome. Such a use of power increases the already considerable probability of an entire range of possible alternatives to it, with little or no regard as to which particular alternative happens to materialize.

The power to increase the probability of a specific positive outcome is the power of *goal attainment* and of *control* over one's environment. Like all goal attainment and control, it implies a high degree of self-control on the part of the actor. A charging elephant can smash down a large obstacle, but he cannot thread a needle. Indeed, he cannot make a right-angled turn within a three-foot radius. The greater the brute power, mass, speed, and momentum

of the elephant, the harder it is for him to control his own motions, and the less precise his control becomes. Driving offers a similar illustration. The bigger, heavier, faster, and more powerful the car, the harder it is to steer. An attempt to measure its power in terms of its performance would give us, therefore, at least two different ratings: a high one for its power to accelerate and a low one for its power to stop or turn.

Does something similar hold for the power of governments and nations? The larger a country is, the more numerous its population, and the larger the proportion of its population and resources mobilized for the pursuit of some policy (and, we may add, the more intense and unreserved their emotional commitment to that policy), the greater is likely to be its power to overcome any obstacles in its path. But national policies usually require more than surmounting obstacles. Often they aim at specific positive results. They may require, therefore, the pursuit of a constant goal through a sequence of changing tactics, or even the preservation or enhancement of a basic value through a succession of changing goals. The more people and resources have been committed to the earlier tactics, policies, or goals, however, and the more intensely and unreservedly this has been done, the more interests, careers, reputations, and emotions have become committed to the old policy, and the harder it may be for any member of the government, or even for the entire government, to propose a change. Unless substantial and timely precautions are taken, therefore, governments may become prisoners of their past policies and power may become a trap.

This danger tends to grow with the amount of national power and with the breadth and intensity of efforts to increase it. Ordinarily, therefore, the danger of losing self-control is greater for large nations than for small ones, for dictatorships than for democracies, and in wartime—hot or cold—than in peacetime. If this danger is not guarded against, the weight of power in the long run may become self-defeating, self-negating, or self-destructive.

D. Societal Sources of Foreign Policy

25. Domestic Structure and Foreign Policy

Henry A. Kissinger, formerly Professor of Government and a member of the Center for International Affairs at Harvard University, was appointed Special Assistant for National Security Affairs in the White House under President Nixon. A leading student of foreign and military policy, his writings include such widely discussed books as *Nuclear Weapons and Foreign Policy* (1957), *The Necessity for Choice* (1961), and *The Troubled Partnership* (1965). In this essay Professor Kissinger provides a brilliant insight into the relationship between a society's historical experience, its shared values, and its social and political structure on the one hand, and its foreign policy behavior on the other. The subtleties of this relationship are difficult to trace and explain, but here they are clearly exposed and persuasively assessed. Especially valuable are the distinctions that Professor Kissinger draws among the dynamics of the relationship in different types of societies. [*Reprinted from "Conditions of World Order,"* Daedalus, *XCV (Spring 1966), 503–29, by permission of the author and the American Academy of Arts and Sciences, Boston, Mass.*]

I. The Role of Domestic Structure

In the traditional conception, international relations are conducted by political units treated almost as personalities. The domestic structure is taken as given; foreign policy begins where domestic policy ends.

But this approach is appropriate only to stable periods because then the various components of the international system generally have similar conceptions of the "rules of the game." If the domestic structures are based on commensurable notions of what is just, a consensus about permissible aims and methods of foreign policy develops. If domestic structures are reasonably stable, temptations to use an adventurous foreign policy to achieve domestic cohesion are at a minimum. In these conditions, leaders will generally apply the same criteria and hold similar views about what constitutes a "reasonable" demand. This does not guarantee agreement, but it provides the condition for a meaningful dialogue, that is, it sets the stage for traditional diplomacy.

When the domestic structures are based on fundamentally different conceptions of what is just, the conduct of international affairs grows more complex. Then it becomes difficult even to define the nature of disagreement because what seems most obvious to one side appears most problematic to the other. A policy dilemma arises because the pros and cons of a given course seem evenly balanced. The definition of what constitutes a problem and what criteria are relevant in "solving" it reflects to a considerable extent the domestic notions of what is just, the pressures produced by the decision-making process, and the experience which forms the leaders in their rise to eminence. When domestic structures —and the concept of legitimacy on which they are based—differ widely, statesmen can still meet, but their ability to persuade has been reduced for they no longer speak the same language.

This can occur even when no universal claims are made. Incompatible domestic structures can passively generate a gulf, simply because of the difficulty of achieving a consensus about the nature of "reasonable" aims and methods. But when one or more states claim universal applicability for their particular structure, schisms grow deep indeed. In that event, the domestic structure becomes not only an obstacle to understanding but one of the principal issues in international affairs. Its requirements condition the conception of alternatives; survival seems involved in every dispute. The symbolic aspect of foreign policy begins to overshadow the substantive component. It becomes difficult to consider a dispute "on its merits" because the disagreement seems finally to turn not on a specific issue but on a set of values as expressed in domestic arrangements. The consequences of such a state of affairs were explained by Edmund Burke during the French Revolution:

I never thought we could make peace with the system; because it was not for the sake of an object we pursued in rivalry with each other, but with the system itself that we were at war. As I understood the matter, we were at war not with its conduct but with its existence; convinced that its existence and its hostility were the same.[1]

Of course, the domestic structure is not irrelevant in any historical period. At a minimum, it determines the amount of the total social effort which can be devoted to foreign policy. The wars of the kings who governed by divine right were limited because feudal rulers, bound by customary law, could not levy income taxes or conscript their subjects. The French Revolution, which based its policy on a doctrine of popular will, mobilized resources on a truly national scale for the first time. This was one of the principal reasons for the startling successes of French arms against a hostile Europe which possessed greater over-all power. The ideological regimes of the twentieth century have utilized a still larger share of the national effort. This has

[1] Edmund Burke, *Works* (London, 1826), Vol. VIII, pp. 214–15.

enabled them to hold their own against an environment possessing far superior resources.

Aside from the allocation of resources, the domestic structure crucially affects the way the actions of other states are interpreted. To some extent of course, every society finds itself in an environment not of its own making and has some of the main lines of its foreign policy imposed on it. Indeed, the pressure of the environment can grow so strong that it permits only one interpretation of its significance; Prussia in the eighteenth century and Israel in the contemporary period may have found themselves in this position.

But for the majority of states the margin of decision has been greater. The actual choice has been determined to a considerable degree by their interpretation of the environment and by their leaders' conception of alternatives. Napoleon rejected peace offers beyond the dreams of the kings who had ruled France by "divine right" because he was convinced that *any* settlement which demonstrated the limitations of his power was tantamount to his downfall. That Russia seeks to surround itself with a belt of friendly states in Eastern Europe is a product of geography and history. That it is attempting to do so by imposing a domestic structure based on a particular ideology is a result of conceptions supplied by its domestic structure.

The domestic structure is decisive finally in the elaboration of positive goals. The most difficult, indeed tragic, aspect of foreign policy is how to deal with the problem of conjecture. When the scope for action is greatest, knowledge on which to base such action is small or ambiguous. When knowledge becomes available, the ability to affect events is usually at a minimum. In 1936, no one could know whether Hitler was a misunderstood nationalist or a maniac. By the time certainty was achieved, it had to be paid for with millions of lives.

The conjectural element of foreign policy—the need to gear actions to an assessment that cannot be proved true when it is made—is never more crucial than in a revolutionary period. Then, the old order is obviously disintegrating while the shape of its replacement is highly uncertain. Everything depends, therefore, on some conception of the future. But varying domestic structures can easily produce different assessments of the significance of existing trends and, more importantly, clashing criteria for resolving these differences. This is the dilemma of our time.

Problems are novel; their scale is vast; their nature is often abstract and always psychological. In the past, international relations were confined to a limited geographic area. The various continents pursued their relations essentially in isolation from each other. Until the eighteenth century, other continents impinged on Europe only sporadically and for relatively brief periods. And when Europe extended its sway over much of the world, foreign policy became limited to the Western Powers with the single exception of Japan. The international system of the nineteenth century was to all practical purposes identical with the concert of Europe.

The period after World War II marks the first era of truly global foreign policy. Each major state is capable of producing consequences in every part of the globe by a direct application of its power or because ideas can be transmitted almost instantaneously or because ideological rivalry gives vast symbolic significance even to issues which are minor in geopolitical terms. The mere act of adjusting perspectives to so huge a scale would produce major dislocations. This problem is compounded by the emergence of so many new states. Since 1945, the number of participants in the international system has nearly doubled. In previous periods the addition of even one or two new states tended to lead to decades of instability until a new equilibrium was established and accepted. The emergence of scores of new states has magnified this difficulty many times over.

These upheavals would be challenge enough, but they are overshadowed by the risks posed by modern technology. Peace is maintained through the threat of mutual destruction based on weapons for which there has been no operational experience. Deterrence—the policy of preventing an action by confronting the opponent with risks he is unwilling to run—depends in the first instance on psychological criteria. What the potential aggressor believes is more crucial than what is objectively true. Deterrence occurs above all in the minds of men.

To achieve an international consensus on the significance of these developments would be a major task even if domestic structures were comparable. It becomes especially difficult when domestic structures differ widely and when universal claims are made on behalf of them. A systematic assessment of the impact of domestic structure on the conduct of international affairs would have to treat such factors as historical traditions, social values, and the economic system. But this would far transcend the scope of an article. For the purposes of this discussion we shall confine ourselves to sketching the impact of two factors only: administrative structure and the formative experience of leadership groups.

II. The Impact of the Administrative Structure

In the contemporary period, the very nature of the governmental structure introduces an element of rigidity which operates more or less independently of the convictions of statesmen or the ideology which they represent. Issues are too complex and relevant facts too manifold to be dealt with on the basis of personal intuition. An institutionalization of decision-making is an inevitable by-product of the risks of international affairs in the nuclear age. Moreover, almost every modern state is dedicated to some theory of "planning"—the attempt to structure the future by understanding and, if necessary, manipulating the environment. Planning involves a quest for predictability and, above all, for "objectivity." There is a deliberate effort to reduce the relevant elements of a problem to a standard of average performance. The vast bureaucratic mechanisms that emerge develop a momentum and a vested interest of their own. As they grow more complex, their internal standards of operation are not necessarily commensurable with those of other countries or even with other bureaucratic structures in the same country. There is a trend toward autarky. A paradoxical consequence may be that increased control over the domestic environment is purchased at the price of loss of flexibility in international affairs.

The purpose of bureaucracy is to devise a standard operating procedure which can cope effectively with most problems. A bureaucracy is efficient if the matters which it handles routinely are, in fact, the most frequent and if its procedures are relevant to their solution. If those criteria are met, the energies of the top leadership are freed to deal creatively with the unexpected occurrence or with the need for innovation. Bureaucracy becomes an obstacle when what it defines as routine does not address the most significant range of issues or when its prescribed mode of action proves irrelevant to the problem.

When this occurs, the bureaucracy absorbs the energies of top executives in reconciling what is expected with what happens; the analysis of where one is overwhelms the consideration of where one should be going. Serving the machine becomes a more absorbing occupation than defining its purpose. Success consists in moving the administrative machine to the point of decision, leaving relatively little energy for analyzing the merit of this decision. The quest for "objectivity"—while desirable theoretically —involves the danger that means and ends are confused, that an average standard of performance is exalted as the only valid one. Attention tends to be diverted from the act of choice—which is the ultimate test of statesmanship—to the accumulation of facts. Decisions can be avoided until a crisis brooks no further delay, until the events themselves have removed the element of ambiguity. But at that point the scope for constructive action is at a minimum. Certainty is purchased at the cost of creativity.

Something like this seems to be characteristic of modern bureaucratic states whatever their ideology. In societies with a pragmatic tradition, such as the United States, there develops a greater concern with an analysis of where one is than where one is going. What passes for planning is frequently the projection of the familiar into the future. In societies based on ideology, doctrine is institutionalized and exegesis takes the place of innovation. Creativity must make so many concessions to orthodoxy that it may exhaust itself in doctrinal adaptations. In short, the accumulation of knowledge of the bureaucracy and the impersonality of its method of arriving at decisions can be achieved at a high price. Decision-making can grow so complex that the process of producing a bureaucratic consensus may overshadow the purpose of the effort.

While all thoughtful administrators would grant in the abstract that these dangers exist, they find it difficult to act on their knowledge. Lip service is paid to planning; indeed planning staffs proliferate. However, they suffer from two debilities. The "operating" elements may not take the planning effort seriously. Plans become esoteric exercises which are accepted largely because they imply no practical consequence. They are a sop to administrative theory. At the same time, since planning staffs have a high incentive to try to be "useful," there is a bias against novel conceptions which are difficult to adapt to an administrative mold. It is one thing to assign an individual or a group the task of looking ahead; this is a far cry from providing an environment which encourages an understanding for deeper historical, sociological, and economic trends. The need to provide a memorandum may outweigh the imperatives of creative thought. The quest for objectivity creates a temptation to see in the future an updated version of the present. Yet true innovation is bound to run counter to prevailing standards. The dilemma of modern bureaucracy is that while every creative act is lonely, not every lonely act is creative. Formal criteria are little help in solving this problem because the unique cannot be expressed "objectively."

The rigidity in the policies of the technologically advanced societies is in no small part due to the complexity of decision-making. Crucial problems may—and frequently do—go unrecognized for a long time. But once the decision-making apparatus has disgorged a policy, it becomes very difficult to change it. The alternative to the *status quo* is the prospect of repeating the whole anguishing process of arriving at decisions. This explains to some extent the curious phenomenon that decisions taken with enormous doubt and perhaps with a close division become practically sacrosanct once adopted. The whole administrative machinery swings behind their implementation as if activity could still all doubts.

Moreover, the reputation, indeed the political survival, of most leaders depends on their ability to realize their goals, however these may have been arrived at. Whether these goals are desirable is relatively less crucial. The time span by which administrative success is measured is considerably shorter than that by which historical achievement is determined. In heavily bureaucratized societies all pressures emphasize the first of these accomplishments.

Then, too, the staffs on which modern executives come to depend develop a momentum of their own. What starts out as an aid to decision-makers often turns into a practically autonomous organization whose internal problems structure and sometimes compound the issues which it was originally designed to solve. The decision-maker will always be aware of the morale of his staff. Though he has the authority, he cannot overrule it too frequently without impairing its efficiency; and he may, in any event, lack the knowledge to do so. Placating the staff then becomes a major preoccupation of the executive. A form of administrative democracy results, in which a decision often reflects an attainable consensus rather than substantive conviction (or at least the two imperceptibly merge). The internal requirements of the bureaucracy may come to predominate over the purposes which it was intended to serve. This is probably even more true in highly institutionalized Communist states—such as the U.S.S.R.—than in the United States.

When the administrative machine grows very elaborate, the various levels of the decision-making process are separated by chasms which are obscured from the outside world by the complexity of the apparatus. Research often becomes a means to buy time and to assuage consciences. Studying a problem can turn into an escape from coming to grips with it. In the process, the gap between the technical competence of research staffs and what hard-pressed political leaders are capable of absorbing widens constantly. This heightens the insecurity of the executive and may thus compound either rigidity or arbitrariness or both. In many fields—strategy being a prime example—decision-makers may find it difficult to give as many hours to a problem as the expert has had years to study it. The ultimate decision often depends less on knowledge than on the ability to brief the top administrator—to present the facts in such a way that they can be absorbed rapidly. The effectiveness of briefing, however, puts a premium on theatrical qualities. Not everything that sounds plausible is correct, and many things which are correct may not sound plausible when they are first presented; and a second hearing is rare. The stage aspect of briefing may leave the decision-maker with a gnawing feeling of having been taken—even, and perhaps especially, when he does not know quite how.

Sophistication may thus encourage paralysis or a crude popularization which defeats its own purpose. The excessively theoretical approach of many research staffs overlooks the problem of the strain of decision-making in times of crisis. What is relevant for policy depends not only on academic truth but also on what can be implemented under stress. The technical staffs are frequently operating in a framework of theoretical standards while in fact their usefulness depends on essentially psychological criteria. To be politically meaningful, their proposals must involve answers to the following types of questions: Does the executive understand the proposal? Does he believe in it? Does he accept it as a guide to action or as an excuse for doing nothing? But if these kinds of concerns are given too much weight, the requirements of salesmanship will defeat substance.

The pragmatism of executives thus clashes with the theoretical bent of research or planning staffs. Executives as a rule take cognizance of a problem only when it emerges as an administrative issue. They thus unwittingly encourage bureaucratic contests as the only means of generating decisions. Or the various elements of the bureaucracy make a series of nonaggression pacts with each other and thus reduce the decision-maker to a benevolent constitutional monarch. As the special role of the executive increasingly becomes to choose between proposals generated administratively, decision-makers turn into arbiters rather than leaders. Whether they wait until a problem emerges as an administrative issue or until a crisis has demonstrated the irrelevance of the standard operating procedure, the modern decision-makers often find themselves the prisoners of their advisers.

Faced with an administrative machine which is both elaborate and fragmented, the executive is forced into essentially lateral means of control. Many of his public pronouncements, though ostensibly directed to outsiders, perform a perhaps more important role in laying down guidelines for the bureaucracy. The chief significance of a foreign policy speech by the President may thus be that it settles an internal debate in Washington (a public statement is more useful for this purpose than an administrative memorandum because it is harder to reverse). At the same time, the bureaucracy's awareness of this method of control tempts it to shortcut its debates by using pronouncements by the decision-makers as charters for special purposes. The executive thus finds himself confronted by proposals for public declarations which may be innocuous in themselves —and whose bureaucratic significance may be anything but obvious—but which can be used by some agency or department to launch a study or program which will restrict his freedom of decision later on.

All of this drives the executive in the direction of extra-bureaucratic means of decision. The practice of relying on special emissaries or personal envoys is an example; their status outside the bureaucracy frees them from some of its restraints. International agreements are sometimes possible only by ignoring safeguards against capricious action. It is a paradoxical aspect of modern bureaucracies that their quest for objectivity and calculability often leads to impasses which can be overcome only by essentially arbitrary decisions.

Such a mode of operation would involve a great risk of stagnation even in "normal" times. It becomes especially dangerous in a revolutionary period. For then, the problems which are most obtrusive may be least relevant. The issues which are most significant may not be suitable for administrative formulation and even when formulated may not lend themselves to bureaucratic consensus. When the issue is how to transform the existing framework, routine can become an additional obstacle to both comprehension and action.

This problem, serious enough *within* each society, is magnified in the conduct of international affairs. While the formal machinery of decision-making in developed countries shows many similarities, the criteria which influence decisions vary enormously. With each administrative machine increasingly absorbed in its own internal problems, diplomacy loses its flexibility. Leaders are extremely aware of the problems of placating their own bureaucracy; they cannot depart too far from its prescriptions without raising serious morale problems. Decisions are reached so painfully that the very anguish of decision-making acts as a brake on the give-and-take of traditional diplomacy.

This is true even *within* alliances. Meaningful consultation with other nations becomes very difficult when the internal process of decision-making already has some of the characteristics of compacts between quasi-sovereign entities. There is an increasing reluctance to hazard a hard-won domestic consensus in an international forum.

What is true within alliances—that is, among nations which have at least some common objectives —becomes even more acute in relations between antagonistic states or blocs. The gap created when two large bureaucracies generate goals largely in isolation from each other and on the basis of not necessarily commensurable criteria is magnified considerably by an ideological schism. The degree of ideological fervor is not decisive; the problem would exist even if the original ideological comment had declined on either or both sides. The criteria for bureaucratic decision-making may continue to be influenced by ideology even after its élan has dissipated. Bureaucratic structures generate their own momentum which may more than counterbalance the loss of earlier fanaticism. In the early stages of a revolutionary movement, ideology is crucial and the accident of personalities can be decisive. The Reign of Terror in France was ended by the elimination of a single man, Robespierre. The Bolshevik revolution could hardly have taken place had Lenin not been on the famous train which crossed Germany into Russia. But once a revolution becomes institutionalized, the administrative structures which it has spawned develop their own vested interests. Ideology may grow less significant in creating commitment; it becomes pervasive in supplying criteria of administrative choice. Ideologies prevail by being taken for granted. Orthodoxy substitutes for conviction and produces its own form of rigidity.

In such circumstances, a meaningful dialogue across ideological dividing lines becomes extraordinarily difficult. The more elaborate the administrative structure, the less relevant an individual's view becomes—indeed one of the purposes of bureaucracy is to liberate decision-making from the accident of personalities. Thus while personal convictions may be modified, it requires a really monumental effort to alter bureaucratic commitments. And if change occurs, the bureaucracy prefers to move at its own pace and not be excessively influenced by statements or pressures of foreigners. For all these reasons, diplomacy tends to become rigid or to turn into an abstract bargaining process based on largely formal criteria such as "splitting the difference." Either course is self-defeating: the former because it negates the very purpose of diplomacy; the latter because it subordinates purpose to technique and because it may encourage intransigence. Indeed, the incentive for intransigence increases if it is known that the difference will generally be split.

Ideological differences are compounded because

major parts of the world are only in the first stages of administrative evolution. Where the technologically advanced countries suffer from the inertia of over-administration, the developing areas often lack even the rudiments of effective bureaucracy. Where the advanced countries may drown in "facts," the emerging nations are frequently without the most elementary knowledge needed for forming a meaningful judgment or for implementing it once it has been taken. Where large bureaucracies operate in alternating spurts of rigidity and catastrophic (in relation to the bureaucracy) upheaval, the new states tend to take decisions on the basis of almost random pressures. The excessive institutionalization of one and the inadequate structure of the other inhibit international stability.

III. The Nature of Leadership

Whatever one's view about the degree to which choices in international affairs are "objectively" determined, the decisions are made by individuals who will be above all conscious of the seeming multiplicity of options. Their understanding of the nature of their choice depends on many factors, including their experience during the rise to eminence.

The mediating, conciliatory style of British policy in the nineteenth century reflected, in part, the qualities encouraged during careers in Parliament and the values of a cohesive leadership group connected by ties of family and common education. The hysterical cast of the policy of Imperial Germany was given impetus by a domestic structure in which political parties were deprived of responsibility while ministers were obliged to balance a monarch by divine right against a Parliament composed of representatives without any prospect of ever holding office. Consensus could be achieved most easily through fits of national passion which in turn disquieted all of Germany's neighbors. Germany's foreign policy grew unstable because its domestic structure did little to discourage capricious improvisations; it may even have put a premium on them.

The collapse of the essentially aristocratic conception of foreign policy of the nineteenth century has made the career experiences of leaders even more crucial. An aristocracy—if it lives up to its values—will reject the arbitrariness of absolutist rule; and it

will base itself on a notion of quality which discourages the temptations of demagoguery inherent in plebiscitarian democracy. Where position is felt to be a birthright, generosity is possible (though not guaranteed); flexibility is not inhibited by a commitment to perpetual success. Where a leader's estimate of himself is not completely dependent on his standing in an administrative structure, measures can be judged in terms of a conception of the future rather than of an almost compulsive desire to avoid even a temporary set-back. When statesmen belonged to a community transcending national boundaries, there tended to be consensus on the criteria of what constituted a reasonable proposal. This did not prevent conflicts, but it did define their nature and encourage dialogue. The bane of aristocratic foreign policy was the risk of frivolousness, of a self-confidence unrelated to knowledge, and of too much emphasis on intuition.

In any event, ours is the age of the expert or the charismatic leader. The expert has his constituency —those who have a vested interest in commonly held opinions; elaborating and defining its consensus at a high level has, after all, made him an expert. Since the expert is often the product of the administrative dilemmas described earlier, he is usually in a poor position to transcend them. The charismatic leader, on the other hand, needs a perpetual revolution to maintain his position. Neither the expert nor the charismatic leader operates in an environment which puts a premium on long-range conceptions or on generosity or on subordinating the leader's ego to purposes which transcend his own career.

Leadership groups are formed by at least three factors: their experiences during their rise to eminence; the structure in which they must operate; the values of their society. Three contemporary types will be discussed here: (a) the bureaucratic-pragmatic type, (b) the ideological type, and (c) the revolutionary-charismatic type.

Bureaucratic-Pragmatic Leadership

The main example of this type of leadership is the American élite—though the leadership groups of other Western countries increasingly approximate the American pattern. Shaped by a society without fundamental social schisms (at least until the race problem became visible) and the product of an environment in which most recognized problems have proved soluble, its approach to policy is *ad hoc*, pragmatic, and somewhat mechanical.

Because pragmatism is based on the conviction that the context of events produces a solution, there is a tendency to await developments. The belief is prevalent that every problem will yield if attacked with sufficient energy. It is inconceivable, therefore, that delay might result in irretrievable disaster; at worst it is thought to require a redoubled effort later on. Problems are segmented into constituent elements, each of which is dealt with by experts in the special difficulty it involves. There is little emphasis or concern for their interrelationship. Technical issues enjoy more careful attention, and receive more sophisticated treatment, than political ones. Though the importance of intangibles is affirmed in theory, it is difficult to obtain a consensus on which factors are significant and even harder to find a meaningful mode for dealing with them. Things are done because one knows how to do them and not because one ought to do them. The criteria for dealing with trends which are conjectural are less well developed than those for immediate crises. Pragmatism, at least in its generally accepted form, is more concerned with method than with judgment; or rather it seeks to reduce judgment to methodology and value to knowledge.

This is reinforced by the special qualities of the professions—law and business—which furnish the core of the leadership groups in America. Lawyers—at least in the Anglo-Saxon tradition—prefer to deal with actual rather than hypothetical cases; they have little confidence in the possibility of stating a future issue abstractly. But planning by its very nature is hypothetical. Its success depends precisely on the ability to transcend the existing framework. Lawyers may be prepared to undertake this task; but they will do well in it only to the extent that they are able to overcome the special qualities encouraged by their profession. What comes naturally to lawyers in the Anglo-Saxon tradition is the sophisticated analysis of a series of *ad hoc* issues which emerge as problems through adversary proceedings. In so far as lawyers draw on the experience which forms them, they have a bias toward awaiting developments and toward operating within the definition of the problem as formulated by its chief spokesmen.

This has several consequences. It compounds the already powerful tendencies within American society to identify foreign policy with the solution of immediate issues. It produces great refinement of issues as they arise, but it also encourages the administrative dilemmas described earlier. Issues are dealt with only as the pressure of events imposes the need for resolving them. Then, each of the contending factions within the bureaucracy has a maximum incentive to state its case in its most extreme form because the ultimate outcome depends, to a considerable extent, on a bargaining process. The premium placed on advocacy turns decision-making into a series of adjustments among special interests— a process more suited to domestic than to foreign policy. This procedure neglects the long-range because the future has no administrative constituency and is, therefore, without representation in the adversary proceedings. Problems tend to be slighted until some agency or department is made responsible for them. When this occurs—usually when a difficulty has already grown acute—the relevant department becomes an all-out spokesman for its particular area of responsibility. The outcome usually depends more on the pressures or the persuasiveness of the contending advocates than on a concept of over-all purpose. While these tendencies exist to some extent in all bureaucracies they are particularly pronounced in the American system of government.

This explains in part the peculiar alternation of rigidity and spasms of flexibility in American diplomacy. On a given issue—be it the Berlin crisis or disarmament or the war in Viet-Nam—there generally exists a great reluctance to develop a negotiating position or a statement of objectives except in the most general terms. This stems from a desire not to prejudge the process of negotiations and above all to retain flexibility in the face of unforeseeable events. But when an approaching conference or some other pressures make the development of a position imperative and some office or individual is assigned the specific task, a sudden change occurs. Both personal and bureaucratic success are then identified with bringing the particular assignment to a conclusion. Where so much stock is placed in negotiating skill, a failure of a conference may be viewed as a reflection on the ability of the negotiator rather than on the objective difficulty of the subject. Confidence in the bargaining process causes American negotiators to be extremely sensitive to the tactical requirements of the conference table—sometimes at the expense of longer-term considerations. In internal discussions, American negotiators—generally irrespective of their previous commitments—often become advocates for the maximum range of concessions; their legal background tempts them to act as mediators between Washington and the country with which they are negotiating.

The attitudes of the business élite reinforce the convictions of the legal profession. The American business executive rises through a process of selection which rewards the ability to manipulate the known—in itself a conciliatory procedure. The special skill of the executive is thought to consist in coordinating well-defined functions rather than in challenging them. The procedure is relatively effective in the business world, where the executive can often substitute decisiveness, long experience, and a wide range of personal acquaintance for reflectiveness. In international affairs, however—especially in a revolutionary situation—the strong will which is one of our business executives' notable traits may produce essentially arbitrary choices. Or unfamiliarity with the subject matter may have the opposite effect of turning the executive into a spokesman of his technical staffs. In either case, the business executive is even more dependent than the lawyer on the bureaucracy's formulation of the issue. The business élite is even less able or willing than the lawyer to recognize that the formulation of an issue, not the technical remedy, is usually the central problem.

All this gives American policy its particular cast. Problems are dealt with as they arise. Agreement on what constitutes a problem generally depends on an emerging crisis which settles the previously inconclusive disputes about priorities. When a problem is recognized, it is dealt with by a mobilization of all resources to overcome the immediate symptoms. This often involves the risk of slighting longer-term issues which may not yet have assumed crisis proportions and of overwhelming, perhaps even undermining, the structure of the area concerned by a flood of American technical experts proposing remedies on an American scale. Administrative decisions emerge from a compromise of conflicting pressures in which accidents of personality or persuasiveness play a crucial role. The compromise often reflects the maxim that "if two parties disagree the truth is usually somewhere in between." But the pedantic application of such truisms causes the various

contenders to exaggerate their positions for bargaining purposes or to construct fictitious extremes to make their position appear moderate. In either case, internal bargaining predominates over substance.

The *ad hoc* tendency of our decision-makers and the reliance on adversary proceeding cause issues to be stated in black and white terms. This suppresses a feeling for nuance and makes it difficult to recognize the relationship between seemingly discrete events. Even with the perspective of a decade there is little consensus about the relationship between the actions culminating in the Suez fiasco and the French decision to enter the nuclear field; or about the inconsistency between the neutralization of Laos and the step-up of the military effort in Viet-Nam.

The same quality also produces a relatively low valuation of historical factors. Nations are treated as similar phenomena, and those states presenting similar immediate problems are treated similarly. Since many of our policy-makers first address themselves to an issue when it emerges as their area of responsibility, their approach to it is often highly anecdotal. Great weight is given to what people say and relatively little to the significance of these affirmations in terms of domestic structure or historical background. Agreement may be taken at face value and seen as reflecting more consensus than actually exists. Opposition tends to produce moral outrage which often assumes the form of personal animosity—the attitude of some American policy-makers toward President de Gaulle is a good example.

The legal background of our policy-makers produces a bias in favor of constitutional solutions. The issue of supra-nationalism or confederalism in Europe has been discussed largely in terms of the right of countries to make independent decisions. Much less weight has been given to the realities which would limit the application of a majority vote against a major country whatever the legal arrangements. (The fight over the application of Article 19 of the United Nations Charter was based on the same attitude.) Similarly, legal terms such as "integration" and "assignment" sometimes become ends in themselves and thus obscure the operational reality to which they refer. In short, the American leadership groups show high competence in dealing with technical issues, and much less virtuosity in mastering a historical process. And the policies of other Western countries exhibit variations of the American pattern.

A lesser pragmatism in continental Europe is counter-balanced by a smaller ability to play a world-role.

The Ideological Type of Leadership

As has been discussed above, the impact of ideology can persist long after its initial fervor has been spent. Whatever the ideological commitment of individual leaders, a lifetime spent in the Communist hierarchy must influence their basic categories of thought—especially since Communist ideology continues to perform important functions. It still furnishes the standard of truth and the guarantee of ultimate success. It provides a means for maintaining cohesion among the various Communist parties of the world. It supplies criteria for the settlement of disputes both within the bureaucracy of individual Communist countries and among the various Communist states.

However attenuated, Communist ideology is, in part, responsible for international tensions. This is less because of specific Marxist tactical prescriptions —with respect to which Communists have shown a high degree of flexibility—than because of the basic Marxist-Leninist categories for interpreting reality. Communist leaders never tire of affirming that Marxism-Leninism is the key element of their self-proclaimed superiority over the outside world; as Marxist-Leninists they are convinced that they understand the historical process better than the non-Communist world does.

The essence of Marxism-Leninism—and the reason that normal diplomacy with Communist states is so difficult—is the view that "objective" factors such as the social structure, the economic process, and, above all, the class struggle are more important than the personal convictions of statesmen. Belief in the predominance of objective factors explains the Soviet approach to the problem of security. If personal convictions are "subjective," Soviet security cannot be allowed to rest on the good will of other statesmen, especially those of a different social system. This produces a quest for what may be described as absolute security—the attempt to be so strong as to be independent of the decisions of other countries. But absolute security for one country means absolute insecurity for all others; it can be achieved only by reducing other states to impotence. Thus an essentially defensive foreign policy can grow indistinguishable from traditional aggression.

The belief in the predominance of objective factors explains why, in the past, periods of détente have proved so precarious. When there is a choice between Western good will or a physical gain, the pressures to choose the latter have been overwhelming. The wartime friendship with the West was sacrificed to the possibility of establishing Communist-controlled governments in Eastern Europe. The spirit of Geneva did not survive the temptations offered by the prospect of undermining the Western position in the Middle East. The many overtures of the Kennedy administration were rebuffed until the Cuban missile crisis demonstrated that the balance of forces was not in fact favorable for a test of strength.

The reliance on objective factors has complicated negotiations between the West and the Communist countries. Communist negotiators find it difficult to admit that they could be swayed by the arguments of men who have, by definition, an inferior grasp of the laws of historical development. No matter what is said, they think that they understand their Western counterpart better than he understands himself. Concessions are possible, but they are made to "reality," not to individuals or to a bargaining process. Diplomacy becomes difficult when one of the parties considers the key element to negotiation—the give-and-take of the process of bargaining—as but a superstructure for factors not part of the negotiation itself.

Finally, whatever the decline in ideological fervor, orthodoxy requires the maintenance of a posture of ideological hostility to the non-Communist world even during a period of coexistence. Thus, in a reply to a Chinese challenge, the Communist Party of the U.S.S.R. declared: "We fully support the destruction of capitalism. We not only believe in the inevitable death of capitalism but we are doing everything possible for it to be accomplished through class struggle as quickly as possible."[2]

The wariness toward the outside world is reinforced by the personal experiences which Communist leaders have had on the road to eminence. In a system where there is no legitimate succession, a

[2] "The Soviet Reply to the Chinese Letter," open letter of the Central Committee of the Communist Party of the Soviet Union as it appeared in *Pravda*, July 14, 1963, pp. 1–4; *The Current Digest of the Soviet Press*, Vol. XV, No. 28 (August 7, 1963), p. 23.

great deal of energy is absorbed in internal maneuvering. Leaders rise to the top by eliminating—sometimes physically, always bureaucratically—all possible opponents. Stalin had all individuals who helped him into power executed. Khrushchev disgraced Kaganovich, whose protegé he had been, and turned on Marshal Zhukov six months after being saved by him from a conspiracy of his other colleagues. Brezhnev and Kosygin owed their careers to Khrushchev; they nevertheless overthrew him and started a campaign of calumny against him within twenty-four hours of his dismissal.

Anyone succeeding in Communist leadership struggles must be single-minded, unemotional, dedicated, and, above all, motivated by an enormous desire for power. Nothing in the personal experience of Soviet leaders would lead them to accept protestations of good will at face value. Suspiciousness is inherent in their domestic position. It is unlikely that their attitude toward the outside world is more benign than toward their own colleagues or that they would expect more consideration from it.

The combination of personal qualities and ideological structure also affects relations *among* Communist states. Since national rivalries are thought to be the result of class conflict, they are expected to disappear wherever Socialism has triumphed. When disagreements occur they are dealt with by analogy to internal Communist disputes: by attempting to ostracize and then to destroy the opponent. The tendency to treat different opinions as manifestations of heresy causes disagreements to harden into bitter schisms. The debate between Communist China and the U.S.S.R. is in many respects more acrimonious than that between the U.S.S.R. and the non-Communist world.

Even though the basic conceptual categories of Communist leadership groups are similar, the impact of the domestic structure of the individual Communist states on international relations varies greatly. It makes a considerable difference whether an ideology has become institutionalized, as in the Soviet Union, or whether it is still impelled by its early revolutionary fervor, as in Communist China. Where ideology has become institutionalized a special form of pragmatism may develop. It may be just as empirical as that of the United States but it will operate in a different realm of "reality." A different philosophical basis leads to the emergence of another set of categories for the settlement of disputes, and these in turn generate another range of problems.

A Communist bureaucratic structure, however pragmatic, will have different priorities from ours; it will give greater weight to doctrinal considerations and conceptual problems. It is more than ritual when speeches of senior Soviet leaders begin with hour-long recitals of Communist ideology. Even if it were ritual, it must affect the definition of what is considered reasonable in internal arguments. Bureaucratization and pragmatism may lead to a loss of élan; they do not guarantee convergence of Western and Soviet thinking.

The more revolutionary manifestations of Communism, such as Communist China, still possess more ideological fervor, but, paradoxically, their structure may permit a wider latitude for new departures. Tactical intransigence and ideological vitality should not be confused with structural rigidity. Because the leadership bases its rule on a prestige which transcends bureaucratic authority, it has not yet given so many hostages to the administrative structure. If the leadership should change—or if its attitudes are modified—policy could probably be altered much more dramatically in Communist China than in the more institutionalized Communist countries.

The Charismatic-Revolutionary Type of Leadership

The contemporary international order is heavily influenced by yet another leadership type: the charismatic-revolutionary leader. For many of the leaders of the new nations the bureaucratic-pragmatic approach of the West is irrelevant because they are more interested in the future which they wish to construct than in the manipulation of the environment which dominates the thinking of the pragmatists. And ideology is not satisfactory because doctrine supplies rigid categories which overshadow the personal experiences which have provided the impetus for so many of the leaders of the new nations.

The type of individual who leads a struggle for independence has been sustained in the risks and suffering of such a course primarily by a commitment to a vision which enabled him to override conditions which had seemed overwhelmingly hostile. Revolutionaries are rarely motivated primarily by material considerations—though the illusion that they are persists in the West. Material incentives do not cause a man to risk his existence and to launch himself into the uncertainties of a revolutionary struggle. If Castro or Sukarno had been principally interested in economics, their talents would have guaranteed them a brilliant career in the societies they overthrew. What made their sacrifices worthwhile to them was a vision of the future—or a quest for political power. To revolutionaries the significant reality is the world which they are striving to bring about, not the world they are fighting to overcome.

This difference in perspective accounts for the inconclusiveness of much of the dialogue between the West and many of the leaders of the new countries. The West has a tendency to believe that the tensions in the emerging nations are caused by a low level of economic activity. To the apostles of economic development, raising the gross national product seems the key to political stability. They believe that it should receive the highest priority from the political leaders of new countries and supply their chief motivation.

But to the charismatic heads of many of the new nations, economic progress, while not unwelcome, offers too limited a scope for their ambitions. It can be achieved only by slow, painful, highly technical measures which contrast with the heroic exertions of the struggle for independence. Results are long-delayed; credit for them cannot be clearly established. If Castro were to act on the advice of theorists of economic development, the best he could hope for would be that after some decades he would lead a small progressive country—perhaps a Switzerland of the Caribbean. Compared to the prospect of leading a revolution throughout Latin America, this goal would appear trivial, boring, perhaps even unreal to him.

Moreover, to the extent that economic progress is achieved, it may magnify domestic political instability, at least in its early phases. Economic advance disrupts the traditional political structure. It thus places constant pressures on the incumbent leaders to re-establish the legitimacy of their rule. For this purpose a dramatic foreign policy is particularly apt. Many leaders of the new countries seem convinced that an adventurous foreign policy will not harm prospects for economic development and may even foster it. The competition of the superpowers makes it likely that economic assistance will be forthcoming regardless of the actions of the recipient. Indeed the more obstrusive their foreign policy the greater is their prospect of being wooed by the chief contenders.

The tendency toward a reckless policy is magnified by the uncertain sense of identity of many of the new nations. National boundaries often correspond to the administrative subdivisions established by the former colonial rulers. States thus have few of the attributes of nineteenth-century European nationalism: common language, common culture, or even common history. In many cases, the only common experience is a century or so of imperial rule. As a result, there is a great pressure toward authoritarian rule, and a high incentive to use foreign policy as a means of bringing about domestic cohesion.

Western-style democracy presupposes that society transcends the political realm; in that case opposition challenges a particular method of achieving common aims but not the existence of the state itself. In many of the new countries, by contrast, the state represents the primary, sometimes the sole, manifestation of social cohesion. Opposition can therefore easily appear as treason—apart from the fact that leaders who have spent several decades running the risks of revolutionary struggle or who have achieved power by a coup d'état are not likely to favor a system of government which makes them dispensable. Indeed the attraction of Communism for many of these leaders is not Marxist-Leninist economic theory but the legitimacy for authoritarian rule which it provides.

No matter what the system of government, many of the leaders of the new nations use foreign policy as a means to escape intractable internal difficulties and as a device to achieve domestic cohesion. The international arena provides an opportunity for the dramatic measures which are impossible at home. These are often cast in an anti-Western mold because this is the easiest way to recreate the struggle against imperial rule which is the principal unifying element for many new nations. The incentive is particularly strong because the rivalry of the nuclear powers eliminates many of the risks which previously were associated with an adventurous foreign policy—especially if that foreign policy is directed against the West which lacks any effective sanctions.

Traditional military pressure is largely precluded by the nuclear stalemate and respect for world opinion. But the West is neither prepared nor able to use the sanction which weighs most heavily on the new countries: the deliberate exploitation of their weak domestic structure. In many areas the ability to foment domestic unrest is a more potent weapon than traditional arms. Many of the leaders of the new countries will be prepared to ignore the classical panoply of power; but they will be very sensitive to the threat of domestic upheaval. States with a high capacity for exploiting domestic instability can use it as a tool of foreign policy. China, though lacking almost all forms of classical long-range military strength, is a growing factor in Africa. Weak states may be more concerned with a country's capacity to organize domestic unrest in their territory than with its capacity for physical destruction.

Conclusion. Contemporary domestic structures thus present an unprecedented challenge to the emergence of a stable international order. The bureaucratic-pragmatic societies concentrate on the manipulation of an empirical reality which they treat as given; the ideological societies are split between an essentially bureaucratic approach (though in a different realm of reality than the bureaucratic-pragmatic structures) and a group using ideology mainly for revolutionary ends. The new nations, in so far as they are active in international affairs, have a high incentive to seek in foreign policy the perpetuation of charismatic leadership.

These differences are a major obstacle to a consensus on what constitutes a "reasonable" proposal. A common diagnosis of the existing situation is hard to achieve, and it is even more difficult to concert measures for a solution. The situation is complicated by the one feature all types of leadership have in common: the premium put on short-term goals and the domestic need to succeed at all times. In the bureaucratic societies policy emerges from a compromise which often produces the least common denominator, and it is implemented by individuals whose reputation is made by administering the *status quo*. The leadership of the institutionalized ideological state may be even more the prisoner of essentially corporate bodies. Neither leadership can afford radical changes of course for they result in profound repercussions in its administrative structure. And the charismatic leaders of the new nations are like tightrope artists—one false step and they will plunge from their perch.

IV. Domestic Structure and Foreign Policy: The Prospects for World Order

Many contemporary divisions are thus traceable to differences in domestic structure. But are there not countervailing factors? What about the spread of technology and its associated rationality, or the adoption on a global scale of many Western political forms? Unfortunately the process of "Westernization" does not inevitably produce a similar concept of reality. For what matters is not the institutions or the technology, but the significance which is attached to them. And this differs according to the evolution of the society concerned.

The term "nation" does not mean the same thing when applied to such various phenomena as India, France, and Nigeria. Similarly, technology is likely to have a different significance for different peoples, depending on how and when it was acquired.

Any society is part of an evolutionary process which proceeds by means of two seemingly contradictory mechanisms. On the one hand, the span of possible adaptations is delimited by the physical environment, the internal structure, and, above all, by previous choices. On the other hand, evolution proceeds not in a straight line but through a series of complicated variations which appear anything but obvious to the chief actors. In retrospect a choice may seem to have been nearly random or else to have represented the only available alternative. In either case, the choice is not an isolated act but an accumulation of previous decisions reflecting history or tradition and values as well as the immediate pressures of the need for survival. And each decision delimits the range of possible future adaptations.

Young societies are in a position to make radical changes of course which are highly impractical at a later stage. As a society becomes more elaborate and as its tradition is firmly established, its choices with respect to its internal organization grow more restricted. If a highly articulated social unit attempts basic shifts, it runs the risk of doing violence to its internal organization, to its history and values as embodied in its structure. When it accepts institutions or values developed elsewhere it must adapt them to what its structure can absorb. The institutions of any political unit must therefore be viewed in historical context for that alone can give an indication of their future.

Societies—even when their institutions are similar—may be like ships passing in the night which find themselves but temporarily in the same place.

Is there then no hope for cooperation and stability? Is our international system doomed to incomprehension and its members to mounting frustration?

It must be admitted that if the domestic structures were considered in isolation, the prognosis would not be too hopeful. But domestic structures do not exist in a vacuum. They must respond to the requirements of the environment. And here all states find themselves face to face with the necessity of avoiding a nuclear holocaust. While this condition does not restrain all nations equally, it nevertheless defines a common task which technology will impose on even more countries as a direct responsibility.

Then, too, a certain similarity in the forms of administration may bring about common criteria of rationality as Professor Jaguaribe has pointed out in his contribution to this volume.[3] Science and technology will spread. Improved communications may lead to the emergence of a common culture. The fissures between domestic structures and the different stages of evolution are important, but they may be outweighed by the increasing interdependence of humanity.

It would be tempting to end on this note and to base the hope for peace on the self-evidence of the need for it. But this would be too pat. The deepest problem of the contemporary international order may be that most of the debates which form the headlines of the day are peripheral to the basic division described in this article. The cleavage is not over particular political arrangements—except as symptoms—but between two styles of policy and two philosophical perspectives.

The two styles can be defined as the political as against the revolutionary approach to order or, reduced to personalities, as the distinction between the statesman and the prophet.

The statesman manipulates reality; his first goal is survival; he feels responsible not only for the best but also for the worst conceivable outcome. His view of human nature is wary; he is conscious of many great hopes which have failed, of many good intentions that could not be realized, of selfishness and

[3] "World Order, Rationality, and Socioeconomic Development," pp. 607–26.

ambition and violence. He is, therefore, inclined to erect hedges against the possibility that even the most brilliant idea might prove abortive and that the most eloquent formulation might hide ulterior motives. He will try to avoid certain experiments, not because he would object to the results if they succeeded, but because he would feel himself responsible for the consequences if they failed. He is suspicious of those who personalize foreign policy, for history teaches him the fragility of structures dependent on individuals. To the statesman, gradualism is the essence of stability; he represents an era of average performance, of gradual change and slow construction.

By contrast, the prophet is less concerned with manipulating than with creating reality. What is possible interests him less than what is "right." He offers his vision as the test and his good faith as a guarantee. He believes in total solutions; he is less absorbed in methodology than in purpose. He believes in the perfectibility of man. His approach is timeless and not dependent on circumstances. He objects to gradualism as an unnecessary concession to circumstance. He will risk everything because his vision is the primary significant reality to him. Paradoxically, his more optimistic view of human nature makes him more intolerant than the statesman. If truth is both knowable and attainable, only immorality or stupidity can keep man from realizing it. The prophet represents an era of exaltation, of great upheavals, of vast accomplishments, but also of enormous disasters.

The encounter between the political and the prophetic approach to policy is always somewhat inconclusive and frustrating. The test of the statesman is the permanence of the international structure under stress. The test of the prophet is inherent in his vision. The statesman will seek to reduce the prophet's intuition to precise measures; he judges ideas on their utility and not on their "truth." To the prophet this approach is almost sacrilegious because it represents the triumph of expediency over universal principles. To the statesman negotiation is the mechanism of stability because it presupposes that maintenance of the existing order is more important than any dispute within it. To the prophet negotiations can have only symbolic value—as a means of converting or demoralizing the opponent; truth, by definition, cannot be compromised.

Both approaches have prevailed at different periods in history. The political approach dominated European foreign policy between the end of the religious wars and the French Revolution and then again between the Congress of Vienna and the outbreak of World War I. The prophetic mode was in the ascendant during the great upheavals of the religious struggles and the period of the French Revolution, and in the contemporary uprisings in major parts of the world.

Both modes have produced considerable accomplishments, though the prophetic style is likely to involve the greater dislocations and more suffering. Each has its nemesis. The nemesis of the statesman is that equilibrium, though it may be the condition of stability, does not supply its own motivation; that of the prophet is the impossibility of sustaining a mood of exaltation without the risk of submerging man in the vastness of a vision and reducing him to a mere figure to be manipulated.

As for the difference in philosophical perspective, it may reflect the divergence of the two lines of thought which since the Renaissance have distinguished the West from the part of the world now called underdeveloped (with Russia occupying an intermediary position). The West is deeply committed to the notion that the real world is external to the observer, that knowledge consists of recording and classifying data—the more accurately the better. Cultures which escaped the early impact of Newtonian thinking have retained the essentially pre-Newtonian view that the real world is almost completely *internal* to the observer.

Although this attitude was a liability for centuries—because it prevented the development of the technology and consumer goods which the West enjoyed—it offers great flexibility with respect to the contemporary revolutionary turmoil. It enables the societies which do not share our cultural mode to alter reality by influencing the perspective of the observer—a process which we are largely unprepared to handle or even to perceive. And this can be accomplished under contemporary conditions without sacrificing technological progress. Technology comes as a gift; acquiring it in its advanced form does not presuppose the philosophical commitment that discovering it imposed on the West. Empirical reality has a much different significance for many of

the new countries than for the West because in a certain sense they never went through the process of discovering it (with Russia again occupying an intermediary position). At the same time, the difference in philosophical perspective may cause us to seem cold, supercilious, lacking in compassion. The instability of the contemporary world order may thus have at its core a philosophical schism which makes the issues producing most political debates seem largely tangential.

Such differences in style and philosophical perspective are not unprecedented. What is novel is the global scale on which they occur and the risks which the failure to overcome them would entail. Historically, cleavages of lesser magnitude have been worked out dialectically, with one style of policy or one philosophical approach dominant in one era only to give way later to another conception of reality. And the transition was rarely free of violence. The challenge of our time is whether we can deal consciously and creatively with what in previous centuries was adjusted through a series of more or less violent and frequently catastrophic upheavals. We must construct an international order *before* a crisis imposes it as a necessity.

This is a question not of blueprints, but of attitudes. In fact the overconcern with technical blueprints is itself a symptom of our difficulties. Before the problem of order can be "dealt" with— even philosophically—we must be certain that the right questions are being asked.

We can point to some hopeful signs. The most sensitive thinkers of the West have recognized that excessive empiricism may lead to stagnation. In many of the new countries—and in some Communist ones as well—the second or third generation of leaders is in the process of freeing itself from the fervor and dogmatism of the early revolutionary period and of relating their actions to an environment which they helped to create. But these are as yet only the first tentative signs of progress on a course whose significance is not always understood. Indeed it is characteristic of an age of turmoil that it produces so many immediate issues that little time is left to penetrate their deeper meaning. The most serious problem therefore becomes the need to acquire a sufficiently wide perspective so that the present does not overwhelm the future.

26. Patterns of Personal Involvement in the National System: A Social-Psychological Analysis of Political Legitimacy*

Herbert C. Kelman is Richard Clarke Cabot Professor of Social Ethics at Harvard University. One of the few social psychologists to apply his skills and training to international phenomena, Professor Kelman is the editor of *International Behavior* (1965) and the author of a number of studies that probe the psychological underpinnings of international attitudes and actions. In this essay he explores the psychological bases of political legitimacy and, in so doing, the dynamics of nationalism. The result is a cogent insight into the processes whereby societies cohere and function. Professor Kelman's analysis does not focus directly on foreign policy, but the connections between the phenomena he examines and the external behavior of societies are virtually self-evident. [*Published for the first time in this volume.*]

Nationalism is widely regarded as a powerful force in the world today. In Europe, where it has been discredited as a result of the Second World War, it seems to be reemerging. In the Communist world, it has led to separate and often conflicting policies in different countries, thus helping to break down the myth of a monolithic world Communism. In the United States, it is at least partly responsible for the international posture of the current administration. In the Middle East, clashing nationalisms are seen as the cause of continuing tension. Nationalism has spread throughout the newly emerging states of Asia and Africa and, according to Whitaker and Jordan (1966), "it has become the greatest single force at work in Latin America" (p. 1).

Nationalism is seen as a major cause of wars and threats of war in our century, and as a barrier to the full development of international institutions and of an integrated world system. In some cases, we speak of nationalism as a threat to the internal cohesion of the nation-state—for example, Serbian or Croatian nationalism in Yugoslavia, or French-Canadian separatism in Canada, or even black nationalism in the United States. In other cases—notably when we are thinking of emerging states in Africa and Asia—we see it as a binding force contributing to economic development and political stability. Thus, the secession of Biafra from Nigeria is regarded as an act of Ibo tribalism threatening Nigerian nationalism.

* This paper is a revised version of an invited address presented at the Eleventh Inter-American Congress of Psychology in Mexico City, December 19, 1967. It is based on a research project carried out collaboratively with Daniel Katz, John DeLamater, and other colleagues. The work is supported in part by the Center for Research on Conflict Resolution at the University of Michigan, and in part by Public Health Service Research Grant MH 07280-07 from the National Institute of Mental Health for a research program on social influence and behavior change.

These examples point to one of the many sources of ambiguity and difficulty of the concept of nationalism, at least as it is often employed. We are being entirely arbitrary when we speak of the Serbs and Croatians in Yugoslavia as nations and of the Ibos and Hausas in Nigeria as tribes. The phenomena are broadly similar in both cases, despite, of course, their many unique features. In both, we have regions within an official nation-state whose populations—or important segments of whose populations—see themselves as culturally distinct and as having competing interests. These conditions cause them to demand a political structure that is, to a greater or lesser degree, separate or autonomous from the larger system and thus presumably more reflective of their identities and interests.

One cannot, in such a case, speak of nationalism as *a* force, with clearly definable universal goals. Rather, we must specify whose nationalism we are speaking of—what is the nation whose interest it is designed to serve. The population unit that is defined as the nation in a given case is, to a large extent, arbitrary. It is, therefore, confusing to speak of what is happening in Nigeria as a conflict between tribalism and nationalism. It would seem more reasonable to describe it as a conflict between Nigerian nationalism and Ibo nationalism—between those who see their interests best served by maintaining Nigeria, with all its vastness and tribal diversity, as a single nation-state, and those who see their interests best served by establishing a nation-state in a smaller, culturally more (though by no means entirely) homogeneous region.

There is another sense in which it is misleading to speak of nationalism as *a* force, with the implication that this carries some special explanatory value. Nationalism, wherever it occurs, draws on certain universal psychological dispositions, and on a set of norms established in the contemporary international system, in order to promote a particular set of goals shared by an identifiable population or segment of such a population. What is common to all cases of nationalism is the attempt to promote these goals by maintaining or establishing a nation-state as an effective political unit. The nature of the goals involved, however, may vary widely from country to country, from period to period, and from group to group within a given country. Nationalism may be mobilized, for example, in the service of economic development, or of military expansion, or of internal democratization; and in each of these cases a different segment of the population is likely to provide the impetus and the leadership for this effort.

Thus, it is more useful to conceive of nationalism not as a force in its own right, but as a vehicle for achieving certain other goals. These goals are usually of special importance to a particular elite within a society, but they must, at some level, correspond to goals widely shared by the population at large, whose support must be mobilized. To cite Whitaker and Jordan (1966) again, ". . . nationalism is a tool, and the things we need to know about it are, who uses it, and why, how, and with what results" (p. 5). Only by distinguishing different types of nationalism can we do justice, for example, to "a phenomenon common to most Latin American countries, namely, the existence of several different and competing varieties of nationalism in the same country at the same time" (p. 6).

Generic Features of Nationalism

Before we proceed to examine different types of nationalism, each with its own particular goals and functions, we must identify the generic features that they all share. We can capture these common elements best, I believe, if we conceive of nationalism as the ideology of the modern nation-state or of movements directed toward the establishment of a new nation-state. Nationalism, whatever its form, is an ideology that provides a justification for the existence or establishment of a nation-state defining a particular population, and that prescribes the relationship of the individual to that state. There are at least three elements that all different forms of modern nationalism seem to have in common.

(1) The ultimate justification for maintaining, strengthening, or establishing a political system with jurisdiction over a particular population—that is, an internationally recognized nation-state—is that this system is most naturally and effectively representative of that population. It is this feature, as we shall see later, that provides legitimacy and cohesiveness to the modern nation-state. In principle, the nation-state—as its name implies—is representative of the population by virtue of the fact that its political boundaries also constitute national boundaries. In other words, the political entity corresponds with an

ethnic, cultural, and historical entity with which at least large portions of the population identify. There is the further presumption that such correspondence also assures the best protection of the interests of the population. In practice, of course, this correspondence often does not exist, in that a state may comprise a variety of distinct ethnic and cultural groups, sometimes with a long history of intergroup conflict. Belgium, Yugoslavia, Canada, and Nigeria are some of the many examples of multicultural and multilingual states. Thus, there is an inherent circularity in the defining characteristic of the nation-state: The state is justified by virtue of the fact that it represents a nation, but often a population is considered or becomes a nation by virtue of the fact that it is part of the same state. Despite these ambiguities —and I shall return to them later—the principle that the political system must in some fashion be representative of the population under its control is central to all forms of nationalism.

(2) The nation-state, according to nationalist ideology, is the political unit in which paramount authority is vested. It is placed at the pinnacle of power and entitled to overrule both smaller and larger political units.

(3) Establishing and/or maintaining the independence, the integrity, and the effective functioning of the nation-state is an essential task to which all members of the system (be it an established state or a nationalist movement) are expected to contribute.

These three elements are universal characteristics of nationalist ideology because they are central to the establishment and the effective operation of a national political system in the modern world. They provide the basic set of assumptions that govern the relationship of a nation-state to other states in the international system, and the relationship of the political leadership to the individual citizen. This set of assumptions is thus built into the system's institutional structures and its constitution, and transmitted to the population through its basic documents and elite communications.

In addition to these common elements, which correspond to the generic functions of all nation-states, any given type of nationalism has unique features, corresponding to the particular functions that a nation-state or a nationalist movement must perform at any given historical juncture. These elements too are built into institutional arrangements

and communicated by political leaders. They determine the special form that nationalist ideology will take, depending—in an established state—on its level of development, its international position, its power and success in the international arena, and its internal political structure; and—in a nationalist movement—on the nature of the changes that it is attempting to produce, on the segments of the population from which it draws its leadership, and on the groups to which it is directing its major appeal.

So far I have spoken of nationalist ideology at the system level as a property of the state or the movement. This system ideology is communicated to individual members in the course of socialization and throughout life and adopted by them as part of their belief systems. The way in which the ideology is interpreted and incorporated into the belief systems of individuals and subgroups within the population may vary widely. Depending on their demographic and personality characteristics and on their positions within the social and political structure, individuals may vary in the components of the ideology that they emphasize or de-emphasize, the intensity of their commitment to the nation-state, their definition of the citizen role and the expectations that go with it, and the way in which they enact this role.

While there may be such variations, it is essential to the effective functioning of the nation-state that the basic tenets of its ideology be widely accepted within the population. This does not necessarily mean a well-articulated, highly structured acceptance of the ideology at the cognitive level. It does mean, however, that the average citizen is prepared to meet the expectations of the citizen role and to comply with the demands that the state makes upon him, even when this requires considerable personal sacrifice.

Legitimacy of the National System

In essence, acceptance of the system's ideology implies that the individual regards the authority of the state and hence its specific demands (within some broadly defined range) as legitimate. In times of national crisis the state demands sacrifices from individual citizens that they would not ordinarily make if they were acting purely in terms of their personal interests—at least their short-run interests.[1] At such times it is expected that the role of national— which in normal times is relatively latent—becomes the paramount role in the individual's hierarchy (cf. Perry, 1957). Its requirements are expected to supersede all competing role obligations, many of which are tied to primary group relationships that are far more central to the person's daily life than his relationship to the national state.

The system cannot, in the long run, depend on coercion for enforcing such demands. To be sure, given the state's control of the ultimate sanctioning power, it can rely on coercion to obtain the compliance of relatively small segments of the population, or even of large segments of the population for relatively short periods of time. But the fear of punishment is not a dependable method of enlisting the sustained support of wide segments of the population, which is necessary to meet a national crisis or to mobilize a nation's energies. There are various psychological and organizational mechanisms through which the role of national attains paramountcy at critical times —such as the use of national symbols to heighten emotional arousal and the co-optation of various groups and institutions within the society into the service of the state. The underlying condition, however, for the effective functioning of the state is its perceived legitimacy in the eyes of the population.

We refer to a system as legitimate when it is perceived as having the right to exercise authority in a given domain and within specified limits. Thus, when the administration of a legitimate political system makes certain demands, citizens accept them, whether or not they like them—unless these demands are seen as arbitrary and outside of the limits of the leader's legitimate authority. Legitimacy always implies that there is an external reference point— such as a constitution—to which both political leadership and the citizenry are subject, and which makes it possible to determine whether or not a given demand is legitimate. But, in the normal course of events, the demand of a legitimate authority is obeyed. An individual citizen may or may not be convinced of the value of the action he is asked to take; he may or may not be enthusiastic about carrying it out; and

he may, in fact, be very unhappy about it. If it is within the limits of legitimacy, however, he willingly meets the demand without feeling coerced, and considers it his duty to do so.

Psychologically, once the demand is seen as legitimate, the individual finds himself in a nonchoice situation. His preferences are irrelevant; the legitimate demand takes on the character of an external reality which defines the dimensions of the situation and the required response. Reactions in a situation of legitimate influence are not so much governed by motivational processes as they are by perceptual ones: The focus is not on what the individual wants to do, given available alternatives, but on what is required of him. Perhaps another way of putting it is that legitimacy of a system is tantamount to its right—within certain limits and via duly constituted leadership—to define reality for its members.

Legitimacy is indeed a property of the system, but it cannot be defined in terms of objective characteristics of the system itself. While it is determined by the nature and the environment of the system, legitimacy has no meaning apart from the individuals who perceive it and the groups who share the norms that define it. It is thus a genuinely social-psychological concept in that it represents the intersection between properties of the social system and properties of individual actors.

The question, "What makes a system legitimate?" is equivalent, at the social-psychological level, to the question, "What ties individual members to the system?" The acceptance of the system's legitimacy implies that the individual is in some fashion personally involved in the system—that he feels a sense of loyalty to it and is integrated into its operations. The specific nature of the involvement may differ for different individuals, different subgroups, and different countries, at different times. It should be possible to distinguish different patterns of involvement in the national system, each of which is conducive to its perceived legitimacy, corresponding to different types of national ideology, each of which fosters the integrity of the nation-state.

A Model of Personal Involvement in the National System

A new and still evolving framework for distinguishing different patterns of personal involvement with the

---

[1] Similar demands are made by nationalist movements at the height of the struggle for national independence, though in most of the following discussion I shall concentrate on the established national state.

national system is summarized in Table 1. The model is intended to yield hypotheses about the specific antecedents and consequents of the different patterns it distinguishes, although at this stage it is possible only to suggest the general form that these hypotheses will take.[2]

As can be seen in Table 1, the model distinguishes six patterns of personal involvement in the national system in terms of two qualitative dimensions. The rows represent two sources of attachment or loyalty to the system—sentimental attachment or instrumental attachment. The columns represent three means of integration of the individual into the

individual is sentimentally attached when he sees the system as representing him—as being, in some central way, a reflection and extension of himself. For the sentimentally attached, the system is legitimate and deserving of his loyalty because it is the embodiment of a group in which his personal identity is anchored. Sentimental attachment may be channeled in three different ways, depending on the manner in which the individual is integrated into the system (as shown in the three columns of Table 1):

(1) *Commitment to cultural values.* The individual may be committed to the values basic to the national culture. He may value the special qualities of his

TABLE 1
Patterns of personal involvement in the National System

		Manner of Integration into the System		
(System requirements conducive to this type of integration)		(Consolidation)	(Mobilization)	(Conformity)
(Influence process characteristic of this type of integration)		(Internalization of system values)	(Identification with system roles)	(Compliance with system demands seen as legitimate)
		Ideological	Role-Participant	Normative
Source of Attachment (Loyalty) to the System	Sentimental	Commitment to cultural values reflective of national identity	Commitment to the role of national linked to group symbols	Acceptance of demands based on commitment to the sacredness of the state
	Instrumental	Commitment to institutions promotive of the needs and interests of the population	Commitment to social roles mediated by the system	Acceptance of demands based on commitment to law and order (principle of equity)

system—ideological, role-participant, or normative integration. In other words, the rows distinguish, essentially, two types of motives of the individual that lead him to cathect the system. The columns, on the other hand, distinguish three components of the system via which members may be bound into it. Let me proceed to examine each of these "dimensions" in turn.

An individual's attachment to the nation-state—or to any other group—may be rooted either in sentimental or instrumental considerations. An

[2] The framework has gradually emerged in the course of some empirical work in the United States that has recently been completed (Katz, Kelman, and Flacks, 1963; DeLamater, Katz, and Kelman, to be published), in the course of planning or projecting studies in a number of other countries, and in the course of a series of theoretical seminars and discussions with a number of colleagues and students.

people, as they have evolved historically and are culturally defined (that is, he attaches importance and personal meaning to "the kind of people we are"). He may value the characteristic way of life of the nation; its cultural products—such as its language, its literature, or its art; its national and often its religious traditions; and the goals for which the nation has stood in its historical development. Thus, he is attached to the system because it represents the people whose values are his own values, and whose national identity is part of his personal identity. He will support the political system because—and whenever—he sees the preservation of the system as crucial to the preservation of these cultural values.

(2) *Commitment to the role of national.* The individual may be identified with the role of the

national in the sense that it enters importantly into his self-definition and that it constitutes a genuine emotional commitment for him. He is attached to the system because his role as system member provides him with a satisfying and important part of his personal identity. He will support the system and carry out—usually with enthusiasm—the requirements of the role of national whenever that role becomes salient. The salience of the role depends on situational factors—most notably on the presence of certain national symbols (such as the national flag or the singing of the national anthem). The role is also brought into salience by authoritative announcements that a serious threat to the nation exists (which is, typically, combined with the display of national symbols); or by travel in foreign countries, where others cast the person into the role of national. For some individuals—the adherents of superpatriotic movements—the role is always salient; they surround themselves with national symbols and perceive a permanent state of external and internal threat to the integrity of the nation. For most individuals who identify with the role of national, however, this role is usually latent, but engages their full emotional commitment whenever the situation brings it into salience.

A person's commitment to the national role may be linked to the cultural values for which the national symbols stand, in which case his sentimental attachment would be channeled both through ideology and role participation (columns 1 and 2 in the table). Identification with the role, however, may also be quite independent of the underlying values of the nation and is, in fact, likely to be most intense under those circumstances. Often this identification is based, in large part, on emotional conditioning—started in childhood and reinforced throughout life —of patriotic responses to national symbols. The concrete content of the values symbolized is quite irrelevant in such cases. For an individual who has a commitment to the national role without a true commitment to the cultural values, the nation is important not because it *reflects* his personal identity, but because he *derives* his personal identity to a significant degree from identification with the nation.

(3) *Commitment to the sacredness of the state.* The individual may be committed to the state as an end in itself. The state has become, for him, a sacred object in its own right, by virtue of the fact that it is the embodiment of the people. He will loyally meet all the demands that are made upon him, as long as it is clear that these reflect the wishes of those responsible for maintaining and operating the system. To do otherwise would be to undermine the authority of the state which, in his view, must be preserved at all costs.

A person may be committed to the sacredness of the state because he shares the cultural values and identity of the people whom the state embodies and/ or because he identifies with the role of national. Commitment to the sacredness of the state, however, may be quite independent of these other commitments. In fact, this type of commitment is purest and most intense when the individual has lost touch with the underlying values of the national culture and even with the sense of excitement and self-transcendence that accompanies performance of the national role. He supports the system not out of ideological conviction, nor out of emotional engagement, but out of unquestioning obedience to the demands of the state. His personal satisfaction derives primarily from the knowledge that he has been a loyal servant to the sacred state and from the recognition of his acts of obedience by the authorities in charge of the state apparatus.

Let us turn now to the second row of Table 1, which refers to an individual's attachment to the nation-state on the basis of instrumental considerations. An individual is instrumentally attached when he sees the system as an effective vehicle for achieving his own ends and the ends of other system members. For the instrumentally attached, the system is legitimate and deserving of his loyalty because it provides the organization for a smoothly running society in which individuals can participate to their mutual benefit and have some assurance that their needs and interests will be met. Instrumental attachment, again, may be channeled in three different ways depending on the manner in which the individual is integrated into the system:

(1) *Commitment to social institutions.* The individual may be committed to the ideology that underlies the particular social and economic institutions through which the society is organized. Typically, he will value these institutional arrangements because

he regards them as maximally promotive of the needs and interests of the society's entire population. The decentralized socialism of Yugoslavia, the African socialism of Tanzania, the welfare economy of the Scandinavian countries, and the New Deal and its successors of the United States are among the many examples of such ideologies to which important segments of their respective populations have been committed. (Such commitments, of course, are also central to many modern nationalist movements and revolutionary states, where the goal is fundamental change in social and economic institutions.) An individual integrated in this manner is attached to the national system because he believes that the way it organizes society is just and effective in maximizing general welfare. He will support the political system because—and whenever—he sees the preservation of the system as crucial to the preservation of its valued social institutions.

(2) *Commitment to social roles.* The individual may be committed to a variety of social roles, whose continued and successful enactment depends on the maximally effective functioning of the larger national system. In a large bureaucratic society, such as the United States, in which there is a high degree of functional interdependence and centralization of power in various areas of life, many of the major institutions of the society are directly dependent on the nation-state. Industrial organizations, for example, depend on government contracts and on government regulations concerning taxes, tariffs, transportation, and other matters; educational institutions depend on government research grants, building grants, and financial support for students; municipal agencies depend on federal government programs in housing, urban planning, and assistance to schools.

Individuals who hold positions within such institutions are, thus, directly hooked into the national system via their roles in subsystems that are bound up with the national system. They are attached to the national system because they see it as a useful means toward the performance of their occupational roles, their community roles, and roles in various other subsystems. They will support the system and help to maintain its integrity because—and to the extent that—they have a vested interest in its continued and adequate functioning; and their support

is often mobilized in a context that brings their other social roles (i.e., their subsystem roles) into salience. Those with especially responsible positions in their respective institutions—such as top business executives, educational administrators, or community leaders—are particularly likely to feel a stake in the national system and are usually among the first to be mobilized in its support.

A person's commitment to the system on the basis of his engagement in subsystem roles may be linked to an ideological commitment to the system's institutions. In such a case, the person would, in essence, be instrumentally attached to the system because he perceives it as an effective means for meeting the needs and interests of the population in general and of himself in particular. It can be reasonably assumed that a person who is ideologically committed to the institutions of the society will also be a well-integrated participant in roles within these institutions. On the other hand, commitment to social roles mediated by the system may very well be independent of ideological commitment. In fact, individuals who are most intensely caught up in their subsystem roles and personally committed to them are less likely to be also committed at the ideological level. Such a pattern may be particularly common in a society that does not provide meaningful roles for large segments of its population. Those who benefit from such a system are likely to have a strong investment in maintaining its institutions, since they meet their own needs; yet they are unlikely to value these institutions in the context of a broader commitment to the public interest.

(3) *Commitment to law and order.* The individual may be committed to law and order as an end in itself. He assumes that, if society is to run smoothly and equitably, certain rules have to be followed by its members and that violation of these rules is a threat to the integrity of the society. He is attached to the national system because it is the arbiter of orderly and consistent procedures. He will readily meet all the demands of the system, as long as it is clear that these are normatively required and that they conform to the principle of equity—that is, that they are not merely arbitrary demands applied in a discriminatory fashion, but obligations to which every citizen is potentially bound. They are particularly likely to conform to demands whenever negative sanctions

are attached to nonconformity. This is not because their behavior is entirely or even largely determined by fear of punishment. If that were so, we could not speak of them as in any way integrated into the system and loyal to it; we would be dealing with response to coercive rather than legitimate power. Rather, it is because the existence of negative sanctions is a clear indicator that the behavior demanded is indeed required by law, or at least by general consensus, and that disobedience is therefore out of the question.

A person may be committed to law and order, as prescribed by the state, because he is ideologically committed to the society's institutions and/or because he is involved in institutional roles, and, for these reasons, has an interest in protecting the system's procedures. Commitment to law and order may, however, be relatively independent of these other commitments. In fact, individuals who are most clearly committed on this basis tend to have little ideological conviction about the society's institutions and to participate in institutional roles only at low levels of responsibility. Their commitment is more passive and disinterested and largely oriented toward keeping the fabric of ordinary life undisturbed.

Sentimental and Instrumental Attachments and the Sources of Political Legitimacy

Whether a person's attachment to the national system is largely sentimental or largely instrumental or some fairly balanced combination of the two depends on his personal and social characteristics—such as his place in society, his education, his residence, his religious and ethnic identifications, his personal history, his personality dispositions. One can also examine, however, characteristics of the system that make one or the other of these two types of attachment more probable in a given society, and at a given point in time. Thus, for example, the source of loyalty that predominates in a system may depend on its stage of development. One is reminded, in this connection, of Durkheim's (1947) distinction between the mechanical solidarity of more traditional societies and the organic solidarity of more industrialized societies, a distinction to which our sentimental-instrumental dichotomy is clearly related. The predominant source of loyalty may also depend on the kinds of appeals that the national leadership makes at a given time; these in turn depend on the major system functions that the leaders attempt to perform, and on the dispositions available within the population on which they can draw for popular support.

Consideration of system characteristics brings us back to the question with which I started this discussion of patterns of personal involvement in the national system: What makes a system legitimate in the eyes of the population? We can distinguish between two sources of legitimacy for the national system, which correspond directly to the distinction between sentimental and instrumental attachment at the level of the individual. A modern nation-state's legitimacy depends on the extent to which the population perceives the regime as (a) reflecting its ethnic and cultural identity, and (b) meeting its needs and interests.

Ultimately, the political system is a way of meeting the needs and interests of the population, and unless it accomplishes this, at least to a moderate degree, it cannot maintain its legitimacy in the long run. However, the legitimacy of the system can be sustained, even if it is not adequately organized or lacks the necessary resources to meet the needs and interests of the entire population, if it is seen as reflective of the cultural identity of the people and thus—by definition—as most capable of representing their interests. Under such circumstances, the hardships experienced by the population will be blamed on external sources, and citizens will continue to place their trust in their national leadership and be prepared to make whatever sacrifices are necessary.

Cultural and ethnic identity as the major source of legitimacy is particularly important in a situation in which different segments of the population have conflicting interests and the system is set up to meet the interests of some groups more fully than those of others. By appealing to the common national identity of the people, the leadership may be able to elicit their loyalty despite internal divisions and inequities. Thus, the perception of the system as representing the national identity of the people can compensate—temporarily and sometimes for extended periods—for the system's failures in meeting public interests and needs, and gives it a continuity it might otherwise lack.

It is not surprising that the correspondence between state and nation is a central component of the ideology of the modern nation-state. The impetus for establishing a new state typically has come—both in earlier periods and today—from certain elites within the population whose interests and needs are best served by a redrawing of political boundaries. Even when these elites are committed to a democratic ideology, which calls for institutions that permit broad participation in social life and promote the welfare of the entire population, they need time before they can come close to achieving such goals. Thus, they are in a position in which they have to mobilize the support of the masses of the population even though, at least in the short run, they have few concrete benefits to offer them. Insofar as they are able to appeal to the national identity of the population, they can overcome this difficulty and attain a broad-based support that will at least see them through the initial stages of political development.

The ideal model of the modern nation-state, therefore, is one that governs a population sharing a common ethnic and cultural identity—in other words, a population that is a nation and presumably was a nation even before the state was established. Such a state derives its legitimacy from the principle that it represents an already existing nation, which provides historical and existential justification for organizing the preeminent political unit on that basis.

This ideal model, of course, as I have already pointed out, is only rarely and approximately achieved in actuality. Political boundaries do not usually follow preexisting cultural and ethnic divisions. Yet, the conception of a state corresponding to a nation remains a central feature of modern nationalist ideology. It become necessary, therefore, to grapple with the very difficult concept of "nation." I am referring here not to nation in the political sense in which it is often used today, i.e., the population of an internationally recognized nation-state, but to nation in the sense of an ethnic-cultural unit—a concept that predates by far the rise of the modern nation-state.

The definition of nation in this sense has occupied many historians and political scientists for many years, and I shall not attempt to enter into this intricate discussion. Following Karl Deutsch's (1953) formulation, I shall simply describe a nation as a community of individuals who—in the absence of personal acquaintance—have little difficulty in finding a common basis for communication. Thus,

the boundaries of a nation represent the line at which a qualitative change in the ease of communication takes place; that is, communication is always easier among individuals within these boundaries than it is across boundaries. Such a community cannot arise unless its members share certain important aspects of culture—a common language, a common history, a common tradition, a common way of life, a common religion, or a common sense of destiny—although the specific aspects of culture held in common may vary from nation to nation. No one aspect is crucial to the definition of a nation; thus, for example, a group may constitute a nation even if its members do not share the same language, as long as they share other important values and experiences that provide a ready-made basis for communication among them.

I would assume, furthermore, that nationhood implies a consciousness among members of a collectivity of the special bonds that tie them to one another. I find very useful, in this connection, Fishman's (1966) suggestion that an ethnic group becomes a nation when it begins to ideologize its customs and way of life. That is, it goes beyond the conception of "this is the way we do things" to a conception of "there is something unique, special, and valuable about our way of doing things." It is ideologizing of this sort that makes it possible to develop allegiance to and invest one's identity in a collectivity that goes beyond—in both space and time—one's primary-group, face-to-face contacts.

Historically, such a process of ideologizing ethnic characteristics is likely to have occurred whenever there were energetic individuals who had an interest in creating loyalty to a wider group—in order, for example, to establish a new religion, or to expand their economic activities, or to broaden the base of their political power. Who was to be included in this wider group depended, in each case, on the particular interests of the nation-builders and on the opportunities available to them. Thus, the boundaries of the newly formed nations and the elements of communality that characterized them tended to be somewhat arbitrary (though not completely so, because there had to be some common cultural characteristics as the starting point for the work of ideologizing).

Once a group has developed a sense of nationality, strong psychological and social forces can be mobilized to sustain and perpetuate it. At the psychological level, I would offer the hypothesis that attachment to the nation gains much of its strength from the fact that it represents the coming together of two important and in some sense contradictory needs: the need to protect those—such as members of one's immediate family—who are close to the self and extensions of it, and the need to transcend the self through identification with distant groups and causes. The nation is close enough to draw on the first of these needs, yet distant enough to satisfy the second.

At the social level, attachment to the nation gains much of its strength from its linkage to sacred objects. Love for the nation is typically taught in the home and closely linked to love for one's family. It is no coincidence that family symbolism is borrowed for such terms as fatherland and mother tongue. In many cases, moreover, the nation is closely linked to religious symbols, and love for the nation is inculcated in parochial schools as part of the child's religious duty. With the nation so intimately tied up with God and mother, it is not surprising that support of the nation is seen as a sacred duty and failure to provide such support can be a source of profound guilt.

It is this national consciousness, then, with all the psychological and social forces that sustain it, which the modern nation-state seeks to utilize as a major source of its political legitimacy. Where it does exist, it can indeed be a very powerful binding force (though not without its dysfunctional side effects). Where it does not exist, political leaders attempt to create a national consciousness with boundaries corresponding to the boundaries of the political system. In some established states this has been accomplished, with a new sense of nationhood developing despite initial ethnic and cultural differences. In many new states, however, and in many old ones as well, such a sense of national consciousness has yet to be achieved. The population may be divided into groups that differ widely in ethnic and cultural characteristics and often have a history of intense conflict with one another, or the mass of the population may be tied only to local communities and not at all integrated into the national system. What we find, in such situations, are efforts at nation-building—at creating, out of ethnically distinct groups and out of unintegrated individuals

and localities, a single nation that corresponds to the political state.[3]

These nation-building efforts involve a type of nationalist movement in which the primary push is from state to nation. That is, a state already exists, but if it is to become an effective and legitimate nation-state, a nation has to be built around it. This type of nationalist movement can be distinguished from the usual independence or separatist movement, in which the primary push is from nation to state. That is, a group, with an already existing national consciousness (and, I should add, a set of special interests) demands a political state that will correspond to the nation. Most nationalist movements involve some combination of these two elements, though with different degrees of emphasis.

The push from state to nation may violate the ideal model of the modern nation-state, which presumably is based on an already existing sense of national identity, but it is not at all inconsistent with historical precedents. Whether such a push will succeed, it seems to me, depends on the extent to which the state contains a well-functioning society, with members who are interdependent and whose needs and interests are adequately met. It is the existence of such a society which has, historically, provided the conditions for unifying diverse cultural elements into a national community.

In sum, the two sources of legitimacy that I have been discussing can reinforce each other in both directions. On the one hand—as I have already pointed out—the perception of the state as representative of national unity can compensate for failures to meet the population's needs and interests. On the other hand, the perception of the state as meeting the population's needs and interests can compensate for a lacking sense of national identity, and can in fact help to create such an identity.

Turning back to Table 1, the close interaction between the two sources of legitimacy leads me to a final point about the distinction between sentimental and instrumental attachment. The two types of attachment are by no means mutually exclusive. Both

[3] Such nation-building efforts are, in principle, not so different from the efforts at transforming an ethnic group into a nation that I mentioned above. In both cases, there is a push toward establishing new boundaries for national identity—in the present case, boundaries that correspond to an already existing, internationally recognized political state.

are likely to be present within a system, and are in fact important to the effective functioning of the system. Similarly, any given individual may well be attached to the system in both of these ways, though probably with different degrees of emphasis on each one.

There are also possible patterns of involvement in the system that combine these two components in unique fashion. For example, an African socialist may favor an approach to modernization that draws on traditional African values, thus combining instrumental and sentimental features into a single ideological commitment. Or, at the level of role participation, various subsystem roles may include, as one of their expectations, the requirement to support the nation-state in times of crisis and to take the lead in mobilizing others to that end. Thus, various social roles may, in effect, be co-opted into the service of the national role. Or, finally, at the normative level, a commitment to law and order may be sentimentalized so that the preservation of certain bureaucratic procedures becomes a sacred end in its own right. In short, sentimental and instrumental attachments may compensate for one another, or reinforce one another, or combine with one another in novel ways.

Integration of Individuals into the National System

Let me turn now, and much more briefly, to the distinction between the three columns of Table 1. I have already touched on most of the relevant points in explicating the six individual cells of the table, and shall now merely try to bring them together in summary fashion.

The columns of Table 1 identify three components of the national system through which an individual may be integrated into it—its values, its roles, and its norms. These components are by no means mutually exclusive, and, in fact, a well-integrated system member will be involved in the system at all of these levels. They may, however, as I have already pointed out, be relatively independent of one another, and for some individuals a particular one of these means of integration may predominate. At the very least, the three means of integration are likely to have different weights for different individuals.

These three paths of integration can be linked to three processes of social influence—internalization, identification, and compliance—that I have distinguished in my earlier work on attitude change (Kelman, 1958, 1961). We would speak of internalization when an individual accepts influence from another individual or a group—that is, changes his behavior or attitude in the direction induced by the other—because he sees the new behavior as congruent with his own value system. We would speak of identification when an individual accepts influence from another in order to maintain a satisfying role relationship to the other, in which his own self-definition is anchored. In other words, he accepts the induced behavior because he sees it as required by a role that has personal significance for him. Finally, we would speak of compliance when an individual accepts influence from another in order to attain specific rewards or avoid specific punishments controlled by the other, or to attain the other's approval or avoid his disapproval.

The three processes of influence are relevant to the present analysis in two senses: They can help us define the way in which a particular type of integration is initially established, and the way in which an individual integrated by each of these means is likely to react to a specific system demand. Linking the three types of integration to my work on social influence also has the advantage of suggesting a series of hypotheses about their antecedents and consequents, derived from the earlier work. With this in mind, then, let me briefly review the meaning of each of the three columns.

(1) *Ideological integration.* An individual who is ideologically integrated is bound to the system by virtue of the fact that he subscribes to some of the basic values on which the system is established. These may be the cultural values defining the national identity, or the social values reflected in the institutions by which the society is organized, or both. The ideologically integrated member has internalized these values and incorporated them into a personal value framework. When he is faced with demands for behavior in support of the national system he is likely to respond positively, because support of the system is generally congruent with his own values. The extent to which he meets specific demands, however, depends on the extent to which he sees these

demands as consistent with the underlying values of the system to which he is committed.

(2) *Role-participant integration.* An individual who is integrated via role-participation is bound to the system by virtue of the fact that he is personally engaged in roles within the system—roles that enter significantly into his self-definition. He may be emotionally caught up in the role of national as such, with its associated symbols, and derive a sense of self-transcendence and compensatory identity from it; or he may be functionally caught up in various social roles that are central to his identity and whose effective performance depends on the national system. His integration into the system is based on identification, in the sense that he has a stake in maintaining the system-related roles and the self-definition anchored in them. When he is faced with demands to support the system he is likely to respond positively, because such support is generally required by the system role to which he is committed. The extent to which he meets specific demands depends, however, on the extent to which the relevant role has been brought into salience by situational factors.

(3) *Normative integration.* An individual who is normatively integrated is bound to the system by virtue of the fact that he accepts the system's right to set the behavior of its members within a prescribed domain. Here we are dealing, one might say, with legitimacy in its pure form, in which the question of personal values and roles has become irrelevant. Acceptance of the system's right to unquestioning obedience may be based on a commitment to the state as a sacred object in its own right, or on a commitment to the necessity of law and order as a guarantor of equitable procedures. The normatively integrated member regards compliance with the system as a highly proper and valued orientation. When he is faced with demands to support the system he is likely to comply without question, since he regards it as his obligation to do so. The extent to which he meets specific demands, however, depends on the extent to which these are authoritatively presented as the wishes of the leadership or the requirements of law. One important indicator of the authoritativeness of a particular demand is the existence of positive or negative sanctions to control proper performance.[4]

The manner of an individual's integration into the system—just like the source of his attachment to the system—depends on his personal and social characteristics. Similarly, the prevalence of one or another type of integration or of some combination of them in a given society depends on such system characteristics as its stage of development and the particular requirements that it must meet at a given point in time. Thus, for example, one might distinguish between three system functions in relation to its population: (a) consolidation of the population, which is crucial during periods of nation-building or, in established nation-states, during periods of serious internal division; (b) mobilization of the population, which is crucial during periods of national crisis or periods of major social and political change; and (c) assuring the conformity of the population, which is crucial to the smooth operation of the system during periods of relative quiet. As indicated in Table 1, I am suggesting that system leaders promote and primarily draw on ideological integration to consolidate the population, role-participant integration to mobilize the population, and normative integration to achieve conformity on a day-to-day basis.

Conclusion

I have presented a six-celled scheme that classifies patterns of personal involvement in the national system on the basis of the source of an individual's attachment to the system and his manner of integration into it. Such a scheme is built on the assumption that individuals and groups within a population can be distinguished in terms of the patterns that they are most likely to adopt; that political systems can be distinguished in terms of the patterns that are most likely to emerge within them;

---

[4] In my original model for the study of social influence, which is meant to deal with choice behavior (in contrast to the nonchoice character of demands from legitimate authorities), sanctions constitute a *motivation* for compliance. That is, the person complies in order to attain a particular reward or avoid a particular punishment. In the context of legitimate demands, sanctions still play an important part in controlling compliance, but primarily as *indicators* that the demands are really authoritative and meant to be obeyed, rather than as motivators for the choice that would be personally most rewarding.

and that stages of development and system functions can be identified that are most likely to bring different patterns to the fore. The potential value of such a scheme, of course, is that it can yield hypotheses about the determinants of different patterns of involvement and about their consequences.

With respect to the rows of Table 1, for example, one hypothesis on which we already have evidence from our United States study (DeLamater, Katz, and Kelman) is that individuals characterized by geographical stability are more prone to be sentimentally attached, while those characterized by geographical mobility tend to be instrumentally attached. On the consequent side, we are now planning an experimental study to test the hypothesis that sentimentally attached individuals are more likely to conceive an intergroup conflict in competitive, zero-sum terms, while instrumentally attached individuals are more likely to see the possibilities for cooperation and a nonzero-sum orientation. We further hypothesize that increasing the intensity of attachment will have opposite effects, depending on the type of attachment involved.

With respect to the columns of Table 1, various hypotheses are suggested by the distinction between the three processes of influence corresponding to them. On the antecedent side, for example, one might hypothesize that the higher an individual's socioeconomic status, education, and political power, the more likely he is to be ideologically integrated; the lower he is on these dimensions, the more likely he is to be normatively integrated. On the consequent side, one might hypothesize that the normatively integrated are most likely to obey specific demands, while the ideologically integrated are most likely to give long-run support to the system.

Various other hypotheses about the antecedents and consequents of types of attachment and integration have been mentioned throughout this paper, although perhaps the most interesting hypotheses are likely to be those that refer to the interaction between these two dimensions. Derivation of such hypotheses represents the next step in the development of this model.

References

DeLamater, J., Katz, D., and Kelman, H. C. "On the Nature of National Involvement: A Preliminary Study in an American Community" (to be published).

Deutsch, K. W. *Nationalism and Social Communication*. New York and Cambridge, Mass.: Wiley and Technology Press, 1953.

Durkheim, E. *The Division of Labor in Society*. New York: Free Press, 1947.

Fishman, J. "Nationality-Nationalism and Nation-Nationism." Paper presented at the Social Science Research Council Conference on "Language Problems of Developing Nations," November 1966.

Katz, D., Kelman, H. C., and Flacks, R. "The National Role: Some Hypotheses About the Relation of Individuals to Nation in America Today," *Peace Research Society* (*International*) *Papers*, 1 (1964), 113–27.

Kelman, H. C. "Compliance, Identification and Internalization: Three Processes of Attitude Change," *Journal of Conflict Resolution*, 2 (1958), 51–60.

Kelman, H. C. "Processes of Opinion Change," *Public Opinion Quarterly*, 25 (1961), 57–78.

Perry, S. E. "Notes on the Role of the National: A Social-Psychological Concept for the Study of International Relations," *Journal of Conflict Resolution*, 1 (1957), 346–63.

Whitaker, A. V., and Jordan, D. C. *Nationalism in Contemporary Latin America*. New York: Free Press, 1966.

Part Four

The Interaction of States: Theories and Approaches

INTRODUCTORY NOTE

Studies of international politics are much less systematized than those which focus on foreign policy. Whereas the elements of state action have been clearly delineated in terms of ends, means, decision-making, and capabilities, the same cannot be said for the interaction of states. There is no widely accepted breakdown of the components of an international relationship, and thus studies in this area tend to be scattered in a variety of directions. Many analysts concentrate on the international system and the various interaction patterns which sustain or modify it. In particular, the stability of the system under varying conditions has been subjected to close scrutiny. Such concepts as balance of power, bipolarization, and deterrence have been developed as means of estimating the resiliency of the system and the prospects of its collapse into world war. Other observers are concerned less with the state of the system and more with specific forms of interaction. Some, for example, specialize in the study of conflict and disintegrative interaction processes, while others analyze such integrative processes as the building of alliances and the maintenance of collective security. Another line of inquiry focuses on what might be called the intellectual dimension of interaction. Increasingly, attention is being paid to how interaction is affected by the images and expectations that the participating actors have of each other. The development and adaptation of game theory has been a major stimulant to analyses of this sort. Still another approach is to combine these several dimensions by organizing analysis around the concept of crisis. Such a focus not only allows for the investigation of systemic stability, integrative processes, conflicting images, and other aspects of international interaction, but it also has the advantage that crises are important phenomena in a policy as well as a theoretical sense, thus enabling the analyst to contribute both to the generation of enduring knowledge and the solution of immediate problems.

Underlying the emphasis on crisis is an assumption that may have relevance for the other approaches and that the reader may wish to ponder at some length. The assumption is that crises are not only the result of underlying strain, but that they also give rise to conditions that are in themselves causal. In other words, students of crisis behavior assume that interaction sequences have a logic of their own and that their outcomes can thus be explained—and perhaps even anticipated—by examining the patterns they form rather than the actors who sustain them. A similar premise guides the investigations of those who probe the dynamics of systemic stability and change. In reflecting on the selections that follow, therefore, the reader may want to consider the question of whether such an assumption is inherent in all the approaches that focus on the interaction of states and, if so, under what kinds of conditions does the logic of an unfolding situation prevail and under what circumstances are actors able to break out of and thus alter the patterns in which they have become locked.

Notwithstanding the possibility that all or most students of interaction processes may proceed on the basis of the same basic assumption, their various approaches are marked more by diversity than coherence. The variability of the interaction perspective is clearly evident in the fourteen selections that follow. The first five share an interest in analyzing the stability of the global system, but the remaining nine pursue scattered and essentially unrelated lines of inquiry.

A. Theories of Balance and Imbalance

27. Variants on Six Models of the International System

Morton A. Kaplan is Professor of Political Science at the University of Chicago. A trail-blazer on the frontiers of theory, he has authored *System and Process in International Politics* (1957), coauthored *The Political Foundations of International Law* (1961), and edited *The Revolution in World Politics* (1962). While all of these works are based on an attempt to comprehend the dynamics whereby the structures of international systems persist and change, the first of them had a particularly significant impact upon the development of international theory. In it Professor Kaplan identified two structural forms that the global international system has taken and noted four others that are logically possible, even though they have yet to occur in history. In the ensuing selection Professor Kaplan reassesses his earlier analysis and finds that while there is no need to replace the six forms of the international system he had originally specified, developments during the 1960s require him to identify several variants of the original models. The result is a clarifying analysis of the changing character of the global system and some of the key variables that determine its nature at any moment in time. [*Originally published in a more extensive form under the title, "Some Problems of International Systems Research," in* International Political Communities: An Anthology (*Garden City and New York: Doubleday and Company, 1966*), *pp. 469–501; reproduced by permission of the author.*]

I

. . . A number of theoretical considerations underlie this essay. One is that some pattern of repeatable or characteristic behavior does occur within the international system. Another is that this behavior falls into a pattern because the elements of the pattern are internally consistent and because they satisfy needs that are both international and national in scope. A third is that international patterns of behavior are related, in ways that can be specified, to the characteristics of the entities participating in international politics and to the functions they perform. A fourth is that international behavior can also be related to other factors such as military and economic capability, communication and information, technological change, demographic change, and additional factors long recognized by political scientists.

Just as it is possible to build alternative models of political systems, e.g., democratic or totalitarian, and of family systems, e.g., nuclear families, extended families or monogamous or polygamous families, so it is possible to build different models of international systems. The models can be given an empirical interpretation and the specific propositions of the models can be tested.

The aspiration to state testable propositions in

the field of international politics is useful provided some degree of caution is observed concerning the kinds of propositions one proposes to test. For instance, can a theory of international politics yield a prediction of a specific event like the Hungarian revolution of October 1956? The answer probably must be negative. Yet why make such a demand of theory?

Two basic limitations upon prediction in the physical sciences are relevant to this problem. In the first place, the mathematics of complicated interaction problems has not been worked out. For instance, the physical scientist can make accurate predictions based on general formulas with respect to the two-body problem, more complicated and less general predictions with respect to the three-body problem, and only very *ad hoc* predictions concerning large numbers of bodies. The scientist cannot predict the path of a single molecule of gas in a tank of gas.

In the second place, the physical scientist's predictions are predictions concerning an isolated system. He does not predict that so much gas will be in the tank, that the temperature or pressure of the tank will not be changed by someone, or even that the tank will remain in the experimental room. He predicts what the characteristic behavior of the mass of gas molecules will be if stated conditions of temperature, pressure, etc., hold.

The engineer deals with systems in which many free variables enter. If he acts wisely—for instance, in designing aircraft—he works within the constraints imposed by the laws of physics. But many aspects of exact design stem from experiments in wind tunnels or practical applications of past experiences rather than directly from the laws of physical science.

A theory of international politics normally cannot be expected to predict individual actions, because the interaction problem is too complex and because there are too many free variables. It can be expected, however, to predict characteristic or modal behavior within a particular kind of international system. Moreover, the theory should be able to predict the conditions under which the system will remain stable, the conditions under which it will be transformed, and the kinds of transformations that may be expected to take place.

II

Six alternative models of international systems are presented in this section. These models do not exhaust the possibilities. They are, however, intended to explore the continuum of possibilities. In their present stage of development the models are heuristic. Yet, if they have some degree of adequacy, they may permit a more meaningful organization of existing knowledge and more productive organization of future research. Only two of the models—the "balance of power" system and the loose bipolar system—have historical counterparts.

"Balance of Power" System

The first system to be examined is the "balance of power" international system. Quotation marks are placed around the term to indicate its metaphoric character.

The "balance of power" international system is an international social system that does not have as a component a political sub-system. The actors within the system are exclusively national actors, such as France, Germany, Italy, etc. Five national actors—as a minimum—must fall within the classification "essential national actor"[1] to enable the system to work.

The "balance of power" international system is characterized by the operation of the following essential rules, which constitute the characteristic behavior of the system: (1) increase capabilities, but negotiate rather than fight; (2) fight rather than fail to increase capabilities; (3) stop fighting rather than eliminate an essential actor; (4) oppose any coalition or single actor that tends to assume a position of predominance within the system; (5) constrain actors who subscribe to supranational organizational principles; and (6) permit defeated or constrained essential national actors to re-enter the system as acceptable role partners, or act to bring some previously inessential actor within the essential actor classification. Treat all essential actors as acceptable role partners.

The first two rules of the "balance of power" international system reflect the fact that no political sub-system exists within the international social system. Therefore, essential national actors must rely upon themselves or upon their allies for protection. However, if they are weak, their allies may

[1] The term "essential actor" refers roughly to "major power" as distinguished from "minor power."

desert them. Therefore, an essential national actor must ultimately be capable of protecting its own national values. The third essential rule illustrates the fact that other nations are valuable as potential allies. In addition, nationality may set limits on potential expansion.

The fourth and fifth rules give recognition to the fact that a predominant coalition or national actor would constitute a threat to the interests of other national actors. Moreover, if a coalition were to become predominant, then the largest member of that coalition might also become predominant over the lesser members of its own coalition. For this reason members of a successful coalition may be alienated; they may also be able to bargain for more from the losers than from their own allies.

The sixth rule states that membership in the system is dependent upon only behavior that corresponds with the essential rules or norms of the "balance of power" system. If the number of essential actors is reduced, the "balance of power" international system will become unstable. Therefore, maintaining the number of essential national actors above a critical lower bound is a necessary condition for the stability of the system. This is best done by returning to full membership in the system defeated actors or reformed deviant actors.

Although any particular action or alignment may be the product of "accidents," i.e., of the set of specific conditions producing the action or alignment, including such elements as chance meetings or personality factors, a high correlation between the pattern of national behavior and the essential rules of the international system would represent a confirmation of the predictions of the theory.

Just as any particular molecule of gas in a gas tank may travel in any direction, depending upon accidental bumpings with other molecules, particular actions of national actors may depend upon chance or random conjunctions. Yet, just as the general pattern of behavior of the gas may represent its adjustment to pressure and temperature conditions within the tank, the set of actions of national actors may correspond to the essential rules of the system when the other variables take the appropriate specified values.

By shifting the focus of analysis from the particular event to the type of event, seemingly accidental events may become part of a meaningful pattern.

In this way, the historical loses its quality of uniqueness and is translated into the universal language of science.

The number of essential rules cannot be reduced. The failure of any rule to operate will result in the failure of at least one other rule. Moreover, at this level of abstraction, there does not seem to be any other rule that is interrelated with the specified set in this fashion.

Any essential rule of the system is in equilibrium[2] with the remaining rules of the set. This does not imply that particular rules can appear only in one kind of international system. The first two rules, for instance, also apply to bloc leaders in the bipolar system. However, they are necessary to each of the systems and, in their absence, other rules of the two systems will be transformed.

The rules of the system are interdependent. For instance, the failure to restore or to replace defeated essential national actors eventually will interfere with the formation of coalitions capable of constraining deviant national actors or potentially predominant coalitions.

The equilibrium of the set of rules is not a continuous equilibrium but one that results from discrete actions over periods of time. Therefore, the possibility of some change operating to transform the system becomes great if sufficient time is allowed.

Apart from the equilibrium within the set of essential rules, there are two other kinds of equilibrium characteristic of the international system: the equilibrium between the set of essential rules and the other variables of the international system and the equilibrium between the international system and its environment or setting.

If the actors do not manifest the behavior indicated by the rules, the kind and numbers of actors

[2] This kind of equilibrium is not mechanical like the equilibrium of the seesaw, which re-establishes itself mechanically after a disturbance. Instead, it is a "steady state" or homeostatic equilibrium which maintains the stability of selected variables as the consequence of changes in other variables. For instance, the body maintains the temperature of blood in a "steady state" by perspiring in hot weather and by flushing the skin in cold weather. The international system is not simply stable but in Ashby's sense is ultrastable. That is, it acts selectively toward states of its internal variables and rejects those which lead to unstable states. See W. Ross Ashby, *Design for a Brain*, p. 99, New York: John Wiley and Sons, 1952, for a precise treatment of the concept of ultrastability (and also of multistability).

will change. If the kind or number of actors changes, the behavior called for in the rules cannot be maintained. Some changes in capabilities and information, for instance, may be compatible with the rules of the system, while others may not. If the value of one variable changes—for instance, the capabilities of a given coalition—the system may not maintain itself unless the information of some of the actors changes correspondingly. Otherwise a necessary "counterbalancing" shift in alignment may not take place. Some shifts in the pattern of alliance may be compatible with the rules of the system and others may not.

The rules, in short, are equilibrium rules for the system. This does not, however, imply that the rules will be followed by the actors because they are equilibrium rules, unless an actor has an interest in maintaining the equilibrium of the system. The constraints on the actor must motivate it to behave consonantly with the rules; or, if one or more actors are not so motivated, the others must be motivated to act in a way which forces the deviant actors back to rule-consonant behavior.[3] Thus the rules may be viewed normatively, that is, as describing the behavior which will maintain the equilibrium of the system or as predictive, that is, as predicting that actors will so behave if the other variables of the system and the environment are at their equilibrium settings. If the other variables of the system and the environment are not at their equilibrium settings, deviant behavior is expected.

It is relatively easy to find historical examples illustrating the operation of the "balance of power" system. The European states would have accepted Napoleon had he been willing to play according to the rules of the game.[4] The restoration of the Bourbons permitted the application of rule three. Had this not been possible, the international system would immediately have become unstable. Readmission of France to the international system after restoration fulfilled rule six.

The European concert, so ably described by Mowat, illustrates rule one. The *entente cordiale* illustrates rule four and the history of the eighteenth and nineteenth centuries rule two. Perhaps the best example of rule three, however, can be found in the diplomacy of Bismarck at Sadowa, although his motivation was more complex than the rule alone would indicate. It is not the purpose of this essay to multiply historical illustrations. The reader can make his own survey to determine whether international behavior tended to correspond to these rules during the eighteenth and nineteenth centuries.

The changes in conditions that may make the "balance of power" international system unstable are: the existence of an essential national actor who does not play according to the rules of the game, such as one who acts contrary to the essential rules of the system; in the example discussed, a player who seeks hegemony; failures of information which prevent a national actor from taking the required measures to protect its own international position; capability changes that become cumulative and thus increase an initial disparity between the capabilities of essential national actors; conflicts between the prescriptions of different rules under some conditions; difficulties arising from the logistics of the "balancing" process, the small number of essential actors, or an inflexibility of the "balancing" mechanism.

An important condition for stability concerns the number of essential national actors. If there are only three, and if they are relatively equal in capability, the probability that two would combine to eliminate the third is relatively great. Although the two victorious nations would have an interest in limiting the defeat of the third and in restoring it to the system as an acceptable role partner, they might not do so. Since this might not happen, the penalty for being left out of an alliance would be high and even the hazards of being in an alliance relatively great. Even if a nation were in one alliance, it might be left out of the next. Therefore this would be a system in which each victorious nation might attempt to gain as much as it could from the war as a protection against what might happen in the next round. Moreover, each victorious nation would attempt to double-cross the other in order to obtain a differential advantage. There would be a premium upon deceit and dishonesty. On the other hand, the addition of

[3] See Morton Kaplan, Arthur Burns, and Richard Quandt, "Theoretical Analysis of the 'Balance of Power,'" *Behavioral Science*, Vol. V, No. 3, July 1960, pp. 240–52, for an account of why consonant motivation is expected.

[4] It is nevertheless true that since Napoleon threatened the principle of dynastic legitimacy, the system would have been strained. The principle of legitimacy, for quite some time, reduced the suspicions that are natural to a "balance of power" system.

some other nations to the system would remove many of the pressures and add to the stability of the system.

Coalitions with many members may thus regard loosely attached members with equanimity. The role of the non-member of the coalition will also be tolerated. When there are a large number of loosely attached actors or non-members of an alliance any change of alliance or addition to an alliance can be "counter-balanced" by the use of an appropriate reward or by the cognition by some national actor of danger to its national interest.

When, however, there are very few loosely attached or non-member actors, a change in or an addition to an alignment introduces considerable tension into the international system. Under these circumstances, it becomes difficult to make the necessary compensatory adjustments.

For the same reasons, coalition members will have more tolerance for the role of "balancer," i.e., the actor who implements rule four, if the international system has a large number of members and the alignments are fluid. Under these conditions, the "balancer" does not constitute a lethal threat to the coalition against which it "balances." If, however, there are only a few essential actors, the very act of "balancing" may create a permanent "unbalance." In these circumstances the tolerance of the system for the "balancing" role will be slight and the "balance of power" system will become unstable.

Instability may result, although the various national actors have no intention of overthrowing the "balance of power" system. The wars against Poland corresponded to the rule directing the various national actors to increase their capabilities. Since Poland was not an essential national actor, it did not violate the norms of the system to eliminate Poland as an actor. The Polish spoils were divided among the victorious essential national actors. Nevertheless, even this co-operation among the essential national actors had an "unbalancing" effect. Since the acquisitions of the victorious actors could not be equal—unless some exact method were found for weighting geographic, strategic, demographic, industrial, material factors, etc., and determining accurately how the values of these factors would be projected into the future—a differential

factor making the system unstable could not easily be avoided.

Even the endeavor to defeat Napoleon and to restrict France to her historic limits had some effects of this kind. This effort, although conforming to rules four, five, and six, also aggrandized Prussia and hence upset the internal equilibrium among the German actors. This episode may have triggered the process which later led to Prussian hegemony within Germany and to German hegemony within Europe. Thus, a dynamic process was set off for which shifts within alignments or coalitions were not able to compensate.

The logistical or environmental possibilities for "balancing" may be decisive in determining whether the "balancing" role within the "balance of power" international system will be filled effectively. For example, even had it so desired, the Soviet Union could not have "balanced" Nazi pressure against Czechoslovakia without territorial access to the zone of potential conflict. In addition, the intervening actors—Poland and Rumania—and possibly also Great Britain and France regarded Soviet intervention as a threat to their national interests. Therefore, they refused to co-operate.

It is possible that a major factor accounting for British success in the "balancing" role in the nineteenth century lay in the fact that Great Britain was predominantly a naval power and had no territorial ambitions on the European continent. These facts increased the tolerance of other national actors for Britain's "balancing" role. As a preponderant maritime power, Great Britain could interfere with the shipping of other powers and could transport its small army; it also was able to use its naval capabilities to dispel invading forces. Even so, Palmerston discovered occasions on which it was difficult to play the "balancing" role either because it was difficult to make effective use of Britain's limited manpower or because other powers displayed little tolerance for the role.

The "balance of power" system has the following consequences. Alliances tend to be specific, of short duration, and to shift according to advantage and not according to ideology (even within war). Wars tend to be limited in objectives. There is a wide range of international law that applies universally within the system. Among the most significant rules of applicable law are those dealing with the rules of war and the doctrine of non-intervention.[5]

The "balance of power" system in its ideal form is a system in which any combination of actors within alliances is possible so long as no alliance gains a marked preponderance in capabilities. The system tends to be maintained by the fact that even should any nation desire to become predominant itself, it must, to protect its own interests, act to prevent any other nation from accomplishing such an objective. Like Adam Smith's "unseen hand" of competition, the international system is policed informally by self-interest, without the necessity of a political sub-system.

The rise of powerful deviant actors, inadequate counter-measures by non-deviant actors,[6] new international ideologies, and the growth of supra-national organizations like the Communist bloc with its internationally organized political parties, sounded the death knell for the "balance of power" international system.

Loose Bipolar System

In its place, after an initial period of instability, the loose bipolar system appeared. This system differs in many important respects from the "balance of power" system. Supranational actors participate within the international system. These supra-national actors may be bloc actors like NATO or the Communist bloc or universal actors like the United Nations. Nearly all national actors belong to the universal actor organization and many—including most of the major national actors—belong to one or the other of the major blocs. Some national actors, however, may be non-members of bloc organizations.

In distinction to the "balance of power" inter-national system, in which the rules applied uniformly to all national actors, the essential rules of the loose bipolar system distinguish, for instance, between the role functions of actors who are members of blocs and those who are not.

In the "balance of power" system, the role of the "balancer" was an integrating role because it prevented any alliance from becoming predominant. In the ideal form of the system, any national actor is qualified to fill that role. In the loose bipolar system, however, the integrating role is a mediatory role. The actor filling it does not join one side or the other but mediates between the contending sides. There-fore, only non-bloc members or universal actor organizations can fill the integrative role in the loose bipolar system.

The functioning of the loose bipolar system depends upon the organizational characteristics of the supranational blocs.[7] If the two blocs are not hierarchically organized, the loose bipolar system tends to resemble the "balance of power" system, except that the shifting of alignments takes place around two fixed points. Such shifting is limited by the functional integration of facilities, since a shift may require the destruction of facilities and the reduction of the capabilities of the shifting national actor. Shifting in alignment tends also to be limited by geographic and other logistic considerations. Nevertheless, the bloc actors constitute relatively loose organizations and the international system itself develops a considerable flexibility.

If one bloc has some hierarchical organizational features and the other is not hierarchically organized, a number of consequences can be expected. The hierarchical or mixed hierarchical bloc will retain its membership, since functional integration will be so great that it would be difficult for satellite members to withdraw or to form viable national entities if they did.[8] The relative permanence of membership in the bloc constitutes a threat to non-members. Therefore, such a bloc is unlikely to attract new members except as a consequence of military absorp-tion or political conquest by a native political party which already had associate membership in the bloc through the medium of an international party

---

[5] For an explication at greater length of the hypo-thetical relationship between system structure and system of norms, see Morton A. Kaplan, and Nicholas deB. Katzenbach, *The Political Foundations of International Law*, New York: John Wiley and Sons, 1961.

[6] Britain and France violated rules one, two, four, five, and six in the 1930s.

[7] Extensional definitions would identify NATO as relatively non-hierarchical and the Communist bloc as mixed hierarchical. If the Communist bloc were to be so integrated that national boundaries and organizational forms were eliminated, it would become fully hierarchi-cal.

[8] In this connection, it is noteworthy that the Yugo-slavs were able to resist the drastic Soviet demands for economic integration. Tito's withdrawal would have been much more difficult—and perhaps impossible—had this not been the case.

organization. The relatively irreversible characteristics of membership in such a bloc constitute a threat to all other national actors, whether associated in a bloc or not.

The non-hierarchical bloc has a looser hold over its members but is more likely to enter into co-operative pacts of one kind or another with non-bloc members. The pressure emanating from the hierarchically organized bloc, however, is likely to force the non-hierarchical organized bloc to integrate its bloc activities more closely and to extend them to other functional areas, or alternatively is likely to weaken and undermine the bloc.

If both blocs subscribe to hierarchical integrating rules, their memberships become rigid and only uncommitted states can, by choosing an alignment, change the existing line-up. Any action of this sort, however, would tend to reduce the flexibility of the international system by eliminating nations not included in blocs. Non-bloc member actors therefore would be more likely to support one or the other of the blocs on specific issues than to support either in general. If both blocs are hierarchically organized, their goals are similar—hierarchical world organization—and incompatible, since only one can succeed in leading such a world system.

With only two major groupings in the bipolar system, any rapid change in military capabilities tends to make this system unstable. For this reason, possession of second-strike nuclear systems by both major blocs is a factor for stability within the system.

The rules of the loose bipolar system follow:

(1) All blocs subscribing to hierarchical or mixed hierarchical integrating principles are to eliminate the rival bloc.

(2) All blocs subscribing to hierarchical or mixed hierarchical integrating principles are to negotiate rather than to fight, to fight minor wars rather than to major wars, and to fight major wars—under given risk and cost factors—rather than to fail to eliminate the rival bloc.

(3) All bloc actors are to increase their capabilities relative to those of the opposing bloc.

(4) All bloc actors subscribing to non-hierarchical organizational principles are to negotiate rather than to fight to increase capabilities, to fight minor wars rather than to fail to increase capabilities, but to refrain from initiating major wars for this purpose.

(5) All bloc actors are to engage in major war rather than to permit the rival bloc to attain a position of preponderant strength.

(6) All bloc members are to subordinate objectives of the universal actor to the objectives of their bloc in the event of gross conflict between these objectives but to subordinate the objectives of the rival bloc to those of the universal actor.

(7) All non-bloc member national actors are to co-ordinate their national objectives with those of the universal actor and to attempt to subordinate the objectives of bloc actors to those of the universal actor.

(8) Bloc actors are to attempt to extend the membership of their bloc but to tolerate the non-member position of a given national actor if the alternative is to force that national actor to join the rival bloc or to support its objectives.

(9) Non-bloc member national actors are to act to reduce the danger of war between the bloc actors.

(10) Non-bloc members are to refuse to support the policies of one bloc actor as against the other except in their roles as members of a universal actor.

(11) Universal actors are to reduce the incompatibility between the blocs.

(12) Universal actors are to mobilize non-bloc member national actors against cases of gross deviation, e.g., resort to force by a bloc actor. This rule, unless counterbalanced by the other rules, would enable the universal actor to become the prototype of a universal international system.

Unlike the "balance of power" international system, there is a high degree of role differentiation in the loose bipolar system. If any of the roles is pursued to the exclusion of others, the system will be transformed. If one bloc actor eliminates another, the system may be transformed into a hierarchical system. If the universal actor performs its functions too well, the system may be transformed into a universal international system. Other variations are possible.

The consequences of the loose bipolar system are as follows. Alliances tend to be long-term, to be based on permanent and not on shifting interests, and to have ideological components. Wars, except for the fear of nuclears, would tend to be unlimited. However, the fears concerning nuclear escalation are so great that there is, in fact, a greater dampening of war than in the "balance of power" system. Thus, wars tend to be quite limited; and even limited wars are rare. In the field of law, there are fewer restrictions on intervention than in the "balance of power" system and the limitations which do exist stem largely from the fear of escalation. The universal organization is used primarily for mediation and to some extent for war dampening.

Tight Bipolar System

The tight bipolar international system represents a modification of the loose bipolar system in which non-bloc member actors and universal actors either disappear entirely or cease to be significant. Unless both blocs are hierarchically organized, however, the system will tend toward instability.

There is no integrative or mediatory role in the tight bipolar system. Therefore there will tend to be a high degree of dysfunctional tension in the system. For this reason, the tight bipolar system will not be a highly stable or well-integrated system.

Universal System

The universal international system might develop as a consequence of the functioning of a universal actor organization in a loose bipolar system. The universal system, as distinguished from those international systems previously discussed, would have a political system as a sub-system of the international social system. However, it is possible that this political system would be of the confederated type, i.e., that it would operate on territorial governments rather than directly on human individuals.

The universal international system would be an integrated and solidary system. Although informal political groupings might take place within the system, conflicts of interest would be settled according to the political rules of the system. Moreover, a body of political officials and administrators would exist whose primary loyalty would be to the international system itself rather than to any territorial sub-system of the international system.

Whether or not the universal international system is a stable system depends upon the extent to which it has direct access to resources and facilities and upon the ratio between its capabilities and the capabilities of the national actors who are members of the system.

Hierarchical System

The hierarchical international system may be democratic or authoritarian in form. If it evolves from a universal international system—perhaps because the satisfactions arising from the successful operation of such a universal international system lead to a desire for an even more integrated and solidary international system—it is likely to be a democratic system. If, on the other hand, the hierarchical system is imposed upon willing national actors by a victorious or powerful bloc, then the international system is likely to be authoritarian.

The hierarchical system contains a political system. Within it, functional lines of organization are stronger than geographical lines. This highly integrated characteristic of the hierarchical international system makes for greater stability. Functional cross-cutting makes it most difficult to organize successfully against the international system or to withdraw from it. Even if the constitution of the system were to permit such withdrawal, the integration of facilities over time would raise the costs of withdrawal too high.

Unit Veto System

Consider a world in which some twenty-odd nations have nuclear systems capable of a not incredible first strike. That is, each nation would have a nuclear system that would not completely reduce enemy forces in a first strike but that might nonetheless reduce the enemy forces so much, if everything went according to plan, that a war begun by a first strike might be contemplated. However, even a successful first strike would then leave a nation launching such an attack, because of its depleted arsenal, quite vulnerable to attack by a third nation—an attack that might not be unlikely either if its own attack had been without provocation or if the other nation were malevolent. In any event, the vulnerability of the attacker to subsequent attack by a third state would tend to inhibit such a first strike except in the most extremely provocative circumstances.

There would be little need for specific alliances in this world. To the extent that alliances did occur, one would expect them to be of a non-ideological nature. Nations might ally themselves in pacts establishing an obligation to retaliate against any "aggressor" who launched a nuclear attack, which exceeded certain specified proportions, against an alliance member.

In this system one does not expect large counter-value[9] or counter-force[10] wars. If nuclear weapons are used at all, they will tend to be used in limited retaliations for purposes of warning or in other strictly limited ways. The wars that do occur will tend to be non-nuclear and limited in geographic area and means of war-fighting. Sub-limited wars will occur more often than actual wars.

The system, however, might seem to have some potentiality for triggering wars or for catalytic wars. That is, if one nation engages in a counter-force attack, this in some views would likely trigger an attack on it by a third state. Or an anonymous attack or accident might catalyze a series of wars. These possibilities cannot be denied, particularly if tensions within the system become high. Nonetheless first strikes and accidental wars are unlikely because credible first-strike forces will not exist and because adequate command and control systems will be available. Thus the nuclear systems will be relatively stable against accidents. An anonymous attack will be a theoretical possibility but not a practicable one unless many nations develop polaris forces—that is, forces such that an attack cannot be attributed to a particular nation. Even so, it would seem difficult to identify the rational motive for attack in such a world. An anonymous attack would not seem to have any reasonable political motive, since, by definition, the aggressor could not identify himself and thus secure the benefits arising from threats. Numerous nervous rivals would remain, and the attack might very well trigger a holocaust.

Because of the adequacy of nuclear systems and the relative unimportance of alliances, when contrasted with the "balance of power" international system, interventions would not be as ominous as in that system and therefore would not be as strongly interdicted. But since the gains resulting from such interventions would be smaller than in the loose bipolar system, they are unlikely to become characteristic of this system. The danger of escalation, moreover, would tend to limit them. If universal organizations exist in this system, they would act as mediators, as would non-involved states whether nuclear or non-nuclear. In general, though, the universal organization would have fewer and less important functions than in the loose bipolar system. Nations equipped with nuclear forces in the unit veto system will tend to be self-sufficient and to reject outside pressures, even if coming from universal organizations. In particular, the functions of the universal organization dealing with political change will tend to be minimized. This will be reinforced by the disappearance of the colonial question as an important issue in world politics.

The foreign policies of the great nuclear powers will tend to be isolationist. Alliances, as specified, will recede in importance. Hegemonial ambitions will be curbed—primarily by an obvious inability to achieve them. Protective functions will tend to be shifted to "other" shoulders, when aggression does occur, since no "natural" assignment of this function will be possible. (That is, almost any one of the nuclear powers could play the role; there is no particular pressure on any particular nation to assume it.)[11]

One would expect nations such as the Soviet Union and China to be less revolutionary, as the prospects for revolutionary solidarity receded even further, and as the frictions between nuclear powers, regardless of ideology, increased. As a consequence nations such as the United States would have less incentive to resist changes in the status quo.

The domestic corollary of the above would involve publics suspicious of foreign nations, relatively uninterested in the morals of quarrels or in social change external to the nation, and lacking the assurance necessary for an articulated goal-oriented foreign policy.

---

[9] A counter-value attack is directed against cities or other non-combatant installations that are of social importance.

[10] A counter-force attack is one directed against military installations. The term usually refers to strikes against nuclear installations.

[11] This is parallel to the situation between the two world wars, when the League of Nations sought to control aggression. The onus of stopping aggression could always be shifted to other shoulders and was not undertaken by any nation or combination of nations until very late in the game. At the time of Korea, on the other hand, in the loose bipolar system, if aggression were to be halted, only the United States was in a position to accomplish this. Thus the fact that the system singled out a particular nation for this role served to reinforce the performance of the role function.

III

A number of models follow which may be considered either variations of the loose bipolar system or of the unit veto system. The variations will occur under conditions that are not consonant with maximum stability for either kind of system. Although perhaps not genuinely equilibrium systems, they correspond with conditions that conceivably might persist for critical periods of time. In this sense they might be considered to have some sort of local stability. They are worth exploration since they indicate some potential lines of development from the existing situation. Indeed the very loose bipolar system is descriptively reasonably close to the existing situation. Still for purposes of model construction we simplify and reduce the number of variables involved. We look for those conditions which make for maximum stability within the limitations of the somewhat destabilizing constraints which we do place on the models. Other variants could easily be constructed.

Very Loose Bipolar System

This is a model that does not appear in *System and Process*. It has elements of great inherent instability and would not be presented at all, except that it has striking resemblances to contemporary international politics. In the loose bipolar system, the nations playing different roles are not differentiated in terms of history, culture, state of economic development, color, and so forth. In the real world, the uncommitted nations, by and large, are ex-colonies, in particular, ex-colonies of nations belonging to NATO, are in bad economic circumstances, are attempting to modernize and develop, belong, by and large, to the so-called colored races, and possess ideologies that make them hostile to much the NATO bloc stands for. Increased nuclear stability has reduced the fear of central war, except as a consequence of escalation. This has tended to dampen international crises of the classical military kind but has created a shelter for guerrilla and sublimited wars as well as for rare limited wars in areas where escalation is not likely. The blocs have weakened, although they still exist. Large areas of accord and common interest between the United States and the Soviet Union appear to have arisen. Meanwhile Communist China has appeared to many as a

potential threat to the U.S. and the U.S.S.R. There has also been a limited extent of nuclear diffusion.

In this system, the universal organization is used in ways consonant, but not identical, with the revolutionary drives of many of the uncommitted nations. Within the universal organization both blocs will compete for the support of the uncommitted states with respect to the issues of decolonization and of racial equality. In this competition the bloc, which for the most part, supports the status quo will, by and large, be outbid. The conservative bloc will be more effective in those areas in which it can intervene directly or even indirectly, with military force and economic support.

Although the conservative bloc has sufficient support to prevent a rapid shift to the left within the universal organization, the competition for the support of the uncommitted nations will be shifted from the two blocs to a competition between the more and less radical wings of the revolutionary bloc. The process adumbrated above will likely coincide with the quasi-legitimization of intervention against existing "conservative" governments by revolutionary governments.[12]

This system will be characterized by the search for arms control, for accommodation between the blocs, and by the opposition to bloc policy by important members of both blocs. There will be a fragmentation, or at least weakening, of bloc structures. In the area of law, the rule of non-intervention will be breached even more than in the loose bipolar system. The universal organization will be used primarily to control the path of political change rather than primarily as a mediatory instrument. As a consequence, it is likely to have forced upon it more and more difficult problems that are not

---

[12] An example of this is given by the announced support for the Congolese rebels by the Egyptian and Algerian governments. According to the New York *Times* of January 2, 1965, after the Security Council's resolution calling for non-intervention in the Congo, the State Department, "believed, for example, that the United Arab Republic and Algeria will no longer be willing to admit that they are shipping arms to the Congolese rebels. The two countries may continue their shipments but at a restricted level that can be kept secret it is believed." This pathetic quotation indicates graphically the extent of the shift involved. (According to the New York *Times* of February 1, 1965, the Algerians announced their support for the rebels and the Egyptians, as a gesture of support to the rebels, asked the Congolese to close their embassy in Cairo.)

unlikely to be beyond the competence of the organization. They will likely involve strong conflicts of interest between the bloc leaders and may reach such a magnitude that the support of the bloc leaders for the universal organization may be called in question. Extreme self-restraint on the part of the bloc leaders will be required if the system is not to become unstable and if, in particular, the universal organization is to remain viable and to continue to perform its mediating functions.

The Détente System

The "détente system" world assumes that some of the favorable projections as to changes within both the Soviet and American systems occur. Soviet society becomes more open and less aggressive and the U.S. less defensive of the international status quo. Although no responsible, reasonable, and cautious social scientist would predict these changes, it still would be interesting to see if we can picture the kind of system which might occur if these changes did take place. In general, we assume the amelioration of the Soviet system, the domestication of the Chinese system, or at least the inability of the Chinese to create difficulty, and stability in much of the uncommitted world.

This is a world in which the U.S. and the U.S.S.R. are still strongly competitive but in which the competition is not conflictful. Tensions are relaxed and important arms control agreements reached. As a consequence Russia and the U.S. support nuclear forces capable only of mostly finite deterrence and there are portents that the forces are being reduced to those required for minimum deterrence only.

As a consequence of this "détente system," the internal organization of the two blocs loosens up. Some of the Soviet satellites begin to take occasional positions on foreign policy agreeing with those of the West rather than with the Soviet Union. Fissures within the Western bloc increase. Although most issues tend to find groupings revolving around the Soviet Union and the United States, the alignments have some tendency to differ from issue to issue. And on some issues the U.S. and the U.S.S.R. are in agreement and differ with China or one or more Western states.

The foreign policies of the U.S. and the U.S.S.R.

tend to liberal interventionism. Anti-colonialism is carried to completion. The U.S. quits backing oligarchical but anti-Communist states. The Soviet Union learns how to live with non-Communist new nations and ceases its support of national liberation movements within genuinely independent nations. Some difficulties attend Chinese attempts to aid national liberation movements.

In the area of law, non-intervention in the internal affairs of other states is stressed. This is a necessary corollary of the "détente system." Although some of the rules of international law are changed to accord with new values—on the subject of expropriation, for instance—in general the rules of international law are strengthened and enforced. They are extended to outer space and celestial bodies.

The universal organization plays a strong role in the governance of space, celestial bodies, and the polar regions. It aids in the extinguishment of colonialism, in the regulation of arms control measures, and takes a leading role in the dampening of international breaches of the peace.

Breaches of the peace—or even wars—may occur in this system, but they will not involve the U.S. and the U.S.S.R., at least in direct confrontations with each other. Such wars will tend to be local, to be strictly limited in objectives, to involve minor nations, and to be strictly non-nuclear. Where this threatens not to be the case, the U.S. and the U.S.S.R. are likely to co-operate within limits to prevent occurrences that might escalate. And, if they do not co-operate in this endeavor, at least they will not seriously interfere with each other's actions toward this end. They will usually work through the universal organization in these cases.

The Unstable Bloc System

The world of "the unstable bloc system" is a world in which developments contrary to those assumed for the "détente system" world have taken place. This is a world in which tension has increased and in which the U.S. and the U.S.S.R. are highly suspicious of each other. Arms control agreements are minimal in this world. Third area conflicts are extensive. There are local outbreaks of violence. And national liberation movements continue to be a problem. Qualitative developments have made nuclear systems cheaper and easier to acquire.

The nuclear systems of the U.S. and U.S.S.R. vary in strength from mostly finite deterrence to not incredible massive retaliation. Four or five other states have nuclear systems but these are good for minimum deterrence only. All nuclear powers possess strategies calling for limited strategic reprisal under appropriate circumstances. But obviously it is easier and safer for the U.S. and U.S.S.R. to use this strategy, even against each other, and certainly against the small nuclear powers, than it is for the small nuclear powers to use it against each other. It is conceivable—but barely so—and not credible that the small nuclear powers would use limited strategic reprisal against one of the large nuclear powers. The chance is much greater that the small power attempting this would be left to its fate and that the retaliation then applied against it would not trigger off the other large nuclear power than that it would. Thus the deterrent value of such a threat by a small nuclear power—unless led by an apparent madman—would not be great.

Alliance policy in this system is highly dependent upon military capability and policy. If the United States' posture, for instance, is clearly not adequate for deterrence against aggression directed at countries other than the United States, the strains on its alliance during periods of crises might prove insuperable, except in those cases where its allies' capabilities, in addition to its own, might produce the requisite deterrence. One would assume that the Warsaw Pact powers would not be as susceptible to splitting tactics as NATO because of the "organic" political relationships among the members and because of the presence of the Russian army on satellite soil. Although this position is debatable, it is nonetheless plausible.

In general, bloc alignments would be subject to two conflicting pressures. The fact of crisis in a basically bipolar world would give the blocs greater reason for being and greater cohesion. The additional fact, however, that the U.S., or any other nation, might hesitate before inviting nuclear destruction on its own territory provides an opening for nuclear blackmail. That such blackmail might be dangerous and that it is unlikely to be practiced except under conditions of very great provocation does not negate this consideration. Moreover, the threat need not be overt. The fact that it is operative in the situation is enough to help shape expectations, attitudes, and national policies. How the two conflicting pressures factor out depends upon an interplay of considerations difficult to consider in the abstract.

The foreign policies of the U.S. and the U.S.S.R. in this model will tend to be interventionist. They will respond to the basic clash of interests and not to a general concordance of interests as in the "détente system." U.S. policy will tend toward conservatism, that is, toward the support of status quo conservative regimes. Change will tend to be viewed as a threat, despite some plausible arguments to the contrary.[13] There will be a consequent alienation of a considerable portion of the intellectual elite within the U.S. and in the other NATO states. Soviet policy will be oriented toward national liberation movements despite a desire not to "rock the boat" in the dangerous nuclear age. Additional "Hungarys" may occur, or other events may occur which disillusion Soviet intellectuals. Relations between Russia and China will influence Soviet policy. If, as at present, they are at odds, China will tend to pre-empt the revolutionary position and this might moderate Soviet policy to some extent. But, by assumption, this would not go too far, or we would be back in the "détente system." It is also possible, but not likely, that with the retirement of Khrushchev and after the death of Mao, the two nations become more closely allied. In this latter case, the conflict and tension between the blocs will increase greatly.

Although most breaches of the peace in this system will not involve direct confrontations between the U.S. and the U.S.S.R., such confrontations are not entirely unlikely in this system. Moreover, there is a distinct possibility that nuclear weapons may be used in some limited fashion. If so, the use will probably be of the limited reprisal variety.

The role of the universal organization will be primarily mediatory and adapted to dampening the consequences of outbreaks of violence. Although each bloc will support political changes contrary to the interests of the opposing bloc, the efforts to secure a constitutional majority in the universal organization will generally prove ineffective. The universal organization will not acquire authority

[13] For some of these arguments, see "United States Foreign Policy in a Revolutionary Age," in Morton A. Kaplan, ed., *The Revolution in World Politics*, New York: John Wiley and Sons, 1962.

over outer space, celestial bodies, and serious arms control measures.

Intervention in the internal affairs of other nations will be rampant in this system and will be limited primarily by the fear of nuclear escalation. This system will not be noted for the growth of international law. If anything, there will be retrogression. Existing standards will erode and will not be replaced by generally agreed-upon norms.

Incomplete Nuclear Diffusion System

We will now consider another variation of the "unstable bloc system." The description of this system is roughly similar to the previously mentioned one, except that fifteen or twenty nations, additional to the U.S. and the U.S.S.R., will have nuclear forces. But these forces will be of the small vulnerable variety. Our analysis will stress only those features of this world that differ from the "unstable bloc system."

The United States and the U.S.S.R. will have nuclear forces that are not capable of first strike but that do give some significant advantage if used first. The smaller nuclear nations will possess what is ordinarily called minimum deterrence. This is similar to the French idea of "tearing an arm off." These forces would, in fact, deter most attacks against the homeland, but not all, and probably not in extremely provocative situations. Their triggering capability would be quite small. And they would be quite vulnerable to surprise attack.

Alliances would be possible between major and minor nuclear powers or among minor nuclear powers. But the former type of alliance would be inhibited by the small state's possession of nuclear arms. Possession would by itself be a sign of independence and distrust. Moreover the large state would fear commitment by the small state's nuclear use. It would desire to insulate itself from a chain of actions that it could not control. And, although a general alliance among most of the small states possessing nuclear forces might create a reasonable

deterrent, unless there were exceptional political or cultural circumstances the alliance would be very susceptible to nuclear blackmail and splitting tactics. Otherwise the discussion of the "unstable bloc system" is applicable with respect to alliance conditions.

Although wars in this system would tend to be limited, as in the "unstable bloc system," the degree of tension would be higher also; and the possibility of escalation would be greater. Limited and direct confrontations between the U.S. and the U.S.S.R. might occur in non-European areas. A central confrontation in Europe might also occur, but here the danger of escalation beyond the limited-war category would be very great. And for this reason the factors operating against central confrontation would tend to be very great.

The mediatory functions of the universal organization would be more important than in the "unstable bloc system" world and would tend to be more stressed, although it would also prove more difficult to use them successfully. Outside of mediatory functions the universal organization would have even fewer functions than in the "unstable bloc system" world and would handle them less successfully on the whole.

The legal system would function even more poorly than in the "unstable bloc system" world, and intervention in the internal affairs of other states would be even more extensive. Foreign policy would be as in the "détente system" world, but the conservative interventionist nature of American policy would be even more pronounced. Soviet policy would tend to be more revolutionary. The alienation of some intellectuals would be increased, but the obvious dangers of the situation would also create a counter-current of chauvinism leading to a highly dangerous bifurcation of intellectual opinion within both blocs and within the leading nation of each. Governments and their supporters would lack assurance and might become susceptible to ill-considered actions. There might be a swing between excessive caution and excessive adventurism. . . .

28. International Structure, National Force, and the Balance of World Power

Kenneth N. Waltz is Professor of Politics at Brandeis University. The author of a number of provocative inquiries into international politics, his *Man, the State, and War* (1959) and *Foreign Policy and Democratic Politics* (1967) are among the outstanding works in the field. In this selection Professor Waltz examines the impact of nuclear weapons upon the structure of a global international system. His conclusion that bipolarity persists as an underlying characteristic of the system stands in sharp contrast to the theme of the three subsequent selections and the reader will doubtless want to return again to Professor Waltz's challenging article after he reads those that follow. [*Reprinted from* Journal of International Affairs, *XXI (1967), pp. 215–31, by permission of the author and the publisher.*]

Balance of power is the hoariest concept in the field of international relations. Elaborated in a variety of analyses and loaded with different meanings, it has often been praised or condemned, but has seldom been wholly rejected. In a fascinating historical account of balance-of-power concepts, Martin Wight has distinguished nine meanings of the term.[1] For purposes of theoretical analysis a tenth meaning, cast in causal terms, should be added.

Balance-of-power theory assumes that the desire for survival supplies the basic motivation of states, indicates the responses that the constraints of the system encourage, and describes the expected outcome. Beyond the survival motive, the aims of states may be wondrously varied; they may range from the ambition to conquer the world to the desire merely to be left alone. But the minimum responses of states, which are necessary to the dynamics of balance, derive from the condition of national coexistence where no external guarantee of survival exists. Perception of the peril that lies in unbalanced power encourages the behavior required for the maintenance of a balance-of-power system.

Because of the present narrow concentration of awesome power, the question arises whether the affairs of the world can any longer be conducted or understood according to the balance-of-power concept, the main theoretical prop of those traditionally called realists. Even many who share the realist concern with power question its present relevance. They do so for two reasons.

It is, in the first place, widely accepted that balance-of-power politics requires the presence of three or more states. Political thought is so historically conditioned that the balance of power as it is usually defined merely reflects the experience of the modern era. In Europe for a period of three centuries, from the Treaty of Westphalia to the Second World War,

[1] Martin Wight, "The Balance of Power," in *Diplomatic Investigations: Essays in the Theory of International Politics*, ed. by Herbert Butterfield and Martin Wight (Cambridge: Harvard University Press, 1966), p. 151.

five or more great powers sometimes sought to coexist peacefully and at other times competed for mastery. The idea thus became fixed that a balance of power can exist only where the participants approximate the customary number. But something more than habit is involved. Also mixed into ideas about necessary numbers is the notion that flexibility in the alignment of states is a requirement of balance-of-power politics. The existence of only two states at the summit of power precludes the possibility of international maneuver and national realignment as ways of compensating for changes in the strength of either of them. Excessive concentration of power negates the possibility of playing the politics of balance.

Second, war or the threat of war, another essential means of adjustment, is said to be of only limited utility in the nuclear age. In balances of power, of course, more is placed on the scales than mere military force. Military force has, however, served not only as the *ultima ratio* of international politics but indeed as the first and the constant one. To reduce force to being the *ultima ratio* of politics implies, as Ortega y Gasset once noted, "the previous submission of force to methods of reason."[2] Insufficient social cohesion exists among states and the instruments of international control are too weak to relegate power to the status of simply the *ultima ratio*. Power cannot be separated from the purposes of those who possess it; in international politics power has appeared primarily as the power to do harm.[3] To interdict the use of force by the threat of force, to oppose force with force, to annex territory by force, to influence the policies of other states by the threat or application of force—such uses of force have always been present at least as possibilities in the relations of states. The threat to use military forces and their occasional commitment to battle have helped to regulate the relations of states, and the preponderance of power in the hands of the major states has set them apart from the others. But, it is now often said, nuclear weapons, the "best" weapons of the most powerful states, are the least usable. At the extreme, some commentators assert

that military force has become obsolete. Others, more cautious in their claims, believe that the inflated cost of using military force has seriously distorted both the balance between the militarily strong states and the imbalance between the strong and the weak ones. National military power, though not rendered wholly obsolete by nuclear weapons, nevertheless must be heavily discounted. The power of the two nuclear giants, it would seem, is then seriously impaired.[4]

A weird picture of the political world is thus drawn. The constraints of balance-of-power politics still operate: each state by its own efforts fends for its rights and seeks to maintain its existence. At the same time, the operation of balance-of-power politics is strangely truncated; for one essential means of adjustment is absent, and the operation of the other is severely restricted. In the nineteenth-century liberals' vision of a world without power, force was to be banished internationally by the growing perfection of states and their consequent acceptance of each other as equals in dignity. The liberal utopia has reappeared in odd form. The limitation of power—or in extreme formulations, its abolition—is said to derive from the nuclear armament of some states; for nuclear armament makes at once for gross inequality in the power of states and for substantial equality among all states through the inability of the most powerful to use force effectively. Those who love paradox are understandably enchanted. To examine the ground upon which the supposed paradox rests is one of the main aims of this essay.

I

The first reason for believing that balance-of-power politics has ended is easy to deal with, for only its relevance, not its truth, is in question.

---

[2] Quoted in Chalmers Johnson, *Revolutionary Change* (Boston: Little, Brown, 1966), p. 13.

[3] I do not mean to imply that this exhausts the purposes of power. In this essay, however, I cannot analyze other aspects of power either in themselves or in relation to the power to do harm.

[4] The point has been made most extensively by Klaus Knorr and most insistently by Stanley Hoffmann. See Knorr, *On the Uses of Military Power in the Nuclear Age* (Princeton: Princeton University Press, 1966). See also Hoffmann, "Obstinate or Obsolete? The Fate of the Nation-State and the Case of Western Europe," *Daedalus*, Vol. XCV (Summer 1965), especially pp. 897, 907; "Europe's Identity Crisis: Between the Past and America," *Daedalus*, Vol. XCIII (Fall 1964), especially pp. 1287–8; "Nuclear Proliferation and World Politics," in *A World of Nuclear Powers?*, ed. by Alastair Buchan (Englewood Cliffs, N.J.: Prentice-Hall, 1966); and two essays in *The State of War* (New York: Praeger, 1965), "Roulette in the Cellar: Notes on Risk in International Relations," especially pp. 140–47, and "Terror in Theory and Practice," especially pp. 233–51.

If the balance-of-power game is really played hard it eventuates in two participants, whether states or groupings of them. If two groupings of states have hardened or if the relation of major antagonism in the world is simply between two nations, the balance-of-power model no longer applies, according to the conventional definition. This conclusion is reached by placing heavy emphasis on the process of balancing (by realignments of states) rather than on altering power (which may depend on the efforts of each state).[5] In a two-power world, emphasis must shift from the international process of balancing to the prospect of altering power by the internal efforts of each participant.

Admittedly, the old balance-of-power model cannot be applied without modification to a world in which two states far exceed all others in the force at their disposal. Balance-of-power analysis, however, remains highly useful if the observer shifts his perspective from a concentration upon international maneuver as a mode of adjustment to an examination of national power as a means of control and national effort as a way of compensating for incipient disequilibria of power. With this shift in perspective, balance-of-power politics does not disappear; but the meaning of politics changes in a manner that can only be briefly suggested here.

In a world of three or more powers the possibility of making and breaking alliances exists. The substance of balance-of-power politics is found in the diplomacy by which alliances are made, maintained, or disrupted. Flexibility of alignment then makes for rigidity in national strategies: a state's strategy must satisfy its partner lest that partner defect from the alliance. A comparable situation is found where political parties compete for votes by forming and reforming electoral coalitions of different economic, ethnic, religious, and regional groups. The strategies (or policies) of the parties are made so as to attract and hold voters. If it is to be an electoral success, a party's policy cannot simply be the policy that its leaders may think would be best for the country. Policy must at least partly be made for the sake of party management. Similarly in an alliance of approximately equal states, strategy is at least partly

made for the sake of the alliance's cohesion. The alliance diplomacy of Europe in the years before World War I is rich in examples of this. Because the defection or defeat of a major state would have shaken the balance of power, each state was constrained to adjust its strategy and the deployment of its forces to the aims and fears of its partners. This is in sharp contrast to the current situation in NATO, where de Gaulle's disenchantment, for example, can only have mild repercussions. Though concessions to allies will sometimes be made, neither the Soviet Union nor the United States alters its strategy or changes its military dispositions simply to accommodate associated states. Both superpowers can make long-range plans and carry out their policies as best they see fit, for they need not accede to the demands of third parties. That America's strategy is not made for the sake of de Gaulle helps to explain his partial defection.

Disregarding the views of an ally makes sense only if military cooperation is relatively unimportant. This is the case in NATO, which in fact if not in form consists of unilateral guarantees by the United States to its European allies. The United States, with a preponderance of nuclear weapons and as many men in uniform as all of the Western European states combined,[6] may be able to protect her allies; they cannot possibly protect her. Because of the vast differences in the capacities of member states, the approximately equal sharing of burdens found in earlier alliance systems is no longer conceivable. The gross inequality between the two superpowers and the members of their respective alliances makes any realignment of the latter fairly insignificant. The leader's strategy can therefore be flexible. In balance-of-power politics, old style, flexibility of alignment made for rigidity of strategy or the limitation of freedom of decision. In balance-of-power politics, new style, the obverse is true: rigidity of alignment in a two-power world makes for flexibility of strategy or the enlargement of freedom of decision.

Those who discern the demise of balance-of-power politics mistakenly identify the existence of balances of power with a particular mode of adjustment and the political means of effecting it. Balances

[5] See, for example, Inis L. Claude, Jr., *Power and International Relations* (New York: Random House, 1962), p. 90; and Morton A. Kaplan, *System and Process in International Politics* (New York: John Wiley & Sons, 1957), p. 22.

[6] See "The Text of Address by McNamara to American Society of Newspaper Editors," *The New York Times*, May 19, 1966, p. 11.

of power tend to form so long as states desire to maintain their political identities and so long as they must rely on their own devices in striving to do so. With shrinking numbers, political practices and methods will differ; but the number of states required for the existence and perpetuation of balance-of-power politics is simply two or more, not, as is usually averred, some number larger than two.

II

The reduction in the number of major states calls for a shift in conceptual perspective. Internal effort has replaced external realignment as a means of maintaining an approximate balance of power. But the operation of a balance of power, as previously noted, has entailed the occasional use of national force as a means of international control and adjustment. Great-power status was traditionally conferred on states that could use force most handily. Is the use of force in a nuclear world so severely inhibited that balance-of-power analysis has lost most if not all of its meaning?

Four reasons are usually given in support of an affirmative answer. First, because the nuclear might of one superpower balances that of the other, their effective power is reduced to zero. Their best and most distinctive forces, the nuclear ones, are least usable. In the widely echoed words of John Herz, absolute power equals absolute impotence.[7] Second, the fear of escalation strongly inhibits even the use of conventional forces, especially by the United States or the Soviet Union. Nuclear powers must fear escalation more than other states do, for in any war that rose to the nuclear level they would be primary targets. They may, of course, still choose to commit their armies to battle, but the risks of doing so, as they themselves must realize, are higher than in the past. Third, in the nuclear age enormous military power no longer ensures effective control. The Soviet Union has not been able to control her Asian and European satellites. The United States has found it difficult to use military force for constructive purposes even against weak opponents in Southeast Asia. Political rewards have not been proportionate to the strength of the states that are militarily most powerful. Finally, the weak states

of the world, having become politically aware and active, have turned world opinion into a serious restraint upon the use of force, whether in nuclear or conventional form. These four factors, it is argued, work singly and in combination to make the use of force more costly and in general to depreciate its value.

Never have great powers disposed of larger national products, and seldom in peacetime have they spent higher percentages of them on their military forces. The money so lavishly expended purchases more explosive power and more varied ways of delivering it than ever before in history. In terms of world distribution, seldom has military force been more narrowly concentrated. If military force is less useful today, the irony of history will have yet another vivid illustration. Has force indeed so depreciated as to warp and seriously weaken the effects of power in international relations? The above arguments make it seem so; they need to be reexamined. The following analysis of the use of force deals with all four arguments, though not by examining them one by one and in the order in which they are stated.

E. H. Carr long ago identified the error of believing "in the efficacy of an international public opinion," and he illustrated and explained the fallacy at length.[8] To think of world opinion as a restraint upon the military actions of states, one must believe that the strong states of the world—or for that matter the weak ones—would have used more military force and used it more often had they not anticipated their condemnation. Unless in a given instance world opinion can be defined, its source identified, and the mode of its operation discerned, such a view is not plausible. To believe in the efficacy of world opinion is to endow a non-existent agent and an indefinable force with effective restraining power. Not world opinion but national views, shaped into policies and implemented by governments, have accounted for past events in international relations. Changes that would now permit world opinion, whatever that might be, to restrict national policies would have to lie not in the operation of opinion itself but in other changes that have occurred in the world. With "world

---

[7] John Herz, *International Politics in the Atomic Age* (New York: Columbia University Press, 1959), pp. 22, 169.

[8] Edward Hallett Carr, *The Twenty Years' Crisis, 1919–1939*, 2nd ed. (New York: Harper & Row, 1964), p. 140.

opinion," as with Adam Smith's "invisible hand," one must ask: What is the reality that the metaphor stands for? It may be that statesmen pay their respects to world opinion because they are already restrained by other considerations.

Are such considerations found, perhaps, in changes that have taken place in the nature and distribution of force itself? If the costs of using military force have lessened its value, then obeisance paid to world opinion is merely a cloak for frustration and a hypocritical show of politeness. That the use of force is unusually costly, however, is a conclusion that rests on a number of errors. One that is commonly committed is to extend to all military force the conclusion that nuclear force is unusable. After listing the changes effected by nuclear weapons, one author, for example, concludes that these changes tend to restrict "the usability and hence the political utility of national military power in various ways."[9] This may represent merely a slip of the pen; if so, it is a telling one. A clearer and more interesting form of the error is found in the argument that the two superpowers, each stalemated by the other's nuclear force, are for important political purposes effectively reduced to the power of middle-range states. The effective equality of states apparently emerges from the very condition of their gross inequality. We read, for example, that "the very change in the nature of the mobilizable potential has made its actual use in emergencies by its unhappy owners quite difficult and self-defeating. As a result, nations endowed with infinitely less can behave in a whole range of issues as if the difference in power did not matter." The conclusion is driven home—or, rather, error is compounded—by the argument that the United States thinks in "cataclysmic terms," lives in dread of all-out war, and bases its military calculations on the forces needed for the ultimate but unlikely crisis rather than on what might be needed in the less spectacular cases that are in fact more likely to occur.[10]

Absolute power equals absolute impotence, at least at the highest levels of force represented by the American and Soviet nuclear armories. At lesser levels of violence many states can compete as though they were substantially equal. The best weapons of

the United States and the Soviet Union are useless, and the distinctive advantage of those two states is thus negated. But what about American or Soviet nuclear weapons used against minor nuclear states or against those who are entirely without nuclear weapons? Here again, it is claimed, the "best" weapon of the most powerful states turns out to be the least usable. The nation that is equipped to "retaliate massively" is not likely to find the occasion to use its capability. If amputation of an arm were the only remedy available for an infected finger, one would be tempted to hope for the best and leave the ailment untreated. The state that can move effectively only by committing the full power of its military arsenal is likely to forget the threats it has made and acquiesce in a situation formerly described as intolerable. Instruments that cannot be used to deal with small cases—those that are moderately dangerous and damaging—remain idle until the big case arises. But then the use of major force to defend a vital interest would run the grave risk of retaliation. Under such circumstances, the powerful are frustrated by their very strength; and although the weak do not thereby become strong, they are, it is said, nevertheless able to behave as though they were.

Such arguments are often made and have to be taken seriously. In an obvious sense, part of the contention is valid. When great powers are in a stalemate, lesser states acquire an increased freedom of movement. That this phenomenon is now noticeable tells us nothing new about the strength of the weak or the weakness of the strong. Weak states have often found opportunities for maneuver in the interstices of a balance of power. This is, however, only part of the story. To maintain both the balance and its byproduct requires the continuing efforts of America and Russia. Their instincts for self-preservation call forth such efforts: the objective of both states must be to perpetuate an international stalemate as a minimum basis for the security of each of them—even if this should mean that the two big states do the work while the small ones have the fun. The margins within which the relative strengths of America and Russia may vary without destroying the stalemate are made wide by the existence of second-strike retaliatory forces, but permissible variation is not without limit. In the years of the supposed missile gap in America's disfavor, Khrushchev became unpleasantly frisky, especially over

[9] Knorr, *On the Uses of Military Power*, p. 87.
[10] Hoffmann, "Europe's Identity Crisis," pp. 1279, 1287–88.

Berlin and Cuba. The usefulness of maintaining American nuclear strength was demonstrated by the unfortunate consequences of its apparent diminution.

Strategic nuclear weapons deter strategic nuclear weapons (though they may also do more than that). Where each state must tend to its own security as best it can, the means adopted by one state must be geared to the efforts of others. The cost of the American nuclear establishment, maintained in peaceful readiness, is functionally comparable to the costs incurred by a government in order to maintain domestic order and provide internal security. Such expenditure is not productive in the sense that spending to build roads is, but it is not unproductive either. Its utility is obvious, and should anyone successfully argue otherwise, the consequences of accepting his argument would quickly demonstrate its falsity. Force is least visible where power is most fully and most adequately present.[11] The better ordered a society and the more competent and respected its government, the less force its policemen are required to employ. Less shooting occurs in present-day Sandusky than did on the western frontier. Similarly in international relations, states supreme in their power have to use force less often. "Non-recourse to force"—as both Eisenhower and Khrushchev seem to have realized—is the doctrine of powerful states. Powerful states need to use force less often than their weaker neighbors because the strong can more often protect their interests or work their wills in other ways—by persuasion and cajolery, by economic bargaining and bribery, by the extension of aid, or finally by posing deterrent threats. Since states with large nuclear armories do not actually "use" them, force is said to be discounted. Such reasoning is fallacious. Possession of power should not be identified with the use of force, and the usefulness of force should not be confused with its usability. To introduce such confusions into the analysis of power is comparable to saying that the police force that seldom if ever employs violence is weak or that a police force is strong only when policemen are swinging their clubs. To vary the image, it is comparable to saying that a man with large assets is not rich if he spends little money or that a man is rich only if he spends a lot of it.

[11] Cf. Carr, *The Twenty Years' Crisis*, pp. 103, 129–32.

But the argument, which we should not lose sight of, is that just as the miser's money may grossly depreciate in value over the years, so the great powers' military strength has lost much of its usability. If military force is like currency that cannot be spent or money that has lost much of its worth, then is not forbearance in its use merely a way of disguising its depreciated value? Conrad von Hötzendorf, Austrian Chief of Staff prior to World War I, looked upon military power as though it were a capital sum, useless unless invested. In his view, the investment of military force was ultimately its commitment to battle.[12] It may be permissible to reason in this way, but it makes the result of the reasoning a foregone conclusion. As Robert W. Tucker has noted, those who argue that force has lost its utility do so "in terms of its virtually uncontrolled use." But, he adds, "alter the assumption on which the argument proceeds—consider the functions served by military power so long as it is not overtly employed or employed only with restraint—and precisely the opposite conclusion may be drawn."[13]

In the reasoning of Conrad, military force is most useful at the moment of its employment in war. Depending on a country's situation, it may make much better sense to say that military force is most useful when it deters an attack, that is, when it need not be used in battle at all. When the strongest state militarily is also a status-quo power, non-use of force is a sign of its strength. Force is most useful, or best serves the interests of such a state, when it need not be used in the actual conduct of warfare. Again, the reasoning is old-fashioned. Throughout a century that ended in 1914, the British navy was

[12] "The sums spent for the war power is money wasted," he maintained, "if the war power remains unused for obtaining political advantages. In some cases the mere threat will suffice and the war power thus becomes useful, but others can be obtained only through the warlike use of the war power itself, that is, by war undertaken in time; if this moment is missed, the capital is lost. In this sense, war becomes a great financial enterprise of the State." Quoted in Alfred Vagts, *Defense and Diplomacy: The Soldier and the Conduct of Foreign Relations* (New York: King's Crown Press, 1956), p. 361.

[13] Robert W. Tucker, "Peace and War," *World Politics*, Vol. XVII (Jan. 1965), p. 324 fn. For a comprehensive and profound examination of the use of force internationally, see Robert Osgood and Robert Tucker, *Force, Order, and Justice* (Baltimore: Johns Hopkins Press, 1967).

powerful enough to scare off all comers, while Britain carried out occasional imperial ventures in odd parts of the world. Only as Britain's power weakened did her military forces have to be used to fight a full-scale war. By being used, her military power had surely become less useful.

Force is cheap, especially for a *status quo* power, if its very existence works against its use. What does it mean then to say that the cost of using force has increased while its utility has lessened? It is highly important, indeed useful, to think in "cataclysmic terms," to live in dread of all-out war, and to base military calculations on the forces needed for the ultimate but unlikely crisis. That the United States does so, and that the Soviet Union apparently does too, makes the cataclysm less likely to occur. But not only that. Nuclear weapons deter nuclear weapons; they also serve as a means of limiting escalation. The temptation of one country to employ larger and larger amounts of force is lessened if its opponent has the ability to raise the ante. Conventional force may be used more hesitantly than it would be in the absence of nuclear weapons because it cannot be assumed that escalation will be perfectly regulated. But force can be used with less hesitation by those states able to parry, to thrust, and to threaten at varied levels of military endeavor.

Where power is seen to be balanced, whether or not the balance is nuclear, it may seem that the resultant of opposing forces is zero. But this is misleading. The vectors of national force do not meet at a point, if only because the power of a state does not resolve into a single vector. Military force is divisible, especially for the state that can afford a lot of it. In a nuclear world, contrary to some assertions, the dialectic of inequality does not produce the effective equality of strong and weak states. Lesser states that decide to establish a nuclear arsenal by slighting their conventional forces render themselves unable to meet any threat to themselves other than the ultimate one (and that doubtfully). By way of contrast, the military doctrine of the United States, to which the organization of her forces corresponds, is one of flexible response. Great powers are strong not simply because they have nuclear weapons but also because their immense resources enable them to generate and maintain power of all types, military and other, at different technological levels.

Just as the state that refrains from applying force is said to betray its weakness, so the state that has trouble in exercising control is said to display the defectiveness of its power. In such a conclusion, the elementary error of identifying power with control is evident. Absence of control or failure to press hard to achieve it may indicate either that the would-be controller noticed that, try as he might, he would have insufficient force or inappropriate types of force at his command; or it may indicate that he chose to make less than a maximum effort because imposition of control was not regarded as very important. One student of international relations has remarked that "though the weapons of mass destruction grow more and more ferociously efficient, the revolutionary guerrilla armed with nothing more advanced than an old rifle and a nineteenth-century political doctrine has proved the most effective means yet devised for altering the world power-balance."[14] But the revolutionary guerrilla wins civil wars, not international ones, and no civil war can change the balance of power in the world unless it takes place in the United States or the Soviet Union. Enough of them have occurred since World War II to make the truth of this statement clear without need for further analysis. Even in China, the most populous of states, a civil war that led to a change of allegiance in the cold war did not seriously tilt the world balance.

Two states that enjoy wide margins of power over other states need worry little about changes that occur among the latter. Failure to act may then not betray the frustrations of impotence; instead it may demonstrate the serenity of power. The United States, having chosen to intervene in Vietnam, has limited the use of its military force. Because no realignment of national power in Vietnam could in itself affect the balance of power between the United States and the Soviet Union—or even noticeably alter the imbalance of power between the United States and China—the United States need not have intervened at all. Whether or not it could have safely "passed" in Southeast Asia, the American government chose not to do so; nor have its costly, long-sustained efforts brought success. If military power can be equated with control, then the United States has indeed demonstrated its weakness. The

[14] Coral Bell, "Non-Alignment and the Power Balance," *Survival*, Vol. V (Nov.–Dec. 1963), p. 255.

case is instructive. The People's Republic of China has not moved militarily against any country of Southeast Asia. The United States could successfully counter such a move, one would expect, by opposing military force with military force. What has worried some people and led others to sharpen their statements about the weakness of the powerful is that the United States, hard though it has tried, has been unable to put down insurrection and halt the possible spread of Communist ideology.

Here again old truths need to be brought into focus. As David Hume long ago noted, "force is always on the side of the governed."[15] The governors, being few in number, depend for the exercise of their rule upon the more or less willing assent of their subjects. If sullen disregard is the response to every command, no government can rule. And if a country, because of internal disorder and lack of coherence, is unable to rule itself, no body of foreigners, whatever the military force at its command, can reasonably hope to do so. If Communism is the threat to Southeast Asia, then military forces are not the right means for countering it. If insurrection is the problem, then it can hardly be hoped that an alien army will be able to pacify a country that is unable to govern itself. Foreign troops, though not irrelevant to such problems, can only be of indirect help. Military force, used internationally, is a means of establishing control over a territory, not of exercising control within it. The threat of a nation to use military force, whether nuclear or conventional, is preeminently a means of affecting another state's external behavior, of dissuading a state from launching a career of aggression and of meeting the aggression if dissuasion should fail.

Dissuasion or deterrence is easier to accomplish than "compellence," to use an apt term invented by Thomas C. Schelling.[16] Compellence is more difficult to achieve than deterrence, and its contrivance is a more intricate affair. In Vietnam, the United States faces not merely the task of compelling a particular action but of promoting an effective political order. Those who argue from such a case that force has depreciated in value fail in their analyses to apply their own historical and political knowledge. The master builders of imperial rule, such men as Bugeaud, Galliéni, and Lyautey, played both political and military roles. In like fashion, successful counter-revolutionary efforts have been directed by such men as Templer and Magsaysay, who combined military resources with political instruments.[17] Military forces, whether domestic or foreign, are insufficient for the task of pacification, the more so if a country is rent by faction and if its people are politically engaged and active. To say that militarily strong states are feeble because they cannot easily bring order to minor states is like saying that a pneumatic hammer is weak because it is not suitable for drilling decayed teeth. It is to confuse the purpose of instruments and to confound the means of external power with the agencies of internal governance. Inability to exercise *political* control over others does not indicate *military* weakness. Strong states cannot do everything with their military forces, as Napoleon acutely realized; but they are able to do things that militarily weak states cannot do. The People's Republic of China can no more solve the problems of governance in some Latin American country than the United States can in Southeast Asia. But the United States can intervene with great military force in far quarters of the world while wielding an effective deterrent against escalation. Such action exceeds the capabilities of all but the strongest of states.

Differences in strength do matter, though not for every conceivable purpose. To deduce the weakness of the powerful from this qualifying clause is a misleading use of words. One sees in such a case as Vietnam not the *weakness* of great military power in a nuclear world but instead a clear illustration of the *limits* of military force in the world of the present as always.

III

Only a sketch, intended to be suggestive, can here be offered of the connections between the present

[15] "The soldan of Egypt or the emperor of Rome," he went on to say, "might drive his harmless subjects like brute beasts against their sentiments and inclination. But he must, at least, have led his *mamalukes* or *praetorian bands*, like men, by their opinion." "Of the First Principles of Government," in *Hume's Moral and Political Philosophy*, ed. by Henry D. Aiken (New York: Hafner, 1948), p. 307.

[16] Thomas C. Schelling, *Arms and Influence* (New Haven: Yale University Press, 1966), pp. 70–71.

[17] The point is well made by Samuel P. Huntington, "Patterns of Violence in World Politics," in *Changing Patterns of Military Politics*, ed. by Samuel P. Huntington (New York: The Free Press of Glencoe, 1962), p. 28.

structure of the global balance of power, the relations of states, and the use of force internationally.

Unbalanced power is a danger to weak states. It may also be a danger to strong ones. An imbalance of power, by feeding the ambition of some states to extend their control, may tempt them to dangerously adventurous activity. Safety for all states, one may then conclude, depends upon the maintenance of a balance among them. Ideally, in this view, the rough equality of states gives each of them the ability to fend for itself. Equality may then also be viewed as a morally desirable condition. Each of the states within the arena of balance will have at least a modest ability to maintain its integrity. At the same time, inequality violates one's sense of justice and leads to national resentments that are in many ways troublesome. Because inequality is inherent in the state system, however, it cannot be removed. At the pinnacle of power, only a few states coexist as approximate equals; in relation to them, other states are of lesser moment. The bothersome qualities of this inevitable inequality of states should not cause one to overlook its virtues. In an economy, in a polity, or in the world at large, extreme equality is associated with instability. To draw another domestic analogy: where individualism is extreme, where society is atomistic, and where secondary organizations are lacking, government tends either to break down into anarchy or to become highly centralized and despotic. Under conditions of extreme equality, the prospect of oscillation between those two poles was well described by de Tocqueville; it was illustrated by Hobbes; and its avoidance was earnestly sought by the authors of the *Federalist Papers*. In a collection of equals, any impulse ripples through the whole society. Lack of secondary groups with some cohesion and continuity of commitment, for example, turns elections into auctions with each party in its promises tempted to bid up the others. The presence of social and economic groups, which inevitably will not all be equal, makes for less volatility in society.

Such durable propositions of political theory are lost sight of in the argument, frequently made, that the larger the number of consequential states the more stable the structure of world politics will be.[18] Carried to its logical conclusion, the argument

must mean that perfect stability would prevail in a world in which many states exist, all of them approximate equals in power.

The analysis of the present essay leads to a different conclusion. The inequality of states, though not a guarantee of international stability, at least makes stability possible. Within the structure of world politics, the relations of states will be as variable and complex as the movements and patterns of bits of glass within a kaleidoscope. It is not very interesting to ask whether destabilizing events will occur and disruptive relations will form, because the answer must always be yes. More interesting are such questions as these: What is the likely durability of a given political structure, whether international or domestic? How does it affect the relations of states, or of groups and individuals? How do the relations of constituent units and changes within them in turn affect the political structure? Within a state, people use more violence than do governments. In the United States in 1965, 9,814 people were murdered, but only seven were executed.[19] Thus one says (with some exaggeration, since fathers still spank their children) that the state enjoys a monopoly of *legitimate* violence. Too much violence among individuals will jeopardize the political structure. In international relations it is difficult to say that any particular use of violence is illegitimate, but some states have the ability to wield more of it. Because they do, they are able both to moderate others' use of violence and to absorb possibly destabilizing changes that emanate from uses of violence that they do not or cannot control. In the spring of 1966, Secretary McNamara remarked that in the preceding eight years there had been "no less than 164 internationally significant outbreaks of violence...."[20] Of course, not only violence is at issue. To put the point in more general terms, strong structures are able to moderate and absorb destabilizing changes; weak structures succumb to them.

No political structure, whether domestic or international, can guarantee stability. The question that one must ask is not whether a given distribution

---

[18] By "structure" I mean the pattern according to which power is distributed; by "stability," the perpetua-

tion of that structure without the occurrence of grossly destructive violence.

[19] U.S. Bureau of the Census, *Statistical Abstract of the United States: 1966* (Washington, D.C.: Government Printing Office, 1966), p. 165.

[20] *The New York Times*, May 19, 1966, p. 11.

of power is stable but how stable different distributions of power are likely to be. For a number of reasons, the bipolar world of the past two decades has been highly stable.[21] The two leading states have a common interest in stability: they would at least like to maintain their positions. In one respect, bipolarity is expressed as the reciprocal control of the two strongest states by each other out of their mutual antagonism. What is unpredictable in such a two-party competition is whether one party will try to eliminate the other. Nuclear forces of second-strike capacity induce an added caution. Here again force is useful, and its usefulness is reinforced in proportion as its use is forestalled. Fear of major war induces caution all around; the Soviet Union and the United States wield the means of inducing that caution.

The constraints of duopolistic competition press in one direction: duopolists eye each other warily, and each is very sensitive to the gains of the other. Working in the opposite direction, however, is the existence of the immense difference in power between the two superpowers and the states of middle or lesser rank. This condition of inequality makes it unlikely that any shifts in the alignment of states would very much help or hurt either of the two leading powers. If few changes can damage the vital interests of either of them, then both can be moderate in their responses. Not being dependent upon allies, the United States and the Soviet Union are free to design strategies in accord with their interests. Since the power actually and potentially at the disposal of each of them far exceeds that of their closest competitors, they are able to control in some measure the possibly destabilizing acts of third parties or to absorb their effects. The Americans and Russians, for example, can acquire the means of defending themselves against the nuclear assaults that the Chinese and French may be able to launch by the mid-1970's. Anti-ballistic-missile systems, useful against missiles launched in small number, are themselves anti-proliferation devices. With considerable expectation of success, states with vast economic, scientific, and technological resources can hope to counter the armaments and actions of others and to reduce their destabilizing effects.[22] The extent of the difference in national capabilities makes the bipolar structure resilient. Defection of allies and national shifts of allegiance do not decisively alter the structure. Because they do not, recalcitrant allies may be treated with indifference; they may even be effectively disciplined. Pressure can be applied to moderate the behavior of third states or to check and contain their activities. The Suez venture of Britain and France was stopped by American financial pressure. Chiang Kai-shek has been kept on a leash by denying him the means of invasion. The prospective loss of foreign aid helped to halt warfare between Pakistan and India, as did the Soviet Union's persuasion. In such ways, the wielding of great power can be useful.

The above examples illustrate hierarchical control operating in a way that often goes unnoticed because the means by which control is exercised are not institutionalized. What management there now is in international relations must be provided, singly and occasionally together, by the duopolists at the top. In certain ways, some of them suggested above, the inequality of states in a bipolar world enables the two most powerful states to develop a rich variety of controls and to follow flexible strategies in using them.

A good many statements about the obsolescence of force, the instability of international politics, and the disappearance of the bipolar order are made because no distinction has been clearly and consistently drawn between international structure, on the one hand, and the relations of states on the other. For more than two decades, power has been narrowly concentrated; and force has been used, not orgiastically as in the world wars of this century, but in a controlled way and for conscious political purposes. Power may be present when force is not used, but force is also used openly. A catalogue of examples would be both complex and lengthy. It would contain such items, on the American side of the ledger, as the garrisoning of Berlin, its supply by airlift during the blockade, the stationing of troops

[21] For further examination of the proposition, see Kenneth N. Waltz, "The Stability of a Bipolar World," *Daedalus*, Vol. XCIII (Summer 1964), pp. 881–909. On the possibility of exercising control, see Waltz, "Contention and Management in International Relations," *World Politics*, Vol. XVII (July 1965), pp. 720–44.

[22] On the limitations of a small nuclear force, see Waltz, *Foreign Policy and Democratic Politics* (Boston: Little, Brown, 1967), pp. 145–48.

in Europe, the establishment of bases in Japan and elsewhere, the waging of war in Korea and Vietnam, and the "quarantine" of Cuba. Seldom if ever has force been more variously, more persistently, and more widely applied; and seldom has it been more consciously used as an instrument of national policy.

Since the war we have seen, not the cancellation of force by nuclear stalemate, but instead the political organization and pervasion of power; not the end of balance of power owing to a reduction in the number of major states, but instead the formation and perpetuation of a balance *à deux*.

29. Multipolar Power Systems and International Stability*

Karl W. Deutsch and J. David Singer combine their talents here to probe the implications of recent changes in the structure of global politics for the stability of the international system. Unlike the previous selection, this one presumes that bipolarity no longer marks systemic structure and that a shift toward multipolarity has occurred. While noting that the short-run implications of this shift may be considerable, Professors Deutsch and Singer are dubious about the proposition that in the long run the shift will result in a more stable world order. [*Reprinted from* World Politics, *XVI (1964), 390–406, by permission of the authors and the publisher.*]

In the classical literature of diplomatic history, the balance-of-power concept occupies a central position. Regardless of one's interpretation of the term or one's preference for or antipathy to it, the international relations scholar cannot escape dealing with it. The model is, of course, a multifaceted one, and it produces a fascinating array of corollaries; among these, the relationship between the number of actors and the stability of the system is one of the most widely accepted and persuasive. That is, as the system moves away from bipolarity toward multipolarity, the frequency and intensity of war should be expected to diminish.

To date, however, that direct correlation has not been subjected to rigorous scrutiny by either abstract or empirical test. For the most part, it has seemed so intuitively reasonable that a few historical illustrations have been accepted as sufficient. This is, on balance, not enough to support a lawful generalization; it must eventually be put to the historical test. This will be done eventually,[1] but in the interim

this hypothesis should at least be examined on formal, abstract grounds. The purpose of this article, therefore, is to present two distinct—but related—lines of formal, semi-quantitative, argument as to why the diffusion-stability relationship should turn out as the theoretician has generally assumed and as the historian has often found to be the case.

I. A Probabilistic Concept of International Political Stability

Stability may, of course, be considered from the vantage point of both the total system and the individual states comprising it. From the broader, or systemic, point of view, we shall define stability as the probability that the system retains all of its essential characteristics; that no single nation becomes dominant; that most of its members continue to survive; and that large-scale war does not occur. And from the more limited perspective of the individual nations, stability would refer to the probability of their continued political independence and territorial integrity without any significant probability of becoming engaged in a "war for

* Research used in this article has been supported in part by the Carnegie Corporation.

[1] Data-gathering on this topic is currently being carried on by David Singer.

survival." The acceptable level of this probability—such as 90, or 95, or 99 per cent—seems to be intuitively felt by political decision-makers, without necessarily being made explicit, but it could be inferred by investigators in the analysis of particular cases. A more stringent definition of stability would require also a low probability of the actors' becoming engaged even in limited wars.

This probabilistic concept of political stability differs from the stability concept used by L. F. Richardson, which was that of classical mechanics. Richardson's stability referred simply to any set of conditions under which the system would return to its equilibrium state; instability meant to him any state of affairs that would not so return, but rather would continue to change until reaching some limit or breakdown point of the system. A low rate of exponential growth of arms expenditures, of two competing powers—say, of 2 to 4 per cent a year—would be "unstable" in Richardson's terms, but might be compatible with a political stability for the indefinite future, as long as national per capita income or other indicators of the system's absorption capacity grew at least at the same rate. In that case, of course, the per cent for defense taken from the average per capita income would remain unchanging or might decline, with no untoward effects upon the internal financial or political stability of the states concerned—or upon the stability of the relation between them, as long as both continued to grow at similar rates.[2]

Richardson's essentially non-political stability concept and the political and probabilistic concept proposed here will lead to more closely similar results, however, if we reformulate Richardson's increments of arms expenditure of two rival states not in terms of dollars but in terms of per cent of national income. An arms race proper would then be defined as one in which the rival states stimulate one another to divert *increasing proportions of their national income* to military preparations—a practice with obvious political and economic limits, well before the entire 100 per cent of national income is consumed by military spending. The chief practical case investigated by Richardson, the arms race

preceding World War I, was in fact of this nature, since the growth rate of the aggregate arms budget of the two main coalitions was of the order of 15 per cent per year, in contrast to income growth rates of the order of only 5 per cent in the principal countries.

The political definition of equilibrium that we have just proposed is quite compatible with the language used by Morton Kaplan.[3] In Kaplan's formulation, equilibrium and stability can be defined only in terms of particular variables, which must be chosen in advance. Thus, if we focus our attention upon the absolute level of armaments—say, in terms of a constant dollar expenditure at constant prices—the system would be stable, and a system in which the rival powers allocated constant proportions of their gross national products to armaments would appear to be unstable in these terms. If, however, these percentages of GNP themselves were chosen as the critical variables, the system would once again appear as stable.

The rest of this article will be presented in four sections. In the first, we link up the independent variable (number of independent actors) with the dependent one (stability of the system) by means of an emphasis on "interaction opportunity"—our intervening variable. In the second section, the interaction opportunity concept is extended to the point where it impinges on the degree of attention that any nation in the system may allocate to all of the other nations or to possible coalitions of nations. In the third, the multipolar and bipolar models are connected with Richardson's model of arms races and similar kinds of escalating conflicts. In the final section, these arguments are subjected to a new

---

[2] This argument does not take into account, of course, the effects of any radical changes in the quantity or effectiveness of weapons, or of the quantitative increase of currently available weapons of mass destruction to very high levels.

[3] Morton A. Kaplan, *System and Process in International Relations* (New York, 1957), 6–8. Kaplan has formalized many classic formulations of balance-of-power theory. For outstanding examples of these, see Hans Morgenthau, *Politics Among Nations* (3rd edn., New York, 1960), 167–226; Inis Claude, *Power and International Relations* (New York, 1962), 11–93; Frederick L. Schuman, *International Politics* (6th edn., New York, 1958), 70–72, 275–78, 577–79, 591–92; Arnold Wolfers, *Discord and Collaboration* (Baltimore 1962), 117–32; and Quincy Wright, *A Study of War* (Chicago, 1942), II, 743–46. For other attempts at formalization, see George Liska, *International Equilibrium* (Cambridge, Mass., 1957), 23–56, 187–202; Edward V. Gulick, *Europe's Classical Balance of Power* (Ithaca, 1955); and, for significant recent contributions, Anatol Rapoport, *Fights, Games and Debates* (Ann Arbor, 1960), and Richard Rosecrance, *Action and Reaction in World Politics* (Boston, 1963).

scrutiny, with the time scale introduced as a limiting factor.

II. The Accelerated Rise of Interaction Opportunities

The most obvious effect of an increase in the number of independent actors is an increase in the number of possible pairs or dyads in the total system. This assumes, of course, that the number of independent actors is responsive to the general impact of coalition membership, and that as a nation enters into the standard coalition it is much less of a free agent than it was while non-aligned. That is, its alliance partners now exercise an inhibiting effect—or perhaps even a veto—upon its freedom to interact with non-alliance nations.

This reduction in the number of possible dyadic relations produces, both for any individual nation and for the totality of those in the system, a corresponding diminution in the number of opportunities for interaction with other actors. Although it must be recognized at the outset that, in the international system of the nineteenth and twentieth centuries, such opportunities are as likely to be competitive as they are to be cooperative, the overall effect is nevertheless destabilizing. The argument is nothing more than a special case of the widely employed pluralism model.

In that model, our focus is on the degree to which the system exhibits negative feedback as well as cross-pressuring. By negative as distinguished from positive or amplifying—feedback, we refer to the phenomenon of self-correction: as stimuli in one particular direction increase, the system exhibits a decreasing response to those stimuli, and increasingly exhibits tendencies that counteract them. This is the self-restraining system, manifested in the automatic pilot, the steam-engine governor, and most integrated social systems, and it stands in contrast to the self-aggravating system as seen in forest fires, compound interest, nuclear fission, runaway inflation or deflation, and drug addiction.[4]

The pluralistic model asserts that the amplifying feedback tendency is strengthened, and the negative feedback tendency is weakened, to the extent that conflict positions are superimposed or reinforcing.

Thus, if all clashes and incompatibilities in the system produce the same divisions and coalitions—if all members in class Blue line up *with* one another and *against* all or most of those in class Red—the line of cleavage will be wide and deep, with positive feedback operating both within and between the two classes or clusters. But if some members of class Blue have some incompatible interests with others in their class, and an overlap of interests with some of those in Red, there will be some degree of negative of self-correcting feedback both within and between the two classes.

This notion is analogous to that of cross-cutting pressure familiar to the student of politics. Here we observe that every individual plays a fairly large number of politically relevant roles and that most of these pull him in somewhat different attitudinal, behavioral, and organizational directions. For example, if an individual is (1) a loving parent, (2) a member of a militant veterans' organization, (3) owner of a factory, and (4) a Catholic, the first and third factors will tend to deflect him toward a "coexistence" foreign policy, the second will pull him toward a "holy war" orientation, and his religious affiliation will probably (in the 1960's) produce a deep ambivalence. Likewise, following Ralf Dahrendorf's formulation, if status difference is a major determinant of conflict exacerbation, and an individual is head of a family, a bank teller, and president of the lodge, he will coalesce with and against different people on different issues.[5] In each of these cases, his relatively large number of interaction opportunities produces a set of cross-pressures such as largely to inhibit any superimposition or reinforcement. The consequence would seem to favor social stability and to inhibit social cleavage; increasing differentiation and role specialization in industrial society has, in a sense, counteracted the Marxian expectation of class warfare.

Thus, in any given bilateral relationship, a rather limited range of possible interactions obtains, even if the relationship is highly symbiotic. But as additional actors are brought into the system, the range of possible interactions open to each—and hence to the total system—increases. In economics, this accretion produces the transformation from

[4] For an application of these and related concepts to a range of political questions, see Karl W. Deutsch, *The Nerves of Government* (New York, 1963).

[5] Ralf Dahrendorf, "Toward a Theory of Social Conflict," *Journal of Conflict Resolution*, II (June 1958), 176–77.

barter to market, and in any social setting it produces a comparable increase in the range and flexibility of possible interactions. Traditionally, social scientists have believed—and observed—that as the number of possible exchanges increases, so does the probability that the "invisible hand" of pluralistic interests will be effective. One might say that one of the greatest threats to the stability of any impersonal social system is the shortage of alternative partners.

If we assume, then, that any increase in the number of independent actors *is* conducive to stability, the question remains as to the quantitative nature of this correlation. Is there any particular level at which the system cannot be made more stable by the addition of new actors, or less stable by the loss of existing actors? Is there, furthermore, some critical level at which small changes become crucial? Our response must be based, of course, on the degree to which each single increment or decrement affects the number of possible dyads, or bilateral interaction opportunities, in the system. That effect is found by applying the standard formula for possible pairs: $\dfrac{N(N-1)}{2}$; thus, in a purely bipolar system, only one dyad or pair is possible, while a tripolar situation produces three pairs, four actors produce six pairs, five produce ten possible pairings, and so on, as shown in Fig. 1.

This figure indicates rather dramatically the degree to which the number of independent actors

affects the possible number of dyads, and thus interaction opportunities. Even as we move from bipolarity to a tripolar system, the interaction opportunities within the system triple, and when another single actor is added the possible dyadic relations increase by three, and so on, with each addition in the actor column producing an increment of N−1 in the interaction opportunity column. Intuitively, the student of international politics would note that until N reaches five, there is an insufficient number of possible dyads, and that beyond that level the stability-enhancing increment begins to grow very sharply.

So far, we have operated from the conservative assumption that all nations have identical interests, concerns, and goals, and though we would not want to exaggerate in the opposite direction, one cannot overlook the diversity that does exist. A landlocked nation can hardly offer fishing rights in its coastal waters, an agricultural surplus nation will seldom purchase those same foodstuffs, two underdeveloped nations are most unlikely to exchange machine tools, and a permanent member of the Security Council cannot be expected to give much for assurance of a seat in that organ. Every nation's needs and supplies differ, and the more nations there are, the greater will be the number and diversity of trade-offs available to the total system. As possible trade-offs increase, the greater the possibility for compensatory and stabilizing interactions to occur. That is, in a system characterized by conflict-generating scarcities, each and every increase in opportunities for cooperation (i.e., to engage in a mutually advantageous trade-off) will diminish the tendency to pursue a conflict up to, and over, the threshold of war.

Finally, membership in an alliance not only exercises a negative quantitative impact on a nation's interaction opportunities, but affects the quality of those that do continue to exist. On the one hand, the pattern-maintenance needs of the alliance will be such as to *minimize* (a) the range of issues over which it will conflict with an alliance partner, and (b) the intensity of such intra-alliance conflicts as are permitted. On the other hand, the establishment of such a clear-cut ingroup-outgroup division can only lead to an *increase* in the range and intensity of any conflicts with non-alliance actors.

To summarize, one logical explanation for the correlation between number of independent actors

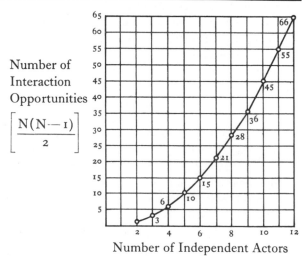

Figure 1. Interaction opportunity

and the probability of armed conflict lies in the realm of enhanced interaction opportunities, observed in terms of their quantity, diversity, and qualities.

III. The Accelerated Diminution in the Allocation of Attention

A second line of argument that should also support the hypothesized correlation between multipolarity and stability revolves around the notion of attention available for conflict. Here we assume that, as the number of independent actors in the system increases, the share of its attention that any nation can devote to any other must of necessity diminish. The argument need not, of course, postulate that each additional actor will attract an equal share of the attention of each of the other actors, or necessarily attract the same share as those already in the system. That share will be a function of many considerations and may vary rather widely. Let us assume, then, that any nation's total external attention—that is, its information-processing and resource-allocating capabilities—will be distributed among all others in the system according to a normal distribution, as illustrated in Fig. 2.

In this figure, we suggest that a very few of the total number of actors in the system receive very little of A's attention, that most of them receive a moderate share of that attention, and that a very few receive an impressively heavy share of it. But regardless of the shape of this attention distribution curve, the fact is that every actor claims *some*.

If those receiving a minimal share of A's attention were to disappear into a coalition, this would have only a minor impact on the amount of attention now left over for A to redistribute among the remaining independent actors. But if coalition were

to occur among some of those receiving a greater share of that original attention, A would then be able to deal with the members of that coalition with fewer demands on its information-processing and energy-allocating capabilities; as a consequence, that remaining for allocation to the other actors in the system would be appreciably increased.

Now the limited attention capability of each nation in the system must be allocated between two different sets of relationships. First priority will tend to go to all of those dyadic relationships in which it is a partner, while the dyads of which it is not a member will receive a lesser, but not insignificant, degree of attention. Some recent illustrations of this latter demand might be found in the attention which the United States has expended on the Soviet-Yugoslavian, British-Egyptian, or Indian-Pakistan dyads, or which the U.S.S.R. devoted to the Arab-Israeli, Cuban-American, or Franco-Algerian pairings. Regardless of membership or non-membership, each nation must spread its attention among most of the dyads in the system.

What, then, is the effect of any trend toward or away from bipolarity upon that distribution of attention? In Fig. 3, we plot that distribution according to the assumption that, with each single addition to the number of independent actors, the total number of dyads in which nation A is a member will also increase by one, following the formula N−1.

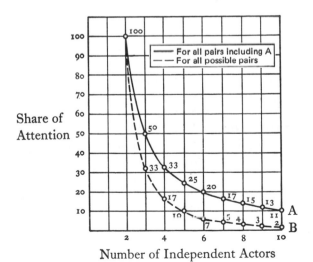

Figure 3. Allocation of attention

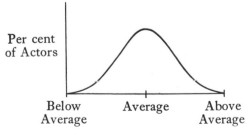

Figure 2. Share of attention

With each increment in the number of dyads of which A may be a member, the amount of attention available for any one such pairing will drop, as shown in the upper (solid line) curve. Thus three actors produce two possible dyads that include A, with an average of 50 per cent of A's attention available for each; four actors produce three such pairs and 33 per cent of A's attention for each; and five actors produce four A-inclusive dyads, with only 25 per cent of his attention available to each.

When we drop the condition that only those dyads of which A (any actor) is a member can constitute a drain on A's attention, and assume that *every* possible dyad will make some such demand, the attention curve responds even more rapidly to an increase in the number of independent actors. As the lower (dotted line) curve indicates, each new actor increases the total number of dyads by the $\frac{N(N-1)}{2}$ formula, as already used earlier in Fig. 1, with the percentage of share of attention available to each dyad dropping even more sharply.

Why should these rapid decreases in percentage of available attention exercise any effect upon the stability of the system? In communication theory, it is generally recognized that below a certain signal-to-noise ratio, the signal is essentially undetectable; that is, it loses prominence as its strength vis-à-vis the noise (or random disturbance) in the system diminishes. The same general principle would seem to apply to social interaction; as Rapoport and Schelling have pointed out, interaction between any two nations may be viewed as a special case of the interchange of messages between them.[6] Each state in this case would have to treat the messages from its most prominent adversary of the moment as the signal relevant to this incipient conflict in or before its early stage of escalation; and it would tend to treat all other messages, concerning all other pairs of states, as noise of relatively little relevance to this particular conflict.[7]

The general requirement of at least a minimal signal-to-noise ratio would then hold for this incipient conflict, as it would hold for any other communication process; and we shall assume that it is approxi-

mated by the ratio of governmental attention to foreign messages from this particular rival, to all other messages concerning other states or pairs of states. Just what this signal-to-noise ratio—or, here, minimal attention ratio—would have to be is a question of empirical fact. Signal-to-noise ratios of 100:1 are not uncommon in electronic communication systems. It is perhaps not excessive to assume that the minimal attention ratio for an escalating conflict would have to be 1:9, since it does not seem likely that any country could be provoked very far into an escalating conflict with less than 10 per cent of the foreign policy attention of its government devoted to the matter.[8]

If we require a minimal attention of 10 per cent for an escalating conflict, the likelihood of such conflicts thus will decline sharply with the decline of the average attention that any one government has available for any one of the remaining actors in the international system.

The decline of this average available attention with an increasing number of actors in the system has been graphed in curves A and B in Fig. 3, as discussed earlier. We can now show on the same graph the lines of minimal attention ratios required to permit average probabilities of, say, 20, 10, or 5 per cent for an escalating conflict between any two actors in the system. Several such lines, at the 10, 20, 30 … per cent levels of an assumed minimum attention ratio, have been drawn in Fig. 3. Their intersections with curves A and B show how quickly the increase of the number of actors will remove an international system from the danger zone, or how fast a diminution in the number of actors will increase the average risk of escalating conflict among the remainder.

As far as it goes, this graphic representation confirms the greater stability of multipolar systems, and it suggests some quantitative findings. It shows that the average share of available attention for any one conflict drops sharply as soon as there are more than three power centers in the system, and more gently after there are more than five such centers; and it further suggests that the stability of the system may depend critically on the *critical attention ratio*— that is, on the proneness of countries to enter into

[6] Rapoport, 213–22; Thomas C. Schelling, *The Strategy of Conflict* (Cambridge, Mass., 1960), 83–118.

[7] Cf. Colin Cherry, *On Human Communication: A Review, a Survey, and a Criticism* (Cambridge-New York, 1957), 42 and *passim*.

[8] For an earlier version of a related argument about mass attitudes to quarrels with a foreign country, see Karl W. Deutsch, "Mass Communication and the Loss of Freedom in National Decision-Making," *Journal of Conflict Resolution*, I (July 1957), 200–11.

escalating conflicts even if only a small part of their government's attention is engaged in this particular quarrel.

Thus, if some minimum percentage of a nation's external attention is required for that nation to engage in behavior tending toward armed conflict, and the increase in number of independent actors diminishes the share that any nation can allocate to any other single actor, such an increase is likely to have a stabilizing effect upon the system.

IV. Some Implications for Richardson's Model of Escalating Conflict

The task of this section will be to correlate the propositions concerning the greater stability of multipolar systems in international politics, especially as recently formalized by Morton Kaplan, with the Richardson model of conflict;[9] and to show that the former proposition can be treated as a special case of the general Richardson model.

In the Richardson model of the arms race, or of similar competitive relations, conflict behavior of each of two parties is seen as growing at an exponential rate, similar to the growth of compound interest or to the progress of an explosion. The rate of this growth is described by a pair of differential equations in which one party's increase in armaments—or of other competitive behavior—is perceived as a threat and becomes the motivating input for the corresponding reciprocal or retaliatory response of the other. Thus, if country A had spent in the previous year $90 million on armaments, while its rival B had spent $100 million, and if A now tries to equal B and increases its armaments budgets from $90 million to $100 million, and if country B, which previously had spent $100 million, tries to maintain the previous ratio of arms budgets, then B must now spend $111 million in the following year; whereupon A, if its rulers still aim at parity with B, will now increase its budget accordingly to $111 million, forcing B to defend its old proportionate lead by raising its arms budget by $12.3 million to $123.3 million, so that not only the absolute amounts but also the *increases* in arms spending on both sides are growing

in every round, and the arms race will accelerate in ever-growing steps until some limit or breakdown is attained.

This simple model would hold equally for bipolar and multipolar systems. In the latter systems, one might imagine that it could apply to every possible pair of nations in rivalry, and thus to 10 pairs in a five-power system, to 15 pairs in a six-power world, and generally to $N(N-1)/2$ powers in an N-power system. If country A wanted at least to keep its proportionate lead against *each* of its rivals, it would have to maintain its level in an exponentially growing arms race with the most quickly growing of these rivals, because this would automatically increase its lead over all the rest. If all powers followed this type of policy, the total pace of arms competition for all countries would be set by the fastest growing competitor.

This model, however, seems too simple. It may be more reasonable to assume that a country is most likely to respond to an increase in the arms expenditure of a rival only in regard to that part which appears likely to be deployed or directed against itself.

In the case of a bipolar world, this consideration would make very little difference. The strongest country, A, would have to fear almost the full amount of the increment in the strength of the next strongest power, B, since in this bipolar world the third and fourth ranking powers, C and D, and all the lesser powers down to N, are almost negligible in their strength in comparison to A and B. These negligible lesser powers would thus not require any significant allocation of B's resources to ensure against the risk of having to fight them, and practically all of B's strength would remain available for use against A, forcing A in turn to increase its own efforts to the full extent required to maintain its own margin of strength in relation to B's growth.

Matters are quite different, however, in a multipolar world. In a four-power system, C and D, the third and fourth ranking nations, are already nearly as strong as A and B, the top and second-rank powers. Accordingly, B may have to allocate more than one-half of its resources—and of its increment in these—to the possibility of having to fight C or D, and thus B may have left less than one-half of its increment for a credible increase in its threat against A. The effect on A's behavior, according to the Richardson model, would be correspondingly

[9] Kaplan, 21–53; Rapoport, 15–47; and the same author's essay, "L. F. Richardson's Mathematical Theory of War," *Journal of Conflict Resolution*, I (September 1957), 249–99. See also L. F. Richardson, *Arms and Insecurity* (Chicago, 1960).

less, since A would have to raise its arms budget only to the extent needed to hold its proportionate lead in regard to one-half or less of B's increment in arms expenditure. The arms race in a completely rational world would thus tend to be slower under multipolar conditions than under bipolar ones.

A different line of reasoning suggests the same result. Richardson's original model assumed that the motivation for a state to try to maintain its proportionate lead over the arms level of another was autonomously generated within the state itself. Once the national subsystems of the international political system had this motivation, in Richardson's model, then the consequences of an escalating arms race followed under the conditions that he specified. It was the competitive motivations of the national states, in Richardson's thought, that produced the competitive character of the international system. Many writers on international politics, from Machiavelli onward, have taken the opposite view. The larger system, they have maintained, is itself competitive to start with, in that it rewards appropriate competitive behavior and penalizes the failure to compete by the pitiless elimination of the laggards and the weak. Machiavelli's princes, Adam Smith's businessmen, and Charles Darwin's animals all must compete for survival in their respective systems, on pain of being wiped out otherwise, regardless of their subjective motivation. In time, each of these systems is expected to select for survival primarily those subsystems that have responded most adequately to its competitive pressure. Which rival subsystem happened to exercise this competitive pressure at the moment is secondary in each of these theories. If this particular rival had been absent, another would have taken his place and served the same function of offering a compelling challenge to competitive behavior.

This type of thinking has remained familiar in the popular rhetoric of arms competition. The world is such, the argument used to run—or the adversary is such, it has run more recently—that "there is no choice" but arms competition or national doom through surrender or defeat. Regardless of the motivations of its own people, its own political system, and its own decision-makers, any state in such a situation must respond to the challenge of an arms race or else perish.

How strong is this externally derived pressure upon a state to increase its own armaments for the sake of survival, regardless of any other values or motivations produced by its domestic political system? Clearly, it is proportional only to that part of the increment in a rival's armament that is not likely to be balanced by a shift in alliances under a balance-of-power policy. In a bipolar world, a 10 per cent increase in the arms spending of power A must be answered by an equal increment in the arms of B, and the escalation process may then proceed at 10 per cent increments for each cycle. In a world of four approximately equal powers, a rise in the arms level of power A from 100 to 110 would give A's coalition, I—consisting, say, of A plus C—only a strength of 210 against the rival coalition II, consisting of B and D, with a strength of 200. The superiority of coalition I over coalition II would thus be not 10 but only 5 per cent; the offsetting armaments needed by coalition II would only have to be of 5 per cent; the subsequent increments of the escalation would likewise be of this lesser order of magnitude; and escalation would proceed more slowly.

In a similar six-power world, a 10 per cent increase in the armament of one power would compel an increment of only about 3 per cent in the arms spending of the three members of the rival coalition. A ten-power world in the same situation would only be forced to a 2 per cent arms rise for each of five powers. Generally, every increase in the number of powers would slow down the speed of Richardsonian escalation.

If we drop the assumption of approximately equal powers in a multipolar world, the same general result follows. So long as most powers are free to move laterally from one coalition or alignment to another, their self-interest will favor such balance-of-power policies as to produce very nearly evenly matched coalitions, each of them composed quite possibly of members of unequal power. In such a mobile multipolar world, no government needs to fear a moderate decline in national power as potentially disastrous. It can survive as a second-class power as safely or precariously as it did as a first-class one, provided only that it joins in time the appropriate new alliance or alignment. Arms increases by a rival power, which in a bipolar world might pose a fatal threat, might call in a multipolar world for little more than a quick adjustment of alliances.

V. Some Implications for the Diffusion of Nuclear Weapons

If an increase in the number and diplomatic mobility of actors may slow down the process of arms escalation, it would by the same reasoning also slow down any process of de-escalation. Here, too, a one-sided arms reduction in a two-power world may elicit an equal response by the other power, while in a multipolar world the effect of any such unilateral initiative would be much weaker.

If we are chiefly interested in rapid de-escalation —that is, in partial or complete disarmament—a multipolar world may prove more intractable than a bipolar one; and we may view the emergence of French, German, Japanese, or Communist Chinese national power with justified alarm. If we are mainly concerned, on the contrary, with preventing any rapid escalation of the two-power arms competition between the United States and the Soviet Union, a shift toward a multipolar world may appear preferable.

At this point, of course, the bare and abstract arguments pursued thus far become quite insufficient. In our analysis of alternative international power systems we have abstracted from all other qualities of the states, governments, and national political systems within them. At the point of policy choice, however, these hitherto neglected aspects may be the decisive ones. A bipolar system in which each of the two rival powers is likely to be moderate and cautious in its policy initiatives and responses might be a great deal safer than a multipolar world containing one or several well-armed powers whose governments or politically relevant strata were inclined to incompetence or recklessness. As elsewhere, so also in international politics a stable general system could be wrecked by the introduction of unstable components.

At the present time, the importance of this latter point may well be decisive. Each of the present major nuclear powers—the United States, Britain, and the Soviet Union—has been politically stable, in the sense that each has retained its particular type of government for over forty years. None of these three countries has been notable for initiating large and reckless military enterprises. Among the middle-level and smaller powers most likely to press for nuclear weapons during the next decade—which

include France, Germany, Japan, Mainland China, Nationalist China, and perhaps Egypt and others—there are several whose recent history lacks any comparable evidence of stability in domestic institutions and caution in international affairs. If this stage should be followed by the dissemination of nuclear weapons among a still larger number of countries, including inevitably at least some with still less stable domestic regimes and less cautious military policies, the instability of the international system would be still more dangerous. For these reasons, any successful efforts by the United States and other powers to slow down the dissemination of nuclear weapons would tend to increase the stability of the international system. In the present article, devoted to an abstract argument, these matters can only be indicated, but they must not be forgotten.

One other problem, however, should be discussed here: the time horizon under which the stability of international systems is evaluated. A multipolar world, though often more stable in the short run than a bipolar one, has its own problem of long-run political stability, and it is to this that we must now turn our attention.

VI. The Long-run Instability of Multipolar Systems

On the basis of these considerations, it might seem that a multipolar system could last forever, or for a very long time, by always opposing the ambitions of its currently top-ranking member; and this is indeed what some writers have claimed as a virtue of the balance-of-power system. In each of the sections above, however, we have dealt with considerations of an essentially short or middle-run nature, with a rather incomplete view as the natural consequence.

There are at least two analytic reasons why this relatively benign long-run outcome cannot be expected. For one thing, if we accept the usual zero-sum assumption of Machiavelli and the classic theory of games—according to which any gain by one contender can occur only through an equal loss by one or more of his rivals—then we must assume that each contending power ordinarily will try to acquire all the territory and population it can at the expense of its rivals, and that it will do nothing to create new rivals for itself. The model thus provides for the possibility of the destruction of states whose rulers misjudged the precise balance of strength at the moment, or whose economies and populations no longer yielded the increasing increments in arms spending and military effort required by the competition, but this model does not provide for the creation of new states. If the probability of states perishing is small, but larger than zero, and the probability of substantial new powers arising is zero in terms of this model, then the model will predict a diminishing number of effective contenders, leading eventually to a two-power world or to the survival of a single power, as in the case of the reduction of the many governments of classic antiquity to the two-power clash of Rome and Carthage, and of Rome's final long monopoly of power in the Mediterranean world until new forces entered from outside the region.

The second line of reasoning is based on considerations of statistics. Thus far we have taken probabilities only in terms of their central tendencies, rather than in terms of the variance of possible outcomes and their distribution. If we assume these outcomes to be normally distributed around some mean, then the usual outcome of an increment in threat by power A against power B in a multipolar system will consist in both A's and B's finding enough allies, respectively, to match the power of their respective coalitions and to produce the relatively moderate outcomes predicted by the classic balance-of-power model. In rare cases, however, corresponding to one tail of the distribution, state A will find a great preponderance of allies and become able to destroy its current enemy, B, completely; and in other rare cases—corresponding to the other tail of the distribution—A must expect to find itself facing an overwhelming coalition of adversaries that will destroy it. In the short run, only the moderate central tendencies of the distribution of outcomes of the coalition-forming process will be frequent enough to be taken into account, but in the long run the balance-of-power world must be expected to produce

eventually dramatic and catastrophic changes, both locally and at last at the system level. The number of years after which long-run rather than short-run phenomena are likely to prevail will depend on the frequency of international crises, and on the shape of the distribution of balanced and unbalanced coalitions, respectively, as outcomes of the coalition-forming process.

This expectation seems in good agreement with the historical data. No balance-of-power system has lasted longer than a few centuries, and most of the original powers contending in such systems have survived as independent powers only for much shorter periods.[10]

The classic descriptive and analytical views of two-power confrontations and of the balance of power among several contenders have been formalized by several writers. The most prominent models, of the tight bipolar and multipolar world, respectively, can be interpreted in terms of the dynamic model of conflict by Lewis F. Richardson. The results suggest that the Richardson model, with very simple assumptions, can be made to include the bipolar and multipolar models as special cases. This combined model then suggests some general inferences in predictions about trends that appear to accord well with historical data. In the long run, according to this model, even multipolar systems operating under the rules of balance-of-power policies are shown to be self-destroying, but both in the short and the long run the instability of tight bipolar systems appears to be substantially greater. It seems plausible that, *if the spread of nuclear weapons could be slowed down or controlled*, a transition from the bipolar international system of the early 1950's to an increasingly multipolar system in the 1960's might buy mankind some valuable time to seek some more dependable bases for world order.

[10] For some historical data, see the discussion of the reduction of Italian city states during the years 1300–1527 from 70 or 80 to 10, in A. J. Toynbee, *A Study of History* (London-New York 1945), III, 355–56; cf. also 301–4, 345–48. In addition, see Wright, II, 762–63 ("The Disappearance of Small States").

30. Bipolarity, Multipolarity, and the Future

Richard N. Rosecrance is Professor of Political Science at the University of California, Berkeley. A leading student of international systems and the dynamics that sustain and transform them, he has authored *Action and Reaction in World Politics* (1963) and *Defense of the Realm: British Strategy in the Nuclear Epoch* (1967), as well as edited *The Dispersion of Nuclear Weapons* (1966). In this selection Professor Rosecrance traces a structure of the global international system that falls midway between the contrasting structures identified in the two previous selections. His invigorating analysis should press the reader to reassess again the prevailing structure and stability of world politics in the nuclear age. [*Reprinted from* The Journal of Conflict Resolution, X (*1966*) *314–27, by permission of the author and the publisher. Copyright 1966 by the University of Michigan.*]

In April 1961 Dr. Stanley Hoffmann of Harvard University reminded us that it was no longer sufficient to design ideal schemes for the preservation of peace on earth (Hoffmann, 1961). World government might be completely desirable, but it was also unattainable. In the future our projected utopias should also be "relevant." Various writers have since taken up Hoffmann's challenge, and we are now told that "bipolarity" on the one hand or "multipolarity" on the other are practical answers to major current difficulties (see Waltz, 1964; Deutsch and Singer, 1964). The purpose of the present essay is to examine these proposed "relevant utopias" and to offer an alternative view. In the end we will discover that neither bipolarity nor multipolarity provides general solutions to basic conflicts in the contemporary international system.

I. Bipolarity

The argument for bipolarity is dual: it is allegedly desirable, as opposed, say, to a multipolar international order; it is also a continuing state of affairs. Four reasons are given to persuade us that a bipolar order will reduce international violence. First, "with only two world powers there are no peripheries" (Waltz, 1964, p. 882). This juxtaposition entails a vital interest and involvement in all the outcomes of world politics. Both the Soviets and the Americans must be concerned with happenings in widely separated areas of the globe—Korea, Cuba, Vietnam, Eastern Europe, to name but a few. Far from leading to violence, however, the commitment on opposite sides has led to a solid and determinate balance. No expansion could be decisively successful; counterpressure is always applied. The very existence of serial confrontation renders the balance more stable. Each counterposition of power discourages the next. There are no realms open to aggrandizement.

Second, not only is the competition extensive, but its intensity has increased. The space race, economic growth, military preparedness, the propaganda struggle, and domestic issues of all sorts have assumed significance in international relations. "Policy proceeds by imitation, with occasional attempts to outflank" (Waltz, 1964, p. 883). Nothing escapes calculation in terms of the international balance. By asserting the interests of the two great powers in even minor equilibrations of the balance, the bipolar international system keeps on an even keel; nice adjustments do not pass unnoticed. A third stabilizing factor is the "nearly constant presence of pressure and the recurrence of crises" (Waltz, 1964, p. 883). Crises are natural and even desirable in a condition of conflict. If crises do not occur, it means that one side or the other is neglecting its own interests. Maintenance of the balance will then require small or large wars waged later on. As long as there are only two major protagonists, there can be no question of the impact caused by a favorable change in the position of one; there also, presumably, can be no uncertainty of an "equal and opposite reaction." "When possible enemies are several in number [however] unity of action among states is difficult to secure." Under bipolar conditions, moreover, "caution, moderation, and the management of crisis come to be of great... importance" (Waltz, 1964, p. 884). One pushes to the limit, but not beyond.

Fourth, and finally, the preponderant power of the two superstates means that minor shifts in the balance are not of decisive significance. The U.S. "lost" China in 1949, the Soviet Union "lost" it in 1962, but neither change drastically altered the Russian-American equipoise. The two states were so strong they could accommodate change. While defection of a major Western European state would be significant, "a five per cent growth rate sustained for three years would add to the American gross national product an amount greater than the entire gross national product of Britain or France or West Germany" (Waltz, 1964, p. 903). Rearmament, economic growth, scientific education—all these were means of internal compensation for international shifts in the balance. The U.S. and the U.S.S.R. confronted each other over each proximate issue, but few of the issues were of decisive importance.

Not only is bipolarity desirable—its proponents claim that it will continue indefinitely; it is a condition to which we must adjust. Patterns of economic growth indicate that the Soviet Union and the

United States will have economic systems more than twice as large as any conceivable competitor until past the year 2000. Nor has the spread of nuclear weapons appreciably influenced the amount of power middle-ranking states can dispose. Britain's nuclear program, so it is argued, is dependent on the U.S., and while France may gain an independent capability, she is likely to find it vulnerable or useless in a crisis. If independent capabilities began to be significant militarily, the nuclear giants would merely increase their offensive or defensive postures (Waltz, 1964, pp. 894–95). As a result of modest exertions, the bipolar world would be restored.

II. Bipolarity: A Critique

There are, in rejoinder, three arguments against bipolarity as a desirable (or even as the best attainable) international system. The first is that bipolarity comprehends only one of the impulses to expansion or aggression. While it may be true that international polarization helps to prevent successful expansion by either side, since it calls forth counterpressure by the opposing camp, it does not reduce motivations for expansion and may even increase them. Since the competition between poles is both intensive and extensive, each action by one will be viewed as a strategic gambit by the other. Even actions which may not be intended to have international reference will be seen in terms of the bipolar competition. This in turn must accentuate the political hostility between camps. The antagonism generated on one side by action of the other will be reciprocated, and the tempo of discord will increase. Since the competition is akin to that of a zero-sum game (see Waltz, 1964, p. 882), this is a quite natural outcome. Any advance in the position of one must take place at the expense of his adversary; hence the slightest improvement in the position of one must provoke the other to new exertions. The respective concern to advance or maintain one's position is realistic in the framework of a two-power competition. The psychological climate in which such a struggle takes place, moreover, is likely to be one of growing ill-will. At some point in this degenerative process one side may think not only of the risks consequent upon striking his opponent, but also of the risks he may suffer if he decides not to strike. Eventually reciprocal fears of surprise attack may grow to such a point that they cannot be endured. Preventive war may be seen to be preferable to war at the opponent's initiative.

A second disadvantage of the case for bipolarity is that two quite different notions of the term appear to be employed. According to one, the Soviet Union and the United States are engaged in a duel for world supremacy or, at minimum, in a struggle to maintain their relative positions. An action by one directly affects the position of the other; all international changes are of vital significance in that they affect the balance between the two. According to the other notion of bipolarity, however, substantial territorial and/or political changes can take place in international relations without impinging on the overarching stability. The U.S. can "gain" or "lose" China without appreciable impact on the balance. If the latter is true, it is because international politics is not analogous to a two-person zero-sum game. The increment (or decrement) to the U.S. is not a simultaneous loss (or gain) to the U.S.S.R. The "gain" is not at the expense of previously Soviet-held territory, the "loss" is not at the expense of previously American-held territory. China is an independent quantity in world politics, not merely a factor in Soviet or Western strength.[1] If this situation prevails, there can be important shifts in the international balance which do not upset the basic relation between the U.S. and the U.S.S.R. That relation, however, is no longer bipolar. All changes are either vital in that they directly affect the bipolar balance, or they are not vital in that they fail to do so.[2]

Thirdly, the prescription "peace by crisis" is a dubious palliative. It seems equivalent to saying that the world's most peaceful place is on the brink of war. Pacific features may be present in one sense, in that nations presumably try harder to avoid war when they are faced with it as an immediate prospect. But if the will to avoid war is greater, the proximity of war is also greater. Cuban and Vietnamese crises may be stabilizing in that they teach techniques of "crisis management," but they are destabilizing in that there is always the possibility that the lessons will not be

learned. When one decides to fight fire with fire, he engages in a policy of calculated risks. At minimum, it is not unambiguously clear that serial crises are the best means to peace.

Bipolarity also seems to have been confused with *détente*. Under conditions of *détente* crises may be manageable, and peace may be preserved. But *détente* is directly contrary to one of the major formulations of bipolarity. *Détente* presumes that the interests of two parties can be advanced simultaneously. The zero-sum notion of bipolarity requires that the interests of one can be advanced only at the expense of those of the other. And if it is then maintained that the looser notion of bipolarity is to be accepted in consequence, one may rejoin that a loose bipolar system does not involve an absence of peripheries. The two poles may then remain partially indifferent and unaffected by even significant changes in the distribution of international power. Immediate countervailing pressures, then, are not called forth by each change in the status quo. Imbalance may emerge. In the result one must choose between two different international systems: a system in which change can be accommodated without drastic action by the two major camps and in which, as a result, disequilibrium can occur; or a system in which there is a taut balance maintained by vigilant employment of counterpressure and in which the antagonism between camps is likely to be very great. The first may permit *détente* but is not strictly bipolar; the second offers stringent bipolarity but rules out accommodation. The two notions are not compatible, and the argument for one undermines the contentions urged on behalf of the other.

III. Multipolarity

If bipolarity does not pass muster as a "relevant utopia" for international relations, what of multipolarity? Does it have special advantages to offer? Again a dual argument may be given. Multipolarity, it is maintained, not only meets the requirements of a reasonable utopia, but it can be approximated in future international politics.[3] Aside from the

[1] It should be noted that it is not pertinent to argue that the magnitude of bipolar power *vis-à-vis* Chinese power is so great that a change in Chinese allegiance is insignificant. If Chinese power is very slight compared with both bipolar powers, the balance between poles is narrow enough to make a switch in alliance of great importance.

[2] Waltz recognizes but does not assign due weight to this contradiction (see Waltz, 1964, p. 903).

[3] Hedley Bull, for example, sees warrant for the view that in the next ten years "the system of polarization of power will cease to be recognizable; that other states will count for so much in world politics that the two present great powers will find it difficult, even when cooperating, to dominate them" (Bull, 1963, p. 21).

feasibility of multipolarity, however, three basic reasons commend it to our attention as a desirable international system. First, multipolarity affords a greater number of interaction opportunities (Deutsch and Singer, 1964, pp. 392–96). The number of possible dyadic relationships in a multipolar system is very great, and it rises in increasing proportion to the number of states (poles). This plenitude of interacting partners means that there is a greatly reduced danger of mutually reinforcing antagonism between two states. Individual states will have associations with a great variety of others; their cross-cutting loyalties will tend to reduce hostility expressed toward one particular state or against one particular cause. Multipolarity, it is claimed, avoids the major disadvantage of a bipolar international order. Since world politics would not be a zero-sum game, action by one nation would not require an offsetting response by its single opponent. Instead of the mutual reinforcement of hostility expressed in terms of "positive feedback" there may be the dissipation of hostility through "negative feedback" (Deutsch and Singer, 1964, p. 393). Multipolarity, then, provides the basis for a stable social system; bipolarity cannot do so. In addition, not only does the need for the expression of augmented hostility fail to appear, but the availability of alternative partners makes possible a response other than direct challenge or military threat. If a state finds itself the object of hostility, it may respond indirectly by firming its connections with other states. This in turn preserves the peaceful atmosphere.

A second argument offered on behalf of multipolarity is that it diminishes the attention paid to other states (Deutsch and Singer, 1964, pp. 396–400); ". . . as the number of independent actors in the system increases, the share of its attention that any nation can devote to any other must of necessity decrease" (p. 396). Since a nation can only actively attend to a certain maximum number of other states at any given time, a large multipolar international system will mean that a number of national actions will not reach the threshold of international significance. Conflicts may be limited in this manner. "It is perhaps not excessive to assume that the minimal attention ratio for an escalating conflict would have to be $1:9$, since it does not seem likely that any country could be provoked very far into an escalating conflict with less than 10 per cent of the foreign

policy attention of its government devoted to the matter" (Deutsch and Singer, 1964, p. 399). An eleven-state world (assuming relative equality of power) would, then, avoid serious conflict (p. 398).

Thirdly, it is contended that a multipolar system, in contrast to bipolarity, has a dampening effect upon arms races. If a state, A, is allocating half of its military strength against B and half against C and D together, and B begins to rearm, A's countervailing increment is only half of what it would be if A and B were the only powers in the system. The typical bipolar model, involving an escalating arms race between two opposed powers, then fails to predict the outcome. Multipolarity is responsible for limiting the arms competition.

The proponents of multipolarity admit that there are circumstances under which an international system of many equivalent powers could become unstable. In present-day international politics there are powers more reckless than the Soviet Union and the United States. If these powers obtained a nuclear weapons capability they might use it in a disruptive fashion (Deutsch and Singer, 1964, p. 404). But "... *if the spread of nuclear weapons could be slowed down or controlled*, a transition from the bipolar international system of the early 1950s to an increasingly multipolar system in the 1960s might buy mankind some valuable time to seek some more dependable bases for world order" (p. 406; authors' emphasis). It is also acknowledged that, while multipolarity is most likely in the near future, in the long run there seems to be a tendency for multipolar systems to break down. "If the probability of states' perishing is small, but larger than zero, and the probability of substantial new powers' arising is zero . . . then the model will predict a diminishing number of effective contenders, leading eventually to a two-power world or to the survival of a single power . . ." (p. 405). Assuming restraint on the dispersion of nuclear weapons and imminent multipolarity in the immediate future, however, one can look forward to a more peaceful international environment.

IV. Multipolarity: A Critique

The case of multipolarity offers remedies for certain of the disadvantages of bipolarity mentioned above. There should be no cause under multipolarity for total international concentration on the reciprocally reinforcing hostility between two states. Alternative interests, antagonisms, and connections should distract attention from a focused bilateral struggle. If two-power arms races develop, they should be of much less consequence than under bipolarity. At the same time, multipolarity has its unique deficiencies. At least three points may be raised against it.

First, it seems highly probable that a multipolar world order will increase the number of international conflicts, though it may possibly reduce their significance. A bipolar system can have but one antagonism; multipolarity, on the other hand, may have virtually numberless frictions. While the attentions of international actors will be dispersed throughout the system, the variety of national interests expressed will multiply. Inevitably, national interests are a complex amalgam of popular attitudes, tradition, geographic situation, economic and military strength, ideological orientation, and governmental structure. Since in a multipolar order a great number of states will be significant actors in the system, a bewildering range of claims and interests must ensue. As the other writers have contended, conflict is partly a function of the degree of particularity in the international system (see Waltz, 1959). The greater the gamut of demands, the harder it must be to accommodate them. Thus multipolarity, by increasing diversity, must also increase conflicts of interest.

This assessment may be countered by the argument that the results of multipolar conflict will be much less catastrophic for the international system than the potential results of bipolar conflict; that:

$$P_{bc} \times R_{bc} > P_{mc} \times R_{mc}$$

where P_{bc} and R_{bc} are the probability and results of bipolar conflict and P_{mc} and R_{mc} are similar quantities for multipolar conflict. The expectation of bipolar conflict (probability times results) would be greater than the expectation of multipolar conflict. This reformulation, however, is open to two difficulties. First, it shows that the advantages of the multipolar system depend on the variable magnitudes assumed. If a multipolar order limits the consequences of conflict, it can scarcely diminish their number. If a bipolar system involves a serious conflict between the two poles, it at least reduces or eliminates conflict elsewhere in the system. The choice between systems, then, depends upon the size of the respective quantities in a given case. Second, if nuclear weapons are widely disseminated in a multipolar environment, bipolarity must be seen to be the better alternative. In such circumstances the greater frequency of multipolar conflict would be accompanied by devastating or disastrous results, and the probability-times-results formula above would suggest that a bipolar system is preferable.

The second major criticism of the case for multipolarity flows directly from these considerations. If a multipolar international order is as harmonious as its proponents claim, even widespread distribution of nuclear weapons should not destabilize the system. As new states enter, the ensuing diminution of national attention should reduce friction. If states really fail to pay attention to their fellows, what differences should diffusion of nuclear weapons make? That the dissemination of weapons is viewed as crucial, however, indicates that multipolar exponents recognize the latent conflict in a multistate system. States are reckless only if they are, or conceive themselves to be, embroiled in conflict. Those features of multipolarity with which we are familiar (in the nationalist, underdeveloped world) are not characterized by lack of interest or attention. They are marked by a highly political awareness of the postures and attitudes of other states. And if some states do not attend to one another, as might be assumed to be the case in the relations of—say—Thailand and Bolivia, this is by no means a general feature of underdeveloped politics. The occasional discontinuities in communication in one part of the system are more than compensated by the range and depth of contacts, both friendly and hostile, which occur in others. Since these contacts link states of very different national interests, they are bound to produce antagonism. And atomic weapons superimposed on antagonism are a recipe for instability.

Thirdly, a multipolar international system, while reducing the significance of any single change of alignment or military posture, inevitably compounds uncertainty. In a bipolar world, an adjustment in relative position of the two poles is important for the entire system. Changes, however, are relatively simple to predict. In a multipower world a single alteration in alliance combination or military prowess may not be decisive for the system as a whole, but its consequences are far more difficult to calculate (see Burns, 1957). The number of tentative combinations is astronomic; military dispositions may take myriad forms. Multipolarity, then, raises the difficulty of policy-making. Results may be altogether unforeseen; choice becomes very complex. Since multipolarity raises incalculability, the system finds it more difficult to achieve stable results. War may occur, not through a failure of will, but through a failure of comprehension.[4]

V. Toward an Alternative System

The respective disadvantages of bipolarity and multipolarity as monolithic images of future international systems should not blind us to their attractive features. Bipolarity provides for well-nigh automatic equilibration of the international balance; in addition, while reinforcing conflict between the two poles, it at least has the merit of preventing conflict elsewhere in the system. Multipolarity reduces the significance of major-power conflict by spreading antagonism uniformly through the system. What we should wish for a future relevant utopia is to combine the desirable facets of each without their attendant disabilities. In practice, even the adherents of one or the other find merit in a wider view. The devotees of bipolarity seem implicitly to include the *détente* (which was a response of the United States and the Soviet Union to their position in a larger international system); the proponents of multipolarity draw back when it is proposed that nuclear weapons be part of the multipolar diffusion of power.

The objective can be accurately described, though it is difficult to give it an appropriate name. The relations between two major powers would be strongly conditioned by the presence and activity of other states. This means that international politics would not be a zero-sum competition between two superpowers. The resources of the international system would not be entirely divided up between the two major states with future outcomes dependent upon a bilateral competition between them. Rather, resources would remain to be appropriated, and the rivalry between the two major protagonists would occur in the external international environment as well as in the national preserves of each. Because

[4] It is possible that the origins of World War I owe something to the inability to calculate policies of other states until it was too late to change them.

external avenues of possible expansion would exist, neither major state need presume that only a direct conflict with its antagonist could decide the issue. The bilateral conflict might be adjusted or equilibrated through actions in the external realm; gains by one power could be made up by countervailing gains by the other. Nor should serial appropriation decide the ultimate fate of the external international world. If the two great powers merely proceeded to apportion slices of the remaining international pie, they would in time be brought back to a strict bipolar confrontation, with all the horrendous consequences which this might involve. The multipolar features of the external sphere should prevent substantial transfers of real estate and political allegiance. Neither hegemony would be acceptable to burgeoning power centers of the external area; changes of alignment or international disposition would not barter the fundamental independence of external states. The bipolar powers would continue to seek advantages in the multipolar realm, but they would fail to eliminate multipolar orientations.

This failure, in turn, might lead to disenchantment with equilibration via the external realm. The bipolar powers might then seek direct advantages in an intensified struggle over the national position of each. If the multipolar challenge were sufficiently great, however, the bipolar states might reduce their own competition for the purpose of making occasional common cause in opposition to external claims. Ultimately, the bipolar states might seek a *détente* based on mutual recognition of two rigidities: (1) the difficulty of achieving preponderance in direct internal competition; (2) the difficulty of making major gains in the external environment. Confronting external challenge, moreover, both might realize that the international *status quo* was preferable to possible foreshadowed deterioration. Since cooperation in international relations tends to be reinforced by conflict elsewhere in the system, resurgence of the multipolar region would produce a tendency toward bipolar agreement.

One of the uncertainties in such a situation would stem from reversals for either of the two major states in the multipolar realm. In order to recoup a lost position of strength, the bipolar states might be tempted to heighten the conflict between themselves to reinsure for a multipolar client the value of past association or alignment. And at present the United States has sought to reaffirm nuclear solidarity with its NATO allies by proposing a counterforce strategy directed against the Soviet Union. If the commitment to Europe is underscored in the one case, the *détente* with Russia is also affected. The multilateral nuclear force, designed to reassure several West European states, also generated Soviet opposition. On the other hand, Soviet attempts to reassure China and North Vietnam of the benefits of the Russian alliance are bound to impinge on U.S. relations. Closer ties with China would inevitably weaken new-found bases of Western accord. In the short run, then, it seems likely that the U.S. will have to accept some erosion of its past position in Europe, while the Soviets will have to adjust to a diminished role in both Eastern Europe and the Far East. If they fail to do so, it will be at the expense of cordiality at the bipolar level.

The maintenance of the *détente* is of fundamental international significance, both theoretical and practical. It is theoretically important because it avoids the antagonism of the zero-sum game in strict bipolar terms. It also obviates a general trend toward multipolarity, with the loss of control and increase in the frequency of conflict that this would involve. A modicum of bipolar cooperation dampens hostility in the external sphere; interventions may be at least partially designed for the purpose of preventing multipolar conflict that could threaten central bipolar stability. In practical terms the *détente* is the means by which the spread of nuclear weapons may be channelled, controlled, or halted. It should be observed that nuclear weapons do not affect the theoretical questions of conflict and cooperation. A measure of bipolar agreement has been achieved despite opposing nuclear weapons systems. The dispersion of weapons is important not because of the new conflicts which it creates, but because it sanctions radical options in the waging of old conflicts. In so doing it threatens the balance attained at the bipolar level. Nuclear weapons may also, over a considerable period of time, give the appearance of transforming a bipolar-multipolar order into a system of general multipolarity. This fundamental alteration would be unlikely to occur in fact, but it is one of a range of possible future outcomes.

If the *détente* is desirable, it is possible to have too much of a good thing. A total bipolar *rapprochement*, an end to the Cold War, would be likely to create a new bilateral tension between major power and multipower spheres. In practical terms it would represent a conflict of rich countries and poor countries, industrial states and agricultural states, European and colored races, northern and southern nations. This emergent bipolarity would demand a rapid spread of nuclear weapons in previously multipolar areas. It would require a hasty amalgamation of economic systems and pooling of industrial resources: the multipolar area would transform itself through a new political coordination. The zero-sum game might be played once again.

A bipolar-multipolar system, on the other hand, would seek to avoid the extremes of either parent form. Enough bipolar control of multipolar realms would take place to prevent extremes of conflict, or, if conflict could be averted, to dissociate bipolar interests from outcomes in the area. At the same time bipolar competition would continue in multipolar as well as bipolar regions. The two major states would act as regulators for conflict in the external areas; but multipolar states would act as mediators and buffers for conflict between the bipolar powers. In neither case would conflict be eliminated, but it might be held in check. Indeed, if hostilities were suddenly eliminated in one realm but not the other, the result would be adverse to general stability. If conflict cannot be eradicated both generally and simultaneously, its abolition in one part is deleterious to the whole.

VI. Bi-multipolarity

It is now possible to list the characteristics of an intermediate international system, a system of bi-multipolarity.

Relationship of Interests

The significant feature of interests in such a system is that they would be partially opposed and partially harmonious. The relation between the bipolar nations would be cooperative in that it would reflect mutual interests in restraining conflict or challenge in the multipolar region. The relation between bipolar powers would be competitive in that each would seek to prevent the other from attaining predominance either militarily or in connections with the multipolar world. The multipolar states would have an equally ambivalent pattern of interests. In regard to one another there would be rivalries stemming from the variety of national perspectives and positions; there would also, however, be common interests in resisting the ambitions of the bipolar powers. In regard to the bipolar states there might be individual interests supporting military guarantees or economic assistance from one (or both) of the major powers. There would also be resistance to big-power encroachment. In no case, however, would the pattern of interests resemble that of a zero- or constant-sum game. Bipolar powers would not directly confront one another; multipolar powers would not develop irrevocable antagonisms among themselves; and the multipolar and bipolar worlds would not be completely opposed. Conflict within each sphere and between spheres would be restrained.

Equilibration

Equilibration, or the redressing of the international balance, will be a more difficult task in a bipolar-multipolar structure than in a strictly bipolar world. Since in the latter system interests are so clearly opposed, any advantage accruing to one evidently must be made up by the other. In a bi-multipolar system where interests are cooperative as well as conflictual, the consequences of a change in the position of one state will be harder to estimate. Since relationships will be more harmonious, on the other hand, the need for equilibration will be significantly reduced.

Predictability

Policy-making in a bi-multipolar system will be more difficult than in a system of bipolarity. A far greater range of separate national decisions must be considered. At the same time, since the bipolar states will exert an important influence on the trend of events in the multipolar fraction of the world, statesmen would not be confronted by the sheer indeterminacy of a strictly multipolar order. While shifts would be harder to predict than under general bipolarity, the momentousness of each shift would be appreciably less.

Probability of Overt Conflict

The probability of war, whether local or general, would be much smaller than in a multipolar system. Conflict would be mitigated on two scores: a multipolar buffer might help prevent the two nuclear giants from coming to blows; and the

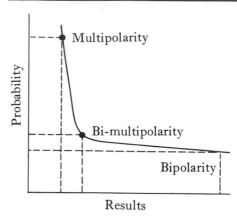

Figure 1. Probability and results of overt conflict in the three different international systems.

restraining influence of the bipolar states might in turn prevent extreme conflict among multipolar powers. While simple bipolarity would not exist, the influence of two superpowers would be crucial in limiting the outcomes of the system.

Results of Overt Conflict

The results of war, whether local or general, would be much more tolerable than in a bipolar system. Overt conflict would most generally take the form of wars among multipolar states, and while crises between bipolar states might not be ruled out, these would be tempered by recognition of significant mutual interests. As long as the *détente* continued, there would be few dangers of major nuclear war.

The probability and results of overt conflict in the three different international systems would be roughly as shown in Fig. 1. The area of the dotted rectangle under the system-point in each instance indicates the amount of violence sustained by the international system. Bi-multipolarity does not eradicate violence, but it holds the prospect of limiting violence to far smaller proportions than does either bipolarity or multipolarity. If peace is the objective, a system combining bipolar and multipolar features may be a means of a reasonable approximation thereto.

VII. Diffusion of Nuclear Weapons

The situation depicted would change considerably if nuclear weapons began to be diffused among

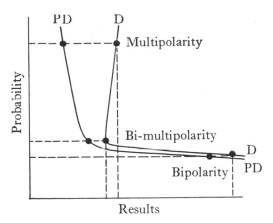

Figure 2. Probability and results of overt conflict before (line PD) and after (line D) nuclear weapons have become available to a large number of states.

quite a number of states. The impact would be greatest on a strictly multipolar system, for the incentives to acquisition would be substantial, and the disincentives involved in having to keep up with nuclear superpowers would be absent. Restraints on acquisition by the larger powers also would be lacking. In a bipolar world nuclear weapons would add least to the dangers already confronted. A cataclysm between two halves of the world would be dangerous enough, even without nuclear bombs, though they would clearly enhance the war's

destructive power. In an intermediate international environment, the process of nuclear diffusion would also raise levels of violence, but bipolar influence within the system would either reduce the scope of diffusion or limit its disruptive impact.

The results would be roughly as shown in Fig. 2. If PD charts the results of international conflict in a prediffusion era, line D describes the outcomes after nuclear weapons have become available options for a large number of states. While bipolarity remains unattractive because of the dire consequences of conflict between the two protagonists, multipolarity has lost most of its previous advantages. Now the probability of conflict not only remains high, but the disastrous results of that conflict are clearly portrayed. Relative to the extremes of bipolarity on the one hand and multipolarity on the other, the intermediate system retains great appeal.

VIII. Bi-multipolarity and the Present International Scene

The system of bi-multipolarity should not be confused with the present international order. One of the major characteristics of the contemporary international scene resides in the difference in attitude and position of the allies of the great powers and neutral states. Two factors seem to account for this. On the one hand, nonaligned nations have received

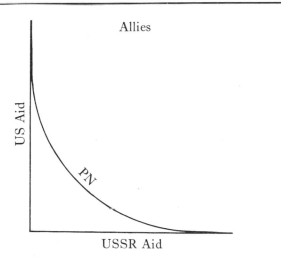

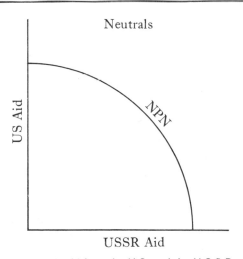

Figure 3. Differential treatment received by allies and neutrals in terms of economic aid from the U.S. and the U.S.S.R. PN is a "penalize neutralism" curve, while NPN is a "not penalize neutralism" curve.

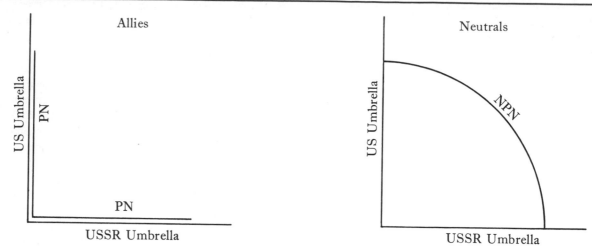

Figure 4. Differential treatment received by allies and neutrals in the nuclear "umbrella" guarantees of the U.S. and the U.S.S.R. As in Fig. 3, PN and NPN indicate policies of penalizing and not penalizing neutralism.

certain of the benefits of alliance protection and assistance without pledging political allegiance to either bipolar camp. This continuing phenomenon has occasioned some disaffection among the formal allies of the two major powers. It has, in a measure, devalued the currency of alliance. On the other hand, the partial attempts at *détente* have made alliances seem less necessary. If a continuing Cold War were not the order of the day, former client powers would have less reason to guard, via great power alliances, against a sudden unfavorable change.

At the moment we seem to be in a phase in which the two major powers are placing enhanced emphasis on their formal alliances. The Soviet Union has come back into Far Eastern international relations, apparently striving to improve its ties with China and to reassert its influence in North Vietnam. Until recently, at least, the United States seemed engaged in an effort to reestablish a strong position within NATO. In both cases it remains unclear whether maintenance of a strong alliance position or an enduring atmosphere of *détente* and/or peaceful

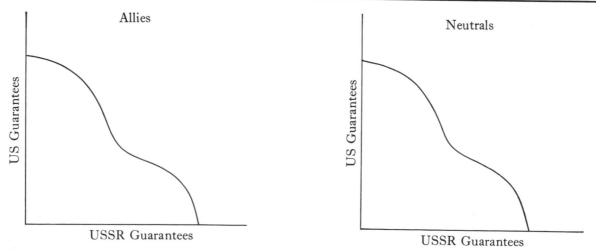

Figure 5. A possible final equilibrium position for allies and neutrals with respect to economic and military guarantees from the U.S. and the U.S.S.R.

coexistence is most important. The issue is a complicated one in practice because any disengagement of interests, justified on grounds of relaxation of tension, may be interpreted by a bipolar opponent as a sign of weakness and a signal for adventure.

In the longer run, however, there are potentialities for the bipolar-multipolar world we have been discussing. It will probably involve treating non-aligned states somewhat less favorably and aligned nations somewhat more favorably than has been the case up to the present. It seems uncertain, however, that the two aligned camps will continue as presently organized into the indefinite future. The reasons for this uncertainty can be seen in Fig. 3.[5] The two diagrams show the differential treatment that allies and neutrals have received in the aid-giving behavior of the United States and the Soviet Union. Among neutrals, roughly speaking, the NPN (not penalize neutralism) curve has been followed, permitting a recipient country to receive sizable quantities of assistance from the opposing bipolar power. Among allies, on the other hand, the PN (penalize neutralism) curve has been followed, providing for substantial reductions of assistance as the ally in question gains additional aid from the opposing camp. If allies suffered in comparison to neutrals in terms of economic and other assistance, they had the compensation of participating in deterrence alliance systems, the protection of which was presumably denied to neutralist nations. As a result of the threatened spread of nuclear weapons today, however, it is no longer certain that allies alone may enjoy the benefits of deterrent protection. India, in particular, may be able to retain her nonalignment

[5] I am indebted to Professor Albert O. Hirschman of Columbia University for the basic notions of the figures which follow (Hirschman, 1964).

while participating in nuclear guarantees of the big powers. If this occurs generally in the neutralist world, an equivalent disproportion in the treatment of allies and neutrals might come to exist in the military sphere, as shown in Fig. 4. Such outcomes would so disadvantage allies and reward neutrals that a considerable movement toward greater neutrality would have to be expected. A final equilibrium might be attained, covering both economic and military guarantees in roughly the form shown in Fig. 5.

In such a case, of course, there would no longer be a difference between allies and neutrals. The growth of multipolar sentiment would presumably reinforce the *détente* between bipolar powers, and an important step in the direction of an intermediate international system would have been taken.

References

Bull, Hedley. "Atlantic Military Problems: A Preliminary Essay," prepared for the Council on Foreign Relations meeting of November 20, 1963, p. 21.

Burns, Arthur. "From Balance to Deterrence: A Theoretical Analysis," *World Politics*, X, 4 (July 1957).

Deutsch, Karl, and Singer, J. David. "Multipolar Power Systems and International Stability," *World Politics*, XVI, 3 (April 1964), 390–406.

Hirschman, A. O. "The Stability of Neutralism: A Geometric Note," *American Economic Review*, LIV (1964), 94–100.

Hoffmann, Stanley. "International Relations—The Long Road to Theory," *World Politics*, XIII, 3 (April 1961).

Waltz, Kenneth N. "The Stability of a Bipolar World," *Daedalus* (Summer 1964).

———. *Man, the State, and War*. New York: Columbia, 1959.

31. Political Discontinuities in the International System

Oran R. Young is Assistant Professor of Politics at Princeton University. An Associate Editor of the influential journal *World Politics*, his work has focused on the dynamics of international systems. His writings include *The Intermediaries: Third Parties in International Crises* (1967) and *Systems of Political Science* (1968). In this selection Professor Young addresses himself to the same question posed in the three previous selections—what is the emerging structure of the global international system?—and comes to still another conclusion. Taking note of the importance of regional systems, he concludes that the global structure is not nearly so coherent as many observers presume, and that instead it is marked by important discontinuities that cannot be ignored by students in the field. Professor Young achieves this assessment through a careful analysis of conditions prevailing in the late 1960s and, while stimulating insights result, the reader may be inclined to wonder whether such a specific focus tends to obscure a basic coherence that underlies the structure of the global system. [*Reprinted from* World Politics, *XX (1968), 369–92, by permission of the author and the publisher.*]

The international political system is currently undergoing changes that are both rapid and extensive. Especially since the early sixties, a number of trends have manifested themselves and become interrelated in such a way that, taken together, they are substantially altering the fundamental postwar patterns of international politics. These indications of change and flux have engendered a substantial debate concerning appropriate concepts for the analysis of the international system. Nevertheless, the resultant debate about the significance of these trends has evolved, for the most part, around the dichotomy between bipolar and multipolar models of the international system.[1] As a result, the debate has been cast in terms of a somewhat narrow conception of essentially structural problems. I submit, however, that the dichotomy between bipolar and multipolar models is clearly inadequate to deal with a number of the principal aspects and axes of change which are becoming increasingly important in international politics in the current period. Nor is the range of mixed types along a spectrum between the poles of bipolarity and multipolarity sufficient for a clear analysis of contemporary shifts.[2] While the notion of a vertically layered system combining elements of bipolarity and multipolarity at the same time, for

[1] For a clear discussion of the bipolar model, see Kenneth Waltz, "The Stability of a Bipolar System," *Daedalus* (Summer 1964), 881–909. A somewhat parallel effort to develop the multipolar model is Karl W. Deutsch and J. David Singer, "Multipolar Power Systems and International Stability," *World Politics*, XVI (April 1964), 390–406.

[2] For various conceptions of the range of mixed types, see Arthur Lee Burns, "From Balance to Deterrence: A Theoretical Analysis," *World Politics*, IX (July 1957), 494–529; and Ciro Elliott Zoppo, "Nuclear Technology, Multipolarity, and International Stability," *World Politics*, XVIII (July 1966), 579–606.

example, is an interesting one, it too fails to capture much of the essence of the contemporary flux.[3] What are needed instead, therefore, are some new modes of conceptualizing the international political system. It is the thesis of this article that a constructive start in this direction can be made by emphasizing the growing interpenetration of the global or system-wide axes of international politics on the one hand and several newly emerging but widely divergent regional arenas or subsystems on the other hand.

The Discontinuities Model

The alternative model I propose for the analysis of international politics in the present period is one that encompasses the concurrent influence of global and regional power processes in patterns that are strongly marked by elements of both congruence and discontinuity. In general, the concepts of congruence and discontinuity refer to the extent to which patterns of political interests and relationships of power are similar or dissimilar as between the global arena and various regional arenas and as between the different regional arenas themselves. There are, however, several more specific characteristics of this model of international politics that should be made explicit at the outset.

First, there are some actors and some substantive issues that are relevant throughout the whole international system, or at least throughout most of its subsystems. The superpowers, though their *effective* influence on many issues is declining, clearly fall into this category in the current international system. Similarly, substantive issues such as communism, nationalism, and economic development have system-wide as well as local aspects. Second, relevant actors, substantive interests, patterns of conflict, and specific power balances differ significantly from one sub-system to another. While global actors and issues are of some importance in each subsystem, the individual subsystems also contain a variety of unique features. Asian and African power balances, for example, are quite different from the more classical arrangements in Europe. And Asian communism is considerably more intertwined with the problems of active

nationalism than is the case with communism in Europe. Third, the regional subsystems of the international system are therefore significantly discontinuous with one another in a number of respects. The degree of discontinuity between any two subsystems may of course vary, but for the moment it is the existence of discontinuities in general that needs to be stressed. Fourth, in all cases the subsystems are by no means totally dis-continuous with one another since each is in fact an amalgam of global and local features. The existence of systemwide actors and issues is not the only source of congruence between the various sub-systems. Several other types of links between sub-systems are of some importance. To begin with, with regard to issues of reputation there is a spread effect that is important in shaping regional manifestations of systemwide issues. For example, the alliance behavior of a superpower in one subsystem can affect the posture of that power's allies in other subsystems. In addition, there are various demonstration effects that exercise a considerable influence on the atmosphere of international politics across subsystems. In other words, there are perceptual links between the subsystems as well as more substantive links. These perceptual links tend to be substantially spread and strengthened through the existence of various universal organizations, such as the United Nations, that serve as channels of communication. The fifth characteristic of the model is that the specific mixture between global and regional elements is apt to differ in a variety of ways from one subsystem to another. In short, levels and patterns of discontinuity are likely to be relatively volatile both horizontally across space and vertically over time.

It is important to clarify the essential differences between the discontinuities model outlined above and the other important models that have appeared in the contemporary discussion of international politics.[4] Bipolar models emphasize the importance of a single, dominant axis of conflict and the tendency for regional actors and issues to be conceptualized in relationship to the underlying bipolar axis of the system. The discontinuities model, on the other hand, stresses the importance of both systemwide

---

[3] This notion of a layered system has been developed by Richard Rosecrance in his article "Bipolarity, Multi-polarity, and the Future," *Journal of Conflict Resolution*, X (September 1966), 314–27.

[4] Perhaps the single most important statement of abstract models of the international system remains Morton A. Kaplan, *System and Process in International Politics* (New York, 1957).

and regional factors and emphasizes the complex patterns of their interpenetration, leaving room for shifting weights with regard to the question of which type of factor is dominant. For its part, the multipolar model tends to stress the existence of a multiplicity of axes of conflict and the phenomenon of cross-cutting relationships among these axes.[5] The discontinuities model differs in several respects from the multipolar perspective: it deals primarily with subsystems rather than with individual actors; it stresses the differences between systemwide and regional axes of conflict; and it focuses on the complex interpenetrations between universal and regional issues rather than on the much less "lumpy" notion of a number of individual actors dealing with each other on a variety of issues in ways that produce numerous intersecting lines of conflict. Next, the distinctions between the discontinuities model and the model based on the notion of a small number of relatively distinct regional blocs are easily discernible.[6] Above all, the discontinuities model emphasizes both the combination of global and regional factors within individual subsystems and the various interconnections between subsystems. Finally, there is a hypothetical model of the international system based on the notion of political fragmentation that would produce a situation somewhat similar to the old conception of atomistic liberalism within individual polities. In this case, the discontinuities model with its repeated stress on interactions and interpenetrations offers a conception of international politics that constitutes one form of direct opposition to the fragmentation model.[7]

One of the most interesting features of the discontinuities model of the international system is the extent to which it contains logical ambiguities that are very much analogous to some of the central problems of international politics in the current era. The sources of these ambiguities fall into several distinct categories. First, the tension between congruence and discontinuity among the various subsystems generates "limited adversary" relationships of a very peculiar nature, especially among the great powers.[8] In short, black-and-white distinctions are impossible in such a situation. The great powers, and especially the superpowers, are increasingly constrained to modify their conflicts in any given subsystem by the fact that they are apt to have important common interests in other subsystems which they do not want to jeopardize. At the same time, these powers are often hampered in the exploitation of common interests both within subsystems and on the global level by the fact that they find themselves engaged in sharp conflicts in other subsystems. There is little doubt, for example, that one important source of change in the postures of the United States and the Soviet Union in Europe is the development of incipient common interests between these powers in the Asian subsystem. Or to take another example, a major barrier to Soviet-American cooperation on the global issues of arms control arises from their conflicting interests in such concrete situations as Germany and Vietnam.

Second, there are important possibilities for manipulation across subsystems which tend to lend further ambiguities to the system, in addition to those emerging directly from the tension between congruence and discontinuity. These possibilities emerge, in essence, from the fact that, while the various subsystems are significantly discontinuous, there are nevertheless important interconnections between them. For this reason, it is sometimes possible to achieve advantages by utilizing political credit and reputation across subsystems. Victories won in a subsystem that is relatively easy to deal with may serve a country in pursuing its interests in other subsystems. Or again, it is sometimes possible to stir up trouble in one subsystem as a means of sowing confusion and of diverting attention from a country's prime area of interest.[9] There are also in a system of this kind some less tangible manipulatory

[5] In its intellectual origins, the multipolar model of the international system really stems from the conceptions of the American group theorists concerning domestic politics. For the original and in some ways clearest statement of these conceptions, see Arthur F. Bentley, *The Process of Government* (Chicago, 1908).

[6] For conceptualizations of models along these lines, see Roger Masters, "A Multi-Bloc Model of the International System," *American Political Science Review*, LV (December 1961), 780–98; and Wolfram Hanrieder, "The International System: Bipolar or Multibloc," *Journal of Conflict Resolution*, IX (September 1965), 299–308.

[7] Another form of direct opposition to fragmentation would be the development of genuine political integration among the units of the international system.

[8] The concept of "limited adversary" relationships is introduced and developed in Marshall D. Shulman, *Beyond the Cold War* (New Haven, 1966).

[9] This particular possibility has always been a major source of American concern with regard to East-West problems in the postwar period.

possibilities arising out of perceptual problems. Especially in a dynamic and fast-changing world, it is sometimes possible to define and conceptualize emerging power balances in terms of perspectives and concepts developed originally for other arenas. Though this effort sometimes leads to dangerous misconceptions and rigidities (more on these problems below), the process can work to the advantage of an actor that can succeed in shaping perceptions about realities and relevant norms in a specific area in ways that work to its own advantage.

Third, the logical ambiguities that can arise from a discontinuities model increase considerably when we begin to move from a world of two important subsystems to one that contains a number of important subsystems. Both the specific issues and the mixture between regional and global concerns will vary from one subsystem to the next. From the point of view of the powers with systemwide interests, the complexities are increased on a straight numerical basis since there are a greater number of combinations of issues and of discontinuities to be dealt with in a situation of multiple subsystems. Moreover, the shift to multiple subsystems raises the possibility of new types of international problems that are not unique to any individual subsystem but that are still not universal problems since they do not arise in all of the subsystems of the overall system. And finally, the number of possibilities for manipulation, mentioned above, rises rapidly as the system shifts from two subsystems to multiple subsystems.

Given the complexities and ambiguities of the system summarized in the discontinuities model, it is hardly surprising that it tends to generate various intellectual problems and confusions that plague the work of analysts and decision-makers alike. In particular, the mixed and interpenetrated nature of the situation seems to go against the grain of very deep-seated psychological needs for clarity and relative simplicity in efforts to conceptualize reality. Perhaps because of these needs, there are two characteristic classes of simplifying devices that tend to crop up repeatedly in efforts to deal with a world of significant discontinuities. Though these classes of devices are, in a sense, opposites, both involve substantial distortions of reality which are apt to generate very serious difficulties for sound analysis and decision-making.

The first class of simplifying devices falls under the heading of *segmentation or compartmentalization* and is based on a form of cognitive dissonance. The main thrust of these devices is an overemphasis on the uniqueness of individual, regional subsystems and a tendency to deny, at least tacitly, the extent of interpenetration and congruence between them. More specifically, segmentation is the characteristic failing of analysts who operate on the basis of area specialization and of decision-makers and bureaucrats who work through the country or regional-office system. This orientation not infrequently leads to an inability to assess the impact of systemwide actors and issues on regional power processes. Even more serious, however, is the extent to which segmentation of this kind tends to result in a failure to take account of interconnections between subsystems in such areas as reputation, demonstration effects, and the problems of manipulation across subsystems.

The second class of simplifying devices falls under the heading of *fusion* or *universalization* and stems from the search for a few underlying dimensions or concepts in terms of which it is possible to conceptualize all of international politics. This device is perhaps even more common than segmentation, especially among the lay public, because it satisfies the felt need for some sense of "understanding" concerning the basic meaning or significance of the whole of international politics. At the same time, fusion is apt to be even more distorting than segmentation, both because it requires simplification on an even more grandiose scale and because it leads to a polarized conception of the whole world rather than, as with segmentation, to a differentially inadequate conceptualization of particular regional subsystems. Even the most cursory consideration of such polarized conceptions as democracy versus communism, capitalism versus socialism, or the world city versus the countryside is ample to demonstrate the extent of distortion that the device of fusion is likely to produce.

The Emergence of Discontinuities in the International System

The problems arising from multiple power balances and political discontinuities are necessarily relatively modern developments in international politics. The fundamental precondition of reasonably extensive contacts between regional subsystems has been met, for the most part, only in the modern era. Within these limitations, however, there are some interesting historical examples of significant discontinuities between regional subsystems. And some concrete examples of the ways in which such problems have manifested themselves in the past may lend perspective to our subsequent discussion of political discontinuities in the contemporary international system.

In the period between the Franco-Prussian War and the First World War several interesting discontinuities began to unfold more or less simultaneously in the international arena. From the 1880s onward, England and France were engaged in a variety of conflicts concerning the division of territories in Africa, a situation that created important rigidities when the common interests of the two countries on the European continent began to grow stronger, around the turn of the century, in the wake of various changes in Germany's posture. During the same period, England and Russia were in almost constant opposition to each other in the Middle East and in the Far East despite the existence of common interests between them in Europe and despite the growing Franco-Russian friendship on European issues. In fact, before the Anglo-Russian arrangement of 1907 concerning Persia, these two powers represented the principal axis of contention in the Middle East. Then, even during the First World War, England maintained a treaty relationship with Japan despite the fact that Russia and Japan were clear opponents in the Far East. Moreover, all of these divergent axes of contention were further complicated by the participation of all the major European powers except Austria-Hungary and Italy in the process of extracting concessions from China. Throughout this period, the lines of conflict in the Chinese arena, in which Japan and the United States also participated, tended to shift along different lines and at a different pace than the evolving pattern of conflict in Europe itself.

It is also possible to find important examples of discontinuities in international politics during the interwar years, though for the most part the complexities of this period seem somewhat less striking than those that characterized the system immediately prior to the First World War. England and France, in this period, developed sharply disparate views concerning the organization of security in Eastern Europe and, especially, concerning the appropriate role for the Soviet Union in this connection. More generally, the extensive and relatively acrimonious disputes between England and France in the Middle Eastern arena during the twenties and thirties clearly played a role in producing the uncertainty and unhappiness that marked Anglo-French efforts to coordinate in response to the resurgence of Germany in Europe. Even into the late thirties, for example, there were no formal alliance commitments or coordination procedures between the two countries. The United States in the interwar period allowed itself to become increasingly involved in the Far East, even while it continued to maintain an insistently isolationist posture with regard to developments in the European arena. Finally, the Second World War itself produced a striking example of political discontinuity in the efforts of the Soviet Union to remain on nonbelligerent terms with Japan long after the opening of the war in the Pacific and the entry of the United States into the European contest had polarized the war on a global basis. The sharpness of this discontinuity is particularly striking in the light of both the clear-cut interdependence of the allied powers in the European arena and the willingness of Britain to join the United States, at least formally, in the war in the Pacific.

Throughout most of the modern history of international politics, however, other types of relationships have tended to be considerably more salient and influential than the patterns of discontinuity under discussion in this article. To a very real extent, in fact, patterns of this kind have emerged on an extensive, worldwide scale and assumed a position of recognized importance only in the present international system. Several significant sets of causal factors underlie this present relevance of a discontinuities model of international politics.

To begin with, the impact of systemwide or global actors and issues is now much more strongly felt than has ever been the case before. The aftermath of the Second World War has seen a sharp acceleration in the rates of development of communications, transportation, and military technologies. As a result, the extent of interdependence of the various components of the overall international system, which has now become a full-fledged world system, has risen dramatically in the contemporary period.[10] Moreover, the period since World War II has witnessed the rise of two superpowers, in contrast to a larger number of great powers, as well as the emergence of several substantive issues that are relevant throughout the international system. Therefore, the contemporary system is not only more interdependent (in the general sense that what happens in any part of it is capable of exercising a very substantial influence on developments in any other part of it), but is also characterized by the existence of several discrete actors and issues of global significance which play very concrete and specific roles in the various regional subsystems.

These developments actually represent the acceleration of a fundamental trend that began in the second half of the nineteenth century. In themselves, however, they are not sufficient to produce an international system such as the one portrayed in the discontinuities model. In the period following World War II, for example, the dominance of the two superpowers became so clear-cut that some version of the bipolar model seemed to be the most accurate representation of reality. During these years, regional subsystems were nonexistent, effectively dominated by the superpowers, or sufficiently peripheral that the conditions of the discontinuities model other than its systemwide features were rarely met. In more recent years, however, a number of important developments in international politics have come together to reduce the salience of the bipolar axis in international politics and to generate a variety of unique features in the power processes of the various subsystems of the international system.

First, a considerable period of time has passed without a large-scale international war to polarize and simplify the patterns of international politics. Because of this, the setting for political discontinuities has been growing increasingly favorable. Second, there has been a gradual diffusion of effective power in the system, despite the superpowers' great superiority in the physical elements of power. Third, the system has witnessed the rise or resurgence of a small number of new power centers that are of major significance even though they are still far less influential than the superpowers. Powers such as France, Germany, China, Japan, and India belong in this category. Fourth, the number of independent states in the system has grown rapidly since 1945, especially in the new regional subsystems of Asia and Africa. Here, the demise of colonialism represented the end of a major simplifying factor of earlier periods of international politics. Fifth, these shifts in the numbers and types of actors in the system have been accompanied by a general rise in levels of political consciousness and by the spread of active nationalism among the "new states." At the present time, even with such an avowedly international movement as communism, it is often difficult to tell whether its specific manifestations in particular states are based more on internationalism or on nationalism. Sixth, as effective influence diffuses in the system and as new lines of conflict emerge, the superpowers themselves are becoming more aware of their own common interests, even while they continue to prosecute a variety of conflicting interests in the various regional subsystems. The upshot of all these developments is that the major simplifying assumptions of the bipolar world of the fifties either are no longer valid or are increasingly hedged about by a variety of complicating relationships on a subsidiary level. The regional subsystems, therefore, are now coming more and more into their own as a complement to the global nature of the overall international system.

Asia and Europe

Let me continue this analysis of contemporary international politics by shifting to some more concrete remarks about the positions of the European and Asian subsystems in the overall international system. Increasingly, the relationships between these two subsystems offer illustrations of a number of the principal aspects of the general discontinuities model outlined above. At the same time, the emerging inter-connections between Europe and Asia in contemporary international politics, which have become the subject of a number of ambiguities and misunderstandings, can be at least partially unraveled by applying the perspectives of the discontinuities model.

During most of the first half of the twentieth

---

[10] Interdependence refers here to the extent to which actions in one part of the system affect the other parts of the system. It is therefore not a measure of common or overlapping interests. Interdependencies may be either positive or negative.

century, the Asian subsystem was essentially subordinate to rather than coordinate with the European subsystem. The degree of European dominance rose and fell in various patterns in the course of this period. Moreover, the various European powers were frequently at odds with one another over particular Asian issues during these years. The fact remains, nevertheless, that a great deal of the tone of Asian politics prior to World War II was set by the participation of various outside, and primarily European, powers in the Asian subsystem. In this perspective, the Second World War constitutes a sharp and decisive break with the previous pattern of relations between Europe and Asia that had, in any case, already begun to deteriorate during the thirties as the influence of Japan expanded.[11] For several reasons, however, the opening of the war did not lead immediately to the development of an independent or fully autonomous pattern of international politics in the Asian subsystem. First, Japan became the dominant political force in Asia during the war years, thereby effectively replacing the European powers in functional terms rather than exerting a significant pressure for the creation of a self-sustaining political system within Asia. Second, the outbreak of the war resulted in a thorough polarization of the patterns of conflict in the overall international system. For the duration of the war, the regional subsystems were effectively merged into a global pattern of dichotomous conflict.

The war itself destroyed the preconditions of the previous pattern of European dominance in Asia, but it did not, in the process, produce the makings of a new and autonomous Asian subsystem. In fact, in the years immediately following the war the Asian subsystem was almost entirely lacking in international relations of an indigenous variety. The individual units of the subsystem were often more deeply involved in bilateral relations with various external powers than in relations with one another. There were several important causes of this absence of local international relations in Asia. On the one hand, the situation was related to the activities of the outside powers. France, Britain, and Holland, for example, attempted to reestablish their former positions of

dominance in Indochina, Malaya, and Indonesia, a posture that led to *inter*regional patterns of interaction as well as to a number of sharp conflicts. At the same time, its dominant role in the war in the Pacific and in the final defeat of Japan made the United States a prominent Asian power almost automatically. As a result, the aftermath of the war found the United States deeply involved in a number of Asian problems, a development that also tended to hinder the emergence of an autonomous Asian political system. On the other hand, this lack of genuine international relations within Asia after the war was also caused by a number of local, Asian factors. First, the most important Asian countries, including Japan and China, had been severely shattered by the war. The principal powers of the subsystem were therefore unable to function effectively as international actors. Second, a number of Asian countries were involved to a great degree with civil wars and a variety of other internal preoccupations during this period. China, Indonesia, Malaya, the Philippines, and various parts of Indochina all belong in this category. Third, many of the new states of Asia had not yet fully emerged from the ties of colonialism at this time. Much of the international effort of these states, therefore, was directed toward breaking the remaining bonds of colonial relationships, an interest that in fact complemented the concurrent attitudes of the European states in producing patterns of *inter*regional interactions. Among those states to which this set of problems was relevant were India, Pakistan, Indonesia, the Philippines, Korea, and the states of Indochina. In summary, then, the aftermath of the war witnessed a sharp break from the previous pattern of unequal relations between Asia and Europe, but it led, in the first instance, only to a peculiar ferment characterized by an absence of local international politics rather than to a new and independent format for international politics in Asia.

Starting from this rather chaotic base, the international politics of Asia have begun to change rapidly and extensively in recent years. The European powers ultimately lost their colonial conflicts. A number of new states appeared on the scene within the Asian subsystem. Though civil strife is still important in Asia, the most important civil war, in China, came to an end relatively early in the postwar period, thereby paving the way for the emergence of

---

[11] It may be appropriate to take the Japanese invasion of Manchuria in 1931 as an important turning point. But the expansion of Japanese influence throughout the Asian subsystem continued on a fairly gradual basis until the actual beginning of the war.

the People's Republic of China as an important force in Asian politics. At the same time, Japan reemerged very rapidly as a dynamic state and a key factor to be reckoned with in any current analysis of the Asian subsystem. In passing, even though these changes have also, to a very great degree, destroyed the physical bases of the tutelary position of the United States in Asia, American perceptions have often been quite slow in adapting to the consequences of this shift.

The unsettled quality of the Asian subsystem clearly remains in evidence today. But a number of fundamental issues have been either settled decisively or thrown into channels whose ultimate outcome is relatively clear. As a result, for the first time in the twentieth century a unique brand of Asian politics is beginning to take its place alongside the long-standing traditions of international politics within the European subsystem. In the contemporary world, of course, there is a great deal of interpenetration among all the regional subsystems in political relationships. And this interpenetration between the European and Asian subsystems is very evident. To an increasing degree, however, the position of the Asian subsystem is becoming coordinate rather than subordinate.

The global features and components of this emerging Asian subsystem are not difficult to locate. Many specific issues in Asian politics still bear the imprint of the dominance of outside states in earlier years. The last vestiges of colonialism are only now disappearing. Many individual states in Asia are presently in the throes of various postcolonial shakedown processes. And the United States has not yet shown itself willing to draw back from its *de facto* emergence as a preeminent Asian power at the end of World War II. At the same time, Asian politics have been shaped in a number of ways by the global contours of the various ideological problems underlying the so-called cold war. Some form of communism has become a dominant, or at least powerful, force in a number of Asian countries.[12] The Asian states in general have become involved in the competition between the superpowers for the political favor of the nonaligned states of the world. And in Asia especially the ideologically tinged debate about

which models of economic development are most appropriate has become virulent.[13] Finally, the global aspects of the Asian subsystem are further emphasized by the fact that the two superpowers have extensive power interests in the area. These interests have manifested themselves both in the extension of alliance systems to Asia and in the efforts of the United States to construct an Asian defense perimeter that is periodically probed and tested by Communist or Communist-influenced forces.[14] The existence of these interests in Asia on the part of both superpowers underlines the interconnection between the Asian subsystem and the overall international system, but it also tends to open up new possibilities for maneuver on the part of various second-order powers in Asia.

The global aspects of the Asian subsystem are therefore quite evident. More interesting perhaps are the unique features of the subsystem which are becoming increasingly evident and influential as Asian politics move away from their formerly subordinate role vis-à-vis the European arena. These unique features are particularly evident when defined in terms of discontinuities between the Asian and European subsystems. First, the Asian subsystem contains a large number of new states that are often lacking in the internal viability that characterizes most of the older and more established states of Europe. As a result, Asian politics are characterized by boundary problems, internal civil strife and shakedown processes, and the dangers of competitive external intervention in internal upheavals. Second, though the dividing lines are not always clear with regard to individual states, the two subsystems operate, for the most part, at very different levels of economic development. While the European states are increasingly interested in the politics of affluence the states of Asia, by and large, are still struggling to reach the stage of sustained economic growth. Third, the brands of communism that have become prominent in Asia are quite different from the mainstream

[13] The models debated range from the pure forms of a free market economy to the pure forms of socialism. At the present time, many of the developing countries are becoming increasingly interested in various mixed forms.

[14] The most obvious cases of testing include (1) the attack on South Korea in 1950, (2) the probes in the Taiwan Strait in 1954–1955 and in 1958, (3) Laos, at least until the Geneva agreement of 1962, and (4) Vietnam from 1959 until the present.

[12] At the present time, some form of communism is dominant in China, North Korea, and North Vietnam. There are, in addition, Communist movements of some significance in a number of the other Asian states.

of European communism. In general, as was suggested earlier, Asian communism is more deeply colored by nationalism and agrarianism in the current period, a fact that has produced great variations in the Communist movements even within the Asian subsystem. Fourth, while European politics in the postwar period have been marked by a relatively clear demarcation between the Soviet and Western blocs, the Asian subsystem has always been rather amorphous with regard to these problems of political delineation. To some extent, this quality is related to geopolitical complexities and to the peculiar features of nonalignment and neutralism in Asia. More fundamentally, perhaps, the quality is also related to the fact that the basic East-West dichotomy essentially originated in Europe and spread only subsequently to the peculiar environment of the Asian subsystem. Fifth, though the superpowers are of critical importance in both subsystems, there are major differences between the second-order powers in the two subsystems. This point relates to such European states as Britain, France, and Germany and to such Asian powers as China, Japan, and India. Among other things, the second-order powers of the two subsystems differ on such matters as the nature of their political alignments, the extent and importance of sources of local conflict among the second-order powers, and the degree of revisionism, directed toward the prevailing international system, manifested by these states.

While the European and Asian subsystems are related to one another in a number of important ways, therefore, they also exhibit a variety of very significant discontinuities. And it is essentially the mixed and complex quality of this relationship that accounts for a considerable amount of the confusion currently evident in efforts to understand the unfolding course of international politics. . . .

Conclusion

The discontinuities model discussed in this article has no particular status as a set of answers concerning international politics. On the contrary, it is offered more as a set of concepts designed to generate fruitful insights concerning the changing state of the contemporary international system. And in this sense, it seems to me that the discontinuities model opens up a number of interesting lines of thought

and problems for analysis which tend to be overlooked by the bipolar and multipolar models underlying most current debate in this area. It leads, for example, to ideas about a variety of types of complex interpenetration among subsystems each of which is sufficiently *sui generis* that it is impossible to assume direct correspondences among them. In this connection, the trade-offs and possibilities for manipulation across subsystems are particularly interesting in the contemporary world. In addition, the discontinuities model offers some useful perspectives on the problems of the actors with systemwide interests. Such perspectives are particularly useful in understanding current developments in international politics. Inconsistencies in Soviet and American behavior, for example, are far easier to explain when it is understood that both of these countries have patterns of interests that diverge substantially and are not infrequently incompatible with one another as between the various subsystems of the overall international system. The contrasts between the European and Asian subsystems, for example, offer illustrations of these problems.

The introduction of concrete material on the European and Asian subsystems also emphasizes some interesting triangular relationships. Here we have two important subsystems that are increasingly coordinate in their influence patterns, even though there are a number of very significant discontinuities between them. At the same time, the global pattern of relations between the superpowers intersects, at a number of points, with the patterns within each of the subsystems as well as with the interconnections between the two subsystems. As a result, an overall pattern of interaction is formed that contains two distinct classes of discontinuities. In addition to the discontinuities between the two subsystems, there are also discontinuities between the conceptually analogous patterns of international politics within the subsystems on the one hand and the global format of international politics focusing on the direct relationships between the superpowers on the other hand. Under these circumstances, it is hardly surprising that a substantive issue influenced simultaneously by several of these divergent patterns of international politics is virtually bound to become extremely complex and ambiguous. For example, a considerable degree of the opaqueness of the problems of Germany and of Southeast Asia at the present time is a result of this phenomenon of several distinct patterns of international politics focusing simultaneously on a given complex of substantive issues.

Finally, it is important to emphasize that the European and Asian problems discussed in this article are, in general terms, illustrative of a broader class of phenomena in contemporary international politics. In short, the relationships between various subsystems as well as between individual subsystems and the global patterns of international politics could be analyzed on a similar basis for such cases as Africa, Latin America, and the Middle East. While the particular substantive problems would vary from case to case, the general perspectives of the discontinuities model are equally relevant throughout the international system. Moreover, a shift from a focus on two subsystems to a consideration of a larger number of subsystems would raise additional questions that could be analyzed profitably. In general, a shift along these lines would open up possibilities for increasingly subtle analyses of the basic power processes of the contemporary international system.

B. Integration Theory

32. The Epigenesis of Political Communities at the International Level*

Amitai Etzioni is Professor of Sociology at Columbia University and one of the very few sociologists to apply the concepts of his discipline to international phenomena. This he has done both in policy-oriented works such as *The Hard Way to Peace* (1962) and *The Moon-Doggle: Domestic and International Implications of the Space Race* (1964), and in highly theoretical treatises such as *Political Unification* (1965) and *The Active Society* (1968). In this article Professor Etzioni engages in the latter form of inquiry and focuses upon the processes whereby integration occurs in international systems. In contrast to the concern of the five previous selections with systemic balance and stability, Professor Etzioni's central concern here is with systemic transformation, with the dynamics whereby international systems acquire new functions and, in so doing, move in integrative directions. [*Reprinted from* American Journal of Sociology, *LXVIII (1963), 407–21, by permission of the author and The University of Chicago Press. Copyright 1963 by The University of Chicago Press.*]

I. A Model for the Study of Political Unification

A. Historical and Contemporary Unifications

So long as international relations are governed by highly calculative orientations, or by the exercise of force, there is relatively little that sociology can contribute to their study. However, during recent decades international relations seem to have changed: Ideology became a major force; non-rational ties among nations were more common; and, recently, institutional bridges became more numerous. Thus, international relations gradually have become more amenable to sociological analysis. Of these trends, probably the most interesting to the sociologist is the formation of new unions whose members are nations (e.g., the European Economic Community [EEC]).

The EEC is by no means an extreme case. There have been many "historical" unions in which units that were previously autonomous merged to such a degree that today they are considered as one unit (e.g., Switzerland, the United States, Italy, Germany); and there are quite a few contemporary unifications where the new community is just emerging and is far from complete (e.g., the Scandinavian community; East European one), exists as a treaty and formal organization rather than as a full-fledged sociological entity (e.g., the Ghana-Guinea-Mali

* This article was written while the author was on the staff of the Institute of War and Peace Studies at Columbia University.

union, the Latin American Free Trade Area), or is so tenuous that it is more likely to collapse than to reach fuller integration (e.g., the Federation of Nyasaland, Rhodesia).

The emerging communities are frequently referred to as supranational communities, a term that is misleading since it implies that the merging units are nations. Actually, many of the historical unifications occurred before the units were sanctified by nationalism (e.g., the Italian cities; the American colonies), and even contemporary unions are not necessarily unions of nations (e.g., the federation of Eritrea with Ethiopia, the formation of the Federation of Nigeria, and the merger of Southern Cameroons with the Cameroon Republic). Moreover, analytically the emergence of a nation state from several tribes, villages, or feudal states—let us say in contemporary Ghana, India, or late medieval France—is in many ways similar to supranational unification. Hence, our concern is with unification of political units that previously shared few or no political bonds. The degree to which these units have been foci of identification for their populations and the degree to which the normative substance of this identification was secular-historical of the kind that marks nationalism are two variables of our analysis, not part of the definition of the concept. Therefore, we refer to the emerging entities simply as political communities and to the process as one of unification. The term "unions" refers to entities that seem to develop in the direction of a political community but have not reached such a high level of integration.

B. Epigenesis Versus Preformism

A strategy often used in sociological studies of international relations is to draw on theories developed in the study of interaction among other social units, bearing in mind the special nature of the subject to which they are applied, and checking whether additional variables have to be introduced or whether the theories require revision in view of the new data. Here we draw on a sociological theory of change.

Most studies of social change presuppose the existence of a unit, and ask: How does it change, why, and in what direction? The analytical framework frequently used for this analysis of social dynamics is the *differentiation model*,[1] which assumes that the

[1] This model is applied to the study of small groups by Robert F. Bales and Philip E. Slater, "Role Differentiation

"primitive" social unit contains, in embryonic form, fused together, all the basic modes of social relations that later become structurally differentiated. While relations originally fused gain their own subunits, no new functions are served or new modes of interaction are molded. There are, for instance, some universalistic relations in the most primitive tribe. According to this viewpoint, every social unit, if it is to exist, must fulfill a given set of functions, those of adaptation, allocation, social and normative integration. On the individual level, the evolution from infancy to maturity can be analyzed in terms of the differentiation of the personality.[2] On the societal level, the evolution of a primitive society, from a traditional into a modern one, is also seen as a differentiation process. All societal functions are fulfilled by the primitive tribe; they merely become structurally differentiated; that is, they gain personnel, social units, and organizational structures of their own. Religious institutions gain churches, educational institutions gain schools, economic institutions gain corporations, and so forth.

Philosophers and biologists have long pointed out that there is an alternative model for the study of change. While Bonnet, Haller, and Malpighi represented the differentiation (or preformism) approach, according to which the first unit or seed possesses in miniature all the patterns of the mature plant, Harvey, Wolff, and Goethe advanced the accumulation (or epigenesis) approach, according to which "adult" units emerge through a process in which parts that carry out new functions are added to existing ones, until the entire unit is assembled.

in Small Decision-making Groups," in Talcott Parsons, Robert F. Bales, and Edward A. Shils, *Working Papers in the Theory of Action* (Glencoe, Ill.: Free Press, 1953); to socialization process by Parsons, Bales, *et al.*, *Family, Socialization and Interaction Process* (Glencoe, Ill.: Free Press, 1953), Chap. IV; to industrialization by Neil Smelser, *Social Change in the Industrial Revolution* (Chicago: University of Chicago Press, 1959); to the study of the family by Morris Zelditch, Jr., "Role Differentiation in the Nuclear Family: A Comparative Study," in *Family, Socialization...*, *op. cit.*, pp. 307–51; and by Smelser, *op. cit.*, Chaps. VIII–X; to the study of elites by Amitai Etzioni, "The Functional Differentiation of Elites in the Kibbutz," *American Journal of Sociology*, LXIX (1959), 476–87; and to the study of underdeveloped countries by Neil Smelser, "Toward a Theory of Modernization," in Amitai and Eva Etzioni, eds., *Social Change: Sources, Patterns and Consequences* (New York: Harper & Row, 1963).

[2] *Family, Socialization ...*, *op. cit.*, Chap. IV.

Earlier parts do not include the "representation" of later ones.

The two processes are mutually exclusive in the sense that new units are either institutional "embodiments" of old functions or serve new ones. They may occur at different times in the same social unit: for example, a unit may first follow a preformistic model of development, then shift to an epigenetic model (or the other way around); or it may simultaneously develop some subunits following one model and some following the other. But unlike the particle and wave theories, which are used to explain the same light phenomena, the change pattern of all sociological units of which we are aware follows at any given period either a differentiation *or* an accumulation model.

Until now sociology focused almost exclusively on differentiation models. There are, however, several social units whose development cannot be adequately accounted for by a preformistic model. This article presents an outline of an alternative model, drawing for illustration on the formation of various social units, in particular, international unions. The following questions are asked: (1) Where is the power located that controls the accumulation process? (2) What form does the process itself take? (3) What sector is introduced first? (4) How does this affect subsequent development of sectors? (5) What sequence does the entire process follow? (6) What kinds of "products" do different accumulation (or epigenesis) processes produce? It is essential to bear in mind constantly the peculiar system reference of this analysis; it is a system that does not exist but which the potential members are gradually building up. It is like studying the effect of social relations among students in their postgraduate life before they have graduated.

II. Power and Epigenesis

A. *Locus of Power: Elitism and Internalization*

The main distinction between preformism and epigenesis is the function that new subunits serve; that is, old functions versus new ones. Determining the structural location of the power that controls the development of a social unit, especially that of new subunits, is essential both for distinguishing between units whose development follows one model and for differentiating between those of one model and those of the other. We need to know whether or not any one, two, or more elite units specialize in control functions; that is, whether or not control is equally distributed among all or most units. This will be called the *degree of elitism*. To the degree that there are elites, the question arises whether they operate from within or from without the emerging union. This dimension will be the *degree of internalization* (of control).[3]

1. *Degree of elitism*. Organizational analysis shows that there are two major ways of forming a new corporate body: An elite unit may construct the performance units, or several existing organizations that have both elite and performance units may merge. On the international level, a new community is formed in the first way when a nation more powerful than the other potential members "guides" the unification process. Prussia played such a role in the unification of Germany; Ghana, in the formation of the Ghana-Guinea-Mali union; Egypt, in the late UAR. The cases in which one nation played a central role are so numerous that Deutsch *et al.* suggest that unification requires the existence of one "core" unit.[4]

While many organizations and communities are established by one or a few elite units, the control center of others is formed through a merger of many units, each contributing a more or less equal part. The power center of the emerging community is a new unit rather than an existing unit subordinating the others. One might refer to the first as elitist, to the second as egalitarian, unification. A study of the Northern Baptist Convention in the United States provides a fine illustration of egalitarian unification.[5] The development of the Scandinavian union appears to follow an egalitarian pattern also. While Norway was initially less supportive of the union than Sweden and Denmark, the differences in their support to,

[3] I found this dimension of much value in analyzing the relationship between specialized units and parent organizations (see "Authority Structure and Organizational Effectiveness," *Administrative Science Quarterly*, IV [1959], 62–67).

[4] Karl W. Deutsch *et al.*, *Political Community and the North Atlantic Area* (Princeton, N.J.: Princeton University Press, 1957), pp. 28, 38–39.

[5] Paul M. Harrison, *Authority and Power in the Free Church Tradition* (Princeton, N.J.: Princeton University Press, 1959).

and in their control of, the emerging union (and the Nordic Council, its formal instrument) comes close to the egalitarian ideal type.[6]

The degree of elitism (or egalitarianism) should be treated as a continuum. In some nation unions one unit clearly plays a superior role (England in the early Commonwealth); in some, two or more countries are superior (Brazil, Argentina, and to a degree Chile, of the seven members in the Latin America Free Trade Area); in others, participation, contribution, and power are almost evenly distributed among all participants (as in the Scandianvian union).

The degree to which one or more units control the unification process versus the degree to which it is an effort of all participants is closely related to the means of control used. At the elitist end of this continuum we find mergers in which one country coerces the others to "unify." It seems that on the international level cases of elitist and coerced unification are much more frequent than egalitarian, voluntary unions, especially if we regard the extensive use of economic sanctions, not just military force, as resulting in a non-voluntary unification.[7] At the egalitarian end, use of normative means, such as appeal to common sentiments, traditions, and symbols, plays a much more central role than coercive means or economic sanctions. Economic factors operate here more in the form of mutual benefits derived from increased intercountry trade than sanctions or rewards given by one country to the others.

This raises an empirical question: How effective are the various means of unification? One is inclined to expect that unification that begins with coercion ends with disintegration. But the Roman empire, despite its coercive techniques, lasted for about five centuries before it finally collapsed. Nor was the German union weak or ineffective because of the methods employed by Bismarck to bring it about. Quite possibly the line that distinguishes effective from ineffective unification efforts lies not between coercion and non-coercion but between high coercion (of the kind used to keep Hungary in the Communist

bloc in 1956 or to hold the Federation of Rhodesia and Nyasaland together in 1961) and lesser coercion.[8] Effectiveness seems also to be highly determined by the degree to which coercion is coupled with other means—for instance, with propaganda.

2. *Degree of internalization.* Collectivities whose developments follow an epigenesis model can be effectively ordered by a second dimension, namely, the degree to which the elite unit (or units, if they exist) controls the emerging union from the outside or from the inside. This is not a dichotomous variable, for there are various degrees to which an elite unit can be "in" or "out." An elite might be completely "out," encouraging or forcing the merger of two or more units into a union which it does not join, sometimes relinquishing control once unification is initiated. Colonial powers brought together, frequently unwittingly, subordinated units, only to have to withdraw once their union was cemented: For example, resisting the British control was a major force in bringing together the thirteen American colonies, the various tribes in the Gold Coast that became Ghana, and the Jewish colonies in Palestine that formed the Israeli society. On the international level, the United States required some degree of intra-European economic co-operation as a condition for receiving funds under the Marshall Plan; it encouraged the union of the six countries that formed the European Economic Community, and is now encouraging the EEC to include Britain, without having joined these unions. Britain was the major force behind the efforts to launch a Federation of the West Indies and the formation of the Federation of Nigeria. In all these cases the center of power was with a non-member, external unit.

In other cases, the elites that initiate and support unification do not stay entirely out of the emerging community, nor are they a fully integral part of it. The United States, for instance, is an "informal but powerful" member of CENTO. It signed bilateral pacts with Iran, Turkey, and Pakistan, the three members of CENTO, which in 1961 showed signs of becoming more than just a treaty.[9] Similarly

[6] Frantz Wendt, *The Nordic Council and Cooperation in Scandinavia* (Copenhagen: Mumsgaard, 1959), pp. 98–100 (see also Norman J. Padelford, "Regional Cooperation in Scandinavia, *International Organization*, XI [1957], 597–614).

[7] The infrequency of voluntary unions is stressed in Crane Brinton, *From Many to One* (Cambridge, Mass.: Harvard University Press, 1949), pp. 49 ff.

[8] For an outstanding discussion of the Soviet bloc from this viewpoint see Zbigniew K. Brzenzski, *The Soviet Bloc* (Cambridge, Mass.: Harvard University Press, 1960), Chap. XII, and his "The Organization of the Communist Camp," *World Politics*, XII (1961), 175–209.

[9] The Ministerial Council of CENTO decided in its meeting in Ankara in April, 1960, that a shared military

France, while not a member of the Conseil de l'Entente (a loose West African custom, communication, and, to a degree, military union of Ivory Coast, Upper Volta, Niger, and Dahomey), still is an active participant in this union through various treaties.[10]

Finally, in still other cases, the elite is a full-fledged member of the union as Britain was in the European Free Trade Area and Prussia in the unification of Germany.

3. *Power, capability, and responsiveness.* The units that control the epigenesis of political communities differ not only in their degree of elitism and internalization but also in their communication capabilities and degree of responsiveness to the needs and demands of participant units.[11] Deutsch pointed out that when all other conditions are satisfactory a unification process might fail because the *communication capabilities* of an elite are underdeveloped. This was probably a major reason why empires in medieval Europe were doomed to fail; they were too large and complex to be run from one center given the existing communication facilities.[12] Sociologists have concerned themselves extensively with communication gaps, but studies frequently focus on the inter-personal and small-group level (even in many of the so-called organizational studies of communication). Sociologists are often concerned with the structure of communication networks (two-step communication systems,[13] as against chain systems[14]) rather than with the articulation of these networks with the

power structure.[15] For students of political systems and of complex organization, ideas such as "overloading" of the elite (presenting it with more communication than it is able to digest; requiring more decisions per time unit than it is able to make) is an interesting new perspective that connects communication studies with power analysis much more closely than the widespread human-relations type of communication analysis.

The concept of *responsiveness* further ties communication analysis to the study of power by asking to what degree does the power center act upon communication received and digested in terms of reallocating resources and rewarding the compliance of sectors.[16]

Thus to analyze epigenesis effectively, we must know not only who has how much power over the process but also what are the communication capabilities and what is the degree of responsiveness of the various power centers.

B. Performance and Control: A Dynamic Perspective

The performance, power, and communication elements of a social unit developing epigenetically do not always develop at the same rate. As the limbs of an infant develop before he has control over them so new performances might be taken over by the accumulating unit before its power center gains control over them. Frequently, part of the performances of an accumulating unit are controlled by another unit, at least temporarily. The industrial capacity of colonies often developed before they gained political control over industry.

New communities, whose development follows the pattern suggested by epigenesis rather than that of preformism, tend to develop new performance abilities first and to internalize control over these activities later.[17] Just as a child first learns to walk, then gains the right to decide when and where to walk, or as military units in basic training first learn to act as units under the control of the training ("parent") unit's instructors and sanction system

command would be developed; intercountry roads and telecommunication improved; and economic and cultural ties increased (*New York Times*, April 29, 1961). Projects already completed include a new Turkish-Iranian railway, a new road linking the CENTO countries, as well as a microwave communication network (*International Organization*, XV [1961], 523).

[10] Immanuel Wallerstein, "Background to Paga," *West Africa*, July 29, 1961, p. 819, and August 5, 1961, p. 861, and Walter Schwartz, "Varieties of African Nationalism," *Commentary*, XXXII (1961), 34.

[11] Karl W. Deutsch, *Nationalism and Social Communication* (New York: John Wiley & Sons, 1953), pp. 65, 143.

[12] Karl W. Deutsch, *Political Community at the International Level* (Garden City, N.Y.: Doubleday & Co., 1954), pp. 13–15.

[13] Elihu Katz and Paul Lazarsfeld, *Personal Influence* (Glencoe, Ill.: Free Press, 1955).

[14] Alex Bavelas, "Communication Patterns in Task-oriented Groups," *Journal of Acoustical Society of America*, XXII (1950), 725–30.

[15] For one of the few studies that successfully ties the two see R. H. McCleary, *Policy Change in Prison Management* (East Lansing: Michigan State University, 1957).

[16] Deutsch, *Nationalism and Social Communication*, p. 143 (see also his *Political Community at the International Level*, p. 37).

[17] "Internalize" means here the transfer of power from external elites to internal elites.

before acquiring their own command, so some countries engage in some collective activity under the control of a superior, non-member power.[18] Later, control is internalized by the evolving supranational system, and a supranational authority is formed, which regulates collective activities previously controlled by the superior external power.

It is the existence of a supranational authority —at first limited, then more encompassing—that distinguishes *unions of nations* from *international organizations*. Unions have at least a limited power center of their own, whose decisions bind the members and are enforcible; they have internalized at least some control. International organizations, on the other hand, are run by intergovernmental bodies, whose "decisions" are merely recommendations to the members and are not enforcible.[19] They have, in this sense, no power of their own.

The special importance of the High Authority, a governing body of the European Coal and Steel Community (ECSC) is that its decisions directly bind the steel and coal industries of the six member nations and it can levy fines on industries that do not conform to its rulings (though national police forces would have to collect the fines, if they were not paid). Moreover, individuals, corporations, and states have the same status before the Court of Justice of the ECSC; they all can sue each other, an individual suing a state, or the High Authority suing a member state.[20]

Until the ECSC was formed in 1952, almost all European co-operation, such as the Organization for European Economic Cooperation (OEEC) and NATO, was intergovernmental. In 1952 the High Authority was formed; this was the first major step toward self-control of the evolving supranational community. (Interestingly, this is also the year NATO developed a supranational authority with the formation of SHAPE, which provided a supranational headquarters for the multination armies.)[21] In the following years functions and powers of the High Authority gradually increased. In 1957 the more encompassing common market (EEC) was established, which has its equivalent of the High Authority, the Economic Commission, except that its supranational powers cover more "performances" —much of the intercountry economic actions—than does the High Authority, which is limited to matters related to steel and coal.[22]

Attempts to develop supranational control over shared political activities, in which the members of the EEC do engage, have not yet succeeded. Whatever collective political action the Six take is based on intergovernment consultations of these countries, not supranational direction. *Thus, in the development of this union of nations, as in the epigenesis of many other social units, collective performances expand more rapidly than collective control.* (It should be noted that while frequently performance accumulation occurs before power internalization, the reversed sequence might occur, too. Power *capabilities* can be built up before performance. Modern armies, for instance, train groups of officers in headquarters work before they are given command of military units.)

We saw that communities are built up by accumulation of *new* performances (e.g., military ones) and control over them. We now turn to the dynamics of accumulation recognizing three problems as basic to the analysis of all accumulation processes: (*a*) Under what conditions does the process start? (*b*) What factors contribute to its expansion and pace? (*c*) What is the sequence in which the functional sectors that make a complete

[18] It should be pointed out that on the international level the power of a new union is more often generalized from its constituent units—"pooling of sovereignty"— than internalized from superior power. From the present viewpoint this distinction is not relevant; the question is: Who controls the collective action—the unit itself or other units (without regard to whether they are outside or constituent units)?

[19] For an outstanding discussion of the differences between intergovernment and supranational decision-making bodies, see Ernst B. Haas, *Uniting of Europe* (Stanford, Calif.: Stanford University Press, 1958), Chaps. XII, XIII. The following discussion of the High Authority draws on Haas's work.

[20] In March, 1961, the Economic Commission— which is roughly, to the EEC what the High Authority is to the ECSC—brought the Italian government before the court of the EEC for violation of an article of the Treaty of Rome concerning a ban on subsidies for trade in pork. This was the first such action taken since the formation of the EEC (*New York Times*, March 27, 1961).

[21] See Andrew J. Goodpaster, "The Development of SHAPE: 1950–1953," *International Organization*, IX (1955), 257–62, and William A. Knowlton, "Early Stages in the Organization of SHAPE," *International Organization*, XIII (1959), 1–18.

[22] William Diebold, Jr., "The Changed Economic Position of Western Europe," *International Organization*, XV (1960), 1–19, esp. p. 12.

community are assembled ? The rest of this artic[...] devoted to these problems.

III. Initiation, Take-off, and Spill-over

A. *Between Initiation and Take-off*

The concept of take-off, borrowed from aerodynamics, is applied to the first-stage of epigenesis to distinguish the initiation point from that where the continuation of the process becomes self-sustained. The image is one of a plane that first starts its engines and begins rolling, still supported by the runway, until it accumulates enough momentum to "take off," to continue in motion "on its own," generating the forces that carry it to higher altitudes and greater speeds. The analogue is that through accumulation, while relying on external support, the necessary condition for autonomous action is produced. Also during "take-off" the pilot, released from airport tower control, gains control of his plane. (This control take-off might occur before or after the performance take-off.)

Economists use this concept in the study of industrialization, especially in reference to foreign aid. An underdeveloped country requires a certain amount of investment before its economy reaches the level at which it produces a national income large enough to provide for current consumption and for increased investment which, in turn, provides for additional growth of the economy.[23] An economy has taken off when additional growth is self-sustained; when no external investment or externally induced changes in saving, spending, or work habits are needed.

The concept of take-off can also be used in studying political, communication, and other social processes. A group of leaders, some labor unions, or "reform" clubs, join to initiate a new political party. Again, "to initiate" has two meanings, to which the concept of take-off calls attention: There is the day the leaders decide to launch the new party, a day that. if the launching is successful, will be known as the party's birthday. However, the new party initially draws its funds, staff, and political power from the founding leaders and groups. Gradually, as

the pa[...] it a[...]lates fo[...]wers and contributors directly committed to it, and if it is successful, it eventually reaches the stage at which it can do without the support of its initiators and continue growing "on its own." While this point is far from being sharply defined, obviously it rarely coincides with the actual birth date. Much insight can be gained by comparing different polities with regard to the lapse between their initiation and their take-off points. For instance, the greater the lapse the more difficult it is for small or new groups to gain political representation. On the other hand, if the lapse is very small, entering the political competition becomes too easy, and it will be difficult to find a majority to establish a stable government.

In many countries there is a formal barrier that has to be surmounted before political take-off. Parties that poll less than a certain percentage of the votes are denied parliamentary representation. Frequently founders' support is given until the election day; then the party either gains representation and becomes a political factor in its own right or it flounders; it either takes off or crashes. One of the special characteristics of the American political system is that the take-off point for participation in national politics is remote from the initiation point. Many "third-party" movements that polled many hundreds of thousands of votes still could not continue to grow and to become permanent participants on the federal level.[24]

Take-off is especially important for the study of social units that are initiated by charter, enactment of a law, or signing of a treaty. While sometimes these "paper" units might be an expression of an already-existing social unit, often the formal structure precedes the development of a social one. While it has been often pointed out that an informal structure is likely to evolve, turning the formal one into a full-fledged social unit, we do not know under what conditions these informal processes take off, as against those conditions under which they never reach such a point. Clearly not all formal structures become functioning social units. This applies in particular to international relations where the supranational take-off, that is, the transition from a formal, inter-governmental structure to self-sustained growth toward a political community, is quite

[23] W. W. Rostow, *The Stages of Economic Growth* (Cambridge: Cambridge University Press, 1960), pp. 4, 7–9, 36 ff.

[24] Daniel Bell (ed.), *The New American Right* (New York: Criterion Books, 1955).

infrequent.[25] Under what conditions, then, does take-off occur?

While these problems still require much research, there appears to be one central factor bringing unification movements to take-off; the amount of decision-making called for by intercountry *flows* (e.g., of goods) and by *shared performance* (e.g., holding a common defense line) that, in turn, is determined by the scope of tasks carried out internationally. If the amount is large, intergovernment decision-making will prove cumbersome and inadequate and pressure will be generated either to reduce the need for international decision-making —by reducing the international tasks—or to build a supranational decision-making *structure*, which is a more effective decision-making body than are intergovernmental ones.

The central variable for the "take-off" of supranational authority is the amount of international decision-making required. This, in turn, is determined largely by the amounts and kinds of flows that cross the international borders (e.g., tourists, mail) and the amounts and kinds of shared international activities (e.g., maintaining an early-warning system). It should be stressed, however, that each flow or shared activity has its own decision-making logarithm. Some flows can increase a great deal and still require only a little increase in international decision-making; others require much more.[26] Moreover, the relationship seems not to be linear; that is, some increases in a particular flow (or shared activity) can be handled by the old decision-making system, but once a certain threshold is passed, some supranational authority is almost inevitable.

It seems also that expanding the power and scope of a supranational authority is easier than to form the first element of such an authority. Initially a supranational authority is often accepted on the grounds that it will limit itself strictly to technical, bureaucratic, or secondary matters, and that the major policy decisions will be left in the hands of a superior, intergovernment body. This was the initial relationship between the High Authority and the Council of Ministers of the ECSC; between the Economic Commission and the Council of Ministers of the EEC; and between NATO's SHAPE and NATO's conferences of ministers.

Once such a bureaucratic structure is established, a process often sets in whereby full-time, professional bureaucrats tend to usurp functions and authority from the part-time, political, "amateur" superior bodies, thereby expanding the scope of the supranational authority. At the same time, the very existence of supranational control in one area tends to promote such control in others. The concept of spill-over, or secondary priming, which is used here to study the epigenesis of nation unions, is applicable to the study of accumulation processes in general.

B. Secondary Priming of Change

"Spill-over" refers to expansion of supranational performances and control from one sphere of international behavior to another. It was introduced by Haas to refer to expansions within the sector in which unification originally started (e.g., from coal and steel industries to transportation) and from sector to sector (e.g., from the economic to the political).[27] Spill-over refers only to secondary priming; that is, to processes—in our case, unifications—that have been initiated or have taken off because of epigenesis in *other* social sectors. NATO, for instance, unifies the military organizations of fifteen nations, and the EEC integrates the economies of six of the NATO countries. While these processes probably support each other, only a little spill-over has taken place. Basically the military unification did not initiate the economic one or vice versa.[28] There was original priming in each area. Both unifications may have had certain common sources (e.g., the conflicts between the United States and Soviet Russia) and may be mutually supportive, but they did not trigger each other. On the other hand, the

---

[25] See Deutsch *et al.*, *op. cit.*, pp. 85–87, on supranational take-off.

[26] Hence the fact that a mere increase in flows is not related to increase in supranationalism does not reject the hypothesis that these variables are positively related. Cf. I. Richard Savage and Karl Deutsch, "A Statistical Model of the Gross Analysis of Transaction Flows," *Econometrica*, XXVIII (1960), 551–72; Deutsch, "Shifts in the Balance of Communication Flows," *Public Opinion Quarterly*, XX (1956), 143–60.

[27] *Uniting of Europe, op. cit.*, Chap. VIII.

[28] Diebold (*op. cit.*) points to the reasons why efforts to base economic integration on NATO have been unsuccessful. Kissinger, on the other hand, believes that NATO could serve as the basis of an Atlantic confederacy (*Reporter*, February 2, 1961, pp. 15–21). Deutsch *et al.* pointed out that where the initial unification efforts were based on military integration half of these efforts failed (*op. cit.*, p. 28).

integration of the economies of the Six generates pressures toward integration of their governments, though so far political unification is mainly a "grand design."[29]

It follows that one can hardly understand supra-national spill-over without studying the internal structure and dynamics of the participating societies. This must be done from a dynamic perspective, for spill-over raises the following questions: Under what conditions and at what level of change does unification of one sector lead to the exhausting of its "degrees of freedom" and trigger unification in other sectors?[30] Which sector is likely to be affected first, second, and nth? Which sector will be affected most, second, and nth?

IV. The Sequence of Epigenesis

A. Clockwise and Counterclockwise Sequences

The concept of take-off suggests that epigenesis has to gain a certain momentum before it becomes self-sustaining. However, it does not suggest in what sector accumulation takes off, or what the effects of the selection of a particular take-off sector are on the probability that general unification will ensue. Similarly, the study of spill-over traces the relation between sectors once take-off in one sector has occurred, but it does not specify either in which sector accumulation is likely to start or in what order other supranational sectors are likely to be built up (since it does not account for primary, simultaneous, or successive priming). To put it in terms of the accumulation model, we still have to determine: Which part is assembled first, which ones later?[31]

A hypothesis defining the sequences most functional for the epigenesis of nation unions can be derived from an application of the Parsonian phase model.[32] Parsons suggests that the most functional cyclical fluctuations in the investment of resources,

personnel, and time follow one of two patterns: either a clockwise sequence (adaptive, allocative, socially integrative, and normative integrative), or a counter-clockwise sequence.[33] The two patterns can be applied to the study of epigenesis. They suggest that it is most functional for a new community to assemble its subunits and its self-control from the adaptive to the normative, or the other way around; and that all other sequences are less functional.[34]

Before we turn to express this hypothesis in more substantive terms the difference between the application of the Parsonian phase model to pre-formism and its application to epigenesis should be pointed out. The phase model, as such, concerns the movement of an existing system, not its pattern of growth or change in its structure. Unless other processes take place, after a full round of the phase movement the system is the same as it started. Moreover, while each system is once accumulated or differentiated, the phase movement can continue ad libitum.[35]

Parsons also suggested a pattern for the analysis of social change, that of differentiation, according to which fused units bifurcate first into expressive and instrumental elements; then, each of these splits. Expressive elements are divided into social and normative ones; instrumental into adaptive and allocative ones. This, like all preformism models, is a pattern according to which functions that were served by one, fused structure, become structurally

---

[29] On spill-over from the economic to the political area see essays by Paul Delouvrier and by Pierre Uri in C. Grove Haines (ed.), *European Integration* (Baltimore: Johns Hopkins Press, 1957).

[30] In other words, up to a point each institutional realm changes independently, but, once that point has been reached, further change affects another institutional realm.

[31] Note that though sector spill-over occurs in the member societies, it leads to expansion in the scope of the supranational community.

[32] Parsons et al., *Working Papers . . ., op. cit.*, pp. 182 ff.

[33] Here, as well as in an earlier work, I found it fruitful to apply Parsons' concepts with a certain amount of liberty. A long conceptual quibble seems unnecessary. The use of allocation instead of "goal attainment" and of normative integration instead of "pattern maintenance and tension-management" may serve as a reminder to the reader concerned with such conceptual subtleties that Parsons is not responsible for my way of using his scheme.

[34] This is one of those statements that sounds tautological but is not. Since there are four phases in the system, the statement suggests that two modes of movement are more functional than twenty-two possible other ones. The first pattern—adaptive to normative—is referred to as clockwise because the convention is to present the four phases in a fourfold table in which the adaptive is in the upper left-hand box, the allocative in the upper right-hand box, the social-integrative in the lower right-hand box, and the normative in the lower left hand box.

[35] Note also that there is no one-to-one relationship between the pattern in which a system is built up (whether accumulated or differentiated) and the pattern in which it is maintained; e.g., the epigenesis of a system might be counterclockwise and the system will "click" clockwise once its epigenesis is completed.

differentiated; that is, they gain their own subunits.[36] The accumulation model, on the other hand, knows no bifurcation, but suggests an order in which new structures serving new functions are conjoined. For example, countries that shared only a common market also establish a common defense line; that is, the union acquires a new function, not just a structural wing. The order we expect to be functional for unification movements to follow is either from the adaptive to the normative or the other way around.

In more substantive terms, the major question raised by the hypothesis concerning the sequence of accumulation is this: Is unification initiated in a particular sector more likely to lead to complete unification (to a political community)? If so, which is it: the military, economic, political, or ideological? Is the probability of success higher if accumulation follows a certain sequence? Which sequence (if any)? And is the most effective sequence the same for all types of unifications? (See below.)

On the basis of the study of ten historical cases Deutsch and his associates reached the following conclusion:

It appears to us from our cases that they [conditions of integration] may be assembled in almost any sequence, so long only as all of them come into being and take effect. Toward this end, almost any pathway will suffice.[37]

They added, however, that:

In this assembly-line process of history, and particularly in the transition between background and process, timing is important. Generally speaking, we found that substantial rewards for cooperation or progress toward amalgamation had to be timed so as to come before the imposition of burdens resulting from such progress toward amalgamation (union). We found that, as with rewards before burdens, consent has to come before compliance if the amalgamation is to have lasting success.[38]

Deutsch's distinction between sequence and order in time seems unnecessary for our purposes. Especially after examining his important book, *Backgrounds for Community*, in which his historical

material is analyzed in great detail and potency, we conclude that Deutsch suggests—if we push the freedom of interpretation to its limit—that the allocative phase tends to come before the adaptive one (rewards before burdens); and that the normative phase (consent) tends to come before the social-integrative phase (compliance). In other words, interpreting liberally, we find Deutsch suggesting that a counterclockwise sequence from normative to adaptive is most common.

Haas compares the findings of his study of a modern unification with the findings of Deutsch *et al.* on historical cases from this viewpoint.[39] He distinguishes between identical expectations (or aims) and converging expectations that make actors cooperate in pursuing their non-identical aims. The distinction comes close to Durkheim's dichotomy of mechanic and organic solidarity and is similar to the dichotomy of expressive and instrumental elements.[40] Haas reports that the ECSC has followed a clockwise sequence in which convergent (or instrumental) expectations preceded the identical (or expressive) ones.[41] Interpreting Haas liberally, one could state that in the case of the ECSC adaptive integration (custom union) came first, followed by allocative integration of economic policies (regarding coal and steel and later the formation of a common market). The union is now on the verge of political integration (election of a European parliament; planning group for federal or confederal institutions) and at the beginning of normative integration. Actually by the time Haas completed his study in 1957, there was hardly any supranational merger of normative institutions, and even attitudes only started to change from convergent to identical.

Any effort to codify Deutsch's and Haas's findings for the benefit of further research on the question of the relative effectiveness of various sequences will have to take into account (1) the nature of the merging units, (2) the nature of the emerging unit (i.e., the kind of union established), and (3) the nature of functional statements.

---

[36] For a later development of this model see Talcott Parsons, "A Functional Theory of Change," in Amitai and Eva Etzioni, eds., *op. cit.*

[37] *Op. cit.*, p. 70.

[38] *Ibid.*, p. 71.

[39] Haas, "The Challenge of Regionalism," in Stanley Hoffmann (ed.), *Contemporary Theory in International Relations* (Englewood Cliffs, N.J.: Prentice-Hall, Inc., 1960), pp. 230–31.

[40] *Ibid.*, p. 229. In Haas's own words: "Converging expectations make for regional unity instrumental in nature rather than based on principle."

[41] *Ibid.*, p. 230.

B. *Merging units*

One might expect the supranational unification of societies that differ in their internal structure will proceed in a different sequence. If, for instance, the merging units are three newly independent states such as Ghana, Guinea, and Mali—states that in themselves are still in the process of building up their "expressive" foundations—the emphasis on normative and social integration on the supranational level might well be higher than when long-established and well-integrated states unify, as in the Scandinavian union, where the instrumental elements of the unification are stressed. These observations support the far from earth-shaking hypothesis that sector integration most responsive to the functional needs of the individual societies that are merging will come first in the unification sequence. After take-off, however, unification is expected to *proceed more and more in accord with the intrinsic needs of the emerging political union, less and less in accord with the internal needs of the merging units.*

The preceding statements should not be read to imply that "political communities develop differently in different historical contexts"; that, for instance, one can account for the difference between Deutsch's findings and those of Haas by pointing to the fact that Deutsch deals with historical cases while Haas is concerned with a contemporary one. Such statements are frequently made by historians who believe that each context is unique, hence what needs explanation is not diversity but uniformity—if ever found. For the sociologist the "historical context" is a shorthand phrase referring to the values of a myriad variables; unless these are specified, little is explained by the statement that "the context is different." In our case the question is: Which contextual variables account for the difference in sequences and for how much of the difference? (Often numerous factors have an effect but a small number accounts for most of the variance.)

"Historical cases," for instance, are often pre-industrial societies; hence it comes to mind that the level of industrialization might account for part of the difference; industrialized societies might tend to merge in an adaptive-first, normative-last sequence; non-industrial ones, in a normative-first, adaptive-last sequence. This formulation seems suggestive because, if valid, it points to the direction in which

these findings can be generalized. We would expect, for instance, contemporary non-industrialized societies to unify in the "historical," not in the "contemporary," fashion. The hypothesis also calls attention to the special importance of historical cases in which unification came after industrialization. If these unifications followed a "contemporary" sequence, the hypothesis on the relation of industrialization to the sequence of unification would be strengthened.

Another variable to be teased out of the undifferentiated phrase, "historical context," is the degree of nationalism. There seem to be three major kinds of unions: pre-nationalist (e.g., the Roman Empire); post-nationalist (e.g., the EEC); and unions that are themselves an expression of rising nationalism (e.g., the unification of Italy). All other things being equal, we would expect the initial phases of pre- and post-nationalist unions to stress the adaptive aspect and follow the clockwise pattern; and those unions that express nationalism to be initiated on the normative side, following the counterclockwise sequence.

C. *Kinds of Union*

The sequence of unification is determined not only by the *initial* needs of the merging units (e.g., industrialization) and the "period" (e.g. advent of nationalism) but also by the function the union fulfills for the various participant units as it is *completed*. Unions of nations differ greatly on this score. The most familiar type is that of custom unions, which keep up the level of international trade among member countries. The new Central American Union, formed in 1959, and the Latin America Free Trade Area, ratified in 1961,[42] are actually oriented at economic development, international division of labor, sharing of information, and even of capital rather than increased regional trade.[43] Wallerstein points to still a different function of unions: Some serve as instruments of subordination, while others serve to bolster independence.[44] Thus the whites,

[42] See "The Emerging Common Markets in Latin America," *Monthly Review* (Federal Reserve Bank of New York), September, 1960, pp. 154 ff.

[43] This point was made by Lincoln Gordon in "Economic Regionalism Reconsidered," *World Politics*, XIII (1961), 231–53.

[44] On these unions see Immanuel Wallerstein, *Africa* (New York: Random House, 1962), Chap. VII.

[?] [?] [?]ger in Southern Rhodesia than in Northern Rhodesia and Nyasaland, use the federation of the three regions to hold the regions in which they are weak.

Functional analysis of social units that develop epigenetically, is more complex than such an analysis of existing social units, for here we deal with functional analysis of change where the system itself is changing. Thus, as unification evolves, it comes to fulfill different (either additional or substitute) functions for the participant units and the emerging union. The West European unification might have been initiated in 1947 as a way to gain capital aid from the United States to reconstruct the postwar economies; soon it acquired the additional function of countering Soviet military expansion; then it came to serve economic welfare and, with the "rebellion" of France since De Gaulle has returned to office, it even serves, to a degree, to countervail United States influence in the Western bloc.[45] (It should be mentioned in passing that at a given stage of development the same union may have different functions for different participants. Thus, Germany supported the EEC partially to overcome its "second" citizen status in the community of nations; allied control of German steel industry, for instance, was abolished when Germany entered the ECSC.[46] France supported the formation of NATO in part to gain some control over a rebuilt and rearmed Germany.)

All functional needs—those of individual members, those common to all members, and those of the evolving community—vary with the various stages of the unification process; and they all seem to affect the sequence in which the "parts" are assembled. It remains for future studies to relate differences in sequence to these functional variations, to validate two hypotheses: (a) the higher the degree of unification the more its pattern of accumulation can be accounted for by common (identical or complementary) needs, rather than by the individual needs of member states, and by needs of the union rather than by common needs of the members, (b) accumulation sequences, whatever their take-off sector, are most likely to complete the process of unification if they follow the clockwise or counterclockwise sequence than any other.

D. Functional and "Real" Sequences

An important difference between the statements about sequences made, on the one hand, by Deutsch and by Haas and the statements made, on the other, by Parsons, his associates, and in the preceding discussion is that the former refer to actual occurrences (the ECSC followed this and that pattern) and empirical frequencies (nine out of ten historical cases followed this sequence), while the latter refer to functional sequences. Functional statements suggest that if epigenesis proceeds in a certain sequence, it will be most effectively completed; if it follows another sequence, certain dysfunctions will occur. The nature of the dysfunctions can be derived from the nature of the stages which are skipped (e.g., high social strain is expected if the expressive elements are not introduced), or incorporated in a "wrong" order (e.g., high strain is expected when allocation of resources is attempted before adaptation has been built up). The fact that a particular unification follows a sequence other than the one suggested by the epigenesis model does not invalidate the latter so long as it is demonstrated that the "deviation" from the model caused dysfunctions. In short, the test of the model lies in its ability to predict which course of action is functional and which one is not, rather than to predict the course of action likely to be followed.[47]

In the construction of epigenesis models for the various kinds of nation unions, the use of two types of functional models must be distinguished: The crude *survival* model and the more sophisticated and demanding *effectiveness* model. The first specifies the conditions under which a structure exists or ceases to exist; the second also takes into account differences in the degree of success. In the case of nation unions, then, while many are likely to continue in existence, some will stagnate on a low level of integration while others will continue to grow in scope, function, and authority.

---

[45] Edgar S. Furniss, Jr., "De Gaulle's France and NATO: An Interpretation," *International Organization*, XV (1961), 349–65.

[46] *Uniting of Europe, op. cit.*, pp. 247–48.

[47] Note that the system this statement refers to is not the existing one but a future state—that of a complete unification—of a community. The use of a future-system reference might prove useful for the general development of the functional analysis of change.

Conclusion

Sociological theories of change tend to be preformist; they provide differentiation models for the analysis of the structural development of existing social units. We presented some elements of an alternative, epigenesis model, which suggests that some social units acquire new subunits that fulfill new functions, do not just provide new subunits for functions served before in a less specialized manner. Since these new elements are incorporated from the environment, epigenesis (or accumulation) models are much more concerned with input from, and articulation with, external units than preformism (or differentiated) models. Hence the first question we asked was: Where does the power lie that controls the process—is it evenly distributed among the participant units or is it concentrated in the hands of elites? Are the power-holders members of the new emerging communities or outsiders? Does increase in self-control of the union precede, follow, or coincide with the growth in its performances?

Turning from the powers that control accumulation to the pattern of accumulation itself, we asked: Where does the process start, what subunit is built up first? Which follows? What effect does the construction of one part have on that of the others? The concepts of take-off and secondary priming proved to be useful in understanding the initiation and progress of accumulating processes. An application of Parsons' phase model served us in formulating a hypothesis concerning the functional sequence of accumulation.

The distinctness of accumulation models should be emphasized: While differentiation models focus our attention on internal processes, accumulation models are concerned with boundary processes; while differentiation models are interested in internal elites, accumulation models ask about the changing power distribution between external and internal ones and their respective impacts on accumulation. Analytically speaking, preformist models see their subject units—even when undifferentiated—as functionally complete, whereas epigenesis models view their units as either partial (to varying degrees) or complete.

We emphasized the need to treat social units and their change as multilayer phenomena, including at least a performance, a power (or control), and a communication layer.[48] If we deal with a phase, differentiation, or accumulation model, we need not assume that changes on one layer are automatically concomitant with changes on the others.

Although the epigenesis model can be applied to many social phenomena, we are interested here primarily in using it to study international unification. There is hardly a subject less frequently studied by sociologists and more given to sociological analysis than the development of political communities whose members are nations. Since the evolution of these communities is likely to be supportive of both the short-run armed truce and the development of the social conditions for lasting peace,[49] and since the processes of social change involved in forming supranational communities are comparatively highly planned, deliberately and frequently drawing on expert advice, the study of supranational unification carries the extra reward of not just better understanding of human society but also of understanding how to better it.

[48] See my *A Comparative Analysis of Complex Organizations* (Glencoe, Ill.: Free Press, 1961), Chaps. V and VII.

[49] These functions of nation unions are discussed in Chap. VIII of my *The Hard Way to Peace* (New York: Collier Books, 1962).

C. Strategic Theory

33. The Calculus of Deterrence*

Bruce M. Russett, whose incisive approach to international phenomena has already been demonstrated in previous Selections (10 and 12), examines here an aspect of strategic theory that is sometimes called deterrence theory and that has been the focus of considerable discussion and analysis in recent years. Unlike many inquiries into the subject, however, Professor Russett employs systematic empirical data to refine theoretical observations. The result is an insightful and valuable glimpse into the dynamics of deterrence as an international process. [*Reprinted from* The Journal of Conflict Resolution, *VII* (*1963*), *97–109, by permission of the author and the publisher. Copyright 1963 by the University of Michigan.*]

A Comparative Study of Deterrence

A persistent problem for American political and military planners has been the question of how to defend "third areas." How can a major power make credible an intent to defend a smaller ally from attack by another major power? Simply making an explicit promise to defend an ally, whether that promise is embodied in a formal treaty or merely in a unilateral declaration, is not sufficient. There have been too many instances when "solemn oaths" were forgotten in the moment of crisis. On the other hand, more than once a major power has taken up arms to defend a nation with whom it had ties appreciably less binding than a formal commitment.

Some analysts like Herman Kahn maintain that the determining factor is the nature of the overall strategic balance. To make credible a promise to defend third areas the defender must have over-all strategic superiority; that is, he must be able to strike the homeland of the attacker without sustaining unacceptable damage to himself in return (Kahn,

* This article is part of the research of the Yale Political Data Program. I am grateful to Paul Y. Hammond for comments on an earlier draft.

1960). This analysis implies, of course, a strategy which threatens to retaliate, even for a local attack, directly on the home territory of the major power antagonist. Advocates of a strategy of limited warfare retort that, in the absence of clear strategic superiority, the capacity to wage local war effectively may deter attack.

Other writers, notably Thomas C. Schelling, have suggested that the credibility of one's threat can be considerably enhanced by unilateral actions which would increase the defender's loss if he failed to keep his promise (Schelling, 1960). One of the best examples is Chiang Kai-shek's decision in 1958 to station nearly half his troops on Quemoy and Matsu. While the islands were of questionable intrinsic importance, the presence of so much of his army there made it virtually impossible for Chiang, or his American ally, to abandon the islands under fire.

All of these explanations tend to stress principally the military elements in what is a highly complex political situation. There are, however, numerous nonmilitary ways in which one can strengthen one's commitment to a particular area. A government can make it a matter of prestige with its electorate. A nation might even deliberately increase its economic dependence upon supplies from a certain area, the better to enhance the credibility of a promise to defend it. W. W. Kaufmann's classic piece identified the elements of credibility as a power's capabilities, the costs it could inflict in using those capabilities, and its intentions as perceived by the enemy. In evaluating the defender's intentions a prospective attacker will look at his past actions, his current pronouncements, and the state of his public opinion (Kaufmann, 1956, pp. 12–38).

Kaufmann's formulation is better than simpler ones that stress military factors almost exclusively, but it needs to be expanded and made more detailed. One must particularly examine the potential costs to the defending power if he does not honor his commitments. In addition, propositions about factors which determine the credibility of a given threat need to be tested systematically on a comparative basis. On a number of occasions, for example, an aggressor has ignored the threats of a major power "defender" to go to war to protect a small nation "pawn" even though the defender held both strategic superiority and the ability to fight a local war successfully. Hitler's annexation of Austria in 1938 is just this kind of case, and one where the aggressor was correct, moreover.

In this paper we shall examine all the cases during the last three decades where a major power "attacker" overtly threatened a pawn with military force, and where the defender either had given, prior to the crisis, some indication of an intent to protect the pawn or made a commitment in time to prevent the threatened attack.[1] A threat may be believed or disbelieved; it may be a bluff, or it may be sincere. Often the defender himself may not be sure of his reaction until the crisis actually occurs. We shall explore the question of what makes a threat credible by asking which threats in the past have been believed and which disregarded. Successful deterrence is defined as an instance when an attack on the pawn is prevented or repulsed without conflict between the attacking forces and regular combat units of the major power "defender."

[1] These definitions are employed purely in an analytical sense with no intention of conveying moral content. The British-French "attack" in 1956, for instance, was certainly provoked to a large extent by the Egyptians themselves.

("Regular combat units" are defined so as not to include the strictly limited participation of a few military advisers.) With this formulation we must ignore what are perhaps the most successful instances of all—where the attacker is dissuaded from making any overt threat whatever against the pawn. But these cases must be left aside both because they are too numerous to be treated in detail and because it would be too difficult to distinguish the elements in most cases. Who, for example, really was the "attacker"? Was he dissuaded because of any action by the defender, or simply by indifference? Such questions would lead to too much speculation at the expense of the careful analysis of each case in detail.

Deterrence fails when the attacker decides that the defender's threat is not likely to be fulfilled. In this sense it is equally a failure whether the defender really does intend to fight but is unable to communicate that intention to the attacker, or whether he is merely bluffing. Later we shall ask, from the viewpoint of the attacker, which threats ought to be taken seriously. At this stage we shall simply examine past cases of attempted deterrence to discover what elements are usually associated with a threat that is believed (or at least not disbelieved with enough confidence for the attacker to act on his disbelief) and therefore what steps a defender might take to make his threats more credible to his opponent. Table 1 lists the cases for consideration.[2]

These cases are not, of course, comparable in every respect. Particularly in the instances of successful deterrence the causes are complex and not easily

[2] Note that we have excluded instances of protracted guerrilla warfare. While preventing and defeating guerrilla war is a major problem, the differences from the matters considered here require that it be treated separately. (See a forthcoming paper by Morton H. Halperin of Harvard University for a comparative examination of these cases.) The current Berlin crisis was not included because, at the time of writing, it was still unresolved. Also excluded are those cases of aggression in the 1930's and 1940's where no particular power had given a previous indication of a readiness to defend the pawn. By "previous indication" we mean either at least an ambiguous official statement suggesting the use of military force, or the provision of military assistance in the form of arms or advisers. The League of Nations Covenant is not considered such an indication because, barring further commitments by a particular nation, it is impossible to identify any one defender or group of defenders.

Data on a number of factors are presented, for all of the cases, in the appendix.

TABLE 1
Seventeen Cases—1935–1961

Pawn	*Year*	*Attacker(s)*	*Defender(s)*
		Success	
Iran	1946	Soviet Union	United States
			Great Britain—Secondary
Turkey	1947	Soviet Union	United States
Berlin	1948	Soviet Union	United States
			Great Britain ⎫ Secondary
			France ⎭
Egypt	1956	Great Britain	Soviet Union[a]
		France	
Quemoy-Matsu	1954–55 1958	Communist China	United States
Cuba	1961	United States (support of rebels)	Soviet Union
		Failure—Pawn Lost	
Ethiopia	1935	Italy	Great Britain
			France
Austria	1938	Germany	Great Britain
			France
			Italy
Czechoslovakia	1938	Germany	Great Britain
			France
Albania	1939	Italy	Great Britain
Czechoslovakia	1939	Germany	Great Britain
			France
Rumania	1940	Soviet Union	Great Britain
Guatemala	1954	United States (support of rebels)	Soviet Union
Hungary	1956	Soviet Union	United States
		Failure—War Not Avoided	
Poland[b]	1939	Germany	Great Britain
			France
South Korea	1950	North Korea (supported by China & Soviet Union)	United States
North Korea	1950	United States	Communist China

[a] Despite its efforts to restrain the attackers, the United States was not a "defender" in the Suez affair. It neither supplied arms to the Egyptians before the crisis nor gave any indication that it would employ military force against Britain and France. In fact, the United States government explicitly ruled out the use of military coercion. See *New York Times*, November 7, 1956.

[b] Possibly the Polish case is not really a failure at all, for Hitler may have expected Britain and France to fight but was nevertheless prepared to take the consequences. A. J. P. Taylor presents an extreme version of the argument that Hitler expected Poland and/or Britain and France to give in (Taylor, 1961).

ascertainable. Nevertheless, a systematic comparison, undertaken cautiously, can provide certain insights that would escape an emphasis on the historical uniqueness of each case.

Deterrence in Recent Decades

First, we may dismiss as erroneous some frequent contentions about the credibility of deterrence. It is often said that a major power will fight only to protect an "important" position, and not to defend some area of relatively insignificant size or population. As we shall see below, this is in a nearly tautological sense true—if, by "important," we include the enmeshment of the defender's prestige with the fate of the pawn, the symbolic importance the pawn may take on in the eyes of other allies, and

TABLE 2

Size (Population and Gross National Product) of Pawn in Relation to Defender(s)

Pawn	Defender(s)	Pawn's Population as per cent of Defender's Population	Pawn's G.N.P. as per cent of Defender's G.N.P.
Success			
Iran	United States	12	*a*
	Great Britain	37	4
Turkey	United States	13	1.7
Berlin	United States	1.5	*a*
	Great Britain	4	3
	France	5	3
Egypt	Soviet Union	12	2
Quemoy-Matsu	United States	*a*	*a*
Cuba	Soviet Union	3	1.5
Failure—Pawn Lost			
Ethiopia	Great Britain	28	1.8
	France	31	2
Austria	Great Britain	14	7
	France	16	8
	Italy	16	17
Czechoslovakia (1938)	Great Britain	30	14
	France	34	16
Albania	Great Britain	2	*a*
Czechoslovakia (1939)	Great Britain	23	11
	France	26	12
Rumania	United Kingdom	33	11
Guatemala	Soviet Union	1.6	*a*
Hungary	United States	6	1.0
Failure —War Not Avoided			
Poland	Great Britain	73	25
	France	82	29
South Korea	United States	14	*a*
North Korea	Communist China	2	3

a Less than 1 per cent

Sources: Population—United Nations (United Nations, 1949, pp. 98–105; United Nations, 1962, pp. 126–37).
     G.N.P.—Norton Ginsburg (Ginsburg, 1962, p. 16). G.N.P. data are approximate and sometimes estimated.

particular strategic or political values attached to the pawn. But if one means important in terms of any objectively measurable factor like relative population or Gross National Product, it is not true.

As Table 2 shows, in all of our cases of successful deterrence—Iran, Turkey, Berlin, Egypt, Quemoy-Matsu, and Cuba—the pawn's population was well under 15 per cent, and his G.N.P. less than 5 per cent of that of the principal defender.[3] (Britain

[3] On the other hand one might argue that they were not of sufficient potential value to the attacker for him to run even a relatively slight risk that the defender might actually fight. A complete formulation involving these factors would have to include both the value of the pawn to the attacker and his estimate of the probability that the defender would fight. See below.

was not Iran's chief protector.) Yet in five of the eleven cases where the attacker was not dissuaded the territory in question represented over 20 per cent of the defender's population (Ethiopia, Czechoslovakia in the Sudeten crisis and again in 1939, Poland, and Rumania). Poland in 1939 constituted the largest prize of all, yet Hitler may not have been convinced that Britain and France would go to war to save it. Nor can one discover any special strategic or industrial importance of the pawn only in cases of success. Austria and both Czechoslovakian cases met these criteria but were nevertheless overrun, and the United States did not expect Communist China to fight for North Korea, despite its obvious strategic significance.

Clearly too, it is not enough simply for the defender to make a formal promise to protect the pawn. Only in one case of success was there what could be described as a clear and unambiguous commitment prior to the actual crisis (Berlin). In the others the commitment was either ambiguous (Iran, Cuba, Quemoy-Matsu) or not made until the crisis was well under way (Turkey, Egypt). The United States' principal precrisis commitment to Iran was the Big Three communique from Teheran in 1943 (written chiefly by the American delegation) guaranteeing Iranian "independence, sovereignty, and territorial integrity."[4] Britain was allied with Iran, but the Russians recognized that any effective resistance to their plans would have to come from the United States rather than from an exhausted Britain. In July 1960 Khrushchev warned that the Soviet Union would retaliate with missiles if the United States attacked Cuba, but this was later qualified as being "merely symbolic" and the precise content of Soviet retaliation was left undefined. Neither Congress nor the President has ever stated the exact circumstances under which our formal guarantees of Taiwan would apply to the offshore islands.

Yet in at least six cases an attacker has chosen to ignore an explicit and publicly acknowledged commitment binding the defender to protect the pawn. Britain, France, and Italy were committed by treaty to Austria, France by treaty to Czechoslovakia in 1938, France by treaty and Britain by executive agreement to Czechoslovakia in 1939, Britain by executive agreement to Rumania, Britain, and France by treaty with Poland, and China by public declaration to North Korea. In three others there was at least an ambiguous commitment on the "defender's" part that might have been more rigorously interpreted. By a treaty of 1906 Britain, France, and Italy pledged themselves to "cooperate in maintaining the integrity of Ethiopia," Britain and Italy agreed in 1938 to "preserve the status quo in the Mediterranean" (including Albania), and in the 1950's American officials made references to "liberating" the satellites that were tragically overrated in Hungary. Of the failures, in fact, only Guatemala and possibly South Korea lacked any verbal indication of their "protectors'" willingness to fight. (In these

instances, the defenders showed their concern principally by sending arms to the pawns before the attack.) The analyst who limited his examination to the present cases would be forced to conclude that a small nation was as safe without an explicit guarantee as with one. At least such guarantees existed in fewer instances of success (one in six) than in cases of failure (six of eleven).

We must also examine the proposition that deterrence is not credible unless the defender possesses over-all strategic superiority; unless he can inflict far more damage on an aggressor than he would suffer in return. It is true that the successful deterrence of attack is frequently associated with strategic superiority, but the Soviet Union had, at best, strategic equality with the United States at the time of the Bay of Pigs affair. While Russia was clearly superior to Britain and France when it threatened to attack them with rockets in 1956, it just as clearly did not have a credible first strike force for use against their American ally.[5]

Furthermore, in at least five cases where the attacker was not dissuaded, it nevertheless appears that the defender definitely had the ability to win any major conflict that might have developed (in the cases of Ethiopia, Austria, Czechoslovakia in 1938, Albania, and South Korea) and in two others (Czechoslovakia in 1939 and Hungary) the defender had at least a marginal advantage. (*Post hoc* analysis of the relevant documents indicates this superiority was more often perceived by the attacker, who went ahead and took the chance it would not be used, than by the defender. Hitler consistently recognized his opponents' strength and discounted their will to use it.)

Even less is it necessary for the defender to be able to win a limited local war. Of all the cases of success, only in Egypt could the defender plausibly claim even the ability to fight to a draw on the local level. In the other instances the defender could not hope to achieve equality without a long, sustained effort, and local superiority appeared out of reach. Yet in at least two failures the defenders, perhaps individually and certainly in coalition, had local superiority (Ethiopia and Austria) and in four

[4] See George Kirk on the Iranian case (Kirk, 1952, p. 473).

[5] In both of these instances we must recognize that the "attacker's" failure to persevere to defeat of the pawn was probably due less to Soviet threats than to pressures from the "attacker's" own allies and world opinion.

others (Czechoslovakia in 1938, Albania, and the Korean cases) the defenders seemed to have been more or less on a par with their prospective antagonists.[6]

Yet if these two kinds of capabilities—local and strategic—are analyzed together, it would seem that a defender may not be clearly inferior in both and yet hope to restrain an attacker. Although the Soviet Union could not dream of meeting the United States in a limited war in the Caribbean, at least in 1961 its strategic nuclear capabilities seemed roughly on a par with America's.[7] And although Russia was inferior to Britain-France-United States on the strategic level, Soviet chances of at least matching their efforts in a local war over Egypt seemed a little brighter. Success requires at least apparent equality on one level or the other—this is hardly surprising —but when we remember that even superiority on both levels has often been associated with failure we have something more significant. *Superiority*, on either level, is not a condition of success. *Equality* on at least one level is a *necessary*, but by no means *sufficient*, condition. The traditionally conceived purely military factors do not alone make threats credible.

Nor, as has sometimes been suggested, does the kind of political system in question seem very important, though it does make some difference. Often, it is said, a dictatorial power can threaten much more convincingly than a democracy because the dictatorship can control its own mass media and present an apparently united front. Democracies, on the other hand, cannot easily suppress dissenting voices declaring that the pawn is "not worth the bones of a single grenadier." This argument must not be overstated—four of our successful cases of deterrence involved a democracy defending against a dictatorship. Yet in all of these cases the democracy possessed strategic superiority, whereas the other two successes, by a dictatorship, were at best under conditions of strategic equality for the defender. And in all but two (North Korea and Guatemala) of the eleven failures the defender was a democracy.

[6] On the military situation prevailing in various crises before World War II see Winston Churchill (1948, pp. 177, 270–1, 287, 336–7).
[7] American intelligence reports were, however, far from unanimous. By the end of 1961 it was clear to those with good information that the Soviets' strategic forces were distinctly inferior to America's.

Thus a totalitarian power's control over its citizens' expression of opinion may give it some advantage, if not a decisive one—particularly under conditions when the defender's strategic position is relatively weak.

Interdependence and Credibility

With some of these hypotheses discarded we may now examine another line of argument, the credibility of deterrence depends upon the economic, political, and military interdependence of pawn and defender. Where visible ties of commerce, past or present political integration, or military cooperation exist, an attacker will be much more likely to bow before the defender's threats—or if he does not bow, he will very probably find himself at war with the defender.

Military Cooperation

In every instance of success the defender supported the pawn with military assistance in the form of arms and advisers. In one of these cases, of course (Berlin) the defenders actually had troops stationed on the pawn's territory. The military link with Iran was somewhat tenuous, for Teheran received no shipments of American military equipment until after the 1946 crisis was past. Yet an American military mission was stationed in the country at the time, and 30,000 American troops had been on Iranian soil until the end of 1945 (Kirk, 1952, p. 150). America had given a tangible, though modest, indication of her interest in Iran. But in only five of the eleven failures were there significant shipments of arms to the pawn. France extended large military credits to Poland, and the British gave a small credit ($20 million) to Rumania. The Americans and the Chinese sent both arms and advisers to their Korean protégés. The Soviets sent small arms to Guatemala but no advisers, and they did not give any explicit indication of an intent to intervene in any American move against the Guatemalan government. A French military mission was stationed in Prague before and during the two Czechoslovakian crises, but no substantial amount of French equipment was sent (in part because of the high quality of the Czechoslovakian armament industry). In none of the other failures was there any tangible military interdependence. Some degree of military cooperation may not always be sufficient for successful deterrence, but it is virtually essential.

Political Interdependence

This is a helpful if not essential condition. Four of the instances of successful deterrence include some kind of current or recent political tie in addition to any current alliance. Western troops were stationed in Berlin and the three Western powers participated in the government of the city by international agreement. America and Nationalist China had been allies in a recent war. Turkey became allied with the Big Three toward the end of World War II. Iran had been occupied by British troops until early 1946 and American troops until the end of 1945. In the case of failures only four of eleven pawns had any significant former tie with a defender. Britain and Rumania were allies in World War I, as were the U.S.S.R. and Guatemala in World War II. Obviously, neither of these ties was at all close. The other two, however, were marked by rather close ties. United States forces occupied South Korea after World War II, and the R.O.K. government was an American protégé. The Communist Chinese had close party and ideological ties with the North Korean regime, and not too many decades previously Korea had been under Chinese sovereignty.

Economic Interdependence

We shall work with a crude but simple and objective measure of economic interdependence. In 1954 all countries of the world, other than the United States, imported a total of $65 billion of goods, of which 16 per cent came from the United States. South Korea, however, took 35 per cent of its total imports from the United States, a figure well above the world average. This will be our measure: does the pawn take a larger than average proportion of its imports from the defender or, vice versa, does the defender take a larger than average proportion of its imports from the pawn? To repeat, this is a crude measure. It does not tell, for example, whether the defender is dependent upon the pawn for a supply of a crucial raw material. But there are few areas of vital economic significance in this sense—almost every commodity can be obtained from more than one country, though not always at the same price— and attention to over-all commercial ties gives a broad measure of a country's general economic stake

in another.[8] In none of the cases where this test does not show general economic interdependence is there evidence that the defender relied heavily on the pawn for a particular product.

In five of the six cases of successful deterrence either the pawn took an abnormally high proportion of its imports from the defender or vice versa. In the remaining case, the Iranian economy was closely tied to Britain if not to the United States, but in only three of the eleven failures was there interdependence between pawn and defender. A higher than average proportion of Austria's trade was with Italy, though not with France and Britain, the other two parties bound by treaty to preserve her integrity. Both Korean regimes also traded heavily with their defenders. Economic interdependence may be virtually essential to successful deterrence.

Divining Intentions

Briefly we may also examine the question from the viewpoint of the attacker. If the defender's threat is not challenged, one may never know whether it truly expresses an intention to fight or whether it is merely a bluff. Perhaps the defender himself would not know until the circumstances actually arose. But we can examine the eleven cases where deterrence was not sufficiently credible to prevent attack. Previously we asked what differentiated the instances when the attacker pressed on from those in which he restrained his ambitions. Now, what distinguishes the cases where the defender actually went to war from those where he did not?[9]

[8] In the cases of Berlin and Quemoy-Matsu we must rely on trade figures for a larger unit (West Germany and Taiwan). West Germany conducted an above-average proportion of her trade with the United States and France in this period, but her trade with Britain was below average. Yet as Allied resolve in the Berlin crisis clearly depended upon American initiative it seems correct to include Berlin in the class of economically interdependent pawns.

[9] Remember that we have been dealing only with those cases in which deterrence was visibly in danger of failing, and not with instances where it was fully successful, i.e., where the attacker was dissuaded from ever making a serious explicit threat. As noted earlier the latter cases are extremely difficult to identify; nevertheless it seems likely that analysis would show similar results to those above. American protection of Western Europe is an excellent example. The political, economic, and military interdependence of Europe and the United States is great enough to make America's threat highly credible (though perhaps not as credible as we might sometimes wish).

"Size," as defined earlier, again is not crucial. Poland, for which Britain and France went to war, was a very large prize but neither North nor South Korea represented a significant proportion of its defender's population or G.N.P. Of the eight instances where the defender's bluff was successfully called, four of the pawns (Ethiopia, Czechoslovakia on both occasions, and Rumania) represented over 20 per cent of the defender's population and four (Austria, Czechoslovakia both times, and Rumania) over 5 per cent of its G.N.P. Proportionately "large" pawns were more often the subject of "bluffs" than of serious intentions. Nor is there necessarily a formal, explicit commitment in cases which result in war. There were such commitments over Poland and North Korea, but South Korea is an obvious exception. And there was such a commitment in the case of half the "bluffs" (Austria, Czechoslovakia twice, and Rumania), and a vague, ambiguous one in three other cases (Ethiopia, Albania, Hungary).

The state of the military balance does not seem to have much effect either. In at least four "bluffs" (Ethiopia, Austria, Czechoslovakia in 1938, and Albania) the defenders were clearly superior *over-all* and in two other cases (Czechoslovakia in 1939 and Hungary) they were at least marginally so. Yet despite their bad military position Britain and France fought for Poland in 1939. And although the Chinese made some bold "paper tiger" talk they really could have had few illusions about their position should the United States counter their move into North Korea with its full conventional and nuclear might. In no instance where a defender fought did he have the ability to win a quick and relatively costless *local* victory. But in the two cases where the defender probably did have this ability (Ethiopia and Austria) he did not employ it. Neither does the defender's political system appear to matter much. The Chinese fought to defend North Korea, but dictatorships did nothing to protect Austria and Guatemala.

Yet bonds of interdependence—economic, political, and military—do turn out to be highly relevant. In every case where the defender went to war he had previously sent military advisers and arms to the pawn. Only four of the eight "bluffs" were marked by either of these activities, and none by a significant level of both. The two Koreas both had important prior political ties to their eventual defenders, but only two of the instances of "bluff" (Rumania and Guatemala) were marked by even very weak ties of previous alliance. The two Korean states also were closely tied economically to their defenders, but of all the seven instances of bluff, only Italy-Austria show a bond of similar strength. Again it is the nature of the defender-pawn relationship, rather than the attributes of either party separately, that seem most telling in the event.

We must be perfectly clear about the nature of these ties. Certainly no one but the most inveterate Marxist would assert that the United States entered the Korean War to protect its investments and economic interests. The United States went to war to protect a state with which it had become closely identified. It was rather heavily involved economically in Korea, and its prestige as a government was deeply involved. It had occupied the territory and restored order after the Japanese collapse; it had installed and supported an at least quasi-democratic government; and it had trained, organized, and equipped the army. Not to defend this country in the face of overt attack would have been highly detrimental to American prestige and to the confidence governments elsewhere had in American support. Even though it had made no promises to defend Korea (and even had said it would not defend it in a general East-West war) the American government could not disengage itself from the fate of the Korean peninsula. Despite the lack of American promises, the American "presence" virtually guaranteed American protection.

Making Deterrence Credible

It is now apparent why deterrence does not depend in any simple way merely upon the public declaration of a "solemn oath," nor merely on the physical means to fight a war, either limited or general. A defender's decision whether to pursue a "firm" policy that risks war will depend upon his calculation of the value and probability of various outcomes. If he is to be firm the prospective gains from a successful policy of firmness must be greater, when weighted by the probability of success and discounted by the cost and probability of war, than the losses from retreat.[10] The attacker in turn will determine whether to press his attack in large part on his estimate of the defender's calculation. If he thinks the chances that the defender will fight are substantial he will attack only if the prospective gains from doing so are great.[11]

The physical means of combat available to both sides are far from irrelevant, for upon them depend the positions of each side should war occur. A defender's commitment is unlikely to be believed if his military situation is markedly inferior to his enemy's. Yet even clear superiority provides no guarantee that his antagonist will be dissuaded if the defender appears to have relatively little to lose from "appeasement." At the time of the Austrian crisis Neville Chamberlain could tell himself not only that appeasement was likely to succeed, but that prospective losses even from its possible failure were not overwhelming. In particular, he failed to consider the effects appeasement would have on Britain's other promises to defend small nations. By autumn 1939, however, it was clear that further appeasement would only encourage Hitler to continue to disregard British threats to fight, as British inaction over Austria in fact had done.

Under these circumstances the effectiveness of the defender's threat is heavily dependent on the tangible and intangible bonds between him and the pawn. If other factors are equal, an attacker will regard a military response by the defender as more probable the greater the number of military, political, and economic ties between pawn and defender. No aggressor is likely to measure these bonds, as commercial ties, in just the way we have sketched them here, but he is most unlikely to be insensitive to their existence.

Strengthening these bonds is, in effect a strategy of raising the credibility of deterrence by increasing the loss one would suffer by not fulfilling a pledge. It illustrates in part why the American promise to defend Western Europe, with nuclear weapons if necessary, is so credible even in the absence of overwhelming American strategic superiority. Western Europe is certainly extremely important because of its large, skilled population and industrial capacity. Yet it is particularly important to the United States because of the high degree of political and military integration that has taken place in the North Atlantic Area. The United States, in losing Western Europe to the Communists, would lose population and industry, and the credibility of its pledges elsewhere. To put the case another way, America has vowed to defend both Japan and France from external attack, and there is much that is convincing about both promises. But the latter promise is somewhat more credible than the former, even were one to assume that in terms of industrial capacity, resources, strategic significance, etc., both countries were of equal importance. The real, if not wholly tangible, ties of the United States with France make it so.[12]

Interdependence, of course, provides no guarantee that the defender's threat will be believed. There have been a few cases where an attacker chose to ignore a threat even when relatively close interdependence existed. But if one really does want to protect an area it is very hard to make that intention credible *without* bonds between defender and pawn. If the United States wishes to shield a country it will be wise to "show," and even to increase, its stake in that country's independence. Because the strength of international ties is to some degree controllable, certain policy choices, not immediately relevant to

---

[10] Formally, the defender will pursue a firm policy only if, in his calculation:

$$V_f \cdot s + V_w \cdot (1 - s) > V_r$$

where

V_f = the value of successful firmness (deterrence without war)
V_w = the value (usually negative) of the failure of firmness (war)
V_r = the value (usually negative) of retreat
s = the probability that firmness will be successful.

Daniel Ellsberg presents a related formulation (Ellsberg, 1960).

[11] Precisely, he will press the attack only if:

$$V_a \cdot s + V_w \cdot (1 - s) > V_o$$

where

V_a = the value of a successful attack (no war)
V_w = the value (usually negative) of an attack which is countered (war)
V_o = the value of doing nothing in this instance (no attack, no war)
s = the probability of a successful attack.

[12] This point is further illustrated by the 1962 Cuban crisis. The American government took great pains to indicate that it was reacting to the threat of Soviet missiles on the island, and only demanded their removal, not the overthrow of the Castro regime. To have directly threatened the existence of a Communist government in which the Soviets had such a heavy military and economic investment would have carried a much greater risk of Soviet military retaliation.

this problem, in fact take on special urgency. Implementation of the Trade Expansion Act, allowing the American government to eliminate tariffs on much of United States trade with Western Europe, will have more than an economic significance. By increasing America's apparent, and actual, economic dependence on Europe it will make more credible America's promise to defend it from attack.

The particular indices of economic, military and political integration employed here are less important in themselves than as indicators of a broader kind of political and cultural integration, of what K. W. Deutsch refers to as mutual sympathy and loyalties, "we-feeling," trust, and mutual consideration (Deutsch, 1954, pp. 33–64). These bonds of mutual identification both encourage and are encouraged by bonds of communication and attention. Mutual attention in the mass media, exchanges of persons (migrants, tourists, students, etc.), and commercial activities all make a contribution. Mutual contact in some of these areas, such as exchange of persons, tends to promote contacts of other sorts, and often produces mutual sympathies and concern for each other's welfare.[13] This process does not work unerringly, but it does work frequently nevertheless. And these mutual sympathies often are essential for the growth of a high level of commercial exchange, especially between economically developed nations rather than nations in an essentially colonial relationship with each other.[14]

In addition to the loss of prestige and of tangible assets, there is yet another way in which a defender may lose if he fails to honor his pledge. New Yorkers would sacrifice their own self-esteem if they failed to defend Californians from external attack; some of the same feeling applies, in lesser degree, to New Yorkers' attitudes toward Britishers. Though broad and intangible, this kind of relationship is nonetheless very real, and knowledge of it sometimes restrains an attacker.

Communication and attention both produce and are produced by, in a mutually reinforcing process, political and cultural integration. The appendix to this paper demonstrates the degree to which economic, military, and political interdependence are correlated. All this raises the "chicken and egg" kind of question as to which comes first. In such a "feedback" situation there is no simple answer; sometimes trade follows the flag, sometimes the flag follows trade (Russett, 1963, ch. 4). Yet these are also to some extent independent, and the correlation is hardly perfect. From the data available one cannot identify any single factor as essential to deterrence. But as more are present the stronger mutual interdependence becomes, and the greater is the attacker's risk in pressing onward.

References

Churchill, Winston S. *The Second World War*, I, *The Gathering Storm*. Boston: Houghton, 1948.

Deutsch, Karl W. *Political Community at the International Level*. Garden City, N.Y.: Doubleday, 1954.

Ellsberg, Daniel. *The Crude Analysis of Strategic Choice*, RAND Monograph P-2183. Santa Monica, Calif.: RAND Corporation, 1960.

Ginsburg, Norton. *Atlas of Economic Development*. Chicago: Univ. Chicago Press, 1962.

Kahn, Herman. *On Thermonuclear War*. Princeton, N.J.: Princeton Univ. Press, 1960.

Kaufmann, W. W. (ed.). *Military Policy and National Security*. Princeton, N.J.: Princeton Univ. Press, 1956.

Kirk, George. *The Middle East in the War: Royal Institute of International Affairs Survey of International Affairs, 1939–46*. New York: Oxford Univ. Press, 1952.

Russett, Bruce M. *Community and Contention: Britain and America in the Twentieth Century*. Cambridge, Mass.: Mass. Inst. Technology Press, 1963.

Schelling, Thomas C. *The Strategy of Conflict*. Cambridge, Mass.: Harvard Univ. Press, 1960.

Taylor, A. J. P. *The Origins of the Second World War*. New York: Atheneum, 1962.

United Nations. *Demographic Yearbook, 1948*. New York: United Nations, 1949.

———. *Demographic Yearbook, 1961*, New York: United Nations, 1962.

---

[13] The theoretical and empirical literature on this point is voluminous and cannot be discussed in more detail here. I have presented elsewhere a general theoretical examination of these problems and their application to Anglo-American relations (Russett, 1963).

[14] Few markets are perfectly analogous to the model of perfect competition, as the products of two sellers are seldom identical, at least in the mind of the buyer. Customs, habits, traditions, and "myths" about the goods or the seller differentiate two seemingly identical products. A seller who speaks the language and understands the mores of his customers has a great advantage over one who does not. Past habits can affect current prices through credit terms. Goods coming across a previously established trade route can be shipped more cheaply than those across one which has not yet developed much traffic.

Appendix: Presence or Absence of Various Factors Alleged to Make Deterrent Threats Credible

| | Attacker holds back | | | | | | Attacker Presses On | | | | | | | | | | |
| | | | | | | | Defender does not fight | | | | | | | | Defender fights | | |
	Iran	Turkey	Berlin	Egypt	Quemoy-Matsu	Cuba	Ethiopia	Austria	Czechoslovakia (1938)	Albania	Czechoslovakia (1939)	Rumania	Guatemala	Hungary	Poland	South Korea	North Korea
Pawn 20% + of defender's population	*						×		×		×	×			×		
Pawn 5% + of defender's G.N.P.								×	×		×	×			×.		
Formal commitment prior to crisis	?		×		?	?	?	×	×	?	×	×		?	×		×
Defender has strategic superiority	×	×	×		×		×	×	×	×	?			?		×	
Defender has local superiority							×	×	?	?						?	?
Defender is dictatorship				×		×	*							×			×
Pawn-defender military cooperation	×	×	×	×	×	×			×		×	×	×		×	×	×
Pawn-defender political interdependence	×	×	×		×							×	×			×	×
Pawn-defender economic interdependence	*	×	×	×	×	×	*									×	×

Key: × Factor present
? Ambiguous or doubtful
* Factor present for one defender

D. Game Theory

34. Game Theory and the Analysis of International Conflict

John C. Harsanyi is Professor of Economics at the University of
California, Berkeley. A leading student of the theory of games, he outlines in this
article its basic premises and suggests some of the ways in which its application
to international politics and foreign policy can facilitate comprehension of the
subject. Game theoretical analyses can be quite technical and highly mathematical, but here Professor Harsanyi portrays in simple terms the logic that
underlies such inquiries. The close connection between game theory and the
strategic theories discussed in the previous selection is also evident in Professor
Harsanyi's account. [*Reprinted from* The Australian Journal of Politics and History,
*XI (December 1965), 292–304, by permission of the author and the University of
Queensland Press, St. Lucia, Queensland, Australia.*]

Game theory is a theory of rational behavior in the
face of opponents expected to behave likewise
rationally. Here by "rational behavior" we mean the
assumption that each participant (or "player") has
a set of well-defined and mutually consistent basic
objectives, and will choose his actual policies in
accordance with these objectives without any
mistake. In technical terms this means that each
player has a well-defined "utility function" expressing the value or "utility" he attaches to various
policy objectives, and that his actual behavior will be
fully consistent with this utility function.

This assumption of rational behavior of course,
if taken quite literally, is certainly unrealistic in many
situations. Policy makers are human and therefore
occasionally do make mistakes. Moreover, their
policy objectives are seldom quite consistent. For
one thing, when people have to choose between two
or more very unpleasant policy alternatives, they
often find it very hard to make up their minds
and follow any of these policies in a consistent

manner. For another thing, every policy maker is
subject to conflicting pressures from his own
constituents, and these may make it very difficult
for him to adopt any unambiguous policy line.

For instance, both in international and in
internal politics, one often has to choose between
trying to reach a mutually acceptable *agreement*
with one's opponents, and trying to keep them in
check by mere superior *strength*. But usually the
worst possible policy is to antagonize and provoke
one's enemies even further without the will and the
ability to face a showdown with them. Yet this is
precisely the irrational policy that many countries
have often been following against countries unfriendly to them.

However, in spite of such occasional inconsistencies and mistakes, if we observe a given
country's foreign policy over long periods, we can
usually discern some fairly stable and consistent
basic policy goals pursued by that country, subject
only to minor deviations. These basic policy goals

seem to undergo only very slow and gradual changes, except possibly at times of major transformations of revolutions in the country's own internal political system. Thus in many cases the assumption of rational behavior in the game-theoretical analysis of international politics can be regarded as a legitimate simplifying assumption, at least for the purposes of first approximation.

Indeed, apart from economic life, there are probably few areas of social behavior where rational calculation plays a more important part than it does in international politics. According to common observation, most foreign policy decisions are strongly influenced by weighing the advantages and the disadvantages likely to result from alternative policies; and this fact makes these decisions eminently susceptible to game-theoretical analysis. (In effect, game-theoretical analysis can be quite useful even in situations where some countries tend to follow rather inconsistent foreign policies as a result of conflicting internal political pressures. But of course in such cases we cannot regard each country as being *one* "player" but rather have to regard it as consisting of that many different "players" as the number of major political groups with radically different attitudes on foreign policy.)

I

Yet even as far as each country does follow a set of reasonably consistent policy objectives, some further problems still remain. It is not enough to know that each country follows consistent policy goals, we must also know *what* these policy goals actually are if we want to make use of game-theoretical analysis. Let us consider an analogy from ordinary parlor games. The game of checkers can be played in two different ways. Normally each player's aim is to "win" the game in the usual sense. But sometimes the game is played with the understanding that the player who "loses" the game (as judged by the usual rules) will win, and the one who "wins" will lose, so that each player's aim becomes to "lose" the game as fast as he can. Now suppose a game theorist wants to analyse the situation, either in order to *predict* what a given player's next move *will* be, or in order to *advise* him what his next move *should* be. Then clearly the predictions or advices of our game theorist will make sense only if he knows what the players'

actual *objectives* are—whether each player's aim is to "win" (as under the usual rules) or whether his aim is to "lose," since these two goals naturally will lead to quite contrary strategies on the part of the players.

Likewise, in international politics we can make predictions about various countries' likely policies, or can give sensible advice to foreign policy-makers, only if we can ascertain what each country's policy objectives actually are. Fortunately, in most cases it is not very hard to find out a given country's policy goals, at least in very general terms. Probably most countries pursue more or less the same general aims, such as national power and military security, as well as certain ideological goals depending on the country's own political creed. The trouble is only that it is not enough if we can simply enumerate all these policy objectives. We also have to know how much *weight* or *priority* a given country will give to its various objectives when it has to *choose* between them: and this is much harder to tell in advance.

For instance, if we want to predict the future behavior of the Soviet Union then the real problem is how much relative importance the Soviet government will actually give to the goal of increasing the standard of living of its own population, how much importance to various military objectives, and how much importance to helping communist parties abroad or to promoting nationalistic or socialistic revolutions in underdeveloped countries, etc. It is reasonable to assume that the Russian government is in fact interested in *all* these policy goals at the same time. But what we do not know is how far it is willing to go in sacrificing any one of these objectives for the sake of another.

Game theory as such can give us little help in predicting how much weight a given country will assign to its different policy objectives because game theory starts with the assumption that the various players' policy goals (utility functions) are *given*, and bases its own analysis on these given policy goals of the different players. Fundamentally, the only way we can infer a particular country's policy objectives is on the basis of its own past behavior (including of course verbal behavior on the part of its leading policy-makers—even though in general naturally we cannot take their policy statements simply at face value). But such inferences are always subject to a certain margin of doubt. On the one hand, a given pattern of past behavior may admit of interpretation in terms of several alternative hypotheses about a certain country's real policy goals. On the other hand, every country's policy goals are subject to continual change, and it may be very hard to judge how far this change has actually progressed at any given moment. For instance, we know that Soviet foreign policy has undergone certain important changes after Stalin's death. But Western experts find it very hard to decide how far these changes have actually gone with respect to the Soviet Union's basic policy objectives, and in particular with respect to the relative importance attached to any particular objective.

III

Let me now, however, leave all these difficulties on one side, and discuss some of the positive contributions game theory can make to our understanding of international politics.

A fundamental distinction in game theory is the classification of games into three main classes: games with *identical interests*, games with *opposite interests*, and games with *mixed interests*.

As an example for a game with identical interests, consider the two-person game having the payoff matrix presented in Example 1:

	B_1	B_2
A_1	(20,20)	(10,10)
A_2	(0, 0)	(5, 5)

Example 1

In this game player 1's strategies are A_1 and A_2 while player 2's strategies are B_1 and B_2. As can be seen from the above payoff matrix, the two players here always obtain equal payoffs: thus the more one player wins the more will the other player win also. Hence the two players' interests are exactly identical. If the two players are rational then player 1 will use strategy A_1 while player 2 will use strategy B_1, so that both players will obtain payoffs of 20 units each. Any other combination of strategies would

make both of them worse off. Thus in this situation there is no real problem. If the two players are rational enough to recognize the identity of their interests then they will surely cooperate in obtaining the highest possible payoffs for both of them.

In real life of course situations where two or more people's interests are *exactly* the same are not very common though there are many situations where they are at least *approximately* the same. But in any case the concept of games with identical interests is theoretically important because it represents one of the two extreme possibilities.

On the other extreme are games where the players' interests are exactly *opposite*. The most important example is that of *two-person zero-sum games*. In such games one player always wins exactly the amount the other player loses and vice versa. If one player's payoff is X then the other player's payoff will be $-X$, and so the two player's payoffs always add up to $X + (-X) = 0$. Hence the name "zero-sum game." Since each player's payoff is always the same as the other player's except for having the opposite sign, it is sufficient to indicate (say) player 1's payoffs in the payoff matrix. (Of course in Example 1 above it would also have been sufficient to indicate only one player's payoffs in the payoff matrix since the other player's payoff was always the same—indeed in that case there was not even a difference in sign.) Consider, for instance, the two-person zero-sum game having the payoff matrix presented in Example 2:

	B_1	B_2	B_3	Row Minima
A_1	15	10	18	10
A_2	9	3	11	3
A_3	20	6	7	6
Column Maxima	20	10	18	

Example 2

Now each player has three alternative strategies, those of player 1 being A_1, A_2, and A_3, while those of player 2 being B_1, B_2, and B_3. The payoff 10 resulting from strategy combination (A_1, B_2) represents both the *minimum* of row A_1 and the *maximum* of column B_2. Such a payoff is called a *saddle point*.

If *both* players act rationally then player 1's actual payoff will be exactly the payoff corresponding to this saddle point, viz. 10 units. For if player 1 acts rationally then his payoff cannot be *less* than that, since by using strategy A_1 he can always assure himself at least that much (as no number in row A_1 is less than 10). On the other hand, if player 2 acts rationally then player 1's payoff cannot be *more* than 10, either. This is so because player 2 by using strategy B_2 can always prevent player 1 from obtaining more than that (since no number in column B_2 is more than 10). But if player 2 *can* prevent this then he *will* (if he is rational), because the lower he can depress player 1's payoff the smaller will be his own loss. Thus player 1's payoff cannot be either less or more than 10: hence it will be *exactly* 10.

This means, however, that—if the two players expect each other to act rationally—then player 1's *best* strategy is A_1. For, as we have seen, he cannot expect to obtain *more* than 10. Hence he must concentrate on assuring at least *that much* for himself. But A_1 is the only strategy assuring him this amount (because rows A_2 and A_3 do contain numbers smaller than 10). For similar reasons, player 2's best strategy is B_2: no strategy can reduce his loss *below* 10 if his opponent acts rationally; but strategy B_2 at least ensures that his loss will not rise *above* this figure.

Two-person zero-sum games, as they represent the extreme case of games with opposite interests, are again a concept of great theoretical importance. But in real life few social situations represent two-person zero-sum games because in almost every case the participants will have *some* common interests. Many parlor games are two-person zero-sum games in that one player can win only if the other loses, and if the game is played for money then one player's money gain is the other player's money loss. (Yet even here the two players do have common interests e.g. in making the game mutually enjoyable.) But, neglecting parlor games, the only important social situation having the nature of a two-person zero-sum game is total war, i.e. a war where both sides are interested only in victory—at all costs whatever. But in practice even so-called total wars are not true two-person zero-sum games because the two sides do have a common interest in limiting the intensity of warfare (so long as this does not shift the balance of power in favor of the other side). For instance, in the second world war, which was called a "total war" and which certainly came closest to a total war among all armed conflicts in modern times, many international agreements were violated by one side or even by both sides. Yet *some* international conventions did enjoy general observance: for instance the use of poison gas was ruled out by mutual consent. Thus even in a "total" war, so called, there may be *some* limited cooperation between the two sides. (This of course means that even so-called "total wars" have not been really total wars in a literal sense.) Hence even in this case the model of a two-person zero-sum game can be applied only with important qualifications.

In any case, most social situations are neither games with identical interests nor games with opposite interests but clearly fall between these two extremes. That is, they are games with *mixed* interests, where the players' interests are similar in some respects and dissimilar in others. Therefore for the purposes of the analysis of real-life social situations the theory of mixed-interest games is the most important part of game theory. But it is also the most difficult part because games with mixed interests raise much harder theoretical problems than does either of the two extreme cases. For this reason the theory of games with mixed interests has been the last part of game theory to achieve a satisfactory analytical framework.

IV

In the case of two-person games we can represent the differences among the three main types of games geometrically as follows. Let us measure player 1's payoff u_1 along the horizontal axis and player 2's payoff u_2 along the vertical axis. Then any point u with coordinates u_1 and u_2 will represent one particular payoff combination, i.e. one particular conceivable outcome of the game. Any such point u in the $u_1 u_2$ plane is called a *payoff vector* and we can write $u = (u_1, u_2)$ where u_1 and u_2 are the coordinates of point u.

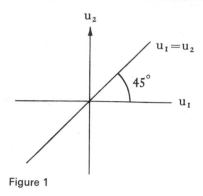

Figure 1

In the case of a game with identical interests, where both players always obtain equal payoffs, all possible payoff vectors will lie on the $u_1 = u_2$ line, which is the 45° line going through the origin (see Fig. 1).

In the case of a two-person zero-sum game, where the two players' interests are completely opposed, all possible payoff vectors lie on the $u_1 + u_2 = 0$ line, which is the −45° line drawn through the origin (see Fig. 2).

Finally, in the case of a game with *mixed* interests, the possible payoff vectors do not lie on the same straight line but are in general dispersed over a certain two-dimensional area. For instance, Fig. 3 represents a game where the possible payoff vectors are the points of the enclosed area ABCD, which we call the payoff space. In this game both players will have a *common* interest in moving out to the upper-right boundary ABC. For instance, *both* of them will increase their payoffs if they move from

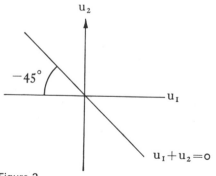

Figure 2

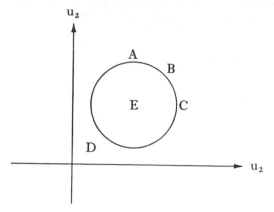

Figure 3

point E to a point like B which lies to the right from E and also lies higher than E. But the two players will have *opposite* interests in choosing among the various points of this upper-right boundary itself. For example player 1 will prefer C to B and will prefer both C and B to A while player 2's preferences will be exactly the other way round. This bears out our statement that the game is one of *mixed* interests: clearly the players' interests are partly similar and partly dissimilar.

In a game with *identical* interests, rational players will always fully cooperate because each of them can only lose by non-cooperation or by less than full cooperation.

In a game with *opposite* interests, such as a two-person zero-sum game, the players cannot usefully cooperate at all because they have no common interests they could promote by cooperation.

In contrast, a game with *mixed* interests usually can be played both as a *cooperative* game and as a *non-cooperative* game. One of the important tasks of game theory is to specify the conditions under which rational players will play a cooperative rather than a non-cooperative game or vice versa. It is at this point, also, where the conclusions of game theory have the most important implications for the analysis of international political situations.

V

Consider the two-person (non-zero-sum) game presented in Example 3:

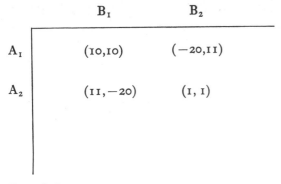

	B_1	B_2
A_1	(10,10)	(−20,11)
A_2	(11,−20)	(1, 1)

Example 3

Player 1's strategy A_1 and player 2's strategy B_1 will be called *cooperative strategies*, whereas player 1's strategy A_2 and player 2's strategy B_2 will be called *non-cooperative strategies*. This terminology is justified by the fact that each player will *help* the other player's interests by using what we call his cooperative strategy, and will *harm* the other player's interests by using what we call his non-cooperative strategy. (For instance, if player 1 himself uses strategy A_1, he will obtain the payoff $+10$ if player 2 uses the cooperative strategy B_1 but will obtain the payoff -20 if player 2 uses the non-cooperative strategy B_2. Again, if player 1 himself uses strategy A_2, he will obtain the payoff $+11$ if player 2 uses B_1 but will obtain only $+1$ if player 2 uses B_2. Thus, whichever strategy player 1 himself uses, he will be better off if player 2 uses the "cooperative" strategy B_1 than if player 2 uses the "non-cooperative" strategy B_2. Likewise, irrespective of the strategy player 2 himself uses, he will be better off if player 1 uses the "non cooperative" strategy A_2.)

The strategy combination (A_1, B_1) under which both players would use their cooperative strategies we call the *cooperative solution* of the game; while the strategy combination (A_2, B_2) under which both players would use their non-cooperative strategies we call the *non-cooperative solution*. Clearly the cooperative solution would be better for both players since it would yield both of them the payoff $+10$ while the non-cooperative solution would yield both of them only the payoff $+1$. In spite of this we shall now argue that the two players will actually use their non-cooperative strategies, so that the outcome will correspond to the non-cooperative solution, less preferred by both of them. We shall

argue that this will happen *in spite* of the fact, and indeed precisely *because* of the fact, that both players are assumed to be very rational individuals. This conclusion which we shall now try to establish is called the *Prisoner's Dilemma Paradox*. This name is used in the game-theoretical literature because the first example (proposed by Professor Tucker of Princeton University) for this paradoxical situation involved two prisoners, who had to choose between a cooperative strategy (not "squealing" on the other prisoner) and a non-cooperative strategy ("squealing"). The argument was that both prisoners will choose to "squeal," even though this will be disastrous for both of them.

The argument runs as follows. First let us consider the situation from player 1's point of view. If he expects player 2 to use the non-cooperative strategy B_2 then he himself will also use the non-cooperative strategy A_2, because by doing so he will obtain the payoff $+1$ instead of -20. But he will use his non-cooperative strategy A_2 even if he expects player 2 to use the cooperative strategy B_1!!! For by doing so he will obtain $+11$ while if he used his cooperative strategy A_1 he would obtain only $+10$. Thus, whatever player 1's expectations about player 2's behavior, he himself will always use his non-cooperative strategy A_2. By similar reasoning, player 2 will always use his non-cooperative strategy B_2. But the strategy pair (A_2, B_2) is the non-cooperative solution. This completes the proof.

Clearly a very crucial point in this argument is the fact that the payoff structure of the game rewards the player who himself uses a *non-cooperative* strategy when the other player uses a *cooperative* strategy. (Numerically in our example this "reward for double-crossing the other player" in this way is $11 − 10 = 1$ unit.) But this payoff structure in itself is insufficient to establish the conclusion. Our argument was crucially dependent on the tacit assumption that the rules of the game do not allow the players to conclude *binding* and *enforceable agreements*. For if the players could make such agreements then both of them could agree to use cooperative strategies, subject to heavy penalties for violating such an agreement. If these penalties were large enough to offset the "reward for double-crossing" inherent in the payoff matrix of the game (which in our case would mean penalties greater than one unit) then double-crossing would become unattractive to the players. Hence in this case each player could feel quite safe in using a cooperative strategy without the danger of being confronted by a non-cooperative strategy on the part of the other player.

Of course, the players' incentives to keeping agreements need not arise from *externally* imposed penalties for violations. The same effect will be achieved if the players' own *internal* moral attitudes are such as to make violations of agreements unrewarding. In this case we may say that violations of agreements are discouraged by the *interiorized penalties* (disutilities) associated with such violations. From a game-theoretical standpoint external and internal penalties represent the same basic mechanism: they reduce the net payoffs (net utilities) connected with strategies involving violations of agreements. (Here we define the "net payoff" as the "gross payoff" *less* the external and/or internal penalty.)

Thus we reach the following important conclusion. In games with mixed interests full cooperation between the players is possible only if they can trust each other's willingness to keep agreements; and this requires that agreements between the players should be fully binding and enforceable by means of external or internal penalties for violations. If agreements are enforceable in this sense then rational players will always play a *cooperative game*, i.e. will try to reach a cooperative solution. But if agreements are not enforceable, i.e. if the players have good reasons to distrust each other's willingness to keep agreements, then they will play a *non-cooperative game* and will reach a non-cooperative solution—in spite of the fact that the cooperative solution would make all of them better off. (Even in what we call a non-cooperative game there may be *some* degree of cooperation between the players, but their cooperation will be restricted to those fields where such cooperation does not require mutual trust.) Accordingly, if the players reach a non-cooperative solution *this may not mean that their behavior is irrational*: it may only mean that they mutually distrust each other, for which they may have very good rational reasons based on past experience. No doubt, acceptance of a non-cooperative solution is in a way always "irrational" when a mutually preferable cooperative solution would be available. But this "irrationality" may not involve any irrationality on the part of the players themselves,

but rather may be the result of their very rational behavior in what may be called an "irrational" social *situation*.

VI

For instance, we can interpret Example 3 as representing an international political situation, say, one involving a cold war between two countries. The cooperative strategies A_1 and B_1 might involve e.g. a substantial reduction in military preparations and other cold-war activities on the part of country 1 and country 2 respectively. The non-cooperative strategies A_2 and B_2 might correspond to maintaining a high level of military preparations and of other unfriendly activities. Both countries would be better off if the levels of their military and other unfriendly activities could be reduced by mutual agreement, tacit or explicit. But this may not be a practicable policy. In particular, it may happen that both countries would be very keen to double-cross each other if they thought they could get away with it, and both countries may know by bitter experience that this is the case. Then it will be perfectly rational for each side to distrust the other so long as the situation described persists.

Of course, it is quite possible that sometimes two countries *think* they must distrust each other though in actual fact this is not true or is true only to a much lesser extent. For instance, the two countries' political leaders may show much more intrinsic reluctance to double-dealing than they would credit each other with. Or alternatively each side's objective political disincentives against double-dealing may be much stronger than the other side might think, etc. In such cases their mutual distrust may possibly yield to increased information about each other's true attitudes and about each other's true political incentives, etc.

But in general we cannot expect that mutual distrust is merely a matter of mutual misunderstanding. Each side may very well find that it could achieve very *real* political advantages in terms of its own political objectives if it could successfully double-cross the other side; and the political leaders of each side may very well follow moral philosophies that make double-dealing quite permissible in international politics—possibly in all cases, or maybe only in the case of double-dealing against one's ideological opponents. (That is, they may take the view that "Promises given to Infidels or to Heretics or to Communists or to Capitalists, etc., do not count.") In such cases the situation cannot be remedied by more information (or by more goodwill) alone. A real improvement can come only from fundamental structural changes in the situation, such as by providing much stronger institutional incentives to keeping international agreements, i.e. by reducing the temptation to violating them; and by changing the basic attitudes of the chief policy makers, as well as those of the general public, toward violations of international agreements and of international law. Of course, such basic attitudinal and institutional changes cannot be achieved from one day to another. The political atmosphere must be prepared for them by first attempting mutual co-operation in minor matters such that do not presuppose a good deal of mutual trust, because they can be reversed without major damage if the other side turns out to be less cooperative or less reliable than one has hoped for.

Clearly, cooperation cannot be achieved merely by one side's willingness to cooperate; and so one must always be prepared for the possibility that the other side may not wish to go further than up to a certain point, at least for the time being. But of course one can never find out how far one can get on the road to mutual cooperation without ever trying a serious start.

To sum up, one of the important contributions of game theory to the analysis of international political situations is realization of the fact that virtually all mixed-interest games, without some mechanism to enforce agreements between the players, lead to a Prisoner's Dilemma Paradox. That is, they are situations where the players *may* have very good reasons to mistrust each other's intentions, so that even very rational players may be driven to the non-cooperative solution, even though the cooperative solution would yield higher payoffs to all of them. The non-cooperative solution will be reached, not because the players act irrationally, but precisely because they act in a rational manner.

This interpretation of international politics sharply contrasts with the view that wars, arms races, and other forms of international conflicts, are merely the results of the policy makers' irrationality, and therefore can be cured by a more rational approach and by better information about the underlying facts. For instance, a famous student of international conflicts, Lewis F. Richardson, who can be regarded as the very Founding Father of the modern analytical approach to the subject, argued that his own theory of international conflicts was "... a mere description of what people would do if they did not stop to think. Why are so many nations reluctantly but steadily increasing their armaments as if they were mechanically compelled to do so? Because ... they follow their traditions ... and their instincts ... and because they have not yet made a sufficiently strenuous intellectual and moral effort to control the situation."[1] If our own interpretation of international conflicts is right then this is an oversimplified and potentially very dangerous view. For it leads to serious underestimation of the political forces actually generating and maintaining international conflicts; and in particular it precludes understanding of the fact that, with the existing subjective attitudes towards violations of international agreements, and with the existing objective payoffs to countries and individuals violating such agreements, non-cooperative behavior may often be the only rational and realistic response to a given international situation. By this means it leads to underestimation of the need for fundamentally *changing* people's *attitudes* towards double-dealing in international politics and for fundamentally changing the *payoff* that people and countries can hope to achieve by such behavior.

VII

In Example 3, strategy pair (A_2, B_2), which we have called the non-cooperative solution, has the following important property. Strategies A_2 and B_2 are mutually the *best replies* to each other; so long as player 2 uses strategy B_2, player 1 will maximize his own payoff by using strategy A_2, and conversely, so long as player 1 uses strategy A_2, player 2 will maximize his own payoff by using strategy B_2. Accordingly, strategy pair (A_2, B_2) represents a *stable* situation: once the two players come to adopt this pair of strategies, neither of them will have any incentive to shift to some other strategy. For this reason we call this strategy pair an

[1] Lewis F. Richardson, *Arms and Insecurity*, Chicago and Pittsburgh: The Boxwood Press and Quadrangle Books, 1960, p. 12.

equilibrium point. More generally, we speak of an equilibrium point whenever each player's strategy is the best reply to the strategies used by all the other players, so that none of the players can gain by changing over to some other strategy so long as the other players do not do so. It is easy to check that in Example 3 the strategy pair (A_2, B_2) is the *only* equilibrium point in this sense. If the players adopted any other strategy pair then at least one (or both) of them could gain by shifting to another strategy, even if the other player did stick to his own strategy without any change. For instance, strategy pair (A_1, B_1), which we have called the cooperative solution, is unstable because e.g. player 1 could gain by shifting from A_1 to A_2 if player 2 used strategy B_2, etc. It is easy to verify that the remaining two strategy pairs (A_1, B_2) and (A_2, B_1) are likewise unstable and do not have the nature of equilibrium points.

We can now state our previous conclusion in the following form. In a non-cooperative game, where the players cannot conclude enforceable agreements, only an *equilibrium point* can represent a stable situation. That is, a stable situation can obtain only if each player's strategy is a *best reply* to the other players' strategies, so that no player will have any incentive to revise his strategy choice. This means that the players cannot adopt a cooperative joint strategy not having the nature of an equilibrium point, even if adoption of this joint strategy would be very advantageous to all of them (such as would be adoption of strategy pair (A_1, B_1) in our example).

As we have already argued, if we want to enable the players to adopt such a more desirable cooperative joint strategy then we must transform the non-cooperative game into a cooperative one by making all agreements fully binding and enforceable—or at least we must change the payoff matrix of the game so as to make the desired cooperative joint strategy an equilibrium point.

This theoretical conclusion may sometimes lead to paradoxical policy proposals. For instance, Professor Morgenstern[2] has made out a strong case for the view that, once the United States has a strong nuclear retaliatory force, it is in her own interest that the Soviet Union should *also* possess one. Otherwise the Soviet Union would feel so

insecure as to be tempted to *start* a nuclear war whenever she had the slightest suspicion that the United States might have offensive intentions. In game-theoretical terminology, if *both* nuclear powers had the capability of striking *first* but only *one* side had the capability of striking back *after* a nuclear attack, this would result in a dangerously *unstable* situation, which both sides have an interest to avoid.

Another implication is that in a non-cooperative game any disturbance may easily destabilize an existing equilibrium situation,[3] and eventually may lead to a new equilibrium situation less favorable to a given player than the old one was. Hence the players will always be wary of changes in the existing situation. For example, if one player demands concessions—even quite minor ones—from another these usually will be bitterly resisted because the other player will fear that any concession he may now grant will be used only to extract still further concessions from him in the future. Therefore a very important aspect of bargaining skill will be always to reassure the other party that one has only *limited objectives*, and that if one's present demands are now granted this will not be used as a leverage for demanding further and further concessions on later occasions.

For instance, in many cases the employers' resistance to recognizing their employees' trade unions was largely due to the fact that the employers did not know how far the unions would try to encroach upon managerial prerogatives and managerial decision making; and recognition was much more readily forthcoming as soon as a union succeeded in convincing the employer that its interests were in fact limited to improving wages and working conditions within the capitalistic institutional framework.

Likewise in international life one of the main purposes of diplomacy must be in many cases to convince the opponent that one's aims are limited to obtaining certain specific concessions, and do not involve any more fundamental changes in the relative power positions—at least when in fact this is the case. This is of course only another aspect of the general conclusion that in a non-cooperative game the most important policy objective is to overcome

[2] O. Morgenstern, *The Question of National Defense,* New York: Random House, 1959.

[3] To a lesser extent this is true also in cooperative games.

the justified mutual distrust existing between the players.

VIII

In a sense all these and other conclusions of game-theoretical analysis are based on one general principle, which can be stated as follows. Rationality requires that each player *himself* should have a set of consistent policy objectives, and should not try to run in two different directions at the same time. Rationality also requires that each player should choose his strategies consistent with the *expectations* he can rationally entertain about *other* players' behavior. For instance, in a two-person non-cooperative game each player must expect that a rational opponent will try to select a strategy that is a *best reply* to his own strategy. Again, in a bargaining game a given player cannot expect that a rational opponent will grant him a certain concession, if in the same situation he himself would refuse a similar concession because, under given conditions, he would not regard it as a rational policy to grant such a concession, etc.

In effect, the main advantage of the game-theoretical point of view is precisely to make us systematically aware of such considerations. It enables us to formulate in more precise terms what it means to act intelligently, and what it means to base our policies on intelligent expectations concerning other intelligent people's reactions to our own policies.

E. Influence Theory

35. Inter-Nation Influence:
A Formal Model*

J. David Singer addresses himself in this article to some of the same problems that concern students of strategy and game theory, but he does so at a more general theoretical level. While strategic and game theoretical analyses tend to be organized mainly around the potential or actual use of force in the interaction of nations, Professor Singer extends the scope of inquiry to all forms of influence. Furthermore, he does not ignore the problem posed by the fact that influence is extraordinarily difficult to trace empirically. He does not solve this problem, to be sure, but his analysis provides methods for resolving it, as well as valuable insights into the operation of influence processes at the international level. [*Reprinted from* American Political Science Review, *LVII (1963)*, *420–30, by permission of the author and the publisher.*]

Students of international politics often state that power is to us what money is to the economist: the medium via which transactions are observed and measured. Further, there seems to be a solid consensus that power is a useful concept only in its relative sense; such objective measures as military manpower, technological level, and gross national product are viewed as helpful, but incomplete, indices. The concept does not come to life except as it is observed in action, and that action can be found only when national power is brought into play by nations engaged in the process of influencing one another. Until that occurs, we have no operational indices of power, defined here as the *capacity to*

* This paper was originally prepared for the International Studies Division of the Institute for Defense Analyses, and is now released for publication. The views expressed are not necessarily those of the Institute, the Arms Control and Disarmament Agency, or the Department of Defense. The author wishes to thank Caxton C. Foster for his assistance both at the conceptual and the graphic level, and Lloyd Jensen for help in surveying the literature on social power.

influence. In this paper, then, my purpose is to seek a clarification of the concept of power by the presentation of a formal, analytical model of bilateral inter-nation influence.

Two caveats, however. First, I am using the word "model" in its most modest sense; I mean somewhat more than a conceptual framework, but considerably less than a theory. If, by theory, we refer to a body of internally consistent empirical generalizations of descriptive, predictive, and explanatory power, it is much less than a theory. And since it is not a theory, there is no need to label it "normative" or "descriptive"; it is merely analytical, with normative or prescriptive implications.

Second, it represents in no sense the result of a systematic search of the historical past from which we might draw empirical generalizations. Nor is it a systematic survey of those other analogous worlds from which such generalizations might be drawn: the experimental or empirical literature of psychology, sociology, or anthropology.[1] Recourse to all of these worlds would be valuable, but would go beyond the task I have set myself here. Moreover, such empirical investigations are best not undertaken until we have a clear picture of the sorts of data we seek. To do so in the absence of such a picture might produce some interesting anecdotes, and an occasionally valuable insight, but it would open no direct path toward a body of empirically "verified" and logically consistent propositions of such explanatory power or predictive reliability as to be useful for either theory building or policy purposes. Until these prior model-building steps have been taken, any comprehensive search of the historical literature would be little more than a fishing expedition, or a ransacking of the past in search of support for *a priori* convictions.

In attempting this preliminary examination of inter-nation influence, I will begin with a search for clarification of the central concepts and variables; then suggest a systematic linking of them; follow this with a search for some general rules about the role of reward and punishment and promise and threat; and conclude with a discussion of the particular limits and uses of threat.

I. Some General Properties of Influence

In trying to clarify what we mean by influence, and to articulate its dominant properties, the first point to be noted is that all influence attempts are *future-oriented*. The past and present behavior of the potential influenc*ee* (whom we will label B) may be of interest to A (the influenc*er*) and will certainly affect A's predictions of B's future behavior, but there is nothing A can do about controlling such actions. He[2] may *interpret* the past and present

behavior of B in a variety of ways, but obviously he can no longer *influence* it.

The second general observation is that influence may or may not imply a modification of B's behavior. While the tendency (there are exceptions) in both political science and social psychology is to define an influence attempt as one in which A seeks to *modify* the behavior of B, or to identify A's influence over B in terms of "the extent to which he can get B to do something that B would not otherwise do," there are several objections to this restricted meaning.[3] One is that it excludes that very common form of influence which we might call perpetuation or "reinforcement."[4] That is, it overlooks the many cases of inter-personal and inter-group influence in which B is behaving, or is predicted to behave, in essentially the manner desired by A, but in which A nevertheless attempts to insure the continuation of such behavior, or the fulfillment of the prediction, by various influence techniques.

The second (and more elusive) objection is that it implies no difficulty in A's prediction of what B will do in the absence of the influence attempt. If A could, with a very high degree of confidence, predict how B will act if *no* attempt to modify or

---

[1] The worlds of the diplomatic past and the experimental present may both be called analogous to that of the diplomatic present in that neither is an exact replication, yet each has a number of important similarities to it. In some respects, one might even find that the small group experiment provides a closer replication of the present international system than does the international system of the 18th or 19th centuries. See J. David Singer, "The Relevance of the Behavioral Sciences to the Study of International Relations," *Behavioral Science*, Vol. 6 (October 1961), pp. 324–35.

[2] Throughout this paper, we will often use the singular personal pronoun to denote a nation, but it will always be understood that the nation is not a person and is not capable

of perceiving, predicting, and preferring in the literal psychological sense. Thus all designations will, unless otherwise specified, refer to those who act for and on behalf of, the nation: the foreign policy decision makers. We are not, however, accepting the proposition of the "methodological individualists," who deny the empirical existence or conceptual legitimacy of the group or nation. Their point of view is articulated in Floyd H. Allport, *Social Psychology* (Boston, 1924), while two persuasive refutations are Ernest Nagel, *The Structure of Science* (New York, 1961) and Charles K. Warriner, "Groups are Real: A Reaffirmation," *American Sociological Review*, Vol. 21 (October 1956), pp. 549–54.

On the choice of the nation-as-actor, see Arnold Wolfers, "The Actors in International Politics," in W. T. R. Fox (ed.) *Theoretical Aspects of International Relations* (Notre Dame, University of Notre Dame Press, 1959) and J. David Singer, "The Level of Analysis Problem in International Relations," *World Politics* Vol. 14 (October 1961), pp. 77–92.

[3] This definition is tentatively employed in Robert A. Dahl, "The Concept of Power," *Behavioral Science*, Vol. II (July 1957) pp. 201–15; Dahl tends to use "power" and "influence" interchangeably. The emphasis on change or modification is also retained by John R. P. French and Bertram Raven, "The Bases of Social Power," in Dorwin Cartwright (ed.) *Studies in Social Power* (Ann Arbor: Institute for Social Research, 1959) pp. 150–67.

[4] We will use this word in its generic sense, rather than in the various specialized ways found in such psychological theories as conditioning, learning, and S-R.

reinforce is made, then reinforcement measures would be unnecessary and influence would only be attempted when changes (from predicted to preferred) are sought. For a multitude of reasons, ranging from the complexity of the international system to the theoretical poverty of the disciplines which study that system, such predictability is a long way off. Consequently, A will tend to seek insurance against the possibility of an error in his prediction as long as he is modest in evaluating his predictive abilities.

This leads in turn to a third difficulty, if not objection, which is the probabilistic nature of all predictions. Even if the "state of the art" in international relations were well advanced, there would still be no *certainty* (probability = 1.0) on the part of A that B will behave in the predicted fashion. Consequently, there will always be some incentive to attempt to influence.

Having made the case for both the modification and the reinforcement types as legitimately belonging in the influence attempt category, however, it would be misleading to suggest that they are of equal significance in international relations. The fact is that if A's decision makers are *reasonably confident* that nation B either *will* behave in a fashion *desirable* to A or *not* behave in an *un*desirable fashion, the incentive to attempt to influence B will diminish, and A may conserve its limited skills and resources for application elsewhere. As the forces at work in A's foreign policy processes move A's decision makers in a pessimistic direction, there will be an increasing application of A's available resources to the influencing of B, until the point is reached where A predicts that *no* influence attempt would be successful.

A third preliminary observation is that internation influence is far from a one-way affair. In the first place, while A is planning or attempting to influence B, B is itself exercising some impact on A's behavior. The very classification of B by A as a potential influencee immediately leads to some degree of influence by B upon A, even when B makes no conscious influence attempt. And in the second place, the international system is neither a dyad (duopoly) nor a multitude of dyads. For analytical purposes, it is often convenient to scrutinize only two nations at a time, but we cannot forget that all are influencing all, directly or indirectly, merely by sharing the same spatial, temporal, and sociopolitical environment. Thus, the system is characterized not only by reciprocity but by multiple reciprocity. For the sake of simplicity, however, we will restrict the analysis which follows to direct bilateral relationships between nations of more or less equal power, in which influence or influence attempts are a conscious effort of the national decision makers.[5]

Finally, we might distinguish between an influence *attempt* and the *outcome* of such an attempt. Not only are they not the same phenomena, but they are described and measured in terms of different variables. An influence attempt is described primarily in terms of: (a) A's *prediction* as to how B will behave in a given situation in the absence of the influence attempt; (b) A's *preference* regarding B's behavior; and (c) the techniques and resources A utilizes to make (a) and (b) coincide as nearly as possible. The outcome of such an attempt will be a function not only of (c) above, but also (d) the accuracy of A's prior prediction; (e) B's own value, utility, or preference system; (f) B's estimate of the probabilities of various contemplated outcomes; (g) B's resistance (or counter-influence) techniques and resources; and (h) the effects of the international environment.

II. The International System as an Influence Environment

Before turning to more refined characteristics of influence, let us place its general properties, as noted above, in their larger setting within the international system.

The fact that nations invest a great deal of their energies in attempts to influence one another is perfectly obvious, but *why* this should be so is somewhat less apparent. One of the most frequently recurring themes among the peace-makers is that all would be well if nations would only "live and let live."

[5] "Power" may be measured in a multitude of ways: relative or absolute, perceived or objective, potential or present; and many criteria may be used in making such measurements. Furthermore, the distinction between "fate control" and "behavior control" made by John W. Thibaut and Harold H. Kelley in *The Social Psychology of Groups* (New York, 1959) is quite relevant here. Thus, the U.S. certainly has the power to decide the ultimate *fate* of Cuba, for example, but lacks the power to exercise effective and continuing control over Cuba's day-to-day *behavior*.

The naïveté of this prescription becomes evident, however, when we recall that such a doctrine can only be effective if one of the following conditions is present: (a) each nation is so completely isolated from all the others that the activities of one have almost no impact on the others; or (b) each is so completely self-sufficient that it has no dependence upon the goals or behavior of the others in order to meet its own "real" and perceived needs. Neither of these conditions characterizes the international system, and it is doubtful whether they ever did. Not only do nations rely heavily upon one another for the commodities (tangible and otherwise) which are sought after, but it is extremely difficult for any nation to trade with or steal from another without this inter-action having some impact on some third party.

But this is only part of the story, and it is the part which is equally applicable to relations among many other forms of social organization. The international system has another characteristic which distinguishes it from other social systems: each actor has the legal, traditional, and physical capacity to severely damage or destroy many of the others with a considerable degree of impunity. In inter-personal, inter-family or other inter-group relations, regardless of the culture, normative restraints and superior third-party governors are sufficient to make murder, plunder and mayhem the exception rather than the rule. But in inter-nation relations the gross inadequacy of both the ethical and the political restraints make violence not only accepted but anticipated. As a consequence, the scarcest commodity in the international system is security—the freedom to pursue those activities which are deemed essential to national welfare and to survival itself.

To be more specific then, we might assert that under the survival rubric the highest priority is given to autonomy—nations are constantly behaving in a fashion intended to maximize their present and future freedom of action and to minimize any present or future restraints upon that freedom. In such a system, no single nation can afford to "live and let live" as long as the well established and widely recognized anarchic norms are adhered to, acted upon, and anticipated by, most of the others. Any social system must contain some inevitable competition and conflict, but in the international system

they are handled in a more primitive fashion. Moreover, there seems to be only the barest correlation between the way a nation pursues its interests and the nature of its leadership or its socio-political institutions. To suggest otherwise would be, to quote an excellent analysis of the problem, to commit the "second-image fallacy."[6] Rather, we might more accurately conclude that the international system itself is the key element in explaining why and how nations attempt to influence the behavior of one another.

III. Perceived Behavior as a Determinant in Influence Attempts

Though the international system is definitely one in which influence and counter-influence attempts are a dominant characteristic, our interest is in analyzing the factors which tend to produce any given such attempt. The first prerequisite for an influence attempt is the perception on the part of A's decision-makers that A and B are, or will be, in a relationship of significant interdependence, and that B's future behavior consequently could well be such as to exercise either a harmful or beneficial impact on A.

Not too long ago, most nations were in such a relationship with only a handful of other nations. Even in today's highly interdependent world, one still finds, for example, little interaction between Paraguay and Burma or Egypt and Iceland. Moreover, no nation has the resources to engage in serious efforts to influence a great many of the others at any given time; we select our influence targets because of the perceived importance of our relationship to, and dependence upon, them. In addition, there is a particular tendency to concentrate such efforts upon those nations with which we are already in a highly competitive and conflictful relationship, devoting far fewer resources to those with whom our relations are either friendly or negligible.

Not only do our perceptions of interdependence and conflict-cooperation strongly determine whom we will attempt to influence, but, as subsequent

[6] See Kenneth N. Waltz, *Man, the State, and War* (New York, Columbia University Press, 1959) and the review article based on it: J. David Singer, "International Conflict: Three Levels of Analysis," *World Politics*, Vol. 12 (April 1960), pp. 453–61.

sections will suggest, they affect the types of influence attempt we will make and the likelihood of success or failure in that attempt.

IV. Predicted Behavior as a Determinant in Influence Attempts

The second determinant is that of the *predictions* which A's decision-makers reach regarding the nature of B's future behavior: what is B likely to do, in the absence of any conscious influence attempt by A? This expectation may be of two rather distinct types. One deals with the affirmative *commission* of an act, and the other deals with the more passive *non-commission* or *omission* of an act. In the first case, illustrations range from the American expectation that, in the absence of any conscious influence attempt by ourselves, India might endorse a troika arrangement for arms control supervision, to the fear that the Soviet Union might employ military force in an effort to drive us out of Berlin. In the second case, we think of such examples of non-commission or failure to act as Germany *not* meeting its ground force commitment to NATO, or mainland China *not* participating in a disarmament conference to which it had been invited. Though one can often describe expected acts of *omission* as ones of *commission* (i.e., Germany *refusing* to draft more soldiers or China *rejecting* the conference bid), and with somewhat greater conceptual straining even describe acts of commission in the semantics of omission (India *not rejecting* the troika, or the USSR *not refraining from* force) one or the other of these two emphases is almost always more obvious and salient to the influencer, as discussed in the next section.

V. Preferred Behavior as a Determinant in Influence Attempts

Finally, and perhaps most important, there is A's *preference* regarding B's future behavior. Without preferences, the perception of B's present behavior and predictions regarding his future behavior have only limited importance to A and would exercise only a minor impact on A's tendency to invest in an influence attempt. Here we might illustrate by reference to the contingent predictions suggested above. The United States prefers that India *not* accept the troika plan, and that the Soviets *not* use force in Berlin; we care much less what administrative arrangements New Delhi *does* accept, or what other techniques the Kremlin *does* apply in Berlin. Our main concern is that they *not* do the specified, but partially likely, act from among a number of possible acts. For us, removing or reducing the likelihood of what they *might* do is much more salient than which one of a host of alternative acts they select in its place. Conversely, the concern of our decision-makers (as the potential influencers) over what the Germans do *not* do with their limited manpower, or what the Chinese do *not* do regarding a disarmament conference is much less than our concern that they *do* engage in the act which we prefer. The salience of what they *do* do is higher for us than the salience of what they do *not* do, because of the nature of our preferences.

To illustrate this crucial distinction further, let us suppose that A predicts that B is about to supply weapons to an insurgent group opposing the government of an ally of A's; A's concern is not so much what else B does with these weapons as with seeing that B does *not* supply them as predicted. B might, at this juncture, scrap them, sell them to a neutral nation outside the immediate conflict area, or give them to an ally, and A would have a much less intense concern over which of these alternatives B selected. In another—and very real—case, A might want desperately to prevent its major adversary B from supplying nuclear weapons to an ally of B with whom A has had a number of disastrous military encounters in the past. Whether B gives these nuclear weapons to another ally, converts them for peaceful uses, or retains them in its own arsenal is of much less moment than that they *not* be supplied to the feared recipient. In both these cases, avoiding or preventing a specific outcome is of considerably greater salience to the influencer than is the remaining range of alternatives open to B.

VI. Perception, Prediction, and Preference: Their Composite Effect

So far, we have discussed individually the way in which A's perceptions, predictions, and preferences will tend to move him toward an influence attempt *vis-à-vis* B. What are the implications of combining these three sets of variables? More particularly, what are the possible combinations, and what is the effect of each upon: (a) the motivation of A to undertake an influence attempt, (b) the relative amount of effort required for success, and (c) the techniques and instruments A will employ?

As the following chart will indicate, there are eight possible combinations of influence situations, four dealing with cases in which A prefers that B *do* a certain act (X) and four in which A prefers that B *not* do a particular act, but do almost anything else (non-X or O) instead. The first four might be called *persuasion* cases, and the latter four *dissuasion*. Since each of these eight cases would seem to pose a different type of influence problem for A and call for varying combinations of techniques, let us list and label them as in Fig. 1.

In cases 1 through 4, A prefers that B do act X, and in cases 5 through 8, A prefers that B *not* do act X, but do O (anything else but act X). Cases 1 and 5 are relatively simple and normally would call for no impressive influence attempt: B not only is already acting or not acting as A prefers, but the prediction is that such behavior will continue into the relevant future. Cases 2 and 6 are, however, slightly more interesting: again B's predicted behavior is seen as congruent to that which A prefers in the future, but A observes that for the moment B's behavior is different from the preferred or predicted. And in cases 3 and 7, B's present behavior *is* what A prefers, but the prediction is that it will *not* remain so without any effort on A's part. Finally, in cases 4 and 8 we have the most difficult situation for A: he perceives B not only as not behaving as preferred, but as unlikely to do so in the future, without some effort on the part of A. These, then, are the eight typical situations confronting a potential influencer, ranged more or less in order of increasing difficulty.

VII. The Influencee's Decisional Calculus

Having examined the varieties of influence situations, we should notice one other consideration prior to evaluating the range of techniques available to the influencer in these situations. This is the influencee's decisional calculus: the abstract dimensions upon which he (*i.e.*, those individuals who, alone or together, act on behalf of the target nation) weighs a range of conceivable outcomes in any influence situation. For every outcome which any decision-maker can conceive of as possible, there are at least two such dimensions. The degree to which he likes or dislikes the prospect is called the *utility* or *disutility*, and the likelihood which he assigns to its ever occurring is called the *probability*. Both of these are, of course, subjective variables: preferences and predictions of the influencee (B).

In the abstract, the combined judgments which the influencee makes along both of these dimensions will determine his contingent expectations and thus his response to the influence attempt. Before combining them, let us examine each in somewhat more detail. As to the subjective utility dimension, we proceed from the assumption that an individual or a group does—implicitly or explicitly—have a set of benchmarks by which it is able to arrange conceivable outcomes (be they threatening, rewarding, or more typically, both) in some order of preference. These benchmarks usually derive from value systems and goal structures and, though they are by no means uniform from nation to nation, those relevant to foreign policy behavior tend to have a great deal in common. For example, outcomes

	Persuasion Situations: A Prefers X				Dissuasion Situations: A Prefers O			
	1	2	3	4	5	6	7	8
Preferred Future Behavior	X	X	X	X	O	O	O	O
Predicted Future Behavior	X	X	O	O	O	O	X	X
Perceived Present Behavior	X	O	X	O	O	X	O	X

Figure 1. Types of influence situations

that appear to restrict short-range freedom of action will almost invariably be placed very low in any such utility scale; they will be assigned a high *dis*utility score. Conversely, those which seem likely to minimize the power of some other competing nation (A, C, or D), and hence reduce that competitor's capacity to restrict one's own (B's) freedom, are normally rated high on utility. If we go much beyond these basic drives of nations, however, we get into the peculiar webs of their secondary goals and their varying formal and informal ideologies.

We may pause, though, to point out that national preferences are by no means fixed and permanent. Not only do successive parties and factions in a particular nation bring differing preference structures into office, but even the same sub-group or individuals undergo value changes while in power. Consequently, we must not overlook the usefulness to A of seeking to induce attitudinal (especially value and preference) changes in B's elites as an alternative means of influencing B's existing preferences, or of seeking to change them now in order to make it easier to appeal to them later.

Nations do not, however, commit themselves to actions merely because one possible outcome of such actions seems to be extremely attractive or because it may avoid an extremely *un*attractive outcome. No nation has the unlimited resources and skills which such behavior would require. They must compare these possible outcomes not only in terms of a *preference* ordering, but also in terms of their estimated *likelihood*. And just as there are important differences between nations in the matter of assigning utilities and disutilities, there are equally important (but more subtle) differences when it comes to assigning probabilities to future events. Some are more willing than others to play the "long shot," and pursue an objective whose probability of attainment may be quite low. On the other hand, there do seem to be strong similarities here, as in preference ordering. A perusal of recent diplomatic history strongly suggests that most nations are remarkably conservative in foreign policy; *i.e.*, they seldom commit resources and prestige to the pursuit of an outcome which seems improbable—no matter how attractive that outcome may be. Individuals, on the other hand, reveal far greater ranges of risk-taking propensities, with many getting a large measure of psychological

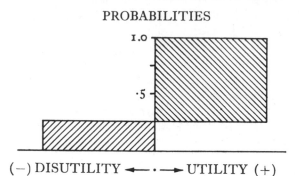

PROBABILITIES

1.0

·5

(−) DISUTILITY ◄— · —► UTILITY (+)

Figure 2. Influencee's decisional calculus

satisfaction from the low-probability-of-success decision.[7]

The point which concerns us here, however, is that—despite idiosyncrasies on one or the other dimension—nations *combine* both sets of considerations in responding to an influence attempt or in any other choice situation. In graphic terms, we might depict this combining process as in Fig. 2.

Suppose that A is attempting to influence B by the use of threatened punishment in order to deter B from pursuing a certain goal (i.e., A is trying to induce *O*). If B attaches a high utility to the outcome which he is pursuing while the threat which A makes would—if carried out—constitute a loss whose disutility is of approximately the same magnitude, these two considerations will tend to cancel out and the important dimension becomes the probability of each outcome actually eventuating. If B estimates that the probability of A carrying out the threatened punishment is quite low (let us say .25) and that he therefore has a .75 probability of pursuing his goal *without* A executing the threat (perhaps its cost to A is seen as quite high) the resultant product would tend to make B adhere to his original intention. Though he realizes that there is *some* chance that A will act to punish him, the combined probability and disutility is so much less than the combined probability and utility of A's *not* acting, that B decides to take the gamble.

This is, of course, a rather abstract model, and it not only deviates from the kinds of articulate, as

[7] See Ward Edwards, "Utility and Subjective Probability: Their Interaction and Variance Preferences," *Journal of Conflict Resolution*, Vol. 6 (March 1962), pp. 42–51.

well as implicit, calculations which policy makers employ, but it over-simplifies the choice situation with which nations are ordinarily confronted. For example, B must normally weigh his utility-times-probability product against not only the disutility-times-probability of A's *threatened* punishment but against a range of greater or lesser punishments which A is capable of inflicting and against the probability of each of these occurring.[8] Furthermore this model assumes that choice situations and influence attempts, as well as their possible outcomes, occur at discrete and identifiable moments in time. The assumption is extremely useful for analytical purposes, but it pays insufficient attention to the overlapping and highly unpredictable time scale along which such situations and alternate outcomes may occur. Finally, it ignores three important quantitative considerations. One of these is the relative weight which a given set of decision-makers might assign to each of the two dimensions; in their implicit fashion, nations do differ in the degree to which they emphasize either the probability or the preference element in their appraisal of an outcome. Moreover, these two dimensions are by no means psychologically independent; the more highly valued an outcome is, the greater the tendency to exaggerate the probability that it can be achieved (the wish is father to the thought), and conversely, when a probability looks very low, the tendency will be to downgrade the attractiveness of the associated outcome. Thirdly, there is the tendency toward polarity: as subjective probabilities move up or down from .5 they will be exaggerated in the direction of either the certainty (1.0) or the impossibility (0.0) end of the scale. Recognizing these limitations does not, however, invalidate this influencee's decisional model. It merely reminds us that it cannot be employed for either descriptive or predictive purposes in a purely mechanical way. But used in a careful, self-conscious fashion it can be helpful to both the study and the execution of the decision process. For the scholar, much of the confusion and mystery of that process could be clarified, and for the policy maker, regardless of the weights and values he attaches, it could identify the range of alternatives and indicate the implications of each. It might even lead to consideration of a larger number of alternatives and hence mitigate one of the greatest causes of diplomatic disaster—the prematurely restricted repertoire.

VIII. Influence Techniques

Up to this juncture, we have delineated some of the general characteristics of inter-nation influence, identified its three major dimensions alone and together, and articulated a sub-model of the influencee's decisional considerations. Now let us turn to the two broad classes of technique available to the influencer: threat and promise. Each may be used either to modify or to reinforce, although, as we shall see later, not with equal efficacy. Each has an appropriate role, but careful choice must be made in determining which is best suited to the various classes of influence situation.

By *threat* we mean the communication to the influencee (B) by the influencer (A) that if a certain preferred act (X) is not taken, or non act (O) is not avoided by B, there is a given probability that A will act to punish B in a particular fashion. That punishment may take the form either of withholding a reward, denying a preference, or positively damaging that which B values.[9]

By *promise* we mean the communication to B that if he complies with A's preference, A will with some given probability, act to reward B. Again, that reward may range from withholding a contemplated punishment to the enhancement of one or more of B's values and preferences.

Threat and punishment and promise and reward go together, but the distinction must be constantly kept in mind. Threat and promise refer to nothing but contingent, probable future events, while punishment and reward are concrete acts that already have taken, or are in the process of taking, place. Thus punishments and rewards may be threatened or promised respectively, and they may be contemplated by both A and B, but they have

---

[8] Among the outcomes to be considered are those which might impinge on the domestic setting or upon one's allies or any Nth powers.

[9] One quite successful attempt has been made to draw an analytic distinction between punishment and denial, but it seems less relevant here. In *Deterrence by Denial and Punishment* (Princeton, Center of International Studies, 1959) and in *Deterrence and Defense* (Princeton University Press, 1961) Glenn Snyder refers to retaliation as punishment, while denial refers to the costs inflicted upon B (the deterree who was not deterred) while trying to gain his military objective.

none of the empirical concreteness in a future situation that they have in past or present situations.

In inter-nation influence, reward and punishment for past or ongoing behavior may be said to serve primarily as a link between B's experiential present and his anticipated future. The outcomes which accompany particular actions in B's past and present serve as predictors of such associations in the future. Therefore, the use of rewards and punishments by A should be devoted, among other aims, to increasing the *credibility* of the promises and threats which he transmits to B. This is not to suggest that credibility-building is the only relevant use for reward and punishment in attempting to influence an opponent of approximately equal power. Present-oriented techniques might also serve the supplementary purposes of (a) hastening an influencee's *shift* from non-preferred to preferred behavior, or (b) reinforcing current preferred behavior if there is some indication that it might not continue.

Be that as it may, we have little evidence at this point to justify any confident generalizations regarding the applicability of the four types of influence technique to the eight classes of influence situations. Let me therefore pause briefly in order to hypothesize, before going on to suggest what next needs to be done to develop a coherent theory of inter-nation influence. Given the speculativeness of these hypotheses and the limitations of space, let me present them in the form of a chart which is merely an extension of Figure 1.

In Figure 3, we have added five rows to the original three. Row 4 emphasizes that cases 1, 3, 5,

and 7 are reinforcement or behavior stabilization situations, in which A, regardless of his predictions, prefers that B's future behavior remain as it is in the present. Conversely, cases 2, 4, 6, and 8 are modification or behavior change situations, again disregarding A's prediction of B's future behavior.

Then in rows 5 and 6 we ask whether punishment and reward (our present-oriented techniques) are relevant to each of these, while in 7 and 8 the question is whether the future-oriented techniques of threat and promise have any applicability. In situations 2 and 6 and 1 and 5, the ambiguous entry (P for "perhaps") is meant to suggest that A's confidence in his prediction regarding B's future behavior will be controlling. If, in the two ambiguous modification situations (2 and 6) A's subjective probability that B will change without any influence attempt is not satisfactorily high, A might consider punishment as an appropriate technique. Likewise, in the two ambiguous reinforcement situations, A's lack of confidence in the prediction that B will continue his present behavior might well impel him to utilize threat as a form of insurance.

IX. Some Experimental Possibilities

Can the hypotheses in Figure 3 be confirmed or disconfirmed? Clearly, the preferable long-run method of proof would lie in direct testing within the international system, and though the bona-fide experiment is hardly a routine matter in this area, some modified form of it seems possible. I refer to the so-called *ex-post-facto* experiment, in which we determine some reasonable and fixed limits in time

	Persuasion Situations: A Prefers X				Dissuasion Situations: A Prefers O			
	1	2	3	4	5	6	7	8
Preferred Future Behavior	X	X	X	X	O	O	O	O
Predicted Future Behavior	X	X	O	O	O	O	X	X
Perceived Present Behavior	X	O	X	O	O	X	O	X
Reinforce or Modify	R	M	R	M	R	M	R	M
Punish?	No	P	No	Yes	No	P	No	Yes
Reward?	Yes	No	Yes	No	Yes	No	Yes	No
Threaten?	P	Yes	Yes	Yes	P	Yes	Yes	Yes
Promise?	Yes	Yes	Yes	Yes	Yes	Yes	Yes	Yes

Figure 3. Hypothesized relevance of influence techniques

and space, and then devise the criteria by which our population of influence situations is selected. From that population we then sample in such a manner as to get a sufficient number of each of our eight classes of influence situation. Of course, the difficulty here is in setting up and refining the operational rules by which we identify each of these situations in the ongoing welter of diplomatic history so as to permit reliable classification by two or more independent coders. Once the experimental cases are selected, we then go on (again with operationally articulated criteria) to determine which influence techniques were used in each. Following that, we measure—with either a simple yes-no dichotomy or (at later stages in the study) a graduated scale—B's compliance with A's preference. By correlating our predicted influence attempt outcomes with those observed in the "experiment" we get a test of the hypotheses generated by the model.

If this particular project worked out satisfactorily, a more nearly "natural" experiment, involving *pre*diction rather than *post*diction, could be attempted. In this case, we would want to ascertain the applicability of our historical findings to the real world of the present, by classifying some sample of influence situations as they unfold, and then actually predicting the attempt outcomes before they are known.[10] The central problem in either of these "real world" types of study is that of developing, pre-testing, and applying measures or indices of an operational and unambiguous nature. Until we have devised a means for recognizing and recording perceived, predicted, preferred, and actual outcomes, such experimental research is impossible.

While the development of measures for the key variables in inter-nation relations goes forward—and it is doing so at much too slow a pace—another possibility remains. Systematic data-gathering with relatively operational classification and measurement criteria has been going on in sociology and social psychology for several decades. As a consequence, these disciplines have accumulated a respectable body of empirical generalizations regarding inter-group and inter-personal influence. These generalizations, moreover, have two possible linkages to a

theory of inter-nation influence in particular and inter-nation relations in general. The more useful one is that of empirical inputs into the inter-personal and inter-group interactions which occur in the foreign policy decision process. There is no reason to expect that the findings in industrial, academic, community, or other social settings should be too disparate for application to the inter-personal and inter-group influence processes which obtain in governmental policy processes. Enough inference is called for, however, to preclude any automatic assumption that the results will be identical in, for example, business firms and foreign ministries.

Requiring a somewhat longer inferential leap would be the effort to analogize directly from our inter-personal and inter-group results to internation influence situations. Though this sort of extrapolation is often more legitimate than the naive critic would have us believe, one must first demonstrate a high degree of isomorphism between the setting which produced our data and that to which the generalizations are to be applied. But whether one employs the indirect or direct application of these psychological and sociological findings, it should be clear that they cannot suffice for confirmation or disconfirmation of our hypotheses. The final test must be made with data from the real world of inter-nation relations.

X. The Limits and Uses of Threat

Despite these caveats, it might nevertheless be useful to examine some of the propositions that emerge from the inter-personal and small group literature, in order to suggest their possible relevance. For these illustrative purposes, let me summarize and speculate upon some of the empirical findings regarding one of the four major influence techniques: threat. First, what do these inter-personal experiments suggest regarding the dysfunctional effects of this future-oriented influence technique?

The most obvious undesirable side effect of threat is that it may often do no more than "modify the form of anti-social behavior which is chosen."[11] In other words, by making one path of behavior which is undesirable to A seem unattractive to B, A

---

[10] Some suggestive versions of such a technique are advocated in Richard C. Snyder and James A. Robinson, *National and International Decision-Making* (New York: Institute for International Order, 1960), pp. 30–34.

[11] Alex Comfort, *Authority and Delinquency in the Modern State* (London, Routledge and Kegan Paul, 1950), p. 74.

may merely drive B into other behavior which, while more attractive to B than the action which has been associated with impending punishment, is equally undesirable to A. And for A to threaten B for so wide a range of anticipated acts could either exceed A's capabilities or create such a dilemma for B that he has no choice but to carry out the action and accept (or retaliate for) the consequences.

As to the effect of threat on B's capacity to respond rationally, a number of disturbing findings appear. First of all, threat often exercises a negative influence on B's capacity to recognize signals and communications accurately. Not only might B become less able to identify and respond to neutral messages, but he may also lose some of his ability to recognize subsequent threats. Thus, threats might well make it difficult or impossible for A to convey the very messages upon which his capacity to influence B must rest.[12] An equally dysfunctional result is that of "cognitive rigidity:" the inability of B to respond efficiently and adequately to changing stimuli, and a consequent breakdown in B's problem-solving capacity.[13] This experiment also suggests that the ultimatum is a particularly dangerous form of threat, inasmuch as the subjects dropped markedly in their capacity to respond appropriately when the experimenter reduced the time allowed for making that response.

Similar results were found when subjects were threatened with a physical shock. The threat of this highly undesirable possibility produced a high level of stress and markedly hampered their problem-solving capacity.[14] The stress induced by threat has also been reported as not only degrading an actor's predictability but his own confidence in that predictability as well.[15]

On the other hand, there is a tendency among some observers of international relations to exaggerate the dysfunctional effects of threat and to ignore the very real role it does and must play in the contemporary international system. These critics forget that most of the influence and social control situations from which they analogize take place in an ordered, hierarchical environment in which influence is normally based on legitimate authority, recognized roles, and accepted norms. To illustrate, one of the more thorough analyses of social power lists five major bases of such power: reward power, coercive power, legitimate power, referent power, and expert power.[16] Of these five, reward often requires more resources than are found in a highly competitive influence relationship between equals, legitimate power can only be exercised through the frail channels of international law or organization, referent power is generally absent between rivals, and expert power is seldom recognized by national decision-makers. Coercion via threat is, by process of elimination, one influence technique upon which we must continue to rely until we have markedly modified the international system.

A point worth noting in this connection has been demonstrated in a number of experiments on group performance under varying degrees of stress. The results "indicated that the performance of the group was best under mild stress."[17] If threat produces stress (as we assume), the absence of threat may often be as detrimental to successful influence attempts as too heavy a dose of it. The lesson seems to be to use enough threat to generate stress, but not so much as to produce high anxiety. If the upper threshold is crossed (and it varies from nation to nation and situation to situation) we are likely to generate the sort of undesirable effects which reduce B's rationality. The less rational B is, the less likely he is to consider the entire range of alternative actions open to him, and the less likely he is to analyze adequately the implications of each such alternative. Anxiety induced by excessive threat may be said to contract B's repertoire of possible responses as well as his ability to predict the payoffs associated with each.

In the same vein, we have some experimental results which indicate the impact of threat upon

[12] Charles D. Smock, "The Relationship Between Test Anxiety, Threat-Expectancy, and Recognition Thresholds for Words," *Journal of Personality*, Vol. 25 (1956), pp. 191–201.

[13] Sidney Pally, "Cognitive Rigidity as a Function of Threat," *Journal of Personality*, Vol. 23 (1955), pp. 346–55.

[14] Robert E. Murphy, "Effects of Threat of Shock, Distraction and Task Design on Performance," *Journal of Experimental Psychology*, Vol. 58 (1959), pp. 134–41.

[15] Alvin Landfield, "Self-predictive Orientation and the Movement Interpretation of Threat," *Journal of Abnormal and Social Psychology*, Vol. 51 (1955), pp. 434–38.

[16] John R. P. French and Bertram Raven, "The Bases of Social Power," in Dorwin Cartwright (ed.), *Studies in Social Power* (Ann Arbor, Institute for Social Research, 1959).

[17] John T. Lanzetta, "Group Behavior Under Stress," *Human Relations*, Vol. 8 (1955), pp. 29–52.

group cohesiveness. While it is generally true that external threat exercises a unifying effect, there are some important exceptions, and when cohesiveness in B is reduced, some serious problems arise.[18] Admittedly, internal divisions may lead to a diminution in B's power *vis-à-vis* A, thus enhancing the credibility of threat even further. But on the other hand, a drop in B's relative power is not necessarily a percursor to compliance. Moreover—and this is a frequently overlooked consideration—the creation of divisions within B may make an intelligent response to A's influence attempt almost impossible. When B's top elites are in firm control of their nations, they are more capable of (a) making rational choices and (b) making the concessions necessary to A's successful influence attempt. Conversely, when they are preoccupied with critics, conspirators, and powerful "inevitable war" factions at home, they must resist influence attempts in order to stabilize their shaky power base.

Another point that seems to emerge in regard to the role of threat, (and to a lesser extent, promise) is that B must be provided with two categories of information. One is the precise nature of the action which A prefers to see B take (X) or avoid (O); without this information B is unable to respond in a mutually advantageous fashion. The other is the availability of alternatives, and this is particularly relevant in the dissuasion situation.[19] For A to try to dissuade B from a given action (to induce O) when B must clearly do X or something similar to X, without helping B to ascertain which O acts are available to B and acceptable to A, is to call for a probable showdown. If B is completely thwarted, he has little choice but to resist.

Also worth considering, in terms of the limitations of threat, is the fact that A may well be able to modify B's decisional calculus in the appropriate fashion and still fail in his influence attempt. Even

though, in the time period implied by the effort to modify or reinforce, B might find A's preferences the most attractive alternative behavior for himself, he may nevertheless refuse to comply. The explanation lies primarily in the context of longer-range considerations on B's part: precedent. B (or A, when in the B role) may be concerned that this compliance under threat will set a precedent. Each time that B does the rational thing and complies with the preferences of A, he increases A's propensity to believe in the efficacy of threat, and to utilize it again and again. As a result, B has an additional reason to do the thing which is, in the specific and discrete influence situation, irrational. Moreover, B must combine his refusal to comply with a more-or-less immediate counter-influence effort, in order to compel A to re-allocate those resources which might otherwise be used to carry out his threat. In a simplified way, this is what an armaments race boils down to: threat and counter-threat coupled with the drive toward ever-increasing military capabilities with which to resist these threats.

XI. Conclusion

Without laboring the need for an empirically based theory of inter-nation influence, it should not be amiss to note that its lack is both a cause of intellectual embarrassment to political science and a menace to the human race. For the policy-maker to select intelligently from among a wide range of alternative decisions, he must be able to predict their outcomes with *some* degree of reliability. Such prediction requires far more than the "hunches" by which we operate today; having no sound criteria for behavior choices, the policy-maker will tend, as he has in the past, to adopt those policies which have the most powerful or persuasive advocates, regardless of the accuracy (or even the existence) of the "theory" upon which those policies are allegedly based. And as long as the nations continue to base their policies on so flimsy a foundation, our understanding will be incomplete, our predictions unreliable, and our policies deficient. I would not want to exaggerate the reliability of any theory we might build, nor minimize the difficulties of injecting it into the policy process, but neither we nor our adversaries of the moment can afford these present deficiencies. The probabilities of error are already much too high, and the disutilities could be disastrous.

[18] For example, Albert Pepitone and Robert Kleiner, "The Effects of Threat and Frustration on Group Cohesiveness," *Journal of Abnormal and Social Psychology*, Vol. 54 (1957), pp. 192–99.

[19] Daniel Katz, "The Functional Approach to the Study of Attitudes," *Public Opinion Quarterly* Vol. 24 (1960), pp. 163–204. Note that this does not preclude the use of influence by ambiguity; it calls for clarity regarding A's preferences but permits ambiguity regarding A's behavior if B does not comply. Highly suggestive in this regard is Thomas C. Schelling, "The Threat That Leaves Something to Chance," in *The Strategy of Conflict* (Cambridge, Harvard University Press, 1960).

36. Stability and Sudden Change in Interpersonal and International Affairs*

Dean G. Pruitt is Associate Professor of Psychology at the State University of New York at Buffalo. The author of a number of important inquiries into the psychological dimensions of international politics, Professor Pruitt probes here the effect of one actor's behavior on another and shows the similarity between the effects experienced by international actors and individuals. Even more significantly, the ensuing analysis reveals that a multiplicity of interaction patterns can mark the relations of states and that the stability of any of the patterns may be more subject to external influence than is often thought to be the case. [*Reprinted from* The Journal of Conflict Resolution, *Vol. 13 (March 1969), by permission of the author, the Center for International Security and Conflict Studies at the State University of New York at Buffalo, and the publisher. Copyright 1969 by the University of Michigan.*]

This paper was developed with the aim of contributing to theory about the relations between pairs of nations. Nevertheless, its focus is considerably broader, involving relations between two parties (i.e., decision-making units) of any kind, whether nations, organizations, groups or individuals. Quite clearly there are differences among the kinds of parties just enumerated. But there are also similarities which, hopefully, make it possible (and if possible indeed desirable) to develop broader generalizations embracing all kinds of parties.

* The ideas in this paper were first presented to and critiqued by a faculty seminar of the Center for International Security and Conflict Studies of the State University of New York at Buffalo. An earlier version, "Reaction Systems and Instability in Interpersonal and International Affairs," appeared in Buffalo Studies, IV (1968), 3–28. Preparation of the manuscript was supported by the Office of Naval Research by means of Contract NOOO 14–67–C–0190.

Reciprocation, Stability, and Sudden Change

Various dimensions can be used to describe the action that one party takes toward another; e.g., amount of smiling, level of attention, number of units of a commodity shipped, level of tariff charged, amount of money spent on armaments. Within certain limits, one end of such a dimension is usually more beneficial to the other party and the other end more costly; e.g., up to some limit, the more one person smiles the happier will be another person to whom he is talking.

Change in one party's level of output on a given dimension often produces *reciprocation* (also called reciprocative change), i.e., a resulting change in the other party's level of output on the same or another dimension. Frequently the other party matches both the direction and the dimension of the first party's movement. For example, research evidence suggests that increases in the intimacy of one person's remarks produce increases in the intimacy of his companion's remarks (Taylor, 1965; Tognoli, 1967). Changes in rate of smiling also tend to be reciprocated in kind (Kendon, 1967). In international affairs, increases in expenditure on arms tend to be matched, and escalation on the battlefield is often met by escalation. Sometimes the other party matches the direction of the first party's movement (i.e., whether benevolent or malevolent) but not the dimension. For example, a reduction in the percentage of his salary which a husband brings home to his wife may be reciprocated by a reduction in the quality of the wife's cooking. In international affairs, military sanctions may be employed in retaliation for economic restrictions. Occasionally, the direction is reversed in reciprocation; e.g., the response to verbal attack is sometimes greater warmth, and military escalation sometimes produces political concessions.

Various efforts have been made to explain reciprocation, particularly the kind in which direction is matched. Gouldner (1960) speaks of a "norm of reciprocity," which requires that "people should help . . . and . . . not injure those who have helped them" (p. 171). Pruitt (1965, 1968) has discussed the strategic and emotional advantages of matching benefits and costs produced by the other party. Homans (1961) has attempted to explain reciprocation in terms of stimulus-response learning theory.

However, even if single instances of reciprocation were well understood, it would still be necessary to explain the various ways in which reciprocative changes are *sequenced over time*. One finds *vicious circles*, in which the two parties alternate providing increased cost to one another. An example would be an arms race. *Benevolent circles* are also found, in which the two parties alternate providing increased benefit to one another. An example might be the sequence of political moves in 1963 which led to the Soviet-American détente (Etzioni, 1967). Vicious and benevolent circles sometimes move rapidly. At other times they slow down and stop or even reverse. An example of a reversal might be a typical lovers' spat. After a period of escalating costs on both sides, one side mismatches the other's most recent initiative by responding in a repentant or

forgiving way. This starts a reverse spiral back to friendly relations. The result of such an excursion may well be a return to the same level of mutual benefit that had previously obtained.

The last example leads into a discussion of the relationship between *stability* and *change* in the level of output on one or more dimensions.

It is important to recognize that stability and change are not totally incompatible in matters that have to do with living organisms. In most stable situations, the level of output on the relevant dimension(s) does not stand perfectly still but rather oscillates around some *equilibrium point*. In the relations between two parties, such oscillation often takes the form of mutually canceling sequences of reciprocative change, i.e., a vicious circle followed by a benevolent circle or a benevolent circle followed by a vicious circle. The lovers' spat described above is a typical example, involving a brief excursion toward unfriendly relations followed by a return to the status quo. Another example, involving the dimensions of trust and responsiveness in international relations, has been given by the author in a previous publication (Pruitt, 1965, p. 421):

During the Suez Crisis, both the United States and Great Britain greatly antagonized one another. First Britain failed to notify the United States of its intention to use arms; then the United States put pressure on the British to halt their invasion. A vicious circle seemed to have begun and, for some time thereafter, trust and responsiveness were at a low ebb. But then the system returned to its earlier level, and trust and responsiveness were fully reconstituted.

Temporary changes of the kind just described, that are part of oscillatory cycles around a stable equilibrium, can be distinguished from basic changes in which the equilibrium point itself is altered, i.e., where the parties do not return to their earlier levels of output on the dimensions involved. Basic changes often develop gradually, but the most interesting kind occurs quite suddenly: a war erupts (e.g., World War 1), lovers abruptly part, a man precipitously leaves the Communist Party. Sudden basic changes seldom come without warning, but they move relatively fast at the appointed hour.

This brings us to a specialized definition of stability and instability which will be employed in the balance of the paper. Instability is defined as the *likelihood of sudden (basic) change* and stability is defined as the opposite of instability.

The ultimate causes of sudden change are often complex and remote, but the immediate antecedent of such change is frequently an excursion by one party *that goes too far along some dimension*, producing a *runaway* vicious or benevolent circle. In common parlance, we say that one party has "gone beyond a point of no return" or has provided for the other a "straw that broke the camel's back." For example, lovers may be unable to return to a mutually rewarding equilibrium in their relationship once one of them has gone to the length of using his fists instead of simply yelling at the other. The international system in 1914 was presumably unable to return to its former equilibrium once Russia had gone so far as to mobilize its troops on the German border (Russett, 1962).[1] It follows that instability can be further defined as the likelihood that a party will move "too far" on a relevant dimension.

The purpose of this paper is to provide a geometric interpretation of reciprocation and the way reciprocative changes are sequenced over time, based on the writings of Richardson and his followers,[2] and to interpret the notions of stability and instability within this framework. Reciprocation is first interpreted in terms of "reaction functions." Then "reaction systems," in which two reaction functions are combined, are employed to interpret sequences over time. Next a particular reaction system, involving *S*-shaped curves, is examined in depth. The dynamics of this system permit an interpretation of sudden change and hence of

[1] The discussion of stability and change in the last four paragraphs is partially inspired by Ashby's (1960) analysis of an adaptive system. Such a system has "feedback" mechanisms that cause "essential variables" to return to their "resting states" when they have been displaced—in other words that produce oscillation around a stable equilibrium. Some of the variables in such a system may behave as "step functions," i.e., when one such variable reaches a "critical state," it may cause other variables to change rapidly and radically, altering the resting states. This resembles our notion of sudden change which results from an excursion that goes too far along a critical variable. It should be noted that Ashby's analysis applies to all adaptive systems, including certain kinds of machines such as the thermostat.

[2] Authors who have been inspired by Richardson's initial analysis of the arms race include Abelson (1963), Boulding (1962), Brody and Vesecky (1967), Caspary (1967), Intriligator (1964), and Smoker (1963). Boulding's work has been especially important in the development of the present paper. Richardson's own presentation of his ideas (Richardson, 1960) is quite technical. A more readable version will be found in Rapoport (1960).

stability and instability. Finally a number of hypotheses are advanced about the determinants of stability, which are based on the dynamics of this system.

Reaction Functions

Figure 1 portrays a variety of generic *reaction functions*. These show the level of action on any dimension which party Y would prefer to emit (i.e., would emit if he had time) in response to party X's level of action on the same or another dimension. The usual convention in such diagrams is for both the abscissa and the ordinate to run from greater benefit for the other party to greater cost for that party. For example, the left-hand end of the abscissa might represent complete economic cooperation from X and the right-hand end might represent extreme economic competition. The bottom end of the ordinate might represent a disarmed Y and the top end a fully armed Y. For the sake of convenience, the curves in Fig. 1 have been drawn in the upper right-hand quadrant, but they can be drawn in any other quadrant or passing through the boundary(ies) between two or more quadrants, depending on the kind of behavior involved.

In his basic analysis of the arms race, Richardson (1960) employed straight-line functions, such as function *A* to represent the effect of one nation's annual armament expenditure on its adversary's preferred annual expenditure.

Caspary (1967) has suggested that negatively accelerated growth curves, of the kind shown in function *B*, may be more appropriate for Richardson's purpose. He argues that economic considerations make it harder to increase military expenditure the larger this expenditure already is. A negatively accelerated growth curve follows logically from this argument. A similar point might be made about two men yelling at each other. The louder person X yells, the louder will person Y respond. But Y's yelling capacity has an upper limit; and the closer he approaches this limit, the harder it will be for him to produce additional volume. Hence, the effect of X's loudness of yelling on Y's loudness of yelling is likely to follow a negatively accelerated growth curve.

Function *C* is a positively accelerated growth curve. Intriligator (1964) has suggested that such a function may be useful for describing the accumula-

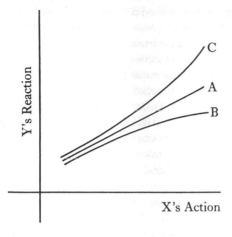
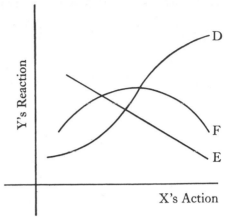

Figure 1. Six reaction functions

tion of nuclear weapons by a nation that seeks a first strike capability, while function *B* may be appropriate to a nation that seeks only to deter such a strike. Function *C* may also be useful for describing the way in which many people (Y) react with verbal or physical expressions of anger in the face of abuse from another person (X). People often react minimally to mild abuse, "taking it in their stride," as it were. But beyond a certain level of abuse, they begin to get angry; and their anger mounts (at least within a certain range) at an increasing rate.

Pruitt (1965) has suggested, in addition, that a positively accelerated growth curve like *C* may be characteristic of defensive reactions (e.g., arming) to challenge from another nation that has previously been trusted. The positive acceleration may result from increasing distrust. At a low level of challenge from nation X (e.g., mobilization of a small number of troops), the trust built up in earlier interactions may prevent the leaders of nation Y from seeing X as a potential threat. Hence their reaction is minimal. But as the level of challenge from X increases, their trust begins to wear thin, and they increasingly interpret X's actions as harbingers of a future threat for which they must prepare.

It should be noted that the sequence of events described in the last paragraph has a *starting point* at the bottom end of function *C*, where X is minimally challenging and Y maximally trusting and hence minimally defended. The slowly rising lower portion of function *C* might be thought of as reflecting a psychological "effort" on the part of the

leaders of state Y to preserve as long as possible their initial picture of nation X. Such psychological conservatism is characteristic of human beings. It satisfies their need to believe in an orderly, predictable world.

This need for predictability also implies the appropriateness of a curve like *function B* if the starting levels of challenge from X and response from Y are at the upper (conflictful-distrustful) end of the curve. A minimal reduction in challenge from nation X would have little effect on basic perceptions (i.e., distrust) in nation Y and, hence, little effect on Y's defensive preparations. It would take a relatively large demonstration of good will from X to cause very many leaders in Y to question their basic distrust of X and significantly change their behavior toward X.

Holsti (1962) has analyzed one example of the psychological conservatism underlying the slowly declining upper portion of function *B* in a striking study of John Foster Dulles' verbal reactions to tension-reducing moves on the part of the Soviet Union after 1953. He argues that Dulles habitually defended himself from recognizing these tension-reducing moves for what they were by attributing them to political or economic weakness on the part of the Soviet Union. In addition, a proposal has been advanced by Osgood (1962) for radical tension-reducing moves on the part of the United States which would break through the distrust that Soviet leaders feel toward the United States and, essentially, move these leaders into the steep lower portion of function B, where they would presumably make decisive reductions in their defensive preparations. In the Holsti example, Dulles is party Y and the Soviet Union is party X. In the Osgood example, the Soviet leaders are party Y and the United States is party X.

S-shaped functions like D may well turn out to be very common because they combine the features of B and C. This point can be illustrated with the example mentioned earlier of the effect of X's abuse on Y's anger in interpersonal relations. This example was given in connection with function C which reasonably describes reactions to low and moderate levels of abuse. But at higher levels of abuse, a curve resembling function B may be more appropriate, since anger must have an upper limit, the closer one gets to that limit the more costly it is to become more angry. Hence, function D, which looks like C at lower levels and B at higher levels, seems the most likely candidate for describing the entire relationship between abuse and anger. Function D will be heavily stressed later in this paper in the discussion of stability.

Functions like E involve an inverse correlation between the cost imposed by X on Y and that imposed by Y on X. Such a function is characteristic of a successful threat; e.g., the more fear-inspiring the punishment proposed by a parent (X), the more rapidly is a small boy (Y) likely to pick up his toys.

Inverted U-shaped functions were employed by Richardson (1960) in his analysis of "submissive" reactions. Boulding (1962) also uses such functions, arguing that one party will often match another's hostility for low levels of hostility, but "as the hostility of the other party increases beyond a certain point, the first party will become cowed and its hostility will diminish" (p. 32).

The material presented in this section can be linked to the first part of this paper by observing that the various reaction functions shown in Fig. 1 imply different patterns of reciprocation. The advantage of employing such functions in our theoretical analysis is that they express the notions of reciprocation a good deal more precisely than we were able to do earlier in words. Such precision is probably necessary for an understanding of the ways in which reciprocative changes are sequenced over time, a topic that will now be discussed.

Reaction Systems

The next step in the analysis is to put two reaction functions together. If Y's actions can be expressed as a function of X's, X's actions can also be expressed as a function of Y's, and the two functions can be presented in the same space, as shown in Figs. 2 and 3. The contents of this space can be called a *reaction system*. Richardson's (1960) basic analysis of the arms race was based on the systems shown in Fig. 2, which employ straight-line functions. The line $y = f(x)$ represents the level of expenditure on arms

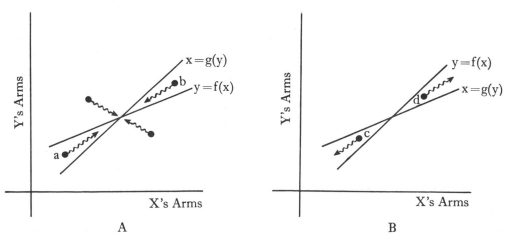

Figure 2. Two Richardson reaction systems. System A has a stable equilibrium and system B an unstable equilibrium

which the leaders of nation Y would consider appropriate for every level of expenditure made by nation X. The line $x = f(y)$ represents the same thing for the leaders of X as they view nation Y's expenditures. It should be recalled that these lines represent the *preferred* expenditure on arms, i.e., the expenditure to which each nation would move if it had time, rather than the *actual* expenditure. The latter can be called the *joint location*[3] and is exemplified by points a, b, c, d. The equations from which Richardson derived his straight lines imply that the joint location moves more rapidly toward a line the further it is from that line.

At the point where the two lines intersect, the leaders of both nations will be satisfied. This point is comparable to an equilibrium in physics in that it can be stable or unstable. If stable, as in Fig. 2A, expenditures on both sides will always move to this point, no matter where they begin. The reader can demonstrate this for himself by starting anywhere in the space shown in Fig. 2A, moving vertically first toward line y (Y's preferred position), then horizontally toward line x (X's preferred position), then vertically again toward y, and so on. Eventually he must reach the equilibrium point. The same point will be reached if he moves first horizontally instead of vertically. The wavy lines in this and subsequent figures illustrate such patterns of movement from various possible points of origin. If the equilibrium is unstable, as in Fig. 2B, joint expenditures will either increase indefinitely or decrease to zero, depending on where they start. The reader can also demonstrate this for himself, using the method described above. Whether the equilibrium is stable or not depends on the product of the slopes of the two lines.[4] If the product of these slopes is less than 1, the system will be stable; if equal to or greater than 1, it will be unstable.

The reaction systems shown in Fig. 2 exhibit all of the sequences of reciprocal changes described in the first section of this paper. Vicious circles, that move toward greater expenditure on arms, can be seen in the movement proceeding from points a and d. In case a, which approaches a stable equilibrium

point, the vicious circle slows down and eventually stops when it reaches the equilibrium. In case d, on the other hand, the circle accelerates over time.[5] Benevolent circles, that move toward reduced expenditure on arms, originate at points b and c. In case b, the circle slows down and stops, while in case c, it speeds up (presumably until it reaches the point at which neither side has arms). The system shown in Fig. 2A is also capable of exhibiting oscillation around a stable equilibrium, in which a vicious circle turns into a benevolent circle or vice versa. This happens if a *momentary force* (i.e., a temporary condition),[6] acting on one party, pushes the joint location away from the equilibrium point. The other party will respond in kind, starting what looks like a vicious or benevolent circle. But as soon as the momentary force is dissipated, a circle will ensue in the opposite direction, and the joint location will return to its former equilibrium point.

Momentary forces, which move the joint location away from an equilibrium point, can be contrasted with *fundamental forces*, which determine the locations and shapes of the reaction functions and hence affect the location of the equilibrium point(s). Actually the distinction is not very sharp, being a matter of degree of permanence. Momentary forces are more temporary and fundamental forces more permanent. The exact interpretation of these terms must vary from one application of the model to another.

Reaction systems are not, of course, limited to joint expenditures on arms. The axes in Fig. 2 might be relabeled "volume of shouting," or one axis might be labeled "amount of spanking by parent" and the other "level of disobedience by child." (In accordance with the convention established earlier, such variables are oriented on the axes so that they run from less to more prejudicial to the interests of the other party.) The shapes of the functions might also, of course, be changed. Any of those shown in Fig. 1 can be used, and others as well. Two differently shaped curves can be included in the same space. Quite a few varieties are presented by Boulding (1962).

---

[3] Richardson's term for the joint location was "representative point." His term for reaction function was "equilibrium line."

[4] The slope of each line is, of course, calculated with respect to its own abscissa.

[5] Richardson believed that the arms race before World War I was of this kind. His data revealed that the rate of growth in expenditures on arms increased linearly over time, as predicted by the model.

[6] Richardson called momentary forces "temporary influences."

S-Shaped-Curve Reaction Systems

In Fig. 3 is shown a system consisting of two S-shaped curves. The reader will recall that we gave reasons earlier for assuming that the S-shaped curve is a very common reaction function. In addition, a reaction system composed of S-shaped curves has the interesting property of permitting an interpretation of sudden change and hence of stability and instability, as defined earlier.

This system has *three* equilibrium points. The ones at the bottom and top are stable, since the products of the slopes of the curves at these intersections are less than 1. The middle point is unstable, since the same product is greater than 1. Hence, there are two locations in the space that are much more likely to be occupied than any other: the upper and lower equilibrium points.

Although the unstable middle equilibrium point is of little intrinsic significance, the dashed lines proceeding from it are noteworthy. These lines can be called *boundaries*. They divide the space into four quadrants, each of which has special characteristics. If, at any time, the joint location is in quadrant 1, the dynamics of the system cause it to move to the lower equilibrium point. A similar conclusion can be reached about quadrant III, where the dynamics of the system cause the joint location to move to the upper equilibrium point. There is less certainty about what will happen in quadrants II and IV, but something can be said about them.

Assume that the joint location is initially at the lower equilibrium point in Fig. 3. Momentary forces may move this location anywhere in quadrant I and it will return to the lower equilibrium point when these forces dissipate. In other words, so long as it stays within the boundaries of quadrant I, the joint location merely oscillates around the lower equilibrium point. But suppose instead that a momentary force, acting on party X, moves the joint location horizontally across the boundary to point *a* in quadrant IV. If this force dissipates rapidly, the joint location may be able to "scramble" back horizontally into quadrant I with nothing lost. But if this force is maintained for a long enough time, party Y will increase its level of action along the path shown moving upward from point *a*, and the joint location will enter quadrant III. There X will react escalatively to Y's reaction, and the (now "runaway") vicious circle will continue until it reaches the upper equilibrium point, *even if the momentary force that started the sequence now dissipates.*

The same conclusion can be reached about a momentary force, acting on party Y, which moves the joint location vertically from the lower equilibrium point to point *b* in quadrant II. Unless this force dissipates rapidly, a runaway vicious circle will develop in which the joint location will move to the upper equilibrium point.

The same kind of reasoning applies, of course, to a process that starts at the upper equilibrium point. So long as the joint location stays in quadrant III, it will return (at least periodically) to the upper equilibrium point. But if a momentary force should move the joint location into quadrants II or IV and keep it there for a while, a runaway benevolent circle will ensue in which the joint location moves into quadrant I and, thence, to the lower equilibrium point.[7]

[7] Richardson's model of the unstable arms race employs a concept "barrier" which is similar in some ways to the concept "boundary" used here. His barrier would be analogous to a straight line running through the unstable equilibrium from somewhere in quadrant II to somewhere in quadrant IV. The dynamics of his system, which are more thoroughly specified (in a set of equations) than the dynamics of the present system, cause the joint location to move downward if it starts on the southwest side of the barrier and upward if it starts on the northeast side. Hence there are no regions of uncertain outcome such as quadrants II and IV in the present system. A model of the trade cycle, put forward by Kaldor (1940), resembles in some ways the S-shaped curve reaction system presented here.

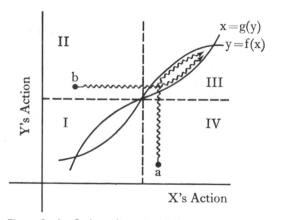

Figure 3. An S-shaped curve reaction system

The reader will undoubtedly have surmised by now that *sudden change* is represented in this system by movement from one equilibrium point to the other. Such change takes place when one party moves too far along a relevant dimension, just as in many real-life cases. Definitions of stability and instability follow logically from this analysis. But first, for greater clarity, two concrete cases will be described that can be construed as illustrating some of the dynamics of this reaction system.

The first case is drawn from an experiment performed in a boys' camp by Sherif and others (1961). The campers were divided initially into two groups. After a getting-acquainted period in which the two groups had no contact with each other, the counsellors arranged for a number of competitive games to be played between the groups. As a result of these games, the groups became very antagonistic toward one another, expressing their feelings by name-calling, arguments, raids, and fights. This mutual antagonism might well have perpetuated itself until the end of the season had it not been for another series of interventions by the counsellors which forced the two teams to work together on common projects. The camp's water system broke down and both groups had to work together to fix it. They also had to work together to pull a "stalled" truck; and on a camping trip, they had to exchange parts before erecting their tents. The result of these interventions was disappearance of the earlier joint antagonism. This "era of good feelings" also perpetuated itself.

To translate this story into theoretical terms, the behavior of each team toward the other might be characterized on a dimension ranging from friendly to antagonistic. The data can be interpreted as reflecting a system with two equilibria and no resting point in between. Either the two teams could be pretty friendly toward each other (lower equilibrium) or pretty antagonistic (upper equilibrium). Hence, the *S*-shaped curve system shown in Fig. 3 may be appropriate.

The sequence of events can be conceived as starting at the lower equilibrium point. By skillful manipulation of the environment, the experimenters produced a series of momentary forces (the competitive games) that pushed the joint level of antagonism into quadrant III (either via quadrant II or quadrant IV or possibly straight across the midpoint),

where it moved quickly to the upper equilibrium point. The mutual antagonism perpetuated itself at that level without further intervention. A return to the lower equilibrium point was made possible by forcing the two teams to reward each other for a period of time, another momentary force. This caused a reentry into quadrant I and a rapid return to the lower equilibrium point, where the joint location remained thereafter.

The second case consists of the international crisis of 1914, which ushered in the First World War. This war was the culmination of a vicious circle, involving two alliances: Germany and Austria-Hungary,[8] on the one hand; France, Great Britain, and Russia, on the other. The crisis began with the assassination of an Austrian archduke in Serbia followed by an ultimatum from Austria to Serbia and a declaration of war. Russia, which was determined to protect Serbia, mobilized against Austria and Germany. Germany, fearing a Russian invasion, warned Russia that continued mobilization would lead to war. When Russia refused to comply, Germany declared war on Russia and France and announced a plan to invade France through Belgium. This brought Great Britain into the war on the side of Russia and France.

It is interesting to compare the crisis of 1914 with several earlier crises, involving members of the same alliances, which did not lead to war. In 1905–06 Germany became involved in a conflict with France over the control of Morocco which looked as if it might lead to war. This crisis was resolved in an international conference. In 1908, Austria-Hungary annexed Bosnia and Herzegovina, and Serbia threatened war against Austria. War was avoided because the leaders of Russia did not feel militarily prepared to support Serbia. In 1911 Germany sent a warship to Morocco, again as a warning to the French. After threats of war on both sides, the crisis was settled through bilateral negotiations.

The system shown in Fig. 3 can be employed to analyze the crisis of 1914 and compare it with earlier crises. The dimensions can be taken as the extent of military threat or action mounted by a member or members of one alliance against a member

---

[8] In 1914, Italy was formally an ally of Germany and Austria-Hungary; but she did not enter the war until 1915, and then on the side opposed to her erstwhile allies.

or members of the other. Each crisis presumably began at the lower equilibrium point. One state made a militarily threatening move, which was matched by a similar move from a member of the opposing alliance. Thereafter, in the first three crises, the vicious circle was reversed, and the action reverted to its previous resting place. Presumably, in those crises, the joint location remained in quadrant I, and, therefore, had to return to the lower equilibrium point when the immediate cause of the crisis (i.e., the momentary force) dissipated. In the crisis of 1914, the joint location can be thought of as having entered quadrant III, where it was doomed to spiral to the upper equilibrium point, which in this case entailed total war. Presumably the actions of one nation (either Austria or Russia) caused the process to cross a boundary into quadrants II or IV and stay there long enough for other states to push it into quadrant III. When the process reached quadrant III, there was no possibility for a return to the lower equilibrium point.[9]

In his analysis of the crisis of 1914, Russett (1962) has written of a "point of no escape," which is "that point in time after which the war cannot be prevented" (p. 6). If the lower equilibrium in an S-shaped curve system is taken as representing peace and the upper equilibrium as representing war, the point of no escape can be thought of as the time at which a joint location that started in quadrant I crosses one of the boundaries into quadrant III.

Instability and Its Causes

We are now ready for a working definition of stability and instability based on the reaction system shown in Fig. 3. As mentioned earlier, instability can basically be defined as the likelihood that sudden change will take place. In the S-shaped curve system, this can be interpreted as the likelihood that the joint location will move from the lower to the upper equilibrium point or vice versa. Hence, instability can be thought of as the likelihood that a momentary force will move the joint location over a boundary and cause it to stay there long enough for the dynamics of the system to carry it to the other equilibrium point. Conversely, stability can be

[9] Later in this paper, it will be hypothesized that a quadrant boundary was crossed in 1914 because the lower equilibrium point was quite close to the quadrant boundaries.

thought of as the likelihood that the joint location will remain in its current quadrant.

There are two basic components of instability, as so defined. One is the likelihood that momentary forces will develop that have sufficient force to push the joint location over a boundary and sufficient duration to keep it there until it moves to the quadrant opposite to that in which it started. The other component can be interpreted geometrically as the *closeness* of the boundaries to the equilibrium point currently occupied. The closer a boundary, the greater the likelihood of crossing it and, hence, the greater the instability of the system. The latter component will be our main concern in the remainder of this paper.

The notion of closeness is illustrated in Fig. 4. This figure portrays two reaction systems (A and B), superimposed on each other to facilitate comparison. The function $x = g(y)$ (which is labeled X) is the same in both systems, but the function $y = f(x)$ is different. In system A, the y-function (which is labeled A) rises very slowly from the lower equilibrium point and falls rapidly from the upper. In system B, the y-function (which is labeled B) rises rapidly from the lower equilibrium point and falls slowly from the upper. As a result, the boundaries are closer to the lower equilibrium point in system B than in system A; hence, B is less stable than A

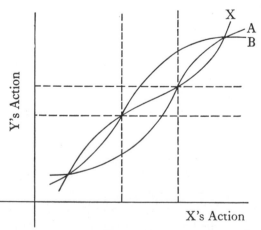

Figure 4. Two superimposed S-shaped curve reaction systems. Both share curve X, which is the function $x = g(y)$. The function $y = f(x)$ differs in the two systems, in one case being curve A and in the other case, curve B.

when the starting point is at the lower equilibrium. Conversely, the boundaries are closer to the upper equilibrium point in system A than in system B; hence, A is less stable than B when action starts at the upper equilibrium point.

Quite clearly, instability is at least partially a matter of the slope of the reaction functions, more precisely, the rate[10] at which they rise or fall from the equilibrium point at which action starts. Hence, to understand instability, we must look for factors that affect this slope. In the next section, we shall discuss factors that may affect the *rate of rise from the lower equilibrium point*. (This is the main concern of our paper, since the problems connected with instability primarily concern the prevention of vicious circles that lead to heightened conflict, i.e., the prevention of migration from the lower to the upper equilibrium point.) After that, a few words will be said about factors affecting the rate of fall from the upper equilibrium point. Finally there will be a brief discussion of the relationship between instability and the location of an equilibrium point.

Instability as a Function of the Rate of Rise from the Lower Equilibrium Point

In discussing determinants of the rate of rise from the lower equilibrium point, we shall deal with a generalized reaction system whose dimensions will be termed "level of provocation directed toward the other party." Referring to Fig. 4, X's output will be provocation of Y and Y's output will be provocation of X. Provocation is a generic term, referring to any kind of behavior that imposes costs on the other party, e.g., withdrawal of love, raising of tariffs, making a threat, or arming. The rate of rise from the lower equilibrium will often be referred to as the extent to which the party overreacts (as against underreacts) to provocation from the other party. Slow rise is termed an underreaction and rapid rise is an overreaction. These terms are only handy labels and are not intended to imply the value-laden assumption that we can specify an "adequate" reaction to any level of provocation.

The first set of hypotheses concerns dependence and interdependence. It seems reasonable to suppose that one party is more likely to underreact to provocations from the other party, the more *dependent* it feels itself to be on the other party's good will. The greater the first party's dependence, the more careful it will be not to alienate the other party. Hence, the first party will be slower to anger, less prone to punish the other for infractions, and less touchy in the face of abuse from the other. In the terms of our model, dependence on the other party reduces the rate at which the first party's reaction function rises; hence, dependence enhances the stability of the system (so long as the first party's dependence does not produce a mirror-image independence in the other party). Dependence on the other party results from that party's possession of the capacity to reward or punish the first party.

If one party's dependence on the other generally contributes to stability, then *interdependence*, i.e., both parties' dependence on one another, should make an even greater contribution. Our source of interdependence is the *possession of a common enemy* under conditions where it is possible to develop a joint strategy for dealing with the enemy. A proverbial illustration of the effectiveness of a common enemy is the stability of most wartime alliances, such as that between the United States and the Soviet Union between 1941 and 1945. This part of the analysis implies that, on the average, *multipolar* (i.e., multiparty) *systems* should be more stable than bipolar systems, since only in the former can a common enemy be found (Deutsch and Singer, 1964).[11]

Anticipation of a common enemy in the future can also contribute to interdependence and hence to stability. This point implies a relationship between

---

[10] The notion of "rate," as used in this context, refers only to the slope of reaction functions and does not imply rate of change over time.

[11] The assumption that multipolarity leads to international stability is not universally shared among students of international relations. Waltz (1964) has argued that a bipolar world is more stable than a multipolar one because the responsibility for deterring aggressive action is unambiguously in the hands of one party rather than being diffused among several. His argument represents a conception of instability which is quite different from the one proposed in this paper. For him, instability results from an underreaction to the other party's aggressive initiatives rather than from an overreaction, as suggested in this paper. He reasons that an underreaction encourages the other party to further aggression and, hence, is destabilizing in the long run. This position, which is closely related to the traditional theories of balance of power and deterrence, will be discussed more fully in the last section of this paper on further theoretical issues. See also Rosecrance (1966) for a discussion of the bipolar-multipolar issue.

the structure of the two parties in a system and the stability of that system. When each of the two parties is made up of subparties whose interests are not completely compatible, members of subparties on one side may anticipate seeking support from members of subparties on the other in some future intraparty conflict and, hence, may be loath to alienate the other side. It follows that *lack of unity in one or both parties*, where there is some possibility of developing interparty coalitions between subparties, should contribute to stability. The stability of relations between the political parties in the United States is a case in point. Members of each political party are so likely to find themselves in need of support from members of the other party in some future political controversy (e.g., over strategy in the Vietnam war) that they dare not risk alienating the other party too greatly by overreacting during interparty controversies. Hence, escalative reactions are strictly limited in conflicts between the political parties in the United States.

Another factor that can affect the steepness with which a reaction function rises is the *availability of resources* for reacting. The harder it is to behave in a defensive or challenging manner to provocations from the other party, the more likely is an underreaction to these provocations, and hence the greater the stability of the system. Again, one can argue that a multipolar system should be more stable than a bipolar system. In a multipolar system, each party must be ready to defend itself against provocation from several other parties. Hence, it cannot afford to divert a large proportion of its resources to conflict with any one party and is, therefore, likely to underreact to provocation from another party.

Third-party pressures for moderation can sometimes reduce the steepness of reaction to the other party's aggressive initiatives and, thereby, contribute to stability. A theory of third-party pressures must distinguish between the *effectiveness* of these pressures (i.e., their capacity to induce moderation) and their *vigor* (i.e., the extent to which they can be mobilized and amplified). The effectiveness of third-party pressures presumably depends primarily on the extent to which the first and/or second parties are dependent on the third party(ies). The vigor of these pressures is presumably a function of at least the following four factors: (a) the extent to which third parties are aware of what is happening between the first two parties, (b) the extent to which third parties feel threatened by instability in the relations between the first two parties, (c) the extent to which third parties can agree on norms of moderation (and, therefore, expect support from one another in putting pressure on belligerents), and (d) the extent to which there exists a forum (like the United Nations) for the mobilization and coordination of third-party pressures. Again, one can argue that a multipolar system should be more stable than a bipolar system, since only the former can have third parties that exert pressures for moderation. Russett (1962) has cited the rejection by Germany of British pressures for moderation as one of the many factors contributing to the outbreak of the First World War.

Certain *social norms* enhance stability by dampening reactions to provocation from another party. In interpersonal relations, in this country, people are encouraged and often required by the law to take their adversary to court rather than punish him personally for hurting their interests. The alternative, as can be seen in certain other countries, may be a long-term and often bloody feud, in which the parties alternate escalating the conflict to punish the other party for the just-previous escalation. In international law, where direct retaliation is considered more permissible than in civil law, there are "proportionality" norms against overreacting to harmful initiatives from another nation. Nations, like Lord High Executioners, are supposed to "make the punishment fit the crime."

The *technology* involved in conflict between two parties may contribute to the stability or instability of their relationship. Under some technologies (e.g., where air power is strong and antiaircraft defense weak), the party that first initiates violence has a decided advantage over the other. The likelihood of overreacting to provocation from the other side is great in these circumstances because of the fear that otherwise the other party will strike first and gain a decided advantage. Hence, reaction functions rise rapidly, and the likelihood of crossing a quadrant boundary is great. The military technology of 1914 is probably a case in point. The advantage of striking first was so great that mobilization by Russia was seen by Germany as an intolerable threat which could only be countered by launching an attack against France while there was still time.

The degeneration into war of the Arab-Israeli crisis of 1967 may also illustrate the instability which is produced when striking first carries an important military advantage.

Another feature of technology is the *existence or nonexistence of intermediate levels of reaction* to provocation from the other party. Sometimes there are no means available for a moderate reaction to the other party's initiatives. One must either overreact or not react at all. Presumably, beyond a certain level of provocation from the other party, one will choose to react and, hence, to overreact. Geometrically speaking, at that level of provocation, the reaction function rises precipitously. Such a rise may contribute to instability. This point can also be illustrated with the events of 1914. It appears that both Germany and Russia had only one viable military plan for reacting to a serious challenge from their adversaries. Russia's plan involved mobilizing on the borders of Germany and Austria. Germany's plan (the Schlieffen Plan) involved invading France through Belgium. Both plans required a considerable overreaction to the events which actually transpired in 1914, and this was apparently perceived at the time at least in Russia, but there seemed to be no reasonable alternative courses of action. In modern times, President Kennedy, apparently mindful of the 1914 tragedy, decided to abandon President Eisenhower's reliance on a "massive retaliation" strategy because it provided no intermediate levels of military reaction to intermediate levels of military challenge from the Soviet Union.

Certain *psychological factors* can also affect the extent of reaction to aggressive initiatives from the other party and, hence, the degree of instability in the system. Research evidence and psychological theory suggest that overreaction to provocation from another party is more likely (a) the more *hostile* one is toward the other party on the basis of previous experience (Coleman, 1957); (b) the less *trust* one bears toward the other party (Pruitt, 1965); (c) the greater one's existing level of *frustration* (Christiansen, 1959, 1965); (d) the more frequently one has previously perceived third parties receiving *rewards for counteraggression* (Walters, 1966); (e) the more *foolish one thinks he looks* in the eyes of third parties as a result of sustaining the provocation (Brown, 1967); and (f) in international affairs, the more *nationalistic* one's outlook (Christiansen, 1959, 1965).

In 1914, hostility and distrust were great between the two contending power blocs and nationalism was strong.

Certain *perceptions of the future* can also have an effect on the steepness of a party's reaction function and, hence, on the stability of his relations with another party. Sometimes individuals or statesmen, looking ahead, conclude that a challenger will be emboldened to launch further provocations if he is not decisively punished in the present. This is one tenet of the *doctrine of deterrence*. Such a conclusion is probably more likely if the challenger is seen as having unlimited goals than if he is seen as having limited goals. Such a conclusion steepens the reaction function and makes a vicious circle more probable in the present, however much it may contribute to greater stability in the future.[12]

Peering into the future, a party may also become *aware of an impending vicious circle*, i.e., of the instability of its own system or of the approach in that system to a critical boundary. Such a conclusion may cause it to "pull back from the brink" and to underreact to provocations from the other side, especially if the upper equilibrium point (e.g., war) is seen as highly undesirable. Russett (1962) has called the moment at which such a perception develops in a crisis the "point of surprise." He reasons that a vicious circle is less likely to develop, the longer the time elapsing between the "point of surprise" and the "point of no escape," because there is more opportunity to devise a strategy to escape disaster. Hence, a "crisis in slow motion" should be more stable than a fast-moving crisis.

In the paragraphs just above, quite a few factors were mentioned that may contribute to a steepening of reaction functions and, hence, an increased instability of reaction systems resembling those shown in Figs. 3 and 4. Each of the proposed factors, or a key word pertaining to it, was italicized for the purpose of clarity. At this point, it is conceivable that the reader may feel himself gasping for air, half-drowned in a sea of unrelated factors. While apologizing for the primitive, list-type nature of this theory, the author would argue that it represents a stage beyond the old one-factor theories that have so often been generated to explain war and related phenomena (human nature, capitalism,

---

[12] See the last section of this paper on further theoretical issues.

power imbalance, etc.). Instead of looking for *the cause* of the First World War, we were able to list in the last few paragraphs a series of possible *causes*: rejection of pressures for moderation, the military advantage of a first strike, the lack of capability for intermediate levels of reaction to provocation, hostility, distrust and nationalism. Each of these factors presumably added its fuel to the fire by increasing the slopes of the reaction functions on both sides of the controversy until, unbeknownst to the participants, the boundaries of quadrant I were exceedingly close to the lower equilibrium point. By 1914, a relatively weak momentary force, Austrian displeasure with the assassination in Serbia, was capable of initiating a wildly escalating vicious circle that culminated in world war.[13]

Instability as a Function of the Rate of Fall from the Upper Equilibrium Point

The stability of systems where activity begins at the *upper* equilibrium point will now be considered. The greater the instability of such a system, the more likely a benevolent circle that will move the joint location to the lower equilibrium point. Little will be said about this matter except to comment on the concept of *lag*. Much earlier in this paper, we mentioned psychological conservatism, the natural human tendency to cling to existing perceptions, including perceptions of the other party (e.g., trust of and perceived dependence on that party). Assume that the other party becomes more rewarding or more punishing than it has been in the past. We would expect some lag in perception of this change.

[13] Small, last-minute events that touch off war, such as the assassination of the Austrian Archduke, have sometimes been called *occasions* of war in distinction to larger *causes*, such as the absence of trust or the military advantage of attacking first. Occasions involve small amounts of energy that somehow release the large amounts of energy embodied in causes, as the pull of a trigger can release the energy stored in a cartridge. The S-shaped-curve reaction system embodies this kind of distinction: the fundamental forces that shape the reaction functions and hence determine the location of the equilibria and boundaries can be thought of as the causes of any vicious circles that ensue, whereas the momentary forces that actually drive the joint location over a boundary and thereby start its journey to the opposite quadrant can be coordinated with the notion of occasions. Actually, as pointed out by Richardson (1960, pp. xix-xx), causes and occasions are simply different kinds of causes.

Holsti's study of the lag in Dulles' recognition that the Russians were becoming more friendly was mentioned earlier as an illustration of this point. The concept of lag implies an underreaction to small changes in the other party's behavior at both the lower and the upper equilibrium points of an S-shaped reaction system. At the lower equilibrium point, a party will be slow to react in a defensive or aggressive manner; and at the upper equilibrium point, slow to react in a conciliatory manner. This implies, in turn, that the shape of the reaction curves may depend on which of the two equilibrium points is currently occupied. More specifically, in Fig. 4, *curve A may be more appropriate for movement upward from the lower equilibrium point and curve B more appropriate for movement downward from the upper equilibrium point.*[14]

Instability as a Function of the Location of the Current Equilibrium Point

In the discussion so far, instability has been treated geometrically as a function of the location of the quadrant boundaries with respect to the equilibrium point currently occupied. But instability can equally well be seen as a function of the location of the current equilibrium point with respect to the boundaries. This is more than a verbal distinction; it has meaning for the way theory is built. Take a look at Fig. 5. This shows two superimposed reaction systems which have the same quadrant boundaries but different lower equilibrium points. Assuming that action starts at the lower equilibrium point, system A is more stable than system B, because the equilibrium point is farther from the boundaries of quadrant I. The main reason for this, as before, is that function X rises more rapidly from this equilibrium point in system B than in A. This has to do not with the shape of curve X, but rather with the *height* of the lower part of the curve, i.e., the function $y = f(x)$.

The height of the lower part of the y-function can be interpreted as that part of Y's aggressiveness toward X that is not attributable to X's provocations, i.e., Y's *basic aggressiveness* toward X. Y's basic aggressiveness is greater in system B than in A.

[14] The factors listed in the last section presumably add their effects to these natural lags.

An analogy can be drawn between this interpretation of Fig. 4 and the phenomenon of *hysteresis* in magnetism.

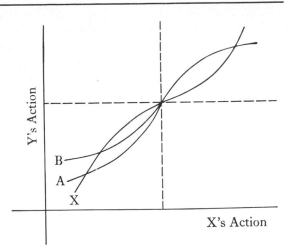

Figure 5. Two superimposed S-shaped reaction systems. Both share curve X, which is x = g(y). The function y = f(x) differs in the two systems, in one case being curve A and in the other case, curve B.

As a result, system B is less stable than system A. The greater the basic aggressiveness, the less stable the system. Many factors produce Y's basic aggressiveness, e.g., past grudges against X, acquisitiveness, perceived divergence of interest, etc. No effort will be made to enumerate the many other contributory factors except to say that "aggressiveness" is being used in its usual sense here.

It is interesting to note that, according to the model shown in Fig. 5, one nation can become so basically aggressive that war is very likely; yet war when it comes may still be the product of a vicious circle, involving escalation on both sides, which quite possibly may be initiated by some momentary force acting on the *other* nation. In such a case, it is hard to say who is "to blame." Is it the first nation whose basic stance produced instability or the second nation whose actions pushed the process over the brink? But, if we are willing to hold the question of blame in abeyance, we can perfectly easily analyze such a situation using the geometric tools shown in Fig. 5.

Further Theoretical Issues

The working definition of instability employed in the last four sections was the closeness of the quadrant boundaries to the equilibrium point currently occupied, in an *S*-shaped curve reaction system. As was indicated earlier, there is another component of instability in this system: the likelihood of a momentary force with sufficient strength and durability to push the joint location over a boundary and keep it there long enough for movement into the quadrant opposite the one in which it started. The theory is incomplete without a discussion of this issue, though no discussion will be attempted here. Furthermore, no discussion is presented of how fast the joint location moves in response to the dynamics of the system, though this issue is critical for understanding how long the joint location can safely remain in quadrants II and IV and still "scramble" safely back to its original location. In addition, there are other kinds of reaction systems which exhibit greater or lesser stability (e.g., systems in which the parties react to one another's rates of change as well as to absolute levels of action), and there are types of instability that are not easily expressed in terms of reaction systems. Hence, this paper is not seen as a definitive statement of the sources of instability but only as one contribution to a much broader theory of instability.

The most prominent theories of instability in international affairs are the traditional balance of power and deterrence theories (Pruitt and Snyder, 1969). In certain ways, these theories are quite opposed to the one presented here. In this paper, stability has been linked to an underreaction to provocations from the other party; whereas, the traditional theories (or theoretical approaches as they might better be called) trace stability to an equal or overreaction to such provocations. "Doves" will probably find the present theory more compatible, while "hawks" are likely to feel more at home with the traditional theories.

There appear to be two basic differences between the assumptions underlying the traditional theories and the one presented here (and, hence, between hawks and doves). One lies in a differing conception of the *shape of the other party's reaction function*. The traditional theories seem to assume that defensive and counteraggressive moves will reduce the likelihood of further provocation from the other party. Hence, they essentially assume that the other party's reaction function is either monotonic decreasing (as in Fig. 1, curve E) or an inverted U (as in Fig. 1, curve F), rather than monotonic increasing as in the present analysis. Both positions about the shape of the other party's reaction function are probably right at times and wrong at others. The issue of which kind of theory is right under what circumstances is an empirical question of considerable importance.

The traditional theories and the one presented here also seem to differ in *time perspective*. Balance of power and particularly deterrence theorists often advocate large reactions to provocations as a way of avoiding further provocations, e.g., to teach the other party that aggression does not pay. They often argue that underreaction encourages the other party to engage in further provocation and, hence, is destabilizing *in the long run*. There is certainly some truth to this contention, at least under certain circumstances, and it needs to be reconciled with the theory presented in this paper, which concerns the causes of *short-run stability*, i.e., stability in the here and now. At present, in practical (e.g., governmental) decisions, the choice between the kind of thinking represented in this paper and traditional theories is made on an ad hoc basis, depending on the facts surrounding the case at hand. At times (e.g., when there may otherwise be no long run) short-run stability is considered more important than long-run stability, and nations make "dovish" underreactions to another nation's initiatives. (One wishes that the Austrians in 1914 had been interested in the short-run goal of preserving international tranquility instead of the long-run goal of teaching the Serbs a lesson they would remember.) At other times, long-run stability may be seen as more important, and nations "hawkishly" escalate in order to reduce the incidence of future provocation from the other nation. Hopefully, in the not too distant future, it will be possible to develop a scientifically based theory that will give us a more reliable answer to the question of whether an overreaction or an underreaction produces greater stability in a given situation. Assuming that such a theory employed reaction functions as an analytical tool, one of its prominent features would have to be an interpretation of the changes in one party's reaction functions that result from the other party's activities.

Two theoretical problems must be mentioned in connection with the S-shaped reaction system model developed in this paper. One concerns the distinction between momentary forces (which push the joint location away from an equilibrium point) and fundamental forces (which determine the shape of the reaction functions). This distinction is not very precise, the assumption being only that momentary forces are more temporary than fundamental forces. Further analysis is needed to clarify this distinction. The other problem concerns the question of what dimensions to include in a reaction system. This is the problem of identifying the dimensions in one party's behavior that react to changes on some dimension in the other party's behavior. Sometimes this problem is fairly simple: as the other party becomes more provocative, the first party's behavior becomes more hostile in all respects. But at other times, one finds a kind of *insulation* between realms of behavior within a single party, such that his reactions in one realm are not highly correlated with his reactions in the other. Thus, a wife whose husband stops exhibiting affection to her may stop exhibiting affection to him but continue making meals that are as good as before and keeping the house as clean as before. The Soviet Union can respond to American military actions in Vietnam by sending supplies and technicians to that country and yet (much to the consternation of China) continue to make efforts in other areas to improve relations with the United States. Some kind of theory needs to be developed about the nature of such insulation and the way it develops.

Finally, a word must be said about *measurement*. It may be possible in laboratory settings to make enough measurements, of sufficient precision, to draw geometric diagrams of reaction functions, though this has not as yet been attempted. But outside the laboratory, in naturalistic settings such as international affairs, such measurement is likely to be much more difficult. Certain predictions can be derived from the theory that will require only rough, ordinal-scale measurement; e.g., that a sudden change is more likely, the greater the frustration of the parties involved, or that bimodal distributions will be found on many dimensions of interpersonal and intergroup hostility (one mode for each of the stable equilibria). But one would hope eventually to be able to make more precise predictions and to test the theory more fully. This capability probably awaits the development of more adequate measurement procedures.

Summary

Change in the behavior of one member of a dyad is often reciprocated by the other member. Hence change in interpersonal and international relations often takes the form of vicious or benevolent circles. Stable relations are usually characterized by oscillations around an equilibrium point, i.e., mutually canceling benevolent and vicious circles. Sudden change in the location of an equilibrium point typically results from one party's moving "too far" along a critical dimension, which initiates a runaway vicious or benevolent circle. Instability can be defined as the likelihood of sudden change and hence as the likelihood that one party will go "too far."

A geometric interpretation of these concepts has been advanced here. A variety of reaction functions can be plotted showing the level of output on any dimension emitted by one party in response to the other party's level of output on the same or another dimension. When both parties' reaction functions are presented in the same space, a reaction system emerges. One such system, consisting of two S-shaped curves, seems particularly interesting. This system has two equilibrium points, a lower "peaceful" one and an upper "conflictful" one. The system also has boundaries separating it into four quadrants. If the relationship between the parties is at one equilibrium point, and a momentary (temporary) force moves one party over a boundary for a long enough period, the relationship will move to the other equilibrium point, despite the subsequent abatement of the momentary force. Such movement is analogous to sudden change. Hence, one interpretation of "instability" is the closeness of the boundaries to the equilibrium point that is currently occupied. Various factors may increase this closeness and, hence, contribute to instability, including the availability of resources for reacting, a military technology that favors first strike or lacks intermediate levels of reaction, the doctrine of deterrence, hostility, distrust, frustration, nationalism, and factors producing aggressiveness. Other factors may reduce this closeness and, hence, contribute to stability, such as dependence and interdependence, the existence of a common enemy, lack of unity in one or both parties, third-party pressures for moderation, the existence of certain social norms, and awareness of an impending vicious circle. Multipolar systems differ from bipolar systems on a number of these factors, all in the direction of greater stability for multipolar systems. In the last section of the paper, the relationship between this theory and traditional approaches to instability drawn from balance of power and deterrence theory is explored.

References

Abelson, R. P. "A 'Derivation' of Richardson's Equations." *Journal of Conflict Resolution*, VII (1963), 13–20.

Ashby, W. R. *Design for a Brain*. New York: Wiley, 1952.

Boulding, K. E. *Conflict and Defense*. New York: Harper, 1962.

Brody, R. A., and Vesecky, J. F. "Soviet Openness to Changing Situations: A Critical Evaluation of Certain Hypotheses about Soviet Foreign Policy Behavior." Unpublished, 1967.

Brown, B. R. "Face Saving in a Two-Person Bargaining Game." Paper presented at the annual meeting of the Eastern Psychological Association, 1967.

Caspary, W. R. "Richardson's Model of Arms Races: Description, Critique, and an Alternative Model." *International Studies Quarterly*, XI (1967), 63–88.

Christiansen, B. *Attitudes towards Foreign Affairs as a Function of Personality*. Oslo: Oslo Univ. Press, 1959.

———. "Attitudes towards Foreign Affairs as a Function of Personality," In H. Proshansky and B. Seidenberg, eds., *Basic Studies in Social Psychology*. New York: Holt, 1965.

Coleman, J. S. *Community Conflict*. New York: Free Press, 1957.

Deutsch, K. W., and Singer, J. D. "Multipolar Power Systems and International Stability." *World Politics*, XVI (1964), 390–406.

Etzioni, A. "The Kennedy Experiment." *Western Political Quarterly*, XX (1967), 361–380.

Gouldner, A. W. "The Norm of Reciprocity: A Preliminary Statement." *American Sociological Review*, XXV (1960), 161–178.

Holsti, O. R. "The Belief System and National Images: A Case Study." *Journal of Conflict Resolution*, VI (1962), 244–252.

Homans, G. C. *Social Behavior: Its Elementary Forms*. New York: Harcourt, 1961.

Intriligator, M. D. "Some Simple Models of Arms Races." *General Systems*, IX (1964), 143–147.

Kaldor, N. "A model of the trade cycle." *Economic Journal*, March 1940, 78–89.

Kendon, A. "Some Functions of Gaze-Direction in Social Interaction." *Acta Psychologica*, XVI (1967), 22–63.

Osgood, C. E. *An Alternative to War or Surrender*. Urbana, Ill.: Univ. Illinois Press, 1962.

Pruitt, D. G. "Definition of the Situation as a Determinant of International Action." In H. C. Kelman, ed., *International Behavior: A Social-Psychological Analysis*. New York: Holt, 1965.

Pruitt, D. G. "Reciprocity and Credit Building in a Laboratory Dyad." *Journal of Personality and Social Psychology*, VIII (1968), 193–47.

———, and Snyder, R. C., eds., *Theory and Research on the Causes of War*. Englewood Cliffs, N.J.: Prentice-Hall, 1969.

Rapoport, A. *Fights, Games and Debates*. Ann Arbor, Mich.: Univ. of Michigan Press, 1960.

Richardson, L. F. *Arms and Insecurity: A Mathematical Study of the Causes and Origins of War*. Pittsburgh: Boxwood Press, 1960.

Rosecrance, R. N. "Bipolarity, Multipolarity and the Future." *Journal of Conflict Resolution*, X (1966), 314–327.

Russett, B. M. "Cause, Surprise and No Escape." *Journal of Politics*, XXIV (1962), 3–22.

Sherif, M., Harvey, O. J., White, B. J., Hood, W. R., and Sherif, C. W. *Intergroup Conflict and Cooperation: The Robbers Cave Experiment*. Norman, Okla.: Univ. Oklahoma, 1961.

Smoker, P. "A Mathematical Study of the Present Arms Race" and "A Pilot Study of the Present Arms Race." *General Systems*, VIII (1963), 61–76.

Taylor, D. A. *Some Aspects of the Development of Interpersonal Relationships: Social Penetration Processes*. Doctoral Dissertation, Univ. Delaware, 1965.

Tognoli, J. J. *Reciprocal Behavior in Interpersonal Information Exchange*. Doctoral Dissertation, Univ. Delaware, 1967.

Walters, R. H. "Implications of Laboratory Studies of Aggression for the Control and Regulation of Violence." *The Annals*, CCCLXIV (1966), 60–72.

Waltz, K. N. "The Stability of a Bipolar World." *Daedalus*, III (1964), 881–909.

37. International Crisis as a Situational Variable

Charles F. Hermann is Assistant Professor of Politics at Princeton University. The author of a number of important articles on research problems in the international field, Professor Hermann has also collaborated with his wife on innovative empirical inquiries into the dynamics of foreign policy behavior (see Selection 51). In particular, his work has focused on behavior in crisis situations and, as such, has contributed to the emergence of crisis as a major concept in the field. Although the reader will doubtless wish to ponder for himself the question of whether crises should be treated as dependent or independent variables—as merely the outcome of underlying processes or as processes that in themselves significantly contribute to the outcome of situations—here Professor Hermann provides a persuasive answer to the question. He examines the possible impact of crises on the behaviour of a single national actor and, in so doing, demonstrates several ways in which crises can influence decisional processes and thus operate as more than the outcome of underlying processes. [*This paper was written especially for this volume.*]

I

Interpreters of international politics have discussed numerous variables in their efforts to understand the variety of actions taken in the name of nation-states and other international actors. Single acts of foreign policy as well as patterns of inter-action have been explained in terms of goals and national interests, the available national capabilities, the type of government, the personalities of national leaders, the influential nongovernmental agents within a country, or the human and nonhuman environment outside the country. One cluster of variables of potential value in explaining the behavior of international actors characterizes the situation that provides the occasion for action. Situational analysis, as it has been applied in other areas,[1] assumes that the action of an agent (in this case an international actor) is a function of the immediate situation it confronts.

With appreciation for the multiplicity of variables operating in international politics and with the availability of multivariate techniques of analysis, students of world affairs have increasingly avoided

[1] For some applications of situational analysis in other fields, see G. W. Allport, "Prejudice: A Problem in Psychological and Social Causation," in T. Parsons and E. A. Shils, eds., *Toward a General Theory of Action* (New York: Harper and Row, 1962) Torchbook edition, pp. 365–87; L. J. Carr, *Situational Analysis* (New York: Harper and Brothers, 1948); R. Boguslow, "Situational Analysis and the Problem of Action," *Social Problems*, VIII, 3, (1960–61), 212–19; D. Cartwright, ed., *K. Lewin's Field Theory in Social Science* (New York: Harper and Brothers, 1951), especially Chap. 10.

reliance on simplistic, single-factor explanations of their subject. No reversal of this trend is intended in this discussion of situational analysis. Rather this essay suggests that for the explication of some foreign policy actions, specific situational variables should be examined together with other factors. Situational variables are among a number of independent variables that can be expected to contribute significantly in accounting for the variation in international actions.

Assuming that a researcher plans to include reference to the immediate situation, what specific variables can he use to characterize the event? Some time ago Snyder and his associates observed: "We ought to recognize that a systematic frame of reference for the study of international politics will require several typologies, one of which will be concerned with situations."[2] As a step in the development of a typology of situations, individual categories of situations can be isolated and defined. Crisis constitutes one possible category if only because it has been analyzed so frequently by observers of international politics.

Secretary of State Rusk gave evidence of the frequency of crises when he told a Senate subcommittee that the world experienced forty-seven international political crises between 1961 and mid-1966.[3] These recurrent situations that often contain far-reaching implications for the future have not gone unexamined. Policy-makers, journalists, and academics all have undertaken descriptions and analyses of international crises. But one remarkable quality about most studies of crises has been their failure to provide cumulative knowledge about the class of events they investigate. Recollections of crises in the autobiographies of statesmen or reconstructions of events by reporters and scholars provide a more or less satisfactory interpretation of a particular crisis, but these analyses prove of limited value in understanding subsequent crises. As a given crisis recedes into history, critical attention shifts to the new, current crises. Because the accounts of the former crisis lack relevance for the most recent

situations, new studies are prepared and replace the previous ones.

A number of reasons can be offered for this state of affairs in the study of crisis. First, only the vaguest common meaning appears attached to the concept. Since many analysts fail to define crisis at all, the reader is left to infer from the context that the situation concerns some "critical" or "urgent" problem. In the attempt to call attention to every important issue, we suffer from the indiscriminate use of the term "crisis." Second, many individuals who write about crisis seem to believe in the uniqueness of every situation. At least they find unique the combination of properties necessary to provide a satisfactory explanation of a specific event. For example, in discussing some implications of economic theory for international relations, Aron observes: "It has not yet been proven that 'crisis situations' are all alike. It is possible that each crisis is unique or, if you prefer, has its own particular story...."[4] If we foster the conviction that each crisis is totally distinct from those encountered in the past and to be encountered in the future, then it is not surprising that we have little accumulated knowledge about crises. Third, the prevailing mode of analysis has been the detailed case history of a single crisis. Despite the satisfaction gained by reading a thorough and well-written case study, this method of analysis makes it unnecessary for the writer to consider how the crisis under examination compares with other situations.[5] Not only is the development of empirically verifiable generalizations by the original author hampered, but the absence of parallel construction between case studies makes it difficult for hypotheses to be abstracted by the reader of several studies.

These difficulties must be overcome if crisis is to be used as a situational variable accounting for certain foreign policy behaviors of nations. Although this essay deals primarily with the problems of definition and analysis, the question concerning the uniqueness of events requires brief consideration.

[2] R. C. Snyder, H. W. Bruck, and B. Sapin, eds., *Foreign Policy Decision-Making* (New York: The Free Press, 1962), p. 81.

[3] Statement of Dean Rusk at Hearing before the Preparedness Investigating Subcommittee of the Committee on Armed Services, United States Senate, 89th Congress, 2nd Session, August 25, 1966.

[4] R. Aron, "What Is a Theory of International Relations?" *Journal of International Affairs*, XXI, 2 (1967), p. 188.

[5] Insightful statements concerning the problems of case studies can be found in G. D. Paige, *The Korean Decision* (New York: The Free Press, 1968), Chap. 1; and J. N. Rosenau, "Moral Fervor, Systematic Analysis, and Scientific Consciousness in Foreign Policy Research," in A. Ranney, ed., *Political Science and Public Policy* (Chicago: Markham, 1968), Chap. 9.

Every situation is novel when all its properties are considered. Even two simple situations—one a carefully executed replication of the other—differ in numerous ways. Between these occurrences, time will have elapsed. The earth and solar system will have moved. Human actors will be older and will have had intervening experiences. Given the novelty of simple, controlled situations, it is clear that countless differences exist between two complex international events such as the Berlin blockade of 1948 and Khrushchev's ultimatum on Berlin in 1958. Man would be unable to cope with his daily existence, however, if he did not treat most new situations as comparable to some situations he has met or learned about in the past. For purposes of evaluation and action, all humans categorize events according to a limited number of properties and ignore the rest. The adequacy of a response to a situation will depend in part upon the quality of the classifying categories and our ability to correctly recognize the situation as a member of a class of events. Having established how the present circumstances are related to some already experienced, man can bring the success or failure of past responses to bear on his present action. Of course, explanation and action are not the same; nor are the simple situations of daily living similar to the complex ones of international events. Nevertheless, if we *correctly* recognize a few critical properties of an international situation which identify it as a member of a general set of situations, we may establish many things about it even without examining many other qualities that make it unique.[6]

II

Definitions of crisis which identify a specific class of situations can be constructed with reference to either of two approaches which are among those prevalent in the contemporary study of international politics. These two are the systemic and decision-making approaches. A set of crisis situations does not automatically emerge once the analyst selects either the decision-making or systemic framework for organizing his research. But the approach helps structure the kind of hypotheses in which crisis can prove to be a significant explanatory variable. The effect of the approach or organizing framework on a situational variable will become more evident upon closer examination of crisis defined from the systemic perspective.

We shall stipulate that a system is a set of actors (for example, nations, international organizations, and so on) interacting with one another in established patterns and through designated structures. In any given international political system, critical variables must be maintained within certain limits or the instability of the system will be greatly increased—perhaps to the point where a new system will be formed. A crisis is a situation which disrupts the system or some part of the system (that is, a subsystem such as an alliance or an individual actor). More specifically, a crisis is a situation that creates an abrupt or sudden change in one or more of the basic systemic variables.

In the present international system the existing military relationships depend in part on the relative superiority of the strategic weapon systems of the two superpowers and their deterrence capabilities with respect to each other. A sudden change in one of the superpowers' ability to deter the other would constitute a crisis for the system. The deterrence crisis might not transform the system or the subsystem comprised of the Soviet Union and the United States, but it has the potential to do so.

Rosecrance identifies nine international political systems between the years 1740 and 1960[7] which indicate the role of crisis in system transformation. In his analysis, system-transforming events includes the French Revolution, the end of the Napoleonic Wars, the revolutions of 1848, the Franco-Prussian War, the dismissal of Bismarck, and the two World Wars of the present century. Although the extended conflicts that Rosecrance describes as the usual transition between systems cannot be considered as crises under the present definition, several of these events were triggered by crises. The long years of World War I, for example, followed the crisis in late June and July 1914.

[6] Of course, policy-makers can get into serious trouble by the misclassification of events. See A. M. Schlesinger, Jr.'s *The Bitter Heritage* (Boston: Houghton Mifflin, 1967). The problem of situation recognition and classification is somewhat different for the art of policy-making than it is for the development of a science of politics. In the latter case new situations provide an opportunity for hypothesis-testing and refinement of categories, whereas in the former an unfamiliar situation introduces the risk of a policy misfortune.

[7] R. N. Rosecrance, *Action and Reaction in World Politics* (Boston: Little Brown and Company, 1963).

The characterization of crisis from the systemic approach suggests the relationship of the concept to such terms as change and conflict. Because crises engage one or more of the critical variables necessary to maintain the existing pattern of relationships between actors, they necessarily can effect significant changes in the international system. Whether or not a crisis actually produces significant change depends on a number of factors such as the nature of the modified variables, the existing destabilizing factors, and the available techniques for crisis management. Just as not all crises lead to important changes, not all significant changes are crises. A gradual shift in the rate of exchange between nations could ultimately have a profound effect on the system, despite small increments of change at any given point in time. The association of crisis with abrupt change also bears on its relationship to conflict. A conflict between parties that continues at a relatively constant level of intensity would not constitute a crisis, but a sudden shift in the level of hostilities—most notably from peace to war—would be a crisis at least for the subsystem comprised of the combatants.

Although the proposed systemic definition of crisis has been an arbitrary one, it is consistent with much of the writing about crisis from a systemic perspective. Thus, crisis has been described as "intensive inputs to the international system . . . unbalancing stabilities,"[8] or as "some kind of boundary or turning point,"[9] or as "involving significant actual or potential international conflict in either a novel form or at an abruptly changing level."[10] One of the more complete systemic definitions of crisis is offered by Young: "An international crisis, then, is a set of rapidly unfolding events which raises the impact of destabilizing forces in the general international system or any of its subsystems substantially above "normal" (i.e., average) levels and increases the likelihood of violence occurring in the system."[11]

If a class of crisis situations can be operationally defined from the guidelines discussed above, what

contribution might this variable make to the analysis of international political systems? The structures and processes that maintain an international system may be more or less subject to the sudden stresses imposed by crisis. The question then arises as to what structures and processes are most "sensitive" to crisis situations. Sensitivity can vary in several ways including the tendency for some parts of the system to be more frequently exposed to crises. For example, interactions between actors who seek alterations in their international status are more prone to crises than interactions between actors who have accepted their status positions. Sensitivity also develops because some elements of a system can vary less than others without exceeding critical thresholds. For example, a system may be able to withstand considerably greater variation in the degree of conflict between smaller states than it can between major states. Essentially these questions concern the effect of crisis on system stability and transformation.

Because international systems differ, the impact of crisis can be expected to vary according to the type of system. This observation leads to such research questions as: Does the nature of the international system influence the frequency with which crises occur? Are certain systems better structured to allow policy-makers to cope with crises without destroying the system? According to Waltz, one "distinguishing factor in the bipolar balance, as we thus far know it, is the nearly constant presence of pressure and the recurrence of crises."[12] In addition to finding crises more frequent in a bipolar system than in a multipolar system, Waltz also contends that in a multipolar world a nation's policy-makers can create a crisis to further their objectives with the hope that opponents of the change will not coalesce in opposition. In a bipolar system, the permanency of opposing polar powers greatly increases the probability that any move to initiate a crisis will be countered.[13] Thus, two relevant hypotheses from the Waltz study are that the type of international system influences (1) the rate with which crises occur, and (2) the probability of direct confrontations

[8] J. F. Triska and D. D. Finley, *Soviet Foreign Policy* (New York: The Macmillan Company, 1968), p. 317.

[9] K. E. Boulding, *Conflict and Defense* (New York: Harper and Row, 1963) Torchbook edition, p. 250.

[10] A. J. Wiener and H. Kahn (eds.), *Crisis and Arms Control*, Hudson Institute, Advanced Research Projects Agency Contract No. SD-105, October 9, 1962, p. 12.

[11] O. R. Young, *The Intermediaries: Third Parties in International Crisis* (Princeton: Princeton University Press, 1967), p. 10.

[12] K. N. Waltz, "The Stability of a Bipolar World," *Daedalus*, XCIII, 3 (1964), p. 883.

[13] It is interesting to note in this context that one of the polar powers in the present system, the United States, was directly or indirectly involved in one-third of the forty-eight crises mentioned by Secretary Rusk.

between actors when any actor attempts to abruptly change significant systemic variables.

Conflicting hypotheses exist concerning the systemic consequences of numerous crises. Wright contends that the probability of war in a given period of time increases with the frequency of crises.[14] McClelland and Waltz make the counter-hypothesis although they use different arguments.[15] The nature of a given international system may be introduced as a mediating variable to resolve this apparent contradiction. In some inherently unstable systems, the appearance of a single crisis might trigger war. In other systems with effective regulatory mechanisms, crises might be repeatedly managed without resort to war. The availability to both the Soviet Union and the United States of a tremendous destructive capability that can be applied even after absorbing an initial nuclear attack may serve as such a regulator of crisis effects in the present international system.

These questions and hypotheses are only a few of those that might be examined using crisis as a systemic variable. To date, however, few empirical studies have been designed to investigate issues of this type which concern the entire international system. Authors with commitment to the systemic framework tend to examine the interaction of a subsystem in a single crisis.[16] The inspection of subsystem interaction or even a single national actor, treated as a system component, undoubtedly

can yield important insights into the role of crisis as a situational variable. But the effect of crisis on the relations within an alliance or between two adversaries may be quite different from the effect of that same crisis on the overall system. A specific crisis may drastically alter a subsystem without having any destabilizing consequences for the total international system. A greater variety of research methods must be employed to examine issues like the role of crisis as an instrument of system change and the effects of alternative systems on crisis management. In order to compare the effect of crises as a class of situations in different international systems we must expand the period of history in which crises are scrutinized. Furthermore, the single case study which describes in detail the interaction between a few parties in a crisis must be augmented by research which (1) views crisis from the perspective of the entire system, and (2) examines a number of crises with attention to comparable structures and processes. The need for additional methods of analysis using the systemic approach parallels requirements that become evident when crisis is defined using the decision-making approach.

III

As the name suggests, central to the decision-making approach is the process by which decisions are made on questions of policy. Also basic to this organizing framework are the persons who, as individuals or in some collective form, constitute the authoritative decision-makers. The decision-makers behave according to their interpretation of the situation, not according to its "objective" character as viewed by some theoretical omnipotent observer.[17] Therefore, in attempting to explain how different kinds of situations influence the type of choice that is made, the analyst must interpret the situation as it is perceived by the decision-makers.

The use of crisis as a situational variable which partially explains the policy-makers' decision is not unlike the stimulus-response model familiar to psychologists. Crisis acts as a stimulus; the decision represents a response. In the usual experimental application of this model, the researcher varies an

[14] Q. Wright, *A Study of War* (2nd ed.; Chicago: University of Chicago Press, 1965), p. 1272.

[15] Charles McClelland proposes that experience is gained with the management of each crisis; therefore, policy makers cope more successfully with subsequent crises. See his "The Acute International Crisis," *World Politics*, XIV, 1 (1961), 187–88. Kenneth Waltz suggests that if continuing hostility exists between two parties, crises may become a substitute for war (*op. cit.*, p. 884). Raymond Aron notes a "trend toward the diminution of the force used" in direct crises between the Soviet Union and the United States, but he does not speculate that this pattern could be generalized to all parties experiencing repeated crises. See his *Peace and War*, translated by R. Howard and A. B. Fox (Garden City: Doubleday and Company, Inc., 1966), p. 565.

[16] Examples of subsystem crisis studies are W. P. Davison, *The Berlin Blockade* (Princeton: Princeton University Press, 1958); C. A. McClelland, "Decisional Opportunity and Political Controversy: The Quemoy Case," *Journal of Conflict Resolution*, VI, 3, (1962), 201–13; A. Wohlstetter and R. Wohlstetter, *Controlling the Risks in Cuba*, Adelphi Paper No. 17, Institute for Strategic Studies, London, England, April, 1965.

[17] Harold and Margaret Sprout are among those who have carefully explicated this point. See their *The Ecological Perspective on Human Affairs* (Princeton: Princeton University Press, 1965), especially pp. 28–30.

event or act which is used to account for any observed variation in the respondent's behavior. Applying this model to the interaction between policy makers of two nation-states, several political scientists expanded the paradigm to include: (1) the stimulus or actual policy of the initiating state, (2) the perception of that stimulus by the decision-makers in the recipient state, (3) the response or actual reply of the recipient state, and (4) the perception of that response by the decision-makers in the initiating state.[18] As in this modification of the stimulus-response model, the definition of crisis required by the decision-making approach must take into account the screening processes of human perceptions.

Those analysts who have studied crisis using the decision-making framework display no more agreement regarding the definition of crisis than do their counterparts who have applied the systemic approach. As before, we stipulate a definition which delimits a class of situations and contains some of the properties frequently associated with crisis. Specifically, a crisis is a situation that (1) threatens high-priority goals of the decision-making unit, (2) restricts the amount of time available for response before the decision is transformed, and (3) surprises the members of the decision-making unit by its occurrence. Threat, time, and surprise all have been cited as traits of crisis,[19] although seldom have all three properties been combined. Underlying the proposed definition is the hypothesis that if all three traits are present then the decision process will be substantially different than if only one or two of the characteristics appear. Contained in the set of events specified by this definition are many that observers commonly refer to as crises for American policy-makers, for example, the 1950 decision to defend South Korea, the 1962 Cuban missile episode, and the 1965 decision to send marines to the Dominican Republic. But other situations would not be considered crises for policy-makers in the United States; the 1958 ultimatum on Berlin, the extended Greek-Turkish-Cypriot dispute, and the mission in 1964 to rescue Europeans in Stanleyville (Congo) are illustrative in this regard. The exclusion of these and other situations that do not contain at least one of the three traits does not deny the importance of these situations or the significant consequences of the resulting decisions. The classification of them as noncrises simply indicates that these situations may be different with respect to the decision process in some systematic ways from those included in the crisis set.

Before hypothesizing how the decision process in crisis differs from noncrisis, we must return to the perceptual problem. The proposed definition clearly refers to the decision-makers' perceptions of crisis situations, but how can this definition be implemented? The ideal answer is as obvious as it is difficult to achieve. Through interviews the researcher would get decision-makers to assess the amount of threat, time, and surprise they thought a given situation involved. Even if interviews should not be feasible, however, perceptual data on each crisis trait can be developed through the use of the public statements of policy-makers, their memoirs, and reports of their perceptions by other political leaders and by journalists.

Once we assume that the decision-makers' perceptions of a situation can be measured, a phenomenological question arises: Do the elements of the definition represent actual properties of situations as well as images in the minds of policy-makers? That is, do these qualities represent measurable stimuli independent of perceptions? Experimental data have been assembled elsewhere that offer an affirmative reply to this inquiry.[20] Without reviewing that evidence we may note that situations do vary in the extent to which they obstruct goals sought by policy-makers, and hence, situations differ in measurable threat. Moreover, most situations contain dynamic elements which lead to their evolution after a measurable period of time regardless of whether these aspects of the situations are recognized by the affected decision makers. Finally, the frequency with which similar events have occurred in the past and the existence of contingency planning are indicators of the amount

[18] O. R. Holsti, R. A. Brody, and R. C. North, "Affect and Action in International Reaction Models," *Journal of Peace Research*, III-IV (1964), 170–90.

[19] See the review of these traits in C. F. Hermann, "Some Consequences of Crisis which Limit the Viability of Organizations." *Administrative Science Quarterly*, VIII, 1 (1963), 61–82 and C. F. Hermann, *Crises in Foreign Policy: A Simulation Analysis* (Indianapolis: Bobbs-Merrill, 1969).

[20] See C. F. Hermann, "Threat, Time, and Surprise," in C. F. Hermann, ed., *Contemporary Research on International Crises*, forthcoming.

of potential surprise contained in a situation. In short, the three crisis traits can be measured directly as properties of the situation or indirectly as perceptions of the decision-makers.

Because situations differ in their degree of threat, in their duration through time, and in their amount of surprise, each of the three traits that define a crisis can be conceived as one extreme on a dimension with scale positions for every possible quantity of each property. When taken together at

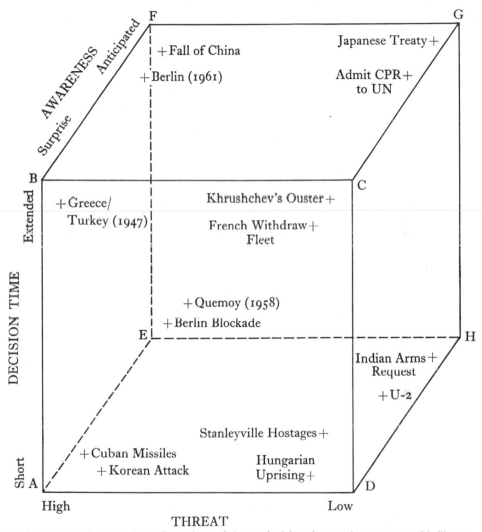

Figure 1. A situational cube representing the three dimensions of threat, decision time, and awareness, with illustrative situations from the perspective of American decision-makers. (*Note:* The representation of a three-dimensional space in a two-dimensional diagram makes it difficult to interpret the locations of the situations; their positions should not be considered exact in any case.)

A. Crisis Situation
   High Threat/Short Time/Surprise
B. Innovative Situation
   High Threat/Extended Time/Surprise
C. Inertia Situation
   Low Threat/Extended Time/Surprise
D. Circumstantial Situation
   Low Threat/Short Time/Surprise

E. Reflexive Situation
   High Threat/Short Time/Anticipated
F. Deliberative Situation
   High Threat/Extended Time/Anticipated
G. Routinized Situation
   Low Threat/Extended Time/Anticipated
H. Administrative Situation
   Low Threat/Short Time/Anticipated

right angles, these three scales form a three dimensional space in which all situations can be located according to their degree of threat, time, and awareness (surprise).[21] In Figure 1, this space has been closed to form a cube, the eight corners of which represent all possible combinations of the extreme values of the three dimensions. Thus, the corners of the cube represent ideal types of situations with respect to threat, time, and awareness.[22] Few, if any, actual situations can be considered to correspond to these ideal types, but as the location in the cube of a specific situation approaches one of the corners, that situation can be treated as influencing decision-making in a manner similar to the ideal type.

To illustrate the location of a situation along a dimension, consider the element of decision time in both the Korean crisis of 1950 and the Cuban crisis of 1962. As the South Korean army crumbled before the North Korean advance, the initial optimism of American decision-makers changed to a realization that unless the United States intervened quickly the invaders would control the entire peninsula. The first meeting with the President to discuss the Korean situation occurred on Sunday evening, June 25. After a series of steps taken in the next several days to support the faltering South Korean army, President Truman decided early Friday morning, June 30, to commit American ground forces. Although Truman and his advisers considered the time to be extremely short, other situations such as the detection of a launched ballistic missile attack could offer even less time for decision. Thus, on the time dimension the Korean decision would be located near the short time end of the scale, but would not be at the most extreme point. The Cuban missile crisis also presented short decision time because, as the American policy-makers observed, once the missiles were operational they would be extremely difficult to remove without the possibility that some of them would be launched in retaliation. With missiles prepared for firing, the

situation facing the leaders of the United States would be drastically altered. The first presidential session on that crisis occurred on the morning of Tuesday, October 26; the following Tuesday President Kennedy issued the "Proclamation of the Interdiction of Offensive Weapons" that ordered the blockade to begin the next morning. In actual time the decision in the missile crisis was more extended than that in the Korean crisis. If the decision-makers' perceptions of available time are used, some evidence indicates that the Korean crisis as compared to the Cuban crisis involved even less time than estimates based on clock or calendar. Despite these differences, the perceived time for both decisions puts them near the extreme of short time and both decision processes could be expected to bear resemblance to ideal type situations involving short decision time.

Hypothesized differences in decision-making introduced by crisis can be indicated by comparing crises with the other types of situations represented by the corners of the cube in Figure 1. The more decision makers perceive a situation to approximate the specified characteristics of crisis, the more applicable the following comments should be.

Crisis Situations

In a crisis, with its extreme danger to national goals, the highest level of governmental officials makes the decision. The time limitations together with the ability of these high-ranking decision-makers to commit the government allow them to ignore usual bureaucratic procedures. Information about the situation is at a premium because of the short time for collecting new intelligence and the absence of the serious data-gathering that precedes expected situations of importance. To a greater degree than in other situations the inputs that provide the basis for choice must be other than information about the immediate situation. For example, decision-makers may have a tendency to rely on incomplete analogies with previous situations or on their prior judgments about the friendliness or hostility of the source of the crisis. Although some substantive disagreements may occur among the policy-makers, personal antagonisms remain subdued because of a felt need for ultimate consensus. Compared to the policies

---

[21] We shall use surprise as one extreme on an awareness dimension in order to permit a construction parallel to that for threat and time. Thus, the complete absence of awareness is surprise; the other extreme is anticipation. Because awareness refers to a condition of the decision-maker (i.e., his perception), the term would be less satisfactory if the remainder of this essay were concerned with the objective properties present in the situation.

[22] An earlier version of this situational cube appears in C. F. Hermann, *Crises in Foreign Policy, op. cit.*

made in response to other situations, crisis decisions tend more toward under- or over-reaction. An extreme response is encouraged by certain constraints imposed by the decision process (e.g., minimal information, increased importance of the decision-makers' personalities). The high stakes of a crisis decision and the uncertainty surrounding the outcome lead the decision-makers to remain quite anxious after the decision. Consequently, they expend considerable energy in the post-decision phase seeking support for their policy from allies and others.

Innovative Situations

A situation perceived to contain high threat and surprise but an extended amount of time can be described as encouraging an innovative decision. The threat to high-priority objectives increases the likelihood that the situation will receive the attention of the most able men available and, similarly, that considerable energy will be devoted to investigating the problem. Unlike a crisis decision, the greater time allows the government to undertake considerable search—a process motivated by the threat. Occasionally individuals in an agency charged with conducting foreign policy have programs or ideas that they have been unable to gain support for under normal conditions. A situation of the innovative type, for which there is no planned response and an openness to new ideas, will be sought by such individuals as an opportunity to obtain acceptance for their proposals. As in crises, ad hoc groups may be organized for the consideration of the situation, but they are not as free as crisis decision-makers to ignore normal administrative procedures.

Consider the following illustrations of innovative decisions. The deteriorating economic and political situation in Western Europe became increasingly visible to policy-makers in Washington during the last months of 1946. Against this background on February 21, 1947, the British surprised American officials by notifying them that beginning the first of April, Britain would be forced to discontinue financial assistance to embattled Greece. The same note also indicated that the British government would be unable to supply all the military assistance required by Turkey. That incident resulted in what Jones has called "the fifteen weeks" that

culminated in the Marshall Plan.[23] A second example of an innovative decision followed Nasser's nationalization of the Suez Canal in July 1956. That situation appears to have been perceived as a high-threat, surprise situation by decision-makers in Britain and France. They apparently felt that the decision time was sufficiently extended to explore several possible alternatives (e.g., the users' conference, a United Nations resolution) while coordinating their military operations that led to the dramatic attack on Egypt, October 31.

Inertia Situations

Situations perceived as involving low threat, extended time, and surprise often lead to inertia decisions, that is, to decisions not to act or to discussions that never result in a decision. The surprise quality of the situation makes less likely the existence of preparations appropriate for coping with it. Being unexpected, no agency or bureau may see the situation as salient to its own plans. As a result the situation may be discussed by the various offices to which it is referred without the commitment of any agency. A decision is further inhibited by the absence of any sense of urgency. Given the number of policy situations at any given time that pose considerable danger to the objectives of policy-makers, this type of situation has difficulty being assigned a place on the crowded agenda of men with the authority to commit the state. Actual situations which, from the American perspective, approach the prototype for inertia decisions include the fall of Khrushchev on October 15, 1964 and De Gaulle's sudden withdrawal of the French Mediterranean Fleet from NATO in 1959. The latter situation was an annoyance to American objectives, but by itself was not recognized as a serious threat. Nor did it seem likely that De Gaulle would soon alter the situation if no American decision was made immediately.

Circumstantial Situations

Circumstantial decisions are increasingly likely in situations that policy-makers recognize as involving low threat, short time, and surprise. Like crises these are situational conditions that require a quick decision

[23] J. M. Jones, *The Fifteen Weeks* (New York: Harcourt, Brace & World, 1964), Harbinger book edition.

if a choice is to be made before the situation is transformed in some manner that makes action more difficult. But unlike crises, and more like inertia decisions, the stakes in the present type of situation are not high. A failure to make the "right" decision in time is not seen as leaving important national goals in jeopardy. Under these conditions whether or not the nation's policy makers reach a decision depends on other circumstances that exist at the time the situation is recognized. In other words, the three situational variables are not likely to be critical determinants in the low threat, short time, and surprise configuration.

The captives held at Stanleyville in the Congo during November 1964 and the Hungarian revolt in November 1956 both created some threat to American objectives. On balance, however, these two situations must be located near the corner of the cube in Figure 1 designated "circumstantial." Both situations illustrate the importance of other factors in determining the response. When the uprising occurred in Hungary, policy-makers in the United States were preoccupied with the Anglo-French-Israeli assault on Egypt and the Suez Canal. They made no decision on the Hungarian issue until after the presence of Soviet troops had radically altered that situation. By contrast, the availability of Belgian troops and the interest of their government in cooperating with the United States to prevent the threatened murder of the European and American hostages resulted in 600 Belgian paratroopers being flown to Stanleyville on November 24, 1964, in aircraft furnished by the United States.

Reflexive Situations

The first four classes of situations involved surprise; the remaining four (located at the back of the cube in Figure 1) mark the opposite end of the awareness dimension. The lower left-hand corner of the cube represents situations that are recognized by policy-makers as containing high threat, short time, and anticipation. This situational configuration increases the probability of reflexive decisions. With decision time at a premium, no elaborate search routines or consultations are possible to disclose methods for coping with the situation. In this sense the decision process is similar to that for crises, the difference being that for reflexive decisions the policy-makers

have expected the situation to occur. Because they will experience a serious threat to their goals if it does develop, the policy-makers probably produce a contingency plan in the period before the situation emerges. Once the situation appears, minor alterations may be made in the proposed plan, but time pressures deny decision-makers the chance to consider major alternatives. In fact, the knowledge that they have already considered the problem may lead policy-makers to an almost reflexive response. Under these circumstances the decision process will be more rapid than in a crisis.

The blockade of Berlin in 1948 provides an example. American decision-makers perceived the threat to their objectives to be severe. They also recognized decision time to be restricted both by the dwindling supply of essential commodities in Berlin and by the need for a rapid response to assure Europeans of the commitment of the United States. As early as January 1948, the Soviets introduced various restrictions on transportation moving through East Germany to Berlin. By early April, General Clay had proposed to Washington an airlift to Berlin—at least for American dependents—if access on the ground were denied. When the Soviets began to stop traffic on June 24, Clay called for an airlift to begin the following day as an interim measure.[24] After a month, the President and his advisers agreed to continue this temporary measure on an increased scale for the duration of the blockade. The confrontation over the Taiwan Straits in 1958 may be another illustration of a situation containing the characteristics that lead to a reflexive decision. Policy-makers in the United States considered the shelling of Quemoy and Matsu islands—which began on August 23—as a serious threat requiring a quick decision if the islands were to be defended. American intelligence detected clues of the forthcoming assault during the first days of August, which added to the sense of anticipation already created by previous encounters. When the shelling of the islands began, the United States quickly responded by reinforcing the Seventh Fleet, which was operating in the area. Although engaging in overstatement, Stewart Alsop revealed the reflexive nature of the American reaction with his observation: "There is little real significance in the

[24] J. E. Smith, *The Defense of Berlin* (Baltimore: Johns Hopkins Press, 1963), p. 107.

inner history of the 1958 crisis, simply because the basic decisions had already been made in 1954 and 1955."[25]

Deliberative Situations

The combination of high threat, extended time, and anticipation often results in a decision process that can be described as deliberative. The reaction of decision-makers parallels that for the innovative decision in many respects. High threat increases the probability that the situation receives careful attention, but unlike a crisis, the deliberations are not limited to a small group of the highest-ranking officials. Consideration of the problem occurs at different levels and in different agencies. The time available for discussion both prior to the actual appearance of the situation (as a result of anticipation) and after it emerges (as a result of extended decision time) can lead to organizational difficulties. Many groups in and out of government may become committed to a particular method of handling the problem. As the following examples indicate, deliberative situations increase the likelihood of hard bargaining between groups with alternative proposals.

In August 1949, the Soviet Union achieved its first nuclear explosion. That threatening event had been anticipated by the American government, but had not been expected until 1952 or 1953. In the next several months it became evident to the American government that the civil war in China would result in a Communist regime on the Chinese mainland. With the background of the Soviet atomic explosion, the actual formation of the Chinese Peoples Republic created an anticipated situation for United States policy-makers of high threat and extended time. The response to the situation included the preparation of NSC-68, a document that makes a series of policy recommendations on the basis of a comprehensive statement of national strategy. These recommendations for rearmament involving large increases in military expenditures became the subject of an extensive debate within the Truman administration during the spring of 1950—a debate that was ultimately resolved by the attack on South Korea. The Soviet ultimatum on June 4, 1961, created a similar type of situation. The Soviet government warned that it would sign a separate peace treaty with East Germany within six months unless the Western powers withdrew their military forces from Berlin which was to become a demilitarized city. The U.S.S.R. had made a similar demand in November 1958. Moreover, Khrushchev for months before the formal note was dispatched had boasted that he would sign such a treaty. Despite the anticipated quality of the situation and the relatively extended period of time for decision, the American decision-makers perceived it as quite threatening. The decision process in response to this situation involved considerable internal dissent among United States policy-makers as well as sharp divisions between the Western allies.[26]

Routinized Situations

A diagonal running through the center of the cube in Figure 1 which has crisis decisions at one end has routinized decisions located at the other extreme. Routinized decisions frequently occur in low threat, extended time, and anticipated situations. Many, but not all, situations of this type are anticipated because they reappear with considerable regularity. Agencies charged with the conduct of foreign policy develop programmed routines for meeting recurrent low threat situations. Because established procedures are available, these situations tend to be dealt with by policy-makers at the lower and middle levels of the organization. The decision process follows one of two general patterns. In the first pattern decision-makers treat the problem in the same manner as they have treated previous situations of the same genus. Execution of the recommended course of action follows prompt agreement, unless temporary delays develop because policy-makers, whose approval is required, are engaged in more urgent business. If the situation lacks precedent or becomes the pawn in an interagency dispute, it follows the second pattern. Under these circumstances it may never come to a decision or may lie fallow until personnel change. Fear of bureaucratic obstruction provides one reason why policy-makers offer strong resistance to proposals for altering the response

---

[25] S. Alsop, "The Story Behind Quemoy: How We Drifted Close to War," *Saturday Evening Post*, CCXXXI (December 13, 1958), p. 88. Evidence that American intelligence had indications of the Chinese move early in August appears in D. D. Eisenhower, *Waging Peace* (Garden City: Doubleday and Company, Inc., 1965), p. 292.

[26] See Smith, *op. cit.*

to an issue for which there are established procedures. For the United States the question of admitting Communist China to the United Nations is a routinized decision regularly considered before the General Assembly convenes. Efforts to change the American response to this situation—as in 1961—have met with opposition in the government. The signing of a peace treaty with Japan offers another example. American policy-makers, some of whom had anticipated the problem since the closing days of World War II, began formulating a response when the situation arose in 1947. But differences developed over the issue. Not until September 1951 was the United States able to call the San Francisco Conference at which forty-eight nations signed the treaty of peace with Japan.[27]

Administrative Situations

The final corner of the situational cube represents low threat, short time, and anticipation—a combination that usually results in a decision process described in this essay as administrative. Administrative decisions engage middle-level officials of foreign policy organizations, men who have the authority to energize selected parts of the decision machinery for quick responses to situations that contain limited threat. Efforts to seek out new information about the situation are limited by the short decision time and by the relatively low priority of low threat situations in gaining access to the government's facilities for search. In a fashion similar to reflexive decisions, the treatment of an administrative decision depends on the extent to which policy-makers have taken advantage of their expectation that the situation is likely to occur. If they anticipate that the situation will involve minimal threat, policy-makers may be reluctant to invest much time in the preparation of a possible response. On the other hand, when a low threat situation materializes they have less of a felt need for some kind of action than do the participants in a reflexive decision. Hence, those engaged in an administrative decision are unlikely to act at all unless they are confident that the proposed response

is appropriate to the situation. In brief, a low threat, short time, anticipated situation will mobilize existing work groups who will not engage in any significant amount of bargaining or search and who will reach a decision only if they are confident in their choice at the time it is made.

On May 1, 1960, when American decision-makers received notification that a U-2 reconnaissance aircraft was missing over the Soviet Union, the situation for them involved low threat, short time, and anticipation. The possibility that a U-2 might be lost over the U.S.S.R. had been considered previously. On the assumption that the Soviets would be unable to produce any substantial evidence regarding the plane's mission, United States policy-makers had prepared a series of guidelines for a cover story. The credibility of the cover story would be weakened if it were held until the Soviets made specific charges rather than being released immediately at the time the plane went down. Thus, a quick decision was made to issue the cover story.[28] That the decision-makers had confidence in the released statement is suggested by their repetition of the story after the Soviets announced they had shot down a spy plane. Once the pilot and other evidence were produced the situation was radically changed. A second illustration of the administrative type of situation is the Indian request for arms during the October 1962 border conflict with China. The issue of military aid to India had been extensively explored during the previous months, especially since May when it appeared that India might turn to the Soviet Union for military support. When

[27] The appointment of John Foster Dulles as a special counselor in the State Department charged with overseeing the task appears to have been a critical step in obtaining a decision on this situation. See B. C. Cohen, *The Political Process and Foreign Policy: The Making of the Japanese Peace Settlement* (Princeton: Princeton University Press, 1957).

[28] The following excerpt provides insight into the level of government at which the U-2 problem was initially handled as well as an indication of the low threat, anticipated quality of the situation: "Cumming [Hugh S. Cumming, Jr., chief of Intelligence and Research] was the only State Department man present. The rest were C.I.A. officials and technical experts. The men who gathered around the table this afternoon were concerned, but not overly so. True, there was every indication that Powers [the U-2 pilot] was down in the Soviet Union, but the chances that the Russians would recover any damning physical evidence of the overflight was slim.... The discussion, therefore, centered on the cover story.... The cover story pulled out of the files on May 1 and under consideration by the men meeting at the clandestine C.I.A. headquarters stated that the U-2 had taken off from Turkey on an upper-altitude-research mission and had, unfortunately, overflown Pakistan without authorization after the pilot reported mechanical difficulty." D. Wise and T. B. Ross, *The U-2 Affair* (New York: Bantam Books, 1962), pp. 23–24.

Prime Minister Nehru made an urgent appeal to the United States on October 29, the United States decision followed with such speed that the first shipments arrived within the week. This American decision was made while the highest levels of the government remained involved in the Cuban missile crisis.

We should reiterate that the statements about the decision processes that develop in response to various types of situations are hypotheses which may or may not be confirmed by further research. Thus, the statement about confidence in administrative decisions could be recast in the customary form for hypotheses as follows: The less threat and decision time and the more anticipation that decision-makers perceive in a given situation, the greater will be their initial confidence in any decision made about that situation. We hypothesize that situational variables increase the tendency for the occurrence of a certain kind of process or decision, but these variables alone may not determine the outcome. Other variables reinforce or alter the influence of the specified situational variables. It is possible, of course, that the effect of some situational configurations—perhaps crisis—is so strong that the impact of other variables seldom changes the situational effect on the decision. The question of how much variance in decisions is accounted for by particular situational variables is a matter for empirical research.

The situational cube offers one technique for increasing the cumulative knowledge about crises using the decision-making approach. The use of any classification scheme encourages the analyst to compare a particular situation with others he believes to be similar in specified qualities and to distinguish it from those assumed to be different.[29]

Many classifications for differentiating crises from other situations may prove to be of little use in explaining various types of decisions and will be discarded in favor of better alternatives. This process itself is valuable in increasing our knowledge about the important attributes of situational variables.

The examples used for the situational cube illustrate that previously written case studies can provide material for evaluating hypotheses about the effect of crises on decisions once these propositions have been advanced. As in the systemic approach, however, certain problems arise in reinterpreting a series of prepared studies, each describing an individual situation. The original authors may have excluded important information necessary for inspection of the hypotheses or they may have attached different meanings to important variables. If the same analyst examines a number of cases with the hypotheses in mind, some of these problems are overcome. Nevertheless, as we move from the statement of hypotheses about crisis as a situational variable to the rigorous testing of these hypotheses, the case study necessarily must be augmented by other methods of analysis. This requirement, together with more exact definitions of the situational variable, seems necessary for further crisis analysis using either the systemic or decision-making approaches.

---

the means to use in the response (the authors refer to this as beliefs about causation) and (2) the ends toward which the response is directed (the authors refer to this as preferences about outcomes). See J. D. Thompson and A. Tuden, "Strategies, Structures, and Processes of Organizational Decision," in J. D. Thompson and associates, *Comparative Studies in Administration* (Pittsburgh: University of Pittsburgh Press, 1959), pp. 196–211. Another fourfold classification is based on the decision-makers' level of understanding of the situation and whether the resulting decision can yield large or small changes in the initial situation. See D. Braybrooke and C. E. Lindblom, *A Strategy of Decision* (New York: The Free Press, 1963), especially pp. 66–79.

[29] Other ways of classifying situations have been proposed. One fourfold scheme separates situations according to whether the decision-makers agree on (1)

H. Image as an Organizing Concept

38. National Images and International Systems*

Kenneth E. Boulding, for many years Professor of Economics at the University of Michigan, is now Director of the Research Program in General Social and Economic Dynamics at the University of Colorado. Interested mainly in an interdisciplinary approach to social phenomena, he has written a number of stimulating articles and books that extend beyond his own field of economics. These include *The Organizational Revolution* (1953), *The Image* (1956), and *Conflict and Defense* (1962). In this selection the international system becomes the focus of Professor Boulding's interests and talents as an interdisciplinarian, and as a result he makes available to the field an important framework for analyzing the interaction of states. [*Reprinted from* The Journal of Conflict Resolution, *III* (1959), 120–31, by permission of the author and the publisher, Copyright 1959 by the University of Michigan.]

An international system consists of a group of interacting behavior units called "nations" or "countries," to which may sometimes be added certain supra-national organizations, such as the United Nations.

Each of the behavior units in the system can be described in terms of a set of "relevant variables." Just what is relevant and what is not is a matter of judgment of the system-builder, but we think of such things as states of war or peace, degrees of hostility or friendliness, alliance or enmity, arms budgets, geographic extent, friendly or hostile communications, and so on. Having defined our variables, we can then proceed to postulate certain relationships between them, sufficient to define a path for all the variables through time. Thus we might suppose, with Lewis Richardson,[1] that the rate of change of hostility of one nation toward a second depends on the level of hostility in the second and that the rate of change of hostility of the second toward the first depends on the level of hostility of the first. Then, if we start from given levels of hostility in each nation, these equations are sufficient to spell out what happens to these levels in succeeding time periods. A system of this kind may (or may not) have an *equilibrium* position at which the variables of one period produce an identical set in the next period, and the system exhibits no change through time.

Mechanical systems of this kind, though they are frequently illuminating, can be regarded only

---

* This paper was presented to a meeting of the American Psychological Association in Washington, D.C., on August 30, 1958.

[1] See Anatol Rapoport, "Lewis F. Richardson's Mathematical Theory of War," *Journal of Conflict Resolution*, I (September, 1957), 249, for an excellent exposition.

as very rough first approximations to the immensely complex truth. At the next level of approximation we must recognize that the people whose decisions determine the policies and actions of nations do not respond to the "objective" facts of the situation, whatever that may mean, but to their "image" of the situation. It is what we think the world is like, not what it is really like, that determines our behavior. If our image of the world is in some sense "wrong," of course, we may be disappointed in our expectations and we may therefore revise our image: if this revision is in the direction of the "truth" there is presumably a long-run tendency for the "image" and the "truth" to coincide. Whether this is so or not, it is always the image, not the truth, that immediately determines behavior. We act according to the way the world appears to us, not necessarily according to the way it "is." Thus in Richardson's models it is one nation's image of the hostility of another, not the "real" hostility, which determines its reaction. The "image," then, must be thought of as the total cognitive, affective, and evaluative structure of the behavior unit, or its internal view of itself and its universe.[2]

Generally speaking, the behavior of complex organizations can be regarded as determined by *decisions*, and a decision involves the selection of the most preferred position in a contemplated field of choice. Both the field of choice and the ordering of this field by which the preferred position is identified lie in the image of the decision-maker. Therefore, in a system in which decision-makers are an essential element, the study of the ways in which the image grows and changes, both of the field of choice and of the valuational ordering of this field, is of prime importance. The image is always in some sense a product of messages received in the past. It is not, however, a simple inventory or "pile" of such messages but a highly structured piece of information-capital, developed partly by its inputs and outputs of information and partly by internal messages and its own laws of growth and stability.

The images which are important in international systems are those which a nation has of itself and of those other bodies in the system which constitute its international environment. At once a major

complication suggests itself. A nation is some complex of the images of the persons who contemplate it, and as there are many different persons, so there are many different images. The complexity is increased by the necessity for inclusion, in the image of each person or at least of many persons, his image of the image of others. This complexity, however, is a property of the real world, not to be evaded or glossed over. It can be reduced to simpler terms if we distinguish between two types of persons in a nation—the powerful, on the one hand, and the ordinary, on the other. This is not, of course, a sharp distinction. The power of a decision-maker may be measured roughly by the number of people which his decisions potentially affect, weighted by some measure of the effect itself. Thus the head of a state is powerful, meaning that his decisions affect the lives of millions of people; the ordinary person is not powerful, for his decisions affect only himself and the lives of a few people around him. There is usually a continuum of power among the persons of a society: thus in international relations there are usually a few very powerful individuals in a state—the chief executive, the prime minister, the secretary of state or minister of foreign affairs, the chiefs of staff of the armed forces. There will be some who are less powerful but still influential—members of the legislature, of the civil sevrice, even journalists, newspaper owners, prominent businessmen, grading by imperceptible degrees down to the common soldier, who has no power of decision even over his own life. For purposes of the model, however, let us compress this continuum into two boxes, labeled the "powerful" and the "ordinary," and leave the refinements of power and influence for later studies.

We deal, therefore, with two representative images, (1) the image of the small group of powerful people who make the actual decisions which lead to war or peace, the making or breaking of treaties, the invasions or withdrawals, alliances, and enmities which make up the major events of international relations, and (2) the image of the mass of ordinary people who are deeply affected by these decisions but who take little or no direct part in making them. The tacit support of the mass, however, is of vital importance to the powerful. The powerful are always under some obligation to represent the mass, even under dictatorial regimes. In democratic societies the aggregate influence of the images of

[2] See K. E. Boulding, *The Image* (Ann Arbor: University of Michigan Press, 1956), for an exposition of the theory on which this paper is based.

ordinary people is very great; the image of the powerful cannot diverge too greatly from the image of the mass without the powerful losing power. On the other hand, the powerful also have some ability to manipulate the images of the mass toward those of the powerful. This is an important object of instruments as diverse as the public education system, the public relations departments of the armed services, the Russian "agitprop," and the Nazi propaganda ministry.

In the formation of the national images, however, it must be emphasized that impressions of nationality are formed mostly in childhood and usually in the family group. It would be quite fallacious to think of the images as being cleverly imposed on the mass by the powerful. If anything, the reverse is the case: the image is essentially a mass image, or what might be called a "folk image," transmitted through the family and the intimate face-to-face group, both in the case of the powerful and in the case of ordinary persons. Especially in the case of the old, long-established nations, the powerful share the mass image rather than impose it; it is passed on from the value systems of the parents to those of the children, and agencies of public instruction and propaganda merely reinforce the images which derived essentially from the family culture. This is much less true in new nations which are striving to achieve nationality, where the family culture frequently does not include strong elements of national allegiance but rather stresses allegiance to religious ideals or to the family as such. Here the powerful are frequently inspired by a national image derived not from family tradition but from a desire to imitate other nations, and here they frequently try to impose their images on the mass of people. Imposed images, however, are fragile by comparison with those which are deeply internalized and transmitted through family and other intimate sources.

Whether transmitted orally and informally through the family or more formally through schooling and the written word, the national image is essentially a *historical* image—that is, an image which extends through time, backward into a supposedly recorded or perhaps mythological past and forward into an imagined future. The more conscious a people is of its history, the stronger the national image is likely to be. To be an Englishman is to be conscious of "1066 and All That" rather than of "Constantine and All That," or "1776 and All That." A nation is the creation of its historians, formal and informal. The written word and public education contribute enormously to the stability and persistence of the national images. The Jews, for instance, are a creation of the Bible and the Talmud, but every nation has its bible, whether formed into a canon or not—noble words like the Declaration of Independence and the Gettysburg Address—which crystallize the national image in a form that can be transmitted almost unchanged from generation to generation. It is no exaggeration to say that the function of the historian is to pervert the truth in directions favorable to the images of his readers or hearers. Both history and geography as taught in national schools are devised to give "perspective" rather than truth: that is to say, they present the world as seen from the vantage point of the nation. The national geography is learned in great detail, and the rest of the world is in fuzzy outline; the national history is emphasized and exalted; the history of the rest of the world is neglected or even falsified to the glory of the national image.

It is this fact that the national image is basically a lie, or at least a perspective distortion of the truth, which perhaps accounts for the ease with which it can be perverted to justify monstrous cruelties and wickednesses. There is much that is noble in the national image. It has lifted man out of the narrow cage of self-centeredness, or even family-centeredness, and has forced him to accept responsibility, in some sense, for people and events far beyond his face-to-face cognizance and immediate experience. It is a window of some sort on both space and time and extends a man's concern far beyond his own little lifetime and petty interests. Nevertheless, it achieves these virtues usually only at the cost of untruth, and this fatal flaw constantly betrays it. Love of country is perverted into hatred of the foreigner, and peace, order, and justice at home are paid for by war, cruelty, and injustice abroad.

In the formation of the national image the consciousness of great *shared* events and experiences is of the utmost importance. A nation is a body of people who are conscious of having "gone through something" together. Without the shared experience, the national image itself would not be shared, and it is of vital importance that the national image be highly similar. The sharing may be quite vicarious; it may be an experience shared long ago but constantly renewed by the ritual observances and historical memory of the people, like the Passover and the Captivity in the case of the Jews. Without the sharing, however, there is no nation. It is for this reason that war has been such a tragically important element in the creation and sustenance of the national image. There is hardly a nation that has not been cradled in violence and nourished by further violence. This is not, I think, a necessary property of war itself. It is rather that, especially in more primitive societies, war is the one experience which is dramatic, obviously important, and shared by everybody. We are now witnessing the almost unique phenomenon of a number of new nations arising without war in circumstances which are extremely rare in history, for example—India, Ghana, and the new West Indian Federation, though even here there are instances of severe violence, such as the disturbances which accompanied partition in India. It will be interesting to see the effect, if any, on their national images.

We now come to the central problem of this paper, which is that of the impact of national images on the relations among states, that is, on the course of events in international relations. The relations among states can be described in terms of a number of different dimensions. There is, first of all, the dimension of simple geographical space. It is perhaps the most striking single characteristic of the national state as an organization, by contrast with organizations such as firms or churches, that it thinks of itself as occupying, in a "dense" and exclusive fashion, a certain area of the globe. The schoolroom maps which divide the world into colored shapes which are identified as nations have a profound effect on the national image. Apart from the very occasional condominium, it is impossible for a given plot of land on the globe to be associated with two nations at the same time. The territories of nations are divided sharply by frontiers carefully surveyed and frequently delineated by a chain of customs houses, immigration stations, and military installations. We are so accustomed to this arrangement that we think of it as "natural" and take it completely for granted. It is by no means the only conceivable arrangement, however. In primitive societies the geographical image is not sharp enough

to define clear frontiers; there may be a notion of the rough territory of a tribe, but, especially among nomadic peoples, there is no clear concept of a frontier and no notion of a nation as something that has a shape on a map. In our own society the shape on the map that symbolizes the nation is constantly drilled into the minds of both young and old, both through formal teaching in schools and through constant repetition in newspapers, advertisements, cartoons, and so on. A society is not inconceivable, however, and might even be desirable, in which nations governed people but not territories and claimed jurisdiction over a defined set of citizens, no matter where on the earth's surface they happened to live.

The territorial aspect of the national state is important in the dynamics of international relations because of the *exclusiveness* of territorial occupation. This means that one nation can generally expand only at the expense of another; an increase in the territory of one is achieved only at the expense of a decrease in the territory of another. This makes for a potential conflict situation. This characteristic of the nation does not make conflict inevitable, but it does make it likely and is at least one of the reasons why the history of international relations is a history of perpetual conflict.

The territorial aspect of international relations is complicated by the fact that in many cases the territories of nations are not homogeneous but are composed of "empires," in which the populations do not identify themselves with the national image of the dominant group. Thus when one nation conquers another and absorbs the conquered territory into an empire, it does not thereby automatically change the culture and allegiances of the conquered nation. The Poles remained Polish for a hundred and twenty-five years of partition between Germany, Austria, and Russia. The Finns retained their nationality through eight hundred years of foreign rule and the Jews, through nearly two thousand years of dispersion. If a nation loses territory occupied by disaffected people, this is much less damaging than the loss of territory inhabited by a well-disposed and loyal population. Thus, Turkey, which was the "sick man of Europe" as long as it retained its heterogeneous empire, enjoyed a substantial renewal of national health when stripped of its empire and pushed back to the relatively homogeneous heartland of Anatolia. In this case the loss of a disaffected empire actually strengthened the national unit.

The image of the map-shape of the nations may be an important factor affecting the general frame of mind of the nation. There is a tendency for nations to be uneasy with strong irregularities, enclaves, detached portions, and protuberances or hollows. The ideal shape is at least a convex set, and there is some tendency for nations to be more satisfied if they have regularly round or rectangular outlines. Thus the detachment of East Prussia from the body of Germany by the Treaty of Versailles was an important factor in creating the fanatical discontent of the Nazis.

A second important dimension of the national image is that of hostility or friendliness. At any one time a particular national image includes a rough scale of the friendliness or hostility of, or toward, other nations. The relationship is not necessarily either consistent or reciprocal—in nation A the prevailing image may be that B is friendly, whereas in nation B itself the prevailing image may be one of hostility toward A; or again in both nations there may be an image of friendliness of A toward B but of hostility of B toward A. On the whole, however, there is a tendency toward both consistency and reciprocation—if a nation A pictures itself as hostile toward B, it usually also pictures B as hostile toward it, and the image is likely to be repeated in B. One exception to this rule seems to be observable: most nations seem to feel that their enemies are more hostile toward them than they are toward their enemies. This is a typical paranoid reaction; the nation visualizes itself as surrounded by hostile nations toward which it has only the nicest and friendliest of intentions.

An important subdimension of the hostility-friendliness image is that of the stability or security of the relationship. A friendly relationship is frequently formalized as an alliance. Alliances, however, are shifting; some friendly relations are fairly permanent, others change as the world kaleidoscope changes, as new enemies arise, or as governments change. Thus a bare fifteen or twenty years ago most people in the United States visualized Germany and Japan, even before the outbreak of the war, as enemies, and after Hitler's invasion of Russia, Russia was for a while regarded as a valuable friend and ally. Today the picture is quite changed: Germany and Japan are valuable friends and allies: Russia is the great enemy. We can roughly classify the reciprocal relations of nations along some scale of friendliness-hostility. At one extreme we have stable friendliness, such as between Britain and Portugal or between Britain and the Commonwealth countries. At the other extreme we have stable hostility—the "traditional enemies" such as France and Germany. Between these extremes we have a great many pairs characterized by shifting alliances. On the whole, stable friendly relations seem to exist mainly between strong nations and weaker nations which they have an interest in preserving and stable hostile relations between adjacent nations each of which has played a large part in the formation of the other.

Another important dimension both of the image and of the "reality" of the nation-state is its strength or weakness. This is, in turn, a structure made up of many elements—economic resources and productivity, political organization and tradition, willingness to incur sacrifice and inflict cruelties, and so on. It still makes some kind of sense to assess nations on a strength-weakness scale at any one time. Strength is frequently thought of in military terms as the ability to hurt an opponent or to prevent one's self from being hurt by him. There are also more subtle elements in terms of symbolic loyalties and affections which are hard to assess but which must be included in any complete picture. Many arrays of bristling armaments have been brought low by the sheer inability of their wielders to attract any lasting respect or affection. No social organization can survive indefinitely unless it can command the support of its members, and a continuing sense of the significance of the organization or group as such is much more durable a source of support than is the fleeting booty of war or monopoly. The Jews have outlasted an impressive succession of conquerors. These questions regarding the ultimate sources of continuing strength or weakness are difficult, and we shall neglect them in this paper.

In order to bring together the variables associated with each nation or pair of nations into an international system, we must resort to the device of a matrix, as in Figure 1. Here the hostility-friendliness variable is used as an example. Each cell, a_{ij}, indicates the degree of hostility or friendliness of nation I

	A	B	C	D	E	Totals
A		−5	+3	0	+2	0
B	−3		−2	−1	−2	−8
C	+2	−4		0	+1	−1
D	−1	−1	0		0	−2
E	+4	−3	+2	0		+3
Totals	+2	−13	+3	−1	+1	−8
X	2	−5	4	+1	−2	0
Y	1	−10½	1	−1½	2	−8

Figure 1

(of the row) toward nation $\mathcal{J}$ (of the column). For purposes of illustration, arbitrary figures have been inserted on a scale from 5 to − 5. − 5 meaning very hostile, 5 very friendly, and 0 neutral.[3] A matrix

[3] The problem of the measurement of hostility (or friendliness) is a very interesting one which we cannot go into extensively here but which is not so hopeless of solution as might at first sight appear. Possible avenues are as follows: (1) A historical approach. Over a period of years two nations have been at war, threatening war, allied, bound by treaty, and so on. Each relation would be given an arbitrary number, and each year assigned a number accordingly: the average of the years' numbers would be the index. This would always yield a symmetrical matrix—that is, the measure of I's relation to $\mathcal{J}$ would be the same as $\mathcal{J}$'s relation to I or $a_{ij} = a_{ij}$. (2) An approach by means of content analysis of public communications (official messages, newspaper editorials, public speeches, cartoons, etc.). This seems likely to be most immediately useful and fruitful, as it would give current information and would also yield very valuable dynamic information about the changes in the matrix, which may be much more important than the absolute figures. The fact that any measure of this kind is highly arbitrary is no argument against it, provided that it is qualitatively reliable—that is, moves generally in the same direction as the variable which it purports to measure—and provided also that the limitations of the measure are clearly understood. It would probably be advisable to check the second type of measure against the more objective measures derived from the first method. The difficulty of the first method, however, is the extreme instability of the matrix. The affections of nations are ephemeral!

of this kind has many interesting properties, not all of which can be worked out here but which depend on the kind of restraints that we impose on it. If we suppose, for instance, the relations of nations are reciprocal, so that I's attitude toward $\mathcal{J}$ is the same as $\mathcal{J}$'s toward I, the matrix becomes symmetrical about its major diagonal—that is, the lower left-hand triangle is a mirror image of the upper right-hand triangle. This is a very severe restriction and is certainly violated in fact: there are unrequited loves and hates among the nations as there are among individuals. We can recognize a *tendency*, however, for the matrix to become symmetrical. There is a certain instability about an unrequited feeling. If I loves $\mathcal{J}$ and $\mathcal{J}$ hates I, then either $\mathcal{J}$'s constant rebuff of I's affections will turn I's love to hate, or I's persistent wooing will break down $\mathcal{J}$'s distaste and transform it into affection. Unfortunately for the history of human relations, the former seems to be the more frequent pattern, but the latter is by no means unknown.[4]

The sum totals of the rows represent the over-all friendliness or hostility of the nation at the head of the row; the sum totals of the columns represent the degree of hostility or friendliness *toward* the nation at the head of the column. The sum of either of these sums (which must be equal, as each represents a way of adding up all the figures of the matrix) is a measure of the over-all friendliness or hostility of the system. In the example of Figure 1, B is evidently a "paranoid" nation, feeling hostile toward everyone and receiving hostility in return; D is a "neutral" nation, with low values for either hostility or friendliness; E is a "friendly" nation, reciprocating B's general hostility but otherwise having positive relations with everyone. In this figure it is evident that A, C, and E are likely to be allied against B, and D is likely to be uncommitted.

In the matrix of Figure 1 no account is taken of the relative size or power of the different nations. This dimension of the system can easily be accommodated, however. All that is necessary is to take

[4] George F. Kennan once said: "It is an undeniable privilege of every man to prove himself in the right in the thesis that the world is his enemy: for if he reiterates it frequently enough and makes it the background of his conduct, he is bound eventually to be right" ("The Roots of Soviet Conduct," *Foreign Affairs*, July, 1947). If for "enemy" we read "friend" in this statement, the proposition seems to be equally true but much less believed.

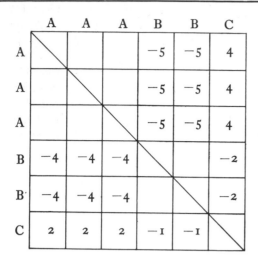

	A	A	A	B	B	C
A				−5	−5	4
A				−5	−5	4
A				−5	−5	4
B	−4	−4	−4			−2
B	−4	−4	−4			−2
C	2	2	2	−1	−1	

Figure 2

the power of the smallest nation as a convenient unit and express the power of the others in multiples of this unit. Then in the matrix we simply give each nation a number of places along the axes equal to the measure of its power. Thus in Figure 2 we suppose a system of three nations, where B is twice as powerful as C and A is three times as powerful as C; A is then allotted three spaces along the axes, B two, and C one. The analysis of the matrix proceeds as before, with the additional constraint that all the figures in the larger boxes bounded by the lines which divide the nations should be the same, as in the figure.

The difference between the sum of a nation's column, representing the general degree of support or affection it *receives*, and the sum of a nation's row, representing the sum of support or affection it *gives*, might be called its *affectional balance*. This is shown in the row X in Figure 1. It is a necessary property of a matrix of this kind that the sum of all these balances shall be zero. They measure the relative position of each nation in regard to the degree of support it can expect from the international system as a whole. Thus in Fig. 1 it is clear that B is in the worst position, and C in the best position, vis-à-vis the system as a whole. Another figure of some interest might be called the *affectional contribution*, shown in the line Y. This is the mean of the column and row totals for each nation. The total affectional contribution is equal to the total of all the

figures of the matrix, which measures the general hostility or friendliness of the whole system. The affectional contribution is then a rough measure of how much each nation contributes to the general level of hostility of the whole system. Thus in the example of Figure 1 we see that nation B (the paranoid) actually contributes more than 100 per cent to the total hostility of the system, its extreme hostility being offset to some extent by other nations' friendliness.

One critical problem of an international system, then, is that of the *dynamics* of the hostility matrix. We can conceive of a succession of such matrices at successive points of time. If there is a system with a "solution," we should be able to predict the matrix at t_1 from the knowledge we have of the matrix at t_0 or at various earlier times. The matrix itself will not, in general, carry enough information to make such predictions possible, even though it is easy to specify theoretical models in which a determinate dynamic system can be derived from the information in the matrix alone.[5]

The difficulty with "simple" systems of this nature is that they are very much more simple than the reality which they symbolize. This is because, in reality, the variables of the system consist of the innumerable dimensions of the images of large numbers of people, and the dynamics of the image are much more complex than the dynamics of mechanical systems. This is because of the structural nature of the image; it cannot be represented simply by a set of quantities or variables. Because of this structural nature, it is capable occasionally of very dramatic changes as a message hits some vital part of the structure and the whole image reorganizes itself. Certain events—like the German invasion of Belgium in 1914, the Japanese attack on Pearl Harbor in 1941, the American use of the atom bomb at Hiroshima and Nagasaki, the merciless destruction of Dresden, and the Russian success with Sputnik I—have profound effects and possibly long-run

[5] As a very simple example of such a system, let $(a_{ij})t$ be a cell of the matrix at the time t and $(a_{ij})t + 1$ be the corresponding value at time $t + 1$. Then if for each cell we can postulate a function of $(a_{ij})_{t+1} = F(a_{ij})_t$, we can derive the whole $t + 1$ matrix from the t matrix. This is essentially the dynamic method of Lewis F. Richardson, and in fairly simple cases it provides an interesting way of formulating certain aspects of the system, especially its tendency toward *cumulative* movements of hostility (arms races) or occasionally of friendliness.

effects on reorganizing the various national images. The "reorganizing" events are hard both to specify and to predict; they introduce, however, a marked element of uncertainty into any dynamic international system which does not exist, for instance, in the solar system!

In spite of this difficulty, which, oddly enough, is particularly acute in short-term prediction, one gets the impression from the observation of history that we are in the presence of a true system with a real dynamic of its own. We do observe, for instance, cumulative processes of hostility. If we had some measures of the hostility matrix, however crude, it would be possible to identify these processes in more detail, especially the "turning points." There is an analogy here with the business cycle, which also represents a system of cumulative stochastic processes subject to occasional "reorganizations" of its basic equations. Just as we can trace cumulative upward and downward movements in national income, the downward movements often (though not always) culminating in financial crisis and the upward movements often leading to inflation and a subsequent downturn, so we can trace cumulative movements in the hostility matrix. We have "prewar" periods corresponding to downswings, in which things go from bad to worse and hostility constantly increases. The total of all the hostility figures (e.g., − 8 on Fig. 1) is a striking analogue of the national-income concept. It might be called the "international temperature." Just as there is a certain critical point in a deflation at which a financial crisis is likely to ensue because of the growing insolvency of heavily indebted businesses, so there is a critical point in the rise of hostility at which war breaks out. This critical point itself depends on a number of different factors and may not be constant. Some nations may be more tolerant of hostility than others; as the cost of war increases, the tolerance of hostility also increases, as we see today in the remarkable persistence of the "cold war." A deflation or downturn, however, *may* reverse itself without a crisis, and a "prewar" period may turn into a "postwar" period without a war. Indeed, in the period since 1945 we might identify almost as many small international cycles as there have been business cycles! The "upturn" may be a result of a change of government, the death of certain prominent individuals, or even a change of heart (or image!)

on the part of existing rulers. The catharsis of a war usually produces the typical "postwar" period following, though this is often tragically short, as it was after the end of World War II, when a "downturn" began after the revolution in Czechoslovakia. The downturn is often the result of the reassertion of a persistent, long-run character of the system after a brief interlude of increasing friendliness. There seems to be a certain long-run tendency of an international system toward hostility, perhaps because of certain inescapable flaws in the very concept of a national image, just as there also seems to be a long-run tendency of an unregulated and undisturbed market economy toward deflation.

In considering the dynamics of an international system, the essential properties of the image matrix might be summed up in a broad concept of "compatibility." If the change in the system makes for greater compatibility the system may move to an equilibrium. The "balance-of-power" theory postulates the existence of an equilibrium of this nature. The record of history, however, suggests that, in the past at least, international systems have usually been unstable. The incompatibility of various national images has led to changes in the system which have created still greater incompatibility, and the system has moved to less and less stable situations until some crisis, such as war, is reached, which represents a discontinuity in the system. After a war the system is reorganized; some national units may disappear, others change their character, and the system starts off again. The incompatibility may be of many kinds, and it is a virtue of this kind of rather loose model that the historian can fill in the endlessly various details in the special situations which he studies. The model is a mere dress form on which the historian swathes the infinite variations of fashion and fact.

In the model we can distinguish two very different kinds of incompatibility of images. The first might be called "real" incompatibility, where we have two images of the future in which realization of one would prevent the realization of the other. Thus two nations may both claim a certain piece of territory, and each may feel dissatisfied unless the territory is incorporated into it. (One thinks of the innumerable irredenta which have stained the pages of history with so much blood!) Or two nations may both wish to feel stronger than, or superior to, each other. It is possible for two nations to be in a position where each is stronger than the other *at home*, provided that they are far enough apart and that the "loss of power gradient" (which measures the loss of power of each as we remove the point of application farther and farther from the home base) is large enough. It is rarely possible, however, for two nations each to dominate the other, except in the happy situation where each suffers from delusions of grandeur.

The other form of incompatibility might be called "illusory" incompatibility, in which there exists a condition of compatibility which would satisfy the "real" interests of the two parties but in which the dynamics of the situation or the illusions of the parties create a situation of perverse dynamics and misunderstandings, with increasing hostility simply as a result of the reactions of the parties to each other, not as a result of any basic differences of interest. We must be careful about this distinction: even "real" incompatibilities are functions of the national images rather than of physical fact and are therefore subject to change and control. It is hard for an ardent patriot to realize that his country is a mental, rather than a physical, phenomenon, but such indeed is the truth! It is not unreasonable to suppose, however, that "real" incompatibilities are more intractable and less subject to "therapy" than illusory ones.

One final point of interest concerns what might be called the impact of "sophistication" or "self-consciousness" on national images and the international system. The process of sophistication in the image is a very general one, and we cannot follow all its ramifications here. It occurs in every person in greater or less degree as he grows into adult awareness of himself as part of a larger system. It is akin almost to a Copernican revolution: the unsophisticated image sees the world only from the viewpoint of the viewer; the sophisticated image sees the world from many imagined viewpoints, as a system in which the viewer is only a part. The child sees everything through his own eyes and refers everything to his own immediate comfort. The adult learns to see the world through the eyes of others; his horizon extends to other times, places, and cultures than his own; he learns to distinguish between those elements in his experience which are universal and those which are particular. Many grown people, of course,

never become adults in this sense, and it is these who fill our mental hospitals with themselves and their children.

The scientific subculture is an important agency in the sophistication of images. In the physical world we no longer attribute physical phenomena to spirits analogous to our own. In the social sciences we have an agency whereby men reach self-consciousness about their own cultures and institutions and therefore no longer regard these as simply given to them by "nature." In economics, for instance, we have learned to see the system as a whole, to realize that many things which are true of individual behavior are not true of the system and that the system itself is not incapable of a modicum of control. We no longer, for instance, regard depression as "acts of God" but as system-made phenomena capable of control through relatively minor system change.

The national image, however, is the last great stronghold of unsophistication. Not even the professional international relations experts have come very far toward seeing the system as a whole, and the ordinary citizen and the powerful statesman alike have naïve, self-centered, and unsophisticated images of the world in which their nation moves. Nations are divided into "good" and "bad"—the enemy is all bad, one's own nation is of spotless virtue. Wars are either acts of God or acts of the other nations, which always catch us completely by surprise. To a student of international systems the national image even of respectable, intellectual, and powerful people seems naïve and untrue. The patriotism of the sophisticated cannot be a simple faith. There is, however, in the course of human history a powerful and probably irreversible movement toward sophistication. We can wise up, but we cannot wise down, except at enormous cost in the breakdown of civilizations, and not even a major breakdown results in much loss of knowledge. This movement must be taken into account in predicting the future of the international system. The present system as we have known it for the past hundreds or even thousands of years is based on the widespread acceptance of unsophisticated images, such as, for instance, that a nation can be made more secure *merely* by increasing its armaments. The growth of a system-attitude toward international relations will have profound consequences for the dynamics of the system itself, just as the growth of a systems-attitude in economics has profound consequences for the dynamics of the economic system.

If, as I myself believe, we live in an international system so unstable that it threatens the very existence of life on earth, our main hope for change may lie in the rapid growth of sophistication, especially at the level of the images of the powerful. Sophistication, of course, has its dangers also. It is usually but a hair's-breadth removed from sophistry, and a false sophistication (of which Marxism in some respects is a good example) can be even more destructive to the stability of a system than a naïve image. Whichever way we move, however, there is danger. We have no secure place to stand where we are, and we live in a time when intellectual investment in developing more adequate international images and theories of international systems may bear an enormous rate of return in human welfare.

I. Learning Theory

39. Learning and Affect in International Politics

John R. Raser, Research Associate of the Western Behavioral Sciences Institute, has authored several analyses of the psychological variables that affect international behavior. In this selection he explores the relevance for international politics of a line of theory that is a central feature of modern psychology. While his inquiry is confined mainly to the work of one learning theorist, the discussion is sufficiently general to allow the reader to assess the utility of any learning theory as a means of gaining insight into the interaction of states. [*Reprinted from the* Journal of Peace Research, *II (1965), 216–26, by permission of the author and the publisher.*]

I. Introduction

This paper is an attempt to formulate the two-factor learning theory of O. Hobart Mowrer in concise terms which can be applied to different levels of systems. In doing so, it will be necessary to neglect many of the implications of the theory which Mowrer sets forth in his two publications of 1960, *Learning Theory and Behavior*, and *Learning Theory and the Symbolic Process*, and to concentrate upon the essential elements.

The second purpose of the paper is to assess the possibility of adapting this theory of learning in biological organisms to other living systems, i.e. to national actors in an international context. If this can be done successfully, it should provide a slightly more accurate and useful model of international behavior than psychology has yet made available. In particular, it should provide a better conceptual base for the study of the role of affect in international reaction models than that provided by the $S - r : s - R$ model used frequently. (See Holsti, Brody, and North, 1964.)

II. Learning Theory—Historical Development and Mowrer Model

Mowrer's two-factor system is constructed upon early experiments and studies of conditioning, primarily work by Thorndike, Pavlov, and Hull. A brief review is in order. About 1898 Thorndike developed his theory of solution learning. According to this theory, all learning (conditioning) can be accounted for in terms of strengthening or weakening the bonds between stimulus (S) and response (R) by a process of reward or punishment. For example, if some drive stimulus S_d produces the instrumental or behavioral response R_i, and if R_i is followed by a reward, then the "bond" between S_d and R_i will be strengthened by reinforcement and the response R_i will become habitual (see Fig. 1).

(a) S_d ———————— R_i: reward

(b) S_d ———————— R_i

Figure 1

(a) S_d ——————————— R_i: punishment

(b) S_d — — — — — — — — R_i

Figure 2

On the other hand, if S_d elicits response R_i, and R_i is followed by punishment, the bond will be weakened, and the behavior R_i will be inhibited (see Fig. 2).

All conditioned behavior can be accounted for in terms of either *reward* or *punishment.*

Pavlov, in his well-known experiments with dogs, developed his theory of learning about 1927. According to this theory, a drive stimulus, such as hunger, can be referred to as an "unconditioned stimulus," or S_u, which will elicit a response R (salivation, for instance). By repeated presentation of a neutral event (such as a ringing bell) contiguous with hunger (S_u) a conditioned stimulus, S_c (the bell), can be developed. This is, S_c will eventually elicit response R in the same way that S_u formerly did (see Fig. 3).

These two types of learning (Thorndike and Pavlov formulations) may be referred to respectively as "solution learning" (Thorndike) and "sign learning" (Pavlov). Or to word it another way, Thorndike was interested in trial and error in responses, finding a solution to the problem of satisfying a drive by making the response which would satisfy the drive without punishment—the conditioning of responses, or "response substitution." Pavlov, on the other hand, was interested in the conditioning of cues, stimuli, or signs, the question of stimuli substitution.

One other point about the difference should be made. Thorndike was concerned with a spontaneous somatic stimulus originating within the organism, resulting in a behavior output, and how that behavior output could be modified. Pavlov, on the other

hand, was primarily interested in external stimuli and their manipulation, with these external stimuli functioning as inputs resulting in turn in organism behavior. I would note that these statements are meant only as a rough outline which will be useful later and not as an accurate picture of reality.

Hull's theory, developed about 1935, is extremely complex, but only one aspect of it interests us here. This is derived from Hull's position that the impulse of the organism is to return to a steady state. Thus, a stimulus consists of a departure from homeostasis, with the response being behavior designed to return the organism to the steady state. The stimulus is a drive, the response an attempt to reduce the drive. Behavior is drive reduction. Punishment consists of inhibiting drive reduction, reward consists of implementing it. This theory can now be superimposed on those of Thorndike and Pavlov, for the organism may be assumed to choose responses which reduce the drive stimulus by trial and error. The organism is rewarded when the drive is reduced, punished when it is not reduced. When the rewarding response is found, the bonds between the drive and this response are habituated, and behavior has become conditioned.

To this homeostatic view of the organism may be contrasted the hedonistic view. This view holds, essentially, that there may be rewards entirely aside from drive reduction (c.f some of the experiments currently being conducted with electric current to the pleasure centers of the brain, in which it appears that satiation does not take place, that reward is not connected with drive reduction). The converse, which will become important in the formulation presented here, is that there may be punishment aside from inhibited drive reduction. It is possible that an organism may be punished for behavior without frustration of that behavior. An example may clarify this concept. Suppose that a dog is hungry. His behavior is to obtain food to reduce the hunger drive. In Hull's formulation, punishment for that behavior would be to frustrate him in his attempts to procure food, that is, to inhibit drive reduction behavior. But it may be that he could be allowed to obtain food, reduce the drive, but at the same time, be punished for the behavior of obtaining food, for example be forced to walk on a charged grid in order to reach the food.

The problem then becomes one of when the reward

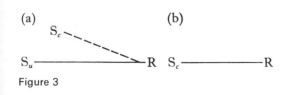

(a)   (b)

S_c ～ ～

S_u———————→R S_c————————R

Figure 3

of drive reduction outweighs the punishment, a problem of weighing utilities. As can be seen, Hull's formulation still obtains, but in a somewhat more complex way than appears at first glance.

As has probably been observed, these theories are essentially mechanistic. They deal with stimuli in terms of somatic, or physiological conditions, with responses as being "instrumental," that is, somehow following mechanically from the stimuli. The organism is seen as nothing more than a transmitter, or a channel. The relationship between stimulus and response would thus be written: $S - R$. Or, to put it in an equation, with (f) as "function of": $R = f(S)$. Woodworth, in 1921, suggested that this might be carrying scientific abstraction somewhat too far, and ventured to insert "O" for organism between the stimulus and response, giving us: $S - O - R$. R. B. Cattell suggested in 1950 that this concept could be written as an equation to read: $R = f(S, O)$. The foregoing is simply an admonition that the organism as an acting and *choosing* entity had best not be ignored in theories of behavior. It is upon this concept that Mowrer's theory of behavior is constructed. His formulation is an attempt to include the *affective* element of the organism in the learning system, an element largely neglected by the Thorndikean and Pavlovian theories.

Mowrer uses the Pavlov sign-learning model when speaking of the input of stimuli into the organism, the Thorndike model when referring to the output of response behavior by the organism, the Hullian concept of reward and punishment as drive reduction or non-reduction. *Feedback* into the organism of reward or punishment acts as a new stimulus, resulting in affective conditions in the organism, that is, hope or fear. These affective elements then become the *primary determinants of behavior*. This concept can be clarified with the use of a diagram.

In Fig. 4, the large circle is the organism. The primary stimulus (such as hunger) is s_d. The organism makes response R_I in order to reduce the hunger drive but is punished by being frustrated in his attempt. This punishment acts as an external stimulus S_I which elicits response r_{fear}. *Response r_{fear} is fear (expectation) that if under stimulus s_d the organism again makes response R_I, punishment will again be the result. This fear is a conditioned response.* It is conditioned under the impact of *punishment*,

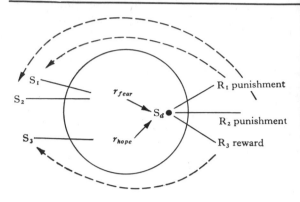

Figure 4

which might be termed "drive increment." By trial and error process, the organism will make another response R_2 to s_d and will again be punished, with S_2 resulting in r_{fear}. Another response will then be made, this time R_3 with *reward* (drive decrement) the result. This reward will act as a stimulus S_3 which will elicit the response r_{hope} (expectation) that if R_3 is again made to s_d, reward will again be the result. Eventually, behavior is conditioned in terms of the R_3 response.

Note that this is a cybernetic model. The determinant of behavior is the emotion of either *hope* or *fear*, with hope being the expectation of reward, fear being the expectation of punishment. These emotions are the result of feeding stimuli back into the system, *stimuli which are a product of a response made by the system*. The essential point to remember is that s_d only insures that *some* behavior will occur, that some response from among many alternatives will be made. *Which* response will be selected depends upon r, the affective, and conditioned variable. So fear is not only a conditioned response, *it is also a conditioned stimulus*. In this formulation, the cybernetic process removes much of the distinction between "sign" learning and "solution" learning, and all aspects of learning take on "sign" characteristics. The two factors of learning become reward (drive decrement or satisfaction) and punishment (drive increment or frustration).[1]

[1] The question has often been asked if Mowrer's theory is not implicit in Thorndike, Pavlov, and others. In answer to this, Mowrer stresses that he is not attempting to build a unique theory, but that he is attempting to find a "*common ground* toward which the thought and

III. The Mowrer Theory and Behavior of National Actors

Two problems immediately emerge when we shift from a discussion of organisms such as those in the experiments used to develop the foregoing theory, into a discussion of living systems made up of an aggregate of organisms, such as national actors. The first problem is that of whether the learning and behavior processes in the single organism system are analogous to those in the multi-organism system. Are there certain characteristics which are common to all living systems on different levels? If so, are learning and behavior among these similar characteristics? These questions have been debated for some time and an answer will not be attempted here. Suffice it to say that enough has been done, both empirical research and inferential reasoning, to indicate that for some purposes we may make useful comparisons between the living national system and the living organism (Kaplan, 1957 and Bertalanffy, 1957). If this is too abstract or speculative, a much more pragmatic type of reasoning may be used. Decisions in foreign policy, or international responses are orginarily made by a small group of persons at the high levels of the governing hierarchy. Thus, it is not really necessary to talk of "national

learning" or "national behavior" to give our discussion meaning; it suffices to talk about learning and behavior in individual men, that is, key decision-makers acting within the constraints of their roles and decision-making groups.

The second problem does not really present difficulties, but must be considered. The learning theories discussed in the first part of this paper consider an organism in a pre-set and *non-social* environment. That is, the environment limits the organism and acts upon him but does not interact with him. In the international system, a given national actor is a member of a *social* environment, is able to manipulate its behavior as it in turn manipulates him. Thus his behavior may be not only a response to internally originating stimuli, but may also be an effort to elicit certain behavior on the part of another national actor.

Traditionally, nations have attempted to control or manipulate the behavior of other nations by the use of punishment or threat of punishment (Morgenthau, 1954, Naroll and Naroll, 1960). This is nearly implicit in any *status quo* approach to international relations, an approach which tends to view any national behavior outside traditional and at least implicitly agreed upon paths as aggressive, expansionist, or threatening to international stability. Thus, there is almost an *a priori* inhibition of any behavior which would tend to alter existing relationships among the actors (Kaplan, 1957). If stimuli experienced by a national actor require behavior for satisfaction conducive to such alteration, this behavior is very likely to be considered threatening and the actor will face punishment, for the other actors will attempt to frustrate drive decremental responses.

Let me use some common examples to illustrate this. The philosophy of military deterrence is based on this idea, emphasizing punishment. "If you attack me, I shall devastate your cities" (North, 1962). This is a generalized statement of common practice in the field of international relations. Raoul and Frada Naroll have studied examples of deterrence postures from that of the Greek States versus Persia in 492 B.C. to the position of Ceylon in the twentieth century. One of the most striking things which emerges from their studies is that while threats of punishment sometimes staved off conflict for a short period, the usual result was a continued

research of *many* workers have for some time been moving" (Mowrer, *Learning Theory and Behavior*, 1960, p. 253, emphasis in original). At the same time, Mowrer attempts to marshal as much evidence as possible to demonstrate that the explanatory power of his two-factor theory is greater than that of the theories of his predecessors. Indeed, much of the volume just cited is an attempt to set forth such experimental evidence. Evidence of particular relevance to the aspects of the theory which are being stressed here may be found in: Mowrer, O.H., "Preparatory set (expectancy)—a determinant in motivation and learning," *Psychol. Rev.*, 45 (1938), pp. 61–91; Mowrer O.H. and Aiken, E. G., "Contiguity vs. drive-reduction in conditioned fear: temporal variations in conditioned and unconditioned stimulus," *Amer. J. Psychol.*, 67 (1954), pp. 26–38; Mowrer, O. H. and Lamoreaux, R. R., "Fear as an intervening variable in avoidance conditioning," *J. Comp. Psychol.*, 39 (1946), pp. 29–50; Mowrer, O. H. and Solomon, L. N., "Contiguity vs. drive-reduction in conditioned fear: The proximity and abruptness of drive-reduction," *Amer. J., Psychol.*, 67 (1954), pp. 15–25; Spence, K. W., "Cognitive versus stimulus-response theories of learning," *Psychol. Rev.*, 57 (1950), pp. 159–72. The burden of the experimental work has been to show that it is possible to condition behavior in animals (usually rats and dogs) which can only be explained by the generation of an anxiety set arising from fear (expectation) of punishment for certain responses, and that this anxiety will become generalized and difficult to extinguish.

deterioration of relations between the deterring powers, with no real resolution of the bases for conflict except through eventual war or the impact of outside influence (Naroll and Naroll, 1960). Current examples are obvious. There is little doubt that both Pakistan and India are following internal policies in terms of military postures which grow from real felt needs. Yet, they attempt to control one another's behavior, not through a dialogue about acceptable courses of action, but through threats of punishment. The United States' decision-makers certainly recognize that much of China's behavior is in response to internal pressures of a very real nature, but the reaction of the United States is almost entirely in terms of punishment threats rather than in terms of an attempt to establish a *mutually* satisfactory relationship. Certainly such threats of punishment are easy to understand and seem to be immediately efficacious. But let us note what this implies in Mowrer's terms by using the deterrence example. We must assume first that the original military buildup to which deterrence is opposed is a response to some felt need, or drive stimulus (s_d). This might be either (a) desire for security, or (b) felt need for aggressive military action. In either case the behavior is punished. If the behavior results from a drive for security, it is punished in the Hullian sense, i.e. by an increment of difference between the need state and the satisfaction state. If the s_d is the latter, that is, felt need for aggressive military action, then punishment again comes by a perception that the costs will be greater than the utilities. In either case, the chain is $s_d - R$: Punishment $- S - r_{fear}$.

Note two results of this chain. First, a relationship has been established between the behaving actor and the punishing actor, a relationship the primary components of which are frustration and fear. A simple Thorndikean explanation of the relationship would involve only frustration, with the presumption that a new set of responses would now be chosen by the actor, presumably with no ill effects from the first "error" of the trial and error sequence. But with the Mowrer model a new factor has been added, the affective, with fear as its dominant element. It becomes evident that *future responses will be made from this affective condition*, not from a sort of *tabula rasa* as implicit in Thorndike's theory. Thus, once this relationship has been es-

tablished, all interaction between actor A and actor B will be carried on within a context of fear, fear based on expectations on the part of A that any given behavior *vis-à-vis* B will result in punishment by B.

The second result of the chain is that s_d still exists unsatisfied and it may be presumed that A will continue making responsive behavior to s_d. If B continues to punish A for its behavior, then we might suppose that the state of fear will become more intensified, the drive stimulus will incrementally become greater and greater, *with the probability of desperation behavior becoming greater and greater*.

Breaking this cycle requires that nation B *reward* nation A for a pattern of behavior which is minimally acceptable to nation B. This will entail satisfaction of A (drive decrement) and will stimulate hope that similar action in the future will result in further reward. Thus, a different affective relationship will be established. But nation B does not need to wait until A hits upon a behavior pattern acceptable to B by simple trial and error, as in the Mowrer scheme. As North has pointed out, state B can open up for A's perception responses acceptable to A and which A will find more rewarding than his previous behavior (North, 1962).

Fear may, however, become institutionalized as a deep-seated response to any contact with B. We might term such fear a general anxiety reaction. Once this has taken place, then it is suggested that *repeated* rewarding behavior patterns would have to be set up before this anxiety could be changed to a hope response and the syndrome broken, before there would be a chance for friendship to replace hostility. An example of this is given in a study of the late Secretary of State, John Foster Dulles, who, under the influence of an institutionalized fear or suspicion reaction to all acts of the Soviet Union, tended to interpret even apparently conciliatory, friendly or rewarding behavior by the Soviet Union as hostile. How long rewarding or friendly behavior would have to persist before such an affective state could be broken is a question which remains to be answered (Holsti, 1962).

The pointing out of minimally acceptable paths of behavior is what Morgenthau conceives to be the task of diplomacy (Morgenthau, 1954), and in this he receives full support from Mowrer. Demands which are not even minimally acceptable (such as the Allied demand for German unconditional surrender during 1944) are not good diplomacy or good applications of Mowrer's principles.[2] State B *should* use diplomacy to indicate to A which of the possible responses B will find it necessary to punish, which she will find it possible to reward, and which, if any, are neutral.

In the deterrence example given, the reward given by B to A will depend on what B perceives the nature of the drive stimulus (s_d) of A to be. We mentioned two possibilities. The first of these is a felt need for security. In this case, if the need for security springs from a sense of military inferiority *vis-à-vis* B, then B's obvious reward action would be to disarm to a level at which A no longer feels insecure, or to illustrate in some other manner that A need not feel insecure. This is not appeasement in the pejorative sense, but is rather reward in order to manipulate, teach, or condition A. It might be objected that we have noted that such reward would result in r_{hope}, that is, hope on the part of A that if A again makes the same response to s_d, A will again be rewarded. The conclusion would now be drawn that A will simply continue to make the same response, that is, continue to arm. But this neglects the fact that in this case, the reward is satisfaction of the need, that is, drive decrement, *removal of* s_d. So this problem need not be encountered. On the other hand, it has been suggested by Mowrer that *the affective condition of hope would persist as a generalized emotion*, facilitating negotiation by creating a condition conducive to friendship. (This presumption will be further elaborated below.)

[2] Certainly the basic tenets of Mowrer's theory are part of the conventional wisdom of diplomacy and Morgenthau is not purporting to be suggesting a new concept. Nor are we. We are rather trying to illustrate that the type of interaction which has long been considered the best diplomacy, receives support in psychological theory from Mowrer in a richer way than it did from the earlier theories of learning. At the same time, this theory offers a more substantial condemnation of the type of diplomacy which tends to characterize a world in which international relations are highly ideological. In this world, ideologies are often seen as either good or evil, and a nation which adheres to a given ideology as either good or evil. Responses to behavior are determined by the ideology of the source of the behavior, not by an objective evaluation of the nature or intent of the behavior itself. Diplomacy becomes, not an attempt to formulate mutually acceptable patterns of interaction, but an attempt to prove that everything done by the ideological opponent is "bad" and should be punished. Mowrer's theory shows us clearly what the results of such practice are apt to be.

If the s_d of A is desire for aggressive military activity, the choices of B are somewhat more difficult. Probably the only possibility is punishment, that is, frustration of the behavior of A. On the other hand, it is here that North's suggestions as to the necessity for B to point out to A modes of behavior that B *can* reward, are the most pertinent. This will not avoid the creation of an affective condition of fear, but it will help to prevent random or desperation behavior as a result of fear.

Lewin notes that the behavior of the system will be a vector of the forces operative upon it (Hall and Lindzey, 1957). We might, then, see the direction of behavior as being a vector of the forces of reward or punishment, frustration or satisfaction, friendship or hostility, and hope or fear. This is related to Boulding's idea that behavior can be *conditioned* by manipulation through controlled feedback of the images held by the system as to the nature of the surrounding environment (Boulding, 1956). Both of these ideas contribute to the concept of *conditioned affect* as we are discussing it here, and its role as a determinant of behavior.

It may have been noted that we have not yet really established a relationship between reward, satisfaction and hope on the one hand, and friendship on the other, and conversely, between punishment, frustration and fear on the one hand, and hostility on the other. The basis for assuming this relationship lies in the fact that the conditions of reward, satisfaction and hope are created by the organism's or system's perception of its environment and the way in which it is being "treated" by the environment. Thus, a rewarding environment would be seen as congenial or sympathetic, a punishing environment as cruel or unsympathetic. When this "environment" is social, another living system, or set of living systems, then the words *friendly* and *hostile* seem descriptive of the way the actor would be apt to perceive the other actors and equally descriptive of the way he, in turn, would react to them. We would like to use a modification of a model developed by George Zaninovich to express this (Zaninovich, 1961).

When the agent of reward or punishment is seen, not as a neutral environment, but as another choosing actor in a social system, fear or hope become translated into hostility or friendship toward that actor. The point here is simply that goal deterrence with the resulting frustration and fear are of much

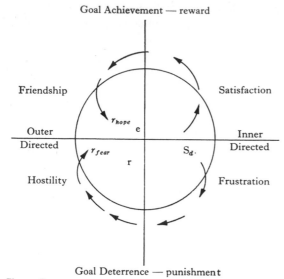

Figure 5

cybernetic model in the true sense of the word. *In the Mowrer model, behavior, unless consciously altered, will tend to remain in the affective hemisphere in which it begins its pattern.*

It should be noted that the direction (on the diagram) of output behavior is determined by whether the behavior is rewarded or punished. We might visualize a series of possible responses (R), some of which will be greatly rewarded, some less rewarded, some slightly punished, some greatly punished. Presumably the friendship or hostility feedback will be of different intensity, as will hope and fear, depending on the intensity of reward or punishment. We can visualize the $s_d - R$ line as being on a pivot at s_d, with the direction determined by the intensity of reward or punishment following various responses and in the conditioned affective state, by expectations as to the results of the responses. The purpose of diplomacy would be to reinforce the cycle as we have described it when on the reward-friendship-hope side by continually pointing out responses (R) which will be rewarded more, or less, or punished (see Fig. 6).

These two factors, the natural tendency of the cycle to be maintained in the same hemisphere due to effective reinforcement, and the use of diplomacy, might be used to encourage the behavior pattern to follow a continued and unbroken, constantly reinforced, reward-friendship-hope cycle and to prevent its running in a figure 8 pattern as it might be expected to do under pure random or trial and

the same genre as hostility (in a social context), while goal achievement with resulting satisfaction and hope are of the same genre as friendship (in a social context). Learned behavior, stemming from hope, resulting in goal achievement and satisfaction, seems likely to result in the system's perception of the outside environment (in this case, the other national actor) in friendly terms. This perception will in turn increase the hope affect, behavior will be characterized by a friendship loading, and a self maintaining cycle will tend to emerge, with the dominant behavior-determining element being what we might refer to as the friendship-hope affect. The same is true, in a converse sense, of the lower hemisphere of the model (see Fig. 5). This is so because the hostility-fear affect will tend to produce aggressive or hostility-laden behavior which is more likely to be punished. Hostility-fear as a response (r) has now also become a stimulus (s_d). On the other hand, in the old Thorndike model, behavior would tend to leave the punishment-hostility-fear hemisphere and go into a satisfaction-friendship-hope pattern and stay there, due to the reinforcing of the "bond" between S and R by reward and its inhibition by punishment. *This difference in expectations as to what will happen to the behavior pattern springs from the fact that in the Thorndike model, the affective element is not considered in turn as a stimulus.* In other words, it is not a

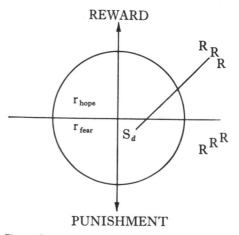

Figure 6

error conditions with no affective reinforcement, outside direction, or Thorndikean "bond" to act as aids in response selection. On the other hand, the affective punishment-hostility-fear condition would tend to make the pattern stay in that half of the hemisphere, once it began there, with diplomacy being a tool which might be used to break into the cycle and direct it into the other hemisphere.

What are some examples of how such a model might be applied to the international arena? Let me elaborate one at some length and then simply mention some others.

The relationship of the United States to the Chinese People's Republic appears to be an excellent example of the perpetually self-reinforcing hostility-fear-hostility cycle. The persistent pattern of communication between these powers consists of punishment threats, condemnation, and frustration of drive reduction. The position of both is one of boycott, verbal hostility in the world forum, and military deployment at the highest state of readiness. There is little or no attempt to tell the other of ways in which they might behave which would meet their own needs and still be acceptable to the speaker.

Discussion among American Sinologists, for instance, usually delineates four possible goals of the Chinese—(1) world domination through Socialism, (2) military expansion into the Asian subcontinent and island area, (3) economic and cultural hegemony in Asia, or, (4) a stable and prosperous regime at home, reasonably secure from outside threat. These can be viewed as four "responses" to the "drive" of national awakening. Now if the historical attitudes of the United States are any indication, the last response would be the most acceptable, the first one the least acceptable. Perhaps the first two would be totally unacceptable, the latter two acceptable. Some particular actions of the Chinese appear to the United States to be clearly aimed at the first two—such as subversion, support to "volunteers" and revolutionary armies, and military aid to nations hostile to the West. Other actions seem to be aimed toward the latter two goals, such as attempts to expand trade in Asia, sending students abroad, as to Canada, and focusing economic development on areas such as agriculture, fertilizer and consumer goods.

Following the Mowrer model, the role of the United States would be to clearly point out to the Chinese which goals were acceptable and which were not, to evaluate given actions as to which goals they seemed, to the United States, to be working toward—to communicate that evaluation to the Chinese—and to punish those actions leading to unacceptable goals and reward those leading to acceptable ones.

The punishment might take much the same forms it now does, trade boycotts, condemnation in the world forums, deployment of weapons into ready positions, withdrawal of aid or technical assistance (as the Soviet Union did with China), or even direct military engagement. *The relevant point is that such punishment should be clearly applied to a given action— not conducted within the framework of an undifferentiated hostility syndrome.*

Rewards can be given in the same way. The United States might say to the Chinese, "If you concentrate on agriculture rather than on nuclear development, we will drop our pressures on Japan not to trade with you," as an example. At the same time, specific actions could be rewarded with a statement that the action had been pleasing and that a reward was being given. The United States could have rewarded the "100 Flowers" campaign with an invitation to Chinese students to come and study in America. A Chinese decision to join the test ban treaty could be rewarded with a switch in U.S. positions about United Nations membership or even an announcement by the United States that it was going to leave the 1,500-mile-range missiles on the Polaris submarines instead of replacing them with the 2,800-mile missiles, and that it would deploy these submarines out of range of China, with some technique for verifying their approximate whereabouts—thus reducing Chinese fear of a surprise attack from that source (Raser, 1964). The Chinese decision to spread birth control measures could have been rewarded by technical and medical assistance from the United States. And so forth.

The Chinese might use the same technique to reward pleasing actions of the United States, or to promise reward for pleasing actions. A withdrawal of U.S. support for the Nationalist positions on the offshore islands might be rewarded by China's opening her doors to American reporters. An American expression of willingness to reduce trade restrictions could be matched by a Chinese move in the direction of respecting the patenting, licensing, quota, most favored nation, and state trading regulations of the General Agreement on Tariffs and Trade. An American offer of technical assistance for agricultural development in China might be rewarded by an increased investment by China in agriculture as opposed to military production.

If even minor steps such as these were taken by either or both powers, it might soon effect a rather drastic change from the current situation when *any* move, by one, even if it is *de facto* in the interests of the other, is met with condemnation and punishment.

Needless to say, in an intensely hostile environment such as that now existing between the United States and Communist China, such a course would be fraught with suspicions, misinterpretations and recriminations. Any progress toward moving the general affective environment from the hostility to the friendship half of the sphere would be slow and laborious. In other cases it might be less difficult. Great Britain's policy for the past half century of allowing her colonies to move toward independence, but rewarding them for moving in directions which would result in some kind of commonwealth status while punishing them for militant anti-British tendencies, appears to have worked quite well. She has, in a sense, provided them with positive incentives for behaving in ways acceptable to her, and in the process created a generally congenial affective environment which acts to a great extent to condition further behavior. In the same manner, the Soviet Union seems to be learning that it had best reward its Eastern European allies for moving along paths which are at least minimally acceptable to it, rather than punishing them for any deviation from its own projected desires, for the punishment creates an affective state eliciting further behavior which must be punished, with the final result being an escalation into a spiral of resistance.

In each of these cases, it is possible to make some judgement as to whether the results of the policy constitute a confirmation or disconfirmation of the theory. The current state of intense hostile affect between the United States and the Chinese People's Republic might be alleviated if the United States applied Mowrer's principles to its communications to the Chinese. If it were (as perhaps indicated by continued content analysis of Chinese

documents of the sort being conducted by Robert North and his associates at Stanford University; Holsti, 1964), this would tend to confirm the theory. If the level of hostility did not change, or increased, it would tend to disconfirm it. We use the word "tend" advisedly, for when we are dealing with a field as complex and as little subject to experimenter control as international politics, it is very difficult to hope to provide adequate "proof" of any hypotheses. The value of such models as that presented here probably depends more on their role as hueristic devices, providers of insights, and points for common communication among disciplines and across national boundaries, than on their "truth" or "falsity."

The relevant point of this entire formulation is that the affective elements of hope-friendship and fear-hostility (a) can be conditioned consciously, (b) are determining factors in choices among possible responses to internal stimuli, and finally (c) that behavior can be altered by the conscious manipulation of reward and punishment, which in turn create affective reinforcing conditions that will tend to establish a milieu in which further behavior will take place, *with the nature of this milieu being in itself a behavior-determining stimulus of the most important kind.*

The policy implications of all this, in terms of international relations, seem fairly clear. If one nation wishes to communicate with and effectively influence another, it must do all in its power to avoid the creation of an environment which is characterized by *generalized* fear and hostility. It must attempt instead to indicate that it is only certain actions which it must punish while others may be rewarded, and not that everything the subject does is reprehensible.

References

1. Boulding, Kenneth. *The Image.* Ann Arbor, Mich: Univ. Michigan Press, 1956.
2. Hall, Calvin S. and Lindzey, Gardner. *Theories of Personality.* New York: Wiley, 1957.
3. Holsti, Ole. *The Belief System and National Images: John Foster Dulles and the Soviet Union.* Stanford University: Ph. D. Dissertation, 1962.
4. Holsti, Ole, Brody, Richard A., and North, Robert C. "Measuring Affect and Action in International Reaction Models," *Journal of Peace Research,* No. 3–4 (1964), 170–90.

5. Kaplan, Morton. *System and Process in International Politics*. New York: Wiley, 1957.

6. Malinowski, Bronislaw. "An Anthropological Theory of War," *American Journal of Sociology*, XLVI (1941), 522–43.

7. March, J. G. and Simon, Herbert A. *Organizations*. New York: Wiley 1958.

8. McLellan, Olson, Sondermann, eds., *Theory and Practice of International Relations*. Englewood Cliffs, N.J.: Prentice-Hall, 1960.

9. Morgenthau, Hans J. *Politics Among Nations*. New York: Knopf, 1954, 2nd ed.

10. Mowrer, O. Hobart. *Learning Theory and Behavior*. New York: Wiley, 1960.

11. Mowrer, O. Hobart. *Learning Theory and the Symbolic Process*. New York: Wiley, 1960.

12. Naroll, Raoul and Frada. "Prospects for the Comparative Study of Deterrence in History: A Phase One Report." San Fernando State College, Nov. 30, 1960, mimeo.

13. North, Robert C. *A Minimal Integration for Avoiding War*. Stanford University: Studies in International Conflict and Integration, First Draft, March 30, 1962, mimeo.

14. North, Robert C. *Some Informal Notes on Conflict and Integration*. Stanford University: Studies in International Conflict and Integration. First Draft, Feb. 15. 1962, mimeo.

15. Raser, John R. "Mobile, Short-Range Missiles: Answer to an Arms Control Dilemma?" Western Behavioral Sciences Institute, La Jolla, California, Dec. 1964.

16. von Bertalanffy, Ludwig, ed., *General Systems, Yearbook of the Society for General Systems Research*, Vol. II, 1957.

17. Zaninovich, George A. *A Suggested Integrative Model for the Study of the Role of Affective Expression in World Politics*. Stanford University: Studies in International Conflict and Integration, August 16, 1961.

40. The Form of a Discipline of International Relations

Quincy Wright is Professor Emeritus of International Law at the University of Chicago, and presently Professor of International Law at the University of Virginia. A leading student of international relations, he was one of the first to approach the field with a broad social science orientation. He has written numerous articles and books, and two of these, *A Study of War* (1942) and *The Study of International Relations* (1955), shall long remain landmarks on the frontiers of theory and research. The following pages, excerpted from the latter work, represent an attempt to identify and synthesize the major variables underlying the actions and interactions of states. Based on the concept of a field, which is considered to be "a system defined by time and space or by analytical coordinates, and by the properties, relations, and movements of the entities within it," this selection is, so to speak, a culmination of Professor Wright's thinking with regard to international phenomena. [*From Quincy Wright*, The Study of International Relations (*New York: Appleton-Century-Crofts, 1955*), *pp. 539–53 and 560–69, reprinted by permission of the author and Appleton-Century-Crofts, Division of Meredith Corporation. Copyright 1955, Appleton-Century-Crofts, Inc.*]

There exists no body of empirically established relations which can provide the basis for a field theory of international relations. However, models utilizing the conception of a field may suggest lines of investigation which might eventually make such a theory possible.

It was pointed out [earlier] that the term *field* has been used in two senses—on the one hand, as the actual time-space in which events take place, and on the other, as an analytical system of co-ordinates within which variables may be located in relation to one another. In developing a discipline of international relations both senses of the term may be usefully employed—the first in the geographical approach, and the second in the analytical

approach. The following discussion has attempted to abstract the most significant concepts and propositions of the various disciplines discussed in earlier sections. . . .

The Geographical Field

The geographical approach locates the people and groups of the world and their characteristics, motivations, actions, institutions, and conditions in actual time and space. It suggests surveys indicating the topics of attention and interest; the direction of attitudes and opinions; the states of tension and unrest; and the policies, laws, and other subjective conditions prevailing among the people at each point of the globe in successive intervals of time. Similarly, changes in objective conditions such as production, trade, technology, population, migration, communication, economy, and polity should be indicated on successive maps in so far as they appear to be relevant to international relations. Such surveys might disclose correlations and suggest hypotheses concerning causal connections among these factors, especially relations between changes in the subjective factors and changes in the objective factors. Social surveys and statistical summaries have appeared in increasing abundance but they have not included many of the most significant factors (14, 16, 22).

In such surveys the importance of political barriers dividing the world into distinct groups would have to be considered. Thus correlations would be made primarily among variables within the same country. Political barriers themselves can be considered from the points of view of (a) their conformity to the "natural" groupings of people and (b) their permeability.

From the first of these points of view, successive maps indicating temporal changes in the geographical extent of systems of communication and transportation, of languages and dialects, of cultures and customs, of religions and ideologies, of producing and trading systems, and of legal and administrative systems might be superimposed to suggest the boundaries between those areas in which many of these factors tend to converge. Studies of nationality suggest that no one of these factors account for national solidarity, nor does the concurrence of many in an area. Such concurrence, however, indicates conditions which permit the realization of national solidarity when active agencies, such as political organizations, patriotic associations, historians, educators, and propagandists have made the public in such an area aware of these conditions, and loyal to symbols, histories, and institutions associated with them (1, 9, 19, 24, 31).

The permeability of existing frontiers can be indicated by mapping the relative obstruction to communication, travel, trade, and invasion across them by natural and artificial barriers, such as mountains, rivers, seas, deserts, fortifications, border patrols, tariff laws, immigration and passport regulations, censorships and prohibitions. Other factors, such as the degree of discontinuity at frontiers of communication and transportation systems; the relative extensiveness of actual communication, trade and travel across frontiers; and the relative abruptness of changes in language, religion, culture, social structure, wealth, and law at frontiers indicate the degree of conformity of existing political boundaries with the "natural" grouping of peoples. All of these factors contribute to the impermeability of iron and other curtains at frontiers (2).

In proportion as the world becomes a more homogeneous field in which national boundaries present less formidable barriers to communication, travel, trade, and migration, and less powerful stimuli to exclusive and hostile attitudes, and in which more abundant transnational communication, travel, trade, and migration moderate the "natural" differences of human groups, the discipline of international relations will be concerned primarily with correlations between the objective and subjective variables mentioned in the first paragraph of this section.

These barriers are, however, today of major importance and hamper the trend in a shrinking world toward a reduction of national differences, consequently factors involved in international relations from the geographic point of view must be divided into two classes—those operating within each of the states and those operating among states. Both types of factors influence the power, the policies, the public opinion, and the attitudes of the leadership of each state, and are the subject matter of the disciplines of international relations, especially of international economics, political geography, diplomatic history, international politics, and the control of foreign relations. These factors are manifested by events and conditions which exist in time and space and can consequently be located on maps or narrated in histories.

The writer has elsewhere sought to define and measure certain changes taking place within a state, such as the tension level, the degree of institutionalization, and the progress of production, population, and education (24, 25, 28): certain aspects of distance between states, technological and strategic, psychic and expectancy, political and social, legal and intellectual (24, 28); and certain processes tending to integrate states and international groups, such as communication and interaction, standardization and acculturation, co-operation and socialization, and organization and administration (12, 24, 26, 27). Karl Deutsch has utilized similar concepts in studying the conditions permitting the integration of nations (1) and security communities (2). The latter are defined operationally as groups, not necessarily politically organized, the participating units of which do not prepare for war against one another, or, more simply, as areas within which there is an expectation of peace. Such a community is distinguished from a political community which is organized to act as a unit to make and maintain internal and external policies. Political integration may or may not increase internal peace and security. Deutsch believes that the historical process of community development is less like that of an incubator (permitting development) than like that of a collective assembly line (implementing plans). He does not consider the possibility that this process (like a conversation) has characteristics of both, synthesizing spontaneous impulses and deliberate purposes by a process of interaction (24). He uses the terms *political integration and amalgamation; psychological identification and assimilation; mutual responsiveness and simple pacification;* and *mutual interdependence and interaction* to describe typical processes which if in proper relation to one another may develop a security community in an area. These appear to be similar, respectively, to the processes which I have described, from the point of view of increasing closeness of groups, as organization, standardization, co-operation, and communication (12, 27), and, from the point of view of increasing separation of groups, as social and political, psychic and expectancy, legal and intellectual and technological and strategic distances (24, 28). Deutsch discusses the intricate relationships between rates of change in these elements affecting the stability of a security community, and emphasizes the importance of a proper balancing of integration loads with capabilities of the parts. He also suggests indicators for measuring rates of change in these variables.

Measurable changes in factors of this kind do not account directly for political decisions, but they tend to influence such decisions by modifying the sentiments, values, goals, and beliefs in the minds of the decision-makers and of the publics on which decision-makers depend for power or for the implementation of their policies (10, 13, 17, 21). These factors can be dealt with analytically and will be considered in connection with the capabilities and values of governments in the next section.

Obviously many of the significant factors, both domestic and international, influencing political decisions, are intangible and difficult to measure or even to describe. Accurate surveys localizing the influence of these factors can be made only if observable and measurable phenomena can be found, so closely correlated with the significant intangible factors, that they can serve as indices. To this end efforts have been made, not only to define significant social and political variables operationally, but also to relate intangible mental dispositions to tangible variables such as physiological types (10, 18), physical conditions (6), economic conditions (8), states of the arts (12), and interactions of all these factors (1, 6).

The object of the study of international relations is not only to understand the factors which account for decisions and actions of governments, but also to facilitate control in order to forward the most generally accepted goals and values. The major problems arise from the diversity of such goals and values among the various nations and governments of the world. Morris and Northrop have suggested that philosophical analysis of the leading ideologies and rational political discussion may lead to synthesis and reconciliation (10, 11). Statesmen have sought to achieve general political agreements on certain goals and values such as those to be found in the United Nations Charter, the Universal Declaration of Human Rights, and other general international instruments. This practical aspect of the study of international relations suggests that a geographical survey should include not only descriptions and statistics of the *factors* significant in international relations and of measurable *indices* disclosing the changes of these variables, but also information concerning the institutions, ideas, procedures, and relations susceptible of human manipulation and the effectiveness of political, administrative, educational, and propaganda activities intended to manipulate these *regulators.*

We may, therefore, conceive of three sets of time series which may be called respectively, *factors, indices,* and *regulators,* continuous survey of which would yield both understanding of, and the power to control, international affairs (14). Determination, however, of the most useful series to survey in each of these categories would depend upon a theory of international relations. Such a theory should be elaborated from the psychological point of view and may be represented by a field defined by certain analytical co-ordinates.

The Analytical Field

The analytical approach to the study of international relations discussed in this section implies that each international organization, national government, association, individual, or other "system of action," or "decision-maker" may be located in a multidimensional field. Such a field may be defined by co-ordinates, each of which measures a political, economic, psychological, sociological, ethical, or other continuum influencing choices, decisions, and actions important for international relations. Much experiment would be necessary to decide what co-ordinates could most usefully be employed. Material factors, relatively easy to measure, such as degree of military strength or weakness, or degree of technical advancement or backwardness, might prove to be indices of important political factors. Moral factors such as degree of reputability or disreputability, or degree of reliability or unreliability are probably important, but difficult to measure and the same is true of intellectual factors such as degree of literacy or of illiteracy, or degree of scientific and philosophical productiveness. Psychic factors, such as degree of satisfaction or dissatisfaction, or degree of anxiety or complacency are undoubtedly important, but not easy to measure. Many other co-ordinates could be suggested. While recognizing the need of balancing measurability against importance in selecting co-ordinates, in this chapter, I have given primary consideration to importance. Further research is necessary to discover accurately measurable indices parallel to these factors. Only after that is done can the hypotheses discussed be verified.

The field might be defined by combinations of alternatives. Parsons has suggested five alternative sets of values or "pattern variables," all possible combinations of which would define a field or matrix of thirty-two cells within one of which each system of action might be located (13). It seems probable

that such subjective values or pattern variables are significant factors in international relations, but estimates of conditions, facilitating or hampering their realization, of the kind suggested by Deutsch (1), are also important. Systems of action are guided by both "wish" and "reality" criteria. Such criteria may, however, be regarded as continuous variables rather than as alternatives. Each decision-maker or system of action judged by its normal criteria in making decisions, can be located at a positive or negative distance from the origin in the field. This method seems preferable to a matrix model. Political decision-makers seldom think theoretically in terms of this or that but practically in terms of more of this and less of that.

The location of systems of action within a field defined by suitable co-ordinates is, however, complicated by the fact that each system of action has different structural levels which may have different criteria of choice. Thus the individual, as Freud pointed out, is influenced at the biological level by basic drives and wishes (the id), at the social level by values internalized in the character (the super ego), and at the psychological level by the personality co-ordinating wishes and values with realities (the ego). At the action level, the other levels struggle against each other in concrete situations resulting in decision and action (the will) (4). Similarly social and political systems of action are influenced at the psychological level by the attitudes and opinions of the people whom they serve, at the cultural level by the values and beliefs accepted by the culture or nationality within which they function, at the social level by the ideology or law of the society or state which regulates them, and at the political level by the policies and skills of the government whose procedures permit them to act. The relationship between these levels, as well as the homogeneity of each and the adequacy of the decision-making process, influence the efficiency of the system of action.

The state of international relations during a period of time may be defined in terms of the power and the policies of each of the principal governments of the world at each moment, and of the trends of change in both power and policy. A decision-maker's power is measured by his capability and his policy by his values, relative to the particular situation. The peculiar characteristics of the situation including communication discontinuities and barriers can only be discovered by geographical and historical study. General tendencies may, however, be indicated by analyzing the values and capabilities of decision-makers, and these general tendencies become increasingly determinative of choice and action as technology advances and the world shrinks. The underlying dynamism of international relations may, therefore, be described, within a field defined by suitable analytical co-ordinates, by vectors, the location of which indicates the values motivating the policy and the capabilities underlying the power of each important government at a given moment. The length and direction of each vector indicates the rapidity and direction of change. The other levels of each of these political systems of action, their relation to the government, and the relative size of the population participating in each, can also be indicated.

The internal conditions and tendencies of a system of action in respect to tension, skill, reliability, security, satisfaction and expansiveness may be indicated by the location and direction of movement of its vector in the capability field, and those in respect to tolerance, rationality, democracy, individualism, tranquility, and optimism may be indicated by the location and direction of movement of its vector in the value field. The relations of friendliness or hostility of two systems of action can be indicated by the direction of their vectors toward or away from one another in the value field. If in the latter field the vectors are headed for a large number of different points, the tendency would be toward a stable balance of power, but, if all the vectors are headed toward two remote points of the field, a tendency toward bi-polarization and instability would be indicated. If all of the vectors are headed toward the center of the field, a trend toward general international organization would be indicated, and if they are headed away from the center, a trend toward international anarchy would be indicated. If the tendencies indicated by such a model were interpreted in the light of empirical knowledge of geographical, technological, and demographic conditions in each state and in the world as a whole, and of the trends of change in these conditions, as suggested by the geographical approach, prediction and control of the future of international relations might be facilitated.

What continua can most usefully be employed as co-ordinates for defining this analytical field? The problem is similar to that of determining the factors which account for mental performance, studied by psychologists. C. E. Spearman assumed a single factor, E. L. Thorndike assumed a great number of independent factors, and L. L. Thurstone devised methods for determining the minimum number of factors necessary to account for the results of numerous tests of mental ability. He found that factors concerning the use of words, numbers, and visual images were sufficient to account for the results of certain tests (20). Application of similar methods to a limited body of data suggested that the psychic relations among certain states could be accounted for by four factors—opinions concerning change, ideology, war, and form of government (14, 24). No such analysis is attempted here. A dozen factors are postulated and relations among them suggested from some familiarity with the field, in the hope that eventually measurement of these factors may permit of correlations to determine the degree of their sufficiency, redundancy, and applicability. Karl Pearson's method of multiple correlation and regression or Sewall Wright's method of "path coefficients" might prove applicable (29, 30). Stuart Dodd has applied such methods to test factors postulated for measuring the progress of peoples toward capacity for self-government (3).

A single multidimensional field including both capabilities and values should be envisaged. It will occasionally be convenient to treat these two aspects of the analytical field separately, but with recognition that they are not entirely independent. Values influence capabilities and vice versa. Furthermore the efficiency of the decision-making process in any system of action influences both aspects of the field as well as the rapidity and direction of that system's movement in the field.

A scheme is suggested in Figures 1–6 with six capability, and six value, dimensions within which systems of action can be located, the rapidity and direction of movement of each depending in considerable measure upon the relation of its four structural levels. This cannot, of course, be represented visually in three-dimensional space but imagination may picture a twelve-dimensional semi-opaque cheese, within which maggots crawl around, the larger ones representing states with the government

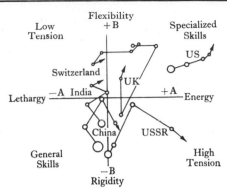

Figure 1. The capability field (a)

at the head and the people at the tail. They vaguely perceive each other as they approach, often changing direction in response to primitive instincts and urges, to sophisticated patterns and policies, and to deliberate appraisals of purposes and powers.

Among general factors influencing the capability of a state, internal, international, and mixed factors have been distinguished. The internal factors may be grouped into those influencing the energy, the rigidity, the tensions and the skills of the state, respectively limiting the vigor, the persistence, the direction and the wisdom of the government's political activity. It may be possible to measure changes in the social energy of a state by using data relevant to economic progress, such as population and production; to measure changes in social rigidity or institutionalization of a state by utilizing such variables as the centralization of government and the pervasiveness of law and custom. Changes in social tensions, probably dependent on changes

in social energy and social rigidity, may be measured by utilizing data on the intensity of public opinion and private attitude, especially in respect to domestic scapegoats and potential foreign aggressors. Changes in the fourth factor, social skill or intellectual progress, may also be related to social energy and social rigidity and may be measured by utilizing data relevant to progress in science and technology and to educational and political adaptability. These variables—energy, rigidity, tension, and skill—appear to be of major importance in influencing the foreign-policy decisions of governments. The last factor, permitting self-correction, modifies the applicability of the analogous formula of an electrical or hydraulic system according to which the rate of change of tension or pressure varies as the product of the rates of change of current strength and resistance (25, 28).

Persistent factors operating among states and influencing their capabilities may be conceived in terms of different aspects of distance between them. In an earlier work (24), the writer defined technological and strategic, legal and ideological, social and political, and psychic and war expectancy distances and suggested means for measuring them. Closely related are the processes of increasing communication, standardization, organization, and co-operation (12, 24, 27). These distances and processes can serve to define international factors in the capability field. Degree of isolation, corresponding to technological distance from other states and manifested by little communication; and degree of military weaknesses corresponding inversely to political distance from other states and manifested by dependence on superorganizations, have been selected as suitable co-ordinates. Unreliability, corresponding to legal distance from other states and manifested by nonstandardization of reaction patterns, appears to be a negative, and insecurity, corresponding to war-expectancy distance and manifested by weakness and aloofness, a positive function of these two variables.

Two other factors, which are both internal and international, have been selected as co-ordinates— relative resource abundance and relative technological advancement. Degrees of satisfaction and expansiveness appear to be respectively positive and negative functions of these variables.

These six co-ordinates have been called an (a) axis measuring degree of social energy or rate of

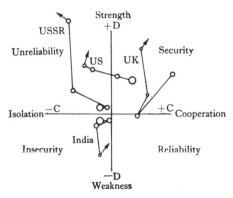

Figure 2. The capability field (b)

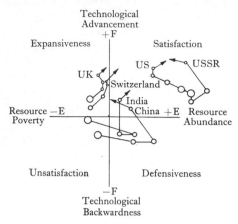

Figure 3. The capability field (c)

economic progress; a (b) axis measuring degree of social flexibility or rate of political decentralization, a (c) axis measuring degree of co-operativeness or rate of development of international trade and communication, a (d) axis measuring degree of power or rate of development of international rivalry, an (e) axis measuring relative resource abundance or rate of development of resources and skills, and an (f) axis measuring relative technological advancement or rate of technological development. Applied to individuals these six axes might be defined as (a) energy and (b) adaptability correlated positively with skill and negatively with tension; (c) sociability and (d) ability correlated positively with security and negatively with reliability; and (e) wealth and (f) education correlated positively with satisfaction and negatively with expansiveness.

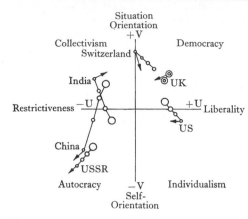

Figure 5. The value field (b)

Recent studies of the values influencing civilizations, religions, ideologies and systems of action suggest that three sets of co-ordinates are of basic importance in the value field. They represent, respectively, objective-subjective, concrete-abstract, and manipulative-contemplative continua.

The first or (x) axis locates systems of action according to the degree in which they evaluate the persons and things with which they deal by objective examination of the capacities or roles in relation to the situation or to the interests of the actor; or by application of subjective categories in the mind of the actor. This axis corresponds to Parsons' "achievement-ascription" pattern variable. Systems of action guided by objective criteria are observant,

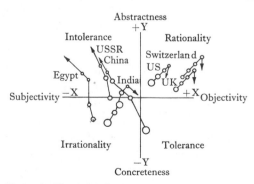

Figure 4. The value field (a)

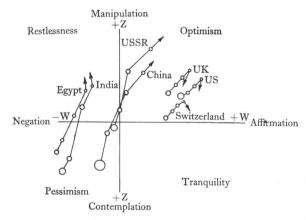

Figure 6. The value field (c)

accurate, realistic, practical, and interested in the effectiveness or ineffectiveness of action, in the strength or weakness of persons, and in the expediencies of action in the existing situation. Systems of action guided by subjective criteria are introspective, vague, idealistic, moralistic, and interested in the rightness or wrongness of actions, in the goodness or badness of persons, and in the principles and standards which should guide actions in general.

The (y) axis (concrete-abstract) locates each system of action according to the degree in which it perceives reality by immediate experience or by deduction from abstract concepts. Northrop emphasizes this distinction and believes it marks the fundamental difference between oriental and occidental cultures (11). Parsons' pattern variable defined as "particularism-universalism" is similar. Systems of action guided by concrete criteria are synthetic, intuitive, inductive, aesthetic, and interested in art, history, and immediate experiences. On the other hand, systems of action guided by abstract criteria are analytical, rational, deductive, mathematical. They are interested in abstract propositions of logic and philosophy, and in the correctness or incorrectness of processes of reasoning.

The (z) axis, (manipulative-contemplative) emphasized by Lasswell (7), locates systems of action according to the degree in which they seek to achieve purposes or to expand understanding—to reform or to comprehend—to do or to know. Morris uses the terms *attachment* and *detachment* in the same sense (10). The pattern variable which Parsons denominates "affectivity-affective neutrality," though related, is different. By affectivity he means reflex, impulsive, or spontaneous behavior. But *action* implies some deliberation upon alternatives. An entity which behaves wholly spontaneously is not a *system of action*. Its behavior is a function of its inherent properties and the environmental stimuli which impinge upon it, and can be entirely explained within a system of geographic co-ordinates. Nor does this criteria correspond to the contrast between active and passive. All systems of action are active in that behavior is internally generated (15). Contemplation is not passivity. Nevertheless there is more of spontaneity in the manipulative than in the contemplative, and the latter may lead to a "passive personality" "sicklied o'er by the pale cast of thought." Systems of action

guided by the manipulative criterion are active, creative, constructive, and interested in the adaptation of means to ends. They tend to build their power and to be militant and authoritarian. Systems of action guided by the contemplative criterion are deliberative, analytic, reflective, and interested in relating causes to effects. They tend to be pacifistic, cosmopolitan, and democratic, and to favor stability, and decentralization of power. This distinction seems to correspond to that between Yin and Yang in Chinese thought (21), related to the rhythms of stability and progress, rest and motion, and to the scientific idea of maximizing or minimizing entropy, or expending or conserving energy (15).

Other co-ordinates of importance appear to be a (u) axis (restrictive-liberal) locating systems of action according to the degree in which they identify themselves and interpret their relations with others narrowly or broadly. This axis corresponds to Parsons' "specificity-generality" pattern variable. Systems of action guided by a restrictive concept of relations are contractual, suspicious, precise, legalistic and interested in the concrete aspects of relationships. Systems of action guided by a liberal concept of relations are tolerant, expansive, accommodating, broad-minded, and inclined to identify themselves with other persons and with organizations.

A (v) axis (self-orientation-situation-orientation) may also be significant, locating systems of action according to the degree in which they guide decisions by self-interest or by consideration of, and reciprocal interest in, others. Such a continuum would correspond to Parsons' pattern variable denominated "self-orientation-collective-orientation." Systems of action oriented by self-interest are competitive, self-assertive, domineering, and, in regard to collective systems of action, nationalistic or imperialistic. On the other hand, systems of action oriented by the situation are co-operative, conciliatory, renunciatory, and, in regard to governments, internationalistic. This axis has often been assumed to be the basic criterion of ethical judgment and has sometimes been considered to define the distinction between *interest* and *principle*, between *realism* and *idealism* or between *egoism* and *altruism* but these terms are all somewhat ambiguous (26).

A (w) axis (affirmation-negation) may also be suggested, locating systems of action according as they guide decisions by a positive or negative attitude toward the world. The first is attracted to the world, and tends to be optimistic, idealistic, extroverted. The latter withdraws from the world and tends to be realistic, pessimistic, and introverted. This axis corresponds to Schweitzer's distinction between affirmation and negation (17). It differs from the (z) axis of manipulation-contemplation in that it refers to the expectations of the actor from the world rather than to his action upon it.

Each of these axes indicates a continuum, positions near the origin indicating neutrality or balance, and those toward the periphery indicating extremes in one direction or the other. They discriminate the criteria by which systems of action evaluate (x), perceive (y), act upon (z), identify themselves with (u), interest themselves in (v), and entertain expectations from (w) the persons, things, and situations with which they are faced....

Movement in the Field of International Relations

General changes in the character of international relations may be interpreted as movements of systems of action in the analytic field and may be attributed to (a) general changes in the field, (b) to interaction between the capability and the value fields, and (c) to interaction between the geographic and the analytical fields.

General changes in the field. The most important general factors which influence both the geographical and analytical fields appear to have been the accelerating progress of science and technology. In respect to the geographical field this progress has on the one hand continually augmented production, communication, and the interdependence of groups, increasing social energy and tending to shrink and unify the geographical field, and, on the other hand, it has augmented the efficiency of administration, education, and propaganda, enlarging and co-ordinating institutions, increasing rigidities, erecting barriers, developing armament races and, tending to increase material distances between groups and to divide the world into a number of artificial geographical fields.

These opposing tendencies have probably been influential since the history of man began, and have had the general tendency to diminish the differentials in values among human groups and to increase the differentials in their capabilities. As a result the more capable groups have absorbed the less, and huge power aggregations, each seeking to impose its values upon the world, have developed. Since these efforts have never been entirely successful, history has chronicled the advance of civilization through a balance between forces of union and division. Sporadic serious disturbances of this balance have resulted in great oscillations marking the rise and fall of civilizations (21). Periods of progress toward the unity of a civilization have been followed by periods of disorganization with intervals of stability between (24, 28).

In recent times, extraordinary scientific and technological advances, augmenting the abundance of communications and the possibilities of profitable trade, have tended to a synthesis of peoples and cultures. By augmenting the vulnerability of all to destruction, this advance has also tended to a synthesis of states and governments in international organizations, thus moving all peoples, nations, states, and governments toward the center of the value field. National systems of administration, education, and propaganda, however, devoted to developing loyalty to traditional national values and institutions have tended to emphasize the distinctiveness of the principal ideologies and to diminish their ambiguities. National culture and popular attitudes have tended to conform to a particular ideology, and governments have become more determined to preserve the one to which they are committed. These factors have tended to move all systems of action away from the center of the value field. The shrinking of distances, the differentials of capabilities, and the resulting increase in the vigor of the power struggle has tended to the assimilation of nations and governments into two great systems in opposing parts of the value field. These opposing tendencies in both the geographical and the analytical fields have made it increasingly difficult for governments in either one of these opposing systems to conciliate those in the other with the result that anxiety and tensions become ever greater (28).

Some relations between capabilities and values. The relative capabilities of states are continually changing under the influence of science and invention, of internal development, and of international politics. What is the effect of these changes in a state's capability in respect to the six dimensions here suggested, that is, its (*a*) energy, (*b*) rigidity, (*c*) co-operativeness, (*d*) strength, (*e*) resources and (*f*) technical advancement upon its values. Other factors influencing capability, such as tension, skill, reliability, security, satisfaction, and expansiveness, are believed to be functions of these six as indicated on the diagram.

Increase in the energy of a people, roughly measured by the average rate of increase in wealth, tends to move a people toward the manipulative ends of the (*z*) axis. Increasing poverty tends to move a people toward the contemplative end. The distribution of wealth may, however, be very unequal. For a considerable period of time a government may be increasing in wealth and energy while the people are becoming poorer. Thus the attitudes of the people may become more contemplative while the policies of the government become more manipulative. Such opposite movements, likely in a totalitarian state, clearly bode ill for the continuous stability of the system of action.

Rigidity refers to the degree of centralization of authority and may be measured by the proportion of the national income administered by central authority, by the degree of mobility of the people in what Lasswell has called the "safety-income-deference pyramid" (7) or by subjective estimates concerning respect for civil liberties and separations of power. A rigid society has a stratification of castes and classes, is permeated by institutions with fixed values, and is regulated by a vigorous system of law. In a flexible society, on the other hand, government is decentralized geographically and functionally; the attitudes of people, the influence of institutions, and the acceptance of values is in continuous flux; and the law is continually changed by central and local legislative processes. Rigidifying systems of action tend to move toward the subjective end of the (*x*) axis, and those becoming more flexible to the objective end. Here again governments may differ from cultures. The two may be moving in opposite directions, again rendering the society unstable.

Increasing energy and increasing rigidity, strengthening allegiance to existing values, tends to increase tensions. Inflexible institutions, especially political institutions, and developing economy, especially if coupled with a system of finance augmenting the capacity of the government, tends to an externalization of these tensions and to aggressive policies.

Tensions may, however, arise from causes other than the relation between the economy and the polity. A challenge of new conditions in the material or social environment, threatening the security or prosperity of the people or the government, if beyond the experience of the existing culture or law, may require significant changes in popular attitudes, in national opinions, in the law of the state, and in the policies of the government if a proper response is to be made. If institutions are rigid, such a response is not likely to be made. As Toynbee has pointed out, only rarely have primitive peoples made a suitable response to such challenges and, thereby, produced a "civilization" (21). Only rarely have civilizations been able to adjust themselves to major changes in their conditions. Adjustments to such challenges require a skillful combination of realism in appreciating the nature of the challenge and the requirements of suitable adaptation, and of idealism, in appreciating the potentialities of the system of action to be preserved from nonessentials and excrescences to be modified.

Tension may also arise because government policies and state laws are unadapted to the attitudes of the people and the opinion of the nation. Such conditions, which lead to political revolution are less likely to occur as the development of democracy decreases the disparity between government and people. If not only the government and the state, but also social institutions and traditional opinions become out of harmony with widespread, but hitherto unvoiced attitudes of the people, social revolution is likely, especially if the government is lacking in skill and resources (28).

From whatever cause, increasing tensions within a system of action tends, up to the point of revolution, to a consolidation of existing values by the government, to a displacement of aggressive dispositions upon an external or internal scapegoat, to an aggressive policy, and to a location on the restrictive end of the (*u*) axis.

Only by the exercise of great skill can a government avoid occasional revolution and war, and a rapid rise of tensions creates conditions unfavorable to the influence of persons with skill. The original mind, capable of solving social problems, becomes suspect with the tendency of both people and government to regress in times of severe crisis to an absolute allegiance to traditional but obsolete values. Such skills are most likely to be used in a system of action near the origin in the (a) (energy), (b) (rigidity) and (y) (abstract-concrete) axes. The sort of skills required involves a combination of techniques arising from specialized abstract thought and of human understanding arising from general concrete experience. A nation of specialists tends to be far out on the abstract end of the (y) axis and to be positively related to high energy and negatively related to social rigidity. A nation of generalists, on the other hand, tends to be far out on the concrete end of the (y) axis and to be negatively related to high energy and positively related to social rigidity. Skill in social and political management is to be found in a culture recognizing both virtues and consequently located near the origin on all these axes (26).

Primitive peoples tend to be at the subjective and concrete ends of the (x) and (y) axes, civilized peoples at the objective and abstract ends. This is because civilization tends to objectivity, abstraction and specialization, to what psychoanalysts call "maturity," modifying the "wish" principle by the "reality" principle, and to division of labor encouraging appreciation of abstract intellectual formulae rather than concrete aesthetic experience. Primitive peoples also tend to be on the low energy and rigid ends of the (a) and (b) axes while civilized peoples tend to be at the opposite ends of these axes. The result is that civilized man has tended to increase his mastery of nature but to decrease his mastery of men. Only if modern culture preserves a supply of generalists, along with the specialists, can political problems be solved. As Northrop and Hsu have pointed out, the aesthetic spirit is less controversial and more conciliatory than the scientific spirit (5, 11).

Movements of governments toward the rigidity, the isolation, and the power ends of the (b), (c), and (d) axes tend to produce autocracy, authoritarianism and a decreasing participation of the people in the state and the government. Movements in the opposite direction tend to produce democracy. The democratic or autocratic organization of a government determines the influence of popular attitudes and public opinion upon the law and policy of the government. Autocratic governments controlling the means of communication tend to decide autonomously upon law and policy and to bring about whatever general consent of the people is necessary by appropriate educational, propaganda, and intimidating methods. Thus the government continually draws the state, the nation, the people to itself, thereby increasing its efficiency and the rigidity of its values. Such a system of action can be represented by a vector with its tail at the location of the people passing through the location of the nation and the state to its head at the location of the government.

In a large state the center of gravity of the people tends to be located near the center of the field in respect to the value co-ordinates because the people usually includes individuals located in all parts of the field. The movement of an autocratic state led by a government which is likely to be further from the center, tends to be away from the center toward more and more extreme positions in the value field. In democratic systems of action, on the other hand, popular attitudes control public opinion. This controls the law, which in turn controls the government policy and action. The people continually draw the government towards themselves. Thus, a democratic government tends to move toward the center of the value field. Democratic governments, therefore, in a shrinking world, tend to cluster near the center of the field and to unite in international organizations, while autocratic governments move toward the periphery and become totalitarian parties, seeking to absorb people, nation, and state. A revolution may suddenly change the autocratic or democratic character of a system of action, and such a change may reverse the direction of movement of the system in the field. Since government policies are likely to be more mobile than the attitudes of a large population of individuals, autocratically governed systems of action are likely to move more rapidly in the field than are democratically organized systems of action. "Autocracy," said Fisher Ames, "is a ship which gallantly sails the seas, but someday it strikes a reef and goes down while democracy is a raft which will never sink, but then your feet are always in the water" (23).

Many other influences of changing capabilities upon values could be explored. For example, a positive relation of resource abundance and technological advancement makes for satisfaction and this induces objectivity, tolerance, and affirmation, characteristic of the United States during most of its history. On the other hand, poor resources and technological backwardness make for dissatisfaction which induces subjectivity, intolerance, and negation, characteristic of the Arabs in recent times. A negative relation of these capability factors (i.e., resource abundance and technological backwardness) makes for aggressiveness as in the Soviet Union, while the opposite relations (poor resources and technological advancement) makes for defensive policies, as in the case of Norway and Switzerland. Figure 7 suggests the direction of influence of many factors affecting international relations.

Some relations between geography and analysis.   As already noticed democracies tend to be located near the center of the value field, to promote common goals, and to co-operate with one another, while autocracies tend to move toward the periphery of the field and to pursue divergent policies.

These relations are, however, affected by relations in actual time and space. States so geographically related that each is vulnerable to attack by the other will, because of this decreasing strategic distance, become increasingly hostile if in psychic relations of opposition. If, on the other hand, geographic relations and technological conditions are such that each is relatively invulnerable to attack, psychic relations of opposition are not likely to lead to conflict.

In the case of states tending to co-operate because moving to the same point in the value field, shrinking geographical distance is likely to augment this tendency. Thus, if between two states psychic distances are diminishing more rapidly than strategic distances, peace becomes increasingly probable. But if strategic distances are diminishing more rapidly than psychic distances, war is probable. As states become less cooperative and more armed, they become less reliable and more belligerent. The writer has examined the relations of changes in different aspects of distance elsewhere. The consequences of changes in these different aspects of distance can be indicated by combined consideration of changes in the analytic and the geographic fields (24).

Negotiations of statesmen might be facilitated if the entire field of international relations were so represented that the negotiators could see the relations of the circles and vectors representing their respective peoples, nations, states, and governments located at particular points both in the geographical and analytical fields, and moving in certain directions in the latter. An observer might calculate with less margin of error the probable outcome of such negotiations by the use of such a model.

The five conceptions of the world, discussed in the preceding chapter, may be interpreted as the attribution of a particular character to the analytical field and to the systems of action within it.

If all systems of action were controlled by a well-articulated law, maintained by an effective government, at one point in the field, the world would appear to be the plan or idea defined by that system of law. Such a system would imply that the attitudes of all people reflect a common culture, uniting all nations, and manifesting the ideology implicit in the universal law. The nature of the idea would, of course, vary greatly according to the point in the field at which the universal state is located.

If all systems of action were controlled by a small number of governments in relations of general opposition to one another, the vector representing each would head toward a different point in the field: each of the governments would regulate the attitudes, cultures, law, and policies of the people within its domain and the domain of its satellites. None would acknowledge any norms of culture, law, or authority except the criteria which guided its own behavior, and the world would appear as a military equilibrium. The stability of the equilibrium would depend upon the number, the power, the relations, and the alliances of the governments.

If collective systems of action were reduced to unimportance, and all individuals guided their behavior by a universal culture maintained, not by coercive laws but by the internalization of the attitudes of all the people, the world would appear to be a universal community. The location of this universal culture in the field would determine the character of the community. A community dominated by Christian love would probably be in the contemplative, subjective, concrete sector of the value field and would differ greatly from a universal commune, dominated by loyalty to the group, giving to each according to his needs and expecting from each according to his capacity, probably located

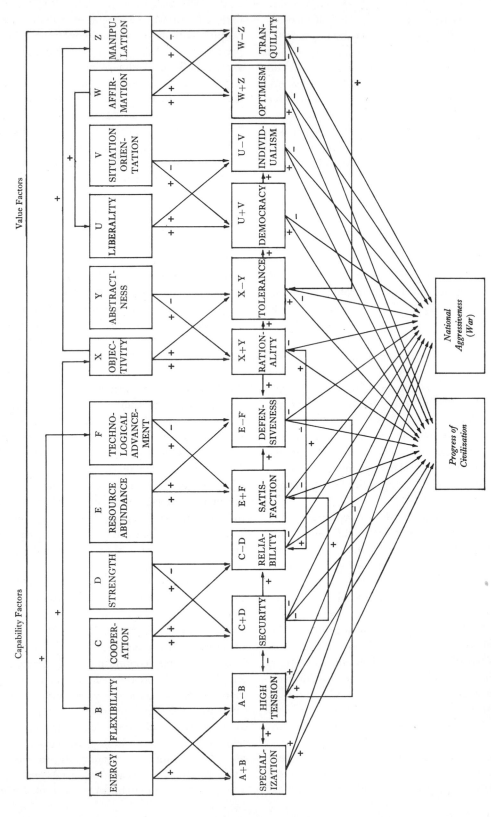

Figure 7. Paths of influence within the analytical field

in the manipulative, objective, abstract sector, from a Buddhistic nirvana of individuals emancipated from all desires in the contemplative, subjective abstract sector, or from an epicurean community of individuals joyfully satisfying their desires without mutual interference in the manipulative, objective, concrete sector. All would differ from a Maitreyan community of individuals at the center of the field (10).

If both individual and collective systems of action existed in all parts of the field; if in each collective system the attitudes of the people, the culture of the nation, the law of the state, and the policies of the government were near the same point thus militating against movement; and if these points were related to certain universal principles of morals and law maintained by a universal organization of limited competency, to prevent sudden or violent changes and to facilitate continuous and gradual adjustments and accommodations among the various systems of action, the world would appear as an organization. Such an organization would imply a certain equilibrium of power among the major systems of action: a degree of international protection of certain spheres of freedom for individuals and less collective systems of action: and a system of law and culture guiding it located near the center of the field.

We may conclude that the world of man, first conceived as a static ideology expressing the origin and destiny of man in fixed symbols revealed by an imperfectly known God, nature, or history, or as a community in which men lived in harmony because they loved one another, has in fact usually resembled an equilibrium resulting from the interplay of forces directed by the government of each of the major groups into which the territory of the world has been divided. As the world shrinks it appears to be becoming an organization designed to maintain the interests of groups and individuals by suitable procedures, by developing certain standards of universal culture, and by enforcing certain rules of universal law. For the scientist, however, the world may be best conceived as a field, a dynamic complex of relations among groups and individuals developing knowledge of which may increase the capacity of man to know his interests and his conditions, and to control his destiny by continually recreating his world in the image best synthesizing the progress and stability of these systems of action as they change under his touch.

References

1. Deutsch, Karl, *Nationalism and Social Communication*. New York: Wiley, 1953.

2. ———, *Political Community at the International Level, Problems of Definition and Measurement*. New York: Doubleday, 1954.

3. Dodd, Stewart C., "The Scientific Measurement of Fitness for Self-Government," *The Scientific Monthly*, Vol. LXXVIII (February 1954), 94 *ff*.

4. Freud, Anna, *The Ego and the Mechanisms of Defense*. New York: International Universities Press, 1946.

5. Hsu, Francis, *American and Chinese, Two Ways of Life*. New York: Schuman, 1953.

6. Huntington, Ellsworth, *Mainsprings of Civilization*. New York: Wiley, 1945.

7. Lasswell, Harold D., *World Politics and Personal Insecurity*. New York: McGraw, 1935.

8. Marx, Karl, *Capital, A Critical Analysis of Capitalist Production*. London: Swan Sonnenschein, 1902.

9. Merriam, Charles E., *The Making of Citizens*. Chicago: Univ. Chicago Press, 1931.

10. Morris, Charles, *Paths of Life, Preface to a World Religion*. New York: Harper, 1943.

11. Northrop, F. S. C., *The Meeting of East and West*. New York: Macmillan, 1946.

12. Ogburn, W. F. (ed.), *Technology and International Relations*. Harris Institute Lectures. Chicago: Univ. Chicago Press, 1949.

13. Parsons, Talcott, and Shils, E. A. (eds.), *Toward a General Theory of Action*. Cambridge, Mass.: Harvard Univ. Press, 1951.

14. Pool, Ithiel de Sola, *Symbols of Nationalism and Internationalism*. Introduction by Quincy Wright, Radir Project. Stanford: Stanford Univ. Press, 1951.

15. Rapoport, Anatol, *Operational Philosophy*. New York: Harper, 1953.

16. Russell Sage Foundation. *A Bibliography of Social Surveys*. New York: The Foundation, 1930.

17. Schweitzer, Albert, "Ethics for a Twentieth Century Man," *Saturday Review* (June 13, 1953).

18. Sheldon, W. H., "Integration in the Biological and Social Sciences," in *Contributions to the Analysis and Synthesis of Knowledge*, Proceedings, American Academy of Arts and Sciences, in cooperation with the Institute for the Unity of Science, Vol. LXXX (July 1951), pp. 31 *ff*.

19. Sulzbach, Walter, *National Consciousness*. Washington: American Council on Public Affairs, 1943.

20. Thurstone, L. L., *The Vectors of Mind*. Chicago: Univ. Chicago Press, 1953, p. 170.

21. Toynbee, Arnold J., *A Study of History*. New York: Oxford Univ., 1934, Vol. I, p. 170.

22. United Nations, Statistical Office, *Statistical Year Book*. New York: United Nations, 1948.

23. Wright, Quincy, *Public Opinion and World Politics*, Harris Institute Lectures. Chicago: Univ. Chicago Press, 1933. p. 9.

24. ———, *A Study of War*. Chicago: Univ. Chicago Press, 1942, pp. 1240 *ff*. 1254, 1433 *ff*. 1471.

25. ———, "Measurement of Variations in International Tensions," in Bryson, Finkelstein, and McIver (eds.), *Learning and World Peace*. Eighth Symposium on Science, Philosophy and Religion. New York: Harper, 1947, pp. 207 *ff*.

26. ———, "Specialization and Universal Values in General International Organization," in *Approaches to Group Understanding*, Sixth Symposium on Science, Philosophy and Religion. New York: Harper, 1947, pp. 207 *ff*.

27. ———, *The World Community*. Harris Institute Lectures. Chicago: Univ. Chicago Press, 1948.

28. ———, *Problems of Stability and Progress in International Relations*. (Berkeley, Univ. California Press, 1954.

29. Wright, Sewall, " orrelation and Causation," *Journal of Agricultural Research*, Vol. XX (Washington, D.C., January 3 1921), pp. 557 *ff*.

30. ———, "The Theory of Path Coefficients," *Genetics*, Vol. VII (May 1923), pp. 239 *ff*.

31. Znaniecki, Florian, *Modern Nationalities*. Urbana: Univ. Illinois Press, 1952.

Part Five

The Actions and Interactions of States: Research Techniques and Orientations

---

INTRODUCTORY NOTE

Methodological innovation in the study of international politics and foreign policy has been no less impressive and widespread in recent years than the progress achieved on the frontiers of theory. Indeed, the advances in theory could not have occurred without corresponding developments at the level of empirical research. The more theorists probed the mysteries of international life, the greater the pressure they created to gather data that would serve to test and refine their theories. In turn, the newly gathered data usually raised as many questions as they answered, thus fostering the need for more theorizing.

This relationship between theory and research is so close and interdependent that one cannot hope to progress as a student of world politics by confining oneself to one or the other forms of inquiry. At the very least it seems necessary to develop a basic familiarity with both the major theoretical orientations and the basic research techniques that are now available. Otherwise the theory that one creates is not likely to be very disciplined or useful and the data one gathers are not likely to be very relevant or meaningful. To be sure, the analyst need not be both theorist and researcher. Division of labor is possible and in fact many analysts do specialize, some preferring to stress theory and others having greater competence at the level of empirical research. Such specialization, however, does not relieve one of the need for some familiarity with the other side of the theory-research relationship. If one is more interested in the development of theory, then one ought to be sufficiently familiar with research procedures both to render one's theories usable by those who engage in empirical work and to evaluate the theoretical utility of the findings that are generated on the frontiers of research. Similarly, if one is more inclined to gather, process, and analyze empirical data, then one ought to be sufficiently knowledgeable about theoretical procedures both to give relevance to one's findings and to facilitate their use by theorists.

This is not to imply that theory must precede research or that research must come before theory. The two are so intertwined that they constitute an endless sequence, each reinforcing the other, and trying to identify where the sequence begins is like asking whether the chicken or the egg came first. The analyst can break into the sequence at any point, depending on whether he starts with some ideas about the dynamics of world politics or with some data that describe their operation.

The interdependence of theory and research is plainly evident throughout the seventeen selections that follow. Most of the previous forty selections have been largely theoretical, and the presentation of empirical evidence was quite incidental to the theoretical concerns of the authors. All those that follow, however, are explicitly oriented toward gathering and analyzing empirical materials. Yet, in no case is this orientation so pronounced that the larger meaning of the materials is ignored. On the contrary, all the selections have a theoretical focus that is either tested by or derived from the data they present. Indeed, if the reader is fascinated by the selections—as seems likely—he will be hard pressed to determine whether his fascination arises out of the intriguing data that have been developed or out of the wider implications to which they point, a problem which again demonstrates the harmony and intimacy of theory and research.

It must be stressed that this balance between theory and research is not easily achieved. Students entering the field frequently tend to see the two as mutually exclusive rather than as reinforcing enterprises. When one first tastes the heady wine of creative theorizing, empirical materials can seem quite mundane and irrelevant, just as theory can seem remarkably farfetched and esoteric when one first applies new techniques of research and experiences the pleasure of discerning central tendencies within seemingly unmanageable data. Consequently, all too often the habit develops of viewing theory and research as competitive, with the theorists contending that the researchers are so enamored of their methodologies that they lose touch with the meaning of data and with the researchers claiming that in the absence of systematic empirical materials the writings of the theorists are little more than guesswork. Such contentions are as regrettable as they are unnecessary. Hopefully the clear-cut way in which theory and research reinforce each other in the ensuing selections will curb any impulse the reader may have to perpetuate these misconceptions or to otherwise assert the superiority of one form of inquiry over the other.

If theory and research are so closely intertwined, the reader might well wonder, why have these seventeen selections been clustered together into a section on research techniques and orientations? Would it not have been better to locate these selections at the appropriate places in the preceding four parts of the book? These are valid questions. The division is an artificial one and it runs the risk of implying that the theory-research relationship has a superior-subordinate dimension. However, while each of the seventeen selections could just as logically have been presented at an earlier point in this volume, the risks of artificially clustering them together have been run in order to indicate the wide range of research techniques available to the student of world politics. Success in achieving an appropriate balance between theory and research depends in large part on a recognition that a multiplicity of techniques for generating and analyzing data can be used, that the techniques vary in terms of the limitations they impose and the opportunities they provide, and that therefore the choice among techniques can be of crucial importance and must be made with care. In other words, the various research methods differ greatly in the kinds of data for which they are suitable and in the kinds of theoretical concerns for which they are appropriate—with the result that both the theory and the research of the analyst will suffer if he is not familiar with these differences. Thus, even as the following selections demonstrate the interdependence of theory and research, so does their juxtaposition allow for an assessment of the differences among the many research strategies that can be adopted.

The variability of the techniques used in these selections also serves to emphasize that there is plenty of room for the exercise of imagination in research. Gathering and processing data can be tedious and routine, but the task of adapting a research strategy to the problem being investigated and the data available can hardly be viewed as dull and boring. On the contrary, it requires a high degree of creativity and constantly challenges the ingenuity of even the most experienced researcher. The charts, tables, and diagrams that pervade these selections suggest orderliness and coherence, but the data did not neatly array themselves into meaningful sequences on their own. Only through the adaptation of disciplined procedures by open and wide-ranging minds could such order and coherence have been brought into being.

Although most of the methods employed in the ensuing selections are designed to create and handle quantified data, quantification is not a necessary tool of research. Much depends on whether one is examining empirical materials in order to test or derive hypotheses relevant to one's theoretical concerns. If one starts with hypotheses about the ways in which some aspect of international behavior is patterned, then quantification would seem to be necessary. Since the hypotheses extend beyond a single historical episode, they can only be confirmed or rejected through the tracing of events that either do or do not recur. To recognize and record recurring instances of a phenomenon is to engage in quantification; and inasmuch as hypotheses normally posit either the presence or absence of recurring patterns, most of the available methods of research consist of some technique for quantifying data. However, if one is interested in an unexplored area of international behavior and thus lacks any basis for framing hypotheses, it may be quite appropriate to probe a single historical episode as a means of deriving hypotheses that can then be tested in other situations. The case study, in other words, can be as important a means of research as the quantitative technique. Indeed, as can be seen in Selection 41, it can be an extremely valuable source of material for those who wish to refine and extend their theoretical models. On the other hand, it must quickly be added that most case studies in the international field are not undertaken for the purpose of deriving testable hypotheses and thus very few can be fitted into the theory-research relationship. An overwhelming preponderance of the available studies consist of little more than historical narrative designed to uncover what happened at a particular time in a particular place under particular conditions, with no attempt whatsoever being made to discern the more general patterns of which the described events may be an instance. Selection 41 is taken from a notable exception to this kind of case study, and it is intended to illustrate that the single historical episode can serve the purposes of scientific inquiry.

The fact that the case method is no less valuable than the quantitative technique is not widely appreciated. Frequently the controversy between those who favor and oppose the application of the scientific method to international politics turns on the mistaken notion that case studies and quantified analyses are antithetical. The scientifically oriented researchers tend to equate the typical case study with the method itself, with the result that they contest the case writers rather than urging them to generate hypotheses and theory from their specific historical episodes. Contrariwise, those oriented toward traditional methods tend to view quantification as obscuring the deeper meaning of events, with the result that they develop such a strong commitment to the disutility of quantified data that they assert the impossibility of deriving any general implications from their case studies. As can be seen in Selection 41, however, this dimension of the controversy is ill-founded and much would be gained if the continuity between the case study and the quantitative inquiry were more widely recognized.*

The failure to appreciate the potential utility of case studies stands in sharp contrast to the imaginative way in which a variety of other research techniques have been developed in recent years. Selections 42 through 57 present a vast array of methods for gathering, processing, and interpreting empirical materials. Taken collectively, these selections demonstrate that the actions and interactions of states are not inscrutable, that they do recur, and that imaginative steps have been taken to quantify the patterns which they form. It is clear, moreover, that techniques are available for the quantification of virtually every aspect of international politics and foreign policy with which a researcher might be concerned. If, as the following pages indicate, such complex phenomena as the capability of states, the attitudes and motivations of decision-makers, and the character of state interactions can be rendered quantifiable and subjected to analysis, then presumably no aspect of the subject lies beyond the reach of the skillful and creative researcher.

This is not to say, of course, that all the mysteries of international life will be unraveled by the newly developed instruments of research in the immediate future. Many of these tools are still crude and unwieldy. Some are still in the early stages of adaptation from sociology and psychology. Others require extensive training in statistics and mathematics. Still others are so costly that they can be employed only by researchers who have large sums of money at their disposal. Furthermore—and to return again to a central theme of this volume—none of these techniques can be perfected without corresponding refinements in theory. Tools of research cannot gather data on their own; they must be guided and manipulated by researchers. If researchers use rudimentary conceptual equipment, the tools cannot produce more than rudimentary data. The fact remains, however, that in spite of their limitations these new methods of quantification have made virtually every aspect of international politics and foreign policy accessible to imaginative researchers.

* For a more elaborate discussion of this point, see James N. Rosenau, "Moral Fervor, Systematic Analysis, and Scientific Consciousness in Foreign Policy Research," in Austin Ranney (ed.), *Political Science and Public Policy* (Chicago: Markham, 1968), pp. 197–236.

A. The Use of Case Studies

41. The Korean Decision

Glenn D. Paige is Professor of Political Science at the University of Hawaii. A leading specialist on the politics of the Far East and particularly of Korea, Professor Paige has also been in the vanguard of those who have sought to render political analysis more scientific. Among his many writings is *The Korean Decision* (1968), which combines his substantive and methodological concerns and from which this selection has been taken. Based on an explicit attempt to apply the decision-making approach (see Selection 19) to the process whereby the United States became involved in the Korean War in late June of 1950, this work is one of the very few case studies that goes beyond a mere narration and interpretation of events. Its concluding chapter, from which the following is excerpted, consists of a series of hypotheses that are derived from the account of the Korean episode in the previous chapters, but that are cast in such general terms that they can be applied to other foreign policy situations. Although Professor Paige's focus is thus confined to one historical sequence of events, his concluding chapter demonstrates that case studies can serve as a method of scientific inquiry. [*Reprinted from Glenn D. Paige, The Korean Decision (New York: The Free Press, 1968), pp. 273–95, by permission of the author and the publisher. Copyright 1968 by The Free Press, A Division of The Macmillan Company.*]

The main objective of this chapter is to present some empirical propositions about foreign policy decision making that have been derived from the narrative of the Korean decision. . . . These propositions link the variables of the decision-making frame of reference and provide an *a priori* set of hypotheses that can be applied in future case studies or in simulation exercises[1] designed to improve understanding of international politics.

Several points about this analytical effort need to be made clear at the outset. First, since there can be an infinite number of analytical aspects for any social object, this attempt at analysis cannot exhaust the possibilities for the insightful positing of theoretical linkages between elements of the single case that has been presented. Thus the present analysis is to be considered not as the last but only as one effort to analyze the Korean decision. In general, the wider the range of theoretical insights that are brought to bear on the case materials, the greater the number of explanatory hypotheses they may be expected to yield. Therefore each reader is urged to exercise his own creative skills on the data that have been presented.

Second, the basic intellectual strategy that has been employed in the present proposition-building effort has been that which might be termed *guided*

[1] Consult Harold Guetzkow, *et al.*, *Simulation in International Relations* (Englewood Cliffs, N.J.: Prentice-Hall, 1963).

retroduction.[2] It neither brings to bear a deductive set of hypotheses from the behavioral sciences that would predict the behaviors found in this case[3] nor seeks solely to induce propositions from the repeated occurrence of related events. Rather, with the decision-making framework as a guide, it approaches elements of the case as factors that can function as referents of correlated dependent or independent variables. Thus the analyst asks, "Given the basic conceptual framework, what might have been the antecedents or consequences of this element of observed behavior?"

A third consideration is that while the following propositions are empirically grounded in the present case, they cannot be accorded a high degree of empirical confirmation. Thus the occasional skeptical query, "I don't know how far you can generalize on the basis of a single case," is met with complete agreement. We cannot know until we can make general statements on the basis of some evidence and then test them against some more evidence.

A fourth characteristic of the present analytical effort is that no attempt has been made to integrate the propositions derived from the Korean decision with a supplementary body of invented propositions into a comprehensive theory of decision making. Neither has a systematic attempt been made to build propositions by speculating about alternative states of affairs. Both exercises, however, would be useful.

[2] This concept has been suggested by N. R. Hanson's discussions of "abductive" or "retroductive" reasoning in *Patterns of Discovery* (Cambridge: Cambridge University Press, 1958), pp. 85 ff.

[3] It is hoped however that the case materials can be used in this way. For example, the behavior of President Truman and Secretary Acheson in the Korean crisis might be cited as illustrations of the performance of "emotional effect" and "task" leadership roles that would be predicted on the basis of small group research. As a further illustration Professor Joseph de Rivera has suggested that the way in which Counselor Kennan's skills were utilized without bringing him directly into the Blair House Conferences seems to follow a pattern for handling "deviant members" that has been discovered in small group research. It has been pointed out that Mr. Kennan could have been summoned to the first meeting by friends or by local police; a side table could have been set for him if there was no place for him at the main dining table at Blair House or he could have been asked to join the group after dinner. Whether correct or not, these things illustrate new perspectives on the case, that can be obtained by invoking external social psychological theory. See de Rivera's *The Psychological Dimension of Foreign Policy* (Columbus, Ohio: Charles E. Merrill, Inc., 1968).

Hopefully the present effort is a step toward increasing the fruitfulness of such endeavors.

The Korean Decision as a Crisis Decision

The decision-making frame of reference originally did not specify a typology of decisions. It may be left an open question whether typologies, themselves capable of infinite invention and based on *a priori* assumptions about crucial variables, will be helpful in building a variable-oriented theory of foreign policy decision making. The same set of parsimonious variables eventually may be found to be differentially loaded but not qualitatively different in the various "types" of decision situations. For the present, however, it may be found helpful to follow the customary experimental practice of stating a set of relevant antecedent conditions under which the theoretical propositions advanced in a study are anticipated to hold.

The Korean decision thus might be classified as a *crisis decision* with the following principal empirical characteristics: *occasion for decision*—thrust upon the decision makers from outside their organization and from outside the territory and population over which they exercise official control; *decision-making organization*—a large complex organization composed of an executive headquarters and a number of subordinate functional departments the heads of which may be called upon by the chief executive for advice; *internal setting relationships*—characterized by the presence of other organizations that can challenge the legitimacy of the decisions taken, influence the kinds of social resources made available to the decision makers, and eventually perhaps bring about their replacement; and *external setting relationships*—characterized by the presence of allies and enemies over whom the decision makers cannot exercise arbitrary control.

A *crisis* is defined after Hermann as "a situation that (1) threatened high priority goals of the decisional unit, (2) restricted the amount of time in which a response could be made, and (3) was unexpected or unanticipated by the members of the decision making unit."[4] A crisis decision is thus taken to be a

[4] Charles F. Hermann, *Crises in Foreign Policy Making: A Simulation of International Politics* (China Lake, California: Project Michelson Report, U.S. Naval Ordnance Test Station, April 1965), p. 29.

response to a high threat to values, either immediate or long range, where there is little time for decision under conditions of surprise.

Crisis Decision Stages

Although not specified in the original decision-making framework (but implied to some extent by the attention given to feedback processes), the Korean decision suggests that it may be useful to think about developmental stages in a decision-making process. Thus analytical attention is drawn to the possibility that there may be similarities and differences among behaviors characteristic of stages within and among decision types. It may be found that decisional sequences are characterized by progressive activation of necessary conditions that in combination serve as sufficient to produce a given decisional outcome.[5]

The Korean decision suggests four stages for a crisis decision as shown in Table 1.

Almost all of the participants in the Korean decision that were interviewed have reported that they experienced a sense of entering into new phases of the situation at the various points of decision during the last week of June 1950. Some variation was noted in their interpretation of the significance of the various stages but this was not completely idiosyncratic; there was greater agreement than disagreement. For example, the majority of participants interviewed thought that the decision to use force taken during the second Blair House conference on Monday constituted a "point of no return" in the decisional sequence from which the decision to use ground troops logically followed. At least two of the decision makers, including the President, however, thought that the determination displayed during the Sunday Blair House conference was the logical precondition from which flowed the subsequent decisions of the week; others agreed that the Sunday conference was marked by such a sense of determination. At least one of the decision makers did not seem to experience a sense of full and complete response to the aggression until the Friday commitment of ground forces; others seemed to experience an earlier sense of complete involvement but agreed

[5] This is suggested in part by Neil J. Smelser's remarks on the "value-added process" in social action in *Theory of Collective Behavior* (New York: Free Press, 1963), pp. 13 ff.

TABLE 1

Crisis Decision Stages

Stage	Korean decision example
I. Stimulus categorization and establishment of general framework of response.	Identification of invasion as "aggression" and decision to make "collective security" response through the United Nations (June 24).
II. Determination of shared willingness to make a positive response and of capabilities to act.	Consensus of the Blair House conference that there should be "no appeasement." President's military questions (June 25).
III. Articulation of a specific positive response and decision to commit new, limited resources.	Decision to provide air-sea support for ROK forces (June 26).
IV. Progressive expansion of the amount and kind of committed resources.	Decision to employ combat troops in the Pusan area (June 29), one RCT in the combat area (early June 30) and to give General MacArthur unlimited authority to use his ground forces (mid-morning, June 30).

that the decision to send in infantry represented a significant new stage. Thus despite some variation there does seem to have been a consensus that the decision did have certain stages as well as upon what those stages were. . . .

The Korean Decision as a Single Decision and as a Sequence of Decisions

Analytically the Korean decision may be viewed either as a single decision or as a sequence of decisions. It may be regarded either as the American decision to resist armed aggression in Korea through military counteraction, or as the set of decisions taken by the United States Government during the period June 24-30, 1950. Both analytical postures will be adopted in the following analysis.

The concept of a sequence of decisions that contributes to a stage-like progression toward an analytically defined outcome calls attention to the possibility that positive or negative reinforcement of the behaviors of officials between occasions for decision may affect their responses during subsequent formal deliberations.[6] The concept of reinforcement can now be added to the concept of feedback along the path of action contained in the original statement of the decision making framework.[7]

A simplified reinforcement pattern for the Korean decision is suggested in Table 2.

TABLE 2

Sequential Reinforcement of the Korean Decision

Decisions	Reinforcement
1. To call for a Security Council meeting (June 24).	Prompt supporting UN action (June 25).
2. To adopt a strong posture of resistance (June 25).	Coinciding editorial opinion (June 26).
3. To commit air-sea forces; to keep conflict limited; and to avoid direct confrontation with the USSR (June 26).	Overwhelmingly favorable Congressional, domestic, and international approval (June 27–28); temperate Soviet response (June 29).
4. To extend operations into North Korea and to employ combat troops as evacuation cover (June 29).	Unfavorable response from General MacArthur as being inadequate (June 30).
5. To commit one RCT to combat (June 30).	Agreement of full meeting of presidential advisers (June 30).
6. To commit necessary ground forces (June 30).	Congressional and press acceptance as "virtually inevitable" (June 30).

It will be noted that primarily positive reinforcement occurred throughout the week of decision and that the reinforcing agent varied from domestic and foreign actors to nonconsulted decision makers themselves.

The reinforcement pattern of the Korean decision suggests the proposition that *the greater*

[6] A stimulating summary of contemporary theory about reinforcement is contained in Albert Bandura and Richard K. Walters, *Social Learning and Personality Development* (New York: Holt, Rinehart, and Winston, 1963).

[7] Snyder, Bruck, and Sapin, *Foreign Policy Decision Making*, pp. 75 ff., 132.

consistency of positive reinforcement, the less the conflict among decision makers about making progressively more costly responses to threat. Thus one way to elicit or to inhibit progressively more costly responses to crisis, where high costs are not immediately acceptable, may be to vary the reinforcement given to the initial low cost commitments that decision makers have approved. This suggests that the analysis of reinforcement patterns may be a fruitful approach to what might be called potentiality analysis in political science, i.e., to the analysis of the possible alternative states of affairs that might have existed other than that which is empirically verifiable.

Conceptualizing the Korean decision as a sequence of subdecisions also suggests that it may be found helpful to entertain a typology of the predominant characteristics of decision-making conferences. Thus it might be found that crisis decisions tend to be made by a sequence of conferences that can be characterized primarily as *stimulus-evaluating* and *response framework-setting* (June 24), *resolution-probing* (June 25), *response-articulating* and *selecting* (June 26), *response-evaluating* (June 28 and 29), and *response deepening* (June 30). Although any concrete decisional conference may be characterized by a number of processes, it may be found fruitful for the decision-making analyst to entertain the possibility that such conferences tend to serve one or more (or at least limited) functions in a complex sequential decision.

The Korean case also includes another kind of meeting that can serve as a positive or negative reinforcer but which is not in itself strictly a decisional meeting. This is what might be called a *response-legitimating* conference. Here the decision makers communicate their decisions to selected influential leaders in the internal and external political settings. Examples are the meeting of the direct participants in the Korean decision with members of the Congress on June 27 and June 30, and the briefings held by State Department spokesmen for NATO and OAS representatives on June 27. It will be noted that official spokesmen at such meetings not only communicate the content of the decisions that have been taken but also defend their appropriateness and legitimacy.

Against the background of these preliminary considerations the Korean decision will now be examined for the purpose of developing a set of empirically grounded propositions that tie together the variables of the decision-making frame of reference and, hopefully, contribute to more explicit understanding of foreign policy decision processes. The analysis will first attempt to show the impact of crisis upon the main variables of the decision-making framework (organizational roles and relationships, communications and information, and motivation and values), and upon the relationships of the decision makers with their internal and external settings. For this part of the analysis, the decision will be viewed both as a single crisis decision and as a set of subdecisions. Secondly, the analysis will return to the idea of a crisis decision sequence in an attempt to show how the variables identified in the previous analysis interacted to produce the sequence of decisional outcomes observed in the present case. Finally, an attempt will be made to begin to relate properties of decisions to their subsequent execution or administration.

Crisis and Decision-Making Variables

Crisis and Organizational Variables

The effect of crisis upon some organizational variables is summarized in Figure 1. Here crisis is conceptualized as an independent variable, while changes in organizational behavior are regarded as referents of associated dependent variables.

The first proposition to be considered is PROPOSITION 1.1: *Crisis decisions tend to be reached by ad hoc decisional units.* This can be appreciated by reviewing the principal decisional units that were active during June 24–30 as shown in Table 3. It will be noted that all of the decisional units except Unit 4, a meeting of the National Security Council, are *ad hoc* units, specially convened to deal with problems arising out of the Korean crisis. The National Security Council, although in its initial stages of development, might have become a focus for decision during the week but it did not in fact become so. The Cabinet was not employed as a decision-making body for purposes of determining the American response to the North Korean aggression.

There appear to be two main reasons for the formation of *ad hoc* decisional units under crisis conditions. The first is a result of formal role expectations plus chance; e.g., Units 1 and 5. Whereas the fact that the news of the North Korean invasion would be channeled to the Assistant Secretary of State for Far Eastern Affairs (given his availability in Washington) can be attributed to the expectations that surrounded his organizational role, the fortuitous presence of the Secretary of the Army at the Alsops' dinner party and the important liaison role he played with the Department of Defense throughout Saturday night has a strong element of chance. So also did the absence from Washington in a telephoneless farm of one of the Administration's principal analysts of Soviet affairs, Counselor George F. Kennan, Jr. Thus chance can operate inclusively or exclusively with respect to the membership of decisional units. A second contribution to *ad hoc* decisional units is the combination of formal role expectations and leader's preference; e.g., Units 2, 3, and 6. Here the President generally seems to have specified those persons whom he wished to have advise him, while allowing his advisers an occasion

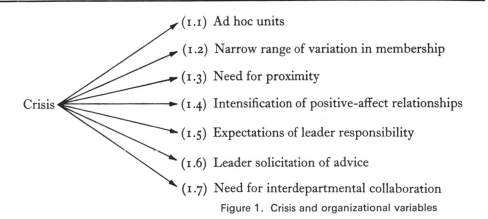

Crisis

(1.1) Ad hoc units

(1.2) Narrow range of variation in membership

(1.3) Need for proximity

(1.4) Intensification of positive-affect relationships

(1.5) Expectations of leader responsibility

(1.6) Leader solicitation of advice

(1.7) Need for interdepartmental collaboration

Figure 1. Crisis and organizational variables

TABLE 3

Sequence of Decisional Units

Decisions	Decisional unit
1. To call for a Security Council meeting (June 24).	1. President Secretary of State Secretary of the Army Assistant Secretary for UN Affairs Assistant Secretary for Far Eastern Affairs Ambassador-at-large
2. To adopt a strong posture of resistance (June 25).	2. President Secretary of State Secretary of Defense Service Secretaries Joint Chiefs of Staff Under Secretary of State Assistant Secretary for UN Affairs Assistant Secretary for Far Eastern Affairs Ambassador-at-large
3. To commit air-sea forces; to keep conflict limited (June 26).	3. Same as (2) minus Secretary of the Navy and Under Secretary of State.
4. To extend operations into North Korea and to employ combat troops as evacuation cover (June 29).	4. President Secretary of State Secretary of Defense Service Secretaries Joint Chiefs of Staff Assistant Secretary for Far Eastern Affairs Special Ambassadors—2 Chairman, NSRB Executive Secretary, NSC
5. To commit one RCT to combat (June 30).	5. President Secretary of the Army Chairman, Joint Chiefs of Staff Chief of Staff of the Army General of the Army
6. To commit necessary ground forces (June 30).	6. President Secretary of State Secretary of Defense Service Secretaries Joint Chiefs of Staff Special Ambassador

to supplement his desired list. Among them, of course, are officials such as the Secretaries of State and Defense who might be expected to participate on the basis of their role responsibilities. On the other hand, there are other participants whose activity, though reasonable, is not so easily explainable solely in terms of formal role expectations; e.g., the participation of the Under Secretary of State in Unit 2 but his absence in Unit 3, the presence of a special ambassador but the absence of the Assistant Secretary for Far Eastern Affairs in Unit 6.

But what is the significance for decision of *ad hoc* units in crisis situations? The significance of the nature of the decisional unit immediately becomes a focus of attention because of the fundamental assumption of decision-making analysis that decisions tend to vary with the composition of the decisional unit. Thus it is of interest that although the threatening stimulus launched by the North Koreans was from the beginning a military action, the initial American response was primarily a diplomatic one based on legal considerations that sought to bring to bear in response the resources of international law and organization. The probability that this response was influenced by the composition of the group that initially articulated it as an alternative is suggested by the fact that this group included (1) the State Department official charged with primary responsibility for United Nations affairs (Assistant Secretary Hickerson), (2) a State Department official who had been the first incumbent in the same post in 1949 and who was known for his strong support of the United Nations (Assistant Secretary Rusk) and (3) a world-renowned specialist in international law (Ambassador Jessup). Confidence in this probability is increased, although to an indeterminate degree, by the conviction of one of Secretary Acheson's principal advisers that if he had been able to reach the State Department on Saturday night, he could have persuaded the Secretary of State not to limit the freedom of United States action by involving the United Nations in the American response to the Korean invasion. The Secretary of State's known preference for realistic power strategies rather than the unrealistic pursuit of principles in international affairs further increased the credibility of this official's conviction that he could have persuaded the Secretary of State to make a response to the Korean crisis that would be unencumbered by the United Nations involvement. Whether the President's great respect for Secretary Acheson's professional judgment would in turn, have led him to accept a recommendation for an initial unilateral American response to the aggression is, of course, speculative but not entirely implausible. The Truman Doctrine had been enunciated without a major role specified for the United Nations in 1947 and the decision to intervene in Formosa that was associated with the Korean decision in 1950 was taken with complete acceptance that it would not and could not be a United Nations action. If the need for direct military intervention in Korea had been clearer on Saturday night the argument for circumventing the United Nations might have been even more acceptable. Nevertheless, the point here is that an experienced decision maker appreciated at the time that it did make a difference who decided what the initial American response to the Korean crisis might be and that there is some evidence tending to support such a view in this case.

A review of the sequence of decisional units presented above suggests a cluster of propositions centering around considerations of size and composition of the decisional units that cope with crisis. Thus PROPOSITION 1.2: *Crisis decisions tend to be made by decisional units that vary within rather narrow limits of size and composition.* Our study has shown that the size of the key decisional units tended to vary between five and fourteen members as indicated in Table 3A.

TABLE 3A
Size of Decisional Units

Decision	Size of decisional unit
1	6
2	14
3	12
4	15
5	5
6	12

It will be noted that four of the six major sets of decisions were made by units having twelve to fourteen members. Two were made by five- and six-man groups. It is suggested that the larger groups can be accounted for partly by PROPOSITION 1.21: *The more costly the commitment anticipated, the larger the unit up to a psychologically and physically acceptable limit.* This is most clearly illustrated by the differences between Units 1 and 2 and between Units 5 and 6. The upper limits on decisional units seem to be influenced by felt need for secrecy and a sense of adequate representation of interests within the executive branch for the matter at hand. It has also been stated by one official who was not invited to the first Blair House conference that he was not invited but would have been except for the seating capacity of the Blair House dining room (said to be fourteen). Whether the capacity of customary facilities for high level face-to-face national decision making is a factor here, or whether it is a sense of adequate representation of interest, or of an upper level in group size in which meaningful participation in discussion can take place, it nevertheless seems possible to suggest that *the principal national crisis decision-making group will tend to vary in size from twelve to fifteen officials.* This possibility is made more intriguing by the fact that the Presidium of the Central Committee of the Communist Party of the Soviet Union tends to have from eleven to fifteen members and that the core group that

President Kennedy involved in the Cuban decision in the fall of 1962 apparently constituted about fifteen officials. Are there organizational qualities of crisis decision in the modern world that transcend size of polity, issue, technological capability, historical background, and cultural context?

It is suggested that the smaller decisional units (1 and 5) can be accounted for by PROPOSITION 1.22: *The more the felt need for immediate action and* (a) *the less costly the commitment, or* (b) *the greater the revocability of a costly commitment, or* (c) *the greater the anticipated acceptance of a costly commitment, the smaller the decisional unit.* In the first case, the decision to call a meeting of the United Nations Security Council was viewed as being a limited commitment that would not foreclose other alternatives. The President's decision to approve the movement of one RCT into combat on Friday combined considerations (b) and (c). The decisional units of the week seemed to vary but little in membership as well as in size. Note that the President, the Secretaries of State and Defense, the Civilian Secretaries, and the Joint Chiefs of Staff served as a kind of core decision-making group (Decisions 2, 3, 4, and 6). But it will also be noticed that, taking the week as a whole, there took place a gradual decrease in the number of participating State Department roles, except for Unit 4 which was not an *ad hoc* unit but rather an augmented National Security Council. The declining role of the Assistant Secretary of State for United Nations Affairs is apparent. Excluding the President, the relative proportions of State and Defense Department officials in the various decisional units is shown in Table 3B.

TABLE 3B

Relative Preponderance of State and Defense Roles in Decisional Units (Excluding the President)

	Per cent State	Per cent Defense
1	80	20
2	38	62
3	36	64
4	29	57
5	0	100
6	18	82

This pattern suggests PROPOSITION 1.23: *The more technical the problems of decision implementation, the greater the role of the appropriate specialists in the decisional unit.* Thus, in the Korean decision, as the problems thrust upon the decision makers more and more came to center around military problems of how to carry out the basic decision to resist the North Korean aggression, the representatives of the military establishment came to play a greater role in the deliberations. This is further supported by Secretary Johnson's later recollection that by the end of the week the center of working-level initiative in dealing with the Korean crisis seemed to have gravitated to his own office.

It was tempting to view the independent variable of Proposition 1.23 as the technical nature of crisis information and to hypothesize that it would be correlated with the composition of the official group that would react to it. However, the striking contrast between the purely military content of Ambassador Muccio's first report (on the Korean fighting) and the nonmilitary composition of Unit 1 for all practical purposes suggest that factors other than the content of information were crucial determinants of the composition of the decision-making group. The factors might have included the shared sense of required speed of action among the State Department officials, the lack of habits of intimate collaboration at high levels between State and Defense Department officials, the Secretary of State's misunderstanding that the Defense Secretary had not yet returned from the Far East, and other chance elements that seem to lead to an initial *ad hoc* assemblage of officials faced with a crisis. But in the implementation phases of crisis response more systematic factors seem to be at work, including official designation as a determinant of the composition of decision-making groups and a comparative decline in the importance of chance and self-selection in decisional participation. Thus it is suggested that the variables that intervene between the technical content of information and the composition of the decision-making group as expressed in Proposition 1.23 are a more regularized mode of designating decision makers and important control over channels of incoming information. For example, whereas military information from Ambassador Muccio that had been received through State Department channels was acted upon primarily by State Department officials (Unit 1), military information from General MacArthur that had been received through Army channels served as the basis for decision by an almost purely Army group (Unit 5).

PROPOSITION 1.3: *The greater the crisis, the greater the felt need for face-to-face proximity among decision makers.* This proposition is suggested by the President's desire to return to Washington on Saturday night and by the whole series of face-to-face deliberations among his advisers that were suggested to him during the week. Thus crisis situations apparently intensify the need for the direct full sharing of information and views among organizational members. Do they also intensify a need to reinforce individual security feelings through group reassurance?

PROPOSITION 1.4: *The greater the crisis, the greater the accentuation of positive affect relationships among decision makers.* The warm personal relationship that existed between the President and the Secretary of State is demonstrated repeatedly during the events of the week by their harmony of views, frequent interaction, and the predominant role of the latter in articulating courses of action for presidential approval. Negative affect relationships, however, seemed not to have been affected in just the same way. Though the coolness at the secretarial level between the Departments of State and Defense may have inhibited somewhat the fullness of departmental collaboration that might otherwise have been accomplished, there is no evidence that these relations worsened. On the contrary, the public praise of the Secretary of State by the Secretary of Defense on Wednesday perhaps illustrates the facilitating effect of crisis, at least in moderate degree, upon group cohesiveness.

PROPOSITION 1.5: *The greater the crisis, the greater the acceptance of responsibility for action by the leader and the more the follower expectation and acceptance of the leader's responsibility.* The President's behavior during the Korean decision and the understanding and respect for his responsibilities shown by his advisers then and afterward enhances the appreciation of leadership behavior as a pattern of interaction between leaders and followers. There is no doubt that the President's own definition of his role as a strong president contributed to his decision to respond to crisis without formal Congressional approval. But it is also likely that he was influenced by the expectations of his advisers that he should act independently and responsibly. Two pieces of evidence suggest support for this interpretation. Apparently only one adviser suggested a discussion of domestic politics during the Blair House conferences and apparently none raised any question about the appropriateness of presidential action. More directly, Secretary Acheson explicitly advised the President after the Monday evening decision not to seek a Congressional mandate for it and this advice was accepted. Both leader and follower definitions of his responsibility for taking positive action in response to crisis are undoubtedly conditioned by past social learning experiences. Thus for those who had observed the President under previous crisis conditions, such as in the Berlin crisis of 1948 when he had been inclined to favor a more drastic response than the airlift that was finally decided upon, his determination to resist the North Korean aggression could be anticipated. Participants in the Korean decision seem agreed that a less strong president might not have responded to the Korean aggression in the firm and timely way in which Mr. Truman did. This, in turn, suggests PROPOSITION 1.51: *The greater the crisis, and the greater the past record of nonavoidant response to crisis by the leader, the greater the propensity to make a positive response.* Thus the intensification of mutual responsibility expectations and the enhancement of the importance of behavior during past crises can be anticipated under crisis conditions.

PROPOSITION 1.6: *The greater the crisis, the more the leader's solicitation of subordinate advice.* This is illustrated in the Korean decision by the way in which President Truman invited each of his advisers to comment upon the situation during both of the Blair House conferences. Although the President was known to have a permissive leadership style, the Korean crisis probably accentuated that pattern. The President's past behavior suggested that the more important the problem, the more likely he was to seek the advice of his advisers in reaching a decision about it.

For this reason, it would have been surprising if he had not demonstrated such a leadership style during the Korean decision. It will be interesting to examine this proposition further in cases where the leader is not habitually permissive in his relationships with advisers.

PROPOSITION 1.7: *The greater the crisis, the greater the interdepartmental collaboration.* The crisis in Korea seemed to draw the Departments of State and Defense into collaboration closer than that which they had experienced for many months. It will be recalled that at one time Secretary Johnson had ordered all interactions should cease except those that were channeled through his own office. But during the crisis, officials at this "working level" appear to have been in especially close collaboration. There was both joint action and intermingling of officials in the field in Korea and in Washington. The need for interdepartmental collaboration that was expressed in practice at lower levels, however, seems not to have overcome the obstacles to cooperation at the secretarial level except for formal confrontations under presidential supervision. This seemed particularly evident in the period between the receipt of the news of the fighting on Saturday and the decision to intervene on Monday.

Crisis and Informational Variables

The main informational bases of the sequence of decisions that made up the Korean decision are summarized in Table 4.

Figure 2 summarizes some effects of crisis upon informational variables.

PROPOSITION 2.1: *The greater the crisis, the greater the felt need for information.* From the State Department duty officer's first efforts to obtain confirmation of the United Press report on the North

TABLE 4

Sequence of Information

Decisions	Information
1. To call for a Security Council meeting (June 24).	Cable from Ambassador Muccio Press reports
2. To adopt a strong posture of resistance (June 25).	MacArthur memo on Formosa Confirming reports on all-out invasion Favorable Security Council action ROK Army might hold Soviet Union backed North Korean action US held military superiority over USSR US had Far Eastern military capability Invasion was like pre-WW II aggressions Acheson recommendations Direct appreciation of mutual attitudes
3. To commit air-sea forces (June 26).	MacArthur report on imminent ROK collapse Acheson recommendations Air-sea support would probably be decisive Soviets would probably not intervene Gross report on strong UN sanction support Shared determination not to appease
4. To extend operations into North Korea and to use combat troops as evacuation cover (June 29).	Reports on military difficulties Johnson recommendations Temperate Soviet response Overwhelmingly favorable domestic and foreign response
5. To commit one RCT to combat (June 30).	ROK Army incapable of more than delaying action MacArthur recommendation
6. To commit necessary ground combat forces (June 30).	Same as (5). Further Soviet aggression not imminent Two divisions probably adequate

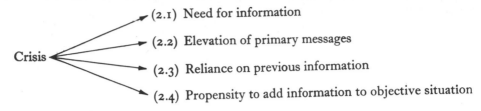

Figure 2. Crisis and informational variables

Korean attack through the President's repeated requests for more information about Soviet intentions in other troublesome areas, the record of the Korean decision illustrated a strong demand for information under crisis. This need for information leads to the directed scanning of the organizational environment. The Sunday decision to ask General MacArthur to send a survey party to Korea is an excellent example of a decision-making group seeking to improve its information about the external setting in a crisis situation. Although the emphasis during the Korean decision seems to have been on scanning the external setting, noteworthy efforts were also made to obtain information about significant aspects of the internal setting—especially information needed to estimate capabilities for action. Thus the President's questions on Sunday night about the size, disposition, and mobility of American military forces in the Far East, as well as relative Soviet strengths, not only exemplify a need for information but also show how information variables can link capabilities analysis and foreign policy decision making.

PROPOSITION 2.11: *The more limited the information, the greater the emphasis placed upon the reliability of its source.* This is suggested by the fact that decision makers at the Department of State on Saturday evening placed great weight upon Ambassador Muccio's estimate of the attack as an "invasion" since he had a reputation for careful and cautious reporting.

PROPOSITION 2.12: *The more varied the organizational sources and channels of communication of similar information, the greater the confidence in its validity.* This may be illustrated by the remark of Senator Connally just prior to the Korean crisis that military, diplomatic, and private reports seemed to indicate a general lessening of international tension. Immediately after the attack the cumulative effect of multiple sources of information on the accepted seriousness of the invasion could be seen as the result of the process of comparing information, especially among Army and Air Force officers in Tokyo and Army and State Department officials in Washington.

PROPOSITION 2.13: *The more prolonged the crisis, the greater the sense of adequacy of the information about it.* In the initial stages of a surprise threat, there are acute feelings of inadequacy of information about it, but as efforts are made to obtain further information, as actions are taken and responses to such actions are observed, and as additional information is thrust upon the decision makers from their environment, the sense of inadequacy begins to diminish. Thus in the early stages of the Korean decision, the Washington officials felt inadequately informed about the progress of fighting in Korea, the relative strengths of the opposing forces, the intentions of Soviet leaders, and other matters. By the end of the week, they felt more adequately informed. Here the eruption of a crisis is unanticipated and the initial feelings of inadequacy are intensified by the lack of contingency planning that would have led to continuous prior monitoring of information deemed necessary for response determination. Although information was viewed as becoming generally more adequate as the situation unfolded, there were some matters on which doubt was high (such as the ultimate costs of repelling the aggression and the possible role of the Chinese Communists) and only a very few things about which information was felt to be more than adequate (such as the domestic American acceptance of the Korean involvement).

PROPOSITION 2.2: *The greater the crisis, the greater the tendency for primary messages to be elevated to the top of the organizational hierarchy.* An example of this is the fact that the duty officer at General Headquarters in Tokyo did not attempt to bring the first fragmentary reports of the Korean fighting to the attention of General MacArthur in the early morning of June 25 until the extreme seriousness of the attack had become clear. In Washington throughout the week, there were a number of primary messages that were communicated directly to the President; e.g., the Muccio report, the Dulles-Allison cable, and the MacArthur recommendations. This pattern of information flow seems correlated both with the need for information at higher organizational levels and with subordinate need for high-level decisions in fast-moving crisis situations. This pattern incidentally suggests qualities required in order to gain top-level organizational attention.

PROPOSITION 2.3: *The greater the crisis, the greater the reliance upon the central themes in previously existing information.* This is illustrated throughout the Korean decision by the persistent tendency to rely upon information about the relative capabilities of the North and South Korean armies that underestimated the capacities of the former and overestimated the abilities of the latter. This lack of appreciation of the actual relative capabilities of the two opposing military organizations was rooted, of course, in the estimate that they were approximately equal in weight. Thus the central, or predominant, theme in this matter was that the Republic of Korea Army could probably contain an invasion unless the North Korean People's Army was reinforced from outside. This theme, however, did not represent the total range of information about the opposing forces that was objectively available in Washington files. It will be recalled that the State Department had released to the press on June 9, 1950, a statement by Ambassador Muccio who asserted that "the undeniable material superiority of the North Korean forces would provide North Korea with the margin of victory in the event of a full-scale invasion of the Republic."[8] Thus the estimates discussed during the Blair House conferences represented selective

recall of the main trend of earlier estimates rather than a rather full exploration of the range of objectively available information. Although this tendency did not prevent timely support of the South Korean forces, it undoubtedly delayed appreciation of its necessity and required scope. One way to compensate for the tendency for crisis comprehension to be narrowed through selective recall of predominant themes in existing information might be to initiate immediate scanning of past records for contrary themes, or to maintain continuing awareness of subdominant interpretations.

PROPOSITION 2.31: *The greater the confidence in existing information, the greater the amount of contrary evidence and the greater the authority of the sources required to bring about a change in interpretation.* It will be recalled that major revisions in previous estimates of South Korean capabilities were made twice during the Korean decision—on Monday just prior to the air-sea commitment and on Friday immediately before the decision to employ infantry. Both of these revisions, it will be noted, were made on the authority of information from General MacArthur, not upon reports emanating from the Korean Military Advisory Group.

PROPOSITION 2.4: *The greater the crisis, the greater the propensity for decision makers to supplement information about the objective state of affairs with information drawn from their own past experience.* This proposition, originally suggested by Richard C. Snyder, is illustrated by the categorization by the decision makers of the North Korean attack as an act of "aggression" similar to German, Japanese, and Italian actions that preceded World War II. Since a crisis involves a threat to values it is likely that the information selectively added from memory by the decision makers will be value-connected as "aggression" is associated with the values of "war" and "peace." Once again the importance of past social learning for response to crisis is suggested, furthermore, the briefer the opportunity for new learning under crisis conditions, the greater its probable importance. . . .

[8] John J. Muccio, "Military Aid to Korean Security Forces," *Department of State Bulletin*, XXII, No. 573 (June 26, 1950) p. 1049.

B. The Use of Comparative Analysis

42. Action Structures and Communication in Two International Crises: Quemoy and Berlin

Charles A. McClelland, whose general orientation toward international phenomena is outlined in Selection 1, has long been committed in his research to the proposition that progress in the field requires a more thorough job of mapping the structure of the patterns of interaction among nations. Thus his empirical work eschews an effort to uncover the strategic considerations that underlie actions and the influence factors that give rise to reactions. Instead Professor McClelland confines his attention to the interaction patterns that actually transpire, hoping thereby to reveal more clearly the structure of international phenomena, whatever their motivational sources. To accomplish this task his research has focused on the structure of crisis situations and the ensuing article is but one of many inquiries that reflect his work along these lines (see also Selection 57). [*Reprinted from* Background, *VII (1964), 201–15, by permission of the author and the publisher.*]

Current international relations theory suggests to the researcher that at least two distinctly different perspectives ought to be brought to bear in the analysis of any major series of international events. Foreign policy analysis—or, more generally, the study of the international behavior of "national actors"—is one focus. The other focus is on the interplay of demands and responses in a series of international events—or, on the operations of the international system. A competent historical narrative utilizes both perspectives and blends "actor" and "system" considerations in order to reveal an ordering of what occurred in a time and place setting. No complaints ought to be raised against good diplomatic histories. They represent one level of approximation of the truth to complex realities. The present interest in international relations research is to develop empirical studies which, by their method and scope, will improve on the historical synthesis and in a cumulative manner. Detailed case studies of particular decisions in foreign policy and calculations of cost-effectiveness ratios in planning military and foreign programs are types of work that are beginning to cluster around the "national actor" perspective. Richardson's (1960) analyses of the patterns of arms races and Deutsch's (1956, 1960) comparative studies of input-output performances of many nations are examples in the development of the systems perspective.

473

The Structures of Action

This paper is within the systems framework although it does not make use of quantitative techniques as most systems analyses do. The approach is, in fact, quite close to that of diplomatic history. The questions that we seek to answer are not the ones usually asked by the historian, however. Thus, it may be well to state what will *not* be taken into account here. No attempt will be made to describe or explain the motives, goals, and policies of the governments that were participants in the Berlin crisis of 1948–49 or in the Quemoy crisis of 1958. The complex international environments which gave these crises their orientation in world politics are neither described nor analyzed. We shall not be concerned here with ideological or ethical questions. As a means of narrowing the scope of the work, we have largely eliminated the data concerned with diplomatic negotiations during the course of the crises. Even a definition of an international crisis will not be attempted; it is contended simply that the Berlin and Quemoy crises took place in recent history and that both had fairly clear beginning and ending dates. Operational definitions and tests of acute crises in the Cold War period are needed but the task is being evaded here.

What then, is the research question? It is, in brief, to examine and evaluate the data of the two crises in that single aspect of "physical acts" that constituted a part of the total of the demands and responses of the contesting parties. For purposes of analysis, we are asserting that the historical events of the Berlin and Quemoy crises can be separated into two arenas, one of which—the diplomatic—is being ignored while the other—the "field" or theater of operations—is being emphasized. The moves made in the field by one side created problems of counter-moves for the other side. A connected sequence of events should be found in the records of these crises, therefore. The question, then, is what phases and stages did these moves and countermoves go through from the beginning to end of the crises? What traits or characteristics of the interaction in the arena of physical events can be discerned? Particularly, what communication phenomena can be found? Can anything be said on how the two crises were alike and different with respect to the "structure" or ordered sequences of action?

Chronologies for each crisis were prepared, mainly from the day to day accounts of American and British newspapers. Items were assembled for the two year period, 1948–49, for the Berlin crisis and for the entire year of 1958 for the Quemoy crisis. All reports reflecting physical acts such as movements of military units, arrests, rioting, road interferences, air incidents, battles, military and naval skirmishes, etc. were then extracted for analysis from the whole chronological compilation. On the order of one-third of the items in the two chronologies belonged in the "physical acts" category. All of the selected items were then arranged in chronological order on charts that indicated the action-response connections between the events reported. Some items were isolated and stood alone without known relationships to other items; a great many were connected in series, resembling "changes of state in the system." Ashby's conception (1957) of sequential behavior and its charting was followed.

The initial charting for the two crises was then modified in two further steps of analysis for the Quemoy crisis (three steps for the Berlin crisis). Sequences were rearranged according to whether individual acts were (1) threats or direct attacks on "the temporary status quo," (2) defense or manipulation of "the temporary status quo," (3) yielding acts or withdrawing from the position of "the temporary status quo." Each of these acts was also placed according to whether it occurred in the "thick of things"—i.e., closely-coupled in the sequence—or at some distance away and thus, representing a "mobilizing" action only. This step of the analysis changed the appearance of the charts so that separate acts could be seen clustered tightly together by type and time period or spread apart and connected by long lines of interaction.

The second analytical operation was a judgment on where to draw lines to mark off stages in the development of the crisis. The concept of a "temporary status quo" was the central influence in guiding the decision. It was conceived that at the active beginning of an acute international crisis, one side or the other would hold a position of such character to put the problem of responding—deciding what to do next—on its opponent. As long as the opponent is unable to cope with his problem of an effective response, it is assumed that a "temporary status quo" is in being and dominated by the initiating government. Once the party upon whom the responsibility for the next move makes good his claim and changes the situation, the problem of the next move is shifted to the erstwhile holder of the initiative. The behavior of the latter must change until he can put the burden of response back on his opponent. The amounts of shift in this see-saw motion were chosen to demarcate the stages of the crises. More will be said below on the subject of "the temporary status quo."

The Berlin material required a further categorization because it proved to cover a much more complex situation than that of Quemoy. It was necessary to reposition groups of items so that they fitted in to four different channels of interactions. These are identified in the discussion of the Berlin crisis.

The charting of interaction sequences with items connected to items by lines and arrows reveals much information through visual inspection. One can get a direct impression of the patterns and structures of a crisis by studying the charts. The main drawback of the technique is that it becomes too extensive to reproduce in a book or article and lacks a means for summarization and compact statement—this being a chief advantage of quantitative techniques. On the other hand, the charting provides a shorthand to support an interpretation that otherwise would be long and choked with small details. A quantitative system that would not obscure the detail of pattern would be preferred.

Communication and Strategy

In analyzing the physical acts of the two crises, we had an active interest to see if evidences of non-verbal communicating would appear in the sequences.

Thomas Schelling, perhaps more than anyone else, has recently made us aware that it might be well to take a fresh look at the details of interaction sequences in diplomatic history. The reason is that reexaminations of some parts of diplomatic history may throw additional light on the strategy of international negotiations, on .international conflict behavior, and, in general, on what Schelling has called "mixed-motive games." Episodes such as international conferences or international crises are very elaborately compounded events. If they are to

be studied in detail in terms of tacit bargaining, coordination of actions, communication effects, and boundary-maintaining behavior, the compounded events must be broken apart. One way to do this, obviously, is to "map" sequences of related actions.

Schelling has very effectively brought attention to how action "talks" in the setting of mixed-motive games and in bargaining. A large amount of tacit communicating occurs in the social millieu. Small children (and some diplomats) understand the powerful effects related to moving into a perilous location where a fall *may* result despite the best efforts of everyone to prevent that outcome (Schelling, 1960, p. 200). Words are not required to draw responses from others. When no amount of verbally-transmitted persuasion or evidence is convincing, an overt act can be persuasive if it is carried out in the right setting and with the right timing. Schelling gives many examples of tacit coordination where persons who cannot talk, write, or signal to one another still manage to collaborate through mutual but independent reading of some element of the system. He also illustrates how tacit negotiations can be carried on, how tacit bargains may be struck, and how tacit threats can be made. Many of these processes are interpreted in terms of variations on behavior that remains within conventionalized limits. Consistently *not* overstepping behavioral boundaries can convey important information.

Schelling notes that the physical character of Korea set "natural" boundaries to the Korean conflict. These boundaries were unmistakable in an area surrounded by water except in the north where a river concisely marked that frontier. "The thirty-eighth parallel seems to have been a powerful focus for a stalemate; and the main alternative, the 'waist' was a strong candidate not just because it provided a shorter defense line but because it would have been clear to both sides that an advance to the waist did not necessarily signal a determination to advance farther and that a retreat to the waist did not telegraph any intention to retreat further" (Schelling, 1960, p. 76).

The physical act of building a block and mortar wall on the dividing line of East and West Berlin "spoke" eloquently. The first Sputnik in October 1957 was only a piece of hardware shot into space but its communicative effect was such to make Khrushchev the commissar of U.S. education, as someone has said. When the Soviet Union set off its first nuclear device in 1949, there was no need to make an announcement because the detection devices in other countries were sure to receive the information of the act. Perhaps, the event had enhanced impact from *not* being announced. What the Berlin airlift in 1948–49 "said" to the world certainly was potent although the content of the message was not explicit.

Not all tacit communications by physical act involve large events. President Eisenhower golfing on a politically-charged day and Premier Khrushchev touring the countryside in a holiday mood after sabotaging a summit meeting are examples of small actions which are capable of speaking loud. The Quemoy crisis was especially rich in the phenomena of communicating by doing, as we shall see.

Yet, we have not really traveled far toward understanding the dynamics of coordinating, focusing, threatening, negotiating, and bargaining by nonverbal means. We merely recognize that such processes have considerable stature in an international system in which no one can afford to believe too much of what another says.

Physical acts such as the East Germans building a wall do not contain the meanings that become attached to them. The meanings are added, presumably, according to the "fit" of the action with pre-existing and shared images or according to ordered memories of past experience. The type of act perceived to have been the immediate cause of an acute crisis does not "communicate" the same way at all times. The immediate "logic of the situation" and the timing of events seem to be crucial. The Chinese mainland artillery bombarded Quemoy before the Quemoy crisis began and it bombarded Quemoy after the crisis was calmed. At Berlin during the early summer of 1949, the blocking of the railways by the stubborn UGO strike against the Soviet-controlled Reichsbahn was as desperate and aggravating as any event in the entire affair, yet this did not reopen the crisis which at the very moment was being "settled" in the aftermath of the Jessup-Malik diplomacy.

To get beyond the present uncertainties about the workings of nonverbal communication in international transactions, we shall need to study real cases from the standpoint of interaction analysis. An initial step is to isolate those happenings which probably were vehicles of non-verbal communications. Let us see, then, what the Quemoy crisis of August-October 1958 and the Berlin blockade crisis of June 1948–October 1949 will yield in the way of interaction sequences of the non-verbal variety.

The Quemoy Crisis

What happened at Quemoy ? For those who may not recall vividly the course of the Quemoy crisis, the following may be helpful: Late in August 1958, the Chinese mainland regime launched a massive attack on Quemoy which was being held by about one-third of the Nationalist Chinese armed forces. The declared intention of the mainland was to capture Taiwan and the other islands held by the Nationalists. The American response was to call the Seventh Fleet and other units to alert but to leave indefinite on the diplomatic front whether or not Quemoy and Matsu would be defended by the United States. The Eisenhower Administration and Secretary of State John Foster Dulles were put under pressure by critics of American foreign policy and the fear of war—particularly nuclear war—was aroused. The allies of the United States, especially Great Britain and France, were reluctant to support U.S. policy while spokesmen in neutralist countries were very critical of the "war-provoking" behavior of the United States and Mr. Dulles.

At Quemoy, the main problem was the cutting of the supply lines of the Nationalists between Quemoy and Taiwan. Before that blockade was finally broken, Mao Tse-tung proposed that ambassadorial talks between Communist China and the United States be resumed and Dulles followed the lead. The tension began to ease toward the middle of September and eventually the crisis was channeled into the Warsaw talks. At the psychological peak of the crisis, Khrushchev sent two notes to Eisenhower accusing the United States of planning aggressive war and threatening nuclear retaliation in return, if the United States moved against the mainland Chinese. The resumption of the ambassadorial talks at Warsaw, the rumors of UN action, discussions of the de-militarization of Quemoy, etc. aroused the ire of Chiang Kai-Shek and this created new problems. No solutions were found for the problem of the off-shore islands and it can be said with confidence that the crisis, itself, was not resolved. It merely deteriorated until the attentive publics and the press were no longer interested in it. The foregoing description contains evidence of several change-inducing events. Let us attempt to analyze these.

Perhaps the most primitive message conveyed by an act concerns what it does, or what it promises to do, to the status quo. An international crisis always is focused on some change or threat of change to the existing situation. During the course of a crisis, events, particularly physical actions, modify the status quo. Hence, we can conceive of a line running through time which traces the trajectory of the status quo. Such a line would change directions; it would reflect a succession of conditions and show a succession of "situations." Some events can be classed as attempts to bend the line—to shift the status quo— while others can be identified as attempts to keep the situation as it is at the moment. Sometimes, there is a "softening" of the status quo or a retreat from it. Further, some events appear to be very close to the center of action and change, both geographically and temporally, while others appear to operate at a distance of future time and/or geographical location.

The detailed charting makes visible some interesting facts about the action of the Quemoy crisis. First, the shifts in the temporary status quo are plainly shown by the occurrence of certain events. This permits the naming of four stages or periods of the crisis: (1) the warning period, opened most fully by the mobilizing action of the Chinese Nationalists on August 6 and closed by the extraordinary bombardment of Quemoy on August 23; (2) the period of the blockade, opened on August 23 and closed with the temporary suspension of bombardment by Peking on September 4; (3) the period of the convoy *versus* the blockade, opened on September 3 or 4 and closed on September 24 with the first use of the Sidewinder missile and the announcement of the breaking of the blockade; and (4) the period of tacit bargaining beginning September 24 and ending October 25 when the Chinese Communists established the pattern of even-numbered day bombardments.

During the warning period, two "signalling" mechanisms were brought into action: (1) the reporting of mobilizing events (the Seventh Fleet alert in July, the movement of aircraft and the activating of military installations on the mainland of China adjacent to Quemoy, and the defensive measures

taken on Taiwan and the offshore islands) and (2) the accelerating of "threshold actions." There existed between 1955 and 1958 a normalized level of violent interaction[1] in the Taiwan Straits which was characterized by sporadic artillery bombardments of the offshore islands, infrequent naval encounters, and occasional air battles between Nationalists and Communist fighter aircraft. During August, these kinds of threshold events simply occurred more frequently than usual. The warning events did not change the status quo; they announced the possibility of change in the status quo, however.

The bombardment of August 23 forecast a change because of its intensity—five times greater than the previous record bombardment. It took several days for the Nationalists to comprehend the intent of the "message" and to ascertain that it was not the initial stage of a major invasion attempt. Whether or not the mainland commanders immediately understood the situation that they had created remains an interesting question not open to answers at the present time. At any rate, the mainland soon controlled a new status quo and faced only the problem of supporting and maintaining the situation they had created. The bombardment cut the supply lines by water and air between Taiwan and the Quemoy islands; the Nationalists were unable to do anything about it.

During the second period—that of the unbroken blockade—the air actions increased but these encounters have appeared to us to be so detached from the main lines of military and naval operations (although Nationalist planes obviously *were* flying cover for the supply vessels trying to reach the offshore islands) that we have, in most cases, classified the air clashes as "holding actions"—maintaining a threshold only in the air space. A definite sequence of interactions can be identified in this second period in the challenge of the status quo of blockade by the Nationalists and the responding defense in the selective artillery fire of the Communists which held off the supply vessels.

The American response to the blockade in the second period was strictly at long-distance. Only a well-publicized gathering of naval and air strength in the Western Pacific and Taiwan took place. In

[1] It is probable that those who took part in these operations saw nothing "normalized" in them and would, understandably, reject the characterization.

effect, the mainland bid into the game with a remarkably intense display of its ability to fire its artillery
pieces and the United States bid in with a remarkably
intense mobilizing of its fighting forces.

The third phase of action opened with a fundamental change in the situation. The United States
initiated a move—the escorting of Nationalist supply
ships to the territorial waters of the mainland at
Quemoy. We are tempted to go beyond the available
data by saying that the response of the mainland to
the U.S. escort move was to halt its own operations
in order to scan for further evidence of the meaning
of the American move. All that can be asserted, however, is that Peking stopped its bombardment for a
few days immediately after the American participation in the convoying began.

The third period of action was the most dangerous with respect to the possibility of the escalation of
violence because the status quo was rendered
extremely unstable. After the point in time when the
blockade was being broken occasionally by improved
techniques of convoying and landing, both sides
were threatening the status quo which was merely a
kind of unsteady equilibrium. It is conceivable that
the mainland Chinese expected the shift from mobilizing to threatening acts on the part of the United
States to extend to the air. The tremendous reputation
of U.S. air power in the fifties may have been more
influential in Peking's image of what would happen
next than the nuclear potential of the fleet. The
introduction of the Sidewinder missile may have
conveyed the meaning to the mainland that the
United States intended to relieve Quemoy from the
air—by bombing raids and an airlift. The unilaterally
declared and executed cease-fire of October 6 by
Peking may have arisen from such an image. Or, it is
possible that the mainland decision-makers were
aware, after a few trials that the status quo had
shifted again and that their bargaining position had
become stronger than their threatening position.

The fourth period of the action of the Quemoy
crisis is extremely instructive in the perspective of
tacit communication. The interaction chart indicates
a definite slackening of activity on both sides. Until
October 6, the mainland actions appear very much
to be probing operations—seeking the intentions of
the other side. There occur, also, further evidences
of the main American response to the crisis in
additional mobilizing actions. The occasional air

battles resemble in their infrequency a return to the
normalcy of the previous "threshold of violence" of
1955–58. Most interesting are the de-mobilizing
events which clearly answered one another, in
sequence.

After a few days, the mainland cease-fire was
responded to by the cessation of Nationalist attacks.
The United States abandoned its naval escort service
on the reasonable ground that, since the blockade had
been lifted, no naval protection for the supply
vessels was any longer needed. After the extension of
the cease-fire by Peking, some ships recently attached
to the Seventh Fleet were sent elsewhere. These
events followed one another to bring about a relaxation of the crisis despite the failure of the diplomatic
negotiations at Warsaw to achieve any agreement or
settlement.

The mainland's resumption of the bombardment of Quemoy on October 20, aimed with the
arrival of Secretary of State Dulles at Taipeh, was
as expressive as any non-verbal communication
could be. Where else in diplomatic history is there
such a greeting—a veritable Bronx cheer in iron?
Finally, the beginning of even-day-of-the-month
bombarding after October 25 by the mainland possibly indicated several things: that the mainland
could still seize the initiative at Quemoy, that there
was to be a return to a normalized pattern of sporadic
and even meaningless violence, and that the affair in
the Taiwan Straits might not be over for good.

The Berlin Crisis

The sequence of actions of the Berlin blockade
provides a second case for interaction study. It
proves to be strikingly more complex than the
Quemoy crisis, even when its verbal and diplomatic
aspects have been cut away to reveal the framework
of non-verbal events. Unlike the Quemoy affair,
the Berlin crisis could not be fitted into a single
channel on the detailed interaction chart. Instead of
one, it required the use of four channels. Further,
it turned out to be more difficult to make the judgments which separate "talk" from "action" and to
distinguish those events that are immediate in their
impact on the status quo and those that are more
distant or indirect. These characteristics make the
Berlin case more demanding but also more interesting
in the technical sense.

The preparations and procedures employed in analyzing the Berlin action remained the same type as for the Quemoy action; the only change was to record four streams of events instead of one. The shifts in the traffic of events from one stream to another are very apparent on the interaction "map." Advantage was taken of these shifts to arrange the periodization of the history of the crisis. What happened in the Berlin crisis will be described according to these shifts; the narrative which would be necessary to establish the broad setting, including such matters as the administration of the occupation, the conditions that led to the currency reform of June 1948, the planning for the merging and self-governing of the Western zones, the London, Prague, and Warsaw conferences of 1948, and, in general, the whole background of the German "question" is omitted.

The status quo at Berlin at the beginning of 1948 featured the chronic conflict in the governing of Berlin by military authorities of the United States, the Soviet Union, Great Britain, and France through the Allied Control Council and the Kommandatura. The situation worsened at the end of March when the Soviet representative walked out of the Control Council and brought these sessions to a close. Occasionally, the strife between the administrators of the three Western zones and the military governors of the Soviet zone was extended to disputes and friction involving members of the Magistrat, the civil executive body of Berlin. This source of potential disruption was joined by the sporadic Soviet interferences with travel and traffic between the West zones of Germany and Berlin to establish what may be interpreted as the threshold of normalized action.

As at Quemoy, the acceleration of action on the threshold during April 1948 heightened sensitivities to possible shifts in the status quo. The Soviet declaration on March 31 of new regulations governing travel into Berlin, followed shortly by the argument that no agreements were in force to permit free and unrestricted access to Berlin from the West through the Soviet zone of Germany created a flurry of interaction. These challenges appear to us to have been tests by the Soviet authorities of the will to resist the new restrictions on travel on the part of the three Western commandants. On the surface, the record shows a mixed response with some considerable amount of yielding to the Soviet pressure but also some determined exchanges in episodes where

the Soviet behavior was to back away from a showdown. The rail, road, and waterway routes were put under this challenge; the record we have used shows no systematic interference with air travel.

The lone event that was the outstanding exception was the aftermath of the collision of a British transport plane and a Soviet fighter on the approach to the Gatow airfield on April 5, 1948. The British and American responses were exceptionally vigorous, to the point of ordering fighter escorts for British and American planes approaching Berlin through the corridors. These orders were rescinded quickly but they created an impression. The supporting documentation is absent but this vigor may well have conveyed to the Soviet side the idea that the air approach from the West to Berlin would be safeguarded at any cost. Davison arrived at that tentative conclusion: "Soviet efforts to restrict air travel appeared to be coordinated with other measures to choke off Berlin's surface communications, but both the British and Americans seemed more sensitive to the air restrictions than to interference with rail and road traffic. The Western powers' readiness to assign fighter escorts, if necessary, may have been one reason why the Soviet made no serious attempt to interfere with the air corridor during the blockade. They apparently wished to avoid any incident that would lead to war . . ." (Davison, 1958, pp. 67–68).

The first period of the crisis has been named here the period of "minor challenges" between January 24 and June 18, 1948. In its speeding up of threshold-type events it corresponds well to the first period of the Quemoy crisis but with the difference that no particular indication of mobilizing actions is in the Berlin picture.

The beginning of the second period between June 18 and July 27 ("blockade and parallel economic conflict") arrived with two dramatic announcements: (1) currency reform for the West zones of Germany and for Berlin and (2) the Soviet imposition of a travel blockade by land and water on Berlin. The blockade was a direct response to the currency reform and was announced that way. The dense and intense interaction sequence that followed is divided on the chart in two channels. First, Soviet and American forces fought to control the new status quo of June 18, the Soviets by harassing the air approaches to Berlin, although in a cautious and limited manner, and the Americans by initiating the airlift. If two cases established a behavioral regularity (and they do not), we could say that the initial, unerring response of the United States to a crisis is mobilization—a series of acts conveying tacitly to the world a threat that massive overwhelming forces are being assembled for possible use at the point of crisis. This is a Spanish Armada kind of mechanism which, at Berlin and Quemoy, enjoyed success.

By July 15, the United States had come into clear control of one sector of the new status quo, for the airlift was already proven to be viable and the military air support for it, in case of serious challenge, was well on its way to the entrance of the arena. The Soviet control of the new status quo on the ground, on the other hand, was equally established and no challenge of importance to the blockade was issued by the West, except in the verbal and legal areas of action.

The second response to the announcements of June 18 is especially interesting. A type of international conflict which seems not to be accounted for adequately by the arms race theory occurred in the second period of the Berlin crisis. So far in our analyses, we have seen mainly asymmetrical responses to threats. A nucleararmed fleet presented its potential against an active bombardment. An airlift answered the cutting off of travel on the ground. Now, we encounter an instance of "equal, opposite, and opposing" conflict behavior that seems not to escalate but rather, to set up dual vacua which subject everything standing between to contrary pulls. This effect has to do with the polarization of conflict. Following Linebarger's naming (1957), we have called the process "conflict by duplication." It is, *par excellence*, a long distance, mobilizing type of behavior, under the definitions given previously.

In the second stage of the Berlin crisis, the Soviet response to the Western currency reform was to establish a counterpart reform, equal in form and opposing. Two parallel structures began to grow. These structures, covering currency regulations and trade control systems, were built in a setting of opposition so that the persons and organizations affected were pulled one way or the other according to particular circumstances. The result was a partitioning, not for the resolution of conflict as the theoretical literature has suggested but as a *means* of carrying on conflict. This is a process deserving further study. In the Berlin situation, the parallel structures were set in place and in later periods of 1948 and 1949 the West launched a new offensive against both the blockade and the economy of the east zone of Germany by means of a progressively tightened economic counterblockade. The second period of the Berlin crisis came to a close with the first appearance of the program of Western economic counterblockade toward the end of July 1948.

The third period of action is traced most easily by following the shift of scene to the "fight for Berlin." By the first of August, temporary status quo conditions had been established in three of the four arenas—access to Berlin from the West on the ground and by water was interdicted, access to Berlin by air was assured by the airlift, and the East-West division of control over economic affairs was a fact. Diplomatic measures were being taken not only toward bargaining out the blockade problem but also with reference to the whole spectrum of unresolved German questions. A waging of cold war for the control of the city took place, according to our somewhat arbitrary dates, between July 27 and October 16, 1948.[2] The reason for establishing the latter date is that the chronology shows a gap—a virtual rest period of a month—in the sequence of events between the middle of October and the middle of November.

The fight for the control of Berlin was violent. It was at this time that the West Berliners made their special bid to maintain a permanent defense of freedom at that particular place in the world. The episode belongs, probably, to the class of traumatic historical experiences. American, British, and Soviet military authorities became embroiled in the political and parliamentary battles for the control of the municipal government, sometimes literally for control of buildings and meeting rooms. There were mob actions, killings, and the most drastic kind of psychological aggressions and back alley blackmailing pressures put on the administrators and representatives of the municipality who were of the West's persuasion. Stalemated tradeoffs took place in the matter of arrests, counterarrests, and releases of political and occupation-duty figures. The climax of this phase of the conflict probably arrived on September 9 with the explosive violence of the crowds and troops in Platz der Republik at Brandenburg Gate.

[2] Davison gives a full account of the struggle.

The fourth period of the Berlin crisis was brought to life at the middle of November by the municipal elections scheduled for December 5, 1948. The anticipated defeat of a majority of the Soviet-backed candidates for the City Assembly was deflected, before the election took place, by the establishment of an East Berlin apparatus of city administration. The tug of war between Soviet-appointed Magistrat officials and the incumbents who stood on the side of the West Berliners soon gave way to conflict by duplication. The physical possession of the east sector of Berlin by the Soviet authority was decisive and the split of Berlin into two opposing municipalities became unavoidable save through a direct contest for territorial possession of the access streets and the city buildings and offices located in the east sector.

The following period from mid-December 1948 to May 1949 was relatively uneventful in terms of physical acts in the four arenas of the crisis. The airlift fought and won its battles with winter weather, the economic pressure on the East's economy was increased, and, despite some passages of renewed strife, the consolidation of the East and West Berlin administration continued. The Berlin crisis was beginning to age perceptibly and the absence of new and highly upsetting events may have made easier the long "quiet negotiations" of the Jessup-Malik diplomacy during the period.

The last phase of the Berlin blockade crisis opened on May 10 on the footing of a new status quo which was built on high-level agreements to end the blockade and the counterblockade and to lift the restrictions imposed earlier by the crisis. Psychologically, the crisis was over; in fact, a strange "post settlement" series of conflicts arose. Almost at once, the Soviet authority began harassments of land and water routes between Berlin and the West, almost identical with those of the initial period of the crisis. Over an ensuing period of months, these interferences lapsed back to a threshold level but, at first, they were serious and provocative. Secondly, a revival of the campaign of "threats by action" to the safety of the air corridors took place. Thirdly, an extremely dangerous and important altercation between East and West occurred over the question of which authority was going to control the railway system in and out of Berlin.

The episode took the form of a strike by the union of railway workers of the West sectors against the Soviet-controlled railway authorities. Among the complications were the involvements, very directly, of the military commandants and of the civil governments of the city in this strike. Thus, the struggle for the control of the city was revived and was merged with the vital question of free access from the West by rail. Two old arenas merged into one. While the crisis was "over," violence reached a higher level than it had achieved in months. The Soviet and American military commandants were finally able to arrange the basis for the settlement of the strike but the problem persisted stubbornly for many weeks after the official ending of the strike.

It is difficult to establish a terminal date for the Berlin crisis because of the late repetitions of series of events of the intensity and type characteristic of the crisis, itself. Thus, the end of the airlift on October 1, 1949 is probably the best closing date.

If not a word had been spoken, written or printed during the Berlin blockade crisis—if it had taken place in a silent world—what might onlookers have understood about it ? The main tacit communication of the Berlin crisis was carried in the series of interactions at three points in time. The first was the Soviet response of the land and water blockade to the "first move" of the West's currency reform in June. The response to the blockade was the airlift with its rich accompanying connotations of American technological strength and political determination. And, the Soviet response to the airlift was largely to let it alone, despite three short series of opposing actions which threatened interference. The second source of tacit communication was the chain of events in the fall and winter of 1948 at Berlin which led to the final rupture of four-power administration and the splitting of the city into an East Berlin and a West Berlin. The manufacture of political symbols, some of great and lasting importance, was notable in this second series of intense interactions. The third major sequence was the official demobilization of the crisis in May 1949 which was followed, however, by a repudiation-in-actions by the Soviets of the psychological contract to call off the crisis.

Tentative Conclusions

The "structures" of two acute international crises have now been traced and described, in part. A number of additional analyses would have to be added to identify the full configurations of sequential behavior in the two crises. The point was made previously that we have been dealing here with a fraction of an analysis and not the whole. One comparative statement will be made, however, because it stands forth with exceptional clarity.

The problems which created the Quemoy and Berlin situations were not solved during the demobilization of the crises. They were shunted aside. In both instances, there was a demobilization process which signalled the passing of the acute crisis. In the comparison of these closing processes, it is the contrast that is most striking. At Quemoy, the demobilization was carried out in the field by a technique that we should not hesitate to call tacit bargaining. At Berlin, the demobilization of the crisis took place by means of explicit, verbal negotiations and discussions at New York and Paris while, in the field, conditions were so far from meeting the terms of demobilization that the conflict flared again, and seriously, on the very heels of the events that signified that the crisis was over. These appear to be modes of action at the polar extremes.

Increasingly speculative remarks might be set forth with respect to the caution exhibited on all sides against increasing the levels of violence toward the break-over to full war. The differences in the location and population of Quemoy and Berlin must account for much of the differences in the complexity of the two crises. What is needed clearly, before other conclusions are drawn, is an improvement in the techniques of handling interaction sequences of international relations. If it is claimed that the approach we have used is better than impressionistic reconstructions, then it would be hoped that improved methods of handling problems of "organized complexity" will be brought to bear on the range of subjects treated above.

References

Ashby, W. Ross. *An Introduction to Cybernetics.* New York: Wiley, 1957.

Davison, W. Phillips. *The Berlin Blockade. A Study in Cold War Politics.* Princeton: Princeton Univ. Press, 1958.

Deutsch, Karl W. "Shifts in the Balance of Communication Flows: A Problem of Measurements in International Relations," *Public Opinion Quarterly,* XX (Spring 1956), 152–55.

———. "Toward an Inventory of Basic Trends and Patterns in Comparative and International Politics, *American Political Science Review,* LIV (March 1960), 34–57.

Linebarger, Paul M. A. "Taipei and Peking: The Confronting Republics," *Journal of International Affairs,* XI (1957), 135–42.

Richardson, L. F. *Arms and Security.* London: Stevens, 1960.

Schelling, Thomas C. *The Strategy of Conflict.* Cambridge: Harvard Univ. Press, 1960.

C. The Use of Anthropological Methods

43. Interaction and Negotiation in a Committee of the United Nations General Assembly*

Chadwick F. Alger is Professor of Political Science at Northwestern University. A leading student of international organization, he has taken advantage of the proximity of the United Nations to undertake on-the-spot investigations of his subject. The ensuing selection is one of a number of unique articles that Professor Alger has written on the basis of this first-hand observation. While he has quantified his observations in order to discern recurrent patterns, the reader will recognize that what follows amounts to a form of anthropological research. The setting is a modern one, but the participant-observer technique of anthropology is nevertheless unmistakably present. However the reader may evaluate the results, he will surely want to ponder whether there are other opportunities for research of this type in the international field. [*Reprinted from the* Papers *of the Peace Research Society* (*International*), *V* (*1966*), *pp. 141–59, by permission of the author and the publisher.*]

Introduction

The careful observer of main committees of the General Assembly, and other public United Nations bodies as well, soon becomes aware that two kinds of activity are taking place simultaneously before

* Data for this paper were collected while the author was Visiting Professor of United Nations Affairs at New York University with generous research support provided by the Rockefeller Foundation. Through a grant to the International Relations Program at Northwestern University, the Carnegie Corporation provided assistance for data analysis. Professor Robert Weiner, Northeastern University, collected the interaction data and Mr. Manus Midlarsky, Northwestern University, assisted with data processing. Professors Harold Guetzkow and Raymond Tanter of Northwestern University provided valuable criticism of an earlier draft. Mrs. Lucille Mayer assisted in all stages of the paper, particularly in the presentation of data in tables and figures.

his eyes. There is a continuous flow of *public* debate heard by all in the room, and there are frequent *private* conversations between two or more delegates that are heard only by those involved. Delegates are seated at two long horseshoe desks, one placed inside the other. Conversations may be carried on by delegates seated next to each other. They also move around the chamber, sometimes sitting down behind another delegate to talk and at other times standing and talking with others who also are circulating. An observer in the press gallery, after he learns to recognize the participants, can make a record of who talks to whom, who initiates the interaction, and how long they talk. Such a record was kept during eighteen of the twenty-two meetings of the Fifth Committee (Administrative and Budgetary Committee) during the Fourth Special Session of the General Assembly in May and June 1963. This paper will be devoted primarily to an analysis of the 1,752 interactions observed during the eighteen meetings.

Like all of the main committees of the General Assembly, the Fifth Committee is a committee of the whole, with all nations in the United Nations as members (111 in 1963). National delegations in the committee range from one to five in size, with most nations having one person in attendance and others rarely having more than two present. During the session analyzed here, the observer was able to identify 130 delegates, eighty-eight by name, and forty-two by designations invented by the observer.

Analysis of 3,475 interactions observed in an earlier session of the same committee has been reported already (Alger, 1967). Systematic observation data have been collected and analyzed as one part of an effort to study the effect of political and social processes in intergovernmental organizations on intergovernmental conflict and consensus development.[1] Field work at the United Nations over a period of seven years has revealed that the voluminous and, to the scholar, highly valuable documentary records of UN proceedings provide only a partial view of the legislative process. The political scientist often finds it necessary to supplement analysis of documentary records with interviews and informal discussion with diplomats. Exploration in the collection and analysis of observation data has been undertaken because of a hunch that such data can offer information complementary to the already mentioned data collecting techniques. In addition, observation data may offer valuable short cuts to the scholar who finds it necessary to interview in the study of legislative processes, as an aid in identifying key participants and in generating hypotheses.

The Seventeenth Regular Session

The earlier analysis of Fifth Committee interactions is based on data collected during fifty-two meetings from October to December 1962 (the Seventeenth Regular Session of the General Assembly). The analysis supported Garland Routt's assertion in 1938, based on observation of interaction in the Illinois Senate, that high interactors play important

[1] See Alger (1961, 1963, and 1965) for studies based on interviews, informal discussions with diplomats, and less systematic observation.

legislative roles (Routt, 1938). High interactors tended to be the ones the observer knew to be most active in drafting resolutions and in obtaining support for them. This conclusion was based on information obtained in contact with committee members outside the committee chamber. Variation in the interaction rate as the committee debated different issues also pointed to a relationship between interaction and the legislative process.

The analysis indicated that observation of legislative bodies may be a source of information about the legislative process that is complementary to records of public debate. Delegates of certain nations known to play key roles in the legislative process ranked much higher in number of interactions than they did in rankings based on the quantity of contribution to public debate. The number of interactions by a nation's delegates was found to be related more to a number of other measures of United Nations participation than was public speaking. Measures of UN participation used were: number in UN permanent mission, number in General Assembly delegation, and financial contributions to the UN. Quantity of a nation's interactions also was related more to GNP and GNP/population than was public speaking, but public speaking was found to be related more to population.

The Fourth Special Session

The analysis of data for another session of the same 111 nation committee offers an opportunity to see if conclusions of the earlier study apply to more than one session. Data for the more recent session also permit a more probing analysis of the relationship between observed interactions in the committee chamber and those aspects of the legislative process that take place elsewhere. This is possible because in the Fourth Special Session the General Assembly had only one agenda item, the financing of peace-keeping operations, instead of the normal load of approximately one hundred items. Therefore, only the Fifth Committee was in session, instead of all seven main committees. Thus, it was possible for the observer to follow in greater depth the less public aspects of the legislative process through conversations with committee members, because their attention was focused primarily on one issue for a longer period of time. In addition, the observer was able to get more information on negotiations outside the chamber in the Special Session, because he had developed more contact with delegates.

The Fourth Special Session of the General Assembly was called by the Seventeenth Regular Session in December 1962 to handle UN financial problems caused by unwillingness of certain members to pay assessments for the United Nations Emergency Force in Suez (UNEF) and the UN Force in the Congo (ONUC). Although it was not expected that the Special Session would solve outstanding financial problems, some hoped that it would be possible to devise a special scale of assessment of peace-keeping operations. Some members believed that a Special Session devoted exclusively to financial problems would highlight the organization's financial difficulties, educate more diplomats in UN financial issues, and, in particular, get heads of missions and their deputies more interested in and more involved in financial problems. The Special Session ran from May 14 to June 27, 1963, and produced seven resolutions which all received between seventy-nine and ninety-five affirmative votes out of a possible 111. The resolutions provided general principles for sharing of peace-keeping costs, authorized expenditures for UNEF and ONUC, appealed to members to pay their arrears, extended the period during which UN bonds (to support peace-keeping activity) could be sold, and established procedures for continuing the effort to find more long-range solutions to problems of peace-keeping finance.[2]

In debate and negotiation in the Special Session the committee tended to divide into three groups. France, the Soviet Union and its Warsaw Pact allies, and a few other nations claimed that the peace-keeping operations violated the UN Charter. They were unwilling to enter into negotiations on how to finance them. Therefore, the legislative struggle was waged between two other groups, referred to by the committee as the developed countries (DC) and the less developed countries (LDC). The major issue was how expenses for past and future peace-keeping operations should be apportioned among the members, with the LDC desiring a scale of assessment with a lesser burden on them than is required by the regular scale of assessment. Lengthy negotiations of the two groups were carried on outside the committee chamber and eventually produced resolutions supported by most members of both groups.

Overall Comparisons of Interaction in the Two Sessions

In the Special Session 1,752 interactions were observed in eighteen meetings, an average of ninety-seven interactions per meeting—length of meetings varied from thirty minutes to three and one-half hours. This is almost one-third more than the rate of sixty-seven in the Seventeenth Session where 3,475 interactions were observed during fifty-two meetings. As was the case in the Seventeenth Session, only eleven nations contributed over one-half of the interactions. Table 1 shows that the number of interactions per nation for the two sessions produce distributions that are quite similar. If the table were more detailed on the lower end, it would reveal that forty-one nations participated in a total of less than three per cent of the interactions in the Seventeenth Session and seventy nations participated in less than three per cent in the Special Session.

Table 2 shows the number and percentage of interactions that were between seatmates for both sessions. With thirty-six per cent seatmate interactions in one session and thirty-two per cent in the other, the percentage is quite constant. With one observer recording interactions for 111 nations it is possible that some seatmate interactions of very short duration were missed. Because delegations shifted five places to the right every week, thus varying the ability of the observer to see them, the bias introduced by missing seatmate interactions is not likely to be great. It is believed that few nonseatmate interactions were missed, because delegates can be observed quite easily as they move from one spot to another.

Deciding whether or not to include seatmate interactions in analyses of interactions is difficult. It is likely that a higher percentage of the nonseatmate interactions are of direct consequence to the legislative process. This conclusion rests on the assumption that a delegate who leaves his seat to talk to another person more often has a legislative goal in

[2] For further details see United Nations, General Assembly, Fourth Special Session, Fifth Committee and Plenary, *Official Records*, 1963. Also see Singer (1961, pp. 96–121) for fuller information on the role of the Fifth Committee in the U.N. General Assembly.

TABLE 1

Total Interactions by Nation for Both Sessions

No. of Interactions Special Session			No. of Interactions 17th Session
300–350	(Canada)	(US)	600–700
250–300			500–600
200–250		(Netherlands, Ireland)	400–500
150–200	(US, Brazil, India)	(Canada, UK, Israel)	300–400
100–150	(Netherlands, UK, Bulgaria, Ireland, New Zealand, Pak., Norway)	(New Zealand, [Secretariat], Iraq)	200–300
50–100	(Nigeria, [Secretariat],[a] Arg., Israel, Australia, Italy, USSR, Yugo.)	(USSR, Australia, Brazil, Norway, Yugoslavia, Czech., Poland, Arg.)	100–200
0–50	93 nations	94 nations	0–100

Number of Nations: 100 90 80 70 60 50 40 30 20 10 0 10 20 30 40 50 60 70 80 90 100

[a] Although Secretariat activity is included in tables, it will not be discussed in this paper.

mind than a delegate who makes a comment to his seatmate. On the other hand, seatmates, such as the United States and the United Kingdom, certainly talk a lot about matters they would discuss even if they were not seatmates. Partially because nonseatmate interaction counts are deemed to be more reliable and because they include a higher percentage of purposeful legislative activity, they alone will be used in the analysis that follows (except where noted otherwise).

TABLE 2

Number of Seatmate Interactions for the Two Sessions

	17th session Interactions		Special session Interactions	
Seatmate	1243	(36%)	560	(32%)
Nonseatmate	2232	(64%)	1192	(68%)
Total	3475	(100%)	1752	(100%)

Analysis of the Seventeenth Session revealed that nation ranks in number of interactions were correlated more closely with seven other measures of UN participation than was nation rank based on number of public speeches. Other measures of UN participation used were: number of resolutions and amendments sponsored, number in General Assembly delegation, number in UN permanent mission, voluntary financial contributions to the UN, regular budget contributions, total UN contributions, and UN contributions as a percentage of gross national product.[3] Table 3 reveals that there is also a closer rank correlation in the Special Session between these measures of nation participation in the UN and number of interactions than is the case with number of speeches. Interaction also was correlated more closely in the Seventeenth Session

[3] All correlations in this paper are Spearman rank correlations.

TABLE 3

Spearman Rank Correlations for Speaking,
Interaction, Nation Investment of Men and
Money in the UN and Nation Characteristics

Variable		NO. OF INTERACTIONS NONSEATMATE $N = 97$		TOTAL LENGTH OF SPEECHES IN MINUTES $N = III$	
		17th	*Special*	*17th*	*Special*
No. in Permanent Mission	$(N = 96)$	.42	.36	.30	.14
No. in General Assembly	$(N = 96)$	.48	.53	.43	.22
Voluntary Contributions	$(N = 96)$	.52	.56	.39	.18
Regular Budget	$(N = 96)$	.59	.59	.45	.28
Total UN Contributions	$(N = 93)$	.59	.60	.46	.25
UN Payments/GNP	$(N = 93)$	.18	.18	.07	−.08
Diplomats Abroad[a]	$(N = 108)$	n.a.	.55	n.a.	.18
Exports	$(N = 106)$	n.a.	.60	n.a.	.20
GNP	$(N = 90)$	.52	.56	.42	.22
GNP/Population	$(N = 90)$	53	.45	.23	.04
Population	$(N = 90)$	.29	.35	.35	.36
Resolutions and Amendments Sponsored	$(N = III)$	.38	.28	.32	.17

[a] Number of diplomats abroad taken from Alger and Brams, "Patterns of Representation in National Capitals and Intergovernmental Organizations" (1967).

with gross national product and GNP/population than was public speaking. This is the case in the Special Session as well. Two variables appear in Table 3 that were not used in the Seventeenth Session analysis: number of diplomats abroad and exports. These also correlate much more closely with interaction than with speaking. Of all the nation measures chosen in the Seventeenth Session, only population related more closely with public speaking than interaction. This is the case in the Special Session as well, although the difference between population correlation with public speaking and interaction is very slight (.36 and .35). Thus, over two sessions there is considerable stability in the comparative relationship of interaction and public speaking to the ten variables. The correlations involving interactions are much more stable than those involving speeches. The average change in interaction correlations is 4.3, whereas the average change in speaking correlations is 16.5, with changes in public speaking correlations almost all downward. There is no obvious hypothesis for this consistent downward pattern. Particularly striking is the high and stable correlation (59) between interaction and regular budget contributions across the two sessions.

Negotiation and Interaction

Differences between the Seventeenth and the Special Session are crucial to analysis of the relationship between interaction in the Fifth Committee and negotiation outside the chamber. During the Seventeenth Session, the Fifth Committee handled a number of administrative and budgetary questions. These included annual problems, such as budget estimates, the scale for assessing members, geographic distribution of Secretariat posts, and also less recurrent items, such as financing of the Congo and Middle East operations and the advisory opinion of the International Court of Justice on financing of these operations. During the Special Session, on the other hand, the Fifth Committee devoted itself completely to the financing of peace-keeping operations.

As a committee with a number of items on its agenda moves from one item to another, there is some change in the list of nations most involved in debate and legislative activity outside the chamber. While public debate proceeds on one item, interaction in the chamber and activity outside may be devoted to others soon to be debated. Thus, normally it is not possible to assume that interaction in committee meetings is concerned with the same item as is legislative activity outside the chamber or public debate. The Special Session provides an unusual opportunity for assessing the relationship between nation participation in public debate, interaction, and negotiation outside the chamber, because the committee is concerned with only one item. Because interaction and public debate data are available on the earlier Seventeenth Session, performance on the Special Session issue can be contrasted with data summarizing Fifth Committee performance across most kinds of issues handled by the committee.

While a one item committee session provides the researcher with a remarkable opportunity for a field experiment, there could be concern that a Special Session could cause crucial variation other than limitation of the agenda. For example, in the Special Session some ambassadors had more opportunity to give personal attention to Fifth Committee activity than is normally the case. While there is no conclusive evidence against that kind of variation, the stability of some dimensions of interaction across the two sessions provide evidence that the Special Session did not vary in basic parameters crucial to the analysis. It has been reported already that frequency curves for interactions per nation are rather similar across the two sessions (Table 1). Number of seatmate interactions is rather constant (Table 2). Correlations between nation interaction and nation contribution to the UN are almost identical across the two sessions (Table 3). There is also a .90 rank correlation between the ranks of eight regional groups in per cent of intragroup interaction across the two sessions.[4]

An important part of the political process in the General Assembly is discussion and negotiation outside the chamber as delegates exchange ideas on issues and pass around, amend, and negotiate the wording of resolutions. The discussions often are quite impromptu, in corridor, lounge and dining room. Sometimes they are a result of a planned strategy. Occasionally they develop into rather informal meetings in small committee rooms at United Nations headquarters and in national missions

[4] In Special Session rank order the groups are: Soviet (2), NATO (3), Latin America (1), Commonwealth (5), Western Europe (4), Asia (6), Sub-Sahara Africa (7), and Arab (8). (Seventeenth Session ranks are in parentheses.)

TABLE 4
Number of Meetings of Negotiators and Regional Groups in Special Session

Negotiators	
Developed Countries	12
Lesser Developed Countries	6
Developed and Lesser Developed Countries	18
Total	36
Regional Groups	
Developed (W. Europe, U.S., Canada, Japan)	7
Latin America	5
Afro-Asia	12
Afro-Asia subgroup (Lesser Developed Countries + Cameroon, Japan, U.A.R.)	3
Commonwealth	2
Arab	4
Total	33
Entire Fifth Committee	
Public Meetings of Fifth Committee	22

scattered around the East Side of New York.[5] During the Special Session, the Fifth Committee utilized highly structured negotiating procedures through which five developed nations and five less developed nations negotiated outstanding issues. The five developed nations were Canada, Netherlands, Sweden, United Kingdom, and United States. The five less developed nations were Argentina, Brazil, India, Nigeria, and Pakistan. The observer collected information in discussions with delegates as negotiations progressed revealing that the negotiators held a total of thirty-six meetings (twelve for the developed nation representatives alone, six for the developing nations alone, and eighteen negotiating sessions attended by both groups). In addition, Table 4 shows that the various regional groups who provided guidelines to their representatives on the negotiating teams held thirty-three meetings. In meetings between the two negotiating teams, the Canadian representative served as the chairman. He is given much credit by both LDC and DC negotiators for what was achieved in the negotiations.

Examination of nonseatmate interaction in the Seventeenth Session (Table 5) reveals that nations chosen as negotiators for the Special Session rank high as interactors in the Seventeenth Session. Seven of the ten rank among the first twenty interactors

[5] See Hadwen and Kaufmann (1962), Chaps. 2 and 3, for informative description of the UN political process.

TABLE 5
*Highest Ranked Nations in Interaction
and Public Speaking for Both Sessions[a]*

NONSEATMATE INTERACTIONS				TOTAL LENGTH OF SPEECHES (IN MINUTES)			
17th		*Special*		*17th*		*Special*	
*U.S.	436	*Canada	315	(Secretariat)	1259	(Secretariat)	160
*Canada	317	*U.S.	149	*U.K.	323	U.S.S.R.	126
*Netherlands	252	*India	140	U.S.S.R.	294	Ukraine	71
(Secretariat)	215	*Brazil	120	*U.S.	287	*Pakistan	61
Ireland	173	*Netherlands	96	Iraq	248	Bulgaria	56
*U.K.	157	*U.K.	93	Australia	209	Indonesia	47
Norway	145	*Pakistan	91	Czech.	167	Hungary	45
*Brazil	137	(Secretariat)	86	Colombia	156	Cameroon	43
Australia	123	New Zealand	86	*Argentina	150	Fed. of Malaya	43
U.S.S.R.	117	Ireland	75	Israel	147	*Nigeria	43
Israel	116	*Nigeria	70	Nepal	122	Poland	43
Czech.	116	Bulgaria	69	*Canada	107	Cyprus	41
Iraq	115	*Argentina	68	Poland	105	Czech.	41
Yugoslavia	109	Norway	63	France	103	*Argentina	39
New Zealand	103	Australia	60	Ivory Coast	99	Ceylon	38
Poland	101	Italy	60	Sudan	98	Jamaica	36
Denmark	84	U.S.S.R.	46	*Brazil	91	Tunisia	36
*Argentina	80	Yugoslavia	39	Romania	91	Iran	35
*India	77	*Sweden	39	Ukraine	89	Ghana	34
Ceylon	75	Hungary	33	Ghana	85	Byelorussia	33
Mexico	67	Israel	30	New Zealand	81	*Canada	33
						France	33

[a] Includes first twenty nations and Secretariat.
* Special Session Negotiator.

(U.S., Canada, Netherlands, U.K., Brazil, Argentina, India) with five negotiators among the first ten ranks. Past performance in interaction was a better indicator of who would be chosen as a Special Session negotiator than public speaking, because only five negotiators are among the first twenty in time spent in public speeches. Canada, the most active in interaction during the Seventeenth Session, with the exception of the United States, chaired the negotiation sessions. (It would not be expected that diplomats from a super power would assume the role of chairman.)

Examination of interaction in the Special Sessions suggests that those who assumed negotiating roles increased their involvement in interaction. In the Special Session all ten negotiators ranked among the first twenty interactors, compared with only seven in the Seventeenth Session. Negotiators hold the first seven ranks, with three others ranked ten, twelve, and eighteen. Also notable is the fact that

Canada moved from second place to first, with double the interactions of the United States.

Table 6 compares the ranks of negotiators in the

TABLE 6
*Negotiator Change in Interaction
Rank Across Two Sessions*

Negotiator	*17th session*	*Special session*	*Change in rank[a]*
Canada	2(317)	1(315)	+1
U.S.	1(436)	2(149)	−1
India	18(77)	3(140)	+15
Brazil	7(137)	4(120)	+3
Netherlands	3(252)	5(96)	−2
U.K.	5(157)	6(93)	−1
Pakistan	26(42)	7(91)	+19
Nigeria	29(35)	10(70)	+19
Argentina	17(80)	12(68)	+5
Sweden	22(215)	18(39)	+4
Total			+62

[a] Plus sign means movement upward in rank.

TABLE 7
Negotiator Nation Nonseatmate Interactions
as Percentage of Total for Both Sessions

Nation	Per cent of total 17th Session	Per cent of total Special Session	Difference
Argentina	3.6	5.7	+2.1
Brazil	6.1	10.1	+4.0
India	3.5	11.8	+8.3
Nigeria	1.6	5.9	+4.3
Pakistan	1.9	7.6	+5.7
Canada	14.2	26.4	+12.2
Netherlands	11.3	8.1	−3.2
Sweden	2.7	3.3	+.6
U.K.	7.0	7.8	+.8
U.S.	19.5	12.5	−7.0

LDC—an average increase per nation of 4.85 per cent
DC—an average increase per nation of .68 per cent
Total—an average increase per nation of 2.78 per cent

two sessions and shows that negotiators moved up a total of sixty-two ranks in the Special Session. The table shows further the developing nations accounted for sixty-one of these, with particularly dramatic moves by India (14 ranks), Pakistan (19), and Nigeria (19). Thus, participation in the negotiation seems to

have stimulated greater involvement of Afro-Asian negotiators in interaction.

Another perspective on the relationship between negotiation outside the chamber and interactions observed in the chamber is gained from Table 7. Here each negotiating nation's interactions are computed as a percentage of total interactions in the committee. All of the Special Session negotiators but Netherlands and the United States increased their percentage of the total in the Special Session. The most dramatic increase was made by Canada, chairman of the negotiating sessions.

Still another view of the shift in negotiator participation in interaction is provided in Table 8 where it is indicated that the negotiators participated in sixty-seven per cent of the interactions in the Special Session but only in forty-seven per cent in the Seventeenth Session. Subtotals reveal that, as negotiators, the diplomats from the ten nations doubled their interaction with each other from thirteen per cent of the total interactions to twenty-six per cent. They also increased their interaction with non-negotiators from thirty-four per cent to forty-one per cent. But interaction between non-negotiators dropped from fifty-three per cent to thirty-three per cent.

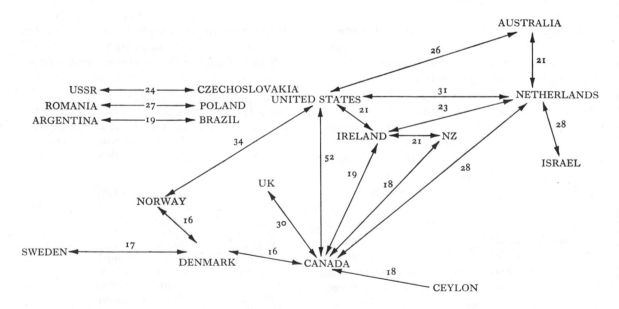

Figure 1. Diagram of interaction between first twenty ranked nonseatmate pairs, 17th Session.

TABLE 8
*Nonseatmate Interactions Between Negotiators
and Non-Negotiators for Both Sessions*

Nonseatmate interactions	17th session		Special session	
	No.	Per cent	No.	Per cent
Negotiator—Negotiator	287	(13%)	313	(26%)
Negotiator—Non-negotiator	764	(34%)	483	(41%)
Non-negotiator—Non-negotiator	1181	(53%)	396	(33%)
Total	2232	(100%)	1192	(100%)

Table 9 lists the first twenty interacting pairs, with seatmate pairs included in one set of rankings and not in the other. As might be expected, seatmate pairs rank high, taking thirteen of the first twenty ranks. It is remarkable, however, that eight of the seatmate pairs include at least one negotiator. Thus, negotiators are involved in all but five of the first twenty pairs. When the pairs from which seatmates have been excluded are examined, the dominance of the negotiators in interaction stands out even more boldly. Negotiator pairs are in the first five ranks with Canada involved in all five. Indeed, Canada is involved in the first ten highest interacting pairs, the second five involving Canada and a non-negotiator. Only four of the twenty pairs do not involve negotiators.

TABLE 9
Highest Interacting Nation Pairs Special Session[a]

Seatmates and nonseatmates			Nonseatmates	
Canada/U.S.		48	Canada/U.S.	48
U.S./U.K.	(SM)[b]	46	Canada/Neth.	31
Ireland/Israel	(SM)	40	Canada/India	27
Brazil/Bulgaria	(SM)	35 ⎫	Canada/U.K.	24
Neth./N.Z.	(SM)	35 ⎭	Canada/Brazil	21
Bulgaria/Burma	(SM)	31 ⎫	Canada/Ireland	19 ⎫
Canad/Neth.		31 ⎭	Canada/New Zealand	19 ⎭
India/Indonesia	(SM)	29	Canada/Pakistan	17
Canada/India		27	Canada/Australia	14 ⎫
Austria/Belgium	(SM)	25	Canada/Italy	14 ⎪
Canada/U.K.		24	India/New Zealand	14 ⎬
Canada/Brazil		21 ⎫	Ireland/New Zealand	14 ⎭
Norway/Nigeria	(SM)	21 ⎭	Argentina/Brazil	13 ⎫
Bolivia/Brazil	(SM)	20	Bulgaria/Byelorussia	13 ⎬
Canada/Ireland		19 ⎫	India/U.S.	13 ⎭
Canada/New Zealand		19 ⎬	Brazil/India	12 ⎫
Norway/Pakistan	(SM)	19 ⎭	Bulgaria/U.S.S.R.	12 ⎬
Canada/Pakistan		17	Nigeria/Pakistan	12 ⎭
Ukraine/U.S.S.R.	(SM)	16	Bulgaria/Hungary	11 ⎫
Iraq/Ireland	(SM)	15 ⎫	Canada/Sweden	11 ⎭
Nepal/Netherlands	(SM)	15 ⎭		

[a] Total interactions for all interacting pairs of nations were compiled by using NUCROS, a general cross-classification program. Janda (1965), Chapter 6, describes this program. On pp. 40–42 he describes how it was used for this study.
[b] (SM)-Designates pairs that are seatmates. Underlining indicates negotiator.

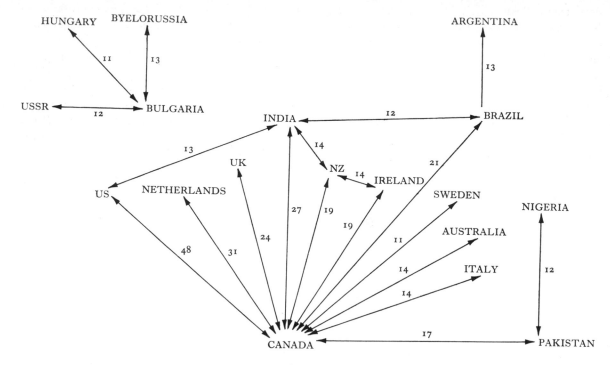

Figure 2. Diagram of interaction between first twenty ranked nonseatmate pairs, Special Session.

If the first twenty interacting pairs are diagrammed, the position of Canada in the interaction system can be seen more clearly. Figure 1 is a diagram of the first twenty pairs in the Seventeenth Session, which includes all pairs with sixteen or more interactions. If the number of links to each nation is counted and all with over two links recorded, the following is obtained:

Canada	7
United States	5
Netherlands	5
Ireland	4
Denmark	3

Thus, Canada, whose delegation was to become the key figure in the Special Session negotiations, was at the hub of the communication wheel that had the most spokes.

Figure 2 diagrams the first twenty pairs in the Special Session, including all pairs with eleven or more interactions. Here Canada's role as chairman of the negotiating sessions seems to have a profound effect, since the number of spokes to each nation having more than two is as follows:

Canada	12
India	4
Brazil	3
Bulgaria	3
New Zealand	3
United States	3

An examination of the nations with which Canada interacted the most in both sessions also suggests a relationship between the negotiation organization and committee interaction. In the Seventeenth Session the only nations that were to be negotiators in the Special Session to whom Canada is linked are Netherlands, U.K., and U.S. But in the Special Session, Canada is linked to seven negotiating nations: Brazil, India, Netherlands, Pakistan, Sweden, U.K., and U.S.

Comparison of the two diagrams also suggests that the negotiating organization tied representatives of the Afro-Asian nations more directly into the main committee interaction system. During the

Seventeenth Session only Western European and North American nations had three or more links, but in the Special Session Brazil and India are added. In addition, the diagrams show that the negotiators, Brazil and Argentina, not attached to the main interaction system in the Seventeenth Session, are connected through a Canada-Brazil link in the Special Session. In contrast, the nations from the Soviet group that appear on the diagram remain outside the main interaction system in the Special Session, as they had in the Seventeenth Session. This is consistent with their refusal to participate in the negotiations. Therefore, the diagrams give rather convincing evidence of the value of interaction observation as a partial reflection of the political process that takes place outside the chamber.

Differences Between Negotiator and Dissenter Interaction and Public Speaking

It has been demonstrated already, in the sessions under analysis that high participation in interaction is a more reliable indicator of nation participation in negotiation outside the chamber than length of public speeches. The relationship between public debate and interaction merits further scrutiny. Table 10 shows correlation between nation rank in number of interactions and nation rank in length of public speeches. In the Seventeenth Session, as contrasted with the Special Session, correlation between nonseatmate interaction and length of public speaking is seventy-two, but in the Special Session it drops to forty-four. How might this change be explained?

Table 5 throws some light on the question. Although all ten negotiators in the Special Session are in the first twenty ranks in interaction, only four are listed in the first twenty ranks for public speaking. On the other hand, a reverse pattern is seen for those nations who refused to participate in the negotiations and who voted against the resolutions. Twelve nations, the Soviet group and France, cast all of the "no" votes against the seven resolutions passed by the committee, with the eleven members of the Soviet group voting against all seven and the French voting against five. Table 5 reveals that eight from this group of nations are in the first twenty ranks for

speaking (five among the first ten), but only three are listed among the first twenty interactors (none among the first ten).

Plotting of interaction against length of public speeches provides a very helpful view of the shifting performance of the negotiators and dissenters across the two sessions. Figure 3 is a plot for the Seventeenth Session and Figure 4 for the Special Session. If the plots are split into three sectors, nations are divided into three groups in terms of the relationship between their public speaking and their interaction:

   A. Nations who speak a lot and interact relatively little.
   B. Nations whose speaking and interaction are relatively equal.
   C. Nations who interact a lot and speak relatively little.

Turning first to the Special Session negotiators, they are found to be almost equally distributed across the three sectors in the Seventeenth Session (four in A, three in B, and three in C), but as negotiators in the Special Session, they have shifted to sectors B and C (five in B and five in C). The dissenters who were active enough to be designated on the plots, those above the tenth percentile on either variable, are clustered primarily in sector A in the Seventeenth Session (six in B and two in A). In the Special Session the dissenters are clustered even more in sector A (eleven in A and one in B). Table 11 recapitulates this data.

Analysis of nation change in position on the plots across two sessions shows that two dissenter nations shifted from Sector B to sector A and one in the reverse direction. The more pronounced clustering of dissenters in sector A is accounted for largely by the addition of four nations to the plot. This means that dissenters spoke relatively more in the Special Session, with all twelve above the tenth

TABLE 10
Spearman Rank Correlation Between Nation Ranks in Public Speaking and Interaction in Both Sessions

	TOTAL LENGTH OF SPEECHES	
No. of interactions	*17th Session* (N = 97)	*Special Session* (N = 111)
Total interactions	.70	.38
Nonseatmate interactions	.72	.44

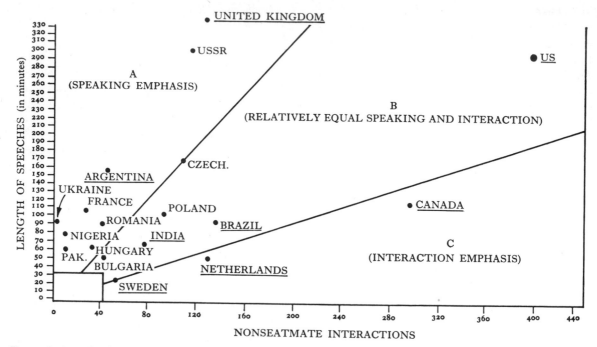

Figure 3. Length of speeches and nonseatmate interaction, seventeenth session. (Negotiators are underlined and all negotiators and dissenters above tenth percentile are identified by name.)

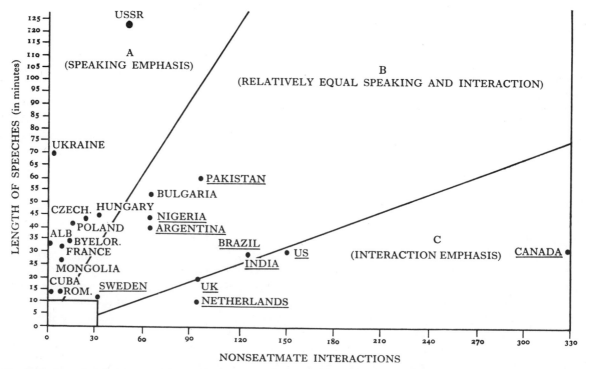

Figure 4. Length of speeches and nonseatmate interaction, special session. (Negotiators are underlined and all negotiators and dissenters above tenth percentile are identified by name.)

TABLE 11
*Recapitulation of Sector Location in Plots of
Negotiators and Dissenters for Both Sessions*

A. Numerical Recapitulation

Sector	NEGOTIATORS		DISSENTERS	
	17th	*Special*	*17th*	*Special*
A (Speaking Emphasis)	4	0	6	11
B (Relatively Equal Speaking and Interaction)	3	5	2	1
C (Interaction Emphasis)	3	5	0	0

B. Nation Recapitulation

Sector	NEGOTIATORS		DISSENTERS	
	17th	*Special*	*17th*	*Special*
A (Speaking Emphasis)	Argentina Nigeria Pakistan U.K.		Bulgaria France Hungary Romania Ukraine U.S.S.R.	Albania Byelorussia Cuba Czechoslovakia France Hungary Mongolia Poland Romania Ukraine U.S.S.R.
B (Relatively Equal Speaking and Interaction)	Brazil India U.S.	Argentina Brazil Nigeria Pakistan Sweden	Czechoslovakia Poland	Bulgaria
C (Interaction Emphasis)	Canada Netherlands Sweden	Canada India Netherlands U.K. U.S.		

percentile in speaking (in contrast to eight in the earlier session). On the other hand, although four of these twelve nations were above the tenth percentile in interaction during the Seventeenth Session, only one ranked above this point in the Special Session. Shifts in negotiator nations from one sector to another were in the direction of greater interaction relative to speaking (i.e., in the A to C direction) with one exception. Sweden's slight shift moved it from C to B.

Thus, it can be seen that dissenters tend to emphasize public speaking and negotiators tend to emphasize interaction. This is found both when examining separate lists of highest interactors and speakers and when analyzing plots that reveal relative participation in both kinds of activity. In interpreting the plots it is important to recognize that the A sector of Figure 4 does not include only dissenters. There are other nations in this sector who go along with the general will of the committee and tend to participate little in the legislative process except for public statements of their nation's views. On the other hand, sector C is inhabited almost completely by negotiators. Thus, sector C would provide the observer who knew nothing about the legislative process outside the chamber with a quite reliable list of important participants in this process.

Summary and Conclusion

Comparison of interaction in two sessions of the Fifth Committee has revealed continuity in the number of nations highly active in interaction. In both sessions the number of interactions by specific nations is correlated more highly with a number of other measures of UN participation than is total length of public speeches. The same is true for a number of other nation characteristics except for population which tends to be correlated more with public speaking in both sessions. Across the two sessions there is less variation in interaction correlations with other measures of UN participation and nation characteristics than there is variation in public speaking correlations with these variables.

In the session where much is known about negotiations outside the chamber, all ten negotiators rank high in interaction and not as high in public speaking. Nations who were relatively high in interaction in one session become negotiators in the next session. After becoming negotiators, these nations ranked even higher in interaction. The chairman of negotiations in the Special Session was chosen from the nation with the most lines of communication to other nations in the earlier Seventeenth Session. In the Special Session the number of lines of communication to this nation greatly increased.

When interaction of individual nations is plotted against public speaking for both sessions, negotiators and dissenting nations (those refusing to participate in negotiations and voting against negotiated resolutions) reveal distinctly different patterns of behavior. In the second session negotiators interact more in relation to their amount of public speaking than they did in the first session. In the second session dissenters move in the opposite direction.

In an earlier analysis of interaction data for the Seventeenth Session, it was concluded that committee interaction provides the observer with important information about the legislative process outside the chamber. Analysis of data for the later Special Session of the same committee gives added support for this conclusion. The information can be useful in helping the researcher to identify important actors in the legislative process that might not be identified through the public debate. Such information can be applied in the use of other field techniques, such as interviewing. In addition, it may offer insights that permit more judicious use of records of public debate. For example, analysis in this paper suggests that records of public debate may be more useful for understanding the public statements of dissenters than for probing the processes of consensus development.

Aspects of continuity in interaction behavior, across sessions and in the relationship between past interaction behavior and the selection of negotiators, offer new insights on the contributions of permanent international organizations to the negotiation of international problems. The permanent organization provides already established communication systems that sometimes can be transformed into negotiation when problems arise. On the other hand, more *ad hoc* conference procedures, for the most part, would have to start building a private conversation system from scratch. It is reasonable to predict that use of *ad hoc* procedures would require longer to achieve a given level of consensus. Furthermore, it would seem appropriate to hypothesize that a permanent organization can achieve a higher degree of consensus than *ad hoc* procedures. This would follow partially from the assumption that lack of established patterns of private conversation would require greater utilization of public debate. Particularly in large bodies, this would bring increased frustration and acrimony because problems would be dumped into the public forum that could be handled more easily in private conversation.

With the exception of the previously cited brief observations by Routt in the Illinois legislature and occasional brief descriptive comments or anecdotes, such as those of Hadwen and Kaufmann (1962, p. 50), there is an intriguing neglect of the fact that conferences and legislative bodies have a simultaneous two-level dialogue.[6] For example, a UNESCO study of *The Technique of International Conferences* (1951) contains a lengthy check list of potential

[6] The work of Wayne Francis is closely related, however. Through interviews with U.S. state legislators, he has obtained information on their interaction with each other outside the legislative chamber.

subjects for systematic study of international conferences that even extends to nonverbal communication, but there is no mention of private conversation in public meetings. A search of the conference literature in other areas of social behavior, including the experimental literature, also reveals no recognition of the simultaneous two-level phenomenon. Therefore, the data reported in this paper are believed to be a contribution to the general field of conference (and legislative) behavior.

References

Alger, Chadwick F. "Interaction in a Committee of the United Nations General Assembly," in Singer, J. D. (ed.) *Quantitative International Politics: Insights and Evidence*. New York: Free Press, 1968.

————. "Personal Contact in International Organizations," in Kelman, Herbert (ed.) *International Behavior*. New York: Holt, 1965, pp. 523–47.

————. "United Nations Participation as a Learning Experience," *Public Opinion Quarterly*, XXVII, 3 (Fall 1963), 411–26.

————. "Non-Resolution Consequences of the United Nations and Their Effect on International Conflict," *Journal of Conflict Resolution*, V, 2 (June 1961), 128–45.

————, and Brams, Steven J. "Patterns of Representation in National Capitals and Intergovernmental Organizations," *World Politics*, XLV (July 1967), 646–63.

Francis, Wayne L. "Influence and Interaction in a State Legislative Body," *American Political Science Review*, LVI, 4 (December 1962), pp. 953–60.

Hadwen, John and Kaufmann, Johan. *How United Nations Decisions are Made*. (2nd rev. ed.) New York: Oceana; Leyden: A. W. Sythoff, 1962.

Janda, Kenneth. *Data Processing: Applications to Political Research*. Evanston: Northwestern Univ. Press, 1965.

Routt, Garland C. "Interpersonal Relationships and the Legislative Process," *American Academy of Political and Social Science Annals*, CXCV (January 1938), 129–36.

Singer, J. David. *Financing International Organizations: The United Nations Budget Process*. The Hague: Martinus Nijhoff, 1961.

UNESCO. *The Technique of International Conferences. A Progress Report on Research Problems and Methods*. Paris, 1951.

United Nations, General Assembly, Fourth Special Session, Fifth Committee and Plenary, *Official Records*, 1963.

44. Toward an Inventory of Basic Trends and Patterns in Comparative and International Politics*

Karl W. Deutsch addresses himself here to the problems of gathering and processing quantitative data. He argues not only that comprehension of international relations will be extended through the use of quantitative methods, but also that their use does not preclude qualitative analysis or the application of "humanistic insight." In order to demonstrate what can be accomplished with quantitative data, Professor Deutsch devotes the second half of the article to the presentation and analysis of empirical materials that are relevant to his theoretical interest in the transactions that underlie integrative processes in international systems. [*Reprinted from* American Political Science Review, *LIV (1960),* *34–57, by permission of the author and the publisher.*]

Recent decades have seen a vast increase of research in international relations, as in all fields of political and social science. We have more facts and many more expressions of opinion, and we are facing increasingly serious problems of reorientation. We know that much in the world of relations among nations has changed and is still changing, but what is the nature of this change? Is the world becoming more international? Is it turning into one world in which even the United States and the Soviet Union are influencing each other ever more, or at least into two worlds of two rival and ever more tightly inte-grated Communist and non-Communist blocs? Is the nation-state being superseded by the rise of new continent-wide or ocean-wide treaty organizations or federations?

And what is happening within most of the old and new nation-states, as they enter upon these new arrangements? Are their governments becoming more stable or less? Are their political and administrative capabilities rising or declining? Are power and prestige within these states shifting toward the elites or toward the masses of their populations? Are political controls of economic life in the long run growing or receding? Are we moving toward a world of "garrison states," or toward a world of "open societies," or is the world moving in uncharted directions for which not even images have yet been found?

Surely, these seem sweeping questions. Scholars

* A draft of this paper was presented at the International Relations Conference, Northwestern University, April 8–10, 1959. Much of the work reported in this paper has been supported by the Carnegie Corporation: and the research summarized in section V, below, was started at the Center for Advanced Study in the Behavioral Sciences.

and men of affairs might be tempted to put them aside, and to turn their attention to the immediate business at hand. They may prefer the study of some particular conflict between two countries, or of the interests of this or that state, or of the merits of this or that policy at some particular moment. All serious questions, it has been argued, are particular and perhaps unique, and any broader and more general answers might be neither warranted nor wanted.

Such a retreat into the exclusive study of small-scale and short-range problems is based upon a fallacy. We cannot think about particular problems without making assumptions about the general context of the world in which they occur. Usually these assumptions are intuitive and vague. We form some indefinite conception of how states of a particular size and type of government and culture are expected to behave at particular times and places, and we feel surprised when some particular country departs strikingly from these half-formed expectations.

Clearly our analysis could gain a great deal if we tried to lift these vague types and models of political behavior into the light of consciousness, and if we used broad surveys of actual data in order to know what has been or is now the "usual" or expectable behavior of states of some particular type under a typical set of circumstances. To do this implies, however, that we also form a more explicit notion as to what constitutes a particular type of state, and what constitutes a typical set of circumstances or a type of situation.

We are thus trying to form three sets of types: types of states (such as small Scandinavian democracies, or middle-sized Asian traditionalistic authoritarian regimes); types of situations (such as a severe business depression or a rapid growth of towns and industries); and a typical behavior when a typical state and a typical situation meet (such as increasing government intervention under constitutional auspices in Scandinavian countries during depression years, or increasing political instability in traditionalistic authoritarian governments under the impact of rapid industrialization). Some of the typical states, situations, and behavior patterns form part of the folklore of political science, or indeed of common sense. Some of our common sense images, however, may not in fact be true, and

there may be characteristic responses which folklore and common sense have overlooked. Moreover, common sense images may well be mutually contradictory; and it might be worthwhile to know the degree to which a particular common sense image applies in fact.

If we are willing, however, to go beyond political intuition and historical narrative, then we may soon risk a split within the community of students of political science. Some of our colleagues may think of themselves primarily as social scientists, studying political behavior by quantitative and experimental methods; others see themselves rooted most deeply in the humanistic literary and historical tradition of scholarship and judgment. These two groups are in danger of losing communication with each other.

It seems vitally important at this time to maintain and restore the unity of the study of politics —to strengthen and revive communication between the bearers of its historical and descriptive scholarship and those practitioners engaged in the more analytic, behavioral and quantitative aspects of political research.

This paper is an attempt to contribute to the process of mutual communication. Its first part will discuss some problems of method in the use of quantitative data. Parts of it may seem familiar to those who have long been engaged in this type of research, although they may perhaps note some shifts in emphasis; but the same discussion of method may seem unfamiliar or inappropriate to scholars who have been approaching the study of international politics from a different tradition. The indulgence of readers from both these groups is asked. The brief discussion of method in the following section seems needed to indicate the setting for the appraisal of the possible usefulness of the data discussed in the rest of this paper.

I. The Interplay of Political Analysis and Data

In order to do better than common sense, we must try to do several things. We must know what we *want* to know about the politics of states. We must formulate criteria of interest: what aspects of domestic or foreign politics have the most interest to us? In the second place we must form some tentative judgments as to what we *need* to know in order to get the knowledge that we want. We must thus formulate criteria of relevance: what kinds of facts do we think have the greatest influence on the political outcomes in which we are interested?

After having formed some general criteria of interest and some general surmises about relevance, we are likely to proceed to the formulation of some tentative hypotheses. By what supposed connections or operations are the supposedly relevant data linked to supposedly interesting outcomes? In other words, what are the interesting but tentative "if—then" relations, the existence of which we suspect?

Given an interesting tentative hypothesis, what data, if found, would confirm or disconfirm it? (If no conceivable data could do either, it is not a hypothesis in any scientific sense.) What kinds of data would be more persuasive in disconfirming it, and exactly at what point would we consider the hypothesis disconfirmed? In other words, what are our criteria of evidence and its relevance, and what are our criteria of verification?

To state even these preliminary questions for a tentative hypothesis may force us to take a careful second look at it. Our original surmise may not have been specific enough to permit a statement of the precise kind of evidence in the light of which it should be judged, and of the precise findings that would confirm or disconfirm it. It may therefore be necessary to reformulate the original surmise or hypothesis in order to bring it to a point where it can be tested: what changes in the original hypothesis are needed to make it thus testable by evidence?

Once we have a sufficiently specific tentative hypothesis—one that still has the relevance and interest for us that it had in the first place—we will ask: Where can existing data be found that will meet our standards for evidence? What are the probable limits of error in these data, and how seriously will they interfere, if at all, with the use to which we are proposing to put them?

How can these data be processed for further analysis? Usually, political scientists and historians still labor heavily under the heritage of the literary tradition. They spend a great deal of time and ingenuity in order to get the data, but very little time and effort in processing them. There are many mathematical techniques available today by which

data can be correlated, trends can be found, or patterns of interaction among many actors can be brought out more clearly through analysis of matrices. The whole field of data processing is just in its beginnings so far as political science and analysis of international relations is concerned; and more careful attention in this step in the analysis may well pay dividends.

If not enough existing data are available to test the hypothesis in which we are interested, where and by what procedures can relevant new data be obtained? Are there survey methods or experiments that are feasible for us, within the range of our means available, and that would fill some of the gaps in the existing material available from government statistics and elsewhere in our libraries? And how can these new data be further processed for analysis, either by themselves, or in conjunction with existing data obtained from earlier publications by scholars or public or private agencies?

Once we have obtained the minimum of data needed, we can test our tentative hypotheses against them. Which of these hypotheses have been confirmed or disconfirmed, and to what degree?

Here we come to a final and important step. It is quite possible that the data we thought would confirm or disconfirm our original hypothesis will in fact do neither, and we may find that our original hypothesis was less adequately formulated than we thought. Our last step may, therefore, have to be a reformulation of some of our original hypotheses in order to make them more effectively testable—and still relevant—in the light of the evidence we now have found.

Finally, once we have come to some sort of result in relation to the hypotheses with which we started, we will end up not with the closure of the inquiry but with the opening up of a new search. What further important questions seem to have been suggested by the inquiry carried out thus far? How fruitful has our inquiry been in generating further significant questions?

Here, of course, we are closing a cycle, or rather we have rounded the feedback loop in the process of inquiry that we call science. We began with a tentative assessment of a situation and some tentative hypotheses about it. We ended with more definite evidence and with more judgments about these hypotheses. We used the results to formulate new hypotheses which will send us in search for more evidence. Much of our search consists of going through this cycle over and over again; but if carried through effectively, the sequence of operations does not constitute a vicious cycle of frustration. On the contrary, it should constitute each time a production cycle of new knowledge.

II. The Interdependence of Humanistic Insights and Social Science Measurements

This production cycle has its qualitative and its quantitative stages. It starts with the problem of recognition —with the tentative and often intuitive identification of important qualities or aspects of the situation which we are trying to understand. It thus begins with a basic qualitative operation the matching of aspects of politics and of types of states and institutions. Without such a preceding qualitative matching no quantitative work is possible. Nothing can be counted that has not been recognized first, counting is repeated recognition.

Out of the quantitative stages of our inquiry, however, should come the recognition of new trends and new patterns. We ask what these data add up to. What is the pattern of behavior which we infer from the quantitative data that we count? and once we are engaged in trying to recognize new patterns that seem suggested by our quantitative work, we are back in the field of recognition and qualitative thinking.

What I have called qualitative and quantitative thinking is often embodied in old and well-known divisions within the fields of political and social science. The student of literature or the humanities, and those practitioners of political and social science who approach the subject matter primarily in literary or humanistic terms, are most often the persons who make major contributions in the realm of qualitative analysis. They recognize new patterns that are just barely beginning to be dimly visible against the dark and chaotic background of miscellaneous, distracting and often trivial detail. Moreover, they may have an excellent intuitive sense for singling out significant details from among the merely trivial. On the other hand, we have the "short-haired" social scientists, the counters and the verifiers, who are too often and too thoughtlessly

identified with the behavioral approach to social science. In fact, of course, the study of human behavior in national and international politics requires ineluctably the use of both approaches. We need to combine the insight of the literary and historical traditions of political scholarship as well as the quantitative skills of analysis and verification, if our understanding of international politics is to become less inadequate than it has been in the past.

It is time now to give a few examples of the role which particular quantitative data and studies can play toward this end. As should be clear from what has already been said, this manner of presentation will slight, of necessity, the equally important and indispensable contribution of intuitive, qualitative, and humanistic thinking, and readers must be urged, therefore, to make the appropriate supplements and corrections in reading the discussion of quantitative operations that follows.

III. Background Data on the Stability and Capabilities of Governments

Two problem areas of obvious concern to the student of international relations lend themselves particularly well to the application of quantitative methods. One deals with questions of stability. How stable is the existence of a state *vis-à-vis* other states, or *vis-à-vis* the possibly disruptive pressures of some sectional interests or nationality groups within it? And how stable is the government of a state—how probable or improbable appears its overthrow—within its national boundaries?

The second problem area deals with the capabilities of a state *vis-à-vis* other states, and with the capabilities of the government within each state *vis-à-vis* the rest of the population. How capable is a country, and its government, to keep international commitments of some given kind (*e.g.*, to pay debts, to supply troops, to furnish legal protection, etc.)? What are its capabilities for inflicting economic, political or military damage upon other countries (*e.g.*, its economic, military or propaganda potential)? What are the capabilities of its government to carry through specific domestic policies or reforms (*e.g.*, to balance the budget, to limit inflation, to maintain full employment, to redistribute land, to slow down population growth, to strengthen the armed forces, to promote education, to accelerate economic development, etc.)? Finally, what are the capabilities of a government or country for co-operating or merging, wholly or in part, with one or several other countries?

Stability and capabilities are doubly interdependent. Without stability a government's capabilities are drastically reduced, in extreme cases to zero; and without adequate capabilities a government may find it difficult to remain stable in the face of foreign or domestic challenges. But any major increase in the capabilities of a country *vis-à-vis* other countries, or in the capabilities of a government *vis-à-vis* its own population, may require changes that may upset stability.

Generally, increases in capabilities require increasing social mobilization of the people, such as increasing participation in national markets for goods and labor, increasing use of money, industrialization, urbanization, social communication, literacy, participation as audiences of mass media, contacts with the government, interest and participation in politics. Such mobilization, however, is usually accompanied by rising needs and expectations which must not be frustrated if stability is to be preserved.

To preserve stability, this increase in social mobilization needs to be accompanied by two things: first, by an adequate increase in per capita income for the country as a whole, or at least for its politically relevant strata—which are themselves broadening in the process of social mobilization; second, by an adequate increase in capabilities of the central government in regard to its rapidly growing domestic and foreign commitments and responsibilities.

In principle, the background conditions for stability—though not stability itself—could be predicted from a ratio of two numbers: one indicating the rising burdens upon a government and upon popular habits of compliance or loyalty toward it; the other indicating the resources available to the government for coping with these burdens. An indicator of rising burdens could be found in the percentages of literacy, L, and of political participation, *pol*, together with data about the extent of inequality in the distribution of incomes, such as the percentage of total national income, Y, in the hands of the top 10 per cent of income receivers, written as y_{10}. A

rough indication of the resources of the government could be found in the per capita national income, y, and perhaps—though this would have to be investigated—in the ratio, g, of the government sector—sometimes approximated by the national budget—to the total national income. Briefly put, the background conditions for stability would thus be indicated by some such ratio as

$$St = \frac{g}{L\,\text{pol}} \times \frac{y}{y_{10}}$$

Where enfranchisement is wide (*i.e.*, the percentage of enfranchised voters, v_e, is close to 100 for men above 20), voting participation, v, may be taken as approximately equal to *pol*.

Capabilities, on the other hand, may be expected to increase with most of these indicators, so that C may rise with y, g, L, *pol* and y_{10}; that is, with the increases in per capita income, literacy and political participation, as well as with the concentration of resources in the hands of the government and perhaps in the hands of an elite, represented by the top 10 per cent of income receivers. This is at most a tentative surmise, however, and much research is still needed.

Needless to say, no single over-all ratio could furnish anything but the roughest kind of indication of some of the background conditions favoring stability. The actual stability or instability of a government—that is, the probability of its overthrow—will depend to a large extent, of course, on its skill in using its resources, and on its opponents' skill in taking advantage of its difficulties. Governmental skill includes both the skill of political leadership and the administrative competence of the bureaucracy.

The background conditions, against which these political skills are exercised, can be described more adequately by data about some 75 categories, and by about two dozen ratios between them. A tentative list of such data and ratios is given in Table I in the Appendix. A very crude typology, based on only two of these sets of data—size and per capita income—is given there in Table II.

Let it be repeated again that these data are proposed as aids to political judgment, not as substitutes for it. (Similarly, blood counts and readings of body temperature aid the diagnosis of the physician but do not supplant it.) Nevertheless, the help we could get from the measurement, comparison and simultaneous exhibition of a larger number of such background data should not be neglected. . . .

IV. Data about Capabilities and Burdens in Political Integration

Estimates of stability and of general capabilities are not, of course, the only things of interest to us. As students of international relations we are interested in data about the conditions for political amalgamation or integration among different countries, or between different sections or ethnic groups within the same countries.

The background for many of these integrative capabilities, as well as for the possible burden or strains upon them, could again be estimated with the aid of data of the kinds listed in Table 1. In the case of integration or amalgamation between two countries, such data would have to be found for each of the two countries separately, and then, wherever possible, for the specific flow of transactions between them. This specific flow of transactions between the two countries would then have to be compared separately for each country with the total volume of comparable foreign transactions for this particular country, as well as with its volume of domestic transactions of the same kind. Changes in these ratios over time would then indicate whether each kind of transaction was growing faster between the two countries than within either or both of them, and than between either country and the rest of the world. Only in the event that growth of transactions between the two countries should be clearly greater than its alternatives, would there be *prima facie* evidence for a growth of conditions favoring integration or amalgamation—provided, furthermore, that this relative growth in transactions should be experienced by the participants as associated predominantly with rewards rather than frustrations.

What are some of the findings that result from investigations of such ratios of national to international transactions?

A study of the changing ratios of foreign trade to total national income in about fifteen countries suggests that British foreign trade grew faster than national income during the middle third of the 19th century; that the ratio between British foreign trade and national income then changed relatively little

between 1870 and 1913; and that it declined thereafter, with some fluctuations, to one-third less than the 1913 level in 1956. Some other countries, such as Denmark and Japan, reached the peak of their foreign trade ratios somewhat later, in 1915 and 1915–19, respectively, but the development for almost all countries surveyed, as well as some data for the world as a whole, suggests that the relative weight of the international sectors of most national economies has been declining over the last 50 years. For the United States, in particular, the ratio of foreign trade to national income declined from 23 per cent in the days of George Washington to 9 per cent in 1956.[1]

Studies of mail flows, references in scientific journals, and similar data confirm the impression that in terms of the relative proportions of actual transactions the international character of the world may have declined rather than increased during the last half-century.[2] At the same time, however, the strategic, political and financial involvement of governments, and the symbolic and vicarious involvement of large numbers of individuals in international affairs, may have increased. If so, we are facing here a problem of cross-pressures on many individuals in terms of their own allocations of attention and support to international as against national and local issues; and we are facing a similar problem of cross-pressures on governments and legislatures, all of which must respond to an increasing and partly competitive flow of domestic and foreign messages and pressures.

One point seems to emerge clearly, however, from these considerations. There is no single, simple and clear-cut process making the world—even the communist world alone—more international, or producing automatically a steady increase in integration or cooperation even among the major democratic countries. What increase there has been in unity among the democratic countries, world-wide or regional, has been wrested by conscious effort and statesmanship from a welter of contradictory underlying trends.

The study of all such data and ratios thus can

[1] *Cf.* K. W. Deutsch and Alexander Eckstein, "National Industrialization and the Relative Decline of Foreign Trade, 1890–1957," *World Politics*, XIII (January, 1961), 267–99.

[2] *Cf.* K. W. Deutsch, "Shifts in the Balance of International Communication Flows," *Public Opinion Quarterly*, XX (Spring, 1956), 143–60, with further references.

indicate at most the background for possible action: What actually happens, within fairly wide limits of probability, will depend on the political actors concerned, such as the governments, leaders, parties, interest groups and elites involved in the situation. Their aims and skills, their strategies, tactics and timing may do much to influence the outcome.

Here again, quantitative data can aid the judgment of the political analyst, but cannot replace it in the evaluation of historical cases or in the assessment of possible future developments. Some aids for qualitative judgments have been given in several studies by Harold Guetzkow, Ernst Haas, and others, including this author, and need not be repeated here.[3]

V. The Matrix Analysis of Transaction Flows

A final word might be said about the analysis of transaction flows among several countries with the help of a somewhat more elaborate mathematical technique than has been usual. In its essence, the method consists in constructing an "indifference model" or "null model" of the flow of transactions of some defined type between many actors, such as countries. The countries are written in matrix form, with the amount of transactions initiated by each country, say country i, written in the i-th row (which bears its name) and that portion of these transactions which ends up in country j written in the j-th column. The row totals thus show the total transactions initiated by each country, and the column totals show the total transactions terminating in each country. The total of the columns equals the total of the rows, and equals the total of transactions in the system of countries for the period under consideration.

If all countries were totally indifferent to each

other, with nothing influencing their behavior—neither proximity nor similarity of resources, nor anything else—except the mere amount of transactions among them, one can construct an "indifference model" or "null model" which would predict for each cell of the matrix (corresponding to each pair of countries) an "expected" amount of transactions *under the assumption of indifference*. The extent to which actual amounts of transactions deviate from these expected amounts or "indifference levels" will show, of course, in what direction and to what extent any two countries are not indifferent to each other.

Accordingly, three matrices are constructed. The first is a matrix of actual transaction data. The second is a matrix of "expected" amounts from the indifference model; and the third is a difference matrix, showing indicators of deviations of the first from the second matrix for each cell.

For the 106 countries for which suitable international trade data have been collected by the United Nations, this procedure yields three matrices of about 10,000 cells each for any one year. With the help of punched cards and a 650 IBM computer, data for such a world matrix for two different years, 1938 and 1954, could be put on a single deck of cards. The inclusion of 18 putative regions with presumably greater intra-regional ties brought the number of cards closer to 20,000.

A smaller matrix for fifteen North Atlantic countries was computed for five different years, covering a span of over two generations: 1890, 1913, 1928, 1938 and 1954.

The results of this international trade study cannot be presented in detail within the framework of this paper.[4] A few of the provisional findings, however, may be summarized, provided that their tentative character is kept in mind:

1. Indices of relative deviation are a sensitive and reliable instrument for measuring regionalism, clustering, and similar special relationships between states.
2. They permit numerical comparisons between different regions or clusters, as well as the measurement of changes within the same region over time.

---

[3] *Cf.* Harold Guetzkow, *Multiple Loyalties, Theoretical Approach to a Problem in International Organizations.* Publication No. 4, Center for Research on World Political Institutions (Princeton: Princeton University, 1955); Ernst B. Haas, *The Uniting of Europe* (Stanford: Stanford University Press, 1958); "Persistent Themes in Atlantic and European Unity," *World Politics*, X (July, 1958), 614–28; and "The Challenge of Regionalism," *International Organization*, XII (Fall, 1958), 440–58; K. W. Deutsch, S. A. Burrell, Robert A. Kann, Maurice Lee, Martin Lichterman, Raymond E. Lindgren, Francis L. Loewenheim, and Richard W. Van Wagenen, *Political Community and the North Atlantic Area* (Princeton: Princeton University Press, 1957), Chaps. 1–3, and Appendix.

[4] A fuller account, with the data, will appear in K. W. Deutsch and I. Richard Savage, *Regionalism, Trade and International Community*, forthcoming.

3. Regions widely believed to be characterized by special regional ties are confirmed in this characteristic by the new data: of 18 putative regions or clusters of this kind, 16 appear to be so confirmed, including the European Coal and Steel Community, the Scandinavian countries, and the Arab League.

4. Efforts to increase regional integration may have had substantial success. The six countries of the European Coal and Steel Community appeared significantly closer to each other in 1954 in terms of our data than they had been in 1938. An even more outstanding case of strong and increasing ties appears to be that of the United States and Canada.

5. The data show the special relationship of particular countries to their regions, such as the persistent orientation of Finland toward Scandinavia, and the persistent separateness of Iraq from most of its Arab neighbors.

6. Geographic proximity has only limited effects on the distribution of international trade. Less than one-half of the pairs of countries with particularly high positive deviations from the indifference model are within 200 miles of each other; many pairs of countries with the highest positive deviations are over 1,000 miles apart.

7. Specialization of a country in specific commodities, and the complementarity of resources between two countries have likewise only limited effects. Of two sugar islands in the Caribbean, one—Haiti—has close trade ties to the United States but not to England; in another—Jamaica—the reverse holds true.

8. The most conspicuous correlation of high deviations from the indifference model seems to be with language, culture and, above all, financial and political association. Colonial empires and spheres of influence, present and to a lesser extent even past, stand out in the matrices. Trade, like credit, does follow the flag and often lingers after it.

9. The matrix analysis method permits a measurement of the trade-distorting effects of colonialism. These turn out to be strikingly high, turning colonial trade in 1954 away from the United States, Germany, Italy and Japan, and favoring very strongly France and the United Kingdom in their respective colonies.

10. Territories recently sovereign, and colonial territories near the point of independence—such as Nigeria, Ghana, Tunisia and Morocco—showed in 1954 markedly less trade distortion in favor of their present or former "mother countries" than did most of the other colonies. It is possible that this method may thus furnish some additional measures of progress toward the emancipation of particular colonial or quasi-colonial territories.[5]

11. For certain areas, the findings suggest the existence of significant cross-pressures on foreign policy. They show a sharp and continuing decline of relative trade levels between some countries which are linked otherwise by close political, cultural and military ties. Conspicuous among these cases of cross-pressure, or contradictory development, is the steady decline of relative trade levels between Britain and the United States. Other instances include the persistently low relative trade levels between Britain and the ECSC countries, particularly France and Germany, but also the Netherlands and Belgium, and the similarly low relative trade levels between the same countries and the United States. Findings in this respect, based on a more refined analysis of the data, supersede some of the earlier surmises published in 1957 in the Appendix to my *Political Community and the North Atlantic Area*. The new data suggest that the task of reconciling contradictory trends and pressures within different ranges of transaction may offer particular challenges to NATO statesmanship.

[5] *Cf.* data on German exports in 1938 and 1954 in Karl W. Deutsch and Lewis J. Edinger, *Germany Rejoins the Powers* (Stanford: Stanford University Press, 1959), pp. 228–31. See also Elliott J. Berg, "The Economic Basis of Political Choice In French West Africa," *American Political Science Review*, LIV (June, 1960), 391–405.

TABLE 1
A List of Desirable Data and Ratios for
Capability and Stability Analysis

	1 *Magnitude or aggregate*		2 *Average change per year* *(1953–57, or nearest* *period) %*		3 *Ratio (per 100 units of denominator* *category, where appropriate)*[a]
Population Data					
1. P	Population	P'	Population growth from all causes		
2. P_{10+}	Population 10 and above				
3. P_{20+}	Adult population (15–64)	P_d	Crude death rate		
4. P_W	Population of working age	P_b	Crude birth rate		
5. P_D	Dependent population ($P-P_W$)	P_n	Natural rate of population growth	P_D/P	Dependency burden
6. P_M	Men in armed forces	P'_W	Growth of population of working age	P_M/P	Gross military participation ratio
7. P_{MW}	Women in military forces				
8. P_{MP}	Total military personnel				
9. P_{MA}	Men of military age (20–50)			P_M/P_{MA}	Net military participation ratio
10. W	Work force (persons working or seeking work, incl. self-employed and family-employed)				
11. W_W	Wage and salary earners, incl. job seekers				
12. W_E	Employed				
13. W_{EG}	Employed by government (all levels)				
14. W_{EGC}	Employed by central government				
15. W_{ag}	Labor force in agriculture			W_{ag}/W	Proportion of work force in agriculture
16. W_{na}	Labor force outside agriculture			W_{na}/W	% share of non-agricultural labor force
17. U	Unemployed			U/W	Unemployment
18. P_u	Urban population			$ur = P_u/P$	Urbanization ratio
19. P_{u20+}	Population in towns of 20,000 and above			$ur_{20+} = P_{u20+}/P$	Urbanization ratio for cities above 20,000
20. P_r	Rural population				
21. P_{ag}	Agricultural population	P'_{ag}	Growth or decline of agricultural population	$ag = P_{ag}/P$	Percentage of population in agriculture
22. P_{na}	Non-agricultural population				
23. P_{ind}	Industrial population (incl. mining and transport)			$ind = P_{ind}/P$	Industrialization ratio
24. P_{lit}	Number of literate population			$lit = P_{lit}/P_{10+}$	Literacy
25. P_s	Population in the subsistence sector of the economy				

TABLE 1—continued

I Magnitude or aggregate		2 Average change per year (1953–57, or nearest period) %		3 Ratio (per 100 units of denominator category, where appropriate)[a]	
26. P_{Mo}	Population in the monetized sector of the economy				
27. P_{em}	Number of emigrants in last 30 years				
28. P_{im}	Number of immigrants in last 30 years				
29. P_{for}	Number of foreign born population			P_{for}/P	Ratio of foreign born
30. Mar	Number of marriages per year			Mar/P	Ratio of marriages
				Mar_{for}/Mar	Ratio of marriages with foreign partner to total marriages
31. P_{min}	Number of members of ethnic or racial minorities of political significance			P_{min}/P	Ratio of ethnic or racial minorities
32. P_{lang}	Speakers of minority languages			P_{lang}/P	Ratio of speakers of minority language
33. P_{bil}	Speakers of both the dominant and at least one minority language				
Area Data					
34. A	Area (mi²)			P/A	Population density
35. A_{ar}	Arable land				
36. A_c	Cultivated land				
37. A_i	Irrigated land				
Income Data					
38. Y	National income	Y'	Income growth	$y = Y/P$	Per capita income
				Y/W	Income per work force member
39. GNP	Gross national product	GNP'	Average change per year	$gnp = GNP/P$	Gross national product per capita
40. E	Exports			$e = E/Y$	Export ratio
41. M	Imports			$m = M/Y$	Import ratio
42. T	Total foreign trade (E + M)	T'	Change in foreign trade	$t = T/Y$	Foreign trade ratio
43. B_T	Foreign trade balance (E − M)				
44. B_P	Balance of payments				
45. Y_{5t}	Income of top 5% of receivers			$y_{5t} = Y_5/Y$	% of national income going to top 5%
46. Y_{10t}	Income of top 10% of receivers			$y_{10t} = Y_{10}/Y$	% of national income going to top 10%
47. Y_{20t}	Income of top 20% of receivers			$y_{20t} = Y_{20}/Y$	% of national income going to top 20%
48. Y_{50B}	Income of bottom 50% of receivers			Y_{50B}/Y	% of national income going to bottom 50%

TABLE 1—continued

1 *Magnitude or aggregate*	2 *Average change per year (1953–57, or nearest period)* %	3 *Ratio (per 100 units of denominator category, where appropriate)[a]*
49. Y_{30B} Income of bottom 30% of receivers		Y_{30B}/Y % of national income going to bottom 30%
50. Y_G Income of government sector of economy (budget + social security + nationalized and municipal industries)		
51. Y_{Gc} Income of central government sector (usually national budget)		$g = Y_{Gc}/Y$ Political centralization ratio of national economy
52. Y_s Income of subsistence sector of economy		
53. Y_{Mo} Income of monetized sector of economy		$mo = Y_{Mo}/Y$ Monetization ratio
54. Y_{Mil} Defense budget		$mil = Y_{Mil}/Y$ Military expenditure ratio
Mail Flow Data		
55. L Number of letters (1st class) per year ($L = D + F$)		$le = L/P$ Letters per capita
56. D Number of letters in domestic mail		
57. F Number of letters sent or received from abroad		$f = F/L$ Ratio of foreign mail D/F Domestic-foreign mail ratio
58. F_s Letters sent abroad		
59. F_r Letters received from abroad ($F = F_s + F_r$)		F_r/F_s Received-sent ratio of mail
Mass Media Data		
60. N Newspaper circulation (daily average)		$n = N/P$ Newpaper circulation ratio (daily)
61. Mv Motion picture theater seats		Mv/P Movie seat ratio
62. Mv_A Motion picture audience (weekly average)		Mv_A/P Movie audience ratio
63. R Radio receivers		R/P Radio set ratio
64. R_A Radio audience (estimated total)		R_A/R Listeners per radio set R_A/P Radio audience ratio
65. Tv Television sets		Tv_A/Tv Viewers per set
66. Tv_A Television audience (estimated total)		Tv/P TV set ratio to pop. tv_A/P Television audience ratio
67. N_{pol} Newspaper circulation under direct political control (*i.e.*, by party or government)		
Attention Data		
News ratios (from content analyses if available; to be compiled separately for each kind of medium)		

TABLE 1—continued

1 *Magnitude or aggregate*	2 *Average change per year (1953–57, or nearest period) %*	3 *Ratio (per 100 units of denominator category, where appropriate)[a]*	
68. N_F Foreign news[b]		N_F/N	Ratio of foreign news to total newspaper space, inc. advertising
69. N_D Domestic news ($N_F + N_D$ = total news)		N_D/N	Ratio of domestic news ($N_F/N + N_D/N = 1$)
70. Ed_F Editorials on foreign topics (only those clearly referring to foreign topics or items)		N_D/N_F	Ratio of domestic to foreign news[c]
71. Ed_D Editorials on domestic topics ($Ed_F + Ed_D$ = total editorials)		Ed_F/Ed	Percentage of editorials devoted to foreign affairs
		Ed_D/Ed	Percentage of editorials devoted to domestic affairs
Attention ratios (from readership surveys of foreign editorials, if available)			
72. N_{Att} Average reader attention paid to all news			
73. N_{FAtt} Attention paid to foreign news			
74. N_{DAtt} Attention paid to domestic news			
75. N_{Fav} Favorable news (*e.g.*, about a certain country)			
76. $N_{non-Fav}$ Unfavorable news		$\dfrac{N_{Fav} - N_{nonFav}}{N_{neut}}$ Bias index	
77. N_{neut} Neutral news			
Voting Data			
78. V Number of votes cast in elections		$v = V/P$	Gross ratio of voting participation
79. V_E Number of eligible voters		$v_a = V/P_{20+}$	Adult ratio of voting participation
80. P_{po} Number of persons loosely involved in political activities (strikes, meetings, riots, civil wars, etc.)		$v_e = V_E/P_{20+}$	Ratio of enfranchisement
		$pol = P_{pol}/P_{20+}$	Ratio of general political involvement (Hyp.: where v_e is high, $v = pol$)
81. P_{ac} Number of persons more intensely involved in political activity (members of parties, trade unions, farm or business organizations, etc.)		$ac = P_{ac}/P_{20+}$	Ratio of intense political involvement. (Since people under 20 years may be in politics, ac could be larger than one.)
82. V_{com} Number of communist votes		V_{com}/V	Ratio of communist votes

TABLE 1—continued

1 *Magnitude or aggregate*	2 *Average change per year (1953–57, or nearest period)* %	3 *Ratio (per 100 units of denominator category, where appropriate)*[a]
83. V_{soc} Number of socialist votes		V_{soc}/V Ratio of socialist votes
84. V_{rel} Number of votes for religious parties		V_{rel}/V Ratio of religious votes
85. V_{sec} Number of votes for secular parties		V_{sec}/V Ratio of secular votes

Value Orientation Data

86. n_{ach} Index of achievement motivation, acc. to McClelland[d]
87. auth   Index of authoritarianism, acc. to Adorno[e]
88. sat   Index of satisfaction, acc. to Inkeles[f]
89. sec   Security index, acc. to Buchanan and Cantril (p. 26)[g]
90. ster   Stereotype score (towards a given country), acc. to Buchanan and Cantril (p. 53)[g]
91. friend   Friendliness score (towards a given country), acc. to Buchanan and Cantril (p. 54)[g]
92. fut   Index of future orientation, acc. to Florence Kluckhohn, if data should become available[h]
93. M_{nat} Index of value of mastery over nature, acc. to Florence Kluckhohn, if data should become available[h]
94. lin   Index of value put on "lineal" relationships, acc. to Florence Kluckhohn, if data should become available[h]
95. Mor_{m-13} Indices of acceptance of different "paths of life" (*i.e.,* configurations of values), acc. to Charles Morris[i]

---

[a] Annual shifts can then be computed from the ratios in Column 3 according to the formula: $\dfrac{R_{t2} - R_{t1}}{t2 - t1}$

[b] N_F and D_D can be compiled on various bases, such as column inches of news space or number of news items. The news ratio N_F/N is likely to be similar in each case so long as the same measurement is used. For further details, see Ithiel de Sola Pool, *Prestige Papers* (Stanford, Stanford University Press, 1952), and Pool, *Symbols of Internationalism* (Stanford, Stanford University Press, 1951); see also International Press Institute, *The Flow of News* (Zurich, 1953); Jacques Kaiser, *One Week's News* (Paris, UNESCO, 1951); and Wilbur Schramm, ed., *One Day in the World's Press* (Stanford, Stanford University Press, 1959).

[c] This ratio follows from the preceding ones but is convenient to list for purposes of comparisons with similar ratios for trade and mail flow data. *Cf.* K. W. Deutsch, "Shifts in the Balance of Communication Flows," *The Public Opinion Quarterly*, Vol. 20 (Spring 1956), pp. 143–60, and "The Propensity to International Transactions," a paper presented to the American Sociological Society, Chicago, September 1959, multigraphed.

[d] Daniel C. McClelland, "The Achievement Motive in the Economic Development of Primitive and Modern Societies," multigraphed, Harvard University, 1959.

[e] T. W. Adorno, Else Frenkel-Brunswick, Daniel J. Levinson and R. Nevitt Sanford, *The Authoritarian Personality* (New York, 1950).

[f] Alexander Inkeles, "Toward a Social Psychology of Industrial Society," multigraphed, Conference on Political Modernization, Social Science Research Council, June 1959.

[g] William Buchanan and Hadley Cantril, *How Nations See Each Other: A Study in Public Opinion* (Urbana, University of Illinois Press, 1953).

[h] Florence Kluckhohn, "Dominant and Variant Value Orientations," multigraphed, Harvard University, n.d. (1957). This manuscript, a chapter in a large forthcoming work, is a revised and substantially expanded version of two previously published papers: "Dominant and Substitute Profiles of Cultural Orientations: Their Significance for the Analysis of Social Stratification," *Social Forces*, Vol. 28, no. 4 (May 1950), pp. 276–93; "Dominant and Variant Value-Orientations," a paper read at the 78th Annual Meeting of the National Conference of Social Work and later published in part in the *Social Welfare Forum* (1951), pp. 97–113. Two slightly different versions of the complete paper have appeared in Hugh Cabot and Joseph A. Kahl, *Human Relations* (Cambridge, Harvard University Press, 1953), Vol. 1, pp. 88–98, and in the second edition of Clyde Kluckhohn and H. A. Murray, *Personality in Nature, Society and Culture* (New York, 1954,) Part Two, Sec. IV. pp. 342–61.

[i] Charles Morris, *Varieties of Human Value* (Chicago, University of Chicago Press, 1956).

TABLE 2
A Primitive Typology: Some Countries Typed
by Classes of Size and Wealth[a]

1955 GNP per cap.	Country	GNP $ billion	gnp $	P million	P' %	P_{na} %	P_{u20} %	lit %	n %	cal %	P_d %
				A. 1956 Pop. under 10 million							
	Switzerland	6	1229	5	1.1		31	98–99	335	+11	10.2
	Australia	11	1215	9	2.3	86	57	98–99	396	+12	9.1
	New Zealand	2	1249	2	2.1			98–99	394	+12	9.1
$900+	Sweden	8	1165	7	0.7	79	35	98–99	459	+11	9.6
	Belgium	9	1015	8	0.6	87	42	97	338	+11	12.1
	Norway	3	969	3	1.0			98–99	435	+11	8.5
	Finland	4	941	4	1.2		24	98–99	269	+11	9.0
	Denmark	4	913	4	0.7		40	98–99	378	+12	8.8
	Venezuela	4	762	6	3.1		31	52	71	−7	9.9
$300–900	Israel	.9	540	2	3.5			94	195		6.6
	Austria	4	532	7	0.1	67	40	98–99	214		12.4
	Portugal	2	201	9	0.8			56	61		12.1
	Iraq	1	195	5				11	21		5.8
$100–300	Guatemala	.6	179	3	3.1		11	29	27		19.8
	Ghana	.6	135	5	1.6			20–25	18		20.8
	Jordan	.1	96	1	2.7			15–20	9		8.4
Under $100	Bolivia	.2	66	3	1.2			32	23		10.1
				B. 1956 Pop. 10–30 million							
$900+	Canada	26	1667	16	2.7	81	35	97–98	242	+11	8.2
	Netherlands	8	708	11	1.2	80	56	98–99	259	+11	7.8
	Czechoslovakia			13	1.1			97–98	191		9.6
$300–900	Poland			26	2.0			90–95	159		9.0
	Argentina	7	374	19	1.9	73	48	86	154	+9	8.2
	Yugoslavia	5	297	18	1.6		13	73	46	+10	11.2
	Turkey	6	276	25	2.9	14	15	32	32	+9	
	Spain	7	254	29	0.8	50		83	85		9.9
$100–300	Philippines	4	201	22	1.9			60	19	−12	9.2
	Egypt	3	133	24	2.3	35	29	20	25	−0.4	18.4
	Thailand	2	100	21	1.9	14		52	4		9.2
	Iran	2	100	19			21	10–15	6		6.8
	Ethiopia	.9	54	20				1–5	.5		
Under $100	Burma	1	52	20	1.4			45–50	8		21.8
				C. 1956 Pop. 30–90 million							
$900+	France	45	1046	43	0.8	72	33	96	246	+11	12.5
	U.K.	51	998	51	0.4	95	69	98–99	570	+12	11.7
	Germ. Fed. Rep.	38	762	51	1.1	79	45	98–99	243	+11	11.2
$300–900	Italy	21	442	48	0.5	58		85–90	107	+11	10.3
	Brazil	15	262	60	2.4	39	20	49	51	−4	20.6
$100–300	Mexico	5	187	30	2.9			57	48	−9	13.6
	Indonesia	11	127	84	1.8			15–20	7		13.2
	Nigeria	2	70	32	1.9			12	5		11.9
Under $100	Pakistan	5	56	83	1.5	20	8	14	9	−5	11.9

TABLE 2—continued

1955 GNP per cap.	Country	GNP $ billion	gnp $	P million	P' %	P_na %	P_u20 %	lit %	n %	cal %	P_d %
				D. 1956 Pop. 90+ million							
$900+	United States	387	2343	168	1.8	87	43	98	339	+12	9.4
$300–900	U.S.S.R.	150	682			57	32	98	247	+11	7.7
$100–300	Japan	21	240	90	1.3	55	42	98	397	−7	8.0
	India	27	72	387	1.3	26	12	19	7	−18	27.4
Under $100	China	35	56	621	2.2			45–50			17.0

 Categories:

GNP—gross national product (billions)
gnp—per capita gross national product
P—population (millions)
P'—population increase (av. p.a.) %
P_{na}—work force in non-agricultural occupations %

P_{u20}—share of population in towns of 20,000 or more %
lit—% literate in population 15 yrs. and above
n—daily newspaper circulation per 1000 population
cal—calory intake above or below estimated requirements %
P_d—crude death rates per 1000 population

E. The Quantification of Historical Materials

45. National Alliance Commitments and War Involvement, 1818–1945

J. David Singer and Melvin Small have long been associated in an effort to uncover the sources of military conflict in the international system. The former is a political scientist at the University of Michigan whose theoretical orientations have already been presented (Selections 3, 7, 29, and 35) and the latter is a historian at Wayne State University who is more interested in probing the past for recurring patterns than for unique occurrences. The combination of their different trainings and common interests has resulted in a series of valuable studies that are filled with theoretical relevance and empirical substance. One of these studies follows. Among its many virtues is the clear-cut illustration it offers of how human history can be used as a vast laboratory by the scientifically oriented student of international politics and foreign policy. Here data are, to use the authors' term, "made" out of a welter of diplomatic facts; and the procedures of data-making are so general and logical that the reader may well be encouraged to apply them to the substantive problems that interest him. [*Reprinted from the* Papers *of the Peace Research Society* (*International*), *V* (*1966*), *109–40, by permission of the authors and publisher.*]

Introduction

In any serious effort to understand the extent to which certain properties of the international system predict the incidence of events such as war, one always has at least two legitimate lines of inquiry. On the one hand, we can conceptualize that particular property as being an attribute of the system itself; and, on the other, we can focus upon the sub-systemic components or actors whose behaviors or relationships may serve as the observed units from which the systemic attribute is inferred. This set of options would seem to be particularly applicable in any study of balance of power phenomena. For example, if our independent or predictor variable were one aspect or another of alliance configuration—a central theme in balance of power paradigms—we would address ourselves to the larger alliance patterns which characterize the system over time, or we could examine the specific alliance involvements of the individual nations comprising the system. To put it another way, we can focus on the *structure of the system* or on the *relationships among its components*.

In an earlier study, we addressed ourselves to the former of these options, inquiring into the co-variation between certain alliance aggregation indicators at the systemic level and the amount of war which the system experienced, with a longitudinal analysis of the period from 1815 to 1945. The purpose of that inquiry was to make a partial test of what we consider to be a central, but implicit, proposition in the theoretical literature: that as the system's members become involved in alliance commitments, they reduce the interaction opportunities available to the system, inhibit the salutary effect of pluralistic cross-pressures, and increase the likelihood that some of the many inevitable international conflicts will escalate into military hostilities (Deutsch and Singer, 1964). Using a number of simple indicators of alliance aggregation and interaction opportunity loss, we found that the classical doctrine has indeed been borne out by the experience of the twentieth century up to the end of World War II. But we also found almost as strong a set of *negative* correlations for the nineteenth century, thus raising serious doubts as to the timelessness of a well-accepted proposition in our literature (Singer and Small, 1967).

Admittedly, no primitive bivariate analysis such as that can be accepted as conclusive evidence, and further examination of several other system properties relating to alliance configuration is now under way. But even as these follow-up studies at the *systemic* level of analysis go forward, it occurred to us that the discipline's understanding of the alliance-war pattern might be furthered by shifting to the other option, away from the systemic to the sub-systemic or *national* level. In this paper then, we shall report our findings on the extent to which the alliance relationships which nations enter into predict to their war-proneness.

Data-Making Operations

In certain sectors of the scientific enterprise, including much of the social science realm, it is no longer necessary to dwell upon the sources of one's data and the procedures by which they were acquired. But in international politics, we find very few of the theoretically interesting phenomena ready-made in quantitative form, and this paucity of such essential indicators is largely attributable to a folklore which holds that "it can't be quantified." Until we *do* operationalize and quantify our key constructs we can have no acceptable evidence for the many plausible and persuasive (but often contradictory) generalizations which abound. Thus, we first summarize the procedures whereby we converted a welter of diplomatic *facts* (recorded in far-flung and fugitive reports) into scientifically useful *data*.

The Empirical Domain

A prior step in that process, however, is the selection of one's empirical domain. What are its spatial-temporal boundaries and what sorts of samples or populations provide the basis for one's generalizations?

As to the time span, we begin with the year 1815 which marked the Congress of Vienna and its abortive attempt to "return to normalcy," and end with the close of World War II.[1] Despite the many changes in the pattern and process of international relations during that 131 year period, we find a remarkable constancy. The national state was the dominant actor and most relevant form of social organization, world politics were dominated by a handful of European powers, the Napoleonic reliance upon the citizens' army endured, with all of its implications for public involvement in diplomacy, the concept of state sovereignty remained relatively unchallenged, and while technological innovation went on apace, the period postdates the smoothbore and predates the nuclear-missile combination. In sum, it seems reasonable to conclude that this period provides an appropriate mixture of stability and transition from which generalization would be legitimate. As to whether such generalization might be extended beyond 1945 and into the present, we would be skeptical, but this is, of course, an empirical question.

Turning to the population of nations which are to be examined during this period, a serious problem arises. No scholar (as far as we can tell) has ever bothered to look at the entire range of political entities existing in the world during this period and to differentiate between those which qualify as nation-members of the system and those which do not. Thus, we undertook the assignment ourselves, along with an analysis of the attributed diplomatic importance of each qualifying member at five year intervals, and the results are now available (Singer and Small, 1966a). Here we shall briefly summarize those coding rules. To qualify as a member of the system, a political entity had to have a population exceeding a half-million and *de jure* diplomatic recognition from the two nations that came closest

[1] The phrase was Harding's, but it summarizes well the motivation of those who arranged and dominated the Congress; see Kissinger (1957).

to being the international community's legitimizers: England and France. These procedures were modified slightly to meet some of the changing circumstances of the post-1920 period. The political entities which we classified as members of the system appear in Table 1, along with their dates of qualification or disqualification.

One further refinement merits attention here. As indicated in Table 1, we did make a distinction between membership in a central system and membership in a total system. In general, from 1815 through 1920, the international system was dominated by a handful of European states; other independent entities, with a few exceptions, while qualifying for membership in the system, took little or no active role in the crucial political and military affairs of the continent. We have therefore distinguished between a total system, including both European and peripheral powers, and a central system conforming to the historian's conception of the states that really "counted" in international relations from the Congress of Vienna to the Paris Peace Conference. This distinction was maintained through 1920 when, with the interdependence of the system considerably increased, we felt that the total system could be merged with the central system.[2]

War Involvement: The Dependent Variable

Since this inquiry into the alliance-war relationship is part of a larger enterprise on the correlates of war, our first task was to sort out, from the sorry record of continuous bloodshed, those episodes which qualify as cases of international war. We hope to publish soon a detailed handbook presenting all of our data on war since the Congress of Vienna, a variety of transformations and distributions of those data, and an explicit description of our operations, but a summary of the latter is clearly in order here.[3]

[2] We also differentiated between major and minor powers as alliance members and war participants, following the intuitive but generally agreed definitions used in diplomatic history. The nations which qualify as majors and the dates of such status are as follows: Austria-Hungary, 1815–1918; Prussia or Germany, 1815–1918, 1925–1945; Russia, 1815–1917; France, 1815–1940; Britain, 1815–1945; Japan, 1895–1945; United States, 1899–1945; Italy, 1860–1943.

[3] An interim report is in Singer, Small, and Kraft (1965), and it summarizes and expands upon the crucial pioneering work of Quincy Wright (1942) and Lewis Richardson (1960).

To begin with, we had to differentiate between international wars and other types of wars, murders, and riot . According to our definition, an international war was one in which at least one participant on each side was a member of the international system. If only one of the participants engaged in the war was a member of the system, then that war was considered a colonial, imperial, or civil war, and therefore excluded. Thus, for the purposes of this study, England's participation in the Sepoy Mutiny, Spain's in the Cuban revolt of 1868, and Russia's in the Polish uprisings of the nineteenth century, are not included. Of course, colonial, imperial, or civil wars can become internationalized, as in the Russo-Turkish war of 1878–79 and the Austro-Sardinian war of 1848–49.

A second order refinement was also necessary to distinguish between armed conflicts which had an appreciable effect on the participants and mere skirmishes or bandit raids. We have therefore excluded those wars in which the best estimate of battle-connected deaths is less than 1,000. Consequently such conflicts as the Aroostok War between Canadians and Americans in 1838 and the Sino-Soviet clash in Manchuria in 1929 have been excluded. Employing these criteria of war type and our casualty threshold, we found a total of 41 international wars for the total system, 24 of which were central system wars. A listing of the wars, their participants, duration in nation-months, and battle deaths appears in Table 2.

Alliance Commitments: The Independent Variable

Generating the various indicators of our predictor variable presented problems of an equally challenging nature, and in this case nothing comparable to Richardson or Wright was available. A basic data report is available (Singer and Small, 1966b) so we will, again, merely summarize our procedures.

In the first place, we coded bilateral and multilateral treaties of alliance into three classes, depending upon the response required by the signatories in certain specified contingencies. Type I, the defense pact, called for military intervention by a signatory on the side of a treaty partner who was attacked; Type II, the neutrality or non-aggression pact, called for the partners to remain neutral if any co-signatory was attacked; and Type III, the entente, called for consultation and/or cooperation by the

TABLE 1
Composition of Total (1815–1945)
and Central (1815–1919) Systems

	Qualifies as nation-member of total system	Loses membership in total system	Qualifies as nation-member of central system		Qualifies as nation-member of total system	Loses membership in total system	Qualifies as nation-member of central system
Afghanistan	1920			Italy (Sardinia)	1815		1815
Albania	1914^b	1939	1914	Japan	1860^b		1895
Argentina	1841^b			Korea	1888^b	1905	
Australia	1920			Latvia	1920	1940	
Austria (-Hungary)	1815	1918		Liberia	1920		
	1920	1938	1815	Lithuania	1920	1940	
Baden	1815	1870		Luxembourg	1920	1940	
Bavaria	1815	1870		Mecklenberg-			
Belgium	1830^b	1940	1830	Schwerin	1843^a	1867	
Bolivia	1848^b			Mexico	1831^b		
Brazil	1826^b			Modena	1842^a	1860	
Bulgaria	1908^b	1944	1908	Mongolia	1921^c		
Canada	1920			Morocco	1847^b	1911	
Chile	1839^b			Nepal	1920		
China	1860^b		1895	New Zealand	1920		
Colombia	1831^b			Nicaragua	1900^a		
Costa Rica	1920			Norway	1905^b	1940	1905
Cuba	1934^c			Panama	1920		
Czechoslovakia	1919^b	1939	1919	Papal States	1815	1860	
Denmark	1815	1940	1815	Paraguay	1896^a		
Dominican				Parma	1851^a	1860	
Republic	1887^a			Peru	1838^b		
Ecuador	1854^b			Poland	1919^b	1939	1919
Egypt	1936^c			Portugal	1815		1815
England	1815		1815	Rumania	1878^b	1944	1878
Estonia	1920	1940		Russia	1815		1815
Ethiopia	1898^b	1936		Salvador	1875^a		
	1941			Saudi Arabia	1927^b		
Finland	1919^b		1919	Saxony	1815	1867	
France	1815	1940	1815	South Africa	1920		
Germany (Prussia)	1815		1815	Spain	1815		1815
Greece	1828^b	1941	1828	Sweden	1815		1815
Guatemala	1849^b			Switzerland	1815		1815
Haiti	1859^b			Thailand (Siam)	1887^b		
Hanover	1838^a	1866		Turkey	1815		1815
Hesse Electoral	1815	1866		Tuscany	1815	1860	
Hesse Grand Ducal	1815	1867		Two Sicilies	1815	1860	
Holland	1815	1940	1815	United States	1815		1899
Honduras	1899^a			Uruguay	1882^a		
Hungary	1920	1944		Venezuela	1841^b		
Iceland	1944			Wurtemberg	1815	1870	
Iran (Persia)	1855^b			Yemen	1934^b		
Iraq	1932^c			Yugoslavia			
Ireland	1921^c			(Serbia)	1878^b	1941	1878

Qualification Key:
^{a} Crossed population threshold
^{b} Recognized by legitimizers
^{c} Released from de facto dependence
No letter—qualified at or before either 1815 or 1902.

TABLE 2
International Wars by Duration
Magnitude and Severity: 1815–1945

Name of war and participants	Dates	INTERNATIONAL SYSTEM			NATIONAL INVOLVEMENT		National dates of participation (if different)
		Duration (months)	Nation (months)	Battle deaths (000)	Duration (months)	Battle deaths (000)	
1. Franco-Spanish	4/7/23–11/13/23	7	14	1			
France					7	.4	
Spain					7	.6	
2. Russo-Turkish	4/26/28–9/14/29	16.5	33	130			
Russia					16.5	50	
Turkey					16.5	80	
3. Mexican War*	5/12/46–2/12/48	21	42	17			
Mexico*					21	6	
U.S.A.*					21	11	
4. Austro-Sardinian	3/24/48–8/9/48, 3/20/49 3/23/49	4.5	9	9			
Austria					4.5	5.6	
Sardinia (incl. Ital. rebels)					4.5	3.4	
5. Danish	4/10/48–8/26/48, 3/25/49 7/10/49	8	16	6			
Denmark					8	3.5	
Prussia					8	2.5	
6. Roman*	4/30/49, 5/8/49–7/1/49	2	7	2.2			
Austria					2	.1	5/8/49–7/1/49
France					1	.5	4/30/49, 6/3/49–
Papal States*					2	1.5	7/1/49
Two Sicilies*					2	.1	5/8/49–7/1/49
7. La Plata*	7/19/51–2/3/52	6.5	13	1.3			
Argentina*					6.5	.8	
Brazil*					6.5	.5	
8. Crimean	10/23/53–3/1/56	28	115.5	264.2			
England					23	22	3/31/54–3/1/56
France					23	95	3/31/54–3/1/56
Russia					28	100	
Sardinia					13.5	2.2	1/10/55–3/1/56
Turkey					28	45	
9. Persian*	10/25/56–3/14/57	4.5	9	2			
England					4.5	.5	
Persia*					4.5	1.5	
10. Italian	4/29/59–7/12/59	2.5	7	22.5			
Austria					2.5	12.5	
France					2	7.5	5/3/59–7/12/59
Sardinia					2.5	2.5	
11. Moroccan*	10/22/59–3/26/60	5	10	10			
Morocco*					5	6	
Spain					5	4	
12. Roman*	9/11/60–9/29/60	.5	1	1			
Italy					.5	.3	
Papal States*					.5	.7	
13. Sicilian*	10/15/60–1/19/61	3	6	1			
Italy					3	.6	
Two Sicilies*					3	.4	

TABLE 2—continued

Name of war and participants	Dates	INTERNATIONAL SYSTEM			NATIONAL INVOLVEMENT		National dates of participation (if different)
		Duration (months)	Nation (months)	Battle deaths (000)	Duration (months)	Battle deaths (000)	
14. Mexican Expedition*	4/16/62–2/5/67	57.5	115	20			
France					57.5	8	
Mexico*					57.5	12	
15. Colombian*	11/22/63–12/6/63	.5	1	1			
Colombia*					.5	.3	
Ecuador*					.5	.7	
16. Schleswig-Holstein	2/1/64–4/25/64, 6/25/64–7/20/64	4	12	4.5			
Austria					4	.5	
Denmark					4	3	
Prussia					4	1	
17. Spanish*	10/25/65–5/9/66	6.5	17	1			
Chile*					6.5	.1	
Peru*					4	.6	1/14/66–5/9/66
Spain					6.5	.3	
18. Austro-Prussian	6/15/66–7/26/66	1.5	15.5 4.5°	36.1			
Austria					1.5	20	
Baden*					1.5	.1	
Bavaria*					1.5	.5	
Hanover*					.5	.5	6/15/66–6/29/66
Hesse-Electoral*					1.5	.1	
Hesse-Grand Ducal*					1.5	.1	
Italy					1.5	4	
Mecklenberg-Schwerin*					1.5	.1	
Prussia					1.5	10	
Saxony*					1.5	.6	
Wurtemberg*					1.5	.1	
19. Franco-Prussian	7/19/70–2/26/71	7	26.5 14°	187.5			
Baden*					4	1	7/19/70–11/22/70
Bavaria*					4	5.5	7/19/70–11/15/70
France					7	140	
Prussia					7	40	
Wurtemberg*					4.5	1	7/19/70–11/25/70
20. Russo-Turkish	4/12/77–1/3/78	8.5	17	285			
Russia					8.5	120	
Turkey					8.5	165	
21. Pacific*	2/14/79–12/11/83	58	170.5	14			
Bolivia*					58	1	
Chile*					58	3	
Peru*					54.5	10	4/5/79–10/20/83
22. Central American*	3/28/85–4/15/85	.5	1	1			
Guatemala*					.5	.8	
Salvador*					.5	.2	

TABLE 2—continued

Name of war and participants	Dates	INTERNATIONAL SYSTEM			NATIONAL INVOLVEMENT		National dates of participation (if different)
		Duration (months)	Nation (months)	Battle deaths (000)	Duration (months)	Battle deaths (000)	
23. Sino-Japanese*	8/1/94–3/30/95	8	16	15			
China*					8	10	
Japan*					8	5	
24. Greco-Turkish	2/15/97–5/19/97	3	6	2			
Greece					3	.6	
Turkey					3	1.4	
25. Spanish-American*	4/2/98–8/12/98	4	8	10			
Spain					4	5	
U.S.A.*					4	5	
26. Boxer	6/17/00–8/25/00	2	18	2			
China					2	1.5	
Austria					2	+	
England					2	|	
France					2	+	
Germany					2	+	
Italy					?	+	
Japan					2	+	
Russia					2	+	
U.S.A.					2	+	
27. Russo-Japanese	2/8/04–9/15/05	19	38	130			
Japan					19	85	
Russia					19	45	
28. Central American*	5/27/06–7/20/06	2	6	1			
Guatemala*					2	.4	
Honduras*					2	.3	
Salvador*					2	.3	
29. Central American*	2/19/07–4/23/07	2	6	1			
Honduras*					2	.3	
Nicaragua*					2	.4	
Salvador*					2	.3	
30. Moroccan*	7/7/09–3/23/10	8.5	17	10			
Morocco*					8.5	8	
Spain					8.5	2	
31. Italo-Turkish	9/29/11–10/18/12	12.5	25	20			
Italy					12.5	6	
Turkey					12.5	14	
32. 1st Balkan	10/17/12–4/19/13	6	20	82			
Bulgaria					4	32	10/17/12–12/3/12, 2/3/13–4/19/13
Serbia (& Montenegro)					4	15	
Greece					6	5	
Turkey					6	30	
33. 2nd Balkan	6/30/13–7/30/13	1	4	60.5			
Bulgaria					1	18	
Greece					1	2.5	
Rumania					.5	1.5	7/11/13–7/30/13
Serbia					1	18.5	
Turkey					.5	20	7/15/13–7/30/13

TABLE 2—continued

Name of war and participants	Dates	INTERNATIONAL SYSTEM			NATIONAL INVOLVEMENT		National dates of participation (if different)
		Duration (months)	Nation (months)	Battle deaths (000)	Duration (months)	Battle deaths (000)	
34. World War I	7/29/14–11/11/18	51.5	606.5	10,000			
Austria					51	1,200	7/29/14–11/3/18
Belgium					51	87.5	8/4/14–11/11/18
Bulgaria					35.5	14	10/12/15–9/29/18
England					51	908	8/5/14–11/11/18
France					51	1,350	8/3/14–11/11/18
Germany					51.5	1,800	8/1/14–11/11/18
Greece					16.5	5	6/29/17–11/11/18
Italy					41.5	650	5/23/15–11/11/18
Japan					50.5	.3	8/23/14–11/11/18
Portugal					32.5	7	3/1/16–11/11/18
Rumania					15.5	335	8/27/16–12/9/17
Russia					40	1,700	8/1/14–12/5/17
Serbia					51.5	48	
Turkey					48.5	325	10/28/14–11/11/18
U.S.A.					19	126	4/17/17–11/11/18
35. Greco-Turkish	5/5/19–10/11/22	41	82	50			
Greece					41	30	
Turkey					41	20	
36. Chaco	5/12/28–12/19/33, 1/8/34–6/12/35	84	168	130			
Bolivia					84	80	
Paraguay					84	50	
37. Sino-Japanese	12/19/31–5/6/33	16.5	33	60			
China					16.5	50	
Japan					16.5	10	
38. Italo-Ethiopian	10/3/35–5/9/36	7	14	20			
Ethiopia					7	16	
Italy					7	4	
39. Sino-Japanese	7/7/37–12/7/41	53	106	1,000			
China					53	750	
Japan					53	250	
40. Russo-Finnish	11/30/39–3/12/40	3.5	7	90			
Finland					3.5	40	
Russia					3.5	50	
41. World War II	9/1/39–8/14/45	71.5	910	16,000			
Australia					71.5	23	9/3/39–8/14/45
Belgium					.5	7.8	5/10/40–5/28/40
Brazil					10	.1	7/6/44–5/7/45
Bulgaria					34.5	10	12/8/41–10/28/44
Canada					71	37.5	9/10/39–8/14/45
China					44	1,350	12/7/41–8/14/45
England					71.5	270	9/3/39–8/14/45
Ethiopia					5.5	5	1/24/41–7/3/41
Finland					39	42	6/25/41–9/19/44
France					19.5	210	9/3/39–6/22/40, 10/23/44–8/14/45[c]
Germany					68	3,500	9/1/39–5/7/45
Greece					6	25	10/25/40–4/23/41
Holland					.5	6.2	5/10/40–5/14/40

TABLE 2—continued

Name of war and participants	Dates	INTERNATIONAL SYSTEM			NATIONAL INVOLVEMENT		
		Duration (months)	Nation (months)	Battle deaths (000)	Duration (months)	Battle deaths (000)	National dates of participation (if different)
World War II (cont.)							
Hungary					43	40	6/27/41–1/20/45
Italy					57	77	6/10/40–9/2/43, 10/18/43–5/7/45
Japan					44	1,000	12/7/41–8/14/45
Mexico					3.5	.1	5/1/45–8/14/45
New Zealand					71.5	10	9/3/39–8/14/45
Norway					2	1	4/9/40–6/9/40
Poland					1	320	9/1/39–9/27/39
Rumania					39	300	6/22/41–9/13/44
Russia					47	7,500	6/22/41–5/7/45, 8/8/45–8/14/45
South Africa					71	6.8	9/6/39–8/14/45
Thailand					45	.1	11/30/40–1/31/41, 1/25/42–8/14/45
U.S.A.					44	292	12/7/41–8/14/45
Yugoslavia					.5	410	4/6/41–4/17/41

* Indicates peripheral system nation or war
° number includes central system nation-months only for Austro-Prussian and Franco-Prussian wars.

\+ All foreign losses insignificant in Boxer Rebellion.
ᵉ Vichy 11/30/40–1/31/41, 11/8/42–11/11/42

signatories in times of specific political or military crises.

Secondly, only those alliances embodied in formal written treaties, conventions, or agreements were included. Of course, this excluded such all-important unwritten commitments as the Anglo-American entente of the twentieth century, and, more importantly, included such "scraps of paper" as the German-Polish non-aggression pact of 1934. While realizing the shortcomings of relying exclusively on the written alliance, and even though it does not always tell the entire story, we have found that the written alliance has usually been treated as a meaningful commitment, rarely entered into lightly (Singer and Small, 1966b, pp. 16–19). Among those written treaties of alliance excluded were: (a) such general collective security arrangements as the Charter of the League of Nations; (b) constitutions of international organizations such as the Universal Postal Union and the International Labor Organization; (c) treaties of guarantee to which all relevant powers registered their assent, such as the Belgian neutrality treaty of 1839;

(d) agreements limited to general rules of behavior such as the Kellogg-Briand Pact; (e) alliances which were consummated during, or less than three months before, a war in which any of the signatories participated; (f) any alliance which did not include at least two members of the international system; and (g) unilateral guarantees such as American "protection" of Panama in the 1903 Canal Zone treaty.

The 112 alliances which met our criteria are listed according to membership, duration and classification in Table 3.[4]

The Data Summarized

Having defined our empirical domain, described the relevant variables, and outlined the operational

[4] Notes on calculation of alliance indicators: (1) Since each alliance is treated as a cluster of bilateral ones, the scores are based on the number of bilateral *links*; (2) Length of time in an alliance is calculated as if it ran during the entire inception and termination years; (3) When a nation had more than one alliance link with another in a given year, only the highest priority one was counted, with defense, neutrality, and entente ranking in that order.

TABLE 3
Inter-Nation Alliances 1815–1939,
with Commitment Class and Dates

Members	Incept.	Termin.	Class	Members	Incept.	Termin.	Class

Austria
Baden*
Bavaria*
Hesse-
  Electoral*
Hesse-Grand
  Ducal*
Prussia
Saxony*
Wurtemberg*
Hanover*
Mecklenberg-
  Schwerin*
	6/1815–1848,
	1850
	
	1838**
	
	1843**
		1866	1	France
				Sardinia
					1/1859	1859	1

				Modena* Parma* Tuscany*	?/1859	1860	1
Austria England Prussia Russia France	11/1815 11/1818	1823	1	Ecuador* Peru*	1/1860	1861 (?)	1
				England France Spain	10/1861	1862	3
England France Russia	7/1827	1830	3	Prussia Russia	2/1863	1864	1
Russia Turkey	7/1833	1840	1	Colombia* Ecuador*	1/1864	1865 (?)	1
Austria Prussia Russia	10/1833–1848, 1850	1854	3	Baden* Prussia	8/1866	1870	1
				Prussia Wurtemberg*	8/1866	1870	1
England France Portugal Spain	4/1834–1840, 1841	1846	1	Bavaria* Prussia	8/1866	1870	1
				Bolivia* Peru*	2/1873	1883	1
Austria England Prussia Russia Turkey	7/1840	1840	1	Austria Germany Russia	10/1873	1878	3
				Austria Russia	1/1877	1878	2
England Russia	6/1844	1846 (1853 ?)	3	England Turkey	6/1878	1880	1
Austria Modena*	12/1847	1859	1	Austria Germany Italy	10/1879 5/1882	1914	1
Austria Parma*	1851	1859	1	Austria Germany Russia	6/1881	1887	2

TABLE 3—continued

Members	Incept.	Termin.	Class
Austria Serbia	6/1881, 1889***	1889 1895	2 1
Austria Germany Rumania Italy	10/1883 5/1888	1914	1
Germany Russia	6/1887	1890	2
Austria England Italy	2/1887	1895 (1897 ?)	3
Austria Italy Spain	5/1887	1895	2
France Russia	8/1891, 1894***	1894 1914	3 1
China Russia	5/1896	1902 (?)	1
Japan Russia	6/1896	1903	3
Austria Russia	5/1897	1908	3
England Portugal	10/1899	1914	1
France Italy	12/1900 7/1902***	1902 1914	3 2
England Japan	1/1902	1921	1
England France	4/1904	1914	3
France Spain	10/1904	1914	3
England Spain	5/1907	1914	3
France Japan	6/1907	1914	3

Members	Incept.	Termin.	Class
Japan Russia	7/1907	1914	3
England Russia	8/1907	1914	3
Japan U.S.A.	10/1908	1909	3
Italy Russia	10/1909	1914	3
Bulgaria Serbia	3/1912	1913	1
Bulgaria Greece	5/1912	1913	1
Greece Serbia	6/1913	1914	1
Czechoslovakia Yugoslavia	8/1920	1933	1
Czechoslovakia Rumania	4/1921	1933	1
Rumania Yugoslavia	6/1921	1933	1
Czechoslovakia Rumania Yugoslavia	2/1933	1939	1
Belgium France	9/1920	1936	1
France Poland	2/1921	1939 (1934 ?)	1
Poland Rumania	3/1921	1939	1
Afghanistan Turkey	3/1921	1939	1
Persia Turkey	4/1926	1937	2
Afghanistan Persia	11/1927	1937	2
Afghanistan Iraq Persia Turkey	9/1937	1939	2

TABLE 3—continued

Members	Incept.	Termin.	Class	Members	Incept.	Termin.	Class
Austria Czechoslovakia	12/1921	1927	2	Greece Rumania	3/1928	1934	2
Estonia Latvia	11/1923	1939	1	Greece Turkey	10/1930	1934	2
Czechoslovakia France	1/1924, 1925***	1924 1939	3 1	Rumania Turkey	10/1933	1934	2
Italy Yugoslavia	1/1924	1927	2	Turkey Yugoslavia	11/1933	1934	2
Czechoslovakia Italy	7/1924	1930	3	Greece Rumania Turkey Yugoslavia	2/1934	1939	1
Russia Turkey	12/1925	1939	2	Italy Turkey	5/1928	1938	2
Germany Russia	4/1926	1936	2	Hungary Turkey	1/1929	1939	2
France Rumania	6/1926	1939	2	Bulgaria Turkey	3/1929	1938	2
Afghanistan Russia	8/1926	1939	2	Bulgaria Greece Rumania Turkey Yugoslavia	7/1938	1939	2
Lithuania Russia	9/1926	1939	2	France Turkey	2/1930	1939	2
Italy Rumania	9/1926	1930	3	England Iraq	1932	1939	1
Albania Italy	11/1926, 1927***	1927 1939	3 1	Finland Russia	1/1932	1939	2
France Yugoslavia	1/1927	1939	2	Latvia Russia	2/1932	1939	2
Hungary Italy	4/1927	1939	2	Estonia Russia	5/1932	1939	2
Persia Russia	10/1927	1939	2	Poland Russia	7/1932	1939	2
Greece Italy	2/1928	1938	2	France Russia	11/1932, 1935***	1935 1939	2 1

TABLE 3—continued

Members	Incept.	Termin.	Class	Members	Incept.	Termin.	Class
England	6/1933	1936 (?)	3	Brazil			
France				Chile			
Germany				Colombia			
Italy				Costa Rica			
				Cuba			
Italy	9/1933	1939	2	Dominican			
Russia				Republic			
				Ecuador			
Argentina	10/1933	1939	2	Guatemala			
Brazil				Haiti			
Chile				Honduras			
Mexico				Mexico			
Paraguay				Nicaragua			
Uruguay				Panama			
Colombia	4/1934			Paraguay			
Panama	11/1936			Peru			
Finland	2/1938			Salvador			
				U.S.A.			
Germany	1/1934	1939	2	Uruguay			
Poland				Venezuela			
Austria	3/1934	1938	3	Italy	3/1937	1939	2
Hungary				Yugoslavia			
Italy							
				Arabia	4/1937	1939	1
Estonia	8/1934	1939	3	Yemen			
Latvia							
Lithuania				China	8/1937	1939	2
				Russia			
France	4/1935	1938	3				
Italy				France	12/1938	1939	3
				Germany			
Czechoslovakia	5/1935	1939	1				
Russia				Portugal	3/1939	1939	2
				Spain			
Mongolia	3/1936	1939	1				
Russia				Germany	5/1939	1939	1
				Italy			
Egypt	10/1936	1939	1				
England				Denmark	5/1939	1939	2
				Germany			
Germany	11/1936	1939	3				
Japan				Estonia	6/1939	1939	2
Italy	11/1937			Germany			
Argentina	12/1936	1939	3	Germany	6/1939	1939	2
Bolivia				Latvia			

1. Classes of alliance are: 1-Defense Pact; 2-Neutrality or Non-Aggression Pact; 3-Entente.
2. Inception dates show month and year, but termination dates cannot be ascertained with the same precision; where no consensus exists for that date, an alternate year (?) is also shown.
3. Comma between dates indicates temporary break in the alliance.
4. One asterisk * indicates that nation belongs to peripheral system only.
5. Two asterisks ** indicate that nation qualified for system membership *after* joining alliance, i.e. data shown.
6. Three asterisks *** indicate that the same nations negotiated a new alliance of another class, effective this date.
7. Brackets indicate that one or more alliances were merged in a new and larger grouping.

procedures, we can now summarize the results of the data-making operation. In Tables 4 and 5 we present the raw data on each of twelve alliance variables and five war variables for the total and the central system members respectively. And even the most cursory examination of these figures suggests that there is *some* positive relationship between the two types of experience over time. If we look, for example, at such major powers as France, England, or Germany with their relatively high scores on the war indicators, we find them to have also accumulated a large amount of alliance experience as well. Likewise such nations as Holland and Sweden show correspondingly low scores on both sets of indicators.

The next step in the interpretation process makes the pattern clearer still. As we see in Tables 6 and 7, when the absolute indicators are replaced by rank order scores,[5] there tends to be a low number (high rank) next to some nations across all the columns, and high numbers all the way across for others. It is the information shown in these tables which now permits us to go beyond visual inspection and to pinpoint the precise strength of the postulated correlations.

Observed Correlations

When these rank-order data are subjected to correlational analysis via the Spearman *rho* (a non-parametric, rank-order correlation), is the visual impression strengthened and is the hypothesized pattern further evidenced? Tables 8 and 9 clearly point toward an affirmative answer. With an N of 83 nations for the total system and 68 for the central system, a one-tailed test (since no negative correlations were predicted) for a significance level of .01 calls for *rho* values of .255 and .281 respectively. Regardless of one's views on the relevance of significance levels when the full population—rather than a sample—is used, these figures certainly permit us to differentiate between what might be called weak relationships and strong relationships. Omitting for the moment the three indicators that warrant sepa-

rate attention,[6] we have ten different alliance involvement indicators and five different war indicators, permitting a maximum of fifty strong (or statistically significant) correlations. For the total system, we find that forty of the pairs exceed the .255 threshold; for the central system membership, thirty-three of the fifty are equally strong.[7]

Among those several alliance involvements which most consistently predict to war for the total system members, the ones showing the strongest *rho* values are: the total years spent in any alliances; those spent in any alliances with major powers; number of any class of alliances with majors; and number of defense pacts with majors. Weaker predictors are mere number of any class of alliances with any system members and number of neutrality pacts involved in; and in the case of ententes, there are even some weak negative correlations along with equally weak positive ones.

Shifting back to the more restricted central system, a highly similar pattern emerges. The only difference is that the positive correlations tend to be a bit stronger, and the predictors more consistent, in that the low correlations show up for *each* of the five war indicators rather than just a portion of them; likewise, the negative value for ententes holds for all of the war indicators.

So far, the evidence points clearly in the direction of the original hypothesis, but additional data remain to be examined. The skeptic might readily argue that over a long period of time certain nations will tend to be more active than others, and will thus experience at one time or another a larger amount of both war *and* alliance involvement. The point is extremely well taken, and in anticipation of it, we computed an additional indicator designed to help meet this dilemma. If our high correlations are little more than statistical artifacts of nations' activity and inactivity, we should not expect to find

---

[5] When two or more nations have the same score in a given variable, they each receive the average of the ranks they would have received had there been no tie. For example if exactly two nations achieved the maximum score on a variable, each would be given rank 1.5—the average of ranks 1 and 2.

[6] One of these is mere duration of membership and the other two are not independent *or* dependent variables, but indicators of a ratio between them; these, in a sense, already *are* correlations, and will be discussed below.

[7] It should, of course, be noted that this basis for inferring a strong positive relationship has its limits, given the fact that each of the war indicators and each of the alliance indicators is getting at essentially the same phenomenon and that inter-correlations within each cluster will tend to be quite high.

In these and following tables *rho* values are rounded off to two places and the decimal point is omitted.

any discernible *sequential* linkage between alliance membership and war involvement. But we do. In Table 10 we show the correlations between war involvement and a much more limited class of alliance memberships: only those alliance commitments which existed three months before the nation's involvement in war. Our concern here was to ascertain the extent to which nations that got into war were members of alliances just prior to that war involvement. In this Table, the correlation between the number of wars a nation experienced during its tenure in the system and the number of times an alliance commitment existed within three months prior to war involvement is shown. That these figures are extremely high should come as no surprise, given the data in Tables 4 and 5. For example: Austria-Hungary experienced seven total system wars in its lifetime, and alliance membership preceded each, as did Germany (Prussia); England was in five wars and four of these were preceded by alliance commitments; Russia's eight wars were preceded by alliances in all but one case, and so on.

The evidence is quite compelling for the international system's membership as a whole, and even more so for those in the central system.[8] The chances of an allied nation staying out of an impending war during the years covered in this study were not particularly good.

Up to this point, the evidence seems to be pointing rather strongly in the direction of the basic proposition. At this juncture, however, it might be wise to refine that proposition somewhat. Quite clearly, we can say that for the duration of the nations' tenure in the system, war involvement is strongly and positively correlated with alliance commitment. But this is not quite a general law in any scientifically useful sense, inasmuch as it is not based on a genuine *rate* criterion. That is, our evidence does not permit us to say that, for any given unit of time (be it a month, year, or decade) alliance involvement predicts to war involvement: our time unit has been the varying one of membership duration.

One obvious ground for caution is found in Table 11, where we note that mere length of time

in the system correlates very strongly with each of the measures of the nations' war involvement, as it does with almost as many of the alliance indicators.[9] This pattern would then suggest that duration of membership is perhaps the factor which accounts for most of the variance here. If so, then we had better rerun our correlations, now controlling for—or eliminating the effect of—the nations' duration of membership in total and central systems.

This we do via the simple expedient of dividing war and alliance indicator by that nation's duration figure, thus permitting a correlation between frequency *rates* rather than merely between frequencies. Do we find (Tables 12 and 13) on controlling for duration of membership, the same strong and positive correlations which appeared earlier? Quite clearly not. Instead of the thirty-seven and thirty significant correlations we found for the total and central systems, respectively, when we did *not* control for duration of membership, we find only nine and ten such values. Moreover, two of these in the total system and five in the central are *negative*. Only neutrality pacts with majors for total system members are consistently strong, and only number of defense pacts with majors are strong for the central system. And a fair number of negative correlations are found for ententes and for all alliances with anyone. On the other hand (Table 14), when we examine the correlations between the number of times the nations had alliance commitments before entering into war and the number of wars experienced, the values are all strong and positive, only a shade lower than those found when we did *not* control for duration of membership.

Conclusion

What do we make of this rather mixed set of results? On the one hand, there is little doubt that, when we examine the nations' complete experience in our 1815–1945 systems, their alliance commitments predict to their war involvement. But we also note that this is essentially a gross *frequency* correlation, and not a correlation among frequency *rates*. Using

[8] When a given pattern of relationships appears quite clearly in the total system and with even greater clarity in the central system, one can be even more confident of the pattern, since the "noise" generated by the peripheral members could well account for the somewhat weaker correlations in the larger and more diffuse setting.

[9] While the correlations are high for both, they are consistently stronger for the war indicators. Does this suggest that wars are a more deterministic phenomenon in the system than are alliances, and that nations enjoy a greater degree of choice when it comes to alliance involvement than when it comes to war involvement?

TABLE 4
*War and Alliance Involvement
by Nation; Total System 1815–1945*

| Nation | Years in system | Years in war | Years in war vs. major | No. of wars | No. of wars vs. major | Battle deaths (in thousands) | Years in alliance | Years allied with major | No. of alliances | No. of alliances with major | No. defense pacts | No. neutrality pacts | No. ententes | With major | | | Pre-war alliances | Pre-war alliances with major |
														No. defense pacts	No. neut. pacts	No. ententes		
Europe																		
Albania	26	.0	.0	0	0	.0	14	14	1	1	1	0	0	1	0	0	0	0
Austria (-Hungary)	123	5.6	4.6	7	3	1238.7	106	98	30	14	20	4	6	7	2	5	7	7
Baden	56	.5	.5	2	2	1.1	55	55	10	3	10	0	0	3	0	0	2	2
Bavaria	56	.5	.5	2	2	6.0	55	55	10	3	10	0	0	3	0	0	2	2
Belgium	111	4.3	4.3	2	2	95.3	17	17	1	1	1	0	0	1	0	0	0	0
Bulgaria	37	6.3	5.8	4	2	74.0	13	0	6	0	2	4	0	0	0	0	2	0
Czechoslovakia	21	.0	.0	0	0	.0	20	19	6	4	4	1	1	2	1	1	0	0
Denmark	126	1.0	1.0	2	2	6.5	1	1	1	1	0	1	0	0	1	0	0	0
England	131	12.7	12.1	5	3	1200.5	71	61	29	20	16	0	13	9	0	11	3	1
Estonia	21	.0	.0	0	0	.0	17	8	4	2	1	2	1	0	2	0	0	0
Finland	27	3.5	3.5	2	2	82.0	8	8	9	1	0	9	0	0	1	0	2	2
France	126	14.2	8.5	9	5	1811.4	69	56	29	18	13	4	12	7	1	10	6	5
Germany (Prussia)	131	11.8	10.7	7	4	5353.5	111	107	38	21	22	7	9	9	3	9	7	6
Greece	114	6.1	1.9	6	2	68.1	15	11	7	1	5	2	0	0	1	0	3	0
Hanover	29	.1	.1	1	1	.5	28	28	9	2	9	0	0	2	0	0	1	1
Hesse Electoral	52	.1	.1	1	1	.1	51	51	9	2	9	0	0	2	0	0	1	1
Hesse Grand Ducal	53	.1	.1	1	1	.1	51	51	9	2	9	0	0	2	0	0	1	1
Holland	126	.1	.1	1	1	6.2	0	0	0	0	0	0	0	0	0	0	0	0
Hungary	25	3.6	3.6	1	1	40.0	13	13	3	1	0	2	1	0	1	0	1	1
Iceland	2	.0	.0	0	0	.0	0	0	0	0	0	0	0	0	0	0	0	0
Ireland	25	.0	.0	0	0	.0	0	0	0	0	0	0	0	0	0	0	0	0
Italy (Sardinia)	131	12.1	10.0	11	6	750.0	50	41	24	14	6	8	10	4	2	8	8	8
Latvia	21	.0	.0	0	0	.0	17	8	4	2	1	2	1	0	2	0	0	0
Lithuania	21	.0	.0	0	0	.0	14	14	3	1	0	1	2	0	1	0	0	0
Luxembourg	21	.0	.0	0	0	.0	0	0	0	0	0	0	0	0	0	0	0	0
Mecklenberg-Schwerin	25	.1	.1	1	1	.1	23	23	9	2	9	0	0	2	0	0	1	1
Modena	19	.0	.0	0	0	.0	14	13	3	1	3	0	0	1	0	0	0	0
Norway	36	.2	.2	1	1	1.0	0	0	0	0	0	0	0	0	0	0	0	0
Papal States	46	.2	.2	2	2	2.2	0	0	0	0	0	0	0	0	0	0	0	0
Parma	10	.0	.0	0	0	.0	10	9	3	1	3	0	0	1	0	0	0	0
Poland	21	.1	.1	1	1	320.0	19	19	4	3	2	2	0	1	2	0	1	1
Portugal	131	2.7	2.7	1	1	7.0	29	28	5	3	4	1	0	3	0	0	0	0
Rumania	67	4.6	4.5	3	2	636.5	51	46	11	5	8	2	1	3	1	1	2	2
Russia	131	13.7	11.2	8	4	9565.0	91	91	40	26	13	15	12	8	6	12	8	8
Saxony	53	.1	.1	1	1	.6	51	51	9	2	9	0	0	2	0	0	1	1
Spain	131	2.6	.6	5	1	11.9	35	34	10	8	3	3	4	2	2	4	1	1
Sweden	131	.0	.0	0	0	.0	0	0	0	0	0	0	0	0	0	0	0	0
Switzerland	131	.0	.0	0	0	.0	0	0	0	0	0	0	0	0	0	0	0	0
Two Sicilies	46	.4	.3	2	1	.5	0	0	0	0	0	0	0	0	0	0	0	0
Turkey	131	13.7	9.5	9	5	700.4	30	26	16	8	9	7	0	5	3	0	0	0
Tuscany	46	.0	.0	0	0	.0	2	0	2	0	2	0	0	0	0	0	0	0
Wurtemberg	56	.5	.5	2	2	1.1	55	55	10	3	10	0	0	3	0	0	2	2
Yugoslavia (Serbia)	64	4.8	4.3	4	2	491.5	38	31	11	4	7	4	0	1	3	0	4	1

TABLE 4—continued

Nation	Years in system	Years in war	Years in war vs. major	No. of wars	No. of wars vs. major	Battle deaths (in thousands)	Years in alliance	Years allied with major	No. of alliances	No. of alliances with major	No. defense pacts	No. neutrality pacts	No. ententes	With major No. defense pacts	With major No. neut. pacts	With major No. ententes	Pre-war alliances	Pre-war alliances with major
Middle East																		
Egypt	10	.0	.0	0	0	.0	4	4	1	1	1	0	0	1	0	0	0	0
Iran (Persia)	91	.4	.4	1	1	1.5	14	13	4	1	0	4	0	0	1	0	0	0
Iraq	14	.0	.0	0	0	.0	8	8	4	1	1	3	0	1	0	0	0	0
Saudi Arabia	19	.0	.0	0	0	.0	3	0	1	1	0	0	0	0	0	0	0	0
Yemen	12	.0	.0	0	0	.0	3	0	1	0	1	0	0	0	0	0	0	0
Africa																		
Ethiopia	44	1.0	1.0	2	2	21.0	0	0	0	0	0	0	0	0	0	0	0	0
Liberia	26	.0	.0	0	0	.0	0	0	0	0	0	0	0	0	0	0	0	0
Morocco	65	1.1	.0	2	0	14.0	0	0	0	0	0	0	0	0	0	0	0	0
South Africa	26	5.9	5.9	1	1	6.8	0	0	0	0	0	0	0	0	0	0	0	0
Asia																		
Afghanistan	26	.0	.0	0	0	.0	19	14	4	1	1	3	0	0	1	0	0	0
Australia	26	6.0	6.0	1	1	23.0	0	0	0	0	0	0	0	0	0	0	0	0
China	86	10.3	9.6	5	4	2161.5	10	10	2	2	1	1	0	1	1	0	2	2
Japan	86	16.1	9.5	7	3	1350.3	30	30	7	7	1	0	6	1	0	6	5	5
Korea	18	.0	.0	0	0	.0	0	0	0	0	0	0	0	0	0	0	0	0
Mongolia	25	.0	.0	0	0	.0	4	4	1	1	1	0	0	1	0	0	0	0
Nepal	26	.0	.0	0	0	.0	0	0	0	0	0	0	0	0	0	0	0	0
New Zealand	26	6.0	6.0	1	1	10.0	0	0	0	0	0	0	0	0	0	0	0	0
Thailand (Siam)	59	3.8	3.8	1	1	.1	0	0	0	0	0	0	0	0	0	0	0	0
Western Hemisphere																		
Argentina	105	.5	.0	1	0	.8	7	4	21	1	0	8	13	0	0	1	0	0
Bolivia	98	11.8	.0	2	0	81.0	15	4	21	1	1	0	20	0	0	1	1	0
Brazil	120	1.4	.8	2	1	.6	7	4	21	1	0	8	13	0	0	1	1	1
Canada	26	5.9	5.9	1	1	37.5	0	0	0	0	0	0	0	0	0	0	0	0
Chile	107	5.4	.0	2	0	3.1	7	4	21	1	0	8	13	0	0	1	0	0
Colombia	115	.1	.0	1	0	.3	8	4	22	1	1	8	13	0	0	1	0	0
Costa Rica	26	.0	.0	0	0	.0	4	4	20	1	0	0	20	0	0	1	0	0
Cuba	12	.0	.0	0	0	.0	4	4	20	1	0	0	20	0	0	1	0	0
Dominican Republic	59	.0	.0	0	0	.0	4	4	20	1	0	0	20	0	0	1	0	0
Ecuador	92	.1	.0	1	0	.7	8	4	22	1	2	0	20	0	0	1	0	0
Guatemala	97	.2	.0	2	0	1.2	4	4	20	1	0	0	20	0	0	1	0	0
Haiti	87	.0	.0	0	0	.0	4	4	20	1	0	0	20	0	0	1	0	0
Honduras	47	.3	.0	2	0	.6	4	4	20	1	0	0	20	0	0	1	0	0
Mexico	115	6.8	5.1	3	2	18.1	7	4	21	1	0	8	13	0	0	1	1	1
Nicaragua	46	.2	.0	1	0	.4	4	4	20	1	0	0	20	0	0	1	0	0
Panama	26	.0	.0	0	0	.0	4	4	21	1	0	8	13	0	0	1	0	0
Paraguay	50	7.0	.0	1	0	50.0	7	4	21	1	0	8	13	0	0	1	0	0
Peru	108	4.9	.0	2	0	10.6	17	4	22	1	2	0	20	0	0	1	0	0
Salvador	71	.4	.0	3	0	.8	4	4	20	1	0	0	20	0	0	1	0	0
Uruguay	64	.0	.0	0	0	.0	7	4	21	1	0	8	13	0	0	1	0	0
United States	131	7.5	5.3	5	2	434.0	6	2	21	1	0	0	21	0	0	1	1	0
Venezuela	105	.0	.0	0	0	.0	4	4	20	1	0	0	20	0	0	1	0	0

TABLE 5
War and Alliance Involvement by Nation;
Central System only 1815–1945

Nation	Years in system	Years in war	Years in war vs. major	No. of wars	No. of wars vs. major	Battle deaths (in thousands)	Years in alliance	Years allied with major	No. of alliances	No. of alliances with major	No. defense pacts	No. neutrality pacts	No. ententes	With major			Pre-war alliances	Pre-war alliances with major
														No. defense pacts	No. neut. pacts	No. ententes		
Europe																		
Albania	26	.0	.0	0	0	.0	14	14	1	1	1	0	0	1	0	0	0	0
Austria (-Hungary)	123	5.5	4.6	6	3	1238.6	105	98	20	14	10	4	6	7	2	5	6	6
Belgium	111	4.3	4.3	2	2	95.3	17	17	1	1	1	0	0	1	0	0	0	0
Bulgaria	37	6.3	5.8	4	2	74.0	13	0	6	0	2	4	0	0	0	0	2	0
Czechoslovakia	21	.0	.0	0	0	.0	20	19	6	4	4	1	1	2	1	1	0	0
Denmark	126	1.0	1.0	2	2	6.5	1	1	1	1	0	1	0	0	1	0	0	0
England	131	12.3	12.1	4	3	1200.0	71	61	29	20	16	0	13	9	0	11	3	1
Estonia	21	.0	.0	0	0	.0	17	8	4	2	1	2	1	0	2	0	0	0
Finland	27	3.5	3.5	2	2	82.0	8	8	9	1	0	9	0	0	1	0	2	2
France	126	9.3	8.5	7	5	1802.9	64	52	29	18	13	4	12	7	1	10	5	4
Germany (Prussia)	131	11.8	10.7	7	4	5353.5	107	107	27	21	11	7	9	9	3	9	6	6
Greece	114	6.1	1.9	6	2	68.1	15	11	7	1	5	2	0	0	1	0	3	0
Holland	126	.1	.1	1	1	6.2	0	0	0	0	0	0	0	0	0	0	0	0
Hungary	25	3.6	3.6	1	1	40.0	13	13	3	1	0	2	1	0	1	0	1	1
Iceland	2	.0	.0	0	0	.0	0	0	0	0	0	0	0	0	0	0	0	0
Ireland	25	.0	.0	0	0	.0	0	0	0	0	0	0	0	0	0	0	0	0
Italy (Sardinia)	131	11.8	10.0	9	6	749.1	50	41	24	14	6	8	10	4	2	8	6	6
Latvia	21	.0	.0	0	0	.0	17	8	4	2	1	2	1	0	2	0	0	0
Lithuania	21	.0	.0	0	0	.0	14	14	3	1	0	1	2	0	1	0	0	0
Luxembourg	21	.0	.0	0	0	.0	0	0	0	0	0	0	0	0	0	0	0	0
Norway	36	.2	.2	1	1	1.0	0	0	0	0	0	0	0	0	0	0	0	0
Poland	21	.1	.1	1	1	320.0	19	19	4	3	2	2	0	1	2	0	1	1
Portugal	131	2.7	2.7	1	1	7.0	29	28	5	3	4	1	0	3	0	0	0	0
Rumania	67	4.6	4.5	3	2	636.5	51	46	11	5	8	2	1	3	1	1	2	2
Russia	131	13.7	11.2	8	4	9565.0	91	91	40	26	13	15	12	8	6	12	8	8
Spain	131	.6	.6	1	1	.6	35	34	10	8	3	3	4	2	2	4	1	1
Sweden	131	.0	.0	0	0	.0	0	0	0	0	0	0	0	0	0	0	0	0
Switzerland	131	.0	.0	0	0	.0	0	0	0	0	0	0	0	0	0	0	0	0
Turkey	131	13.7	9.5	9	5	700.4	30	26	16	8	9	7	0	5	3	0	0	0
Yugoslavia (Serbia)	64	4.8	4.3	4	2	491.5	38	31	11	4	7	4	0	1	3	0	4	1
Middle East																		
Egypt	10	.0	.0	0	0	.0	4	4	1	1	1	0	0	1	0	0	0	0
Iran (Persia)	26	.0	.0	0	0	.0	14	13	4	1	0	4	0	0	1	0	0	0
Iraq	14	.0	.0	0	0	.0	8	8	4	1	1	3	0	1	0	0	0	0
Saudi Arabia	19	.0	.0	0	0	.0	3	0	1	0	1	0	0	0	0	0	0	0
Yemen	12	.0	.0	0	0	.0	3	0	1	0	1	0	0	0	0	0	0	0
Africa																		
Ethiopia	22	1.0	1.0	2	2	21.0	0	0	0	0	0	0	0	0	0	0	0	0
Liberia	26	.0	.0	0	0	.0	0	0	0	0	0	0	0	0	0	0	0	0
South Africa	26	5.9	5.9	1	1	6.8	0	0	0	0	0	0	0	0	0	0	0	0

TABLE 5—continued

Nation	Years in system	Years in war	Years in war vs. major	No. of wars	No. of wars vs. major	Battle deaths (in thousands)	Years in alliance	Years allied with major	No. of alliances	No. of alliances with major	No. defense pacts	No. neutrality pacts	No. ententes	With major No. defense pacts	With major No. neut. pacts	With major No. ententes	Pre-war alliances	Pre-war alliances with major
Asia																		
Afghanistan	26	.0	.0	0	0	.0	19	14	4	1	1	3	0	0	1	0	0	0
Australia	26	6.0	6.0	1	1	23.0	0	0	0	0	0	0	0	0	0	0	0	0
China	51	9.6	9.6	4	4	2151.5	10	10	2	2	1	1	0	1	1	0	2	2
Japan	51	15.4	9.5	6	3	1345.3	30	30	7	7	1	0	6	1	1	0	6	5
Mongolia	25	.0	.0	0	0	.0	4	4	1	1	1	0	0	1	0	0	0	0
Nepal	27	.0	.0	0	0	.0	0	0	0	0	0	0	0	0	0	0	0	0
New Zealand	26	6.0	6.0	1	1	10.0	0	0	0	0	0	0	0	0	0	0	0	0
Thailand (Siam)	26	3.8	3.8	1	1	.1	0	0	0	0	0	0	0	0	0	0	0	0
Western Hemisphere																		
Argentina	26	.0	.0	0	0	.0	7	4	21	1	0	8	13	0	0	1	0	0
Bolivia	26	7.0	.0	1	0	80.0	4	4	20	1	0	0	20	0	0	1	0	0
Brazil	26	.8	.8	1	1	.1	7	4	21	1	0	8	13	0	0	1	1	1
Canada	26	5.9	5.9	1	1	37.5	0	0	0	0	0	0	0	0	0	0	0	0
Chile	26	.0	.0	0	0	.0	7	4	21	1	0	8	13	0	0	1	0	0
Colombia	26	.0	.0	0	0	.0	6	4	21	1	0	8	13	0	0	1	0	0
Costa Rica	26	.0	.0	0	0	.0	4	4	20	1	0	0	20	0	0	1	0	0
Cuba	12	.0	.0	0	0	.0	4	4	20	1	0	0	20	0	0	1	0	0
Dominican Republic	26	.0	.0	0	0	.0	4	4	20	1	0	0	20	0	0	1	0	0
Ecuador	26	.0	.0	0	0	.0	4	4	20	1	0	0	20	0	0	1	0	0
Guatemala	26	.0	.0	0	0	.0	4	4	20	1	0	0	20	0	0	1	0	0
Haiti	26	.0	.0	0	0	.0	4	4	20	1	0	0	20	0	0	1	0	0
Honduras	26	.0	.0	0	0	.0	4	4	20	1	0	0	20	0	0	1	0	0
Mexico	26	.3	.3	1	1	.1	7	4	21	1	0	8	13	0	0	1	1	1
Nicaragua	26	.0	.0	0	0	.0	4	4	20	1	0	0	20	0	0	1	0	0
Panama	26	.0	.0	0	0	.0	4	4	21	1	0	8	13	0	0	1	0	0
Paraguay	26	7.0	.0	1	0	50.0	7	4	21	1	0	8	13	0	0	1	0	0
Peru	26	.0	.0	0	0	.0	4	4	20	1	0	0	20	0	0	1	0	0
Salvador	26	.0	.0	0	0	.0	4	4	20	1	0	0	20	0	0	1	0	0
Uruguay	26	.0	.0	0	0	.0	7	4	21	1	0	8	13	0	0	1	0	0
United States	47	5.4	5.3	3	2	418.0	6	2	21	1	0	0	21	0	0	1	1	0
Venezuela	26	.0	.0	0	0	.0	4	4	20	1	0	0	20	0	0	1	0	0

TABLE 6
*Ranks of Nations on War and
Alliance Variables, Total System*

	Years in system	Years of war	Years war vs. major	No. of wars	No. of wars vs. major	Battle deaths	Years allied
Albania	59.5	69.0	63.0	69.0	63.0	69.0	31.5
Austria (-Hungary)	14.0	19.0	16.0	6.0	8.0	6.0	2.0
Baden	39.0	35.5	30.0	25.5	16.5	38.5	7.0
Bavaria	39.0	35.5	30.0	25.5	16.5	33.0	7.0
Belgium	19.0	24.0	18.5	25.5	16.5	14.0	25.5
Bulgaria	51.0	13.0	13.0	13.5	16.5	17.0	34.5
Czechoslovakia	71.5	69.0	63.0	69.0	63.0	69.0	21.0
Denmark	12.0	32.5	25.5	25.5	16.5	31.0	64.0
England	5.5	5.0	1.0	10.5	8.0	7.0	4.0
Estonia	71.5	69.0	63.0	69.0	63.0	69.0	25.5
Finland	54.0	27.0	22.0	25.5	16.5	15.0	39.5
France	12.0	2.0	8.0	2.5	2.5	4.0	5.0
Germany (Prussia)	5.5	7.5	3.0	6.0	5.0	2.0	1.0
Greece	18.0	14.0	24.0	8.0	16.5	18.0	28.5
Hanover	53.0	50.0	39.0	44.0	33.0	47.5	19.0
Hesse Electoral	43.0	50.0	39.0	44.0	33.0	52.5	10.5
Hesse Grand Ducal	41.5	50.0	39.0	44.0	33.0	52.5	10.5
Holland	12.0	50.0	39.0	44.0	33.0	32.0	74.0
Hungary	66.5	26.0	21.0	44.0	33.0	20.0	34.5
Iceland	83.0	69.0	63.0	69.0	63.0	69.0	74.0
Ireland	66.5	69.0	63.0	69.0	63.0	69.0	74.0
Italy (Sardinia)	5.5	6.0	4.0	1.0	1.0	8.0	13.0
Latvia	71.5	69.0	63.0	69.0	63.0	69.0	25.5
Lithuania	71.5	69.0	63.0	69.0	63.0	69.0	31.5
Luxembourg	71.5	69.0	63.0	69.0	63.0	69.0	74.0
Mecklenberg-Schw.	66.5	50.0	39.0	44.0	33.0	52.5	20.0
Modena	75.5	69.0	63.0	69.0	63.0	69.0	31.5
Norway	52.0	43.5	34.5	44.0	33.0	40.0	74.0
Papal States	47.5	43.5	34.5	25.5	16.5	35.0	74.0
Parma	81.5	69.0	63.0	69.0	63.0	69.0	36.5
Poland	71.5	50.0	39.0	44.0	33.0	13.0	22.5
Portugal	5.5	28.0	23.0	44.0	33.0	29.0	18.0
Rumania	32.0	23.0	17.0	16.0	16.5	10.0	10.5
Russia	5.5	3.5	2.0	4.0	5.0	1.0	3.0
Saxony	41.5	50.0	39.0	44.0	33.0	45.0	10.5
Spain	5.5	29.0	28.0	10.5	33.0	26.0	15.0
Sweden	5.5	69.0	63.0	69.0	63.0	69.0	74.0
Switzerland	5.5	69.0	63.0	69.0	63.0	69.0	74.0
Two Sicilies	47.5	39.0	33.0	25.5	33.0	47.5	74.0
Turkey	5.5	3.5	6.5	2.5	2.5	9.0	16.5

| Years allied with major | No. of alliances | No. of alliances with major | No. of defense pacts | No. of neutrality pacts | No. of ententes | With major | | |
						No. of defense pacts	No. of neutrality pacts	No. of ententes
25.0	61.0	43.5	35.5	58.0	59.5	25.0	52.5	58.0
2.0	3.0	5.5	2.0	16.0	27.5	4.5	7.5	7.0
7.0	32.5	15.0	7.0	58.0	59.5	10.0	52.5	58.0
7.0	32.5	15.0	7.0	58.0	59.5	10.0	52.5	58.0
23.0	61.0	43.5	35.5	58.0	59.5	25.0	52.5	58.0
72.0	43.5	72.0	26.0	16.0	59.5	57.0	52.5	58.0
21.5	43.5	11.5	19.5	30.0	33.0	16.0	16.0	20.5
60.0	61.0	43.5	63.0	30.0	59.5	57.0	16.0	58.0
4.0	4.5	3.0	3.0	58.0	18.0	1.5	52.5	2.0
34.5	48.5	22.0	35 5	24.5	33.0	57.0	7.5	58.0
34.5	37.5	43.5	63.0	2.0	59.5	57.0	16.0	58.0
5.0	4.5	4.0	4.5	16.0	23.5	4.5	16.0	3.0
1.0	2.0	2.0	1.0	12.5	26.0	1.5	3.0	4.0
30.0	41.5	43.5	18.0	24.5	59.5	57.0	16.0	58.0
17.5	37.5	22.0	11.5	58.0	59.5	16.0	52.5	58.0
10.0	37.5	22.0	11.5	58.0	59.5	16.0	52.5	58.0
10.0	37.5	22.0	11.5	58.0	59.5	16.0	52.5	58.0
72.0	74.0	72.0	63.0	58.0	59.5	57.0	52.5	58.0
28.0	53.5	22.0	63.0	24.5	33.0	57.0	16.0	20.5
72.0	74.0	72.0	63.0	58.0	59.5	57.0	52.5	58.0
72.0	74.0	72.0	63.0	58.0	59.5	57.0	52.5	58.0
13.0	6.0	5.5	17.0	7.0	25.0	7.0	7.5	5.0
34.5	48.5	22.0	35.5	24.5	33.0	57.0	7.5	58.0
25.0	53.5	43.5	63.0	30.0	30.0	57.0	16.0	58.0
72.0	74.0	72.0	63.0	58.0	59.5	57.0	52.5	58.0
20.0	37.5	22.0	11.5	58.0	59.5	16.0	52.5	58.0
28.0	53.5	43.5	22.0	58.0	59.5	25.0	52.5	58.0
72.0	74.0	72.0	63.0	58.0	59.5	57.0	52.5	58.0
72.0	74.0	72.0	63.0	58.0	59.5	57.0	52.5	58.0
32.0	53.5	43.5	22.0	58.0	59.5	25.0	52.5	58.0
21.5	48.5	15.0	26.0	24.5	59.5	25.0	7.5	58.0
17.5	45.0	15.0	19.5	30.0	59.5	10.0	52.5	58.0
12.0	29.5	10.0	15.0	24.5	33.0	10.0	16.0	20.5
3.0	1.0	1.0	4.5	1.0	23.5	3.0	1.0	1.0
10.0	37.5	22.0	11.5	58.0	59.5	16.0	52.5	58.0
14.0	32.5	7.5	22.0	20.0	29.0	16.0	7.5	8.0
72.0	74.0	72.0	63.0	58.0	59.5	57.0	52.5	58.0
72.0	74.0	72.0	63.0	58.0	59.5	57.0	52.5	58.0
72.0	74.0	72.0	63.0	58.0	59.5	57.0	52.5	58.0
19.0	28.0	7.5	11.5	12.5	59.5	6.0	3.0	58.0

TABLE 6—continued

	Years in system	Years of war	Years war vs. major	No. of wars	No. of wars vs. major	Battle deaths	Years allied
Tuscany	47.5	69.0	63.0	69.0	63.0	69.0	63.0
Wurtemberg	39.0	35.5	30.0	25.5	16.5	38.5	7.0
Yugoslavia (Serbia)	34.5	22.0	18.5	13.5	16.5	11.0	14.0
Egypt	81.5	69.0	63.0	69.0	63.0	69.0	54.5
Iran (Persia)	27.0	39.0	32.0	44.0	33.0	36.0	31.5
Iraq	78.0	69.0	63.0	69.0	63.0	69.0	39.5
Saudi Arabia	75.5	69.0	63.0	69.0	63.0	69.0	61.5
Yemen	79.5	69.0	63.0	69.0	63.0	69.0	61.5
Ethiopia	50.0	32.5	25.5	25.5	16.5	23.0	74.0
Liberia	59.5	69.0	63.0	69.0	63.0	69.0	74.0
Morocco	33.0	31.0	63.0	25.5	63.0	25.0	74.0
South Africa	59.5	17.5	11.5	44.0	33.0	30.0	74.0
Afghanistan	59.5	69.0	63.0	69.0	63.0	69.0	22.5
Australia	59.5	15.5	9.5	44.0	33.0	22.0	74.0
China	29.5	9.0	5.0	10.5	5.0	3.0	36.5
Japan	29.5	1.0	6.5	6.0	8.0	5.0	16.5
Korea	77.0	69.0	63.0	69.0	63.0	69.0	74.0
Mongolia	66.5	69.0	63.0	69.0	63.0	69.0	54.5
Nepal	59.5	69.0	63.0	69.0	63.0	69.0	74.0
New Zealand	59.5	15.5	9.5	44.0	33.0	28.0	74.0
Thailand (Siam)	36.5	25.0	20.0	44.0	33.0	52.5	74.0
Argentina	22.5	35.5	63.0	44.0	63.0	41.5	44.5
Bolivia	24.0	7.5	63.0	25.5	63.0	16.0	28.5
Brazil	15.0	30.0	27.0	25.5	33.0	45.0	44.5
Canada	59.5	17.5	11.5	44.0	33.0	21.0	74.0
Chile	21.0	20.0	63.0	25.5	63.0	34.0	44.5
Colombia	16.5	50.0	63.0	44.0	63.0	50.0	39.5
Costa Rica	59.5	69.0	63.0	63.0	69.0	69.0	54.5
Cuba	79.5	69.0	63.0	69.0	63.0	69.0	54.5
Dominican Republic	36.5	69.0	63.0	69.0	63.0	69.0	54.5
Ecuador	26.0	50.0	63.0	44.0	63.0	43.0	39.5
Guatemala	25.0	43.5	63.0	25.5	63.0	37.0	54.5
Haiti	28.0	69.0	63.0	69.0	63.0	69.0	54.5
Honduras	45.0	41.0	63.0	25.5	63.0	45.0	54.5
Mexico	16.5	12.0	15.0	16.0	16.5	24.0	44.5
Nicaragua	47.5	43.5	63.0	44.0	63.0	49.0	54.5
Panama	59.5	69.0	63.0	69.0	63.0	69.0	54.5
Paraguay	44.0	11.0	63.0	44.0	63.0	19.0	44.5
Peru	20.0	21.0	63.0	25.5	63.0	27.0	25.5
Salvador	31.0	39.0	63.0	16.0	63.0	41.5	54.5
Uruguay	34.5	69.0	63.0	69.0	63.9	69.0	44.5
United States	5.5	10.0	14.0	10.5	16.5	12.0	48.0
Venezuela	22.5	69.0	63.0	69.0	63.0	69.0	54.5

Years allied with major	No. of alliances	No. of alliances with major	No. of defense pacts	No. of neutrality pacts	No. of ententes	With major		
						No. of defense pacts	No. of neutrality pacts	No. of ententes
72.0	56.5	72.0	26.0	58.0	59.5	57.0	52.5	58.0
7.0	32.5	15.0	7.0	58.0	59.5	10.0	52.5	58.0
15.0	29.5	11.5	16.0	16.0	59.5	25.0	3.0	58.0
47.5	61.0	43.5	35.5	58.0	59.5	25.0	52.5	58.0
28.0	48.5	43.5	63.0	16.0	59.5	57.0	16.0	58.0
34.5	48.5	43.5	35.5	20.0	59.5	25.0	52.5	58.0
72.0	61.0	72.0	35.5	58.0	59.5	57.0	52.5	58.0
72.0	61.0	72.0	35.5	58.0	59.5	57.0	52.5	58.0
72.0	74.0	72.0	63.0	58.0	59.5	57.0	52.5	58.0
72.0	74.0	72.0	63.0	58.0	59.5	57.0	52.5	58.0
72.0	74.0	72.0	63.0	58.0	59.5	57.0	52.5	58.0
72.0	74.0	72.0	63.0	58.0	59.5	57.0	52.5	58.0
25.0	48.5	43.5	35.5	20.0	59.5	57.0	16.0	58.0
72.0	74.0	72.0	63.0	58.0	59.5	57.0	52.5	58.0
31.0	56.5	22.0	35.5	30.0	59.5	25.0	16.0	58.0
16.0	41.5	9.0	35.5	58.0	27.5	25.0	52.5	6.0
72.0	74.0	72.0	63.0	58.0	59.5	57.0	52.5	58.0
47.5	61.0	43.5	35.5	58.0	59.5	25.0	52.5	58.0
72.0	74.0	72.0	63.0	58.0	59.5	57.0	52.5	58.0
72.0	74.0	72.0	63.0	58.0	59.5	57.0	52.5	58.0
72.0	74.0	72.0	63.0	58.0	59.5	57.0	52.5	58.0
47.5	14.0	43.5	63.0	7.0	18.0	57.0	52.5	20.5
47.5	14.0	43.5	35.5	58.0	7.5	57.0	52.5	20.5
47.5	14.0	43.5	63.0	7.0	18.0	57.0	52.5	20.5
72.0	74.0	72.0	63.0	58.0	59.5	57.0	52.5	58.0
47.5	14.0	43.5	63.0	7.0	18.0	57.0	52.5	20.5
47.5	8.0	43.5	35.5	7.0	18.0	57.0	52.5	20.5
47.5	23.0	43.5	63.0	58.0	7.5	57.0	52.5	20.5
47.5	23.0	43.5	63.0	58.0	7.5	57.0	52.5	20.5
47.5	23.0	43.5	63.0	58.0	7.5	57.0	52.5	20.5
47.5	8.0	43.5	26.0	58.0	7.5	57.0	52.5	20.5
47.5	23.0	43.5	63.0	58.0	7.5	57.0	52.5	20.5
47.5	23.0	43.5	63.0	58.0	7.5	57.0	52.5	20.5
47.5	23.0	43.5	63.0	58.0	7.5	57.0	52.5	20.5
47.5	14.0	43.5	63.0	7.0	18.0	57.0	52.5	20.5
47.5	23.0	43.5	63.0	58.0	7.5	57.0	52.5	20.5
47.5	14.0	43.5	63.0	7.0	18.0	57.0	52.5	20.5
47.5	14.0	43.5	63.0	7.0	18.0	57.0	52.5	20.5
47.5	8.0	43.5	26.0	58.0	7.5	57.0	52.5	20.5
47.5	23.0	43.5	63.0	58.0	7.5	57.0	52.5	20.5
47.5	14.0	43.5	63.0	7.0	18.0	57.0	52.5	20.5
59.0	14.0	43.5	63.0	58.0	1.0	57.0	52.5	20.5
47.5	23.0	43.5	63.0	58.0	7.5	57.0	52.5	20.5

TABLE 7
*Ranks of Nations on War and Alliance
Variables, Central System Only*

	Years in system	Years of war	Years war vs. major	No. of wars	No. of wars vs. major	Battle deaths	Years allied
Albania	38.0	51.0	50.0	51.0	50.0	51.0	21.0
Austria (-Hungary)	13.0	17.0	15.0	7.0	8.0	6.0	2.0
Belgium	15.0	21.0	17.5	16.5	14.0	14.0	17.0
Bulgaria	21.0	11.0	13.0	10.5	14.0	17.0	23.5
Czechoslovakia	59.5	51.0	50.0	51.0	50.0	51.0	13.0
Denmark	11.0	26.5	24.5	16.5	14.0	27.0	53.0
England	5.0	4.0	1.0	10.5	8.0	7.0	4.0
Estonia	59.5	51.0	50.0	51.0	50.0	51.0	17.0
Finland	23.0	24.0	21.0	16.5	14.0	15.0	26.5
France	11.0	8.0	8.0	4.5	2.5	4.0	5.0
Germany (Prussia)	5.0	5.5	3.0	4.5	5.0	2.0	1.0
Greece	14.0	12.0	23.0	7.0	14.0	18.0	19.0
Holland	11.0	32.5	30.5	26.0	25.0	28.0	61.0
Hungary	54.0	23.0	20.0	26.0	25.0	20.0	23.5
Iceland	68.0	51.0	50.0	51.0	50.0	51.0	61.0
Ireland	54.0	51.0	50.0	51.0	50.0	51.0	61.0
Italy (Sardinia)	5.0	5.5	4.0	1.5	1.0	8.0	7.0
Latvia	59.5	51.0	50.0	51.0	50.0	51.0	17.0
Lithuania	59.5	51.0	50.0	51.0	50.0	51.0	21.0
Luxembourg	59.5	51.0	50.0	51.0	50.0	51.0	61.0
Norway	22.0	31.0	29.0	26.0	25.0	29.0	61.0
Poland	59.5	32.5	30.5	26.0	25.0	13.0	14.5
Portugal	5.0	25.0	22.0	26.0	25.0	25.0	12.0
Rumania	16.0	20.0	16.0	13.5	14.0	10.0	6.0
Russia	5.0	2.5	2.0	3.0	5.0	1.0	3.0
Spain	5.0	29.0	27.0	26.0	25.0	30.0	9.0
Sweden	5.0	51.0	50.0	51.0	50.0	51.0	61.0
Switzerland	5.0	51.0	50.0	51.0	50.0	51.0	61.0
Turkey	5.0	2.5	6.5	1.5	2.5	9.0	10.5
Yugoslavia (Serbia)	17.0	19.0	17.5	10.5	14.0	11.0	8.0
Egypt	67.0	51.0	50.0	51.0	50.0	51.0	43.0
Iran (Persia)	38.0	51.0	50.0	51.0	50.0	51.0	21.0
Iraq	64.0	51.0	50.0	51.0	50.0	51.0	26.5
Saudi Arabia	63.0	51.0	50.0	51.0	50.0	51.0	51.5
Yemen	65.5	51.0	50.0	51.0	50.0	51.0	51.5
Ethiopia	56.0	26.5	24.5	16.5	14.0	23.0	61.0
Liberia	38.0	51.0	50.0	51.0	50.0	51.0	61.0
South Africa	38.0	15.5	11.5	26.0	25.0	26.0	61.0
Afghanistan	38.0	51.0	50.0	51.0	50.0	51.0	14.5
Australia	38.0	13.5	9.5	26.0	25.0	22.0	61.0

| Years allied with major | No. of alliances | No. of alliances with major | No. of defense pacts | No. of neutrality pacts | No. of ententes | With major | | |
						No. of defense pacts	No. of neutrality pacts	No. of ententes
17.0	49.0	34.0	21.5	50.0	51.5	16.0	45.0	50.0
2.0	20.0	5.5	5.0	15.0	26.5	4.5	7.5	7.0
15.0	49.0	34.0	21.5	50.0	51.5	16.0	45.0	50.0
59.5	34.5	59.0	14.5	15.0	51.5	44.5	45.0	50.0
13.5	34.5	11.5	11.5	29.0	32.0	10.5	16.0	20.0
50.0	49.0	34.0	48.0	29.0	51.5	44.5	16.0	50.0
4.0	2.5	3.0	1.0	50.0	17.5	1.5	45.0	2.0
24.5	39.5	16.5	21.5	23.5	32.0	44.5	7.5	50.0
24.5	31.0	34.0	48.0	2.0	51.5	44.5	16.0	50.0
5.0	2.5	4.0	2.5	15.0	22.5	4.5	16.0	3.0
1.0	4.0	2.0	4.0	11.5	25.0	1.5	3.0	4.0
21.0	32.5	34.0	10.0	23.5	51.5	44.5	16.0	50.0
59.5	60.5	59.0	48.0	50.0	51.5	44.5	45.0	50.0
19.5	43.5	16.5	18.0	23.5	32.0	44.5	16.0	20.0
59.5	60.5	59.0	48.0	50.0	51.5	44.5	45.0	50.0
59.5	60.5	59.0	48.0	50.0	51.5	44.5	45.0	50.0
7.0	5.0	5.5	9.0	6.5	24.0	7.0	7.5	5.0
24.5	39.5	16.5	21.5	23.5	32.0	44.5	7.5	50.0
17.0	43.5	34.0	48.0	29.0	29.0	44.5	16.0	50.0
59.5	60.5	59.0	48.0	50.0	51.5	44.5	45.0	50.0
59.5	60.5	59.0	48.0	50.0	51.5	44.5	45.0	50.0
13.5	39.5	13.5	14.5	23.5	51.5	16.0	7.5	50.0
11.0	36.0	13.5	11.5	29.0	51.5	8.5	45.0	50.0
6.0	28.5	10.0	7.0	23.5	32.0	8.5	16.0	20.0
3.0	1.0	1.0	2.5	1.0	22.5	3.0	1.0	1.0
8.0	30.0	7.5	13.0	19.0	28.0	10.5	7.5	8.0
59.5	60.5	59.0	48.0	50.0	51.5	44.5	45.0	50.0
59.5	60.5	59.0	48.0	50.0	51.5	44.5	45.0	50.0
12.0	27.0	7.5	6.0	11.5	51.5	6.0	3.0	50.0
9.0	28.5	11.5	8.0	15.0	51.5	16.0	3.0	50.0
37.5	49.0	34.0	21.5	50.0	51.5	16.0	45.0	50.0
19.5	39.5	34.0	48.0	15.0	51.5	44.5	16.0	50.0
24.5	39.5	34.0	21.5	19.0	51.5	16.0	45.0	50.0
59.5	49.0	59.0	21.5	50.0	51.5	44.5	45.0	50.0
59.5	49.0	59.0	21.5	50.0	51.5	44.5	45.0	50.0
59.5	60.5	59.0	48.0	50.0	51.5	44.5	45.0	50.0
59.5	60.5	59.0	48.0	50.0	51.5	44.5	45.0	50.0
59.5	60.5	59.0	48.0	50.0	51.5	44.5	45.0	50.0
17.0	39.5	34.0	21.5	19.0	51.5	44.5	16.0	50.0
59.5	60.5	59.0	48.0	50.0	51.5	44.5	45.0	50.0

TABLE 7—continued

	Years in system	Years of war	Years war vs. major	No. of wars	No. of wars vs. major	Battle deaths	Years allied
China	18.5	7.0	5.0	10.5	5.0	3.0	25.0
Japan	18.5	1.0	6.5	7.0	8.0	5.0	10.5
Mongolia	54.0	51.0	50.0	51.0	50.0	51.0	43.0
Nepal	38.0	51.0	50.0	51.0	50.0	51.0	61.0
New Zealand	38.0	13.5	9.5	26.0	25.0	24.0	61.0
Thailand (Siam)	38.0	22.0	19.0	26.0	25.0	32.0	61.0
Argentina	38.0	51.0	50.0	51.0	50.0	51.0	30.5
Bolivia	38.0	9.5	50.0	26.0	50.0	16.0	43.0
Brazil	38.0	28.0	26.0	26.0	25.0	32.0	30.5
Canada	38.0	15.5	11.5	26.0	25.0	21.0	61.0
Chile	38.0	51.0	50.0	51.0	50.0	51.0	30.5
Colombia	38.0	51.0	50.0	51.0	50.0	51.0	34.5
Costa Rica	38.0	51.0	50.0	51.0	50.0	51.0	43.0
Cuba	65.5	51.0	50.0	51.0	50.0	51.0	43.0
Dominican Republic	38.0	51.0	50.0	51.0	50.0	51.0	43.0
Ecuador	38.0	51.0	50.0	51.0	50.0	51.0	43.0
Guatemala	38.0	51.0	50.0	51.0	50.0	51.0	43.0
Haiti	38.0	51.0	50.0	51.0	50.0	51.0	43.0
Honduras	38.0	51.0	50.0	51.0	50.0	51.0	43.0
Mexico	38.0	30.0	28.0	26.0	25.0	32.0	30.5
Nicaragua	38.0	51.0	50.0	51.0	50.0	51.0	43.0
Panama	38.0	51.0	50.0	51.0	50.0	51.0	43.0
Paraguay	38.0	9.5	50.0	26.0	50.0	19.0	30.5
Peru	38.0	51.0	50.0	51.0	50.0	51.0	43.0
Salvador	38.0	51.0	50.0	51.0	50.0	51.0	43.0
Uruguay	38.0	51.0	50.0	51.0	50.0	51.0	30.5
United States	20.0	18.0	14.0	13.5	14.0	12.0	34.5
Venezuela	38.0	51.0	50.0	51.0	50.0	51.0	43.0

the latter form (by controlling for duration of membership) we find a less compelling picture. This finding, however, need not be thought of as seriously disabling, since it is largely accounted for by those nations whose duration of membership in the system is relatively brief. Thus, if we were to look only at the major powers—whose tenure is generally much longer—we would find that controlling for duration does not appreciably reduce the strength of the relationship. Moreover, when we shift from the entire period to a frequency rate analysis, we make two implicit assumptions. One is that all of the years in our 131 year span are diplomatically and militarily

equivalent. As our earlier work (Singer and Small, 1966b; Singer, Small and Kraft, 1965) has demonstrated, this is clearly an incorrect assumption. That is, if we divide the total span into four or five periods, we find certain ones characterized by a low level of alliance involvement and moderately high war activity (1815–1870), and others by high alliance levels and very low war levels (1871–1900). Thus the second implied assumption would be equally incorrect: that the specific period during which a given nation was in the system does not matter. Quite obviously, it does. Nations which entered the system in different periods will exercise differential effects

Years allied with major	No. of alliances	No. of alliances with major	No. of defense pacts	No. of neutrality pacts	No. of ententes	With major No. of defense pacts	With major No. of neutrality pacts	No. of ententes
22.0	45.0	16.5	21.5	29.0	51.5	16.0	16.0	50.0
10.0	32.5	9.0	21.5	50.5	26.5	16.0	45.0	6.0
37.5	49.0	34.0	21.5	50.0	51.5	16.0	45.0	50.0
59.5	60.5	59.0	48.0	50.0	51.5	44.5	45.0	50.0
59.5	60.5	59.0	48.0	50.0	51.5	44.5	45.0	50.0
59.5	60.5	59.0	48.0	50.0	51.5	44.5	45.0	50.0
37.5	9.5	34.0	48.0	6.5	17.5	44.5	45.0	20.0
37.5	20.0	34.0	48.0	50.0	7.5	44.5	45.0	20.0
37.5	9.5	34.0	48.0	6.5	17.5	44.5	45.0	20.0
59.5	60.5	59.0	48.0	50.0	51.5	44.5	45.0	50.0
37.5	9.5	34.0	48.0	6.5	17.5	44.5	45.0	20.0
37.5	9.5	34.0	48.0	6.5	17.5	44.5	45.0	20.0
37.5	20.0	34.0	48.0	50.0	7.5	44.5	45.0	20.0
37.5	20.0	34.0	48.0	50.0	7.5	44.5	45.0	20.0
37.5	20.0	34.0	48.0	50.0	7.5	44.5	45.0	20.0
37.5	20.0	34.0	48.0	50.0	7.5	44.5	45.0	20.0
37.5	20.0	34.0	48.0	50.0	7.5	44.5	45.0	20.0
37.5	20.0	34.0	48.0	50.0	7.5	44.5	45.0	20.0
37.5	20.0	34.0	48.0	50.0	7.5	44.5	45.0	20.0
37.5	9.5	34.0	48.0	6.5	17.5	44.5	45.0	20.0
37.5	20.0	34.0	48.0	50.0	7.5	44.5	45.0	22.0
37.5	9.5	34.0	48.0	6.5	17.5	44.5	45.0	20.0
37.5	60.5	59.0	48.0	50.0	51.5	44.5	45.0	50.0
37.5	20.0	34.0	48.0	50.0	7.5	44.5	45.0	20.0
37.5	20.0	34.0	48.0	50.0	7.5	44.5	45.0	20.0
37.5	9.5	34.0	48.0	6.5	17.5	44.5	45.0	20.0
49.0	9.5	34.0	48.0	50.0	1.0	44.5	45.0	20.0
37.5	20.0	34.0	48.0	50.0	7.5	44.5	45.0	20.0

on our correlations when we control for duration and make the all-years-are-the-same assumption.

These correlational differences may be interpreted in one of three ways. First, we can assume that if the late-comers *had* been in the system from 1815 on, their alliance and war involvement patterns would have been essentially similar to those which they *did* experience once they entered on the scene. Second, we can assume that they would have been essentially similar to the experiences of those other minor nations (whom the late-comers most frequently resemble) who were already on the scene in the early nineteenth century. Third, we can assume that they

would have experienced an alliance and war involvement pattern typical of the *modal* nation during the period.

Each assumption is plausible on the surface, but each requires further analysis. Thus, the first assumption would have such minor members as Serbia, Thailand, or Korea (which qualified in 1878, 1887, and 1888 respectively) showing as much diplomatic and military activity in the early nineteenth century as they did from the 1880's on. Given the fact that the system revealed markedly different (i.e. considerably less) activity in that earlier period than in later ones, and that the minor nations were seldom active

TABLE 8
Correlations between War and Alliance Indicators
for Total System Members (N = 83)

	Years of war	Years war vs. majors	No. of wars	No. wars vs. majors	Battle deaths
No. of alliances	35	11	43	17	33
No. alliances with major	35	37	46	46	43
No. of defense pacts	25	34	36	44	31
No. defense pacts with major	29	45	39	54	36
No. of neutrality pacts	33	26	32	27	35
No. neutrality pacts with major	28	38	35	42	40
No. of ententes	15	−17	17	−19	09
No. ententes with major	35	10	37	08	32
Years allied	36	36	46	47	42
Years allied with major	29	35	40	45	36

TABLE 9
Correlations between War and Alliance Indicators
for Central System Members (N = 68)

	Years of war	Years war vs. majors	No. of wars	No. wars vs. majors	Battle deaths
No. of alliances	10	11	16	16	15
No. alliances with major	32	36	40	42	43
No. of defense pacts	44	47	51	52	51
No. defense pacts with major	47	52	53	55	55
No. of neutrality pacts	21	26	32	34	28
No. neutrality pacts with major	35	39	46	47	45
No. of ententes	−17	−19	−17	−18	−15
No. ententes with major	15	16	17	16	18
Years allied	39	38	46	45	48
Years allied with major	33	33	40	40	43

TABLE 10
Number of Times Allied Before War
as Correlate of War Involvement

		Years of war	Years war vs. majors	No. of wars	No. wars vs. majors	Battle deaths
Total	No. of times allied before war	51	58	62	68	59
	No. times allied with major	39	53	52	63	48
Central	No. of times allied before war	64	66	72	72	72
	No. times allied with major	56	60	61	64	66

TABLE 11

*Duration of Membership as a Correlate of
Alliance Commitment and War Involvement*

		Years of war	Years war vs. majors	No. of wars	No. wars vs. majors	Battle deaths	No. of alliances	No. alliances with majors	No. defense pacts with alliances	No. defense pacts with majors	No. neutrality pacts with alliances	No. neutrality pacts with majors	No. ententes with alliances	No. ententes with majors	Years allied with alliances	Years allied with majors
Total	Years in system	60	44	67	47	58	50	35	18	22	30	19	35	48	31	27
Central	Years in system	60	62	66	66	62	27	35	34	42	25	28	02	28	36	35

TABLE 12

*Correlations between War and Alliance Indicators,
Modified for Duration of Membership, Total
System (N = 83)*

	Years of war	Years war vs. majors	No. of wars	No. wars vs. majors	Battle deaths
No. of alliances	−02	−17	−08	−04	02
No. alliances with major	05	14	24	28	18
No. of defense pacts	−03	17	21	38	14
No. defense pacts with major	28	25	25	45	21
No. of neutrality pacts	18	15	19	11	24
No. neutrality pacts with major	15	25	27	19	28
No. of ententes	−11	−41	−18	−47	−16
No. ententes with major	19	−05	25	−01	24
Years allied	−01	12	17	30	12
Years allied with major	02	13	19	30	14

TABLE 13

*Correlations between War and Alliance Indicators,
Modified for Duration of Membership, Central
System (N = 68)*

	Years of war	Years war vs. majors	No. of wars	No. wars vs. majors	Battle deaths
No. of alliances	−23	−24	−12	−20	−18
No. alliances with major	00	−04	14	07	21
No. of defense pacts	16	22	29	21	37
No. defense pacts with major	21	27	29	26	43
No. of neutrality pacts	04	10	20	18	13
No. neutrality pacts with major	14	19	26	23	30
No. of ententes	−31	−37	−31	−35	−36
No. ententes with major	03	02	08	02	12
Years allied	04	04	17	08	22
Years allied with major	04	05	15	07	24

TABLE 14
Number of Times Allied Before War as Correlate
of War Involvement, Modified for Duration of
Membership

		Years of war	Years war vs. majors	No. of wars	No. wars vs. majors	Battle deaths
Total	No. of times allied before war	45	53	65	58	58
	No. times allied with major	31	44	54	53	46
Central	No. of times allied before war	50	55	70	59	72
	No. times allied with major	41	45	58	52	64

in the earlier period, this assumption cannot stand. The second would have such late-comers as Finland, Poland, or Paraguay experiencing the same pre-1890's pattern as Denmark or Portugal, which were in the system almost from the beginning; a glance at Table 4 shows this to be an erroneous assumption.

The third assumption, on the other hand, seems to contain no empirical or logical pitfalls; the late-comers did indeed range from major to minor states, high to low activity levels, and relatively mixed alliance vs. war correlation patterns. We can, therefore, accept the third assumption as the most reasonable, and treat the correlations which did control for duration of membership as if the late-comers' pattern would have been close to that of the modal system member of the earlier period. When we do this we must recall one of the key findings in our earlier study (Singer and Small, 1967), concerning the striking disparity between the nineteenth and twentieth centuries: only the latter showed, for the system as a whole, the strong positive relationship between alliance aggregation and the onset of war; in the earlier of our two periods, the correlations were strongly *negative*. What holds for the *system* must also hold in general for the *nations*, since *they* generate the behavior from which our systemic properties are inferred. Therefore, when we introduce hypothetical (i.e. not yet existent) nations into the earlier of our periods, via the involvement-per-year computation, it is statistically inevitable that

the correlations will be pushed in the negative direction. As a consequence, the strong positive correlations will become weaker, and the weak ones will cross over the zero threshold and become moderately negative in direction. This seems to be what occurred when we controlled for duration of membership.

References

Deutsch, Karl W. and J. David Singer. "Multipolar Power Systems and International Stability," *World Politics*, XVI (April 1964), 390–406.

Kissinger, Henry. *A World Restored: Metternich, Castlereagh and the Problems of Peace, 1812–1822.* London: Weidenfeld and Nicolson, 1957.

Richardson, Lewis F. *Statistics of Deadly Quarrels*, edited by Quincy Wright and C. C. Lienau. Pittsburgh: Boxwood Press, 1960.

Singer, J. David and Melvin Small. "Alliance Aggregation and the Onset of War, 1815–1945," in J. David Singer (ed.), *Quantitative International Politics: Insights and Evidence.* New York: Free Press-Macmillan, 1968. [Vol. VI of the *International Yearbook of Political Behavior Research*, Heinz Eulau, General Editor.]

———. "The Composition and Status Ordering of the International System, 1815–1940," *World Politics*, XVIII (January 1966a) 236–82.

———. "Formal Alliances 1815–1939: A Quantitative Description," *Journal of Peace Research*. I (1966b) 1–32.

———. *International War, 1815–1965: A Statistical Handbook* (forthcoming).

Wright, Quincy. *A Study of War.* Chicago: Univ. Chicago Press, 1942 (2 vols.) and 1965 (1 vol.).

F. The Use of Content Analysis

46. The Belief System and National Images: A Case Study*

Ole R. Holsti, formerly associated with the Stanford University Studies in International Conflict and Integration, is presently Associate Professor of Political Science at the University of British Columbia. He has written a number of works either assessing or employing content analysis methods in the study of international politics. Most notable in this regard are his many contributions to the conflict studies of the Stanford group (see, for example, Selection 55). In this article Professor Holsti applies the content analysis technique to the pronouncements of a single foreign policy official. In addition to the interesting insights into the dynamics of international phenomena that are thus provided, this article has the virtue of demonstrating that content analysis techniques can be put to fruitful use by the individual student whose resources may consist only of his own time and the documents available in a nearby library. Much time and effort can be saved by those whose resources allow for computerized content analyses (see Selection 54), but here it can readily be seen that a wide range of problems can be investigated through content analysis procedures by the student who is willing to allocate his time to their use. [*Reprinted from* The Journal of Conflict Resolution, *VI (1962), 244–52, by permission of the author and the publisher. Copyright 1962 by the University of Michigan.*]

I. The Belief System and National Images

Even a cursory survey of the relevant literature reveals that in recent years—particularly in the decade and a half since the end of World War II—students of international politics have taken a growing interest in psycho-attitudinal approaches to the study of the international system. It has been proposed, in fact, that psychology belongs at the "core" of the discipline (Wright, 1955, p. 506). Two related problems within this area have become particular foci of attention.

1. A number of studies have shown that the relationship between "belief system," perceptions, and decision-making is a vital one (Rokeach, 1960; Smith *et al.*, 1956; Snyder *et al.*, 1954).[1] A

* The author wishes to express his deep gratitude to Professors Robert C. North, James T. Watkins, IV, and Thomas A. Bailey for their advice and encouragement on the larger study from which this paper is derived; to Charles A. McClelland and Richard Fagen for their useful comments on this paper; and to Mrs. Helen Grace for preparing the figures.

[1] Although in the literature the terms "belief system" (Rokeach, 1960, pp. 18–9), "image" (Boulding, 1956, pp. 5–6) and "frame of reference" (Snyder *et al.*, 1954, p. 101) have frequently been used synonymously, in this paper "belief system" will denote the complete world view, whereas "image" will denote some subpart of the belief system.

decision-maker acts upon his "image" of the situation rather than upon "objective" reality, and it has been demonstrated that the belief system—its structure as well as its content—plays an integral role in the cognitive process (Boulding, 1956; Festinger, 1957; Ray, 1961).

2. Within the broader scope of the belief-system-perception-decision-making relationship there has been a heightened concern for the problem of stereotyped national images as a significant factor in the dynamics of the international system (Bauer, 1961; Boulding, 1959; Osgood, 1959b; Wheeler, 1960; Wright, 1957). Kenneth Boulding, for example, has written that, "The national image, however, is the last great stronghold of unsophistication. . . . Nations are divided into 'good' and 'bad'—the enemy is all bad, one's own nation is of spotless virtue" (Boulding, 1959, p. 130).

The relationship of national images to international conflict is clear: decision-makers act upon their definition of the situation and their images of states—others as well as their own. These images are in turn dependent upon the decision-makers' belief system, and these may or may not be accurate representations of "reality." Thus it has been suggested that international conflict frequently is not between states, but rather between distorted images of states (Wright, 1957, p. 266).

The purpose of this paper is to report the findings of a case study dealing with the relationship between the belief system, national images, and decision-making. The study centers upon one decision-maker of unquestioned influence, John Foster Dulles, and the connection between his belief system and his perceptions of the Soviet Union.

The analytical framework for this study can be stated briefly. The belief system, composed of a number of "images" of the past, present, and future, includes "all the accumulated, organized knowledge that the organism has about itself and the world" (Miller et al., 1960, p. 16). It may be thought of as the set of lenses through which information concerning the physical and social environment is received. It orients the individual to his environment, defining it for him and identifying for him its salient characteristics. National images may be denoted as subpart of the belief system. Like the belief system itself, these are "models" which order for the observ-

er what will otherwise be an unmanageable amount of information (Bauer, 1961).

In addition to organizing perceptions into a meaningful guide for behavior, the belief system has the function of the establishment of goals and the ordering of preferences. Thus it actually has a dual connection with decision-making. The direct relationship is found in that aspect of the belief system which tells us "what ought to be," acting as a direct guide in the establishment of goals. The indirect link—the role that the belief system plays in the process of "scanning, selecting, filtering, linking, reordering, organizing, and reporting," (McClelland, 1962, p. 456)—arises from the tendency of the individual to assimilate new perceptions to familiar ones, and to distort what is seen in such a way as to minimize the clash with previous expectations (Bronfenbrenner, 1961; Ray, 1961; Rokeach, 1960). Like the blind men, each describing the elephant on the basis of the part he touches, different individuals may describe the same object or situation in terms of what they have been conditioned to see. This may be particularly true in a crisis situation: "Controversial issues tend to be polarized not only because commitments have been made but also because certain perceptions are actively excluded from consciousness if they do not fit the chosen world image" (Rapoport, 1960, p. 258). These relationships are presented in Figure 1.

The belief system and its component images are, however, dynamic rather than static; they are in continual interaction with new information. The impact of this information depends upon the degree to which the structure of the belief system is "open" or "closed." According to Rokeach,

At the closed extreme, it is new information that must be tampered with—by narrowing it out, altering it, or constraining it within isolated bounds. In this way, the belief-disbelief system is left intact. At the open extreme, it is the other way around: New information is assimilated as is . . . thereby producing "genuine" (as contrasted with "party-line") changes in the whole belief-disbelief system [Rokeach, 1960, p. 50].

Thus while national images perform an important function in the cognitive process, they may also become dysfunctional. Unless they coincide in some way with commonly-perceived reality, decisions based on these images are not likely to fulfill expectations. Erroneous images may also prove to

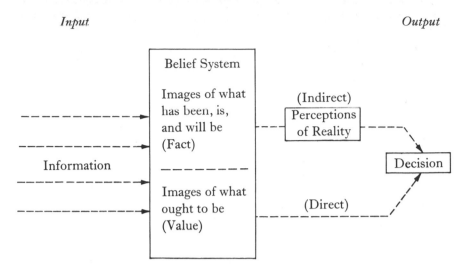

Input   *Output*

Figure 1. The dual relationship between belief system and decision-making

have a distorting effect by encouraging the reinter-
pretation of information that does not fit the image;
this is most probable with rigid "models" such as
"totalitarian communism" or "monopolistic capitalism" which exclude the very types of information
that might lead to a modification of the models
themselves (Bauer, 1961; Wheeler, 1960).

II. John Foster Dulles and the Soviet Union

The selection of John Foster Dulles as the central
figure for my study fulfilled a number of historical
and research requirements for the testing of hypotheses concerning the relationship between the belief
system and perceptions of other nations. He was
acknowledged as a decision-maker of first-rate
importance, and he held office during a period of
dramatic changes in Soviet elites, capabilities, and
tactics. In addition, he left voluminous public
pronouncements and writings on both the Soviet
Union and on the theoretical aspects of international
politics, thus facilitating a reconstruction of salient
aspects of both his belief system and his perceptions
of the Soviet Union.

The sources used in this study included all of
Dulles' publicly available statements concerning the
Soviet Union during the 1953–1959 period, derived
from a content analysis of 434 documents, including

Congressional testimony, press conferences, and
addresses.[2] These statements were transcribed,
masked, and quantified according to the "evaluative
assertion analysis" technique devised by Charles E.
Osgood and his associates (Osgood *et al.*, 1956;
Osgood, 1959a).[3]

All of Dulles' statements concerning the Soviet
Union were translated into 3,584 "evaluative assertions" and placed into one of four categories:

1. *Soviet Policy:* assessed on a friendship-hostility
    continuum (2,246 statements).
2. *Soviet Capabilities:* assessed on a strength-
    weakness continuum (732 statements).
3. *Soviet Success:* assessed on a satisfaction-
    frustration continuum (290 statements).

[2] The author has corresponded with a number of
Dulles' close associates. They almost unanimously stated
that Dulles' public assessments of various characteristics
of the Soviet regime were identical with his private beliefs.

[3] The method involves the translation of all statements
into one of two common sentence structures: 1. Attitude
Object$_1$ (AO$_1$)/Verbal Connector (c)/Common-meaning
Evaluator (cm); 2. Attitude Object$_1$ (AO$_1$)/Verbal Connector (c)/Attitude Object$_2$ (AO$_2$). For example, the sentence, "The Soviet Union is hostile, opposing American
national interests," is translated to read: 1. The Soviet
Union/is/hostile (form 1); 2. The Soviet Union/opposes/
American national interests (form 2).

The value of AO$_1$'s are computed on the basis of values
assigned to the cm's, c's and AO$_2$'s. These range from +3
to −3, depending upon their direction and intensity.

4. *General Evaluation of the Soviet Union:* assessed on a good-bad continuum (316 statements).

The resulting figures, when aggregated into time periods, provide a record of the way in which Dulles' perceptions of each dimension varied. From this record inferences can be made of the perceived relationship between the dimensions.

Dulles' image of the Soviet Union was built on the trinity of atheism, totalitarianism, and communism, capped by a deep belief that no enduring social order could be erected upon such foundations.[4] He had written in 1950, for example, that: "Soviet Communism starts with an atheistic, Godless premise. Everything else flows from that premise" (Dulles, 1950, p. 8). Upon these characteristics—the negation of values at or near the core of his belief system—he superimposed three dichotomies.

1. The "good" Russian people versus the "bad" Soviet leaders.[5]
2. The "good" Russian national interest versus "bad" international communism.[6]
3. The "good" Russian state versus the "bad" Communist Party.[7]

That image of the Soviet Union—which has been called the "inherent bad faith of the Communists" model (Kissinger, 1962, p. 201)—was sustained in large part by his heavy reliance on the

[4] "Dulles was an American Puritan very difficult for me [Albrecht von Kessel], a Lutheran, to understand. This partly led him to the conviction that Bolshevism was a product of the devil and that God would wear out the Bolsheviks in the long run, whereas many consider it a perversion of Russian qualities" (Drummond and Colbentz, 1960, p. 15).

[5] "There is no dispute at all between the United States and the peoples of Russia. If only the Government of Russia was interested in looking out for the welfare of Russia, the people of Russia, we would have a state of non-tension right away" (Dulles, 1958a, p. 734).

[6] "The time may come—I believe it will come—when Russians of stature will patriotically put first their national security and the welfare of their people. They will be unwilling to have that security and that welfare subordinated to the worldwide ambitions of international communism" (Dulles, 1955b, p. 329).

[7] "The ultimate fact in the Soviet Union is the supreme authority of the Soviet Communist Party. . . . That fact has very important consequences, for the State and the Party have distinctive goals and they have different instruments for getting those goals. . . . Most of Russia's historic goals have been achieved. . . . But the big, unattained goals are those of the Soviet Communist Party" (Dulles, 1948, pp. 271–2).

study of classical Marxist writings, particularly those of Lenin, to find the keys to all Soviet policies (Dulles, 1958b).

In order to test the general hypothesis that information concerning the Soviet Union tended to be perceived and interpreted in a manner consistent with the belief system, the analysis was focused upon the relationship Dulles perceived between Soviet hostility and Soviet success, capabilities, and general evaluation of the Soviet Union. Specifically, it was

TABLE 1

Period	Hos-tility	Suc-cess	Capabil-ities	General evalu-ation
1953: Jan.–June	+2.01	−1.06	+0.33	−2.81
July–Dec.	+1.82	−0.40	−0.30	−2.92
1954: Jan.–June	+2.45	+0.46	+2.00	−2.69
July–Dec.	+1.85	−0.25	+1.93	−3.00
1955: Jan.–June	+0.74	−1.81	−0.80	−2.83
July–Dec.	+0.96	−1.91	−0.20	−2.33
1956: Jan.–June	+1.05	−1.68	+0.37	−2.91
July–Dec.	+1.72	−2.11	−0.22	−3.00
1957: Jan.–June	+1.71	−2.10	−0.28	−2.79
July–Dec.	+2.09	−1.01	+0.60	−2.93
1958– Jan.–June 1959	+2.03	+0.02	+1.47	−2.86
July–Feb.	+2.10	−1.20	+1.71	−2.90

Correlations[8]

	N	r	P
Hostility–Success (Friendship–Failure):			
6 Month Periods (Table Above)	12	+0.71	0.01
12 Month Periods	6	+0.94	0.01
3 Month Periods	25	+0.58	0.01
Hostility–Strength (Friendship–Weakness):			
6 Month Periods (Table Above)	12	+0.76	0.01
12 Month Periods	6	+0.94	0.01
3 Month Periods	25	+0.55	0.01
Hostility–Bad (Friendship–Good):			
6 Month Periods (Table Above)	12	+0.03	n.s.
12 Month Periods	6	+0.10	n.s.
3 Month Periods	25	+0.10	n.s.

[8] Correlations, based on rank ordering of variables, were computed using Spearman's formula:

$$r = 1 - \frac{6 \Sigma D^2}{N(N^2 - 1)}$$ (McNemar, 1955, p. 208).

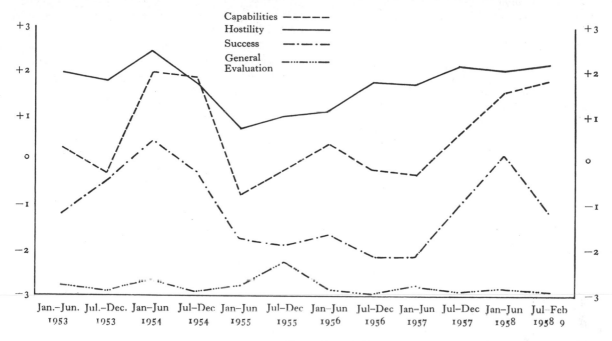

Figure 2. Dulles' perceptions of the Soviet Union, 1953–1959

hypothesized that Dulles' image of the Soviet Union would be preserved by associating decreases in perceived hostility with:

1. Increasing Soviet frustration in the conduct of its foreign policy.
2. Decreasing Soviet capabilities.
3. No significant change in the general evaluation of the Soviet Union.

Similarly, it was hypothesized that increasing Soviet hostility would be correlated with success and strength.

The results derived through the content analysis of Dulles' statements bear out the validity of the hypotheses. These strongly suggest that he attributed decreasing Soviet hostility to the necessity of adversity rather than to any genuine change of character.

In a short paper it is impossible to include all of the evidence and illustrative material found in the full-length study from which this paper is derived. A few examples may, however, illuminate the perceived relationship presented in Table 1.

The 1955–1956 period, beginning with the signing of the Austrian State Treaty and ending with the dual crises in Egypt and Hungary, is of particular interest. As shown in Fig. 2, Dulles clearly perceived Soviet hostility to be declining. At the same time, he regarded that decline to be symptomatic of a regime whose foreign policy had been an abysmal failure and whose declining strength was forcing Soviet decision-makers to seek a respite in the Cold War. That he felt there was a causal connection between these factors can be suggested by numerous statements made during the period.[9]

The process of how Soviet actions were re-

[9] "It is that [United States] policy, and the failure of the Soviet Union to disrupt it, and the strains to which the Soviet Union has itself been subjected which undoubtedly require a radical change of tactics on the part of the Soviet Union" (Dulles, 1955a, p. 914).

"Today the necessity for [Soviet] virtue has been created by a stalwart thwarting of efforts to subvert our character. If we want to see that virtue continue, I suggest that it may be prudent to continue what produced it" (Dulles, 1955c, p. 8).

"The fact is, [the Soviets] have failed, and they have got to devise new policies. . . . Those policies have gradually ceased to produce any results for them. . . . The result is, they have got to review their whole creed, from A to Z" (U.S. Senate, 1956, p. 19).

interpreted so as to preserve the model of "the inherent bad faith of the Communists" can also be illustrated by specific examples. Dulles clearly attributed Soviet actions which led up to the Geneva "Summit" Conference—notably the signing of the Austrian State Treaty—to factors other than good faith. He proclaimed that a thaw in the Cold War had come about because, "the policy of the Soviet Union with reference to Western Europe has failed" (U.S. Senate, 1955, p. 15), subsequently adding that, "it has been their [Soviet] system that is on the point of collapsing" (U.S. House of Representatives, 1955, p. 10).

A year later, when questioned about the Soviet plan to reduce their armed forces by 1,200,000 men, he quickly invoked the theme of the bad faith of the Soviet leadership. After several rounds of questions, in which each reply increasingly deprecated the value of the Soviet move in lowering world tensions, he was asked, "Isn't it a fair conclusion from what you have said this morning that you would prefer to have the Soviet Union keep these men in their armed forces?" He replied, "Well, it's a fair conclusion that I would rather have them standing around doing guard duty than making atomic bombs." In any case, he claimed, the reduction was forced by industrial and agricultural weakness: "I think, however, that what is happening can be explained primarily by economic factors rather than by a shift in foreign policy intentions" (Dulles, 1956, pp. 884–5).

There is strong evidence, then, that Dulles "interpreted the very data which would lead one to change one's model in such a way as to preserve that model" (Bauer, 1961, p. 227). Contrary information (a general decrease in Soviet hostility, specific non-hostile acts) were reinterpreted in a manner which did not do violence to the original image. In the case of the Soviet manpower cuts, these were attributed to necessity (particularly economic weakness), and bad faith (the assumption that the released men would be put to work on more lethal weapons). In the case of the Austrian State Treaty, he explained the Soviet agreement in terms of frustration (the failure of its policy in Europe), and weakness (the system was on the point of collapse).

The extent to which Dulles' image of the Soviet Union affected American decision-making during the period cannot be stated with certainty. There is considerable evidence, however, that he was the primary, if not the sole architect of American policy *vis-à-vis* the Soviet bloc (Adams, 1961; Morgenthau, 1961; Davis, 1961). Moreover, as Sidney Verba has pointed out, the more ambiguous the cognitive and evaluative aspects of a decision-making situation, and the less a group context is used in decision-making, the more likely are personality variables to assert themselves (Verba, 1961, pp. 102–3). Both the ambiguity of information concerning Soviet intentions and Dulles' *modus operandi* appear to have increased the importance of his image of the Soviet Union.[10]

III. Conclusion

These findings have somewhat sobering implications for the general problem of resolving international conflict. They suggest the fallacy of thinking that peaceful settlement of outstanding international issues is simply a problem of devising "good plans." Clearly as long as decision-makers on either side of the Cold War adhere to rigid images of the other party, there is little likelihood that even genuine "bids" (North *et al.*, 1960, p. 357) to decrease tensions will have the desired effect. Like Dulles, the Soviet decision-makers possess a relatively all-encompassing set of lenses through which they perceive their environment. Owing to their image of "monopoly capitalism," they are also pre-conditioned to view the actions of the West within a framework of "inherent bad faith."

To the extent that each side undeviatingly interprets new information, even friendly bids, in a manner calculated to preserve the original image, the two-nation system is a closed one with small prospect for achieving even a desired reduction of tensions. If decreasing hostility is assumed to arise

[10] "Nor was the Secretary of State, in either his thinking or his decisions, much affected by what the Department of State knew and did. Dulles devised the foreign policies of the United States by drawing upon his own knowledge, experience and insight, and the Department of State merely implemented these policies" (Morgenthau, 1961, p. 305).

"He was a man of supreme confidence within himself. . . . He simply did not pay any attention to staff or to experts or anything else. Maybe in a very subconscious way he did catalogue some of the information given him but he did not, as was characteristic of Acheson and several others of the Secretaries of State with whom I have worked, take the very best he could get out of his staff" (Anon., 1961).

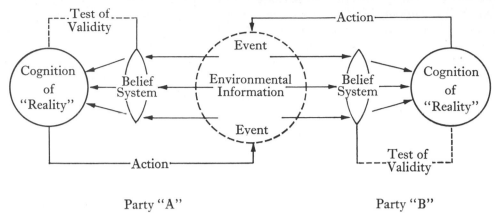

Figure 3. The indirect relationship between belief system and action   (*Source:* Ray, 1961, p. 21)

from weakness and frustration, and the other party is defined as inherently evil, there is little cause to reciprocate. Rather, there is every reason to press further, believing that added pressure will at least insure the continued good conduct of the adversary, and perhaps even cause its collapse. As a result, perceptions of low hostility are self-liquidating and perceptions of high hostility are self-fulfilling. The former, being associated with weakness and frustration, do not invite reciprocation; the latter, assumed to derive from strength and success, are likely to result in reactions which will increase rather than decrease tensions.

There is also another danger: to assume that the decreasing hostility of an adversary is caused by weakness (rather than, for example, the sense of confidence that often attends growing strength), may be to invite a wholly unrealistic sense of complacency about the other state's capabilities.

In such a closed system—dominated by what has been called the "mirror image"—misperceptions and erroneous interpretations of the other party's intentions feed back into the system, confirming the original error (Ray, 1961).[11] Figure 3 depicts such a system.

[11] "Herein lies the terrible danger of the distorted mirror image, for *it is characteristic of such images* that they are self-confirming; that is, each party, often against its own wishes, is increasingly driven to behave in a manner which fulfills the expectations of the other. . . . Seen from this perspective, the primary danger of the Soviet-American mirror image is that it impels each nation to act in a manner

If this accurately represents the interaction between two hostile states, it appears that the probability of making effective bids to break the cycle would depend upon at least two variables:

1. The degree to which the decision-makers on both sides approach the "open" end of Rokeach's scale of personality types (Rokeach, 1960).

2. The degree to which the social systems approach the "pluralistic" end of the pluralistic-monolithic continuum. The closer the systems come to the monolithic end, the more they appear to require the institutionalization of an "external enemy" in order to maintain internal cohesion (North, 1962, p. 41; Wheeler, 1960).

The testing of these and other hypotheses concerning the function of belief systems in international politics must, however, await further research. Certainly this looms as a high priority task given the current state of the international system. As Charles E. Osgood has so cogently said,

Surely, it would be tragedy, a cause for cosmic irony, if two of the most civilized nations on this earth were to drive each other to their mutual destruction because of their mutually threatening conceptions of each other—without ever testing the validity of those conceptions [Osgood, 1959b, p. 318].

which confirms and enhances the fear of the other to the point that even deliberate efforts to reverse the process are reinterpreted as evidence of confirmation" (Bronfenbrenner, 1961, p. 51).

This is no idle warning. It has been shown empirically in this paper that the characteristics of the reciprocal mirror image operated between the two most powerful nations in the international system during a crucial decade of world history.

References

Adams, Sherman. *Firsthand Report*. New York: Harper, 1961.

Anon. "Letter to Author by an Associate of Mr. Dulles." August 25, 1961.

Bauer, Raymond A. "Problems of Perception and the Relations Between the United States and the Soviet Union," *The Journal of Conflict Resolution*, V (1961), 223–9.

Boulding, Kenneth E. *The Image*. Ann Arbor: Univ. Michigan Press, 1956.

———. "National Images and International Systems," *The Journal of Conflict Resolution*, III (1959), 120–31.

Bronfenbrenner, Urie. "The Mirror Image in Soviet-American Relations: A Social Psychologist's Report," *The Journal of Social Issues*, XVII (1961), 45–56.

Davis, S. R. "Recent Policy Making in the United States Government." In D. G. Brennan (ed.). *Arms Control, Disarmament, and National Security*. New York: Braziller, 1961.

Drummond, R. and Coblentz, G. *Duel at the Brink*. Garden City: Doubleday, 1960.

Dulles, John F. "Interview," *Department of State Bulletin*, XXXIX (1958a), 733–9.

———. "Not War, Not Peace," *Vital Speeches*, XIV (1948), 270–3.

———. "Our Foreign Policies in Asia," *Department of State Bulletin*, XXXII (1955b), 327–32.

———. "Reply to Bertrand Russell," *Department of State Bulletin*, XXXVIII (1958b), 290–3.

———. "Tenth Anniversary of the U.N.," *Department of State Bulletin*, XXXIII (1955c), 6–10.

———. "Transcript of News Conference, May 24, 1955," *Department of State Bulletin*, XXXII (1955a), 914.

———. "Transcript of News Conference, May 15, 1956," *Department of State Bulletin*, XXXIV (1956), 880–6.

———. *War and Peace*. New York: Macmillan, 1950.

Festinger, Leon. *A Theory of Cognitive Dissonance*. Evanston, Ill.: Row, 1957.

Kissinger, H. *The Necessity of Choice*. Garden City: Doubleday, 1962.

McClelland, Charles A. "General Systems and the Social Sciences," *Etc.: A Review of General Semantics*, XVIII (1962), 449–68.

McNemar, Q. *Psychological Statistics*. New York: Wiley, 1955.

Miller, G. A., Galanter, E., and Pribram, K. H. *Plans and the Structure of Behavior*. New York: Holt, 1960.

Morgenthau, Hans J. "John Foster Dulles," In N. A. Graebner (ed.). *An Uncertain Tradition*. New York: McGraw, 1961.

North, Robert C., Koch, Howard, and Zinnes, Dina. "The Integrative Functions of Conflict," *The Journal of Conflict Resolution*, IV (1960), 353–74.

North, Robert C. "Some Informal Notes on Conflict and Integration." Unpublished manuscript, 1962.

Osgood, C. E., Saporta, S., and Nunnally, J. C. "Evaluative Assertion Analysis," *Litera*, III (1956), 47–102.

Osgood, C. E. "The Representational Model," In I. Pool (ed.). *Trends in Content Analysis*. Urbana, Ill.: Univ. Illinois Press, 1959a.

———. "Suggestions for Winning the Real War with Communism," *The Journal of Conflict Resolution*, III (1959b), 311–25.

Rapoport, A. *Fights, Games, and Debates*. Ann Arbor: Univ. Michigan Press, 1960.

Ray, J. C. "The Indirect Relationship Between Belief System and Action in Soviet-American Interaction." Unpublished M.A. Thesis: Stanford University, 1961.

Rokeach, M. *The Open and Closed Mind*. New York: Basic Books, 1960.

Smith, M. B., Bruner, J. S., and White, R. W. *Opinions and Personality*. New York: Wiley, 1956.

Snyder, R. C., Bruck, H. W., and Sapin, B. *Decision-making as an Approach to the Society of International Politics*. Princeton: Princeton Univ. Press, 1954.

U.S. House of Representatives. Committee on Appropriations. *Hearings*. (June 10, 1955), Washington, 1955.

U.S. Senate. Committee on Foreign Relations. *Hearings*. (May 5, 1955), Washington, 1955.

———. *Hearings*. (Feb. 24, 1956), Washington, 1956.

Verba, Sidney. "Assumptions of Rationality and Non-Rationality in Models of the International System," *World Politics*, XIV (1961), 93–117.

Wheeler, H. "The Role of Myth System in American-Soviet Relations," *The Journal of Conflict Resolution*, IV (1960), 179–84.

Wright, Quincy. "Design for a Research Project on International Conflict and the Factors Causing Their Aggravation or Amelioration," *Western Political Quarterly*, X (1957), 263–75.

———. *The Study of International Relations*. New York: Appleton, 1955.

G. The Use of Survey Techniques

47. Foreign Policy Opinion as a Function of Social Position*

Johan Galtung is Director of the International Peace Research Institute, Oslo, and editor of its quarterly, the *Journal of Peace Research*. One of the most prolific and stimulating writers in the international field, his articles always reflect an impressive mixture of creative theory and disciplined research. The ensuing selection is no exception in this regard. It begins with a highly original thesis as to how, why, and when opinions about foreign policy matters circulate in a society, and then it submits the resulting hypotheses to the test of empirical data. Thus one is here provided not only with an illustration of how survey methods can be used to investigate international phenomena, but, even more importantly, also with a clear-cut demonstration of how theory and research can enhance each other. [*Reprinted from the* Journal of Peace Research, *II (1965), 206–30, and the* Papers *of the Peace Research Society (International), I (1964), pp. 206–30, by permission of the author and the publishers.*]

I. Introduction

There are several approaches to the study of public opinion and international relations, but many of them are of only marginal interest to the student of international relations in general, and to the student of peace research in particular.

* Paper presented at the First Nordic Conference on Peace Research, Oslo, 4–8 January 1963 and at the meetings of the Peace Research Society (International), Ghent, 18–19 July 1964, here published as PRIO publication no. 16–1. The author wishes to express his gratitude to mag. art. Nils Halle and cand. mag. Ståle Seierstad for excellent assistance, to the Institute for Social Research for financing most of the data-collection; to the Campaigns against atomic weapons in Norway (in 1961, "De 13") and against full membership in the Common Market (in 1962, "De 143") for permission to use their data, to the Norwegian Gallup Institute for its helpful cooperation, and to the Norwegian Research Council for Science and the Humanities for general support. Björn Christiansen, Thomas Mathiesen and James N. Rosenau gave important substantive criticism of an earlier version.

First of all, there is the obvious approach of *description*: What *is* public opinion concerning this or that issue? Democratic ideology has stimulated interest in this question, and modern survey techniques—including sophisticated sampling procedures—have perfected the means so that reasonably accurate answers can be given.[1] The answer, given as a set of percentages, may reflect more or less accurately the distribution of attitudes to an issue at a given point in time and space, much like election results of which they are a non-institutionalized imitation. The best recent study comes from the

[1] Surveys, like most human endeavors, can be made by professionals and by amateurs, and the former are very often blamed for the mistakes made by the latter. For some still valid comments on the state of modern survey techniques, see the chapter "Problems of Survey Analysis" by Lazarsfeld and Kendall in Lazarsfeld, Merton (Eds.), *Continuities in Social Research. The American Soldier* (New York: Free Press, 1950), pp. 133–96.

Canadian Peace Research Institute, John Paul and Jerome Laulicht's *In Your Opinion*,[2] which describes Canadian foreign policy opinion. Such data are actually published frequently[3] and would be of considerable research interest if they could be systematically exploited for analysis.[4] The more sophisticated presentations would also give the distributions for suitably selected background categories. But by themselves these distributions give us no basis for inferences since there is no simple relationship between the distribution of attitudes in the population and the foreign policy of the nation; they belong to different levels of social organization.

Secondly, there is the problem of *explaining* the distribution. There are at least three different ways of attacking this problem: in terms of the opinion-holder's *personality*, in terms of his *social position* and in terms of the *communication and influence structure* of his social system. Needless to say, these three approaches in no way exclude one another, and really good research on this problem would use all three, and probably be forced into such methodological improvements on the traditional survey techniques as sociometric sampling[5] and contextual analysis.[6] Thus one could attack the problem of how personality, social position and communication structure interact, and more particularly the problem of whether the same personality type follows the same attitudinal patterns under different conditions where social position is concerned. The most important work so far in this category is Björn Christiansen's *Attitudes Towards Foreign Affairs as a Function of Personality*,[7] although it is limited by theoretical framework and sampling procedure to the use of personality as the independent variable.

Thirdly, there is the problem of relationship between the foreign policy *of* a nation and the distribution of attitudes *within* the nation. Leaving aside all kinds of normative considerations derived from democratic ideology as to a correspondence between foreign policy and public opinion, one is left with the intricate problem of describing the feed-back loops between the two, as a function of political, social and personality structure. By far the most important work here is the attempt by James N. Rosenau in his *Public Opinion and Foreign Policy*,[8] but this work is theoretical and mainly taxonomic, not empirical.

We have listed the three research problems in order of increasing relevance to peace research, but also in order of increasing difficulty. Typically, the first problem engages pollsters and statisticians. The second problem is a frequently chosen point of attack for psychologists and sociologists who want to do peace research, but fail to make it directly relevant to international affairs by falling too easily prey to the idea that a peaceful public opinion is a necessary or sufficient condition for a peaceful policy. They fail, also, to see that international affairs at least to some extent are *sui generis*. The problem of peace becomes defined to suit one's own professional competence, not according to political reality.

On the other hand, political reality certainly does not warrant total neglect of the public opinion factor. One may reject the *model* of a strong coupling between opinion structure at the individual level and international action at the national level, but not the *ideal* of public opinion as a constraint or impetus on national policy. But the problem is intricate because

[2] Clarkson, Ontario: Canadian Peace Research Institute, 1963.

[3] The most useful and regular review is found in the poll section in the *Public Opinion Quarterly*. Also see yearbooks etc. from the public opinion institutes, e.g. *Jahrbuch der Öffentlichen Meinung* (from Inst. für Demoskopie) or the excellent monthly bulletin from the Indian Institute on Public Opinion (Monthly Public Opinion Surveys) or the bulletins from DIVO and DOXA, and the French *Sondages* (with special attention to issue no. 1–2, 1958, devoted to "La Politique étrangère de la France et l'opinion publique," and issue no. 1, 1963, devoted to "L'opinion publique et l'Europe des six"). A special survey is found in Puchala, D. J. (comp.), *Western European Attitudes on International Problems, 1952–1961* (New Haven: Yale Political Science Research Library, Research Memorandum no. 1). Also see Rosenau, J. N., *National Leadership and Foreign Policy* (Princeton: Princeton Univ. Press, 1963).

[4] A mimeographed proposal is available from the Peace Research Institute.

[5] According to this way of sampling respondents would not be selected randomly but in clusters connected by chains of interaction in order to get more systematically at the communication process.

[6] For a good presentation, see Lazarsfeld, Menzel, "On the Relation Between Individual and Collective Properties," in Etzioni, A. (Ed.), *Complex Organization. A Sociological Reader* (New York: Holt, 1961), pp. 422–40.

[7] Oslo: Oslo University Press, 1959. For a good discussion of the work, see review article by William A. Scott, *Journal of Conflict Resolution*, 1960, 458–67.

[8] New York: Random House, 1961, 1964. For another discussion with interesting data, see Fagen, A. R., "Some Assessments and Uses of Public Opinion in Diplomacy," *Public Opinion Quarterly*, 1960, 448–57.

it combines two classical problems in social science theory: the problem of relationship between attitudes and actions, and the problem of the relation between the system and subsystem levels.

Our long-term goal is a better understanding of the third problem, but this presupposes a knowledge of the answers both to the first and the second problem (in addition it would require extensive research on decision-makers). And here we believe more in using social position than personality as the independent variable, though admitting that the ideal would be to use both. Apart from the methodological reason that it is easier to get valid data about social position, we have also some theoretical reasons. Social position is visible, it is a basis for institutionalized social interaction. As long as personality is private and not made public (e.g. by wearing tags with diagnoses) it serves less as a focus for social organization, and hence is less suited to be a predictor of political behavior. Hence, more political implications can be drawn from knowing, for example, that young people or rural people favor a certain policy than that "authoritarians" favor it, or people "with a closed mind." Moreover, propositions using personality as an independent variable are often useless from the point of view of application, since efforts to manipulate personality, at best, presuppose a long time-perspective, and, at worst, are rather uncertain.[9]

We then turn to our major task, that of clarifying the relationship between a person's social position and his foreign policy orientation.

II. A Theory of Foreign Policy Attitudes and Social Position

We need a simple and forceful axis to classify social positions, and for our purposes we shall divide society into three parts: a decision-making *nucleus* (DN), surrounded by the *center* (C) of the social structure, which again is surrounded by the *periphery* (P). On occasions we shall make a distinction between "periphery" and "extreme periphery" (EP),

but the understanding is always that there is a continuum from the extreme periphery via the periphery and intermediate positions to the center of the social structure. As a matter of fact, we shall use a nine-point scale from 0 to 8 to measure how centrally located a person is. The composition of this scale and its rationale will be given in the next section on methodology. At this point it is sufficient to say that *the social center occupies positions that are socially rewarded, and the social periphery positions that are less rewarded and even rejected.* In the center are the topdogs of the society, in the periphery the underdogs. Thus, our model of society is simply this:

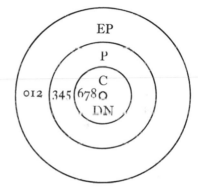

Figure 1. The model of social structure

Our concern is with the difference in foreign policy orientation between the social center and the social periphery within any one country. To construct a theory of this kind we have to single out the basic differences between the two, and apart from the definition above the basic distinctions are given in Table 1.

TABLE 1
Structural Differences Between Center and Periphery

	Center	Periphery
Social participation, particularly secondary (associations) and tertiary (mass media)	High	Low
Knowledge, particularly about policies	High	Low
Opinion-holding, particularly about policies	High	Low

[9] See comments made by Else Frenkel-Brunswick in Jahoda, Christie, (eds.) *Continuities in Social Research, the Authoritarian Personality* (New York: The Free Press, 1954), pp. 226–75. But to manipulate organizations may be difficult, and they may also be formed on the basis of personality, perhaps, particularly in situations of crisis ("the Nazi mind").

The society belongs to the center, it is visible and conceivable in its entirety mainly from the center, and this holds *a fortiori* for foreign policy since it is so far removed from the periphery. Since the center possesses access to the media of communication (associations, mass media) and besides has something to communicate (knowledge and opinions; cognitions and evaluations), *the process of communication will have to be mainly from the center towards the periphery.* This goes only for the sending of communications, not necessarily for their reception—the low levels of knowledge and opinion in the periphery are ample indications that the communication process for policies is mainly contained within the social center. The lack of participation, knowledge and opinions in the periphery mutually reinforce one another. But the periphery will nevertheless be attached to the communication system via more informal contacts with the center: like the father communicating the news to his family with appropriate comments.

This basic structural characteristic must have implications for attitudes, and it is our basic thesis that the difference shows not so much in the opinions held and expressed, as in the way in which these opinions are held. Examination of a great variety of opinion data makes us doubt that any simple formula can be found for relating social position to attitude. The periphery, or the "lower classes," may be peaceful and they may just as well be belligerent, and the same applies to the center. More particularly, data give no basis for any general belief that the "people" should be particularly in favor of "peace" and so represent a bulwark against the "military-industrial complex," or armament capital or nationalist governments, or similar "sinister forces."[10]

[10] The discrepancy between the resolutions passed at the universal Peace Congress in Geneva in 1912 and the Second Socialist International Congress in Stuttgart in 1907 and the working class participation in the 1914–18 war is but one example here. It would have been easy if one could identify "center" with "upper classes" and "periphery" with "lower classes" and hypothesize belligerent attitudes in the former and peaceful attitudes in the latter. The underlying theory might be one of vested interests: in a society where the center sends the periphery to the battlefields to fight and die for them, war might be a paying proposition for the center and a losing one for the periphery. But this kind of theory neglects (1) that the center has the command of the media of communication and can turn nationalist sentiment into belligerent attitudes, and (2) that modern societies are much more complicated than this two-class system mentioned above. Dimensions of stratification interlock in a complex web, and the result is a

But even if little or nothing may be said in general about its content, we can say quite a lot about the nature of foreign policy opinion in the center and the periphery, and our basis is some simple reasoning about how attitudes arise.

An attitude has a cognitive and an evaluative component; it is a question of perceiving alternatives and choosing between them. It is possible to perceive and not select, but not to select without any perception; evaluation presupposes cognition. Thus, we get three types (see Table 2).

TABLE 2
Stages in Attitude Formation

		EVALUATION OF ALTERNATIVES	
		Absent	*Present*
Cognition of alternatives	Absent	Stage 1	Impossible
	Present	Stage 2 ⟶	Stage 3

At one extreme are people to whom international policy is virtually non-existent, and even the national level is hardly perceived: they are chiefly found in the extreme periphery. On the other hand are people in the center to whom a range of foreign policy alternatives is known and who select some and reject others. The selected (or "cathected") alternatives will be clustered in sets and bundles and tied together by ideologies—there are political *tastes* in the social center.

There are probably many possible paths of transition from premature-periphery pre-cognitive thinking about foreign policy to mature-center thinking. One such path is the ideal-democratic, where the individual develops a set of alternatives, and then makes his choice (stage 2 in the Table). Another, and probably more realistic, model would use another intermediate step (step 2*) where perception and selection go hand in hand. The young person, or the periphery person in general, is taken directly from his ignorance to a ready-made set of policies that he is taught to prefer. Alternatives are not spelt out and only later may he develop sufficient autonomy to extend his cognitive basis, and even to shift from one evaluation to another (perhaps accompanied by a rejection of the person(s) who took

much less clear relationship between social position and the distribution of pay-offs from a war.

him into step 2*). According to this model ignorance is followed by cognition and positive or negative evaluation combined; only later (stage 3) does the individual learn how to distinguish between "is" and "ought."

But regardless of which model is more realistic they have two characteristics in common. They are *models of imperfect communication or imperfect internalization*, and apply to the genesis of foreign policy orientation in the young person as he grows older, or the genesis of new orientations when he is already grown-up. We also feel that social space is similar to individual time in the sense that we will find stage 1 above in the extreme periphery, stages 2 or 2* in the periphery and stage 3 in the center, generally speaking.

Moreover, stages 2 or 2* have this in common: the foreign policy alternatives perceived are not evaluated differentially; they will either all be accepted or all rejected. A person emerges from stage 1 as far as foreign policy is concerned and discovers a new world, the international system. But he is still a victim of incomplete communication. He is not yet caught up in the web of competing ideologies and will therefore react according to more global feelings in terms of either rejection or acceptance of this new world. If the former, he becomes what is known as an isolationist, if the latter he comes out in wholesale favor of engagement; any policy will be a fascinating link to the external world. But then he may grow more solidly into the world of politics and develop tastes, and of the many policies appearing on this mental horizon he will choose some and reject others.

Thus, we have a model for the genesis of foreign policy orientation in the individual, for an individual's relation to new issues, for an individual exposed to social mobility (anticipated or real) with special allegiance to new reference groups, and for the static distribution of attitudes in the population, along the center-periphery axis. Since we shall use only social position as an independent variable, what we now need is a way of giving some dynamic life to this model. For even though we assume that individual mobility will be accompanied by a change in mode of orientation, this will only explain individual changes, not changes in the total distribution over time.

First of all, we deduce from the above that attitudes will be more stable in content at the center than at the periphery, for in the former they will be protected by the anchoring influence of ideologies, and the pressure from organizations built around the ideologies. Thus, in the center people may subscribe to "tough" or to "soft" orientations, and make changes within these frameworks, but only rarely jump from a soft to a tough attitude or vice versa. In the periphery, however, this is entirely possible. The jump from isolationism to engagement may be a difficult one, but if engagement is chosen, then the transition from soft to tough or vice versa is much easier. Such differences exist only in the light of political ideology, and foreign policy ideology, we feel, is a center phenomenon.

How then, do new ideas or alternatives appear so as to provoke real changes in the attitude distributions? In general it is unlikely that such ideas are generated in the periphery itself. For even if they are, ideas emerging from the periphery proper will not be discovered and will only be accepted at the idea market under extraordinary circumstances, e.g. when they are linked to extraordinary charisma. "Who said it, not what was said" is probably a fairly valid principle of communication.

Thus, we assume that new ideas are generated in the social center (or imported from abroad, with which only the center has good pipe-lines) and then communicated downwards in the structure, towards the periphery. In a sense this is nothing but the Lazarsfeld-Katz two-step flow of influence hypothesis,[11] only that we try to identify the steps in the structure. In the first step, the idea is received by a person in the center, and in the second step this person communicates the idea to people in the periphery. Thus, a veritable downward communication pressure is established.

Inevitably, there will be a lag in the communication process in the sense that the periphery will be impressed by ideas emanating from the center some time ago, and insensitive to new developments in the idea-structure of the social center. One implication of this is quite far-reaching: *the periphery will very often tend to favor the* status quo. Ideas held by the center long ago and implemented by the center may

---

[11] Lazarsfeld, P. and Katz, E. 'The Two-step Flow of Communication. An Up-to-date Report on an Hypothesis." *Public Opinion Quarterly*, 1957, 61–78.

have reached the periphery and be internalized in the periphery long after the center has lost its real interest in the issue and started looking for new solutions. Thus, a typical sequence is probably: (1) ideas emerge in the center and are communicated to the periphery, (2) the center starts a discussion, the periphery remains apathetic, (3) ideas are implemented and new social structures emerge; their effects are felt by the periphery, (4) the center starts searching for new ideas, the periphery starts internalizing what has already been institutionalized and accepted, (5) the center proposes new solutions, the periphery resists them and defends the *status quo*, (6) the center goes ahead and implements the idea and the periphery comes around to acceptance once the idea is built into social institutions. Thus, a vote in parliament may change their mind, and attune their ideas in consonance with the new *status quo*.

This model emphasizes the *status quo* orientation of the periphery. However, there should be other models, since it is obvious that the periphery is not always lagging behind and imitating the center, nor is it always in favor of the *status quo*. We shall present one alternative model.

According to this model the periphery is short on information, on knowledge of foreign policy alternatives, etc., but long on morality. Very basic moral ideas permeate the thinking of the periphery, derived from religious or heavily ideologized thinking. If these ideas are used to legitimate the *status quo*, then the conservatism of the periphery will be even more deeply entrenched, so much so, even, that the internalization of the ideas of the periphery after new institutions have been created will not take place, and a sector of the periphery will be alienated and have to encapsulate itself in protest, if society so permits. Religious sects and monasteries are good examples.

But the moral ideas may also define a new social or world order by such slogans as "Thou shalt not kill," "one world," "world government," "the triumph of our system," "the kingdom of God on earth," "the abolition of government," etc. In principle this is very close to what politics is about, for goals are formulated, the present state of the world is found wanting relative to the ideals, and efforts are made to transform the socially real and existing into the socially ideal and hypothetical. And here a major distinction can be made, for people have, more or less explicitly, *social cosmologies*,[12] and their foreign policy attitudes have somehow to be compatible with them. The social cosmologies are fundamental conceptions of social reality and social change and we have found the typology shown in Table 3 to be very useful.

These modes of orientation are well known. On the one hand there stands the advocate of "everything now"—everything or nothing, now or never— on the other hand stands the advocate of "something later." The former will say that we have to do it all at once to produce a real effect, that the old and the new orders are completely incompatible, that change to be real must be absolute change. The latter will say that change to be real must be real, and whether it is or not is an empirical problem solved by proceeding gradually, experimentally. More important than this, however, is the total rejection of the *status quo* by the absolutist, as contrasted with the gradualist's only partial rejection. The absolutist works with black and white, the gradualist with shades of gray. Thus, their models of the transition from an old to a new order are as in Fig. 2.

[12] The best known discussion of cosmology on change is still found in Sorokin, P., *Social and Cultural Dynamics* (Boston: Porter, Sargent, 1957). But his distinction between ideationals and sensates is less useful here, since most of these Norwegians are change-oriented sensates.

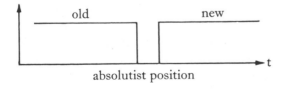

absolutist position

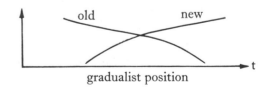

gradualist position

Figure 2. Normative models of social transitions

TABLE 3
Orientations Towards Social Change

	Absolutist	Gradualist
Scope of change	Total	Partial
Duration of change	Quick	Slow
Initiation of change	Now	Later

TABLE 4
Conditions Conducive to Orientation to Change

	Absolutism	Gradualism
Intellectual styles	Deductive moralist subsumption	Inductive pragmatist means-end
Social position	Periphery	Center

The absolutist abolishes the old system and establishes the new order overnight; for the gradualist it is a question of a decline of the old and rise of the new as the new "proves itself." The absolutist will not tolerate the ambivalence implied when two social orders, deduced from incompatible ideologies, co-exist. For the gradualist co-existence will be an empirical, not an ideological problem and he will be better trained for tolerance of the ambivalence of the real world.

The crucial problem now is under what conditions one or the other of these orientations is likely to arise. Table 4 contains our major hypotheses.

The links between *intellectual styles* given by the catchwords above and the modes of orientation are almost tautological. A person trained in and believing in a highly deductive system with unchanging standards, which defines for him the social order as it ought to be, is also a person for whom this order is not merely one among many, but *the* order. A change, to be real, must involve a wholesale commitment to the social order defined by the system — if not there will be contamination and impurities in the order.

There are three deductive systems of particular relevance here: Religion, Ideology and Law.[13] The first system usually defines a transcendental existence and stresses the importance of *conversion*, which is nothing but an absolutist conception of individual change. Our thesis is that it will predispose the individual for a similar attitude to social change. The second system, Ideology, usually defines a social order to be realized in the future; and the more complete the ideology, the tighter will be the deductive framework and the more absolutist the attitude towards change, for the less will the system permit a mixture of two social orders. There will be one social order defined as Right and the other social orders as

[13] For more extensive comments on this, see Galtung, Johan, "Development and Intellectual Styles: The Case of the Lawyer" (paper delivered at the International Social Science Council and the Center for Comparative Sociology Council in Buenos Aires, September 7–16, 1964).

Wrong. And finally there is Law, which as a deductive system serves to sanctify the existing social order insofar as it conforms to the law. Needless to say, Religion and Ideology may also have this effect, in which case a *status quo* orientation will result. The distinction between absolutism and gradualism will be irrelevant, for change as such will be rejected.

On the other hand, there is the inductive and pragmatist style found, among others, in the professionals of an empirical persuasion, e.g. among physicians, engineers, some politicians, etc. Change is seen as an experiment where hypotheses are tested; and if the hypothesis does not work it is partly retained and partly rejected and new approaches are tried. This piecemeal approach as opposed to global thinking is fundamental for the gradualist. If he does not reach his goal he tries again, for change is a process, not a transition. The pragmatist also has goals, but built into his gradualism he has a kind of methodology that makes it possible for him to pick his means according to whether they really lead to the ends. For the person working with a strongly deductive system, often of a moral nature, social transitions are judged according to how they accord with dogma, whether they are correctly performed. "Correctly" here means precisely "according to the prescripts," where the prescripts are retained come what may. And this is tested by examining whether an action can be subsumed under the scriptures or dogma of the religious, ideological, or legal system.

We have mentioned this relationship to intellectual style because it also sheds some light on the basic hypothesis that absolutism will prevail in the periphery and gradualism in the center, and we can now give a set of reasons for this basic hypothesis.

First of all, the discrepancy between the real and the ideal is likely to be greater for the periphery than for the center, for a number of reasons. The center is, by definition, rewarded by its society; it has vested interests in it as a going concern. The periphery is institutionally rejected by society and may reject society in return. Hence, the periphery will more easily fall prey to sensate or ideational ideologies that promise rapid salvation of one's soul, of one's children or one's grandchildren or one's society under certain conditions of sustained work and deep beliefs; for the periphery has more to gain and less to lose. The center will be more preoccupied with the immediate problems facing them, since the society is theirs and its problems are there for them to solve.

But there are more subtle reasons why center and periphery should perceive the transition from present reality to future goals so differently. To map out a path between present and future states of the society presupposes something which is scarce in the periphery but less scarce in the center: precise knowledge of (1) what society *is*, which is better seen from a central than from a peripheral position, (2) what are the possible *means*, in the sense that they are (*a*) instrumental, (*b*) technically feasible and (*c*) socially acceptable. There is no idealization of the center implicit in this. The center may also be deficient in this and so oriented to the *status quo* that the problem of which means to select for implementing a change does not even arise. All we say is that the center is more likely to possess knowledge of that kind, since this is the kind of knowledge it is likely to apply in its day-to-day activities, when it is working with matters of far-reaching social importance.

Thus, for the center a social change is likely to be seen as a problem of using the correct means-end relationships, i.e. as a problem of instrumentality. For the periphery this kind of instrumental thinking will probably be used in their private life or in general at the level where they have knowledge and experience of causal relationships—e.g. at the level of local affairs. But this does not necessarily extend to an area so functionally remote as international affairs; hence the thinking in this field is likely to be of a very different kind. Utopia is used not so much to generate good ideas about means, first steps, and feasible trajectories in general as it is used as a yardstick to judge and blame the dismal present. The language becomes that of protest, of denial, of accusation and not the language of concrete proposal. That change may be problematic is denied; it is defined as "easy

once people are willing and really want peace/disarmament/harmony/salvation/utopia." Change is defined as essentially a moral problem of will and want and conversion of mind, and once these conditions obtain the transition is seen as a very rapid one, almost automatic. This is often the young person's perspective on foreign policy change, and acquaintance with the perspective of the center may come as a shock that kills all dreams of utopia forever.

According to these hypotheses it is easily seen where *revolutions* should draw their support from: a combination of the absolutism of the periphery with the absolutism of one of the intellectual elites, e.g. ideologized lawyers.[14] It is also easily seen how *revisionism* is furthered structurally; i.e. by excluding the periphery from the decision-making process and leaving it to de-ideologized pragmatists. This is done in modern democracies by stipulating that the person from the periphery must pass through central positions before he can take part in decision-making (he must be of a certain age, education, etc.). It should be noticed, in passing, that a parliamentary democracy, by its very nature, has to be gradualist since it proceeds by compromises that are impure; no model of future society is bought wholesale in a multi-party system. For that reason there is limited space in a working democracy for deductive-system oriented, ideologized intellectuals, and also for global planning—both of these go better together with more autocratic and absolutist forms of government where change can be made according to the rules of absolutism.

The absolutist will map future society, the gradualist will map the first steps on the roads leading from present society. The absolutist will be concerned with brilliant analyses of present as well as future society. Nobody will be able to reject present society so forcefully as he. To depict clearly a future society is more difficult and when it comes to the path between them the absolutist is silent. This is where the gradualist enters and our thesis is that the closer he is to the decision-making nucleus, the smaller the steps he envisages, for then the higher becomes the pressure to solve immediate problems. From the gradualist mind analyses of "what is wrong" will be

[14] See the section on "The conditions for revolutions," in Galtung, Johan, "A Structural Theory of Aggression," *JPR*, 1964, 95–119, particularly, 108–9.

partial and "constructive" in the sense of suggesting policies, while from the absolutist mind such analyses will be total and very often stop at the protest itself. Hence, the two will have severe difficulties in establishing a dialogue, their social cosmologies are too different.

And this, in a sense, is probably the story of the relationship between the peace movement and the establishment; it is a variation on the general theme of the relation between periphery and center, between absolutism and gradualism. To the extent that a particular peace organization is recruited from the periphery, we would predict absolutist orientations, and to the extent that it is recruited from the center gradualist orientations should dominate. What remains is only to spell this out in more detail with reference to the specific issues of today.

Leaving aside the isolationist part of the periphery, let us look in Table 5 at the concrete policies that will be advanced. We limit the discussion to two broadly defined foreign policies, "soft" and "tough," and spell out their gradualist and absolutist versions. Many more examples could be given of hypotheses of this kind.[15]

One important hypothesis is the distribution of attitudes towards the adversary, another the distribution of attitudes towards defense. The *tough gradualist* wants arms so that he can deter by careful calculation, but the *tough absolutist* wants arms, not for deterrence but for fighting, and may be an advocate of taking up the fight now. The *soft gradualist* wants carefully executed disarmament, but for the

soft absolutist nothing short of "unilateralism now" will do.[16] We shall have occasion to test some of this, but leave for future research the exploration of such themes as how statistically infrequent categories (according to our hypotheses) such as the tough absolutist in the center will be oriented.

Let us then emphasize: we do not think we can tell from knowledge of a person's social position the *content* of his foreign policy orientation. Rather, we feel that whether he is more tough or more soft is more a question of personality than of social position. But we feel something can be said about the relationship between the *form* of his foreign policy orientation and his social position.

Thus we have essentially presented two perspectives on the difference between center and periphery, derived from the difference between them given by the definition and the consequences spelt out in Table 1. On the one hand there is the difference due to the lag in communication between center and periphery, where the periphery is pictured as lagging behind, and its response to initiatives from the center is apathy and "go along with it" and a tendency to favor the *status quo*. According to the second perspective the periphery asserts itself; it has its own political philosophy which we term absolutism with its many facets and an urge towards radical change. These two perspectives should now be considered in combination.

Absolutism combined with a low degree of access to the channels of communication yields a kind of

---

[15] For one systematic distinction between soft and tough attitudes see Galtung, Johan, "Balance of Power and the Problem of Perception," *Inquiry*, 1964, 277–94, particularly 281–82.

[16] All four attitudes are well known in the contemporary debate, and the soft, gradualist attitude is found in the McCloy-Zorin principles for disarmament. For a book making "gradualism" its focus, see Etzioni, Amitai, *The Hard Way to Peace* (New York: Collier, 1962).

TABLE 5
A Survey of Engagement Policies

	Gradualist (center)	Absolutist (periphery)
"Tough"	1. Armament-oriented 2. Deterrence through strength 3. No contact with adversary	1. Preventive or pre-emptive war 2. Fighting capacity through strength 3. Hatred of adversary
"Soft"	1. Disarmament-oriented; multilateral, balanced 2. International cooperation; technical assistance 3. Contact with adversary	1. Immediate disarmament; unilateral 2. Renunciation of sovereignty; sacrifice for developing countries 3. Love of adversary

pre-political thinking, usually unsuited to political action; the periphery either wants too little or too much. But there exists also a kind of post-political thinking characterized by excessive gradualism and too easy access to information, which together can have a paralyzing effect on imagination and readiness for action. Thus, the politically useful person for social change is probably the person in the transition period between the two forms; before the world looks so complicated that he dares develop neither ideas nor actions to change it. This is the stage between the excessively ends-oriented absolutist in the periphery and the excessively means-oriented gradualist in the center.

We can now conclude with some remarks on a theme we mentioned but left undeveloped: the forms of political action. The decision-makers emit words and deeds; the problem is what kind of feed-back they get from the public. It will have to be different in center and periphery: "urbane" discussions in the center, protests and demonstrations from the periphery, or plain apathy. We shall elaborate this a little further.

The center has its organization network to draw upon and its ready access to the media of mass communication. The implication of this is not only that it has permanent mechanisms for making itself heard, seen, and felt by the decision-makers, whereas the periphery has to improvise, to make *ad hoc* organizations that are dissolved "when the crisis is over" and then have to be rebuilt from the scraps again. More important, in a sense, is the factor of *pluralistic ignorance*. Since the center associate and communicate more with one another they meet more and know better what other people stand for, which means that a person who feels opposed to official policy can relatively easily find others with whom he can share his position (or opposition). Not so for the person in the periphery; he is much more likely to develop a feeling of loneliness around his attitudes and hence be discouraged from expressing them. To the extent that this is the case it explains not only how low participation is its own cause through contributing to pluralistic ignorance which in turn contributes to low participation (ignorance about where the "plurality" stands), but also the *form* of participation when it comes. When pluralistic ignorance is broken down in the politically undernourished periphery, i.e. by means of efficient

propaganda, it is likely to produce a chain-reaction in the opposite direction: people feel that this is the thing to do and join the bandwagon, and those who are against the movement may nevertheless join because they think they are the only ones against. And this is one more factor contributing to inconsistency in the periphery.

In Table 6 we summarize in an easily surveyable form the difference between center and periphery as developed in this theory.

III. Methodology

To test these hypotheses the ideal would be crossnational, longitudinal surveys covering many structural, social background, personality and attitudinal dimensions. Our data are limited relative to this ideal, however. First of all, they cover only Norwegian public opinion and only in the period 1959–64. Moreover, to obtain the data the Norwegian Gallup agency was used. This agency conducts monthly surveys on samples with about 2,000 respondents and has a remarkable record of representativity, as witnessed, for instance, by the close coincidence between voting records from the last parliamentary election and what the respondents report.[17] The surveys give a rich variety of background data, but, since the interviewers are not easily trained for this purpose, no personality variables. And as to attitudinal questions, one is limited to questions that are simple and phrased in the terminology of current and important issues.

The ideal would have been, as in most social science research, to arrive at the usually neglected time dimension by following the *same* respondents (the panel) through a period of, say, five years to get at a basis for understanding how personality, social position and communication structure interact in producing an opinion structure. We have data from 1959 (August), 1961 (January and June), 1962 (May), 1963 (July) and 1964 (June), but they are not panel data since respondents have not been reinterviewed. But trend data can also shed some light on problems of change and development.

Data have been obtained about attitudes concerning the invitation of former Premier Khrushchev

---

[17] The discrepancies in terms of percentage differences ranged for January 1961 between 0.4 and 2.4 points, for June 1961 between 0.2 and 3.1 points.

TABLE 6
The Theory: Differences Between Center and Periphery

	Center	Periphery
Definition	Rewarded (topdog)	Rejected (underdog)
General consequences		
H_1: Social participation	High	Low
H_2: Knowledge	High	Low
H_3: Opinion-holding	High	Low
H_4: Communication	Sender, initiator	Receiver, imitator
Attitude-formation		
H_5: Mode of orientation	Differential evaluation "soft v. tough," *taste*	Total evaluation engagement v. isolation
H_6: Consistency,		
1. Between attitudes	High	Low
2. Attitudes v. behavior	High	Low
3. Over time, stability	High	Low
H_7: Internalization of new policies	Before institutionalization	After institutionalization
Social cosmology		
H_8: Perspective on change	Gradualist	Absolutist
H_9: Style of thought	Inductive, pragmatic, means-end, means-oriented	Deductive, moralist, subsumption, ends-oriented
H_{10}: Attitude to existing social order	Partial acceptance and rejection, revisionism	Total acceptance or rejection *status quo* or revolution

For a list of hypotheses about which foreign policies will be advocated in center and periphery see Table 5.

Feed-back to decision-makers		
H_{11}: Content	Discussion, low on pluralistic ignorance	Protest or apathy, high on pluralistic ignorance
H_{12}: Form	Through existing organization or communication networks	Through *ad hoc* demonstrations or no expression

to Norway (asked August 1959, July 1963 and June 1964); about the stationing of atomic weapons on Norwegian territory (January 1961, June 1961, May 1962); about NATO membership (same samples); about the Norwegian campaign against nuclear armament (June 1961); about Norwegian technical assistance and peace corps (January 1961, June 1961 and May 1962); and about attitudes to EFTA (August 1959) and EEC (September 1961, February, April, May 1962). Thus, a number of issues have been used, tapping the two major dimensions of the quest for peace (armament-disarmament, and development-integration) at different points in time. The questions were simple and straightforward; the issues had been (except in the case of the peace corps) known for some time, so that the

DK-rates were reasonably low, and the questions did not exceed the capacities of the interviewers (see Appendix).

The main methodological task was to translate into operational terms the ideas of "center" and "periphery." Since the idea is to include in the center the parts of the society that are favored or rewarded and in the periphery the parts that are less rewarded or even rejected, center and periphery clearly have to do with social *rank*. But is it a question of the rich v. the poor, or the occupationally high v. the occupationally low, or the educated v. the uneducated or the geographical center v. the geographical periphery? We saw no reason to favor any one of these or other dimensions of rank in the social order and for that reason made two decisions: (1) to make a

TABLE 7
The Composition of the Index of Social Position

	Topdog or central (Score 1)	*Underdog or peripheral (Score 0)*
1. Sex	Male	Female
2. Age	30–59	Below 30, Above 60
3. Education	More than primary	Primary or less
4. Income	Above median	Below median
5. Location ecologically	Urban, suburban	Rural
6. Location, geographically	Central	Peripheral
7. Occupation, position	White-collar, Self-employed	Blue-collar, Foreman
8. Occupation, sector	Secondary, tertiary	Primary

reasonably complete list of the dimensions that are used to rank all members of a nation, (2) to make a composite measure so as to use all the information obtained about the individual.

We have used eight rank-dimensions and combined them in an additive index (see Table 7). Read horizontally these eight criteria are dimensions along which individuals are not only placed, but also ranked on a national scale. Thus, to be president of a local organization does not count here since the system reference is not to the nation but to a subsystem. That they are rank-dimensions and not only dimensions of classification can best be established by asking members in the system what they would like to be, giving them the choices above. The topdog position is then, by definition, the position around which the wishes cluster. This has been done,[18] and the Table seems to reflect wishes and values fairly well. Another method would take as a point of departure the institutionalization of rewards, e.g. to which position on the seven other variables does the highest income accrue? Again, the categories seem reasonable—but we shall not give the details here.

There are methodological and theoretical problems related to the location of the cuts once the decision to use dichotomies has been taken. Thus, even though one may agree that the very young and

the very old are both underdogs relative to adults at their best working age, the transition is by no means a sharp one. Hence, there are problems that are solved most easily by invoking other criteria, such as the desirability of relatively equal cuts, in the sense of having about the same number of underdogs and topdogs. This has been used systematically, and for the Norwegian social structure this is relatively compatible with the more theoretically derived cuts indicated above.

Read vertically the two columns give us the two social extremes, the complete topdog to the left and the complete underdog to the right.[19] The additive index gives them the scores of 8 and 0 respectively, and in between are all the combinations. For practical purposes we shall sometimes use this nine-point scale in a simplified form with only three values: periphery (0–2), medium (3–5) and center (6–8). It should be noticed that this index of social position is not the same as the classical division in terms of social classes used in social and political theory and common-sense social thinking. That classification is likely to use only one of the eight dimensions (e.g. position in a work organization) and presents a much too narrow picture of the social situation of a person.[20] Besides, its meaning depends very much on the degree of correlation or crystallization of all the rank-dimensions. Clearly, occupation is much more meaningful in a society that essentially consists of two groups, the complete topdog (bourgeoisie) and the complete underdog (proletariat), than in a society where these two groups are numerically insignificant and most of the society is located in between.

No doubt better scales of degree of centrality can be devised, based on better conceptualization and more thorough work with the items. And the index blurs many important distinctions. For some issues and variables the trend found with the index may be replicated for each item, but for other variables some items may show trends in the opposite direction or no trend at all. Nevertheless we shall use the index with two rationales. It gives a first approximation where the details on each item can be explored later. And secondly, it is meaningful in its

[18] With data from two Norwegian communities, to be published. Also for sex and age the wishes clustered on the topdog positions.

[19] These are the TTTTT and UUUUU positions from the article by Galtung, Johan, in *JPR* II, 1964, 97.

[20] It should be noticed that industrial workers score rather high on the index, they easily make "7" and are in the "center," not in the "lower classes."

own right. It measures the total social position of the individual, and for that reason gives us insights that could never be obtained using one item at a time—and in most cases much higher correlations than could be obtained for any one single item. Thus, the index is essentially an interval scale variable: it counts the number of topdog statuses a person has.

IV. Testing the Theory

We can now test the ideas in Table 6 at a number of points, sometimes in the core and sometimes more on the edge of the theory, with the data we have. For this purpose we may start with the first hypotheses H_1 to H_4 that are really for validation and not substantive since we would never reject the thinking behind the hypotheses if they did not predict the data, but rather reject the index of social position. We shall use data from the 1959 and the 1961 investigations since these data are easily comparable (Tables 8 and 9). The three criteria are participation, knowledge and opinion-holding. It is so crucial for our analysis that the index actually gives a measure of centrality in the social structure that we present corresponding data from 1961 (no knowledge questions included). There are very few irregularities in the 17 columns of Tables 8 and 9. With a total of 128 steps ($7 \times 8 + 9 \times 8$) from one percentage to the next, only 13 (10%) are against the trend and seven of the percentage columns are entirely monotone (undirectional). Further, the

range in meaning for the indicators of the three validation criteria is considerable, so we feel satisfied that the index does the job we have asked it to do. He who feels that sports constitute a compensation for the periphery should study the percentages in the relevant columns to get an impression of how general and forceful the center/periphery factor is. The periphery is deprived and deprives itself of opportunity; that is the true meaning of the periphery. Particularly significant are the columns for organization and board membership, where 85% are isolated from this kind of participation in the periphery.

Unfortunately, we have no direct test in these data of the communication hypothesis, H_4. But we have much data pertaining to the hypotheses about attitude-formation in center and periphery, although they are not ideal data. Actually the whole idea is summarized in the key concept of H_6, consistency, since H_5 essentially defines two different concepts of consistency, one for center and one for periphery, and H_7 deals with factors that make for stability (consistency) or change over time.

To test this idea about consistency examination of one attitude will not do; one has to study how attitudes cluster as a function of social position. And there is no reason to restrict this to attitudes; it is just as, or even more interesting to study how the relation between attitude and attitude-relevant action varies as a function of social position.

TABLE 8
Validation of the Social Position Index, 1959 Data. %

	NO PARTICIPATION			NO KNOWLEDGE		NO OPINION		
Index level	In election	Reading newspapers	Interest in football	About EEC	About EFTA	About Khrushchev visit	About free trade	About daylight saving time
0–1[a]	29	24	91[b]	98	96[b]	39	86[b]	45
2	19	17	88	94	92	34	76	25
3	17	10	82	91	87	20	63	20
4	12	6	77	84	84	22	59	19
5	13	10	65	84	79	17	51	11
6	12	8	61	77	75	11	56	8
7	14	4	51	66	64	8	33	7
8	10	10	40	58	54	4	27	2

[a] Combined since there were too few in the 0 category.

[b] 100% at the 0 level.

TABLE 9
*Validation of the Social Position Index,
1961 Data, %*

	NO PARTICIPATION					NO OPINION			
Index level	*In election*	*Reading newspapers*	*As a member of organizations*	*As a board member*	*Interest in sports*	*About NATO membership*	*About atom bombs in Norway*	*About what is worse, occupation or atomic war*	*Foreign aid*
0	31	54	85	85	85	46	38	77	39
1	20	45	68	75	70	44	36	47	29
2	15	43	58	74	57	43	35	31	26
3	13	34	48	65	55	31	24	19	21
4	12	27	41	62	39	20	14	15	14
5	13	18	44	62	33	24	21	20	16
6	14	10	43	54	35	16	15	14	9
7	9	6	33	43	30	14	10	18	9
8	5	3	27	38	27	0	2	0	6

For the first test of the theory at the crucial point H_5 all we need is a set of questions about foreign policies; some of them about "tough," some of them about "soft" policies. In the center of society the tendency will then be to choose, so that being in favor of a tough policy predisposes one to oppose a soft policy, and vice versa. In other words, in the center there will be a negative correlation between the attitudes to soft and tough positions. But in the periphery, according to the theory, one should either be engaged, and be for both policies, or be an isolationist, and be against both. In other words again, in the periphery there should be a positive correlation between the two positions.

But what if both items are tough or both soft? We should expect positive correlation all the way (one is either for both or against both), *but for different reasons.* In the center one would be for both NATO and the stationing of atomic weapons because of a general tough orientation; in the periphery this would be because of a general engaged orientation. Correspondingly one would be against both because of a soft orientation in the center and an isolationist orientation in the periphery.

We can now formulate the hypothesis H_5 in an easily testable form:

$H_{5,1}$: The correlation between the attitudes to soft and tough foreign policy measures will decrease from periphery to center.

$H_{5,2}$: The correlation between the attitudes to two soft or to two tough foreign policy measures will be positive and relatively independent of social position.

The formulation in $H_{5,1}$ actually weakens the hypothesis somewhat: we no longer assume that the correlation will be negative in the center and positive in the periphery, only that there will be a decrease when we move from the periphery towards the center. The reason for this is that there will be a general level of correlation in society between a soft and a tough policy measure, depending on how it has been launched. It will probably be neither high and positive nor high and negative but somewhere in between. Thus, a trend from a positive correlation down to zero, or from zero down to a negative correlation would also be in conformity with the hypothesis.

We have relevant data from the January 1961 and the June 1961 surveys and shall use both since the hypotheses are so crucial to our theory. For January 1961 we have data about attitudes to NATO (tough), atomic weapons (tough) and technical assistance (soft); for June 1961 we have data about NATO (tough), atomic weapons (tough) and peace corps (soft). Unfortunately, we cannot test the hypothesis that there will be a strong and positive and relatively constant correlation between the attitudes to two soft items; but all the other tests

TABLE 10
*Correlations Between Foreign Policy Attitudes as a
Function of Social Position, Yule's Q*

Index level	Periphery (0–2)	Medium (3–5)	Center (6–8)	Type
January 1961 data				
NATO/atomic weapons	+.85	+.94	+.77	Tough-tough
TA[a]/NATO	+.65	+.20	−.11	Soft-tough
TA[a]/atomic weapons	−.15	−.23	−.37	Soft-tough
June 1961 data				
NATO/atomic weapons	+1.0	+.74	+.89	Tough-tough
Peace corps/NATO	+.85	+.33	−.12	Soft-tough
Peace corps/atomic weapons	+.65	−.09	−.33	Soft-tough

[a] TA stands for technical assistance.

could be carried out (see Table 10). All six rows of correlations corroborate the hypotheses and are explained by our theory, though this of course does not preclude some other theory from explaining the data equally well or better.[21] As a matter of fact, the tendency is so strong that for the last line the correlations are actually +1.0, +.56, +.31, +.20, +.31, −.18, −.52, −.50 when we calculate them for all levels of social position (except the 0 level—nobody had any attitude at this level). The total correlation is .03, which means that a zero correlation is elaborated using the index as a third variable to give us insights of theoretical significance. And for the correlation between attitudes to peace corps and NATO the range is actually from +1.0 for the extreme periphery to −1.0 for the extreme center —but the series is not so regular as the one given above.

Thus we have a strong indication that what is "consistent" in the sense of "going together in the same mind" in the center is not necessarily consistent in the periphery and vice versa. Attitudes are kept in clusters according to very different organizing principles in the periphery and in the center. We then turn to the relation between attitudes and action. Fortunately, an excellent occasion occurred in Norway in 1961. A campaign against nuclear weapons (i.e. against having any stationed on Norwegian territory) was organized and obtained, among other items, 220,000 signatures on a letter of protest to the Storting (Parliament). This was somewhat

[21] Thus, the correlations in Table 10 were tested for the influence of response-set, in the Cronbach-tradition, and found to stand the test.

below 10% of the adult population and of a sample of 2,000 we would expect 200 to report that they had signed. Actually, there were 199 signers in the sample, and 91% of them still had in June 1961—some months after they had signed, if their report was truthful—a clear attitude against atomic weapons. Eighteen persons were inconsistent.

We are interested in inconsistency between attitude and action and this cannot be tested on so few respondents, so we have to use another question to represent the action, not "Did you do it?" but "Would you have liked to have done it?" 846 said yes, which brought the total number of "protestants" to 54% and hence the number of potential signers with a more efficient campaign above the magic 50%. Of these 846, however, 54 or 6% declared that they felt atomic weapons to be advantageous! Depending on which side one is on oneself one can say that the "protestants" are unconvincing since some of them are *for* what they protest *against*, or that the adherents of atomic weapons are strange people since some of them protest *against* what they are *for*. The social scientist would regard this as a natural social phenomenon, and perhaps blame some of the inconsistency on the data-collection. But we shall explore inconsistency in the light of our theory.

Instead of describing the periphery as inconsistent—which is a value judgment since it is an application of what the center considers to be consistent—we shall rather emphasize what the theory says about the kind of consistency the periphery has. We have mentioned absolutism as a central element in periphery ideology, and absolutism as compatible both with the protest attitude, with kicking

TABLE 11
*Attitude/Action Inconsistency as a
Function of Social Position*

Index level	0	1	2	3	4	5	6	7	8	SUM
In favor of atomic weapons, *total*	0	8	32	64	73	55	68	44	11	355
Would have liked to sign protest against atomic weapons, *total*	0	5	10	23	10	3	2	1	0	54
Percentage of adherents who would have liked to sign	—	62%	31%	36%	14%	6%	3%	2%	0%	15%

the center in the rear so to speak, and with absolute weapons that can bring about absolute changes. To test this hypothesis adequately we would need independent indicators of absolutism which we do not have. However, the hypothesis

$H_{6,2,1}$: The tendency to be in favor of atomic weapons and also want to sign a protest against them will decrease from periphery to center.

is well confirmed by the data (see Table 11).

Thus the 15% inconsistents distribute themselves nicely according to the hypothesis. If we are to trust the data, this kind of inconsistency is almost completely absent in the center, and very much present in the periphery. Thus, parts of the periphery have the best of two worlds: they protest against the center, *and* the attachment to absolute weapons. This is a kind of consistency, though not according to the ideological criteria of the center. The social mechanism producing this phenomenon

is probably the combined operation of pluralistic ignorance and susceptibility to propaganda in the periphery.

We then turn to the section in our theory about social cosmology where, according to our hypotheses H_{8-10}, the periphery should have a more moralist, a more absolutist orientation in general, and be more inclined to reject the society in which it lives. The methodological difficulty lies in establishing this in spite of the lack of participation, knowledge and opinion in the social periphery. Thus, even weak trends indicating moralist and absolutist tendencies in the social periphery strongly corroborate the hypothesis since they have compensated for the general trend towards apathy and withdrawal characteristic of the periphery.

We get the data set forth in Table 12. For the two value-items contrasting success for oneself in this life with success in the after-life and success of one's children, the periphery effect is very

TABLE 12
*Morality and Absolutism in Center and
Periphery, 1961 Data, %*

Index level	After-life more important than this life	Success of children more important than own success	Fundamental change of Norway necessary	Consider myself a personal Christian
0	69	54	46	39
1	65	48	46	28
2	65	56	28	30
3	51	47	18	25
4	41	42	19	25
5	39	40	21	32
6	39	39	17	28
7	33	30	23	28
8	32	29	19	27

TABLE 13
Periphery Absolutism, "Soft" Orientations.
January 1961 Data, %, Respondents with
Clear Answers

Social position	Periphery (0–2)	Middle (3–5)	Center (6–8)	Difference, Center–Periphery
Advantageous not to be member of NATO	30	27	24	+6
Advantageous not to have atomic weapons	85	85	77	+8
Preference for (unilateral) disarmament to conventional or atomic defense	67	60	51	+16
In favor of increased aid to India	14	10	11	+3

conspicuous. Whether one chooses to interpret this in terms of rejection of the present or firm attachment to a transcendental or mundane future that can compensate for present deprivations, is less important; the importance lies in the very marked trend. This is also found, though less so, for the very absolutist value-item "a really fundamental change is necessary if Norway is to be a good country to live in." But where self-identification as a "personal Christian" is concerned we do not get as much of a trend as expected, possibly because the periphery feels it will satisfy less the institutional criteria, such as active church or sect participation. Nevertheless the general thesis seems relatively well substantiated.

But most important in this context is the distribution of attitudes hypothesized in Table 5. We do not have data to test all this, but we can make tests at some crucial points.

One such point is the hypothesis that the more absolutist ideas will differentiate most clearly between center and periphery.

In Table 13 we present some relevant data. The periphery is in general more in favor of the soft orientations against NATO and atomic weapons when we correct for the influence of increasing ignorance towards the periphery (DK-answers) and increasing ambivalence towards the center (both-and answers), but this may also be an expression of isolationism. On the other hand, the periphery is more generous, more willing simply to give money away in a TA-project like the Indo-Norwegian project in Kerala (the center probably prefers a better contract). And, as predicted, the difference is much more pronounced for the most radical "soft" solution, that of unilateral disarmament. The most absolutist idea is found more in the periphery.

Let us then see to what extent this also holds for tough orientations. We examined among adherents of atomic weapons in Norway what reasons they subscribe to for having such weapons, and obtained the results shown in Table 14. Thus, deterrence is a center argument and "good weapons for our soldiers" is more of a periphery argument, but the trends are not strong. The really strong trend is for the engagement and international loyalty argument in the third column, and this is only one more expression of the more international orientation in the center.

Finally, there is the hypothesis about different kinds of feed-back. More concretely, the hypothesis is that the extreme periphery will not show any sign of participation, the center will use their organization and communication network and sometimes extend it to fit the exigencies of a new issue, and the middle sector, which is close to the extreme periphery, will use *ad hoc* methods such as demonstrations and mass signatures. To test the hypothesis the data about the campaign against nuclear armament mentioned above were studied. We concentrated on the respondents who were against atomic weapons, in order to avoid contamination from the factor mentioned in $H_{6,2}$ and demonstrated in Table 11. Respondents were asked (1) whether they had wanted to sign, (2) whether they had had the opportunity to sign, and (3) whether they had actually signed, and the four possible combinations were tabulated against social position in Table 15.

Table 15 actually gives a corroboration of a number of the hypotheses advanced about the difference between center and periphery. Thus, the last line gives a good indication of the difference in opportunity between center and periphery. Even in

TABLE 14
Periphery Absolutism, "Tough" Orientation.
May 1962 Data, %

Social position[22]	*Atomic weapons will deter an enemy*	*Atomic weapons are efficient if a war comes*	*Atomic weapons are an obligation to our allies*
0–2	60	7	20
3	56	6	66
4	73	6	73
5	70	6	76
6	83	4	96

the center there was a certain lack of opportunity; the organization was not big enough to reach all corners of the society—but the trend is indicative of the isolation of the periphery even from an organization of this kind. This is reflected in the second row of percentages: a monotone decline in lack of opportunity or awareness.

But the line corresponding to "could but would not" is most interesting. It shows a marked increase towards the center of people opposed to translating their attitude into an action of protest, as predicted. Thus, the hypothesis is confirmed in a general sense, and this is reflected in a little dip at the center end of the curve of those who actually did sign. But the general tendency to participate in the center almost overrides the predicted tendency to withdraw from *ad hoc* protest organizations.

[22] Unfortunately, in the sample from May 1962 educational level was not asked by the Gallup agency, so it could not be included in the index. When we constructed the new index it was also decided to omit the geographical aspects of location since the ecological aspect seems to be the important factor. This means that the social position index for May 1962 has a range from 0 to 6, and that it is not comparable with the other points in time. However, it is nevertheless of interest.

That concludes our testing of the theory, so far. It remains to see whether it stands up against cross-national comparisons, and some attempts in that direction will be made.[23]

And there is no compelling reason to limit this kind of theory to the level of individuals. The international system is also a multi-dimensionally stratified system where the 140-odd members, nations with varying degrees of autonomy, distribute on a dimension running from center to periphery. *One* aspect of this dimension, one item so to speak, is center-periphery as used by economists in the Prebisch/ECLA tradition; another aspect is purely geographical as measured by transport networks; a third aspect is in terms of per capita income, and so on. The only significant difference between the structure of international community and that of, say, Norwegian social structure is that the former is more feudal, with a higher correlation between the indicators of social position in the international system. But our theory would be that foreign policy orientations of

[23] In a three-nation study of France-Norway-Poland now under way. In two forthcoming PRIO monographs on Norwegian data the theory will be much elaborated.

TABLE 15
Could You Sign, Would You Sign,
Did You Sign? June 1961 Data, %

Social position	0–1[a]	2	3	4	5	6	7–8[a]	*Total*
Could, would and did sign	7	8	14	17	24	26	23	18
Would, but could not	80	77	69	67	56	53	36	63
Could, but would not	9	1	10	8	13	14	27	11
Neither would, nor could	4	14	7	8	7	7	14	8
SUM	100	100	100	100	100	100	100	100
(N)	(44)	(137)	(194)	(225)	(215)	(126)	(74)	(1016)
% signers among those who would	8	10	15	20	30	33	39	22

[a] Combined to avoid too small bases for the calculation of percentages.

(the leaders of) periphery nations will be very like what we have described as periphery orientation in general—making the span in social cosmology between the centrally located person in a center nation and a peripherally located person in a periphery nation almost inconceivably wide. But this will be explored in another context.

V. Discussion and Policy Implications

After this effort to explain the social structure of foreign policy opinion in Norway in the beginning of the sixties, let us return to the problem of how this ties in with the process of decision-making. Since we have no direct data, e.g. reports from foreign office deliberations where the impact of public opinion can be ascertained, we have to limit ourselves to theoretically guided speculations.

A major thesis of our paper has been the volatility and relative unpredictability of the content of public opinion in the social periphery. We may predict that it is pre-political and absolutist, but not whether it is soft or tough. Thus, it may *look* as if the periphery is against atomic weapons and for "peace" when an equally good or better interpretation would be that the periphery is against change and for isolation. The distance between the periphery and the decision-makers exceeds the range of mutual visibility; they become strangers to each other. The impact of foreign policy opinion from the periphery is probably very limited. The decision-makers will either be ignorant about it or ignore it even if they know—for if they get to know it it will probably be because opinion has expressed itself in an eruptive way, in demonstrations, slogans and protests. This will increase the estrangement and activate the usual psychological techniques to reduce the significance of the demonstration (they were all youngsters, it was inspired from the outside, a bunch of intellectuals, etc.). Decision-makers will probably limit their contact to very centrally located segments of public opinion and interact with them—newspaper editors, pressure groups, establishment oriented and composed meetings, etc. These groups will give them a feeling of continuity and predictability, the terms of the discussion will be the same and disagreement will be contained within frames of reference that will be similar enough. The decision-makers will not be left with a feeling of confronting a superficially informed public that has picked out one issue from the hyper-complex web of foreign policy issues and made a cause of it.

But this does not mean that public opinion in general and periphery opinion in particular cannot have an impact on foreign policy decisions. We shall distinguish between the *direct impact*, the *constraining influence* and the *bargaining function*. The direct impact, if it occurs, is probably usually of a negative character if we are right in assuming that periphery opinion is usually *status quo* oriented. An overwhelming demonstration against a specific proposal may force a parliament or a government not to go ahead, at least not overtly, with a proposal. But in addition to the direct focus on one issue, public opinion may also function as a general constraint—as vaguely defining a vast region of admissible policies, surrounded by a belt of inadmissible policies. The trial and error strategies politicians engage in to locate the border-line are too well known to be commented on here.

Probably much more important in a practical sense than either of these effects of public opinion is the bargaining function.[24] The foreign minister sits at the conference table and wants to back up his own position. He cannot say "I will not"—for he is there as a target of persuasion; he has to say "I cannot" and refer to sources of authority outside himself. But these sources will have to be unmanipulable by him. If he refers to his ministry officials or even to his government, his parliament or his party, his colleagues may insist: "How much time do you need to persuade them?" He can escape by portraying them as unmanipulable, at least for a period sufficient for the purpose at hand. But public opinion can serve this function better. First of all, since public opinion on foreign policy issues is very often unknown, at least in a reasonably scientific sense, the foreign minister is free to present it to outsiders as it suits him. Secondly, *its volatility now becomes its force:* the foreign minister can, with sincerity, plead that there are limits to his capacity of manipulation. He can refer to demonstrations, etc., and create an image of being a victim.

To what extent this is done we do not know.

24 See the essay by Thomas C. Schelling, "An Essay on Bargaining," in his *The Strategy of Conflict* (Harvard: Harvard Univ. Press, 1960), pp. 21–52.

Clearly this is not the ideal method from the point of view of democratic ideology, for it leaves it to the highest decision-making level to decide when public opinion should be heeded, and there is no way in which public opinion can give explicit, direct or constraining, directives. Elections are usually no answer to the problem. This is completely clear where elections at the local, municipal level are concerned; but at the national level too it is interests and ideologies with regard to domestic issues much more than foreign affairs that parties are likely to reflect in a non-superficial way. And if decision-makers say that they cannot listen too much to public opinion on foreign affairs because of its volatility, we would say that they are, more often than not, right. There is nothing in the theory and data we know that makes it unlikely that opinion in the periphery can change from, say, unilateralism to belligerent nationalism very quickly. Hence there is not only the problem of institutionalizing public opinion by coupling it more strongly to foreign policy decisions, but also the problem of stabilizing it, particularly public opinion in the periphery. And how is that possible?

One answer to this, glancing at Table 6, is rather obvious: everything that reduces the distance between center and periphery will also reduce the differences in attitude-formation: better diffusion of information, more organizations, more meetings, more knowledge, more opinions in the periphery. This is known as democratization and is an ongoing process; but there are other aspects to stability of a more subtle nature.

Thus one general perspective on how to obtain stabilization is probably as follows. An expressed opinion is an output from a person and an input to others, to fellow members of an organization, to kins and peers, to mass meetings, to newspapers, to pressure groups, to decision-makers. *Unless there is a feed-back to the opinion-holder that can function as a reinforcement the emission will die out.* For public opinion to be expressed relatively continuously, it must be nurtured by an input, by some kind of reflection that the opinion-holder can interpret as an effect.

This is well known to leaders of the many organizations built around foreign policy ideologies, usually of the single factor variety. The input that the opinion-holder receives in return from his opinion output is rarely more than the normative support from his organizational surroundings, the feeling of effervescence in the Durkheimian sense. This effect is known to taper off unless it is constantly reinforced and backed up by ritual, e.g. the kind of ritual in which churches specialize. The breakdown of the organization surrounding and stimulating the individual will also be the breakdown of an important source of feed-back, and the opinion-emission will fade out. Concretely, since only few pacifist organizations will withstand nationalist pressure in times of crisis, that kind of opposition to belligerent policy will easily die out. This is very different from domestic policy where the individual may register direct effects of his opinion-holding.

Even if the organizational surrounding is kept alive there is a limit to the stabilizing effect of this normative feed-back. It will probably suffice only for relatively few individuals; others will either have to be rewarded on a more direct *quid pro quo* basis or be *forced* to emit opinions in a stable pattern. Others again will need the feeling of being influential, if not by observing how their expressed opinion is translated into foreign policies and enacted, then at least by having their parliamentarians repeat their ideas at regular intervals, thus acknowledging receipt of the opinion pressure.

Leaving aside coercive methods where people are forced to express certain opinions we are left with "contractual" measures. The following may serve as an extreme illustration. An individual expresses attitudes in favor of "disarmament now," his signal is pooled with others of the same kind, is channeled via a party and a parliament structure to the decision-makers, the nation engages in disarmament and the individual gest his feed-back not only as acts of acknowledgment on the road from him to the top, but directly and concretely as a tax-cut made possible by reduced expenses for defense. In this case the feed-back will probably reinforce his attitude unless negative consequences of the policies are reported and believed in. Merely believing in this feed-back may serve as a stabilizer.

But the feed-back will usually not be so direct as in this hypothetical case. And this is a general problem in the relation between foreign policy and individual opinion: most benefits at the international level are likely to accrue to the nation or the collectivity as a whole—not as in social security where the individual may see direct results for himself personally. Usually the maximum that can be expected in the way of feed-back is a quotation in a speech by a member of parliament. But this can be combined with what we mentioned above about normative support from the organizational environment and the importance of ritual through organizing parties and elections with special reference to foreign policy. This would establish a direct pipeline between periphery and policy, whether the individual has voted for a party in power or in opposition.

Short of this there is still a particular structure that probably has a stabilizing effect. Imagine that we classify political parties according to two criteria: as to whether they are in power or opposition, and according to their social basis. For simplicity we distinguish between parties recruited mainly from the periphery, mainly from the middle categories and mainly from the center. Of the six combinations one is unlikely: a party mainly from the periphery will hardly be in power for a long time in any country. Imagine that a party with its social basis in the center is in position. This would add political alienation to the structural alienation we have discussed for the periphery and make the differences in Table 6 even much more pronounced—we assume. Hence one way of integrating the periphery, or at least the middle sectors, consists in having in power a party

with a solid basis in the middle category between center and periphery—high enough on social position to rule efficiently despite opposition from the center, yet low enough to integrate a sizeable fraction of the periphery.

In conclusion let us summarize conditions that would probably contribute to a stable, peace-oriented and effective public opinion in the field of foreign policy:

1. Elimination of the periphery from influence on foreign policy, for instance through a party-structure that does not adequately reflect periphery foreign policy orientations.
2. Stronger and less absolutist peace organizations that could decrease the distance between center and periphery where attitude-formation and social cosmology are concerned.
3. Ways of linking peaceful foreign policies to the self-interest of the individual.
4. A peaceful government party with strong links to the periphery, so that the periphery becomes engaged through party adherence.
5. A political structure that permits the expression of foreign policy attitudes regardless of attitudes towards domestic policy, provided these attitudes are "stabilized for peace."

APPENDIX

The reader might be interested in the wording and the marginals on some of the survey questions:

1. *Would you have preferred that Khrushchev's visit had taken place or do you prefer that it did not take place?*
   1963 } *Do you think it right or wrong to invite Premier Khrushchev to make a state visit to*
   1964 } *Norway?*

	In favor of invitation	Not in favor of invitation	Undecided	SUM
	%	%	%	%
August 1959	29	31	40	100
July 1963	45	31	24	100
June 1964	69	23	8	100

2. *Everything taken into consideration do you think it would be advantageous to have atomic weapons in Norway or do you think it is an advantage not to have atomic weapons in Norway?*

	Advantage to have atomic weapons in Norway	Depends, both-and	Advantage not to have atomic weapons	DK	SUM
	%	%	%		%
January 1961	11	12	56	21	100
June 1961	17	9	49	25	100
May 1962	8	10	57	25	100

3. *Everything taken into consideration do you consider it an advantage for Norway to be a member of NATO, or would it be an advantage if Norway were not a member of NATO?*

	Advantage to be in NATO	Depends, both-and	Advantage not to be in NATO	DK	SUM
	%	%	%	%	%
January 1961	46	11	17	26	100
June 1961	50	9	12	29	100
May 1962	42	16	12	30	100

4. *What do you think about Peace Corps or Peace Brigades, should Norway carry it out, should we wait and see what other countries do or should we not carry it out?*

	Should be carried out	Wait and see, etc.	Should not be carried out	DK	SUM
	%	%	%	%	%
June 1961	17	20	6	51	100
May 1962	13	18	5	64	100

5. *Do you or do you not think that Norway should tie itself to the Common Market?*

	In favor	Not in favor	DK	SUM
	%	%	%	%
September 1961	26	15	59	100
February 1962	31	28	41	100
April 1962	35	37	28	100
May 1962	30	24	46	100
August 1959 (EFTA)	10	60	30	100

Comments: (1) Khrushchev was invited to come in July 1959 but cancelled the visit, was then re-invited before the second poll. Figures show steady increase in acceptance with cold war depolarization. (2) Between the first two polls a heavy campaign *against* atomic weapons was organized, which may have mobilized the *adherents* of atomic weapons. Afterwards the campaign subsided and the original distribution was restored. (4) Peace Corps was suggested spring 1961, but between the two polls nothing much happened. The data probably reflect erosion of good-will for an idea when nothing happens. (5) Data for EEC first show polarization eroding the DK-rates, then comes parliament decision to open negotiations with EEC, and the ratio in favor to not in favor among the decided increases, but there is more increase among the DK. EFTA never gained great acceptance.

H. The Use of Mathematics

48. Fear in the Arms Race: A Mathematical Study*

Paul Smoker is affiliated with the Peace Research Center at Lancaster, England, and has authored a number of important inquiries that apply modern techniques of research to international phenomena. In this article he subjects data bearing on the postwar arms race to mathematical analysis and comes up with a number of interesting insights. That these insights are then shown to have considerable relevance for policy-making argues against the idea that applying mathematics to such problems is farfetched. [*Reprinted from the* Journal of Peace Research, *1 (1964), 55–63, by permission of the author and the publisher.*]

I. Introduction

"There have been only three great arms races. The first two of them ended in wars in 1914 and 1939; the third is still going on." So said Dr. Richardson, a pioneer in the study of arms race mechanics, in September 1951 at the beginning of an article in *Nature* (1, pp. 567–8). In that article, written shortly before his death, Richardson asked the important question "Can an arms race end without fighting?" The present article asks the same question in the light of world events before and after 1951.

The studies by Richardson of the first two arms races are now collected together in *Arms and Insecurity* (2). The present work can only be fully understood against the background of his work. While this study has much in common with the former work of Richardson, there are two major differences.

The first of these concerns nuclear weapons, which have introduced a new dimension of fear into world politics. The "Classical" Richardson theory

(2, pp. 12–16), which was able to describe the first two world arms races, is not suitable for examining the present arms race unless it is modified to allow for what Richardson in 1951 called *submissiveness*. Submissiveness, a fear factor, causes both sides to cool off when the international temperature becomes too hot.

The previous two arms races were able to break down into war without fear of complete extinction of life. Today this is not the case. It is recognized by leading politicians that a nuclear war would be disastrous, that it must be avoided, that in certain political circumstances it is better to draw back than to go on. This very human sense of fear has to be included in any theory which attempts to describe a nuclear arms race. The Richardson studies show that it was absent during the two non-nuclear arms races.

The second major difference concerns methodology. Richardson was the first to apply mathematical models to the arms race.[1] By means of equations he attempted to describe the behaviour of large groups

---

* This paper is a revised version of a paper first presented at the European Conference on Peace Research at Voksenåsen, Oslo, 22–25 September 1963, and subsequently published in *General Systems*, VIII, 61–76.

[1] The world "model" is used here in the loose sense, the correct word being "analogue."

of people.[2] He assumed that both nations in a two-nation arms race, being large groups, would behave in the same way. Thus he said (2, p. 12):

"The equations are merely a description of what people would do if they did not stop to think. Why are so many Nations reluctantly but steadily increasing their armaments as if they were mechanically compelled to do so? Because, I say, they follow their traditions, which are fixtures, and their instincts, which are mechanical and because they have not yet made a sufficiently strenuous intellectual and moral effort to control the situation. The process described by the ensuing equations is not to be thought of as inevitable. It is what would occur if instinct and tradition were allowed to act uncontrolled. In this respect the equations have some analogy to a dream. For a dream often warns an individual of the antisocial acts that his instincts would lead him to commit, if he were not wakeful."

The assumption made in this paper is that the common property of the two nations considered, that of being a national group, gives rise to some common patterns of group behaviour. These common patterns of behaviour are partly described by the deterministic differential equations. At the same time there are important differences in group behaviour in the present study between the two groups concerned (the United States and the Soviet Union). These differences in group behaviour are mainly the products of recent history. The classic example in the present study is the profound effect on the Soviet Union of the German Federal Republic entering the NATO defence organization in 1954. The massive mutual slaughter between these two nations during the still recent Second World War has left its mark on the group psychologies of both parties.

These differences in group behaviour are outside the scope of any single deterministic model but can be illustrated by constructing a number of different models. Some models give more weight to Russian behaviour, others more to American behaviour. All of the models give the same general

picture of the arms race, which corresponds to the common group patterns of behaviour, and all the models exhibit certain differences, which correspond to differences in group behaviour between the two groups.

This study does not try to construct the "most accurate model." Rather, a battery of models are used which give a better total picture of the arms race than any one model would on its own, and enable us to view the international situation from different angles.

It is this aspect of the present study which shifts the emphasis from the determinism of the differential equations to a vaguer broader picture of the whole situation. The whole picture could only be drawn using an infinite number of models and is therefore indeterminate. Nevertheless we feel that an understanding of the few models presented here provides a picture of the arms race.

II. The Richardson Theory

The fact that only two nations, the United States and the Soviet Union, are included in this paper is an important limitation.[3] A later analysis could attempt to extend the sample to, say, the top five or six powers.

Richardson's two-nation theory for the growth of an arms race assumes that the rate at which the first side arms depends on the amount of armament the other side has, the colossal costs of armaments, and the feelings towards the other side (for instance as expressed in treaties and trade).

This is represented mathematically as

$$(1) \qquad \frac{dx}{dt} = ky - \alpha x + g$$

where y is the amount of armaments the second side has, x is the amount the first side has, $\frac{dx}{dt}$ is the rate at which the first side arms, and g is the feelings of the first side. The positive constant k is called the defence coefficient, while the positive constant α is called the fatigue and expense coefficient. The higher k the more the first side is influenced by the amount

[2] In so doing he assumed that large-scale human events can be viewed in the deterministic framework, the determinism being the determinism of large numbers. The same determinism can be used to predict the number of road casualties next year, or the population of the world in the year 2000. An excellent discussion of Richardson's scientific philosophy is given in the *Journal of Conflict Resolution* by Anatol Rapoport (3, pp. 249–58).

[3] German (4, pp. 138–44) estimates on geopolitical indices that the Soviet Union and United States together possess more than twice the power of the next 17 most powerful nations.

of armament of the second side; the higher α the greater the fatigue effect due to the level of armament already attained.

A similar state of affairs holds for the other side. This is expressed as

$$(2) \qquad \frac{dy}{dt} = \text{I}x - \beta y + h$$

where h is the feeling of the second side towards the first side, I is the defence coefficient, and β is the fatigue and expense coefficient. Richardson argued that these equations are correct for low level arms races where there is a low level of fear, for example the previous world arms races and the early part of the present one. Obviously a high level arms race cannot go on forever without fighting. Something would have to cause the two nations to reduce their defence expenditures, or at least keep them constant. In the equations this would make $\frac{dx}{dt}$ and $\frac{dy}{dt}$ negative, or zero. But the cost of armaments x and y must be positive. So this change in sign must come from other coefficients, as h and l, α and β, g and h are assumed constant. These other coefficients would have to overcome the increasing net effect of $ky - \alpha x$ and $lx - \beta y$ as x and y become larger.

We shall now analyse this in terms of submissiveness. The effect of submissiveness depends not only on y or x absolutely, but also on the difference between y and x. Today the United States may have ten more bombs than the Soviet Union, but this would not make the Soviet Union submit to United States demands. An imbalance of ten bombs is insignificant in relative terms when y and x are as high as they are today—but significant at low levels of armament. Thus we assume the submissiveness effect to be proportional to the absolute level of armament of the other party and to the difference between levels.

If these conditions are incorporated in both equations the result is

$$(3) \qquad \frac{dx}{dt} = ky[\text{I} - \sigma(y-x)]\text{I} - \alpha x + g$$

$$(4) \qquad \frac{dy}{dt} = \text{I}x[\text{I} - \rho(x-y)] - \beta y + h$$

where σ and ρ are positive measures of submissiveness. When σ and ρ are zero, equations (3) and (4) become equations (I) and (2).

If these equations are added we get:[4]

$$(5) \qquad (k-\alpha)(x+y) - \frac{d}{dt}(x+y) = k\sigma(y-x)^2 - (g+h)$$

This is the general form of the submissiveness model which is tested in this paper. Particular forms of this model, which attempt to illustrate differences in behaviour between the two groups, are constructed by using different measures for x and y. In order to test this model $(k-\alpha)$ must be known. The left-hand side of the equation can then be plotted on the X axis against $(y-x)^2$ on the Y axis. For the model to represent the arms race a straight-line graph should result, except at times when a group behaviour pattern peculiar to one group dominates the general common group pattern.

III. The Calculation of x and y

One method of measurement of x and y would be to express the defence expenditure as a percentage of government expenditure. This would show its relative importance compared with other expenditure, such as health, education or welfare.

Unfortunately to do this both Governments would have to balance their budgets. The United States never does. For example, in 1953 the United States defence expenditure was 79.9 per cent of Government Revenue as against 67.9 per cent of Government Expenditure.

To make x and y comparable, a defence ratio must be worked out which takes into account defence expenditure, Government Expenditure and Government Revenue.

An arithmetic ratio could be used:

(6) *Arithmetic Defence Ratio =*

$$= \frac{\text{Defence Expenditure} \times 100}{\frac{1}{2}(\text{Govt. Expend.} + \text{Govt. Revenue})}$$

However, in an earlier paper (5, p. 57) it was shown that the arithmetic defence ratio, when used with equations (1) and (2) to describe the first few

[4] German (4, pp. 138–44) also showed that on geopolitical indices the U.S.A. and Soviet Union can be regarded as of equivalent strength. For equal groups, the various coefficients can be regarded as equal. Thus to obtain equation (5) it has been assumed that $k = l$, $\alpha = \beta$, $\sigma = \rho$.

years of the present arms race, did not provide as accurate a representation as the geometric defence ratio, for the Richardson theory to describe the arms race.

The geometric defence ratio, R, is defined thus:

$$(7) \quad R = \frac{\text{Defence Expenditure} \times 100}{\sqrt{\text{Government Expenditure} \times \text{Government Revenue}}}$$

The values of x and y used in this paper have been calculated using the geometric defence ratio.

Unfortunately the United States' budget is for fiscal years, i.e. July 1st to June 30th. An average is taken to get a defence ratio for calendar years by letting

$$(8) \quad x = \tfrac{1}{2}(R_1 + R_2)$$

where R_1 and R_2 are the defence ratios of the United States for the fiscal years 1 and 2. x is then the measure used in all models to represent the behaviour of the United States during the year (calendar) 1.

The measure of Soviet behaviour, y, is exaggerated in one model and played down in another. A third more central model is also constructed. The period of exaggeration taken has been 1952–60.

For the model which exaggerates American behaviour during the period 1952–60, the Soviet defence ratio, as defined by equation (7), is used as the measure for y. It is well known that the Soviet economic system is different from the American system. In the United States, defence expenditure since the Second World War has never been lower than a defence ratio of 29.7, and has at times reached levels of over 70. On the other hand the Soviet ratio has varied between 12.8 and 24.8. Thus by using unweighted Soviet ratios the American defence expenditure is played up.

For the model which exaggerates Soviet behaviour during the period 1952–60 the Soviet defence ratio is made equal to the American ratio for the years 1948 and 1952. When this is done the American ratio has a value of 72.1 in 1952 and never, during the period 1952–60, has a value different by more than 14.5 units from 72.1. On the other hand the Soviet measure, which also has a value of 72.1 in 1952 has a value of 1.9 in 1960, a change of some 70.2 units. Thus this model is greatly influenced by the change in Soviet defence expenditure and the American changes are relatively small.

The third model gives a picture between the two which still exaggerates the Soviet behaviour. In this model y is defined as follows:

$$(9) \quad y_m = \frac{x_{52} - x_{48}}{R_{s52} - R_{s48}} \times R_{sm}$$

Here y_m is the behaviour measure used for the year m. R_{sm} is the Soviet defence ratio for the year m, R_{s48} and R_{s52} are the Soviet defence ratios for the years 1948 and 1952.

During the period from 1952 to 1960 the Soviet ratio changes by 63.8 units for this model as against the 14.5 units of the United States. On the other hand, relative to the size of the Soviet ratio, 208.3 units in 1952, the change does not have as great an effect as the change of 70.2 units in the Russian model. This model is called the "Inbetween Model."

IV. Finding a Value for $(k - \alpha)$

To test the general submissiveness model, equation (5), $(k - \alpha)$ must be known.

α is a measure of what an economy can afford, and k is a measure of what armaments decision-makers think they need. The difference between k and α is a measure of the acceleration of the arms race providing submissiveness is very small.

To calculate $(k - \alpha)$ a period near to the origin, 1948–52, is examined using the "Classical" Richardson theory, equations (1) and (2) expressed in the form

$$(10) \quad \frac{d(x+y)}{dt} = (k - \alpha)(x + y) + (g + h).$$

For reasons given above the various constants have been assumed equal. This equation corresponds to equation (5) without the effects of submissiveness. Close to the origin these effects should be small, but should increase as we move away from the origin.

If the left-hand side of equation (10) is plotted on the Y axis of a graph, and $(x + y)$ is plotted on the X axis, a straight line should result of slope $(k - \alpha)$. In order to test this bit of the theory the Inbetween Model has been used (equation (9)).

Unfortunately the Korean War broke out in June 1950, and obviously a theory of arms races cannot be applied to a state of war. If the budget of the United States is examined for the period 1949–50, it is noticeable that the defence ratio is considerably

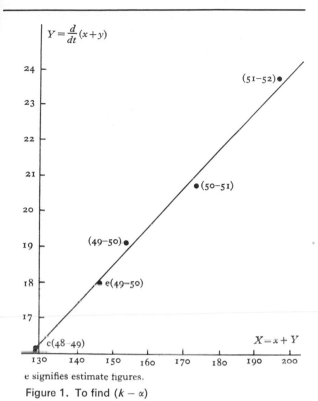

$Y = \dfrac{d}{dt}(x+y)$

(51–52)

(50–51)

(49–50)

e(49–50)

c(48–49)

$X = x + Y$

e signifies estimate figures.

Figure 1. To find $(k - \alpha)$

line with a very high correlation ($r = .97$). The slope of the line is very close to 0.1. Hence this is the value of $(k - \alpha)$ used throughout the rest of this study, as both k and α are assumed to be constants.

The plot also shows that the period 1948–52 follows the same pattern as the two previous world arms races, the "acceleration,"

$$\frac{d(x+y)}{dt},$$

being proportional to the "velocity," $x + y$.

If the line in Fig. 1 is taken back to the X axis, $Y = 0$, the point where it cuts plots the hostility when the arms race began. On this scale hostility equals thirty-two units. This means that there was already hostility between the great powers in 1948 and the arms race should have started sooner. Perhaps it didn't because of the effect of war-weariness (2, Chapter XXIII).

V. Testing the Submissiveness Model During the Whole Period 1948–60

In equation (5) $(k - \alpha)$ is now known, and three weighting procedures have been suggested which respectively accentuate the Soviet behaviour to a greater extent, the American behaviour, and the Soviet behaviour to a lesser extent (the Inbetween Model). For each of these particular models the left-hand side of equation (5) is plotted as X against $(y - x)^2$ as Y. A straight-line graph should result for those periods which are not disturbed by a particular group behaviour pattern.

The Russian Model

Figure 2 shows the submissiveness model which accentuates the Soviet behaviour most.

The figure is in two parts: 1948–52 and 1952–60. In part two seven points are close to a straight line ($r = .843$, $p < .02$). One point, 1954–5, is away from the straight line. This is the German entry into NATO at the end of 1954, which the Russians viewed seriously. As Sir Anthony Eden remarks (6, p. 301):

"The West, and in particular the United States, has never clearly understood the terrible significance of the German invasion of Russia. A nation of eighty million had invaded a nation of one hundred and sixty million, devastated its western provinces and

higher during the fiscal year 1950 than the previous year's official governmental estimates for 1950 had expected. The official estimates and the actual expenditure differed by ten units when measured as a defence ratio. In 1949 and 1951 no such effect was present.

For the Soviet Union a similar jump is found spread over two years (calendar). In 1949 there is a jump of two units, while in 1950 there is a jump of eight units. This is consistent with a change taking place during the fiscal year 1950. This in turn is consistent with the assumption that a subsidiary arms race took place during the fiscal year 1950, in the same year as the outbreak of the Korean War.

To eliminate this effect, official governmental estimates have been used for the fiscal year 1950. With this estimate included in the model, Figure 1 shows $(x + y)$ as X, and

$$\frac{d(x+y)}{dt}$$

as Y. Both the estimate and actual points are marked for the period 1949–50. The points lie on a straight

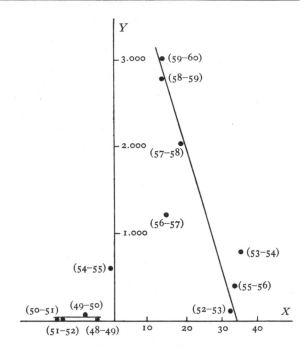

Figure 2. The Russian model

almost reached its capital. The Russian people could not forget this. They had no Atlantic between them and Germany, not even a Channel. They would not run such risks again. In much that is false in the stream of comment which flows from the Soviets, there is one cry that is real. It is that of a nation which has nearly bled to death, not for the first time in Russian history. The Napoleonic War, World War I, both tolled the same experience. Russians have long memories, they would be feckless not to take precautions."

Speaking in Moscow on August 8th, 1953, just over a year before the German entry into NATO took place, Mr. Malenkov is reported in *Keesing's Contemporary Archives* as saying:

"The German question which is of primary importance can and must be settled. This is necessary in the interests of strengthening the security of all European countries—in the first place the security of Germany's western and eastern neighbours—and in the national interests of the German people. For this purpose it is necessary to abandon the policy of dragging Germany into aggressive military blocs, or restoring an aggressive militarist Germany. Our

people did not shed the blood of millions of its sons and daughters in order to restore once more this dangerous hotbed of war in Europe. The Great Powers have assumed the obligation to preserve Germany's national unity and to ensure the transformation of Germany into a peace loving democratic state, not to facilitate the birth of German militarism. The German people have drawn serious conclusions from their history. They do not want to shed their blood once again in the interests of the military clique, which has already brought catastrophe upon Germany more than once."

A report by the Population Register of Washington, D.C., concluded from a survey of a recent Russian census of population by age that the estimate of Russian losses in World War II should be increased from 7 to 20 millions (7, p. 292). The United States of America have lost less than a million people in major wars during the last 100 years (8). This figure includes the total deaths in the American Civil War, The Spanish American War, World War I, World War II and the Korean War. It is therefore understandable that there should be differences in group behaviour of the sort demonstrated by the (53–54) point in this model.

The other slightly displaced point, apart from (53–54) which is also displaced by the German entry into NATO, is that for 1956–7. Here things are not so simple. On February 24th, 1955, Turkey and Iraq signed a pact of mutual co-operation in Baghdad. Just before the now well-known Middle East crisis Britain became involved in the pact, together with Iran, Pakistan and Turkey and with the support of the United States of America. Changes of organization of this sort are bound to influence one side or the other in a polarized world.

The American Model

Figure 3 shows the American model, that is the one model of the three drawn which exaggerates the American behaviour. This model is also in two parts, but the 1951–2 point lies between the two. In the second part seven points lie near a straight line ($r = .925$, $p < .01$). The (55–56) point is displaced from the line. On May 14th 1955 a Treaty of Friendship, Co-operation and Mutual Assistance was signed in Warsaw between the Soviet Union and its European Allies (Albania, Bulgaria, Eastern Germany, Hungary, Poland, Romania,

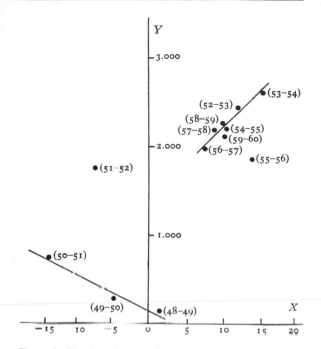

Figure 3. The American model

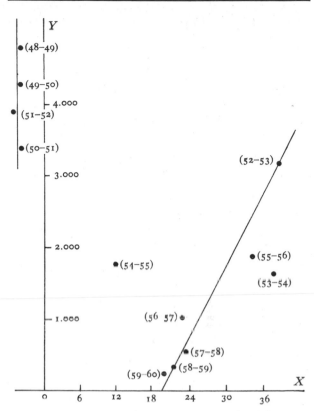

Figure 4. The "inbetween model"

and Czechoslovakia) to serve as a counterpoise to NATO. A unified military command was set up in Moscow.

The United States would almost certainly regard the Warsaw pact as a threat to her and it is reasonable to suppose that she would respond to such an event. The response is seen in the displaced point, which represents a particular behaviour pattern of the United States. The general pattern of behaviour dominates before and after this event.

The Inbetween Model

Figure 4 shows the Inbetween Model.

As $(k - \alpha)$ was calculated for this model the slope of the graph gives us a value for $1/k\sigma$.

In this model, the slope of the first section is infinity, indicating that submission suddenly appeared in 1952 but was previously absent ($\sigma = 0$ gives a slope infinity). This sudden submission is something which was not expected, for the model in equation (5) assumes that submission is always present but is small at first.

It could be argued that the Soviet and American defence policies softened as a result of the death of

Stalin. At the same time there is another possibility. Mr. Maynard Smith has suggested that (9):

"A pecking order with ritual rather than real fighting is often found. The winner ceases to attack as soon as surrender is made. The surrender ceremonies are better developed and more obvious in birds than in humans."

Ignoring the stimulating analogy between "ritual rather than real fighting" and the arms race, it would seem that the existence of this mutual submissiveness effect, which comes into being quite suddenly between members of the same species, is a well-established fact of the biological sciences. It is my contention that this safety mechanism, which like a thermostat, operates when things are becoming too hot, is well enough developed in human beings to slow the arms race when the fear experienced by both sides becomes too great. It is also my contention that when the international climate cools off sufficiently, when there is less tension, then the thermostat will switch off and the arms race will accelerate once again. This will lead to a cyclic arms race with defence ratios oscillating between maximum and minimum values. Whether or not the maximum and minimum values are constant or not is a complex question best left for further research. Coupled with the accidental war risk (10, pp. 8–24) this presents a very black picture if survival is our aim.

VI. Some Policy Implications

(i) The most obvious policy implication which has to be recognised if the above study is valid is the limitations in time of deterrent theory. As long as this theory provides the basis for foreign policy, the arms race will at best oscillate between upper and lower levels. The arms race since 1960 has followed such a course, reaching a maximum at the end of 1963. The fact that there is a finite probability of accidental war makes deterrence as a long-term policy insanity. Alternative policies must be formulated.

(ii) A second policy implication concerns viewing the arms race as a whole system. If the arms race is understood as a system to be controlled, decision makers would not aggravate it during times of stress. If it is viewed as a reasonable way to conduct international relations, regardless of the danger, then the high long-term probability of nuclear war will remain.

(iii) An understanding of this paper makes it very likely that alliance formation shocks the system. Examples are the German entry into NATO, the Warsaw Pact formation, and American involvement in CENTO. Alliances are intended to prevent war, but in fact such shocks could disrupt the system and cause the war which they are trying to prevent. Decision makers should consider the effect on the whole system before forming, strengthening or expanding alliances.

(iv) A positive side to the arms race concerns submissiveness. When submissiveness first sets in, decision makers should do everything in their power to keep the system moving in the disarmament direction. Positive peace measures are more likely to bite during this phase than at any other time.

(v) The logical extension of continuing the submissiveness trend is the evolution of a peace race. Such a race would involve international friendship on a scale currently reserved for international hostility. If the measures taken during the submissiveness section of the arms race were strong enough and positive enough, a peace race might be started. Once started it would have to be kept going, lest rearmament occur.

References

1. Richardson, L. F. "Could an Arms Race End Without Fighting?" *Nature*, September 29, 1951.

2. Richardson, L. F. *Arms and Insecurity*. London: Stevens and Sons Ltd., 1960.

3. Rapoport, Anatol: "Lewis Fry Richardson's Mathematical Theory of War," *Journal of Conflict Resolution*, I. 3.

4. German, F. Clifford. "A Tentative Evaluation of World Power," *Journal of Conflict Resolution*, IV, 1.

5. Smoker, Paul. "A Mathematical Study of The Present Arms Race," *General Systems*, VIII, Ann Arbor.

6. Eden, Sir Anthony. *The Memoirs of Sir Anthony Eden, Full Circle*. London: Times Publishing Co., 1960.

7. Richardson, L. F. *Statistics of Deadly Quarrels*. London: Stevens, 1960.

8. Information Please Almanack. New York: Macmillan, 1959.

9. Smith, J. Maynard. *Conference on the Pathogenesis of War*. London: Medical Association for the Prevention of War, September 1961.

10. COUND (Campaign in Oxford University for Nuclear Disarmament). *Accidental War, Some Dangers in the 1960's. The Mershon Report*. London: Housemans, 1962.

[*Editor's Note:* The response to the preceding article was such that the following appeared in the *Journal of Peace Research*, Vol. II (1965), pp. 94–95, and is reprinted by permission of the author and the publisher.]

Research Communication:

On Mathematical Models in Arms Races

From Paul Smoker

I have had some valuable comments and criticisms of my article in the first issue of the *Journal of Peace Research*, pages 55–64, which should be brought to the attention of the readers of the *Journal*.

Comment. The infinite slope in Figure 4 is an inevitable consequence of the facts of Figure 1, if it is assumed that the slope in Figure 1 gives a value for $(k - \alpha)$.

Author. This is quite true, as is the converse. That is, the mathematical form of equation (5) is such that it can only be consistent with the facts in Figure 1 if the submissiveness constant is zero during the period 1948–52. This is assuming, as stated in the article, that k and α are positive constants.

The discovery that, for fact and theory to agree, the submissiveness constant is zero up to 1952 belongs to Figure 1 and not to Figure 4. Figure 4 shows that if k and α are constants then the submissiveness constant is not zero after 1952.

The argument and conclusions of the article remain the same, and are as valid.

Comment. A value for $(k - \alpha)$ should have been calculated for each model.

Author. This is quite true and is pointed out in my earlier papers.

Comment. A mathematical model which has to assume a change in value of a "constant" is not very satisfactory.

Author. This may be true from a pure mathematical point of view, but the phenomena of submission in the animal world seem to follow the sudden appearance pattern, which mathematically speaking implies discontinuity.

Professor Penrose pointed out to me an interesting article by Mr. Maynard Smith [1] which talks about this change in value of the submissiveness constant in animal behaviour. In one section Mr. Smith says:

A pecking order with ritual rather than real fighting is often found. The winner ceases to attack as soon as surrender is made. The surrender ceremonies are better developed and more obvious in birds than in humans.

Comment. The form of equation (3) could mean that if x is greater than y, when submission is acting the bigger power increases its rate of arming while the smaller power decreases its rate. Without saying this is good or bad, it would not be so if the first minus in the bracket was made a plus.

Author. This is true, and altering the sign would not alter the general form of the final equation (5). The article was testing Richardson's theory rather than trying out other models. Certainly alternative models should be tried.

For example, it has been suggested that instead of $(y - x)$ in equation (3), the rationale leading to that equation might be better expressed by having $\left[\dfrac{y - x}{x}\right]$. Of course this would make things more complicated and, in general, I have tried to keep things as simple as possible.

Comment. It seems to me that defence expenditure, however it is measured, is not a very good measure of level of armament. Surely there can be a steady increase in level of armament of a nation while its defence expenditure is constant. For example, the defence expenditure of Norway has remained at about 16.5% of total expenditure for some years, but one may nevertheless have the impression that the level of armament has increased.

Author. This is probably true, even allowing for the effects of obsolescence, but my main concern in using the defence ratio was to get a measure of "feeling about defence" rather than assume nations make decisions on these matters which are influenced by the actual level of armament. The fact that we continue to rationalize into overkill capacity casts serious doubts upon the rationality of current defence decision making. As the stimulating article by Hansen and Ulrich [2] illustrates so well, there are no destruction capabilities beyond overkill.

The defence ratio tries to gauge how much of the available money goes into defence, rather than how much actual defence capacity a nation needs or has.

References

1. Smith, J. Maynard. *Conference on the Pathogenesis of War*. Medical Association for the Prevention of War, September 1961.

2. Hansen, Erland B. and Ulrich, J. W. "Some Problems of Nuclear Power Dynamics," *Journal of Peace Research*, 1964, pp. 137–49.

49. The Structure of Influence Relationships in the International System*

Steven J. Brams is Assistant Professor of Political Science at Syracuse University. The author of several highly innovative studies that seek to uncover the structure of international phenomena through quantitative analysis, Professor Brams employs in this selection algebraic procedures to probe the structure of a phenomenon—influence—that is both extremely crucial to the comprehension of world politics and highly resistant to empirical observation. The result is a lucid exposure of the nature of international influence relationships as well as a clear-cut illustration of how modern mathematics can usefully be adapted to the research needs of the field. [*Published for the first time in this volume.*]

As a preliminary report on the application of the theory of directed graphs (digraphs)[1] to the study of international relations, this article has two purposes: (1) at a descriptive level, to show how digraph theory can help one simplify and bring order out of the myriad transactions that occur between many pairs of nations; (2) at an explanatory level, to suggest how this order might be related to the behavior of nations in the international system. Clearly, the articulation of the structural order or form of a system whose actors have nondesultory relations with each other is a logical precondition for the explanation of recurring patterns of behavior within it.

More specifically, an attempt will be made to show how influence relationships, conceptualized as something immanent in the transactions nations have with each other, can be abstracted from the flow of these transactions and operationally defined for all pairs of nations. Balances in these flows will then be used to distinguish symmetrical from asymmetrical influence relationships between pairs of nations, and procedures for simplifying the digraph structures of nations connected by these influence relationships will be outlined. From a graphical description of influence structures for all nations in the world and a comparison of these structures over time, we shall advance certain empirical generalizations about the overall pattern of influence relationships in the international system, the nature of superpower alignments and the cross-pressures they create, and the stability of membership in subsystems at different hierarchical levels. Then, on the basis of the kind of influence at a

* Research on this article was supported by the Institute for Defense Analyses under ISA/SA Exploratory Research Contract DAHC 15 67C 0013. I gratefully acknowledge the support and encouragement of William A. Niskanen, Jr., and the valuable advice of James N. Rosenau, Wade P. Sewell, and Oliver R. Smoot, Jr. I especially wish to thank Sally P. Taylor, whose unfailing research assistance proved invaluable to the completion of this study. The views expressed in this article are entirely those of the author and are not necessarily those of any agency of the United States Government.

[1] For a very clear introduction to digraph theory and some of its applications in the social sciences, see Frank Harary, Robert Z. Norman, and Dorwin Cartwright, *Structural Models: An Introduction to the Theory of Directed Graphs* (New York: John Wiley and Sons, Inc., 1965).

conceptual level that our empirical measure seems to tap, we shall suggest some possible linkages between the behavior of nations and their positions in the influence structures. Finally, we shall conclude with an assessment of the reliability of our influence measure and the validity of our analysis of influence structures.

Because a digraph model allows one to differentiate symmetrical from asymmetrical relations between the actors in a system, it enables one to preserve information that other data-reduction techniques, such as factor analysis, which permit only single-valued interrelationships for each pair of variables (or actors), rule out. Since there is no reason to assume that symmetrical relations between nations have the same meaning as asymmetrical relations, this model offers an especially important advantage in studies of international relations. What meaning and significance symmetrical or asymmetrical relations *do* have, of course, will depend on the nature of the relations under consideration and how the symmetry/asymmetry distinction is made.

International Visits and the Exercise of Influence

The kind of international relations data analyzed here is visits between heads-of-state and other high-level government officials for all nations in the world in 1964 and 1965. These data were chosen because they probably come as close as any comparative and publicly available information to reflecting the flow of influence between the major decision-makers of nations. When a high-level government official travels to a foreign nation, he usually does so because he wishes to convey information or exert influence *in a manner and to a degree* which could not be done otherwise.[2] If it could, he would be much more likely to try to communicate or exert influence through other channels, such as through his ambassador or a representative to an international organization. There seems good reason, therefore, to believe that most high-level government officials visit their counterparts in foreign nations to discuss

matters on which they think they can be more influential than their representatives.[3]

To be sure, the parties to a visit may not succeed in influencing each other, in the sense of getting the other party to do something he would not otherwise do. In fact, it is probably rare that representatives from competing blocs meet with the expectation of changing each other's behavior in major policy areas. Even when changes do occur, it is hazardous to ascribe these changes to a prior meeting on which reliable information may at best be sketchy.

Given that we are not generally privy to meetings between high-level government officials from different nations, the task of trying to measure the exercise of influence in such meetings would appear to be nearly impossible. If we forget for the moment about what transpires in such meetings, however, and instead focus on who visits whom, the pattern of communications might provide a clue to the influence process.

Although the relationship between communication flows and influence flows at the international level is at this stage only speculative, the correlation between these two different flows at the interpersonal level is reasonably well-established: the greater a person's influence over other persons in small groups (by a number of different measures), the higher the proportion of communications he tends to receive from them rather than send to them.[4] As Thibaut and Kelley explain, the possession of superior (or asymmetrical) power tends to relieve an actor in a dyadic relationship of the necessity of paying close attention to his partner's actions.[5]

---

[2] He may also travel abroad to increase the strength of his position at home. In such cases we may interpret the flow of influence to be back to the official's government, though it is questionable whether we may properly label the source of this influence as the foreign nation visited.

[3] More broadly, J. David Singer argues that ". . . the international system itself is the key element in explaining why and how nations attempt to influence the behavior of one another." "Inter-Nation Influence: A Formal Model," *American Political Science Review*, LVII (June 1963), 423.

[4] See Jacob I. Hurwitz, Alvin F. Zander, and Bernard Hymovitch, "Some Effects of Power on the Relations among Group Members," in Dorwin Cartwright and Alvin Zander, eds., *Group Dynamics: Research and Theory* (2nd ed.; New York: Harper and Row, 1960), 800–809; Arthur R. Cohen, "Upward Communication in Experimentally Created Hierarchies," *Human Relations*, XI (February 1958), 41–53; and David L. Watson, "Effects of Certain Social Power Structures on Communication in Task-Oriented Groups," *Sociometry*, XXVIII (September 1965), 322–36.

[5] John W. Thibaut and Harold H. Kelley, *The Social Psychology of Groups* (New York: John Wiley and Sons, Inc., 1959), p. 125.

In this sense, power is "the ability to afford not to learn."[6]

Transferred to international relations, this proposition would suggest that a nation has influence over another nation to the extent that it receives rather than sends visits to it. (Note that the proposition says nothing about nations whose leaders do not visit each other.) Influence is thus conceived not as a substance or possession but as a relational property that appears in the transactions of nations. In particular, we have conceptualized it as a property associated with the recurring movements of government officials. From the symmetrical or asymmetrical pattern of such movements, we shall seek to infer the responses of these officials and their governments to each other's actions.[7]

Two nations will be considered to be in an influence relationship if their meetings with each other exceed a specified number. If an approximately equal number occurs in each nation, their influence relationship will be considered symmetrical; otherwise, the nation receiving the preponderant number of visits will be considered the nation exercising asymmetrical influence over the other. Later in this article we shall seek to clarify at a conceptual level the meaning that the exercise of influence, based upon visit data, seems to have in international relations.

Selection and Coding of the International Visit Data

The source of the visit data for the 121 nations included in this study, all of which were independent or gained their independence in 1964 (see Table 1), were reports of visits gleaned from the *New York Times Index* for 1964 and 1965.[8] The rules which were

applied in the coding of the visit data, with the rationales for their adoption, are as follows:

1. Two levels of officials involved in visits have been distinguished:

> (a) head(s)-of-state (including president, prime minister, premier, chancellor, or leader of dominant political party in parliamentary or Communist political system), deputy head(s)-of-state, and foreign minister;

> (b) other cabinet or subcabinet minister, leader of political party, other government-connected official.

The foreign minister is differentiated from other cabinet ministers and placed in category (a) because of his generally influential role in the determination of a nation's foreign policy. "Government-connected" officials in category (b) refer to high-level officials (e.g., General Maxwell Taylor) who are sent on officially sanctioned missions but are not necessarily full time employees of their governments; this category does not include the visits of private citizens (e.g., ex-Vice President Nixon). Since the influence of royalty in different nations varies enormously, visits of royalty are counted at the level of the hosting government officials, if any, with whom they confer.

2. Visits to multilateral conferences have not been counted, since the host nation may be the location for a conference for purely idiosyncratic reasons

---

[6] Karl W. Deutsch, *The Nerves of Government: Models of Political Communication and Control* (New York: The Free Press, 1963), p. 111.

[7] For an extended treatment of this idea, see Charles A. McClelland, *Theory and the International System* (New York: The Macmillan Company, 1966), Chap. 3. In a recent paper, McClelland has used digraph theory to study international crises. See his "The Beginning, Duration, and Abatement of International Crises: Comparisons in Two Conflict Areas," in Charles F. Hermann (ed.), *International Crises*, forthcoming.

[8] (New York: The New York Times Company). The reliability of this source was checked informally against several other English-language sources: *Deadline Data on World Affairs* (New York: Deadline Data, Inc.); *Facts on*

File Yearbook (New York: Facts on File, Inc.); *News Dictionary: An Encyclopedic Summary of Contemporary History* (New York: Facts on File, Inc.); and *Keesing's Contemporary Archives* (London: Keesing's Publications Limited). On the reporting of international visits, the *Times Index* was the most comprehensive of all these sources. A formal comparison of combined-level visits reported in the *Times Index* for 1964 and those reported in the French newspaper, *Le Monde*—as indexed in the English-language "Index of *Le Monde*" (Washington, D.C. Joint Publications Research Service, U.S. Department of Commerce)—showed a high coincidence in reports for almost all nations. Although *Le Monde* reported 63 percent fewer visits than did the *Times Index* for 1964, the 193 visits between pairs it did report were also reported in the *Times Index* for all but twenty-two nations receiving visits, only eight of which (Algeria, France, West Germany, Morocco, Tunisia, U.A.R., U.S.S.R., and Yugoslavia) had two or more visits reported in *Le Monde* that were not reported in the *Times Index*. Some of the implications of only a single data source on the reliability of the data and the validity of the analysis which follows are discussed later in the article.

TABLE 1
*Code Abbreviations of the
121 Nations in the Study*

Abbreviation	Nation	Abbreviation	Nation	Abbreviation	Nation
1 AFG	Afghanistan	42 GUA	Guatemala	83 NOR	Norway
2 ALB	Albania	43 GUI	Guinea	84 PAK	Pakistan
3 ALG	Algeria	44 HAI	Haiti	85 PAN	Panama
4 ARG	Argentina	45 HON	Honduras	86 PAR	Paraguay
5 AUL	Australia	46 HUN	Hungary	87 PER	Peru
6 AUS	Austria	47 ICE	Iceland	88 PHI	Philippines
7 BEL	Belgium	48 IND	India	89 POL	Poland
8 BOL	Bolivia	49 INS	Indonesia	90 POR	Portugal
9 BRA	Brazil	50 IRN	Iran	91 RUM	Rumania
10 BUL	Bulgaria	51 IRQ	Iraq	92 RWA	Rwanda
11 BUR	Burma	52 IRE	Irish R.	93 SAU	Saudi Arabia
12 BUU	Burundi	53 ISR	Israel	94 SEN	Senegal
13 CAM	Cambodia	54 ITA	Italy	95 SIE	Sierra Leone
14 CAO	Cameroun	55 IVO	Ivory Coast	96 SOM	Somali R.
15 CAN	Canada	56 JAM	Jamaica	97 SPN	Spain
16 CEN	Central African R.	57 JAP	Japan	98 SUD	Sudan
17 CEY	Ceylon	58 JOR	Jordan	99 SWD	Sweden
18 CHA	Chad	59 KEN	Kenya	100 SWZ	Switzerland
19 CHL	Chile	60 KON	Korea (Dem. R.)	101 SYR	Syrian Arab R.
20 CHN	China (People's R.)	61 KOS	Korea (R.)	102 TAN	Tanzania (Tanganyika & Zanzibar)
21 CHT	China (R.)	62 KUW	Kuwait		
22 COL	Colombia	63 LAO	Laos	103 TAI	Thailand
23 CON	Congo (Braz.)	64 LEB	Lebanon	104 TOG	Togo
24 COP	Congo (Lep.)	65 LBR	Liberia	105 TRI	Trinidad & Tobago
25 COS	Costa Rica	66 LBY	Libya	106 TUN	Tunisia
26 CUB	Cuba	67 LUX	Luxembourg	107 TUR	Turkey
27 CYP	Cyprus	68 MAD	Malagasy R.	108 UGA	Uganda
28 CZE	Czechoslovakia	69 MWI	Malawi (Nayasaland)	109 UNS	Union of S. Africa
29 DAH	Dahomey	70 MAL	Malaysia	110 USR	U.S.S.R.
30 DEN	Denmark	71 MLI	Mali	111 UAR	United Arab R.
31 DOM	Dominican R.	72 MLT	Malta	112 UNK	United Kingdom
32 ECU	Ecuador	73 MAU	Mauritania	113 USA	United States
33 ELS	El Salvador	74 MEX	Mexico	114 UPP	Upper Volta
34 ETH	Ethiopia	75 MON	Mongolia	115 URU	Uruguay
35 FIN	Finland	76 MOR	Morocco	116 VEN	Venezuela
36 FRN	France	77 NEP	Nepal	117 VTN	Vietnam (Dem. R.)
37 GAB	Gabon	78 NTH	Netherlands	118 VTS	Vietnam (R.)
38 GME	Germany (Dem. R.)	79 NEW	New Zealand	119 YEM	Yemen
39 GMW	Germany (Fed. R.)	80 NIC	Nicaragua	120 YUG	Yugoslavia
40 GHA	Ghana	81 NIR	Niger	121 ZAM	Zambia (N. Rhodesia)
41 GRC	Greece	82 NIG	Nigeria		

(e.g., warm climate) that are unrelated to its "political" influence or importance. Furthermore, the significance of a nation's receiving bilateral visits of officials from, say, twenty nations over the course of a year is probably quite different from the significance of its receiving these officials for a multilateral conference at a single time. For these reasons, data on visits to multilateral conferences have not been considered comparable to data on bilateral visits.

3. When officials of two nations meet for talks in a third nation (e.g., meeting of Kennedy and Khrushchev in Austria in 1961), each of the visiting nations is considered to have visited the other (i.e., the visit is symmetrical). However, when the dispute

between two nations is mediated in a third nation (e.g., mediation of Indian-Pakistan dispute over Kashmir in Russia in 1966), officials from each of the disputing nations are considered to be visiting the mediating nation instead of visiting each other. Our assumption in this latter case is that the primary political force at work will be the influence of the mediating nation on the disputing nations, and secondarily the influence of the disputing nations on each other.

4. Visits, even from more than one nation, on commemorative occasions (e.g., a national anniversary) or ceremonial occasions (e.g., an inauguration or funeral) are counted if they result in private talks or meetings between officials of the visiting and host nations.

What we have attempted to exclude from our data are visits that do not reflect the flow of influence between nations, such as those occasioned by private or personal reasons (e.g., medical care in another nation). To be sure, this rationale alone would not admit our exclusion of visits of high-level government officials to major multilateral conferences, or even some visits of prominent private citizens to foreign nations. In the case of the former, however, the inclusion of multilateral conference visits would greatly inflate the influence it seemed reasonable to impute to nations which happened to host such conferences; in the case of the latter, visits of private citizens do not allow ready comparability across all nations. Neither for that matter, do visits of heads-of-state (some nations have one head-of-state, others have two or three by our definition), but judgments about where the "real power" in different nations lies—and, on this basis, who is comparable to whom—seemed an even more precarious, and certainly more arbitrary, way to aggregate the data.

Since the *Times Index* generally reports only the barest details of visits, it was often necessary to check the original *Times* newspaper story to ascertain the nature of the visit in order to decide how it should be coded. A brief stopover of a government official in a foreign nation, for example, was not counted as a visit if he did not confer with any government leaders in the stopover nation.

The visit of a party of government officials to a foreign nation was coded as either a highest-level category (a) or a lower-level category (b) visit depending on the level of the highest government official in

the party. We have analyzed the structure of influence relationships (defined below) separately for the highest-level visits in category (a) and for the combined-level visits in both categories (a) and (b). These analyses have been performed for the years 1964 and 1965 separately, as well as on the combined data for 1964 and 1965.

In all the analyses, two nations were considered to be in an *influence relationship* for a given time period if their officials visited each other two or more times. Their influence relationship was considered *symmetrical* if the nations exchanged an equal number of visits, plus or minus one. On the other hand, if one nation in the pair sent at least two more visits than the other nation sent, the nation receiving the greater number of visits (by at least two) was considered to have *asymmetrical* influence over the nation sending the greater number of visits. In effect, these criteria specify a minimum of two visits for a pair of nations to be in an influence relationship and a difference of at least two visits between the number which each sent to, or received from, the other for the relationship to be asymmetrical.[9]

Although these two-visit cutoff points are arbitrary, they at least exclude (1) two nations from being in an influence relationship because of a single visit, which may, for example, routinely occur in the course of a visiting official's extended goodwill trip that is quite divorced from the international political process, or (2) their relationship from being asymmetrical because of an imbalance of one visit, which may be simply a function of when the sampling period started and ended. Raising the influence relationship visit minimum above two will enable us later to probe more deeply into the structural properties of the digraphs with the two-visit cutoff points.

[9] We could have used the transaction-flow model to compute threshold criteria for each pair of nations on the basis of the total number of visits each nation sent to and received from all other nations in the world. Since the frequency with which high-level officials visit each other is probably little influenced by the financial cost of such visits, however, the model did not seem particularly relevant to eliminating the "size effect" that often renders gross comparisons of transaction flows between large and small nations incomparable. For a description of the transaction-flow model, see Steven J. Brams, "Transaction Flows in the International System," *American Political Science Review*, LX (December 1966), 882–86; and "Trade in the North Atlantic Area: An Approach to the Analysis of Transformations in a System," *Peace Research Society: Papers*, VI (1967), 144–48.

TABLE 2
*Summary of Combined-Level Visit Data
in 1964, 1965, and 1964–65*

Visit data	1964	1965	1964–65
Number of visits	515	428	943
Number of pairs visited	298	255	429
Number of visits to pairs in influence relationships (two or more visits)	328	258	694
Number of pairs in influence relationships (two or more visits)	111	85	183
Symmetrical	55	41	92
Asymmetrical	56	44	91

Construction of the Influence Structures

Given these criteria for the measurement of symmetrical and asymmetrical flows of influence between pairs of nations, how can we represent graphically the structure of influence relationships in the international system? From the magnitude of the combined-level visit data for both categories (a) and (b) which is summarized in Table 2, it is immediately apparent that some simplifying scheme will be necessary to make sense out of the 111 influence relationships in 1964, the 85 influence relationships in 1965, and the 183 influence relationships in 1964–65. These influence relationships do not include the 187 pairs of nations visited in 1964 (63 percent of the total), the 170 pairs visited in 1965 (67 percent of the total), and the 246 pairs visited in 1964–65 (57 percent of the total) that had only one visit and thus did not qualify as being in influence relationships.

For each time period, the symmetrical and asymmetrical influence relationships, and the nations which they connect, define a digraph with the nations as points and the symmetrical and asymmetrical influence relationships as directed lines between pairs of points. (An asymmetrical relationship is represented by a directed line going from the influencing nation to the influenced nation, a symmetrical relationship by two directed lines going in opposite directions between two nations.) Of the 121 nations in the study, the digraphs connect 60 different nations to each other in 1964, 50 different nations to each other in 1965, and 75 different nations to each other in 1964–65. Because these digraphs

are very complicated, however, it is virtually impossible to give a coherent and meaningful schematic picture of the structure of influence relationships in any of the time periods that preserves *all* individual influence relationships between pairs of nations.

Fortunately, however, certain strategic simplifications can be made in a digraph to highlight its underlying structure (see Figs. 1 and 2). To begin with, we can group together into *mutual influence sets* those nations which can directly or indirectly influence, and be influenced, only by every other member in their sets. (Graphically, these sets, whose members are the boxed-in nations at each level in Figs. 1 and 2, can be represented by a closed sequence of points and directed lines.) These mutual influence sets are disjoint, for if there were a common member of two different sets this member would connect together all members of the two sets into a single mutual influence set.

After grouping nations into mutual influence sets, these sets become our new units of analysis and can be treated as points of a reduced digraph, which is acyclic (free of cycles) since the mutual influence sets subsume all instances of cycles of influence between nations. The acyclic reduced digraphs can then be organized into hierarchical structures by assigning each mutual influence set to a level in such a way that it receives influence only from higher levels and transmits it only to lower levels. We can do this by a unique assignment of each mutual influence set to a level one above that of the highest set which it influences, with those sets whose members do not influence members of any other set being placed at the bottom level of the hierarchy, the sets whose members influence the members of the bottom-level sets and none higher at the next level, and so on up to the top-level mutual influence sets whose members are not influenced by members of any other mutual influence sets.[10]

---

[10] Actually, mutual influence sets whose members do not influence any other mutual influence sets will not be assigned to the bottom level of the hierarchy if they are not the terminal points of a longest path in the digraph. Instead, such sets will be assigned to a level one below that by which they are influenced, as, for example, are those sets at level 3 in Fig. 4 whose members do not influence members of either of the two sets at level 4. For a more detailed explanation of the level-assignment procedure, see Steven J. Brams, "Measuring the Concentration of Power in Political Systems," *American Political Science Review*,

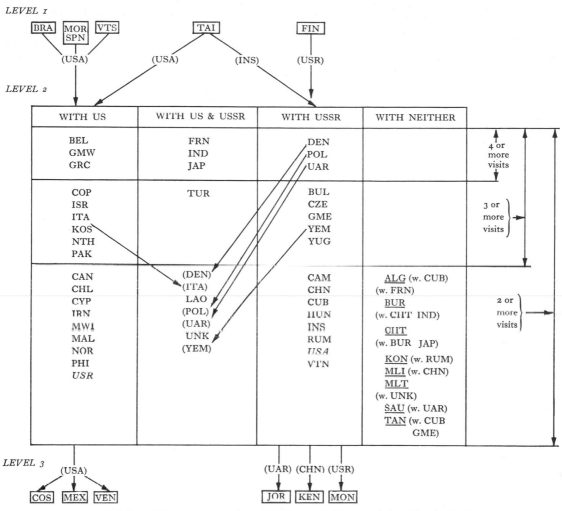

Figure 1. Hierarchical structure of combined-level influence relationships in 1964 for sixty nations

In this way, an economical structure of hierarchical levels of influence can be obtained, with the mutual influence sets the building blocks of the structure. These sets have a clear and unambiguous

substantive interpretation which clusters of units generated by statistical (e.g., factor analysis) and iterative grouping and ordering procedures often do not possess.[11] The only information from the original

LXII (June 1968), 465–66. Since all of the influence structures presented in this article have few levels (either three or four) and are structurally similar, the power concentration index developed in *ibid.* would have limited utility as a comparative measure and thus has not been computed for the structures analyzed here. Elsewhere I have computed a measure of *hierarchization,* based on the graph-theoretic concept of "path-consistency," for the highest-level and combined-level influence relationships in 1964, 1965, and 1964–65. See Steven J. Brams, "The Search for Structural Order in the International System: Some Models and Preliminary Results" (unpublished paper, November 1968).

[11] For reviews of some of the recent literature on clustering techniques see Geoffrey H. Ball, "Data Analysis in the Social Sciences: What about the Details?", *Proceedings—Fall Joint Computer Conference, 1965,* 533–59; J. J. Fortier and H. Solomon, "Clustering Procedures," in Paruchuri R. Krishnaiah (ed.), *Multivariate Analysis* (New York: Academic Press, 1966), 493–506; Stephen C. Johnson, Hierarchical Clustering Schemes," *Psychometrika,* XXXIII (September 1967), 241–54; and Hayward R. Alker, Jr., "Statistics and Politics: The Need for Causal Data Analysis" (paper presented at the Annual Meeting of the American Political Science Association, September 5–8, 1967, Chicago).

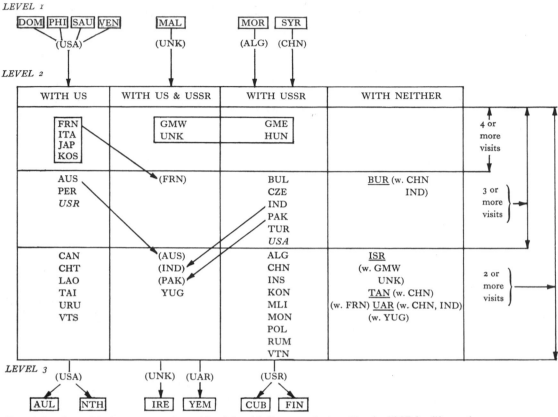

Figure 2. Hierarchical structure of combined-level influence relationships in 1965 for fifty nations

digraph which is not depicted in the hierarchical structure is the configuration of influence relationships *within* each mutual influence set.[12]

Influence Structures in the International System

The hierarchical structures of combined-level influence relationships for sixty nations in 1964, and for fifty nations in 1965, are illustrated in Figs. 1 and 2.[13] Although not given here, the hierarchies of the highest-level influence relationships based only upon the highest-level category (a) visits are quite similar to the combined-level hierarchies, except that they embrace thirteen fewer nations in 1964 and sixteen fewer nations in 1965 than the combined-level hierarchies.

In both the 1964 and 1965 combined-level structures there are only three hierarchical levels with one very large mutual influence set, comprising forty-eight nations in 1964 and thirty-seven nations in 1965, occupying level 2 in each structure. Each of

[12] A write-up and source deck of a computer program called DECOMP, which operates on the adjacency matrix of a digraph to produce a hierarchically ordered structure of the elements of that matrix, are available from the Syracuse University Computer Center, Syracuse, New York. For a description of the program, see Steven J. Brams, "DECOMP: A Computer Program for the Condensation of a Directed Graph and the Hierarchical Ordering of Its Strong Components," *Behavioral Science*, XIII (July 1968), 344–45. Most of the theorems from digraph theory on which the program is based are given in Harary, Norman, and Cartwright, *op. cit.*, Chaps. 5 and 10.

[13] In 1965 Argentina influenced Chile, and Belgium, the Congo (Leopoldville), but because none of these nations was connected to nations in the main hierarchy, they were not included in Fig. 2. In none of the other influence structures presented in this article are there pairs of nations in influence relationships not connected to the main hierarchies.

these large sets includes virtually all major and middle-level international powers as well as an assortment of smaller nations whose leaders were active in international negotiations in each year. Ninety-two percent of all the directed lines forming symmetrical or asymmetrical influence relationships between pairs of nations in the 1964 structure, and 88 percent of all the directed lines in the 1965 structure, fall within these mutual influence sets and thus are not shown in the influence structures in Figs. 1 and 2.

To give some organizational structure to the nations in the large mutual influence sets at level 2 in each hierarchy, each of these sets has been successively pared down by raising the minimum number of visits necessary for two nations to qualify as being in an influence relationship from two visits to three and four visits, while leaving unchanged in each case the asymmetry criterion of an imbalance of two or more visits sent or received. Further, the nations in these large sets have been classified according to whether or not they had influence relationships (symmetrical or asymmetrical) at each visit level with the United States, the Soviet Union, both superpowers, or neither. The nations in these mutual influence sets that are connected to neither the United States nor the Soviet Union are underscored, with the nations in the mutual influence set to which they are connected (symmetrically or asymmetrically) given in parentheses. These connecting nations are listed to the left, the right, or underneath the nations which they connect depending on whether the connecting nations fall in the United States column, the Soviet Union column, or both or neither columns.

At the tops of the hierarchies at level 1 are those mutual influence sets—generally containing only one nation—which influence (i.e., receive an asymmetrical number of visits from) one or more nations in the large mutual influence sets at level 2. Similarly, the mutual influence sets which are influenced by (i.e., send an asymmetrical number of visits to) one or more nations in the large mutual influence sets at level 2 are placed at the bottoms of the hierarchies at level 3. In each case, the connecting nations from the large mutual influence set, which elsewhere have been termed "linkage" actors,[14] are listed in parentheses along the directed lines connecting nations at

[14] Brams, "Measuring the Concentration of Power in Political Systems," *op. cit.*, 468.

levels 1 and 3 to nations at level 2. The directed lines *within* the large mutual influence set indicate which nations move from connections exclusively with the United States or the Soviet Union at the three- or four-visit level to connections with both at the two- or three-visit level.

An examination of the nations in 1964 and 1965 that start off in the U.S. and U.S.S.R. column, or make the switch from either the U.S. or U.S.S.R. column to the U.S. and U.S.S.R. column at a lower level, suggests at least three reasons for their dual associations that perhaps reflect the cross-pressures on them:

1. They are ostensibly nonaligned nations (Austria, India, U.A.R.);
2. They are nations aligned with one bloc but favoring closer ties with the other bloc (Britain, Denmark, France, Japan, Italy, Pakistan, West Germany, Turkey, Yugoslavia);
3. They are centers of conflict between the two blocs or their proxies (Laos, Yemen).

These characterizations probably also fit the nations in a large mutual influence set which, though connected with neither superpower, are connected with column entries of both. The U.A.R. in 1965 is a case in point (see Fig. 2), with connections to France on the one hand, Communist China and India on the other, and Yugoslavia in the middle.

The nations which are connected exclusively with either the U.S. or the U.S.S.R. in both years occasion few surprises. One peculiarity in the 1965 structure (Fig. 2) which should be noted is the breakdown into two four-member mutual influence sets of the eight nations (ten including the U.S. and U.S.S.R.) at the four-visit level. Of the four hierarchical structures presented in this article, only in the 1965 structure does the paring down of the large mutual influence set through the raising of the visit level produce more than one reduced mutual influence set at the higher level.

It is striking that no Latin American nations, and only three African nations (Algeria, Mali, and Tanzania, which are all connected with Communist nations), are in the large mutual influence sets at level 2 in both 1964 and 1965. In contrast, levels 1 and 3 in both 1964 and 1965 include no major world powers but instead a preponderance of small nations, several of which are from Africa and Latin America.

The appearance of mostly small nations at the top and bottom levels of the hierarchies is in all cases but one (Thailand in 1964) due to the fact that each of these nations sent to or received from just one other nation, usually a major power, an asymmetrical number of visits. These asymmetries are probably largely a function of the period of time sampled and not an enduring feature of the position of these nations in the international system. Indeed, by our measure of influence Finland is a sender of influence to the Soviet Union from level 1 in 1964 but a receiver of influence from the Soviet Union at level 3 in 1965.

The instability in membership of nations at levels 1 and 3 is confirmed by the data in Table 3. In 1964 only one of the six nations at level 1, and none at level 3, showed up at the same level in 1965. By comparison, thirty-one of the forty-eight nations in the large mutual influence set at level 2 in 1964 had renewed memberships in this set in 1965. In fact, only 16 percent of the thirty-seven members of this set in 1965 were not members of the set in 1964. The nations in the influence structures at level 2, each of which could influence and be influenced by every other nation at that level in a sequence of influence relationships of length five or less (i.e., through no more than four other nations) in 1964, and a sequence of length two or less (i.e., through no more than one other nation) in 1965, appear to form a pretty stable lot.[15]

So do the nations outside the influence hierarchies, whose numbers are given in the dashed row and dashed column of Table 3 but are not cumulated in the intersection of the two totals. (These two totals in the lower right-hand corner of the table include only the nations in the hierarchical structures in each year.) The excluded nations for the most part stay excluded from the influence hierarchies, as indicated by the fact that 89 percent of the sixty-one nations not in the 1964 structure were not in the 1965 structure either.

What structural changes can we discern over time *within* the large mutual influence sets at level 2? Not unexpectedly, the data in Table 4 reveal that only one out of the thirty-four nations (Pakistan)

[15] The length of the shortest sequence through which influence can be exerted by each nation on every other in a mutual influence set could serve as one possible indicator of the "density" of influence relationships in the set.

TABLE 3
Turnover of Nations Between Levels from 1964 to 1965

FROM *1964* LEVEL	TO *1965* LEVEL				
	One	*Two*	*Three*	*Not in 1965 structure*	*Total*
One	1	2	1	2	6
Two	3	31	3	11	48
Three	1	1	0	4	6
Not in 1964 structure	2	3	2	54	61
Total	7	37	6	71	60 / 50

in either the U.S. or U.S.S.R. columns in 1964 makes the switch to the column of the other superpower in 1965. Far more interesting than this, however, is the fact that while only four out of eighteen nations (22 percent) with the U.S. in 1964 stay with it in 1965, ten out of sixteen nations (63 percent) with the U.S.S.R. in 1964 are with it again in 1965. United States attention to, and influence over, a particular set of nations would appear to be less institutionalized, and probably more ephemeral, than that of the Soviet Union. For nations like the Soviet Union our empirical measure of influence probably tends better to reflect interdependence between nations that may persist over time rather than control specific to a particular time and place. This point will be considered further in the next section.

Nations which moved to their dual affiliations with both the U.S. and U.S.S.R. from the three or four-visit level with just one superpower have been classified in Table 4 with the superpower with which they started out. The only nation that achieves a perfect visit balance by starting out *and* remaining in the U.S. and U.S.S.R. column in both 1964 and 1965 is the U.K. Two underdeveloped nations, Burma and Tanzania, are the only nations in the influence structures that have no associations with either the

TABLE 4
*Turnover of Nations Within Level Two from
1964 to 1965*

FROM *1964* LEVEL TWO	TO *1965* LEVEL TWO					
	With U.S.	*With U.S.S.R.*	*With both*	*With neither*	*Not in 1965 level two*	*Total*
With U.S.	4	1	1	1	11	18
With U.S.S.R.	0	10	1	1	4	16
With both	3	2	1	0	0	6
With neither	1	3	0	2	2	8
Not in 1964 level two	5	1	0	0	67	73
Total	13	17	3	4	84	48 / 37

U.S. or the U.S.S.R. in both 1964 and 1965 but instead maintain their memberships in the mutual influence sets in both years through other nations.

The 1964–65 hierarchy of combined-level influence relationships embraces a total of seventy-five nations, fifteen more than were included in the 1964 hierarchy and twenty-five more than were included in the 1965 hierarchy (see Fig. 3). Only seven nations in this structure (Ceylon, New Zealand, Nepal, Albania, Zambia, Afghanistan, and Somalia), however, were not in either the 1964 structure or the 1965 structure—none had more than one visit with another nation in either year—again suggesting the relative exclusiveness over time of membership in an influence system based upon visits of high-level government officials.

The only nation associated exclusively with one of the superpowers in both 1964 and 1965 that made the switch to associations with both in the 1964–65 structure is Rumania, which is perhaps a reflection of the increasingly independent policy its leaders began to pursue in the mid-1960's. Also interesting is the appearance in the 1964–65 structure of both

Bulgaria and Mongolia—the two Communist nations with probably the closest ties with the Soviet Union —as recipients of Soviet influence.

Thirteen nations drop out, and a fourth level is added, to the 1964–65 structure of highest-level influence relationships based only on category (a) visits (see Fig. 4). Whereas each nation in the large mutual influence set of the combined-level structure for 1964–65 can influence every other nation through at most two other nations, no nation has to go through more than one other nation to exercise influence in the large mutual influence set of the highest-level structure for 1964–65. Moreover, the large mutual influence set in the combined-level structure subsumes 95 percent of all directed lines in the digraph, but in the highest-level structure only 81 percent of the directed lines, accounting for the higher proportion of nations at the bottom levels in the latter structure that are influenced by nations in the large mutual influence set.

The two nations at level 4 in the highest-level structure, the Congo (Leopoldville) and Cyprus, both received influence from several Western nations at levels 2 and 3, which seems indicative of the efforts

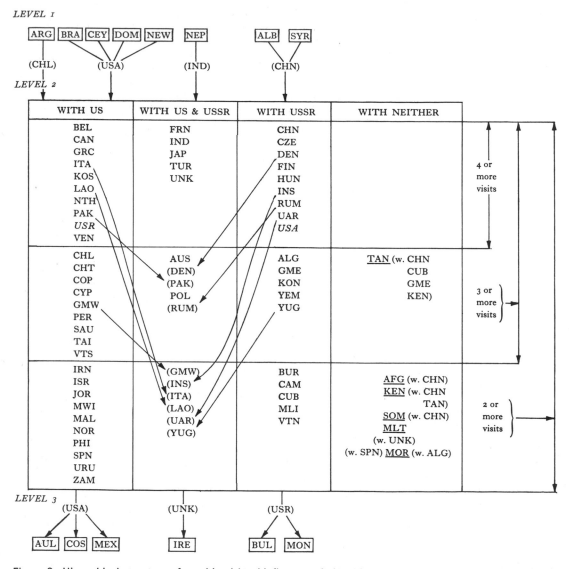

Figure 3. Hierarchical structure of combined-level influence relationships in 1964–65 for seventy-five nations

of leaders of these influenced nations to rally support in Western capitals to prevent the outbreak of major conflicts in their nations during the 1964–65 period. Similarly, Laos at level 3 received influence from no less than three Communist nations (China, North Vietnam, and the Soviet Union) and two Western nations (Britain and France) in this period, clearly attesting to the support competing leaders of this nation sought from foreign powers.

The Behavior of Nations and Their Positions in the Hierarchy

It is tempting to hypothesize that those nations which show up at the bottom levels of a structure that is based upon "high-level" visits over a "sufficient" period of time tend to be those nations that, for a variety of reasons, most actively seek the approval and support of other nations. If they receive the

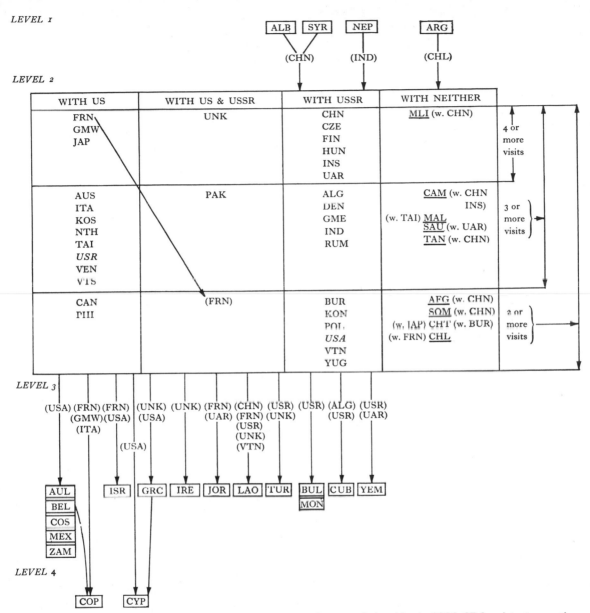

Figure 4. Hierarchical structure of highest-level influence relationships in 1964–65 for sixty-two nations

approval and gain the support they seek, then we might say that, contrary to our definition of influence flows, they influence the nations they visited. However, while this might be true in the short-run, in the long-run we suspect that the nation which is visited, when it boosts its "credit" with the nation seeking support, tends to exercise continuing direction over that nation's foreign policy. Our measure of asymmetrical (as well as symmetrical) influence, therefore, probably comes closer to reflecting long-term and continuing control in broad policy areas than short-term and absolute control over specific actions—especially those which a nation links to its vital national interests. Nations may go to war despite the admonitions of big powers, but the big powers which the leaders of these nations regularly visit probably have greater control over their policies and behavior, short of war, than vice versa.

Needless to say, not all international visits reflect the presence of this kind of control. Some visits are designed to build up goodwill or prevent its erosion, others to stabilize an official's position at home, and still others to maintain the stability of the system by narrowing or widening the range of options available to nations in conflict. Thus, when we say influence is "exerted" it is important to realize that it may take different instrumental forms and have different effects. It seems reasonable to assume, nevertheless, that the erratic properties of visits are distributed more or less randomly in the international system and, when aggregated for purposes of comparison, form a less erratic and more coherent whole. Yet, exactly what theoretical coherence is reflected in the whole, besides the fact that international relations are not random, must remain largely speculative until attempts are made at validating a concept of relational influence in international relations (to be discussed below).

If nations at the bottom of a hierarchy, because they frequently seek the approval and support of the big powers on specific matters, tend to be the nations most responsive to the efforts of big powers on long-term matters, then the same reasoning would suggest that nations at the top of the hierarchy would tend to be the most unresponsive and recalcitrant members of the international system. They neither experience the stabilizing influence of the several members of a large mutual influence set nor do they attempt through visits to curry the favor of other nations. When such nations as Albania and Syria receive a preponderance of visits from a revolutionary nation like Communist China (see Figs. 3 and 4), then what probably results is a reinforced recalcitrance unmitigated, in the case of Albania and Syria, by significant contacts with nations in the large mutual influence set at level 2.

We hasten to add that our speculation about the behavioral characteristics of nations associated with membership in the top and bottom levels of hierarchical structures is applicable only to nations with "permanent" asymmetries and not to nations that happen to have asymmetrical relationships because of the particular time period (e.g., 1964–65) sampled.

Trying to determine "stable" time periods will require much further investigation. We shall explore this and other methodological questions connected with the research reported in this article under the headings of the reliability and validity of a hierarchy of influence relationships in the international system.

The Reliability of a Hierarchy of Influence Relationships

A measurement procedure is reliable to the extent that independent but comparable measures of the same phenomenon or event give the same results. For example, the consistency with which news sources report the same information about visits between world leaders would be a measure of the reliability of news accounts of such visits. The extent to which accounts differ about the details of visits is only serious, however, if such information is relevant to one's analysis. Our preliminary examination of different sources of information on international visits (see footnote 8) suggests that there are no substantial discrepancies in the reporting of details of visits by different sources that would affect the coding of the visit data that were collected.

The concept of reliability has another dimension besides the degree of equivalence of observations of the same event. In addition to variations due to differences in the reporting of events, measurements may vary because of fluctuations over time in the phenomena being measured (e.g., fewer or more visits between world leaders) or because of random errors due to transient factors or conditions (e.g., crises). Indeed we did find a substantial variation in the number of visits that were reported in the *Times Index* for 1964 and 1965: highest-level category (a) visits decreased by 20 percent, and lower-level category (b) visits by 29 percent, from 1964 to 1965.[16]

Situational variables like crises are an inescapable feature of international politics and will affect the phenomena (visits) we are attempting to measure.

[16] This decline is probably in part attributable to the 1965 newspaper strike in New York, which caused suspension of the *New York Times* from September 17 to October 10, inclusive. During this period news from the international edition of the *Times* and other sources was indexed. Although news on international visits was more compendious at this time, the reporting of visits was probably not so unrepresentative during this period as to bias seriously the data on which the 1965 influence structure is based.

Sources of unreliability due to such situational variables may be controlled for in at least two different ways: (1) by trying to take account of and separate out visits attributable to "random" disturbances, or (2) by trying to choose periods of time long enough so that transient fluctuations do not significantly affect the relatively enduring differences one is attempting to measure.

Since it is not at all obvious what constitute random disturbances in the international system (When is a crisis "random," or when are situational factors "transient"?), the comparison of changes that occur over sampling periods of different duration would seem to be the best procedure to distinguish genuine fluctuations in the phenomena being measured from random fluctuations due to the failure of the measuring procedure to exclude variations caused by transient situational factors. Generally speaking, the greater the *consistency* of trends over three or more sampling periods, the more likely the sampling periods will reflect permanent shifts in the structure of influence relationships between nations.

Unfortunately, limitations on time and resources did not permit our doing trend analyses of the visit data. Our comparison of the 1964 and 1965 data did indicate, however, that the stability of membership in the large mutual influence sets at level 2 is far greater than the stability of membership at either levels 1 or 3. Further, the ties of the Soviet Union to a particular group of nations in the large mutual influence sets seem to be more enduring than the ties of the United States to any particular group of nations.

So far we have identified as sources of unreliability the lack of equivalence in observations (i.e., news reports) of the same event and random fluctuations in the occurrence of different events over time. To measure the equivalence of observations of the same event, the reporting of visits by different news sources has been compared; to measure fluctuations over time, a procedure has been suggested, and some tentative calculations have been made, to compare positional shifts of nations in the hierarchical structures. Establishing, however, whether particular sampling periods are representative of a longer time frame, or whether changes in the hierarchical structures over several sampling periods are enduring, will require more detailed and extensive future analyses.

The Validity of a Hierarchy of Influence Relationships

In contrast to errors due to random fluctuations, systematic errors tend to one direction or the other according to the particular distorting factor at work. An example of such a distorting factor might be a tendency on the part of Western news sources not to report visits between leaders of Communist nations or small nations. Another example of a systematic error might be that caused by the failure of these sources to pick up information on visits intentionally kept secret. Because a valid measuring procedure reflects true differences in the phenomena being measured, errors which systematically affect the phenomena being measured lower the validity of the measuring procedure.

Although the sources of information used in this study allow us no direct way for testing for such a bias, the results of our analysis furnish some clues as to the direction of a possible bias. Since all of the hierarchical structures contain almost the same number of nations associated exclusively with the United States, on the one hand, and with the Soviet Union, on the other, we suspect that there is not a great bias in the *New York Times* or other Western news sources against reporting visits to or from Communist nations. Some of these visits are undoubtedly kept secret, but if these are randomly distributed they would not greatly affect the results of the analysis.

There might, on the other hand, tend to be a systematic exclusion in the Western press of reports of visits between small nations. Even in the combined-level structure for 1964-65, there were forty-six nations for which the *Times Index* did not report their having even two visits with one other nation. Though two-thirds of all the visits recorded in 1964-65 were highest-level category (a) visits, many visits at even the highest level between small nations probably go unreported in the Western press. Further, our exclusion from the visit data of multilateral conferences undoubtedly knocked out a substantial portion of the visits made by officials from small nations.

In future analyses, many of the excluded nations might be included in the structures of influence relationships by lowering the visit cutoff point for these nations to only one visit. Successively raising the cutoff point, as we did for the large mutual influence sets, shows up the order in which nations drop out of a structure, but it is questionable how much significance can be attributed to a nation's maintaining its association with a superpower at, say, the two-visit level, but not at the three- or four-visit level.

Apart from any systematic bias which may be present in news reports, the kind of phenomena being measured (i.e., visits) may not necessarily be relevant to the theoretical construct (i.e., influence) with which it is identified. "Construct" validity involves validation not only of the measurement procedure but the theory underlying it. Evidence from many sources may be used to estimate the validity of the relationship between the measurement procedure and the construct; the previously cited experimental evidence (see footnote 4) bearing on the connection between the symmetry/asymmetry of responses between two actors and the symmetry/asymmetry of influence relationships certainly needs confirmation in the field of international relations.

The validation of a theoretical construct like influence may also proceed by using the operational measure in question as a correlate, or predictor, of a different measure of influence. Yet, while influence and power are much talked about in the international relations literature, there is no body of empirical data which has been assembled on *relational* measures of these concepts (as opposed to measures of possession, like GNP, which say nothing about the *exercise* of influence between nations).

Although no measure is valid in an absolute sense—that is, there is no direct way of determining the "true" measure of a theoretical construct—the closeness of association of the measure of influence used here with independent measures of the construct based on perhaps different kinds of international relations, could be used as a test of its "concurrent" or "predictive" validity. These independent measures might in turn suggest conceptual refinements in the aspects of influence that we have argued the visit data seem to tap. Different measures of influence may produce different findings, but these will be a matter of concern only if one insists that influence is a unidimensional concept whose essence can be revealed by some single best method of analysis.[17]

[17] On this point, see James D. Barber, *Power in Committees: An Experiment in the Government Process* (Chicago: Rand McNally and Company, 1966), p. 129.

To recapitulate, the study of reliability consists in determining whether measurements by different forms or at different times give similar results; the study of validity demands inquiry into the nature and meaning of the phenomena under consideration. Moving from theoretical constructs to valid operational measures requires one to identify possible distorting factors (systematic errors) in the measurement procedure, demonstrate the congruence of the construct with the properties being measured, and show that the measure is correlated with or can predict some independently arrived-at outcome or state of affairs. These considerations imply a need for gathering different kinds of international relations data in order to determine those aspects of the empirical process most relevant to the study of influence relationships in the international system.

Summary and Conclusions

In this article, I have attempted to show how the theory of directed graphs can be used to construct hierarchical structures of nations based on symmetrical and asymmetrical relationships between pairs of nations. These hierarchical structures, which enable us to summarize graphically very complex behavioral patterns, can be formally described as systems obtained by imposing a set of ordering principles on digraphs composed of a set of points (nations) and a set of directed lines (visits) relating pairs of points.

From the pattern of international visits between high-level government officials of all nations in the world in 1964 and 1965, symmetrical and asymmetrical influence relationships were operationally defined for pairs of nations. The connected nations were then grouped into mutual influence sets, which were assigned unique levels in influence hierarchies according to which sets they influenced and were influenced by.

For the influence structures based on the combined-level visits in 1964 and 1965, longitudinal comparisons were made of the turnover of nations at all levels in the hierarchies. Composite structures for 1964–65 were then obtained using both the combined-level and highest-level visits for this two-year period.

Several tentative findings, all of which need further investigation, emerged from the study:

1. The hierarchical structures of influence relationships for the combined-level visits connected less than half of all nations to each other in 1964 and 1965, somewhat more than half in 1964–65. The high coincidence of memberships in the 1964 and 1965 structures suggests that an influence system based on international visits has quite stable boundaries over time.

2. The hierarchical structures of influence relationships spanned very few levels (three to four) in 1964, 1965, and 1964–65. This finding was not affected by the level of officials involved in visits.

3. One large mutual influence set at a middle level in each structure, comprising almost all major and middle-level powers and several smaller nations, constituted the core of each influence system. (In 1964, 1965, 1964–65, these sets varied in the length of the shortest sequences through which each nation could exercise influence over every other nation in the set, suggesting differences in the "density" of influence relationships in these sets.)

4. In the large mutual influence sets, nations connected with both superpowers, and thus under apparent cross-pressures, were either nonaligned nations, nations aligned with one bloc but favoring closer ties with the other bloc, or centers of conflict between the two blocs or their proxies.

5. In the large mutual influence sets, the group of nations connected with the Soviet Union was more stable in membership between 1964 and 1965 than the group of nations connected with the United States, suggesting a greater institutionalization of visit relations (and influence relationships) on the part of the Soviet Union with its allies than on the part of the United States with its allies.

6. The top and bottom levels of the influence structures were occupied primarily by small nations with asymmetrical ties principally to major powers in the large mutual influence sets.

7. The membership of nations at the top and bottom levels was not stable between 1964 and 1965. There are reasons to believe, however, that over longer periods nations that occupy the top level(s) of a hierarchy will be more prone to behavior provocative to other nations than nations which occupy the bottom level(s).

No extensive reliability checks have been made on the visit data, though the equivalence in the reporting of relevant details of the visits by different news sources appears high. Measuring the consistency of shifts in the hierarchical structures over time was suggested as a means for distinguishing random fluctuations caused by transient situational factors from relatively enduring changes in the influence structures.

The strong underrepresentation of small nations in the hierarchical structures suggested the possibility of a systematic bias against the reporting of visits of officials from small nations in Western presses. Such a bias would call into question the validity of finding (1) but would not probably upset findings (2) through (7).

Our identification of an operational concept of influence, based on international visits, with the theoretical construct of influence as control over broad policy areas (but not specific actions related to vital national interests) remains unvalidated. Hopefully, the eventual linkage of systemic patterns, based on different relational measures of influence, to characteristics of the nations forming them will shed further light on the exercise of influence in the international system and its effects on the behavior of nations.

I. The Use of Factor Analysis

50. Some Dimensions in the Foreign Behavior of Nations*

Rudolph J. Rummel is Associate Professor of Political Science at the University of Hawaii and Director of the Dimensionality of Nations Project. The latter is a large and long-term effort to chart and explain behavior within and between nations on the basis of sophisticated statistical treatment of recurrent patterns. The source of many of Professor Rummel's original and important studies, the Dimensionality of Nations Project is distinguished by the many variables for which quantitative indicators have been derived and by the manipulation of these variables through a technique known as factor analysis. Although the merits and limits of factor analysis are the focus of considerable debate among statisticians, Professor Rummel's presentation here plainly demonstrates that its application to international phenomena can be extremely stimulating. If an attempt is made to take the limits of the technique into account (say, by numbering, as Professor Rummel does, the uncovered factors rather than labeling them), the findings generated by this method of inquiry can hardly be ignored. Certainly those generated in the ensuing analysis provoke thought and indicate the need to undertake further investigation. [*Reprinted from the* Journal of Peace Research, *III (1966), 201–23, by permission of the author and the publisher.*]

I. Introduction

In any one day a nation is involved in multitudinous activities. It may import and export various goods, vote in the United Nations, sign treaties, give or receive aid, join international organizations, dispatch or receive messages, deploy troops in a foreign land, make threats, sever or establish diplomatic relations, exchange tourists and migrants, and so on. The magnitude and nature of these activities vary from one nation to another. For some, trade may be the central interest around which other activities group.

* Prepared in connection with research supported by the National Science Foundation, Contracts NSF–G24827, NSF–GS224, and NSF–GS–536. Many thanks are due to Helga Shen and Dennis Cook for helping to collect the data, and to Richard W. Chadwick for helping in the former task and preparing and overseeing numerous runs through the computer at Northwestern University. Thanks are also due to Raymond Tanter, who handled the correlation and factor analyses runs at Indiana University. A debt of gratitude is owed the computer centers of Northwestern and Indiana Universities, whose patience and considerate help made this study possible. Moreover, with thanks the author would like to acknowledge particularly his debt to Harold Guetzkow and Jack Sawyer, in collaboration with whom the variables used in this study were selected and many of the judgments involved in their analysis were made, and his debt to Raymond Cattell, Richard W. Chadwick, Ivo Feierabend, Harold Guetzkow, Dean Pruitt, Bruce Russett, and Raymond Tanter for their many helpful comments on an earlier draft of this paper. They should, however, be absolved of any guilt by association for this final product. This paper is a revision of "Some Dimensions of International Relations" (Dimensionality of Nations Project, 1964, mimeo).

For some other nations, the immediate concern may be actions stemming from a border dispute or long standing grievance. And for still others, activities primarily may revolve around a threat to their regional or global power positions.

Although varying from nation to nation, several of these activities may be correlated with each other. Nations that trade a great deal may also belong to many international organizations, make many protests, and give economic aid; nations that trade little may belong to few international organizations, make few protests, and give little economic aid. These several activities may thus form a continuum—a *dimension*—along which nations may be distributed. Nations that trade a lot, belong to many international organizations, and so on, would be at one end of the continuum; at the other would be nations that have few of these activities.

The conceptual and analytical capacity of students and practitioners of international relations would be overwhelmed by an indigestible mass of data if the myriad activities of nations did not group themselves into dimensions. These dimensions function to classify these activities and to summarize and group them in a way which allows for the description of present and prediction of future activities. A dimension may be of interest in itself as representing an underlying influence bringing about the correlations it represents. A hypothetical dimension involving trade, international organizations, etc., for example, might well be the result of economic development. But a dimension also may be of interest in summarizing a variety of different activities and indicating which of them best can be used to represent this cluster or pattern of correlated activities. If trade were to have the highest average correlation with the other behavior in a pattern, then, in data collection, analysis, and projection, trade might well be used to represent all these activities. Trade employed in this sense would become a *basic* indicator defining a particular pattern in the foreign behavior of nations.

There need not be one dimension of variation among nations, of course. Although there well could be a trade cluster, there also might be an independent cluster of conflict activities that may vary similarly in magnitude for different nations. Such behavior might consist of the number of threats a nation makes, the number of accusations, and its troop movements.

The *basic* indicator here could be threats. It is important to note that these conflict activities would form a pattern if they were more highly correlated among themselves than each is with those activities forming the above-mentioned hypothetical trade pattern.

Besides trade and conflict, the correlations between the activities of nations might group into a number of other patterns. Thus, one might be able to resolve international relations into groups of highly correlated activities, each represented by a dimension along which nations are distributed and can be compared.

As part of a larger study,[1] research was undertaken by the author to determine empirically and systematically what some of the dimensions in the foreign behavior of nations were for the mid-1950's. In brief, the design consisted of collecting data on 94 foreign behavior variables, transforming their distributions to normality (where possible), eliminating extreme data values, assessing the correlations between the 94 variables, factoring the correlations, and rotating the results to an orthogonal solution. This essay is a report on the results.

II. Methodology

Factor analysis

With the increase in the number, capacity and speed of computers, researchers are directing more attention to the quantitative determination of the major dimensions in their substantive areas. The primary tool used in this research is factor analysis. The technique is now based on a considerable number of methodological studies,[2] and has a

[1] R. J. Rummel, "The Dimensionality of Nations Project" in Richard L. Merritt and Stein Rokkan, eds., *Comparing Nations* (New Haven: Yale University Press, 1966), pp. 109–29.

[2] See, for example, Raymond B. Cattell and William Sullivan, "The Scientific Nature of Factors; A Demonstration by Cups of Coffee," *Behavioral Science*, VII (1962), 184–93; Sten Henrysson, *Applicability of Factor Analysis in the Behavioral Studies: a Methodological Study* (Stockholm: Almquist and Wiksell, 1957); Henry F. Kaiser, "The Application of Electronic Computers to Factor Analysis," *Educational and Psychological Measurement*, XX (1960), 141–51; Charles I. Mosier, "Influence of Chance Error on Simple Structure: An Empirical Investigation of the Effect of Chance Error and Estimated Communalities on Simple Structure in Factorial Analysis," *Psychometrika*, IV (1939), 33–44.

number of textbooks devoted to it.[3] Although hundreds of major and minor applied studies have used factor analysis,[4] and it can be easily applied to a set of data by employing already prepared computer programs,[5] cross-national studies have little benefited by its use.[6] Yet cross-national data seem well suited

to the application of factor analysis, as do the questions scholars frequently direct to such data. The units are precisely delimited in terms of national boundaries, the universe of nations at a point in time can be dealt with (avoiding sampling problems), the variables (e.g., telephones, newspaper circulation, electricity production, number of years independent, coups, etc.) can be operationalized, and data are readily available.[7] And the question often asked of such data, "How are the economic, political, social, and behavioral characteristics of nations interrelated?" is the question for which factor analysis is best qualified.

Although the same is true of international relations, there have been even fewer factor analyses in this area.[8] Some students of international relations have tried to deduce the dimensions of international relations,[9] or to fit such relations into an *a priori* conceptual scheme.[10] One has tried an intuitive factor analysis.[11] With the data, methods, and computer facilities available today, however, a scholar can work more directly with his data in a more systematic way than heretofore has been the fashion in studying international relations.

What factor analysis attempts to do, in short, is to identify the patterns of variation in the data in terms of those variables (acts; behavior; characteristics) that are highly interdependent. The results of factor analysis, the *factors* defining the different patterns, are often spoken of as "dimensions." The

[3] A very good conceptual introduction to the nature of factor analysis is given by Raymond B. Cattell in the introductory chapters of *Factor Analysis* (New York: Harper and Brothers, 1952). For an elementary technical introduction, see Benjamin Fruchter, *Introduction to Factor Analysis* (New York: D. Van Nostrand and Company, 1954). An excellent text which covers factor analysis in all its technical aspects is Harry Harman, *Modern Factor Analysis* (Chicago: University of Chicago Press, 1960). For the philosophy and research design of factor analysis, see R. J. Rummel, *Applied Factor Analysis* (Evanston, Ill.: Northwestern University Press, 1967).

[4] Some applied studies outside of psychology that one might point out in particular are E. F. Borgatta, L. S. Cottrell, Jr., and H. J. Meyer, "On the Dimensions of Group Behavior," *Sociometry*, XIX (1956), 223–40; Harold E. Driver and Karl F. Schuessler, "Factor Analysis of Ethnographic Data," *American Anthropologist*, LIX (1957), 655–63; E. P. Godfrey, Fred E. Fiedler, and D. M. Hall, *Boards, Management and Company Success* (Danville: Interstate Printers and Publishers, 1959); P. R. Hofstaetter, "Factorial Study of Culture Patterns in the U.S.," *Journal of Psychology*, XXXII (1951), 99–113; Christian T. Jonassen and Sherwood H. Peres, *Interrelationships of Dimensions of Community Systems* (Columbus: Ohio State University Press, 1960); Charles Morris, *Varieties of Human Value* (Chicago: University of Chicago Press, 1956); Glendon Schubert, "The 1960 Term of the Supreme Court; A Psychological Analysis," *American Political Science Review*, LVI (1962), 90–113; Robert C. Wood, *1400 Governments* (Cambridge: Harvard University Press, 1961). Rummel, 1967, *op. cit.*, has a bibliography of applications in the social sciences.

[5] Such as the Biomedical Programs BIMD 17 and its revision BMD 3M, that are found at many university computer centers.

[6] Some of the exceptions are Raymond B. Cattell, "The Dimensions of Culture Patterns of Factorization of National Characters," *Journal of Abnormal and Social Psychology*, XLIV (1949), 443–69; "The Principal Culture Patterns Discoverable in the Syntal Dimensions of Existing Nations," *Journal of Social Psychology*, Vol. XXXII (1950), 215–53; Raymond B. Cattell, H. Breul, and H. Parker Hartman, "An Attempt at More Refined Definition of the Cultural Dimensions of Syntality in Modern Nations," *American Sociological Review*, XVII (1951), 408–21; Brian Berry, "An Inductive Approach to the Regionalization of Economic Development," *in* Norton Ginsburg (ed.), *Essays on Geography and Economic Development* (Chicago: University of Chicago Press, 1960), pp. 78–107, and "Basic Patterns of Economic Development," in Norton Ginsburg, *Atlas of Economic Development* (Chicago: University of Chicago Press, 1961), pp. 110–19; Leo F. Schnore," The Statistical Measurement of Urbanization and Economic Development," *Land Economics*, XXXVII (1961), 209–45. For a bibliography of applications to nations and other political units, see Rummel, 1967, *op. cit.*, Chap. 21.

[7] After having used such statistical and event sources as the *Statistical Yearbook*, *Demographic Yearbook*, *Encyclopedia of Nations*, *New York Times Index*, and *The Annual Register of the Year*, the author cannot help but feel that students interested in international relations and cross-national research are, indeed, data rich.

[8] Some of the exceptions are Hayward R. Alker, "Dimensions of Conflict in the General Assembly," *American Political Science Review*, LVII (1964), 642–57; R. J. Rummel, "Dimensions of Conflict Behavior Within and Between Nations," *General Systems Yearbook of the Society for General Systems Research*, VIII (1963), 1–50; Raymond Tanter, "Dimensions of Conflict Behavior Within and Between Nations 1958–60," *The Journal of Conflict Resolution* (March, 1966), 41–64.

[9] See, for example, Morton Kaplan, *System and Process in International Relations* (New York: John Wiley and Sons, Inc., 1957).

[10] See, for example, Richard N. Rosecrance, *Action and Reaction in World Politics* (Boston: Little Brown, and Company, 1963).

[11] Quincy Wright, *A Study of International Relations* (New York: Appleton–Century–Crofts, 1955), pp. 543–603.

method can be applied directly to data[12] or the data first can be intercorrelated and then factored, the approach most often used and the one employed here. Since the initial factors found by a factor analysis define variance rather than patterns, a rotation of the factors is subsequently carried out to delineate the clusters of interdependent variables.

Variables and nations

Ninety-four variables were selected for this analysis according to the following criteria: (1) theoretical relevance; (2) coverage of a wide number of activities of nations; (3) data availability; and (4) use in other systematic studies. The variables selected cut across a number of levels of analysis. Some of them refer to official decisions, such as diplomatic protests, number of UN representatives, or UN votes; some to private decisions, such as number of visitors, and membership in non-governmental international organizations; some to characteristics of the nation as a whole, such as air distance from U.S.; and some to characteristics of the citizens of a nation, such as ratio of immigrants to population. This catholicity allows the possible identification of dimensions with the widest substantive meaning.[13]

Organized into domains on the basis of content for easier reading, the variables are given in Appendix I.

The number of nations used in the analysis is 82. This includes all nations that were legally sovereign in 1955 (that is nations which had a foreign ministry and exchanged ambassadors with other nations) and which had a population greater than 750,000. In alphabetical order, the nations thus included are: Afghanistan, Albania, Argentina, Australia, Austria, Belgium, Bolivia, Brazil, Bulgaria, Burma, Cambodia, Canada, Ceylon, Chile, China, Colombia, Costa Rica, Cuba, Czechoslovakia, Denmark, Dominican Republic, Ecuador, Egypt, El Salvador, Ethiopia, Finland, Formosa, France, Germany (D.D.R.), Germany (Fed. Rep.), Greece, Guatemala, Haiti, Honduras, Hungary, India, Indonesia, Iran, Iraq, Irish Republic, Israel, Italy,

Japan, Jordan, Korea (Dem. Rep.), Korea (Rep. of), Laos, Lebanon, Liberia, Libya, Mexico, Nepal, Netherlands, New Zealand, Nicaragua, Norway, Outer Mongolia, Pakistan, Panama, Paraguay, Peru, Philippines, Poland, Portugal, Rumania, Saudi Arabia, Spain, Sweden, Switzerland, Syria, Thailand, Turkey, Union of South Africa, U.S.S.R., U.K., U.S.A., Uruguay, Venezuela, North Vietnam, South Vietnam, Yemen, and Yugoslavia.

Technical details of the analysis are given in Appendix II.

III. Results

The rotated factor matrix, communalities, and percent of variances are given in Appendix III.[14]

The communalities denoted by h^2 (proportion of variation of each variable in common with all the others) exceeds 1.00 for some of the variables, due to their level of missing data.[15] The percentages of variance at the foot of the table indicate the amount of variation among the variables accounted for by a factor (a pattern) in terms of the *total* possible variation, and in terms of the total *common* variance among all the variables. The variance accounted for by a factor indicates its importance in delineating the major patterns of covariation among the variables being analyzed.

Only those loadings greater or equal to an absolute value of .30 are given in the table. Smaller loadings have less than 10 per cent of their variation in common with a factor, and are thus of little importance in its description and identification. For the unrotated and orthogonally[16] rotated factors, a "loading" represents the correlation of a variable with the factor. By looking at the loadings one can see how much of the variation (where the proportion

[12] See, for example, Berry, *op. cit.*

[13] Within the scope of this paper it is hardly possible to touch on the many methodological issues and considerations involved in the selection and transformation of the variables. Those interested in pursuing these questions further are referred to R. J. Rummel, 1967, *op. cit.*, Chaps. 6–8.

[14] The correlations between the 94 international relations variables will be given along with their correlations with 142 intra-nation characteristics in R. J. Rummel, Jack Sawyer, Harold Guetzkow, and Raymond Tanter, *Dimensions of Nations* (forthcoming).

[15] See the technical appendix for number of correlations at various ranges of missing data.

[16] Orthogonal rotation means fitting the factors to the patterns (clusters) of variables with the restriction that the correlations (cosines) between the factors must remain zero. Thus, in doing an orthogonal rotation independence among the dimensions may be forced on the data. The size of the loadings (see below for a discussion of "loading") and the substantive meaning of the factor are an indication of the degree to which the data fit the orthogonal scheme.

TABLE 1
Factor 1: Participation

Domain	Variable no.	Variable[a]	Rotated factor 1	Rank
Military	1.	High defense expenditure	.85	6
	4.	Large production of population × energy production	.86	5
	5.	Many military personnel	.62	23
International collaboration	20.	Small ratio of aid received to GNP² per cap (N = 47)	−.65	21
	23.	Small ratio of balance of donations to gold stock	−.45	29
	25.	Large technical assistance contributions	.81	7.5
	26.	Small ratio of technical assistance received to GNP² per capita	−.66	20
	28.	Many treaties	.74	12
	29.	Many military treaties	.47	27.5
	30.	Many multilateral treaties	.67	18.5
Colonialism	33.	Has colonies	.47	27.5
	34.	Small ratio of national area to national and territorial area	−.40	31.5
	36.	Large national and territorial population	.68	16.5
International communication	37.	Much foreign mail (N = 48)	.81	7.5
Diplomatic	41.	Many embassies and legations in other nations	.92	3.5
	42.	Many embassies and legations in nation	.73	13
International organization	43.	Many UN representatives	.76	11
	44.	Many IGO's of which a member	.70	14.5
	45.	Many NGO's of which a member	.77	10
	46.	Many International Organization's HQ in country	.70	14.5
	49.	Large ratio of UN assessment to total UN assessments	.94	2
	50.	Large ratio of science NGO to NGO	.64	22
International politics	56.	Prominent in bloc politics	.40	31
International population movement	72.	Many immigrants	.42	30
	76.	Many foreign visitors	.68	16.5
	79.	Many T&R fellowship recipients in country	.61	24
	80.	Many foreign college students in country	.78	9
International trade	82.	Much trade	.95	1
	83.	Many exports	.92	3.5
	85.	Small ratio of raw material exports to exports	−.67	18.5
	89.	Small ratio of agricultural exports to exports	−.55	25
	91.	Small ratio of import duties to imports	−.49	26

Per cent common variance	22.2	
Per cent total variance	19.1	

[a] Double underlining of a variable indicates data on less than 30 nations and/or a correlation involving that variable on between 10 and 20 nations. Single underlining signifies data on between 30 and 50 nations. The number of nations for these variables is given in parentheses. Adjectives are attached to all variables to indicate the direction of relationship with the factor. Only loadings ≥ |.40| are shown.

of variation accounted for equals the square of the correlation) of each variable is accounted for by the factor (i.e., the extent to which each variable is involved in the pattern). Those variables that have a high correlation with the factor form a pattern of interdependent behavior identified by the factor—the strength of the correlation represents the degree to which a variable (behavior) is part of the pattern. *Different* factors therefore define *different* patterns.

Before turning to the particular factors, it should be noted that the 16 factors extracted and rotated account for 85.6 percent of the total possible variation

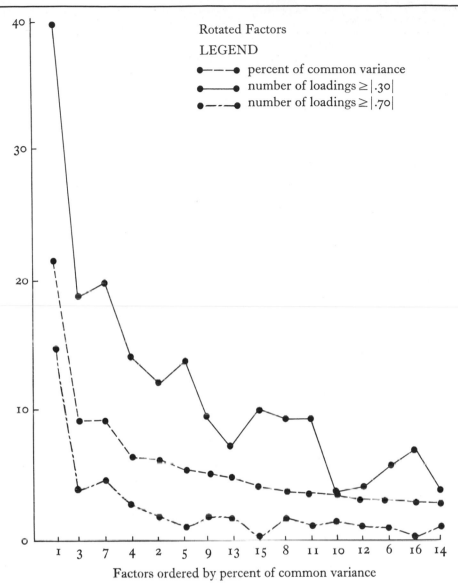

Figure 1.

among all the variables. Although inflated to a certain extent by the effect of missing data for some of the variables,[17] the percentage is still remarkable, even if the inflation were to amount to a most unlikely increase of 10 per cent. Even more remarkable is the finding from the unrotated factor variances in Appendix III that the first four factors extracted account for more than 50 per cent of the total possible

[17] The effect of missing data on a factor analysis is discussed in Rummel, 1966, *op. cit.*, Chap. 7.

variation. These figures mean that the activities of nations, as indexed by the 94 variables used here, *are highly patterned behavior. They mean that nations generally act similarly to each other and that these similarities can be resolved into a few basic dimensions. In other words, international relations is structured behavior.* If such activities were essentially unique to a nation, unpatterned, and explicable only within the context of that nation's milieu, then the communalities down the right side of Table 1 generally would be low (say about .30 or .40), the first factor (which is responsible for the greatest variance) would have accounted for something less than around 10 per cent of the total variance, and the sixteen factors together would have accounted for hardly more than 30 or 40 per cent of total variance.

Figure 1 gives a plot of the percent of common variance among all the variables for which each rotated factor accounts, as well as plots of the number of high loadings. This enables one to gauge the importance of each of the factors. Referring to the Figure, factors 1, 3, and 7 are obviously important in terms of variance accounted for and number of high loadings. Factors 4, 2, 5, and 9 are of lesser importance, and difficult to rank among themselves. Nonetheless, they account for more variance and have higher loadings than do the remaining factors, 13, 15, 8, 11, 10, 12, 6, 16, and 14. The factors will be discussed in their ordering by percent of common variance; the discussion will be confined to those that comprise the most variance and are readily interpretable. Variables loading on the factors will be given adjectives to indicate their direction of magnitude associated with the factor.

Rotated factor 1 is given in Table 1. For ease in locating a variable by content, variables are ordered in terms of domain; the rank of variables with a loading equal to or greater than an absolute value of .40 is given. So that the possible influence of missing data on the dimension may be gauged, variables with data on less than twenty or fifty nations are indicated as shown in the table. As can be seen, out of 32 variables loading on this factor only two have data on less than 50 nations.

This is the most important factor of the sixteen. It accounts for almost 20 per cent of the total possible variation among the variables and cuts across a number of domains. The trade domain is represented by much trade (.95) and many exports (.92); the international organization domain by the large ratio of UN assessment to all assessments (.94), membership in many NGO's (.77) and IGO's (.70); the diplomatic domain by the large number of embassies and legations in other nations (.92), and in the nation (.73); the military domain by large defense expenditures (.85), and Wright's power index of population times energy production (.86); the collaboration domain by large technical assistance contributions (.81) and many treaties signed (.74); the communica-

tions domain by much foreign mail (.81); and the population movement domain by a large number of foreign college students in the country (.78).

Further study of the loadings indicates that two very interesting domains are missing. The foreign conflict domain does not have any of its thirteen variables loading on the first factor, and the international politics domain has only high bloc prominence loaded (.40). Such conflict variables as threats, military action, and negative sanctions, and such international politics variables as bloc membership, Western bloc trade as a ratio of Western plus Communist bloc trade, and net percent votes with the U.S. in the UN are missing from this factor.

Thus, when one considers the nature of the variables loading highly on the factor and the nature of those missing altogether, the factor appears to be a *participation* pattern.[18] This does not place participation at one end of a continuum and cold war politics and international conflict at the other end. Rather, this dimension indicates that participation by nations in the international system, as defined by the variables loading on the factor, generally took place independent (see footnote 22) of bloc politics and international conflict.

Table 2 shows factor 3. Out of thirteen measures of international conflict included in the analysis, only one (number of ambassadors expelled or recalled) is missing from this factor. The variables with the highest loadings are large number of threats (.87), accusations (.85), killed in foreign conflict (.84), and presence of military action (.82). There is no doubt that this factor is a *conflict pattern*.[19] The

---

[18] In naming a dimension one can use *descriptive* labels to identify the variables in the cluster, such as participation, or *causal* labels to indicate the influence bringing about the clustering. The author prefers a descriptive label at this stage in the early exploration of a field by factor analysis, leaving to later analysis the identification of the underlying causes.

[19] It might be argued that this is a method factor, resulting from systematic bias in the sources used to collect the data. Since these sources were not consulted for other variables, a method factor is a distinct possibility. Fortunately, however, the data for several of the variables are such that we can reasonably expect them to be correct without source bias. These variables are the number of wars, presence or absence of military action, and severance of diplomatic relations. With less confidence one might also include mobilizations, and negative sanctions. Given these *marker* variables and their high correlations with the factor, the possibility of the latter being a result of method appears unlikely.

TABLE 2
Factor 3: Conflict

Domain	Variable no.	Variable[a]	Rotated factor 3	Rank
International conflict	6.	Many anti-foreign demonstrations	.44	10.5
	7.	Many negative sanctions	.52	9
	8.	Many protests	.67	5.5
	9.	Many severances of diplomatic relations	.44	10.5
	11.	Many expulsions or recalls of minor diplomats	.41	12
	12.	Many threats	.87	1
	13.	Involved in military action	.82	4
	14.	Involved in war	.66	6
	15.	Many troop movements	.67	5.5
	16.	Many mobilizations	.64	7
	17.	Many accusations	.85	2
	18.	Many foreign killed	.84	3
International politics	56.	Prominent in bloc politics	.58	8

Per cent common variance	9.6
Per cent total variance	8.2

[a] All variables had data on more than 50 nations and correlations with all variables on more than 20 nations. Adjectives are attached to all variables to indicate direction of relationship with factor. Only loadings $\geq |.40|$ are shown.

existence of this dimension suggests that international conflict behavior can be considered a continuum in international relations. At right angles to this continuum and through its center should be put a participation continuum to indicate the first dimension (pattern) found. In terms of the distribution of nations along these two continua, then, some nations during the mid-1950s were actively involved in the international system but had little conflict, while others no less involved had much conflict behavior. Some nations neither participated in the system nor had foreign conflict, while for some conflict was the major international activity.

Table 3 gives the loadings for factor 7. While factor 1 is surely the most important of the sixteen factors extracted in terms of variance and high loadings, on the basis of Figure 1 factors 3 and 7 appear of approximately equal importance. The variables with the high loadings on factor 7 are large number of technical assistance and relief fellowships received (.85), large ratio of IFC plus IBRD subscription to GNP² per capita (.79), much U.S. aid received (.77), much technical assistance received (.75), and large ratio of technical assistance contributions to GNP² per capita (.71) and technical assistance contributions to GNP² per capita. In

terms of high loadings this dimension well might be labelled an *aid* pattern. There are a number of international politics variables loaded on this dimension, although with the exception of U.S. aid received (.77), the loadings are generally low. The contrast can be seen in terms of technical assistance and relief fellowships received (.85), and the international politics variable of bloc allegiance (.57), that have 72 per cent and 33 per cent, respectively of their variation in common with the factor. What these loadings seem to indicate is that those nations which are involved in more than average aid activities, whether it be giving or receiving technical assistance and economic aid or subscribing to international lending institutions, are more often than not the Western and neutralist countries.

Factor 2 is given in Table 4. The pattern of behavior identified by this factor mainly involves large net percent votes with the U.S. (.79), low percent with the U.S.S.R. in the UN (−.76), and acceptance of the ICJ (.65). The positive loading for votes with the U.S. and negative loading for votes with the U.S.S.R. suggest that this is a bipolar factor, indexing behavior associated with opposing ideological positions. In view of the high loadings of the UN voting variables it seems more appropriate to

TABLE 3
Factor 7: Aid

Domain	Variable no.	Variable[a]	Rotated factor 7	Rank
International conflict	9.	Many severances of diplomatic relations	.44	13
International collaboration	20.	Large ratio of aid received to GNP^2 per cap	.42	14
	21.	Large ratio of IFC and IBRD subscription to GNP^2 per cap	.79	2
	24.	Large ratio of technical assistance contributions to GNP^2 per cap	.71	5
	26.	Large ratio of technical assistance received to GNP^2 per cap	.69	6
	27.	Much technical assistance received	.75	4
International organization	51.	Large ratio of membership in law NGO to NGO	.41	15
International politics	57.	Western bloc allegiance	.57	8
	61.	Large ratio of U.S. aid to U.S. and U.S.S.R. aid	.56	9
	62.	Much U.S. aid received	.77	3
	63.	Large ratio of English titles translated to all translations (N = 27)	.58	7
	64.	Small ratio of Russian titles translated to all translations (N = 35)	−.45	11.5
	65.	Large ratio of English titles translated to English and Russian (N = 25)	.45	11.5
International population movement	78.	Many T&R fellowships received	.85	1
	79.	Many T&R fellowships recipients in country	.49	10

Per cent common variance	9.5
Per cent total variance	8.1

[a] Double underlining of a variable indicates data on less than 30 nations and/or a correlation involving that variable on between 10 and 20 nations. Single underlining signifies data on between 30 and 50 nations. The number of nations for these variables are given in parentheses. Adjectives are attached to all variables to indicate the direction of relationship with the factor. Only loadings ≥ |.40| are shown.

name this an *ideology* pattern, rather than a cold war one.[20] That this dimension discriminates more along ideological lines than cold war alliances and oppositions is indicated by the relatively low loading of bloc allegiance (.48) in contrast to the higher loading of acceptance of the ICJ (.65)[21] and the complete lack of loading on this dimension of such cold war variables as ratio of Western bloc trade to trade with the Western and Soviet bloc, of U.S. aid

to U.S. plus Soviet aid, and neutrality (if this were a cold war dimension then neutrality should have a negative loading). Considering the stress put on ideology in the literature it is interesting that it should *account for less than a third of the variance of the largest dimension, participation, and be generally unrelated to participation, conflict, and aid.*[22]

Table 5 shows the loadings for factor 4. Here, the high loadings are for many foreign visitors (.62)

[20] Compare Hayward Alker's factor analysis, *op. cit.*, of UN General Assembly votes, in which a major factor extracted was an East–West, or cold war dimension.

[21] The contrast in variance is 23 per cent to 42 per cent. The variance of the highest loaded variable on this factor is 62 per cent. Hence, bloc allegiance contributes about one-third the variance of the highest loading variable and half the amount of acceptance of the ICJ.

[22] The high loadings of the variables on these dimensions, their interpretability and, to anticipate the discussion below, the lack of correlation between the basic variables selected to index them argue that the orthogonality of these dimensions fit the data—that independence in the sense of near zero correlation is not wholly an artifact of the orthogonal rotation.

TABLE 4
Factor 2: Ideology

Domain	Variable no.	Variable[a]	Rotated factor 2	Rank
International collaboration	32.	Accepts jurisdiction of ICJ	.65	3
International politics	57.	Western block allegiance	.48	6
	63.	Large ratio of English titles translated to all titles (N = 27)	.46	7
	65.	Large ratio of English titles translated to English plus Russian (N = 25)	.50	5
	66.	Large net percent of votes with U.S. in UN	.79	I
	67.	Low net percent of votes with U.S.S.R. in UN	−.76	2
Political geography	68.	Few contiguous nations	−.59	4

Per cent common variance	6.6
Per cent variance	5.7

[a] Double underlining of a variable indicates data on less than 30 nations and/or a correlation involving that variable on between 10 and 20 nations. Single underlining signifies data on between 30 and 50 nations. The number of nations for these variables are given in parentheses. Adjectives are attached to all variables to indicate the direction of relationship with the factor. Only loadings ≥ |.40| are shown.

TABLE 5
Factor 4: Popularity

Domain	Variable no.	Variable[a]	Rotated factor 4	Rank
International communication	38.	Large ratio of foreign mail to pop (N − 47)	.78	3
International organization	53.	Small ratio of membership in religion NGO to NGO	−.41	7.5
International politics	63.	Large ratio of English titles translations to all titles (N = 27)	.43	5
	65.	Large ratio of English titles translations to English and Russian (N = 25)	.42	6
International population movement	76.	Many foreign visitors	.62	4
	77.	Large ratio of foreign visitors to population	.81	1.5
	81.	Large ratio of foreign college students to college students	.81	1.5
International trade	94.	Large ratio of trade to GNP	.41	7.5

Per cent common variance	6.8
Per cent total variance	5.8

[a] Double underlining of a variable indicates data on less than 30 nations and/or a correlation involving that variable on between 10 and 20 nations. Single underlining signifies data on between 30 and 50 nations. The number of nations for these variables are given in parentheses. Adjectives are attached to all variables to indicate the direction of relationship with the factor. Only loadings ≥ |.40| are shown.

and the ratios of foreign visitors to population (.81), foreign college students to college students (.81), and foreign mail to population (.78). One might be tempted to call this a communication dimension at first, but the high loadings for visitors and foreign students points to a pattern of activities associated with nations that have an attraction for foreigners. This dimension might be labelled, therefore, a *popularity* pattern.

Factor 5, which is given in Table 6, appears to be a South American pattern. The two distance measures, air distance from the U.S. (−.75) and small ratio of air distance from the U.S. to air distance from the U.S. and U.S.S.R. (−.69), have the highest loadings. These distance measures indicate that the variation accounted for by the dimension is mainly common to nations close to the U.S., and far from the U.S.S.R.—that is, South American nations. The activities associated with the dimension are expelling or recalling many ambassadors (.68), large ratio of membership in medicine NGO to total NGO of which a member (.64), large ratio of agricultural exports to exports (.44), relatively low level of aid received (−.44) and small ratio of aid received to GNP^2 per capita (−.44).

Table 7 gives factor 9, which has highly loaded ratio of immigrants to population (.77), immigrants (.73), and ratios of emigrants to population (.64) and immigrants to migrants (.41). This factor seems to define, therefore, activities associated with world migration patterns. Other activities involved in this *migration* pattern are ratio of membership in peace and friendship NGO (.58) and religion NGO (.51) to total NGO, and ratio of Western bloc to Western plus Soviet bloc trade (.48). The last ratio implies that those nations mainly involved in world migration patterns are non-Communist.

The dimensions discussed account for 56.0 and 65.3 percent of the total and common variance, respectively, among the 94 variables. The remaining nine factors only account for a third more of the variation, have relatively low loadings, and are not readily interpretable. Therefore, no discussion of them will be offered here.

IV. Discussion

In interpreting the results it should be kept in mind that the factor analysis yields only what was put into the study in the first place. The technique essentially

TABLE 6
Factor 5: South American

Domain	Variable no.	Variable^a	Rotated factor 5	Rank
International conflict	10.	Expulsion and recall of many ambassadors	.68	3
International collaboration	19.	Little economic aid received (N = 47)	−.44	6
	20.	Small ratio of aid received to GNP^2 per cap (N = 43)	−.44	6
International organization	54.	Large ratio of medicine NGO to total NGO	.64	4
International politics	59.	Neutral bloc	.42	8
Political geography	69.	Short air distance from U.S.	−.75	1
	71.	Small ratio of air distance from U.S. to air distance from U.S. and U.S.S.R.	−.69	2
International trade	89.	Large ratio of agriculture exports to exports	.44	6

Per cent common variance   5.5
Per cent total variance   4.7

^{a} Double underlining of a variable indicates data on less than 30 nations and/or a correlation involving that variable on between 10 and 20 nations. Single underlining signifies data on between 30 and 50 nations. The number of nations for these variables are given in parentheses. Adjectives are attached to all variables to indicate direction of relationship with factor. Only loadings $\geq$ |.40| are shown.

TABLE 7
Factor 9: Migration

Domain	Variable no.	Variable[a]	Rotated factor 9	Rank
International organization	52.	Large ratio of membership in peace and friendship NGO to NGO	.58	4
	53.	Large ratio of membership in religion NGO to NGO	.51	5
International politics	60.	Large ratio of Western bloc trade to Communist and Western trade	.48	6
International population movement	72.	Many immigrants	.73	2
	73.	Large ratio of immigrants to population	.77	1
	74.	Large ratio of emigrants to population (N = 43)	.64	3
	75.	Large ratio of immigrants to migrants (N = 33)	.41	7

	Per cent common variance	5.1
	Per cent total variance	4.4

[a] Double underlining of a variable indicates data on less than 30 nations and/or a correlation involving that variable on between 10 and 20 nations. Single underlining signifies data on between 30 and 50 nations. The number of nations for these variables are given in parentheses. Adjectives are attached to all variables to indicate direction of relationship with factor. Only loadings ≥ |.40| are shown.

describes the relations among the variables *selected*. Thus, if one does an analysis of variables, over half of which are conflict, then it is almost a foregone conclusion that the first and most important dimension will be conflict. If one overloads his set of variables with measures defining various aspects of the cold war, a cold war dimension will probably emerge. It is hoped that this danger was avoided here by the conscious choice of measures that were as catholic as possible. Only replications of this study, however, will give a definite answer to such a possibility.

Moreover, the dimensions found are specific to nations employed in the analysis. If there are data on very few newly emerged nations in the analysis, then a dimension related to number of years independent cannot be extracted. Caution here is particularly important, since this study was done on data for the mid-1950s. The dimensions for this period may have undergone some change by today, since current international relations involve over a 30 per cent increase in the population of nations. It should also be mentioned that the dimensions of this study are patterns of activities of nations *directed toward and received from all other nations*. That is, they define various patterns of involvement *in* the international *system*. These dimensions do not refer to interactions *between* countries. Hence, although the amount of trade of a nation and the number of international organizations of which it is a member were found related in this study, nothing can be said from this as to whether the trade between two countries and their co-membership in international organizations is related.

Turning to the substantive results, an interesting aspect of the patterns found is that participation in the international system and conflict behavior form distinct patterns. Conflict does not appear as a necessary consequence of greater involvement in foreign affairs. This is surely contrary to expectations. One would expect that as nations are more involved with a larger range of activities in the system, there would be more contact with the diverse goals and ideologies of other nations. A higher level of conflict behavior would then exist for the nation as a reflection of its attempts to arrive at explicit accommodations and informal understandings to govern the issues arising from its greater participation. This would then mean, empirically, that conflict behavior on the one hand and on the other, treaties, trade, membership in international organizations, number of embassies and legations, mail, immigrants, tourists, etc., would be found as part of the same pattern of activities. But this is not the case. Why?

First, I will argue that participation in the international system is internally derived behavior.

Participation is a resultant of the properties of the nation. Specifically, the level of involvement in the system depends on the economic development of a nation and its power capability. Economic development brings with it the need for markets and resources. The higher level of education and internal communications that is a concomitant of economic development enables knowledge about, contact with, and travel to other nations. Migration, student exchange, and tourist travel is encouraged and facilitated. Most importantly, these transactions and private international activity require official agreements and administration. The nation will therefore enter into treaties governing these activities, join more international organizations related to these activities, and exchange embassies and legations with other nations to ease and administer them.

Participation in the system, however, appears not to be wholly a consequence of economic development. The power capability of a nation is also and even more important. The more powerful become the power brokers within the international system. They not only have a greater capacity for satisfying and protecting their own national interests, but they also play a role in deciding international issues related to the community of nations. Their power necessarily casts them in the role of actively protecting the current officially sanctioned international configuration of power and rewards (e.g., U.S.; U.K.), attacking it (e.g., U.S.S.R.; China), or moderating between *status quo* and non *status quo* powers (e.g., India; Egypt). Let me denote the economic development of a nation by E, its power capability by C and its participation in the system by P. Then the theory is that $P = \alpha E + \beta C$, where α and β are constants.

In contrast to participation, foreign conflict behavior, however, is not internally derived. Its genesis lies outside the nation. It is a *relational* phenomenon depending on the degree of economic, social, and political similarity between nations, the geographic distance between them, and their power parity.[23] Participation in the system may increase the *potentiality* for conflict only. Whether conflict

actually occurs depends in part on the social and value *distances* between the nations in contact and their relative power. Even nations that participate very little in the international system may have great conflict with each other if they are contiguous while having a great social and value distance between them (e.g., Israel and Syria).

Some evidence for this theory is found when the variables used in this study are included in a matrix with 146 domestic attributes of nations and factor analyzed.[24] Two of the major patterns to emerge were economic development (E) and power capability (C). The major variables defining participation in the international system were found with significant loadings on both E and C, but on no other patterns determined by the analysis. That is, this analysis found that $P = \alpha E + \beta C$. In other words, the level of participation of a nation in the system could be highly predicted by knowing only its level of E and C. In terms of the loadings of P on both E and C, the constant β seems slightly larger than that of α, i.e., power capability plays a slightly larger role in determining participation than economic development.

In this same analysis, however, the foreign conflict variables form a pattern of behavior independent of any of the domestic attributes. This lends credence to the theory that conflict is relational and therefore not necessarily related to participation. Further evidence for this was obtained by regressing conflict between nations onto relational measures of their economic and value distances, geographic distance, joint power to span distance, and power parity. This regression was found to significantly predict to conflict between nations.[25]

Therefore, the finding here of independent patterns of level of system participation and conflict behavior is theoretically explicable. And the theory itself has empirical validity in the results of other studies that have been done.

Besides participation and conflict, several other patterns of system involvement were found. The finding of all these patterns and the amount of variation in the activities of nations (proportion of variance of the variables) they describe indicates

---

[23] These ideas are discussed in greater length and tested in R. J. Rummel, "A Social Field Theory of Foreign Conflict," *Papers IV* [Peace Research Society (International)], 1965. The theory that conflict is relational is also involved in Galtung's concept of "rank disequilibrium" between nations. See Johan Galtung, "A Structural Theory of Aggression," *Journal of Peace Research*, II (1964), 15–38.

[24] This is reported in Rummel *et al.* (forthcoming), *op. cit.* In an already overlong paper it is not possible to give these findings in detail here.

[25] Rummel, *Papers IV*, 1965, *op. cit.*

that the international relations of the mid-1950s is highly structured.

This structuring indicates that more systematic analyses of international relations can be carried out than has heretofore been seen, and that scientific explanation and prediction are more possible in this area than students of international relations have been wont to believe.

This structuring of international relations can be indexed (operationalized) by several *basic* indicators that are selected in terms of the highest loading on the factors. The most important of these indicators is a nation's *trade*, which is an index to a nation's degree of *participation* in the international system. With this factor trade has a .95 correlation, which means that it has a 90 per cent fit (i.e., the factor accounts for 90 per cent of the variation in trade) to the pattern identified by the factor. Trade does not stand alone, however, as a measure of participation. The loading of trade (.95) on the factor has no meaningful difference from that of ratio of UN assessments to total UN assessments (.94). As a consequence of its greater theoretical significance and the large number of studies that have been done on it, however, the choice between the two measures has been made in favor of trade as the *basic* indicator.[26]

Second in importance as a *basic* indicator is the number of *threats* a nation makes, which is an index to the *conflict* pattern. The correlation of .87 with the dimension (76 per cent fit) signifies that the number of threats of a nation is a very good indicator of the amount of international conflict in which it is involved.[27] A nation's threats, however, are no

measure of a nation's participation, or lack thereof, in the international system of the mid-1950s. As shown below, in terms of the *basic* indicators, threats and trade are uncorrelated.

A third *basic* indicator, indexing the *aid* pattern, is the *technical assistance and relief fellowships received* by a nation. This variable has 72 per cent fit to the aid dimension. Next in line with a 58 per cent fit is the amount of U.S. aid received.[28] The two previous basic variables, trade and threats, have received much study in the literature; T. & R. fellowships have received relatively little. Yet, if the research reported here is valid, the variable demands more attention.

With regard to the *ideological dimension*, the *basic* indicator with 62 per cent fit is *net percent votes with the U.S. in the UN*. Given the bipolar nature of much of mid-1950 international politics, the importance of this variable is clear. It is rewarding, however, to have what is "self evident" confirmed by systematic analysis. The popularity pattern, that accounts for slightly less of the variation among the 94 variables, can be defined by either the *ratio of foreign visitors to population* or *foreign college students to college students* (both have 66 per cent fit to the pattern). The latter variable, however, seems to offer slightly less trouble in data collection and will be the choice for the *basic* indicator here.[29] The *South American* pattern can be indexed by *air distance from the U.S.* (56 per cent fit) and the

---

[26] Another solution is to standardize each variable and then sum these scores. The composite would then constitute the index of the factor. In defining the dimensions, however, I have resisted the temptation to make such compound indices. They may be appropriate when one is dealing with dimensions resulting from a factor analysis of psychological tests, which have little meaning in themselves. Here, however, each variable is well defined, has considerable substantive meaning, and in the case of many of the variables, considerable research into its nature. To sum these variables, then, would give a composite which is unique to this study and thus has no history to aid in interpretation when the index is used elsewhere. Consequently, although using single measures to define the factors results in less than an ideal definition of the dimensions, the long run research payoff of keeping the measures *simple* and *well known* will be probably much greater.

[27] A nation's threats or their perception has been gaining research attention as a crucial conflict measure. See, for example, T. C. Schelling, *The Strategy of Conflict* (Cambridge: Harvard University Press, 1960); Richard A.

Brody, "Some Systemic Effects of the Spread of Nuclear Weapons Technology: A Study Through Simulation of a Multi-nuclear Future," *The Journal of Conflict Resolution*, VII (1963); Dina Zinnes, *Expression and Perception of Hostility in Inter-State Relations* (Ph.D. Dissertation, Stanford University, 1963); and Lewis Fry Richardson, *Arms and Insecurity* (Pittsburg and Chicago: The Boxwood Press and Quadrangle Books, 1960).

[28] With a better fit, U.S. aid received would be the natural choice to index the factor. It has much substantive meaning, has been studied considerably, and presents little problem in data collection. But its fit is 14 percent less than that of T and R fellowships received which is a meaningful difference in allowing extraneous variation to enter future studies which may use these *basic* indicators as input. For example, if a correlation between T and R fellowships, as an index to the aid dimension, and GNP per capita is exactly zero, using U.S. aid received as the index and correlating it with GNP per capita could raise the correlation to .37! Thus, one might come to opposite conclusions depending on which of the measures one selected. Since T and R fellowships received has the better fit to the aid dimension, it is the indicator which should be used.

[29] See footnote 26, above.

TABLE 8
Coefficient of determination (r^2)
between basic indicators

Variable no.	Basic indicators	Basic variable no.[a]						
		82	12	78	66	77	69	73
82.	Trade		.044	.073	.012	.040	.000	.005
12.	Threats	71		.012	.048	.010	.010	.002
78.	T&R fellowships	73	77		.026	.017	.003	.017
66.	Net per cent votes U.S.	54	56	56		.240	.090	.138
77.	Visitors/Population	50	49	51	37		.152	.049
69.	Air distance U.S.	72	76	80	55	50		.000
73.	Immigrants/Population	50	51	52	39	38	51	

[a] Variable numbers are the same as those given in the Variable List. The values in upper right hand triangular matrix are the coefficients; those in the lower left matrix are the number of nations on which these coefficients were calculated. The coefficient of determination measures the proportion of variation two variables have in common. See Mordecai Ezekiel and Karl A. Fox, *Methods of Correlation and Regression Analysis* (New York: Wiley, Third Edition, 1959), pp. 130–32.

migration pattern by the *ratio of immigrants to population* (58 per cent fit).

Table 8 gives the percent of variation that these indicators have in common with each other, and thus the degree to which they index the independence of the patterns delineated. The matrix is derived by squaring the product moment correlations between these indicators. Ideally, if the indicators were perfect indices to the patterns (100 per cent variation in common with the factors) the matrix would have all zeros. The extent to which it does not is a measure of the departure of the variables from the pattern they are supposed to index. Since the indicators to the right and bottom of the matrix are the ones that have higher amounts of variation in common with each other, they thus have poorer fits to the pattern they were chosen to index. Nevertheless, the overall low values in the matrix argue that the *basic* indicators selected do sufficiently index the basic structure of international relations in the mid-1950s as derived from this study.

A number of usages for these basic indicators is possible. They may serve as variables to be used in simulation to index the structure of international relations in which participants will interact.[30] They may be used as predictors in a regression equation when one is concerned about how a nation's position on the dimensions of international relations in the mid-1950s will predict particular international activities.[31] Moreover, the equation can be turned around and a nation's position on these dimensions can be regressed on domestic attributes (such as the organizational structure for decision making) to see how well they predict international structures. In addition, these indicators should serve as foci for data collection and individual variable analyses, and should certainly be used as markers in studies attempting to replicate or extend in whole or in part the findings of this study.

[30] See Harold Guetzkow *et al.*, *Simulation in International Relations*, (Englewood Cliffs, N.J.: Prentice-Hall, Inc. 1963).
[31] For an example of this, see Rudolph J. Rummel, "Predictors of Conflict Behavior Within and Between Nations," *Papers I* (Peace Research Society, 1964), pp. 79–111.

APPENDIX I

Variable list

No.	Variable[a]	Nations	Year(s) of data[b]	Transformation[c]
Military Domain				
1.	Defense expenditure	65	1955	Log X
2.	Defense expenditure/government expenditure	69	1955	$\sqrt{X}$
3.	Military personnel/population	79	1955	Log $(X + 1)$
4.	Population X energy production[d]	76	1955	Log $(X + 1)$
5.	Military personnel	80	1955	Log X
International Conflict Domain[e]				
6.	Anti-foreign demonstrations	77	1955–57	None
7.	Negative sanctions	77	1955–57	Grouping[j]
8.	Protests	77	1955–57	Grouping[j]
9.	Countries with which diplomatic relations severed	77	1955–57	None
10.	Ambassadors expelled or recalled	77	1955–57	None
11.	Diplomatic officials of lesser than ambassador's rank expelled or recalled	77	1955–57	None
12.	Threats	77	1955–57	Grouping[j]
13.	Military action, or not[f]	77	1955–57	None
14.	Wars[g]	77	1955–57	None
15.	Troop movements	77	1955–57	None
16.	Mobilizations	77	1955–57	None
17.	Accusations	77	1955–57	Log $(X + 1)$
18.	Killed in foreign violence	77	1955–57	Log $(X + 1)$
International Collaboration Domain				
19.	Economic aid received	47	1954–57	Log $(X + 326)$
20.	Economic aid received/GNP² per cap	43	1954–57	Log $(X + 1)$
21.	IFC and IBRD subscription/GNP² per cap	79	1957	Log $(X + 1)$
22.	Balance of official donations	61	1954–56	Log $(X + 74)$
23.	Balance of official donations/gold stock	60	1954–56	Log $(X + 7, 274)$
24.	Contributions to technical assistance/GNP² per cap	78	1954–57	Log $(X + 1)$
25.	Contributions to technical assistance	79	1954–57	Log $(X + 1)$
26.	Technical assistance received/GNP² per cap	77	1955	Log $(X + 1)$
27.	Technical assistance received	82	1955	Arcsine $\sqrt{X}$
28.	Treaties	82	1954–56	Log $(X + 1)$
29.	Military treaties	82	1954–56	Log $(X + 1)$
30.	Multilateral treaties	82	1954–56	Log $(X + 1)$
31.	Military treaties/treaties	82	1954–56	Log $(X + 1)$
32.	Acceptance of jurisdiction of International Court of Justice[h]	82	1959	None
Colonialism Domain				
33.	Possession of colonies	82	1955	None
34.	National land area/national and colonial land area	82	1955	None
35.	National population/national and colonial population	82	1955	None
36.	National and colonial population	81	1955	Log $(X + 1)$
International Communication Domain				
37.	Foreign mail	48	1955	Log $(X + 1)$
38.	Foreign mail/population	47	1955	Log X
39.	Foreign mail sent/foreign mail	48	1955	None
40.	Foreign titles translated/book titles	36	1955	None

Variable list—continued

No.	Variable[a]	Nations	Year(s) of data[b]	Transformation[c]
Diplomatic Domain				
41.	Embassies and legations in other nations	67	1955	None
42.	Embassies and legations from other nations	67	1950	None
International Organization				
43.	Representatives to UN	57	1955	$\text{Log}\,(X+1)$
44.	IGO (intergovernmental international organizations) of which a member	80	1954	None
45.	NGO (private international organizations) of which a member	80	1954	$\text{Log}\,(X+1)$
46.	International organization headquarters in nation	80	1954	$\text{Log}\,(X+1)$
47.	Arts and culture NGO/NGO	79	1954	$\text{Log}\,(X+1)$
48.	UN payment delinquencies/UN assessment	56 as of	1955	$\text{Log}\,(X+1)$
49.	UN assessment/total UN assessment	56	1955	$\text{Log}\,X$
50.	Engineering, technology and science NGO/NGO	80	1954	None
51.	Law NGO/NGO	79	1954	None
52.	Peace and friendship NGO/NGO	80	1954	$\sqrt{X}$
53.	Religion NGO/NGO	80	1954	None
54.	Medicine NGO/NGO	80	1954	None
55.	Education and youth NGO/NGO	80	1954	None
International Politics				
56.	Bloc prominence[i]	82	1955	None
57.	Bloc membership	82	1955	None
58.	Membership in British Commonwealth	82	1955	None
59.	Membership in neutral bloc	82	1955	None
60.	Trade with Western bloc/trade with Communist bloc and Western bloc	69	1955	None
61.	U.S. aid received/U.S.S.R. and U.S. aid received	68	1955–58	None
62.	U.S. aid received	63	1955	$\text{Log}\,(X+1)$
63.	English titles translated/foreign titles translated	27	1955	None
64.	Russian titles translated/foreign titles translated	35	1955	$\text{Log}\,(X+1)$
65.	English titles translated/Russian and English titles translated	25	1955	X^b
66.	Percent of votes in agreement with minus percent of votes in opposition to U.S. votes in UN General Assembly	56	1955	None
67.	Percent of votes in agreement with minus percent of votes in opposition to U.S.S.R. votes in the UN General Assembly	56	1955	None
Political Geography				
68.	Nations contiguous to colonies and national territory	82	1955	$\sqrt{X}$
69.	Air distance from U.S.	81	1960	None
70.	Air distance from U.S.S.R.	81	1960	$\sqrt{X}$
71.	Air distance from U.S./air distance from U.S.S.R. and U.S.	80	1960	Arcsine $\sqrt{X}$

Variable list—continued

No.	Variable[a]	Nations	Year(s) of data[b]	Transformation[c]
International Population Movement				
72.	Immigrants	52	1955	Square Root
73.	Immigrants/population	52	1955	$\text{Log}\,(X+1)$
74.	Emigrants/population	43	1955	$\text{Log}\,(X+1)$
75.	Immigrants/migrants	33	1955	None
76.	Foreign visitors	51	1955	$\text{Log}\,(X+1)$
77.	Foreign visitors/population	51	1955	$\text{Log}\,X$
78.	UN technical assistance fellowships received	81	1955	$\sqrt{X}$
79.	UN technical assistance fellowship recipients in country	80	1955	$\text{Log}\,(X+1)$
80.	Foreign college students in country	55 1956 or 1957		$\text{Log}\,(X+1)$
81.	Foreign college students/college students	55 1956 or 1957		$\sqrt{X}$
International Trade Domain				
82.	Trade	73	1955	$\text{Log}\,X$
83.	Exports	76	1955	$\text{Log}\,X$
84.	Imports/trade	75	1955	$\sqrt{X}$
85.	Exports of raw materials/exports	73	1955	X^b
86.	Balance of payments/gold stock	59	1954–56	$\sqrt{X}$
87.	Exports/GNP	71	1955	None
88.	Leading export/exports	75	1955	None
89.	Agricultural exports/exports	59	1955	Arcsine $\sqrt{X}$
90.	Agricultural exports/agricultural trade	53	1955	Arcsine $\sqrt{X}$
91.	Import duties/imports	54	1955	$\sqrt{X}$
92.	Balance of investments	62	1954–56	$\text{Log}\,(X+1826)$
93.	Balance of investments/gold stock	58	1954–56	X^b
94.	Trade/GNP	69	1955	None

[a] The univariate statistics for the raw and transformed data and for nations lying at or more than three standard deviations from the mean are given in R. J. Rummel, Jack Sawyer, Harold Guetzkow, and Raymond Tanter, *Dimensions of Nations* (forthcoming).

[b] See Rummel *et al., op. cit.*, for the definitions and the sources of the data for each variable.

[c] Transformations were applied to each variable until the best transformation was found to increase the fit of the distribution to normality, as determined by the Chi-Square test, and to reduce or eliminate data extremes of more than three standard deviations from the mean.

[d] Suggested by Quincy Wright, *The Study of International Relations* (New York: Appleton-Century-Crofts, 1955), p. 599, as a measure of a nation's "power."

[e] Extensive definitions of the conflict variables along with their data are given in R. J. Rummel, "Dimensions of Conflict Behavior Within and Between Nations," *General Systems: Yearbook of the Society for General Systems Research*, Vol. 8 (1963), pp. 1–50.

[f] Any military clash of a particular nation with another involving gunfire, but short of war.

[g] Any military clash of a particular nation with another in which more than .02 percent of its population are militarily involved in the clash.

[h] Rating: 0 = not listed in *Status of Multilateral Conventions in Respect of which the Secretary-General Acts as Depository* (UN, 1959, Chapter I, pp. 8–31), as declaring acceptance of the jurisdiction of the ICJ, 1 = declares acceptance of jurisdiction with reservation, 2 = declares unconditional acceptance.

[i] Rated zero for non-prominence and unity for prominence in terms of a nation being a recognized spokesman for a bloc or a faction therein, of organizing conferences within or between blocs, and of independently tabling major proposals for the solution, resolution, or control of political problems or conflict.

[j] Data are grouped in a geometric progression with the common ratio after zero being 2, as follows:

Data	Transformed Value
0	0
1	1
2–3	2
4–7	3
8–15	4
etc.	etc.

APPENDIX II

Some technical aspects of the analysis

Data and preliminary screening. Data were generally collected from UN statistical sources. In tabulating and punching the data a number of error screening devices were used to avoid clerical and source error. Non-ratio data were collected by one assistant and then double-checked against the source by two working together. Ratios were calculated independently by assistants and then compared. And data were finally screened visually for unreasonable values. Data punching was inspected for extreme errors through the calculation of distribution statistics and then extreme values of more than three standard deviations from the mean were double-checked.

Transformations were applied to data for each variable until a transformation was found which maximized the fit of the distribution to normality, as tested by Chi-Square, and minimized data extremes of greater than three standard deviations. Extremes in the data that could not be reduced through transformation usually were eliminated and the distribution statistics recalculated. The purpose of the normalization and reduction of extremes here was to lessen the effect of skewed data and of outliers on the correlation coefficient. Of the 94 variables, 54 per cent were normalized with a Chi-Square fit at the .05 level.

Correlations. Product moment correlations were calculated between all the variables, including five that were dichotomous. In the latter case, the marginals were calculated to insure that in no instance did the frequency of occurrence of a 0 or 1 fall below a frequency of 10 per cent. Because of missing data, correlations were calculated only for data present for both variables for each nation. The number of nations for each correlation thus varied from correlation to correlation. In the 94 variable correlation matrix, the percent of the 4,371 correlations that fell within the following ranges for the number of nations involved were: $(21-30) = 1.6$ per cent; $(31-40) = 7.1$ per cent; $(41-50) = 15.3$ per cent; $(51-60) = 24.2$ per cent; $(61-70) = 16.9$ per cent; $(71-82) = 34.8$ per cent. Four correlations had between 10 and 20 nations. They were between aid received and ratio of immigrants to migrants, between aid received and ratio of migrants to population, between ratio of immigrants to migrants and ratio of aid received to GNP^2 per capita, and between ratio of emigrants to population and ratio of aid received to GNP^2 per capita.

Curvilinearity. Because of the large number of variables plots to assess the degree of curvilinearity in the over 4,000 relationships were not made. The large number of high correlations found in the study, however, suggest that extreme curvilinearity was either not a general problem to begin with or generally was linearized by the transformations applied to the data. A low product moment correlation is a necessary, though not sufficient, condition for a curvilinear relation that would distort a factor analysis.

Factor analysis. Principal components technique was used. Unities thus were inserted in the principal diagonal of the correlation matrix. Factoring was stopped at the 17th factor because of negative eigenvalues resulting thereafter. All but the last factor were rotated. In the extraction of 17 factors employing Hotelling's iterative technique, 328 iterations were calculated at a precision level of 1.00009.

Rotation. Orthogonal rotation was performed using Kaiser's varimax criterion. The number of iteration cycles was 29; an accuracy check on the original and final communalities and their difference was computed. Both factor analysis and rotation were carried out in single precision arithmetic.

Significance tests. No significance tests were calculated for the correlations or the factor results. Such tests were considered ambiguous in the case where one is dealing with the universe and not a sample. All independent nations for the mid-1950's were used, although in the case of individual correlations the number of nations involved dropped below the universe size of 82. Yet in about 50 per cent of the correlations, the number of nations employed was at least 74 per cent of the universe.

Computer. All, except minor calculations, were carried out on IBM 709's at Northwestern and Indiana Universities using a program prepared especially for the project of which this study is a part.[a]

[a] Thanks are due to Harry Harman for making available his 236 variable correlation factor analysis and orthogonal rotation programs, Robert Sandsmark for linking these programs together and rewriting the correlation program to handle missing data, and Norman Swartz for the final debugging of the correlation program and its linkages with the factor analysis routine.

APPENDIX III

Orthogonally rotated factors

No.	Variable abbreviation	1	2	3	4	5	6	7	8	9	10	11	12	13	14	15	16	h^2
1.	DEFEXP	85																96
2.	DX/EXP			37					−41							33		77
3.	MIL/PP			32			−32									64		83
4.	E × PP	86																95
5.	MILTRY	62		32	−35													94
6.	F-DMST			44		−35												65
7.	NEGSAN			52										35				70
8.	PROTST	36		67														74
9.	SEVDIP			44				44										67
10.	ER-AMB					68												65
11.	ER-LES	33		41													−57	73
12.	THREAT			87														85
13.	MILACT			82														81
14.	WAR			66														67
15.	TRPMVT	30		67										35				82
16.	MOBILI			64														64
17.	ACCUSA			85														87
18.	F-KILL			84														79
19.	AIDRVD				−44			35					35				38	81
20.	AID/GP	−65			−44			42							31		34	129
21.	TFC/GP							79										81
22.	DONBAL														69			82
23.	BOD/GO	−45													61			80
24.	FTR/GP							71										75
25.	CNT-TR	81																88
26.	DTR/GP	−66						69										100
27.	D-TR							75										87
28.	TREATY	74						39										95
29.	MIL-TR	47												66				86
30.	M-TRET	67						35										87
31.	MT/TRE													76				77
32.	AC-ICJ		65															57
33.	COLONY	47											−59					74
34.	NA/TAR	−40											75					79
35.	NP/TPP	−30											73					71
36.	POL-PP	68	−33		−39													96
37.	F-MAIL	81			37													102
38.	EML/PP	30			78													98
39.	MSNT/M										−35		−66					81
40.	TRSL/T						47		−39							58		99
41.	F-EMBS	92																96
42.	D-EMBY	73				33												89
43.	UN/REP	76		37														87
44.	IGO	70				33							−35					95
45.	NGO	77						32										99

Factors[a]

Orthogonally rotated factors—continued

No.	*Variable abbreviation*	\multicolumn{16}{c}{*Factors*[a]}	h²
		I	2	3	4	5	6	7	8	9	10	11	12	13	14	15	16	
46.	IO–HQ	70											−38					77
47.	ART/NG	36						33	−33			43						65
48.	UNDE/C																66	65
49.	(CT–UN	94																112
50.	SCI/NG	64										−48						88
51.	LAW/NG					32		41										69
52.	PCE/NG										58	36						83
53.	REL/NG				−41					51								75
54.	MED/NG					64	51											78
55.	ED/NG											75						79
56.	BLOCPR	40		58														74
57.	BLOC		48			34		57										94
58.	CMWLTH		35													−40		67
59.	NEUTRL				−34	42												79
60.	WTR/TR									48					31		42	77
61.	US/AID					38		56										86
62.	US/AID							77	−31									97
63.	E/TRSL		46	−31	43			58	31			60						155
64.	R/TRSL	−38						−45	53			−41				−39		119
65.	E/E + RU		50		42			45	−37			52	−57					161
66.	US–SUP	79																94
67.	RU–SPT	−76																95
68.	CNT–NA		−59															58
69.	US–DIS				−75													85
70.	RU–DIS											−79						70
71.	USD/DT		−33		−69													83
72.	IMMIGR	42								73								91
73.	IMM/PP									77								85
74.	EMG/PP					36				64			−38					111
75.	IM/I + E			32					60	41								86
76.	VISITR	68			62													96
77.	VIS/PP		31		81													98
78.	FEL–RC							85										82
79.	D–FELL	61						49										85
80.	FORSTU	78														−34		99
81.	FST/ST				81											−36		89
82.	TRADE	95																100
83.	EXPORT	92																98
84.	IP/TRD						−51									37		82
85.	RM/EPT	−67																88
86.	BOP/GO								−79									73
87.	EP/GNP										−77							86
88.	EX/EPT						70											71
89.	A–EX/X	−55				44						32	−37					92
90.	AX/ATR	−35			−33		34					48						82
91.	DU/IMP	−49			−35												46	75

Orthogonally rotated factors—continued

No.	Variable abbreviation	1	2	3	4	5	6	7	8	9	10	11	12	13	14	15	16	h²
																		Factors[a]
92.	INVBAL										57							53
93.	BOI/GO								−70									71
94.	TR/GNP	−32			41						−73							93
	% Total variance	19.1	5.7	8.2	5.8	4.7	3.0	8.1	3.4	4.4	3.3	3.4	3.1	4.3	2.7	3.6	2.8	85.6
	% common variance	22.2	6.6	9.6	6.8	5.5	3.5	9.5	4.0	5.1	3.9	4.0	3.6	5.0	3.2	4.2	3.3	100.0
	Unrotated factor variances[b]	22.1	13.3	9.3	5.5	5.1	4.3	4.0	3.5	2.8	2.9	2.7	2.4	2.0	2.0	1.9	1.8	

[a] Only loadings ≥ |.30| are shown. Decimals are omitted. See Appendix II for details on the factor analysis. For ease of identification, horizontal lines are drawn to separate variable domains. The complete factor matrix is given in R. J. Rummel, Jack Sawyer, Harold Guetzkow, and Raymond Tanter, *Dimensions of Nations* (forthcoming).

[b] These are the percent of total variance figures for the unrotated factors. They are given under the factor number for convenience, but it should be kept in mind that the rotated factor numbers may not correspond to the number of the factor in the unrotated case.

51. An Attempt to Simulate the Outbreak of World War I*

Charles F. and Margaret G. Hermann, a political scientist and psychologist trained at Northwestern and now associated with Princeton University, have pooled their talents in a number of inquiries. Their substantive interests have converged on foreign policy behavior in crisis situations (see Selection 37), and methodologically they have found common ground in the experimental research technique known as simulation. This technique differs from all others in that it attempts to probe the phenomena of world politics by simulating them under controlled conditions in a laboratory. While the success of the technique depends on the degree to which the simulate world is made to correspond to the real world, it has the great advantage of allowing the researcher to manipulate the variables in which he is interested. By systematically holding some conditions constant and altering others in successive "runs" of a simulation, the researcher can observe and measure the potency of variables in a way that can never be matched by the more conventional methods of inquiry. In this article the Hermanns seek to explore the discrepancies between the real and simulate worlds by simulating a well-documented and important historical episode. As can be seen in Selections 52, 53, and 54, this is but one kind of use to which the technique of simulation can be put. [*Reprinted from* American Political Science Review, *LXI (1967), 400–16, by permission of the authors and the publisher.*]

Political games and simulations are models or representations of particular political systems and their associated processes. They are techniques for reproducing in a simplified form selected aspects of one system, A, in some independent system, A'. Games and simulations have a dynamic quality produced by the complex interaction of properties in the model. This feature enables them to generate states of the system that differ radically from those present originally. The kinds of transformations that may occur between the initial and final states of a simulation or game are difficult to represent by

* This research was conducted under Contract N123(60530)25875A from Project Michelson, U.S. Naval Ordnance Test Station, China Lake, California. An earlier report on this project was distributed by the contractor as *Studies in Deterrence X: Validation Studies of the Inter-Nation Simulation*, NOTS Technical Paper 3351, De-cember, 1963. The authors wish to acknowledge their indebtedness to Harold Guetzkow, principal investigator and mentor; Thomas W. Milburn, director of Project Michelson; and Robert C. North and his colleagues at the Stanford Studies in Conflict and Integration who generously shared their document collection and data analysis on the outbreak of World War I. The Center of International Studies at Princeton University supported the first author during the preparation of the present article.

other means, despite a diversity in modeling procedures ranging from verbal descriptions to differential equations. Because of their apparent applicability to many problems of politics, as well as their novelty, games and simulations have been developed in a variety of areas in political science.[1] They have been used in research, instruction, and policy formation. Although the application of these techniques has been increasing, systematic evaluation of their performance is only now beginning. This essay reports one type of evaluation.

The researchers sought to structure a simulation of international politics so it would reproduce features of the political crisis that preceded the beginning of the First World War. Two separate trials or runs of the simulation were performed as a pilot project. With two runs, the data are sufficient only to illustrate what might be done in an expanded research program.[2]

[1] In addition to the studies cited elsewhere in this paper, the variety is suggested by the following illustrations: Oliver Benson, "A Simple Diplomatic Game," in James N. Rosenau, ed., *International Politics and Foreign Policy* (New York: The Free Press, 1961), 504–11; William P. Davison, "A Public Opinion Game," *Public Opinion Quarterly*, XXV (1961), 210–20; Robert P. Abelson and Alex Bernstein, "A Computer Simulation Model of Community Referendum Controversies," *Public Opinion Quarterly*, XXVII (1963), 93–122; Lincoln P. Bloomfield and Barton Whaley, "The Political-Military Exercise: A Progress Report," *Orbis*, VIII (1965), 854–70; Andrew M. Scott with William A. Lucas and Trudi M. Lucas, *Simulation and National Development* (New York: John Wiley and Sons, Inc., 1966); J. David Singer and Hirohide Hinomoto, "Inspecting for Weapons Production: A Modest Computer Simulation," *Journal of Peace Research* (1965), 18–38; James A. Robinson, Lee F. Anderson, Margaret G. Hermann, and Richard C. Snyder, "Teaching with Inter-Nation Simulation and Case Studies," *American Political Science Review*, LX (1966), 53–65.

[2] The simulation runs were conducted in the summer of 1961 at Northwestern University. The exploratory nature of these runs led the authors to question whether the pilot study should be published. The supply of the original Navy report, however, is now exhausted. Moreover, no more complete set of historical runs has been conducted to date. Because a number of other published materials have discussed these pilot runs, it seems appropriate to make a fuller description of the World War I simulation more widely available. In doing so, the authors wish to caution that the work is primarily an examination of a means of evaluating simulations rather than a direct validation of the Inter-Nation Simulation. For examples of how this pilot project has been discussed elsewhere, see Arthur Herzog, *The War-Peace Establishment* (New York: Harper and Row, 1963), esp. 183–84; Sidney Verba, "Simulation, Reality, and Theory in International Relations," *World Politics*, XVI (1964), esp. 507–15; James A. Robinson and Richard

The study was undertaken to investigate the use of a historical situation as a means of validating simulations. The problems of model validity are critical in determining the value of the simulation-gaming technique not only to political science, but to all the social sciences. In a fuller discussion of simulation validity elsewhere,[3] one of the authors has indicated that model validity is always a matter of degree and is affected by (1) the purpose for which the model is used, (2) whether or not human participants are involved, and (3) the types of criteria employed. The World War I simulation explores the third area—criteria for estimating validity. It focuses on possible standards or criteria for establishing the goodness of fit between the simulation and the system represented. To what extent do features of a political system or its processes correspond to their simplified representation in a model? One means of investigating this question is to ascertain if a simulation produces events similar to those reported in a historical situation. Another approach is to determine whether the simulation supports more general hypotheses about political phenomena which previously have been confirmed by independent methods. Both events and hypotheses are used as validity criteria in the simulation of the 1914 crisis.

Although the validity issue is the primary reason for conducting the simulation of World War I, several other purposes are served by the exercise. First, it provides a milieu in which to explore the relative effect on political actions of personality characteristics as compared to variables more frequently associated with political analysis. Second, the simulation of past events offers a possible device for teaching and studying history.

I. Procedure

The Inter-Nation Simulation

Researchers differ as to the distinction between games and simulations. A number of experimenters, however, have associated "games" with operating

C. Snyder, "Decision-Making in International Politics," in Herbert C. Kelman, ed., *International Behavior* (New York: Holt Rinehart and Winston, 1965), 445, 512; and J. David Singer, "Data-Making in International Relations," *Behavioral Science*, X (1965), p. 77.

[3] Charles F. Hermann, "Validation Problems in Games and Simulations with Special Reference to Models of International Politics," *Behavioral Science*, XII (1967), 216–31.

models that involve human participants and "simulations" with models which do not.[4] Usually human participants are involved when the procedures or rules for designating the interplay of all components in the model have not been explicitly determined. When the model's relationships are incompletely programmed, human players and administrators are required to make judgments during the game. If the relationships are programmed, the need for human decision makers is reduced. In this essay an operating model will be defined as a simulation rather than a game, if a separate staff or computer is required to execute the programmed features. Thus, it is possible to have a simulation that is partially programmed and partially determined by human participants.

The model of international politics used in this study is such a hybrid. Developed by Harold Guetzkow and his associates,[5] the Inter-Nation Simulation incorporates both human participants and programmed calculations. In its usual format the Inter-Nation Simulation involves five or more nations. The government of each simulated nation is represented by human participants who asssume one of several decision-making positions. During the 50 to 70-minute periods into which the simulation is divided, the decision makers allocate the military, consumer, and natural-industrial resources available to their nation. These various types of resources have different functions in domestic and international affairs. Using their resources the participants make decisions about internal matters such as economic growth, government stability, defense preparations, and research and development programs. At the international level nations may enter alliances, negotiate trades or aids, engage in various kinds of hostilities, and participate in international organizations.

Every period, which represents approximately one year of "real" time, the decision makers record their actions on a standardized decision form. Then either a calculation staff or a computer applies the

programmed rules to the decision form to determine the net gain or loss in the various types of resources. The structured part of the model also establishes whether the decision makers have maintained the support of the politically relevant sectors of the nation whose endorsement is required for them to remain in office. The calculated results are fed back to each nation, thus beginning a new period of interactions and decisions by the participants.

Adapting the Simulation

Five nations were represented in the simulation runs of the 1914 crisis. Each government was staffed by two decision makers. A third participant in each nation acted as a messenger. The five simulated nations were intended to replicate features of Austria-Hungary, England, France, Germany, and Russia. Italy was excluded altogether and Serbia was represented symbolically by the researchers without participants. Several reasons can be offered for this treatment of Italy and Serbia. Reliable records of their diplomatic communications (a major input in the simulation of the other nations) were not available. Secondly, one can argue that although Serbia seemingly precipitated the immediate conflict and Italy was a member of the Triple Alliance, both nations were on the periphery in determining the question of world war when compared to the five other countries. Their exclusion, therefore, did not hinder the purposes of the exploratory runs. Although frequently other runs of the Inter-Nation Simulation have included more nations and more participants per nation, these changes are not as fundamental as several others.

Two major modifications were made in the basic simulation model. The first alteration established the initial conditions which the experimenters deemed important to characterize the international situation in the summer of 1914. Participants were introduced to some of the attributes of the historical setting by means of (1) a brief history of selected international affairs prior to the beginning of the crisis, (2) a statement of the current domestic and foreign policies of the participant's nation and the reasons they were being pursued, (3) a sketch of several personality traits of the historical policy maker whose role the participant occupied, and (4) a set of relevant historical diplomatic messages, conversations, and newspapers for the time between the assassination of the

[4] For a discussion of the distinctions made between games and simulations, see Charles F. Hermann, "Simulation: Political Process," *International Encyclopedia of Social Sciences*, XIV (1968), 274–81.

[5] Harold Guetzkow, Chadwick F. Alger, Richard A. Brody, Robert C. Noel, and Richard C. Snyder, *Simulation in International Relations* (Englewood Cliffs, N.J.: Prentice-Hall, Inc., 1963).

Austro-Hungarian Archduke on June 28 and the Serbian reply to the ultimatum on July 25, 1914. In addition, an effort was made to fit the programmed parameters and variables of the simulation to the national profiles of the countries involved.[6]

Several of these inputs require elaboration. Values for most of the components in the programmed part of the simulation were based on 1914 statistical indices (e.g., population, gross national product, size of armed forces) that approximated the meaning of the model's parameters. The 1914 indices were multiplied by an arbitrary constant to convert them to amounts convenient for use in the simulation. Individuals familiar with recent European history were asked to estimate decision latitude, the parameter that indicates how sensitive policy makers must be to the politically-relevant segments of their nation. These judges rated the decision latitude of each nation on a 10-point scale. Higher values were assigned to nations whose policy makers enjoyed greater freedom of action. Table 1 displays the values of each nation's basic parameters as they were reported to the simulation participants at the beginning of both runs. The historical diplomatic materials used in the simulation were compiled from hundreds of communications and documents which had been translated, edited, and verified by the Stanford Studies in Conflict and Integration under the editorship of Howard Koch.[7] The procedures for determining the personality characteristics are described in the section on participants and their historical counterparts.

All of the structured inputs were masked to avoid revealing to the participants that an actual historical situation was being modeled. Proper nouns, e.g., the names of individuals, countries, and alliances, were falsified. Misleading cues casting events in the future were introduced into the world history. In addition, after a pretest the assassination

at Sarajevo was modified to avoid disclosing the identity of the historical setting. In the revised simulation account, several major Austro-Hungarian officials were killed by a strafing aircraft while they were on a reviewing stand in Serbia. These precautions were taken in order that the participants' knowledge of history would not bias their responses. The introduction of an extensive amount of structured material in the initial phase of the operating model represented an important modification of the usual practice in the Inter-Nation Simulation.

The second major alteration in the Inter-Nation Simulation affected the time units represented in the

TABLE 1
Four Simulation Parameters for 1914 National Profiles

Nation	Basic capability units[a]	Force capability units[b]	Validator Satisfaction[c]	Decision latitude[d]
Austria-Hungary	45,540	14,560	4	7
England	86,940	25,000	6	3
France	62,100	20,800	4	3
Germany	120,000	24,500	7.5	8
Russia	78,660	23,000	4.5	9
Serbia	less than 4,140	less than 1,700	not given	not given

Note.—With the exception of decision latitude, the 1914 data and procedures for estimating these parameters were derived from James A. Winnefeld, "The Power Equation Europe, 1914," Stanford University (1960).

[a] Basic capability units represent the human, natural, and industrial resources available in a country. For the 1914 period the following indices were combined: steel production, national income, and total population weighted by the rate of male literacy.

[b] Force capability units are the military component in the simulation and were calculated by combining two indices, regular peacetime armies and capital ships.

[c] Validator satisfaction is the degree to which a decision maker's policies are acceptable to those elite groups with power to authenticate his office holding. A "crisis coefficient" composed of the frequencies of certain types of events (e.g., civil disturbances and insurrections, assassinations) in a given country in the 50 years preceding 1914 was combined with an indicator of national security (relative military strength). The integrated estimates of satisfaction were placed along a 10-point scale. Higher values represent more satisfaction with the government.

[d] Decision latitude is an ideological element. It is defined as the degree to which probability of office holding is responsive to changes in validator satisfaction. To estimate decision latitude, judges rated the nations on a 10-point scale. Higher values represent greater latitude for the government (i.e., less sensitivity to the demands of validators).

[6] The international history, the statements of domestic and foreign policy, and the personality sketches appear as appendices in Technical Paper 3351, *op. cit.* A complete set of the diplomatic messages in the form in which they were used in the simulation is on file with the contracting agency and with the International Relations Program, Northwestern University. For values assigned the basic parameters, see Table 1.

[7] Howard E. Koch with the staff of the Stanford Studies in Conflict and Integration, *Documentary Chronology of Events Preceding the Outbreak of the First World War: 28 June–6 August, 1914* (Stanford University, mimeo., 1959).

model. Usually the simulation is divided into 50 to 70-minute periods which constitute the equivalent of a year in the "real" world. These intervals are associated with a year because of the programmed calculations. Every period the policy makers allocate their national resources. The consequences of their allocations are determined by the relationships between a number of variables in the programmed part of the simulation. Examples of these variables include the rate of depreciation in existing military equipment, the amount of lead time required for a new research program, and the extent of shift in popular support for the government. The equations used to calculate these and other variables are designed to reflect changes that might occur on roughly an annual basis. As a result, decisions taken by the participants and submitted for calculation normally represent the allocation of resources for approximately twelve months.

The present exercise, however, required the representation of not years, but the few critical days in late July, 1914. This reduction in time necessitated several seemingly contradictory changes. On the one hand, the existing programmed calculations had to be made relevant to the participants. If the basic model was to be maintained, persons involved in the exercise had to experience the constraints and demands imposed on their immediate behavior by the programmed features of the simulation as it is usually constituted. On the other hand, participants required a time framework that would allow them to deal with the kinds of decisions that policy makers might encounter on a daily rather than annual basis. In sum, the individuals in the simulation had to be able to make short-term decisions, while being aware of the long-term consequences as represented in the programmed calculations.

To meet these requirements only individuals who had previous experience with the Inter-Nation Simulation were invited to participate in the exercise. These experienced participants were told that the first few simulation periods would represent days. Moreover, there was the implication that these short time frames would be followed by periods which would be equivalent to years as in previous simulations. To further the impression that the initial periods were to be embedded in a series of longer time units, the participants received an annual decision form and were instructed to submit an updated version for calculations when the simulation periods began to represent years. These arrangements were made to encourage the participants to take account of the basic programmed variables and parameters in conducting their immediate interactions. A decision maker is more likely to act in a short-term situation so as not to damage such programmed variables as the probability of his continuing in office or the annual amount of consumer goods available to his nation, if he believes that the simulation is going to continue for "years." Notwithstanding the information given the participants, both simulation runs were terminated before the anticipated conversion to the longer time units had occurred. Hence no calculations were made in any of the programmed components of the model.

In addition to designating the periods as days, the shortened character of the time units was promoted by the diplomatic messages. These historical documents reflected events and decisions that were developing day by day, if not hour by hour. Finally, as an aid to short-term decision-making, a new form was introduced into the simulation. On the new instrument each nation's decision makers were able to indicate more immediate changes in the intensity of their action toward other nations. Participants were advised that daily variations in their nation's level of commitment would influence such annually computed variables as total available resources and the likelihood of office-holding. Thus, the intensity scale provided an explicit link with the long-term elements presented in the programmed calculations of most Inter-Nation Simulation exercises.

Historical Figures and Their Simulation Counterparts

An attempt was made to select participants with personality traits similar to some of those manifested by political leaders in the crisis of 1914. This task involved three subproblems. First, a restricted number of historical figures who were active in the crisis had to be selected. Second, a judgment had to be made regarding which personality characteristics of these men were salient in their political behavior. Finally, a method had to be devised for selecting simulation participants with similar personality profiles.

The resources available to the researchers necessitated that the total number of decision makers in each run be limited to 10—two participants for each nation. Consequently, we sought the two policy makers in each of the five European nations who were major contributors to the critical decisions during the crisis. More specifically, three criteria guided the selection: (1) which persons had a dominating influence on the foreign policy decisions of their nation at the time of the crisis? This criterion recognizes that the loci of decision making may not correspond with the "legitimate authority" to make such decisions. (2) Which persons received and dispatched (or at least read) diplomatic cables and related foreign policy documents? The historical figures whom the simulation participants represented should have occupied a reasonably central position in the diplomatic communication net because diplomatic messages acted as a major source of simulation inputs. (3) About which persons was autobiographical and/or biographical material available to help in the assessment of personality traits? Utilizing these criteria, the following historical personages were chosen for representation in the simulation:

Austria-Hungary
    Berchtold (Minister for Foreign Affairs)
    Conrad (Chief of General Staff)
England
    Grey (Secretary of State for Foreign Affairs)
    Nicolson (Permanent Under-Secretary of State for Foreign Affairs)
France
    Poincaré (President of the Republic)
    Berthelot (Acting Political Director of Foreign Ministry)
Germany
    Wilhelm II (Kaiser)
    Bethmann-Hollweg (Chancellor)
Russia
    Nicholas II (Czar)
    Sazonov (Minister for Foreign Affairs).[8]

Once the political leaders judged to have assumed critical roles in the crisis were selected, it was necessary to establish which personality characteristics were salient to their political behavior. This determination was made by a cursory content analysis of personal letters, autobiographies, and biographies of the chosen policy makers.[9] Each document was content analyzed for psychological characteristics or traits identified by one of several tests for measuring personality.[10] On the basis of the content analysis, dominance, self-acceptance, and self-control appeared to be characteristics which differentiated among all 10 of the political leaders. Furthermore, the personality of one or more of the selected individuals was strongly characterized by his attitude toward such concepts as fate, frankness, making decisions, his own country, peace, self-confidence, success, suspicion, and war. No claim is made that these traits provide a complete personality profile of the historical individuals under examination. Undoubtedly some important characteristics have been overlooked. This list of traits, however, yielded a distinctive profile for every leader which was consistent with features stressed in documents describing that individual.

Two psychological tests were used to measure the personality characteristics that the researchers

relied heavily on Berthelot. For further evidence on the role of Berthelot, see Richard D. Challener, "The French Foreign Office: The Era of Philippe Berthelot," in Gordon A. Craig and Felix Gilbert, eds., *The Diplomats: 1919–1939* (Princeton, N.J.: Princeton University Press, 1953), 49–85. The third criterion was important in the choice of Conrad. Far less autobiographical and biographical material is available on the Austro-Hungarian political leaders than on those from the other countries. Most information concerns Emperor Franz Joseph, a logical selection in addition to Berchtold for the simulation. However, because Franz Joseph was quite old and recovering from a serious illness, he was not as influential on the decisions as other officials. Among the key figures, Conrad had the most available material.

[9] No inter-coder reliability was performed in the content analysis of the personality traits. For this reason, as well as because of the very limited sample of materials that could be examined for each figure, the selected traits must be considered only as tentative approximations. A list of the sources used in the content analysis appears in Technical Paper 3351, *op. cit.*

[10] Sources for the personality categories were Raymond B. Cattell, *The Sixteen Personality Factor Questionnaire*, rev. ed. (Champaign, Ill.: IPAT, 1957); Allen L. Edwards, *Edwards Personal Preference Schedule* (New York: Psychological Corp., 1953); Harrison G. Gough, *California Psychological Inventory* (Palo Alto, Calif.: Consulting Psychologists Press, 1956).

[8] Some illustration of how the criteria were employed is appropriate. The selection of Berthelot provides a good example of the application of the first two criteria. Although Berthelot did not have the legitimate authority to make binding decisions for his government, he nevertheless extensively influenced French foreign policy during July of 1914. With the president, premier (who was also the foreign minister), and political director of the foreign ministry on a mission to Russia in July, Berthelot was placed in charge of the foreign ministry. He became the chief advisor during this time to Bienvenu-Martin, acting Premier and Foreign Minister. Bienvenu-Martin, officially the Minister of Justice, was a novice at foreign affairs, and

associated with the selected historical figures. The California Psychological Inventory (CPI)[11] not only measured the three traits judged to be relevant to all the policy makers, but it also contained measures of some secondary characteristics identified in the content analysis. The second instrument was the semantic differential.[12] The nine attitudes were estimated with this testing device. Utilizing a suggestion made by Gough,[13] one of the researchers responded to both instruments as if she were the historical policy makers. The tests were completed after the biographical and autobiographical material on each of the chosen figures had been read. Test profiles for all 10 individuals were made in this way. These 10 profiles provided a standard against which to compare the responses of potential simulation participants on the same personality tests.

Some 101 high school students, who had participated in the Inter-Nation Simulation experiment in the summer of 1960,[14] were tested. As previously noted, persons already acquainted with the operation of the simulation were used in order to facilitate the shift in the time dimension. Furthermore, experienced participants freed the experimenters from training participants in basic simulation skills. The CPI profile of each prospective participant was compared with that of each historical figure. Particular attention was paid to profiles that matched exactly on dominance, self-acceptance, and self-control and were within one standard deviation of the other traits measured by the CPI. The semantic differential was utilized as a final selection step. In other words, those individuals chosen through the CPI matching were screened further by means of the semantic differential until three individuals per role were selected. Of the 10 individuals best matched to the historical figures, six were able to participate in the runs—five in the first run and one in the second. The balance of the participants in each run were second and third choices.

[11] Harrison G. Gough, *California Psychological Inventory.*

[12] Charles E. Osgood, George J. Suci, and Percy H. Tannenbaum, *The Measurement of Meaning* (Urbana, Ill.: University of Illinois Press, 1957).

[13] Personal correspondence from Harrison G. Gough, dated July 25, 1961.

[14] For a description of this earlier simulation research, see Richard A. Brody, "Some Systemic Effects of the Spread of Nuclear Weapons Technology: A Study through Simulation of a Multi-Nuclear Future," *Journal of Conflict Resolution,* VII (1963), 663–753.

Because of the interest in using individuals whose profiles most closely corresponded to those prepared for the actual leaders, the participants were not controlled on sex. Four women participated in the first run and three in the second.

Conducting the Revised Simulation

To provide an overview of the procedures used in the modified Inter-Nation Simulation, we will describe the operations in the two attempted replications of the pre-World War I crisis. Both simulation exercises were conducted in two days. On the first day, the participants in the runs assembled together for a general introduction and review of simulation procedures. After these activities, the remainder of the first day was used to introduce the structured input for each run.

At the beginning of the input phase, each participant was assigned to a separate cubicle. There they started by reading a disguised statement of pre-1914 "world history" and a description of the individual whose role they would assume. Upon completing this material, every participant was given a set of masked diplomatic communiques, newspapers, and memoranda which might reasonably have come to the attention of his historical counterpart. To the extent that such information was available, messages were ordered in the sequence in which they were received by the historical figure. For example, although the simulation began with an incident representing the assassination of the Archduke on June 28 (known to the participants as Day 1), some participants learned about that event the same day; others did not. In general, a participant received an incoming message and then the recorded reaction, if any, which his counterpart had made to that message. If evidence indicated that the historical figure had been aware of responses made to a message by other members of his government, the simulation participant also received this information. Thus, the Kaiser's marginal notes on diplomatic communiques were seen by the individual assuming the role of the German Chancellor, Bethmann-Hollweg. The input phase terminated with the Austro-Hungarian ultimatum on July 25 (Simulated Day 28). As the historical events became more rapid and complex in the latter part of the input phase, the order in which participants received information took on considerable importance.

The participants were allowed to read the set of messages available to them at their own pace. They were encouraged to write their reactions to each communication in a space opposite the message. The researchers believed that the participants would become more involved in the situation if they recorded their thoughts about the messages as they read. Moreover, these reactions provided a source of data. For the same reasons, after Day 15 and again after Day 28, every individual was required to write a summary of the events that had occurred. On these two simulated days, the participants also were provided sheets of paper and asked to draw a map of the world as they conceived it at that time.[15] After completing the second history and map, the participants were dismissed until the following day. They were cautioned not to discuss the material they had read.

The first run was concluded on the morning of the second day (hereafter designated the M-run) and the second was finished that afternoon (the A-run). When the participants returned to their respective simulations, they were informed that the world would continue with the situation as it had evolved up to that point. They were told that there would be no more structured messages. Thereafter, the situation could be handled in whatever manner they chose. Each nation's decision makers were given an annual decision form and an intensity of action scale to indicate their country's resources and commitments at the beginning of the free activity phase of the simulation. They were instructed to designate each 50-minute period as one simulated day, but the number of such periods that would occur remained unspecified. Following, these initial instructions, the two participants in each nation were assigned to a room in which they were separated by a partition. A messenger or courier sat at one end of the partition to prevent unauthorized conversations, to relay messages, and to operate a tape recorder during conferences between the decision makers. Written messages and periodic conferences were used as means of communication both within and between nations.

At the end of three periods (representing July 26–28, 1914), each participant was asked to draw another map and update his statement of world events. Much to the surprise of the participants, upon completing this task they were informed that the simulation was over. A post-mortem or debriefing session was held with each simulation run. The participants first completed a questionnaire and then described their plans and reactions to events in the simulation.

II. Results

Two different standards or criteria were employed in estimating the validity of actions taken by the decision makers in the free activity phase of the simulation runs. First, both macro and micro level events in the 1914 crisis were used as standards with which to compare incidents that occurred in the simulation. Second, two general hypotheses, previously tested with documents from the outbreak of the First World War, were explored using simulation data. Findings on the hypotheses from the two data sources were checked for comparability.

Macro and Micro Events

In the present context, "macro event" refers to the occurrence of general war. Did war break out in the simulation runs as it had in Europe in 1914? In neither run did war—or more accurately, the representation of war—occur during the last three periods. Historically, Austria-Hungary declared war on Serbia on July 28th, the final day represented in the simulation runs. In 1914, the declarations of general war between the other European nations did not occur until after the last time period portrayed in the simulation.[16] Although no war had been declared

---

[15] Geographical features are not incorporated in the Inter-Nation Simulation and no explicit geographical statements were included in the masked historical communiques. Therefore, the participants' maps provided data about the changing conception of relationships among nations. The distance between allied and hostile nations as well as the relative size of the nations represented in the maps were analyzed. Although the measuring device is worthy of further exploration, the results from these pilot runs proved to be quite ambiguous and are not reported here. They are included in Technical Paper 3351, *op. cit.*

[16] The chronology of hostilities during this critical period in 1914 was as follows: July 28—Austria-Hungary declares war on Serbia; July 29—Russia orders and then cancels general mobilization; July 30—Russia again orders general mobilization, France alerts troops along German border; July 31—Austria-Hungary begins general mobilization, Germany issues ultimatum demanding Russia stop mobilizing within 12 hours or Germany will mobilize; August 1—France and Germany start general mobilization, Germany declares war on Russia. After August 1, formal declarations of war follow in quick succession from the other major European states.

when the simulations were terminated, hostilities were imminent in the M-run.

In the researchers' opinion, if the M-run simulation had been continued for another 50-to-100 minutes (one or two more simulated days), war would have been declared along lines similar to the historical situation. This position is confirmed by 10 of the 15 M-run participants and messengers in their debriefing questionnaires. Throughout the free activity phase of that run the two alliance structures held. Germany[17] was prepared to give secret aid to Austria-Hungary for an attack on Serbia while signing neutrality pacts with England and France to keep them out of the war. This effort was intended to localize the conflict and to assure victory for the Dual Monarchy. If Russia then considered assisting Serbia, she would lack the support of her allies—a fact which Germany and Austria-Hungary believed would deter such action. France and England, however, had plans to go to war if Austria-Hungary attacked Serbia. That attack by Austria-Hungary was being planned at the close of the simulation run. An internal conference between the German participants on the next to last simulated day illustrates the direction in which the M-run was moving.

Central Decision Maker [Kaiser]: Is their war started yet? [Austria-Hungary's attack on Serbia]

External Decision Maker [Bethmann-Hollweg]: I don't think so.

CDM: Here's the problem—we can certainly give them [Austria-Hungary] the aid but the aid must be kept secret because if monetary aid isn't kept secret then the promises—written promises—which I am giving to Bega [England] and Colo [France] will mean absolutely nothing; total war is bound to break out. . . . If Enuk [Russia] enters it, we have to send secret aid; If Enuk [Russia] doesn't enter it, then he [Austria-Hungary] can defeat Gior [Serbia] by himself and that will be a thorn out of our side. We have already driven a wedge into the Tri-Agreement [Triple Entente].

EDM: Another question: Suppose Colo [France] enters, then we go in?

CDM: If Colo [France] enters the war we go in. . . .

In the A-run the participant representing Lord Grey of England called for an international confer-

ence on the first simulated day of the free activity phase. Thereafter, most of the simulation time was spent in obtaining agreement from all nations to attend this meeting. At the conference Austria-Hungary was charged with making far too extreme demands against Serbia and was pressured into withdrawing them. This retraction resulted in substantial conflict among the decision makers in Austria-Hungary as well as a bitter dispute between Germany and the Dual Monarchy. Germany had pledged complete support to Austria-Hungary and was highly irritated at the failure of Austria-Hungary to consult privately before changing its policy.

Two observations should be made about these developments in the A-run. First, some historians have expressed the opinion that England should have taken a stronger position more quickly, forcing moderation upon the Triple Alliance.[18] Second, and perhaps of greater importance, if the input phase had been extended for one more historical day, the participants would have received England's diplomatic communiques proposing an international conference and the prompt rejection of this suggestion by several nations. Thus, an alternative actually considered and subsequently excluded by the historical figures provided the avenue which the simulation participants followed for the resolution of the imposed situation.

Several major divergences from the outbreak of World War I developed in the A-run. Least parallel to historical events is the indication in some messages that England was considering the initiation of war on Germany while the advantage appeared on her side. This war was represented in communications as a defensive strategy resulting from the military and economic threat of Germany. A second significant variation was the agreement of Austria-Hungary to withdraw her ultimatum. The Austro-Hungarian decision maker, intended to represent Conrad, revealed pacifistic tendencies and readily accepted the objections to his nation's militaristic actions. This behavior suggests a need to match more closely the social-political attitudes of the historical figures and the simulation participants.

This account of the A-run's divergences fittingly

---

[17] It is to be understood that the references to nations here are to the student decision makers in the simulated nations.

[18] See, for example, Luigi Albertini, *The Origins of the War of 1914*, edited and translated by Isabella M. Massy (London: Oxford University Press, 1953), Vol. 2, p. 514; and Sidney B. Fay, *The Origins of the World War* (New York: The Macmillan Company, 1930), II, p. 556.

introduces the analysis of smaller, more specific events that occurred in the simulation and in the last days of July, 1914. By comparing numerous micro occurrences, validity depends not on the correspondence between isolated events (war or no war) but on the overall goodness of fit between a distribution of events. In other words, we are interested in whether the overall pattern of simulation occurrences is more or less like the pattern of reported incidents prior to World War I.

To illustrate this approach a sample of micro events was drawn from the simulation (the M-run) that at the macro level displayed a higher degree of correspondence to 1914. In this analysis an action mentioned by the participants in their written communication constituted a micro event. Eighteen separate micro events were identified in the M-run messages during the first simulated day of the free activity phase. A somewhat longer series of events would probably have been discovered for that day if transcripts of conferences had been examined in addition to the written communications. No reason, however, has been found to suggest that the types of events produced in face-to-face interactions differ for validity purposes from those indicated in written messages.

After the simulation events had been abstracted, a major historical study of the beginnings of the First World War was examined for comparable events.[19] In Table 2 the simulation events are indicated in the left-hand column and the reported historical events are listed in the corresponding space in the right-hand column.

Several alternative means of comparing the events were identified. Comparable activity is one way to match events in both the pre-World War I crisis and the simulation. We describe this as occurrence similarity. A second basis of comparison involves intent or purpose. Men's purposes in initiating or manipulating events may be similar, regardless of differences in format or activity. For example, in Item 16 in Table 2 the simulation action is the reverse of that reported in the observable world of 1914, but the intentions of the decision makers in both actions were probably similar. Germany was concerned that any war between Austria-Hungary and Serbia be kept localized without the intervention of other countries. To achieve this objective the

[19] Luigi Albertini, *ibid.*, II.

simulation decision makers chose to elicit pledges of neutrality from two important nations. In actuality, the German decision makers decided that quick action, before commitments and reactions could be made, was the preferable policy. Another way of comparing events is through temporal equivalence. The timing of some simulation events closely matches that of similar events in reality; others deviate sharply in this temporal aspect.

One of the researchers rated the 18 simulation events on each of the three bases of comparison. For each simulation event, temporal equivalence was given a score of one (i.e., assumed similarity) if it occurred within one day on either side of the reported 1914 event to which it was compared. If the time disparity was greater than the arbitrary threshold, it was coded as nonsimilar and assigned a zero. The same zero or one scoring was used for comparing events on intention and on occurrence similarity. The estimated scores for each event are presented in the center column of Table 2.

If the scores for the three categories are combined for the 18 events, the highest possible goodness of fit score is 54. The overall score for the distribution of events in the first simulated day of the M-run is 31. More specifically, all 18 events were judged similar in intent to developments that occurred in the 1914 crisis. Weighed against the significance of this finding must be the recognition that it is difficult to ascertain the intent of simulation participants, to say nothing of historical policy makers. Rules for guiding such coding are exceedingly hard to devise. For half of the simulation events (9 to 18), the researchers were able to find historical actions which seemed to be equivalent in physical format. Four of the 18 simulation events took place at approximately the point in time that the simulation was intended to replicate. One possible explanation for the low correspondence on temporal equivalence involves the problem of equating intervals in the simulation to actual days. The simulation may not have been adequately structured to provide the participants with the impression that each 50 minute period represented 24 hours of "real" time.

Hypotheses

In one sense the comparison of simulation and historical events includes the investigation of a hypothesis. The hypothesis is that a macro event or a

TABLE 2
Comparison of Sample of Simulation Events with Historical Events

Simulated July 26, M-run	Estimated Score[a]	Reported Historical Events[b]
1. Germany requests Russia to demobilize.	T = o I = 1 O = 1 — 2	*July 29:* German note to Russia: "... further progress of Russian mobilization measures would compel us to mobilize and then European war would scarcely be prevented" (p. 491).
2. Russia notifies Germany that no demobilization will occur until safeguards are established for Serbia.	T = 1 I = 1 O = o — 2	*July 26:* Russian foreign minister informs German ambassador that Russia is ready to assist in "procuring legitimate satisfaction for Austria-Hungary without abandoning the standpoint, to which Russian must firmly adhere, that Serbia's sovereignty must not be infringed" (p. 404). There is no explicit mention of making demobilization conditional on such safeguards.
3. In a conference Russia asks England and France to mobilize; both refuse.	T = o I = 1 O = o — 1	*July 24:* Conversation between Russian foreign minister and ambassadors from France and England. France agrees to fulfill all obligations of her treaty. England more evasive but conciliatory (pp. 294–96).
4. In a conference England and France inquire as to Russian military needs.	T = o I = 1 O = 1 — 2	
5. Germany notifies Russia that the latter's support of Serbia would be aggression.	T = o I = 1 O = o — 1	*July 28:* No evidence found of direct communication between Germany and Russia on this matter; however, Albertini concludes that this was a German objective. In support he cites several telegrams emanating from the German foreign office on July 28 including a note from the Kaiser: "It is an imperative necessity that the responsibility for a possible extension of the conflict to the Powers not immediately concerned should in all circumstances fall on Russia" (p. 474 and p. 476).
6. Austria-Hungary warns Russia not to mobilize further.	T = o I = 1 O = 1 — 2	*July 29:* There is some suggestion that the Austro-Hungarian ambassador warned the Russian foreign minister against Russian intervention on this date, although the conversation was interrupted by information that Austria-Hungary had bombed Belgrade (pp. 552–53). On July 26 Austria-Hungary's alliance partner, Germany, issued warnings through her ambassador to the Russian foreign minister: "I made detailed and urgent representations to the Minister about how dangerous it seemed to me to attempt to strengthen diplomatic action by military pressure" (p. 481).
7. Discussion on need for attack on Serbia in Austro-Hungarian internal conference.	T = o I = 1 O = 1 — 2	*July 7:* Austro-Hungarian Council of Ministers for Joint Affairs: one of a number of internal conferences before delivery of the Serbian ultimatum in which plans for attack on Serbia and the expected Russian reaction were discussed.

TABLE 2—continued

Simulated July 26, M-run	Estimated Score[a]	Reported Historical Events[b]
8. Discussion in Austro-Hungarian internal conference on making Russia appear the aggressor in an expansion of hostilities.	T = 0 I = 1 O = 0 — 1	No explicit program to make Russia appear the aggressor is mentioned although this appears to have been part of the Triple Alliance strategy. (p. 166.)
9. Austro-Hungarian note to Russia charges Russia's action is aggressive.	T = 0 I = 1 O = 1 — 2	*July 30:* Austro-Hungarian foreign minister tells Russian ambassador: "Austria-Hungary had mobilized solely against Serbia, not against Russia. . . . By the fact that Russia is obviously mobilizing against us we should also have to extend our mobilization. . . ." (p. 662).
10. Austro-Hungarian note to Russia states Austria-Hungary must hold Serbia accountable.	T = 0 I = 1 O = 1 — 2	*July 30:* On the basis of above conversation with Berchtold, the Russian ambassador telegraphs his own foreign minister: "[Berchtold] is of the opinion that it is impossible for Austria to stop her operations against Serbia without having received full satisfaction and solid guarantees for the future" (pp. 662–63).
11. In note France assures England of friendship.	T = 0 I = 1 O = 0 — 1	*July 29:* France appears to have repeatedly probed England on the issue of unified action and support. For example, the July 24 three-way conversation in St. Petersburg (pp. 294–96) or the inquiry to the British ambassador by his French colleague in Berlin, July 29 (p. 520n). A major discussion on this point took place between the British foreign minister and the French ambassador on July 29. In a follow-up conversation on July 31, the ambassador asked Grey if England would "help France if Germany made an attack on her" (p. 646). However, the type of military aid was not specified.
12. France requests military aid in note to England.	T = 0 I = 1 O = 1 — 2	
13. France urges a united front in a note to England.	T = 0 I = 1 O = 1 — 2	
14. Germany makes internal decision to give secret aid to Austria-Hungary.	T = 0 I = 1 O = 1 — 2	*July 5–6:* The Hoyos mission occurred, and Germany agreed to the so-called "blank check." Subsequent conversations between the Kaiser, his Chancellor, and military staff also reveal a discussion of military assistance to Austria-Hungary (pp. 133–59).
15. Germany's internal decision to seek neutrality pact with France and England to keep them from aiding Russia should latter intervene in Austria-Hungary's war against Serbia.	T = 0 I = 1 O = 0 — 1	While no direct documentation was found for verifying this internal decision, Albertini concludes: "The study of the German documents shows beyond all shadow of doubt (1) that in allowing Austria to attack Serbia, Germany started from the assumption, that if the attack developed into a European war, England would remain neutral; (2) that Grey's conduct until the afternoon of July 29 . . . strengthened the German leaders in this opinion. . . ." (p. 514).

TABLE 2—continued

Simulated July 26, M-run	Estimated Score[a]	Reported Historical Events[b]
16. Germany urges Austria-Hungary not to attack until neutrality of France and England is assured.	$T = 1$ $I = 1$ $O = 0$ — 2	*July 26:* Austria receives Germany's message urging military operations against Serbia as quickly as possible: "Any delay in coming military operations is regarded here as a great danger because of the interference of the other Powers" (p. 453).
17. Decision in Russian internal conference not to reveal, at present, their plan to attack Austria-Hungary if she attacks Serbia.	$T = 1$ $I = 1$ $O = 0$ — 2	*July 25:* Russian crown council decides on mobilization to be followed by war if Serbia is attacked (p. 762).
18. Decision in Russian internal conference to announce their intention to give Serbia full military aid.	$T = 1$ $I = 1$ $O = 0$ — 2	

[a] "T" stands for temporal equivalence, "I" for intention, and "O" for occurrence similarity. Each of the three categories was assigned a "1" if the simulation and 1914 event were judged as similar on that criterion; or a "0" if they were judged dissimilar. Simulation and historical events rated as similar on each of the criteria received an overall score of three.

[b] The source for the reported historical events is Luigi Albertini, *The Origins of the War of 1914*, edited and translated by Isabella M. Massy (London: Oxford University Press, 1953), Vol. 2. All page references are to this volume.

distribution of events in system A is comparable in a specified characteristic to a given event or distribution of events in system A'. Such a proposition, however, is oriented exclusively to the two systems involved—in the present case, the outbreak of World War I and the simulation of those events. In this section, attention is directed to more general hypotheses. These statements of relationship are intended to apply not only to the situation as it existed in Europe in the summer of 1914, but to other configurations of nations in international politics. Two hypotheses which have been tested with data from the 1914 crisis will be explored with the simulation data.

The three researchers who have studied the first hypothesis in the 1914 context have stated it as follows:

If a state's perception of injury (or frustration, dissatisfaction, hostility, or threat) to itself is "sufficiently" great, this perception will offset perceptions of insufficient capability, making the perception of capability much less important a factor in a decision to go to war.[20]

[20] Dina A. Zinnes, Robert C. North, and Howard E. Koch, "Capabilities, Threat and the Outbreak of War," in Rosenau, *op. cit.*, p. 470.

To explore their hypothesis, the members of the Stanford Studies in Conflict and Integration content analyzed 1,165 communications exchanged between the European states in the weeks prior to the beginning of the First World War. The purpose of this analysis was to determine the frequency of perceptions of capability and hostility. In the content analysis a perception of capability was defined as an assertion "concerning the power of another state or a coalition of states, or a statement with regard to the changing power of either a state or a coalition of states." A perception of hostility was defined as "a statement by one country about the hostility directed toward it by a second country, or about the hostility directed by a second country toward a third country. . . . Statements of hostility are defined to include statements of threat, fear and injury."[21]

The number of hostility and capability statements that the Stanford group found for the nations subsequently represented in the simulation are reported in the first columns of Table 3. Perceptions of hostility exceed those of capability for every nation. The overall difference is statistically significant

[21] *Ibid.*, p. 472.

TABLE 3

Number of Hostility and Capability Statements for Nations in 1914 and in Simulation

Nation	1914[a]		M-RUN		A-RUN	
	Hostility	Capability	Hostility	Capability	Hostility	Capability
Austria-Hungary	179	26	91	38	63	28
England	32	16	17	13	24	7
France	26	18	41	36	21	5
Germany	138	34	53	35	107	26
Russia	50	28	30	16	69	20

[a] The 1914 data are in Dina A. Zinnes, Robert C. North, and Howard E. Koch, "Capabilities, Threat and the Outbreak of War," in James N. Rosenau (ed.), *International Politics and Foreign Policy* (New York: Free Press, 1961), p. 476.

($p < .05$) by a sign test. Using the same definitions of hostility and capability, the messages written during the two simulation runs were content analyzed in a similar fashion.[22] As shown in the second and third sections of Table 3, the perceptions of hostility were significantly greater ($p < .05$) than those of capability in both runs. Thus, the simulation runs and the 1914 data produce comparable results on this general hypothesis.

A further check was made on the goodness of fit between the simulation and the 1914 data. The difference between the number of hostility and capability statements was determined for each nation. Within each of the three sets of data these differences were placed in rank order, that is, with the nation having the largest difference being given the first rank, etc. Then the order of the ranks for each of the simulation runs was compared with the order produced by the 1914 data. The resulting rank-order correlation (.90) between the 1914 data and that of the M-run was statistically significant ($p = .05$). The correlation for the A-run was not significant, however.

The second general hypothesis asserts that when opposing alliances or blocs emerge in international politics, the communication between blocs will be

[22] The inter-coder reliability for the simulation content analysis of hostility was .82 and for capability .83. For a description of the statistics used in this paper (the sign test, rank-order correlation, and Mann-Whitney U test) see Sidney Siegel, *Nonparametric Statistics for the Behavioral Sciences* (New York: McGraw-Hill Book Company, 1956).

TABLE 4

Effects of Alliance Structure on Communication in 1914 and in Simulation

Source of data	Number of intra-bloc dyads (n_1)	Number of inter-bloc dyads (n_2)	Mann-Whitney U[a]	Significance
1914	8	12	15	< .01
M-Run	8	12	10.5	< .01
A-Run	8	12	43	—

[a] It should be noted that for a given n_1 and n_2, the smaller the U the greater its likelihood of being significant.

much less than that among alliance partners. Zinnes, who has tested this hypothesis with the 1914 data, states the relationship as follows: "Frequency of interaction within the bloc will be greater than the frequency of interaction between blocs."[23] To explore this hypothesis, a count was made of the number of communications that each nation dispatched to the other four nations primarily involved in the 1914 crisis. The number of messages exchanged between each possible combination of two nations was established. Rates of communication in dyads composed of nations in the same bloc were compared with those in dyads consisting of nations from opposing blocs. A Mann-Whitney U test applied to the rank-order positions of these dyads supports the hypotheses.[24] The results are shown in the first row of Table 4. Identical procedures were followed for the M- and A-runs using the message sent by the decision makers to other nations. The results for the M-run, shown in the second row of Table 4, are statistically significant. By contrast, as indicated in the third row of Table 4, the findings for the A-run are not significant. Once again, the data from the M-run appear to be a better fit with that drawn from 1914 than do the data produced in the A-run.

[23] Dina A. Zinnes, "A Comparison of Hostile Behavior of Decision-Makers in Simulate and Historical Data," *World Politics*, XVIII (1966), 477. This article is one of the few efforts to explore simulation validity by what we have described as the hypothesis approach. Statistical tests are conducted on hypotheses using data from World War I and from another series of Inter-Nation Simulation runs which made no attempt to replicate those historical events.

[24] The 1914 data for this analysis were obtained from Zinnes, *ibid.* She performed a similar statistical test using Serbia as well as the five nations represented in the simulation. It is interesting that with the addition of Serbia, the result is not significant.

III. Evaluation

Replication of the 1914 Crisis

Can the Inter-Nation Simulation replicate occurrences in the observable universe such as the outbreak of World War I? Regardless of how intriguing this question is, for a number of reasons we cannot fully answer it with the present data. The exploratory nature of this initial research as been emphasized. A more complete study would require many more runs. It would be desirable to engage more mature participants whose previous experiences and backgrounds might lend themselves to the simulation problem. Moreover, the calculations used to set the beginning values of the parameters and the procedures used to code the simulation data need further refinement.

Even if one were tempted to make rough judgments on validity based exclusively on this pilot study, the divergence between the two runs imposes constraints. Using both events and general hypotheses to check the "fit" between 1914 and simulation data, the M-run approximates the political crisis prior to the First World War more closely than the A-run. At the macro event level, the M-run appeared on the verge of war with the same alliance commitments as observed in 1914. On the other hand, the A-run averted the immediate threat of war and involved several incidents in sharp contrast to those reported in the historical situation. In data from both runs, as in the material from 1914, perceptions of hostility were significantly more frequent than perceptions of capability. Only in the M-run, however, did the differences between these two kinds of perceptions correlate with similar data from the actual nations of 1914. Furthermore, the hypothesis that communication would be greater within alliances than between them was supported both by the 1914 data and the M-run data; but it was not confirmed in the A-run. These differences occurred despite a common introductory briefing, identical materials in the input phase, and the same set of initial values for the simulation parameters.

The two runs, however, did not share the same human participants. Although an effort was made to select participants in both runs with similar personality characteristics, it will be recalled that the matching was limited to a few traits. Moreover, on those characteristics for which an attempt at correspondence was made, the personality profiles of some individuals more closely matched their historical counterparts than others. As we noted previously, five of the six individuals whose profiles corresponded most completely with those designed to represent the historical figures participated in the M-run and only one in the A-run. In other words, half of the participants in the run that best approximated the 1914 crisis were first choices on the personality matching, whereas only one of the 10 decision makers in the more divergent run was a first choice. (In the A-run, six participants were second choices and three were third choices. Of the other five participants in the M-run, three were second choices and two were third choices.) Correspondence between a simulation and its reference system appears to have been facilitated by closer matching of the personalities of the participant and the historical figure.

Procedural Issues

These initial runs do not establish whether the Inter-Nation Simulation can replicate aspects of historical events, but they do uncover several procedural issues that a more complete study would confront. One problem is the participants' awareness of the historical events being simulated. We have described the efforts to mask the historical clues to avoid biasing participant responses. Despite these attempts, the disguise was not fully successful. On the debriefing questionnaire, the participants were asked to check from a list of historical situations those incidents that appeared "somewhat similar" and those that seemed "almost exactly like" their simulation run.[25] Table 5 indicates that five of the 10

[25] In retrospect, this questionnaire item was not totally satisfactory. Estimating the difference between situations rated "exactly alike" and those rated "somewhat alike" is difficult. Because most participants checked several historical situations, it is not clear how much more the simulation resembled the 1914 crisis than, for example, Hitler's ultimatum to Poland. Furthermore, participants were not asked to state when they became aware of the apparent similarity between the simulation and a past event. Some evidence indicates that a messenger suggested the parallel to World War I to several individuals near the end of the M-run. An unstructured question, which provided no list of historical events, might have reduced the number of references to World War I. The alternative situations in the questionnaire item were selected from events mentioned by high school students who pretested the material for the input phase.

TABLE 5
Situations Viewed as Similar to the Simulation on the Debriefing Questionnaires

Situation	M-RUN DECISION MAKERS (N = 10)		A-RUN DECISION MAKERS (N = 7ᵃ)		TOTALS (N = 17)		
	Similar	Almost exact	Similar	Almost exact	Similar	Almost exact	Overall total
World War I	3	2	1	1	4	3	7
Hitler's ultimatum to Poland	1	2	2	1	3	3	6
Berlin crisis	2	2	1	1	3	3	6
Hitler's ultimatum to Sudetenland	2	1	2	1	4	2	6
Israeli-Arab conflict	3	0	2	1	5	1	6
French-Algerian conflict	1	1	2	1	3	2	5
Korean war	3	0	1	1	4	1	5
19th century colonialism	4	0	0	1	4	1	5
Spanish-American war	1	0	2	1	3	1	4
Attack on Pearl Harbor	1	0	0	0	1	0	1
World War II	1	0	0	0	1	0	1

ᵃ Three of the A-run participants were unable to attend the briefing session.

participants in the M-run and two of the seven who completed the questionnaire in the A-run perceived some degree of similarity between their simulation and World War I. No other historical situation was identified by seven participants, but four others were each chosen by six individuals.[26]

Even though the results from this questionnaire item are not conclusive, they suggest the need for more vigilance in making past events unrecognizable. When, however, the content of historical situations is changed or misleading clues are added, there is the danger that essential attributes of the actual events will be so distorted they will not provide a validity check. This difficulty can be handled by selecting a less well-known situation—providing sufficient information exists on it to construct the necessary inputs. Alternatively, means of comparing the simulation and the actual event can be chosen which are unlikely to be affected if the participants identify the general situation. For example, in the present runs even those participants who saw a similarity to World War I were less likely to know the relationship between perceptions of hostility and capability, or to

be aware of the micro events that occurred on July 26, 1914.

Another issue is the distinction between "self-structured activity" and "role playing." Should a simulation participant be required to play the role of a historical decision maker whose characteristic behaviors have been described to him or should the participant be free to structure his own activity? This problem is illustrated by an incident in one of the runs. A participant confronted a decision which he felt his assigned historical figure would answer one way, but he personally would answer another. Should he assume the role or play himself? Given difficulties in constructing profiles of historical figures and problems in matching participants on numerous characteristics, role playing may supplement incomplete personality correspondence. On the other hand, without detailed information one individual's interpretation of the probable behavior of another individual is likely to produce major distortions. Supplying such information would disclose the identity of the historical figure. Investigations probably should be limited to a few personality traits that are part of the natural disposition of the participant. In the event, however, that participants are asked to "play" a historical personality, selection procedures might include some indicators of the empathic qualities required for role playing or acting.

[26] The messengers in both runs also completed this questionnaire item. Six out of nine messengers reported a similarity to World War I. It may be that the overall view of events provided by this role increased their awareness of the similarities.

Some explicit reference should be made to the procedural problem of selecting the kind of historical situation that the simulation is intended to represent. All models—including games and simulations—are simplifications of the systems they are designed to replicate. This simplification is achieved in part by completely excluding certain properties of the reference system from the model or by combining numerous detailed elements in an aggregated form. Obviously, a simulation cannot be validated by comparing its output with historical phenomena the model was not designed to represent.

In several ways the effectiveness of the present research for validating the Inter-Nation Simulation is reduced because the 1914 crisis was selected as the historical situation to be replicated. The conversion of the basic time units in the simulation from years to days furnishes one example. With the time units scaled-down, the components in the programmed part of the model acted as constants, though many of them normally operate as variables. In these exploratory runs, then, the part of the simulated world contained in the structured programs affected the behavior of the participants only insofar as they recalled its impact on their previous simulation experience. The 1914 crisis did not provide a means of investigating the programmed relationships as they operate in the usual Inter-Nation Simulation. Although such short-term crises may be excellent for determining the validity of other simulation models, they seem somewhat less appropriate for the Inter-Nation Simulation.

The micro event analysis provides a second illustration of the problem. The variables in the programmed portion of the simulation are broad representations of properties within a nation (e.g., the sum of all human and natural resources, or overall military capability). The events in the micro analysis however, were at the more specific level of a diplomatic conference or a decision to mobilize ground forces in a certain district. The Inter-Nation Simulation was able to produce events at this level of specificity, but it is not clear that they are produced by the aggregate variables that compose the model.[27]

[27] For further discussion of the level of specificity issue, see Harold Guetzkow, "Simulation in International Relations," in *Proceedings of the IBM Scientific Computing Symposium on Simulation Models and Gaming*, December, 1964, Thomas J. Watson Research Center, Yorktown Heights, New York, esp. pp. 264–67.

IV. Historical Situations as an Approach to Validity

The procedural problems that emerged in the exploratory attempts to replicate the 1914 crisis are not insurmountable obstacles to the use of historical situations as validity tests for simulations. With careful attention to the selection of both participants and the past occurrences to be simulated, these difficulties can be minimized. Broader concerns about the use of historical data for verifying models, however, also must be considered. One challenge to this validity technique is raised by the developers of a simulated underdeveloped economy.

When a simulation of a particular economy has been formulated, it should be subjected to shocks and exogenous trends like those that have impinged on the actual economy in the past so that its responses may be compared with historical records. It would seem that such tests would yield an independent verification of the model. Actually, in most cases it is unlikely that this ideal can be fully realized. . . . The difficulty, fundamentally, is that the information available in almost all countries is insufficient to establish a model without using all the relevant historical data in the formulation and in the adjustment of parameter values.[28]

The economic model mentioned above is a completely programmed computer simulation and, accordingly, requires more data for establishing its initial values. Nevertheless, the problem is applicable to all historical validation attempts. Clearly, a simulation cannot be validated against the same historical material used to determine its parameters and beginning variable values. Historical replication always will be limited by the record of past events. Not only must there be a detailed account of decisions and actions, but the sequence of events must continue over a sufficient period of time without major changes which require resetting the model's parameters. For this reason historical verification may be more feasible for some types of simulations than others. The smaller the number of variables and parameters which require historical data, the more uncommitted historical material is available for establishing the goodness of fit. Moreover, if the content of the simulation deals with the kind of phenomena that recur frequently in the observable world, then historical validation is more applicable. Thus, a simulation of American judicial decision making is more readily verified with

[28] Edward P. Holland, with Robert W. Gillespie *Experiments on a Simulated Underdeveloped Economy* (Cambridge, Mass.: MIT Press, 1963), 207–08.

historical data than an operating model of disarmament processes.

Let us assume for the moment that sufficient historical data exist and that the content of a given simulation model permits the use of the validity approach described in this essay. Furthermore, let us assume that a comparison of events in simulation and in history reveals a high degree of correspondence. This correspondence does not demonstrate that the simulation correctly represents the structure and processes that were operative in the historical occurrence. We are speculating on the similarity between the historical and simulated inputs on the basis of the similarity of their outputs. Different relationships among various combinations of properties in the simulation conceivably could produce outcomes like those in the historical situation.

A simulation of the 1960 national Presidential election predicted the percentage of the vote for each candidate—the outcome—with considerable success. The designers of that simulation observe, however, that "it may legitimately be asked what in the equations accounted for this success, and whether there were parts of the equations that contributed nothing or even did harm."[29] Further analysis of the equations in the simulation revealed that the outcome was predicted despite the fact that at least one equation misrepresented aspects of voter turnout. Part of the structure of the simulation was incorrect, but the simulated result still matched the actual outcome. Despite this difficulty, our confidence that the simulation has captured some aspects of the voting process is greater than it would have been if the simulation had failed to replicate the campaign outcome. Confidence in the simulation would increase further as the operating model demonstrated ability to produce outcomes that corresponded with various elections. In sum, the similarity between simulation and historical events can provide at best only indirect and partial evidence for the correctness of the simulated structures and processes that produced the outcome.

Historical material can be used for validity purposes in other ways than by providing events for simulations to reproduce. In the exploratory runs, two validation techniques were tried—event comparisons and hypothesis testing. Although general hypotheses can include events as variables, they also can involve the processes by which events are produced. When events do become variables in a hypothesis, they tend to be more the micro events that occur with sufficient frequency to permit an adequate test. Hypothesis testing, therefore, is less susceptible to the criticisms of event comparisons made above. Verba has argued that difficulties in validly simulating a macro event (such as the outbreak of war) may exceed a model's potential contribution to theories of international politics. "Even if one could design a successful simulation in that respect, it might not be useful for future situations, which would not match the historical one in many important ways." Instead, he proposes that "if the situation can be decomposed into many subprocesses, such as communications flows, emotional states of decision-makers, and so forth . . . it may be possible to develop more widely applicable principles that can deal with many political situations."[30] Historical material may prove more useful for simulation validity explorations if it yields frequency distributions of events and processes that can be employed in hypothesis testing.

We have described some important procedural problems as well as two major limitations to using the replication of historical situations as a means of validating political simulations. In addition to event comparisons and hypothesis testing, alternative ways of verifying simulations are available. But they also have substantial liabilities.[31] In part because no one approach can fully establish the correspondence between a simulation and its intended referent system, simulation validity is always a matter of degree. Yet we cannot abandon the efforts to determine the goodness of fit between verifiable empirical observations and our conceptualizations— be they stated as verbal theories, mathematical equations, or simulation models. To improve our estimates of simulation validity, a strategy is required that includes multiple methods for discerning the degree of correspondence. In such a multi-method strategy one approach is historical replication. Until more validation exercises are conducted, it is premature to accept or reject simulation as an important new tool for studying political phenomena.

[29] Ithiel Pool, Robert P. Abelson, and Samuel L. Popkin, *Candidates, Issues, and Strategies* (Cambridge, Mass.: MIT Press, 1965) rev. ed., p. 64.

[30] Sidney Verba, *op. cit.*, 511, 513.

[31] For a survey of various validity approaches and a discussion of their assets and liabilities, see Charles F. Hermann, *Behavioral Science, op. cit.*

52. Alliances and the Theory of Collective Action: A Simulation of Coalition Processes*

Philip M. Burgess and James A. Robinson are members of the Political Science Department at Ohio State University, where the former is also Director of the Behavioral Sciences Laboratory and the latter is also Director of the Mershon Center for Education in National Security. Professor Burgess' writings include *Elite Images and Foreign Policy Outcomes: A Study of Norway* (1967) and Professor Robinson's many works include *Congress and Foreign Policy-Making* (1967). Part of a much larger project on which Professors Burgess and Robinson have collaborated, this selection uses the same technique of research as the previous selection, but it has a very different focus and purpose. While the former tests the utility of simulation techniques through a re-creation of actual historical events, here the techniques are used to test substantive theoretical propositions about international behavior. In addition, this article constitutes one of the few attempts to use the factorial analysis of variance model as a statistical means of assessing political data generated in a laboratory. The result of this combination of creative theory and innovative research is a stimulating insight into both the dynamics of international systems and the potentialities of simulation techniques. [*Reprinted from Philip M. Burgess and James A. Robinson, "Alliances and the Theory of Collective Action: A Simulation of Coalition Processes," Midwest Journal of Political Science, XIII (May 1969), by permission of the authors and the Wayne State University Press. Copyright by Wayne State University Press, Detroit, Michigan.*]

Introduction

That research on coalitions has been conducted in a variety of ways indicates that interest in coalitions is not limited to specialists in international politics nor to practitioners of a single mode of analysis. Dahl has examined the formation of political coalitions around "issue areas" with survey and participant-observer techniques,[1] and Riker[2] has mathematically described

26th Annual Meeting of the Midwest Political Science Association in Chicago, May 2–4, 1968.

* We acknowledge our debt to the staff of the Behavioral Sciences Laboratory at The Ohio State University whose technical assistance facilitated our research and particularly to Lawrence S. Mayer of the Department of Mathematics and the Behavioral Sciences Laboratory for his invaluable advice and assistance in the statistical analysis of our data. Through the initiative of the late Edgar S. Furniss, Jr., the Mershon Center for Education in National Security sponsored the research. This paper was prepared for the

[1] Robert A. Dahl, *Who Governs?* (New Haven: Yale University Press, 1961).

[2] William H. Riker, "A New Proof of the Size Principle," in Joseph L. Bernd (ed.), *Mathematical Applications in Political Science* (Dallas: Southern Methodist University Press, 1966); and William H. Riker, *The Theory of Political Coalitions* (New Haven: Yale University Press, 1962).

the formation, size, and maintenance of coalitions. Singer and Small[3] and Zinnes[4] have relied on historical data to study the effects of alliance aggregations on the stability of the international system. Brody[5] has examined inter- and intra-bloc behavior under conditions of nuclear proliferation through a quasi-experimental simulation. Hovet[6] using roll call techniques, and Alker and Russett,[7] combining factor analysis with roll call techniques, have studied international voting coalitions in a quasi-legislative body, the United Nations. Liska[8] has explored intuitively and imaginatively the political functions of international coalitions. These efforts show clearly that research on coalitions emphasizes different contextual foci, represents both macro- and micro-levels of analysis, and examines coalitions both as dependent and independent variables.

Our research concerns coalitions at the micro-level of analysis and coalition behavior as a dependent variable. The research was stimulated, topically, by the apparent disintegration of the Atlantic alliance and, theoretically, by the economic theory of "public goods" elaborated by Mancur Olson.[9] Like some of the research cited above, this study regards coalitions as generic in conception and is applicable to the formation and maintenance of voluntary human associations, i.e., associations of people and/or groups of people who share common interests, who communicate about achieving their shared interests, and who pool their resources by some arrangement in order to achieve these shared interests. Our

principal objective is to test a theory of collective action that Olson has developed and that we have elaborated. This theory applies to all types of voluntary associations: internation coalitions and alliances; domestic political coalitions; loosely organized intranation associations such as civil rights groups, professional associations, and labor unions in "right-to-work" states; and other associational interest groups.

The Theory

Olson classifies associations by the *types of benefits* they produce—not by their size or complexity, their functions, the substance of their activities, their location, or their membership. The benefits produced by an association may be *collective* or *private*.[10] Collective benefits are such that their use or enjoyment cannot feasibly be denied any potential consumer, whether the consumer is a member of the association or not. Moreover, most collective benefits are such that their use or enjoyment by one consumer does not reduce the availability of the benefits to others. In the terminology of economics, these characteristics of collective benefits are called respectively "nonexcludability" and "jointness of supply," although the latter is a common though not a necessary attribute of collective benefits.

Private benefits, by contrast, do not have the nonexcludability characteristic and may not have the jointness of supply attribute. First, private benefits are available only to the members of the association

[3] J. David Singer and Melvin Small, "Alliance Aggregation and the Onset of War, 1815–1945," in J. David Singer, ed., *Quantitative International Politics* (New York: The Free Press, 1968); and J. David Singer and Melvin Small, "Formal Alliances, 1815–1939: A Quantitative Description," *Journal of Peace Research*, III (1966), 1–32.

[4] Dina Zinnes, "Testing a Balance of Power Theory" (Bloomington, Ind.: Department of Government, Indiana University, 1966), (mimeo).

[5] Richard A. Brody, "Some Systemic Effects of the Spread of Nuclear Weapons Technology: A Study Through Simulation of a Multi-Nuclear Future," *Journal of Conflict Resolution*, VII (December 1963), 663–753.

[6] Thomas Hovet, *Bloc Politics in the UN* (Cambridge: Harvard University Press, 1960).

[7] Hayward Alker and Bruce Russett, *World Politics in the General Assembly* (New Haven: Yale University Press, 1965).

[8] George Liska, *Nations in Alliance* (Baltimore: Johns Hopkins Press, 1962).

[9] Mancur Olson Jr., *The Logic of Collective Action* (Cambridge: Harvard University Press, 1965).

[10] Economists use the terms "collective (or public) and private (or exclusive) goods." "Benefits" has been substituted for "goods" as a term less ambiguous for political scientists. For elaborations of the theory of collective benefits, see Mancur Olson, *ibid*; John G. Head, "Public Goods and Public Policy," *Public Finance*, XVII (1962), 197–219; Gerhard Colm, "Theory of Public Expenditures," *Annals of the American Academy of Political and Social Science*, CLXXXIII (January 1936) 1–11; Julius Margolis, "A Comment on the Pure Theory of Public Expenditure," *Review of Economics and Statistics*, XXXVII (November 1955) 347–9; Richard Musgrave, *The Theory of Public Finance* (New York: McGraw-Hill, 1959); Paul A. Samuelson, "Aspects of Public Expenditure Theories," *Review of Economics and Statistics*, XL (November 1958) 332–8; Paul A. Samuelson, "Diagrammatic Exposition of a Theory of Public Expenditure," *Review of Economics and Statistics*, XXXVII (November 1955), 350–6; Paul A. Samuelson, "Pure Theory of Public Expenditure," *Review of Economics and Statistics*, XXXVI (November 1954), 387–90.

that creates them. Nonmembers are excluded. Second, the use or enjoyment of private benefits may result in a reduction of benefits available to others.

This theory, it should be emphasized, assumes or implies nothing about whether benefits are political social, economic, or military. Some theories of international organization emphasize that economic functions undergird political functions, or vice versa. Other theories stress differences between single-function and multifunction organizations. The theory of collective action should not be confused with a theory of mixed (political, economic, and military) functions or with a theory of multiple functions. Likewise, the theory applies to economic, political, and military coalitions. Regardless of the number or the substance of functions, the *theory of collective action predicts differences in organizational performance only with regard to whether benefits are collective or private.* Organizational performance may be measured by its effectiveness in satisfying the demands of its members, by arrangements for sharing burdens among the members of the organization, by the ability of the organization to influence the behavior of its members, and by the cohesiveness of the organization, the absence of hostility among members, and a manifest capacity to work together to achieve shared aims.

Discussion of the Theory

Collective benefits include many of the services that national and provincial governments furnish those who reside within their territorial boundaries. Among these are common defense, police and fire protection, highways and streets, sanitation, and antipollution controls. Both aliens and citizens enjoy these services; both indigents and taxpayers benefit from them. When organizations such as governments are committed to providing collective benefits, it is in no one's self-interest to share the cost of producing them. Voluntary contributions are not "rational" because one person's proportionate contribution to national defense, internal security, and well-being bears no relation to the small, indeed infinitesimal, increment he receives in added defense, security, or health. Nor is it practicable (because of the non-excludability attribute of collective benefits) to

induce contributions by selectively providing defense, security, or well-being only to those who bear their share of the burden. In others words, certain collective benefits cannot be offered as private benefits. For example, policemen cannot protect citizens and ignore aliens; firemen cannot distinguish between those who have paid their taxes and those who have not; public health inspectors do not certify the purity of milk for one class of people and not for another. Governments, therefore, typically rely on coercion to extract contributions to bear the cost of providing collective benefits.[11]

Voluntary associations, like coercive organizations, have the same problems in enlisting support among those who may use or enjoy the collective benefits that are produced. Voluntary and coercive associations differ, of course, in that the voluntary association cannot compel potential users to support the production of the collective benefits they provide. For example, manufacturing groups cannot exclude noncontributors from enjoying benefits resulting from successful lobbying on a tariff bill; labor unions in "right-to-work" states cannot withhold from nonmembers wage increases extracted from a firm. And great powers that provide protection to client states cannot compel the clients to contribute politically or financially to the collective benefits they enjoy.

The theory of collective action that applies most generically to voluntary associations is, thus, applicable to coalitions among nations, as well as to other coalitions. Alliances are in the class of voluntary associations because of the absence of authoritative means for compelling participation and, like other associations, alliances may produce collective and private benefits. Alliances in the nuclear age are particularly interesting when viewed through the theory of collective action because one member

[11] Of course, other motives may induce cooperation, but governments and other nonvoluntary associations always have ultimate recourse to methods that can compel compliance. See William A. Gamson, *Power and Discontent* (Homewood, Ill.: Dorsey Press, 1968); Morris Janowitz and Dwaine Marvick, "Competitive Pressure and Democratic Consent," in Eulau, *et al.*, *Political Behavior* (New York: The Free Press, 1956), pp. 275–85; Harold D. Lasswell, *Politics: Who Gets What, When, How* (New York: McGraw-Hill, 1936); Harold D. Lasswell and Abraham Kaplan, *Power and Society* (New Haven: Yale University Press, 1950); Talcott Parsons, "'Voting' and the Equilibrium of the American Political System," in Eugene Burdick and Arthur J. Brodbeck, *American Voting Behavior* (New York: The Free Press, 1959).

frequently is able and has the incentive to provide the collective benefit unilaterally.

How, then, can voluntary associations induce potential users to support the association's production of collective benefits? Political science theories suggest an answer: people have "propensities to join."[12] Stimulating as these theories are, however, attribution of behavior to gregarious "instincts" or "propensities" does not permit explanation of observed variance in behavior, for people (and associations) often fail to combine when collective interests would appear to demand otherwise. Moreover, theories that include variables like "instincts" do not apply well to the behavior of coalitions of aggregates to which the theory of collective action is intended to apply.

Group theories suggest another answer. As societies develop, a transfer of functions from primary to secondary groups is observed. Structural differentiation involves the assumption of kinship group functions by larger associations: class and caste groups, neighborhood groups, and occupational groups,[13] and other secondary groups such as states, churches, business firms, and professional societies.[14] The group theorists, however, are more concerned with describing the evolution of the "webs of affiliation" than with the "logic of affiliation."[15]

The theory of collective action also suggests an answer. Voluntary associations induce support (i.e., membership) from potential users of collective benefits they make possible by providing private benefits, benefits that either cannot be obtained elsewhere or that can be obtained less expensively through an association, the *raison d'être* of which is the provision of collective benefits. This is, of course,

what cooperative associations do. They make it rational to join and support the association by offering commodities at lower prices to members than to nonmembers or by excluding nonmembers from making purchases. Persons or groups of persons who would, in any event, member or not, enjoy the collective benefits produced by an association, are thus induced to join and support the association's efforts in producing collective benefits in order to avoid exclusion from valued private benefits.

The Research Problem

While the theory of collective action is intuitively appealing and persuasive, it wants for compelling evidence to support it. Only Olson and Zeckhauser[16] have provided supporting empirical evidence, but their findings on cost-sharing in the NATO infrastructure program are hardly conclusive and admit the appropriateness of further testing of hypotheses derived from the theory. Because of the absence of other findings, we undertook experimental research to facilitate control over confounding factors so that relationships among variables in the hypotheses could be subjected to unambiguous disconfirmation.[17] Failure to disconfirm the theory in the laboratory would then provide strong justification for moving into "richer" and more subtle field research situations. Meanwhile, in view of weak evidential support for the theory, more conventional research methods were considered inappropriate because of their inability to control confounding variables.

The theory of collective action consists of a number of elements. The research reported here emphasizes only one of the conditions of the theory (albeit the most significant one), namely the relationship between private benefits and the cohesion and effectiveness of a voluntary association or coalition.[18]

---

[12] See Daniel Bell, *The End of Ideology* (New York: The Free Press, 1960); Arthur Bentley, *The Process of Government* (Evanston, Ill.: Principia Press, 1949); James Bryce, *The American Commonwealth* (New York: The Macmillan Company, 1910); Alexis de Tocqueville, *Democracy in America* (New York: New American Library, 1956); David B. Truman, *The Governmental Process* (New York: Alfred A. Knopf, 1958); Sidney Verba, *Small Groups and Political Behavior* (Princeton: Princeton University Press, 1961).

[13] R. M. MacIver, "Interests," *Encyclopedia of the Social Sciences*, VII (New York: The Macmillan Company, 1932).

[14] Talcott Parsons, Robert F. Bales, James Olds, Morris Zelditch, and Philip E. Slater, *Family, Socialization and Interaction Processes* (New York: The Free Press, 1955).

[15] Georg Simmel, *Conflict and the Web of Group Affiliations* (New York: The Free Press, 1950).

[16] Mancur Olson and Richard Zeckhauser. "An Economic Theory of Alliances," RAND Corporation Paper No. 2992, Santa Monica, Calif., 1964.

[17] See Donald T. Campbell and Julian C. Stanley, "Experimental and Quasi-Experimental Designs for Research on Teaching," in N. L. Gage, ed., *Handbook of Research on Teaching* (Chicago; Rand McNally and Company, Inc., 1963); and Sidney Verba, "Simulation, Reality, and Theory in International Relations," in *World Politics*, XVI (April 1964), 490–519.

[18] We expect to release a full report of our tests of the theory of collective action in Philip M. Burgess and James A. Robinson, *Nations in Alliance: A Simulation of Coalition Processes* (Columbus, Ohio: The Ohio State University Press, 1969).

Two major hypotheses, stated in the null form were tested.

> H_{o1} Coalition *cohesion* is not affected by supplementing collective benefits with private benefits.
>
> H_{o2} Coalition *effectiveness* is not affected by supplementing collective benefits with private benefits.

Multiple indicators of the two dependent variables were used to avoid confirmation on the basis of a single kind of evidence. As is well known, social science measures rarely have the "index stability" of more advanced sciences; hence, the value of many indices. Consistent findings on several indicators obviously claim greater credibility than those founded on one or a few indicators. Among these measures are *both* "behavioral" and "attitudinal" or "perceptual" indices. Frequently, social science research must confine itself to attitudes, because behavior, or action, is inaccessible to direct observation. Surrogate measures of behavior are unfortunate because attitudes are not always predictive of actions. Fortunately, however, experimental techniques made possible the measurement of both behavior and attitudes.

Because of the complexity of the variables and interactions in the theory, simulation techniques were used to represent the major conditions prescribed by the theory.[19] The simulation was a modi-

fied version of the Inter-Nation Simulation (INS). Because the INS has been described in detail elsewhere,[20] it will not be reviewed here. It is only necessary to remember that INS is a "man-machine" simulation in which participants are organized hierarchically into role-differentiated, decision-making teams ("nations"). Participants make decisions about the allocation of resources and about their relations with other "nations" and with internation organizations. Decisions are made periodically (in one-hour "decision periods") and are expressed quantitatively. The decisions affect the political, economic, and military standing of the nation. They are computed hourly and the effects of the decisions are returned as inputs or conditions for subsequent rounds of decisions. Consequently, any INS "run" (constituted by a set of decision periods) is a dynamic, unfolding process. Finally, it should be recalled that INS "nations" and decision-making roles are prototypic. Nations typically bear names such as Amra or Colo, and roles refer to functional responsibilities like Central Decision-Maker (CDM), External Decision-Maker (EDM), and Internal Decision-Maker (IDM). These three roles are included in all decision-making teams, and the interactions among these roles constitutes the "nation."

INS was selected as the research method because nearly all the essential conditions of the theory are already found or can rather easily be represented in the Inter-Nation Simulation model. To wit:

INS with its three-man decision-making teams (nations), permitted the examination of coalitions constituted by groups or organizations, not individuals.

The mathematics of the computations for "national security" for each nation (referred to in INS as "Validator Satisfaction–national security" or

---

[19] It should be noted that *conditions or properties of a theory were simulated*. No attempt was made to simulate coalitions or alliances as such. To the extent that the conditions of the theory are typical occurrences in the referent, then to that extent (but only to that extent) we simulated the behavior of coalitions. Unlike other useful and insightful theories of coalitions (e.g., Riker's theory of minimum winning coalitions), the conditions or properties of the theory of collective action appear to be typically found in referent arenas. These points will be elaborated in Burgess and Robinson (1969) *op cit*. For similar discussions of the above assertions about the applications of simulation techniques, see also Richard C. Snyder, "Experimental Techniques and Political Analysis: Some Reflections in the Context of Concern over Behavioral Approaches," in J. C. Charlesworth, ed., *The Limits of Behavioralism in Political Science* (Philadelphia: American Academy of Political and Social Science, 1962); E. W. Kelley, "Techniques of Studying Coalition Formation," *Midwest Journal of Political Science*, XII (February 1968), 62–84. For an alternative view that stresses the study of "events" and "concrete" variables, see J. David Singer, "Data-Making in International Relations," *Behavioral Science*, X (January 1965), 68–80.

[20] See Harold Guetzkow, Chadwick F. Alger, Richard A. Brody, Robert C. Noel, and Richard C. Snyder, *Simulation in International Relations: Developments for Research and Teaching* (Englewood Cliffs, N.J.: Prentice-Hall, 1963); Harold Guetzkow, "The Use of Simulation in the Study of Inter-Nation Relations," *Behavioral Science*, IV (1959), 183–91; Richard A. Brody (1963), *op. cit.*; Richard A. Brody and Robert C. Noel, *Inter-Nation Simulation Participant's Manual*, Program of Graduate Training and Research in International Relations (Evanston, Ill., 1960); Hayward Alker and Ronald D. Brunner, "Simulating International Conflict: A Comparison of Three Approaches" (1966, mimeo); Philip M. Burgess and James A. Robinson, *Inter-Nation Simulation Participant's Manual* (Columbus, Ohio: The Ohio State University, Department of Political Science, 1966).

"VSns") met exactly the conditions for "collective benefits" described by the theory.[21]

By supplementing the functions of the coalition (and employing a participant-observer to serve as the administrative head of the coalition), it is possible to represent "private benefits" as described by the theory.

Because macro-level and interaction theories in the social and behavioral sciences suggest a strong relationship between "in group" cohesion and "out-group" threat, participant-observers were used to staff a large, powerful, threatening nation. In addition, systematic monitoring and selective manipulation of the perceptions of the members of the experimental coalition were undertaken in order to control external threat perceived by the members of the coalition. Thus, external threat was removed as a variable.

The Experimental Design

The design for the experiment called for ten independent simulation runs with five replications of a coalition producing only collective benefits and five replications of a coalition that supplemented collective benefits with private benefits. Five three-man "nations" constituted the experimental coalition, or 150 different participants for the entire experiment.[22] Each of the ten simulations consisted of a seven-nation "world" of twenty-two participants, three hierarchically organized decision-makers in each nation, and one permanent secretary for the coalition. Each simulation run was divided into six sixty-five minute decision periods run continuously. Runs alternated between treatment conditions on successive Saturdays.

The five-nation experimental coalition was led by a sixth nation manned by three participant-observers who were instructed to maintain the coalition (under *both* treatment and control conditions)

[21] See Harold Guetzkow, "Structured Programs in Inter-Nation Simulation," in Massarik and Ratoosh, eds., *Mathematical Explorations in Behavioral Science* (Homewood, Ill.: Richard D. Irwin, 1965); and Carl D. Frantz, "OSU/INS Calculations Procedures" (Columbus, Ohio: The Ohio State University, Department of Political Science, 1968, mimeo).

[22] Participants were drawn from Army, Navy, and Air Force ROTC units at The Ohio State University. Most were juniors or seniors. Within runs, participants were stratified by test scores and randomly assigned to decision-making roles. *Post hoc* examination indicated that participants were normally distributed on most measures of class, culture, interests, and personality. Details concerning participants' characteristics will be reported in the full report of our study.

"at all costs." The coalition staff was challenged by a nonmember hostile nation, also manned by participant-observers. This threat to the coalition was created for control purposes: it insured a minimally viable coalition because of the threat-cohesion principle noted above and it permitted the establishment of experimental control over threat perception, so that observed variance could be attributed to the treatment effect. In the absence of this control procedure, the coalition might have disintegrated or wide variations in perceived threat might have occurred. Neither development could be tolerated if the theory were to be tested. The participant-observers were guided by a set of written instructions, a program of minute-by-minute directives that determined the content of speeches, messages, and initiatives and responses in order to reduce as much as possible variance in their behavior within and between replications.

With seven participant-observers (three each manning two nations: the leading nation of the six-nation coalition and the nonmember nation that was hostile toward the coalition; and the coalition itself), and with their behavior, actions, and styles guided and, to the extent possible, controlled by detailed directives, we attempted to control variables that might otherwise confound the outcome of the experiment. By employing these procedures, the benefits produced by the coalition (collective or collective coupled with private) were isolated to permit a test of their effects on the variance in cohesion, effectiveness, and the behavior of the coalition itself as well as in the behavior and attitudes of the individual members of the coalition.

The Data

As noted earlier, simulation permits the examination of both attitudes and behavior, and we exploited this advantage. Indicators of coalition cohesion and effectiveness under both the treatment and the control conditions include attitudinal indicators and behavioral indicators. Data are gathered on "game forms," some of which are used in the operation of the simulation and some of which are relayed directly to the experimenter.

The most important source of attitudinal or perceptual data included responses to nine questions administered at the end of each decision period.

Each participant was asked to rate the friendliness, the trustworthiness, the cooperativeness, the helpfulness, and the likelihood of war with each of the other six nations on an eight-point Likert-type scale. In addition, each participant in a nation that was a member of the experimental coalition rated the effectiveness of the coalition, its efficacy in maintaining peace, and its contribution to both the domestic and national security goals of the nation. Responses to these questions yielded nine hundred repeated measures[23] of attitudes and perceptions of the coalition itself and of the other members of the coalition. These responses also provided the procedure for monitoring threat perception in order to control external threat.

Behavioral data include information from game forms that serve as directives among decision-makers or as means of interaction among nations. In addition, a substantial number of the actions of participants were recorded and can be evaluated against the predictions of the theory. Some of the behavioral measures, such as the data from a form on which each nation's representative in the coalition informed his superior of his evaluation of the coalition's activities, can be summarized and subjected to tests of statistical significance. Others, such as withdrawals from the coalition or communication with the nonmember hostile nation, are events or actions of low frequency, but which nevertheless can be evaluated as consistent or inconsistent with the predictions from the theory.

The Analysis: Perceptual Data

The main purpose of the analysis was to test the propositions that coalitions facing a common and constant threat are more cohesive and more effective if they supplement collective benefits with private benefits than if they produce collective benefits exclusively.

The construction of the analysis model included a desire to perform the most appropriate tests for the major and minor hypotheses and appropriate tests for the attitudinal and behavioral data. In addition, we also wanted an analysis technique that

would offer opportunities to explore the operation of simulation and particularly the effects of the simulation model (as contrasted with the experimental treatments) on the results obtained.

At first glance, the hypotheses appear to fit a correlational or analysis of covariance model. Correlations between cohesiveness and the production of private benefits might have been examined while statistically controlling for the effect of threat. The major objection to that was that private benefits in the experimental design was a dichotomous variable, thus permitting only the examination of the cohesiveness of coalitions that produce private benefits with those that do not. We were not concerned with degrees or levels of private benefits, which implies an analysis of covariance model. That, however, was rejected because of the need to test the efficacy of the procedures instituted to control the threat to the coalition. Instead, a factorial analysis of variance model was selected.[24]

The analysis model is a $2 \times 5 \times 6$ analysis of variance with repeated measures. The independent variables in the model are as follows:

A = Treatment
  A_1 = collective benefits only
  A_2 = private benefits supplementing collective benefits

B = run set = two paired runs
  B_1 = run set No. 1
  B_2 = run set No. 2
  B_3 = run set No. 3
  B_4 = run set No. 4
  B_5 = run set No. 5

C = decision period within a run
  C_1 = decision period No. 1
  C_2 = decision period No. 2
  C_3 = decision period No. 3
  C_4 = decision period No. 4
  C_5 = decision period No. 5
  C_6 = decision period No. 6

The .05 alpha level was selected as the rejection region. Because of the absence of evidence support-

---

[23] 5 nations $\times$ 3 decision makers $\times$ 6 decision periods $\times$ 10 replications. For each run we had 90 repeated measures. For each treatment we had 450 repeated measures, or 900 for the entire experiment. (Although each "world" consisted of seven nations, data were not analyzed from the two nations manned by participant-observers.)

[24] See W. G. Cochran and G. M. Cox, *Experimental Designs* (New York: John Wiley and Sons, Inc., 1957); William L. Hays, *Statistics for Psychologists* (New York: Holt, Rinehart, and Winston, 1963); B. J. Winer, *Statistical Principles in Experimental Design* (New York: McGraw-Hill, 1962); and Henry Schaffe, *The Analysis of Variance* (New York: John Wiley and Sons, Inc., 1959).

ing the theory, we regarded .01 as too severe. While Type I errors were tolerable, the .10 alpha level was rejected as excessively lenient in view of the large sample size and the number of replications.

Five dependent measures of cohesion were measured on an eight-point Likert-type scale. These included each participant's perception of the (1) Friendliness, (2) Trustworthiness, (3) Helpfulness, and (4) Cooperativeness of each of the other nations in the simulation. In addition, (5) the Likelihood of War item required each participant to assess the chances of violence between his nation and every other nation in the simulation.

Four dependent measures of effectiveness of the coalition, also measured on an eight-point Likert-type scale, were used. These included each participant's assessment of (1) the effectiveness of the coalition, (2) the likelihood that the coalition would succeed in maintaining peace, (3) the contribution of the coalition in maintaining national security, and (4) the effectiveness of the coalition in the attainment of domestic goals.

Data on these nine dependent measures were collected at the end of each decision period from each participant. Participants responded to the questions without consulting with each other. Consequently, nine hundred observations of the attitudinal measures are available for both of the treatment conditions (A_1, A_2).

Before the analysis of variance was performed on the dependent variables, the efficacy of the control procedures was tested. Threat was measured on the same scale as the previously mentioned five dependent measures of cohesion. For this test, each participant's rating of the threatening nation overall decision periods $(C_1...C_6)$ over all runs $(B_1...B_5)$ under both experimental conditions (A_1, A_2) was

examined. These scores were not combined into a single measure of threat perception because excessive variance within treatment groups on any indicator could not be tolerated. A single indicator might well have concealed those differences that were essential to be eliminated by the control procedures.

There were ten treatment groups with respect to the threat variable. They were A_1B_1, A_1B_2, A_1B_3, A_1B_4, A_1B_5, $A_2B_1,...A_2B_5$. First, our major interest was whether a significant difference existed between the combined A_1 groups and the combined A_2 groups on any of the five indicators. If the mean perception of threat within the A_1 group differed significantly from the mean perception of threat within the A_2 group, further analysis would have been unnecessary because the control procedures would have been shown to have failed. Second, we were interested in whether the control variable (threat) was successfully manipulated from run to run regardless of which treatment a group received. In order to test for any A_1-A_2 difference with as much power as possible and still retain the option of an omnibus F-test, a planned comparison followed by an F-test with n-2 degrees of freedom was used. This combination focused power exactly as we wanted it and was, therefore, more appropriate than an F-test followed by post-hoc testing. The results obtained from the planned comparison and the F-test are displayed in Tables 1 and 2.

As Tables 1 and 2 indicate, no significant differences are found between the A_1 and A_2 groups, and there are no significant differences between any runs on any of the five indicators of threat. Moreover, the reciprocal of the omnibus F-test shows that the between-treatment variance is significantly less than within treatment variance (error variance). This finding gives confidence that the control procedures

TABLE 1

Means on Control Variable

	TREATMENT/RUNS									
Variable	A_1B_1	A_1B_2	A_1B_3	A_1B_4	A_1B_5	A_2B_1	A_2B_2	A_2B_3	A_2B_4	A_2B_5
Friend	41.9	42.6	43.1	43.9	42.1	41.4	43.1	42.6	43.1	44.7
War	38.3	36.3	38.8	41.9	36.4	39.5	40.9	34.9	35.4	38.1
Trust	42.7	43.1	43.1	44.5	40.5	41.7	43.9	42.1	43.7	43.1
Help	42.3	42.9	41.7	44.1	41.5	42.3	43.9	42.5	42.8	43.3
Coop	42.9	43.7	42.4	43.7	41.9	42.2	44.1	42.5	42.5	43.4
Weights	1	1	1	1	1	−1	−1	−1	−1	−1

TABLE 2
Result of Planned Comparison and Omnibus F-test

Variable	MSe	ψ	F	F^{-1}
Friend	21.84	.12	.04	25.0*
War	33.96	.40	.14	7.1*
Trust	24.90	.03	.05	20.0*
Help	24.38	.35	.02	50.0*
Coop	23.64	.01	.02	50.0*

* F^{-1} indicates $p < .05$

for holding threat constant in order to avoid confounding the effects of private benefits on coalition effectiveness and cohesion were successful.

These results justified the testing of the major hypotheses. Because the B and C factors are artifacts of the simulation technique, a simple one-way analysis of variance was used to test the effects of A on the nine dependent measures. Cohesiveness and effectiveness measures were summed over decision periods and run sets to examine the total independent effect of the presence or absence of private benefits. On all measures except the Likelihood of War, the F-ratio was significant ($p < .0001$). Consequently, the null hypotheses that predicted no treatment effects were, with one exception, rejected below the .05 level.

The one variable that failed to be affected by the experimental treatment was the assessment of the Likelihood of War (variable No. 2), although this variable behaved in all respects like the other eight variables. This result was not surprising inasmuch as it has a quality different from the other variables. The mere existence of a coalition would appear to

reduce the likelihood of war within the coalition. This variable also failed to yield significance in the subsequent analysis.

The failure to obtain significance on this single variable coupled with the weak correlations between the two sets of five and four variables intended to measure cohesion and effectiveness, respectively, is indication that the participants were discriminating in their responses to the questions. Some evidence for this interpretation is displayed in Tables 3 and 4.

Because of the size of the F-ratio and because of the relatively little experience with the effects of the complex interactions of roles, the open-ended nature of any given simulation run, and the use of participant observers, we subjected our data to the more demanding $2 \times 5 \times 6$ analysis of variance. The analysis of variance employed is a fixed-effects model (Model II) consisting of six repeated measures. The measures were summed over all participants within a coalition to determine the mean score for each coalition.

Main Effects

As the results displayed in Tables 5 and 6 indicate, the coalition that supplements collective benefits with private benefits (experimental treatment A_2) is perceived as more effective and the individual members of such coalitions perceive the other members of the coalition as more friendly, trustworthy, helpful, and cooperative.

The factorial design indicates no significant independent B-effect on the cohesion measures, suggesting that no significant differences existed

TABLE 3
Correlations of Dependent Measures

Variables	COHESION (1–5)					EFFECTIVENESS (6–9)			
	1	2	3	4	5	6	7	8	9
1 Friend		.48	.70	.70	.73	.36	.26	.32	.31
2 War			.59	.46	.51	.31	.22	.30	.24
3 Trust				.71	.74	.39	.31	.37	.34
4 Help					.83	.43	.32	.37	.39
5 Coop						.46	.34	.38	.41
6 Effective							.71	.73	.65
7 Peace								.73	.55
8 Security									.65
9 Goals									

TABLE 4
Correlations of Dependent Measures by Treatment

Variables	A_1								
	1	2	3	4	5	6	7	8	9
1 Friend	—	.44	.66	.69	.72	.33	.29	.30	.23
2 War	.54	—	.55	.43	.48	.27	.20	.27	.16
3 Trust	.73	.63	—	.73	.74	.39	.38	.38	.30
4 Help	.68	.50	.67	—	.83	.40	.36	.36	.35
5 Coop	.71	.55	.72	.81	—	.45	.39	.38	.39
6 Effective	.34	.37	.36	.39	.40	—	.70	.70	.61
7 Peace	.15	.24	.17	.21	.21	.69	—	.75	.55
8 Security	.29	.36	.31	.31	.31	.74	.65	—	.59
9 Goals	.33	.33	.33	.37	.38	.64	.50	.68	—
	1	2	3	4	5	6	7	8	9
	A_2								

between run sets. An early concern was experienced with respect to the effect on the experimental outcome of increased proficiency among the participant-observers. The absence of a significant B-effect gives confidence that the procedures instituted to control the behavior of the participant-observers were successful. Main effects probably cannot be attributed to their behavior.

A significant C-effect, particularly evident in Table 6, was obtained on the cohesion measures but not on the effectiveness measures. This is interpreted as the "scenario effect." Fifteen minutes prior

TABLE 5a
F-Ratios of Main Effects: Cohesion Variables

	1	2	3	4	5
A (Treatment)	10.2^a	<1	5.3^a	12.8^a	13.0^a
B (Run)	1.7	<1	<1	<1	<1
C (Decision Period)	13.5^a	2.6^a	5.1^a	9.7^a	4.8^a

[a] F ratio indicates $p < .05$

TABLE 5b
F-Ratios of Main Effects: Effectiveness Variables

	6	7	8	9	d.f.
A (Treatment)	28.1^b	13.3^b	14.9^b	22.1^b	1, 140
B (Run)	3.0^b	2.3^b	2.0	3.4^b	4, 140
C (Decision Period)	<1	3.4^b	1.1	<1	5, 140

[b] F ratio indicates $p < .05$

to the beginning of each simulation run, participants are methodically introduced to the "history" of their "world." This "game culture" included several indicators of the impending and imminent threat to the coalition which is immediately reflected in the scores obtained at the conclusion of the first decision period. The emphasis in the scenario is on the hostile intentions of the nonmember nation toward the coalition. The scenario does not, on the other hand, emphasize private benefits, which would be reflected in the effectiveness measures. Moreover, after the first decision period C-effects are reduced, a result that might be explained by the fact that the effects of the production of private benefits would not be expected to "take hold" until sometime after the first decision period. In this regard, it is noteworthy that after the first decision period measures of cohesion tend to stabilize.[25]

Interactions

As Table 7 indicates, no AC interactions were obtained on either of the two sets of dependent measures. The absence of an AC interaction was reassuring, for it means that the A treatment was uniform in its effects across decision periods. Had an AC interaction emerged, it would have been necessary to qualify rather seriously the interpretation of the significant A effect.

[25] This interpretation was validated by post hoc testing.

TABLE 6
Marginal Means

	COHESION VARIABLES					EFFECTIVENESS VARIABLES			
	1	2	3	4	5	6	7	8	9
A_1[a]	12.1	8.9	11.0	12.5	12.0	5.7	5.7	6.1	5.5
A_2[a]	10.6	8.5	9.9	10.7	10.1	6.6	6.3	6.8	6.3
B_1	10.4	8.6	9.9	11.3	10.9	5.9	5.8	6.1	5.6
B_2	11.9	9.0	10.8	11.6	11.1	6.4	6.2	6.7	6.1
B_3	12.1	9.2	10.9	12.4	11.9	5.8	5.6	6.3	5.7
B_4	10.8	8.2	10.0	11.2	10.6	6.3	6.1	6.5	5.5
B_5	11.5	8.4	10.6	11.4	10.7	6.6	6.3	6.7	6.3
C_1	13.2	9.4	11.5	13.2	12.1	6.2	6.0	6.4	5.8
C_2	11.4	8.1	10.0	11.5	10.9	6.1	6.1	6.5	5.8
C_3	11.0	8.4	10.1	11.4	10.7	6.2	5.9	6.4	5.9
C_4	11.3	8.6	10.4	11.1	11.0	6.1	6.0	6.4	5.9
C_5	10.6	8.7	10.1	10.8	10.7	6.3	6.3	6.6	6.0
C_6	10.6	9.1	10.5	11.4	10.8	6.2	5.7	6.4	5.9

[a] Lower values on the A_2 runs represent confirmatory findings for the five cohesion variables. Higher values on the A_2 runs represent confirmatory findings for the four effectiveness variables.

Significant *BC* interactions were obtained on four of the five measures of cohesion, although none emerged on the four measures of effectiveness. It was expected that *BC* interactions would be discovered on all measures because of the "richness" and "uniqueness" of each simulation run. These interactions are probably best interpreted as representing the relative stability of the effectiveness measures over runs and decision periods compared to the less stable, more sensitive sociometric cohesiveness measures.[26]

A significant *AB* interaction, reflected in Table 7, was obtained. It should be recalled that all ten runs occurred on different weeks and that the pairing of the two runs in the third run set merely reflects that A_1B_3 and A_2B_3 occurred one week apart. Although a number of alternative explanations exist for this interaction effect, it will be necessary to re-examine the notes on each of the runs and to explore the data further before confident interpretations can be offered.

Finally, a significant *ABC* interaction was obtained. It will be recalled that each nation consisted of three people occupying three different roles.[27] These three roles meant that the experience of each of the participants within a nation was somewhat different from the experience of each of his cohorts.

[26] Albert Pepitone and Robert Kleiner, "The Effects of Threat and Frustration on Group Cohesiveness," *Journal of Abnormal Psychology*, LIV (1957), 192–200.

[27] In simulation terminology, the Central Decision-Maker, the Internal Decision-Maker and the External Decision-Maker.

TABLE 7
F-Ratios of Interactions

	COHESION VARIABLES					EFFECTIVENESS VARIABLES				d.f.
	1	2	3	4	5	6	7	8	9	
AB	5.3[a]	2.9[a]	5.0[a]	4.8[a]	4.9[a]	3.3[a]	2.7[a]	1.8	3.8[a]	4, 140
AC	1.7	< 1	< 1	< 1	< 1	1.8	1.1	2.0	1.7	5, 700
BC	2.6[a]	1.9[a]	2.6[a]	1.3	2.2[a]	1.5	< 1	1.4	< 1	20, 700
ABC	2.3	1.7[a]	2.7[a]	1.8[a]	3.2[a]	1.7[a]	1.5	< 1	< 1	20, 700

[a] F ratio indicates $p < .05$

It is therefore interesting to note that when "role effects" are statistically controlled the strength of the *ABC* interactions is reduced.

These data indicate considerable variance between roles and remarkable consistency within roles. If these initial observations hold up under more rigorous analysis, it is likely that the *ABC* interaction will be eliminated. In the meantime, Table 7 displays the *ABC* interactions on all nine variables in order to reveal the idiosyncratic behavior of the treatment/run set/decision period interactions.

In summary, the evidence obtained from the perceptual data indicates that the presence of private benefits increases cohesion among the members of a coalition and results in higher ratings of coalition effectiveness by its constituent members. The interactions do not significantly weaken the main effect of the experimental treatment. Moreover, further analysis of the interactions promises to reveal the combination of simulation and experimental design methodologies. They indicate the ability of the researcher to represent complex variables in a theory by the use of simulation. They indicate the ability of simulated environments to produce discriminating and differential effects between treatments, through time, between participants, and within participants over different variables. Also, the analysis justifies confidence in the experimenter's ability to isolate and control variables by the use of participant-observers without confounding the treatment effects. Finally, the analysis indicates the stability of simulated environments with respect to participants and the relative strength of role behavior over idiosyncratic behavior.

The Analysis: Behavioral Data

Behavioral data include voting in the coalition and in the international organization, recommendations among decision-makers within "nations," and the content of communications between "nations." Below we present a sample of these data from two sources: voting in the coalition and recommendations with respect to the coalition communicated between the Central Decision-Makers (CDM's) and External Decision-Makers (EDM's).

Coalition Voting

Each decision period the coalition met for ten minutes. All nations were free to send agenda items to the

TABLE 8
Per Cent Unanimity in Coalition Voting

Run set	Total votes A_1	A_2	Total unanimous votes A_1	A_2	% unanimous A_1	A_2
B_1	16	23	10	22	62.5	95.8
B_2	14	20	10	16	17.4	80.0
B_3	6	20	5	17	83.3	85.0
B_4	11	21	10	18	90.9	85.7
B_5	12	23	11	23	91.7	100.0

Overall %
$A_1 = 77.96$
$A_2 = 89.07$

coalition secretariat and items were tabled in the order they were received. Issues before the coalition were resolved by voting. The cohesion of the coalition may be measured by the frequency with which unanimous votes are obtained. These data are displayed in Table 8 and show that the coalition which provided its members with private as well as collective benefits was more likely to act with unanimity in recording its decisions in formal votes.

Voting, it hardly need be said, reveals only part of any decision-making body's activities and behavior. Other behavioral data available to us included the assessment of the policies and role of the coalition made by the External Decision Maker at the conclusion of each coalition meeting. This appraisal and recommendation was then forwarded to his Central Decision Maker and served as his channel of information about the role of his nation in the coalition as assessed by his delegate to the coalition. At the end of each decision period, the Central Decision-Maker completed a form statement of his "nation's" coalition policy. On this form he indicated his agreement or disagreement with the basic policies of the coalition and his desire to continue to support the coalition and its policies or to attempt to modify the policies of the coalition.

When the responses of the EDM's and the CDM's are combined, we find, as predicted by the theory, significantly more dissatisfaction with the policies of the coalition in the A_1 than in the A_2 treatment. As Table 9 shows, coalitions that produce collective benefits only, evidence greater desire for moderate or radical change in policies than coalitions that produce both collective and private benefits.

Also included on the EDM's appraisal and

TABLE 9
Desire for Change in the Policies of the Coalition

Treatment	No change	Some change	Severe change
A_1	242	49	9
A_2	285	14	1

$$X^2 = 29.34$$
$$P < .001$$

recommendation to his CDM was his judgment with respect to the "correctness" of the coalition's policies. Once again, the coalition that supplemented collective benefits with private benefits was viewed more favorably. Table 10 displays data that indicate greater approval of policies when the coalition offers both collective and private benefits than when it offers only collective benefits.

The consistency of this result for all runs can be seen in Table 11.

No coalition that confined its output to collective benefits scored as high as any coalition that produced both kinds of benefits when measured by decision-makers' appraisals of coalition policies.

Implications

The results of one experiment should not be carried too far, even if the design did involve five replications of two experimental treatment conditions. Nevertheless, additional evidence now supports a theory of collective action, a theory that has substantial "face" validity, that appears to be supported by the analysis of the behavior of NATO members' support for the infrastructure program, and that seems to "explain" or account for many of the typical problems faced by voluntary associations. The support for the theory given by the results encourages, at the very least, continued work with different research strategies in

TABLE 10
Approval of Coalition Policies

Treatment	Basically correct	Require modification
A_1	124	26
A_2	147	3

$$X^2 = 20.2$$
$$P < .001$$

TABLE 11
Approval of Coalition Policies: Per Cent Appraisals "Correct"

Run	Appraisals judged "correct"		% Appraisals "correct"	
	A_1	A_2	A_1	A_2
B_1	24	30	80.0	100.0
B_2	26	30	86.6	100.0
B_3	24	29	80.0	96.6
B_4	22	29	73.3	96.6
B_5	28	29	93.3	96.6

Overall %
$$A_1 = 82.7$$
$$A_2 = 98.0$$

different arenas, including "real world" political, social, and economic arenas.

The research appears to have a number of theoretical, methodological and policy implications. Time and space permit only a summary account of these. Theoretically, the findings suggest that much that goes under the functionalist heading might be reviewed with heightened cognizance for the type of benefits (collective or private) that the function represents for members and nonmembers alike.[28] With respect to prescriptions, the theory has a number of obvious implications for alliances, for labor unions, for voluntary associations of individuals, and for voluntary aggregates of organizations. With specific reference to NATO, for example the policy implications clearly run counter to many current recommendations. Given the desirability of NATO's continuation as an institutionalized alliance beyond 1969 and presuming, therefore, the desire to see more substantial collaboration, more equitable sharing of financial burdens, and more commitment to the well-being of the organization, the theory of collective action suggests increasing the number of private benefits produced by the organization formed within the framework of the North Atlantic Treaty. Recommendations based on this theory do not require (nor do they discourage) administrative or decisional reorganization,[29] or expanding *per se* the functions of the organization, or limiting the functions of the

[28] See Ernst B. Haas, *Beyond the Nation-State* (Stanford: Stanford University Press, 1964).

[29] See Alastair Buchan, *NATO in the 1960's* (New York: Frederick A. Praeger, 1963).

alliance to those strictly related to military-security.[30] Rather, the theory supports recommendations that call for expanding private benefits to supplement the collective benefits. Whether these recommendations are supplemented by an administrative reorganization or an expansion of the functions of the alliance into matters less clearly concerned with military-security affairs is much less crucial than whether private benefits supplement collective benefits.

Methodologically, we think we have demonstrated an appropriate way in which man-machine simulation can be used in social and policy science research namely the examination of micro-processes. Simulation and experimental procedures were resorted to as a way to obtain evidence about the behavior of extremely complex human associations under specified conditions. In this particular study, the theory that generated the hypotheses that were tested appeared to be highly relevant to basic theoretical interests as well as to policy issues that are widely shared, yet it has very little rigorously accumulated evidence to support it. The conditions or properties of the theory could not have been easily or inexpensively isolated or manipulated in order to test the theory in the "real world" for example by a "prototyping" effort.[31] Moreover, prototyping, a not inexpensive research method, would seem to require substantially more confidence in the theory than is presently justifiable. A field study, while possible to be sure, would probably have been inconclusive because of the "messiness" of the real world coupled with the complexity of the theory. The man-machine simulation experiment is not, quite

clearly, as asceptic and neat as the psychologist's Skinner Box or even the social psychologist's small-group experiment, yet it is considerably neater, much more susceptible to control and observation, and much more conclusive *at least with respect to the variables under examination* than is the field study. As Verba[32] has pointed out, artificial confirmation of an hypothesis in the laboratory (always a possibility, to be sure) is less likely than is artificial disconfirmation, while the converse holds for research in the real world. The difference, of course, is the investigator's control over the processes that lead to the results.[33]

The substantial emphasis on simulation in the social sciences as a "heuristic" is undoubtedly justified, but it is an expensive heuristic. The emphasis in the research reported here, however, is on the use of simulation for hypothesis-testing, for examining under the controlled conditions of the laboratory the relationships between properties in a theory and the causes of variance in the behavior of complex systems. As the process of evaluating gaming and simulation techniques continues, more emphasis might be given to combining experimental procedures with simulation techniques for the purposes of hypothesis-testing and for subjecting the many variables (particularly the analytical variables) of verbal theories to the rigors of the experimental method.

---

[30] See Senator Henry M. Jackson. "The Atlantic Alliance," Hearings before the Subcommittee on National Security and International Operations, The Committee on Government Operations, U.S. Senate, 89th Congress, 1966.

[31] See Harold D. Lasswell, *The Future of Political Science* (New York: Atherton Press, 1963).

[32] See Sidney Verba. "Simulation, Reality, and Theory in International Relations," *World Politics*, XVI (April 1964), 490–519.

[33] Disagreements concerning the place of simulation in research in the social sciences can be appreciated by comparing Sidney Verba (1964), *op. cit.*; Harold Guetzkow, ed., *Simulation in Social Sciences: Readings* (Englewood Cliffs, N.J.: Prentice-Hall, 1962); E. W. Kelley, *op. cit.*; David Schwartz. "Problems in Political Gaming," *Orbis*, IX (Fall 1965), 677–93; Richard A. Brody, *op. cit.*; and J. David Singer, *op. cit.*

53. The Political-Military Exercise: A Progress Report

Lincoln P. Bloomfield and Barton Whaley were associated with the Massachusetts Institute of Technology when they collaborated on this summary of a long-standing project conducted at that institution. The second author has written several studies on psychological warfare, while the first author's writings include *The United Nations and U.S. Foreign Policy* (1967). In this essay they report the results of actual experience in applying simulation techniques to problems of foreign policy. Also known as political gaming, this method of applied research should not be confused with game theory (see Selection 39), which is substantive rather than methodological in nature and which may or may not be developed through the use of simulation. [*Reprinted from* Orbis (*a quarterly journal of world affairs published by the Foreign Policy Research Institute of the University of Pennsylvania*), *VIII* (*Winter 1965*), *854–70, by permission of the authors and the publisher.*]

Revolutions are few in the study and understanding of foreign policy. Rarer still are techniques for methodically anticipating events in the realm of diplomacy—a trade which traditionally relies on a combination of unscientific hunch-playing and an educated sense of history. In recent years the search has intensified for ways of bringing to foreign policy planning some of the imaginative analytical techniques employed by military planners and operations analysts. As a result, a variety of experimental techniques has been developed with a view to increasing knowledge of the policymaking process and—the ultimate objective—trying to improve our ability to make predictions about the future. If these new methods are to serve a useful purpose, they should provide us new insights into the wisdom and feasibility of national strategies and policies. They should help us make better guesses about the probable reactions to American initiatives by other actors on the international stage. They should help the weapons designer understand better the likely political context of his product, and the civilian planner the impact of force structures and capabilities on national policy in crises. Most of all, they should help us "stockpile" some useful conclusions about the options open to the United States in a crisis-ridden world.

Some of these attempts to make foreign policy "more scientific" seem useful. Others—such as the attempts to reduce international relations to numbers —too often seem to remove the very essence of the process, those elements which in many ways constitute the real world of international relations, such as temperament, history and irrationality. Some of the new techniques have impinged profoundly on the consciousness of policymakers; others are as remote to them as Sanskrit. Diplomacy has by no means enthusiastically welcomed the invasion of its sacred precincts by operations research or game theory. Many professional diplomats persist in viewing their trade as an art—evanescent, fragile, and not susceptible to scientific (or pseudo-scientific) approaches. And in some ways they are right.

At least one of these experimental devices—the political-military exercise[1]—has caught the attention and imagination of scholars and responsible government officials. Indeed, there is a danger that too much might be expected of it as an aid to contingency planning. Clearly it remains highly experimental and of unproven value in the science (or art) of prediction. Furthermore, it may or may not be worth the cost and effort compared with more conventional forms of research and planning. Yet as an interesting intellectual innovation it is worth investigating. This paper is a report on the political-military exercises conducted at the Massachusetts Institute of Technology.[2]

The initial M.I.T. policy-type exercise—the so-called POLEX—was held in the fall of 1958 as a part of the Center for International Studies' UN project. Its *mise en scène* was a hypothetical future crisis situation in Poland, and the participants drew heavily on the role-playing, political gaming technique developed in 1954–56 by the RAND Corporation's Social Science Division.[3] In 1959 two additional games using undergraduates as players laid the foundation for the use of simulation in the teaching of foreign policy, strategy and international relations to both undergraduates and graduate students—a method that continues to be used at M.I.T.[4]

The second Center experiment—POLEX II—employing as players senior specialists in and out

of government, was held in 1960 and focused on a crisis in the Middle East.[5] This game was noteworthy both for demonstrating the feasibility of incorporating a substantial element of simulated theater-level military operations in an international political crisis and for developing the general technique to a point where the professional participants recognized it as having heuristic value even for themselves.

Pure experimentation gave way to a fairly concrete policy-research focus in four games conducted under contract with the Institute for Defense Analyses in 1962–63 as part of Project DAIS sponsored by the Office of the Assistant Secretary of Defense for International Security Affairs. The participants were concerned with the possible future employment of United Nations military forces under conditions of increasing disarmament. Interest also centered on the strains to which the disarmament process itself might be subjected by major international crises. Finally, as with all M.I.T. games, the focus was on crisis management per se: each of the four hypothetical crises was chosen to represent a type of crisis and a regional problem which was thought to be of potential concern to U.S. policymakers.

The first game in this "POLEX-DAIS" series was set in the present arms environment and involved a typical ambiguous situation of Chinese communist indirect aggression and subversion in Southeast Asia. The second was set at the mid-point of Stage I[6] of a disarming world and concerned a colonial-racial civil war in a newly independent African nation. The third simulated a classic small-power war in the Near East under conditions midway through Stage II in a disarming world, and the fourth simulated a Castro-type revolution in Latin America in mid-Stage III.

The most recent application of the method at M.I.T.—a series of similar exercises undertaken in 1963–64 under Project Michelson of the U.S. Naval Ordnance Test Station, China Lake, California—centered on the possible role of sea-based strategic deterrent weapons systems, notably the Polaris missile-firing nuclear submarines and the proposed MLF, in the future conduct of U.S. strategy and

[1] This term might be defined as a simulation of foreign policymaking under conditions of international crisis. The term "exercise" is used here as the formal rubric for this specific category of political or political-military simulation. For informal usage the terms "game," "gaming" and "simulation" are suitable alternatives.

[2] Dr. Bloomfield has served as the project director at M.I.T. and Mr. Whaley since 1962 as his deputy. The Joint War Games Agency of the Pentagon conducts comparable games, and the Department of State ran such an exercise internally in the fall of 1963 which Dr. Bloomfield directed.

[3] See *Experimental Research on Political Gaming* (Santa Monica: The RAND Corporation, Memorandum P-1540-RC, November 10, 1958).

[4] POLEX and the two student games of 1959 are described in Lincoln P. Bloomfield and Norman J. Padelford, "Three Experiments in Political Gaming," *American Political Science Review*, December 1959, 1105–15, and Bloomfield, "Political Gaming," *United States Naval Institute Proceedings*, September 1960, 57–64.

[5] See Lincoln P. Bloomfield, *The Political Exercise: A Progress Report* (Cambridge: Center for International Studies, M.I.T., March 1961).

[6] The disarmament stages were taken from the U.S. disarmament proposals of April 18, 1962.

diplomacy. The research objective here was particularly challenging for it sought to evaluate the roles of certain strategic military systems in the larger context of high-level decision-making in complex international crisis situations. (The deterrence games have been nicknamed "DETEX" and the lower-level experimental parallel simulations using students as subjects have been labeled "EX-DET.") Before suggesting some of the tentative conclusions drawn from these games it might be helpful to review briefly the state of the art of the policy-level political-military game as now practiced at M.I.T. A later section discusses briefly the equally important and interesting educative uses of the technique.

The Policy-Type Political-Military Exercise

The policy-type political-military exercise is basically a device for crudely simulating the decision-making process at the top governmental level.[7] It employs the technique of role-playing, with the roles of senior policymaking officials of government and international organizations taken by professionally qualified political, military and academic specialists, preferably men with either decision-making experience at higher levels of government or close working relations with policymakers. Typically, the exercise takes a problem generating high levels of international tension and threatening, if not actually involving, the use of significant military force—in short, a major crisis.

The chief purposes of the policy-type game are, first, to throw additional light on hypotheses about foreign policy and strategy arrived at by more conventional methods of research; second, to "pretest" strategies of action; third, to discover unanticipated contingencies, alternatives or possible outcomes as a consequence of the interaction between conflicting strategies in the simulation; and

[7] For the theory and taxonomy of political simulations see Richard A. Brody, "Varieties of Simulations in International Relations Research," in Harold Guetzkow et al., *Simulations in International Relations* (Englewood Cliffs, N.J.: Prentice-Hall, Inc., 1963), 190–223. For the theoretical limitations of "simulations" as contrasted with both "operational gaming" and "analytic game theory" see Clayton J. Thomas and Walter L. Deemer, Jr., "The Role of Operational Gaming in Operations Research," *Operations Research*, February 1957, 1–27.

fourth, to examine closely one particular line of policy action that in its development and impact illustrates vividly what a single plausible outcome might resemble in detail.

This kind of simulation is related only indirectly to the theory of games, which applies mathematical formulas, laws of probability or bargaining theories to determine outcomes of formalized conflict situations. The political exercise has parental roots in the classic military war game, but like diplomacy does not usually lend itself to the precise and numerically expressed wins and losses of the latter.

How is a game organized? The participants in the Center's games have been divided among two to five teams and a Control Group. In all games played to date there has been, at a minimum, a U.S. and a Soviet team. (Some of the War College and Defense Department exercises often limit themselves to "Red" and "Blue," in the possibly too simple fashion of "aggressor" and "defender" in military war games.) Each of the four POLEX-DAIS games also included a UN Team representing the quasi-autonomous role of the UN Secretary-General and his military advisor. Several games in the recent series incorporated additional teams representing China or the U.A.R., or such collectivities as Western Europe or the Afro-Asian bloc.

The Control Group has several functions. It represents "Nature," introducing unexpected events; it is umpire, ruling on the plausibility and outcomes of moves; it is, as it were, "God," requiring the players to live with the implications of their chosen strategies. Since only a fraction of the political world can be represented by playing teams, the Control Group customarily furnishes the needed inputs on behalf of any other nations or international organizations whose actions may be relevant to the crisis problem or to which the teams may be sending messages. If matters reach a point where UN Assembly or Security Council action is the plausible real-world response, the Control Group can count probable votes and stipulate the action taken.

The games have employed from eighteen to twenty-four full playing participants (not counting the Game Director and Game Historian). This number depends upon the number of teams, three to five members per team probably representing the limits for efficient operation. A team with only two members may be unable to act if they regularly disagree and does not provide enough manpower for the necessary production of messages; more than five may produce near-paralysis in the team. The POLEX-DAIS and DETEX series employed two- to six-man teams, and the control groups ranged in size from five to nine men with a single chairman; the 1958 and 1960 games experimented with twin umpires supported by consultants. Five seems to be the optimum number for Control, although the number here is more flexible than on the teams. (With increased experience in game administration, we believe that by better controlling the message flow the technique can cope effectively with at least five teams, the main limiting factors being finance and physical facilities rather than increased complexity of communications.)

The Game Director usually appoints one member of each playing team as Chairman, who is then expected to assign further roles or responsibilities within his group, e.g., defense minister and foreign minister. It often follows that games take place within the teams in the process of arriving at their own collective decisions. The Control Group is generally selected on the basis of anticipated specialized assignments, such as intelligence officer, UN expert, Asian inputs and local area expertise. Moreover, each team and the Control Group has one or more military advisors assigned to it. A Game Historian serves the Control Group as its rapporteur, maintains the game archives, and subsequently writes the narrative history of the game. Each team is assigned a rapporteur, usually a young instructor or company grade military officer, who assists the Historian's subsequent task by keeping an account of the alternative strategies considered by the teams (and who may also be co-opted by the team chairman to perform an active playing role).

One key to the operation is the requirement that every move of whatever sort, whether diplomatic messages, public speeches, troop movements or secret strategic plans, is always committed to writing on standard printed message forms and channeled by a message center to, through or from Control. There is no objection to face-to-face negotiations or discussions between delegated members of teams, but experience shows their value in policy-games to be questionable. If permitted, they are monitored by Control and subsequently summarized as standard game documents.

The 1958 POLEX exercise ran for three days, and the participants concluded at the time that five days were needed. But it has proven possible to reduce exercises to two days without loss of quality and with the virtue of making it more convenient for busy men to take part. At the suggestion of one government agency an experiment was run in late 1963 with a one-day exercise that, with only a minimum of planning and overhead, could on short notice be focused on an impending crisis situation. Experience indicates, however, that such an abbreviated exercise does not permit sufficient time for the indispensable sequential interaction which alone permits the unfolding of climaxes and denouements of crises that can teach something significant about their anatomy.

The physical arrangements for the games can vary widely but must ensure privacy of team discussions by assigning each team to a separate room. The Control Group requires space sufficient for both plenary meetings and the message center.

Adequate administrative staff consists of the Game Director, an administrative assistant, two message center clerks (usually graduate students or comparable personnel), a duplicating machine operator, and one secretary-typist for each team. Although this is a rather large administrative group —POLEX-DAIS III with five teams plus Control had an administrative staff of eleven— it has helped minimize intrusive procedural incidents and has ensured prompt handling of messages. In one exercise the Game Director doubled as Control Chairman; this is feasible if he has a competent deputy, but otherwise little modification in the administrative roster is possible.

Given this setting and structure, how is a game actually played?[8] First, the substantive event with which the players must deal is set forth in a basic

[8] For a now dated but still excellent compression of the history, technique and theory of political games, see Herbert Goldhamer and Hans Speier, "Some Observations on Political Gaming," *World Politics*, October 1959, pp. 71–83. For a highly critical evaluation of the "reality games" see Bernard C. Cohen, "Political Gaming in the Classroom," *Journal of Politics*, May 1962, 367–81. For an informal discussion of the definitions, utilities and limitations of the various forms of political-military gaming see Ithiel de Sola Pool, "Cold War Modeling," *Proceedings of the Military Operations Research Symposia (MORS)*, Fall 1961, 17 pp. For a recent survey of the more theoretical models, see Thomas C. Schelling, "War Without Pain, and Other Models," *World Politics*, April 1963, 465–87.

document, the "Scenario-Problem," which specifies such details as prior history, capabilities and military dispositions, and concludes with the unfolding crisis situation up to the moment play begins. The document must be carefully written so as not to preempt the strategies the teams may wish to adopt, and not to encourage the participants to play their hands excessively. Unlike formal or highly structured political, military and business games, the political-military exercise does not necessarily proceed according to any predetermined program or script. Indeed, the operative question is "what is going to happen?" Subsequent moves and countermoves are improvised by the teams.

In the most recent games, profiting from experiment, some pre-programmed messages were fed by Control to the teams after the game commenced. But in general the Control Group is not constrained by a fixed program, although it has in mind that the game tends to work best if certain lines of action are stressed. For example, it may be desirable for the teams to be pushed deliberately toward the "brink," or for the UN to play an active part in the crisis, or for certain naval capabilities to figure prominently in simulated Presidential decision-making. Generally Control will limit itself to meshing the moves of the playing teams in such a way as to keep them focused on the central research problems posed for the exercise.

Play proceeds through a series of discontinuous move periods ranging from three to six in number, the precise number subject to change by Control in the light of developing events. Each move cycle begins with Control inputs, the scenario counting as the initial Control move. In each move period the teams go through a one and one-half to three hour process of defining and redefining their basic strategies, assessing the motives underlying the moves of other teams, trying to predict future events and the courses of action which might subsequently open, and then determining their moves in relation to those alternatives. At the end of the allotted time, while individual team members are engaged in drafting portions of collective team output, it has been found extremely useful to have team chairmen orally brief Control (separately, of course) so that Control can commence work without waiting for the detailed papers. The exceptions to the "packaged" team output are simulated "hot-line" messages which are hand-carried without delay.

The relationship of game time to actual time is determined by Control after considering the plausible time-lags required to accommodate the events generated by the teams. The time clock is adjustable, each move period reflecting whatever time period Control may stipulate. The POLEX-DAIS and DETEX games simulated from eight to 195 days, the length of the exercise depending on the level of intensity of the crisis at the time it was presented to the players, the complexity of diplomatic negotiations involved in formulating responses to the crisis, the speed with which escalation may have developed, and other factors.

A fairly lengthy, highly informal interaction process of this sort is bound to generate a rather large number of events. Of the many possible methods by which such data can be collected and analyzed, four have been found useful.

First, the standard message forms on which all final team decisions and formal team interactions were recorded comprise the basic record of the game, providing the raw material for the game summary prepared for each game by the Game Historian, and remaining as promising data to be refined at leisure.

Second, the team rapporteurs record data about team consideration of choices, strategies opted for and rejected, internal conflicts, and the like. Their occasional dual role as playing members has tended to interfere with the systematic collection of data on intra-team activities, but this problem should be readily solvable.

Third, a verbatim record is made of the post-game plenary critique session—the general debriefing for all participants. A full account of the exercise is thus available in the words of all players.

Fourth, following the game each participant is given a questionnaire to be completed at his leisure. So far, 88 per cent have been returned and provide a valuable basis for analyzing both the participants' reactions and their suggestions for improvements in the technique.

Implications for Policy

The questions raised by employing the technique of gaming for serious policy purposes are almost self-evident. Can Americans, however knowledgeable, really simulate the actions and reactions of people bred and trained in wholly different cultures or steeped in hostile ideology? Can reality ever be reproduced or even approximated under laboratory conditions, however skillfully attempted? Does what happens in a game bear any demonstrable relationship to what will happen in real life?

The answers to these questions vary. The first one, on the evidence, can be answered with a qualified affirmative. (It would nonetheless be fascinating to run a game with real Soviet officials simulating the reactions of the Soviet Union to a potential crisis; it might even be highly therapeutic to have them play the role of Western policymakers!)

To the second question we must answer that reality can never be reproduced exactly. But in gaming, as in any intellectual undertaking, reality is represented by a model that reduces to manageable proportions the infinite number of variables. The relevant question is whether this particular model teaches what other models of reality—whether pieces of paper, discussions or computer simulations—do not. Our impression is that on some issues—but not on all—it comes closer to reality than many other methods by isolating an impressive number of the significant variables that condition fundamental strategic decisions.

As to the third question, there is no sure way to relate the events of the game with the future until the future reveals itself. The interesting point here, however, is that within this obvious limit the game may illuminate better than other methods some possibilities regarding the future that have not been examined in such depth before. For example, in some situations involving major policy choices the alternatives are not really infinite; they might even be limited to "yes" or "no." In such cases we can learn a good deal about the factors that influence our choice of alternatives and about the kinds of reaction that might be expected on the part of allies and opponents, Congress and public opinion, State Department and military services, intelligence community and scientific advisors.

By exposing those options to simulated reactions and eliciting some of their potential effects, an exercise can supply useful information about policy alternatives that have not hitherto been tested. This also enables us to study the choice-points that arise to confront the policymaker in the life of a given strategy, and the possible consequences to be ex-

pected from each, developing one or more to their logical conclusion.[9] As one colleague put it, the game does not create new knowledge of the world, but it does supply a unique way to put existing knowledge to work. Above all, it forces one to consider all alternatives, including the most terrifying as well as the more pleasant ones. Conventional research and planning have always sought to do this job, but they cannot do it in precisely this way. Thus gaming is a useful adjunct to both.

Role-playing should not be misunderstood as requiring faithful emulation of the policymaking style of a given statesman or politician under given constraints. For the teaching purposes discussed later, that form of role-playing may be most instructive. But in the policy-type game each team is usually free to choose the broad strategy it wishes to follow, an "optimal" strategy which is not rigidly confined to actual past strategies of the assigned country. The team, of course, is required to evolve a strategy which is plausible given the constraints imposed by vital national or ideological interests. It is usually specified that the Soviet team should play a "representational" strategy, duplicating as best it can the responses of current Soviet policymakers to analogous situations. On the other hand, in some games the U.S. teams are free to be as imaginative as desired, unrestrained by fears of the reactions of various world political leaders or world public opinion.

The M.I.T. games, while conducted in connection with government-sponsored research studies, have been unclassified. At the same time we have felt it essential to protect the privacy of the participants, particularly those occupying sensitive positions in the government who ought under no circumstances to be identified publicly with either the roles they played or the outcome of particular games. Nothing could more quickly put an end to this promising area of collaboration than a sensational news story that puts two and two together and comes up with an inaccurate or irrelevant answer. The details of the hypothetical crisis, as well as its specific outcome, have in some cases not been made public because of the possibility that such an exercise might be misconstrued as actual contingency planning.

[9] We have recently commissioned a systems analysis of the games during and after play with a view to more systematic study of the action flow.

It *is* possible to suggest the types of policy inferences one can derive from this species of game. Seven examples from analyses made of the POLEX-DAIS and Project Michelson series are illustrative:[10]

In general it appeared that an international military force (IMF) can be helpful to both U.S. and general peace-keeping interests in the present world; in Stage I of General and Complete Disarmament (GCD) an IMF appears somewhat more indispensable if the action is a considerable distance from the U.S. power base. The games' investigation of altered U.S. strategic "reach" in a disarming world indicated that, while U.S. naval and sea power can still be projected with relative ease through Stage I, in Stage II it pinches. In the Stage III game U.S. residual power appeared adequate to deal with a single hemispheric crisis but U.S. relations with "client" states elsewhere would certainly have to alter radically, and international military and political action substitute therefore. On balance, Stage II looked more attractive than Stage III in terms of a responsible U.S. capacity to act even marginally. U.S. disarmament planning might well consider whether an appropriate plateau for the GCD process can be found somewhere in Stage II, and how to structure the GCD process so that terminal points can be established in equilibrium without endangering the entire process.

The games demonstrated that if international forces are going to be used for such politically delicate operations as racial war in Central and Southern Africa one quickly runs out of neutral countries or forces of the right national complexion (which may argue for considering the desirability of an internationally recruited police unit). The African game (like the real-life Congo) emphasized the Secretary General's problems of internal authority, specifically his ability to discipline units which become ideologically committed to one side or the other in a civil-war situation. It also suggested to some the desirability of looking again at a regionalization of peace-keeping arrangements in order to avoid some of the complications of policy escalation, as it were, in a highly complex internal situation.

In the games there was less concern for escalation than today. The Soviet teams in the advanced stages of disarmament reported that they felt less constrained, thanks to the absence of American forces in Europe and the general diminution of strategic power. But the several U.S. teams estimated that they were not particularly disadvantaged by a disarmament agreement as they examined their strategic options; their view suggested that a new equilibrium had been established in the world by GCD, embodying a system

[10] The analyses in question were prepared by Professor Bloomfield. The conclusions drawn are entirely his own and not necessarily those of the sponsoring agencies.

which was possibly less dangerous than that of the past.

In the crisis the need to communicate to and from the Polaris system was greater than the need to protect the strategic capability by maintaining complete radio silence. The reason for this may well be the existence of other strategic weapons, particularly the Minuteman missiles in hardened sites, which made the element of compromise somewhat less absolute.

The game brought out rather vividly some of the radical options that might be pressed upon Soviet policy by factions in the Soviet leadership in circumstances of great strain and external pressure. In the simulated Soviet leadership group three distinct positions took shape as the hypothetical world situation deteriorated. The hardest line was taken by a military faction which urged a disarming strike against the IRBM's and other military targets in Western Europe. The second faction felt that Eastern Europe was a lost cause and that the Stalinist position was the only solution, and urged that Soviet losses be cut and Mao re-embraced with concentration thenceforth on the underdeveloped world. The third group, which prevailed by a thin majority, embodied the standard Khrushchevian mixture of pressure and conciliation.

Some were struck with possibilities they had not considered before of the existence of more possible political "fire-breaks" and restraints on strategic weapons deployment than appear on the surface (for example, keeping airplanes over national airspace rather than letting them proceed to a fail-safe line).

By the end of the game the Soviet team had come privately to see the MLF as a lesser evil with which it could live in preference to a European nuclear force, as the various alternatives to MLF began to become more visible. One curious feature was the rather natural way in which the European teams moved toward renewed interest in disengagement of allied and Soviet forces in Central Europe as they appraised the positions in which they found themselves prior to the North Atlantic Treaty.

The Educative Uses of the Policy-Type Exercise

So far this discussion has concentrated on the professional use of the game technique for policy research. But the teaching and training possibilities of this method may actually outweigh its obviously moot predictive values.

One highly promising use of gaming is to teach students of international relations and foreign policy more about the process of making and executing foreign policy than they can learn from books or lectures. At its best, it brings sharply into focus the more formal learning material. Colleges and universities such as M.I.T., Northwestern, Columbia, West Point, the Air Force Academy and others have in recent years used political games in both undergraduate and graduate courses with considerable success.

Another use of potential value is to help train military and diplomatic officers at mid-career and senior levels by having them act out the stresses and strains typical of real-life crisis diplomacy, the decisions made under pressure of time and events, the unexpected overturn of established plans, and the necessity for evaluating a multitude of factors and of having available alternative courses of action. Gaming is intended to highlight the complex of factors, subtle and otherwise, that weigh in on the policymaker but which are not always apparent in the neat strategic plan, the routine policy paper or the self-assured theory. It is hard to think of a better short-run device for the military officer who with increasing rank will face growing involvement in diplomatic situations, an involvement for which his academy training, his years with the troops or the fleet, his correspondence courses and his professional readings have inadequately prepared him. In an attempt to fill this serious gap some U.S. military colleges, through which pass those officers eligible for high command, have begun to look at gaming with a primarily political emphasis as a way of making better use of limited training time. The diplomatic trainee can also benefit from practice runs, so to speak, through a variety of crises involving global, regional or individual country situations for which he might one day have policy responsibility.

The senior policy-type game, not primarily designed as a training device, has nevertheless proven itself an important educational technique. Indeed, this, rather than anything else, may be its principal enduring payoff. For, wholly apart from the policy lessons, questionnaires returned by participants have revealed that responsible officials and, to a slightly lesser extent, scholars, place a uniformly high value on the special benefits the games provide, particularly in sharpening their perceptions of alternatives that could arise in crisis situations. The responses of military officers were, interestingly, the most explicit in this respect. Officers from all services have commented on the unique usefulness of this device in training senior officers in the sophistication of modern crisis diplomacy, with its richness of non-military as well as military factors.

Leading specialists on Soviet policy have come out of an M.I.T. game with strikingly fresh ideas about their specialty, including such things as a more acute awareness of the detailed constraints imposed on Soviet policymaking by the communist alliance system, and the conditions under which a Sino-Soviet *rapprochement* might surprisingly take place. Senior U.S. policymakers who have taken part in simulation exercises have been struck by the extraordinary difficulty encountered in communicating serious intentions to one's opponents in a fully convincing way. This difficulty arose under laboratory conditions, but it mirrored some comparable problems of real-life diplomacy.

In sum, the only sure value of the political-military exercise may be the not inconsiderable one of providing not only students but also policymakers and scholars with one or more crucial lessons not learned before, indelibly recorded in an important personal experience.[11]

Some Problems for Future Research in Gaming

A number of problems for further research on the application of gaming to foreign policy problems have been flagged in the above discussion of past experiences; others are equally worthy of study. The 1963–64 series of simulations sought to combine the substantive focus on problems of deterrence with the equally compelling research objective of making more explicit and systematic some of the theoretical aspects of the gaming technique.

For example, nearly all participants in past games have remarked on the highly realistic nature of the exercises, yet the games, as noted earlier, represent a considerable abstraction from reality. Further work is required to identify specifically the reasons for this sense of realism. Experimentation has shown that it does not in fact depend on such superficial atmospherics as appropriate national symbols, i.e., flags or pictures of Lenin for the

[11] Mr. Whaley is currently engaged in a follow-up project, sponsored by Project Michelson, seeking to develop more systematic data concerning the impact of these games on the growing number of responsible officials who have taken part in the M.I.T. exercises.

Soviet teams. Rewarding games can be played in bare rooms containing only the essential reference and writing materials.

To what degree does a realistic simulation depend on the participants' personal involvement in their assigned roles, their conscientious professional interest in the subject matter of the game, or their enjoyment of a game for its own sake? These three modes of involvement should be investigated to determine whether they lead to decisions which occur in games but not in actual political-military crises. The man who cannot become thoroughly absorbed by the assigned role may easily produce responses inappropriate to that role; the man who remains uninvolved in the subject matter may lack incentive to consider the full range of alternatives; and the man who plays only the game itself may be tempted to accept higher risks than he would if the situation were real.

In this general connection one might experiment with the extent of role involvement by drawing out and reintroducing the "control rods," as it were, to keep the role-playing effect alive while still permitting the participants to discuss out of role as appropriate. It should be remembered that, unlike student games in which role-playing may produce the desired pedagogic result, role-playing in professional games is strictly a means to an end, not an end in itself. For example, the game might be stopped after each move and the decisions analyzed before going on— although experience suggests that the "chain reaction" might stop abruptly and even permanently if this were done. Alternatively, play might end when one side had identified all the alternatives open to it at a given choice-point, without waiting to see how it came out. Or it might be decided to stop and replay a crucial move with different strategies.

One unresearched phenomenon apparently common to virtually all games has been the high degree of consensus among team members that *their* team had won or had come out ahead of their adversary. A tendency to euphoria permeates teams as they begin to play out their initial strategy, remains despite setbacks, and even persists into the post-game plenary critique sessions when the teams assess the outcome.

This unanticipated situation is as striking as it is consistent. Although each game in our series realistically yields a non-zero-sum outcome, it was almost as if some participants perceived themselves in zero-sum situations—even though their own generally-held concept of international relations is that one side's gain is not necessarily another's loss, or, put differently, that both may win or both may lose. Although this point also should be a commonly recognized inference from non-zero-sum game theory, it does not appear to be uniformly applied in the literature on international relations, arms control or deterrence strategy.

Another area of research interest relates to the causes for the misperception of messages received by the teams in games observed to date. First and probably most important, the teams—particularly the U.S. and Soviet—have sometimes tended to assess prematurely the other's initial messages concerning its goals, strategies and contingency plans, and then have adhered to this false reading despite further inputs of contradictory signals from other teams and Control. This may result from human tendencies to optimism, to denial of the unpleasant and, in a more precise operational sense, to blocking out relevant information in a mounting crisis situation. This particular type of misperception is closely related to the faulty assessments of wins and losses discussed above, and closely simulates some real-life situations.

Misperception of communications may also be attributed to the artificial aspects of the game. For example, the compressed time period of the crises and the small size of the teams seem to reduce below realistic levels the volume of relevant information and staff evaluations that reach the top policymaking echelon within the teams.

A third source of misperception of messages arises from administrative errors. These resulted either from faulty messages that were constructed in haste or from the failure of Control to be responsive to all requests or needs on the part of the teams for follow-on intelligence. Fortunately, these types of misdirection seem to have produced only insignificant alterations in the course of the games played so far.

Another promising area for research involves the possible effects on game outcomes of varying the quality and experience of the persons selected to play. For example, it might prove fruitful to use non-Americans on teams to avoid the possibly significant predispositions of culture-bound Americans. As suggested earlier, one of the most interesting future topics for experimentation, if protocol and other inhibiting obstacles could be overcome, would be the interchange of roles—e.g., Russians on a U.S. team playing opposite Americans on a Soviet team—to explore the efficacy of this technique for teaching mutual perceptions of the constraints that operate on one's adversary. We conducted some experiments with the replication of the same games using different levels and types of personnel. One of our tentative findings shows an amazing uniformity of "U.S." responses to dangerous situations, reassuring us of characteristic American sobriety and devotion to peace, but raising again some old questions about our national capacity for orchestrated national strategies, long-range planning and ability quickly to exploit tactical opportunities.

Conclusion

The art of the political exercise is in its infancy, but it has a modestly promising future. While it is not a magic shortcut to knowledge of the future, neither is it purely social science fiction. It can be very expensive in time, manpower and money to organize on any substantial scale; but it can also be done for virtually nothing, requiring only willing—and able—participants. In a time when nations and individuals are communicating more but understanding the messages less, it can be only helpful to get a glimpse of ourselves as others see us, or of others as they may see themselves.

It is clear from recent games, as well as seminar experiments, that the gaming technique can be applied with special benefit to the field of disarmament and arms control for the simple reason that agreements about limiting armaments, if they take place, will occur in an environment that by definition differs from the one we now live in. The game technique is a particularly good way to move people from the present to a different political or arms environment, setting a hypothetical situation and requiring them to act in ways consistent with it. On the other hand, its values are less clear if one's interest is in a rather specific military system and the relevance of that system in a broad-spectrum crisis situation.

It was suggested earlier that possibly the most crucial feature of the enterprise is that it requires the players to live with the implications of their chosen strategy. Contrasted to what happens in a planning operation around a table or in the brain of a single individual, however gifted, the game sets up a process that by its nature produces a dynamic sequence of actions, responses and counteractions. This sequential process, once set in motion, moves ahead under a momentum of its own, often in quite logical and plausible directions not always foreseen. A kind of chain reaction takes place beyond the capacity of a single mind to anticipate. The reason for this takes us back to role-playing itself, for the heart of this process is the interaction of antagonistic wills; the same effect can be produced solo only by a schizophrenic.

In summary, the political-military exercise may be rated as excellent for training, useful for teaching, and potentially valuable—within limits that have been only tentatively probed—for policy research and planning.

54. The Kaiser, The Tsar, and the Computer: Information Processing in a Crisis*

Ithiel de Sola Pool and Allen Kessler were affiliated with the Massachusetts Institute of Technology, the former as Professor of Political Science and the latter as a Ph.D. candidate, when they collaborated on this article. Their account of a simulation based on a use of computers rather than humans affords an interesting insight into the potentialities and limits of research that employs high-speed machines for processing data. Just as in the case of the research described in Selection 51, this article seeks to test a basic model through a simulation of the outbreak of World War I, thus providing an opportunity to contrast directly the behavior of human subjects with the behavior traced by a computer. The result demonstrates that computers can be of considerable value to researchers, enabling them to explore the implications and consequences of a wide range of problems of international politics that might otherwise require thousands of man-hours to complete. At the same time the article clearly illustrates that there is nothing magical about computers, that they are useful as aids to, not as substitutes for, research. The machine carries out only the operations that it is programmed to perform, and it is the researcher who designs the program. [*Reprinted from* The American Behavioral Scientist, *VIII, 9 (May 1965), 31–38, by permission of the authors and the publisher, Sage Publications, Inc.*]

Summary

Crisiscom is a computer simulation of national decision makers processing information during a crisis. The project has several purposes:

1. It is designed to increase our understanding of the process of deterrence by exploring how far the behavior of political decision makers in crisis can be explained by psychological mechanisms. This is done by comparing the output of the highly simplified computer model based on principles of individual psychology with records of actual political behavior.

2. It is designed to put together a good deal of what we know about the psychology of deterrence into a rigorous and formal system and thus to serve as an integrating device for that body of knowledge.

3. It is designed to be used in human games of

* This work was supported by the Naval Research Laboratory under a contract to the Simulmatics Corporation and by the Advanced Research Projects Agency of the Department of Defense under Contract 920F-9717 with the Center for International Studies, M.I.T. This contract is monitored by the Air Force Office of Scientific Research. We have made use of the computer time sharing system of Project MAC, an M.I.T. research project sponsored by the Advanced Research Project Agency, Department of Defense, under of Office of Naval Research, contract Nonr. –4102(01).

the type represented by Bloomfield's political-military games to provide inputs for teams that cannot be staffed with humans and to represent aspects of the environment that are not played out by the human players.[1]

4. It is designed perhaps ultimately to provide a way of simulating a variety of possible crises. It will be some time before we have enough confidence in the model to use it in such a semi-predictive fashion, but that cannot be ruled out.

In the Crisiscom computer model two human decision makers are represented (the number is easily expansible). Each of them receives a large number of messages which enter into his cognitive system.

The elements of the cognitive system of each simulated decision maker are messages that represent interpersonal relationships among international actors. For example, "President Johnson" (an actor, A_1) "visits with" (a relation, R_x) "the Prime Minister of Great Britain" (an actor, A_2). The set of relations, R, is at present limited to two — affect and salience. Affect refers to the attitude or feelings which an actor, A_i, has toward another actor, A_j, or toward an interpersonal relationship. Salience describes the importance of an actor or interpersonal relationship for another actor. The cognitive system A_n (the world he knows) is thus comprised of elements A_1, A_2, . . ., A_m, and affects or saliences which relate them *as perceived by* A_n.

A_n came to perceive these relationships as a result of receiving messages about the actors and their interpersonal relationships. However, the total information conveyed in these messages is too great for any one human to handle. Not all the information is absorbed by A_n. Psychological mechanisms restrict his input and distort it. As a result each decision maker has an incomplete and imperfect picture of the relationships among all actors. As the simulation has been run recently, both actors have been fed the same set of messages about the world but by the end of a week's crisis they have quite different perceptions.

In the present program the cognitive systems of only two of twenty four actors are completely represented, namely the cognitive systems of

decision makers J and K. J and K receive information about themselves and about the other actors in the form of messages written by a scenario writer. Each message has the format A_n, R_a, A_m. For example: The King of Ethiopia confers with President Nasser of Egypt. These messages are written in natural English and as long as the sentence order is A_n, R_a, A_m, the computer accepts them.

The scenario consists of a large number of messages of the kind just described about interpersonal relationships among the actors. The decision maker does not pay attention to all messages. In accordance with well-established psychological principles, he "selectively attends" to a subset of them. He pays attention to some, ignores others.

These incoming messages that are selected not only enter into the decision maker's attention space; they also change his basic image of the world with which he started the simulation. This basic image is represented by an affect matrix which tells how each actor feels about each other actor. New messages alter slightly this continuing perception of the relationships in the world.

In our present simulation the following hypotheses about selective perception operate on the messages in the scenario:

1. People pay more attention to news that deals with them.
2. People pay less attention to facts that contradict their previous views.
3. People pay more attention to news from trusted, liked sources.
4. People pay more attention to facts that they will have to act upon or discuss because of attention by others.
5. People pay more attention to facts bearing on actions they are already involved in, i.e., action creates commitment.

In its present stage the model is thus a rather simple representation of a number of the major mechanisms that come into play in crisis, but clearly not of all of them. In the future a number of additional mechanisms of decision making will be grafted onto the model. The model is modular permitting continued growth and refinement.

We have been utilizing historical crisis events to test our simulation, even in its present simple form. We have written a scenario of messages representing

[1] L. P. Bloomfield and B. Whaley, "The Political Military Exercise: A Progress Report," *Orbis*, Vol. VIII (1965), pp. 854–70.

the week of the outbreak of World War I. This week was chosen because it is extensively written up by historians and has also been replicated by gaming procedures. Thus comparison is possible between what seemed important to national decision makers as described by historians, as played by game players, and as put out by the simulation.

The scenario messages were written by going through historical documents about the week, but most of all from the newspapers of that week. The two key decision makers we have represented are the Kaiser and the Tsar. Appended to this report are a sample of the list of messages they received, a sample of the list of messages that went into the attention space of each one on each day, and part of the final affect matrix (representing their basic picture of the world).

The results are intuitively very satisfactory. The Kaiser and Tsar behave as we think they would. Each pays attention to those events that affect him particularly. They each miss some key cues that if they had been mutually perceived might have prevented war. Instead each sees the overt military acts of the other unmitigated by his moderating intents, while remaining conscious of his own moderate intentions that he must have (wrongly) assumed equally obvious to the other.

Readers not interested in the computer processes can turn to the next to the last section headed, A Test of the Crisiscom Model Against A Real World Crisis. It deals with the World War I experiment.

Purpose of the Project

Crisiscom is a computer simulation of the behavior of national decision makers in international crisis. More specifically it is designed to represent the ways in which psychological mechanisms enter into their processing of the information they receive. It is designed to simulate the process whereby two different decision makers acquire in their own minds quite different pictures of the world in which they are interacting. A flow of messages representing the real world comes to the decision makers. They selectively attend to different messages in this flow leaving each decision maker with a quite different image of the world from that of the other. This in a nutshell is the process simulated by the Crisiscom program.

There were several reasons for developing such a simulation. First among them is the desire to explore how far a limited set of psychological relations can take us in understanding the behavior of national decision makers in a crisis. We are attempting by the simulation to push to the limits the hypothesis that the basic principles of individual psychology which describe how individuals behave in personal crises also account for the behavior of national decision makers in a world political crisis. We do this not because we believe this proposition to be true. On the contrary, it is perfectly clear that individual psychology accounts for only a small part of international politics. However, the best way to ascertain what part, if any, individual psychology plays in the determination of political behavior is to postulate the truth of the extreme proposition and then see what conclusions it leads us to. We can then compare those conclusions with reality. We are, in short, engaged in a kind of experiment—the kind sometimes called a Gedanken experiment—in which we press an idea to see where it breaks down.

Our procedure corresponds to the ideas of the philosopher Hans Vaihinger in his book *The Philosophy of As If*.[2] We model a hypothetical world based on certain propositions to ascertain just what the consequences of these propositions would be; we look at the world *as if* they were true.

Various devices have been developed to explore hypothetical futures of which computer simulation is only one. Gaming is at present an increasingly popular and effective tool for answering that what if question. It is effective because it forces each player to specialize on thinking about a particular set of roles and particular aspects of the situation. The same player trying to write an essay predicting how things would be in some specified hypothetical future would miss many of the eventualities which other players force onto his attention as they play out their own required roles.

Human gaming, however, has certain limitations as well as some enormous advantages. One of its limitations is that it is expensive and time consuming. For the results to be useful the players should be experts on the roles they are representing. There are limits to the numbers of experts one can collect and

[2] H. Vaihinger (tran. C. L. Ogden) *The Philosophy of As If* (New York: Barnes & Noble, 1952).

to the periods of time for which one can commandeer them. Furthermore, in the time available it is usually possible to play out only one alternative out of the many branches that history could follow depending on eventualities.

Computer simulation gets around both these disadvantages of human gaming though at its own price. The computer runs fast and can run the same game over many times with minor variations. However, in all candor, it is necessary to recognize that no computer program ever written contains as much expertise as is stored in the heads of a group of specialists.

Thus an intelligent approach to the problem of exploring strategic futures is to use both human gaming and computer simulation and also combinations of them. Computer simulation should be developed to assess how far it can approximate the results achieved in human games. It should be used to play out many variants of situations that one can game with experts only once. Finally, the two procedures can be linked. A computer can be used to produce the results of minor teams or of nature or other factors for which players themselves cannot be provided.

With these considerations in mind, we can now summarize the purposes that the Crisiscom project has set out to achieve. It set out to explore how realistic a simulation could be produced with a relatively constricted and simple model arising entirely from the propositions of social psychology about human behavior in crisis. Secondly, it set out to produce a program that would provide messages that could be used in mixed human-machine games. Thirdly, in the process of achieving these objectives it served to advance our understanding of the psychological system known as deterrence by working out the interactions of various propositions about behavior in a crisis. Finally perhaps it advanced us a few steps toward the point where such computer simulations might have some predictive value.

The Model

We now proceed to describe the Crisiscom model by three successive elaborations, each covering the same ground, but each more fully and accurately than the last.

The Crisiscom Model in Sketchy Form

The Crisiscom simulation represents the interaction of national commanders in a crisis in which they confront each other.

(a) Each receives information about the world.
(b) Each handles this information in ways which are determined by his own background and by the principles of psychology.
(c) Each then reacts by originating new messages.

This happens each time period, so the model cycles through those three steps over and over. The messages put out by the commanders become part of the input of messages at the next period.

A skeleton basic flow chart is presented in Figure 1. The two commanders are designated $DM(J)$ = decision-maker J, and $DM(K)$ = decision-maker K. In the present version of the model this is a man-machine simulation rather than a pure machine simulation. The decision making portion of the model is done by human simulation, the bias and distortion portion by the computer.

We now describe the model in greater detail.

The Crisiscom Model Somewhat Elaborated

In the real world decision-makers receive information about their world from various sources and through various media. In most cases the volume of information they receive is too large for them to attend to, so they use a variety of techniques of selective attention, forgetting and distortion, in order to limit this information to proportions they can handle.

Let us consider the selective attention and distortion processes. Two decision-makers, J (let's say for Mr. Johnson) and K (let's say for Mr. Kosygin) receive messages from a human scenario writer as to the events and relationships occurring among 24 countries or country blocks. For example, associated with the recent Guantanamo affair, messages of the following nature would come to J and K.

Guantanamo affair. U.S.A. arrests Cuba's fishermen. Each message is a statement related to some event having two actors and a relationship between them. Another message related to Guantanamo would be: *Cuba cuts water supply to U.S.A. military base.*

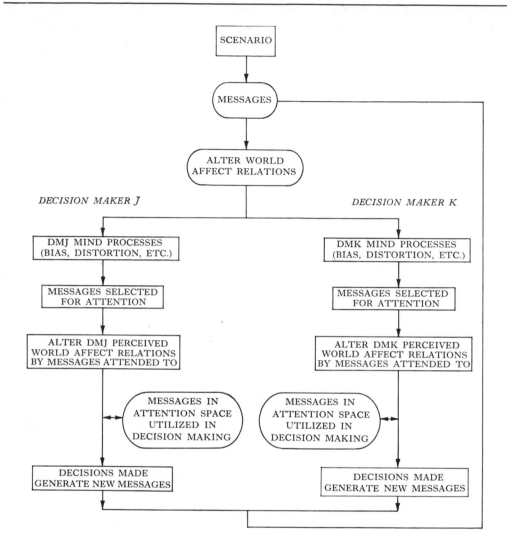

Figure 1. Crisiscom general flow chart

The importance of the message to each decision maker, their feelings about the reliability of the source of the message, their attitudes toward the particular countries' relationship, and the importance of the relationship to the countries involved all are important in determining the probable nature and extent of distortion of the message.

Underlying the distortion processes is the decision-maker's perception of the world, his perception of the attitudes and feelings—or affect—existing between each pair of countries. For example, J may perceive that the Soviet Union has negative feelings toward Communist China while France has a more positive affect toward Communist China. A decision-maker's perceptions tend to remain stable and change significantly only when new information about countries' relationships is greatly at variance with his present perception. Similarly, a decision maker will pay less attention to messages that differ from his present perception of the relationship between the countries involved. However, relationships *that do come to his attention*, and that differ from his present perception, will alter that perception. Emphasis has been placed on "relationships that do come to his attention" because, on a given day, the decision-maker cannot attend to all messages. Some must be put aside as pressing problems, some are ignored and some forgotten. The most important events are attended to, that is, they are placed in the decision-maker's attention space. On some days, a decision-maker who is concerned with very important events may put aside events that would have come into attention space if they occurred on another day. What the decision-maker attends to is a function of the importance of the messages in his present attention space. This importance, or salience, is itself altered by the distortion processes. Thus, what J attends to may differ from what K attends to. In turn, the information to which K and J attend differentially alters their perception of the world. Once events have been attended to they are placed in the decision-maker's memory where they are subject to forgetting. This classification and ordering of messages and events is illustrated in detail in Figure 2.

At present, decisions based on the information in J's and K's attention spaces are made by humans who receive this information at the end of a decision day. Later, this output will be the input to simulated decision processes which will generate messages to be placed in the environment.

The Crisiscom Model More Fully Elaborated

Figure 2 is a flow chart of the computerized portion of the simulation for a single time period.

Crisiscom Input

Messages from a scenario writer are the input for Crisiscom. Every message is a combination of two countries and a relationship between them [CONE(REL)CTWO].

Messages are associated with a unique event. At present the scenario writer must specify the following values for each message.

AFFT — The affect (-1 to $+1$) of the (REL) between CONE and CTWO

SLCONE — The salience (0 to $+1$) or (REL) for CONE

SLCTWO — The salience (0 to $+1$) of (REL) for CTWO

SALJ — The salience (0 to $+1$) of the message for DM(K)'s Public Opinion

SALK — The salience (0 to $+1$) of the message for DM(J)'s Public Opinion

SALPOJ — The salience (0 to $+1$) of the message for DM(J)

SALPOK — The salience (0 to $+1$) of the message for DM(K)

ASOURJ — J's affect (-1 to $+1$) toward the message source

ASOURK — K's affect (-1 to $+1$) toward the message source

Examples of messages can be found in the Appendix.

Every message received by a decision-maker is distorted according to the following saliency bias routines.

1. *People pay more attention to information that deals with them.* When the actor, or ego, is one of the elements in the structural configuration under evaluation, salience is weighted more heavily.

2. *People pay less attention to facts that contradict their views.* This hypothesis interacts with both semantic and affect relations. A message can be found to be completely incredible, or in some degree semantically explicable but having an affect relations which is unbalanced. Rather than attempt to balance the relations, the actor may avoid or ignore the message.

3. *People pay more attention to information from trusted, liked sources.* Whenever the source of a message is identified in the scenario it is included in the structural configuration under evaluation. In addition to testing the credibility of the source generating such a message, the actor's affect toward the source alters the salience of the message—positive affect increases salience.

4. *People pay more attention to information that they will have to act on or discuss because of attention by others.* Ego considers in his evaluation not only the actors in the message, but also other actors whom he thinks show interest in the relationship. He even considers the attitudes of actors who might attend to the information because of their relations to ego or to the actors in the message. As an example, the low salience of the uprising in Zanzibar for the President may have become increased because Communist decision makers might have and then did demonstrate their attention to the event.

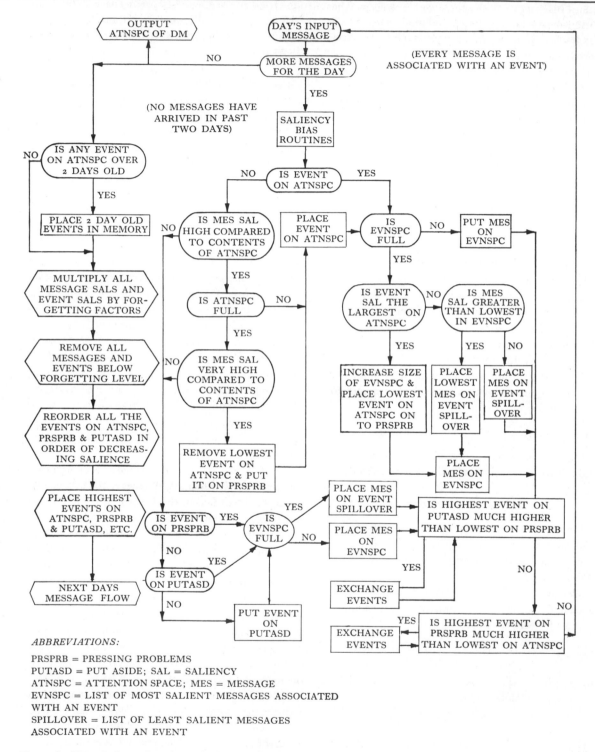

Figure 2. Message input flow for a decision maker on a decision day (third approximation)

5. *People pay more attention to information bearing on actions they have already taken, i.e., action creates commitment.* When information is being fed back to the actor about information he has previously generated, he evaluates this information higher. The consequences of his actions which he learns through messages from others may involve him to a greater degree.

Decision makers are concerned with events that occur in their world. George Miller has hypothesized that a person can attend to 7 ± 2 things at a time.[3] Decision makers can attend to 7 ± 2 events, i.e., his attention space has 7 ± 2 events in it. Associated with each event the decision maker can attend to 7 ± 2 messages. An event space has these 7 ± 2 messages in it. Other associated messages are placed on the event spillover. The selection of input events and messages for attention is a function of the number and importance of the events and messages presently in the decision-maker's attention space. In the long run the decision maker will attempt to attend to the messages and events he perceives as most salient to him. However, in the short run this may not be feasible as there is a certain amount of inertia which tends to give precedence to the events the decision maker is presently attending to over the new events that arrive.

The decision maker keeps his attention space and event spaces as full as possible, and continually seeks information to keep them full. He may attend to few very important events, many unimportant events, or some number in between these extremes depending on the salience of the messages he is receiving as he perceives them. If an event is very important to him, he will seek as many messages as he can attend to. If an event is unimportant to him, he will not attend to a large number of messages. Unimportant events have up to 5 messages in their event spaces. The decision maker will attend up to 5 very important events. Normally an important event may hold up to 9 messages. However, very important events may hold many more messages at the expense of attending to fewer events. It is possible for the decision maker to attend to only one extremely important event having a large

number of messages in its event space. Therefore a continuum of few events with many messages to many events (9) with few messages is specified for the selection of information for the attention space.

Events not attended to immediately are placed aside as pressing problems or put aside according to their importance.

When a very important message compared to the contents of attention space arrives, and its event is not in attention space, the event associated with this message may displace an event in attention space.

At the end of the day the attention space of each decision maker is made available to the programmer.

To bypass the decision processes, any event which has its most recent message over two days old is placed in memory. The salience of an event is exponentially reduced over time until it is below the forgetting level at which time it is deleted.

Each day the mind spaces are reorganized by placing the events and messages in the hierarchy of the mind spaces in order of importance ignoring all inertia factors.

A Consideration of the Psychological Principles

The decision-maker's "mind" represented in the Crisiscom simulation consists of two main parts: one representing the kind of stable backlog of experience that each person carries with him into any new situation; the other representing the flow of new messages and information which the decision maker processes. The first of these is represented by the affect matrix (and in principle in later versions of the model in the matrices representing other relationships besides affect). The affect matrix is part of the initial condition of the simulation at t_0. It states how the decision maker perceives each actor (in the present runs actors are countries) in relation to each other actor. Not all cells in the affect matrix need be filled out. In some instances the decision maker may have no idea how two actors feel about each other. The matrix is not symmetric. Actor One may have an affect of $-.3$ toward Actor Two while Actor Two has an affect of $+.1$ to Actor One. Such sharp differences are, of course, unusual. The affect

[3] G. Miller, "The Magical Number Seven plus or minus Two: Some Limits on Our Capacity for Processing Information," *Psychological Review*, Vol. 63 (1963), pp. 81–97.

matrix summarizes the way in which each decision maker views the world. It thus provides the base line against which he tests incoming messages.

The other part of the decision-maker's mind is a hierarchical set of list structures, the items on the lists being messages. This hierarchy is composed of: (1) an attention space, (2) a pressing problems list, (3) a put-aside list, and (4) memory. The put-aside list acts as a buffer for the memory. Onto it go the messages that are hardly considered. The pressing problems list is used for important messages that could not be considered on the day of their arrival, important things that have to be put off until tomorrow. At the beginning of the day some pressing problems may go immediately into the attention space for those things being considered on the given day.

In memory are stored all messages that have been considered and have managed to avoid being deleted by the forgetting deletion operations.

It is in this framework that the selective process of retention takes place and in which the affect matrix gets modified by the flow of new information.

This model conforms rather closely to what we know about the actual characteristics of human information handling. It has to be a rather complex model to do so. Powerful as the pleasure principle may be in guiding human behavior, the algorithm people use in conforming to it is a complex one.

The simple algorithm, that people pay attention to what they like to hear and disregard what they do not like to hear, does not work. There are contradictory experimental results as to whether people are more likely to see good news or bad news. Sometimes it is one; sometimes it is the other. So this is *not* one of the determinants of bias in our model. The process is a more purposeful one. The determinant seems to be an unconscious pleasure maximizing calculation that takes into account the consequences of inattention. An unpleasant story that has no action consequences for the hearer may be disregarded because that way pain is minimized. But a "danger, live wire" sign will get high attention because, by taking note of that unpleasant fact, the pain can be minimized. Experiments show that most people do not read newspaper stories that contradict their political views, but debaters read carefully statements that disagree with their stand because they thereby

increase the probability of a pleasant outcome, winning the debate.

Our model handles information in ways that conform to this complexity of human rationality. It does pay less attention to facts that contradict prior views, but more attention to action relevant facts.

A Test of the Crisiscom Model Against a Real World Crisis

We have run the seven days from 25 July through 31 July, 1914, through the Crisiscom simulation. A seven-day crisis will do very little to the basic image of the world that a decision maker holds. The affect matrix which represents that image of the world should remain quite stable. When the events are as world shaking as those of 1914 there may indeed be deeper effects drastically changing his views in the future, i.e., a sleeper effect. That could be the case even if nothing else happened, but it takes time for such attitude changes to occur. Nonetheless in a crisis of any intensity some perceptible shift in the image of who is good and who is bad and who loves whom should be visible, even if not large. That is what happens if one compares the affect matrices from beginning to end of the week.

The place where big changes may be expected in a short period is in what the decision maker is attending to.

Both the changes in attention and the changes in the affect matrices are recorded in the computer output describing our major test of the Crisiscom simulation so far. That test is a replication of the minds of the Kaiser and the Tsar in the seven days of the outbreak of World War I. We picked that crisis because it has been widely used in other kinds of gaming and other kinds of research. It has been the subject of a Project Michelson study by Professor Robert North of Stanford University[4] and of human gaming using the device of Harold Guetzkow's internation simulation.[5] At the end of this article the reader will find a sample of the messages that were fed into and the calculations performed by the computer. There are approximately 1400 of them,

[4] R. North, *et al.*, *Content Analysis: A Handbook with Application for the Study of International Crisis* (Evanston, Ill.: Northwestern University Press, 1963).

[5] H. Guetzkow, *et al.*, *Simulation in International Relations: Developments for Research and Teaching* (Englewood Cliffs, N.J.: Prentice-Hall, 1963).

200 per each day of the crisis. To the reader of ordinary history books what is fascinating is the amount of chaff in the communications channel which the historians forget. We collected our messages from the daily newspapers of that time plus the North collection of documents which includes later revelations that at that time were secret to the public. (About one per cent of the message input was secret.) These were the messages that might normally have come to the attention of the decision maker as he lived and worked in that particular week. They included vast numbers of casual events in the sporting world, in the business world, progress in the development of airplanes, crime, etc. A volcano erupted in the U.S.A.; the English bought a Rembrandt; suffragettes pawned their jewels for funds; there were riots in Russia; strikes in the U.S.A.; a mutiny in Mexico; etc. The historian filters out these irrelevancies before he reports to the reader on the subject of his essay. But in the real decision process competition for attention is an important fact. It is handled in our computer simulation. With its speed and large memory a computer can do what an essay writer cannot, i.e., it can analyze the interaction between the crisis that interests us and the rest of what was going on. This is a unique advantage the full significance of which we did not realize until we actually became involved in this sample simulation.

But needless to say as war is breaking out the Tsar and the Kaiser did not give much of their energies to the trial run through the Panama Canal or terrorism in Ireland. They selected a few events to which they gave attention. The attention space, it will be recalled, contains material on 7 ± 2 events with each having the capability of having 7 ± 2 messages considered. However, it will also be recalled that terribly important events reduce the number of things to which attention is paid (a psychological proposition that is well confirmed). That is what happened in the period with which we are concerned. It was normally the case that less than 49 messages were in the heart of the attention space.

The computer also has stored other messages on a pressing problems list, a set-aside list and memory. We save the reader the tedium of reproducing this vast mass of data.

It is clear that the computer has selected for the attention space a reasonable set of the most important messages. The reader should recognize that this is partly but not wholly a reflection of the initial coding of saliency. That coding is subsequently modified by reactions to the salience of the message to the other side; by its salience to public opinion; and by the passage of time. The reasonableness of the output is therefore by no means guaranteed. In our simulation we sent each decision maker J and K almost the same set of messages. This need not have been done but we chose to do it that way for experimental purposes.

The way in which the psychological processes in our model work may be well illustrated by looking at the difference in the messages accorded attention in the course of Day one. Both the Tsar and the Kaiser gave more attention to Austria's ultimatum to Serbia. The fact of the ultimatum was the primary message for both men. For the Kaiser, however, almost as important was the fact that Germany's mobs rallied for war. For the Kaiser, Serbian reaction was the *third* ranking message closely followed by Germany's fears that Austria's ultimatum was too harsh. The Tsar ranked the messages in a somewhat different order. Behind the bald fact of the ultimatum, the *second* most significant fact for him was the reaction to the ultimatum in Serbia. That Germany's mobs rallied for war was also important although *third*, but that Germany feared that Austria's ultimatum was too harsh was a much less credible and therefore less salient news event. The fourth most important event was Russia's own reaction.

The event of the Austrian ultimatum to Serbia was one that both men could not dismiss from attention, but much of the rest of what they saw in the world was quite different. The Tsar preoccupied himself with the visit of the French President to Russia and with Russia's alliance with France. He worried about England's possible noncommitment to what later became the Allied cause and requested a show of England's support.

The Kaiser did not concern himself with the Tsar's alliance problems but rather with some of his own. He attempted to localize the Serbian conflict and paid a lot of attention to that. He concerned himself with Belgian neutrality and also with a purely domestic financial matter, ordering banks to hold 10 per cent of their assets.

By the end of the seven days J and K are not

looking at the same world although reality impinges itself on each. Three events, Russia's mobilization, Germany's mobilization and the secret treaties, are in the attention space of both men. But two events, the collapse of Europe's stock markets and Germany's military precautions, are also in the attention of the Kaiser, while two other events, Serbia's Balkan allies and the Russian press, are in the attention of the Tsar.

Even when the same event is in both men's mind, the picture of it differs. Let us look at Russia's mobilization. The Kaiser is primarily concerned with the facts: "Russia orders complete mobilization," "Russia's Tsar declares war is inevitable," "Russia calls up reserve troops," "Russia's troops are near Germany's border." The Tsar, on the other hand, who has administrative responsibility for the mobilization is, in addition, concerned with various political aspects of it. Most notably included in his list is the message "England confers with Russia on mobilization measures." Also included is that "France advises Russians to speed up military preparations" and that he as "Tsar orders general mobilization." (The last is a different message from the fact that Russia as a country had ordered complete mobilization. It identifies the Tsar's personal role.) The relation to France is particularly interesting. The Kaiser reflecting wishful thinking pays attention to the message that "France asks Russia to cut down mobilization." He neglects the message which the Tsar retains that "France asks Russia to speed up preparations." Here is the kind of reversed perceptions that causes the breakdown of international discourse.

The differences in the material in attention space devoted to German mobilization is in some respects a mirror image of that just noted for the Russians. Here we find the Russians paying attention merely to the bald fact "Germany mobilizes." (Note that this is repeated as three different messages. The program permits this for messages of truly extraordinary importance; they thus fill much of the attention space.) The Kaiser, on the other hand, also pays attention to such administrative aspects as "Germany's war chiefs confer on mobilization" and "Germany's officers press for mobilization." The Kaiser also thinks about his justification that Germany has threatened to mobilize if Russia continues arming. Here again we find the expectable psychological aspects of the situation well represented in the

simulation. The Tsar gives no thought to the process which justifies German mobilization in the mind of the Kaiser, only to the fact.

Further Development of the Crisiscom Simulation

The Crisiscom simulation is now a working model. It has been used on the gaming of one crisis and can be used on others, but it is not at the end of development. We would like to see it further developed, further tested, and further used.

The development of a model of this sort is partly an open-ended matter. More and more aspects of reality can be built into it. Right now we have a very small model representing a limited range of the psychological mechanisms that are relevant to crisis. Specifically, we represent the processes of selective attention and very little more.

There are a number of obvious next steps. One of them is to introduce distortion processes. Right now a message that is received can be rejected or accepted. It cannot be changed by the receiver. We know that receivers do distort messages. We wish to introduce balancing processes whereby, though the message sent to J and K might be the same, the message that appeared in attention space could be different.

Another important direction of development is to introduce more relations than just affect. Some specific relations of military and naval reference would be useful, i.e., mobilizing forces. A relatively small dictionary of relational terms would give the model greatly enhanced flexibility and perhaps some predictive power.

Another important development permits J and K themselves to generate messages as well as receiving them. In the process of generating messages they would be programmed to reflect the character of their countries and perspectives. These messages would then become part of the message flow, making Crisiscom a truly dynamic model whose ultimate play of a game would be hard to predict *a priori*.

Finally, we plan to replace much of the initial coding of saliency now done by a human with computer operations based on Robert Abelson's Hot Cognition model.[6]

[6] R. Abelson, "Computer Simulation of Hot Cognition," in S. Tomkins and S. Messick (eds.), *Computer Simulation of Personality* (New York: Wiley, 1963), p. 282.

Appendix

Explanatory Notes

1. In the Affect Matrix (Table 1) the row label is the country which feels a certain way about the country named in the column label.
2. In the listing of messages in Attention Space:

The first number under each message is a current saliency measurement.

The second number under each message is an affective significance measure relating to the subject's treatment of the object.

The third number under each message indicates the day the message first appeared.

Lines without numbers label an event. The messages about that event follow it.

TABLE 1

A Partial Listing of the Initial (I) and Final (F) Affect Matrix Values of the Kaiser and the Tsar[a]

Kaiser

	AUSTRIA		ENGLAND		FRANCE		GERMANY		RUSSIA		SERBIA	
	I	F	I	F	I	F	I	F	I	F	I	F
Austria	0/0		−0.31/−0.330		−0.38/−0.399		0.65/ 0.670		−0.48/−0.480		−0.69/−0.820	
England	−0.21/−0.264		0/0		0.63/ 0.630		0.34/ 0.321		0.36/ 0.363		0.12/ 0.159	
France	−0.47/−0.504		0.66/ 0.657		0/0		−0.38/ 0.380		0.68/ 0.677		0.28/ 0.318	
Germany	0.68/ 0.682		0.38/ 0.395		−0.33/−0.330		0/0		−0.36/−0.295		−0.41/−0.399	
Russia	−0.67/−0.839		0.39/ 0.426		0.69/ 0.690		−0.38/−0.615		0/0		0.63/ 0.720	
Serbia	−0.70/−0.738		0.13/ 0.13		0.31/ 0.310		−0.46/−0.46		0.71/ 0.742		0/0	

Tsar

	AUSTRIA		ENGLAND		FRANCE		GERMANY		RUSSIA		SERBIA	
	I	F	I	F	I	F	I	F	I	F	I	F
Austria	0/0		−0.31/−0.326		−0.38/−0.396		0.65/ 0.65		−0.48/−0.48		−0.69/−0.869	
England	−0.21/−0.257		0/0		0.63/ 0.613		0.34/ 0.352		0.36/ 0.337		0.12/ 0.133	
France	−0.47/−0.491		0.66/ 0.663		0/0		−0.38/−0.38		0.68/ 0.68+[b]		0.28/ 0.307	
Germany	0.68/ 0.671		0.38/ 0.378		−0.33/−0.33		0/0		−0.36/−0.30		−0.41/−0.398	
Russia	−0.67/−0.968		0.39/ 0.466		0.69/ 0.742		−0.38/−0.763		0/0		0.63/ 0.810	
Serbia	−0.70/−0.729		0.13/ 0.13		0.31/ 0.310		−0.46/−0.460		0.71/ 0.754		0/0	

[a] Both decision makers have same initial matrix in this example.
[b] Error in scenario.

```
DATE JULY 25 1914 ..                                              00010
( 1$ )                                                            00020
ENGLAND'S MUSEUM .. ENGLAND OPENS NEW MEMORIAL MUSEUM ..          00030
(  .00  .18  .00  .05  .03  .04  .03  .75  .68  0    )            00040
USA TREATY WITH JAPAN .. USA SENATE DELAYS SIGNING JAPAN  LAND TREATY..  00050
(- .18  .18  .25  .11  .18  .06  .08  .57  .65  0    )            00060
CANADA'S RAILROAD .. CANADA MEETS WITH USA TO DISCUSS RAILROAD LOANS..   00070
(  .31  .35  .21  .09  .08  .07  .06  .71  .48  0    )            00080
USA HYDROPLANE .. USA HYDROPLANE PREPARES FOR TRIAL RUN ..        00090
(  .00  .21  .00  .13  .13  .15  .15  .82  .64  0    )            00100
HAITI'S REVOLUTION .. USA SENDS WARSHIPS TO HAITI ..              00110
(- .41  .48  .52  .28  .20  .23  .18  .76  .72  0    )            00120
AUSTRIA'S ULTIMATUM TO SERBIA .. AUSTRIA SENDS ULTIMATUM TO SERBIA ..    00130
(- .68  .73  .75  .68  .70  .58  .58  .91  .88  0    )            00140
RUSSIA'S ALLIANCE WITH FRANCE ..FRANCE'S MINISTER GOES TO RUSSIA TO      00150
STRENGTHEN ALLIANCE ..                                            00160
(  .57  .53  .68  .49  .68  .24  .39  .59  .81  0    )            00170
CRISIS IN IRELAND .. ENGLAND FEARS CIVIL WAR IN IRELAND ..        00180
(- .48  .67  .63  .23  .22  .20  .19  .48  .36  0    )            00190
PROHIBITION .. USA WITNESSES MORE PROHIBITION DEMONSTRATIONS ..   00200
(  .00  .29  .00  .09  .07  .06  .06  .43  .45  0    )            00210
DEATH OF LORD WEMYSS .. ENGLAND'S LORD WEMYSS DIES ..             00220
(  .00  .37  .00  .12  .10  .08  .08  .81  .89  0    )            00230
AUSTRIA'S ULTIMATUM TO SERBIA .. ENGLAND DENOUNCES SEVERITY OF    00240
AUSTRIA'S ULTIMATUM ..                                            00250
(- .38  .36  .40  .31  .42  .24  .21  .63  .71  0    )            00260
RUSSIA'S ALLIANCE WITH FRANCE .. FRANCE GIVES RUSSIA FULL DIPLOMATIC     00270
SUPPORT ..                                                        00280
(  .63  .51  .61  .41  .61  .28  .45  .61  .90  0    )            00290
PRINCE OF WALES .. ENGLAND'S PRINCE INHERITS FOUR MILLION POUNDS ..      00300
(  .00  .19  .00  .05  .04  .07  .08  .56  .58  0    )            00310
BICYCLE RACES .. ITALY BEATS USA IN BICYCLE RACE ..               00320
(  .08  .11  .08  .04  .03  .06  .07  .41  .31  0    )            00330
USA IMMIGRATION .. USA RAISES QUOTA FOR RUSSIA'S IMMIGRANTS ..    00340
(  .39  .21  .32  .12  .32  .25  .34  .32  .75  0    )            00350
MEXICO'S CIVIL WAR .. PEASANT MOBS STORM MEXICO'S CAPITAL ..      00360
(  .00  .63  .00  .26  .20  .21  .14  .51  -.20  0   )            00370
AUSTRIA'S ULTIMATUM TO SERBIA .. GERMANY DENIES FOREKNOWLEDGE OF  00380
AUSTRIA'S ULTIMATUM ..                                            00390
(- .27  .45  .38  .45  .31  .41  .25  -.73  -.56  0  )            00400
AUSTRIA'S ULTIMATUM TO SERBIA .. RUSSIA ACCUSES AUSTRIA OF PLOTTING      00410
INTERNATIONAL WAR ..                                              00420
(- .51  .46  .48  .38  .46  .40  .32  -.14  .42  0   )            00430
RUSSIA'S ALLIANCE WITH SERBIA .. SERBIA ASKS RUSSIA FOR FULL SUPPORT ..  00440
(  .32  .62  .53  .49  .53  .55  .39  .43  .82  0    )            00450
SERBIA'S REPLY .. AUSTRIA ALLOWS TWO-DAY TIME LIMIT FOR SERBIA'S REPLY ..  00460
.                                                                 00470
(- .29  .44  .51  .42  .48  .28  .31  .73  .75  0    )            00480
AUSTRIA'S ULTIMATUM TO SERBIA .. FRANCE DENOUNCES SEVERITY OF     00490
AUSTRIA'S ULTIMATUM ..                                            00500
(- .42  .39  .41  .40  .43  .32  .38  .55  .51  0    )            00510
MEXICO'S CIVIL WAR .. MEXICO'S LEADERS SIGN ARMISTICE ..          00520
(  .00  .73  .00  .28  .22  .23  .21  -.31  -.42  0  )            00530
HAITI'S REVOLUTION .. NEW VIOLENCE BREAKS IN HAITI'S CAPITAL ..   00540
(  .00  .68  .00  .31  .30  .26  .26  .66  .43  0    )            00550
JEWEL ROBBERY .. THIEVES STEAL JEWELS FROM GERMANY'S DUTCHESS ..  00560
(  .00  .11  .00  .11  .06  .27  .09  .81  .35  0    )            00570
GERMANY'S STEAMSHIP LINES..GERMANY'S STEAMSHIP LINES RAISE PRICES TO USA  00580
                                                                 00590
```

Figure 1. Partial list of messages inputted to the Kaiser and the Tsar on Day 1

LOCALIZATION HOPES .

GERMANY ASSERTS NEED FOR LOCALIZATION OF SERBIA'S CONFLICT .
(0.67195   0.24999   1$)
ENGLAND REQUESTS LOCALIZATION OF CONFLICT IN SERBIA .
(0.42719   0.27999   1$)

AUSTRIA'S ULTIMATUM TO SERBIA .

AUSTRIA SENDS ULTIMATUM TO SERBIA .
(0.66989   −0.67999   1$)
GERMANY'S MOBS RALLY FOR WAR .
(0.66759   0$ 1$)
ULTIMATUM AROUSES ALARM IN SERBIA'S CAPITAL .
(0.58053   0$ 1$)
GERMANY FEARS AUSTRIA'S ULTIMATUM TOO HARSH .
(0.35165   −0.10999   1$)
RUSSIA'S COUNCIL MEETS TO DISCUSS AUSTRIA'S ULTIMATUM .
(0.34117   −0.12999   1$)
FRANCE DENOUNCES SEVERITY OF AUSTRIA'S ULTIMATUM .
(0.34065   −0.41999   1$)
RUSSIA DENOUNCES SEVERITY OF AUSTRIA'S ULTIMATUM .
(0.33717   −0.42999   1$)
ENGLAND DENOUNCES SEVERITY OF AUSTRIA'S ULTIMATUM .
(0.26801   −0.37999   1$)
RUSSIA ACCUSES AUSTRIA OF PLOTTING INTERNATIONAL WAR .
(0.21981   −0.50999   1$)
GERMANY DENIES FOREKNOWLEDGE OF AUSTRIA'S ULTIMATUM .
(0.20505   −0.26999   1$)
USA FEARS WAR IMMINENT IN SERBIA .
(0.13231   −0.09999   1$)

BELGIUM'S NEUTRALITY .

BELGIUM REASSERTS NEUTRALITY STATUS .
(0.65695   0$ 1$)

GERMANY'S BANKS .

GERMANY ORDERS BANKS TO HOLD TEN PERCENT OF ASSETS .
(0.65637   0$ 1$)

RUSSIA'S ALLIANCE WITH SERBIA .

RUSSIA ASSURES SERBIA FULL SUPPORT .
(0.63795   0.71999   1$)
SERBIA ASKS RUSSIA FOR FULL SUPPORT
(0.58353   0.31999   1$)

Figure 2. The attention space of the Kaiser at the end of Day 1

RUSSIA'S MOBILIZATION .

RUSSIA ORDERS COMPLETE MOBILIZATION .
(0.57841   0$ 6$)
RUSSIA'S TSAR DECLARES WAR INEVITABLE .
(0.44883   0$ 6$)
RUSSIA'S MINISTERS PRESS TSAR FOR GENERAL MOBILIZATION .
(0.40561   0$ 6$)
RUSSIA CALLS UP RESERVE TROOPS .
(0.37247   0$ 6$)
RUSSIA'S TROOPS NEAR GERMANY'S BORDER .
(0.36109   −0.46999   6$)
FRANCE ASKS RUSSIA TO CUT DOWN MOBILIZATION .
(0.19053   −0.10999   6$)

GERMANY'S MOBILIZATION .

GERMANY MOBILIZES .
(0.67266   0$ 6$)
GERMANY MOBILIZES .
(0.56733   0$ 6$)
GERMANY MOBILIZES .
(0.55425   0$ 6$)
GERMANY ARMS FRONTIER TOWNS .
(0.47609   0$ 6$)
GERMANY PREPARES TO MOBILIZE .
(0.46127   0$ 6$)
GERMANY'S WAR CHIEFS CONFER ON MOBILIZATION .
(0.46127   0$ 6$)
GERMANY CALLS IN RESERVES .
(0.38351   0$ 6$)
GERMANY'S OFFICERS PRESS FOR MOBILIZATION .
(0.35681   0$ 5$)
GERMANY THREATENS MOBILIZATION IF RUSSIA CONTINUES ARMING .
(0.33943   −0.39999   5$)

EUROPE'S STOCK MARKET .

GERMANY'S MARKET NEARS PANIC .
(0.46681   0$ 6$)
AUSTRIA'S MARKET SUSPENDS ALL DEALINGS .
(0.35665   0$ 6$)
ENGLAND CALLS STOCK SITUATION CRITICAL .
(0.32907   0$ 6$)
ENGLAND'S MARKET NEARS PANIC .
(0.32683   0$ 5$)
ENGLAND'S MARKET SUSPENDS DEALINGS .
(0.32627   0$ 6$)
INVESTORS DUMP STOCKS ON FRANCE'S MARKET .
(0.29591   0$ 6$)
WAR PARALYSES ENGLAND'S MARKET .
(0.28347   0$ 5$)
ENGLAND SUFFERS WORSE STOCK DECLINE IN A GENERATION .
(0.26975   0$ 5$)
FRANCE DUMPS AUSTRIA'S SECURITIES .
(0.19811   −0.27999   6$)

GERMANY'S MILITARY PRECAUTIONS .

GERMANY CALLS UP RESERVE TROOPS .
(0.45829   0$ 6$)

SECRET TREATIES .

SERBIA ENLISTS GREECE'S AID .
(0.45189   0.47999   6$)
SERBIA ENLISTS MONTENEGRO'S AID .
(0.39135   0.44999   6$)

Figure 3. The attention space of the Tsar at the start of Day 7

RUSSIA'S ALLIANCE WITH FRANCE .

FRANCE'S MINISTER GOES TO RUSSIA TO STRENGTHEN ALLIANCE .
(0.79365   0.56999   1$)
FRANCE GIVES RUSSIA FULL DIPLOMATIC SUPPORT .
(0.74821   0.62999   1$)
FRANCE REAFFIRMS SUPPORT TO RUSSIA .
(0.67997   0.60999   1$)

OFFICIAL VISITS .

FRANCE'S PRESIDENT VISITS RUSSIA .
(0.74521   0.60999   1$)
RUSSIA GIVES WARM GREETING TO FRANCE'S PRESIDENT .
(0.63807   0.52999   1$)
ENGLAND'S FLEET VISITS GERMANY .
(0.46999   0.34999   1$)
RUSSIA'S PRINCE VISITS USA
(0.35217   0.19999   1$)
CANADA'S MINISTER TOURS FRANCE .
(0.35153   0.40999   1$)
USA HOTEL BARS PRINCE OF RUSSIA'S DOGS .
(0.11149   −0.07999   1$)

RUSSIA'S ALLIANCE WITH SERBIA .

RUSSIA ASSURES SERBIA FULL SUPPORT .
(0.74293   0.71999   1$)
SERBIA ASKS RUSSIA FOR FULL SUPPORT .
(0.67237   0.31999   1$)

AUSTRIA'S ULTIMATUM TO SERBIA .

AUSTRIA SENDS ULTIMATUM TO SERBIA .
(0.68683   −0.67999   1$)
ULTIMATUM AROUSES ALARM IN SERBIA'S CAPITAL .
(0.59349   0$ 1$)
GERMANY'S MOBS RALLY FOR WAR .
(0.58215   0$ 1$)
RUSSIA'S COUNCIL MEETS TO DISCUSS AUSTRIA'S ULTIMATUM .
(0.44521   −0.12999   1$)
RUSSIA DENOUNCES SEVERITY OF AUSTRIA'S ULTIMATUM .
(0.43935   −0.42999   1$)
ENGLAND DENOUNCES SEVERITY OF AUSTRIA'S ULTIMATUM .
(0.38237   −0.37999   1$)
RUSSIA ACCUSES AUSTRIA OF PLOTTING INTERNATIONAL WAR .
(0.37687   −0.50999   1$)
FRANCE DENOUNCES SEVERITY OF AUSTRIA'S ULTIMATUM .
(0.36287   −0.41999   1$)
GERMANY FEARS AUSTRIA'S ULTIMATUM TOO HARSH .
(0.27159   −0.10999   1$)
GERMANY DENIES FOREKNOWLEDGE OF AUSTRIA'S ULTIMATUM .
(0.20225   −0.26999   1$)
USA FEARS WAR IMMINENT IN SERBIA .
(0.09753   −0.09999   1$)

ENGLAND'S NON-COMMITMENT .

RUSSIA REQUESTS SHOW OF ENGLAND'S SUPPORT .
(0.63713   0.17999   1$)
FRANCE REQUESTS SHOW OF ENGLAND'S SUPPORT .
(0.59293   0.19999   1$)
ENGLAND DECLINES SUPPORT TO RUSSIA .
(0.40303   −0.27999   1$)
ENGLAND DECLINES FULL SUPPORT TO FRANCE .
(0.36305   −0.30999   1$)

Figure 4. The attention space of the Tsar at the end of Day 1

RUSSIA'S MOBILIZATION .

RUSSIA ORDERS COMPLETE MOBILIZATION .
(0.57923   0$ 6$)
RUSSIA'S TSAR ORDERS GENERAL MOBILIZATION .
(0.51195   0$ 6$)
RUSSIA'S TSAR DECLARES WAR INEVITABLE.
(0.47123   0$ 6$)
RUSSIA'S MINISTERS PRESS TSAR FOR GENERAL MOBILIZATION .
(0.45593   0$ 6$)
ENGLAND CONFERS WITH RUSSIA ON MOBILIZATION MEASURES .
(0.43455   0.28999   6$)
FRANCE ADVISES RUSSIA TO SPEED UP MILITARY PREPARATIONS .
(0.42073   0.27999   6$)
RUSSIA CALLS UP RESERVE TROOPS .
(0.40359   0$ 6$)
RUSSIA'S TROOPS NEAR GERMANY'S BORDER .
(0.33711   −0.46999   6$)
FRANCE ASKS RUSSIA TO CUT DOWN MOBILIZATION .
(0.18155   −0.10999   6$)

GERMANY'S MOBILIZATION.

GERMANY MOBILIZES .
(0.53429   0$ 6$)
GERMANY MOBILIZES .
(0.49571   0$ 6$)
GERMANY MOBILIZES .
(0.49027   0$ 6$)
GERMANY ARMS FRONTIER TOWNS .
(0.44373   0$ 6$)
GERMANY CALLS IN RESERVES .
(0.35381   0$ 6$)
GERMANY PREPARES TO MOBILIZE .
(0.27357   0$ 6$)

SERBIA'S BALKAN ALLIES .

MONTENEGRO RAISES ARMY TO AID SERBIA .
(0.45699   0.51999   6$)
MONTENEGRO PROMISES MILITARY AID TO SERBIA .
(0.36609   0.40999   6$)

SECRET TREATIES .

SERBIA ENLISTS GREECE'S AID .
(0.43413   0.47999   6$)
SERBIA ENLISTS MONTENEGRO'S AID .
(0.42581   0.44999   6$)

RUSSIA'S PRESS .

RUSSIA'S PRESS URGES MILITARY AID TO SERBIA .
(0.42915   0.32999   6$)

Figure 5. The attention space of the Tsar at the start of Day 7

55. Measuring Affect and Action in International Reaction Models: Empirical Materials from the 1962 Cuban Crisis*

Ole R. Holsti, Richard A. Brody and Robert C. North were the prime movers of the aforementioned Stanford Studies in International Conflict and Integration. As previously noted (in the introduction to Selection 46), Professor Holsti has since left Stanford University, but Professors Brody and North continue to be members of that institution's Political Science Department. Collectively and individually, these three researchers have provided the field with a large number of valuable inquiries on conflict processes. Many of these were based on a mediated stimulus-response model that was applied to the outbreak of World War I through a content analysis of the relevant historical documents. In this article the same model is applied to a more recent international crisis. It thus provides an excellent opportunity for comparative analysis—which the authors do not hesitate to exploit—across different situations. It is also noteworthy that they do not rely exclusively on perceptual indicators of crisis, but rather bulwark these materials with financial data derived from other, more behavioral, indicators. Equally notable is the fact that their content analysis was accomplished through the use of a computer programmed to sort and tabulate recurrent themes in the published documents of the Cuban missile crisis. The advent of automated content analysis opens up vast areas of research that heretofore seemed beyond exploration and the reader may thus wish to consult one of the sources listed here (Item 33 in the references) for a more elaborate discussion of the possibilities along this line. [*Reprinted from the* Journal of Peace Research, *I (1964), 170–89, and the* Papers of the Peace Research Society (International), *II (1965), 170–89, by permission of the authors and the publishers.*]

I. The Background—The Cuban Crisis

In October, 1962 the first nuclear confrontation in history was precipitated by the establishment of Soviet missile sites in Cuba. For a period of approximately one week, the probability of a full-scale nuclear exchange between the United States and the Soviet Union was exceedingly high. Speaking of the events of the week of October 22, Attorney General Robert Kennedy recalled: "We all agreed in the end that if

* This study was supported by the United States Naval Ordnance Test Station, China Lake, California, Contract N60530-8929. The authors wish to express their gratitude to Mrs. Marian Payne for her research assistance in collecting the financial data analyzed in this paper.

the Russians were ready to go to nuclear war over Cuba, they were ready to go to nuclear war, and that was that. So we might as well have the showdown then as six months later."[1]

An examination of the events immediately surrounding the crisis, analyzed in four rather distinct periods, offers the clear-cut case history of a conflict that escalated to the brink of war—and then de-escalated. This presents a useful contrast with another great crisis in history—which spiralled into major war. The two are almost classic patterns of international conflict.

During the 1962 pre-crisis period President Kennedy had been under considerable domestic pressure to take action against Cuba. In addition to attacks on Administration policy by Senators Cape-hart,[2] Bush, Goldwater, and Keating,[3] the Republican Senatorial and Congressional campaign committees had announced that Cuba would be "the dominant issue of the 1962 campaign. . . . Past mistakes toward Cuba could be forgotten if the Administration now showed itself willing to face reality. But there is little evidence of willingness to recognize the developing danger and to move resolutely to cope with it" [6, p. 35]. Public opinion polls revealed an increasing impatience with American policy toward Communist influence in the Caribbean [37, p. 184]. When the President arrived in Chicago on a campaign tour in mid-October, one "welcoming" sign read: "Less Profile—More Courage" [37, p. 186].

There had been a number of rumors regarding the emplacement of Soviet missiles and troops in Cuba, but "hard" evidence was lacking; those most critical of administration policy were not, in fact, willing to reveal their sources of information. Although Cuba had been under surveillance for some time, the first active phase of the crisis, from October 14 to October 21, began with the development of photographic evidence that Soviet missiles had indeed been located in Cuba. It was during this period that—according to President Kennedy—"15 people, more or less, who were directly consulted"

[1] 1, p. 16.
[2] "He [President Kennedy] said to Mr. Khrushchev you go ahead and do whatever you want to in Cuba, you arm in any way you wish, and do anything you want to. We'll do nothing about it..." [20, p. 8].
[3] "I am sure the administration must have been fully aware of what has been going on for the past month and yet they have remained silent on the threat to our security now festering in Cuba" [20, p. 8].

developed "a general consensus" regarding the major decision to invoke a limited blockade [4, p. 2]. Unfortunately for the purposes of this analysis, there are no publicly-available documents from either Soviet or American decision-makers for the period.

The second and third periods—October 22–25 and October 26–31 respectively—might be described as the "period of greatest danger of escalation" and the "bargaining period." The present paper is confined to this time span, and is not concerned with the final period, during which the agreements reached between President Kennedy and Premier Khrushchev were assertedly carried out and in which further questions regarding verification were raised.

The period of most acute danger of escalation began with President Kennedy's address to the nation on October 22 regarding recent events in Cuba and announcing the institution of certain policies designed to compel the withdrawal of Soviet missiles from the Caribbean. The President announced:

Within the past week unmistakable evidence has established the fact that a series of offensive missile sites is now in preparation on that imprisoned island. The purpose of these bases can be none other than to provide a nuclear strike capability against the Western Hemisphere.

Additional sites not yet completed appear to be designed for intermediate-range ballistic missiles capable . . . of striking most of the major cities in the Western Hemisphere.

This urgent transformation of Cuba into an important strategic base—by the presence of these large, long-range, and clearly offensive weapons of mass destruction—constitutes an explicit threat to the peace and security of all the Americas, in flagrant and deliberate defiance of the Rio Pact of 1947, the traditions of this nation and hemisphere, the Joint Resolution of the 87th Congress, the Charter of the United Nations, and my own public warning to the Soviets on September 4 and 13.

The United States would, according to the President: (1) impose a "strict quarantine" around Cuba to halt the offensive Soviet build-up; (2) continue and increase the close surveillance of Cuba; (3) answer any nuclear missile attack launched from Cuba against any nation in the Western Hemisphere with "a full retaliatory response upon the Soviet Union"; (4) reinforce the naval base at

Guantanamo; (5) call for a meeting of the Organization of American States to invoke the Rio Treaty; and (6) call for an emergency meeting of the United Nations. At the same time he stated that additional military forces had been alerted for "any eventuality." James Reston reported "on highest authority" that,

Ships carrying additional offensive weapons to Cuba must either turn back or submit to search and seizure, or fight. If they try to run the blockade, a warning shot will be fired across their bows; if they still do not submit, they will be attacked [21, p. 1:4].

In accordance with the Joint Congressional Resolution passed three weeks earlier, the President signed an executive order on October 23 mobilizing reserves. It has been reported that decision-makers in Washington also wanted the North Atlantic Treaty forces placed on a maximum missile alert, which meant putting American-controlled nuclear warheads on the NATO-controlled missiles aimed at the Soviet Union. This would prepare them for instant firing. General Lauris Norstad, Supreme Commander of NATO, is reported to have objected successfully, on the basis that in the absence of secrecy, such preparations could bring war when neither side wanted it, by way of "the self-fulfilling prophecy" [2, p. 6].

In its initial response the Soviet government denied the offensive character of the weapons, condemned the blockade as "piracy," and warned that Soviet ships would not honor it.[4] It was also reported that Defense Minister Malinovsky had been instructed to postpone planned demobilization, to cancel furloughs, and to alert all troops. Although the issue was immediately brought before the United Nations and the Organization of American States, the events of October 22–25 pointed to a possibly violent showdown in the Atlantic, in Cuba, or perhaps in other areas of the world. President Kennedy apparently expected some form of retaliation in Berlin. In his October 22 address he specifically warned the Soviet Union against any such move: "Any hostile move anywhere in the world against

the safety and freedom of people to whom we are committed including in particular the brave people of West Berlin—will be met by whatever action is needed."

The blockade went into effect at 10 a.m. Eastern Standard Time on October 24. At that time a fleet of 25 Soviet ships nearing Cuba was expected to test the American policy within hours. Statements from Moscow and Washington gave no immediate evidence that either side would retreat, although the Soviet Premier dispatched a letter to Bertrand Russell in which he called for a summit conference. The next day rumors of an American invasion of Cuba were strengthened by the announcement by Representative Hale Boggs that if the Soviet missiles were not removed the United States would destroy them: "if these missiles are not dismantled, the United States has the power to destroy them, and I assure you that this will be done" [21, Nov. 3, 1962, p. 6:1–2]. At the same time American intelligence sources revealed that work on the erection of missile sites was proceeding at full speed.

The first real break in the chain of events leading to an apparently imminent confrontation came on October 25 when twelve Soviet vessels turned back in mid-Atlantic. It was at this point that Secretary of State Dean Rusk remarked, "We're eyeball to eyeball, and I think the other fellow just blinked" [1, p. 16]. Shortly thereafter the first Soviet ship to reach the blockade area—the tanker *Bucharest*—was allowed to proceed to Cuba without boarding and search.

By the following day the crisis appeared to be receding somewhat from its most dangerous level. The Soviet-chartered freighter, *Marucla* (ironically, a former American Liberty ship now under Lebanese registry), was searched without incident and, when no contraband was discovered, allowed to proceed to Cuba. In answer to an appeal from Secretary General U Thant, Soviet Premier Khrushchev had agreed to keep Soviet ships away from the blockade area for the time being. President Kennedy's reply to the Secretary stated that he would try to avoid any direct confrontation at sea "in the next few days." At the same time, however, the White House issued a statement which said: "The development of ballistic missile sites in Cuba continues at a rapid pace.... The activity at these sites apparently is directed at achieving a full operational capability as soon as

[4] William Knox, Chairman of Westinghouse Electric International, was told by Premier Khrushchev on October 24—the day the blockade went into effect—that "as the Soviet vessels were not armed the United States could undoubtedly stop one or two or more but then he, Chairman Khrushchev, would give instructions to the Soviet submarines to sink the American vessels" [20, p. 36].

possible." The State Department added that "further action would be justified" if work on the missiles sites continued. Photographic evidence revealed that such work was continuing at an increased rate and that the missile sites would be operational in five days.

The "bargaining phase" of the crisis opened later in the evening of October 26. A secret letter from Premier Khrushchev acknowledged the presence of Soviet missiles in Cuba for the first time.[5] He is reported to have argued they were defensive in nature but that he understood the President's feeling about them. According to one source, "Never explicitly stated, but embedded in the letter was an offer to withdraw the offensive weapons under United Nations supervision in return for a guarantee that the United States would not invade Cuba" [21, Nov. 3, 1962, p. 6:3]. A second message from Premier Khrushchev, dispatched twelve hours later, proposed a trade of Soviet missiles in Cuba for NATO missile bases in Turkey; the United Nations Security Council was to verify fulfillment of both operations, contingent upon the approval of the Cuban and Turkish governments.

In his reply to Khrushchev's secret letter of Friday evening, the President all but ignored the later proposal to trade bases in Turkey for those in Cuba. At the Attorney General's suggestion, the President simply interpreted Premier Khrushchev's letter as a bid for an acceptable settlement [1, p. 18].

As I read your letter, the key elements of your proposal —which seems generally acceptable as I understand them—are as follows:

(1) You would agree to remove these weapons systems from Cuba under appropriate United Nations observation and supervision; and undertake, with suitable safeguards, to halt the further introduction of such weapons systems into Cuba.

(2) We, on our part, would agree—upon the establishment of adequate arrangements through the United Nations to ensure the carrying out and continuation of these commitments—(a) to remove promptly the quarantine measures now in effect and (b) to give assurance against an invasion of Cuba.

He added, however, that,

...the first ingredient, let me emphasize, ... is the cessation of work on missile sites in Cuba and measures

to render such weapons inoperable, under effective international guarantees. The continuation of this threat, or a prolonging of this discussion concerning Cuba by linking these problems to the broader questions of European and world security, would surely lead to an intensification of the Cuban crisis and a grave risk to the peace of the world.

In responding to Khrushchev's proposal to trade missile bases in Turkey for those in Cuba, a White House statement rejected that offer: "Several inconsistent and conflicting proposals have been made by the U.S.S.R. within the last 24 hours, including the one just made public in Moscow.... The first imperative must be to deal with this immediate threat, under which no sensible negotiation can proceed."

Despite the advent of negotiations, the probabilities of violence remained high. On October 27 an American U-2 reconnaissance plane had been shot down over Cuba, and several other planes had been fired upon. The Defense Department warned that measures would be taken to "insure that such missions are effective and protected." At the same time it was announced that twenty-four troop-carrier squadrons—14,000 men—were being recalled to active duty. The continued building of missile sites, which would be operational by the following Tuesday, was of even more concern. Theodore Sorensen, speaking of the events of October 27, said, "Obviously these developments could not be tolerated very long, and we were preparing for a meeting on Sunday [October 28] which would have been the most serious meeting ever to take place at the White House" [20, p. 42].

On the following morning, however, Moscow Radio stated that the Soviet Premier would shortly make an important announcement. The message was broadcast in the clear to shortcut the time required by normal channels of communication.[6] Premier Khrushchev declared that,

I regard with great understanding your concern and the concern of the United States people in connection with the fact that the weapons you describe as offensive are formidable indeed.... The Soviet Government, in addition to earlier instruction on the discontinuation

[5] This is apparently the only communication between the United States and the Soviet Union during the crisis period which is not publicly available (cf. Larson, 1964).

[6] "During the Cuban crisis, it took four hours, with luck, for a formal message to pass between Kennedy and Khrushchev. Any such message had to be carried physically from the head of state to the local embassy, translated, coded, transmitted, decoded on the other side, and carried to the other leader" [2, p. 6].

of further work on weapons construction sites, has given a new order to dismantle the arms which you describe as offensive, and to crate and return them to the Soviet Union.

The statement made no reference to the withdrawal of American missiles from Turkey.

In reply, President Kennedy issued statement welcoming Premier Khrushchev's statesmanlike decision." He added that the Cuban blockade would be removed as soon as the United Nations had taken "necessary measures," and further, that the United States would not invade Cuba. Kennedy said that he attached great importance to a rapid settlement of the Cuban crisis, because "developments were approaching a point where events could have become unmanageable." According to one source, all agreed that the Soviet missiles had to be removed or destroyed before they were operational; thus, an air strike against the missile sites was planned by no later than Tuesday, October 30 [1, p. 18].

Although Khrushchev stated that the Soviet Union was prepared to reach an agreement on United Nations verification of the dismantling operation in Cuba, Fidel Castro announced on the same day that Cuba would not accept the Kennedy-Khrushchev agreement unless the United States accepted further conditions, including the abandonment of the naval base at Guantanamo. But the critical phases of the Soviet-American confrontation seemed to be over. Despite the inability to carry out on-site inspection, photographic surveillance of Cuba confirmed the dismantling of the missile sites. The quarantine was lifted on November 21, at which time the Pentagon announced that the missiles had indeed left Cuba aboard Soviet ships.

II. The Interaction Model

What research questions does the Cuban crisis suggest? The crisis may be analyzed from several perspectives. From one point of view, it was a unique event, and not comparable to previous situations. In relation to either World War, the weapons systems of the adversaries were of incomparable magnitude. The nations, as well as their leaders, were different. And certainly in its potential consequences, the Cuban crisis surpassed all previous cold war confrontations and, for that matter, any previous crisis

in history. Even the alerting and mobilization of armed forces, which were so crucial to the escalation into war in the summer of 1914, resulted in a different outcome in October 1962. From this perspective the investigator may focus his attention on the unique characteristics of the situation.

The analyst of international relations may, on the other hand, examine the events of October 1962 in such a manner as to permit relevant comparisons with other crisis situations, both those resolved by war and those eventually resolved by non-violent means. Are there, for example, patterns of behavior that distinguish the situation which escalates into general war—as in 1914—from those in which the process of escalation is reversed? This concern for comparable, replicable, and cumulative studies requires a model and research techniques which permit the student to investigate international transactions, examine how they were initiated and received and compare those of October 1962 with others as widely separated in time and circumstance as the events leading to world war in 1914, and the continuing Arab-Israeli conflict.

A conceptual framework developed for such analysis is a two-step mediated stimulus-response model [26]; $S - r : s - R$. Within the model the acts of one nation are considered as inputs to other nations. The nations are information processing and decision-making units whose output behavior (responses), in turn, can become inputs to other nations (Figure 1). The basic problem is this: given some action by Nation B, what additional information is needed to account for Nation A's foreign policy response?

Within the model a stimulus (S) is an event in the environment which may or may not be perceived by a given actor, and which two or more actors may perceive and evaluate differently. A stimulus may be a physical event or a verbal act.

A response (R) is an action of an actor, without respect to his intent or how either he or other actors may perceive it. Both S's and R's are non-evaluative and non-affective. For example, during the early autumn of 1962, the Soviet Union began erecting launching sites for medium range ballistic missiles in Cuba (R). Regardless of the Soviet motives or intent behind this act, it served as an input or stimulus (S) to the United States, which responded by a series of steps, including the blockade of Cuba (R).

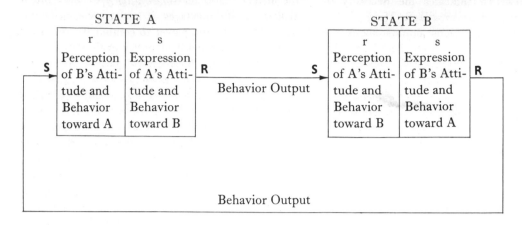

Figure 1. The interaction model

In the model the perception (r) of the stimulus (S) within the national decision system corresponds to the "definition of the situation" in the decision-making literature [31] [18]. For example, the Soviet missile sites in Cuba (S) were perceived by President Kennedy as a threat to the security of the Americas (r). Finally, the "s" stage in the model represents the actor's expression of his own intentions, plans, actions or attitudes toward another actor, which becomes an action response (R) when carried out. Both "r" and "s" carry evaluative and affective loadings.[7] Thus, irrespective of Russian intent, the Cuban missiles were perceived as a threat (r) by President Kennedy, who expressed American intent (s) to remove them from Cuba. This plan was put into effect by the blockade (r), which then served as an input (S) to the Soviet decision-makers.

Operationally it would be much simpler, of course, to confine oneself to an analysis of actions (S and R) as do many classical formulations of international politics [29, p. 2]. In some situations the one nation's actions may be so unambiguous that there is little need to analyze perceptions in order to predict the response; consider, for example, the case of the Japanese attack on Pearl Harbor. Unfortunately, as Kenneth Boulding and others have pointed out, it is clear that rewarding actions will lead to reciprocation.

[7] A number of factors—including those of personality, role, organization and system—will affect the perceptual variables in the model. A further elaboration may be found in [11, Chaps. 1–2].

In any case, not all—or even most—foreign policy behavior is consistent or unambiguous. For political behavior, what is "real" is what men perceive to be real. Boulding [3, p. 120] has summarized this point succinctly:

We must recognize that the people whose decisions determine the policies and actions of nations do not respond to the "objective" facts of the situation, whatever that may mean, but to their "image" of the situation. It is what we think the world is like, not what it is really like that determines our behavior.

At this point one might protest that surely well-trained statesmen will find little difficulty in interpreting the facts as they pertain to foreign policy. Yet one can cite example after example to the contrary. Consider, for example, the various interpretations —even among foreign policy professionals—which in the U.S.A. and other NATO countries almost inevitably follow nearly every turn in Soviet policy. Such problems of interpretations are encountered at every point in the stream of decisions which constitute foreign policy, and *mis*perceptions may have behavioral consequences as "real" as more accurate perceptions do.

If the real world for a President, Prime Minister or Foreign Secretary—and for their counterparts in friendly and hostile nations—is the world as they perceive it, perceptual variables are crucial in a conflict situation [22]. Thus, since all decision-making is rooted in the perceptions of individuals, our model attempts to assess both objective and subjective factors. Our research indicates the necessity of accounting for perceptual variables [23] [12].

There have been serious doubts about the feasibility of quantifying perceptual and affective data, and the inclination, until recently, has been to emphasize "hard" variables and aggregate data; to measure gross national products and populations, or to count troops or planes or ships or megatons and assume that decision-makers respond to the "objective" value assigned to these capabilities by the investigator.

As important as these "objective" data are, they may fail to take into sufficient account how human beings react to these factors. Moreover, objective data are usually compiled on an annual, quarterly, or monthly basis. Thus, while these indices may well be relied upon to reveal the existence of an environment conducive to crisis [28] [36] [8] such as Europe in 1914 or the Cold War since 1945—they may prove less useful for the intensive study of a short time period and for identifying human factors giving rise to conflict. Thus it is particularly important for the investigator who seeks to analyze short term changes in the international system—such as the crisis situation—to incorporate subjective data into his model.

Some objective indices—such as commodity futures, exchange rates and securities prices—are available on a day-to-day basis. A study of the 1914 data had revealed a striking correlation between fluctuations of the economic indices and such psycho-political variables as perceptions and expressions of hostility [10]. These indices are particularly useful as an independent check on the validity of one's techniques of measurement, and will be incorporated into this analysis of the Cuban crisis.

III. Methodology and Data

The premise that the analysis of political behavior is enriched by the incorporation of perceptual data poses special problems for the student of international relations. Clearly the standard method of attitude measurement—the personal interview, the questionnaire, or the direct observation of decision-makers in action—can rarely be used by the social scientist who seeks to study human behavior at the international level. What he needs are instruments for measuring attitudes and actions "at a distance." This is perhaps the primary rationale for settling upon the content analysis of the messages of key decision-makers—those who have the power to commit the resources of state to the pursuit of policy goals at the international level—as an important research tool.

Source materials used for the analysis of perceptions (s and r in the model) consist of 15 United States, 10 Soviet, and 10 Chinese documents, a total of approximately fifty thousand words, from the ten-day period opening on October 22—the day of President Kennedy's address on the Cuban crisis—and closing on October 31.[8] Whereas all Soviet and American documents focus on the situation in Cuba, five of the Chinese documents are concerned solely with the border fighting in India. After relevant decision-makers had been selected, *all publicly-available documents*, rather than a sample, were used. For example, President Kennedy, Secretaries Rusk and McNamara, Ambassador Stevenson, and Attorney General Kennedy were selected as the key American decision-makers. *The entire verbatim text of every available document* authored by these five persons during the ten-day period was included.

These documents were subjected to analysis by means of the General Inquirer system of automated content analysis via the IBM 7090 Computer [33]. The Stanford version of the General Inquirer includes a dictionary which can be used to measure changes in verbalized perceptions—the "r" and the "s" sectors in the basic model—in terms of both frequency and intensity [9] [11].

The scaling of action data (S and R in the model) resulted in the ratings in Table 1 (1 is the highest level and 10 is the lowest level of violence or potential violence).[9]

The perceptual data generated by the General Inquirer are combined with the scaled action data into the S − r : s − R model for the United States and the Soviet Union in Tables 2 and 3. It is apparent that Soviet and American actions during the period are closely correlated; that is, the actions for both sides are most violent or potentially violent in the

---

[8] The present analysis is concerned primarily with Soviet-American interactions during the crisis period. Data from the Chinese documents will be introduced at appropriate points, however, for the purpose of comparing Chinese and Soviet attitudes.

[9] A more complete description of the research techniques may be found in the Methodological Appendix at the end of this paper.

TABLE 1
Sealing of Action Data

	22	23	24	25	26	27	28	29	October 30	31
United States	2	3	1	4	5	6	7	9	10	8
Soviet Union	3	1	2	5	6	4	3	8	9	10

TABLE 2
Active and Perceptual Data—The United States

Oct. 1962	S	Posi- tive	Nega- tive	Strong	Weak	Ac- tive	Pas- sive	Posi- tive	Nega- tive	Strong	Weak	Ac- tive	Pas- sive	R
22	3[a]	1.3[b]	33.5	37.2	5.5	16.2	6.3	11.9	11.2	29.5	4.4	31.8	11.2	2
23	1	0.3	30.3	26.1	3.6	32.3	7.4	11.6	9.7	35.7	2.0	35.7	5.3	3
24	2													1
25	5	17.8	15.6	31.1	0.0	24.4	11.1	16.0	9.0	21.0	5.0	32.0	17.0	4
26	6	13.5	8.1	21.6	2.7	35.2	18.9	30.3	0.0	30.3	3.0	12.1	24.3	5
27	4	10.7	16.1	21.4	8.9	19.6	23.3	24.3	1.7	28.6	6.7	22.7	16.0	6
28	7	25.3	13.4	33.3	2.7	18.6	6.7	16.4	21.7	23.1	3.7	21.7	13.4	7
29	8													9
30	9													10
31	10													8

S — Soviet action
r — U.S. perceptions of Soviet action
s — U.S. statements of intent
R — U.S. action
[a] The values for S and R are rank-order figures.
[b] The values for r and s are percentages of the total loading on the three dimensions.

TABLE 3
Action and Perceptual Data—The Soviet Union

Oct. 1962	S	Posi- tive	Nega- tive	Strong	Weak	Ac- tive	Pas- sive	Posi- tive	Nega- tive	Strong	Weak	Ac- tive	Pas- sive	R
22	2[a]													3
23	3	2.4[b]	27.2	28.8	1.6	34.0	5.0	17.7	13.6	31.2	6.4	22.8	8.3	1
24	1	5.9	19.6	21.6	3.9	31.4	17.6	24.5	10.5	27.8	3.5	15.1	18.6	2
25	4	0.0	16.7	22.2	2.8	30.5	27.8	22.2	7.4	22.2	3.7	7.4	37.1	5
26	5	0.0	29.7	21.6	0.0	48.7	0.0	21.2	1.9	26.9	0.0	32.7	17.3	6
27	6	15.9	12.9	22.1	9.8	27.0	12.3	24.7	6.9	20.1	9.2	20.7	18.4	4
28	7	12.6	16.6	23.4	4.0	30.3	13.0	24.6	8.1	25.9	4.5	21.4	15.5	7
29	9													8
30	10													9
31	8													10

S — U.S. action
r — Soviet perceptions of U.S. actions
s — Soviet statements of intent
R — Soviet actions
[a] The values for S and R are rank-order figures.
[b] The values for r and s are percentages of the total loading on the three dimensions.

first three days, followed by a relatively steady decline through October 31. The Spearman rank-order correlation between Soviet and American actions ($r = .89$) is significant at the .01 level [30, Table P]. The correlation coefficient should not be interpreted to indicate that the level of violence in the actions of each of the two parties was of equal magnitude; the separate scaling of Soviet and American actions precludes such an inference. Rather, it indicates that as the level of violence in the actions of one party increased or decreased, the actions of the other party tended to follow a similar pattern.

The input (S) and output (R) action may also be compared with the perceptual General Inquirer data (r and s). The pattern of perceptions was relatively consistent with the course of events surrounding the Cuban crisis.[10] In each case October 25–26—

[10] The reader may wonder why, in Table 2, the highest level of negative affect in the "s" sector of the model is found on October 28, the day of the Kennedy-Khrushchev agreement. This result is due primarily to President Kennedy's expressions of regret about an American weather airplane straying over Soviet territory; many of the words used by the President are "tagged" for negative affect in the General Inquirer dictionary.

previously identified as the point dividing two phases of the crisis—was the point at which mutual perceptions appeared to change. The rigidly negative-strong-active perceptions of the period of highest danger became somewhat modified at this point. Perceptions along the evaluative dimension became more neutral and, in some cases, actually became positive. As one would expect, during the latter days of the crisis there was also an increase in perceptions of passivity. The potency dimension, on the other hand, remained predominantly on the strong side throughout the crisis period.

Spearman rank-order correlation coefficients across various steps in the model are presented in Table 4.[11] The evaluative dimension is the most sensitive to behavioral changes; the highest correlation coefficients are consistently those for positive affect (positive correlation with decreasing violence).

Table 4 also reveals that there is a relatively close correspondence between the actions of the other party (S) and perceptions of the adversary's actions (r). By themselves these findings are hardly conclusive. When compared with a similar analysis of the crisis which escalated into World War I [12], however, one interesting point emerges. The members of the

[11] Because there are no United States perceptual data for October 24, the average of the values of October 23 and 25 has been used for the purpose of calculating the correlation coefficients in Table 4.

Dual Alliance (Germany and Austria-Hungary) consistently reacted at a higher level of violence than did the members of the Triple Entente (Britain, France and Russia). At the same time, they also consistently overperceived (r) the level of violence in actions (S) taken by members of the Triple Entente. British, French and Russian decision-makers, on the other hand, underperceived (r) the level of violence in the actions of the Dual Alliance. In terms of the S − r : s − R model, this relationship between one coalition's actions (S), the other coalitions' perceptions of those actions (r), and the resulting policies (R) was apparently the crucial one.

In the Cuban crisis, however, both sides tended to perceive (r) rather accurately the nature of the adversary's actions (S), and then proceeded to act (R) at an "appropriate" level; that is, as the level of violence or potential violence in the adversary's actions (S) diminished perceptions of those actions (r) increased in positive affect and decreased in negative affect, and the level of violence in the resulting policies (R) also decreased. Thus, unlike the situation in 1914, efforts by either party to delay or reverse the escalation were generally perceived as such, and responded to in a like manner. Whether the different patterns of action and perception found in the 1914 and Cuban cases will be found consistently to distinguish crises that escalate and de-

TABLE 4
Rank-Order Correlations Across S — r : s — R Model

	SOVIET UNION (n = 6)		UNITED STATES (n = 7)	
	U.S. action (S)	Soviet action (R)	Soviet action (S)	U.S. action (R)
Perceptions of other state (r)				
Positive	+ .70	− .07	+ .93	+ .71
Negative	− .43	− .20	− .82	− .79
Strong	− .13	− .13	+ .11	− .25
Weak	+ .54	+ .09	− .24	+ .17
Active	− .43	− .20	− .18	− .14
Passive	− .31	+ .03	+ .18	+ .32
Self-perceptions (s)				
Positive	+ .66	+ .32	+ .79	+ .71
Negative	− .31	− .60	− .11	− .11
Strong	− .31	− .49	+ .46	+ .21
Weak	+ .20	− .32	+ .29	+ .29
Active	+ .37	+ .14	− .86	− .71
Passive	− .37	+ .03	+ .79	+ .54

escalate, of course, can only be determined through continuing research.

Up to this point Chinese actions and attitudes have not been considered. As an observer rather than direct participant in the crisis, there are few, if any, Chinese actions with respect to the Cuban situation. Despite China's peripheral role, however, the analysis of its attitudes has considerable significance. The suggestion has often been made that while the antecedents of the Sino-Soviet schism predate the Cuban crisis, the gulf between Moscow and Peking widened considerably as a result of it. China, of course, was deeply involved in a concurrent crisis with India, but a number of Chinese documents during the period relate to the events in Cuba.

One immediate indication of differences is the seemingly calculated manner in which the Chinese ignored the role of the Soviet Union. A frequency count of the appearance of various nations in the documents (Table 5) reveals the extent to which Soviet and American decision-makers perceived the Cuban situation almost immediately as a Soviet-American issue, rather than one involving Cuba. The Chinese, on the other hand, referred constantly to Cuba as a primary actor in the crisis, and only rarely mentioned the Soviet Union. This, of course, renders impossible any direct analysis of Sino-Soviet attitudes, although there are occasional veiled references to the Soviet Union. After the Kennedy-Khrushchev agreement of October 28, for example, *Renmin Ribao* editorialized that, "The peoples of

the world cannot under any circumstances lightly put their trust in the empty promises of United States aggressors," implying that Premier Khrushchev had done so. The same editorial went on to praise Fidel Castro for the "justified and absolutely necessary" opposition to the on-site inspection agreed to by the United States and the Soviet Union.

The data do not permit a direct comparison of Chinese and Soviet perceptions of each other, but some indirect analyses are possible. For the purposes of comparison, all documents have been divided into two periods—October 22–25 and October 26–31. The data are further divided to distinguish between perceptions of one's own actions toward others (s in the model), and the actions of others toward oneself (r in the model). From the General Inquirer output it was determined whether these actions were perceived as positive or negative, strong or weak, and active or passive, together with the intensity level of each. The results yielded a series of fourfold contingency Tables.[12] Tables 6a and 6b reinforce the earlier finding that both the United States and the Soviet Union regarded *each other* as significantly less negative during the latter stage of the crisis period. They also regarded *themselves* as

[12] The cell entries, which are based on a weighted (frequency × intensity) total, are independent of each other. The frequency and intensity of positive actions, for example, have no bearing on the number of actions which are rated negative. Nor can a single action word be entered in both the positive and negative cells; no dictionary entry is tagged for both ends of a single dimension.

TABLE 5
Frequency of Appearance of Actors in Documents Relating to Cuban Crisis

| | UNITED STATES DOCUMENTS | | | SOVIET DOCUMENTS | | | CHINESE DOCUMENTS | | |
Date	United States	Soviet Union	Cuba	United States	Soviet Union	Cuba	United States	Soviet Union	Cuba
	%	%	%	%	%	%	%	%	%
Oct. 22	54.5	37.2	8.3	—	—	—	—	—	—
Oct. 23	45.8	34.6	19.6	59.6	29.8	10.5	—	—	—
Oct. 24	—	—	—	27.5	71.0	1.5	79.7	0.0	20.3
Oct. 25	61.1	38.9	0.0	60.5	39.5	0.0	75.7	2.0	22.3
Oct. 26	40.9	59.1	0.0	53.9	46.1	0.0	—	—	—
Oct. 27	41.0	59.0	0.0	41.8	48.2	10.0	—	—	—
Oct. 28	57.8	41.4	0.8	30.8	65.7	3.5	63.5	1.0	35.5
Oct. 29	—	—	—	—	—	—	—	—	—
Oct. 30	—	—	—	—	—	—	—	—	—
Oct. 31	—	—	—	—	—	—	50.2	0.9	48.9

TABLE 6a

United States Perceptions in the Early and Late Periods of the Crisis

United States Perceptions of Soviet Actions

	October 22–25	*October* 26–31		*October* 22–25	*October* 26–31		*October* 22–25	*October* 26–31
Positive affect	13[a]	40	Strong	153	57	Active	153	47
Negative affect	203	36	Weak	28	13	Passive	39	38
$X^2 = 80.3$		$P = .001$		$X^2 = 0.1$	$P = $ n.s.		$X^2 = 15.7$	$P = .001$

United States Perceptions of United States Actions

	October 22–25	*October* 26–31		*October* 22–25	*October* 26–31		*October* 22–25	*October* 26–31
Positive Affect	106	61	Strong	149	75	Active	280	60
Negative affect	90	31	Weak	31	14	Passive	79	45
$X^2 = 4.2$		$P = .05$		$X^2 = 0.1$	$P = $ n.s.		$X^2 = 15.9$	$P = .001$

[a] Figures are weighted (frequency × intensity) total.

TABLE 6b

Soviet Perceptions in the Early and Late Periods of the Crisis

Soviet Perception of United States Actions

	October 22–25	*October* 26–31		*October* 22–25	*October* 26–31		*October* 22–25	*October* 26–31
Positive affect	16[a]	50	Strong	176	85	Active	216	115
Negative affect	163	61	Weak	12	23	Passive	46	43
$X^2 = 52.1$		$P = .001$		$X^2 = 14.4$	$P = .001$		$X^2 = 5.2$	$P = .05$

Soviet Perceptions of Soviet Actions

	October 22–25	*October* 26–31		*October* 22–25	*October* 26–31		*October* 22–25	*October* 26–31
Positive affect	76	128	Strong	127	127	Active	92	117
Negative affect	56	35	Weak	21	29	Passive	46	85
$X^2 = 18.5$		$P = .001$		$X^2 = 0.6$	$P = $ n.s.		$X^2 = 2.6$	$P = $ n.s.

[a] Figures are weighted (frequency × intensity) total.

less negative toward the adversary than during the first four days of the crisis.[13]

[13] The figures in Table 6a and 6b support other studies which have found the evaluative dimension of cognition to be the most important (Osgood *et al.*, 1957; Levy and Hefner, 1962). It is also true, however, that the activity dimension provides rather consistent discrimination between the early and later periods of the crisis. Inasmuch as there was little, if any, actual change in Soviet and American capabilities during the short period under investigation, it is not surprising that perceptions of potency show little variation.

Chinese perceptions of the Cuban crisis, on the other hand, differ markedly from those of both the Soviet Union and the United States (Table 6c). There is no change (at the .05 level of statistical significance) in Chinese perceptions of American actions during the two periods; the proportion of negative affect to positive affect remains relatively constant. Nor is there any difference in perceptions of Chinese and Cuban actions toward the United States during the two periods in question. Thus, despite

TABLE 6c
Chinese Perceptions in the Early and Late Periods of the Crisis

Chinese Perceptions of United States Actions

	October 22–25	October 26–31		October 22–25	October 26–31		October 22–25	October 26–31
Positive affect	3^a	20	Strong	110	306	Active	120	413
Negative affect	96	300	Weak	14	41	Passive	14	63
$X^2 = 1.5$	P = n.s.		$X^2 = 0.0$	P = n.s.		$X^2 = 0.9$	P = n.s.	

Chinese Perceptions of Chinese-Cuban Actions

	October 22–25	October 26–31		October 22–25	October 26–31		October 22–25	October 26–31
Positive affect	11	88	Strong	39	291	Active	20	231
Negative affect	35	129	Weak	13	22	Passive	8	48
$X^2 = 2.9$	P = n.s.		$X^2 = 9.7$	$P = .01$		$X^2 = 1.8$	P = n.s.	

^{a} Figures are weighted (frequency × intensity) total.

the lack of data for direct comparison, the available data do suggest a considerable difference in evaluation of the course of events in October 1962. Subsequent direct Chinese attacks on Soviet policy during the crisis have confirmed these differences.

As indicated earlier, certain financial indications were used in a study of the 1914 crisis as a validity check against the measurement of other variables. A strictly analogous study—in which data are gathered from all nations involved in the crisis—is not possible for the Cuban crisis, owing to the absence of free markets in either Cuba or the Soviet Union. Data were gathered from major American markets, however, for a number of financial indices. As indicated in Table 7, there is a significant correlation between Dow-Jones average of industrial securities and the level of violence or potential violence in both Soviet and American actions; as the crisis intensified, the value of stocks fell sharply, followed by an even greater rise in stock prices as the crisis receded. The pattern for wheat futures was the reverse, with a significant increase in prices corresponding with the heightened tensions. Although the value of the American dollar—in relation to the Swiss franc—fluctuated in the predicted direction, the correlation coefficient is quite low.

The relationship between the financial indices and decision-maker's perceptions are roughly similar to those for the action data, although not significant at the .05 level for n = 6.

While the movements of the financial indices *by themselves* cannot be used as indicators of international crisis—the stock market crash of 1962 is a good case in point—the results during the Cuban crisis add to the confidence with which the other quantified data may be employed.

IV. Discussion

Having utilized the $S — r : s — R$ model to examine the pattern of Soviet and American interaction, it may be useful to attempt at least a partial explanation for the patterns with some comparisons with the 1914 crisis. Such an analysis will be concerned primarily with what might be called "styles of decision-making," and must of necessity be based on incomplete data. Although there are several accounts of the process by which American policy was formulated, such data with respect to the Soviet Union are much more fragmentary and inferential [14] [13].

One major characteristic of Soviet policy during this period is clear. Unlike German leaders in 1914, Premier Khrushchev did not irrevocably tie his policy to that of a weaker—and perhaps less responsible—ally. The Cuban response to President Kennedy's address of October 22 was stronger and more unyielding than that of the Soviet Union. Premier Castro in fact ordered a general war mobilization *prior to* the delivery of the President's

TABLE 7
Relationship of Selected Financial Indices to Soviet and American Actions and Perceptions

October	Dow-Jones average	December wheat futures	Swiss franc
Average 8–21	585.55	2.04 1/2	23.13 1/4
22	568.60	2.07 1/2	23.14
23	558.06	2.10 1/2	23.17 1/4
24	576.68	2.08	23.17 5/8
25	570.86	2.07 3/8	23.17 1/2
26	569.02	2.07 7/8	23.17 1/2
27	—	—	—
	(Exchanges closed for weekend)		
28	—	—	—
29	579.35	2.05 1/4	23.16 1/2
30	588.98	2.06 3/4	23.17
31	589.77	2.06 7/8	23.17

Rank-order correlations

	Dow-Jones average	December wheat futures	Swiss franc
U.S. Action (n = 8)	+ .83[a]	− .83[a]	− .37
Soviet Action (n = 8)	+ .69[b]	− .76[b]	− .36
+			
U.S. Perceptions:			
U.S. Action (n = 6)	+ .71	− .54	− .24
Soviet Action (n = 6)	+ .54	− .38	− .39

[a] Significant at .01 level
[b] Significant at .05 level
+ Net Affect (Positive − Negative)

speech. The following day Premier Castro in effect left no room for either Cuba or the Soviet Union to maneuver: "Whoever tries to inspect Cuba must come in battle array! This is our final reply to illusions and proposals for carrying out inspections on our territory" [7, p. 42]. Premier Khrushchev, on the other hand, like President Kennedy, almost immediately chose to interpret the crisis as one involving the United States and the Soviet Union alone. In his correspondence with President Kennedy during October 26–28, it is also apparent that the Soviet Premier was unwilling to let the intransigence of Dr. Castro stand in the way of a possible solution of the crisis. In his letter of October 28, in which Khrushchev offered to withdraw the missiles, there was, in fact, no acknowledgment of the necessity to obtain Cuban agreement on the terms of the settlement.

American decision-making in regard to the missiles in Cuba was characterized by a concern for action based on adequate information. The resistance of the Administration against action—despite public pressure—until photographic evidence of the missile sites was available, has already been noted.[14] As late as Thursday, October 18 a series of alternatives was being considered pending more accurate information, and while the decision to institute a blockade was being hammered out, open discussion of the alternatives was encouraged. The President recalled that "though at the beginning there was a much sharper division . . . this was very valuable,

[14] McGeorge Bundy recalled that upon receiving the first news of the photographic evidence, "his [President Kennedy's] first reaction was that we must make sure, and were we making sure? And would there be evidence on which he could decide that this was in fact really the case" [20, p. 14].

because the people involved had particular responsibilities of their own" [4, p. 4]. Another participant in the decision-making at the highest level wrote: "President Kennedy, learning on his return from a mid-week trip in October, 1962, that the deliberation of the NSC [National Security Council] executive committee had been more spirited and frank in his absence, asked the committee to hold other preliminary sessions without him" [32, p. 60]. Thus despite the very real pressure of time—the missile sites would be operational by the end of the month—the eventual decision was reached by relatively open discussion. Group decision-making does not ensure the emergence of sound policy, of course, but it does limit the probability of a decision performing a personality-oriented function [35, p. 103].[15]

Actually, it was not until Saturday, October 20—almost a week after the photographic evidence became available—that the general consensus developed. The President himself acknowledged that the interim period was crucial to the content of the final decision: "If we had had to act on Wednesday [October 17], in the first 24 hours, I don't think probably we would have chosen as prudently as we finally did, the quarantine against the use of offensive weapons" [4, pp. 2–3].[16]

Another characteristic of the decision process in October 1962 was the very conscious concern for action at the very lowest level of violence—or potential violence—necessary to achieve the goals. J. William Fulbright and Richard B. Russell, both Democratic policy leaders in the Senate, were among those who urged immediate invasion of Cuba, a suggestion against which the President stood firm

[20, p. 30].[17] According to Kennedy, the decision to impose a blockade was based on the reasoning that: "the course we finally adopted had the advantage of permitting other steps, if this one was unsuccessful. In other words, we were starting, in a sense, at a minimum place. Then, if that were unsuccessful, we could have gradually stepped it up until we had gone into a much more massive action which might have become necessary if the first step had been unsuccessful" [4, p. 4]. By this step, no irrevocable decisions had been made—a number of options remained.

The concern of the President and his advisers with maintaining a number of options was based at least in part on an explicit differentiation between a violent "bid" or threat (such as the blockade), and a violent commission. The use of threats has become a more or less accepted tool of international politics in the nearly two decades of cold warring. The United States and the Soviet Union, on the other hand, had systematically abstained from direct violent action against each other. The desire to avoid killing Soviet troops was an important factor in the decision to refrain from an air strike against Cuba [20, p. 22]. Instead the blockade shifted the immediate burden of decision concerning the use of violence to Premier Khrushchev. Even if Soviet ships refused to honor the blockade, the initial American plan was to disable the rudders of the vessels, rather than to sink them [2, p. 6].

The flexibility provided by a number of plans requiring less than the use of unlimited violence stands in marked contrast to the situation in 1914. One factor in the rapid escalation in 1914 was the rigidity of various mobilization plans. The Russian attempt to mobilize against only Austria was anathema to the Russian generals because no such formal plan had been drawn up. According to General Dobrorolski, "The whole plan of mobilization is worked out ahead to its final conclusion and in all its detail. . . . Once the moment is chosen, everything is settled; there is no going back; it determines mechanically the beginning of war" [5, p. 343].

Similarly the Kaiser's last-minute attempt to reverse the Schlieffen plan—to attack only in the east—shattered Moltke, who replied: "That is impossible, Your Majesty. An army of a million cannot be improvised. It would be nothing but a

---

[15] In this respect the contrast to many of the crucial decisions made in 1914 is striking. That the German Kaiser underwent an almost total collapse at the time he made a series of key decisions—the night of July 29–30—is evident from a reading of his marginal notes [19].

[16] Despite the relative lack of speed—with the possible exception of the German army—with which European weapons systems could be mobilized in 1914, decision-makers in the various capitals of Europe perceived that time was of crucial importance—and they acted on that assumption. The Kaiser, for example, immediately upon learning of Russia's mobilization (which had been intended only to deter Austria-Hungary), ordered: "In view of the collossal war preparations of Russia now discovered, this is all too late, I fear. Begin! Now!" [19, p. 368]. One can only speculate on the outcome had there been some delay in the making of such decisions in 1914.

[17] According to one top official, "invasion was hardly ever seriously considered" [21, Nov. 3, 1962, p. 6:3].

rabble of undisciplined armed men, without a commissariat. . . . It is utterly impossible to advance except according to plan; strong in the west, weak in the east" [5, pp. 248–9].

American decision-makers also displayed a considerable concern and sensitivity for the position and perspective of the adversary as a vital variable in the development of the crisis. Unlike some of the key decision-makers in the 1914 crisis, those in October 1962 thought in terms of linked inter-actions—closely tied reciprocations—rather than two sides, each acting independently, *in vacuo*. Theodore Sorensen described the deliberation as follows: "We discussed what the Soviet reaction would be to any possible move by the United States, what our reaction with them would have to be to that Soviet reaction and so on, trying to follow each of those roads to their ultimate conclusion" [20, p. 17].[18]

This sensitivity for the position of the adversary was apparent in a number of important areas. There was a concern that Premier Khrushchev should not be rushed into an irrevocable decision; it was agreed among members of the decision group that "we should slow down the escalation of the crisis to give Khrushchev time to consider his next move" [20, p. 19]. There was, in addition, a conscious effort not to reduce the alternatives of *either* side to two—total surrender or total war. According to one participant, "President Kennedy, aware of the enormous hazards in the confrontation with the Soviets over Cuba in October, 1962, made certain that his first move did not close out either all his options or all of theirs" [32, pp. 20–21].

Sorensen added that:

The air strike or an invasion automatically meant a military attack upon a communist power and required almost certainly either a military response to the Soviet Union or an even more humiliating surrender . . . The blockade on the other hand had the advantage of giving Mr. Khrushchev a choice, an option, so to speak, he did not have to have his ships approach the blockade and be stopped and searched. He could turn them around. So that was the first obvious

[18] President Kennedy and others were aware of the possibility of misperception by their counterparts in the Kremlin, "Well now, if you look at the history of this century where World War I really came through a series of misjudgments of the intentions of others . . . it's very difficult to always make judgments here about what the effect will be of our decisions on other countries" [4, p. 3].

advantage it had. It left a way open to Mr. Khrushchev. In this age of nuclear weapons that is very important [20, p. 22].

Thus, unlike the 1914 situation, in which at least one ultimatum was worded so as to be incapable of execution, there was no demand which the Soviet Premier could not understand, none that he could not carry out, and none calculated to humiliate him unduly. During the summer of 1914, by way of contrast, there were numerous instances of failure on all three of these important points. The Austro-Hungarian ultimatum was deliberately worded in such a manner as to humiliate Serbia and to provoke rejection. The policy of the other powers, on the other hand, was hardly characterized by clarity. Russian decision-makers failed to communicate their initial desire to deter Vienna rather than to provoke Berlin. This was matched by England's inability to convey to German leaders their intention to intervene should the local conflict engulf the major continental powers.[19] And, in the culminating stages of the crisis, decision-makers in the various capitals of Europe made the very types of demands upon their adversaries—notably in regard to mobilizations—which they admitted they could not reciprocate.[20]

References

1. Alsop, Stewart and Charles Bartlett. "In time of Crisis," *The Saturday Evening Post*, Dec. 8, 1962, 15–20.

2. Bagdikian, Ben H. "Press Independence and the Cuban Crisis," *Columbia Journalism Review*, (Winter, 1963), 5–11.

3. Boulding, Kenneth E. "National Images and International Systems," *The Journal of Conflict Resolution*, III (1959), 120–31.

4. C.B.S. News. "A Conversation with President Kennedy," Dec. 17, 1962. (Mimeo. transcript.)

5. Cowles, Virginia. *The Kaiser*. (New York: Harper, 1964.)

[19] The failure of communication was not, of course, solely attributable to the sender. The Kaiser, for example, consistently dismissed the warnings of his able ambassador in London, Prince Lichnowsky.

[20] For example, both the Kaiser and the Tsar demanded that the other stop mobilizing. Nicholas replied that, "it is technically impossible to stop our military preparations" [19, p. 402]. At the same time Wilhelm wrote: "On technical grounds my mobilization which has already been proclaimed this afternoon must proceed against two fronts, east and west" [19, p. 451].

6. Data Digest, *Cuban Crisis*. (New York: Keynote Publications, 1963.)

7. Draper, Theodore. "Castro and Communism," *The Reporter*, Jan. 17, 1963, 35–40.

8. Holsti, K. J. "The Use of Objective Criteria for the Measurement of International Tension Levels," *Background*, VII (1963), 77–96.

9. Holsti, Ole R. "An Adaptation of the 'General Inquirer' for the Systematic Analysis of Political Documents," *Behavioral Science*, IX (October, 1964), in press.

10. ―――― and Robert C. North. "History as a 'Laboratory' of Conflict," in Elton B. McNeil, ed., *Social Science and Human Conflict*. (Englewood Cliffs, N.J.: Prentice-Hall, in press.)

11. ――――, Richard A. Brody and Robert C. North. *Theory and Measurement of Interstate Behavior: A Research Application of Automated Content Analysis*. (Stanford Univ. mimeo.) 1964a.

12. ――――, Richard A. Brody and Robert C. North. "Violence and Hostility: The Path to World War," Paper read at American Psychiatric Association Conference, Los Angeles, Calif. (May, 1964b).

13. Horelick, Arnold L. "The Cuban Missile Crisis: An Analysis of Soviet Calculation and Behavior," *World Politics*, XVI (1964), 363–89.

14. Kolkowicz, Roman. "Conflicts in Soviet Party-Military Relations: 1962–1963," RAND Corp. Memo., RN-3760-PR, 1963.

15. Kumata, H. and Wilbur Schramm. "A Pilot Study of Cross-Cultural Methodology," *Public Opinion Quarterly*, XX (1956), 229–37.

16. Larson, David L. *The "Cuban Crisis" of 1962*. (Boston: Houghton, 1963.)

17. Levy, Sheldon G. and Robert Hefner. "Multi-dimensional Scaling of International Attitudes" (unpublished: mimeo.), Center for Research on Conflict Resolution (November 1, 1962). Working paper no. 201.

18. March, J. G. and H. A. Simon. *Organizations*. (New York: Wiley, 1958.)

19. Montgelas, Max and Walther Schücking, ed., *Outbreak of the World War, German Documents Collected by Karl Kautsky*. (New York: Oxford Univ. Press, 1924.)

20. N.B.C. "Cuba: The Missile Crisis," Feb. 9, 1964.

21. *New York Times*. October–November 1962.

22. North, Robert C. "International Conflict and Integration: Problems of Research," in Muzafer Sherif, ed., *Intergroup Relations and Leadership*. (New York: Wiley, 1962.)

23. ――――, Richard A. Brody and Ole R. Holsti. "Some Empirical Data on the Conflict Spiral," *Peace Research Society Papers* (1964), 1–14.

24. Osgood, Charles E. "Studies on the Generality of Affective Meaning Systems," *American Psychologist*, XVII (1962), 10–28.

25. ――――, George J. Suci and Percy H. Tannenbaum. *The Measurement of Meaning*. (Urbana, Ill.: Univ. Illinois Press, 1957.)

26. ―――― and Robert C. North. "From Individual to Nation: An Attempt to Make Explicit the Usually Implicit Process of Personifying International Relations," an unpublished manuscript. (Urbana and Stanford, 1963.)

27. Rapoport, Anatol. *Fights, Games and Debates*. (Ann Arbor, Mich.: Univ. Michigan Press, 1960.)

28. Richardson, Lewis F. *Arms and Insecurity*, ed., by Nicolas Rashevsky and Ernesto Trucco. (Pittsburgh, Pa.: Boxwood Press, 1960.)

29. Rosenau, James N. "Pre-Theories and Theories of Foreign Policy." Paper prepared for the Conference on Comparative and International Politics, Northwestern Univ., April 2–4, 1964.

30. Siegel, Sidney. *Non-Parametric Statistics for the Behavioral Sciences*. (New York: McGraw-Hill, 1956.)

31. Snyder, Richard C., *et al.*, edd., *Foreign Policy Decision Making*. (New York: Free Press, 1962.)

32. Sorensen, Theodore C. *Decision-Making in the White House*. (New York: Columbia Univ. Press) 1963.

33. Stone, Philip J., Robert F. Bales, J. Zvi Namenwirth and Daniel M. Ogilvic. "The General Inquirer: A Computer System for Content Analysis and Retrieval Based on the Sentence as a Unit of Information," *Behavioral Science*, VII (1962), 484–94.

34. Suci, George J. "An Investigation of the Similarity between the Semantic Space of Five Different Cultures." Report for the Southwest Project in Comparative Psycholinguistics, 1957.

35. Verba, Sidney. "Assumptions of Rationality in Models of the International System," *World Politics*, XIV (1961), 93–117.

36. Wright, Quincy. "Design for a Research Proposal on International Conflict and the Factors Causing Their Aggravation or Amelioration," *Western Political Quarterly*, X (1957), 263–75.

37. ――――. "The Cuban Quarantine of 1962," in John G. Stoessinger and Alan F. Westin, eds., *Power and Order*. (New York: Harcourt, 1964.)

Methodological Appendix

The Stanford General Inquirer is programmed to measure perceptions—as found in written documents—along three dimensions: strength—weakness, activity—passivity, positive affect—negative affect. These dichotomized dimensions correspond to the evaluative, potency, and activity dimensions which have been found to be primary in human cognition in a variety of cultures [25] [34] [5] [24]. The dictionary thus reflects the assumption that when decision-makers perceive themselves, other nations, events—

or any stimulus—the most relevant discriminations are made in a space defined by these three factors. The computer can be used to analyze perceptual units defined in terms of the following elements: the *perceiver*; the perceived *agent* of action; the *action* or *attitude*; and the *target* of action. The components may be illustrated in a statement by President Kennedy (perceiver): "Soviet missiles [agent] threaten [action] all the Americas [target]". For the present analysis the computer has been instructed to measure the *action-attitude* component within a specified set of agent-target relationships involving the United States, Soviet Union, China and Cuba.

The scaling of action data (S and R in the model) was accomplished by the following technique. Three judges were given a set of cards concerning Soviet and American actions for the ten-day period October 22–31—the same period which encompasses all the publicly available documents by key Soviet and American decision-makers. Each action was typed on a separate card and these were then aggregated on a day-to-day basis. Thus each judge was given a set of cards for both United States and Soviet actions, each set being subdivided into ten periods. The judges were instructed to rank order the events—using the day as the unit of analysis—for the degree of violence or potential violence. The Soviet and American actions were scaled separately largely because of the disparity of available data; published chronologies of American actions during the crisis period are detailed to almost an hourly basis, whereas the action data for the Soviet Union are relatively sparse.

The level of agreement between each pair of judges for scaling both Soviet and American actions was:

Judge	A	B
C	.800	.883
	.891	.842
B	.967	
	.939	

The top figure is level of agreement for the scaling of Soviet action; the bottom figure is that for the scaling of United States action. All figures are significant at beyond the .01 level.

56. Supranationalism in the United Nations[*]

Hayward R. Alker, Jr. is Professor of Political Science at the Massachusetts Institute of Technology. An expert in quantitative research techniques as well as political science, Professor Alker's work includes authorship of *World Politics in the General Assembly* (1965) and *World Handbook of Political and Social Indicators* (1964). In this article he demonstrates that the various methods of inquiry depicted in the previous fifteen selections are not mutually exclusive and that insight into important problems can often be achieved through an imaginative strategy that makes combined use of several research methods. Professor Alker employs four different methods to probe the same problem and his success in this regard should encourage other researchers to be creative in combining the many research techniques that are available. [*Reprinted from the Papers of the Peace Research Society (International), III (1965), 197–212, by permission of the author and the publisher.*]

I. Introduction

In his *The Uniting of Europe*, Ernst Haas comments that "The 'good Europeans' [e.g. Jean Monnet] are not the main creators of the regional community that is growing up; the process of community formation is dominated by nationally constituted groups with specific interests and aims, willing and able to adjust their aspirations by turning to supranational means when this course appears profitable."[1] Applying the same perspective to the world arena, one may observe that "good universalists" such as Dag Hammarskjold and U Thant are not by themselves the main builders of a world community. Community formation is more the result of nations and groups of nations, willing and able to adjust their own aspirations, when such adjustments seem profitable, by turning to supranational means.

International community is a condition of international society in which existing attitudes and institutions assure peaceful adjustments of differences among nations.[2] It is a task of considerable importance

[*] This research has been supported, in part, by the Yale Political Data Program. The author gratefully acknowledges the research assistance of Raymond Hopkins and Douglas Condie.

[1] Ernst B. Haas, *The Uniting of Europe: Political, Social and Economic Forces, 1950–1957* (Stanford: Stanford University Press, 1958), p. xiv.

[2] I have purposely avoided distinguishing between amalgamated and pluralistic international communities because I do not want to rule out the possibility of peaceful adjustment of policy differences between sovereign nations under UN auspices. As a full-grown supranational organization, the United Nations may at some time foster and guide an amalgamated world polity. Before then, we can still talk about the peace-keeping contributions of partially supranational organization with nearly universal membership. Relevant literature on the definition of international or supranational political community includes E. B. Haas, *op. cit.*, K. W. Deutsch *et al.*, *Political Community and the North Atlantic Area* (Princeton: Princeton University Press, 1957); K. W. Deutsch, P. E.

to describe and explain the extent of supranational readjustments of national aims and practices and of resulting developments in international community.

The problem breaks down into several distinctive parts; each of which I shall briefly discuss. Specifically, if the United Nations is the major world-wide supranational mechanism involved in the satisfaction and readjustment of national aims, what indications do we have of a willingness to use supranational means for achieving readjusted national goals? Is supranationalism a factor in Assembly decisions? Secondly, if some evidence of supranational inclinations can be found, among which nations and for what reasons do such inclinations or predispositions occur? In other words, what considerations of profit lead to readjustments of national policies along supranational lines? Thirdly, since calculations of supranationalism are of necessity influenced by the environment in which they are made, what kinds of situations have led to supranational political responses? Finally, when supranational means have been used for achieving readjusted national goals, to what extent have these nations succeeded in laying the foundations of a world community?

Data and Methods

Inevitably, data for answering such ambitious questions as these are not adequate. Nonetheless the records of the United Nations General Assembly are unusually valuable because they contain the official positions of a large number of nations on a large number of situations in which supranational activity is likely to occur. The institutional requirements in several ways aid the behaviorally oriented peace researcher: for example, all nations have to vote on exactly the same resolutions, copies of which are permanently available; whenever any one nation at any time calls for a permanent record of such positions, a roll-call vote is taken. Such roll calls force a nation to choose among four possible responses: Yes, Abstain, No, or nonparticipation in the roll call. Extensive verbatim and summary records indicate policy justifications of nations and

Jacob, H. Teune, J. V. Toscano and W. L. C. Wheaton, *The Integration of Political Communities* (Philadelphia: J. B. Lippincott and Company, 1964); and recent articles by Amitai Etzioni, especially "The Epigenesis of Political Communities at the International Level," *American Journal of Sociology*, LXVIII, 4 (January 1963), 407–21.

their allies, *as well as* competing explanations offered by less charitable observers of these policies.

A body of records that are particularly suited to the search for the rudiments of supranationalism at the United Nations are those for the eight special and emergency special sessions of the General Assembly.[3] Such sessions have been called to deal with a variety of major threats to international peace; as such they may be considered an important test of the United Nations' peace-keeping capability, the core element, if not the main cause of international community.[4]

Emergency special sessions are called for by the Security Council (ironically, Yugoslavia first invoked the Uniting for Peace Resolution in the Suez crisis), "regular" special sessions are convened by a majority of Assembly members at the call of any one of them (as was done by the United Kingdom at the First Special Session on the future of Palestine). In chronological order these sessions are briefly described in Table 1. Fortunately, for all but one special session (the Third Emergency Special Session, which discussed Lebanon) one or more roll-call votes on final resolutions are readily available.[5]

Methodologically, I should like to illustrate a different research procedure for dealing with each of the four main substantive questions previously discussed. To see if predispositions to use UN peacekeeping mechanisms are a regularly distinguishable component of Assembly roll calls, I have applied the principal component method of factor analysis to a matrix of correlations among voting

[3] The role of the Security Council on these matters has also been significant especially in Korea and in the first Congo crisis, when the Soviet Union did not veto the establishment of ONUC. But even before, and especially since the Korean War and the Uniting for Peace resolution, the Assembly has initiated or supported the major peacekeeping efforts of the United Nations.

[4] Korea, Cuba and Berlin, prime Cold War crises, have not been the subject of special Assembly sessions; the omissions are significant ones in any over-all analysis of the United Nation's role. For a more detailed analysis of noncrisis Assembly sessions see H. R. Alker, Jr., "Dimensions of Conflict in the General Assembly," *American Political Science Review*, LVIII, 3 (September 1964), 642–57, and H. R. Alker, Jr., and B. M. Russett, *World Politics in the General Assembly* (New Haven: Yale University Press, 1965).

[5] United Nations, *Official Records of The General Assembly*. Resolutions may generally be found in the Annexes of these documents.

TABLE 1

*A Chronology of Special and Emergency Special Sessions
of the General Assembly*

Session	Date	Topic	Result
First Special Session (SS 1)	Summer, 1947	Future of Palestine	Set up committee that recommended partition
Second Special Session (SS 2)	Spring, 1948	Future government of Palestine	Established UN Mediator
First Emergency Special Session (ES 1)	November, 1956	Suez Crisis	United Nations Emergency Force
Second Emergency Special Session (ES 2)	November, 1956	Hungarian Revolt	UN unable to enter Hungary; aided refugees.
Third Emergency Special Session (ES 3)	Summer, 1958	Lebanon and Jordan	Arabs pledged non-intervention; UN observation grouping set up by Security Council; troops withdrawn.
Fourth Emergency Special Session (ES 4)	September, 1960	Congo	Resolutions backed territorial integrity, asked for voluntary support of Congo operation.
Third Special Session (SS 3)	Summer, 1961	Tunisia	Urged negotiations for the withdrawal of French troops.
Fourth Special Session (SS 4)	Spring, 1963	Financial Crisis	Extended bonds; appropriated $33 million for ONUC through December, 1963

ranks on all non-unanimous special session roll calls. Even after the voting ranks of a very small number of absent states have been estimated, the main problem with such a correlation matrix is that the number of observations varies considerably from correlation to correlation. At the First Special Session 55 members were present; by the Fourth Special Session, Assembly membership had increased to 111. Nevertheless, the stability of UN voting alignments through the years allows for greater certainty as to the usefulness of this procedure.[6]

After the factor analysis, correlational analyses

can be used to test various possible determinants of supranationalist predispositions, if at least to some extent, they appear to underlie Assembly voting alignments. Correlating national characteristics with supranationalism factor scores will help explain why UN instrumentalities are voted for.

Content analysis of Assembly resolutions may suggest answers to a missing link in the relationship between particular votes and general supranational predispositions: why particular resolutions do or do not evoke supranationalist responses. Such a technique has rarely if ever been applied to General Assembly resolutions or debates. Nevertheless, I shall try to demonstrate how, in conjunction with factor analyses of final roll calls, it can shed light on diplomatic procedures for shaping perceptions of ambiguous crisis situations.

Finally, in a more historical and impressionistic vein, I would like briefly to comment on the characteristics of international crisis situations associated

[6] A more lengthy technical discussion of the factor analysis methods used below may be found in Henry Harmon, *Modern Factor Analysis* (Chicago: Chicago University Press, 1960) and Alker and Russett, *op. cit.*, Chap. 2. As a justification for using roll-calls from different sessions with different memberships, I am relying on the similarity of many of the voting factors identified below with those found in the previously cited analyses of votes in separate General Assembly sessions.

with greater national compliance with supranational initiatives.[7]

II. Is Supranationalism a Factor in Assembly Decisions?

Supranationalism means commitment to use and to be bound by political institutions transcending the nation state. In studying the European Coal and Steel Community, Ernst Haas suggested several structural characteristics of supranational institutions which, when joined to the supranationalism of national policies, lead to the sustained growth of supranational political communities. An international organization has become supranational, Haas believes, to the extent that it: (1) performs a wide range of governmental functions including peace-keeping and law enforcement, independent of those performed by nation states, (2) relies less on weighted majorities and national vetoes, (3) legislates on the recommendations of popular representatives independent of national governmental control, (4) produces a set of binding decisions that can effectively be carried out, (5) enlarges the scope of supranational power without requiring the consent of all member states, and (6) disallows unilateral termination of membership.

Assuming for the present that such a theory is relevant to a larger international context, we shall look for supranationalism, commitment to United Nations supranationality, in the decisions of the General Assembly sessions described above.

[7] An important refinement of each of these procedures would be explicitly to allow for the interaction of individuals and subnational interest groups. See E. B. Haas, *op. cit.*, and C. F. Alger, "Personal Contact in Intergovernmental Organizations," to appear in H. Kelman (ed.), *International Behavior* (New York: Holt, Rinehart and Winston, 1965).

The Unrotated Factor Matrix

The conventional literature on factor analysis suggests two strategies for identifying principal voting components, exemplified in the unrotated and rotated factor matrices of Table 2 and Table 3. Entries in both factor matrices may be thought of either as *correlations* between these hypothetical voting alignments and particular concrete roll-calls, or as *factor loadings* in the *factor model* that is assumed to explain particular voting alignments.[8]

The first strategy for identifying voting components emphasizes *frequent voting behavior*. The loadings in Table 2 are derived from uncorrelated hypothetical voting alignments, each explaining as

[8] If subscripts i refer to countries, j's refer to roll calls and k's indicate voting components (factors), the model assumes that the vote of a particular country i on roll-call $j(V_{ji})$ results from a linear additive combination of national positions on a small number of voting components ($F_{ik's}$, called "factor scores"). Factor loadings ($a_{ik's}$) may be thought of either as correlations between roll calls and factors or as coefficients of the factor model in Equation (1):

$$V_{ji} = \sum_k a_{jk} F_{ik} + U_{ji} \qquad (1)$$

The $U_{ji's}$ represent the part of voting ranks that cannot be explained by identifiable factors. In the present analysis only factors with variances equal to that of one roll call or more, and with loadings of 0.50 higher are considered identifiable. Even these relatively strict identification rules have produced communalities (h^2's. roll-call variance accounted for by factor loadings in the factor matrix) averaging around 80 per cent of their maximum value (which is 1.0 or 100 per cent in the case of no missing data).

Dynamically, Equation (1) suggests several ways of influencing national votes ($V_{ji's}$) on a particular roll call (j). Given relatively stable cold war and supranationalist predispositions (respectively, F_{i1}, F_{i2}), the neutralist diplomat, for example, tries to shape resolutions about a particular crisis so as to evoke favorable, supranationalist responses. His success would be indicated by a high supranationalism factor loading (a_{j2} bigger than a_{j1}) and by small particularistic voting components (negligible $U_{ji's}$).

TABLE 2
Unrotated Factor Matrix for 52 Special Session Roll Calls

Roll-Call Description		Factors					
		I	II	III	IV	V	h^2
SS1:	1 Omit Palestine future	70	35	04	17	09	65
	2 Omit religious concerns	−49	−07	−12	44	30	54
	3 Note religious concerns	42	14	29	−31	30	47
	4 Immediate independence	−83	−32	04	−02	10	81
	5 Consider independent Palestine	−67	−21	24	−11	14	58

TABLE 2—continued

Roll-Call Description		Factors					
		I	II	III	IV	V	h^2
	6 Committee of SC members	− 77	− 05	12	22	48	88
	7 Committee of SC members	− 76	− 04	17	24	51	93
	8 Add 1 African member	− 75	− 05	15	19	48	85
	9 Committee of small powers	48	− 35	06	02	− 32	45
	10 End mandate	− 72	− 35	00	− 14	− 03	66
	11 Hear Jewish viewpoint	− 46	39	23	− 05	10	42
	12 Hear all viewpoints	46	69	32	− 11	09	81
	13 Small power committee	91	14	13	− 10	11	89
	14 Power to investigate	44	63	38	− 09	12	75
	15 Palestine resolution	44	63	38	− 09	12	75
SS2:	16 Jerusalem urgent	52	46	52	12	− 04	76
	17 Charter OKs UN admin.	56	46	44	21	− 01	75
	18 Use regular UN budget	53	57	26	35	− 14	82
	19 OKs Unforseen expenses	69	45	23	27	− 24	81
	20 UN Commissioner	60	57	28	30	− 16	89
	21 UN administer Jerusalem	58	58	29	29	− 16	87
	22 UN Mediator in Palestine	66	− 08	− 01	35	03	57
ES1:	23 Urges Suez cease-fire	− 29	− 40	69	− 38	03	81
	24 SG arrange cease-fire	− 35	− 38	48	− 53	− 21	81
	25 Asks SG for UNEF plan	44	− 64	38	− 17	− 10	78
	26 Establishes UNEF	45	− 58	48	− 13	− 15	81
	27 Organizes UNEF	66	− 55	07	04	− 08	74
	28 Withdraw forces	− 29	− 43	69	− 38	10	90
ES2:	29 Notes Soviet repression	93	− 04	− 15	− 17	17	94
	30 Hungary desires freedom	93	− 04	− 15	− 14	18	93
	31 Intervention intolerable	93	− 03	− 17	− 18	18	95
	32 Soviets violate Charter	92	− 03	− 14	− 21	15	93
	33 Withdrawal necessary	93	− 04	− 15	− 14	18	94
	34 USSR withdraw now	92	− 05	− 13	− 15	16	92
	35 UN auspicies for elections	79	− 12	− 15	− 05	06	65
	36 Favors free elections	94	01	− 11	− 13	16	94
	37 Requests SG investigate	91	− 07	− 08	− 11	12	86
	38 SG report compliance	92	− 07	− 10	− 11	15	87
	39 Hungary resolution	91	− 03	20	− 15	21	93
	40 Help refugees	92	− 06	− 10	− 10	15	89
	41 Hungarian relief	55	− 50	− 23	03	− 11	61
	42 Omit references to USSR	− 83	− 35	05	26	− 13	89
	43 Withdrawal and relief	93	03	− 09	− 14	15	91
SS3:	44 Tunisia and France	− 61	− 36	24	16	39	73
ES4:	45 Noninterference: Congo	61	− 72	− 03	04	06	89
SS4:	46 UNEF financing	65	− 42	26	35	09	80
	47 Collective responsibility	54	− 72	11	18	− 01	85
	48 ONUC financing	68	− 43	24	33	04	81
	49 Appeals for arrears	71	− 37	26	32	06	81
	50 Bond sales extension	46	− 72	08	35	00	86
	51 SG consider peace fund	49	− 74	07	27	− 01	86
	52 Continue working group	54	− 73	12	20	− 00	87
% Roll-Call Variance Explained		47.6	16.9	6.9	5.1	3.5	
(5 factors together explain 79.5%)							

much voting variance as possible. Factor loadings for the first five hypothetical factors (voting components) form the columns of Table 2. Note how the *most frequent voting factor contains nearly half (48 per cent) of all special session non-unanimous roll-call votes*. The second, third, fourth and fifth most frequent distinctive voting components underlie 17, 7, 5 and 3.5 per cent of these roll calls. Three other factors, none of which had any loadings above 0.50 or explained more than 3 per cent of the voting variance, have been omitted from the table.

Using the maximum voting variance approach, do we find common supranational voting predispositions across the different special sessions of the General Assembly? Unrotated Factor I certainly cuts across these different sessions, but seems to consist primarily of issues on which East and West disagree: Hungary, Soviet and Arab initiatives on Palestine, French attacks on Tunisia, and payment of Congo arrears. Thus half of special session votes reveal *"East-West"* alignments. If East-West issues could be solved in a United Nations context, international political community would be increased, but there is no striking evidence that such a trend has occurred or that commitment to a greater United Nations has played a dramatic role in such developments. Once East-West predispositions are taken into account, however, the second and third most frequent voting factors consist of issues showing a greater degree of commitment to use the UN and to obey its decisions.

Because of the content of the issues loading heavily on it, I would call the second most frequent voting predisposition, *"North-South"* inclinations. These predispositions have appeared in issues on which many "Northern powers" including the United States, the United Kingdom, France and the Soviet Union, have either positively agreed or negatively been forced into voting together: setting up adequate machinery for investigating the Palestine problem without crippling restrictions (especially votes 2, 12, 14 and 15), disagreeing (except for the United States) with Southern attempts to use the Secretary-General and the United Nations Emergency Force to prevent Northern intervention in the Suez crisis (especially vote 25), hesitating to support (except for the United States and to a lesser extent the United Kingdom) United Nations Congo operations (votes 45, 47, 50, 51 and 52).

As the major alternative alignment to the East-West conflict in the General Assembly, we should expect the North-South alignment to have differing substantive implications, including the possibility of greater use of and commitment to United Nations decision-making machinery. The UN's role in Palestine's partition and its aftermath, its intervention in the Suez and Congo crises do evidence a considerable degree of supranational activity. Because several roll calls from these crises do load on the North-South factors, supranationalism is clearly a major part of this voting component; but because several apparently constructive roll calls on these situations also appear to load more on the East-West factor, it would be premature at this point to identify supranationalism with the North-South conflict.

The third most frequent voting component reveals a different set of supranationalist aspirations. The three highest loadings on the third unrotated factor (votes 16, 23 and 28) have in common a desire to prevent *"Arab-Israeli conflict."* Vote 16 is a vote on Mexican text referring to the civil strife that broke out before Palestine's independence: "Whereas the maintenance of order and security in Jerusalem is an urgent question which concerns the United Nations

TABLE 3
Rotated Factor Matrix for 52 Special Session Roll Calls

Roll-Call description	Factors								
	I	II	III	IV	V	VI	VII	VIII	h^2
1 Omit Palestine future	45	− 15	− 19	− 41	− 09	56	24	10	88
2 Omit religious concerns	− 13	02	− 24	39	56	08	− 16	01	58
3 Note religious concerns	18	03	40	− 43	− 01	29	13	57	80
4 Immediate independence	− 45	14	16	53	34	− 49	− 14	− 07	91
5 Consider independence	− 27	14	26	39	31	− 69	06	− 05	89

TABLE 3—continued

Roll-Call Description	I	II	III	IV	V	VI	VII	VIII	h²
6 Committee of SC members	− 20	22	06	46	78	− 15	− 04	− 04	93
7 Committee of SC members	− 15	21	08	46	81	− 15	− 04	− 01	97
8 Add 1 African member	− 18	23	10	44	76	− 12	− 05	− 02	88
9 Committee of small powers	18	− 44	08	− 27	− 38	− 36	− 28	09	67
10 End mandate	− 41	16	23	42	17	− 51	− 31	00	81
11 Hear Jewish viewpoint	02	38	00	35	16	− 28	47	− 08	60
12 Hear all viewpoints	50	21	− 02	− 28	− 15	20	69	03	91
13 Small power committee	39	− 28	− 02	− 73	− 22	05	32	02	91
14 Power to investigate	48	13	− 00	− 25	− 13	08	76	07	92
15 Palestine resolution	48	13	− 00	− 25	− 13	08	76	07	92
16 Jerusalem urgent	83	− 00	16	− 24	− 01	11	22	− 11	85
17 Charter OKs UN admin.	83	− 05	06	− 26	00	18	19	− 06	83
18 Use regular UN budget	87	01	− 22	− 19	− 12	− 02	14	05	87
19 OKs Unforeseen expenses	84	− 10	− 14	− 30	− 25	14	06	− 06	91
20 UN Commissioner	90	01	− 16	− 25	− 16	01	10	08	95
21 UN administer Jerusalem	90	03	− 13	− 24	− 17	03	08	16	95
22 UN Mediator in Palestine	43	− 43	− 22	− 42	− 05	− 13	− 21	28	74
23 Urges Suez cease-fire	− 09	− 11	90	24	13	05	− 03	08	92
24 SG arrange cease-fire	− 27	− 00	78	27	18	− 23	02	− 00	84
25 Asks SG for UNEF plan	03	− 62	53	− 78	− 09	82	− 12	− 35	88
26 Establishes UNEF	10	− 64	54	− 20	− 13	04	− 00	− 35	89
27 Organizes UNEF	05	− 70	13	− 43	− 14	08	− 11	− 33	84
28 Withdraw forces	− 12	− 13	91	20	18	− 08	00	06	94
29 Notes Soviet repression	19	− 28	− 08	− 89	− 18	07	03	− 02	95
30 Hungary desires freedom	19	− 30	− 09	− 88	− 17	08	04	00	94
31 Intervention intolerable	19	− 25	− 08	− 91	− 18	06	02	− 01	98
32 Soviets violate Charter	20	− 24	− 03	− 90	− 19	08	00	− 03	95
33 Withdrawal necessary	19	− 30	− 09	− 88	− 17	08	04	00	94
34 USSR withdraw now	20	− 30	− 07	− 87	− 19	07	05	− 01	93
35 UN auspices for elections	15	− 34	− 08	− 67	− 20	22	− 06	03	69
36 Favors free elections	24	− 29	− 09	− 86	− 20	09	11	03	95
37 Requests SG investigate	21	− 35	− 06	− 81	− 20	08	08	− 02	88
38 SG report compliance	20	− 35	− 07	− 83	− 19	08	08	00	90
39 Hungary resolution	18	− 25	− 10	− 90	− 15	08	− 01	05	95
40 Help refugees	21	− 35	− 08	− 82	− 18	09	07	00	90
41 Hungarian relief	− 14	− 57	− 11	− 41	− 22	− 07	− 17	− 22	65
42 Omit references to USSR	− 34	− 04	04	79	26	− 18	− 20	− 12	90
43 Withdrawal and relief	24	− 28	− 08	− 84	− 22	08	12	06	92
44 Tunisia and France	− 29	− 10	25	43	60	− 14	− 08	21	77
45 Noninterference: Congo	− 15	− 80	08	− 40	− 16	03	− 14	− 21	92
46 UNEF financing	20	− 84	− 03	− 28	− 01	− 03	17	13	87
47 Collective responsibility	− 07	− 86	12	− 27	− 04	10	− 13	− 11	87
48 ONUC financing	20	− 84	− 02	− 28	− 08	− 04	13	21	90
49 Appeals for arrears	23	− 82	− 03	− 31	− 09	− 02	19	21	91
50 Bond sales extension	− 07	− 92	− 00	− 13	− 02	05	− 14	13	90
51 SG consider peace fund	− 10	− 90	04	− 19	04	04	− 14	03	88
52 Continue working group	− 07	− 88	12	− 25	− 03	10	− 12	− 08	90
% Roll-Call Variance Explained (8 factors explain 87%)	14.2	18.5	7.0	28.3	7.5	4.0	5.3	2.2	

as a whole." Votes 23 and 28 requested the cessation of hostilities and the withdrawal of French, British and Israeli forces nine years later during the Suez crisis. Once again, however, the substantive significance of this unrotated factor needs to be sharpened, a task for which factor rotation is especially appropriate.[9]

The rotated factor matrix

A second strategy for identifying voting components is to construct hypothetical voting alignments producing a substantively interpretable, *simply structured* factor matrix. Such a matrix ideally consists of only very high factor loadings and very low ones. It can be approximated by applying what is known as Kaiser's "normal Varimax procedure" to the unrotated factor matrix. A factor can then be simply identified from roll-calls with high loadings on no other voting component.

Hopefully, the rotated factor matrix will help distinguish more clearly among the rather varied set of rollcalls loading on the unrotated voting components. Comparing the rotated factor matrix (Table 3) with Table 2, clearer substantive interpretations are indeed possible. Note, however, that the percentage of variance explained by these rotated factors does not correspond to the analogous figures for the unrotated matrix.

Rotated Factor 4, consisting almost completely of Hungarian roll-calls, seems quite similar to the East-West conflict, although Palestine and Congo questions no longer make sizeable contributions. I would use a *Cold War* label for it. Rotated Factor 3 appears to be a "cleaned up" version of unrotated Factor 3: it consists only of the Suez related Arab-Asian conflicts. Because previously noted votes 23 and 28, urging a cease-fire and troop withdrawal, now have extremely high loadings, perhaps an *anti-intervention* label is appropriate. Only colonial powers—France, Belgium, Britain, Portugal and South Africa among them—did not vote against

Israeli-British-French intervention in the Middle East.

In a similar fashion, the second rotated factor seems to bring out more clearly the *United Nations supranationalism* predispositions contained in North-South alignments. *All* Congo and UNEF votes from two different sessions load heavily on this factor. Two other votes (No. 22 on a UN Palestine mediator and No. 41 on Hungarian relief) also have their highest loadings on this factor. In a modest way, like other supranationalist votes, they evidence national willingness to use and obey supranational instrumentalities.

The Palestine related votes loading on the unrotated factors can be distinguished into a number of substantively distinct components. Rotated Factor 5, like the fifth unrotated factor, pinpoints votes 6, 7 and 8, Soviet Bloc resolutions calling for a Palestine committee similar in composition to the Security Council. This attempt to keep Assembly decisions within a great power framework was resisted by Western states, while Arabs and Asians mostly abstained. The peculiar cross-pressures on Afro-Asian states in the Palestine context suggest, however, that Russian reluctance concerning what might be called *Security Council competence* might in other contexts appear on supranationalism issues.

A few of the remaining Palestine votes, appear on rotated Factors 6, 7 and 8. Only Factor 1 contains enough of these votes to require particular comment. Centered as it is on votes 16 through 21, the first rotated factor might be identified as *Palestine settlement* concerns. Voting alignments similar to these have regularly occurred in the General Assembly.[10] Because the main resolutions loading on this factor failed to achieve the required two-thirds majority, they failed to achieve even the status of internationally sanctioned recommendations.

The general effect of rotating the factor matrix (according to what is called the normal varimax criterion) was to sharpen the factor interpretations

[9] The remaining unrotated factors do not seem to have appeared frequently enough to warrant detailed discussion. Factor 4 seems to catch a lesser aspect of both the Palestine and Congo situations, issues loading more heavily on the North-South and Arab-Israeli factors. Factor 5 distinguishes a special aspect of votes 6, 7 and 8. Unlike typical East-West alignments, Arab states and some Asians abstained on these Soviet initiatives, to compose the committee considering the future of Palestine in a manner similar to the Security Council.

[10] At the Sixteenth Assembly, for example, Palestine Cold War, UN supranationalism and anti-intervention factors can be identified, as well as unrotated East-West and North-South alignments. The most significant omission of data from special session voting has been straight anti-colonial or self-determination resolutions such as occur on resolutions on the self-determination of natural resources or sanctions against South Africa and Portuguese Angola. See Alker, *op. cit.*

given to the first four unrotated factors.[11] Five such rotated factors were identifiable: Palestine settlement, UN supranationalism, the Cold War, "anti-interventionism" regarding Suez, and Security Council competence concerning Palestine's future.

Supranationalism in UN Voting

Given complementary pictures of "frequent behavioral" and "simply structured" components of General Assembly voting, we are now able to assess the extent of UN supranationalism. Implied by the definition of "supranationalism" as the "commitment to use and to obey supranational means" is the need to establish the degree to which the UN has acted as a supranational institution on these issues loading heavily on the supranationalism factor. The significance of such activities goes beyond the mere frequency of such votes to the resulting changes in the structure of the UN.

In Haas' terms, both United Nations activities in recommending and overseeing the consequences of Palestine partition and its extended role in the Suez and Congo crises exemplify important increases in the range of functions performed and the scope of power exercised, often in spite of strong national opposition. Russia's decision not to veto the Congo operation, the extensive reliance of the Secretary-General on his advisory bodies for UNEF and ONUC, and the effective role of the General Assembly in both these situations once the veto had been exercised, are all radical departures from the 1-nation veto principle of the League of Nations in the direction of majoritarian rule.

If most UN representatives cannot legislate independently of their government's control, most supranationalism issues have nonetheless shown UN delegations and related interest groups in England, United States, and other countries to be significant influences on national policy-making. It is significant also, that none of the principal powers involved in these crises has publically announced its considera-

tion of withdrawal from the UN because of the injustices it has suffered. Retaliatory action has always been less severe (often financial) and generally less successful.

A distinguishing characteristic of supranationalism resolutions has been the extent to which they have been binding decisions effectively carried out. After rotation, the Security Council competence factor "split" off from "supranationalism": it did not even receive a two-thirds Assembly majority—such a majority did obtain, however, on the UN mediator vote. Anti-intervention votes also reflected supranational *aspirations*, but to become *effective*, resolutions establishing the requisite peace force were necessary; these roll-calls evoked a supranational alignment. Of the many votes on Hungary loading with exasperating futility on East-West and cold war factors, only the humanitarian issue evoked supranational responses and led to an effective charitable mission.

In sum, we find Haas' criteria of institutionalized supranationality remarkably appropriate for describing the intermittent strengths and the reoccurring weaknesses of supranationalism in the United Nations. Special Session majorities have not been able to legislate a new world order into being, but to varying degrees they have readjusted national policies on each of the main conflicts in the Assembly; cold war calamities have been humanized; Arab-Israeli conflicts have on certain occasions been radically transformed; nations have been successfully born in the struggle for self-determination.

III. What Determines Supranationalist Predispositions?

The world is not ruled by votes in the General Assembly. Effective supranational decisions in the Assembly have resulted from readjusted calculations of national advantage.

Whatever progress may be possible toward the evolution of a larger role for such civilized devices in international life will be furthered by the development of a tradition of vigorous and meaningful contests for voting support by rival leaders, operating within the context of a General Assembly which is nobody's tool.[12]

---

[11] This conclusion is greatly strengthened by intercorrelation among the appropriate factor "scores" defined as noted in Table 4: East-West and Cold War factors, North-South and Supranationalism factors, Arab-Israel and anti-intervention factor "scores" reveal paired correlations above 0.90. The rotated Palestine settlement factor correlates 0.62 with East-West alignments and about 0.60 with rotated Factors 5, 6, 7 and 8, all on different aspects of the Palestine situation.

[12] I. L. Claude, Jr., *Swords into Plowshares* (2nd ed.; New York: Random House, 1961), p. 459.

Granting the realities of General Assembly politics, what kinds of states have evidenced supranationalist predispositions at its special sessions? Keeping with the above interpretation of the supranationalism alignment as the major evidence of such predispositions, one can test various possible voting determinants using correlational and related techniques. The discussion below will be only suggestive, not exhaustive.

National Characteristics Related to Supranationalism

Among the noblest ideals of Western civilization is the belief that nations with competitive political systems, democracies, are more peaceful than communist, autocratic or totalitarian regimes: "[Woodrow] Wilson, following the thesis laid down more than a hundred years earlier by Immanuel Kant in his essay on *Perpetual Peace* (*Zum ewigen Frieden*), believed that world peace could be established only by a compact among democratically governed nations."[13]

A somewhat less classical argument embodied in the Covenant of the League and the Charter of the United Nations, is that Great Powers ought to be primarily responsible for the maintenance of international peace, presumably because they have both the required capabilities and intentions. Ever since two "International Peace Conferences" held at the Hague under the impetus of Russia's Czar Nicholas II in 1899 and 1907, smaller powers have taken a different view. Seeking voting positions equal to those of great powers, such states could argue that international organizations benefit appreciably from small power detachment and their real desire not to be destroyed by great powers.[14]

Three other national characteristics might also account for supranationalism predispositions. If we believe supranational issues to originate in Cold War debates then supranationalism voting may represent an extension of the Cold War into the General Assembly. Perhaps, too, ex-colonial states and underdeveloped states are using the Assembly for their collective security and economic development needs.[15]

The correlations and average supranationalism scores in Table 4 serve to test these various hypotheses. More than anything, supranationalism predispositions seem to be anti-communist ones. As Woodrow Wilson would have us believe, democracies are supranationally predisposed, but to a much lesser extent than communist states are anti-supranationalist. Western military allies, not all notable for their democratic systems, seem also to have moderately positive supranational inclinations.

Great powers (as defined by a crude indicator, Gross National Product) appear to be resisting the supranationalism visible in the United Nations. Perhaps smaller powers are in fact more willing to use and to obey General Assembly resolutions.

Finally, although economic development (as measured by per capita G.N.P.) does *not* seem related to supranationalism, ex-colonial background does. Not a little of the incisiveness of Suez and Congo resolutions comes from the anti-colonial as well as anti-communist feelings of newly independent countries.[16]

---

[13] I. L. Claude, *op. cit.*, pp. 55–6.

[14] *Ibid.*, pp. 28–35. Small power attempts to enlarge General Assembly functions (the Uniting for Peace resolution) and to keep great powers ("members of the Security Council") off Assembly Committees indicate such feelings still exist.

[15] Ernst Haas, for example, has suggested the eventual possibility that revolutionary (usually anti-colonial) states will channel their collective security demands (as now done regarding South Africa) through the General Assembly. Beneficiaries of UN technical assistance programs have also submitted to supranational authority on numerous occasions in order to receive the desired assistance. The use of UN peace-keeping capabilities by the United States and its allies might also be considered in Haas' terming as "permissive enforcement." See E. B. Haas, "International Integration: The European and the Universal Process," *International Organization*, XV, 3 (Summer 1961), 366–92; E. B. Haas, "Dynamic Environment and Static System: Revolutionary Regimes in the United Nations," in M. A. Kaplan, *The Revolution in World Politics* (New York: John Wiley and Sons Inc.), 1962, pp. 267–309. Other references, as well as descriptions and justifications of the dichotomous coding procedures are given in Alker, "Dimensions of Conflict," *op. cit.*

[16] I would like to illustrate only one of the many ways in which further multivariate explanatory relations among the variables in Table 4 could be developed. Consider the problem of adequately relating regional correlations to universal ones. Among Western allies (roughly, the "West" when OAS members are included), a correlation between communism and anti-supranationalism is meaningless because none of these states are communist. Among non-Western countries communism correlates − 0.92 with supranationalism, even higher than the universal 0.84 figure. For all 111 states ex-colonial status correlates only moderately ($r = 0.29$) with supranationalism, but belies a much higher relationship *among* non-Western countries

TABLE 4

Relations Between National Characteristics and Supra-nationalism Voting (Positive supranational scores represent high supranationalism predisposition)

National characteristic	Average supranationlism score[b] of state sharing the characteristic	Correlation of national character with supra-nationalism score[b]
Political democracy (N = 40)	0.34	0.29
National power (dichotomized at $10 billion GNP, N = 20)	[a]	− 0.30 (estimate)
Economic underdevelopment (per capita GNP below $700 N = 95)	0.00	0.06
Western military ally (N = 43)	0.29	0.23
Recent ex-European colony (since 1919) (N = 52)	0.31	0.29
Communist State	2.38	− 0.84
All Countries (N = 111)	0.02	[a]

[a] Not computed.

[b] Supranationalism scores are a weighted average of standardized scores for three different sets of Assembly resolutions: votes 1–22, votes 23–43 and votes 44–52. For each period standard scores have been computed from standardized voting ranks multiplied by factor loadings above 0.40 taken from the second column of the rotated factor matrix. Final scores are the result of weighting these period scores according to the amount of supra-nationalism roll-call variance for each period. These resulting scores are themselves nearly standardized (with a mean of 0.02 and a standard deviation of 0.93).

IV. Why Do Particular Resolutions Evoke Supranationalist Alignments?

The factor model (given in Equation 1 above) implies that two sets of information are necessary to explain or predict voting positions on a particular roll call. First, one must know the various possible general voting predispositions, and why they are

($r = 0.61$) than it does among Western countries ($r = 0.16$). In sum, *within* the West supranationalism is not an anti-communist reaction while among non-Western states supranationalism is both an anti-communist and an anti-colonial disposition. For more detailed examples of relations among regional and universal correlations, see Alker, "Regionalism versus Universalism in Comparing Nations," in Russett, Alker, Deutsch and Lasswell, *World Handbook of Political and Social Indicators* (New Haven: Yale University Press, 1964).

held. The previous sections of this paper have tentatively answered some of these questions. Before we can say that a particular resolution will evoke general supranationalist predispositions, however, another crucial piece of information is necessary. Looking at a factor matrix both the anti-behavioralist and the diplomat are likely to ask the same valid question: why did vote such and such (e.g. vote 48) load on the supranationalism factor? Factor analysis only allows us to say, *after the fact*, that such a loading did occur. We still need to know what characteristics of the resolution and of the situation it refers to to determine particular kinds of voting responses.

If we stress the determinative importance of reality *perceptions*, one fruitful area of investigation is to try and understand why and how certain situations are viewed in supranationalist terms. Interviews with diplomats and content analysis of their speeches and documents would be appropriate strategies. A preliminary study of the resolutions themselves may tentatively serve to indicate the usefulness of such an approach.

Distinguishing characteristics of supranationalism resolutions

Table 5 contains data for testing several plausible hypotheses about the distinguishing characteristics of supranationalism resolutions. On the basis of the existing literature we might expect, for example, that resolutions must draw heavily on neutralists, democracies and ex-colonies as sponsors in order to achieve resounding supranationalist majorities.[17]

Several stylistic or wording characteristics of supranationalist resolutions have also been suggested: increased Charter references on successful task expansions tend to increase the legitimacy of the UN; the concept of supranationality implies more references to the role of the executive, the Secretary General, and/or to UN legislative bodies. One would also suppose that supranationalist resolutions avoid criticisms of specific states. Universalism of language and application is a definitional characteristic of the "rule of law."

Finally, concerning the objectives of supranationalist resolutions, we would expect increased task requirements in peacekeeping and other areas of international activity. Because of the UN's limited competence, such activities are not likely to occur in direct confrontations of the two super-powers.[18]

Despite the judgmental element of the content analysis categories used in Table 5 (two coders always agreed on more than 80 per cent of the category

---

[17] Conor Cruise O'Brien, *To Katanga and Back* (London: Hutchison, 1962), refers to all of these characteristics of "good sponsorship" in Assembly politics. Ernst Haas, "Dynamic Environment," *op. cit.*, has stressed the need for support from revolutionary (anti-colonial) states on new tasks that increase the legitimacy and authority of the United Nations.

[18] The above hypotheses have been drawn from previously cited literature or from conversations with UN diplomats. Most scholars seem to expect peacekeeping functions to grow more slowly than other informational economic and social ones. See in particular the fascinating varieties of this argument in terms of Parsonian functionalism in A. Etzioni, *op. cit.*; the present data is inadequate to test such theories about stages of supranational development.

assignments), these results tentatively corroborate most of the above mentioned hypotheses. Neutralist and excolonial sponsorships do seem to help produce supranationalist responses when such sponsors can be obtained. Democratic sponsorship is generally desirable in the Assembly on both supranationalism and Cold War alignments (note that democracies, although they form less than two-fifths of the membership, account for nearly three-fifths of the sponsorship).

Supranationalism resolutions, as expected, do have a larger number of Charter references than most other votes (Cold War votes do too), while references to Secretariat and legislative roles are also especially high. Supranationalism resolutions, although they *imply* criticisms of specific states, also usually do not use abusive language when referring to particular states.

Regarding the kinds of task expansion and the geographic areas appropriate for supranationalism responses, the sending of troops and the commitment of finances have obviously been important. Geographically, Hungarian aid, Middle Eastern and African peace-keeping forces have been possible in supranationalism terms.

VI. Supranationalism and International Community

Even though supranationalist predispositions have been formed and invoked with considerable success on several crucial occasions in the short period since the United Nations began, the above analysis does *not* prove that international community—peaceful relations among nations has been brought closer to realization. The problems facing peaceful international cooperation and competition have also multiplied in the post-war period—perhaps even more rapidly the United Nation's limited supranationalist capabilities, which even now are being seriously challenged by great powers from both the East and the West.

Historically viewed, however, certain encouraging characteristics of the UN's modest supranational capability should be mentioned. First of all, it is sometimes said that the UN can only help settle disputes of small powers (such, in general, was the League's experience). The UN's record is a considerable improvement on such expectations: Britain

TABLE 5
A Content Analysis of the Sponsorship, Wording and
Objectives of 52 Special Session Roll-Call Resolutions[a]

A. Sponsorship characteristics

Predominant alignment:	COLD WAR ALIGNMENT			DEMOCRACY		COLONIAL PAST		
	US ally	Neutral	Soviet	Yes	No	Colonial power	None	Ex-colony
UN supranationalism	7[b]	8	0	8	7	6	8[b]	7[b]
Cold War	9	3	0	7	6	4	6	3
Palestine settlement	5	0	0	5	0	3	2	0
Anti-interventionism	3	2	0	2	1	1	2	2
Other (Palestine, etc)	7	4	7	9	10	5	10	3
Total	31	17	7	31	24	19	28	15

B. Wording characteristics

Predominant alignment:	LEGAL REFERENCE			UN REFERENCES			SPECIFICITY		CRITICAL	
	Char- acter	Other UN	No	SG	Other	None	Yes	No	Yes	No
UN supranationalism	4	7[b]	1	12	12	2	5	12	2	11
Cold War	3	3	11	6	9	6	12	4	9[b]	6
Palestine settlement	2	1	3	2	5	0	3	1[b]	0	6
Anti-interventionism	1	3	0	3	2	0	1	2	1[b]	2
Other (Palestine, etc)	1	0	13	2	10	3	9	6[b]	1	14
Total	11	14	28	25	38	11	30	25	13	39

C. Objectives characteristics

Predominant alignment:	ACTION REQUIRED					REGION			
	$	Troops	Info	Organize Discuss	Other	Europe	N. East	Africa	Other
UN supranationalism	7	3	7	6	4[b]	1	6	6[b]	0
Cold War	0	0	4	1[b]	8	14	1[b]	0	0
Palestine settlement	3	0	0	3	0[b]	0	6	0	0
Anti-interventionism	0	1	2	0	3	0	3	0	0
Other (Palestine, etc)	1	0	6	9	2[b]	0	14	1	0
Total	11	4	19	19	17	15	30	7	0

[a] Data in tables above are frequencies of references to particular categories of sponsorship, wording and objectives. Because one resolution may have several kinds of sponsor, as well as require several kinds of action, it might be counted under more than one characteristic.

[b] Table entries marked by [b] were these most significantly increased on a subsequent recoding of the above information.

was centrally involved, in partitioning Palestine, Britain and France attacked at Suez, France fought with Tunisia at Bizerta, and Communist China battled the United Nations in Korea. The UN was unable significantly to affect outcomes only in major superpower confrontations, such as Cuba, Berlin and Hungary. Some small power problems, such as the current Arab-Israeli refugee problem, have remained intractable, but other crises in which great powers have been indirectly involved (such as the Congo) have been met satisfactorily. Significant UN successes have occurred on both small power and great power threats to peace.

Secondly, the analysis above does not take into account all community building capabilities of regional and universal supranational organizations: I have purposely limited myself primarily to General Assembly activities at special and emergency special sessions. The Secretary-General's individual intervention in the Cuban crisis must be remembered.

Many of the less dramatic political, economic and social activities of the United Nations and of its affiliated organizations may also be helping to build foundations for world community.[19]

Finally, nonsupranational modes of moderating international conflict, however inadequate, must also be mentioned. American and Soviet calculations of advantage prevented the escalation of the Cuban, Berlin and Hungarian crises, even though justice was not always served. It is appropriate, therefore, to consider the United Nations' General Assembly as only one of several significant weapons in the arsenal of peace.

[19] Many observers have taken the view that economic development and technical assistance programs have, indirectly, been the United Nation's chief contributions to international community. When both Soviet and Western great powers have objected (as at the Sixteenth Regular Session of the General Assembly), these programs have also evoked North-South alignments. UN Supranationalism seems to be the more general phenomenon, embracing both peace-keeping and major developmental aspirations and achievements.

57. Conflict Patterns in the Interactions Among Nations*

Charles A. McClelland and Gary D. Hoggard, respectively a professor and graduate student at the University of Southern California, here employ several quantitative techniques to carry forward Professor McClelland's interest in developing a detailed map of the structure and operation of the international system (see Selections 1 and 42). The result of their collaboration affords not only a clearcut demonstration of the various ways in which different research techniques can be used in combination, but it also provides some impressive and imposing insights into the basic processes of international politics. [*Published for the first time in this volume.*]

Definition of the Research Area

The daily news of the world is the most common source of our information about international developments. Unless we are prepared to wait for extended periods of time until state papers and compilations of documents of international relations are released by governments, we have no real alternative but to base our knowledge of contemporary world affairs mostly on day-to-day reporting of the wire services, newspapers, and other mass media agencies.

Government officials, perhaps even more than ordinary newspaper readers, make extensive use of the public reporting of the daily news. Almost universally criticized for being biased and inaccurate, the news media continue to provide most of the information most people have about current international relations.

For more than a generation, academic journalism and communication research have been accumulating

systematic findings about the mass media. We have now the benefit of a body of knowledge, much of it based on statistical analyses, about the characteristics of public communication. There is a growing body of reliable knowledge about the flow of the news and about communication behavior. International communication is an important aspect of this expanding field of knowledge, albeit there is a lag in the study of international political behavior from the perspective of the communication approach. There is no question however, that such an approach can be taken to the analysis of the way in which the countries of the world act toward one another. Communication materials, orientations, and methodologies are as applicable to the international political system as to any other type of social system. Much of the world news is devoted to the reports of the actions and responses passing between the governments of the world. If we wish to understand more thoroughly and exactly how the contemporary international system operates, one way to go about the task is to analyze the content of action and response in the news.

The customary practice has been to take note of international news items as they appear in their temporal sequence and to synthesize the items

* An earlier version of this paper was presented at the Annual Meeting of the American Psychological Association in San Francisco, September 1968. The program of research on which the paper is based is supported under the Office of Naval Research contract N00014-67-0269-004.

"intrapsychically" into classes and patterns of meaning, more or less as anyone does in studying any organized historical account. The communication approach differs from the usual procedures of historical reconstruction by requiring a coding of reported items of information into an explicit system of categories and a subsequent interpretation of the data according to quantitative analyses of the frequencies and the distributions of the coded materials contained in the category structure.

The World Event/Interaction Survey (WEIS) is a research program on international system characteristics and processes. This paper is the first substantive report from the WEIS program and it follows the communication approach. The data developed in the WEIS program are a collection of public events reported day by day reflecting the flow of action and response between countries. We assume that there are continuities and regularities in the international political behaviors of nations and, therefore, that our basic theoretical orientation is tenable: that the past behavior of a given country in the international system is a source for the prediction of its present and future behavior. Thus, a country's external "performance characteristics" in dealing politically with a wide variety of situations and with other countries are conceived to be made up of combinations of "primary actions" that we categorize explicitly. These combinations of primary actions are expected theoretically to fit together with those of other countries in patterns of interaction. The purpose of the research is to discover if these theoretically expected characteristics and patterns make regular appearances in international relations.

Particular attention is being given to the phenomenon of international conflict. Conflict generally has been considered to be the dominant ingredient in the contemporary international system. It is a matter of widespread concern, within as well as outside government circles, to devise some means to control international conflict at least to the extent of keeping it off a nuclear collision course. Conflict patterns of international interaction are of fundamental interest. From the standpoint of interaction patterning, we adopt the proposition that any particular international conflict may be identified according to the combination and sequences of primary actions that compose it.

The primary actions of conflict in international relations are, in part, verbal and are readily recognized as protests, accusations, complaints, warnings, threats, demands, etc. Conflict includes also acts of a physical character such as seizures, confiscations, armed attacks, and some other depriving and punishing behaviors.

A conflict pattern might consist only of a combination of verbal and physical acts but it is possible that the primary actions of conflict may be "mixed in" in various ways in association with many co-occurring nonconflict types of actions. In any case, any international conflict pattern will be found to be embedded within the whole range of actions and responses of countries for some given time period.

Once a body of interaction data, gathered for all countries over a period of time such as a year and categorized according to primary actions, becomes organized and available for analysis, certain basic questions of a general nature become answerable. For instance, the matter of the general relationship of verbal conflict to physical conflict can be investigated. Other questions may be approached. What is the relationship between conflict behavior and cooperative behavior for all nations? Which countries are the originators of most of the conflict activity? Which countries are the recipients or targets of the most conflict actions? What types of action and response tend to group together? Is there a difference in the actions of the group of countries that are more prone to conflict compared to the action pattern of all countries? These are the kinds of queries that are most readily answerable from a collection of interaction data and that are raised earliest by the analyst as he approaches a first "cut" at his data.

Such descriptive and classificatory matters are the subject of this paper. Findings are set forth from the initial analyses and they are, in the main, descriptions of the volume and distribution of conflict activity in the international system for a single recent year. These findings are subject to a number of limitations with respect to both the data and the methods of analysis. It is to be borne in mind that the interpretations stem from one particular collection of interaction data.

Nature of the Research

Several constraints must be imposed when one sets out to do a worldwide survey of the details of the actions and responses of governments and regimes in international relations. A comprehensive statement on the rationale of the interaction survey and a description of research rules and definitions in the collection and organization of data is being prepared separately. It will set forth more fully the basis of the present paper. The important methodological and data restrictions which one should keep in mind in judging the findings set forth below are as follows:

1. The conclusions and interpretations in this paper are based on analyses made of interactions for the year 1966 only, but on a worldwide basis. A total of 5,550 event/interaction items constitutes the data base.

2. The daily *New York Times* is the sole source of the data. "National bias" and other validity problems in connection with the survey are discussed elsewhere.[1]

3. As far as possible, motivational interpretations and the implicit intentions of the participants in the international system have been eliminated in the data collection. The objective is to identify the sociological structure of the international system rather than to develop causal or psychological interpretations.

4. A distinction has been made between *transactions* and *interactions*. Transactions are defined as items of action that have at some point in time become so numerous, so commonplace, and so normal to their situation that they are accounted for conventionally in an aggregated form, usually by some unit other than item frequency (i.e., dollar values of trade, numbers of troops in the field, etc.). Interactions are, by our definition, single action items of a nonroutine, extraordinary, or newsworthy character that in some clear sense are directed across a national boundary and have, in most instances, a specific foreign target. One important qualification is that under the data gathering rules, the specific military events and acts of the Vietnam war in 1966 were excluded from the data collection although all other reported international events bearing on the war were included.

[1] A series of comparisons with non-United States sources for two months of the daily news of public international events has been undertaken. For example, a comparison of *Le Monde* and the *New York Times* for January and February 1968 generally supports the ratios between the volumes of interaction of the major participants as identified in the *New York Times* collection.

5. The 1966 world survey data have been ordered in a category system of sixty-three types of actions and responses. These were elaborated from a list of twenty-two more general classes of behavior. The coding system was developed over a period of years and extends across both the general cooperation and conflict dimensions. Table 1 shows the sixty-three types and the various aggregations of the category system that have been used in the paper. Although the sixty-three categories are listed according to a cooperation-through-conflict ordering (on *a priori* and "logical" grounds) the important point is that the interaction categories have *not* been assumed to be locations of a single continuum of conflict or of conflict and cooperation. The categories have been regarded initially as separate variables whose independence from one another has been assumed until analyses of the data indicate otherwise. The categories of primary actions cited earlier (accusations, threats, warnings, force, etc.) appear in the category system and are joined by others with face validity in the direction of cooperative behavior such as promise, grant, reward, request, explain, propose, etc.

6. Intercoder reliability tests have been conducted periodically and the coded materials represent an 83 per cent level of agreement among ten assistants who worked on the 1966 data.

Findings

The most general yield of information that can be obtained from the data for 1966 is in the answers to the following questions:

1. What kinds of action were most and least prominent?
2. What were the proportions among several types of actions?
3. Which countries initiated the larger numbers of actions?
4. Which countries were recipients (targets) of the larger number of actions?

1. Accusations are the most prominent single type of behavior transmitted in the international system. This is in accord with the findings of Rummel and Tanter for the period of the late 1950s.[2] Items

[2] For example, see Selection 50 of this volume.

TABLE 1
World Event/Interaction Category System

Cooperative/Collaborative Behavior Types:

Verbal Cooperation	Approve	041	Praise, hail
		042	Give verbal support
	Promise	051	Promise policy support
		052	Promise material support
		053	Promise future support
		054	Assure; reassure
	Agree	081	Make substantive agreement
		082	Agree to future action
	Request	091	Request information
		092	Request policy assistance
		093	Request material assistance
		094	Request action
		095	Appeal to
	Propose	101	Offer proposal
		102	Urge action or policy
Cooperative Action	Yield	011	Surrender, submit
		012	Yield position; retreat
		013	Retract statement
	Grant	061	Express regret; apologize
		062	Give state invitation
		063	Grant asylum
		064	Grant privilege
		065	Suspend sanctions
		066	Return persons or property
	Reward	071	Extend economic aid
		072	Military assistance
		073	Other assistance
Participation	Comment	021	Decline to comment
		022	Pessimistic comment
		023	Neutral comment
		024	Optimistic comment
		025	Explain policy position
	Consult	031	Consult—neutral site
		032	Visit
		033	Host meeting

Conflict Behavior Types:

Verbal Conflict—Defensive	Reject	111	Reject proposal, demand, etc.
		112	Refuse, oppose
	Protest	131	Complain
		132	Formal protest
	Deny	141	Deny accusation
		142	Deny policy, action
Verbal Conflict—Offensive	Accuse	121	Criticize, charge
		122	Denounce
	Demand	150	Demand
	Warn	160	Warn
	Threaten	171	Threat—not specific
		172	Threat—nonmilitary
		173	Threat—force specified
		174	Ultimatum

TABLE 1—continued

Conflict Action	Demonstrate	181	Nonmilitary demonstration
		182	Military mobilization
	Reduce relationship	191	Cancel planned event
		192	Reduce international activity
		193	Suspend aid
		194	Halt negotiations
		195	Break relations
	Expel	201	Expel personnel
		202	Expel organization
	Seize	211	Seize position
		212	Arrest persons
	Force	221	Destructive act
		222	Nonmilitary injury
		223	Military engagement

reflecting blame, criticism, excoriation, and denunciation make up 10.5 per cent of the total reported traffic of international interactions. The explanation of a country's own foreign policy (8 3 per cent) and official commentary on international situations and events (7.1 per cent) are the next most frequently occurring action-types. Reported agreements are 4 per cent of the total. The discrete events of sporadic military combat and organized violence are 1 per cent of the total (the reminder is necessary here that when the acts of military violence become virtually continuous and occur in large volume per short time period (a week or a month)—as in the Vietnam conflict in 1966—they are defined as transactional and are excluded from the interactional data collection). The least employed type of international act in 1966 was the ultimatum—an explicit threat with actions specified within a stated time limit—and was reported only twice (.04 per cent of the total).

2. The proportion of cooperative type actions to conflict type actions has a small complication in it that was resolved in the following way. It is possible to argue that explaining one's own foreign policy and making comments on prevailing conditions are more collaborative in nature than combative. The same may be said for the actions of going to meetings, hosting conferences, conferring, and making arrangements for exchanges and communications between countries. It happens that all these activities sum up to a large fraction of all interactions. One can contend also that conferring and delineating foreign policy positions are not invariably expressions of cooperative behavior.

These questions can be seen in still another light with the consequence that it appears appropriate to group comments, explanations, and consultations as within neither the cooperation nor the conflict domains. They constitute a separate grouping of actions. Such talking and meeting probably serves several functions: expediting affairs, filling in the intervals of potential silence, informing other participants and publics, etc. We call these *participatory acts* and regard them tentatively as functioning as a kind of "overhead" expenditure to help keep the system in motion. The 1966 data divide this way among the three groupings:

	Per cent
Cooperation	33
Conflict	31.5
Participation	35.5

Another way to approach the proportions of activities in the international system is to consider the amount of "talk" compared to the amount of "action." Verbal activity is a reasonably straightforward category; "action activity" is an awkward term to cover a more complex grouping of behaviors. Under action we would include rewards which are consequent to and different from the promises, which are verbal only. Punishments are actions that compliment threats, on some occasions. Also to be included under an action heading would be those type of "physical deeds" that governments are capable of undertaking: arrests, confiscations, withdrawals of assistance, impositions of penalties, armed attacks, intrusions, etc. When the 1966 data are divided between these two classes of activity, the result is 65.5 per cent verbal behavior and 34.4 per cent action behavior.

When conflict, cooperation, and participation are considered in terms of the verbal and physical action distinction, the distribution is as follows:

	Per cent
Verbal cooperation	24.2
Cooperative actions	8.8
Defensive/reactive verbal conflict	7.7
Offensive verbal conflict	16.4
Conflict actions	7.5
Verbal participation	17.4
Participatory actions	18.0

The data suggest that international relations are not quite as conflict-ridden as some have supposed, although the objection can be raised readily that other more important indicators, such as the size of armies and military budgets, have not been taken into account.

3. The most interesting statistic about the initiators of the most activity in the international system is that the twenty most active parties contribute just short of 70 per cent of the total volume of reported acts. The five most active countries account for 40 per cent of the total: U.S.A. (18 per cent), U.S.S.R. (9 per cent), mainland China (5.5 per cent), United Kingdom (4.7 per cent), and France (3.5 per cent). That the United States initiates twice as many events in the international system as the Soviet Union may appear to be an artifact and the self-attending bias of an American newspaper. A *Le Monde* sample shows smaller percentages for the U.S.A. and the U.S.S.R. and a larger percentage for France (6 per cent) but the same general relationship holds among the five countries. More study of this validity problem is needed.

The countries that contribute between 1 per cent and 2 per cent of the output of initiated actions are Syria, Indonesia, Pakistan, Canada, Japan, Cuba, and Cambodia. In the middle range between the 1 per cent group and the "big five" are Israel, United Arab Republic, West Germany, and North Vietnam.

Only twenty-six countries initiated ten or more actions with at least one other country during 1966, according to the data. The United States maintained this level (or higher) relationship with seventeen other countries; the U.S.S.R. achieved the ten or more level with nine other countries; West Germany and the United Kingdom maintained the relationship with four other countries each; and India, Indonesia, and France show a record of relating at the ten or more interactions level with three other countries each. Again, the reminder is in order that the data are for reported interactions and do not reflect, therefore, either transactional flows or anything like the total exchanges among nations.

The recipients of the greater volume of international actions are, by and large, the same parties that initiate the greater volume of international actions. There are a few differences between intake and output of activity. The United States initiated 18 per cent and received 15.7 per cent; the Soviet Union was the originator of 9 per cent of the 1966 action and was the target of 15 per cent; West Germany initiated 2.7 per cent and received 2.2 per cent; and Cuba initiated 1 per cent and did not make the list of the twenty top targets of international acts.

The main conclusion to be drawn from the foregoing findings is the observation that the nations in the international system are unequal in the extreme. There is much other evidence of the unequal distribution of almost everything among the countries. One might expect a different picture for international interaction since words are cheap and the leaders of a number of the smaller countries have projected themselves in recent years with high effect on the world stage. The data for 1966 do not support the expectation except for North Vietnam with a record of initiating 3 per cent of the total actions of the year.

The Results of Factor Analysis

The preceding discussion of the general character of international behavior in 1966 leaves some questions for further investigation. The interplay between types of behavior involved in the process of action and response by national actors is of interest. The above discussion has pointed out that comments, consultations, and accusations are frequently used behavior types. It does not, however, describe the relationships between the use of comments, consultations, and accusations, for example. The co-occurrence of patterns or types of interaction which consistently appear in the international system is one of our major research interests. Therefore, further analysis sought answers to the following questions:

1. What were the overall patterns of behavior present in the international system for 1966, reflected in the data collection?
2. Specifically, what were the patterns of *conflict* behavior?
3. Were the patterns of interaction for countries whose behavior is largely conflict significantly different from those present in the complete data collection?

Principal component factor analysis was used to answer these questions.[3] It was chosen as an appropriate technique for bringing about data reduction and for developing a first rough approximation to dimensionality in the data. It should be pointed out that the findings presented below were produced by orthogonal rotation of the factor matrix. The patterns identified are thus unrelated to each other.

For the purpose of the factor analyses we removed those actors having entries in less than 10 per cent of the interaction category cells, to eliminate statistically nonsignificant data. Further, those interaction categories which did not have entries in at least 10 per cent of the cells were combined with associated categories to produce a revised forty-seven-category system (see the first column of Table 2).

The deleting of the nonsignificant data reduced the number of participants included in the analysis from 137 to 83 and resulted in a reduction in the amount of interaction items from 5,550 to 5,334, or 96.2 per cent of the original data collection.

Factor analysis of the 1966 data indicates six patterns of behavior. Because of the exploratory and classificatory nature of this analysis, no attempt was made to label the patterns or to determine those groupings of actors responsible for their emergence. Rather, the following discussion simply attempts to characterize the behavior patterns in terms of behavioral variables. The patterns of behavior for 1966 presented in Table 2 are:

1. Cooperation and collaboration
2. Verbal conflict
3. Military force

[3] The factor analyses reported in this section of the paper were done at the University of Southern California Computer Sciences Laboratory.

4. Diplomatic conflict
5. Non-military force
6. Espionage

The first rotated factor suggests routine international behavior. It is characterized by almost the entire range of cooperation and collaboration variables plus nonformal complaints and denials of accusations and attributed policies. The verbal conflict pattern is characterized by high factor loadings for reject, accuse, demand, and protest behavior. The third factor is characterized solely by military engagements.

What has been termed a diplomatic conflict pattern suggests a nonmilitary threat and punishment type of behavior. The co-occurrence of threats of nonmilitary negative sanctions and reductions of relations between nations in the form of suspensions of aid and negotiations, recall of officials, and breaks in diplomatic relations, etc., is characteristic.

The fifth pattern is characterized solely by the presence of nonmilitary force behavior. These events usually involve destruction of property and/or injury to nationals of a foreign government and take place within the national boundary of the originator.

The espionage pattern suggests a common concern for internal security. Detention, arrest, expulsion, and return of foreign nationals or organizations are characteristic of this pattern.

Conflict patterns were more specifically identified by the deletion of those categories originally designed to encompass non-conflict interaction. The patterns indicated by this analysis are:

1. Verbal conflict
2. Diplomatic conflict
3. Military force
4. Demonstrations

With the exception that the espionage pattern is not identified, the patterns suggested by the focus on conflict behavior appear to be elaborations of those identified in the first analysis.

The verbal and diplomatic conflict patterns of rotated factors I and II in Table 3 are similar in structure to those of the first analysis. However, the military force pattern is characterized by the presence of threats to use force, ultimata, and seizures of possessions or physical position in addition to the military engagement variable of the first analysis.

TABLE 2
Patterns of 1966 International Behavior of 83 Countries[a]

Variables	\multicolumn{6}{c}{Orthogonally rotated factors}
	I	II	III	IV	V	VI
1. Yield 011–3	(94)	08	− 06	01	13	11
2. Comment 021–4	(95)	19	00	12	10	05
3. Comment 025	(91)	22	− 01	14	18	06
4. Consult 031	(82)	15	01	26	04	− 01
5. Consult 032	(90)	24	− 02	21	10	11
6. Consult 033	47	46	13	08	22	10
7. Approve 041	(82)	45	08	− 08	02	04
8. Approve 042	(87)	24	09	10	14	08
9. Promise 051–4	(86)	35	04	16	03	16
10. Grant 061–3	(85)	12	00	28	12	06
11. Grant 062	(84)	07	− 12	02	− 08	13
12. Grant 064	(84)	06	06	15	22	− 00
13. Grant 065	(89)	06	− 18	19	10	12
14. Grant 066	10	27	− 20	− 04	11	(71)
15. Reward 071	(95)	11	08	13	00	05
16. Reward 072	(79)	25	07	01	− 02	19
17. Reward 073	(78)	15	16	23	02	04
18. Agree 081	(69)	42	− 06	11	20	12
19. Agree 082	(76)	25	01	22	21	11
20. Request 091–2	(76)	13	03	(55)	01	10
21. Request 093	16	12	− 13	09	− 00	22
22. Request 094	(85)	14	− 17	14	06	11
23. Request 095	(58)	06	07	− 10	− 11	− 04
24. Propose 101	(93)	14	01	15	00	18
25. Propose 102	(72)	24	06	22	− 01	02
26. Reject 111	44	(80)	05	16	00	10
27. Reject 112	(56)	(59)	10	− 05	03	13
28. Accuse 121	23	(84)	− 13	− 01	− 01	26
29. Accuse 122	− 03	(82)	− 05	− 02	− 06	19
30. Protest 131	(76)	32	11	03	05	02
31. Protest 132	(61)	(68)	− 06	01	01	19
32. Deny 141	(89)	15	− 24	10	01	19
33. Deny 142	(95)	18	− 02	07	02	10
34. Demand 150	32	(80)	05	26	22	− 01
35. Warn 160	(67)	(54)	− 12	10	01	26
36. Threaten 171, 173–4	45	30	− 11	07	01	06
37. Threaten 172	28	10	− 13	(71)	− 03	− 10
38. Demonstrate 181	12	40	18	06	42	15
39. Demonstrate 182	42	10	− 04	16	15	01
40. Reduce Rel. 191	06	44	00	05	− 09	28
41. Reduce Rel. 192	(57)	18	10	(50)	21	33
42. Reduce Rel. 193–5	(51)	02	16	(69)	14	14
43. Expel 201–2	30	39	03	15	07	(53)
44. Seize 211	− 04	24	− 21	08	− 02	08
45. Seize 212	25	18	02	00	− 00	(73)
46. Force 221–22	22	03	− 05	05	(81)	04
47. Force 223	05	02	(− 86)	00	02	06

[a] Decimals are omitted from the factor loadings and loadings equal to or greater than 0.50 are indicated by parentheses. Only orthogonally rotated factors are provided, owing to the size of the factor matrix. Per cent of total variance and eigenvalues for the six unrotated principal component factors are 55.8, 8.8, 4.5, 3.6, 3.0, 2.7 per cent and 26.3, 4.1, 2.1, 1.7, 1.4, 1.3 respectively. Squared multiple correlation coefficients were used as communality estimates for the correlation matrix diagonal.

TABLE 3
Patterns of 1966 Conflict Behavior of 83 Countries[a]

Variables	Variable communality[b]	Unrotated factors				Orthogonally rotated factors			
		I	II	III	IV	I	II	III	IV
1. Reject 111	.82	(85)	28	12	− 01	(79)	29	− 03	04
2. Reject 112	.76	(84)	14	18	− 02	(58)	08	− 05	26
3. Accuse 121	.95	(82)	(51)	− 14	− 04	(80)	− 00	28	16
4. Accuse 122	.82	(61)	(58)	− 31	11	(81)	− 03	35	16
5. Protest 131	.67	(77)	− 22	16	01	34	25	− 09	29
6. Protest 132	.80	(88)	10	05	− 09	(60)	17	08	18
7. Deny 141	.91	(78)	− 44	− 05	− 32	08	32	22	14
8. Deny 142	.91	(79)	− 45	12	− 26	14	34	02	13
9. Demand 150	.68	(77)	24	06	15	(75)	33	− 03	14
10. Warn 160	.92	(93)	01	02	− 23	49	26	18	12
11. Threaten 171, 173–4	.64	(62)	− 15	48	03	30	23	(51)	38
12. Threaten 172	.23	39	− 27	− 03	08	13	(50)	04	07
13. Demonstrate 181	.63	(53)	11	02	(59)	36	06	− 04	(76)
14. Demonstrate 182	.47	(51)	− 27	− 16	33	14	22	14	(56)
15. Reduce Rel. 191	.53	47	44	33	− 07	47	− 07	− 17	04
16. Reduce Rel. 192	.70	(73)	− 39	− 03	10	15	(72)	15	25
17. Reduce Rel 193–5	.61	(54)	(− 52)	03	22	03	(82)	01	23
18. Expel 201–2	.44	(61)	11	20	− 14	29	27	02	05
19. Seize 211	.36	26	13	(− 52)	06	27	19	(52)	07
20. Seize 212	.26	46	10	19	− 16	16	18	10	09
21. Force 221–22	.25	28	− 21	02	35	− 02	16	− 03	(51)
22. Force 223	.47	09	− 02	(− 58)	− 34	− 07	− 07	(67)	− 10
Per cent total variance		42.8	9.6	5.7	4.9				
Eigenvalues		9.4	2.1	1.3	1.1				

[a] Decimals are omitted from the factor loadings and loadings equal to or greater than 0.50 are indicated by parentheses. Squared multiple correlation coefficients were used as communality estimates for the correlation matrix diagonal.

[b] Communality of individual variables equals sum of squared factor loadings for each variable.

Thus, a second threat-punishment pattern characterized by physical violence is suggested, which exists separate from the nonviolent threat and punishment pattern of diplomatic conflict.

The nonmilitary force pattern of the overall analysis is expanded substantially by the focus on conflict behavior. A "demonstration" pattern is suggested as an elaboration of the nonmilitary force pattern previously identified. It is neither verbal, diplomatic, nor military conflict, but rather a pattern of attention-getting involving physical action. Nonmilitary demonstrations, military mobilizations, and nonmilitary injury and destruction are characteristic of this pattern. Again, it appears that a reasonable interpretation of this pattern is that although it is aimed at eliciting a response from a second national actor, it is expressed almost entirely within the national boundary of the originator. The categories involved specifically reflect demonstrations in front of embassies, military maneuvers and mobilizations, and terrorist bombings, etc., of foreign government buildings.

To determine whether the interaction patterns for countries whose behavior is largely conflict are significantly different from those present in the complete data collection, a subset of the data was extracted for "belligerent" actors.

The "belligerents" listed in Table 4 were defined as those actors with greater than 25 per cent of their actions and responses in the conflict group of variables (protest, accuse, deny, demand, demonstrate, warn, threaten, force, etc.). Further, in order to eliminate the unnecessarily high ratio of variables to cases for this analysis, the behavioral variables were reduced to the twenty-two general types of Table 1 within which the sixty-three categories had originally been elaborated.

This focus on the "belligerent" actors provides

TABLE 4
Actors with High Percentage Conflict Behavior

Actor	Per cent conflict behavior	Actor	Per cent conflict behavior
China	65.34	Vietcong	50.00
South Africa	64.70	Albania	47.82
Cambodia	57.14	Poland	45.65
Syria	55.20	Zambia	43.18
Spain	54.34	Israel	42.42
Rhodesia	53.70	Czechoslovakia	38.70
Cuba	53.33	East Germany	38.63
Jordan	52.83	Ghana	38.29
United Arab Republic	51.56	Soviet Union	36.92
North Vietnam	51.16	India	29.13
Portugal	51.16	United States	25.03

the opportunity to investigate conflict behavior in a more concentrated form.

The factor analysis of the twenty-two general behavior variables, presented in Table 5, suggests four major patterns of behavior as follows:

1. Cooperation and collaboration
2. Verbal conflict
3. Military force
4. Diplomatic conflict

The rotated factors of Table 5 show alignments for the twenty-two major categories similar to those produced by the more specific forty-seven category system. Again, the uniform nature of the cooperation variables plus high loadings for the deny and reduce relationship variables, suggest routine international behavior.

The verbal conflict and military force patterns are similar to those of the analysis of eighty-three actors. The fourth pattern, characterized by high loadings for expulsions and seizures, suggests a combination of the diplomatic conflict and non-military force patterns identified for the eighty-three countries. It is not possible to determine from this analysis whether this suggested combination of patterns results from an actual difference in behavior patterns of the "belligerents" or whether it results from use of the twenty-two general rather than the forty-seven more detailed variables.

An even more concentrated example of international conflict behavior is provided by a separate analysis of the behavior of the "belligerent" actors

for the twelve general conflict categories. The rotated factors of Table 6 indicate conflict patterns similar to those suggested by Table 3, as follows:

1. Verbal conflict
2. Threats of conflict
3. Diplomatic conflict
4. Military force

The verbal conflict pattern is again clearly indicated. The threat-punishment combinations, characteristic of the diplomatic conflict and military force patterns of the eighty-three country analysis, do not appear. Rather, the second pattern is characterized only by the threaten variable. The third pattern is again a combination of verbal and diplomatic action of a nonviolent nature, and the force variable again stands alone as characteristic of the fourth pattern.

Considering the influence that the use of the twenty-two general rather than the forty-seven more specific categories may have produced, the conclusion is that the patterns of interaction for countries whose behavior is largely conflict are not substantially different from the patterns of

1. Cooperation and collaboration
2. Verbal conflict
3. Military force
4. Diplomatic conflict
5. Demonstrations
6. Espionage

present in the entire data collection.

Other opportunities for describing the character

TABLE 5
*Factor Analysis of 22 Behavioral Variables for 22
"Belligerent" Countries*[a]

Variables	Variable communality[b]	Unrotated factors				Orthogonally rotated factors			
		I	II	III	IV	I	II	III	IV
1. Yield	.93	(88)	39	08	00	(96)	02	07	− 00
2. Comment	.99	(95)	29	− 02	− 03	(96)	20	02	04
3. Consult	.97	(98)	07	− 08	00	(88)	39	− 01	19
4. Approve	.97	(97)	10	− 12	− 08	(91)	37	− 07	05
5. Promise	.99	(99)	06	− 07	02	(89)	36	− 05	20
6. Grant	.99	(93)	33	09	07	(95)	07	07	13
7. Reward	.74	(85)	13	− 03	02	(80)	25	− 02	14
8. Agree	.93	(96)	− 01	− 08	01	(82)	45	− 02	24
9. Request	.93	(92)	28	01	01	(93)	23	13	09
10. Propose	.97	(97)	15	− 06	06	(91)	29	− 02	20
11. Reject	.91	(79)	− 47	− 17	− 19	47	(83)	− 10	18
12. Accuse	.94	(54)	(− 74)	20	− 24	06	(82)	09	32
13. Protest	.93	(92)	− 24	02	− 17	(69)	(63)	06	12
14. Deny	.99	(94)	32	02	02	(96)	14	05	09
15. Demand	.79	(62)	− 49	− 22	− 34	30	(87)	− 10	03
16. Warn	.89	(92)	− 20	09	04	(67)	(51)	06	40
17. Threaten	.59	(59)	21	28	− 35	48	11	10	− 06
18. Demonstrate	.55	(56)	− 41	21	− 18	28	36	− 11	11
19. Reduce Rel.	.95	(87)	− 03	06	43	(76)	15	− 16	(56)
20. Expel	.82	(59)	− 38	− 12	(56)	35	29	− 20	(80)
21. Seize	.86	27	(− 52)	(54)	47	− 00	13	30	(72)
22. Force	.75	05	25	(82)	− 12	09	− 06	(97)	− 03
Per cent total variance		66.5	10.8	5.9	5.3				
Eigenvalues		14.6	2.4	1.3	1.2				

[a] Decimals are omitted from the factor loadings and loadings equal to or greater than 0.50 are indicated by parentheses. Squared multiple correlation coefficients were used as communality estimates for the correlation matrix diagonal.

[b] Communality of individual variables equals the sum of squared factor loadings for each variable.

of international behavior are available from our data collection.

For example, a logical step in the use of factor analysis is to provide approximations of dimensionality of the data using the actors as variables. Combined with other descriptive statistics, the derivation of actor classes or individual country profiles is possible.

Table 7 presents a first attempt to identify actor classes using the twenty-two "belligerent" countries of Table 4. Factor analysis of the countries as variables for each behavior category suggests four actor classes. In order to relate meaningfully the groupings of countries as diverse as those present, a review of the raw data was accomplished to attempt a labeling of the factors identified. The following names for the rotated factors are suggested as descriptive of

the classes of actors present (the naming is somewhat fanciful and not to be taken too seriously):

1. Movers and shakers
2. Self-justifiers
3. Hosts and travelers
4. Side changers

Table 7 allows the reader to identify the countries that are characterized by the preceding classification.

The strong appearance in the factor analyses of a pattern of routine cooperative activity in the international system lends support to an observation that almost any seasoned analyst of international affairs is likely to support: the flow of events through the international system is subject to sharp fluctuations. This effect has virtually a meterological characteristic. Flurries of international activity appear suddenly

TABLE 6
Factor Analysis of Conflict Variables for 22 "Belligerent" Countries[a]

Variables	Variable communality[b]	Unrotated factors				Orthogonally rotated factors			
		I	II	III	IV	I	II	III	IV
1. Reject	.94	(90)	25	15	−22	(89)	13	38	−08
2. Accuse	.91	(78)	41	30	22	(74)	23	04	01
3. Protest	.91	(94)	−03	16	−07	(76)	35	47	10
4. Deny	.98	(78)	(−59)	−07	−14	30	(55)	(72)	18
5. Demand	.76	(73)	29	26	−27	(86)	10	19	−11
6. Warn	.91	(94)	−15	−04	05	(56)	38	(62)	12
7. Threaten	.64	(52)	(−52)	31	04	17	(82)	18	14
8. Demonstrate	.50	(65)	15	17	15	40	49	10	−17
9. Reduce Rel.	.96	(82)	−22	−49	−05	23	26	(89)	−10
10. Expel	.77	(67)	16	(−54)	01	27	−09	(72)	−17
11. Seize	.73	44	28	−27	(62)	11	−06	27	18
12. Force	.55	−00	−36	25	(60)	−06	10	−05	(82)
Per cent total variance		52.8	10.5	8.5	8.1				
Eigenvalues		6.3	1.3	1.0	1.0				

[a] Decimals are omitted from the factor loadings and loadings equal to or greater than 0.50 are indicated by parentheses. Squared multiple correlation coefficients were used as communality estimates for the correlation matrix diagonal.

[b] Communality of individual variables equals sum of squared factor loadings for each variable.

TABLE 7
Factor Analysis of 22 "Belligerent Actors" for 22 Behavioral Variables[a]

Variables	Variable communality[b]	Unrotated factors				Orthogonally rotated factors			
		I	II	III	IV	I	II	III	IV
1. China	.98	(86)	43	20	11	(85)	01	40	03
2. South Africa	.87	(86)	21	27	10	(79)	13	21	08
3. Cambodia	.94	(84)	08	35	−33	(85)	44	08	11
4. Syria	.67	(80)	16	03	−05	(64)	25	33	18
5. Spain	.72	(74)	09	−37	−15	37	24	(50)	(54)
6. Rhodesia	.74	(59)	(−53)	−27	20	−06	49	29	33
7. Cuba	.95	(91)	32	11	−11	(84)	18	37	22
8. Jordan	.95	(83)	27	16	−40	(87)	30	14	28
9. UAR	.94	(94)	18	−11	11	(61)	25	(58)	20
10. North Vietnam	.92	(92)	−02	26	06	(70)	40	32	04
11. Portugal	.75	(73)	−20	31	29	46	31	18	−04
12. Viet Cong	.90	(80)	−37	35	01	(52)	(63)	04	−02
13. Albania	.95	(86)	40	01	22	(70)	02	(61)	06
14. Poland	.81	(83)	11	−27	18	39	25	(79)	22
15. Zambia	.89	(86)	−32	−03	−21	45	(67)	16	33
16. Israel	.85	(86)	−21	01	−26	(53)	(67)	30	23
17. Czechoslovakia	.88	(83)	−07	−35	25	27	41	(59)	16
18. East Germany	.67	(60)	26	−48	13	27	08	25	26
19. Ghana	.75	44	07	(−58)	−46	16	10	11	(90)
20. USSR	.90	(92)	−08	−08	22	46	46	(58)	06
21. India	.88	(84)	−41	−07	05	29	(75)	(50)	08
22. USA	.86	(58)	(−71)	03	−14	08	(93)	09	05
Per cent total variance		64.5	9.3	7.1	4.7				
Eigenvalues		14.2	2.0	1.6	1.0				

[a] Decimals are omitted from the factor loadings and loadings equal or to greater than 0.50 are indicated by parentheses. Squared multiple correlation coefficients were used as communality estimates for the correlation matrix diagonal.

[b] Communality of individual variables equals sum of squared factor loadings for each variable.

and then recede. Most of these flareups are easily connected with the strong conflicts that are called international crises. Such conflicts are analogous to storm fronts and appear to override the usual pattern of international action and response. These fronts are marked by sharp increases in interaction including the cooperative types of behavior.

Figure 1 shows how the volume of action increased in some international crises of earlier years. The WEIS data for 1966 to the present show two sharp peaks of international activity in the period. The first in the summer of 1967 is accounted for readily by the outbreak of the June war in the Middle East. The second peak is more surprising since no major international crisis occurred in the spring of 1968. Inspection of the world survey data leads to the conclusion that several streams of events rising in the same period of time account for the sharp rise in the volume of activity: the Paris negotiations on

Vietnam, the renewal of threats to the access to Berlin, the Biafran–Nigerian conflict, and the onset of opposition in the Soviet world to the Czech liberalization movement.

How often these noncrisis co-occurrences take place on the average and whether or not they are simply chance phenomena are matters to be decided on the basis of a larger and longer record of quantitative observation and analysis of the operations of the international political system.

Summary Interpretations

The principal characteristics of international behavior for 1966 that this study emphasizes are:

1. The unequal distribution of the interactions of nations, exemplified by the finding that the twenty most active participants contribute almost 70 per cent of the total volume of reported acts.

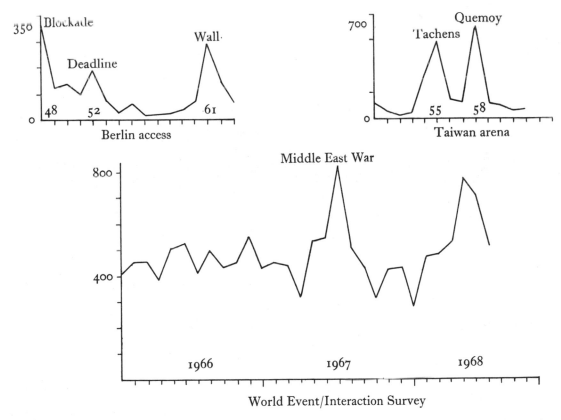

Figure 1. Fluctuations of international interaction

2. The prominence of the United States and the Soviet Union as both originators and recipients of interaction.

3. The highly organized and unitary pattern in the routine flow of international politics that is primarily cooperative and collaborative in character.

4. The more complex ordering of international conflict, which provides more patterns for nations to follow alternatively and divides military violence from other configurations of conflict.

5. Conflict behavior in the international system is not shown to be dominating. Rather, there is an approximate balance of three general classes of behavior: cooperation, conflict, and participation.

Name Index

Subject Index